MW01631212

An Uncommon Common Pioneer

The Journals of
James Henry Martineau
1828–1918

Edited by Donald G. Godfrey
& Rebecca S. Martineau-McCarty

Published by the Religious Studies Center, Brigham Young University, Provo, Utah

http://religion.byu.edu/rsc_rec_pub.php

ISBN 978-0-8425-2697-5

TO

THE DESCENDANTS OF JAMES HENRY MARTINEAU

James H. Martineau

JAMES HENRY MARTINEAU
1828-1921

Courtesy of James Henry Martineau Family Organization

CONTENTS

PREFACE

JAMES HENRY MARTINEAU'S JOURNALS ARE A RICH historical resource. They represent the life of a Latter-day Saint convert, a pioneer, and an individual dedicating his life to serve his family, his country, and his church. These records reflect not only the life of one man but also the everyday struggles of a people whose lives were in transition as they set the foundations of a new society.

The records have passed from James Henry Martineau through several Martineau families over the generations. The originals remain with the Glen Bothwell Martineau family, great-great-grandchildren of James Henry Martineau. The journals were accessed for the family through the work of Anne Martineau Moulton, Alice Anne Martineau, and Paul S. Martineau, who photocopied them and placed two copies with the James Henry Martineau Family Organization; one at the Huntington Library, Manuscripts Division, San Marino, California; and one at the Church History Library in Salt Lake City.

The challenges of transcribing and editing the journals for publication are worthy of mention so that readers may understand the framework from which this publication grew as well as more fully profit from them as a historical resource. There were several challenges in transcribing the diaries: reading Martineau's handwriting (especially as he aged), attaching meaning, and documenting historical details.

Facing these challenges, the editors worked to maintain the historical integrity of the diaries. First, the complete set of diaries were transcribed by family members and then combined and cross-checked by Mollyanne Hopkins, Paul S. Martineau, and Rebecca Martineau-McCarty. The work of this published transcription was again cross-checked by the editors for accuracy with both the family and the Church History Library copies.

Second, in preparing the manuscript for publication, we noted that Martineau's entries were not always standard. They were written and organized by Martineau in two copybooks, typical of the era, with the pagination printed in the corner of each page. Dates entered by Martineau in the margins were not always chronological; they were abbreviated and often inconsistent. It will be evident to the reader that Martineau was not only recording current events of his life but also reviewing his entries and adding information. The editors have retained the chronology as it was entered by the author. For ease in reading, the editors have standardized date headings for each entry.

In dealing with the major preservation challenges and preparing the journals for publication, the editors utilized Mary Jo Klein's *A Guide to Documentary Editing* (Baltimore: Johns Hopkins University Press, 1987) and formatting precedents set in Donald G. Godfrey and Kenneth W. Godfrey's *The Diaries of Charles Ora Card: The Utah Years, 1871–1886* (Provo, UT: Religious Studies Center, Brigham Young University, 2006). Card's diaries are from the same time period, and, in fact, Card and Martineau were acquainted. Professor Klein provided practical advice in dealing with unusual matters of editing and preserving the diaries as historical documents. The Godfreys provided a formatting template.

Third, in transcribing and editing for publication, square brackets [ ] were used where the transcribers and the editors wrote their best interpretation of a word or phrase, made a needed correction, or provided an abbreviated interpretation. If something was illegible or missing, it was explained in brackets or with ellipses [. . .].

Fourth, the transcribers included Martineau's provincial spellings, abbreviations, and word usage exactly as in the original. With these measures, we have worked to preserve the totality of the original journals.

Fifth, the page numbers printed in the original copybooks were retained in square brackets [page no.] within a few lines of the original.

The final challenge in this publication was that of attaching meaning, providing context, and adding documentation. Martineau was a wonderfully descriptive writer, so much of the context is already in the text. He is responsible for the organization of the journals. The editors have sought to provide context where needed through annotations. They have also included the graphics Martineau drew in the journals as well as additional family photos. The publication includes a selected bibliography and an extensive index facilitating future research.

The appendices contain family history of extended family and include documents Martineau inserted into the journals. The inserts are transcriptions or copies of letters, notes, and certificates that Martineau had placed in the journals but not written into the narrative.

Martineau's letters, surveys, and Church reports are mentioned only briefly in the journals. It is noticeable in many places that he had taken notes and documents and then later used these to write more extensively on his experiences. Martineau was a topographer and a good sketch artist, and he included these in his journals.

The journals sum up Martineau's life but are not the complete record. Scattered about the family collections and in various archives are other writings, letters, photographs, reports of his railroad and survey work, and newspaper and magazine articles. In his later years, he wrote extensively for the various Church magazines and published articles in newspapers. In this work the editors have referenced these materials when possible. He kept his "Book of Pearls" and his "temple book." The "Book of Pearls" is his collection of inspirational thoughts. His "temple book" is a record of his temple activities.

Martineau often referred to familiar subjects that he simply expected his reader to understand. However, now more than 130 years later, we do not always understand. To remedy this challenge, the editors have provided overall context in our introduction to the diaries. For ease in reading, the editors have divided the entries as parts 1 through 10, with subject headings taken from the narrative topics. Footnotes provide documentation and context wherever possible. The footnotes are added at the first mention of an individual or topic, thus providing context, clarification, and corrections for progressive reading. The editors relied on scholarly documentation where possible, as well as other Church and online works.

The main Church-related sources used for the annotations included Leonard J. Arrington, *Great Basin Kingdom: An Economic History of the Latter-day Saints 1830–1900*; Leonard J. Arrington and Davis Bitton, *The Mormon Experience: A History of the Latter-day Saints*; Leonard J. Arrington, Feramorz Y. Fox, and Dean L. May, *Building the City of God: Community & Cooperation Among the Mormons*; Martha Sonntag Bradley, *A History of Kane County*; Juanita Brooks, *The Mountain Meadows Massacre;* Brigham Y. Card, ed., *The Mormon Presence in Canada*; Helen R. Cole, ed., *One Hundred Years in Thatcher, 1883–1983*; Arnold K. Garr, Donald Q. Cannon, and Richard O. Cowan, eds., *Encyclopedia of Latter-day Saint History*; Donald G. Godfrey and Brigham Y. Card, eds., *The Diaries of Charles Ora Card: The*

Canadian Years, 1886–1903; Donald G. Godfrey and Kenneth W. Godfrey, eds., *The Diaries of Charles Ora Card: The Utah Years, 1871–1886*; Richard Neitzel Holzapfel, *A History of Utah County*; Andrew Jenson, ed., *Encyclopedic History of the Church of Jesus Christ of Latter-day Saints* and *Church Chronology*; Daniel H. Ludlow, ed., *Encyclopedia of Mormonism*; James H. McClintock, *Mormon Settlement in Arizona*; Myron W. McIntyre and Noel R. Barton, eds., *Christopher Layton*; Frederick M. Muchel, *A History of Box Elder County*; Nolan Porter Olsen, *Logan Temple: The First 100 Years*; F. Ross Peterson, *A History of Cache County*; Norma Baldwin Ricketts, *Arizona's Honeymoon Trail and Mormon Wagon Roads* and *The Mormon Battalion: U.S. Army of the West, 1846–1848*; Joel E. Ricks and Everett L. Cooley, eds., *The History of a Valley: Cache Valley, Utah–Idaho*; Richard C. Roberts and Richard W. Sadler, *A History of Weber County*; Thomas Cottam Romney, *The Mormon Colonies in Mexico*; Janet Burton Seegmiller, *A History of Iron County: Community above Self*; Morris A. Shirts and Kathryn H. Shirts, *A Trial Furnace: Southern Utah's Iron Mission*; Linda Sillitoe, *Welcoming the World: A History of Salt Lake County*; A. J. Simmonds, *The Gentile Comes to Cache Valley*; Ray Somers, *History of Logan*; Clifford L. Stott, *Search for Sanctuary: Brigham Young and the White Mountain Expedition*; F. LaMond Tullis, *Mormons in Mexico*; and Clarence F. Turley and Anna Tenney Turley, *History of the Mormon Colonies in Mexico.*

In general, few scholars have used these journals. Related studies provide a wealth of information about Martineau's environment but have not had access to his journals. Ricketts provided details related to the members of the Mormon Battalion, while Martineau lived around many of them during the first years after his conversion to the Church. Ricks and Cooley briefly mention Martineau in their work on Cache Valley. The same is true in the writings of Romney, Seegmiller, Shirts and Shirts, Tullis, and Turley and Turley. Similarly in the scholarly journals, Mills wrote about the colonies in Chihuahua; Kenneth W. Godfrey wrote on Moses Thatcher; Naylor wrote about Colonia Morelos; and Wasserman wrote on the social origins of the revolution. The work of Noel A. Carmack, "Running the Line: James Henry Martineau Surveys in Northern Utah, 1860–1882," gives us significant insight into the importance of Martineau's early surveying activities.

Common online sources included www.familysearch.org, www.lds.org, www.saintswithouthalos.com, the Utah State Historical Society site, www.arizonastatehistoricalsociety.org, the Mormon Literature Database, the Utah History Encyclopedia site, Utah Collections Browser, and www.lib.utah.edu/digital/unews.

Ldslibrary.com is a subscriber-based service containing a wealth of historical material; however, nonsubscribers still have access to a great deal of free content. Online searches at university libraries for Utah and Arizona towns were also significant identification sources. In the majority of the online research, the search value (s.v.) or key word was taken from the diary entry. For the Utah Digital Newspaper, the search value was simply "Martineau" connected to the diary by date and content. References to online sources appear at the first mention in the footnotes. Online addresses often change over time, so key words are given to provide clues to find revised locations.

A good deal has been written about prominent Church leaders. There are extensive biographies on all the prophets and many pioneer leaders. Yet so little has been written about the pioneers who served quietly in Church history. Martineau was one of those tranquil servants. The purpose of this publication is to make these primary records available to the public, the family, and future researchers. This publication provides a starting point for whatever direction future researchers may follow.

The Martineau journals describe the issues faced by converts of the era. They describe Mormon and non-Mormon relationships from an individual who could be classified as both at different points in his life and who was always looking for common ground. They describe, in detail, the daily life of a common pioneer as he aged within the Church.

This publication provides opportunities. The answers are in future research made possible by the preservation of this primary historical source.

—Donald G. Godfrey

ACKNOWLEDGMENTS

THE FAMILY AND THE EDITORS WISH TO EXPRESS appreciation to all who have contributed to this work. A special thanks to Anne Martineau Moulton, Alice Ann Martineau, and Paul S. Martineau, who were instrumental in securing the journals of James Henry Martineau and making them available for this work; to Ray Glen Martineau, chairman, and Leland Kent Martineau, president, and members of the Board of Trustees of the James Henry Martineau Family Organization; to Mollyanne M. Hopkins and other family members who transcribed parts of the journal; to Loni G. Gardner and Paul S. Martineau, who assembled the chronology of significant events on the life of James Henry Martineau; to Paul J. McCarty, vice president of the James Henry Martineau Family Organization and the family organization officer in charge of this journal publication project and the research at the Church History Library of The Church of Jesus Christ of Latter-day Saints; to Richard E. Turley Jr., managing director of the Family and Church History Department, for his direction, encouragement, and support; to Marilyn Claire Overfelt Franke, for her permission to use the Charles Freeman and Eva Rice Martineau family photographs; to the many family members who provided direction and pictures; to Beverly Fraser, for her expertise in editing the footnotes; to Janet Soper, who assisted in editing and formatting the journals for publication; to Becky Rogers, who helped with southern Arizona history; to Richard Neitzel Holzapfel, Christy M. Bigelow, Elizabeth N. Hixson, Rachel A. Grover, Heather C. Jacobsen, Devan Jensen, Elisabeth R. Sutton, and Stephanie H. Wilson at the Religious Studies Center, Brigham Young University; A. J. Rich, BYU Publications and Graphics; and Stephen Hales, Kelly Nield, Spencer Hales, and Matt Davis at Stephen Hales Creative, Inc. This publication would not have been possible without their work. We are especially grateful to our spouses and families, who share in all that we do.

INTRODUCTION

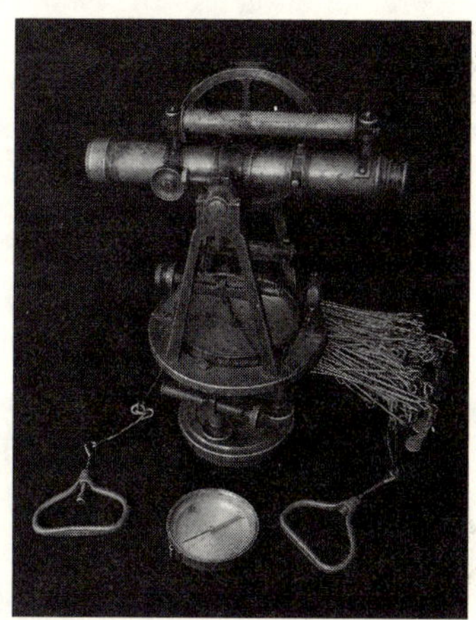

James Henry Martineau's original survey equipment. Photos courtesy of Richard Crookston and Anthony Ray Martineau.

THE JOURNALS OF JAMES HENRY MARTINEAU ARE comparably the most descriptively written diaries of their period. They comprise the records of the common Latter-day Saint pioneer. They shed light on the historical events of the era, the lives of average people, and the impact of Church leaders. At times they read more like a novel than a journal. They are exciting, testimony building, and detailed. The reader will see clearly what Martineau is picturing and feel what he is experiencing. His focus was on his family and his work, while the result is a reflection of a common, yet uncommon, Latter-day Saint pioneer.

The journals describe Martineau's conversion to the Church. He was on his way to California following the gold rush immigrants. He had planned on taking a global tour after arriving in California. On the first part of this journey west, he "wanted in future years to say I had 'seen the Mormons.'" His companions were afraid to pass through Mormon Territory, so he ventured out. Arriving in Salt Lake City on July 22, 1850, Martineau went no further. Staying with the Mormons, he was baptized in January 1851. The journals illustrate his compassion and patience as he worked throughout his life providing the foundations for settlement, an understanding of the Church, and support for his family. His life was quite a contrast from what he had first heard about the Mormons in the eastern press.

Martineau's contributions to the settlements of northern and southern Utah, southern Idaho, southeast Arizona, and northern Mexico are monumental. He was a civil engineer whose survey work left a lasting impression. The productivity of his work can be seen today. He was on the mountaintops of the Western Rockies working for the railroads.[1] He laid out thirty-five townships in Cache Valley and Bear Lake in Utah. He conducted surveys in the Snake River area of Idaho, the settlements along Upper Gila River in Arizona, and the Mexican colonies of the Sonora and Chihuahua provinces.[2] Martineau was an assistant engineer for the Union Pacific Railroad, making the transcontinental railroad dream a national reality. He labored on several of the Utah railroad spurs; he was the chief engineer for the Utah Northern Railroad.[3] He described the challenges, the toil, the workers, the daily tasks, the contrasts, and the progress.

Martineau was not a prominent religious leader, but he served in the locales where he lived. He surveyed their settlements, roads, irrigation, and major buildings, including the Logan Temple. He served in the stake presidency while living in Parowan, Utah, and St. David, Arizona. He was a patriarch during the latter stages of his life and blessed the lives of many. He walked shoulder to shoulder with the prophets and apostles of his era. He was a traveling companion with Brigham Young, John Taylor, Moses Thatcher, Lorenzo Snow, and others. Nearly every general Church officer, or General Authority, of the era is mentioned in these records.

In 1882 Moses Thatcher asked Martineau to accompany him to Mexico to help explore the area. True to the spirit of the times and loyal to his Church leaders, he was on the train two days later with Thatcher and Snow. It was a journey that took them through Sacramento, San Francisco, Los Angeles, Phoenix, the Mormon townships of eastern Arizona, and the future territories of the Mormon colonies in Mexico. During his Arizona travels, the Martineau journals are full of descriptions of the West and dotted with personal sketches.

These records reflect a common Saint who was true to the gospel under trials today's reader cannot imagine. He was criticized by the family of his childhood for converting to the Church but returned their criticism only with love and patience, doing their temple work. He felt the persecution for the practice of polygamy, but he sought only to follow the leaders of the Church and preserve his family. These were difficult frontier times. Today's traveler drives with ease through areas such as the Box Elder and Logan canyons and past Old Cove Fort. If we go back a few years, we can imagine riding through these canyons on horseback or in a covered wagon. The wheels of your covered wagon may break, the temperature could be well below freezing, and the axle of your wagon may sink deep into the mud. You must huddle together with your spouse for the night or you will freeze. Imagine trying to make it home for Christmas when you have been in the mountain country on horse and foot. The weather is prohibitive. There is no room at the local hotel, so you spend the night in the stable. These journals illustrate a father's love for his wives and family, a love for his church, and an undying testimony. Challenges occurred with the approach of Johnston's Army, the attacking natives, and the flow of persecution from the federal government, and while some grew bitter leaving the Church at the onslaught of a trial, Martineau's experiences strengthened his character, his will, and his testimony.

The Martineau journals provide the reader an understanding of the average Latter-day Saint. Martineau knew the primary figures in the Mountain Meadows Massacre and was a character witness at the trial. He was part of a scouting party who watched for the rumored approach of Johnston's Army at the time of the massacre. He and the Saints were just as afraid of the intruders as the intruders were afraid of the Mormons. These records stand as testaments to the strength of an individual and the blessings this

1 Noel A. Carmack, "Running the Line: James Henry Martineau Survey's in Northern Utah, 1860–1882," *Utah Historical Quarterly* 68 (Fall 2004): 66–83.

2 "Funeral to Be Held at Residence of Son," *Deseret News,* June 24, 1921; Journal History of the Church of Jesus Christ of Latter-day Saints, Church History Library, Salt Lake City. This specific collection is something of a news clipping service related to press coverage of the Church.

3 "Pioneer J. H. Martineau Celebrates 82nd Birthday," *Deseret News,* Saturday, n.d.; Journal History.

strength can bestow to a posterity because of one man's faith, stalwartness, and testimony.

Consider the following events described in detail and the reader has a glimpse of the value of these records: the early Mormon settlements are organized, the transcontinental railroad is completed, the California gold rush brings the world to Utah, the Mountain Meadows Massacre occurs, Johnston's Army marches into Utah, life and relations with the Native Americans are recorded, Chief Walker's funeral is witnessed, the Mexican territory is explored, and members are persecuted because of polygamy and the Manifesto of 1890. Each of these events brought trials and growth. Martineau's journals in effect provide the reader a glimpse of these events from two settings—non-Mormon and Mormon. For Martineau, the non-Mormons were both patient opportunists and persecutors, and the Mormons were his brothers and sisters. Whether living in Logan or Colonia Juárez, it was the same. He reached out to those who would detract from his faith, and he worked to support his faith and convictions. Martineau's journals are detailed, but there are no smoking guns recorded. Instead the reader finds an articulate, testimony-building, sometimes humorous, record of the trials of the times.

The purpose of this introduction is to provide the reader with an appreciation for the significance of these journals and overview of the primary settings: the Great Basin, the Iron Mission, Cache Valley, Arizona, and Mexico. These were the areas where his influence was felt most significantly. The Great Basin provided the Mormon context of his frontier life. Parowan, Utah, was the locale providing his family foundations. He thrived in Logan as an experienced engineer. An aging Martineau in Arizona and Mexico struggled to provide for his family and to establish these distant settlements. He spent his final years as a patriarch, back in the center of the Great Basin, working on his genealogy and serving in the temple.

THE GREAT BASIN OF THE 1880S

The Great Basin setting of the early 1800s had seen only a transient population. It was arid, isolated, and, until the mid-eighteenth century, virtually unknown. This changed abruptly in 1847 when the Saints arrived in the Salt Lake Valley. When Brigham Young declared, "This is the right place," it became unique, with a rapid influx of settlers who established their own structural institutions, culture, government, and social arrangements.[4] Historically, the area was bordered on the west by the Sierras and on the east by the Wasatch Mountains and the Colorado Plateau; to the south it tapered off into the Mojave Desert, and its natural northern boundary was the Columbia River watershed, where it merged into what became the Oregon Territory.[5] In 1822 the newly independent Mexico included the Great Basin as part of the province of California. The Great Basin became part of the United States on February 3, 1848, by the Treaty of Guadalupe Hidalgo. This was just seven months after the Saints arrived.[6] It was but three years prior to Martineau's entry into the Salt Lake Valley.

The discovery of gold in California increased the visibility and awareness of the Great Basin.[7] Until then most of the westward immigration had been headed toward Oregon and took a northern route that bypassed the Great Basin. However, the few bound for Oregon were completely outnumbered by the tens of thousands heading for California, many of whom went right through the Mormon settlements.

Few historical records for the area were kept before the Saints arrived. In the 1820s fur traders, trappers, and mountain men began coming, and they were followed by explorers. In 1845, Miles Goodyear settled on the Weber River; it was called Fort Buenaventura at the time. Three years later his holdings were sold to the Mormon leaders who made it a permanent site.[8] Goodyear left following the gold rush to California. The area was named Ogden after Peter Skene Ogden, a

4 Leonard J. Arrington, *Brigham Young: American Moses* (Urbana: Univ. of Illinois Press, 1986), 130–52.

5 Leland Hargrave Creer, *The Founding of an Empire: The Exploration and Colonization of Utah, 1776–1856* (Salt Lake City: Bookcraft, 1947), 312–13.

6 Leonard J. Arrington, *Great Basin Kingdom: An Economic History of the Latter-day Saints, 1830–1900* (Cambridge, MA: Harvard Univ. Press, 1958), 68, 141.

7 Creer, *Founding of an Empire,* 312–13.

8 Richard C. Roberts and Richard W. Sadler, *A History of Weber County* (Salt Lake City: Utah State Historical Society, 1997), 38–43.

Hudson's Bay Company trader in the Snake River and Great Basin.[9]

In the aftermath of the gold rush, the Great Basin experienced periods of transformation. The majority of the Mormon immigrants were true to their faith, their church, and its leadership, busy creating a livelihood and developing colonies where they could be free of persecution.[10] The Utah settlements and the general colonization process were coordinated through the central Church leadership, which carefully directed the mission and purpose. For example, Martineau lived in Parowan and Logan, Utah, various settlements in Arizona, and the Mexican colonies at his leaders' request.

The transformation during this period was critical. Mormon leaders and members had conceived the Great Basin as an area suitable for the creation of a large independent state in its own right. However, this aim was redefined as a result of conflict and the need for accommodating the federal authorities. Instead of approving the State of Deseret proposed by the Mormons in 1849, Congress created the federal Territory of Utah in 1850.[11] Utah was reduced to its present size when the Great Basin was politically divided by the creation of the states of Nevada, Colorado, and Wyoming.[12] But the Intermountain West, especially Utah, had become a homeland with a heartland. The heartland was establishing along the Wasatch Front. Here the settlements of Salt Lake City, Ogden, and Provo were established with farms and smaller communities reaching out from these focal points. This was the cultural core and the center of Church governance, which would reach throughout the West.[13]

THE IRON MISSION

Parowan was Martineau's first permanent home, where he spent almost a decade. This was plateau country in southern Utah and what is called Iron County today. Geographically, it is a complex of western basins and mountain ranges, with plateaus on the east.[14] Native Americans were the first to the area, followed by Spanish traders and travelers moving west. All were attracted to the mountain streams and cool springs fed by the winter snows.[15] The first Native American camps and later Mormon settlements were located at these watering spots.[16] The western half of the overland route from St. Louis, Missouri, to southern California passed through the Mormon settlements of Parowan and Cedar City in Iron County and St. George in Washington County.[17]

Martineau settled in Parowan on April 8, 1851, shortly after the first Mormon exploration party had traversed the territory. The settlement was surveyed and laid out, in accordance with the typical Mormon settlements, by William H. Dame, who was a later associate of Martineau.[18] Parowan had a twofold purpose. First, it was the halfway point in the Mormon Corridor between Salt Lake City and San Diego, where the Mormon Battalion came to its end. It was on the route home for battalion volunteers, and it was a good place to stop for gold rush immigrants headed the other direction. From 1851 through 1855, the settlements of San Bernardino, California (a transition point for the Mormon Battalion); Las Vegas, Nevada (the Lead Mission); and St. George and Cedar City, Utah (the Iron Mission), received settlers from

9 Peter Charles Newman, *Caesars of the Wilderness* (Markham, Ontario: Viking, 1987), 278–83.

10 Arrington, *Great Basin Kingdom,* 84–85.

11 The name "Deseret" persisted as a Mormon regional term even after the Territory of Utah was created. The name comes from the Book of Mormon, Ether 2:3; it means "honeybee."

12 Creer, *Founding of an Empire,* 303–38.

13 D. W. Meinig, "The Mormon Culture Region: Strategies and Patterns in the Geography of the American West, 1874–1964," *Annals of the Association of American Geographers* 55 (1965): 191–221; Dean R. Louder and Lowell Bennion, "Mapping Mormons Across the Modern West," in *The Mormon Role in the Settlement of the West,* ed. Richard H. Jackson (Provo, UT: Brigham Young Univ. Press, 1978), 135–67.

14 Janet Burton Seegmiller, *A History of Iron County: Community above Self* (Salt Lake City: Utah State Historical Society, 1998), 7–15.

15 Seegmiller, *History of Iron County,* 20–40.

16 Seegmiller, *History of Iron County,* 1–6, 41–55; Morris A. Shirts and Kathryn H. Shirts, *A Trial Furnace: Southern Utah's Iron Mission* (Provo, UT: Brigham Young Univ. Press, 1991), 3–8.

17 See maps in Shirts and Shirts, *Trial Furnace,* 7; Juanita Brooks, *The Mountain Meadows Massacre* (Norman, OK: Univ. of Oklahoma Press, 1991), 71.

18 Seegmiller, *History of Iron County,* 51.

Parowan to work these areas.[19] These various missions were created to provide economic stability and the independence of the growing Mormon territory. Parowan's second purpose was to provide agricultural support for those working in the Iron Mission, soon to be formed in Cedar City.[20]

By the summer of 1852, farming had begun in southern Utah, and the pioneers fought with the grasshoppers for their crops. The first families lived in crude dwellings, clearing the land, sowing the crops, and preparing for the harvest. Joel Hills Johnson, who became Martineau's father-in-law, introduced cattle to the region in the spring of 1851. By the winter of 1852, Parowan had completed a long council house, a schoolhouse, and a stockade around the settlement for protection from the Native Americans.[21]

The Native Americans of the area were the Piutes, with the Utes and Navajo often crossing into the area. The Utes and the Navajo were on hunting raids looking for horses, cattle, and women and children who could be sold or traded into slavery in Mexico. It would be an error to picture the natives as ignorant savage vagabonds. More correctly, their society was quite different from the Christian heritage of the Saints. These natives were an intelligent people. Chief Walker of the Utes, who came to know Martineau, spoke several languages—Spanish, English, and several native dialects. Walker and Brigham Young often convened councils to establish peace between the Mormons and the Native Americans.[22] To Brigham Young and members of the Church, the natives were the perfect potential converts. It was believed that the Book of Mormon was a history of these people. President Young urged the settlers not to fight the natives for stealing horses and sustenance. "The truth is," he declared, "their sense of matter and things differs so much from ours that we often find it difficult to bear with their indignities and ignorance, . . . what to us is a deep insult and outrage, to them is a small matter of little consequence; on the other hand a thing of minor importance to us becomes to them of great importance."[23] In contrast to confrontations, in 1850, Brigham Young preached "patience and forbearance."[24] Native American farms were created to teach the natives an agricultural lifestyle. Natives were actively proselytized and baptized. People were called to serve missions to the Indians and learn the languages, all in hopes that the Native Americans could be civilized. Housing was constructed, clothing donated, and educational assistance was encouraged. President Young approved of the Mormon missionaries who married the daughters of tribal leaders, and he sanctioned the adoption of Native American children into Mormon families.[25] The reader will see these policies reflected in the Parowan life of James Henry Martineau. He adopted a native daughter, Cora Colorado Martineau.

CACHE VALLEY

From Parowan in 1860, Martineau moved north to a new setting—Logan. Cache Valley was at the opposite end of the state—three-hundred and seventy-one miles by today's maps. This valley, at the northeastern end of the Great Basin, was at first thought to be too cold for successful farming.[26] However, the Mormons began settling the valley in 1859–60, and it was transformed into a successful agricultural area, Logan being the hub. The influence of the Logan settlement eventually reached throughout Cache Valley, into western Wyoming, southern Idaho, and later Canada and Mexico.

The Cache Valley immigration of 1859–60 was something of a population boom for the area—with over twenty-five hundred people initiating the movement, working together and building communities. On July 19, 1860, Martineau conducted a survey for the city of Franklin, Idaho. Over the next several decades, twenty townships were established in the valley near Logan, and Martineau was the surveyor laying

19 Arrington, *Great Basin Kingdom,* 84–88; Shirts and Shirts, *Trial Furnace,* 117–35.

20 Arrington, *Great Basin Kingdom,* 87.

21 Seegmiller, *History of Iron County,* 53–54.

22 Arrington, *Brigham Young,* 212–18.

23 Arrington, *Brigham Young,* 211.

24 Arrington, *Brigham Young,* 217.

25 Arrington, *Brigham Young,* 220–22.

26 F. Ross Peterson, *A History of Cache County* (Salt Lake City: Utah State Historical Society, 1997), 1–24; Joel E. Ricks and Everett L. Cooley, eds., *The History of a Valley: Cache Valley, Utah–Idaho* (Logan, UT: Cache Valley Centennial Commission, 1956), 1–32.

out many of them. The valley quickly became a productive agricultural area and was soon connected by railroad to Salt Lake City. Logan also functioned as a supply station for wagon freight and workers who were headed toward the mines in Montana. Later the railroads reached northward, and the Mormon contractors and laborers, including Martineau, followed the railroad throughout Utah and into the north. During Cache Valley's first two decades of settlement, cooperative enterprise, private business, and local wards were organized. These provided the foundation for the development of elementary and secondary schools, a college, a tabernacle, and a temple.[27]

From a Mormon perspective, Cache Valley was a very successful settlement. It had an intensive and varied agricultural base. It had local industry. And it had produced local leaders who were called to Churchwide positions. Marriner W. Merrill became the first president of the Logan Temple and an Apostle. Moses Thatcher was called as an Apostle and encouraged movement into southern Arizona and the Mexican colonies. William B. Preston served as Presiding Bishop of the Church. Charles Ora Card, president of the Cache Valley Stake, led Saints northward into Canada. Martineau had grown with the community and was living comfortably when he received the request to accompany Moses Thatcher on an exploration venture that would change his life once again. Martineau's northern Utah roots were deep, but they were pulled up when he was asked to accompany an exploratory party into Arizona and Mexico.

ARIZONA AND MEXICO

The Mormon Battalion provided the first Church presence in the Arizona territory when they arrived at the southeastern corner of the region which is now the state of Arizona.[28] The trek took the soldiers from southeastern Arizona northward along the San Pedro River, east toward Tucson, and along the Santa Cruz River. South of Phoenix they turned, following the lower Gila River toward Yuma and California. They were not colonizing at this time, but colonies would later be created in the San Pedro area of the route. Jacob Hamblin, considered an Apostle to the Native Americans, also traveled the area. He acted as a missionary, guide, interpreter, and liaison for groups traveling to California over the southern route.[29] It was Hamblin who created the practical route from Utah to the colonies of Arizona.

Pipe Springs and Fredonia were among the earliest northwestern settlements. Pipe Springs was a popular watering hole for Native Americans and travelers alike. Fredonia was a farming community not far east of the spring. Both communities were located within a few miles of the southern Utah border.[30] The route south then took pioneers to Lee's Ferry, which provided Colorado River crossings. John D. Lee was the first ferryman and was later convicted for his role in the Mountain Meadows Massacre. Lee's ferry was something of a hiding place for Lee, who was being pursued by the authorities.[31]

The Mormon settlements in northeastern Arizona were near the Little Colorado River. Later southern Arizona settlements grew along the former Mormon Battalion route near the San Pedro, Santa Cruz, and Gila Rivers.[32] Martineau became a member of the St. Joseph Stake presidency in this same area.[33] Explorations along the Little Colorado River led to settlements in Arizona known today as Joseph City, Holbrook, St. John's, Springerville, Eager, and Alpine; and in New Mexico, just across the Arizona border, Luna. Snowflake and Show Low, Arizona, would spring up southward. Settlements in the Salt River Valley, today's Maricopa County, consisted of Lehi and Mesa.

27 S. George Ellsworth, "Political Developments," in Ricks and Cooley, *History of a Valley,* 111.

28 James H. McClintock, *Mormon Settlement in Arizona: A Record of Peaceful Conquest of the Desert* (Phoenix, AZ: Manufacturing Stationers, 1921), 13.

29 McClintock, *Mormon Settlement in Arizona,* 59–86; P. T. Reilly, *Lee's Ferry: From Mormon Crossing to National Park* (Logan, UT: Utah State Univ. Press, 1999), 4–5; Norma Baldwin Ricketts, ed., *Arizona's Honeymoon Trail and Mormon Wagon Roads* (Mesa, AZ: Cox, 2001), 1–3.

30 Reilly, *Lee's Ferry,* 7–9, 102.

31 Ricketts, *Arizona's Honeymoon Trail,* 3–4.

32 Norma Baldwin Ricketts, *The Mormon Battalion: U.S. Army of the West, 1846–1848* (Logan, UT: Utah State Univ. Press, 1996), 103–30.

33 Myron W. McIntyre and Noel R. Barton, *Christopher Layton* (Salt Lake City: Christopher Layton Family Organization, 1966), 146.

The Arizona territory familiar to Martineau was that along the San Pedro and upper Gila rivers in southeastern Arizona—St. David, Pima, Thatcher, and Safford comprised the St. Joseph Stake, in which Martineau was second counselor with Christopher Layton as president and David Patten Kimball as first counselor.[34] These were appointments made by Apostle Moses Thatcher following the explorative excursion taken by Thatcher, Martineau, and Snow.

Despite its desolation, southeastern Arizona attracted the Mormon settlers in the late 1870s and early 1880s. Many saw the area only as a harsh, rocky, waterless desert full of greasewood and mesquite trees. This was where animals, bandits, and horse thieves harbored to take advantage of any travelers. The upper Gila and San Pedro rivers provided the only moisture and fertile areas for farming.

Pima, Thatcher, and Safford were settlements a few miles apart along the upper Gila River. St. David was to the south along the San Pedro River. Mormon leaders saw the potential in these areas for canals and extended farmland. In 1874, Safford drew ranchers and farmers, who spread along the Gila River. Smithville, today's Pima, was the first to be settled. In 1878, Erastus Snow and Jesse N. Smith saw the potential for irrigated farmland in both areas. John M. Moody purchased the Conley Ranch in 1881, and Thatcher officially became a townsite three years later, in 1883. St. David had a townsite laid out in 1880. Its proximity to Tombstone provided a diversity of employment opportunities in mining and timber.

These southern Arizona townsites grew much like their Utah counterparts toward the common goals of establishing business, industry, educational enterprise, and religious freedom. Here once again Martineau helped draw the official maps of the towns, planned the irrigation routes, and participated in the governing councils.[35] McClintock described St. David as the "scene of one of the most notable councils of the church," where President John Taylor and other notables, including Martineau, met in January 1885 to discuss the persecution which was beginning to unfold against polygamy.[36] The conclusion was the beginning of another southward movement: the Latter-day Saints ventured into Sonora and the Chihuahua areas of Mexico.

In 1874, Brigham Young had established a mission in Mexico. The goals were to proselytize as well as evaluate opportunities for future settlement. As missionaries worked with the native people, exploration groups were sent into the areas of northern Mexico. The explorers found the land monopolized by large landowners, so the required approach and planning were somewhat different. Moses Thatcher, one of the Mexico Mission presidents, worked to smooth out potential political concerns. Mexican leaders looked at the progress of Utah and Arizona settlements and hoped their immigration to Mexico would bring stability to the areas.[37] A later inquiry to Mexican president Porfirio Díaz concerning polygamy brought an unexpected response: "It makes no difference to Mexico whether you drive your horses tandem or four abreast."[38]

The geography of the Mormon colonies in Mexico was not much different from that in Utah and particularly Arizona. There were high mountain plateaus and valleys with interior drainage. Water flowed from the mountain in the major streams but quickly disappeared underground. There were three regions: the basin country that produced most of the typical southwestern desert plants; the foothills that included timber and grass lands; and the mountains, some of which reached six thousand feet.

Life in Mexico was not easy for the Mormon settlers. The difference in culture and changing politics created the constant need for negotiations. At the high point of settlement activity, colonies dotted the region and bandits pestered the settlers, stealing food and cattle. Colonia Díaz was the first permanent col-

34 McIntyre and Barton, *Christopher Layton,* 146.

35 See the original map of Thatcher drawn by Martineau, December 1885, in *One Hundred Years in Thatcher, 1883–1983,* ed. Helen R. Cole (Thatcher, AZ: Town of Thatcher, 1993), 13.

36 McClintock, *Mormon Settlement in Arizona,* 237.

37 F. LaMond Tullis, *Mormons in Mexico: The Dynamics of Faith and Culture* (Logan, UT: Univ. of Utah Press, 1987), 37–43.

38 Clarence F. Turley and Anna Tenney Turley, *History of the Mormon Colonies in Mexico (The Juarez Stake), 1885–1980,* 2nd ed. (Salt Lake City: Publishers Press, 1996), 14.

ony.[39] It furnished settlers for the other areas such as Colonia Juárez, which became the cultural center of the Mormon settlements and the place Martineau resided. Colonia Dublán became the largest of the colonies. The mountain colonies have all but disappeared: Cave Valley, Colonia Pacheco, Round Valley, Colonias Garcia and Chuichupa. The colonies in Sonora included Oaxaca, Morelos, and Colonia Morelos.

Following the Mexican revolution and the Mormon exodus from the colonies, only a handful of Mormons returned to Mexico. Many families remained in the settlements of Arizona. The Saints who moved to Mexico retained their Mormon cultural heritage and adopted the cultural heritage of their new land. They endured many hardships and became Mexican as well as Mormon pioneers.

LEGACIES REFLECTED IN THE JOURNALS

The Martineau journals are a special legacy. They are a primary record of an ordinary Mormon who made an extraordinary contribution to history and the settling of the West. These journals transcend regions and borders—whether secular, religious, or international. They invite the study of a multitude of topics.

The Great Basin, the Iron Mission, Cache Valley, southeast Arizona, and the Mexican colonies were all settings in which James Henry Martineau lived and recorded his experiences. Each of these carried distinct differences. Martineau bridged these differences through his travels, his surveying work, his explorations, his religious faith, and his own ideology. Understanding the Martineau journals necessitates understanding the broader historical context of each of these settings as he passed through them in his life. The journals reflect the Church during critical periods and provide primary data for local histories of communities in Utah, Arizona, Idaho, and Mexico. These journals portray how Martineau and others adapted to the climates, the soil, and the toils and how they developed settlements, railroads, industry, education, and governments. They reveal the intricacies of life. The journals especially relate the story of a common man from the story of his conversion to his aging years. They reveal the human side of pioneering: great successes and failures, fatigue, illness, and pain. They reveal an unwavering faith and determination to persevere.

The legacies of James Henry Martineau stem from a man who stood firmly for what he believed. They amount to more than the story of the pioneering Latter-day Saint. They are about more than exploration, surveys, the development of towns, military protection, church and civic service, railroads, and irrigation. Martineau's writings enrich our understanding of the religious, industrial, economic, and settlement growth of the American West and northern Mexico. The Martineau diaries are personal to his family, yet they are still a public record; they are inspiring yet challenging; they are individualistic yet international in scope. They are all about the life of an uncommon common pioneer.

—Donald G. Godfrey

39 Thomas Cottam Romney, *The Mormon Colonies in Mexico* (Salt Lake City: Univ. of Utah Press, 2005), 74–84.

BIOGRAPHICAL NOTE

JAMES HENRY MARTINEAU WAS UNIQUE AMONG MEN and within his church. He was born at Port Jackson, New York, on March 13, 1828.[1] His ancestors were descendants of the French Huguenots who had left France and come to America in order to exercise their religious freedom. His father was John Martineau, his mother Eliza Mears. John was a practicing physician and surgeon for years before turning to engineering, where he made his wealth building bridges, creating water systems for various cities, and developing railroads. John Martineau lost most of that wealth in the depression of 1837, and young James Henry was forced into working for himself. He later wrote about this experience, "I was compelled at an early age to engage in the battle of life, . . . and thus I became in a measure courageous, persevering and independent."[2]

In his youth, James Henry was an industrious student. He worked his way through school, at the

James Henry Martineau.

1 Differing biographical sketches have different dates, March 13 and 22. Familysearch.org confirms the date of March 13, 1828.

2 Preston Nibley, "James H. Martineau Led an Interesting Life," *Deseret News*, January 24, 1953; Journal History.

Monroe Academy in Elbridge, New York, doing janitorial work. He studied "English, Latin grammar, chemistry, geology, philosophy, history and algebra."[3] Upon graduation, he took a job with the newspaper in Auburn, New York. When war broke out between Mexico and the United States, James Henry enlisted. At the conclusion of the war and before he could return home, he learned that his mother had passed away—Martineau was now alone.

Working his way toward the California gold fields and his planned global tour, he taught school for a year in St. Joseph, Missouri. In 1850 he joined with a group of Missouri immigrants heading west. These associates told him, "The mormons were guilty of every kind of wickedness . . . and would surely kill us or at least rob us" if their route went through Salt Lake. As a result of extended debate and Martineau's desire to see the Mormons, he and a friend parted ways from the majority of the party and made their way to the Salt Lake Valley.[4] He arrived in Salt Lake City on July 22, 1850. He came through Parley's Canyon and described the scenery as sublime. He was baptized six months later on January 8, 1851, by William McBride; Martineau would not make it to California until many years later when he was on his way to Mexico.

Martineau was active in church and civic affairs from the beginning. His family recalled him saying, "In civic affairs I have always been busy."[5] He was ordained a seventy on February 8, 1851, by Jedediah M. Grant and started for his first home in the territory at Parowan, Utah. He records that he spent about a third of his time in various military capacities preparing and defending the new settlement against the hostile natives. His journals tell of being surrounded by a raiding party, getting to know Chief Walker, and adopting a little native girl to keep her from being sold into slavery in Mexico. In civic affairs he served as the city recorder, county clerk, schoolteacher, notary public, city councilor, and clerk of the Representatives Territorial Legislature. He helped organize the Parowan and Logan Dramatic Associations. In the Church he served as tithing clerk, counselor to the bishop, counselor in the stake presidency, patriarch, and was ordained a high priest by Elder George A. Smith.

His surveying began with the association with William H. Dame, whom Martineau assisted in the work of the Iron and Washington counties. Martineau was later elected as the surveyor for Iron County. It was his work as a surveyor that took him to his next destination, Logan, Cache Valley, Utah. Here he surveyed the townsites of almost every new settlement. His practice of sketching led him to an interest in photography. In 1869 he began surveying for the Union Pacific Railroad and later the Utah Northern Railroad, which connected the northern settlements with the city of Salt Lake. He was chief engineer for the Utah Northern Railroad until 1875. Martineau's survey work placed him in positions with every developing railroad, canal, road, and townsite in northern Utah and southern Idaho. In the spring of 1876, he assisted Jesse W. Fox in laying out the foundation for the Logan Temple. He spent a great deal of time in the mountains and on the mountaintops triangulating the elevations of the area. Much of his time was spent in the exploration necessary in his work.

In 1884, Martineau moved to Arizona. He was second counselor in the new St. Joseph Stake, which at the time included the upper Gila River, San Pedro River areas, and settlements in Mexico. He lived in Pima and St. David and later moved to the Mexican colonies. In Arizona and Mexico, he surveyed for these and other settlements including Curtis, Grafton, St. Thomas, Thatcher, Solomonville, and in Mexico for Colonias Juárez, Chuichupa, and Dublán.[6] Part of his family remained in Mexico until 1912 when they were driven back to the United States by bandits calling themselves Mexican soldiers. "I lost all of the savings of a life time," he recalled, because of the instability of the area and the chaos created by the Mexican Revolution.[7] In time, part of his family returned to Mexico and continued there for the next three generations.

3 "Martineau, James Henry, 1828–1921, Autobiographical Sketch," Church History Library, Manuscript 14584.

4 "Col. James H. Martineau," *Tullidge's Histories, Volume II*, 60, Church History Library, Manuscript F 832 A15 T9 C.4. See Martineau Journals, [26].

5 Larry D. Christiansen and Marcella Martineau Roe, "Biographical Sketch of James H. Martineau," http://www.rootsweb.com/~utcache /martineau/.

6 Preston Nibley, "James H. Martineau Led an Interesting Life," *Deseret News*, January 24, 1953; Journal History.

7 Christiansen and Roe, "Biographical Sketch," para. 21.

James Henry Martineau worked on the Utah and Northern Railroad in Eagle Rock, Idaho. Courtesy of James Henry Martineau Family Organization.

In 1903 he returned to the Salt Lake Valley, and by 1908 the move was permanent. He spent his time in the Logan and Salt Lake temples. As he was now a patriarch, he blessed the lives of everyone within his reach. At the age of ninety-three, he passed away on June 24, 1921. Church President Heber J. Grant eulogized Martineau at his passing, stating, "He had been in western life, a pioneer, an explorer, a military, church and civic leader along with being a writer, photographer and above all surveyor—par excellence."[8]

8 Christiansen and Roe, "Biographical Sketch," para. 21.

TIME LINE

March 13, 1828—Born in Montgomery, Port Jackson, New York, James Henry Martineau (hereafter Martineau) was the second child born to John and Eliza (Mears) Martineau. He had an older sister, Emily Henrietta, and two older half sisters, Julia and Lucretia.

January 19, 1831—His brother Charles Augustus Martineau was born in New York City. He died a month later on February 27, 1831.

September 30, 1831—His sister Frances Eliza Martineau was born in Elbridge, Onondaga County, New York.

May 26, 1835—His sister Harriet Martineau was born in Elbridge. She died October 16, 1837, when almost two and a half years old. She was buried in the Rural Cemetery at Elbridge.

April 6, 1838—Father's death and probate in Elbridge; John Martineau died and was buried in the Rural Cemetery at Elbridge.

August 10, 1838—His sister Lois Elleanor Martineau was born in Elbridge four months after her father's death.

February 7, 1841—Martineau was christened in the Baptist Church in Elbridge.

1843—Martineau attended Monroe Academy and graduated with credits in English, Latin, chemistry, geology, philosophy, history, and algebra.

February 21, 1844—Mother remarried in Victory, Cayuga County, New York; Eliza (Mears) Martineau married William G. Babcock, a widower with one son, Edward.

1844—At age sixteen Martineau clerked in his Uncle Peter Martineau's store in Cayuga County.

1845—At age seventeen Martineau became a compositor and ran the power press for the *Cayuga Tocsin*, a weekly newspaper printed between 1839 and 1847 in Auburn, New York.

1846—Martineau, at age eighteen, was given an appointment as midshipman in the navy; it was declined at his mother's request. He later enlisted for the Mexican War with the Mounted Rifles, destined at the time for California or Oregon. His enlistment was canceled because he was under age.

1846—He was engaged at the Milwaukee *Sentinel* office as compositor and ran the power press.

June 15, 1847—His sister Frances Elizabeth Martineau died at age fifteen and was buried in Elbridge.

January 4, 1848—At age nineteen he enlisted in the navy in Milwaukee.

June 1848—Enlisted for the Mexican War and traveled to Newport Barracks, Kentucky; he worked in the recruiting service and as a drill sergeant and clerk. When peace was declared, he was honorably released and mustered out of the service.

July 6, 1848—Mother died at age forty-two in Elbridge.

1848—Resided in Milwaukee and was engaged as a clerk in the bookstore of Hale and Chapman until the spring of 1849, when he determined to go around the world via California, China, India, Persia, and Europe.

1849—At age twenty-one, he left Wisconsin and traveled to Missouri, where he taught school near St. Joseph.

May 15, 1850—Left St. Joseph and crossed the Missouri River with immigrants on his way to California. He traveled with a group from Missouri who filled his mind with curiosity about the Mormons as well as with a lot of false information. He started keeping a journal and making sketches of his observations.

July 22, 1850—At age twenty-two he arrived at the Great Salt Lake Valley, Utah Territory.

September 1850—He was hired to work for William Walker, a resident of Farmington, and later went to Ogden with the militia to rescue people from an attack by the Native Americans.

1850—During the 1850 census, he was numbered with the family of a farmer, William K. Rice of Utah County.[1]

January 8, 1851—He joined The Church of Jesus Christ of Latter-day Saints and was baptized at the Temple Block by William McBride.

February 8, 1851—Ordained a seventy by Jedediah M. Grant and joined the Twenty-seventh Quorum of Seventy.

March 1851—Left Salt Lake City for Iron County with Parley P. Pratt's company of missionaries and arrived in Parowan.

April 13, 1851—At age twenty-three he enlisted in the war against the Utes, Piutes, and Navajos in the Territory of Utah. Served in the cavalry as third sergeant in Captain James Little's Company. In November he became a sergeant major in George A. Smith's Regiment in Parowan, Utah.

September 15, 1851—He was elected city recorder of Parowan and appointed as an Iron County Clerk.

January 8, 1852—At age twenty-three he married Susan Ellen Johnson, age fifteen, daughter of Joel Hills Johnson and Anna Pixley Johnson. They were later sealed on May 13, 1852.

August 28–29, 1852—At a special conference in Salt Lake City, the doctrine of plural marriage was first publicly announced.

November 4, 1852—His first son, Henry Augustus Martineau, was born to Susan Ellen Johnson.

March 1853—Martineau helped organize the Mutual Improvement Society. He was also appointed one of the school examiners and helped construct a protective wall around Parowan.

April 10, 1853—Along with twelve others, he was taken prisoner by Chief Walker, but he escaped.

1854—Became a notary public in Parowan. Helped form a dramatic company, painting scenery and leading the choir. He also became a second lieutenant and regimental adjutant.

May 7, 1854—He received his temple ordinances in the Salt Lake Endowment House.

May 21, 1854—Ordained a high priest by George A. Smith and was made a counselor to John C. L. Smith in the stake presidency.

September 12, 1854—His second son, Moroni Helaman Martineau, was born to Susan Ellen Johnson. Averted Native American plot to take Parowan.

February 4, 1855—Chief Walker died.

June 7, 1855—Took a fishing trip to Fish Lake.

July 1855—Began teaching the Deseret Alphabet and served as sheriff of Iron County.

October 28, 1855—Isaac Whitehouse murdered.

December 9, 1855—Elected clerk of the Representative Territorial Legislature in Fillmore (later moved to Salt Lake City).

1856—Assisted in surveying the Washington and Iron County lines. Surveyed Beaver City townsite and became the assessor of Parowan.

February 15, 1856—At age twenty-eight, after five years of service, he was discharged from the military.

1 1850 Utah County, Utah Census (FHL 25, 540), 243.

August 14, 1856—His third child and first daughter, Susan Elvira Martineau, was born to Susan Ellen Johnson.

January 5, 1857—A memorial to Congress.

January 18, 1857—At age twenty-eight, he married his second wife, Susan Julia Sherman, age nineteen.

January 27, 1857—Appointed captain of topographical engineers of the Nauvoo Legion. Elected alderman of Parowan.

July 1857—Received news of the approaching U.S. Army.

September 1857—Watched for the U.S. Cavalry at the time of the Mountain Meadows Massacre.

November 27, 1857—Daughter Delcena Diadamia Martineau was born to Susan Julia Sherman.

1858—Explored Nevada seeking a place of refuge. Elected surveyor of Iron County. Surveyed Summit Creek and Fort Johnston.

May 1, 1858—Explored Meadow Valley and saw a Native American cannibal. Ascended Mount Greyhead and the Golden Gate.

August 1858—The trial of William H. Dame was held. Martineau did his first work as county surveyor.

January 4, 1859—Elected alderman of Parowan.

January 7, 1859—His fifth child, John William Martineau, was born to Susan Ellen Johnson.

April 21, 1859—His sixth child, Lyman Royal Martineau, was born to Susan Julia Sherman.

May 2, 1859—U.S. soldiers camped close to town, and authorities went into hiding.

September 10, 1859—Traded a rifle to save the life of Cora Colorado, a Native American later adopted into the family.

January 3, 1860—Move to Salt Lake City began.

March 15, 1860—Accused of wrongdoing in Iron County.

May 24, 1860—His grandmother Lois (Sprague) Mears died in Dane, Madison County, Wisconsin.

June 5, 1860—At the 1860 census, Martineau's family was numbered as follows:

James H. Martineau, age thirty-two, born New York

Real Estate $800 [$17,327]

Personal Property $500 [$10,829]

Susan Ellen, age twenty-three, born Ohio

Susan Julia, age twenty-one, born Missouri

Henry A., age eight, born Utah

Moroni H., age five, born Utah

Susan E., age three, born Utah

Delcena, age two, born Utah

John W., age one, born Utah

Lyman R., age one, born Utah

Cora C., age four, born Utah

July 1860—Surveyed in Franklin, Idaho. Horse thieves discovered. A narrow escape in Box Elder Canyon.

September 12, 1860—He was sealed in the Endowment House by Brigham Young to Susan Ellen Johnson, Susan Julia Sherman, and Mary Elvira Sherman (deceased).

January 19, 1861—Now living in Logan, he was appointed Cache County clerk, elected county surveyor, and received an appointment as notary public for Cache County.

July 24, 1861—His eighth child, Charles Freeman Martineau, was born to Susan Julia Sherman in Logan.

October 1861—Logan Dramatic Association was founded.

April 1862—Exploring, he crossed the mountains in the snow to Bear Lake Valley.

May 11, 1862—His ninth child, Nephi Martineau, was born to Susan Ellen Johnson in Logan.

July 10, 1862—Exploring, he crossed the mountains east of Cache Valley.

August 1862—Moses Thatcher's horses stolen. Thieves pursued.

September 1862—The Battles of Providence and Bear River.

April 6, 1863—His tenth child, Jesse Nathaniel Martineau, was born to Susan Julia Sherman in Logan.

May 4, 1863—Martineau's fifth child, John William Martineau, died in Logan.

July 1863—Martineau takes an interest in the art of photography.

March 22, 1864—Son George Albert Martineau was born to Susan Ellen Johnson in Logan.

September 15, 1864—Surveyed Clarkston, Petersburg, and Paradise. Swam the Bear River with a yoke of oxen.

February 4, 1865—Surveyed Weston, Idaho. A daughter, Julia Henrietta Martineau, was born to Susan Julia Sherman in Logan.

October 23, 1865—Daughter Delcena Diadamia Martineau died of typhoid and was buried in the Salt Lake City Cemetery.

June 12, 1867—A son, number thirteen in the family, Joel Hills Martineau, was born to Susan Ellen Johnson in Logan.

August 13, 1867—A daughter, number fourteen in the family, Elizabeth Martineau, was born to Susan Julia Sherman in Logan.

July 7, 1868—Surveyed in Cache County as well as for the Union Pacific.

May 1869—Brigham Young asked Martineau to help survey a new railroad from Ogden to Salt Lake City, and he was made assistant engineer to Jessie W. Fox, chief engineer.

July 16, 1870—Daughter Virginia Martineau was born to Susan Julia Sherman in Logan. She was number fifteen in the family.

July 22, 1870—At the 1870 census, Martineau's family was numbered as follows:

Logan 1st Ward[2]
James Martineau, age forty-two, born New York
Civil Engineer
Real Estate $2000 [$29,231]
Personal Property $100 [$1,462]
Susan J., age thirty-five, born Missouri
Henry A., age seventeen, born Utah
Moroni H., age fifteen, born Utah
Susan, age thirteen, born Utah
Lyman R., age eleven, born Utah
Charley F., age nine, born Utah
Nephi, age eight, born Utah
Jesse, age seven, born Utah
George A., age five, born Utah
Joel H., age four, born Utah
Elizabeth, age three, born Utah
Susanna S., age thirty-four, born Ohio.

September 28, 1870—Daughter Gertrude Martineau was born to Susan Ellen Johnson in Logan. She was the sixteenth in the family.

1871—He became the chief engineer for Utah Northern Railroad.

2 1870 Cache County, Utah Census (FHL 553,109), 139.

September 8, 1872—His seventeenth child, Theodore Martineau, was born to Susan Ellen Johnson in Logan.

April 23, 1873—His eighteenth child, Joseph Herbert Martineau, was born to Susan Julia Sherman in Logan.

May 10, 1873—Son Joseph Herbert Martineau died and was buried in the Logan City Cemetery in Logan.

January 28, 1874—After an extended illness, his second wife, Susan Julia Sherman Martineau, died and was buried in the Logan Cemetery. James Henry was forty-five years of age.

November 2, 1874—Daughter Susan Elvira Martineau married Benjamin Samuel Johnson, son of Benjamin Franklin Johnson and Mary Ann Hale, in the Endowment House, Salt Lake City.

May 4, 1875—Daughter Annie Sariah Martineau was born to Susan Ellen Johnson in Logan.

June 1875—Coal was discovered. Governor S. B. Axtell visited Logan.

September 15, 1875—Uncle Peter Martineau died. This is the man who cared for Martineau after his father passed away.

November 29, 1875—Henry Augustus Martineau married Melissa Editha Johnson, daughter of Sixtus Ellis Johnson and Melissa Editha Merrill, in Salt Lake City.

1877—Martineau assisted Jessie W. Fox in laying out the foundation of the Logan Temple and its ground by the request of President Brigham Young.

May 5, 1877—Son James Edward Martineau was born to Susan Ellen Johnson in Logan. Martineau was forty-nine, and James Edward was number twenty in the family.

December 27, 1877—Martineau married Mary Elizabeth Brown Jones for time only in the Endowment House. She was the widow of Nathaniel Jones, a soldier in the Mormon Battalion.

February 1879—At age fifty-one, Martineau, his son Lyman R., Moses Thatcher, and William Jennings spent about three months visiting Washington; New York; St. Paul, Minnesota, and other eastern and northern cities. This was his first visit since 1849.

October 1879—Surveyed at Eagle Rock, Idaho.

December 17, 1879—Son Moroni Helaman Martineau married Sarah Sophia Johnson, daughter of

Sixtus Ellis Johnson and Melissa Editha Merrill, in St. George, Utah.

January 1880—Surveyed the eleven-mile canal from Logan to Smithfield.

June 2, 1880—At the 1880 census, Martineau's family was numbered as follows:

Logan, Cache, Utah[3]
Jas H. Martineau, age fifty-two, born New York
Susan E., wife, age forty-three, born Ohio
Lyman R., son, age twenty-one, born Utah
Charles F., son, age eighteen, born Utah
Nephi, son, age eighteen, born Utah
Julia V., dau, age fifteen, born Utah
Joel H., son, age thirteen, born Utah
Elizabeth, dau, age twelve, born Utah
Gertrude, dau, age eleven, born Utah
Theodore, son, age seven, born Utah
Annie S., dau, age five, born Utah
James E., son, age three, born Utah

October 17, 1880—Son James Edward Martineau died and was buried in the Logan City Cemetery.

1881—He surveyed land near Cedar City and became president of the American Bible Society for Cache County.

December 29, 1881—Son Lyman Royal Martineau married Alley Preston in the Endowment House.

September 5, 1882—He and Susan Ellen adopt Dora.

November 1882—At age fifty-four, Martineau went with Elders Erastus Snow and Moses Thatcher to Arizona and Sonora, Mexico, to find a refuge for the Saints.

March 1883—Martineau moved to Pima, Arizona.

June 14, 1883—Son Nephi Martineau married Emmaline Pamelia Knowles in the Endowment House.

1883—Martineau was called to be second counselor to President Christopher Layton, St. Joseph Arizona Stake.

May 17, 1884—Martineau attended the Logan Temple dedication.

September 11, 1884—Left Logan for Arizona and surveyed for Thatcher, Pima, and Graham.

3 1880 Cache County, Utah Census (FHL 1,255,335), 134B.

January 9, 1885—Daughter Julia Henrietta Martineau died of dropsy and was buried in the St. David City Cemetery, Cochise County, Arizona.

January 21, 1886—Son Charles Freeman Martineau married Eva Rosetta Rice in the Logan Temple.

April 18, 1887—Martineau was sealed to Jessie Helen Russell Anderson Grieve in Salt Lake City.

1887—Martineau became the mayor of Pima, Arizona, but because of his travels, he resigned the office within a few months.

August 18, 1887—He began compiling his "Book of Pearls."

September 13, 1887—Son George Albert Martineau married Emma Paulina Allred in St. George.

February 8, 1888—At age fifty-nine, he filed for a Mexican War Pension.

1888—He moved to Mexico and surveyed the town plats of Chuichupa, Dublán, and others.

June 27, 1890—Son Henry Augustus Martineau married Mary Ann Spendlove as a polygamist wife, Colonia Juárez, Chihuahua, Mexico.

October 6, 1890—Ending polygamy, the Manifesto was unanimously accepted by a vote in the general conference of the Church.

June 10, 1891—Daughter Elizabeth Martineau married Frank Knowlton Nebeker in Logan.

September 16, 1891—Daughter Virginia Martineau married Edward E. Sudbury in Logan.

November 23, 1891—Son Joel Hills Martineau married Mary Ann Thurston in Colonia Juárez.

November 18, 1892—Daughter Annie Sariah Martineau married Henry Samuel Walser in Colonia Juárez.

April 6, 1893—The Salt Lake Temple was dedicated by President Wilford Woodruff.

January 4, 1896—Utah entered the Union as the forty-fifth state.

April 22, 1896—Son Moroni Helaman Martineau died in Colonia Chuichupa, Chihuahua, Mexico.

October 26, 1896—Jessie Helen Russell Anderson Grieve died and was buried in the Salt Lake City Cemetery.

November 30, 1898—At age seventy, Martineau was ordained a patriarch by Elder Marriner W. Merrill.

October 20, 1900—Daughter Dora Martineau, age eighteen, died in Mexico.

January 6, 1901—Daughter Annie Sariah (Martineau) Walser married Edward Franklin Turley in Colonia Juárez.

March 23, 1901—Daughter Gertrude Martineau married Ernest Guy Taylor in Mexico.

March 23, 1902—Son Theodore Martineau married Josephine Thurston in Colonia García, Chihuahua, Mexico.

1908—As his age was beginning to show its toll, he returned to Utah.

September 30, 1913—Son Lyman Royal Martineau married Emmeline Cannon in Salt Lake City.

September 5, 1916—Daughter Virginia Martineau Sudbury married John S. Murphy in Salt Lake City.

July 13, 1917—At age eighty-nine, he applied for a military pension and received thirty dollars a month. His personal description was five feet ten and one-half inches tall, dark complexion, blue eyes, medium dark hair, occupation—printer.

November 12, 1918—Daughter Annie Sariah Martineau Walser Turley married Alvin James Hawkes in Salt Lake City.

December 5, 1918—Wife Susan Ellen Johnson Martineau died of bowel obstruction and was buried in the Salt Lake City Cemetery.

June 24, 1921—Martineau died at age ninety-three in the home of daughter Virginia Martineau Sudbury Murphy in Salt Lake City. Age ninety-three years, three months, six days, the death certificate reads: James Henry Martineau born March 13, 1828, at Mansfield, New York, son of John Martineau born NY and Eliza Mears born NY, died June 24, 1921, at 235 Iowa St., Salt Lake City, UT, of Uremia, Chr Nephritis, contributory senility and Hypostatin pneumonia; occupation—Civil Engineer; buried June 26, 1921, at Logan, UT; Undertaker, Carl Eddington. Informant—L. R. Martineau, 918 Logan Avenue.

Obituary, *Improvement Era*, August 1921:

Colonel James Henry Martineau, oldest civil engineer in Utah, veteran of the Mexican War, and pioneer of 1850, died at the home of his daughter in Salt Lake City, Friday, June 24, 1921. He was born in Amsterdam, Montgomery County, New York, March 13, 1828, and was the son of Doctor and Mrs. John Martineau. Coming to Utah as a non-"Mormon," in 1850, he taught school in Farmington that winter. Through the study of "Mormonism," he joined the Church shortly after. He later followed his profession as civil engineer, and laid out thirty-five towns and cities in Utah and Idaho, besides roads and canals, and many surveys of the public domain. In 1851 he was called to Iron county with President George A. Smith, remaining there until 1860. In July, 1860, he moved to Logan, occupying there various responsible positions in civil and religious affairs. In early days he was an Indian fighter and rendered active service in a number of campaigns in Utah. In 1884 he moved to Arizona and the next year to Mexico, where he continued in his professional labors, returning to Salt Lake City in 1903, where he spent the remainder of his life. He wrote a number of articles for home magazines, and was a fair writer of both prose and poetry. He filled with credit a number of offices in the Church, and during his later years, was a Patriarch. Impressive funeral services, at which remarks were made by Presidents Heber J. Grant and A. W. Ivins, were held Sunday, June 26, at the residence of his son, Hon. Lyman R. Martineau, one of his thirteen surviving children, and a member of the General Board of the Y. M. M. I. A. He leaves also numerous grandchildren, great-grandchildren, and great-great-grandchildren who are living. His body was buried at Logan.

JAMES HENRY AND SUSAN ELLEN JOHNSON MARTINEAU FAMILY

First wife: Susan Ellen Johnson
Born: 11 Jul 1836, Kirtland, Geauga County, Ohio
Married: 8 Jan 1852, Fort Johnson (near Parowan), Iron County, Utah
Died: 5 Dec 1918, Salt Lake City, Salt Lake County, Utah
Buried: 7 Dec 1918, Salt Lake City, Salt Lake County, Utah
Father: Joel Hills Johnson
Mother: Anna Pixley Johnson

Children:

1. Henry Augustus Martineau

Birth: 4 Nov 1852, Parowan, Iron County, Utah
Married: Editha Melissa Johnson, Mary Ann Spendlove
Death: 10 Oct 1941, Prescott, Yavapai County, Arizona
Buried: 12 Oct 1941, Prescott, Yavapai County, Arizona

2. Moroni Helaman Martineau

Birth: 12 Sep 1854, Parowan, Iron County, Utah
Married: Sarah Sophia Johnson
Death: 22 Apr 1896, Colonia Chuichupa, Chihuahua, Mexico
Buried: 23 Apr 1896, Colonia Chuichupa, Chihuahua, Mexico

3. Susan Elvira Martineau (Elvira)

Birth: 14 Aug 1856, Parowan, Iron County, Utah
Married: Benjamin Samuel Johnson
Death: 15 Oct 1942, Prescott, Yavapai County, Arizona
Buried: 18 Oct 1942, Prescott, Yavapai County, Arizona

4. John William Martineau

Birth: 7 Jan 1859, Parowan, Iron County, Utah
Death: 4 May 1863, Logan, Cache County, Utah
Buried: 1863, Logan, Cache County, Utah;
reburied with James Edward Martineau, 19 Oct 1880, Logan City Cemetery

5. Nephi Martineau

Birth: 11 Mar 1862, Logan, Cache County, Utah
Married: Emmaline Pamelia Knowles, Evelyn Eliza Holman
Death: 26 Feb 1951, Newdale, Fremont County, Idaho
Buried: 2 Mar 1951, Logan, Cache County, Utah

6. George Albert Martineau (Albert)

Birth: 22 Mar 1864, Logan, Cache County, Utah
Married: Emma Pauline Allred, Mary Ellen Kohlhepp, Emmeline Olin, Ida Billingsley
Death: 23 Jun 1957, Phoenix, Maricopa County, Arizona
Buried: 26 Jun 1957, Mesa, Maricopa County, Arizona

7. Joel Hills Martineau

Birth: 12 Jun 1867, Logan, Cache County, Utah
Married: Mary Ann Thurston
Death: 2 Jun 1955, Douglas, Cochise County, Utah
Buried: 6 Jun 1955, Douglas, Cochise County, Utah

8. Gertrude Martineau

Birth: 28 Sep 1870, Logan, Cache County, Utah
Married: Ernest Guy Taylor
Death: 9 Feb 1927, Phoenix, Maricopa County, Arizona
Buried: Date unknown

9. Theodore Martineau

Birth: 8 Sep 1872, Logan, Cache County, Utah
Married: Josephine Thurston, Nellie Ann Gurr, Celia Johnson
Death: 10 Jul 1954, Kanosh, Millard County, Utah
Buried: 12 Jul 1954, Salt Lake City, Salt Lake County, Utah

10. Annie Sariah Martineau (Anna, Annie, Anita)

Birth: 4 May 1875, Logan, Cache County, Utah
Married: Henry Samuel Walser, Edward Franklin Turley, Alvin James Hawkes
Death: 7 May 1963, Phoenix, Maricopa County, Arizona
Buried: 11 May 1963, Mesa, Maricopa County, Arizona

11. James Edward Martineau (Eddie)

Birth: 5 May 1877, Logan, Cache County, Utah
Death: 17 Oct 1880, Logan, Cache County, Utah
Buried: 18 Oct 1880, Logan, Cache County, Utah

12. Cora Colorado Martineau, adopted

Birth: abt 1842, near Parowan, Iron County, Utah
Death: 2 March 1867, Plain City (near Ogden), Weber County, Utah
Buried: Ogden City Cemetery, Ogden, Weber County, Utah

13. Dora Martineau, adopted

Birth: abt 5 Sept 1882, Logan, Cache County, Utah
Death: 18 Dec 1901, Colonia Juárez, Chihuahua, Mexico
Buried: 20 Dec 1901, Colonia Juárez, Chihuahua, Mexico

JAMES HENRY AND SUSAN JULIA SHERMAN MARTINEAU FAMILY

Second wife: Susan Julia Sherman
Born: 21 Oct 1838, Far West, Caldwell County, Missouri
Married: 18 Jan 1857, Salt Lake City, Salt Lake County, Utah
Died: 28 Jan 1874, Logan, Cache County, Utah
Buried: 29 Jan 1874, Logan City Cemetery, Logan, Cache County, Utah
Father: Lyman Royal Sherman
Mother: Delcina Diademie Johnson

Children:

1. Delcina Diadamie Martineau (Dellie)

Birth: 27 Nov 1857, Parowan, Iron County, Utah
Death: 23 Oct 1866, Salt Lake City, Salt Lake County, Utah
Buried: 24 Oct 1866, Salt Lake City, Salt Lake County, Utah

2. Lyman Royal Martineau

Birth: 21 Apr 1859, Parowan, Iron County, Utah
Married: Alley Thatcher Preston, Emmeline Cannon
Death: 4 Jan 1926, Salt Lake City, Salt Lake County, Utah
Buried: 7 Jan 1926, Logan, Cache County, Utah

3. Charles Freeman Martineau (Charley, Charlie)

Birth: 24 Jul 1861, Logan, Cache County, Utah
Married: Eva Rosetta Rice
Death: 20 Dec 1935, Logan, Cache County, Utah
Buried: 23 Dec 1935, Logan City Cemetery, Logan, Cache County, Utah

4. Jesse Nathaniel Martineau

Birth: 6 Apr 1863, Logan, Cache County, Utah
Married: Eliza Belle Johnson
Death: 19 Apr 1928, Chicago, Cook County, Illinois
Buried: 25 Apr 1928, Addison, DuPage County, Illinois

5. Julia Henrietta Martineau (Netta, Nettie)

Birth: 4 Feb 1865, Logan, Cache County, Utah
Death: 9 Jan 1885, St. David, Cochise County, Arizona
Buried: 10 Jan 1885, St. David, Cochise County, Arizona

6. Virginia Martineau (Jean)

Birth: 16 Jul 1870, Logan, Cache County, Utah
Married: Edward Sudbury
Death: 5 May 1947, Provo, Utah County, Utah

7. Joseph Herbert Martineau

Birth: 23 Apr 1873, Logan, Cache County, Utah
Death: 10 May 1873, Logan, Cache County, Utah
Burial: 11 May 1873, Logan City Cemetery, Logan, Cache County, Utah

8. Elizabeth Martineau (Lilla)

Birth: 13 Aug 1867, Logan, Cache County, Utah
Married: Frank Knowlton Nebeker
Death: 8 Apr 1953

MAPS

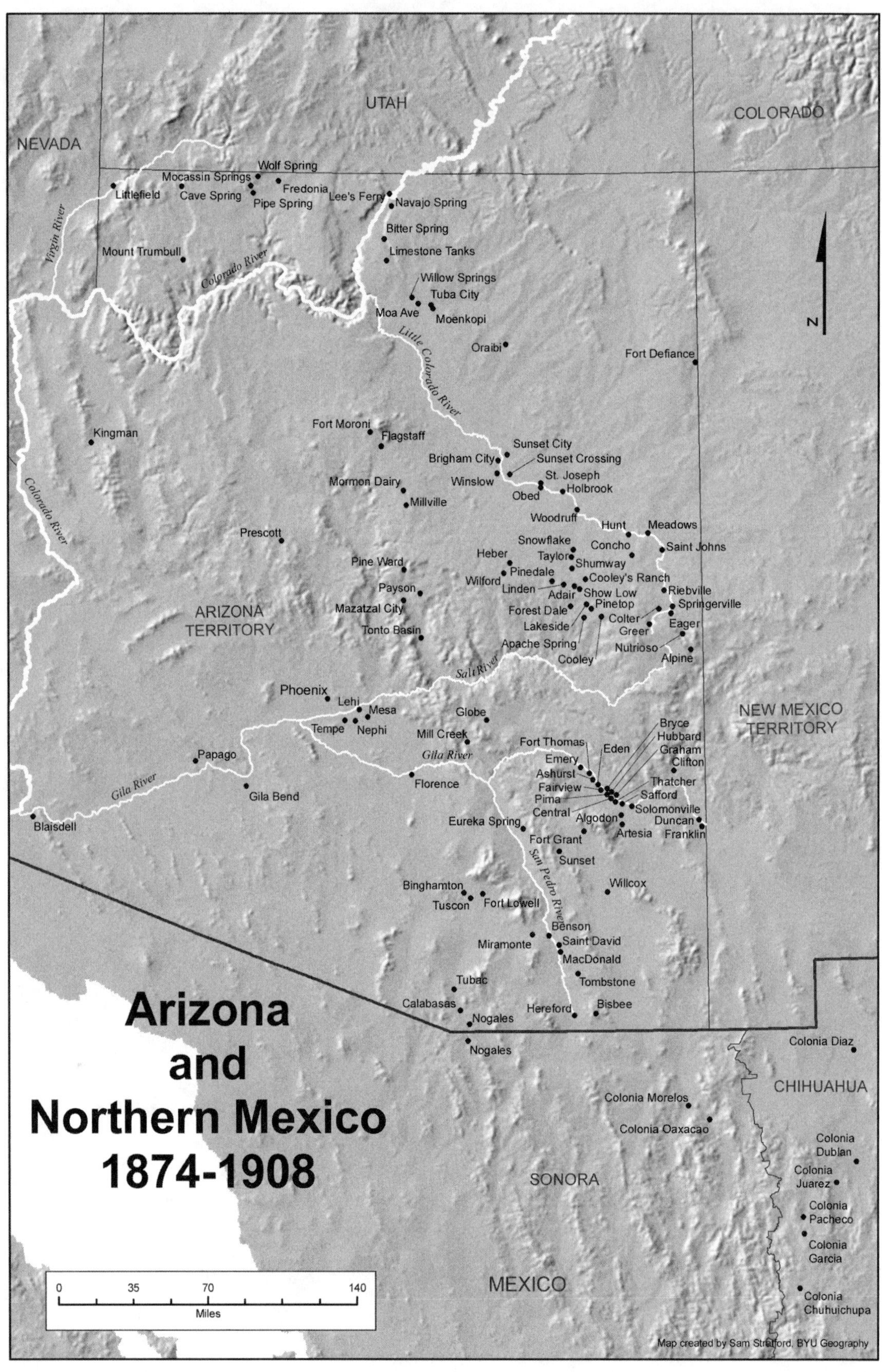
Arizona
and
Northern Mexico
1874-1908
UTAH
COLORADO
NEVADA
ARIZONA TERRITORY
NEW MEXICO TERRITORY
SONORA
CHIHUAHUA
MEXICO
N
Wolf Spring
Mocassin Springs
Fredonia
Littlefield
Cave Spring
Pipe Spring
Lee's Ferry
Navajo Spring
Bitter Spring
Limestone Tanks
Mount Trumbull
Virgin River
Colorado River
Willow Springs
Tuba City
Moa Ave
Moenkopi
Little Colorado River
Oraibi
Fort Defiance
Kingman
Fort Moroni
Flagstaff
Sunset City
Brigham City
Sunset Crossing
St. Joseph
Winslow
Mormon Dairy
Obed
Holbrook
Millville
Woodruff
Hunt
Meadows
Prescott
Concho
Saint Johns
Snowflake
Heber
Taylor
Shumway
Pine Ward
Pinedale
Cooley's Ranch
Wilford
Linden
Payson
Adair
Show Low
Riebville
Pinetop
Springerville
Mazatzal City
Forest Dale
Colter
Lakeside
Greer
Eager
Tonto Basin
Apache Spring
Nutrioso
Cooley
Alpine
Salt River
Phoenix
Lehi
Mesa
Globe
Tempe
Nephi
Mill Creek
Bryce
Hubbard
Fort Thomas
Eden
Graham
Gila River
Emery
Clifton
Papago
Ashurst
Thatcher
Florence
Fairview
Safford
Pima
Gila Bend
Central
Solomonville
Algodon
Duncan
Eureka Spring
Artesia
Franklin
Blaisdell
Fort Grant
San Pedro River
Sunset
Willcox
Binghamton
Tuscon
Fort Lowell
Benson
Saint David
Miramonte
MacDonald
Tubac
Tombstone
Calabasas
Bisbee
Hereford
Nogales
Nogales
Colonia Diaz
Colonia Morelos
Colonia Oaxacao
Colonia Dublan
Colonia Juarez
Colonia Pacheco
Colonia Garcia
Colonia Chuhuichupa
0
35
70
140
Miles
Map created by Sam Strafford, BYU Geography

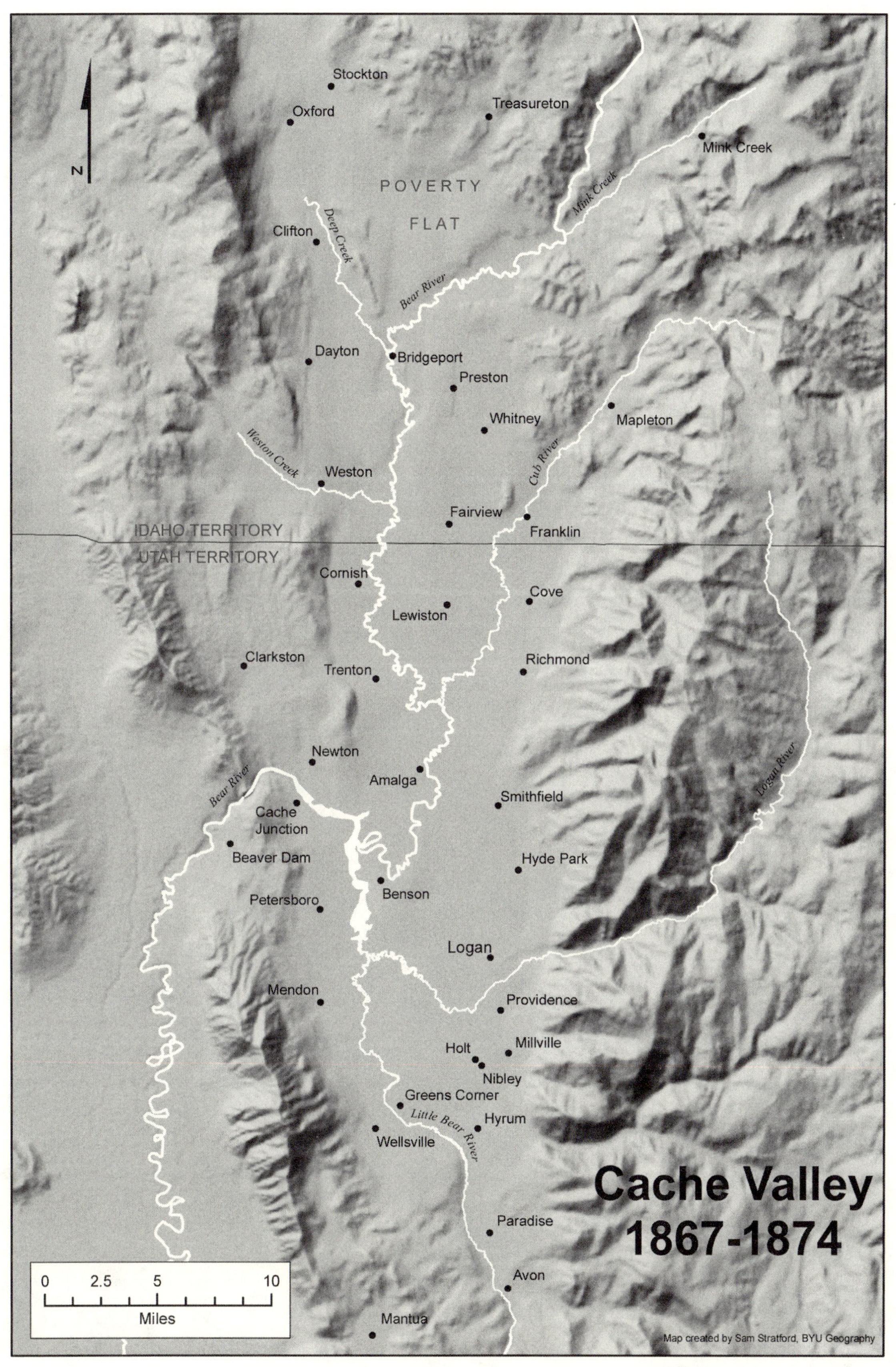
N
Stockton
Oxford
Treasureton
Mink Creek
POVERTY
FLAT
Mink Creek
Clifton
Deep Creek
Bear River
Dayton
Bridgeport
Preston
Mapleton
Whitney
Weston Creek
Weston
Cub River
Fairview
Franklin
IDAHO TERRITORY
UTAH TERRITORY
Cornish
Cove
Lewiston
Clarkston
Trenton
Richmond
Newton
Amalga
Bear River
Cache
Junction
Smithfield
Logan River
Beaver Dam
Hyde Park
Benson
Petersboro
Logan
Mendon
Providence
Holt
Millville
Nibley
Greens Corner
Hyrum
Little Bear River
Wellsville
Cache Valley
1867-1874
Paradise
Avon
0 2.5 5 10
Miles
Mantua
Map created by Sam Stratford, BYU Geography

Great Basin
1851-1867
Egan Range
Schell Creek Range
Snake Range
Sevier River
Deseret
Sevier Lake
Snake Creek Farm
Fillmore
Meadow
Hatton
Kanosh
Cove Fort
NEVADA
UTAH TERRITORY
Manderfield
North Creek
Adamsville
Lincoln
Beaver
Minersville
Greenville
Lower Beaver
Circleville
Spring Valley
Eagle Valley
Meadow Valley Farm
Paragonah
Parowan
Enoch
Summit
Panguitch
Cedar City
Hebron
Old Irontown
Hamilton Fort
Pinto
Kanarraville
Hamblin
New Harmony
Fort Harmony
Alton
Mountain Meadows Massacre
Pine Valley
Anderson
Pintura
Leeds
Little Zion
Gunlock
Glendale
Silver Reef
Toquerville
Mount Carmel
Washington
Springdale
Harrisburg
Virgin
Middleton
Northrup
Dalton
Santa Clara
Shonesburg
St. George
Duncans Retreat
Rockville
Tonaquint
Price
Grafton
Kanab
Virgin River
NEVADA
ARIZONA TERRITORY
N
0 15 30 60
Miles
Map created by Sam Stratford, BYU Geography

Western United States
1875-1900
MONTANA
OREGON
IDAHO
WYOMING
NORTHERN SHOSHONE
EASTERN SHOSHONE
KLAMATH
Eagle Rock
Pocatello
Soda Springs
Oregon Trail
Snake River
Marsh Valley
Grouse Creek
Paris
California Trail
Great Salt Lake
Evanston
NORTHERN PAIUTE
SHASTAN
Transcontinental Railroad
Locomotive Springs
Ogden
Mtn. Green
Farmington
Mormon Trail
Salt Lake City
Tooele
Coalville
Johnston's Army (1858-60)
Provo
Utah Lake
COLORADO
Camp Floyd
Santaquin
Harper
NEVADA
WESTERN SHOSHONE (GOSHUTE)
UTAH
Lake Bigler
Sacramento
UTE
Fillmore
San Francisco
Colorado River
MONO
Parowan
St. George
CALIFORNIA
SOUTHERN PAIUTE
Lee's Ferry
NAVAJO
HOPI
Las Vegas
APACHE
NEW MEXICO TERRITORY
HAULAPAI
Brigham City
St. Joseph
ZUNI
Snowflake
Saint Johns
San Bernardino
Los Angeles
ARIZONA TERRITORY
GILA
SALT RIVER
SERRANO
Phoenix
Mesa
San Diego
Mormon Battalion
PAPAGO
Saint David
Colonia Diaz
Colonia Morelos
Colonia Oaxacao
Colonia Dublan
Colonia Juarez
Colonia Pacheco
Colonia Garcia
Colonia Chuhuichupa
N
0 75 150 300
Miles
MEXICO
Map created by Sam Stratford, BYU Geography

PART

1

FAMILY HISTORY AND CONVERSION

Fig. 1.1—Heading to Volume 1.

[page 11][1]

PART FIRST,

containing my history from the beginning until my baptism into the Church January 19. 1851.

CHAPTER 1ST.

1828[2]—I, James Henry Martineau, son of John Martineau and Eliza Mears, was born on Thursday, March 13th 1828, I think near midnight, in the village of Port ~~Jackson~~, Florida, Amsterdam, Montgomery County, State of New York.

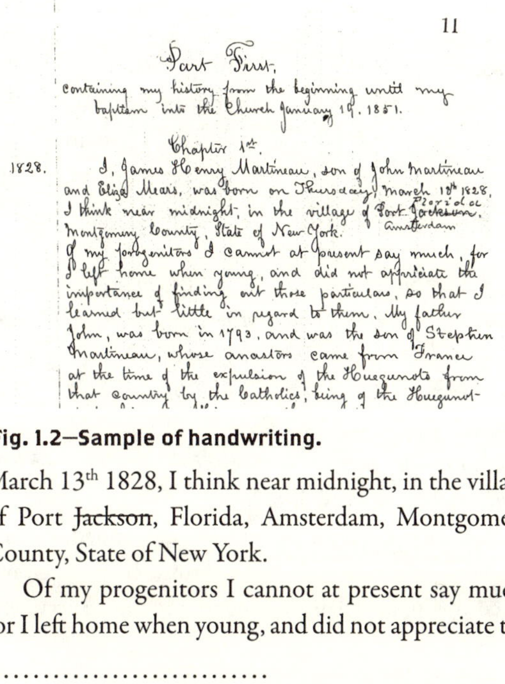

11

Part First,
containing my history from the beginning until my baptism into the Church January 19. 1851.

Chapter 1st.

1828. I, James Henry Martineau, son of John Martineau and Eliza Mears, was born on Thursday, March 13th 1828, I think near midnight, in the village of Port ~~Jackson~~, Florida, Amsterdam, Montgomery County, State of New York.
Of my progenitors I cannot at present say much, for I left home when young, and did not appreciate the importance of finding out those particulars, so that I learned but little in regard to them. My father John, was born in 1793, and was the son of Stephen Martineau, whose ancestors came from France at the time of the expulsion of the Huguenots from that country by the Catholics, being of the Huguenot-

Fig. 1.2—Sample of handwriting.

Of my progenitors I cannot at present say much, for I left home when young, and did not appreciate the

1 Bracketed page numbers represent numbering in the original journals. These numbers allow researchers to cross-check the transcription with the original. Numbering starts at page 11 because the first ten pages are letters from leaders of the Church (see Appendix 2). Martineau periodically inserted documents into the journal that he apparently later intended to write about. The editors have noted where these documents were and have placed the documents in the appendices.

2 While Martineau provides this date to give context to the period about which he is writing, it will become obvious that this was not written at this date but likely after his conversion to the Church. It appears he is thinking about more than short entries as he begins here with the heading "chapter"; however, this is the only place in the records where this heading appears.

importance of finding out those particulars, so that I learned but little in regard to them. My father John, was born in 1793, and was the son of Stephen Martineau, whose ancestors came from France at the time of the expulsion of the Huegunots from that country by the Catholics, being of the Huegunot stock himself.[3] His grandfather married a woman from Holland, also a Protestant expelled for religious faith, so that my father came of a well defined and sturdy stock. Stephen Martineau was a farmer living near New York City while it was occupied by British, and an anecdote is related of his putting Sir Henry Clinton[4] and his suit of officers to flight in revenge for being made at sundry times to stand beside the road hat in hand while the cortege of his Lordship passed by. Returning home from New York City with a large wagon and a splendid pair of horses, he saw Sir Henry and his staff about to meet him in a narrow cut of the road. With a slight motion of the reins he started his team on a furious run, pretending at the same time to try to restrain them. The officers supposing he would turn out, as usual, kept the road until he was almost upon them, and only escaped being run over by suddenly spurring up the hill on each side in very undignified fashinon, uttering oaths loud and fierce.

[page 12]

An officer threatened to shoot him, but Sir Henry interposed saying it was easy to see the Provincial was not to blame, because of his team running away.

[written in margin]

My g. grandfather was a major in Washington's army, and his father an officer in the "French & Indian War. his wife (my grandmother) was descended from the Hutchinson family, her grandfather being Lord Hutchinson His son (Lord Hutchinson's) my grand mother's Uncle, was an officer in the French & Indian War. and was killed by Indians at the Massacre of Fort William Henry. in N. Y. in Sept. 1754.

My Mother, Eliza Mears, was descended, on her mother's side from the Allen family, being a Grand niece of Ethan Allen of Ticonderoga notoriety. She was born in ~~Vermont~~ Fabius N. Y. April 13. 1806. (Died July 6. 1848.) Her father and mother, James and Lois Mears, were born in Berkshire County (I believe) Massachusetts, and moving in early life to Elbridge, Onondaga County, N. Y., then a wilderness, lived there many years, and raised a family of sixteen sons and daughters, all of whom married, except one son who died at about the age of twenty one or two.

He served a short time as a Militia man in the war of 1812, and was at the battle of Sackett's Harbor.[5] He was a contractor on the Erie Canal, where Syracuse, now a thriving city had then only a few shanties. In politics he was a "Whig," in religion, a Universalist, as was also his wife. He was emphatically an honest man and a good specimen from "the land of steady habits." Somewhere near 1860 he and his wife removed to Madison, Wisconsin, where many of his children lived, and in a few years they died, he at the age of 93 and his wife 91. When my Grandmother died, my name was on her lips: she said "Poor Jimmie." I was always a favorite with her, and many were the hours of planning between us, for the future. She was always saying that I would become a great man—and would be a preacher; which last proposition I always opposed

My mother being left a widow in 1838, we lived much after that with my Grandparents, who, though not wealthy, lived in comfort, having a small farm, and receiving some help from their sons, who were all well-to-do. They were very intelligent and well informed people, my Grandmother, especially being quite a politician. My Grandfather was the hero of the following adventure with a "ghost":—

[page 13]

He had been absent from home several weeks, and on returning he had traveled all day and most of the night, so as to get home. When within about a mile of home, at midnight, he was passing the grave yard, when by the light of the moon he saw an object in white passing among the tombstones, and finally sitting upon the roadside-fence. His horse saw it first,

3 Huguenots were French Protestants who fled their country to Germany and America.

4 Sir Henry Clinton was a British general in the American Revolution. His father was the governor of New York.

5 The Battle of Sackett's Harbor was part of the War of 1812 and was a significant victory for America's freedom. Sackett's Harbor was a main shipping port, naval base, and shipbuilding area on Lake Ontario in northwestern New York.

and was frightened. His first thought was that some one wished to scare him, but as no one knew of his coming, he dismissed that idea at once. He was no believer in ghosts, but as he slowly drew near, the thought arose—"perhaps there are such things—and this may be one." To go back was out of the question, and so, both he and his horse keeping a good look-out, he passed by. Seeing it did not follow him, he rode up to see what it was, and gave it a cut with his riding whip. With a scream of terror it fell to the ground, and with surprise he discovered it to be a neighbor's daughter, whose mother had died a few weeks before, and she had been to her grave in her sleep, and in her night clothes. He escorted her home, soothing her agitation as best he could. Had he not returned to her after he had gone by, he might have conscientiously declared he had seen a "ghost."

On another occasion while riding through the woods, accidentally looking up, he saw a catamount just in the act of springing upon him. Giving his horse a cut, the animal, instead of alighting on his shoulders fell upon the horse's rear and was soon dislodged, but pursued him some distance.

[page 14]

My father, who had been apprenticed to a Hatter, desiring to get a better education, ran away at the age of nineteen and went to England, where he remained seven years, and studied hard. He finally married Mrs. Hawkins widow of the Captain Hawkins who left 2 chil^{n} Samuel and Elizabeth. he had by her 4 children. He returned to America and landed at Baltimore, where he lost two children. The remaining two, Julia and Lucretia, remained with him until they married. Julia, the elder, married a Boston printer, named Winslow, and I never saw her again, and to this date, March 14. 1871, know not if she be living or dead, but I suppose she is dead. She was fiery, passionate and self willed, but of a generous noble nature. Lucretia was a mild, sweet-tempered, lovely girl, who married my Uncle Charles at the age of nineteen and died aged twenty-~~one~~ three, of Consumption,[6] and was buried at Elbridge, where also repose the remains of one or two grand uncles, my father, mother, my sisters Harriet and Frances Eliza. Many a pleasant summer evening she Lucretia used to sit on the porch with a flock of us children sitting around her knees, while she sung songs for us, as "the Carrier Dove," "Fading Still fading" and many other choice pieces.[7] She had no children.

[written in margin]

My father's first wife—Widow Hawkins, was ~~grand~~ daughter to the Earl Stanhope, who bequeathed her £18,000 [$1,912,826] and £1000 [$106,268][8] *to each of her children, but this money they never got. of her 2 children, Samuel & Elizabeth, Samuel became an under officer in the U. S. Navy & was in Com. Wilkes exploring expedition in 1840. I do not know what became of Elizabeth. Mrs Hawkins was related by marriage to the Earls of Bedford,*[9] *Earl Chatham, Earl Russell and Earl Chesterfield & E. Mints. My father's ancestors came to France from Italy, and were related to the Colonna family. They ran back into the old Roman Empire, and one, a young girl of our family—Martina, 15 years old, was burned alive as a Christian martyr in the year 235. Our family name in Latin is Martinus, (male,) and Martina (,female.)*

On the death of his first wife, my father married my mother, while his ~~only and~~ younger brother Peter, married my mother's sister Mary. Mother was married Apr. 29. 1824

My father practiced for years as a Physician and Surgeon,[10] until railroading attracted attention in the United States, when he followed Civil Engineering.

6 Consumption is a medical term from the eighteenth and nineteenth centuries. It is a progressive disease where the body wastes away. Today it is called pulmonary tuberculosis.

7 These songs are early American secular inspirational ballads.

8 The dollar amount in brackets represents the equivalent dollar amount for the pounds given in text at this writing. The pounds were converted using the conversation calculator at http://measuringworth.com/exchange/.

9 Earl of Bedford is a British title of honor.

10 The practice of medicine in the eighteenth and nineteenth centuries was mostly an art mixed with a little herbal science. There were no formal lengthy education or degree programs. To practice, the doctor gathered the common knowledge of the day and hung out a shingle. Children were delivered by midwives. The doctors were often involved in other enterprises. Patients were treated at their bedsides under constant care of their physicians. They brought as much compassion to the bedside as they did actual medicine (Robert F. Karolevitz, *Doctors of the Old West, A Pictorial History of Medicine on the Frontier* [Seattle: Superior Publishing, 1967]).

He was an Engineer on some of the first railroads in the United States built large bridges and finally acted as an Engineer on the New York Croton Aqueduct.[11] Through exposure he contracted the consumption, of which he died in 1838. He had at one time accumulated property to the amount of about $65.000 [$1,150,586];[12] but in 1837 lost nearly all in the great collapse which then occurred. When he died he was worth about three thousand dollars. leaving his family a house and lot, with a few acres of land in Elbridge, and 80 acres of Land in Branch county, Michigan: also two patent rights;—for a horse power, which for many years was the best, and for a "centre vent" water wheel, which was the best until the invention of the Turbine wheel.

[page 15]
These inventions brought him some money but more vexations from the constant infractions of his rights. He also invented a most deadly invention, to throw balls with great rapidity and precision, at the rate of about 60 a minute. He had a working model, which worked finely. It used no powder, but the balls entering at the centre of a wheel revolving with great velocity, were thrown by centrifugal force from its peripery. But thinking that there were already too many engines of death, he destroyed the model before he died. Until I left home I kept the fragmentary wheels &c.

He was well educated, and emphatically a self-made man, of the Methodist church, and a Whig, but never much of a politician. He was a very good, moral and honorable man. He died at Elbridge, in my Grandfather's house, in which also Lucretia and Harriet died.

[written in margin]
Raritan & Delaware Canal.[13] *began 1831—contracts ~~then~~ let for work by letter Nov. 7, 1831. Same letter—father was Chf. Engineer on Camiden & Amboy R.R.*[14] *at date Nov. 7. 1831 & uncle Chauncey Asst. Eng. on same*

[written in margin]
She married Apr. 29. 1824.

My mother was born in 1806, in [left blank] in Vermont. I do not know the year she married my father. She had six children by my father, viz:—

Emily Henrietta, born in 1825; myself, born 1828; Charles Augustus born in 1831 Jan. 19 who died 1831 Feb. 27; Francis Eliza, born in 1831, Sept. 31, who died 1847 June 15, aged 15½ years; Harriet born 1835 May 26, died 1837 Oct. 16 and Lois Elenor born in Aug 10 1838. After father's death she lived a widow several years, and then married William Babcock, a widower with one son Edward, a little younger than myself. By him she had a son—Charles, who, at the age of 17 died a soldier near Murfreesboro, of measles.

She was a Baptist, and a good woman, but did not live very happily with her husband who was a straight-laced Presbyterian, and endeavored to prevent her from attending her own church. After her marriage she lived near the small town of Victory. Cayuga County, New York, her husband having a good farm there. She died 1848, July 6, and was buried at Elbridge.

[page 16]
My sister Emily H. married a Presbyterian Minister, David C. Lyon—and now (1871,) lives at St Paul, Minnesota, having two children, John and Fannie. Lois, married a Hollander, John Voswinkel; and now lives in Chicago, having also two children.

My Uncle Peter, also a Civil Engineer, now quite an old man lives in Milwaukee, Wisconsin with my Aunt Mary never having had any children.

11 The Croton Aqueduct was important to the development of New York City. It was a brick tunnel that delivered water to the growing metropolis from 1842 to 1955. Construction of the aqueduct began in 1837 and ended in 1842 with the first flow of water. Today it is one of the New York state parks.

12 To give meaning to Martineau's dollar figures throughout the journals, the editors have utilized an online inflation calculator at http://www.westegg.com/inflation/. The dollar amount in brackets represents the equivalent dollar amount at this writing. This data is extracted from the *Historical Statistics of the United States* from 1975 and allows comparisons of the 1837 dollar to the current value.

13 Today this system is known as Delaware and Raritan Canal State Park. Most of the system constructed still remains. After it opened it was a busy navigation route, delivering Pennsylvania coal to New York.

14 The Camden and Amboy Railroad was the first railroad to operate in New Jersey.

MYSELF.

Having thus spoken of my relatives, I now proceed with my own history.

1828—Born in 1828, when two years old my little baby-brother Charles died, and I remember my mother as she held him on her knee, weeping, and of two men bringing in his coffin which they placed on two chairs in a corner of the room.

While very young, my parents resided two years at Georgetown District of Columbia, having in the family two negroes, a mother and her son, whom my father brought north from Huntsville Alabama—slaves—and set free. He started with the father also, a very fine man—but on the journey north the Captain of the boat knocked him overboard before the eyes of his wife and son, without trying to save him or to let any one else do so, notwithstanding all my father could say. All the redress the law allowed, was his price as a chattel. The son afterwards became a burglar and when last I saw him in 1846 was in the Auburn State Prison for ten years. Although only about 26 years old, having been in prison five years, his wool was as white as that of a sheep.

In 1835 we lived on Staten Island, and I remember seeing the Great Fire in New York City at that time, living ten miles from the city.[15] I also remember the great display of the Aurora Borealis in 1837. In this year my father failed through the fall of real estate in which he had invested heavily, and we returned to live in Elbridge where he soon died.

[written in margin]

1837

[page 17]

1840—In 1840 my uncle William Mears, a merchant living at Fultonville, Montgomery County N. Y. sent for me to come to him, and my journey of 143 miles by rail, alone, was my first experience in traveling. The journey occupied three days, on account of the snow, which was deep in places.

1843—I lived with him about a year and returned home. and in 1843 went to live with him again, remaining another year, then returning home. I went to Munro Academy[16] with my sister Henrietta until 1845 when I went into my Uncle Peter's store as clerk in the village of Sennett, Cayuga County, N. Y. He and I used to play chess, and I often beat him, which annoyed him. Once I detected him making a false move, accused him of it, had a fuss, and ended by determining to leave him, but finally gave it up.

When I left the Academy which I had attended since I was nine years of age at intervals, I had a good knowledge of English and Latin Grammar, Arithmetic, Geography, History, Natural Philosophy, Algebra, Chemistry and Geology, and at the yearly examinations always received prizes, as did also Henrietta.

One year, my mother being unable to pay my tuition, I made fires and swept the rooms of the building, often jeered by my more wealthy schoolmates. Being fully determined to get an education, I did not allow this to hinder me.

After my father died, an intimate friend of his, named Pearson, very wealthy, deliberately robbed my mother of her property in Michigan, and of the benifits of my father's inventions. She trusted him implicitly. This made us poor.

When about 12 years old there was a revival of religion in Elbridge, by the Baptists and Presbyterians, my mother and I joined the Baptists, on account of their doctrine of immersion. For this I was subjected to much ridicule from my young companions.

[page 18]

1846—In 1846 I went to Auburn to learn the art of printing working in the office of the "Cayuga Tocsin." I remained for some time in this business, making myself useful as a hand, until I was overcome by the desire I had from my youth to become a Soldir, and enlisted as such to serve in the Mexican war. I was to start for the seat of war on the train at 2 P.M. and at noon my mother walked into the tavern where I was

15 The Great Fire of New York took place December 16–17, 1835. It destroyed hundreds of homes and buildings, both public and private, in the heart of the city (Kim Taylor, *The Great New York City Trivia and Fact Book* [New York: Cumberland House Publishing, 1998]).

16 This is likely the Munro Collegiate Institute, then simply called the Munro Academy, Elbridge, New York. It was founded in 1835 by Nathan Munro (Dwight H. Bruce, *Onondaga's Centennial* [Boston: Boston Publishing, 1896], 700).

and demanded my release from the Recruiting officer. Being under age, he had to give me up, much against my wish. I had enlisted unknown to my mother, but she had accidentally ascertained the fact, living 20 miles north at Victory, and came for me just in time.

I can now see that I was a brute to do as I did; but I did not see it then. I had always wanted to be a soldier. I subsequently got a chance to enter the navy as Midshipman, but through her tears, gave up the idea.

Feeling that the ridicule of my office mates was too much to bear, I left the office, spent a few month at home on the farm, and then went to Milwaukee to live with my uncle Peter. I traveled with Henrietta on the Erie Canal some days together, she going to visit her uncle Chauncey Mears, living in Western New York.

[written in margin]

Enlisted May 7, 1847

I did not live long with Uncle Peter, not liking him, and went to work in the office of the "Milwaukee Sentinel." I could not resist the sound of the drum and fife, however, and soon enlisted again, for the General Service, for the war, under Lt. A. W. Wright. Being very ardent in my new profession, I soon mastered the Tactics and was made "Lance Corporal." I also served as clerk, making out enlistment papers, pay rolls, and other returns.

January 8, 1848—at noon I had my picture taken.

Early in March our party of recruits, 130 in number, started to Newport Barracks, Ky; by way of Lake Michigan, Huron, St. Clair & Erie to Toledo, Ohio, whence we went by Canal to Cincinnatti, Ohio, thence crossing the River to the Barracks. Being highly recommended by Lt. Wright, I was attached to the permanent party at the Post.

[page 19]

1848—This Post was the point to which all infantry recruits were sent for instruction from all the northern states west of New York, and there was always a large number of recruits there, being sent down to Mexico as they became drilled and equipped, their places being filled with new faces.

Here I served as drill sergeant, as clerk in the Commissary office and finally as clerk in the Superintendents office, Cincinnatti. This was a good place, which I held until I became very sick and had

Fig. 1.3—Army officer James Henry Martineau at age twenty years. Courtesy of James Henry Martineau Family Organization.

to go to the Hospital, where I nearly died. On coming out of the hospital, being to feeble to drill, I was sent on the recruiting service to Cleveland, Ohio, traveling from Cincinnatti to Xenia, 80 miles, by railroad, that being the only railroad in the state. About two miles from Cincinnatti the Locomotive ran off the track on a high embankment about 60 feet high, and we narrowly ~~we~~ escaped destruction. Two passengers went back to the city on foot, thinking it was because we started on Sunday.

From Xenia I traveled by coach to Cleveland, being three days and nights on the road. I had a rough ride over the "Corduroy roads" and was almost shaken to death, but on arriving at Cleveland found myself well. The next day after my arrival, Gen[l] Cass made his famous "noise & confusion" speech, which killed him politically.[17] In a few days orders came to break up the

17 This is likely Lewis Cass, a statesman who was elected to the United States Senate in 1845 but resigned his seat prior to service when he was nominated as a Democratic candidate for the presidency (Frank B. Woodford, *Lewis Cass: The*

station, and we started for Cincinnatti by way of the Akron and Beaver Canal, thence down the Ohio to Newport Barracks. I had a very pleasant trip of about 1000 miles.

Soon after arriving, peace was declared, and we were mustered out of service, and paid of [off], being cheated out of considerable of our pay by the officers. I procured citizens clothes, and started for Milwaukee via St. Louis, the Illinois Canal and Chicago. I had a pleasant trip.

[page 20]

July 6, 1848—This day, while I was at St. Louis on my way home, my mother died. I did not know it until I arrived at Milwaukee, and then I felt as if almost all ties to Earth [were] severed. Had there been a chance I should then have enlisted again as a soldier for life.

I went into the large bookstore of Hale & Chapman as Clerk, where I remained awhile, until the spring of 1849, in March.

March 1849—I determined to go to california to the gold mines,[18] thence to travel round the world. This my relatives opposed, but as I was resolved, Uncle Peter bought the land I had received of Government as Military bounty, 160 acres, giving me $160 [$3,599] for it. It was located near Madison, Wisconsin. I started across the plains with a Mithodist preacher and his wife, and an Irish gentleman named Russell. I left Milwaukee by steamer to Chicago, where I arrived at the time of the great destruction of shipping by the ice. From Chicago we traveled by ox team through Illinois, crossing the Mississippi at Quincy to Palmyra in Missouri: thence by Gallatin to Andrew County, near St Joseph. We had a very tedious journey, the roads being almost bottomless, and all the prairie flooded with water. Add to this our total inexperience in driving cattle, and our plight may be imagined but not described.

Arriving at St. Joseph, we found all the emigrant companies had left the frontiers, and all the citizens advised us not to think of attempting to cross the plains alone, so we all concluded to remain until next spring.

I soon got a situation to teach school, but the trustees told me they thought I might not be able to go through the quarter, as the big boys had a habit of running off or thrashing the teachers. I however accepted, and had very good success. I first tried to win the love and esteem of the scholars, and by joining to this a little just severity at the start, got along very well. The worst scholars became my best ones. One little incident I will relate. About christmas, on going to the school house, which stood in the woods alone, I found the door shut, and on trying to enter, found it barricaded inside, and could hear the partially suppressed tittering of the pupils trying in vain to keep still.

[page 21]

1849—I inwardly was amused, but put on a show of wrath and bluster. After a little, a paper was poked under the door to me, being a notice, that unless I would treat the school to a bushel of apples and five pounds of candy, they would duck me in the creek. I pretended I would break in, and told them I would not treat. They piled more benches against the door, and I, intimating I would get help to break in, went home, saddled my horse and went about five miles to the Settlement and spent the day amusing myself. Going home about sundown, I saw my scholars just going home, having waited all day for me to come back. Seeing me at the same time, coming home from town, they saw they were sold, and felt so cheap that none of them ever hinted at the circumstance again.

While in Missouri, I taught school three quarters in the same place, and had offers from several other and larger districts at the same time. I had a fine horse, and I enjoyed myself much riding over the prairies and hunting rabbits, prairie chickens and squirrels. I also learned to dance, and took great pleasure in it. On one occasion, some of "our set" of boys proposed to go across the prairie 8 miles to an acquaintance, and have a dance. Accordingly four of us, each with a girl

Last Jeffersonian [New Brunswick, NJ: Rutgers University Press, 1950]).

18 The California gold rush created one of the largest westward migrations in the history of the nation. It began with the discovery of gold in January 1848 near Sacramento. A crew of men, under the supervision of James Marshall, were building a sawmill along the American River for John Sutter when gold was discovered. Six of those men were members of the Mormon Battalion working their way back home to Utah (Eugene E. Campbell, "The Mormon Gold Mining Mission of 1849," *BYU Studies* 1, no. 2 [Autumn 1959/60]: 20–31).

riding behind him, rode over to the man's house, asked for permission to dance there, which he readily granted; turned his bed and chairs out of the room, (he had but one) invited him and his wife to join in, and went at it. We danced that day, (Saturday) all that night, next day, and all next night, till ten o'clock Monday morning. I left at 6 [A.M. or P.M.—the A & P are on top of each other] in order to be home in time for my school. There were six boys and five girls in all, and we were trying to see which could out-dance the others, boys or girls. The girls beat, and would, I believe, have cheerfully danced another day and night.

I made my home with Mr. Isaac Todd, who lived near Rochester, who had two daughters. Rachel and Ellen the latter of whom seemed to like me very well, but she was too uneducated for me to marry although I liked her very well.

[page 22]

1849—But I never gave her cause to think I wanted her, lest she might lose a chance for an offer from some one else.

In the spring myself, Russell, and a man living there named Peter Keener, got ready to start for California. We bought our bacon, the very best quality, for 1¼ cents per pound. We crossed the Missouri river on the 13th of May 1850, and waited a day, during which we cut down an immense Cottonwood tree for honey, or which we got two lubs full. The tree was about 8 feet in diameter.

We left the River May 15th on our long march. When out about ten days, I took the cholera,[19] from eating too much dried beef and bathing in Wolf creek while warm. I was taken at noon, and fainted away before I knew I was sick. I took treble doses of cholera medicine, of which we had plenty, but all to no purpose—it had no effect, and by bed time I was given up to die. I was not afraid, but felt lonesome at the thought of lying there alone in the desolate prairie, where my sisters could never see even my grave. I made disposition of my property among my companions, and at midnight as I lay thinking, having long ceased to take any medicine a ~~thought~~ voice came to me "plainly, "You will not die," and I said in answer "if so, I will take it as a sign from the Lord that He has a work for me to do; if not, and I die, all right." The voice said again "you will not die". I surely heard the voice and knew it was from some messenger of the other world. My disease ceased at once, and in the morning I was perfectly well, except weakness, from which I did not recover until two weeks. On the road I often wondered what work I would have to do, feeling that I had a work to perform because I had recovered, but finally concluded my work would be that of a Missionary to the heathen.

We passed up on the south side of the Platte, and saw some most terrible thunder storms, for which that valley is justly celebrated.

I visited Chimney Rock and engraved my initials upon it, and also Independence Rock.[20] At the Devil's Gate, I narrowly escaped death, in the following manner: I had been to the top of the rock—four hundred feet in perpendicular height, and thought I would come down another way.

[page 23]

I commenced climbing down a narrow gully, and I suddenly found myself on a narrow ledge 350 feet above the ground—a perpendicular precipice. I tried to go back, but could not. My train had gone on and I was alone with no one to help me. I found it impossible to go back. Arond [around] a sharp corner of the rock was a ledge, which, if I could reach, would lead me to safety; but how to reach it! My only chance was to swing by a small root growing in a crevice about as thick as my finger. I pulled on it, to try its firmness, but it seemed not very firm, and I was afraid my weight would pull it out as I should swing round over the precipice. But there was no other way, and if I fell, my death would be quick. So I grasped it, swung around the crag, and just succeeded in catching the ledge with my foot—and I was safe. Thanking God for my escape, I hastened down, and got to camp about 9 o'clock P.M. They thought I was lost.

19 Cholera is an infectious disease characterized by diarrhea, vomiting, and cramps.

20 Martineau's party is following the Mormon Pioneer and Oregon-California Trail on his route. Chimney Rock is in southwestern Nebraska and Devil's Gate in south-central Wyoming. Both locations are prominent in the Mormon migration.

At the next-to-the-last crossing of the Sweetwater, our company lay by a day to fix the wagons, lighten up, &c, as our teams were getting weak and giving out. I went south to hunt, and after traveling about 3 or 4 miles, I saw an antelope. He was too far off, so I lay down, and used my red handkerchief to toll him up to me. He came about 100 yards nearer and I fired, but missed him. I followed him about five miles, and almost gave him up, when I came to some large rocks, among which I hid until I got a good shot and killed him. I took the four quarters and some of the tender loin. Being hungry and very thirsty, I built a fire, and tried to cook some meat on the end of my ramrod, but the wind blowing hard, the fire spread and got so hot I could not come near it, and had to eat my meat raw. I started back to camp, but suffered greatly with thirst. One quarter fell to the ground, and I left it. Next I threw away the tender loin. I looked all round for some sign of moisture, but could see nothing but a small green spot of grass about a mile off.

[page 24]
I went to it, and eat some of it in hope to dampen my mouth, but the grass stuck all round my mouth as though glued there, and I worked long to get it out again. I started back again for camp, but soon threw down another quarter. By this time my tongue was swelled very much, and was as dry as a chip. Finally, almost given out, I reached the river and lay down to drink. I knew the danger of drinking too much, but did not care for the consequence. I drank as long as I could,—rested a little, and drank again, then forded the river and got to camp with two hind quarters of my antelope.*

[written in margin]

**After supper, as I sat on the front end of the wagon, talking with a companion, I suddenly fainted and fell forward into his arms, remaining insensible until the next day as we journeyed onward. I was sick until near G. S. Lake. It was caused by my hunting adventure's hardships.*

Another day previously, on the sweetwater,[21] I crossed a high range of hills on the south, and pursued four buffalo until finally I got ahead of them in a hollow up which they were coming, led by a magnificent bull. As I lay there in weight [wait], my heart almost failed me. I could see the ferocious glare of his eye—and he looked the incarnation of fury and strength. He weighed about 1200 lbs, was fat and glossy. I knew that when wounded they often turn upon their assailant, and there was not the slightest place of refuge for me—not a rock or bush. If I wounded him, and he should turn on me my death was sure, for my rifle carried a small ball just right for rabbits, squirils &c. But to follow game nearly a day,—and then not shoot—I could not stand it; and as he came within about four rods, I shot him through his ribs, but too high to hit his heart. Away he and the rest dashed,—I after them, but they soon got out of sight. When I got back to camp, the men gave me a severe reprimand for my foolhardiness, saying it was a wonder they did not turn and trample me to death.

Thousands of wagons crossed the plains this season, and probably a million dollars worth of cattle, wagons, provisions, clothing, goods, and in fact, almost everything was strewn along the road. Sometimes we would see a huge pile of good bacon and other things. Our company and I also, threw away much property, as our team weakened.

[page 25]
I kept a journal, and had in it many sketches which I made, but before reaching Salt Lake City, some one stole it. I took and wore a jacket, which had belonged to a cholera dead man.

We arrived at the South Pass July 7th 1850, and in the night had a heavy snow storm. Here we debated hours as to our future route;—whether to go by Fort Hall or by Salt Lake City. I and Mr. Peter Keener, a Pennsylvanian with whom I boarded some time in Missouri, wished to go through the latter place; all the rest being Missourians, advocated the Fort Hall route, saying the Mormons would surely kill or at least rob us. I argued that if we minded our own business and were careful, we would not be molested, and I wanted in future years to say I had "seen the Mormons." We traveled on, and at the junction of the Fort Hall road, we halted and argued for several hours, until Keener and I carried our point, and we took the Salt Lake Road. Soon after this, I was taken sick, and was hauled about 150 miles.

21 This would be the Sweetwater River in Wyoming, not far from Devil's Gate.

We entered Salt Lake Valley through Parley's Cañon, a new and wretched road. The scenery through the Wahsatch Mountains was sublime. In some places towering cliffs rose perpendicularly a thousand feet. When we entered the valley, it seemed as if we had entered fairy-land. We got in on the 22nd of July, and the fields of waving grain, of fine gardens and flowers,—after seeing nothing but grass and sage plains for three months—were charming to the senses. We entered the city, which was stragglingly built, drove through Emigration Street west to near the Old Fort in the 6th Ward,[22] and camped near the Jordan to rest a week and recuperate. The Old Fort was still inhabited. While driving through town people came out to know if we had any thing to sell, as Cows, clothing, provisions, wagons, oxen, &c offering to sell us vegetables, butter &c.

I had been told on the journey that the Mormons lived in common together, like cattle, and were all thieves and murderers. But I could see nothing of all this, but on the contrary, the people impressed me very favorably indeed; so much so, that after staying two or three days I determined to remain with them until the next spring to study their religion and customs, so as in after years to have an opinion of them of my own.

[page 26]

I accordingly settled with Keener and Russell, and stayed. They went on to California in a few days, and I never heard from them since. I hired out to Mrs. Danl Jones[23] for a few days to help in haying, at $1.50 [$33.74] per day and board. She lived on the west side of Jordan in a dug out.[24] I worked a week and then hired to William Walker,[25] of Farmington for the season, for $25.00 [$562] per month and board & mending. I worked with him all summer, helping him harvest his wheat, which was selling for $10.00 [$225] per bushel in gold when I entered the valley. I reaped about ten acres. I also helped him to build a house, dig a well, &c.

In September an express came from Brown's settlement (now Ogden) with news of an indian raid, and the killing of a white man. We got the word at midnight, and by nine o'clock next morning there were three companies of Cavalry and one of artillery on the ground. The indians had fled, taking 17 horses and considerable plunder besides. We followed them as far as Bear River (North) but did not come in sight of them. We camped on Box Elder creek where Brigham City now is. Going back, we had a false alarm and chased what we thought a party of indians for about two miles, when we found they were a scouting party of our own. We got back home again without further incident. I went in place of William Walker, in Capt. Burton's company of Life Guards, of which James Furguson was a 1st Lieutenant.[26]

At the beginning of winter I went to live with William Rice, and began to inquire seriously into the truth of Mormonism.[27] I went to the city to get some clothes made, and the woman to whom I was directed, finding I was not a Mormon began preaching to

22 A *ward* is a local governing branch of The Church of Jesus Christ of Latter-day Saints presided over by a bishop. It is comparable to a parish in a Catholic setting. Weekly worship, general meetings, and neighborhood activities are organized around a ward. A ward is often named and numbered by location. Multiple wards make up a *stake,* a regional governing unit.

23 There are several Daniel Joneses in Mormon history. Daniel W. Jones was one of the most noted. He was a leader of an independent wagon company during the migration. In 1856 his party suffered greatly at Devil's Gate. Later he was sent by Brigham Young to the Mexico-Arizona Mission (F. LaMond Tullis, "Early Mormon Exploration and Missionary Activities in Mexico," *BYU Studies* 22, no. 3 [Summer 1982]: 289–92, 300, 303).

24 Dugouts were common dwellings used while the early pioneers moved and settled throughout the West. A dugout was a temporary home constructed simply by excavating a hole from the side of a hill or riverbank. The hole was covered with planks or available shrubbery and provided shelter.

25 This is likely William H. Walker. He was among the first missionaries sent to South Africa in 1853.

26 These are likely Robert T. Burton and James F. Ferguson. Burton arrived in the Salt Lake Valley in 1848 and served in the Utah Militia. He was captain of the cavalry. Later he would serve as counselor to William B. Preston, the Presiding Bishop of the Church. Ferguson served in the Mormon Battalion and was an adjutant general in the Utah Militia. He was guarding the Beehive House when Johnston's army arrived in 1858 (Norma Baldwin Ricketts, *The Mormon Battalion: U.S. Army of the West, 1846–1848* [Logan, UT: Utah State University, 1996], 21).

27 William K. Rice accompanied Martineau to Parowan.

me. I argued against her until near night when I had to return home. She lent me "Spencer's Letters," which I took home and read, believing it all as I read.

[page 27]

Baptized

1850—It seemed as though it was good sense, and as if I had always known it to be true. Mrs. Picket,—widow of Don Carlos Smith,—lent me "The Voice of Warning."[28] This I thought was a wonderful book—I believed Mormonism all but one thing—I could not think Joseph Smith a Prophet. I believed him a good man, like Luther, Calvin or Wesley, but Prophets, I thought were no more. I could hardly believe the Book of Mormon—one word was my stumbling block—Isabella—

January 19, 1851—This name I thought, was a native of Europe, and could not have been known to the aborigines. I afterwards got a book from Martin H. Peck on the Authenticity of the Book of Mormon (by Winchester) and desired to be baptized.[29] We went to the Tabernacle block, and after looking up and down some time, found a place deep enough to baptize me in, and thus on the 19th of January 1851 I became a member of the Church of Jesus Christ of Latter Day Saints, being baptized by William McBride.[30] I was confirmed at the water's edge. All my thoughts now were—I'm a Mormon—a feeling of joy and thankfullness that I had been made a partaker of the truth of the Gospel. I knew I should incur the displeasure of my relatives, but for this I cared not. Money is nothing when placed in the balance against truth.

[written in margin]

*Jan. 19 Bapt^d^*

As I expected, my relatives were angry, and all of them, except my two sisters Henrietta and Lois, ceased to correspond with me. I also had one letter from my cousin Napoleon B. Van Slyke.

About this time I resolved to move to Iron County, to help make a settlement there, in company with Wm K. Rice. At this time people were invited to migrate there, and Geo. A. Smith was appointed to preside over the undertaking.

I was baptized at noon, [blank] Jan. 19, 1851, by W^m McBride and confirmed by him where temple later stands

February 8, 1851—This day I was ordained a Seventy, under the hands of Jedediah M. Grant,[31] in company with over a hundred others.

March 5, 1851—Myself and Wm K. Rice this day started for Iron County distant about 260 miles from Salt Lake City.[32]

[page 28]

March, 1851—We had a wagon and three yoke of oxen, with grain, potatoes &c. for seed. We stopped all night at Salt Lake City and I went to Father John Smith, Patriarch,[33] and received the following blessing:—

March 6, 1851—A blessing by John Smith, Patriarch, upon the head of James Henry Martineau, son of John and Eliza, born Montgomery Co. N.Y. March 13th 1828.

Beloved brother, I lay my hands upon thy head in the name of Jesus of Nazareth, and seal upon you a father's blessing. Thou hast received the Gospel in lieu of gold, and the Lord is well pleased with the choice

28 Don Carlos Smith was a brother to the Prophet Joseph Smith.

29 Little is known about Martin H. Peck. He was baptized in Dannville, Vermont, in 1833. The Winchester book Martineau read could have been one of several books authored by Benjamin Winchester. Winchester wrote *The Gospel Reflection: In Which the Doctrine of the Church of Jesus Christ of Latter-Day Saints Is Set Forth, and Scriptural Evidence Adduced to Establish It* (Philadelphia: Brown, Bicking & Guilbert, 1841). The book is of pamphlet size and published while Winchester was in Philadelphia heading a branch of the Church. Copies are rare; one was found in the L. Tom Perry Special Collections, Harold B. Lee Library, Brigham Young University, Provo, Utah.

30 William McBride was a patriarch of the Richfield Utah Stake. He served as a missionary in Hawaii and on his way home from his mission he was commissioned to purchase a printing press.

31 Jedediah M. Grant was the father of Church President Heber J. Grant and second counselor to President Brigham Young from 1854 to 1856.

32 The Iron Mission was organized in 1850 to meet the needs for iron ore in building the State of Deseret. These mines were located near what today is known as Cedar City, Iron County (Morris A. Shirts and Kathryn H. Shirts, *A Trial Furnace: Southern Utah's Iron Mission* [Provo, UT: Brigham Young Univ. Press, 1991]).

33 This is likely John Smith, who was the Church patriarch from 1849 to 1854.

thou hast made. He hath given his Angels charge over you, they will minister unto thee and teach thee great things. Thou art of the blood of Joseph, and a lawful heir to the priesthood, which shall be sealed upon you in fulness in due time, teaching you all the hidden mysteries of the Redeemer's kingdom, giving you power to do miracles, even to rebuke the waves of the sea, and to cause the blind to see, the deaf to hear, and the lame to walk, and the dumb to speak, and to do all things that is necessary for the prosperity of thy work. Thou art Called to go to the nations of the earth, thou shalt bring thousands to a knowledge of the truth, and lead them to Zion. The great and the wise shall submit themselves unto thee. They shall consecrate their gain to the Lord, and their substance to the God of the whole earth. Thou shalt lead them to Zion with their riches. Thou shalt have a companion to assist thee, and raise up a posterity that shall be mighty among the Hosts of Israel. Inasmuch as you live faithful and seek for it, thou shalt see all things fulfilled which the prophets have spoken, concerning Zion, and enjoy all the blessings of the Redeemer's kingdom, for ever and ever. Amen.

PART

SETTLING IN SOUTHERN UTAH: INDIAN WARS AND THE GOLD RUSH

[page 29]

WM. K. RICE AND I GO TO IRON COUNTY

March 1851—We left Salt Lake City and traveled through Provo, which was a small fort. I attended a ball in the Log Meeting house, and saw three of the sisters so drunk that they fell down upon the floor. Alex Williams, who sold liquor close by, gave them wine mixed with brandy; they, thinking it only wine, drank too much.

There was also a small settlement just beginning at Springville, and also at Petieetneet Creek, there were three or four houses just building. Here we lay by for several days, waiting for the rest of the Company to arrive. This settlement was afterwards called Payson, in honor of Capt. James Pace, one of the first settlers. Here I was sick for several days, with the piles,[1] so I could hardly turn in bed.

Elders. C. C. Rich and Amasa M. Lyman,[2] with a large number of saints arrived on their way to San Bernardino, in Southern California to found a new settlement, also several men bound like myself to Little Salt Lake. Pres^t^ B. Young, with H. C. Kimball Willard Richards and others also came up to give the saints their final instructions. They did not wish to see so many people leaving the country, with their flocks and herds, and tried to dissuage them from going, but to no purpose. Also Parley P. Pratt & company.[3]

We were organized in companies of tens and fifties, and we set out in the first company, consisting of the first California ten, and eight wagons going to Little Salt Lake. We left March 24, 1851, with P. P. Pratt & Co.

On Wednesday April 9th 1851 we arrived at the new settlement on Center Creek (now called Parowan) and

1 These are hemorrhoids.

2 Charles Coulson Rich was an Apostle from 1849 to 1883. He resided in Paris, Idaho (Leonard J. Arrington and Davis Bitton, *The Mormon Experience: A History of the Latter-day Saints* [Urbana, IL: Univ. of Illinois Press, 1992], 103–5). Amasa Mason Lyman was an Apostle from 1842 to 1867. He was influential in the settlements of San Bernardino, California. Excommunicated in 1867, Lyman had become involved in an experimental spiritual movement (F. Ross Peterson, *A History of Cache Valley* [Salt Lake City: Utah State Historical Society, 1997], 135).

3 Parley P. Pratt (1807–57) was a leading Apostle and prolific writer.

found Elder Geo. A. Smith and about 100 souls, who had got there in the December previous. Our journey was accomplished without any accident, or incident worthy of notice. The settlement was called Louisa, in honor of Louisa Beeman, ~~one of~~ the first who entered into polygamy. in this dispensation.[4]

[page 30]

April 1851—All the companies halted a few days at Summit Creek seven miles south of Louisa, and a general meeting was held, at which Elders Rich, Lyman, and Smith spoke, and tried to persuade some to stop and settle at Louisa, but without effect, and they all passed on.

Rice and myself took thirty acres of land, but only put in 12½ acres, in wheat and potatoes, on account of the scarcity of water. The ground was so dry, that the water went right down and would not spread much, except with a large stream.

During the summer, the indians annoyed us much, stealing our stock. They stole a horse from Rice. We often followed them up, but never caught any of them. Some Ute indians brought news of the fight at Tooele, which caused the indians to behave better. During the Summer Geo. A. Smith resigned his presidency to return to Salt Lake City, and Elisha H. Groves was appointed in his place.[5]

April 13, 1851—I joined Capt. James A. Little's[6] company of cavalry as a private, but was immediately elected 3d Sergeant, which position I held until November, when Geo. A. Smith came back to Parowan, as it was now called, and organized a Regiment. Geo. A. Smith was elected Colonel; James A. Little Lieut. Col; and Mathew Caruthers Major; John L. Smith Adjutant,[7] and myself Sergeant-Major.

May 11, 1851—I omitted to state that on May 11th Prest B. Young[8] and the leading men, came down to Louisa, and spoke highly of the labors performed. At a public meeting held in the unfinished log meeting house, the name of the place was named Parowan, an Indian word The night before he arrived, snow fell six inches deep, but soon melted away again.

[written in margin]

First name of Parowan was Louisa

September 15, 1851—This day the first Territorial election was held, at which I officiated as Clerk of Election.

November 17, 1851—I was elected City Recorder of Parowan City, and clerk of the County court.

[written in margin]

Dance

In the summer Walker came one Sunday and had us all dance on the dusty ground in clouds of dust. He said we did not know how and he would show us. His men then danced, & he told us "now you see how men should dance."

[page 31]

1851—I taught school about a month, and gave it up near christmas, much to the indignation of Judge Lewis who tried to brow-beat me in a public meeting.

January 8, 1852—This day at a quarter past 9 P.M. myself and Susan Ellen Johnson[9] were married by John L. Smith, at Fort Johnson, situated twelve miles west of Parowan. There were a few couples invited besides. When we retired to rest, our bed was made on the floor, bedsteads being scarce. The next night we slept in a wagon box, and on Jan. 12th began keeping

4 Beeman is said to have been one of Joseph Smith's first plural wives. She was also sealed to Brigham Young.

5 George Smith was an Apostle from 1839 to 1875. He served as Church historian and counselor to President Brigham Young (Glen R. Stubbs, "A Biography of George Albert Smith, 1870–1951" [PhD diss., Brigham Young Univ., 1974]; Daniel H. Ludlow, ed., *Encyclopedia of Mormonism* [New York: Macmillan, 1992], 3:1326–29). Little is known about Elisha Groves. He was born in Kentucky in 1797 and ordained a high priest on September 10, 1833.

6 James Amasa Little (1822–1906) was a pioneer in southern Utah. He joined the Church in St. Louis in 1849 and migrated to Utah in 1850. He lived in Parowan, Cedar City, and Kanab, Utah.

7 Mathew Caruthers was a member of the stake high council. John Lyman Smith was likely the brother of George Albert Smith and was the first counselor to Elisha H. Groves, president of the Iron Mission in 1851 (Morris A. Shirts and Kathryn H. Shirts, *A Trial Furnace: Southern Utah's Iron Mission* [Provo, UT: Brigham Young Univ. Press, 1991], 124, 229).

8 Brigham Young (1801–77) was the second President of the Church.

9 Susan Ellen Johnson was fifteen years old at the time of her marriage. She was the daughter of Joel H. Johnson. They were married for sixty-seven years.

Fig. 2.1—Susan Ellen Johnson Martineau, first wife of James Henry Martineau. Courtesy of James Henry Martineau Family Organization.

house in a building I rented in Parowan. I had only known Susan a few weeks, but could see no use for a long courtship. I rented a one room log cabin, dirt floor.

January 12, 1852—Our stock of household goods was not very extensive, mine consisted of two iron spoons and a Serape, or Mexican blanket. She had two quilts, a towel, a few pounds of feathers and a few other little things, and a few cooking utensils borrowed. We also had one chair, and a hen. In the spring we went to live by the farm 2½ miles from town, having made a kind of dug-out in which to eat and cook, with a wagon box for a bed room. We lived there for several weeks, when one night I was away Susan heard some one prowling around, and in the morning we found tracks made by some one. We moved back into town again.

I boarded Urban Van Stewart for several weeks, and when we came to settle, he managed to bring me in debt, greatly to my astonishment.[10] He was a regular skinner, and once when he owed me, gave me some wheat rotten and stinking. He it was he who caused the indian fuss at Ogden,—I have before mentioned, by his killing White-Cloud, the Shoshone chief, for taking some of his garden stuff.

May 13, 1852—This evening, at about 8½ P. M. Susan and I were sealed by Elder Geo. A. Smith, in company with Jesse N. Smith and others.[11]

May 7, 1852—Pres^{t} B. Young & Company arrived and gave us much praise for our labors. I was introduced to him.

[page 32]

1852—During the winter I acted as Tithing Clerk, recieving but little pay;[12] I also served as Sergeant Major, Recorder for Parowan city, Clerk of the Municipal Court, and Clerk of the Probate and County Courts. For most of this I received but very little pay, and spent a great deal of time for the public, but I considered I was doing good, and did not grumble. I also studied Astrology under John Sanderson,[13] and had made considerable progress. Abut spring, I concluded to give up that study, also that of magic, thinking it too sharp tools for me to work with.

Abut [about] this time I had thoughts of going down to the Rio Virgin[14] to help build a new settlement, being coaxed to do so by John D. Lee.[15] Cotton, grapes and fruit can there be grown in profusion.

10 Urban Van Stewart was married to Mary Ann Jones. They lived in Beaver, Utah.

11 Jesse N. Smith was noted for his good judgment and knowledge of the gospel. He was first counselor to John Calvin Lazelle Smith, president of the Parowan Stake in 1855. Martineau was second counselor (Shirts and Shirts, *A Trial Furnace*, 125).

12 Tithing today is a contribution made by members of the Church that fund activities. In pioneering days, a tithing clerk was the individual within the stake appointed for collecting the tithes.

13 Not a lot is known about English immigrant John Sanderson. In 1852 he was forty years of age and a member of the choir (Shirts and Shirts, *A Trial Furnace*, 51, 438).

14 This would be one of the numerous settlements along the Virgin River in southern Utah. Today, Zion's Canyon, Hurricane, Washington, and St. George are in this area.

15 John D. Lee was a prominent southern Utah colonizer. He is notorious for his involvement in the Mountain Meadows Massacre, which took place in September 1857. In this incident a group of Missourians and Arkansans migrating across the plains was massacred. Lee would later be tried and executed for his involvement (Leonard J. Arrington, *Brigham*

June 3, 1852—I ~~joined~~ organized a club to lecture, on being solicited, not because I thought I could do much, but to improve myself in speaking, so that when called to go as a missionary, I can do some good.

About this time I had a dream, as follows:—

I thought I stood on the bank of a very wide river, clear, deep and with an even current, with a vast multitude of men and women who were being baptized by a fine portly man, with a good countenance and hair about half gray. As he looked round he saw me, and beckoned me to come and assist him. My duty was, as each person was baptized, to reckon up the value of the various items of their property, and sum it all up. I saw that as each person went forward, he gave in a list of his property, which I was to reckon up as before stated. This dream surely means something. The interpretation, as I had it, is, that I shall have much to do in the business affairs of the church, and that to a certain extent, it is my Calling. This dream I had before I was called to assist in any public business.

I also think that the time will come, when a person who joins the church will at the same time give in all his property.

[page 33]

June 18, 1852—Moved up from the field, and rented Benj. Jone's[16] house for $1. [$23] per month.

Being very poor, and spending so much of my time for the public for nothing, and seeing others working for themselves, I had thoughts as to whether I ought to still do so or quit it. I finally reasoned thus, that although I did not get much available pay, I gained a rich experience, and I would still try to be useful to the church and do all the good I can, trusting to the Lord for my reward.

Saturday, September 4, 1852—To day it rained hard, reminding one of the States. Last year hundreds of acres of grain were lost because of the scarcity of water. We made a canal about 6 miles long to bring the waters of Red Creek into our field, but the ground was so dry that we never could get the water to run into the field. It all soaked away or else it evaporated before it got there, although at the upper end there was a large stream constantly running in.

When Pres[t] Young and the Twelve first came to Parowan, Pres[t] Kimball prophesied, that the water would increase in this country as the necessities of the people require it; and said "write it down."[17] I do so.

[written in margin]

He said, "As the people increase in these vallies, and their necessity for water increase so shall the waters increase. Write it down, for it is true." It was true.

This season many persons apostatized from this mission on account of the hardships and privations, scarcity of water &c. There were no stores, no market, no money, no medicines, and not much of anything except hard work. We had, in the first season (1851) to fence our fields, make many miles of water ditch, put in and raise and harvest our crops, build houses, make cañon roads, build mills, herd and guard our cattle and horses and make frequent expeditions after thieving indians. No one can imagine what a burden of labor this was, except those who have the experience. Add to this, standing guard every three or four nights, and no wonder people got tired of it.

My own experience in 1851, was something like this:—After working hard all day, with nothing but dry bread and water, to come home to camp at night, milk the cow then make a pot full of thickened milk, or take a cup of bread and milk.

[page 34]

1852—This diet, continued for weeks and months, finally became so tiresome, that I often vomited as soon as I ate.

How did we get our meal! One of the settlers had a large kind of Coffee mill, in which we could grind a peck of wheat in about 20 minutes. Round this would stand eight or ten tired and hungry men, waiting for their turn to grind. The meal when ground, was very coarse—only fit for mush.

Young: American Moses [Urbana, IL: University of Illinois Press, 1986], 176, 259, 279–81, 285–86; Juanita Brooks, *The Mountain Meadows Massacre* [Norman, OK: Univ. of Oklahoma Press, 1991]).

16 At this writing, no Benjamin Joneses match this entry.

17 This is likely Heber Chase Kimball, first counselor to Brigham Young.

In 1851 William Rice bought an indian girl, a prisoner—from a band of Utahs,[18] and just before leaving the settlement, they stole her away, in order to sell her again at some other place. We went up to their camp to demand her, one Sunday morning. There were about a dozen of us, armed with rifles. They had sent off all the squaws and pack animals, except the wife of the chief and her pony, which she had not finished packing, leaving fifteen warriors well mounted and armed to bring up the rear. They denied all knowledge of her, and were about to leave, when John Steele, our leader, told Bob Gillispie to go and seize the squaw's horse.[19] He did so, and I was then sent to help him keep it. An indian rode up and struck the pony to make it break loose, but both Bob and the squaw held tight—the squaw trying to drag the horse away, jabbering all the time. The Chief had not yet mounted, but stood under a Cedar, with two of our men watching him, with finger on trigger and looking him in the eye. His men had surrounded us, each behind a bush or tree, with rifle leveled and cocked, waiting for the word from the chief. In his tight fix he could not give it, and as he stood there, looked like a very demon, his eyes flashing fire and his lip quivering. Once he made a motion as if to raise his gun, but Wm Rice lowered his muzzle a little, to cover him better, and he became quiet again.

Meantime the other indian, determined to get the pony, tried to ride his horse over me, but knowing he could not if I stood straight up like a post, I did so and the horse sheered off one side.

[page 35]

1852—I yelled at him, for my patience was giving out, and he also took to a tree with rifle cocked. Seeing we could do nothing by talk we started for Camp, about ¾ of a mile off, taking the pony with us,—keeping our rifles cocked and leveled on the indians, ready for battle. The squaw went along with the horse, holding him back by the halter all the way. Several times the indians seemed about to fire on us, but would give it up again. The Chief shot his own horse, he was so mad. When we got to the fort, I was told to keep the horse, but the squaw almost got him away from me before I knew it, although surrounded by fifty people. She tied a knot in his tail for a stirrup, and had almost mounted him, whip in hand, ready to dash away, when my attention was called to her just in time to prevent her daring feat.

The indians found we would not give up the horse unless we got the girl, and as she was miles away, and not come-at-ible, they brought another little indian, a boy about three years old, and gave him in place of the girl and went away. Two days after the girl came back, having escaped from her abductors. So Rice had two indians. The girl—about 13 years old—I named Cora; the boy William named Mosheim, and he kept and raised them in his family.[20]

In this adventure, our lives hung on a hair. Nothing saved us but the awkward position of the Chief. When we got home, Rice thought he would clean his gun, but found he could not shoot it off, it being empty. He was in a pretty fix, but did not know it until all danger was over. My own gun, (a borrowed one) was about as bad.

Rice moved back this fall to Farmington, and sold me an old, lazy yoke of oxen, for $130. [$3,040] on credit. I had borrowed a wagon of Father-in-law Johnson.

We built a two story adobie house, making the adobies ourselves; we also got our own lumber, and rock. I laid the foundation. Rice sold the house to Edward Dolten in the fall.

[page 36]

1852—A settlement was made on Coal Creek called Cedar City, for the purpose of making Iron, and settled mostly by poor English saints.[21] We in

18 This could be William R. Rice or William K. Rice. The tribes of Utah included the Utes, Shoshones, Paiutes, Goshutes, and Navajos. The Church worked to maintain positive relationships, but it was not always easy (Shirts and Shirts, *A Trial Furnace*, 437; Ludlow, *Encyclopedia of Mormonism*, 2:981–85; Ronald W. Walker, "Toward a Reconstruction of Mormon and Indian Relations, 1847–1877," *BYU Studies* 29 [Fall 1989]: 23–42).

19 This is likely Robert Hemphill Gillispie (1829–65), also a newly married resident of Parowan.

20 This is Cora Rice, born circa 1842 in Washington, Utah. There was little information related to her family or her life in the source material. A search for Mosheim Rice revealed no information.

21 The Martineau journals are of critical historical importance as illustrated here because they provide a firsthand account of the development of southern Utah. Parley P. Pratt was

Parowan, were called upon to labor in helping build a furnace &c.

Brigham prophesied on his first visit, that this would be the richest part of the Territory eventually.

September 1852—A few weeks since Br. Philip K. Smith[22] found another vein of coal in Coal Creek cañon, better than the other, and in a better place. He was repairing the road and found it by an accident. We rejoiced much at this discovery.

August 29, 1852—I was appointed Tithing Clerk again, in place of Chapman Duncan.[23]

September 24, 1852—We learned that at a Conference held in August, over 100 Elders were appointed to go on foreign missions, among them Chapman Duncan and James Lewis[24] were appointed to go to China. I felt quite a desire to go too, because I expect to go at <u>some</u> time, and now I have but little family to hinder. But I do not wish to go, unless called by authority.

A few days since Bishop Tarlton Lewis appointed me one of his counsellors; but I declined, because I felt that I was too young and inexperienced. This was on Sept. 18th/52. As he still said he desired me to act, I consented.

Friday, October 1, 1852—To day I bought some valuable books to the amount of $24. [$562] of Mrs. Carter, wife of A. W. Babbit, now on her way to California.[25] I gave a silver lined six keyed flute, bowie knife, 100 gun caps and some other small items. I also traded oxen with her and got a good wagon to boot, for which I was very thankful. I can now let my father-in-law have his again.

This day Richd Harrison and Geo. Wood of Cedar started for Salt Lake City with a pig of iron,—the first fruits of the iron works.[26]

Sunday, October 17, 1852—To day John D. Lee baptized fifty eight indians—Pah-Eeds and four whites, who were confirmed in the evening. We had considerable trouble to get their names. Nearly all the tribe have now been baptized

Monday, November 1, 1852—To day I was appointed Church Recorder in place of James Lewis, who is going on a Mission to China.[27]

[page 37]

December 15, 1852—Yesterday forty Elders arrived from the north on their way to San Diego, California, among whom was Benj. F. Johnson, Susan's uncle, on his way to the Sandwich islands.[28]

As I was helping to measure oats for the missionaries, I stood in the mud and snow barefooted, having

the first to camp in Parowan, during the winter of 1849–50. Exploring the area he found a significant deposit of iron ore (Janet Burton Seegmiller, *A History of Iron County: Community above Self* [Salt Lake City: Utah Historical Society, 1998], 23). Brigham Young was quick to organize the Iron Mission and called missionaries to develop and settle the area (Seegmiller, *History of Iron County*, 57–71). In December 1850, George Albert Smith led the first group from Provo to Parowan (Seegmiller, *History of Iron County*, 44–54). Cedar City was first called Little Muddy, then Coal Creek, and then named for the "cedar" (actually juniper) trees prevalent in the area. There were many attempts to process the iron and coal from the area, and a good deal of ore was shipped to California, Colorado, and other Utah smelters, but none of the Iron Mission efforts fulfilled expectations (Shirts and Shirts, *A Trial Furnace*, 409–20).

22 Philip K. Smith is more than likely Philip Klingersmith. He was a Cedar City bishop and a leader in the Iron Mission (Shirts and Shirts, *A Trial Furnace*, 124, 156, 390–91).

23 Chapman Duncan (1812–1900) was born in Bath, New Hampshire. He joined the Church when he was twenty years old. He wrote a brief account of Parowan's settlement in 1852. He was the clerk in the Parowan Canal Company (Shirts and Shirts, *A Trial Furnace*, 127, 244, 429).

24 James Lewis was the county recorder (Shirts and Shirts, *A Trial Furnace*, 74).

25 This is likely Almon W. Babbitt, one of the leaders of the Saints in Kanesville, Iowa. During the effort to establish the State of Deseret, Babbitt was appointed a representative to Congress with the charge to carry the cause of statehood (Ludlow, *Encyclopedia of Mormonism*, 1:371; Dale L. Morgan, "The State of Deseret," *Utah Historical Quarterly* 8 [1940]: 65–251; Arrington and Bitton, *Mormon Experience*, 53, 163; Arrington, *Brigham Young*, 234–35).

26 Richard Harrison and George Wood were among the original settlers of Cedar City (Shirts and Shirts, *A Trial Furnace*, 172–73, 178–79).

27 Four brethren were selected to go to China. They were James Lewis, Hosea Stout, Walter Thompson, and Chapman Duncan. They left for the mission from San Francisco on March 8, 1853, and arrived in Hong Kong on April 27, 1853. Their mission was cut short due to the Taiping Rebellion.

28 Benjamin F. Johnson (1818–1905) was one of the original members of the Council of Fifty.

no shoes, Uncle Benjamin gave me an old pair of his, for which I pray God to bless him forever. They were about four inches too long for me, with high heels. After wearing them a few weeks, the heels stuck out behind like a rooster's spur. There were no shoes to be bought in Parowan, those having leather or shoes being able to keep them.

Thursday, November 4, 1852—This day my son Henry Augustus was born at 20 minutes past 12 (at night)[29] The moon was in the last quarter, and not up yet. He weighed 8½ pounds. Before retiring to rest, we named, blessed and consecrated him to the Lord.

For a good while before Henry was born, we had been very destitute of clothing and food. I had only one old shirt, an old ragged pair of pants, no coat or vest. Susan had no dress even, and no shoes. As the time for her confinement drew near, and we had not the slightest article to cut up or make for the expected one, and could buy nothing for want of money, we knew not what to do. A rich man owed me $11.00 [$257] for work I had done to be paid in lumber. I stated my extreme circumstances, and as he had a great abundance of all kinds of goods,—flannels, domestics, Calicoes, &c I tried to get some. He refused me any. I then offered to give him the whole amount for one half the value in goods. No. I then offered the whole debt if he would give me two or three dollars worth of flannel. He refused, saying he would pay lumber as agreed, but would pay nothing else. His wife also owed my wife for washing, three yards of domestic, but she also refused to pay even that, although she knew our peculiar circumstances.[30]

[page 38]

1852—At the last, I had the good fortune to borrow .95¢ of Father, with which I got a little flannel just in time. Susan lost her courage but once, and cried a little. I said "Did you ever know a child born and go naked? She said "No". Well, said I, I don't think ours will be the first to do so". She said she guessed not, and dried her eyes.

Fig. 2.2—Henry Augustus Martineau, son of James Henry and Susan Ellen. Courtesy of James Henry Martineau Family Organization.

I cannot help thinking that the Lord will reward that rich man and his wife some time. as he deserves.

When Henry was born, there was a furious snowstorm raging, and the room was full of fine sifting snow which fell all around in the room. But by the blessing of the Lord, my wife did not take cold.

Sunday, November 21, 1852—To day Geo. A. Smith returned to Salt Lake city, having organized the Iron Company, consisting of 13 members, each of whom are to pay $100. [$2,338] for a share.

In the evening Erastus Snow and Franklin D. Richards arrived and preached in the hall. Br. F. D. Richards and ~~Ephraim~~ Tarlton Lewis blessed my son Henry, giving him the promise of great blessings.[31] It

29 Henry Augustus Martineau later lived in Prescott, Arizona. He passed away October 12, 1941. He is the first of thirteen children born to James Henry Martineau and Susan Ellen Johnson.

30 Martineau began to write for the newspaper on November 6, 1852. Eventually he would be considered a frontier reporter (*Deseret News*, November 6, 1852). Martineau's articles are online at http://www.lib.utah.edu/digital/unews/; hereafter referred to as Utah Digital Newspapers.

31 Tarlton Lewis (1805–90) was bishop of the Parowan Ward (Seegmiller, *History of Iron County*, 50).

was prophesied that Henry should live long, his days be filled with usefulness, Should prophesy, bring thousands to a knowledge of the truth, and be shining ornament in the Kingdom of God.

Monday, November 22, 1852—A severe snow storm began to day, lasting until noon of the following day. It fell 8 inches deep—unprecedented in this part of the country

Before Geo. A. Smith went, he counseled me to continue clerking for the church, and trust in the Lord, which I intend to do if I can.

Thursday, December 2, 1852—This day a party of brethren drove out 150 horses of Walker's band of Utahs, which they had turned into our field of grain, some of which was gathered in and some still in the shock. They (the Utes) said the land was theirs, and they should put their horses where they pleased. We told them if they put them in our field we would turn them out. They said if we did, they will destroy our settlement.

[page 39]

1852—It blew over for the time, but on the next Sunday they turned in about 200 horses again, declaring to the brethren who tried to hinder them, that they would put their horses where they pleased, adding many threats. After turning out their horses, the indians spent the night in the war-dance and yelling like devils. We spent the night in preparing for battle, running bullets &c. On the following morning, the indians seeing that we would not give in, did so themselves, and went away with their animals. Our decision had a good effect—the indians never again tried to brow-beat us. We dreaded the result, but felt that if we showed weakness, they would run over us more than ever.

December 7, 1852—To day C. C. Rich and A. Lyman with a small party arrived from San Bernardino, and we had a party in the evening. Br. Grouard[32] was also there, just returning from a seven years mission in the Pacific. Br. John Murdock[33] was also there, just returning [from] a mission to Australia.

December 25, 1852—Had a party to night.

In the latter part of this month, we received the printed revelation on marriage.[34] Pres^t J. C. L. Smith and John Steele[35] preached on it, and Mrs. Samuel West also spoke in favor of it, being the first woman who ever advocated the plurality of wives in Iron County.[36] May she be forever blessed.

January 10, 1853—To day, at the request of the authorities, I began teaching school, at the rate of one bushel of wheat pr day, which we call $2.00, [$47] but in reality only about $1.50 which is a very small price.

Sunday, January 16, 1853—To day Bp. Henry Lunt of Cedar,[37] gave us a good discourse, followed by Pres^t J. C. L. Smith, who cautioned us to be on our guard against the Utahs, who make great threats. We also received the Deseret News, brought by three men.[38]

A few days ago the Utahs fell upon a band of Pah-Eeds near the iron spring, killed 15 or 20 and captured

32 Benjamin Grouard was a missionary in French Polynesia.

33 John R. Murdock served in the Mormon Battalion and at one time directed the mail service between Independence, Missouri, and Fort Laramie, Wyoming. At this time he was serving on the high council of the Beaver Stake (Andrew Jenson, *Latter-day Saint Biographical Encyclopedia: A Compilation of Biographical Sketches of Prominent Men and Women in the Church of Jesus Christ of Latter-day Saints* [Salt Lake City: Andrew Jenson History Company, 1901–36], s.v. "John Murdock").

34 This a reference to the first public announcement of the practice of plural marriage. That announcement became official on August 29, 1852 (David J. Whittaker, "The Bone in the Throat: Orson Pratt and the Public Announcement of Plural Marriage," *Western Historical Quarterly* 18 [July 1987]: 193–314).

35 J. C. L. Smith served as stake president in Iron County. He worked as a local attorney as well as superintendent of the iron works (Shirts and Shirts, *A Trial Furnace*, 217, 416, 464). John Steele was a member of the Mormon Battalion. His journals are in the L. Tom Perry Special Collections, Harold B. Lee Library, Brigham Young University, Provo, Utah.

36 Samuel West was among the early Cedar City settlers who participated in the exploration for iron ore (Shirts and Shirts, *A Trial Furnace*, 263, 453).

37 Henry Lunt was among the Iron Mission settlers. He later became a bishop in Cedar City (Brooks, *Mountain Meadows*, 180).

38 The weekly *Deseret News* began June 15, 1850 (Monte Burr McLaws, *Spokesman for the Kingdom: Early Mormon Journalism and the* Deseret News, *1830–1898* [Provo, UT: Brigham Young Univ. Press, 1977]).

a number of squaws and papposes, which they will probably sell somewhere.

[page 40]

January 23, 1853—To day Dr. Wm A. Morse died, being the first in any of the settlements south of San Pete.[39] At the request of Prest Geo. A. Smith I collected items of his life, and forwarded to the Historian's office for record.

Monday, February 7, 1853—To day I moved into my new house. It is a small one, 16 feet square, with a lumber roof. It is built of adobies. I built it in the face of many difficulties, and thank the Lord for being able to do even so much. Susan helped me lay the adobes.

Wednesday, February 16, 1853—To day an indian brought word that two brethren had been killed by the Big-Muddy indians seven sleeps previously.[40] But we found they were two gentiles that were killed. They started for California with no animals or arms, and probably intended to steal an outfit. On the 17th 17 men went south to learn full particulars, and found it as above stated.

Saturday, February 19, 1853—To-day was organized a Branch Council of Health. Prest J. C. L. Smith was chairman and myself Secretary of the meeting. Much good instruction was given. About forty persons became members.

Monday, February 21, 1853—To-day John Steel and five others, who had been south to the Rio Virgen for emigrant iron returned, having gathered up nearly three tons of iron, in tire, bolts, &c. Most of it they left at Cedar to help on the iron works.

Tuesday, March 1, 1853—This evening, myself and nine other young men met at my house and organized into a society for improvement in speaking and composition. We called it the Parowan Excelsior Society.

Friday, March 4, 1853—To day, the County Court appointed W. H. Dame, J. H. Martineau and Henry Lunt a board of School-teacher examiners for Iron County.[41]

Friday, April 1, 1853—To day I received ten dollars in gold for services as County Clerk—the first gold I have received since I came into the Church.

Sunday, April 3, 1853—Nephi Johnson came to day for Dr. P. Meeks, for his father who is very sick with dropsy.[42]

[page 41]

1853—For a good while past he has been in very poor health, and has spent much time in writing poetry.

Sunday, April 10, 1853—This evening, about an hour before night, a party of thirteen men, I being one, started to take a company of emigrants who were camped at the Iron Spring, thirty miles distant. They had been trading arms and ammunition to the Utahs, and had stolen a span of fine horses from Parowan. About dark we arrived at Summit creek, where Walker and his Utes were camped, about 300 in number. Walker and Ammon rode out to meet us, and we all stopped to "talk." While all in a huddle together, Walker's indians completely surrounded us in a triple circle. About thirty feet from us was a circle of 25 indians on horseback, armed with rifles and bows, with arrows having heads 3 inches long: next behind them was a circle of indians on foot with bows and arrows;

39 William A. Morse was among the oldest of the Iron Mission settlers. He was sixty-four and a physician (Shirts and Shirts, *A Trial Furnace*, 437, 446). Sanpete County is located in central Utah. Manti and Ephraim are its largest cities today.

40 Located in southwest Illinois, the Big Muddy River is a tributary of the Mississippi River.

41 William H. Dame was among the early settlers of Paragonah. He was a Parowan major and stake president (Shirts and Shirts, *A Trial Furnace*, 123–24).

42 Nephi Johnson would have been nineteen years of age during this visit. He was a farmer, delivered the mail between Parowan, Cedar City, and Kane County, and later was a selectman (Martha Sonntag Bradley, *A History of Kane County* [Salt Lake City: Utah State Historical Society, 1999], 134; Shirts and Shirts, *A Trial Furnace*, 434). Selectmen were town officers chosen to manage the affairs of the settlement and provide for the poor. These people were often organized as a board and constituted a kind of executive authority (*The Diaries of Charles Ora Card: The Utah Years, 1871–1886*, ed. Donald G. Godfrey and Kenneth W. Godfrey [Provo, UT: Religious Studies Center, Brigham Young Univ., 2006]). Priddy Meeks (1795–1886) was a physician and fifty-seven at this writing. He was part of the Nauvoo exodus and volunteered in 1851 to help in the settlement of Parowan (Shirts and Shirts, *A Trial Furnace*, 436). Dropsy is swelling caused by an unusual accumulation of water in the body.

and then a circle of indians on foot armed with rifles. Besides this, having halted between two deep ravines, they were filled with indians with bows and arrows. They could not have selected a better spot to stop us, and they surrounded us in such a way that we had no idea that they intended any mischief. We thought they were coming up to listen to the talk.

Soon we noticed the order they stood in, and that they kept their eyes fixed on us. In the mean time, Walker, the Great War Chief, the "King of the mountains" as he was styled, was talking in a very menacing manner.[43] He asked what we were there for—we told him. He said we lied, the Emigrants had stolen no horses. It was our business to raise wheat, and not be there with guns in our hands at that time of the day. All at once all the indians cocked their guns and leveled at us. Our lives hung on a hair. Some of us had our guns in one position, some in another, but none had them in a position to use, and two of us were unarmed. There we were, all in a huddle, and if they fired, there would be no chance for us.

We thought if we could get outside the circle, we would have a better chance for our lives.

[page 42]

1853—So we told them may-be they were right, and we would go home. Walker said if we would go home, we might, so they let us out. We rode off some distance, and at first, thought to fight them, but concluded to go back and acquaint the settlers with what was in the wind. They sent spies who followed us home. The authorities immediately set sentinels and held a council, while the people spent the night making balls and preparing for fight.[44] The indian spies seeing our preparations hastened to Walker, and they all fled into the mountains, except one indian they left to watch.

The result of deliberations was, to send an express to Brigham and ask his counsel. Accordingly, Samuel Lewis was sent, starting before daylight.[45] He reached Salt Lake City in four days, a distance of 260 miles. Brigham told him to tell us to keep peace with the indians at any price. Sam got back, having been gone eight days, and riding 520 miles.

The names of those who formed this Company were James A. Little, E. Curtis, myself, S. F. Howd [Howard], Jesse B Lewis, Sidney Burton, B. Carter, Sam Lewis, J. S. Hyatt, A. W. Clyde and E. Ward, armed; and S. Gould and P. Shirts unarmed.[46] I had only a rifle, hard to load, and a restive horse. In the time when we expected every moment to feel their bullets tearing through us, my fear was, not of death, but of falling wounded in their hands to be tormented.

The fuss all arose from a little boy telling an indian that we were coming out to fight Walker. He believed it and took measures accordingly.

The emigrants who had stolen our horses heard we were coming after them, and let the horses go, and they came back to Parowan. So it all came right at last. About an hour before we were taken, old Dr. Meeks on his way to see my father-in-law, was taken by them but at his earnest entreaty they let him go again.

Saturday, April 30, 1853—To day C. C. Rich and A. Lyman came to Parowan, with a company of 30 mounted men commanded by Capt. William W. Wall who were sent from Salt Lake City to scour all the Southern vallies, and be on the watch for either hostile indians or Mexicans, who, we have reason to think, meditate hostilities against us.[47]

[page 43]

1853—A few days ago I was appointed Adjutant of the Cavalry Battalion commanded by Lt. Col. James A. Little.

43 Walkara, or "Walker," was a chief of the Paiutes who played a prominent part in developing friendships between the Saints and the Native Americans. He was an intelligent leader as well as having a reputation as an accomplished horse thief. He spoke Spanish, English, and several of the Indian languages (Arrington, *Brigham Young*, 212–18; Shirts and Shirts, *A Trial Furnace*, 317–41).

44 This refers to making ammunition for their guns.

45 Samuel Lewis was a sergeant in Militia, Company C, Parowan, First Platoon (Shirts and Shirts, *A Trial Furnace*, 493).

46 These are members of the Militia, Company C, Parowan, which had five platoons (Shirts and Shirts, *A Trial Furnace*, 492–98).

47 William W. Wall was a missionary who served in Australia and upon his return with immigrants in 1856 provided an account of the Indians (Brooks, *Mountain Meadows*, 132–33).

June 13, 1853—Yesterday morning there was a frost on the ground, but it did not injure vegetation much.

To day our cow calved, and we feel much blessed in having milk to use.

The iron works at Cedar are prospering, and the road to the new 8 ft vein of coal is rapidly progressing.

June 29, 1853—This evening Pres[t] J. C. L. Smith appointed me to be chorister of the choir, a position I do not desire.

July 4, 1853—We all went into the cañon and got a new liberty pole 88 feet long, and very straight.

Wednesday, July 20, 1853—This night at about 11½ P.M. an express arrived from Payson, bringing news that the indians had begun hostilities, killing a young man named Dabney Neel, while on picket guard. They also stole the horses of the settlement.[48] Elder F. D. Richards came with the Express.

Saturday, July 23, 1853—To day had a good celebration at Parowan.

July 25, 1853—While returning from Cedar, where we had been to spend the 25th July (the 24th happening on Sunday) we met an express from the ~~news~~ north with important news.

Pres[t] Young had sent orders to all persons living outside of forts, to at once move in and take means to secure their stock. Another man had been wounded at Payson, and Br. G. A. Smith had his horses stolen by the indians at Nephi. A force of 150 men pursued the indians as far as Uinta valley, near Green River, but without success, and were recalled by the Governor, as being too weak.

August 10, 1853—Many things have transpired since my last entry. Some of which I will speak of. Several expresses have arrived from the north, bringing word of the killing of more of our brethren in Utah County.

[page 44]

1853—George A. Smith was given extraordinary authority by Gov. Young and was appointed Colonel, commanding all the Country South of Salt Lake County.

The settlers of Allred's settlement, San Pete Co. had been counseled to move into the fort for protection, but they declined, saying they were able to take care of themselves, and of the whole Ute nation.[49] The next day after sending back the above answer, at 10 A.M. the indians drove off all their cattle herd, 175 in number, and 15 horses.

The Allredites then concluded to take the Counsel given and move in, and sent to Brigham for help. He answered, that as they were able to take care of themselves and the Utes too, they did not need any help, and declined sending any.

A few days afterwards, Edson Whipple with 6 men retook 26 head of stock from the indians.[50]

The people of Utah County would not move into forts, until many had been shot. Br. Geo. A. Smith advised the people of Springville to move in. They did so and that night one man on guard was shot. It was afterwards found that Walker had intended to attack the place with 400 warriors, and was only deterred by the timely precautions taken.

On Tuesday Aug. 2, Col. G. A. Smith, accompanied by Lt. Col. W. H. Kimball and 36 men arrived.[51] Orders were immediately given to abandon and destroy Paragoonah, five miles from Parowan, inhabited by about 25 families. Those who had Log houses, moved them in, but those who had adobie dwellings had to destroy them, so as not to give cover for the indians.

48 Accommodating the Native Americans in Utah was a challenge for the settlers and leaders of the Church. Here in the Martineau journals, we see a firsthand account of the significance of these struggles in daily life. For an overview of the conflicts, see Arrington and Bitton, *Mormon Experience*, 145–60; Arrington, *Brigham Young*, 210–22; for the local perspective of these events, see Shirts and Shirts, *A Trial Furnace*, 317–41.

49 James Allred was among the first Danish settlers in central Utah (Andrew Jenson, *Encyclopedic History of the Church of Jesus Christ of Latter-day Saints*, 2nd rev. ed. [Salt Lake City: Deseret News, 1914], s.v. "James Allred").

50 Edson Whipple (1805–94) was among the first settlers to journey to the Salt Lake Valley in 1847. He was a captain in the 1850 Iron County Militia. He would have been forty-eight years old at this mention in the journal. He was a tinsmith (Shirts and Shirts, *A Trial Furnace*, 440).

51 William H. Kimball was the son of Heber C. Kimball. He was a member of the Mormon Militia as a lieutenant colonel. He started a stagecoach business and later served a mission in England (Shirts and Shirts, *A Trial Furnace*, 237, 320, 324).

Br. W. H. Dame had a fine house, just finished, costing $3000 [$70,150], which had to be leveled.

Fort Johnson had been evacuated, but 15 families were about to move back, to keep the place as a herd-ground, when Col. Smith arrived and countermanded it, as it was thought best to keep but two posts in the County.[52]

Col. Smith also brought orders that all surplus stock be sent to Salt Lake for protection, and if necessary the women and children also.

[page 45]

1853—On Sunday. Aug. 7. an express from Cedar brought word that a large portion of the people of Cedar had rebelled, and refused to let their surplus stock be sent north: some even got their guns, and swore they would blow him through before their stock should go north. Lt. Col. Kimball's Command were at once sent to Cedar, to quell the mutiny, and eight men were arrested, and placed under guard. The people still being refractory, an express was sent to Gov. B Young, and the next night, (Aug 10) an express came to Parowan from Col. Smith for ammunition stored there.

On Wednesday the 10th Col. Smith and the officers had decided to leave the people to their own fate, but Geo. A. determined to try once more, and this time his efforts were successful, and the stubborn ones gave in promising to do as they were told. The military were camped half a mile from the settlement, not feeling safe in it.

A. J. Stewart then laid out a fort for them, the other not being deemed secure.[53]

Col. Smith spoke to us at Parowan Aug. 10, and said he considered the people of Cedar in a dangerous situation, on account of their disobedience, but he felt as safe in Parowan as in Salt Lake City, and said if we would do as we were told, not one of us should be killed or wounded. This was fulfilled [Last sentence added in shaky handwriting, presumably when he was old.]

August 11, 1853—A court of inquiry convened to day to try the mutineers, and Capt. Jacob Hofheines being detailed to go, leaves me in temporary command of the post until he returns.[54]

Sunday, August 14, 1853—This evening Robt H. Gillespie arrived with news from the north, that the indians had burned Hamilton's Mill, with 20,000 feet lumber and six dwelling houses.[55] They had also attacked some men going north with a herd of cattle, wounding one man, killing 2 horses and wounding some other animals.

[page 46]

Tuesday, August 16, 1853—Elders G. A. Smith and F. D. Richards spoke to day.

August 17, 1853—To day G. A. Smith started north with the militia driving 280 head of surplus cattle from Parowan and Cedar. Col. Smith left orders to build a wall round Parowan four feet thick and sixteen high, with bastions.

August 19, 1853—Saw a comet this evening, continuing in sight for several nights.

Monday, August 29, 1853—To day Edd Williams reported he had seen Utahs chasing horses on the bottoms.[56] John Steel, myself and ten men went out to see if we could find them. We found tracks of 4 or 5 mounted indians, and tracked them Towards Summit, a few miles. When about to return home, we came across a hare, which, instead of running away, squatted down. We all began shooting at it, but missed it all the time, firing over it. We fired about forty shots before it was killed. When we got back to the Fort, we found the walls and roofs of houses covered with people, who had been witnessing our firing, and thought a battle was in progress. They anxiously inquired who was killed or wounded. We had a good laugh over it.

The same evening an express was sent to Cedar, with the information, which returned next day, with orders to send out a party of ten men to reconnoitre.

52 Fort Johnson was located just outside of Cedar City where Enoch is today.

53 This could be A. L. Stewart, who was a settler in Kane County.

54 Jacob Hofheines (1812–90) was a bricklayer and captain of the Iron County Artillery. He was a bodyguard to Joseph Smith and witnessed his martyrdom (Shirts and Shirts, *A Trial Furnace*, 77, 432).

55 Hamilton's Mill was south of Cedar City on Shirts Creek.

56 Edward Williams was among the Iron Mission workers. He was a tailor (Shirts and Shirts, *A Trial Furnace*, 440).

Tuesday, August 30, 1853—To-day an Express (A. Henry, of Fillmore) arrived from Salt Lake City, bringing the Governor's proclamation forbidding trade with the Indians in arms or ammunition. I went with A. Henry and Ed. Williams, as Express to Cedar, starting about midnight. Returned the same morning with the reconnoitreing party.

Sunday, September 4, 1853—To day Jo[s] Chatterly accidentally shot himself in the arm with the rifle.[57] He died on the 7th inst.

Tuesday, September 6, 1853—To day, Capt. Jacob Hofhiens, commander of the post, was voted down by the Battalion, in consequence of his incapacity, and placed in arrest, to await the action of a court of Inquiry. Capt. John Steele was placed in temporary command.

[page 47]

Saturday, September 10, 1853—To-day the first Conference ever held in Iron County was convened in Parowan. The Stake at Parowan numbered 11 High Priests, 38 Seventies, 28 Elders, 2 Priests, 1 Teacher, and 122 members; total, 201.

I was clerk of the Conference, and it is the first I ever attended. All the authorities of the Church were unanimously sustained, and much good counsel given. The next day, the Conference was held in Cedar.

Saturday, October 9, 1853—To day the mail arrived from the north, bringing news that on Saturday, Oct. 1, five men from San Pete were killed in San Pete canyon, while feeding. Their throats were cut and they were otherwise horribly mutilated. The next day, (Sunday 2) the men of Nephi became so enraged when the bodies were brought in, that they attacked and killed eight indians in the town. The indians they killed were friendly, so far as I can learn. At any rate they were not concerned in the murder of the five whites. Rob[t] H Gillispie, of Parowan, was one who participated in this deed.

Our crops are gathered in without molestation from the indians, for which we feel thankful to our God.

Two large companies of emigrants have lately passed through here, on their way to California.[58] They had about 1500 Cattle and 15,000 sheep. At Pine Creek, near Fillmore, the first company had a fight with the Pauvan indians, in which one white man was shot, and several indians killed. The next night they were attacked again, and several indians killed or wounded.

Wednesday, October 26, 1853—This morning Lieut. Gunnissons party were attacked in their camp on the Sevier, about 30 miles west of Fillmore, and of twelve, eight, including Gunnisson, were killed. The guide, W[m] Potter, of San Pete, was also killed. The ball did not cut his garments, but passed through the mark over the nipple. The men lately killed in San Pete Canyon, also, had their garments uncut or penetrated by any balls.

[page 48]

1853—Of Gunnisson's company that were killed, all but Potter were horribly mutilated. He was attacked by the Pauvans, in revenge for the attack made on them by Hildreth Company of emigrants, as mentioned just before

Monday, October 31, 1853—This evening Elders Erastus Snow and F. D. Richards arrived from the north, with news that Walker had gone to the Navahoes for assistance: that Pres[t] Young was trying to make peace with them, and says the time has come for the gospel to be preached among them.[59] A hundred elders have been sent to Iron County, with their families, to preach among them

57 Joseph Chatterley was among the early pioneer educators. Cedar City's first school was held in his cabin (Seegmiller, *History of Iron County*, 191).

58 The California gold rush had numerous effects on the Saints. Thousands of travelers heading for California stopped and purchased provisions in Utah; thus, the Church prospered from this migration. Charles C. Rich, a member of the Quorum of the Twelve, was in California between 1846 and 1857. He established the Church in San Bernardino, California. Some members of the Mormon Battalion who were released in San Diego stayed there to earn the money necessary for their return to Utah. Others went to northern California and participated in the construction of Sutter's Mill, where gold was first discovered (Kenneth J. Davies, *Mormon Gold: The Story of California's Mormon Argonauts* [Salt Lake City: Olympus, 1984]).

59 These were Navajos in southeastern Utah. Brigham Young described them as settled Indians who cultivated the land (Arrington, *Brigham Young*, 210, 218).

November 4, 1853—To night, at 12.20 A.M. my son Henry A. Martineau is one year old. He is handsome, smart, has six teeth, and can walk alone across the house.

Many of the people of Cedar, and some few from Parowan, have apostatized and gone to California. They were afraid they would go naked, they said. Poor fools. God is just as able to clothe his people now, as He ever was.

Monday, November 21, 1853—To day, a Conference was held in Cedar, presided over by E. Snow and F. D. Richards.[60] It was decided to locate a new settlement at Summit Creek, 6½ miles south of Parowan. There is a dense body of willows, which would conceal hundreds of indians, making it dangerous to pass there while indians are hostile.

At this conference Joel H. Johnson was appointed to farm, and teach the indians to work; also to preach to and instruct them in all good things. He should do these things, and all his children forever, after him.[61]

Nephi's mission and ordination is to go to school, preach to the Lamanites, take up a school for the instruction of indian children: and his mission shall extend throughout all North America, and he is to travel among and live with them from time to time.[62]

Saturday, November 26, 1853—To day C. C. Pendleton[63] finished my pistols for which I paid him $25.00 [$585] My wife's uncle Geo. W. Johnson arrived here, on his way to Cedar city to settle, being one of those sent to preach to the Indians.[64]

[page 49]

Friday, November 25, 1853—Hosea Stout and James Lewis returned to day from China. They found no favorable opening there to preach.

Sunday, December 25, 1853—To day Col. C. Reese's train, going to California for goods arrived, also two small companies of emigrants. We had good meetings to day. The weather has been very good thus far, no snow nor cold weather, which is fortunate for the people of Cedar, who are, many of them, living in wagons, tents, and booths.

December 6, 1853—To day the first city election was held in Cedar to elect city officers. I. C. Haight was elected Mayor, and John D. Lee, William Miller (Bogus Brigham) George S. Clark & Philip K. Smith Aldermen, James Lewis Recorder.[65]

1854.

Sunday, January 8, 1854—To day we have been married two years. It seems like a dream, but our Henry, now 14 months old, is a substantial proof of the reality of our marriage. He is a perfect rowdy. Our health has been good all the time, and the Lord has greatly blessed us, for which I thank him.

Thursday, January 12, 1854—To day Patriarch Elisha H. Groves[66] blessed me and my wife with the following blessings:—

60 Erastus Snow (1818–88) was an Apostle. Franklin D. Richards (1821–99) was an Apostle and President of the Quorum of the Twelve Apostles.

61 Joel H. Johnson settled in Parowan in 1851. He established a cattle herd near Elk Horn Springs, which afterward was called Johnson's Ranch and Johnson's Springs. It is today known as Enoch. He was also a prolific songwriter known for the authorship of "High on the Mountain Top" and hundreds of other hymns (Seegmiller, *History of Iron County*, 53–54, 170, 240).

62 The Native Americans hold a significant place in Mormon history. The Book of Mormon presents the message of Christ to them. Brigham Young taught fairness and kindness as the best approach to improve relations and worked to establish educational programs for improvement (Arrington, *Brigham Young*, 210–22).

63 Calvin C. Pendleton moved to Parowan in 1854 and established a gun and machine shop. Before joining the Church, he had some medical training; thus he performed minor surgeries and set broken bones (Seegmiller, *History of Iron County*, 222–23).

64 George W. Johnson was born in 1823. Little is known of his life other than what is found in his autobiography at the L. Tom Perry Special Collections.

65 Isaac C. Haight was president of the Cedar City Stake and the Deseret Iron Works manager (Seegmiller, *History of Iron County*, 43–44, 69, 267; Shirts and Shirts, *A Trial Furnace*, 346–47, 371). William Miller, alias Bogus Brigham, was a close associate of Brigham Young. The two apparently looked alike. In April 1846 when government officials sought to arrest Brigham Young, they arrested William Miller by mistake because Miller was wearing Brigham's hat and coat. They took him to Carthage before they realized this was the "bogus Brigham." It was a humorous incident passed through generations. George Clark was a local bishop (Arrington, *Brigham Young*, 126; Shirts and Shirts, *A Trial Furnace*, 214, 346).

66 Elisha H. Groves was a Cedar City bishop, high councilor, and patriarch. He was president of the Iron Mission. Patriarchal blessings are given to declare the recipient's heritage as well as provide guidance to the individual.

Br. James. In the name of Jesus of Nazareth, by virtue of the holy priesthood in me invested, I lay my hands upon thy head to bless thee with a patriarchal or father's blessing. I say unto thee that thou shalt be blessed, and the blessings of thy Heavenly Father shall attend thee. Thou art of the seed of Abraham, of the house of Israel, the greater portion of the blood of Ephraim through the descent of thy fathers. Thou hast a right to all the gifts, blessings, privileges and powers that pertain to the fulness of the Holy priesthood. Thou shalt receive thine annointings, the fulness of the holy priesthood, the power of redemption, that thou mayest officiate in the ordinances of the house of the Lord, in behalf of thy progenitors. Thou shalt receive houses and lands.

[page 50]

1854—Thy posterity shall be numerous in the Earth. Peace and comfort shall dwell in thy habitations, thy bread shall be sure unto thee. Thy Father hath suffered thee to be brought into privation and want, that thou mightest have the powers of appreciation. Thy granaries shall yet be filled, plenty shall be in thy habitations. Thou shalt do much in the records which is necessary to be kept and handed down to future generations. The holy angels shall be with thee, and shall minister unto thee. Inasmuch as thou desirest it with all thy heart, keeping all the Commandments of the Lord thy God, thou shalt not sleep in the dust: thou shalt behold the winding up scene of this wicked generation. Thou shalt behold thy Savior come to dwell with the Saints on earth. Thou shalt see the completion of the temple which shall be built in Zion, on which the cloud shall rest by day and the glory of the Lord shall come into it: thou shalt receive blessings and privileges therein. Thou shalt receive a dispensation of the Gospel, that thou mayest teach the nations that are afar off, the principles of life and salvation, and many shall be made to rejoice therein. Thou shalt be an instrument in the hand of the Lord of bringing many of thy kindred into the kingdom of thy Heavenly Father, although they are many of them, far from the knowledge of the truth. Thou shalt receive thy inheritance, thy blessing, thy kingdom and dominion with the 144.000 who shall stand upon Mt. Zion as Saviors of men. Let thy heart therefore be comforted; be thou faithful, and these blessings are sure unto thee: for what I seal on earth shall be sealed in heaven. In the name of Jesus of Nazareth I seal these blessings upon thee, even so. Amen.

My wife's blessing:—

[page 51]

Sister Susan, in the name of Jesus of Nazareth, by virtue of the holy priesthood in me invested, I lay my hands upon thy head to bless thee with a patriarchal or father's blessing. I say unto thee that thou shalt be blessed, for thou art a daughter of Abraham, of the house of Israel, of the tribe of Joseph, and hast a right to all the gifts, blessings, privileges and powers, that pertain to the holy priesthood, according to the blessing of thy father upon thy sex. Thou shalt receive thine endowments, the holy anointing, the power of redemption, that thou mayest stand in connexion with thy husband, in the redemption of thy dead. Thy life shall be long upon the earth. The holy angels shall minister unto thee, and in their hands they shall bear thee up. Thou shalt enjoy the blessing of posterity, for children's children are the crown of fathers. Thy children and thy children's children shall arise after thee and shall minister unto thee.—shall be a blessing unto thee. Thy name shall be had in honorable remembrance to the latest posterity: Thy sins are remitted unto thee. Thy name is written in the Lamb's Book of Life. Peace and quietness shall dwell in thy habitations, for a quiet spirit inhabiteth thy tabernacle. Thou shalt be blessed with the precious blessings of the earth in common with thy husband. Thou shalt live to be a good old age, until thou art satisfied with life: thou shalt rest for a little season, but shalt not suffer the pains of death. Thou shalt come forth in the morning of the ressurrection of the just, and shall receive thy crown, thy kingdom, dominion, power, and glory: Eternal increase shall be thy joy. Thou shalt receive these blessings in common with thy husband. Be thou therefore faithful, keep all the commandments of the Lord thy God, and thou shalt obtain and realize the fulfillment of those blessings.

The history of such blessings can be traced to antiquity (Shirts and Shirts, *A Trial Furnace*, 26, 124, 275; Ludlow, *Encyclopedia of Mormonism*, 3:1066–67).

[page 52]

SUSAN'S BLESSINGS

1854—I seal thee up unto everlasting life. In the name of Jesus of Nazareth I seal these blessings on thy head, even so Amen and Amen.

February 5, 1854—To day I and my wife were rebaptized, the word of the Lord being that it was pleasing in his sight.[67] I was confirmed by John Steele, who said I should do much good, bring thousands to Zion, should go and preach to a nation I have not yet heard of, have visions and dreams, and ministering of angels, be a very mighty man, and a great leader of the armies of Israel, be a terror to evil doers: no hand, tongue, or weapon raised against me should prosper, to be meek, humble and submissive.

February 20, 1854—This morning myself, wife and baby started for great Salt Lake city, to receive our endowments in company with ten or twelve other brethren.[68] Arrived at Fillmore on Thursday, and at Salt Lake city on Saturday March 4th after a very toilsome and hard journey. It snowed upon us the greater part of the time, also while in the city. Bro. Geo. A. Smith very kindly took me in charge and introduced me to Gov. Young, Orson Hyde, Orson Spencer and others, and assisted me all in his power: he also enabled me to obtain our endowments without delay, for which I feel very thankful.[69] I attended two lectures in the endowment house given by Elder H. C. Kimball, where I learned much.[70] We also went to Father John Smith, the presiding Patriarch, and received the following blessings on the 13th of March 1854:—

Sister Susan, beloved of the Lord, in the name of Jesus Christ I place my hands upon thy head and seal upon you the blessing of a father, even all the blessings and priesthood that was sealed upon the daughters of Joseph. You are entitled to every favor which your heart desires. God will give you wisdom to conduct all your affairs in righteousness, and according to his will.

[page 53]

HENRY'S BLESSING BY JOHN SMITH

1854—You shall be blessed in your family with health, have power to heal the sick. Your children shall become very numerous and mighty in the priesthood. They shall extend their dominions from Sea to Sea. You shall live to see the winding up scene of wickedness, have faith to do any work which your heart desires, see and converse with your Redeemer, and inherit all the blessings and glories of his kingdom, with all your father's house, even so, Amen.

(Recorded in Book G [or C], page 686. № 1595)

My son Henry's blessing:—

Brother Henry, in the name of Jesus Christ I lay my hands upon thy head, notwithstanding you are very young, I seal upon you a patriarchal or father's blessing, even all the blessing and priesthood that was sealed upon Abraham, Isaac and Jacob. God hath given his angels charge over you they will defend you from every danger, give you power to do any miracle that ever was done on the earth. You shall control the waves and the winds and the warring elements. You shall shine forth in the splendor and brightness of the glory of the Sun. You shall inherit all the blessings which your heart desires, and all things shall be subject to your word if you live, and I intend you shall, to see the winding up scene of this generation, and inherit all the blessings and glories of Zion, in a world without end, even so, Amen.

---

67 The practice of rebaptism taking place here is one of rededication. Rebaptisms began in Nauvoo, and the practice continued into the early Utah Church. It was discontinued in 1897 (Ludlow, *Encyclopedia of Mormonism*, 3:1194).

68 The endowment is an important part of Latter-day Saint theology. These symbolic ceremonies are conducted in the temples, in this case the Salt Lake Endowment House. The temple ceremonies include washing and anointing, the endowment, marriages, sealings, and proxy ordinances for deceased family members. The washing and anointing symbolizes the "cleansing power of Christ." The endowment is instruction based on the plan of salvation. The marriages are performed for "time and all eternity." The ordinances are sacred to the members of the Church (Ludlow, *Encyclopedia of Mormonism*, 4:1444).

69 Orson Hyde was an Apostle. Orson Spencer was a missionary. He published numerous missionary tracts with Elders Parley P. Pratt and Lorenzo Snow (Ludlow, *Encyclopedia of Mormonism*, 2:686, 3:1175).

70 The Endowment House was where members of the Church could obtain their temple ordinances before the Salt Lake Temple had been constructed. At this time it was located on the northwest corner of the Temple Block in Salt Lake City.

March 14, 1854—I received a commission from the Governor and Legislative Assembly, as Notary Public, also a commission as 2nd Lieutenant, and one as Adjutant.

I also attended the funeral of Willard Richards who died on Sat. March 11. 1854. of dropsy.[71]

[page 54]

IN SALT LAKE CITY.

March 12, 1854—The day was raw and cold, wet, snowy, muddy. He was buried in his city lot near his house

Tuesday, March 7, 1854—On Tuesday March 7th we received the ordinances of the temple. I felt amply paid for my toilsome journey to the city, through snow and frost. While traveling to the city we suffered great hardships. During the day the snow melted enoung [enough] to let the horses through. In the night it froze very hard, so that the snow would bear up the horses and wagons. We started each day about 2 A.M. and it seemed as if Sunrise would never come, as through intense cold and darkness we traveled slowly along. Samuel West and wife also went in the same wagon with us, and it was close packing for us four to sleep in a small wagon box. Our team, too, was very poor. Four little, lazy, weak indian ponies, which belonged to Samuel Gould.[72] We camped out night after night in the snow. Henry was very sick with the canker in the bowels and diarrea, and no one thought he would ever live to get home again. When we got to Nephi, he was cured by a woman there, who gave him a weak lye of whiskey on ashes.

I saw Prest Young, who gave me permission to take another wife. I saw the new alphabet in Prest Young's office, and copied it. Also saw some of the new type, which were cut by Robt Campbell.[73]

When we started to return home, we traveled a few days to Nephi with H. D. Bayliss and wife, having left our team there to recruit.[74] The traveling was dreadful. Mud, snow and water, in about equal proportion. The first day we had to walk several miles, the team being unable to haul us, and we had to wade through the mud, water and snow, carrying Henry. We came at dark to a house belonging to a man named Caspar, who refused us shelter for the night, although he had plenty of room and everything else. Rendered desperate by our situation, Mrs. Bayless and I determined to storm the enemy's stronghold, and stay whether or no.

[page 55]

JOURNEY HOME

1854—We each took our bedding and marched up to the house, while Bayless and Susan, more timid waited to see the result. We entered a room, built a fire, called them in and made ourselves welcome. Our hosts did not come near us for a long time, and then the man came in for a few minutes, looking as sour as vinegar. In the morning he looked in again; asked who we were and where we were going, but did not press us to stay. This was a christian welcome for a rich man to give!

Friday, March 24, 1854—After a very toilsome journey we arrived home on the 24th at 4 P.M. much rejoiced to be in our own home in Parowan, which city, Prest Young said while we were in Salt Lake city, is the only one built in Utah according to Counsel. He also said that Salt Lake city and Parowan were the only two safe places in the Territory this year, because the only two places where counsel was obeyed, and the people did just right. Prest Young also gave me his approval to practice Astrology, so long as I should do good, and do no hurt.[75]

71 Willard Richards was second counselor to Brigham Young.

72 Samuel Gould was part of the original southern Utah exploring expedition from 1849 to 1850 and an early Cedar City settler (Shirts and Shirts, *A Trial Furnace*, 10, 400).

73 This is a reference to the Deseret Alphabet, which was an attempt to create phonetic symbols for the sounds of the English language, thus helping new immigrants learn English (Arrington, *Brigham Young*, 238). Robert Campbell was part of the early southern Utah exploring expedition from 1849 to 1850. He estimated the area would support settlements of 50,000 to 100,000 people (Shirts and Shirts, *A Trial Furnace*, 11, 13).

74 This could be a reference to Herman B. Bayles, who had a carpenter's shop in Parowan (Shirts and Shirts, *A Trial Furnace*, 400, 426; Seegmiller, *History of Iron County*, 181).

75 According to the *American Heritage Dictionary of English*, the study of astrology here means the same as it does today. It was "the study of the positions and aspects of celestial bodies in the belief that they have an influence on the course of natural earthly occurrences and human affairs." Note

March 29, 1854—<u>Wednesday</u> <u>evening</u>. This evening I for the first time attended a prayer circle, which was held in the upper room of the meeting house, which had been fitted up for the purpose.[76]

Sunday, April 12, 1854—I first assumed garments on the day on which Dr. Richards was buried.[77]

April 14, 1854—To day began sowing my wheat.

April 30, 1854—To day Thos D. Brown preached on "Consecration" which was taught the last Conference. I shall be glad to conform to this law as soon as possible.[78]

I this day made a schedule of my property, and was surprised to find it amounted to $900.00 [$21,045] which I have accumulated in three years. through the blessing of God.

Wednesday, May 24, 1854—To day Pres^{t} Young and party arrived from Salt Lake City. A meeting was held in the evening, and on the next day they proceeded to Cedar.

[page 56]

1854—The Presidency were highly pleased with our labors, good order and industry, and pronounced many blessings upon us.

The Ute Chiefs Walker, Grosfun and Squash-head accompanied Pres^{t} Young, and were well pleased, Pres^{t} Young having made a treaty with them. A company of missionaries under direction of Elder P. P. Pratt, destined for the islands of the Pacific also accompanied President Young. Among them were Silas S. Smith, John A. West and Sixtus E. Johnson, of Iron County.[79] They all went in good spirits trusting in the Lord.

Pres^{t} Young said the war, was over "He had the war with him." He counseled us to build a wall round our town six feet thick and twelve feet high, or of earth and straw well rammed together. He recommended kindness towards the indians, together with firmness. I asked Bishop Ed^{d} Hunter why the company could not make us a longer visit.[80] He said "It is a day of hurrying and warning, and we have not time to stop to talk." I talked much with Lt. Genl Wells, who was pleased that I said I would study Military Engineering and fortification, and promised me all the assistance in his power.[81]

A committee was appointed to take charge of the building of the Fort Wall, and I took a contract to furnish the hewn timbers for five culverts or bridges to support the wall where the creek and canals passed under it. I was to furnish 130 sticks for $660.00 [$14,030] the timbers being from sixteen inches

the word of caution that President Brigham Young gives to Martineau.

76 Prayer circles were held in dedicated buildings and at times in family residences. Participants dressed in white temple clothing and formed a circle symbolizing unity and perfection. Prayers were offered by inspiration with no specific dialogue for the prayer. Today's prayer circles are conducted only in temples.

77 The temple garment has special meaning to those who have participated in temple ordinances. The garment is white underclothing symbolizing purity and acts as a reminder of the temple ordinances and promises.

78 Thomas Dunlap Brown was active in the Southern Indian Mission. He was a bookkeeper (Shirts and Shirts, *A Trial Furnace*, 75). The law of consecration being preached here originated with the Prophet Joseph Smith and was in reaction to the individualistic economic order of the Jacksonian Era. Consecration assumed that everything belongs to the Lord and members of the Church were asked to consecrate, or deed, their property and worldly goods to the bishop, who would then grant back an inheritance to every family who were acting as stewards to what had been received. Thus the poor and younger members of the Church were cared for (Leonard J. Arrington, Feramorz Y. Fox, and Dean L. May, *Building the City of God: Community & Cooperation Among the Mormons*, 2nd ed. [Urbana, IL: Univ. of Illinois Press, 1976], 15). It is interesting to note that Martineau was "appointed to make out the deeds" at this meeting (69).

79 Silas Smith was a bishop at Paragonah (Seegmiller, *History of Iron County*, 78). The John West that Martineau writes about could be John Weston, who was a resident of Cedar City and a shareholder in the Deseret Iron Company (Shirts and Shirts, *Trial Furnace*, 255–57, 476). Sixtus E. Johnson was an early settler and farmer in Parowan. He would have been around twenty-three years of age at the time of this journal entry (Shirts and Shirts, *A Trial Furnace*, 85, 434).

80 Traveling with the company, Edward Hunter was among Brigham Young's inner circle of advisers and administrators. He was also the Presiding Bishop of the Church (Arrington, *Brigham Young*, 193, 303).

81 This is likely Daniel H. Wells, a lieutenant general of the Nauvoo Legion. At the time of this journal entry he would be working to reconstruct the territorial militia (Shirts and Shirts, *A Trial Furnace*, 381; Arrington, *Brigham Young*, 214).

square to two feet. Th[e] earth wall was contracted for at from $20. to $40. [$468–$935] pr rod

Monday, June 19, 1854—To day I was notified by James Lewis, Probate Judge, that he no longer wished my services as County Clerk. He did this from personal enmity. I am not enough of a sycophant to please him.

[page 57]

1854—I have been county clerk of Iron County ever since its organization in 1851, about three years, during which time I have received for my services $161.93 [$4,490]. During this time there has been issued in County scrip $935.81 [$21,887].

Saturday, June 24, 1854—To night the Parowan Dramatic Association, which was organized April 5, 1854, performed for the first time.[82] The plays were "Slasher and Crasher" and "The Village Lawyer," with songs. It went off very well. Admittance 25¢ Total receipts $6.75 [$5.86–$158] I painted the scenery. Nearly all the audience were dead heads.

During this month I wrote a Drama entitled "The Missouri Persecution." In four acts, occupying 52 closely written pages. I wrote it to commemorate the sad scenes of Missouri, and to improve myself in composition.

June 27, 1854—To day a conference was held, at which 14 missionaries were called to go to the States. About this time Walker, the Utah Chief, commanded the people of Nephi to cease building any more of their wall, and forced them to comply. They sent an express to Prest. Young, who sent a letter to Walker reprimanding him severely, and telling him he did not know his own friends. After this Walker allowed the people to go on with their wall. He started to San Pete vally and forced three interpreters, viz:—O. P. Rockwell,[83] and two others, to go with him under pain of death, and trade with him on his own terms. They went, expecting to be killed, but as a sacrifice to save the rest of the people. They were not harmed.

The Utahs, describing the destruction of the Moquich indians, say a man dressed in blue & fifty others dressed in pure white, appeared from heaven, and finding them disposed to fight the whites, destroyed three towns.

[page 58]

1854—The fourth town they spared, because the people were friendly to the whites.

July 4, 1854—We found the Pah Eeds feeling quite hostile to us, because our wall runs through their garden. They had blocked the road with tree tops.

Our theatre again performed to a full house, The receipts were $22.00 [$514].

July 14, 1854—To day, while going up the kanyon with my oxen, I composed the following verses in view of the warlike state of Europe, and the desolations soon to spread over the United States:—

1

All the world is in commotion
Fearfulness and pain,
And all beyond the briny ocean
Is one vast battle plain.

2

There is heard the cannon's thunder
There the bayonets gleam,
While smiling cities without number
In midnight flames are seen.

3

There is heard the widows wailing
And the orphan's cry
While through the clouds of battle flaming
The deadly bullets fly.

4

Columbia's land will soon be sleeping
Oer myriads of her slain
While thousands of her sons are Sleeping
~~Towards~~ On many a bloody plain

[page 59]

1854—

82 Drama and theater were common modes of entertainment among the early Utah settlers. Not long after the Parowan settlement was established, dramas began to be performed (Seegmiller, *History of Iron County*, 249).

83 This could be Orrin Porter Rockwell. He was a bodyguard to the Prophet Joseph Smith (Arrington, *Brigham Young*, 103; Seegmiller, *History of Iron County*, 38).

5

Pestilence and famine stalking
Throughout all the land
And o'er ten thousand corpses walking
Bestrown on every hand

6

But here in Deseret together
We'll rest secure from harm
While clouds of saints begin to gather
From every foreign clime.

July 24, 1854—To day we celebrated as usual: —firing of guns, parading of the Iron Regiment, speeches, and dancing. In the evening the Dramatic Association performed "The Soldier's Daughter" and the "Two Bonny Castles." to a crowded house. Calvin C. Pendleton and James Lewis were Orators of the Day.

To day I played my new Bass viol in the Choir. It was made in Parowan by Barney Carter, and I paid him $30.00 [$702] for it.[84] I think this is the first Base viol made in Utah.

Thursday, August 3, 1854—To day is fast day, which I observed, as usual.[85]

July 26, 1854—Bp W H Dame returned from S. L. City with word that all shirts should be marked, even buckskin ones. I had mine marked on the 27th. Most of the people had theirs marked August 1st.

I have secured about 3 tons of hay this summer.

Monday, September 4, 1854—Today I bought a cow of the city for $40.00 [$935], the first I ever owned. She had only three teats, the other having been spoiled. I feel rich.

Tuesday, September 12, 1854—A son was born to me, this evening at 8 o'clock and 24 minutes P.M. We dedicated him to the Lord and named him Moroni Helaman.[86] I prophesied he should be like Moroni and Helaman of old, in building up the Kingdom of God.

Fig. 2.3—Moroni Helaman Martineau, son of James Henry and Susan Ellen. Courtesy of James Henry Martineau Family Organization.

[page 60]

INDIAN PLOT TO TAKE PAROWAN

1854—At the muster and drill yesterday, we subscribed $45.00 [$1,052] to mount our cannon anew, and a sum to get a flag. Also to get instruments for a brass Band $325.00 [$7,600] I was appointed to get and paint the new flag. I subscribed $1.00 [$23] for the flag, and $5.00 [$117] for the Band.

Friday, September 22, 1854—An indian took a horse belonging to Beason Lewis to day, but was pursued by Beason and Samuel Lewis John Henderson[87]

84 Barney Carter was among the early settlers of Beaver, Utah (Allan Kent Powell, ed., *Utah History Encyclopedia* [Salt Lake City: Univ. of Utah Press, 1994], s.v. "Beaver").

85 J. H. Martineau, "Extracts," August 3, 1854; Utah Digital Newspapers.

86 The FamilySearch International Genealogical Index lists Moroni Helaman Martineau as the third child. The birthday correlates with this record. However, this same record also indicated a second child, a daughter named Cora Colorado Martineau, was born two days earlier, "about 10 September 1854."

87 At the time of this journal entry, John Henderson would have been twenty-three. He served as a private in the Utah Territorial Militia, Company C., Parowan, First Platoon (Shirts & Shirts, *A Trial Furnace*, 432). Beason Lewis was

and a Spaniard. After a ten mile chase they captured him, and brought him back to the fort. When at the gate he refused to enter, and Sam. raised his gun as if to strike him. The other indians then cocked their guns and twanged their bows strings. The same evening, while the matter was still undecided, the indians laid a plan to take the fort, all the men but 6 or 8 being out to work in the fields or up in the mountains. They stationed ten in the field near the field gates to kill those in the field as they should return home, posted others at the fort gates and posted others in the kanyon to kill the men there, as they should return home one by one. One Indian fired at John Steele, but missed him. I was in the kanyon and came home at dark. I might easily have been killed, not knowing anything of the matter.

The difficulty was finally settled amicably.

Monday, September 25, 1854—Ja[s] Williams,[88] mail carrier, arrived from the north with news of the killing of two little boys 7 and 9 years old, who had gone for wood, by the indians, and the hanging of two indians for the murder. There were several thousand spectators and two military Companies present. Also Squash-head and the Utes.

[page 61]

HANGING OF TWO INDIANS, GRASSHOPPERS.

1854—This is the first execution in Utah. The indians are very mad about it.

Col. Steptoe with his dragoons had lately entered the Territory, making the indians fearful.[89]

Word also came of the burning of Fort Laramie and the killing of 30 of the garrison by the indians

Tuesday, September 26, 1854—Pres[t] G. A. Smith had a talk with the indians, who were very saucy, owned to their misdeeds, even to an attempt to kill him, and demanded tribute of us in future. The Spaniard started for California with the mail carrier, and several indians started ahead of him to kill him

Wednesday, September 27, 1854—A mass meeting was held in relation to building of the wall. It was unanimously resolved to drop all work, except saving the grain, and finish the wall.

Sunday, October 8, 1854—To day Br. Dixon gave his first lessons in the Deseret Alphabet to a class of fifty.

In the evening Col. W. H. Dame appointed me the Regimental Adjutant

Monday, October 9, 1854— Finished my thrashing. Had 65 bushels of wheat.

About this time immense swarms of grasshoppers came flying from the north, sometimes obscuring the sun.[90] They flew as high as we could see them, and came for several days, going south.

On Sunday Oct. 8, we had the severest hail storm ever known here. In a few minutes, the earth was covered with ice, and the next day with dead grasshoppers, after which they were no more seen. They visited the whole Territory, and did immense damage, eating almost all the crops left.

Tuesday, October 10, 1854—Bought a clock of E. Curtis[91]

[page 62]

MORONI'S BLESSING BY E. H. GROVES.

Wednesday, October 18, 1854—This day W[m] C. Mitchell arrived from Salt Lake City with 13 brass instruments for the Band.[92] There are also some other

also a private in the same company (Shirts and Shirts, *A Trial Furnace*, 335, 493).

88 This is James S. Williamson, who was a member of the Utah Territorial Militia in Parowan and Cedar City. He was a miner in the Iron Mission (Shirts and Shirts, *A Trial Furnace*, 348, 453, 493–94).

89 Lieutenant Colonel Edward J. Steptoe led an army engineering unit working with the transcontinental railroad. He brought troops into the valley, which worried the Saints (Arrington, *Brigham Young*, 246–48; Arrington, *Great Basin Kingdom*, 148).

90 Grasshoppers were a plague to the entire Great Basin agricultural life. This was not just one isolated incident as recorded here (Arrington, *Great Basin Kingdom*, 148–51).

91 There are several Curtis families in Church history. At this writing no "E. Curtis" fitting the context of this entry could be found. A Uriel Curtis was active in the iron mines and in building the furnace (Shirts and Shirts, *A Trial Furnace*, 348).

92 William C. Mitchell Jr. and Sr. were active in early pioneering musical activities. Both were involved in the early settling of Cedar City. Later William Sr. helped settle Las Vegas (Shirts and Shirts, *A Trial Furnace*, 51, 177–78, 400).

instruments here. Brought news of probable indian hostilities this winter.

[written at top of page]

Called to this place

Tuesday, November 7, 1854—To day, Walker's whole band came with a herd of horses, cattle, sheep and goats. Of course they are Tu-e-je tik-a-boo (very friendly)

Patriarch E. H. Groves this evening blessed my son Moroni H. with the following blessing:—

Moroni Helman, In the name of Jesus of Nazareth, and by virtue of the holy priesthood in me invested, I place my hands upon thy head to seal upon thee a patriarchal ~~ble~~ or father's blessing, which shall rest upon thee and thou shalt realize the fulfillment thereof. Thou art in the days of thy infancy, yet a noble spirit inhabiteth thy tabernacle, and inasmuch as thy parents do their duty by thee, the Spirit of the Lord shall rest upon thee from thy infancy, and thou shalt grow up mighty in faith like unto Moroni of old. Thy days shall be many upon the Earth; thou shalt be a blessing unto thy parents and unto all with whom thou shalt be associated by virtue of the holy priesthood. Thou art of the seed of Abraham, of the loins of Joseph, a lawful heir to the fullness of the priesthood, which thou shalt receive in due time, through which thou shalt ~~do~~ perform a mighty work. [. . .] the redemption of thy progenitors, both the living and the dead. The Destroyer shall seek to take thy life away to deprive thee of thy blessings and of performing thy work, yet thou shalt be delivered from the hand of the Destroyer, becoming a father in Israel.

[page 63]

1854—Thy posterity shall multiply and become numerous upon the earth Thou shalt have great knowledge, ~~of many things~~ and wisdom shall be given unto thee; Thou shalt have knowledge of many things that yet lay in darkness, becoming a mighty prophet, obtain the riches of heaven and of earth; Thou, like unto Moroni of old, shall behold the downfall of many people and the overthrow of many cities; the reign of peace established upon the Earth; the glory of Zion; the coming of the city of Enoch or the New Jerusalem:—receive thy inheritance among the faithful in Zion; become a King and a Priest unto the Most High God; receive thy crown, kingdom, dominion, power, and eternal increase. These blessings I seal upon thy head, and seal thee up unto everlasting life, in the name of Jesus, Even so, Amen.

Wednesday, November 8, 1854—To day I finished my contract on the wall, in connexion with Benjamin Cluff and another,[93] It amounted to $590.$^{\underline{00}}$ [$13,796] of which my part was $201.$^{\underline{00}}$ [$4,910].

December 25, 1854—Christmas. The weather mild and warm. Judge Styles (U. S. Judge) held a court here.[94] I paid my jurors fees, $10.$^{\underline{00}}$ [$234] to Jo^{s} L. Heywood, for a set of mathematical instruments made for F. D. Richards, in England.[95] Two days ago I sold my yoke of oxen to J. H. Johnson for $100. [$2,338] cash and $25.~ [$585] in wheat,

[page 64]

1855

Monday, January 1, 1855—A strong gale of wind all day, causing clouds of dust. Last week I bought a pair of andirons (home made) for $6.50 [$142], which were my first ones.[96] Winter set in today, cold and stormy.

A few days ago I received a letter from my aunt Mary Martineau, enticing me to come home (to Milwaukee) and offering me a large amount of land.

To day I subscribed for two numbers of the "Mormon," one for myself, and one to send to my uncle Peter Martineau; also two copies of the "Luminary,"

....

93 Benjamin Cluff was a member of the Parowan Dramatic Association along with Martineau. The "wall" referred to was being constructed around the city for protection from the natives (Seegmiller, *History of Iron County*, 249).

94 This is likely George P. Stiles, who was one of three non-Mormon judges to head the Utah judiciary (Arrington and Bitton, *The Mormon Experience*, 165).

95 This could be Bishop Joseph L. Heywood of Salt Lake City. He was a proponent of the principle of consecration (Arrington, Fox, and May, *Building the City of God*, 68). Franklin S. Richards was a prominent Mormon attorney. He would go on in history to establish the articles of incorporation for the Church, to work in the women's suffrage movement, as well as to defend polygamy (Ludlow, *Encyclopedia of Mormonism*, 2:824; see also Powell, *Utah History Encyclopedia*, s.v. "Women's Suffrage in Utah").

96 Andirons are a pair of metal supports used to hold the wood for the fireplace.

intending to send one copy to my sister Henrietta, in Indiana. Price $2.00 [$43] Each.[97]

Friday, January 12, 1855—To day Pres[t] Steele desired me to commence teaching school, in connexion with Ja[s] Lewis.

The mail arrived from the north with news of a row between the U.S. troops and citizens of Salt Lake city, in which several hundred were engaged. It began in a quarrel between a fiddler—Hophender—and two drunken soldiers who were abusing him.[98] Friends to each side rallied until a large number were engaged on each side. The soldiers fired many pistol shots, without hurting anyone, however; the Mormons used stones, with good execution. The U.S. officers had to use their swords freely on their men, before they could drive them back to their barracks. There were two or three of them killed. Before the row ended, the soldiers had begun to run for their yaugers, and the Mormons for their rifles.

Miss Susan J. Sherman, who afterwards became my wife was on the sidewalk at the time, and took refuge in a barber shop until it was over.[99] She witnessed it all.

[page 65]

WALKER'S DEATH.

Saturday, January 13, 1855—To day is the anniversary of the settlement of Iron County. It was not celebrated, however.

Sunday, January 21, 1855—I paid to I. C. Haight $50.[00] [$1,083] for the iron works. The Iron Company attempted to make iron to day, but there was too much sulphur in the coke, it proving destructive to the iron. It was therefore determined to use Charcoal in future, until a hot blast furnace can be erected.

Fig. 2.4—Susan Julia Sherman married James Henry, January 18, 1857. Courtesy of James Henry Martineau Family Organization.

There is a great feeling of coldness among the saints, and it has been said that unless they repent, they will be severely scourged.

Sunday, February 4, 1855—To day the Utahs arrived with information that Walker, the great Chieftain,—the "King of the Mountains." was dead. He was taken ill at Corn Creek, and was removed to Fillmore by the Saints, and died there. When the tribe buried him, they killed his first wife for company for him in the other land, also two indian prisoners, for servants, and fifty fine horses, so that he could go into the "happy hunting grounds" as became a great Chieftain. One of the prisoners was buried uninjured up to his neck; leaving his head sticking out, to be picked at by the crows in the day time, and gnawed by the foxes and wolves and indian dogs in the night. The poor wretch endured unutterable agony of hunger, thirst, insects and ravenous animals before he died, and as an indian is entirely devoid of all pity or compassion, this sacrifice was regarded by them as a complete success, for the more the victim suffers, the better.

97 The *Luminary* was a newspaper published in St. Louis, Missouri, by Erastus Snow. The purpose was to inform immigrants as to their needs for traveling west. Snow was a member of the Quorum of the Twelve. In 1854 he directed the emigration of the Saints from Scandinavia. Snow was also a leader in southern Utah for many years.

98 At this writing no mention of Hophender was located fitting this entry.

99 Susan Julia Sherman would marry James Henry Martineau on January 18, 1857. It is apparent this entry was either edited or written years later.

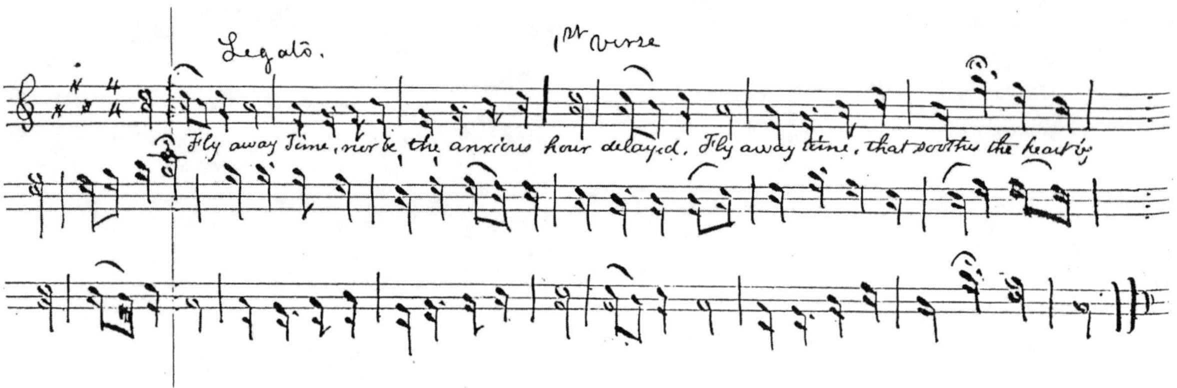

Fig. 2.5–Music that Martineau composed for a scene in *Pizarro.*

[page 66]

February 4, 1855—I have engaged to copy a manuscript, book of 500 pages, of poetry by my father-in-law Joel H. Johnson; who intends to publish it. I am to have $50.00 [$1,083]

Tuesday, February 6, 1855—A dish of oysters! The first I have tasted for a long time—since 1849. What recollections fill my mind, as I think of it.

Thursday, February 8, 1855—First tried surveying, a little, under the direction of Surveyor W. H. Dame. I did quite well, and was approved by him.

We lately had word that, the U.S. Soldiers were filling the city with whoredom and abominations. Also that several women and girls had been detected in the Soldiers quarters, dressed in men's clothing, and that they had been stripped by the police and sent home in that condition.

Tuesday, February 18, 1855—I composed the following music for a scene in "Pizarro"[100] which is preparing for the stage, Act 3 Scene 1:—

[page 67—see Appendix 3 for handwritten note inserted between pages.]

Friday, March 7 9, 1855—This evening the Parowan Dramatic Association performed "Pizarro" to a good house, successfully.

March 10, 1855—Received a letter from Sister Henrietta, urging me to come home (!) and saying uncle Peter will give me $5.000 [$108,256] if I will do so.

Mormonism cannot be estimated in dollars and cents, and in comparison the whole world is valueless. I said this in answer.

Tuesday, March 13, 1855—My birth day. Just one year ago since I assumed garments.[101]

The members of the "Mormon Battalion" gave a fine party to day, to which I was invited. About 50 tickets were issued.[102]

Wednesday, March 21, 1855—Started on horseback to Salt Lake City, with Uncle B. F. Johnson and Brs T. Carrens & Lawson all of whom have just returned from a 3½ years mission to the Sandwich Islands.[103] Last Sunday, the 18th I was sent to Fort Johnson with Elijah Elmer to preach. This was my first preaching mission. The Congregation was small, there being only 6 or 7 families living there.

100 *Pizarro* was a popular play written by Thomas A. Lyne. Lyne is credited with taking the Mormon pioneer theater beyond the amateur level (Ludlow, *Encyclopedia of Mormonism*, 2:837).

101 This is a reference to his participation in his first temple ordinances.

102 These would be former members of the Mormon Battalion who had settled in the area. The battalion was formed in 1846 in the war with Mexico. Although they never fought a battle, they suffered numerous hardships in clearing the wagon trail between Santa Fe and San Diego (Norma Baldwin Ricketts, *The Mormon Battalion: U.S. Army of the West, 1846–1848* [Logan, UT: Utah State University Press, 1996]; see also James H. Martineau, "Mormon Battalion Festival at Parowan," *Deseret News*, March 13, 1855; Journal History).

103 This could be James Lawson, who was among the early southern Utah explorers and settlers. At this writing no "T. Carrens" could be located. Elijah Elmer was a millwright, age fifty-five at this entry (Shirts and Shirts, *A Trial Furnace*, 430).

To day I made application to Gen[l] Wells for enrollment in the Topographical Corps, which was endorsed by Col. W. H. Dame.

March 22, 1855—Was disappointed yesterday, and did not start to Salt Lake city till to day. Camped on Beaver creek at 6 P.M. a distance of about 36 or 37 miles from home.

March 23, 1855—Traveled to Cove Creek

March 24, 1855—Camped 2½ miles beyond Fillmore. The Missionaries had expected to be welcomed at Fillmore, and provided with supper, beds and breakfast, as is usual for Missionaries but the Bishop extended no such hospitalities and we had to "move on" having no money.

[page 68]

SALT LAKE CITY

1855—We camped in the cedars, our sole provisions being some cracker dust and water, with two eggs each.

Sunday, March 25, 1855—Camped on Chicken Creek

March 26, 1855—Arrived at Nephi at noon , and had a good dinner. Camped at the "Crying Spring." This name was given it by the indians, because a squaw once drowned her baby in it, and the indians say they can sometimes hear it crying. It is like a deep well, about two feet across, and of unfathomable depth. The water is level with the surface.

March 27, 1855—Arrived at Payson, where B. F. Johnson lives. Dined, and went on two miles beyond Provo.

March 28, 1855—Drove to Big Cottonwood.

Tuesday, March 29, 1855—Arrived at Salt Lake City. Got barbered and went to A. W. Babbitts house, introduced myself, took breakfast, and did some business with him, and afterwards called on Geo. A. Smith, Church Historian. I first saw Susan J. Sherman here, as I came to the door. She stood there in the doorway, jumping up and down laughing. She was dressed in blue—~~denims~~ tweed, I think.

Friday, March 30, 1855—Took a bath, and called to see Gen[l] Wells, and presented my recommendation for a place in the Topographical Corps. He was well pleased, and promised to remember me when the Corps should be organized.

Saturday, March 31, 1855—Called on Pres[t] Young. Talked with him on the subject of Astrology. He discouraged me somewhat, as being a dangerous thing to meddle with. I finally told him I would let it alone, until he might say—go ahead. I told him I would study Engineering.[104] He said <u>that</u> was right, <u>that</u> was something useful.

[page 69]

Sunday, April 1, 1855—Went to meeting with Susan Sherman, who wore a light blue silk bonnet.

April 2, 1855—Quite a stir today about the three Pah vant Indians, arrested for the murder of Capt Gunnison, who have just escaped from prison.[105]

April 3, 1855—Went to the top of Ensign Peak. Drove through town in A. W. Babbitt's carriage with Susan and J. L. Heywood.

April 4, 1855—The U. S. troops left the city today, on their way to California. Some of the Mormon girls felt very bad.

April 5, 1855—Arrapeen, the Utah Chief, had a talk with Col. Steptoe to day, who tried to prevail upon the indians to sell their lands. Arrapeen refused; he said he was willing the whites should live with the Utahs in unity, and he prayed and dedicated himself and his tribe to the Lord. Col. Steptoe was greatly astonished. Barney Ward was interpreter.[106] Col. Steptoe had previously been administered to and healed by Arrapeen, Ammon and two other indians, at Nephi, and he testified to it himself.

April 6, 1855—Conference. The Tabernacle densely crowded. Several bishops were dropped for incapacity, and young men placed in their stead.

April 7, 1855—To day several women were cut off for their dealings with the Soldiers. A statement

104 Eighteenth-century engineering was a craft profession for the design and building of structural works. This included everything from irrigation to better fireplaces and land surveying. The latter would establish Martineau's reputation.

105 This was army captain John W. Gunnison, who was killed by Pahvant Paiutes. He and his company were on the Sevier River surveying for a railroad route (Shirts and Shirts, *A Trial Furnace*, 326).

106 Arrapeen was the brother of former Chief Walker (Shirts and Shirts, *A Trial Furnace*, 318). Barney Ward was among the early pioneers and an explorer during the early settlement times (Shirts and Shirts, *A Trial Furnace*, 32, 215).

of Church finances was read in Conference, by which it appears that the total amount of Church property in Salt Lake City is $614,000 [$13,293,775] Buildings in the city belonging to the Church $259,762 [$5,624,133], Cattle and Horses $59,077 [$1,277,566]. Total receipts of Salt Lake city Tithing office $58,000, Business done by P. Emigrating Company last year $35,000 [$757,789] this year $71,000[107] [$1,537,228]

[page 70]

CONFERENCE. HOME AGAIN. RUN OVER.

Sunday, April 8, 1855—The number of missionaries sent by this Conference is 153. There was about 8000 people present at the meetings.

I was ordained into the 27th Quorum of Seventies today by Thos Bullock and Stephen Goddard.[108]

April 9, 1855—Transacted some business.

Tuesday, April 10, 1855—Went to Tho. Bullocks house to a quorum meeting.

April 11, 1855—This morning a wagon load of women went off with the soldiers to California, riding in the U. S. Wagons. Some of the people threw stones at them, when the officer in charge drew a pistol to shoot them, but it would not go.

April 12, 1855—Hunted uncle Benjamin's horses all day.

April 13 & 14, 1855—Still hunting them. Br. Callister finally got them.[109]

Sunday, April 15, 1855—Started home, with B. F. Johnson. A. W. Babbitt gave me considerable paper, quills, sand box &c While riding homewards, driving, the lines got hitched, and I went out on the wagon tongue to fix them, when the horses ran away, I trying in the mean time to keep my footing on the pole, which I did for some time, trying first to mount one horse, then the other. Finally crossing a ditch, the jerk threw me off, dragging some time under the horses feet, by the lines. They broke, and I prepared for the striking of the wheel, not knowing but that it might run over my head or nick and kill me. But it did not. It went over my back, and I got up and ran after the team, not feeling hurt any, although it was a heavy wagon with quite a heavy load in it. I felt no pain until night, when stopping at Lehi. I suddenly fainted for a few moments. Next day I was somewhat sore and lame and that was all. It was considered a narrow escape.

April 16, 1855—Arrived at Payson at dark.

[page 71]

JOURNEY HOME.

April 17, 1855—Found Susan's cousin, Susan Julia Sherman, quite ill with toothache. Felt much sympathy for her. I liked her very much, and she seemed to like me. I put her on Uncle Benjamin's horse "Ranger" which he had just brought from California, and which no man but him could ride, not knowing his character. She rode him around on the run, till Uncle Benj. happened to see her, when he was much frightened and took her off. I remained several days waiting for company home, it being dangerous to travel alone on account of indians.

I exchanged rings with Susan before starting home.

April 20, 1855—Started home, riding to Nephi, 25 miles in a wagon, having left my mare at that place.

April 21, 1855—Started alone, to travel about 200 miles alone through an indian Country. I took no provisions except about 8 or 9 biscuits, not wishing to be bothered to carry much baggage with me. I camped at Pioneer Creek, a few miles from Fillmore.

April 22, 1855—Went to Fillmore and breakfasted with Mulford. Went on and camped at Pine Creek.

April 23, 1855—Got home, very tired; my mare also, having rode nearly 70 miles a day for three days in succession.

To prevent being surprised sleeping, I would stop about half an hour before sun set, turn out my horse, make my bed, eat a biscuit, and make all preparations for sleeping there. But about an hour after dark, I got

107 The Perpetual Emigrating Fund utilized Church assets and private contributions to help early members emigrating from Europe and the eastern United States.

108 Thomas Bullock was the clerk to President Brigham Young as well as a frequent traveling companion (Shirts and Shirts, *A Trial Furnace*, 117–18). A "Stephen Goddard" is listed by Ludlow as one of the early conductors of the Mormon Tabernacle Choir, 1854–56 (Ludlow, *Encyclopedia of Mormonism*, 2:950).

109 At this writing no reference to Callister was located.

up silently saddled up and quietly left, generally riding six or 8 miles further. I would then turn aside into the prairie, lie down and go to sleep, listening to the wolves howling all round me, keeping one end of my mare's rope where I could quickly grasp it if she should try to run away.

[page 72]

April 1855—By this means I concealed my sleeping place from the indians. In the morning at daylight I would start, ride 7 or 8 miles to some good open grounds, then stop and eat my biscuit, feed my mare, and then go on. I eat only one biscuit for a meal.

At Corn creek my mare suddenly took a scare, and nearly got away from me, when I was many miles from any settlement. I grasped the rope as she started to run off, and as she drew it through my hand, it took the flesh off my hand and fingers almost to the bone. After I got on her back she ran with me five miles before I could stop her. I then made her run another five miles to pay for it, tying her finally to a cedar tree beside the road.

Found my family all well.

Friday, April 27, 1855—Attended City Council for the first time as a Councillor.

Wednesday, May 9, 1855—Bought half a city lot adjoining mine of Elijah Elmer, for $30.00 [$650] of Wall tax credit.

Monday, May 14, 1855—Was appointed by Pres^{t} J. C. L. Smith to make out the Consecration deeds for the brethren. I consecrated my property, amounting, on paper to $1300 [$28,796], but it would not have cashed that. [Added in shaky handwriting.] amount.

Friday, May 18, 1855—Pres^{t} Young and Company arrived and held meeting the same evening

May 19, 1855—I received a Commission as 2nd Lieutenant and one as Adjutant.

Monday, May 21, 1855—Pres^{t} Young returned from Cedar City.

[page 73]

ORDAINED A HIGH PRIEST.

Monday, May 21, 1855—He had caused a new city to be surveyed out, near the iron works.

In the evening, at 9½ P.M., I was ordained a High Priest under the hands of Geo. A. Smith and John C. L. Smith, and set apart as First Councillor to Pres^{t} J. C. L. Smith, presiding over the Parowan Stake. Jesse N. Smith was also ordained and set apart as 2nd Councillor.[110]

Wednesday, May 22, 1855—Pres^{t} Young and party returned to S. L. City.

May 23, 1855—Attended a party given to John Steel and W. C. Mitchell, who are appointed to go on a mission. Zilpha, wife of Elder G. A. Smith spoke in tongues with great power: also Job P. Hall: and Pres^{t} J. C. L. Smith sang in tongues. Pres^{t} Smith gave the interpretation of Sister Zilpha's tongue, which was to encourage the missionaries; and warned and reproved the sisters for their non-compliance with the law of celestial marriage, and predicted many things that should come upon them, and the trials shortly to come upon the saints.

Thursday, May 24, 1855—Spent the forenoon with Pres^{t} Smith in counselling, and in the afternoon fitted up the middle upper room of the meeting house for an office. Father Johnson and Nephi arrived on their way to Salt Lake City.

Friday, May 25, 1855—Wrote the following verses for the Missionaries:—

1

Go, messengers of Zion
    And publish truth abroad
Be cheerful, and rely on
    The Mercy of our God.
For He will not desert you
    But ever be your friend

[page 74]

May 1855—
Your Leader and Protector
    Till time and Earth shall end.

2

Go, hunt the sons of Nephi:
    Go, search the caves and holes:
Search ~~for~~ out the seed of ~~Nephi~~ Lehi

110 See *Deseret News*, May 21, 1855, for the record of Martineau's being set apart as a counselor in the stake presidency; see also *Deseret News*, June 30, 1855, 69; Journal History.

And sons of Laman bold
Go, preach to them salvation
And tell them that their God
Has heard their lamentations
And will withhold the rod.

3

The bonds that long have galled them
Shall ~~be~~ soon, in sunder brake
And those that have oppressed them
In fear and anguish quake
While on them the Almighty,
The vials of his wrath
Shall pour, with curses weighty
And in their trouble laugh.

4

Then shall the Lord's anointed
Lead forth a chosen band
And in the place appointed
By God's divine command,
A temple rear most glorious
In which the Lord will meet
Those who have proved victorious
To worship at his feet.

5

Go forth ye chosen servants
The saints full armor wear
Have faith and perseverance
And shun each deadly snare.
Fulfill your glorious mission
And when your work is done.

[page 75]

May 1855—
You then will have permission
To meet your friends at home.

Saturday, May 26, 1885—To day I wrote the following:—

TRUST IN GOD

1

The God who has blessed us, in days that are past
Will never forsake us, but prove to the last
That He is our Father, in truth and in deed
And will not deny us the things that we need.

2

In faith, then, we'll ~~look to~~ trust in the God whom we serve
To bless us in spirit, in body and nerve
With blessings eternal, with children and wives,
And power most glorious—of eternal lives.

3

With blessings unstinted of fruit, oil and wine.
With gems from the ~~ocean~~ caverns—with gold from the mine,
With servants and cattle—with houses and land
Which He will bestow with a bountiful hand.

4

Though clouds dark as midnight—the heavens shall veil,—
Though crickets and locusts our harvests assail—
Though pest'lence and famine, with fire and sword
Shall stalk through the land, we'll trust in the Lord.

5

For judgment begins at the house of the Lord
~~From which it will~~ And there shall it spread to ~~the~~ all nations abroad;
And if those who are righteous shall scarcely escape
To what shall the wicked and filthy awake?

6

Then let us rejoice in the work of the Lord
And live by the whole of his excellent word;
The clouds will soon vanish—the heavens grow bright—
And ~~we will~~ saints shall then dwell in ~~continual~~ heavenly light.

[page 76]

Sunday, May 27, 1855—To day, the meeting was turned into a special conference, and several persons were cut off from the church for immorality. Some of the sisters were then set apart to act as nurses for the sick, and to teach the sisters the principles of their organizations, and to doctor by faith and mild herbs: Sisters Mary Smith, Margaret West and Hannah Fish were unanimously chosen for that calling, and in the evening were blessed and set apart by the president and council.[111]

I was unanimously sustained by the people as recorder and reporter for the Stake.

Pres[t] Smith then presented me as his first Councillor and Jesse N. Smith as his second Councillor to the meeting, and both were unanimously sustained by vote.

This evening, Thomas Whitney, a young Pah Eed indian, who had been appointed Chief by desire of Pres[t] Young, was blessed and set apart as a chief, by Pres[t] J. C. L. Smith and Council: being the first chief ever appointed and blessed by the authority of the priesthood in this part of the Territory.

May 28, 1855—Attended a party.

May 29, 1855—Finished my part of the public square fence, & afterwards spent the day reading this history of the stake to Pres[t] Smith

May 30, 1855—Wrote to Elder G. A. Smith: also sent my genealogy to Pres[t] Pettigrew of the High Priests Quorum.[112]

Thursday, May 31, 1855—The sisters held their first meeting to day.

Sunday, June 3, 1855—My son Moroni H. was blessed in meeting to day by Pres[t] J. C. L. Smith. Samuel Lewis and his wife were rebaptized, having confessed in meeting to their crime of adultery before they married.

[page 77]

TRIP TO FISH LAKE

June 5, 1855—To day, for the first time in several months we had a good shower of rain.

Thursday, June 7, 1855—Attended fast meeting. Spoke, and felt well. I resigned the post of Choir leader, and appointed Rich[d] Benson chorister.[113]

June 8, 1855—The mail arrived, bringing me some letters, and the first five numbers of the "Mormon."

June 22, 1855—Bp. Evans and Company arrived from an exploring tour at the White mountains, west of here.[114]

Monday, June 25, 1855—Started to go to Fish Lake with J. N. Smith and six others. Camped in the canyon.

June 26, 1855—Started this morning at 6¼, arrived at the summit at 7¼ A.M. and at the lake at 8¾ A.M. and after obtaining permission of the indians to fish, we went round to the east side of the lake, which is nearly round, and about a mile across. We camped on the shore of the lake among some tall pine trees. A band of indians was on the other side of the lake, catching and drying fish. They had two captive eagles, which they keep to get beautiful white plumes from, which they sell.

We cut down a large tree, and began to make a canoe.

June 27, 1855—Worked at our canoe. While I was chopping the ax glanced on a chip, flew out of my hand to where the boys were sitting, talking, and struck Atha Carter, edge first, on his hand, as he was whittling. The ax cut his hand, turned over and struck him on the breast knocking the breath out of him. I was much scared. We administered to him, and he soon got better.

[page 78]

Fish Lake.

May 1855—We finished the canoe, which will hold 8 men, and launched her at 9½ A.M. naming

111 Mary Amelia Smith was the daughter of George Albert Smith. She married Peter Wimmer (Shirts and Shirts, *A Trial Furnace*, 132). This is likely Margaret T. Smith, wife of Jesse N. Smith. Hanna Fish was the wife of Horace Fish, both early southern Utah settlers (Seegmiller, *History of Iron County*, 89).

112 This is likely David Pettigrew, who served in the Mormon Battalion with James R. Pettigrew (Ricketts, *The Mormon Battalion*, 28).

113 Richard Benson, age thirty-nine at this entry, was a Parowan carpenter (Shirts and Shirts, *A Trial Furnace*, 426).

114 This could be William Evans, who participated in the early mining explorations and settled in Cedar City (Shirts and Shirts, *A Trial Furnace*, 150, 331, 354).

her the "White Canoe." As the water was too rough to fish we spent the day in paddling our canoe over it. The water is very clear, and very deep, being apparently the mouth of a volcano. Myself & John Davis started in the canoe to go to the mouth of the outlet,[115] J. N. Smith and A. Carter going along the shore, on account of the roughness of the water. The waves increased so that we were in danger of swamping, and had to go close in shore, and finally to return to Camp.

May 28, 1855—Went over to the indian camp and bought fish of them, getting two fish for a biscuit. Started home at 10½ A.M. and at 11 A.M. were overtaken by a hail storm, and rain. Arrived at the Summit at noon, and were closely enveloped in a cloud. We were soon wet to the skin with rain and snow and we got very cold. We rode fast all the way home in a storm of rain, until we got below the cloud and got home, tired wet and cold.

The country on the summit is delightful, being covered with timber, pine, aspen, fir and underbrush. The ground was covered with strawberries, which are now in bloom. The nights are very cold,—water froze in our tin cups at night. This lake is the head of the Sevier river, south [fork].

May 29, 1855—Watered my potatos, first time, They are injured by the grasshoppers.

Sunday, July 1, 1855—Attended the Sunday School, and spoke to the Children. Pres. Smith desired me to teach the Deseret Alphabet. In the evening myself and J. N. Smith were appointed orators of the day for the celebration on the 24th inst. which I was loth to accede to.

July 2, 1855—Some of the brethren went up the Canyon to get a new liberty pole.

[page 79]

July 4, 1855—We raised our new liberty pole, and saluted it with discharge of fire arms and music by the Cedar Brass Band[116]

July 7, 1855—The California mail came, bringing me a letter from Henrietta, and one from Sixtus E. Johnson, my brother-in-law, now preaching in the Sandwich Islands.

July 9, 1855—Began teaching a large school in the Deseret Alphabet, gratis.

July 10, 1855—Father and Nephi arrived from the north with Salt, which they obtained about 35 miles up the Sevier river above the Territorial Bridge. There is a mountain of it, solid as a rock and clear as glass.

July 11, 1855—Susan's birth day.—nineteen years old.

July 14, 1855—The Sunday School children had a party, and marched around the Square, led by the Parowan Brass Band.

July 16, 1855—The militia were out, and had a good drill. They agreed to drill every Saturday afternoon under my charge.

July 17, 1855—Began haying today. I got two loads.

July 20, 1855—Haying every day.

July 24, 1855—Had a celebration as usual. Myself and J. N. Smith were orators of the day, but did not display any wonderful oratorial efforts.[117] At noon, Beason Lewis came from Salt Lake City, and brought word that Brigham ~~That~~ on Sunday, the 8th inst. had proclaimed our independence of the U. S. rule. He said he was not afraid of the soldiers—not 500.000 of them. Also that after this year we would raise plenty of grain. Also that all who are fearful can go to California, or take Seven years provisions and go into the mountains and hide up.

[page 80]

FIND SALT IN THE LITTLE SALT LAKE.

July 1855—I am glad, if this is so. Our liberty may be bought with blood, but that is a small price. I am willing to spend mine for that end.

Saturday, August 4, 1855—Made out my regimental report, and in the afternoon taught my military school as usual.

115 This could be John J. Davies, who was a noted choir director in Iron County (Seegmiller, *History of Iron County*, 239).

116 At this celebration Martineau writes in defense of Mormonism to an unidentified eastern newspaper that has run an article on *The Mormon* (James H. Martineau, "To the Editor of the Mormon," July 14, 1855, 3; filed under July 5, 1855, in the Journal History).

117 "Celebration of July 24th, in Utah," August 26, 1854, *Deseret News*; Utah Digital Newspapers.

Monday, August 6, 1855—To day, nearly all Parowan went down to the dry bed of Little Salt Lake to get salt, it having been lately found there.[118] We went, and found thousands of tons of excellent salt, lying on the bottom of the lake, under about an inch or two of water. We, men and women, waded into the mud up to our knees until we came to the water and salt; and then scraped up the salt into heaps of about a bushel, and let the water drain out of it; then carried it to our wagons on the lake shore, from 40 to 80 rods off. It was very toilsome work, carrying the salt through mud so deep and sticky we could hardly pull our legs and feet out at each step. Afterwards, people brought boards to lay on the mud, to walk on. The Lake had not been so dried up before, since the valley was settled, and no one thought there was any salt there. Consequently, all the salt for Iron County had been brought from Salt Lake—nearly 300 miles—and sold for 25 cents pr pound. This new discovery in one day reduced the price to a cent a pound!

At the ~~south~~ north end of the Lake, I saw wagon tracks deeply imprinted in the mud, extending as far as I could see. Who or when that wagon crossed the dry bed of the lake, no one knows.

August 8, 1855—The full election returns having come in, it appears that Br. C. C. Pendleton was elected Recorder.

[page 81]

August 11, 1855—Went to Cedar City to sit on a regimental Court Martial, as Judge Advocate.

August 12, 1855—The people agreed to day, to open a new road into the 2^{d} Left hand Kanyon for timber.

August 13, 1855—Went with Susan E. to the Lake for salt. The Salt Mud made my legs smart so bad that we only got about 400 lbs.

August 14, 1855—Acted to day as clerk to H. D. Bayless Justice of the Peace, in a case between John ~~Steele~~ Smith and Sam. Lewis, about a mule. Smith got the mule.

August 18, 1855—Spent the day in session of the City Council.

August 19, 1855—Quite a rain last night, wetting the earth about an inch deep. There has been only one other shower this year, so far.

August 21, 1855—To day, two indians from Cedar city came to warn us that the Pahvants intend to steal our cattle and horses. We had our loose stock driven in from the range, so that people could take care of their animals.

August 26, 1855—At meeting to day, the people agreed to repair the field fence forthwith or be disfellowshipped in a week. They agreed to fix the fence of John Steele and Wm Burston, absent on missions.[119]

August 28, 1855—Went and repaired my fence. A few others also went.

September 4, 1855—Attended the wedding of Ed. Ward and Miss Elizabeth Parker, at Richd Benson's[120]

September 5, 1855—Hunted my two cows, which the herdsman had left out. Went out to an island in the lake, prayed, and determined and covenanted to preserve my body better. My cows were brought home by an indian. They had been gone about three days.

September 9, 1855—The meeting to day was turned into a Special Conference, at which the authorities of the Church were sustained, and also of this stake of Zion as follows:—

[page 82]

September 1855—Presidency. John C. L. Smith, J. H. Martineau, 1st Councillor and Jesse N. Smith, 2nd Councillor.

Bishop, Tarlton Lewis, and Councillors C. C. Pendleton and O. B. Adams.

High Council, Saml Goold, Elijah Newman, P. Meeks, S. West, F. T. Whitney, W. H. Dame, M. Ensign, Job P. Hall, E. Elmer, H. M. Alexander, Ja^{s} Lewis and Charles Hall.[121]

---

118 Parowan Valley was also known as the Little Salt Lake Valley. *Parowan* is a Paiute word meaning "bad, salty or harmful water" (Shirts and Shirts, *A Trial Furnace*, 11, 14).

119 William Burston (also spelled Burstone) is listed in familysearch.org. He was the husband of Maria Walker.

120 Richard Benson is listed as one of Parowan's early dentists (Seegmiller, *History of Iron County*, 224). Edward Ward and Elizabeth Parker-Ward later had two children that were born in San Bernardino, California.

121 Orson B. Adams was a settler in the Iron Mission. He was an engineer, age forty-one at this writing (Shirts and Shirts, *A Trial Furnace*, 425). Samuel Goold is misspelled here; it should be Samuel Gould. Elijah Newman, too, was an iron

September 15, 1855—Worked at home to day, making out deeds of Consecration for several of the brethren. Also wrote in my journal. Also made out the Bishop's Report, for next October Conference, and recorded minutes of our special Conference.

September 17, 1855—The Parowan Dramatic Association began operations again to day, for the coming season. I was appointed Caster of Characters.

September 20, 1855—To day Pres^t Smith started to Conference, leaving me to preside in his absence. He also appointed me deputy postmaster. I spent the time writing up the history of this stake since its reorganization May 20th 1855 in the new alphabet. I have labored to teach it to the people here, gratis, but they do not seem to appreciate it much.

To day Tarlton Lewis and others went up the canyon, to where they think they have found coal. Moroni has been sick for several days.

September 21, 1855—Moroni is better, to day. I rely entirely upon the ordinances, of washing, anointing, and the laying on of hands, instead of depending on doctors.

[page 83]

MY COW KILLED.

September 22, 1855—Br. E. Luddington arrived thus far on his journey home from his India and China Mission.[122] He preached and told us of his travels and hardships in that heathen country.

September 25, 1855—Engaged C. C. Pendleton to make me a Minnie rifle.[123] Price, $67.^00 [$1,451] to be paid in credit on the city wall. It is to be finished in six weeks.

September 26, 1855—Measured my wheat, and found I have 14¼ bushels, which, with 3½ bushels due me G. Wood, and 9 bushels engaged for a steer I have sold, is all the show I have for my family until next harvest, if we have one. But I trust in the promise that "my bread shall be sure" to me.

The grasshoppers have destroyed all our grain, all through the Territory, but I think we will live, somehow.

September 28, 1855—Went with my family to Johnson's Ranch.

September 29, 1855—I went to Cedar City. Attended the rehearsal by the Dramatic Association of "the Vicar of Wakefield." They made a poor show.

September 30, 1855—Got my 9 bushels of wheat for a two year old steer, and engaged 20 more. Got home at 4 P.M. and learned that my best cow was killed by the indians. H. D. Bayless went with me , and we skinned her. An indian had shot her, because she knocked down a net he had set to catch rabbits, as she was grazing along.

October 1, 1855—Some indians told about the killing of my cow to day. After consultation, I told the indians if they would bring the offender and whip him, we would let it all go.

[page 84]

October 1855—They agreed, and in about an hour, the indian came to be whipped, accompanied by the chief and others. They tied him to the liberty pole, and whipped him well with a birch, the Chief administering the blows, and talking to him all the time.

After the whipping, I gave him (the whipper) the shirt I had on, some tobacco and some other small articles, and thus this matter was settled. But this did not bring back my only milk cow.

missionary laborer. He would have been fifty-seven at this writing (Shirts and Shirts, *A Trial Furnace*, 473). Francis T. Whitney was an Iron Mission settler. He was a blacksmith, age forty-nine at this writing (Shirts and Shirts, *A Trial Furnace*, 440). William H. Dame was another iron missionary. He was a surveyor, age thirty-five at this entry (Shirts and Shirts, *A Trial Furnace*, 429). Marius Ensign was an iron missionary and a farmer, age thirty-three at this entry. This is likely Job P. Hall, who was an iron missionary. He was a cooper, meaning he worked making and repairing barrels and casks. He would have been thirty-four at this writing (Shirts and Shirts, *A Trial Furnace*, 432). There is a Horace M. Alexander listed as a corporal in the Mormon Battalion. He served a mission to the southern states and is the only one in this group not to be among the original iron missionaries (Ricketts, *Mormon Battalion*, 23). Charles Hall was a member of the original iron missionaries. He was a cooper and at this writing was thirty-two years old (Shirts and Shirts, *A Trial Furnace*, 432).

122 Elam Luddington was a first lieutenant in the Mormon Battalion, Company B (Ricketts, *Mormon Battalion*, 22).

123 The Minnie rifle was a famous Civil War weapon.

October 5, 1855—Bought a cow to day of Mrs. Steele for 15 bush[s] of wheat. She is old, poor, and blind of one eye.

October 8, 1855—Began with E. Ward to make adobies to make my house.[124] We have made a pug mill.

October 11, 1855—Quit making adobies to day. Having made 4800 in all of which my portion is 1800.

October 19, 1855—To day I began to lay the foundations of the addition to my house. There will be a bedroom built on the end, and a kitchen and bed room behind. I shall also raise the old walls about two feet higher.

October 20, 1855—Began to lay the adobies for my house. Not having any crop, consequently not much to hire labor with. I do it myself.

In the afternoon Pres[t] Smith and others arrived from the Conference, to my great joy. Editha Johnson, my sister-in-law, also arrived from Lehi.

October 25, 1855—Began to dig my potatoes. They were much hurt by the grasshoppers: and after that by army worms and afterwards by the large tobacco worms, of which incredible numbers were killed each day on the vines.[125] They seemed to increase faster than they were killed off, no one knowing where they came from.

[page 85]

MURDER OF ISAAC WHITEHOUSE BY BAKER & WIFE.

October 28, 1855—Ja[s] Lewis was rebaptized to day. He has long been disaffected with the authorities. Also Rich[d] Benson who has been the same. I heard of the sudden death and burial of an orphan boy named Izaac Whitehouse. He died last night and was secretly buried in the night.

October 29, 1855—To day the body of the boy, who was an orphan about 11 years of age, was dug up, brought to the hall, and an inquest held by H. D. Bayless, Justice of the Peace. When the body was examined it was a horrible sight to see. He had been buried in his dirty clothes and excrement, and showed evident signs of violence. His hands and feet had been tied with a cord (the marks of which were still shown in the flesh) and then he had been placed in a water ditch, and partly chilled and partly drowned. The sand had washed into and settled in the folds of his clothing. His body had large purple spots where he had been kicked or struck, the skin being badly abrazed and broken. Baker denied all, but his wife confessed, and got the cord with which he had been tied. The testimony of the people revealed a long course of the most inhuman cruelty, perpetrated on the poor boy, whose father and mother, dying while on their way here, left him to the care of Mrs. Baker, the sister of his mother. After she got him, she herself became a mother, and hated the boy most intensely, and incited Baker to his cruel deeds.

Baker was cool and defiant throughout. The verdict of the jury is, that deceased came to his death through the cruelty of Sam[l] G. Baker and his wife.[126]

[page 86]

October 29, 1855—To day, Thomas Davenport opened his kiln of Pottery.[127] This is the first ever made south of Provo. I got two jars, some bowls and two meat dishes.

Tuesday, October 30, 1855—This day S. G. Baker and his wife were cut off from the church for their crime, by a unanimous vote of all the people.

October 31, 1855—My wife is sick to day. Pres[t] Smith and I administered to her, and she was immediately healed.

November 2, 1855—This morning, found it cold and snowing.

Sunday, November 4, 1855—Still snowing, and thawing. To day Henry is three years old, Attended Council in the evening, as usual.

To day, William Heap, desired to be rebaptized, having been cut off for the church for apostasy. He

124 A common building product of the Southwest, adobe bricks were made of sun-dried clay.

125 An army worm is a yellow caterpillar that travels in large groups devouring crops. The tobacco hornworm is a large green caterpillar that normally feeds on tobacco plants.

126 At this writing no information could be located about this family or the child Izaac Whitehouse.

127 Thomas Davenport was a potter and songwriter (Shirts and Shirts, *A Trial Furnace*, 400; Seegmiller, *History of Iron County*, 182, 240).

was allowed to do so, after having made a humble confession.

November 7, 1855—Settled with Wm Aston for his labor, he having worked 2½ days for me, and put in only 7 or 8 hours each day for a full day.

Was clerk to day in a Bishops trial. Wm Heap charged W. C. Mitchell with trying to get his (Heap's) wife to leave him, and marry Mitchell. The Bishop decided that Mitchell be cut off from the Church.

Thursday, November 8, 1855—This afternoon the Presidency of the Stake went to the new town of Paragoonah to dedicate the place.[128] Spent some time in looking at the fort and took supper at 7 P.M. The fort is built square, of adobies, 105 feet square, two stories high, outside walls three feet thick without any doors or windows, except, the gateway, which has a room over it.

[page 87]

November 1855—About fifty persons sat down to supper, which was a bountiful one; and afterwards we enjoyed ourselves in the dance until about 2 A.M.

November 13, 1855—S. G. Baker & wife had an examination before Justice Hopkins[129] of Cedar City, for the death of the boy Whitehouse. He and his wife had tried to escape to California previously, but failed. They were bound over to be tried before the next District Court in Parowan.

November 17, 1855—John Steele and W. C. Mitchell returned from the Las Vegas Mission, and on the 18th

November 18, 1855—gave an account of their missionary labors.

November 19, 1855—Began to write off the parts of plays for our D. Association for distribution. Finished "Box & Ox Married and Settled."

November 21, 1855—This evening Elder Amasa Lyman arrived from San Bernardino on his way to S. L. City. accompanied by some returning elders from the Sandwich Islands.

Some elders arrived from S. L. City the same evening, with the word that Prest J. C. L. Smith was quite sick at Fillmore when they came through that city.

The Deputy U. S. Marshall also arrived from Fillmore, with papers for the arrest of Baker and for witnesses. I am subpoenaed as a witness, much against my will.

November 22, 1855—Started with others for Fillmore, hiring my passage with E. Ward, $10.00 [$217]. Camped at Beaver Creek. Snowed in the night.

November 23, 1855—Traveled to Cove Creek.[130] Snowed all day.

November 24, 1855—Arrived at Fillmore, and went at once to see Prest Smith, who was very glad to see me.

November 25, 1855—Went to meeting

November 26, 1855—Went to Court. The Baker Case came up and the trial began, before Judge W. W. Drummond beside him on the bench sat a strumpet, calls wife falsely.[131]

[page 88]

December 1, 1855—To day the Baker trial was finished. He was sentenced to ten years imprisonment in the penitentiary.

December 2, 1855—We started home this morning, with Prest Smith on a bed in a carriage. I rode with him to help take care of him.

I got goods to the amount of $34.00 [$736] for which I feel thankful indeed. Went to Cove Creek.

December 3, 1855—Camped at Beaver Creek, and on the 4th

December 4, 1855—arrived at home, and found all well and feeling thankful to God for my safe journey. The Court was held by Judge W. W. Drummond.

128 First known as Red Creek, the town of Paragonah is located just north of Parowan.

129 This could be Charles Hopkins, who was among the first southern Utah exploration teams. He settled in Cedar City (Shirts and Shirts, *A Trial Furnace*, 10).

130 Cove Creek—or Cove Fort, as it was called—was a major stop for travelers. It offered protection as well as food and rest. It is just north of Beaver, Utah, and today has been restored as a historical site.

131 William W. Drummond was a territorial Superior Court judge appointed by President James Buchanan. He did not like the Mormons and was openly immoral in his conduct. Brigham Young described Drummond as an "infernal, dirty, sneaking rotten-hearted pot-house politician" (Arrington, *Brigham Young*, 233; Shirts and Shirts, *A Trial Furnace*, 383; Seegmiller, *History of Iron County*, 65).

He had a whore with him, whom he claimed as his wife, she sitting with him in Court. He had left a wife and children at his home in Illinois. He is a bitter enemy to us as a people, and is constantly sending lies to Washington about us. He sent his slave Cato to whip a little Jew Merchant while at Fillmore, who nearly killed the poor Jew. He had Drummond arrested for it, and it made much amusement, to see a great U. S. Judge, sent to judge the Mormons, himself under arrest. Hosea Stout was an Attorney at this court.

December 5, 1855—By request of Pres^t Smith, I anointed him all over and prayed for him.

December ~~6~~ 7, 1855—Snowed about four inches last night. We had "the Jacobite" and "Box & Cox" to night.

December 14, 1855—To night saw a remarkable sight in the sky:—

A large circle around the moon, as we often see; the bottom of the circle being below the horizon, the rest of it having three bright spots one on each side and one at the top: another horizontal circle, passing around the heavens, passing through the moon and the two spots at the sides, the zenith being the center of it.

[page 89]

December 1855—This horizontal circle also had, including the moon, four bright spots, like moons, at equal distances apart. The following gives an idea of it:—

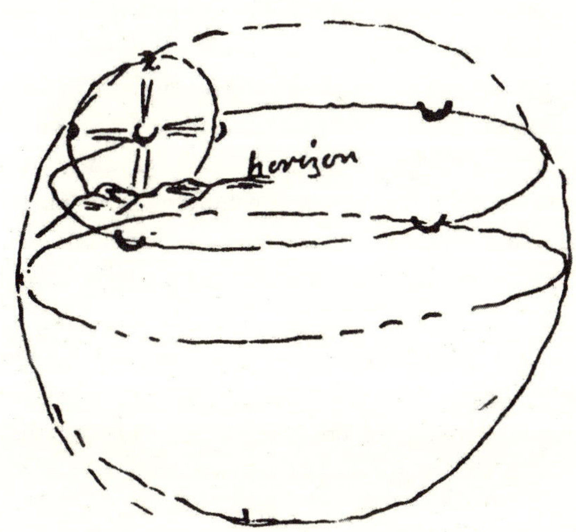

Fig. 2.6—Orbit circle around moon.

There were also broad bands of light passing from the moon to the three moons surrounding it, and one to the horizon below, where the other moon would have been if the circle had been entirely above the horizon.

[See Appendix 3, letter from George Albert Smith inserted here.]

December 15, 1855—A quarterly conference at Cedar to day. Pres^t Smith still continues very low, but I hope he will recover.

~~Sunday~~ Thursday, December 20, 1855—Went to Meeting as usual. The report of the amount of grain in Parowan was presented, by which it appears we have but 1080 bushels of wheat, and 1860 bushels of potatoes to last the people until next harvest, which will allow but a half pound of flour apiece to a population of about 400 souls per day. and leaving nothing for seed.

Friday, December 21, 1855—To day a Conference was held in Parowan at which I presided. Pres^t Smith being unable to come. Speaking by O. B. Adams, W. H. Dame and myself. The meeting adjourned until tomorrow at 10. A.M.[132]

December 22, 1855—Blowed hard all night, and snowed all day. To day Brs. Wallace and J. B. Nobles spoke. Br. Wallace organized the High Priests into a quorum (mass) and on my motion Pres^t Smith was appointed to its presidency. In the afternoon Pres^t E. Snow and Jacob Gates spoke. Pres^t Smith rather worse to day. Adj. until tomorrow.

December 23, 1855—Conference met at 10 A.M. We had much good instruction from Elder E. Snow and others. Br. E. Snow prophesied Calvin should recover, and all the people said "Amen."

[page 90]

December 1855—Pres^t Snow adjourned the Conference to the 23^d of March next.

December 25, 1855—Had a good meeting to day. Wm Lefever was married in meeting this evening, and Pres^t E Snow gave instructions on marriage, &c. He said that when parents begot children, they only

132 For a report on the conference, see Journal History, December 22, 1855, 1–2; see also James H. Martineau, "Singular Phenomenon," *Deseret News*, December 23, 1855, 5:357; Journal History.

repaid the gift of their own bodies: and therefore had no claim upon their children. But if their children wished to be sealed to their ~~children~~ parents, it was all right; if to be sealed to some one else, it was equally right, and that this was the key to the principle of adoption. Also said that God himself began in this way, first taking one wife, afterwards, more.

Br. Nobles blessed me before he started home.

Br. Calvin still remains very sick, although we administer to him every day. He says he has not a particle of faith to be healed by the laying on of hands, although when he lays hands on the sick they are almost always instantly healed. Last night he had such a pleasant dream, of preaching in the spirit world.

Sunday, December 30, 1855—Went to meeting as usual. Appointed next Tuesday—New Years—as a day of fasting and prayer for Pres^t Smith, and to humble ourselves before the Lord. I also attended the Quorum meeting as usual. At a little after 9 P.M. I was sent for to come to Pres^t Smith. I found him in great pain about the heart—intense agony. We administered to him, but no benefit followed. At 20 minutes to 11 P.M. he departed in peace. His wife, who sat on the bed feeling his pulse cease, dropped senseless to the floor. I raised and half carried her into the next room.

Br. Smith was a lovely man, one who had no thought save for the advancement of the cause of God.

[page 91]

December 1855—To sum up his character—he was loved by, and a lover of God and righteousness. He was appointed to preside over this stake in May, 1852.

With his death I cease to be a president of this branch, and do not regret to be relieved of the labors and responsibilities of that office. I can say truly, that while in this position, I have tried to the best of my ability to carry out all the counsels of the authorities, and to work for the good of the saints. I have never given any one bad counsel, knowingly, and feel that altho' I have probably made some mistakes and some enemies, it has been through ignorance and the weakness of humanity.

May my last end be that of the righteous.

December 31, 1855—To day is cold and gloomy, rendered doubly so by the death and funeral of our beloved President. He was buried at about 4 P.M. and was followed to the grave by nearly all the people.

JANUARY 1856

Tuesday, January 1, 1856—This day we observe in fasting and prayer, and we had a good meeting.

January 7, 1856—In shouldering a sack of grain, I hurt my neck so I can hardly move it or myself.

January 8, 1856—To day Susan and I have been married four years. We have two fine boys, and I pray that we may be able to bring them up in the faith of the gospel.

January 9, 1856—Went to Paragoonah

January 10, 1856—Started to day to attend court at Fillmore as a grand Juror, in the place of Br. Calvin Smith.[133] Went to Beaver and camped.

January 11, 1856—Camped at Cove Creek.

[page 92]

AT FILLMORE,—A GRAND JURYMAN.

January 12, 1856—Arrived at Fillmore. Went immediately to call on Elder G. A. Smith, with Jesse N. Smith

We went to Br. S. P. Hoyt's, where he was stopping during the session of the Legislature, knocked, and were invited in.[134] As the door opened we found the room full of Company, there being a dinner-party given to the Presidency and Twelve. We could not help it, and so went in, dusty with travel as we were, and we were introduced individually to all the Company, ladies and gentlemen. Pres^t Young treated us very kindly. Dinner being announced presently, all went in but Elder Geo. A. Smith, who remained to keep us company. In a few moments, however, Representative Isaac C. Haight came out saying the President wished him to give his place at table that we might eat. So we went in and sat down. The President said he thought we would be quite hungry and tired after our tedious journey, and had therefore asked us in. Nothing could exceed his kindness and attention to us. We spent a very pleasant hour. I then found where father J H Johnson is stopping he being Chaplain of the Legislative Assembly,

133 This could be Charles P. Smith, who was a resident of Cedar City and among the early settlers (Shirts and Shirts, *A Trial Furnace*, 11).

134 Silas P. Hoyt was a resident of Cedar City and among the early settlers (Shirts and Shirts, *A Trial Furnace*, 331).

and, took my lodgings with him and his wife Janet. Had a lesson on practical home manufacture by Father and others, which I enjoyed with them.

Sunday, January 13, 1856—Went to meeting, Pres[t] B. Young preached. Among other things he said that the spirits of those who die without the priesthood are tormented after death by the Devil, while those who have the priesthood, are not. The 1000 years will be used in sealing man to man.

He also told us not to bow to the Gentile Judges then holding Court.

January 14, 1856—Attended Court as one of the Grand Jury.

January 15, 1856—Attended again this day. There being no more business, we were discharged

[page 93]

January 16, 1856—Sold my order for Jury fees, amounting to $82.00 [$1,712] (except $20.05 [$418] due sundry persons) for goods amounting to $62.00 [$1,294]. This I think I will divide with the widow of my loved friend J. C. L. Smith. I received a very comforting blessing from Patriarch Isaac Morley,[135] as follows:—

Br. James Henry. I place my hands upon thy head by the authority of the holy priesthood, and I ratify the seals and blessings of the fathers and patriarchs upon thy head. Be comforted, for the seals of promise are extended unto thee. Thou art numbered by covenant with the seed of Abraham. Thou hast a right to claim equal blessings with them. Thou art of Ephraim, and a lawful heir to the seals of the priesthood, and to administer in the holy ordinances for the redemption of thy father's household. Greatly will thy blessings be increased, for the keys of the everlasting gospel that will be committed to thy trust. With them thou wilt administer to thy progenitors, who have passed behind the vail and by promise I seal upon thee the keys and the gifts to understand the influences that operate upon thy mind. The Comforter will instruct thee by the influences of peace, and if uneasiness of or fearfulness are the influences of thy mind, exchange them for love, for this is the attribute of deity, and thou hast a right to enjoy its influence. It is thy privilige to cultivate in thy bosom the attributes of a kind providence, who is thy friend and benefactor, and it will produce in thy bosom love, joy and peace in the Holy Ghost. Mercy will become the monitor and dictator of thy mind. Thy trials will pass away, and thou shalt be blessed with an understanding of the principles that emenate from light, and those that proceed from the source of darkness. Thou shalt be blessed in the domestic circle, and rear sons and daughters in honor to they creator, who shall hand thy name to posterity from generation to generation. Let all thy forbodings of mind be turned to joy, for thou shalt be blessed in every gift that shall be conferred upon thee. Thy table shall flow with the bounties of the earth, flocks and herds will flow unto thee, and thou wilt be numbered with those who have labored for the redemption of Israel. By the authority of the holy priesthood, I seal thee up to enjoy the blessings of immortality and eternal lives, in the name of Jesus, even so, Amen and Amen.

Laura A. Morley, Scribe

[page 94]

January 17, 1856—Started for home. Camped at Cove Creek, the weather intensely cold. Elder G. A. Smith was with us, going to visit his family in Parowan. To pass away the evening, he organized us into a political meeting, to speak in reference to the calling of a convention to frame a Constitution for a state government, for the purpose of admission into the Union. W[m] H. Dame was chairman, myself, secretary. All present, 15 in number, made speeches (!) on the subject, which I shall try and put into form for publication.

We had an immense fire, but could only keep warm by constantly turning before it like a turnspit. At bed time we laid cedar boughs on the snow, and coiled up in our blankets upon them, keeping warm as best we could.

January 18, 1856—Drove to Beaver and Camped. The wolves being very numerous around, one of our party Lyman Woods—went about a hundred feet and lay down on his belly, pistol in hand, to get a shot at a wolf, his straw hat lying at his feet.

135 Isaac Morley was called by Brigham Young to be one of the earliest settlers in Manti (Arrington, *Brigham Young*, 177; Shirts and Shirts, *A Trial Furnace*, 9).

While thus watching, another wolf snatched his hat and started off with it, but was soon settled by a shot from Wood's pistol. We had quite a laugh at him.[136]

January 19, 1856—Got home, after an absence of ten days. I let sister J. C. L. Smith have all the goods she wanted, for which she was very thankful. I, myself, feel well paid, in letting her have them, although we are very destitute, ourselves.[137]

January 20, 1856—At meeting, to day, W. H. Dame was unanimously sustained as President of the stake.

January 21, 1856—Traded for an indian boy for Dr. Meeks.

On Tuesday, Jan. 8. 1856, I wrote the following verses for Sister Smith, on the death of her husband. Tune "Sweet Afton.":—

[page 95]

1856—

IN MEMORY OF
PREST J. C. L. SMITH.

[Title added later in shaky handwriting.]

1

He has gone—he has left us, for a few fleeting years.
He's relieved from affliction, from all trouble and cares,
He has finished his labors on this planet below
And now moves in such glory as the just only know.
While on earth he was with us, he delighted to do
All the works of his Father, as a just man and true,
And though he is absent, yet he labors to spread
All the truths of the Gospel, to the living tho' dead.

2

Yes, his work is not ended—it is, hardly begun:—
He will do as his Father in Heaven has done:
His labors extended, will never be o'er
Though he reign over planets as the sands on the shore.
Do not weep for him, Sarah, though he's severed from thee,
From temptation and sorrow, he forever is free
He has fought the good fight, and stood up for the truth,
Both in health and in sickness—in manhood and youth.

3

O'er the wife of his youth, and his children so dear
He ~~still~~ watches with all of a husband's fond care,
Disiring [divining] that they still his work will pursue,
Performing all things that the righteous should do.
He will come and instruct thee, and comfort thy heart,
So thou shalt not sorrow, though called to part,
In the bright ressurrection, you once more shall you meet,
And through ages eternal, dwell in union ~~most~~ sweet.

On the 12th of January 1856, while on my journey to attend the Court, I composed the following, showing the order in which the saints travel on their journeys:—

THE TRAVELER

Oh, a mountain life is the life for me.
So wild so joyous, and so free,
With naught to vex or make us fear
We'll serve the God of Israel here

[page 96]

January 21, 1856—

2

When morning dawns, tis time to rise
We move—look round—then rub our eyes.
Then up we spring, with cheerful heart
Each one resolved to do his part

136 This could be Lyman Wood, who was an interpreter for the Native Americans.

137 For a report related to the convention, see James H. Martineau, "Tremont House, Cove, Beaver County," *Deseret News*, January 19, 1856; Journal History, filed under January 18, 1856, 1–3.

3

Then first of all, our horse we feed
For truly he's a friend indeed;
Then we our breakfast plain prepare,
With heart so free, and void of care.

4

We kneel around the smould'ring fire
And thank our Father for his care;
His aid implore throughout the day,
To keep us safely on our way.

5

All ready now—we mount—we're off!
And now we wind through valley soft,
And mountains rough, and stern and wild—
The hunting grounds of Laman's child

6

The day is past, and now we meet
Around the Camp fire's genial heat;
Our horses graze—our meal we spread
Beneath the spreading pine tree's cedar's shade.

7

And now the tale, the jest, the song,
Enliven all the circling throng;
Till we prepare the scanty bed
Beneath the arching heav'ns o'rehead

8

Then once again our prayers ascend arise
To Him who rules and gives our lives,
And then, beneath the stars cold ray
We sleep, till dawns another day.

[page 97]

Thursday, January 24, 1856—This evening C. C. Pendleton and Jesse N. Smith were ordained or set apart as counselors to Pres^t^ W. H. Dame.

January 26, 1856—By request of G. A. Smith I copied for him a map of Utah Territory.

January 28, 1856—Made a copy of the Territorial map for Hon. John M. Bernhisel, our Delegate in Congress, to be presented there by him.[138] Also read my drama "The Missouri Persecution to Pres^t^ G. A. Smith, who seemed pleased with it.

January 29, 1856—Attended the dedication of the new meeting house in Parowan.

February 5, 1856—Wrote most of the day for Pres^t^ G. A. Smith.

February 7, 1856—Spent the day in making a report for publication of a convention at Cove, Beaver County. This was an enlarged report of our camp speeches when we camped there last. Sent copies, by Elder G. A. Smith's desire, to the "Deseret News."[139] "Mormon" and "Luminary." Br. Smith was highly pleased with it.

February 8, 1856—We played "Pizarro" tonight with great success. I had the part of the King. Made a ridiculous speech in the last scene. Where I should have said:—

"Let tears of gratitude and woe
For the brave Rolla ever flow."

having forgotten it, I said, (being obliged to say something on the instant.

"Let tears for the brave Rolla fall
For he was God and Lord of all."

No one in the audience noticed it, but Rolla, lying dead, and the Priests and Priestesses of the Sun, who stood round the bier shook with laughter.

February 9, 1856—We played to night, "Sweethearts and Wives."

138 John Milton Bernhisel (1779–1881) represented the Territory of Deseret in the U.S. House of Representatives. He was a close associate of Joseph Smith and Brigham Young. He was a doctor practicing in Salt Lake City (Swynn W. Barrett, "Dr. John Bernhisel: Mormon Elder in Congress," *Utah Historical Quarterly* 36 [Spring 1968]: 143–67).

139 The *Deseret News* began as a weekly publication on June 15, 1850. Its first editor was Willard Richards.

February 10, 1856—Elders G. A. Smith and J. N. Smith started for Salt Lake city. The weather begins to moderate.

[page 98]

Monday, March 3, 1856—This evening my play "The Missouri Persecution" was performed for the first time, and was greatly applauded. I had the part of "Gily."

Thursday, March 13, 1856—To day I am 28 years old. Having just received news of fresh Indian hostilities at the north, we organized a company of "mounted rangers" for service as spies and minute men. Ja^{s} Lewis, Captain Chas Y. Webb 1st Lieutenant and myself 2nd Lieut. and clerk; This is only a temporary organization.[140]

March 25, 1856—Went to Harmony, and assisted Col. W. H. Dame to locate and survey the line between Iron and Washington counties. Got home the 26th

Wednesday, April 16, 1856—Went to Beaver to survey a city plat, by request of Col. Dame, who is about sick.

April 17, 1856—Labored this day laying out Beaver City, 64 lots.

April 18, 1856—Surveyed several fields, in all amounting to 275 Acres.

April 19, 1856—Returned home. Beaver is 37 miles from Parowan.

April 27, 1856—Bought of Marius Ensign 10 acres of land for $50.– [$1,044][141]

Thursday, May 8, 1856—Received a letter from S. S. Smith and Sixtus E. Johnson, from the Sandwich Islands.

May 16, 1856—Traded my mare and colt and $50.00 [$1044] to Nephi for a yoke of oxen. Up to this time I have been putting in potatoes, oats, wheat, &c. and have had no team, only as I could work for one.

May 27, 1856—Finished sowing wheat, having sown 7¼ acres and 2¼ of oats.

June 11, 1856—Began to raise my house higher.

July 14, 1856—To day was our general muster. I drilled them, as usual.[142]

[page 99]

August 9, 1856—To day I begin teaching a juvenile company military tactics. There are about thirty in the company.

Thursday, August 14, 1856—At 6 P.M. a daughter was born, weighing 8 pounds. The moon was full next day. Susan was much blessed in her confinement. We blessed the little baby, and dedicated her to the Lord, and named her Susan Elvira Martineau.[143]

Fig. 2.7—Susan Elvira Martineau, daughter of James Henry and Susan Ellen. Courtesy of James Henry Martineau Family Organization.

140 Charles Y. Webb was among the original iron missionaries. He was a "joiner," meaning he was a woodworker specializing in joints. He was thirty-seven at this entry (Shirts and Shirts, *A Trial Furnace*, 439; "Mass Meeting," *Deseret News*, March 12, 1856; Utah Digital Newspapers).

141 On this date James H. Martineau writes about a false report in the eastern press about an earthquake in the greater Salt Lake region (James H. Martineau, "Iron County, Parowan," *Deseret News*, April 27, 1856; Journal History).

142 James H. Martineau, "Iron County," *Deseret News*, July 14, 1856; Journal History. For a copy of the July 24 program, see James H. Martineau, "Literary and Musical Festival—Anniversary of July 24th," *Deseret News*, July 24, 1856; or "Celebration of July 24, 1856, at Parowan," August 10, 1856; Utah Digital Newspapers.

143 Susan Elvira Martineau (1856–1942) would later marry Benjamin Samuel Johnson. She passed away in Prescott, Arizona. Martineau describes the Parowan harvest as "sufficient for ourselves" (*Deseret News*, August 11, 1856; Journal History).

August 15, 1856—To day Susan is not so well, having taken a violent diarrhea which soon turned to the bloody flux.

August 16, 1856—Worse to day. Considered in danger.

August 17, 1856—Getting worse. She is now very low. I called in Drs. Pendleton and Meeks, who recommended charcoal, and injections of raspberry tea, with a portion of composition in it. This checked the disease for a time.

August 20, 1856—Susan, who had been getting better the last two days, is worse this morning. Dr. Meeks staid (stayed) with her nearly all day; he steamed her, and gave her much hot drinks, which did her much good. Moroni is still sick. I can get no hired help, and taking the almost sole care of Susan and her baby, and attending to Moroni, keeps me pretty busy. I therefore sent for Editha to come up to help me. Susan is hardly expected to live. Who can tell my feelings? None but those who have had the experience. Everything I see calls her to mind.[144]

August 21, 1856—Editha, Nephi and Janet came up to see us.

August 22, 1856—Nephi and Janet returned, taking Henry with them, to take care of him while his mother is sick Moroni is still worse, with a bad diarrhea and vomiting. Got better towards evening. Susan also is some better. Editha is taking care of her. I sat and read all day to Susan, and fanned her and kept away the flies, which are very troublesome.

[page 100]

August 23, 1856—Susan is better to day: Moroni also. His bowels come out many times during the day, and have to be carefully worked back. Mother came up to see Susan.

August 24, 1856—Mother went home again to day. Susan and Moroni are better.

August 25, 1856—Editha came up from the Springs to day to see Susan, who is now about well.

August 27, 28, 29, 1856—I hauled wood and poles for three days past.

August 30, 1856—Editha went home to day. I wrote up minutes in the Bishops book of trials: in the stake record and in my journal

September 1, 1856—Began my harvesting. Broke my cradle.

September 2, 1856—Cut some grain with a sickle and cut my left little finger to the bone severing the chord or sinew. A felon began on my left for-finger.[145]

September 4, 1856—Had an excellent meeting (fast) to day. Sister Zilpha Smith, wife of Geo. A. Smith spoke powerfully in tongues. I had to some extent the gift of interpretation for which I have long prayed.

September 5, 1856—My felon is much worse, and very painful.

September 11, 1856—To day my felon came to a head, so that it could ~~not~~ be opened. I have suffered terribly from it, not being able to sleep or rest, day or night.

September 12, 1856—My finger is a little easier to day.

September 13, 1856—John D. Lee brought me a Spanish Testament which some one sent to me.

September 14, 1856—Filed my official bond as sheriff, in the sum of $5.000 [$104,393]. Received a letter from my sister Henrietta with a gold ring, which was once my mothers. It is a plain circlet

September 15, 1856—Having been appointed Assessor & Collector of "Fortification District N° 1" embracing Parowan, I filed my bonds, in the amount of $15.000 [$318]

September 16, 1856—Wrote out orders for the next muster.

[page 101]

October 4, 1856—Hauled a load of sage brush to burn, the first work I have done for a long time. I cannot use my left hand yet, on account of the felon. I have lost the use of my forefinger on the left hand, the cord having rotted off and the joint become stiff.

October 5, 1856—Last night it snowed. I sowed timothy in my door yard to day, hoping I shall have a nice green plat of grass to gladden the eye.[146] This is the first hay seed sown in Parowan.

144 Martineau was ordained a seventy and set apart as a member of the stake presidency this year ("Report of the Twenty-seventh Quorum of Seventy," *Deseret News*, August 20, 1856; Utah Digital Newspapers).

145 A felon is an infected painful abscess at the end of a finger or toe near the nail.

146 Timothy is a dense European grass.

October 7, 1856—This day Patriarch E. G. Groves blessed my little daughter Susan Elvira, as follows:—

Susan Elvira, in the name of Jesus of Nazareth, by virtue of the holy priesthood in my invested, I place my hands upon thy head, and seal upon thee a patriarchal or father's blessing, which shall rest upon thee, and thou shalt realize the fulfillment thereof. Thou art in the days of thy infancy, yet a noble spirit inhabiteth thy tabernacle, and inasmuch as thy parents will use wisdom, doing their duty by thee, thou shalt grow up to mature ~~years~~ age. Thy guardian angel shall be round about thee, he will not leave nor forsake thee, yea thy life shall be precious in the sight of thy Heavenly Father. Thy days shall be many upon the earth. Thou shalt be a blessing unto thy parents,—a blessing and ornament in the Church and Kingdom of God on earth; that thou mayest be able to fill up the measure of thy creation, according to the design thereof. The Evil One will seek to destroy thee, but thou shalt be delivered, that thou mayest fill up the measure of thy creation. Thou art a daughter of Abraham, of the loins of Joseph, and blood of Ephraim, a lawful heir to all the blessings, privileges and powers of the priesthood that pertain to thy sex, which thou shalt receive in due time, that thou mayest be able to stand in thy proper lot and station, in the redemption of thy progenitors. Thou shalt be connected with a man of God, through whom thou shalt receive thy priesthood, exaltation, power and eternal glory, become a mother in Israel, thy children and thy children's children rising after thee shall bless ~~thee~~ and comfort thee in the decline of life.

[page 102]

ELVIRA'S BLESSING, BY E. H. GROVES.

October 7, 1856—Thou shalt receive of the fruits of the earth in great abundance, and all things necessary to render life happy and agreeable. The holy angels shall minister unto thee, revealing unto thee the genealogy of thy fathers. Thy children, many of them, shall be born without the sting of sin,—thou shalt witness the birth thereof in the millennium. Thou shalt receive many blessings in the temple in Zion, being anointed a Queen and Priestess unto the Most High God. Thou shalt receive thy crown, dominion, power and eternal increase, thy inheritance with the faithful in Zion. These are thy blessings. I seal them upon thy head, sealing thee up to everlasting life, in the name of Jesus of Nazareth, even so, Amen.

October 20, 1856—It having been taught that we should be re-baptized (the people at large) myself and wife were baptized by Bishop Tarlton Lewis, and confirmed by C. C. Pendleton.

November 5, 1856—Threshed my wheat.

November 6, 1856—Cleaned my wheat, putting up 122 bushels. After paying my debts, I had about 90 bushels.

November 8, 1856—Threshed my oats, and have 90 bushels.

November 14, 1856—Sister A. Barton, saying I do a great deal of writing for the public, gave me a pint of Molasses. May she be blessed by our Father in Heaven for it.

November 23, 1856—The company of poor, just arrived from Europe. 20 in number, arrived to day, in the midst of a severe snow storm. They came in wagons, sent from this place to receive them at Salt Lake City.

November 25, 1856—Gave 150 lbs of flour, as an offering for the poor. I took a little Danish girl to keep through the winter. Her name is Metta Kirstena Mortensen.[147]

December 4, 1856—Having received the appointment of Clerk in the Legislature, about to convene at Fillmore, I this day start for that place, in company with I. C. Haight, R. Harrisson, Jas Lewis and W. H Dame.

[page 103]

JOURNEY TO FILLMORE—TO SALT LAKE CITY

December 1856—After a hard trip on account of deep snow and the intensely cold weather. We stopped at S. P. Hoyt's.

December 7, 1856—Preached to day, and felt well. Heard of the death of Prest J. M. Grant.

Monday, December 8, 1856—The Legislature convened to day. I was elected Clerk of the Representatives Branch, and being the only clerk

147 Metta K. Mortensen was born May 2, 1845, and married Christian Rasmussen of Parowan on May 30, 1863.

present, had it all to do and attend to. This and a want of experience, bothered me somewhat, but I got along very well. A resolution was adopted, changing the capital to Salt Lake city, and on the 9th[148]

December 9, 1856—they all started for that place. The weather was very cold, and snow deep, making travel very toilsome and tedious. Our company of five staid [stayed] two days in Fillmore, to rest our team, stopping with Father. He charged us each $4.75 [$99]. We started, and camped in the cedars, in Round Vally, the snow being two feet deep.

December 10, 1856—Arrived at Nephi. The day we got here, I lost my straw hat out of the wagon, and had to enter the city bareheaded. I soon found a second hand one but, the next wagon that came in, brought mine to me.

December 11, 1856—Got to Santaquin, and put up with Uncle B. F. Johnson. I here met Susan J. Sherman again. She was glad to see me, and have some one to pour out some of her girlish troubles to. I felt sorry for her, being fatherless and motherless. I preached in the evening.

December 12, 1856—Drove to Springville, and on the 13th

December 13, 1856—To American fork: and on the 14th

December 14, 1856—Arrived in Salt Lake City. All well. I stopped at the house of Aunt Julia A. Babbitt.

December 18, 1856—To day the Legislature re-convened.

December 20, 1856—Attended a meeting of High priests from all parts of the Territory.

[page 104]

LORENZO SNOW'S REMARKS TO HIGH PRIESTS.

December 20, 1856—I had my name enrolled in the general Quorum. I also spoke in the meeting.

Elder Lorenzo Snow said: It will not be forgiven you High Priests if you are content to be always led. You must be leaders of the people. Take a firm and powerful stand, and let your influence be felt wherever you go. Thunder to the people, teach them and lead them. The High Priests are the mighty men of Israel, and from this Quorum are all the Apostles, Bishops and Councillors taken. Some men will hear others rail out against Mormonism and our authorities, and say nothing. I want you to be sanctified, and so filled with the holy ghost that you cannot be restrained, but like lions of old, put an end to iniquity, if need be, shedding the blood of the wicked. The Spirit whispers to me that we shall be an independent people. The Lord will make us his, if we repent and sanctify ourselves, in spite of all the Devils in hell: and I feel that the people will listen. We shall be a strong and mighty people, and it is not so far off as some think. The high priests are all guilty of not striving to get the spirit and power of their priesthood upon them. They do not realize their position. When the people do repent, we shall make the nations fear and tremble. The reformation could not begin with the people, it must begin at the head,—the High Priests. As the wickedness increases among the people of the earth, so will the Spirit of god gather with us.

Much teaching and counsel was given on the subject of plural marriage, all men being commanded to obey that revelation. When I left home, last, my wife said to me, that I must bring another wife home with me. She said she knew it would be a trial to her, but come it must, and better now than to wait. May our Father in Heaven bless her forever for her integrity.

[page 105]

MY WIFE SHOWN IN A DREAM OF A TREE, &C

December 20, 1856—Having for a considerable time felt it my duty to obey the law of celestial marriage, I felt quite a degree of anxiety in regard to the matter, wishing to marry, if at all, one whom it would please the Lord for me to have; and knowing my own inability to choose properly without the Spirit of the Lord, I prayed much and fasted, that I might be led in the right direction.

148 For these election results and the organization of the legislative assembly, see "The Legislative Assembly," *Deseret News*, December 8, 1856; Journal History. Utah Digital Newspapers lists the publication date as December 24, 1856.

A few nights ago I dreamed that I was in a beautiful grove belonging to Uncle Benjamin F. Johnson, who directed me to a beautiful tree. I stood admiring it, and saw it was a locust, in full bloom and fragrance. I admired the beauty of the tree, its good timber, and fragrant blossoms, but perceived that it had thorns, as do the locust trees. I wished in my mind it had been a tree bearing fruit. While I looked again, I saw it was now a beautiful hickory tree, bearing good fruit to eat, and its timber was very excellent, which made me rejoice much. I reached up to the branches and plucked seven or eight bunches of fruit, and lay them down upon the ground. I then awoke, and lay for some time thinking over the dream and its interpretation until I again fell asleep, and dreamed that Uncle Benj. F. held up a woman in the air, to my view, for my acceptance. I saw that she was beautiful and desirable in every respect, except that she had no strength in her ankles, her feet hanging limp and weak. I awoke immediately and pondered the dreams until morning. The interpretation seemed to me that I should take some woman who was at heart good, but filled with weaknesses; or perhaps I would be required to take one of the hand cart girls then coming in from the plains, with her feet frozen off, as so many of them were. I dreaded this, in my poverty, to be burdened with a cripple, but finally thought I would do it if it was required.

[page 106]

A PROPOSAL OF MARRIAGE.

December 20, 1856—I thought in the second dream, the man said if I would take her and do my duty to the end, I should receive "Sixty bushels of wheat," which seemed an immense sum. I found the first interpretation was the right one.

I thought of Susan J. Sherman, and asked her guardian, Benj. F. Johnson, if he was willing for me to marry her if she was willing. He said yes, but had no idea she would accept, having already refused some advantageous offers:—but I might try. I therefore determined to write to her, and did, as follows:—

"Great Salt Lake City, Saturday, Dec. 20. 1856.

Miss Susan Sherman.

With the consent of Uncle Benjamin, your Guardian, I address you this letter to ascertain if you are willing to join your destiny with mine through time and all eternity. You are somewhat acquainted with me, but perhaps you do not know my circumstances in life. I am not rich, neither am I poor, I do not know that I ever shall be very well off, nor do I wish to be, but rather to spend myself with all I have, if necessary, for the good of the Kingdom. My interests and feelings and hopes are all identified with Mormonism, and consequently, if the church prospers, I hope to prosper with it; if the church suffers persecution, distress and poverty, I hope to suffer with it. These are my principles in short. If they suit you,—if you are perfectly willing to accept and to be guided by them:—if you are willing to become my wife according to the order of heaven, you can inform me by return of mail, or at your earliest convenience. If not, be perfectly free in your feelings:—let me know without fear of ~~hurting~~ injuring my feelings, and rest assured that I will still feel the same friendship and respect as ever.

Yours Truly

James H. Martineau."

[page 107]

LEGISLATIVE PREACHING, &C

December 20, 1856—Having written this, I prayed that if it is according to the will of God that I should have her, that her heart and feelings may be turned to mine, and mine to her. If not His will, that the contrary may be the case, and sent it in full faith and confidence that whatever may be the result, it will be just right.

Uncle Benjamin also wrote to her at the same time speaking in my favor and advising her to accept my offer.

Sunday, December 21, 1856—Went to meeting and heard Pres[t] H. C. Kimball preach. He said "Punctuality is integrity. We have got to be better disciplined than any army in Europe or America. Those who honor the priesthood, are gentlemen and ladies,—no others. If a woman commits adultery, and her husband knows her again as a wife, he is guilty also of adultery. An Elder in Israel who gets a woman to agree to marry him in Zion, and he is on a mission, without leave to get more wives, is guilty of shedding innocent blood.

Monday, March 22, 1856—Went to Seventies meeting, and voted to cut off Geo. P. Stiles for adultery.

Elder Lorenzo Snow said:—

the spirit of God influences a man to kick a—es: and hew down the wicked as Samuel did Agag and to kick guts out, as Peter did the bowels of Judas, and the time will soon come that we must purify Israel in the same way.[149]

March 23, 1856—To day the Legislature met as usual, in the Social Hall, the House of Representatives on the Stage, and the Council under it in the Green Room. The House attempted to do business as usual, but we heard Br. Kimball speaking below, and finally the council sent a message to us, saying that they could do no business till they had repented and got the Spirit of the Lord, and invited us to meet with them, which we did.

[page 108]

THE LEGISLATURE REFORMATION.

December 23, 1856—Br. Kimball spoke much on Reformation, and ridding ourselves of the wicked in our midst of the saints, speaking with great power. He gave all liberty to speak, and we all did. It was one of the most glorious times ever witnessed in the church. The Spirit of God was like fire in our hearts. Great and mighty teachings were given, which it is not wisdom to write. It was said, "We will always be rode, as long as we will submit to it." We will no longer submit to it.

In the evening I went to a meeting of the Bishops and Missionaries, and heard mighty things.

Thursday, December 25, 1856—Went to the 17th Ward meeting, and heard that a conspiracy had been discovered to kill Pres^t^ Ja^s^ C. Snow and Bp. Blackburn, in Provo.

Orson Hyde said "If you have refractory wives, pray with and bless them, and they will melt before you."

Saturday, December 27, 1856—Went to the High Priests meeting, and heard much mighty teachings. Lorenzo Snow said we will have to lay down our lives for each other. Wilford Woodruff said—the day of Judgment is come, and it will not be lengthened. When a man sheds innocent blood, if the President releases him for a week or a month, it is all right. A man cannot be forgiven for that sin.[150]

Sunday, December 28, 1856—In the Tabernacle meeting to day Elder Woodruff said "there are scores of women who ought to have their throats cut."

December 29, 1856—Went to the Seventies meeting as usual. Br. F. D. Richards said "I want the Quorums to be more active and not to spend all winter in trying to rouse their heads to life, for if you do, the armies of the aliens will be upon us, and when we ought to be defending our rights up to the hilt, we will have to be doing something else.

[page 109]

BR. BRIGHAM'S SERMON.

December 30, 1856—The two branches of the Legislature met to day to preach and to get the spirit of the reformation, that the fire may go forth to all the people. Br. Kimball said—"Br. Brigham, you are the master of the house, and have a right to wear your hat here."

Br. Brigham said, "Yes, I have a right to wear my hat. Instead of this reformation waking me out of a deep sleep, and putting thunder and lightning into me, it has a contrary effect, and the spirit has subsided in me. I am resting. When the first Twelve were called, then the thunder of the Almighty was in me; but Mr. Heber and I were only the 'titmen' Bless you, we could hardly reach up high enough to tie the shoes of Br. Hyde and John E. Page. I was just high enough to do that. But this did not infringe upon my priesthood. In the first days of the Twelve, there was much throwing of snot and wiping of faces, but I could never associate with such a spirit. The Twelve knew nothing about their priesthood—do they know anything about their priesthood now? They know no more about it than a boy four or five years old would, if we were to ordain him here to day. That has been the burden upon me,—that the Twelve did not know their duty and calling. I bore it as long as I could, until it seemed as if I should die, and I said to Br. Jeddy, 'I'll take my valise and I'll travel through the country; I'll not be caught riding

149 Lorenzo Snow was an Apostle and counselor to President Brigham Young.

150 Wilford Woodruff was then serving as an Apostle.

either: and I'll preach and cry.' "if there is any man who will be for God, let him come out." and if I cannot find any one to build up and bear off this kingdom, I will go into the wilderness, and raise up a church among the Lamanites.' Br. Jeddy got it ~~it~~ immediately, and it killed him. If the Twelve have got the Spirit, I am glad of it. and will rest,—but not in death. I am not going to die, but if I don't live 130 years as I have sometimes said, I will live as long as I want to.

[page 110]

BRIGHAM'S SERMON

December 30, 1856—How have I been situated since the death of Br. Joseph. I have had no one to stand ~~good~~ guard for me—I have been like a man standing guard every night, but if you will stand guard for me I will rest. I will here digress a little. The brethren have thought I have used myself up with women, but it is not so. I do not use my women as much as you do yours. I do not do so so much as I did when I had but one wife. (Heber, That's a fact.) I do not do it.) I have had to stand on guard every night since Br. Joseph died, without any one to keep the dogs out of the flock. Had it not been for that, I could not have stepped forth as I did at Nauvoo, but I did step forth, and drove the dogs and wolves out of the flock.

There are some here who do not think there is any necessity for a reformation. When they hear anything said about cleansing out iniquity, they start back, they are scared! I want you to get the Holy Ghost upon you, and then you can do more business in one hour than you can in two weeks without. And you will make laws that no gentile power can break. There is more wisdom in our laws, than in all the United States laws, although they have got some good things in them. We can do more business in one week than they can in six months, and it will be better and plainer, though Almon Babbitt used to call our laws 'the Primer' and the 'first and second reader.' What is the law? A mere nothing. You can twist it and turn it any way you please. Look at our State Constitution. It was not what Judge Kinney, Dr. Hurt, T. F. Williams or Orson Pratt wanted. I wrote it myself, with the help of two or three others. What was said about it in the states? They could not find much fault with it, except that it gives us the right to change it by the vote of two thirds, and that is what the constitution of every state and Territory has. I want you to bid farewell to every fear, and say God will take care of his kingdom.

[page 111]

BRIGHAM'S SERMON.

December 30, 1856—Dont worry about it. Let me be right, and I'll know when and what to do. I desire you to get the power of God upon you, so that you can know all things. The Lord is waiting to pour out great blessings upon you. In the days of Joseph the Lord poured out more than you can live up to for years to come. It will take you years to get where you should have been years ago.

Can you divide between wild fire and true fire? You will see bushels of wild fire if this reformation continues. The devils will be on hand to pray, to teach, to exhort,—and you will find the fire mixed—heaven and hell mixed. You may keep heaven or hell in you ~~if~~ as you please. There are devils here—in this room—millions of them—I will say legions, because that is not so many. Look out and be upon the alert. There are plenty who will have wild fire. If you have true fire, you will have wisdom, integrity and knowledge. Every man will be endowed according to his calling, if you will apply your hearts to wisdom. If not, you will have the bitter and the sweet—storm and calm. Select out the things of God, and let the things of the Devil alone.

Do not contend about anything. No man can serve God acceptably who has one particle of the love of the world in him. No man that loves this world has the Spirit of God in him. I dont want you to call me a God to you: you dont know the meaning of that ~~name~~ term. Br. Heber always will keep calling me President Young—if you don't stop calling me President Young, Br. Heber, I'll stick it onto you, and call you President Kimball all the time.

If you'll do as I tell you, I'll lead you into the celestial kingdom, so help me God. You have got to put on the armor of Christ, and keep it on, and you'll grow to be mighty men. I dont believe men can become stationary. I belong to the growing kingdom. I want to be where Joseph is, and He is advancing, and we shall never catch up. with him, for while we advance, so will he.

[page 112]

BRIGHAM'S SERMON.

December 30, 1856—The love of gold or of women has nothing to do with the love of God. Dont get scared if you get the Holy Ghost. and say Br. Brigham is in the back ground. Just come and see if I can't teach you you're A.B.Cs. No man has ever felt as I have felt. Br. Jeddy felt a little of it, and it killed him. He was dear to me as the apple of my eye. He is under the dictation of Joseph; he is under that of Peter, I suppose; he is under Christ, and he is under God: and He is dictated by his father, and there never was a time when there was no God. Joseph said he wouldn't worship a God without father and mother.

The thing is, to have the Lord for our right hand: it is he who has preserved us—not we. We are threatened daily by those in our midst, with soldiers, &c &c. They say, "we will have our whore houses, and our dram shops, and we'll do as we d——n please." I will tell you the characters of a few of them. General Burr was sent here: he was a poor miserable stink. He kept a boarding house and kept hanging round whore houses till his wife got him appointed to Utah. There is T. R. Peltro who pretends to be an officer! He is no more an officer than my dog. He tells us about the army! Mogo, the Surveyor, threatens the Mormons with utter destruction if they dont let him alone. He knows nothing about Surveying. I could do more with a sunflower and a red dog's tail than all of them. I can tell you what they are doing—they are cheating the United States Government by making plots of thousands of miles that they never saw. Let them howl. They will break out among themselves next summer, and call each other d——d rascals, and they'l ~~edge~~ eat each other up—you'll see [it] and they'll have no influence in Washington. Dr. Hurt is as mean as Thos Sharp, of Warsaw, and he'l lose all his influence as sure as the Lord lives. They are destroying themselves as fast as they can, like the Kelkenny cats. Don't fear about things—God is here—and you mus'nt steady the ark."

[page 113]

THE LEGISLATURE BAPTIZED IN THE FONT AND CONFIRMED.

December 30, 1856—If I can sleep for one night, I shall feel thankful. If I have men who will keep watch for me, I will live 130 years, or long enough. I have sanctioned all that Br. Heber has done, and he has all I have done—we never come in contact.

Pres^{t} H. C. Kimball said:—I want to be called "Br. Heber"—not "Mr. President." I have called Br. Brigham a God to me—well, he is a son of God. I wont do so any more—or if I do I will take it back again. If we all do right, Br. Brigham can rest. (Br. Brigham I have rest~~ing~~ed more in two months than in ten years before.) The Holy Ghost is like a tallowed rag—(Brigham, And like a lion.) not like Br. Clapp—tear a pulpit to pieces—that's wild fire. It is high time for this Legislature to repent, and begin to make restitution this very afternoon, if it takes all you have got. (Brigham, Repent of your religion—I mean your forms.) We don't want no forms. Go and get the font filled, and the Twelve will be on hand to baptize you this night.

The Legislature then adjourned in a body to the Temple block, and began about sun set to fill the stone font with buckets, having formed a line to the nearest stream, passing the water from hand to hand for a long time—until dark. We were wet and cold, and then were baptized in the ice-cold water, going thence to the endowment house to be confirmed. Elders Orson Hyde and Lorenzo Snow confirmed us.

While waiting for my turn to be confirmed I prayed that I might have conferred upon me, power to do much good in this Kingdom, I did not dare to pray for riches, or honor and power, fearing it might not be good for me, but I felt safe in asking to be useful to the Cause of God, and felt full faith I should be blessed as I desired. Elder Snow was mouth in confirming me, at a quarter to 7 P.M. I was baptized by James W. Cummings.

[page 114]

MY CONFIRMATION BLESSING. PROMISE OF ETERNAL LIFE.

December 30, 1856—

He said:—

You shall be mighty in doing good in this kingdom. You shall not be a whit behind any of those who seek to do good: you shall attain to the desire of your heart in doing good. You may ~~desire~~ aspire, to as great a degree of usefulness as you desire; and you shall attain to it. You shall have all the desires of your heart, even all the greatest blessings you desire in righteousness. In whatever thing you desire to be useful, you shall be blessed in whatever you put your hands to do in righteousness."

This was a precious blessing, and if I had told Elder Snow my desires, he could not have answered them more pointedly and plainly. It was a strong testimony to me, and I thanked God fervently for it. The Twelve were filled with the Holy Ghost, and the building and those in it almost trembled at the power of God there displayed. It was a time never to be forgotten.

Wednesday, December 31, 1856—Pres^{t} H. C. Kimball said:—If you will live your religion, you can ask the Lord for any thing you want, and it shall be given to you. Then what can the gentile world do with us? Nothing. Where there is order, there will be the abode of the Holy Ghost. All [him] that are not of God should be removed as nuisances, and I move that there be a destructive or distributive committee appointed to attend to such things.

We are now in joint session, and we will never dissolve again,—we will never be dissolved forever, and there is not a man here to day but what I shall see in the celestial kingdom, with every good wife and child he has got, and a thousand more at his heels." Write it down, if you please, whether it comes true or not, but I know it is true. I could not say this yesterday, for there were some present that are not here to day.

PART

3

MOUNTAIN MEADOWS AND THE APPROACHING FEDERAL ARMY

[page 115]

MEMORIAL TO CONGRESS.

Thursday, January 1, 1857—To day I went to the 16th Ward meeting, with Eliza Brown and Antoinette Kesler, daughter of Bp. Kesler.

January 3, 1857—Went to High Priests meeting. The Twelve said we must not use the cudgel so much—pour in the oil and the wine.[1]

January 4, 1857—Snowed last night 1½ feet deep.

Monday, January 5, 1857—Met in joint session to day, Pres^t Kimball announced that last night he and Br. Brigham ordained and set apart Daniel H. Wells to fill Br. J. M. Grant's place.

He said—As the Lord liveth, that man will go under who will not labor with his hands, he will go under."

A Memorial to Congress, praying that no more wicked men be sent here as officers, and expressing a firm determination on the subject, was read by James Ferguson, Chief Clerk of the House. It is one of the most spirited remonstrances ever penned; it was produced by inspiration of the Holy Spirit. I felt gloriously, and as if I could willingly lay down my life, if necessary, for my brethren and for the gospel, and to sustain the declarations of the memorial, which is almost another declaration of independence. It was signed by all the members and officers of the Legislature, for which privilege I felt most thankful. Br. Brigham Said—Boys, we must stick together, or we will sink together." Br. Heber Said—What we have done, we have got to stand up to, do you know it."

Brigham said—"This Memorial was got up in Committee of the Whole on the state of the nation." (a voice—"of the Territory")

Brigham—"No, of the nation, and if any body inquires by what authority this special committee was instituted, you may tell him it was "by the authority of the Great Jehovah and the Continental Congress" I have done that that must be sustained, if it takes my life blood to do it, and I am glad to do it.

[page 116]

ARRIVAL OF SUSAN J. SHERMAN

January 5, 1857—Br. G. A. Smith said, "If we dont all hang together now, we will hang, separately."

1 A cudgel is a club used as a weapon.

Many other speeches of like nature were made by the leading members, and heartily concurred in by all. Truly "the Spirit of God like a fire is burning."

I signed my name with my gold pen (made by Josephi, of Cincinnatti) in a large plain hand, thus

"James Henry Martineau"

so there may be no mistaking my identity.

Tuesday, January 6, 1857—Brigham said to day—"If we live our religion, we shall retain our lands, and the gentile world can have no power over us—they have forfeited all their rights."

To day I attended the Legislative Dinner, in the Globe restaurant.

January 7, 1857—Spent the evening with Eliza Brown.

January 10, 1857—Went to High Priests meeting.

January 11, 1857—Went to meeting, and heard Br. Kimball preach.

January 12, 1857—To day Br. Cannon took my likeness—ambrotype.[2]

January 13, 1857—I dreamed to night that the church is going to another location, and after taking from our houses what we could, we destroyed the rest. Br. Brigham said—Laws made by the children of men do not affect their salvation.

Thursday, January 15, 1857—This evening Susan J. Sherman arrived from Santaquin, having been three days traveling, through the snow, which is about two feet deep. She had a bad cold, caused by breaking the ice of Provo river and getting her foot and leg wet. I was glad to see her.

In the evening I had a talk with her upon the subject of marriage with me, and frankly told her my circumstances in life, and my feelings and principles relative to Mormonism.

[page 117]

SHE AGREES TO MARRY ME. MARRIED.

January 15, 1857—We sat for a while in Aunt Julia's bed room, by the fire, until Aunt Julia wished to retire. We then sat in the dining room for some time, talking over matter. I was very sorry for her. She seemed almost alone in the world—her father and mother dead, and living first with one and then another of her relations. I felt as if I could take her to my heart and shield her from the cold world.

I told her that it would be well for us to pray to the Lord, that our minds might be guided aright: that if it is right for us to be united, that our hearts and feelings may be turned to each other; if not right, that our feelings may be turned away from each other. She said it would be best, too, she thought. She also said she had done so from the time of receiving my letter, to know for a surety if it would be for the best. I had also done the same, and now felt it was right for us to be united. She then promised to be my wife. I wished to kiss her, but thought best to wait until we are married and have a right to do so. I feel that I have done as near right in this proceeding as I know how, from the first, and therefore hope that the blessings of God may be with us.

Sunday, January 18, 1857—To day Susan Julia Sherman and I were married by Pres[t] Heber C. Kimball, according to the order of the priesthood, about 2 o'clock P.M. Joseph B. Nobles, T. D. Brown and Geo. D. Grant were witnesses, and D. Mackintosh clerk.[3] The snow was almost three feet deep. When Br. Kimball took the paper on which was written our names, he read Susan's name and said—Are you the daughter of Lyman R. Sherman![4]

2 There are numerous Cannons in Church history. At this writing none were connected with this context. An ambrotype is a photograph of the time. It was a glass negative that looks like a positive.

3 George D. Grant was a leader of the October 7, 1856, rescue party that went to assist the James G. Willie company (Daniel H. Ludlow, ed., *Encyclopedia of Mormonism* [New York: Macmillan, 1992], 2:571).

4 Lyman Royal Sherman was called to be an Apostle but passed away before his ordination (Leonard J. Arrington, *Brigham Young: American Moses* [Urbana: Univ. of Illinois Press, 1986], 69; Ludlow, *Encyclopedia of Mormonism*, 4:1645).

[page 118]

START FOR PAROWAN WITH E. DOLTEN.

January 18, 1857—"Now I look at you, I see you have his eyes exactly—and his hair. He was a good man—Joseph's right hand man. He was a most beautiful singer, especially in singing in tongues—the finest I ever saw. He died a martyr to the Gospel, and will receive a Martyr's crown."

I was much rejoiced to hear Br. Kimball say this, for it shows to me that a truly good man will never be forgotten, in time, nor in eternity.

My stay this winter has been full of interest, joy and stirring incident. I have spent many pleasant evenings at the house of Ezra T. Benson,[5] who is now in England. Mrs. P. S. Benson[6] reminds me very much of my mother, in her appearance and manners. I have enjoyed myself much in the society of her eldest daughter, Emma, who is just budding into womanhood, though she still wears a girl's dress. We have sung and played the melodeon[7] together, and held arguments on grammar. Mrs. Benson had seven or eight boarders—Br. Dame. P. Maughan,[8] Isaac Bullock,[9] Robt S. Kelton and others, who almost every evening would get up some kind of argument or other.

Aunt Julia has treated me very kindly all winter, for which may the Lord bless her.

January 19, 1857—This morning we start for home in Ed^d^ Dolten's wagon.[10] The weather is cold and snow deep. We traveled 18 miles to Draperville, and stopped at the house of a Br. Smith, in company with a large number of others, who are returning home. The floor was covered with beds, Susan and I having an old pole bedstead to lie on.[11] We had an uproarious evening, laughing and singing songs, much to the scandal of Br. Smith, whose face is as long as a mule's and solemn as an owl.

[page 119]

JOURNEY HOME.

January 20, 1857—Traveled to Provo, and stopped with Joseph Clark.[12]

January 21, 1857—Arrived at Santaquin, and stopped with Uncle B. F. Johnson, who blessed us both, and said we should have a prosperous journey home.

Uncle Benjamin and his wives were glad that I had married Susan, though they thought it strange she had consented, for she had had much better offers in a financial point of view, and from some high in the priesthood. When she first got my letter she made fun of it:—but she afterwards told me it was the first letter from a man she ever received that made her respect the writer. Mine, she said, was plain, straight forward, and to the point, without any great (and unlikely) promises of what things I would do for her, as some would write.

January 22, 1857—Drove to Nephi, and stopped at the house of Br. Wm Cazier, Patriarch. (Note. Wrong. it was with John Cazier.)

[written in margin]

Susan was Blessed by W. Cazier.

January 23, 1857—Started in good time, but after toiling along for about four miles, had to turn back again. The snow as about 1½ feet deep, with a hard crust on top hard enough to bear up a man most of the time. We went to Br. Bryant's to stop this time, who treated us very kindly. Made a sled this afternoon to put the wagon on, and got all ready for tomorrow.

5 Ezra T. Benson (1811–69) was an Apostle at this writing.

6 P. S. Benson is likely Phoebe Benson, the wife of Richard Benson, who served in the Iron Mission.

7 The melodeon was a small organ that used bellows and metal reeds.

8 This could be Peter Maughan, who was a bishop and stake president in Cache Valley.

9 Isaac Bullock was sent by Brigham Young in 1853 to colonize Fort Supply, which was twelve miles south of Fort Bridger, Wyoming (Juanita Brooks, *The Mountain Meadows Massacre* [Norman: Univ. of Oklahoma Press, 1991], 145n).

10 This is likely Edward Dalton, a second lieutenant in the Utah Territorial Militia, Company C, Parowan (Morris A. Shirts and Kathryn H. Shirts, *A Trial Furnace: Southern Utah's Iron Mission* [Provo, UT: Brigham Young Univ. Press, 1991], 493).

11 A pole bedstead consisted of corded strips of bark strung between two poles and a tick filled with dry grass, cotton, feathers, or hair.

12 Joseph Clark (1828–95) was a member of the Mormon Battalion and would later be convicted of polygamy and serve time in the penitentiary (Norma Baldwin Ricketts, ed., *Arizona's Honeymoon Trail and Mormon Wagon Roads* [Mesa, AZ: Cox, 2001], 21).

[written in margin]

See p. 122

January 24, 1857—Started again, and found our sled was a great improvement over the wagon wheels in the snow, sliding along over it nicely. We traveled to about 4 miles beyond the Sevier River, and camped in the cedars. We had a jolly company, composed of the Representatives from Iron County and the South of Utah. We had a large fire under a big Cedar tree, and spent a lively evening. We had no canopy above our beds but the clear cold starry heavens, and the flat sled for a bedstead. The night was very cold.

[page 120]

JOURNEY HOME. GO TO CONFERENCE AGAIN.

January 25, 1857—Traveled to Fillmore to day, and found bare ground. We stopped at the house of a Br. King, and had a fine nights rest, and kind hosts, which were doubly grateful after our cold journey.

January 26, 1857—Went to Cove Creek.

January 27, 1857—Drove to Beaver, and stopped with S. F. Howd [Howard].

Wednesday, January 28, 1857—Got home, and found all well as usual. On the way I had prayed that my wife at home might be prepared to receive me with another wife, as I had no chance to apprize her that I had taken another. When we drove up to the gate, Susan came out to welcome us, and greeted Susan J. with a kiss of friendship which was a joy to me for I did not know how she would meet her. She said she knew or felt sure I would bring another wife home with me. The Spirit of God had warned and prepared her mind for it. Moroni was sick with the croup. I administered to him and he immediately got better, through the blessing of our Father.

On our way home we preached in almost all the towns as we came along.

[written in margin]

Jan. 30. 1857. Susan J. was blessed to day by E. H. Groves, Patriarch, in Parowan for which, accidentally omitted here, see page—129

Sunday, February 1, 1857—Preached to day, on the principles of reformation.

February 4, 1857—Went to Johnson's Springs and preached.

February 7, 1857—Pres^t Dame appointed me to preside over the Choir, much against my feelings.

March 1, 1857—Up to this time I have spent most of my time in the tithing business and in fencing my city lot with a picket fence. Susan J. was sick about a week with a severe cold.[13]

March 27, 1857—Started for Conference with all my family but Mette Stena. We had S. Gould's wagon and team. We arrived in Salt Lake City without accident and stopped with Aunt Julia Babbitt. on the Thursday evening ~~March~~ April 2.

April 8, 1857—Attended Conference every day.

[page 121]

April 8, 1857—While here, John Eager and his wife Sariah, sister to Susan E. arrived from San Pete valley, and these I had the pleasure of meeting them for the first time.[14] I presented my claim to W H Hooper[15] of extra pay, mileage and subsistence for our Legislative trip from Fillmore to Salt Lake City.

I bought 36 seeds of Sorghum of L. Bertrand for ten cents.[16] Before leaving the city for home, I wrote the following lines to Aunt Julia, who expects to start for the States on business soon to settle the estate of her husband Almon W. Babbitt who was killed by the indians on the plains last year, as he was returning from Washington with $20,000 [$433,166] belonging to the Territory:—

LINES

Dearest Aunt, to day we sever.
Life has many changes ever;
Lights and shadows oft succeeding—
Fondest hopes of life receding:

13 Martineau writes the *Deseret News* this month reporting good weather and the planting of trees and "other improvements" ("Parowan," *Deseret News,* April 1, 1857; Utah Digital Newspapers).

14 John Eager was Martineau's brother-in-law.

15 William H. Hooper was an experienced tradesman. He was the merchant who set the foundations for the ZCMI and the Bank of Deseret (Leonard J. Arrington, *Great Basin Kingdom: An Economic History of the Latter-day Saints, 1830–1900* [Cambridge, MA: Harvard Univ. Press, 1958], 166, 294, 311, 316).

16 Sorghum is a grass grown for grain and syrup.

Yet from far
There shines a star

THE STAR OF HOPE—

The hope of bliss and joy forever
~~When friends in peace shall dwell together.~~
When loving friends are parted never.

April 6, 1857—I was this day elected Alderman of Parowan city by a unanimous vote. Paid H. C. Kimball 130 lbs flour for sealing Susan J. to me.

April 10, 1857—Started home, having had a pleasant visit. My wives have had a good spirit, and felt well towards each other.

On arriving at Santaquin, Susan E. wished to go to San Pete County to visit her relatives there, and so I left her and her children at Uncle Benjamin's until she could go there with John Eager's team.

April 12, 1857—Left Santaquin, and arrived at Nephi, stopping at Bryant's.

[page 122]

SUSAN JULIA'S BLESSING, BY Wm CAZIER.[17]

April 12, 1857—I there got Susan's trunk and some other things we left there last winter. I also left my likeness for Susan E. when she should come along.

April 15, 1857—Arrived home at 11 P.M. Found the currents in full bloom.[18]

April 17, 1857—To day Charles Hall's baby died suddenly, choked with a bean. He died in my arms, having gone in to see her as I heard her (his mother) crying as I passed by.

April 21, 1857—Watered my land, to be ready for plowing.

April 22, 1857—Made a chicken house.

April 23, 1857—Began plowing and sowing.

[written in margin]
(see p. 119)

MEMORANDUM.

While bringing Susan J. home for the first time, she was blessed in Nephi by Father William Cazier, a patriarch, as follows:—

January 23, 1857—A patriarchal blessing by William Cazier, upon the head of Susan Julia Martineau, daughter of Lyman Royal Sherman and Delcena Diadamie Sherman, born in Far West, Missouri, October 21st 1838. Nephi Juab Co Jan. 23. 1857.

Sister Susan. In the name of Jesus Christ I place my hands upon thy head to bless thee in the stead of thy father, with a patriarchal blessing. Thou art truly blest ~~my sister~~, inasmuch as thou hast embraced the gospel in thy youth. Thou art entitled to the blessings of Abraham; and of Isaac and of Jacob, and inasmuch as thou art faithful, my sister, thou art entitled to the blessings of the heavens above and of the Earth beneath,—the blessings of the new and everlasting covenant, and inasmuch as ~~thou~~ you have embraced the principles that lead unto life and exaltation, Thou shalt be comforted my sister under all circumstances and troubles wherein you may have to pass. Thy life shall be with pleasantness and with much joy and satisfaction to thyself and to those of thine associates in thy family circle, and thou shalt truly be blessed, ~~my sister~~, with long life and partake of the holy priesthood in connexion with thy husband, which will be thy staff and thy strength. even to the putting aside or the frustrating of all the works of darkness, for thy lineage is that of Joseph, and thy priesthood is like unto his, which is after the order of Melchisedec.

[page 123]

SUSAN J'S BLESSING CONTINUED. ANOTHER—A GIRL'S.

1857—Blessed shalt thou be, my sister, in all thine associating with the saints, for the way of the Lord shall not be hid from thee; and inasmuch as thou wilt reflect with soberness and be faithful to thy husband in all things, the candle of the Lord shall not be hid from thee, day nor night, and thy hearts desire shall be

17 William Cazier (1794–1874) was a patriarch. He was among the first settlers in Juab County (Andrew Jenson, comp., *Church Chronology: A Record of Important Events Pertaining to the History of the Church of Jesus Christ of Latter-day Saints*, 2nd rev. ed. [Salt Lake City: Deseret News, 1914], 82–89).

18 The currant is a small, hardy, fruit-bearing shrub. The berry was used by the pioneers for jam and jelly.

accomplished in all things in righteousness, and thine offspring shall be mighty and many in number, and as for principle and the priesthood, none shall be greater in Israel. Thou shalt see Zion redeemed, and the holy city Sanctified before the Lord; and in the ordinances of the house of the Lord thou shalt officiate for thy dead, even from generation to generation back to that of Abel. Thy life shall be preserved, though many shall seek to interrupt and vex and perplex thee, notwithstanding the angels of the Lord have charge concerning thee, and thou shalt be conqueror over all thine enemies. Thou shalt have the gift of healing, and administer to the afflicted of thy family, in the absence of thy husband, and they shall be healed. Indeed thou art blessed, my sister, because of the honesty and integrity of the heart to do good, and thy life shall pass with much pleasantness to thyself—have part in the first resurrection, exaltation and eternal lives. In the name of Jesus Christ I seal thee up to come forth in the first resurrection, even so, amen.

This blessing was highly prized and very precious to her, and she derived great comfort in thinking of these things. Before I knew her she was blessed by Patriarch Isaac Morley, at Santaquin, as follows:—

Sister Susan, I, by virtue of the holy priesthood, place my hands upon thy head to bless thee, and I seal the blessings of thy father upon thee.

[page 124]

1857—He has stepped behind the vail, thou art left to tarry for a season upon the earth, for a wise purpose in the bosom of thy creator. Thou art in the morning of life, enjoying the period in which thou mayest become useful, Thou art enjoying the light in this last dispensation of the everlasting gospel, that many good men have desired to see, who have stepped behind the vail: Thou art permitted to enjoy the blessing. Thou art endowed with gifts with perceptions which have been lavishly bestowed upon thee by the God of Nature. As thy genius have been increased, so have thy responsibilities, whereby very few will excel thee if thou art wise and prudent with these gifts. And let me seal this impression upon thy mind—thou wilt attain them by humility and prayer. In this principle thou hast been neglectful, yet the love of thy Creator is extended toward thee. Hearken to the voice of wisdom, and none shall excel thee, for thy choices in life shall be among the anointed of the Lord. Thou shalt enjoy the blessings of posterity that shall bear the keys of priesthood from generation to generation. Thy habitation shall become a dwelling of peace. Thy gifts shall be in fine needlework, whereby thy garments will be decorated with the workmanship of thine own hands. Thou art from the Patriarchal family, and that order shall become thy order: and let this seal and caution be committed to thy memory,—Let thy mind often be arrested by thy agency upon the covenants that do and will exist between thee and thy Creator, and thou shalt be endowed with glory, immortality and eternal lives. I ratify them in the name of Jesus. Even so. Amen.

This blessing was given at Santaquin, January 21, 1856 nearly a year before I married her.

[page 125]

[Top half of page is blank.]

April 13, 1857—

LINES WHAT SHALL WE DO TO BE SAVED?

1

"What shall we do to be saved" is a question
Often propounded the Prophets of old,
And if you have no deep rooted objection
I will endeavor the truth to unfold.

Chorus.

Take up you armor—burnish it brightly
Put it on tightly, no more to lay down
Arm you with Truth's glitt'ring sword which is mighty
Fight till you conquer and wear a bright crown.

2

Husbands, your Father to you has intrusted
Spirits most noble to bring unto Him;
Teach them that Sin should be always detested—
Be as a father indeed unto them.

Chorus

3

Wives, love you husbands and honor their counsel
Be unto them truly help meets indeed,
Train up your children as mothers in Israel
Fitting their hearts to receive the ~~glad~~ good seed.

Chorus.

[page 126]

QUARREL BETWEEN KANOSH AND FLINTY-HEART.

April 13, 1857—

4

Children, your parents obey in all meekness,
Strive to gain knowledge of all that is good,
Learn to be mighty in spite of your weakness
Rev'rence the name and the words of your God.
Chorus

5

Saints, let me say to you—live your religion,
Honor the priesthood wherever 'tis found:
Publish the truth, although cast into prison,
Till all your brethren have heard the glad sound.
Chorus.

6

Then let us all as a vine be united—
All of our feelings and interests in one,
Till all that is wrong, shall again be all righted
And Father shall say to his Children "Come home."

Thursday, May 2 7, 1857—Susan J. quite unwell all night

May 14, 1857—At this date I have the following amount of crop in. 9 acres of wheat, 1¼ of corn, ¾ of potatoes and 1/10 peas Susan helped me to plant the potatoes. Spring is very cold and backward.

Rec[d] a letter from John Eager, and one from Susan E. informing me that Moroni had fallen into a deep cellar and got badly hurt.

This evening, Kanosh, a Pah vant Chief and a Pah–eed Chief had a fierce quarrel just in front of our door, surrounded by members of their tribes to the number of about 200.[19] Both parties drew knives and flourished guns &c. but finally parted without a fight. The quarrel was about a disputed gun. I was somewhat alarmed, fearing if they got to fighting that some of my family might get shot Susan and the little girl were much frightened at the uproar.

[page 127]

LINES TO AUNT SALLY.

Sunday, May 24, 1857—This morning, Patriarch Isaac Morley arrived from the north to give patriarchal blessings.

June 1, 1857—To day Br. Morley blessed us, a copy of which will be found further on, Page 252 & 253

June 6, 1857—To day, Col. Dame organized a part of our militia into Tens, for active service.

June 12, 1857—Rec[d] a letter from England wishing me to become a correspondent of the "Millennial Star."[20]

June 14, 1857—Wrote the following lines for Aunt Sarah Tuttle:—

1

Many days are past and gone
Since the one when thou wast born
Yet the years that are in store
Shall be full as many more.

2

Thou hast felt affliction's rod,—
Felt the chastening hand of God
But thou shalt his mercy see
Wide extended unto thee.

3

Heavenly blessings on thy head
In abundance shall be shed;
Life shall full of blessings be
Here, and in Eternity.

4

Children's children shalt thou bless—
Thou their offspring shalt caress:

19 Kanosh was a Pahvant Ute chief (Shirts and Shirts, *Trial Furnace*, 146, 286; Arrington, *Brigham Young*, 210).

20 The *Latter-day Saints' Millennial Star* (1840–1970) was an official publication of the Church. Parley P. Pratt was the first editor. The purpose of the *Star* was to spread the gospel. Today's counterpart would be the *Ensign* (Ludlow, *Encyclopedia of Mormonism*, 2:906; Arrington, *Brigham Young*, 81).

They in priesthood shall be great,—
Great in wisdom and faith.

5

Thy husband's words thy guide shall be:—
He will comfort take with thee.
His counsel will be of great worth
While he shall dwell upon the Earth.

[page 128]

TRIP TO SALT LAKE CITY, WITH ALUM.

June 14, 1857—

6

Let thy hopes be strong and bright
And thy soul be filled with light.
If affliction thou shalt see
A blessing it shall turn to thee.

7

And so, united heart and soul
Thy years full pleasantly shall roll.
Till time shall end, and thou shalt see
The glories of Eternity.

Wednesday, June 17, 1857—Started with Nephi Johnson, for Salt Lake City, and arrived there on the ~~24th~~ 27th in time to be present at a general muster held on the 16th Ward Square, there being three Regiments on the ground. Genl Wells received me very kindly on the ground. I brought a cannon that had been in Parowan ever since its first settlement—a brass 6 lb Carronade howitzer

June 27, 1857—which I delivered to the military authorities here. They wish to put all arms in order for Service, as affairs begin to look squally.

June 28, 1857—Was appointed Captain in the Corps of Topographical Engineers.

June 29, 1857—Went to a special meeting of officers of the Legion called at request of Prest Young, which was held in the social hall. The house was full, and Prest Young spoke like a Lion. We had a glorious time. I sold the alum I had brought down, some at 20¢ and some at 15¢ pr pound.[21]

July 1, 1857—Started for home

July 4, 1857—Arrived at Santaquin and found uncle Benjamin quite sick. I remained here three days. He blessed me with a good blessing: he said I Should do much good—be a terror to evil doers—have more strength of body than ever, and have a safe journey home.

He then asked me to bless him. I did so, also blessing his wives, six in number:—Aunt Jane, and two others.

[page 129]

SUSAN J.'S BLESSING BY E. H. GROVES.

July 7, 1857—Started for Manti, to get Susan E. and family, with a cow and calf belonging to Susan J. Camped in Salt Creek Cañon.

July 8, 1857—Went to Manti—36 miles,—a good days travel for oxen to make. I found all well, and John Eager living in a good stone house two stories high. I here staid six days, visiting: preached on Sunday, and was clerk in a trial of Warren Snow before Isaac Morley.

Br. E. H. Groves gave S. J. the following blessing, which was reported by me, as scribe:—It was given Jan. 30. 1857 at Parowan, but accidentally omitted:—

Sister Susan, in the name of Jesus of Nazareth and by virtue of the holy priesthood in me invested I place my hands upon thy head and seal upon thee a patriarchal or father's blessing, which shall rest upon thee and thou shalt realize the fulfillment thereof. Thou art in the days of thy youth, having been born and raised a natural member in the Church and kingdom of God, and inasmuch as thou wilt be faithful in keeping all the commandments of the Lord thy God, hearkening to the counsels of thy husband, thou shalt be a blessing and a help meet in very deed to him, a blessing unto thy sister with whom thou art associated by virtue of the law of the holy priesthood. Thy life shall be precious in the sight of thy Heavenly Father, thy days shall be

21 "Head Quarters Nauvoo Legion," *Deseret News*, June 30, 1857; Journal History. Utah Digital Newspapers has the publication date of this article as July 1, 1857.

many upon the earth. Thy guardian angel shall be with thee, and in his hands thou wilt be borne up and delivered from the temptations of the Evil One. Thou art a daughter of Abraham, of the loins of Joseph and blood of Ephraim through the descent of thy fathers, a legal heir to all the blessings, privileges and powers which pertain to the holy priesthood according to thy sex, which thou shalt receive in due time, that thou mayest be able to stand in connexion with thy husband in the redemption of thy progenitors, many of whom shall be made known to thee by the visits of heavenly messengers who shall come unto thy habitation revealing the genealogy of thy fathers.

[page 130]

NEWS OF THE APPROACH OF THE UNITED STATES ARMY.[22]

1857—Thou shalt become a mother in Israel. Thy posterity shall multiply and become numerous upon the earth. Thou shalt obtain power over the Destroyer, that he take not thy children from thee. Thy children and thy children's children rising after thee shall bless and comfort thee in thy old age. Thy name shall be handed down to the latest generation as an honorable mother in Zion. Thou shalt enjoy the blessings and fruits of the earth, a sufficiency for thee, participating in all the blessings of thy husband. It is thy privilige to behold the winding up scene, the coming of thy Redeemer—the reign of peace established upon the earth—to receive many blessing and priviliges in the temple in Zion. Thou shalt be anointed a Queen and Priestess to the Most High God, receive thy crown, dominion power and eternal increase—thy inheritance with thy benefactor in Zion. Be thou faithful, yield not to temptation, and these blessings shall be sure unto thee. I seal them upon thy head, in connexion with thy former blessings in the name of Jesus of Nazareth, our Redeemer, even so, Amen.

Wednesday, July 15, 1857—Started for home, by way of the Sevier River, and arrived at home on the 21st and found all well, but Susan J. whose health is quite poor.

July 24, 1857—Attended the celebration.[23]

July 25, 1857—Susan J. very sick to day. Father's folks came.

Monday, July 27, 1857—Much worse. Conversed for hours with her sister Elvira, who died in Nauvoo. I could not hear what the latter said, but from what Susan said, asking and answering questions, I could tell what they were talking about, almost as well as if I could hear both parties. Elvira taught and cheered her much. Susan was quite sick nearly all the week.

Sunday, August 2, 1857—To day a man arrived from S. L. City with news that the Gentile army is on its way here to teach the Mormons morality. They are determined to kill Brigham and all who have more than one wife. They have taken the mail at Laramie, and the mormons at the Stations had to say they were mountaineers in order to save their lives.

[page 131]

G. A. SMITH ARRIVES, ON WAR MATTERS. WE GO SOUTH.

August 5, 1857—Built a cattle shed to day.

August 6, 1857—To day Col. Dame appointed me Regimental Adjutant, with the rank of Major, my commission to date from July 28. 1857. Attended officer drill to day. Also went to fast meeting, which was very dull. I feel as though something will soon quicken our ideas. In the evening some men arrived with news that 2500 men are near the city, 1500 at Ft. Laramie and 1000 beyond that post—all coming to teach us morality. Let them come.

August 7, 1857—Spent most of the day in preparing Muster Rolls for the 9 Companies of our Regiment, and in writing in our Military history and Journal.

Saturday, August 8, 1857—Sent muster rolls to their proper destination, and sent instructions for drilling, immediately. Also sent directions regarding officers uniforms. Had a drill in the afternoon, and while marching around, Geo. A. Smith arrived from

22 President James Buchanan sent approximately twenty-five hundred soldiers and support personnel to Utah. The Latter-day Saints feared the approaching army and their preparations for the army's arrival are reflected in these pages. The context of this "invasion" is described in Arrington, *Brigham Young*, 250–71.

23 James H. Martineau, "Celebrations of the 24th of July," *Deseret News*, July 24, 1857; Journal History.

S. L. City, with news of the approach of the invading army, with orders to be prepared for the worst. If necessary, to lay down our lives in defense of the Kingdom of God. Bro. Smith was glad to see us drilling; as it showed him that we had the spirit of the times.

Sunday, August 9, 1857—Pres^{t} Smith preached a regular war sermon.

August ~~10~~ 13, 1857—Went up into the Mountains, to the head of Red Creek to get a load of hay. We found a small vally full of good hay. There is a spring of water so cold we could take only one swallow at a time.

August 14, 1857—Returned with a load of hay. I was told Br. Dame had invited me to go on a tour through Southern Utah, and Br. G. A. Smith asked me to go along as historian of the trip.

August 15, 1857—We started South to day. Our Company consists of Pres^{t} G. A. Smith and wife. Pres^{t} Dame and wife myself, Capt.^{s} C. C. Pendleton, S. S. Smith, Jesse N. Smith, Captains of tens, E. Dolten, Chas Hall and F. T. Whitney. ~~Besides, these were Jesse's wife and Susan J.~~

[page 132]

TRIP TO THE SOUTH WITH G. A. SMITH

August 15, 1857—Went to Cedar, visited the iron works, attended a muster of the 2^{d} and 3^{d} Battalions, and slept by a haystack.

August 16, 1857—Went to meeting twice, and started south, taking tea at Hamilton's (Joined by Maj. Haight,) and arrived at Harmony at 10.30 P.M. Stopping at J. D. Lee's where we were hospitably entertained.

August 17, 1857—This morning drilled Capt. Ingram's Company, went to meeting, dined, and started for Washington. Went down "Peter's Leap," which is a narrow road down the side of a deep gulch about 100 or 200 feet deep, the sides being perpendicular. The wagons were let down by ropes and men holding behind, the wheels sometimes dropping down two or three feet at a time. Got safely down. Stopped at Grape Vine Springs for the night. Maj. John D. Lee went with us from Harmony.

August 18, 1857—Arrived at Washington at noon. Dined, swam in the Rio Virgin, visited the Cotton fields, and saw cotton in bloom and boll, and corn 15 feet high, attended meeting, eat some half ripe melons, and started for Fort Clara, distant—[empty space] miles, at dark. Went 8 miles and camped at midnight.

August 19, 1857—Arrived at the Fort, dined, drilled the men, attended meeting, eat melons, and sweltered—the thermometer standing at 103° in the shade and 136° in the sunshine. It was rather warm, but the brethren there said it is not so warm as usual owing to the wind then blowing.

At 3½ o'clock P.M. Started for Pinto Creek, distant fifty miles. Passed down a narrow rocky pass, which I named "Jacob's Twist." after Jacob Hamblin.[24] This pass is between perpendicular rocks, and so very narrow as barely to allow a wagon to pass through.

[page 133]

August 1857—I named "Peter's Leap" after Peter Shirts, who first made the road there. We arrived at the Santa Clara and traveled up it about 5 miles and Camped. The valley of the Santa Clara—a small, clear stream—is very narrow, bounded on each side by high, rocky cliffs.

August 20, 1857—Traveled 35 miles to Pinto Creek, took supper and attended meeting. Very cold and rainy. This settlement has a great altitude, causing a great change in temperature.

August 21, 1857—Frost on the ground this morning. Breakfasted, drilled the men, and started for Cedar, distant 27 miles. Arrived there in a rain storm, stopped awhile until the rain ceased and then went on home, 18 miles further, arriving there at 7.45. In this trip we traveled 185 miles. I drilled the men at every settlement, and G. A. Smith and the others preached war sermons to the people.

August 22, 1857—Prepared dispatches for the north[25]

August 23, 1857—Prepared a history of our trip for publication.

---

24 Jacob Hamblin was a convert from Ohio. He was famous for his Indian missionary service and would become a witness in the Mountain Meadows trial (Leonard J. Arrington and Davis Bitton, *The Mormon Experience: A History of the Latter-day Saints* [Urbana: Univ. of Illinois Press, 1992], 153–55; Brooks, *Mountain Meadows*, 99–107).

25 James H. Martineau, "Trip to Santa Clara," *Deseret News*, August 22, 1857; Journal History.

August 24, 1857—Sam[l] Lewis and four others went out on a scout on Gunnisson's trail, in the Mountains East, to be gone several days, to watch indian movements, and to see if there were any U. S. troops on the way south, as reported.

Friday, September 4, 1857—Myself, Saml Lewis, M. Anderson, and Joseph Fish went on a scout, upon the upper Sevier, to watch for signs of troops approaching, we having heard that the Cavalry under Col. Sumner would enter the country that way.[26] We took 8 days rations. We went up Little Creek Cañon, and crossed the ridge of mountains, thence descending to the Sevier River Valley. 25 miles.

September 5, 1857—Next day we reached the Sevier River, and then traveling 8 miles down it (the South fork) and camped. having traveled 35 miles.

September 6, 1857—Crossed the South Fork to the Middle Fork, and proceeded up it 14 miles to the mouth of a small stream coming in from the north, which I named Otter Creek, because of the many otters living in it.

[page 134]

SCOUTING UP OTTER CREEK AND THE SEVIER

September 6, 1857—I killed one, and S. Lewis one. The stream is about 20 feet wide and 20 inches deep, literally full of fish—chubs and suckers—very fat. We found many lying on the banks partially eaten by the otters, and some they had just caught, which we, being the stronger party—ate. We proceeded up this stream 12 miles and camped on a small creek flowing in from the west, which we called 1st Creek. 32 miles. Saw many antelopes and a mountain lion.

September 7, 1857—Traveled up Otter Creek 12 miles to 2nd Creek, then six miles farther to 3[d] Creek, thence 8 miles to West Fork of Otter, where there is a fine grove of tall cedars, of about 5 or 6 acres: thence two miles to the narrows; thence 4 miles to the head of Spring Branch, thence 2 miles to camp = 34 miles.

Tuesday, September 8, 1857—Went 10 miles further to the top of the Divide, Saw Mt. Nebo in the distance to the northwest, many miles. Also the mountains east of San Pete Valley. We dined at the head of Bear Creek, where we saw fresh bear tracks.

Our provisions began to grow small, and as we were ordered not to be gone more than eight days we reluctantly turned homeward again, where we arrived on Friday the 11th all well. Before we got home our provisions gave out, and I tried to cook a little otter meat, which was uneatable, on account of its rancid, fishy taste. We had orders to have no fire on the trip, to avoid being tracked by indians, who were known to be hostile, having been bought up by the U. S. Army officers. But hunger made us determine to cook some meat, but a sudden puff of wind took the fire into the tall meadow grass which extends as much as 40 miles up the stream, and averages about a quarter of a mile wide.

[page 135]

WATCHING FOR THE U. S. CAVALRY. MOUNTAIN MEADOWS.

1857—Here was a dilemma. No time was lost, but all began to fight the fire, and finally extinguished it after half an hour's severe exertion. This stopped all our idea of cooking. Fearing that the Indians had seen the smoke, we traveled rapidly for home, making that day a march of over 50 miles.

The days were pleasant, but the nights clear and cold, the ground being covered with white frost every morning. As we only had one blanket each,—one to be on the ground and one over us, as we lay two and two, our sleep was none of the most comfortable—in fact, we nearly froze. Fire would have been a great blessing, if we could have had it.

On arriving home I found Col. Dame had just gone south to Mountain Meadows to try and stop the slaughter of a company of emigrants who had been attacked there by the Indians. We afterwards learned that when he arrived there he found them all killed but 15 or 20 little children the eldest about eight years of age, which had been saved by the whites. The company numbered over a hundred souls.[27]

26 Watching for the approaching federal troops. Miles Anderson and Joseph Fish were pioneers of the Iron Mission (Shirts and Shirts, *Trial Furnace*, 193, 269).

27 At his first mention of the Mountain Meadows Massacre, it is interesting to note that the approaching U.S. Army

The company had ~~poisoned~~ poisoned six Pahvants at Corn Creek, which greatly enraged all the Indians from that place south, which was the cause of the Massacre. Two or three indians were wounded. The indians had the Company surrounded for four days. This took place, (the massacre) on Monday Sept. 7th it was said.

Another large Company of emigrants had also been attacked at indian creek, and kept up a running fight for Six miles until they were rescued by brethren from Beaver. They finally made peace at Beaver, by giving the indians five head of cattle.

[page 136]

COMPANY OF EMIGRANTS FURNISHED WITH GUARDS

September 1857—The Second Company were also attacked by the indians for the same cause as the first, to wit;—the death of the six indians at Corn Creek.

Of the last Company two were badly wounded by the indians, one of whom afterwards died. One of them had hold of an indian and tried to shoot him with a pistol, firing it six times at the red man without hitting him once, although he had hold of him all the time. The indian kept jumping around all the time, and stabbed him twice in the abdomen with an arrow, which soon after caused his death.

Saturday, September 12, 1857—To day James Haslam arrived from S. L. City having been gone only six days from Cedar city having traveled during that time 560 miles—over ~~90~~ 93 miles a day, stoppages and all.[28] His actual riding time was over 100 miles a day. He was sent as Express to inform Pres^{t} Young of the dangerous state the emigrants were in, besieged by the indians. He sent word to prevent their death by all means, if possible. When he returned to Iron County, the deed was done. The party killed were from Arkansas and Missouri. They had been making threats against the Mormons all the time saying they would help kill off all the Mormons, men, women, and children.

Haslam brought word that most of the troops had been recalled to Kansas, and that indians had taken 800 of their cattle.

September 14, 1857—The Second party of emigrants arrived and Col. Dame Sent five of our brethren with them as interpreters and guards through the worst of the road. Nephi Johnson was one of them.

[page 137]

MARTIAL LAW.

September 24, 1857—To day Col. Dame started to Conference, leaving me in Command of the District, including our Regiment—the 10th Inf. I. C. Haight[29] was also in the Company, driving stock to W H Hooper. As I owed Hooper, Haight demanded a cow, and as I could not find the dry one, I had to let "Rosa" go, a cow worth \$50.$^{\underline{00}}$ [\$1,083] for which Haight would only [no word here] me \$20.$^{\underline{00}}$ [\$433]. Thus I was left without milk. I think some time he will have to repay me for it.

September 26, 1857—Have raised this year 140 bushels of wheat. I had 106 left after paying my debts, and 14 bu. of old wheat, besides 30 bu. due me. Truly the Lord has greatly blessed me since I have taken another wife.

September 26, 1857 [This date is in the journal twice.]—This day Jacob Hamblin arrived Express

troops had precedence to Martineau over the report of the massacre. The massacre was of a party of Arkansas immigrants making their way to California led by John T. Baker and Alexander Fancher. Tensions mounted between the Baker-Fancher party and the Mormon settlers and their allies. The Mormon settlers and their Native American allies were spurred by rumor and memories of Mormon persecution and felt compelled to act. The Mormon settlers sent a rider, identified here as James Haslam, to seek advice from Brigham Young, but before the rider could return, the majority of the Baker-Fancher party was dead. Years later John D. Lee was executed for the crime. Volumes have been written about the massacre. See Ronald W. Walker, Richard E. Turley, and Glen M. Leonard, *Massacre at Mountain Meadows* (New York: Oxford Univ. Press, 2008); see also Juanita Brooks, *The Mountain Meadows Massacre*, rev. ed. (Norman, OK: Univ. of Oklahoma Press, 1991).

28 Most of what we know of James Haslam was his infamous ride to seek advice from Brigham Young. Shirts and Shirts add that Haslam was sent by Isaac C. Haight, stake president. Haslam's occupation prior to his fame was that of an Iron Mission furnace keeper (Shirts and Shirts, *Trial Furnace*, 388).

29 This was likely Isaac C. Haight.

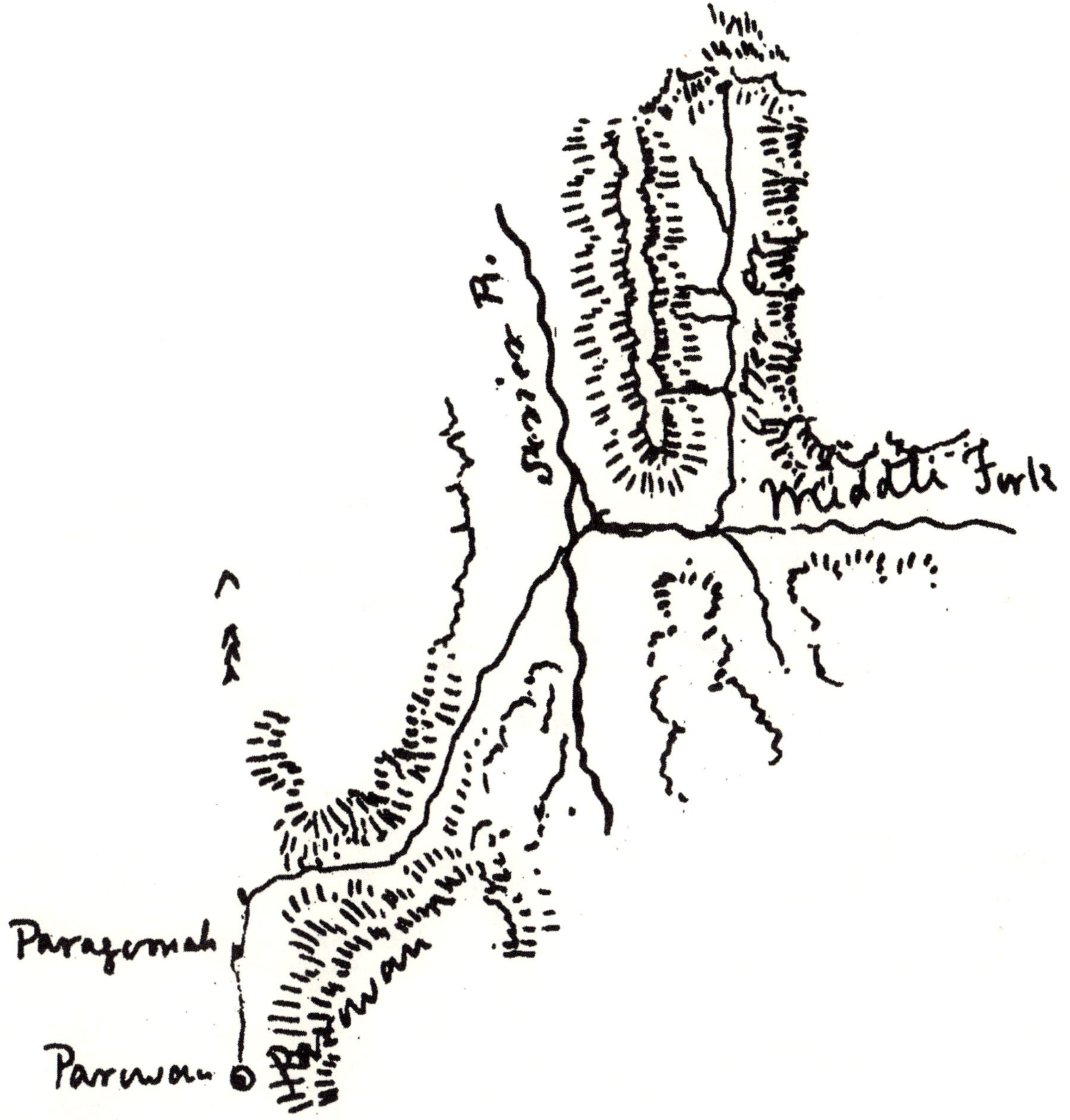

Fig. 3.1—Parowan area.

from G. S. L. City bringing Gov. Young's proclamation of Martial Law. and an order for a general muster on the 10th of October next. I sent copies of the order together with the necessary Regimental orders for its fulfillment, to all the settlements.

Several brethren came to me for passes to go to S. L. City and back, which I gave as follows:—

Parowan Sept. 26. 1857

Let John Jacobs go to Salt Lake City and back without hindrance.[30]

Maj. Ja^{s} H. Martineau Reg$^{\underline{d}}$ Adj.
Com^{r} Iron Mil. District

I gave orders to the Majors to give all necessary passes to the brethren.

30 John Jacobs was an early Cedar City settler (Shirts and Shirts, *Trial Furnace*, 331, 477).

September 27, 1857—At meeting today gave notice for officer drill and muster. Go morning and evening to administer to Sister Cha[s] Hall's sick child

September 28, 1857—Susan J. has been nine days without speaking above a whisper, cause, a bad cold.

October 1, 1857—Susan J. is again able to talk aloud to day. I Cut some wheat.

[page 138]

September 28, 1857—To-day composed the following verses:—

1

What sound is that which now we hear
Re-echoing from the plains!
The troops, they say, are drawing near
With all their wagon trains.
They come with sword and rifle too
And deadly bayonet
And swear to exterminate the few
Who dwell in Deseret.

Chorus. Then we'll fight for God and Liberty
Our powder keep from wet
And when we've gained the victory
We'll rule in Deseret.

2

They know not that a God of power
Will for His people fight
If they, in every trying hour
Will only do what's right,
For Satan has them in his chain
And all his plans are set,
To shed the blood of those who reign
In peaceful Deseret. Chorus.

3

They say, "Your prophets are all false
Their teachings all a sham
They've got your money in their hands
And do not care a d—n.
They're traitors to the Government
With blood their hands are wet,
And soon the gallows we'll erect
In peaceful Deseret. Chorus.

4

But these are lies that they have told
For we have broke no law;
The constitution we uphold

[page 139]

1857—

For it our swords we draw
Then come, ye hireling sons of hell,
Your dues you'll quickly get
Whene'er you venture on the soil
Of peaceful Deseret. Chorus.

5

For God has said you shall not come
To persecute his saints,
For He has heard the Martyr's groan
The widow's sad complaints.
There's guiltless blood upon the ground
That smokes for vengeance yet,
Oh God! avenge thy servants wrongs
Thyself in judgement set. Chorus.

6

Ye sons of God, your weapons take
And stand for Zion's rights!
We'll make the wicked fear and quake
And put them all to flight
We'll stand, our leaders lives to save—
For heaven's celestial law,—
For Wives and Children whom we love
For truth the sword we'll draw. Chorus.

October 3, 1857—Officer drill to day, superintended by me. Examined two men from California, whom we suspected of being horse thieves.

October 8, 1857—To day U. V. Stewart and W[m] Adams were cut off from the Church for selling diseased beef.[31] I bought 47 lbs of his beef, but did not eat any of it—returned it to him.

October 9, 1857—Went to Fort Johnson

31 Stewart and Adams were both settlers in the Iron Mission. Urban V. Stewart was a farmer. At this entry, he would have been forty years old. William Adams was a stonecutter and would have been thirty-six years of age (Shirts and Shirts, *Trial Furnace*, 425, 439).

October 10, 1857—Walked six miles to Cedar to drill the men there. Drilled all day, and walked back to Fort Johnson.

October 11, 1857—Came home. This day, all the pieces of Stewart's beef were gathered up and publicly burned.

[page 140]

October 17, 1857—Attended officer drill at Parowan,

October 23, 1857—Finished my harvesting and thrashing. Susan J. and Susan E. both sick.

October 24, 1857—Officer drill to day, Both my wives sick.

October 25, 1857—Susan E. still sick: Susan J. very sick. I Gave her several lobelia emetics. Rained last night and mountains white with snow this morning.

October 31, 1857—Went to Cedar with Col. Dame to drill the Battalions there.

Sunday, November 1, 1857—Returned home. Was present at the marriage of Alex. Orton and Jane Holmes.[32] Nephi gave the wedding dinner. Determined to have a Batt$^{\underline{n}}$ flag.

November 2, 1857—Officer drill to day.

November 9, 1857—Began to paint over Regimental flag.

Tuesday, November 12, 1857—Had a drill to day. I bought a ram's horn bow and 4 arrows of an indian. I intend to learn to use the bow.

November 13, 1857—Drilled some men from Beaver all day, in the Council house in the forenoon; in the snow and mud in the afternoon. Learned a few motions of British Infantry Sword exercise of Br. Betinson.

November 14, 1857—Drilled all day, in mud and snow.

November 16, 1857—Susan J. taken violently sick about noon to day with violent pains in her head and abdomen. Br. Dame came and administered to her and she at once got better.

November 17, 1857—Susan J. worse again to day. Mother Carter came to nurse her up, and Br. Dame administered to her.

November 21, 1857—During the week several persons came from Salt Lake city with further news from the troops. They reported that Col. Johnson had got to Ham's Fork with about 2000 men, their line of march extending seven miles in length. Br. Brigham had sent 1600 men to meet them, on the 16th and 17th inst, which would make our force about 2000.

[page 141]

DELLIE BORN. NOV. 27.

Tuesday, November 24, 1857—Attended officer drill to day.

Bought needles, thread, buttons, &c of Henry Lunt to the amount of $3.60 [$78] to be paid in wheat at $1.^{00} [$22] bu.

Wednesday, November 25, 1857—Elvira fell into the fire to day, burning her left arm and hand, Applied a paste of flour and water which drew out the fire in about half an hour.

Set out 18 Locust trees.

November 26, 1857—This morning Henry A. was standing by the fire place, when his pantaloon leg caught fire, burning his whole leg severely.[33] Administered to him, and applied flour as before, until the pain ceased. Examined four men, packers, just in from California, who had no passes. They professed to be Mormons and said a Company would soon be in.

Friday, November 27, 1857—Susan Julia presented me with a fine baby to day which was born at 10.45 P.M. after a sickness of six hours. She weighed 9¼ lbs. We named her <u>Delcena Diadamie Martineau</u> after Susan's mother and dedicated her to the Lord.[34]

Susan E. is quite unwell to day, and, with the two burned children, keeps our hands pretty full to take care of all of them.

November 28, 1857—Had Battalion drill to day, with skirmishing.

Monday, December 7, 1857—Bought a short artillery sword for $5.00 [$108] of Seth Johnson, intending to sell my Cavalry Sword to get a horse, so

---

32 Alexander Orton (1837–1915) and Jane Holmes (1839–1909) were both residents of Parowan.

33 Pantaloons are tight pants or trousers fastened just above the ankle or in the boot.

34 According to familysearch.org, Delcina D. Martineau (1857–65) was the last child of James and Susan Julia Sherman-Martineau.

I can go into active service.[35] My family all sick with colds.

December 8, 1857—Got each of my wives a pair of good shoes, and myself some boots. Delcena still very sick. Nearly choked with phlegm. Gave her a few drops of Lobelia tincture, which relieved her at once.

Monday, December 14, 1857—The northern mail arrived with news that the U.S. troops have gone into winter quarters at the ruins of Fort Bridger and Supply, Also that all our troops have come in except 50. and that Amasa Lyman is coming with teams to help the San Bernadino families into Utah.

[page 142]

December 18, 1857—Elder Lyman arrived and took 6 wagons and 23 horses and mules from Parowan.

Wednesday, December 23, 1857—This evening, Andrew Barton died suddenly of quick Consumption.[36]

December 26, 1857—Officer drill to day. Elder Lyman sent for 3 more wagons and 15 yoke of oxen to help the people from San Bernadino.

Tuesday, December 29, 1857—Quite sick today with the "distemper." Took a sweat, but sat too long and fainted several times.[37] The Elders administered and I got better. My family much alarmed.

Friday, January 1, 1858—Susan E. taken sick to day from a bad cold.

January 3, 1858—Susan still sick, but getting better, having been administered to by the Elders.

January 4, 1858—Bought a wild-cat skin quiver and 4 arrows for a butcher knife. I practice with my bow.

Friday, January 8, 1858—We have now been married six years. We had a good dinner provided, at which were present Father's three wives, Orton and wife and Seth Johnson. Jannett was taken quite sick.

January 10, 1858—To day Col. Dame and several others started South on an exploring tour, ~~south~~. The object is to discover water at a distance from the road, so that scouts and guerillas may have places to rally to, and come unawares upon an invading army. Br. Dame intimated to me that he might send me, on his return, to a trip to the Colorado. I wished to see him and bless him before he started but did not have an opportunity to do so.

January 11, 1858—Sick all day. My wives gave me a sweat.

January 12, 1858—To day both my wives are sick, with hot fever, chills &c They were unable to cook or do anything. Martha Hyatt came and cooked supper for us at my request.

[page 143]

ARRIVAL OF COL. KANE FROM WASHINGTON[38]

January 13, 1858—To day I have taken care of the women as well as I can. There are six of us sick. Henry alone is well but the hand of the Lord is in it, and all is right. Jo^{s} L. Heywood and others arrived from the north.

January 14, 1858—Br Heywood administered to us, Susan E. was instantly healed, and we were all helped a good deal.

January 22, 1858—Received a letter from Col. Dame instructing me to go to Cedar and drill the brethren there, but I am too unwell to go.

January 27, 1858—Our Band and Choir gave a concert this evening, in which Americans, English, Welsh, Danish and Hawaiians Sung pieces, in their native tongues.

January 30, 1858—Went to Cedar and drilled the militia in the skirmish drill. Returned as far as Fort Johnson that night.

Monday, February 1, 1858—Began to fix the back rooms, so that Susan J. Can live in it.

35 There was a Seth Johnson who would later become the postmaster at Summit, Utah. Familysearch.org also lists a Seth G. Johnson (1839–1927) of Parowan.

36 This is likely Andrew Baston (not Barton). He was a farmer, a convert from Maine, and one of the iron missionaries (Shirts and Shirts, *Trial Furnace*, 99, 425).

37 Martineau could mean dysentery, an inflammation of the intestine. Distemper is an illness usually associated with animals, particularly dogs and cats.

38 This is Colonel Thomas L. Kane, a non-Mormon friend of the Saints who was later instrumental in negotiating a peaceful settlement to what was called the Utah War (Martha Sonntag Bradley, *A History of Kane County* [Salt Lake City: Utah State Historical Society, 1999], 55–59).

Thursday, February 4, 1858—Susan J. moved into the new rooms.

February 12, 1858—To day Susan E. finished putting a piece of flannel in the loom, and wove a little. It is the first we have ever done, since our marriage.

February 14, 1858—Col. Dame preached to day and counseled us to begin at once making boxes to Cache flour, seeds &c in, to be kept for a time of need.[39]

February 20, 1858—To day Elder A. Lyman arrived from the south accompanied by a man direct from Washington upon Urgent business, the purport of which is unknown to us. He went to Salt Lake City with great expedition, changing horses at every town.

[written in margin]

Col. Kane's arrival

On Tuesday last the people assembled in mass meeting to express their views relative to the present position of the Church. S. S. Smith, J. N. Smith, Ja^s Lewis, C. C. Pendleton and J H Rollins were appointed a Committee, and myself secretary, to adopt resolutions upon the subject, which were unanimously adopted.

[page 144]

A COMPANY CALLED TO THE DESERT.

February 21, 1858—To day Col. Dame informed me that I am appointed to be one of a party of 20 men who are going on a trip among the I-ats (Om-a-há-ves as they call themselves) on the Colorado river. My outfit is to be two mules, arms, and two month provisions.

Up to this date, many persons have come in from San Bernadino, Lower California, having been driven from their homes and beautiful farms by the gentiles and apostates under the name of the "Richabites." Many of them had to be helped here. Frequently, a valuable farm, worth thousands of dollars, was sold for a horse or mule. One man let a house go, costing him $1100.^00 [$23,824], for a small hammer.

Thus was fulfilled the prophesies of the leaders of the Church, when San Bernadino was first settled. Only a small number of persons was called to go there, but hundreds would go, in hopes of getting rich. After laboring for years, they came back stripped of almost everything.

March 7, 1858—Let out my land to Br. Christiansen on shares. I am to have half of all produce, in the stack, except potatoes, which are to be delivered at my house.

March 10, 1858—Mail arrived from S. L. City with news that a Company is to be sent to the desert, to explore for a place of refuge for the Saints. They are to go to the white or Lost Mountains.

The Council met at 8½ P.M. and called the following persons from Parowan and Paragoonah:—O B Adams, and son, L. Barton, John S. Hyatt, James McGuffie, L. Guymon, B. Lewis, A. Carter and U. V. Stewart.[40]

March 19, 1858—Amasa Lyman arrived from the north. He is appointed our Military leader for the South. Our duty is to hold the South part of the Territory for the Saints.

[page 145]

MY DREAM.

March 20, 1858—To day I was honorably released from the trip to the Colorado, on account of having no mules.

March 22, 1858—Was clerk at the sealing of Ansel Twitchell and his two wives.[41]

March 30, 1858—To day news came from the city, with particular of proceedings of a special conference, at which the President announced the policy adopted, to save the shedding of blood. We will retreat south, and burn and destroy everything behind us as we go, leaving nothing for our enemies to profit by.

---

39 Martineau reports on a mass meeting held on February 16, where resolutions were passed regarding persecution and religious freedom ("Mass Meetings: Parowan and Paragonah," *Deseret News*, March 3, 1858; Journal History).

40 Many of these people were a part of the original Iron Mission. Lorenzo Barton was a carpenter by trade and forty-one years old at this time. James McGuffie (also spelled Guffy) was a coal merchant and forty-three at this entry (Shirts and Shirts, *Trial Furnace*, 425, 436).

41 There are two possible Anciel Twitchells who fit this time period. One was a private in the D Company of the Mormon Battalion (Ricketts, *Arizona's Honeymoon Trail*, 27), and the other (1825–98) resided in Beaver, Utah.

The women and children are to be removed south, no crops to be put in, north of Utah County, and Parowan will be head Quarters.

This cast something of a damper over us—the thought of retreating without a fight, and killing some of the infernal scoundrels, but I suppose it is all right, and will carry out the programme.

In the evening, meeting was held, and Bishop Tarlton Lewis called for all the teams and wagons to help the removal South. Twelve wagons were sent—more will be soon.

Thursday, April 8, 1858—Snowing to day. Advised my wives to cook and eat together again, to which they agreed.

April 9, 1858—Still snowing—snow six inches deep.

April 12, 1858—Dreamed last night that Pres^{t} Dame came home in a great hurry from the city and said he had a mission for me—would I fill it. I said Yes, what is it. He said it was to get ready at once ~~for the desert~~ to go somewhere, but where I did not know. I thought I had an acre and ¾ of land yet to plow before I could go, and then I would have nothing to hinder me.

I awoke and thought it over. I worked hard plowing all that day, and finished my land, plowing and sowing 1¾ acres of wheat land, and got home about 9 o'clock P.M.

[page 146]

I AM CALLED ON A MISSION TO THE DESERT.

April 13, 1858—Pres^{t} Dame arrived unexpectedly from S. L. City, being only four days on the journey with orders to get a company of 60 men to explore in the desert for a place of refuge. I was harrowing in my grain and got home late, so I did not see him, but on

April 14, 1858—he told me in the morning he had a mission for me—would I fulfill it? I said yes, what is it? He said, I cannot tell you now, but get ready as soon as you can. Thus was my dream fulfilled to the very letter, For I do not know where I am going, nor how long, just as it was in my dream.

April 15, 1858—Col. Dame came home and told me what we have to do. We are to take, each, a horse, 150 lbs flour, meat, seeds, tools &c including one bushel of seed wheat each.

I feel thankful to be considered worthy to fill such an important mission.

Sunday, April 18, 1858—To day those who are called for the desert all spoke, giving their testimony for the gospel, myself one among the number.

Monday, April 19, 1858—To day Patriarch Elisha H. Groves gave the following blessings:—

Br. James, in the name of Jesus Christ our Redeemer and by virtue of the holy priesthood in me invested, according to the desire of thy heart, I place my hands upon thy head and bless thee and thou shalt be blessed, for the Lord hath said to thy servant "whomsoever thou blessest, they shall be blessed." Thou shalt enjoy health on this mission whereunto thou art called. The vision of thy mind shall be opened unto thee; thou wilt increase in wisdom and understanding, and thou shalt be able, in connexion with thy brethren to lay the foundation for the gathering of the people of God into the the Chambers of the Almighty, where they shall be secure while the indignation of the Lord shall pass over our enemies.

[page 147]

MY BLESSING.

April 19, 1858—Thy guardian angel shall be with thee,—he will not leave nor forsake thee. Thou shalt return in due time, and lead thy family forth as it were to fountains of living waters. All the blessings of the holy priesthood which have been pronounced upon thy head thou shalt realize, and stand firm and unshaken in the trying scenes that the servants of God have got to pass through. Doors of prosperity shall be opened unto thee, in the which thou wilt realize the hand of God over thee for thy good. These blessings I seal upon thy head, and seal ~~upon thy head, and seal~~ thee up to eternal life in the name of our Redeemer. Even so. Amen.

DELCENA'S BLESSING:—

Delcena, in the name of Jesus Christ our Redeemer, and by virtue of the holy priesthood in me invested, I place my hands upon ~~thy head~~ thee, and seal upon thee a patriarchal or father's blessing, and thou shalt be blessed. Thou art in the days of thy infancy, yet a chosen spirit inhabiteth thy tabernacle, and inasmuch as thy parents will be wise, doing their duty by thee, thou shalt grow up to mature age, mighty in faith. The Holy Spirit will rest upon thee from thy infancy, though Satan may seek to take thy life from thee, it shall be precious in the sight of thy heavenly father. Thy days shall be multiplied upon the Earth: thou shalt be a blessing unto thy parents. Thou art of the seed of Abraham, a descendant of Ephraim, entitled to all the blessings, privileges, and powers which pertain to the holy priesthood according to thy sex, which thou shalt receive in due time, that thou mayest be able to stand in thy proper lot and station in the redemption of thy progenitors, many of whom will be made known to thee by holy messengers, who will reveal the genealogy of thy fathers.

[page 148]

DELLIE'S BLESSING. (CONTINUED)

April 19, 1858—Thou wilt be connected with a man of God, through whom thou wilt receive thy priesthood, exaltation, power, and eternal glory. Thy posterity will multiply and become numerous in the Earth. Peace and quietness will rest in thy habitations,—joy and comfort will crown thy days. Thy table will be filled with the precious fruits of the earth for thy comfort and the convenience of thy family. Thou shalt become a teacher of thy sex; the spirit of inspiration ~~shall~~ will burn in thy bosom. Thou shalt behold the winding up scene—the establishment of the principles of truth upon the earth. Many of thy posterity shall be born in the millennium. Thou shalt receive thy endowments, and blessings in the temple in Zion, be anointed a queen and a priestess, receive thy crown, power, dominion and eternal increase, thy inheritance with the faithful in Zion These are thy blessings. I seal them upon thy head in the name of Jesus Christ our Redeemer. Even so. Amen.

Friday, April 23, 1858—To day the Company for the desert started, all but me, who had instructions to wait until tomorrow and bring further word from the north.

This afternoon myself and wives went upon a hill and had a beautiful view of Parowan. We prayed and came home.

I blessed all my family, and told them if they would be united and do right, they should have power to bless and heal their children, if they should be sick. We felt Comforted.

Christiansen did not take my farm, but Br. H. M. Alexander did, on the same terms.

I wrote the following lines:—

1

A blooming flower in beauty bright
A dew-drop-glittering in the light
May fade or vanish from the sight
Nor leave a trace behind.

[page 149]

EXPLORING EXPEDITION TO THE DESERT.

April 23, 1858—
But Truth—eternal, priceless truth—
The brightest gem thats found on earth
Tho' ages roll—yet still in youth
Will shine with light divine.

[Written vertically in margin to the right of other verse with an arrow to show it goes between verses 1 & 2.]

It gives a knowledge of the past—
The present, and the future vast;
It lives and will forever last
Though Time may pass away

2

Then ~~If we are~~ we're wise, this gem we'll seek
And when tis found, securely keep
Nor ~~shut~~ close our eyes in slumber deep
Nor shun its heavenly ray
~~Then let us all in truth be one~~
~~Cleave to the truth~~, ~~but evil shun~~
~~And then in Truth we will be one~~
~~And dwell in light~~

Saturday, April 24, 1858—To day I started to overtake our company, which is camped at the Iron Springs, about 30 miles from here. May God keep and bless my family. Amen.

I had a wild mare belonging to James McGuffie, and came to the Company in the afternoon, and found nearly all the Company gathered, and about ready to start tomorrow. There are 60 men, with 20 wagons, there being three men to each wagon. Two stay with the wagon, and one man on horseback, to act as front or rear guard Scouts or explorers. Each wagon has a large ~~wagon~~ barrel for hauling water for ourselves and teams.

April 25, 1858—Before leaving we organized into two Tens (wagons) Col. W. H. Dame being Captain, and myself Historian and Clerk, Saml Sheppard Sen. Chaplain, Ross R. Rogers, Sergt of the Guard; J. Ward Christian, Capt. of 1st Ten; Geo. W. Sirrine, Capt. 2nd Ten; Nephi Johnson Chief Interpreter; Thos Durham, Chief of Music (Band & Choir.)[42]

I was called on to speak at meeting, and did so, feeling thankful to be thought worthy to be called on so important mission as this is.

Monday, April 26, 1858—Camp started this morning upon our journey all our Company having arrived, 20 wagons with 5 horses or mules to each.

[page 150]

WESTWARD HO! SHOAL CREEK

April 5, 1858—Arrived at Antelope Springs about noon, and watered our animals; distance 15 miles. Went on to Pinto Creek, arriving there at Sunset. Found no water there, so we went up the dry bed for a mile and a half and found water and good feed. Br. Dame and I took observations of the Country from the top of a high hill. Distance to day, 27 miles. and 57m from Parowan. I stood camp guard to night.

Tuesday, April 27, 1858—Started at 8 A.M. Col. Dame, Nephi, myself and seven others started from the road across the valley west, ten miles to the hills, and tried to find a cut off for a road, but found no chance. We descended from the hills to a small stream flowing from the west, called Shoal Creek and Struck "Bennett's trail," so called from the Company that passed this way on their journey to California in 1849. Of 30 wagons and families, having about 150 or 160 souls, only seven—six men and one woman arrived in California, all the others having died, as well as all their cattle. One of the Survivors was Bennett, who is now in our exploring company. He remembers the road and the Country well.

We camped at the first water above Pilot Hill, the water, grass and willows plenty for Camp. At about midnight Barney Carter and Sam. Lewis arrived at Camp, with letters from our friends, and stating that two more wagons which we expect to overtake us from Parowan will be unable to do so, their teams being poor.[43] I wrote a letter to each of my wives. Distance to-day 18 m, total 75.

Wednesday, April 28, 1858—The road from this point passes about 8 miles up a broad, smooth, grassy cañon, with springs at intervals; then through a narrow, rocky, bushy, difficult cañon 3 miles, when it suddenly opens into a beautiful broad, smooth and grassy one, with two good springs and good feed, cedars on the side hills.

[page 151]

April 28, 1858—Camped at 1 P.M. distance 11 miles. Total 86. It began raining hard in the afternoon, and continued all night. In the morning it turned to snow. While lying in bed in the dark, I composed the following:—

LINES.

Come all who're for the desert bound
Let's make these vallies all resound
With sounds of mirth and joy and glee
And thank our God we still are free.

2

We will no longer wear the yoke
of Gentile bondage, for 'tis broke
Our rulers shall be of our own—
For them we'll seek a desert home.

42 Little is known of Samuel Sheppard or George W. Sirrine (see note 41). Ross R. Rogers was among the settlers in Beaver. He left Parowan in February 1856, at the request of George A. Smith, who suggested Beaver would be good pastureland. There is a Dr. J. Ward Christian listed as defending William W. Stewart for his participation in the Mountain Meadows Massacre (Brooks, *Mountain Meadows*, 67). Thomas Durham migrated to Utah with the Martin handcart company. He was noted for his fine furniture and cabinetry making. He was among the first iron missionaries (Shirts and Shirts, *Trial Furnace*, 400; Janet Burton Seegmiller, *A History of Iron County: Community Above Self* [Salt Lake City: Utah State Historical Society, 1998], 182).

43 Barney Carter was among the first settlers in Beaver.

3
Long we've been driven and oppressed,—
On Earth we've scarcely found a rest:—
Our leaders they have basely slain—
Their blood still smokes upon the plain!

4
Our enemies are not a few,
But they have got enough to do.
The north and south, in arms arrayed
Will soon unsheathe the battle blade.

5
We fled to Utah's distant vale
That they no more might us assail;
We left our houses and our lands
Which fell into their greedy hands.

6
But we increased in wealth and power
And blessings on our heads did shower,
But now again we're forced to roam
And in the desert find a home.

[page 152]
April 1858—

7
We here behold a chosen band
Sent by our prophet's high command
To go and find a place of rest
Among the deserts of the west.

8
Then let our hearts be firm and true
Our duty let us nobly do
And ere we do disgrace our trust
Let's rather slumber in the dust.

9
The angels of our God will be
Our constant guard and Company.
And guide us safely on our way
While we his counsels do obey.

10
But if we do His words reject
What can we then but death expect?
For perils dark will hedge our path
And we will feel His righteous wrath.

11
The Lord can send the drops of rain
To wet the Sandy, desert plain.
And show us fountains cool and clear
Our thirst to quench—our hearts to cheer.

12
Then let our hearts be light and free
For Zion's children still are free
And though we may in Deserts roam
We'll find a new and desert home.

Thursday, April 29, 1858—This morning found ice in a cup of water. We set out this morning in a heavy snow storm, which lasted all day, making traveling very disagreeable. Traveled all day in the summit of the mountains, and in the afternoon descended the outer side of the rim of the "Great Basin."

[page 153]
April 1858—Camped at Cave Springs having traveled 22 miles Total 108. About 17 miles back, we passed a bed of chalk.

April 30, 1858—Rained nearly all day and our camp did not move. I went to see if a road can be made through the cedar hills to the right of the road, got caught in the rain, and came in wet and cold.

May 1, 1858—Camp started this morning. Nephi and I, with several others and our indian guide, started for the top of a high mountain, in order to get the lay of the Country. We arrived at the summit after a toilsome ascent, and had a good view of the Country, of about 150 miles in every direction. I could see the Beaver Range, also the Wahsatch from about Parowan to Harmony; Lone Mountain, near Pinto; and a snow covered range to the northwest, about 125 miles. There is snow on the mountain where we now stand. I named this Lookout Mountain. Saw a large valley to the northwest about 15 miles containing grass and water. We descended and met our train at the western foot of the mountain and traveled down a kanyon to the large valley we had seen, which we named "Meadow Valley." We camped by a large meadow, extending about 12 miles N30°E. Found 4 large wagon tires which had been left by the Last Company of 1849. Our train did not come up, and we had rather poor fare. Frost in the night.

While on guard this morning I composed the following lines:—

1

We've left our quiet, peaceful homes
Among these hills and vales to roam
To find a place where saints may come
And leave our foes behind, Sir

[page 154]

April 31 & May 1, 1858—

But though we've left our friends so dear
A hundred miles or more from here
There's nothing that should make us fear
Because we're on the track, sir.
Then let us make these vallies ring
While on our way we're traveling
Let's joke or preach or laugh or sing
And keep our spirits up. sir.

2

The Gentiles now may laugh and scoff
And Say "We've drove the Mormons off
And now we'll take their goods, and stuff
Our pockets to the full, sir
But they will find out their mistake
When they our ruined cities take
And in their ashes poke and rake
To see what they can find, sir.
They'll wish that they had never come
A thousand miles away from home
To fight against us, who have done
No harm at all to them, sir.

3

Buchanan now feels rather bad
For Brigham's got him by the beard
And he seems to be quite ill prepared
To carry on the war, Sir.
For Congress won't sustain his plan
To send his 40,000 men
To march across the western plain—
They've other fish to fry, sir.
For Kansas is the battle ground
Where men in deadly strife are found
And Civil war's discordant sound
Is echoing far and near, Sir

[page 155]

May 1, 1858—

ENTER AND EXPLORE MEADOW VALLEY.

4

Then while our foes with fury rage
~~In better work will we engage~~
And make a blot on history's page
In better work will we engage
And let them whip themselves, sir.
Our prophet's eyes upon us rest
In hope that we will do our best
And find a place far in the west
Where we can rest in peace, sir.
Then let us cheerily travel on
Towards the setting of the Sun
And when our journey we have done
We'll go and bring our wives, Sir.

Distance from Cane Springs to Cave Springs 6 miles; then to Meadow valley 27, distance today 33 miles, total 141.

Sunday, May 2, 1858—Camp arrived this morning. Nephi and some others went northward exploring. On their return they Reported the vally 6 miles to head of brook. It breaks out from a large blue rock, very clear, tepid, and slightly mineral, with fishes 4 inches long in it. I killed a pig for bait, and the boys caught about a dozen fish. At the same time another party explored southward about six miles to its lower end. There is much grass fit for mowing.

About a dozen indians came to camp, one of whom had never seen a white man before. He was much frightened at every little thing at first. We gave them bread to eat, also some flour, with which they made a mush. When it was done they ate it out of the iron pot, boiling hot, while we looked on in amazement.

We had meeting in the forenoon and also in the evening.

[page 156]

CAMP WITHOUT WATER.

May 3, 1858—Camp moved across the valley and up hill for 12 miles to near the top of the divide to Bennett's Spring, which is slightly warm. Here our two indian guides went back, and we wrote to our friends. I wrote to Pres[t] Young for Br. Dame, also to my family and a public letter to C. C. Pendlton. We here got an indian to go on with us. Br. Dame and I, and two others went to the top of the ridge 4½ miles to find how the country lies beyond as we saw strong indications of gold.

May 4, 1858—Each wagon took a barrel of water this day, as our next water is very uncertain. Going west 4½ miles to the top of the ridge, we began to descend, and crossed a wide dry valley leading to Las Vegas. This valley is about 9 or ten miles wide

While riding along slowly, the sun poured down with a great heat upon us, and made me so sleepy that I could not keep awake, but slept for miles on my horse, every now and then partially awaking in time to keep from falling off, and to straighten up again. We ascended another ridge, & descended to Desert Springs. There are no springs here, but we found water by digging holes in the sandy bottom of a dry gulch, into which water slowly percolated, so we could dip it out by a table spoonful at a time. We did not find water here today, however, not knowing where or how to look for it but camped without any water or feed.

We sent out a party to explore for water, who came back saying they could find none, but saw an indian wickiup, but could not talk with the indian, who ran away from them, being frightened at the glancing of their shovels in the sun light. Their revolvers did not frighten him, he not knowing their use. Distance 34 miles

May 5, 1858—Started early, hoping to find water, as there must be some for the indian to subsist upon. Went 6 m. to his Wickiup, by the side of the dry gulch before mentioned.

[page 157]

AN INDIAN CANNIBAL.

May 5, 1858—In a short time our indian guide induced him to come to our camp, where plenty of provisions soon made him feel at home with us, and he showed us how to get water. Near his little hut lay the bones of his wife scattered round, her long black hair lying by her skull. He said she had died, or been killed by other indians, and he had eaten her. From all we could gather, he must have killed her himself to eat. The last winter many of the indians had died of starvation. We gave the poor fellow a large quantity of bread, sufficient, we thought, to last him three or four days, but he began eating and continued until he had eaten it all! Then, as he saw us free with our provisions, he doubtless thought he could afford to be extravagant with his, for he went and brought his own store, which he cooked and ate. The following was what he had:—A mouse, (which he ate raw, guts, hair and all) two large rats, 5 Lizards, 1 horned toad, and 4 large Rattlesnakes! These latter he coiled up nicely in the hot embers, covered, and roasted: they swelled as large as a man's arm, and he began eating at the tail, biting off mouthful after mouthful, the oil running down his face, forming a most disgusting picture. Some of our party had to vomit. The other vermin he also roasted and ate, leaving nothing. The Lizards, when cooked looked very white and nice, like fish meat.

We spent most of the day and the night in dipping water for ourselves and animals, and in trying to fill our barrels for tomorrow's journey. While lying here a party of us—about 14—ascended to the top of the mountain, and amused ourselves by rolling down huge rocks, one of which was as large as a common log house. It was just balanced, and by working vigorously for about an hour, we started it down the steep, smooth mountain side, for about half a mile.

[page 158]

DESERT SWAMP.

May 5, 1858—It was a grand sight, making huge leaps of 4 or 500 feet at a time. Finally it struck a solid rock, with a shock that seemed to jar the mountains, and flew into a million fragments.

Thursday, May 6, 1858—Started at 7 A.M. Cool and cloudy. Traveled all day through a desert country, 27 miles, and encamped without water.

May 7, 1858—Traveled today 11 miles, and camped by Desert Swamp, where there is wire grass, and alkali water. Our total distance from Parowan is

225 miles. Br. Dame seemed disheartened at our prospect—a high mountain barring our progress west, unless we can discover a pass through it. I felt strong and tried all I could to Cheer him up. The mountain before us is crowned with snow, and it inspired me to compose these lines:—

1

The mountains white
Are now in sight
Which we have been sent forth to find
Their tops with snow
Are covered now,
And with the storm-cloud grandly crowned.

2

Through deserts drear
We've wandered here
And God hath led us on our way:
And by His Grace
We'll find the place
Where for a time the saints may stray.

3

Our foes now strive
To take the lives
of those now standing at our head.

[page 159]

ASCEND M^T GREYHEAD.

May 7, 1858—
They oft have mobbed
The Saints of God
And we before their face have fled.

4

Welcome the day
When we can say—
"Thus far—no farther shalt thou come."
Our rights divine
We will maintain,
~~And~~ Or in the desert find a home.

After dinner Br. Dame, myself, Nephi and eleven others, started west exploring. We traveled 22 miles and camped at the foot of the mountain, without water, cold night.

May 8, 1858—Traveled along the base of the mountain southward 9 miles to onion spring—good water—many wild onions growing around it. After resting awhile, we began to go up the mountain. Some of the men gave out, and Br. Dame, myself and Nephi leaving them in charge of the horses, proceeded on foot up a peak still higher, over snow about six feet deep. I was first at the top. A magnificently dreary prospect met they. All round us nothing but desert, no grass to be seen; sand and white alkaline and salty plains all round, with short isolated ranges of barren mountains all around us. West of our mountain lises [lies] a great mud flat, a lake in winter, about 20 by 40 miles in extent, white at this time with alkali. To the east, about 250 miles lies the snowy outline of the Wahsatch; about the same distance west lies the Sierra Nevada; to the northwest high peaks as also to the south. But we looked in vain to the north for the White Mountains, although the air and sky was perfectly clear. We looked long and earnestly to the north for our mountains, but could not see them

[page 160]

GOLDEN GATE

May 8, 1858—We felt as though we were very near Heaven. We built an alter of large flat stones, then I sang a hymn
"For the Strength of the Hills we bless Thee,
Our God; our fathers God"—
after which we prayed in circle, dedicating the country to the Lord, and feeling heavenly.

As soon as we ceased praying, we looked to the north, and there, just as plainly visible as any of them, was the White Mountains we had so long looked for in vain! It seemed as if our eyes had been miraculously opened.

We rejoined our comrades, and descended the mountains still further south, coming into a cañon leading east, full of good grass, and a good clear stream of water, enough to water about 150 acres. We traveled down it till we came to a narrow gap, between perpendicular walls of solid Quartz, about 15 or 20 feet wide. Most of our party having been for years in the gold mines of California, say they never saw such a good show for gold, as here. They wanted to stop and get some gold, but we have no time to think of hunting gold, with the enemy pressing on the front, and thousands of people fleeing to the south from before them. We went on through the pass, which I named the "Golden Gate" and camped, having traveled about 30 miles.

Fig. 3.2—"Golden Gate."

Sunday, May 9, 1858—Started early for camp, and got there about 4 P. M. (85^{m}) having traveled since leaving camp about 85 miles. We passed a huge rock to our left as we came back that looked very much like a huge dog couchant.[44] This we named "Dog Rock." While traveling, we saw a fine mirage—a lake, beautifully blue and calm, in which could be seen reflected mountains and clouds. Feeling very tired, I lay down and slept a little.

An Exploring party was sent south to find a spring said to be about 40 miles south (7 men) Also a party of 8 men northward.

[page 161]

May 10, 1858—Lay in camp, waiting the return of our explorers.

May 11, 1858—Both parties returned, the one from the south having found only two small springs: the northern one had found two large collections of springs.

May 12, 1858—Camp started north, and went 18 miles to Desert Swamp Springs. Dame, myself and five others went on ahead to explore northward. We camped in Pine Cañon, ~~springs~~ about a mile above its mouth. To day we passed miles over an alkali plain, our horses sinking knee deep in fine, floury, alkali, which almost smothered us.

May 13, 1858—Proceeded up the Cañon some 5 miles and found a good spring of water. We unsaddled, and while our horses were eating, Nephi, Dame and I ascended a high mountain. We knelt and prayed. While going up the kanyon we suddenly came upon an indian camp of an indian, squaw and ~~two~~ 3 children who were much scared. The children ran to the cedars, screaming, & beckoning their parents to come. The squaw was sitting on the ground, when suddenly we heard a child cry, and underneath her rabbit skin we found her baby which she had hidden. We gave them bread, and tried to cheer them up. They had never seen a white man before. We arrived at Willow springs, expecting the Camp to overtake us here. Soon the camp came up. We have traveled in these two days 50 miles: the Camp 35. Our distance from Parowan is 260 miles. Dame, Nephi, myself, and a few others, have traveled 360 miles at this date.

May 14, 1858—This morning Col. Dame sent Nephi and a party of five others to hunt for a spring said to exist 75 miles south. At the same time Myself, Dame and 8 others started north, with 8 days rations. We found a good cool spring about 12 miles north, in the bottom and about 12 miles further came to a large meadow, formed by the sinking of a large creek which we named Eureka.

[page 162]

VISIT OF BEAVER COMPANY EXPLORERS.

May 14, 1858—We think it will water 2000 acres. We saw an indian, and ran him down after a hot chase, but we could not talk much with him. He carried an old gun, without any lock on it. We went on about 16 miles, and camped at 9 P.M. in the Cedars, having come 40 miles.

May 15, 1858—Started early, and crossed the rim of the Great Basin, about 25 miles. Found high snow covered mountains. We passed down a kanyon, which we named Lone Rock Cañon, from a lone rock in it, about 40 feet high, 10 or 15 feet thick and 75 long like this:

Fig. 3.3–Lone Rock Canyon.

44 *Couchant* means lying down or crouching.

There is a stream in this, enough to water 1000 acres. There are currants along its banks and a very pretty cascade about 10 feet high.

Here we found recent tracks of men and horses, and supposing some of our camp had been exploring the Country beyond, we returned towards camp a few miles and camped for the night.

May 16, 1858—Continued on our way back, and camped on the banks of Eureka creek, at 8 P.M. Water froze in a canteen.

May 17, 1858—Hunted for some good land. Found a spring large enough to water 300 acres. On getting to Camp, we found that some of the Beaver Company of Explorers had been in our Camp. This accounted for the tracks we had seen, and which we thought were made by some of our own party. We heard some news from home;—We are not to explore any further North or west, but South and Southwest.

I have now traveled 500 miles, including 140 miles on our last trip north, being 240 miles extra traveling, having been in the saddle every day, but four, since I left home,—two Sundays, and two days at desert swamp Camp. I have so far realized the blessings of Br. E H Groves, wherein he promised me health and strength, having been well all the time, and able to eat my allowance whenever I can get.

[page 163]

THE CAVE

1858—I have not been troubled in my mind about my family, although my first thought on waking has always been a prayer for them, and the last thing at night, is a prayer that they may live in peace and unity, to honor me, themselves, and the holy order of marriage: and that I may be able to preside over my family in righteousness, teach them the principles of ~~the~~ truth, and lead them unto Thee, oh Father in heaven.

May 18, 1858—To day had a good game of ball. In the afternoon some men from Parowan, belonging to the Beaver Company came to our camp. It was a most joyful meeting. They told us of a large cave they had found near their Camp, which is about 15 miles east of us on the other side of the range of mountains. They had explored the Cave, but found no end. John S. Hyatt shot off the end of his finger.

May 19, 1858—This morning our visitors returned to their Camp. I went over to see the Camp, and take my mare to Br McGuffie, who has sent for her. Found a good spring at the eastern base of the mountain. We reached the White Mountain Mission Camp after 18 miles travel, and were much pleased to see our friends. I gave the mare to McGuffie and explained how she was taken. He said he was satisfied, and was pleased to see her in such good condition, after riding her 530 miles over high mountains and dreary deserts, and she is now in better order than when she started.

I visited the cave with R. R. Rogers, and spent 4 hours in it, until our candles gave out. We went in about ¾ of a mile but saw no signs of any ending. It enters the S. W. Side of the mountain, the opening being about 12 feet wide by three in height. For 100 feet it is straight and slightly descending, after which it opens into large rooms, then narrows so you have to crawl along, twists and turns every way, sometimes up and sometimes down hill.

[page 164]

INDIAN TRADITION.

May 19, 1858—There are many side passages and apertures. It was a wild looking place. At one place there is a deep and bottomless Chasm, into which we threw stones but could not hear them strike any bottom. Several hundred yards from the mouth of the Cave is a large room, about 70 feet in diameter, in which is a good clear, cool, spring, of water, which drips from the roof into a little basin. We found bones of some large animals—perhaps of horse or ox kind—and in the peculiar stiff, greasy clay forming the bottom of the Cave I found prints of large claws—probably of a Bear. The indians told us the following tradition:—

Many generations ago, two squaws ventured into it one spring when the grass was about four inches high, and did not appear again until the next fall, when they said that when they went in they traveled many miles, the cave becoming wider and more open, until it opened out into a large country inside the earth, with streams, forests, hills, deer and other game. They were taken by the people living there, and taken many days journey farther on until they came to a large city like the Mormon Cities, where people lived like the whites, with wagons, horses, cattle and sheep. There they remained for some months, until they found a chance to escape again to their friends.

The indians all believe this most religiously, and nothing will induce them to enter the cave. Only one of them ever did so, except one, the Warchief of the Pahvants—he who led the party that killed Lt. Gunnisson's Party—He went in with some of our party, after they had repeatedly been in, in order to get a reputation for courage with his tribe.

I returned to our Camp by another pass, 24 miles. Br. Rogers and I preached in the evening at the request of the brethren, dined with U. V. Stewart and supped and slept with Beason Lewis. I took a mare that McGuffie let me have in place of the one I had, and got to our camp on the 20th

[page 165]

BACK TO MEADOW VALLEY.

May 20, 1858—In the afternoon Nephi and his party arrived, having found plenty of water and good land. Geo. Bean's party also arrived.

May 21, 1858—This morning Col. Dame and 12 others started back to Meadow valley by a new route. We went over to the other Camp at the Cave, 25 miles. Preached in the evening. Went into the Cave about a mile, and brought out some specimens of Spar but found no end to the Cave.

Saturday, May 22, 1858—We started early, passed through "package (cave) pass" and nooned at a good spring. I ascended to the top of a high mountain with Nephi and Br. Dame, to see the country south of us. When near the top, the ascent was very dangerous, climbing along a sharp ridge, one side of which was perpendicular for about 1000 feet in depth, and so narrow I could embrace it with my arms. The wind blew in strong gusts almost blowing me off, and down into the gulf below. At such times I had to lay close as I could to the rock, embracing it tightly until the violence of the gale passed by. It was with difficulty I got safe to the top of the mountain which was about 40 feet square, flat as a floor and of solid rock. When on top, I felt well repaid for my toil and danger. A grand view of 150 miles in any direction, of barren plains and desolate mountains. But I could also [no word] the best direction to take to reach Meadow Valley, which seemed about 80 or 90 miles South 10° East.

After dinner we proceeded South, and camped at 10 P.M. without water.

Sunday, May 23, 1858—Started early and found a spring within a mile of Camp, which we named Cricket Spring, and about 5 miles further came to another, which we named Rose Spring. We proceeded until nearly 11 P.M. and camped on the side of the mountain, in a beautiful cove. This I called Cove Spring. Here is plenty of good grass, high up.

[page 166]

MEADOW VALLEY.

May 23, 1858—To day we traveled about 45 miles, through the best of grass, this being on the Rim of the Great Basin.

Monday, May 24, 1858—Arrived at Meadow Valley Springs, 18 miles.

May 25, 1858—To day myself, John Lewis and one other, R. R. Rogers started south to explore down the Meadow Valley creek. We found a beautiful pass, covered with tall grass, with high precipices on each side. About 1500 or 2000 acres of good meadow grass, wire grass, mostly. There were many beautiful flowers, such as I never saw before. The following shows a new plant, the stalks of which are hollow like an onion stalk, hollow, and of the same color:—

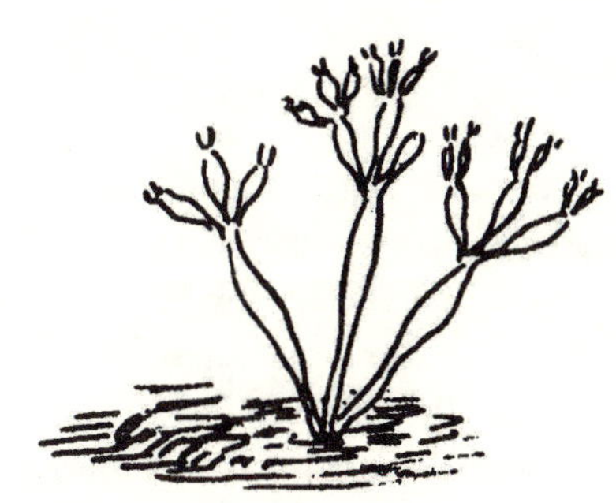

Fig. 3.4—Flower in Meadow Valley.

There is plenty of large cottonwood timber and some Ash growing in the Cañon, and willows a foot in diameter. We traveled 30 miles and camped in an open bottom. We were riding along about 9 P.M. in the dark when we came to some fire burning. We got off our horses, felt around on the ground with our hands, and found corn cobs. Knowing there must be indians around, we silently retreated about a mile, until we came to the open place before mentioned, and lay down one of us watching while the other two slept. I here, as in many other cases, observed the great superiority of a mule over a dog as a watchman at night. A mule will hear noises that a dog will not notice, and by watching the motion of their ears, one can tell just where to look for danger. To night I lay down in the long grass while on guard, and just watched the mules ears. We thought we might perhaps be attacked in the night, but all passed off quietly.

May 26, 1858—Went down the cañon about 5 miles, passing by an indian farm where was wheat knee high and corn just coming up. Found two indians, one of whom came back to Camp with us. I nearly lost my life in trying to climb up the precipitous side of the mountain. I had got ~~within~~ within about ten feet of the top when I came to a shelf a little higher than I could reach, which I could not surmount, although I tried about an hour.

[page 167]

BEGIN TO MAKE A CANAL.

May 1858—I was afraid to try to descend by the way I got up, but was finally compelled to do so, narrowly escaping being dashed to the bottom of the precipice, while my two companions stood watching me below. I had been trying to get where I could see the country round.

We returned to camp, 35 miles, our indian running along by our side as easily and unconcerned as a dog would by a team, and apparently as easy. This trip was 70 miles. I wrote to my family, to Pres^{t} Young and to C. C. ~~Parowan~~ Pendleton

Thursday, May 27, 1858—This morning Ansel Twitchel, G. W. Sirrine, A. Bennett and C. Carter started for Parowan, to carry our mail, two of them to come back immediately, and two to remain for a while longer, to await news from Salt Lake City. In the afternoon Pres^{t} Dame, Nephi, and six others went on a short exploring tour south.[45]

May 28, 1858—Began to make a Chart of our journeys.

May 29, 1858—Continued work on my map. Br. Dame and party returned, having found that Mt. Lookout is west of the mouth of Pinto Creek.

I showed my map to Br. Dame, who was highly pleased with it, which was gratifying to me, as it is my first attempt, and made under great difficulties.

Sunday, May 30, 1858—To day we began work, making a dam, hauling stone, cedars, &c and making a ditch. We made the dam and half a mile of ditch, and got the water running in it. Towards evening we had a good swim in the pond we had made. The water is just warm, wonderfully clear, and strongly mineral.

May 31, 1858—Continued our work on the canal.

June 1, 1858—Began to survey the land into 5-acre lots, and laid off seven of them. Br. Dame was taken sick.

[page 168]

CHARMING A LIZARD.

June 2, 1858—Resurveyed the field, making the lots of 3 acres each. Finished my map.

Thursday, June 3, 1858—To day I began to clear our lot of Sage brush, which grows high as a man's head. The land is quite Sandy. While resting in the shade of a sage brush, I was whistling, and observed a large Black and white lizard about a foot long, that would come out of his hole when I whistled to listen, seemingly pleased. As soon as I stopped he would come out again.

In camp our mess consists of Br. F. T. Whitney, John Osborn and myself, and each mess (of 3 persons) has a Three-acre lot to plant.[46] We have all kinds of seeds. Last night, while on guard, I composed the following:—

45 George W. Sirrine helped settle Mesa, Arizona. Asahel Bennett was a witness to the Mountain Meadows Massacre (Brooks, *Mountain Meadows*, 192). C. Carter could be Charles Carter, who was among the early Beaver settlers.

46 Francis T. Whitney was one of the early iron missionaries and was fifty-two years old (Shirts and Shirts, *Trial Furnace*, 440).

LINES.
THE NIGHT ~~WATCH.~~ GUARD

[*Guard* is written in very shaky handwriting.]

Tis night, My duty is to watch, while others sleep,—
To guard with ~~anxious~~ watchful care their silent slumbers deep;
And while with measured tread I pace my lonely round
With sharpened sense I watch for each unusual sound.

2

Ah What ~~sound~~ is that I hear! ~~ah~~ tis but the tinkling bell
Placed on some Master-mule by which the guard may tell
If all the band is right: for, should some wily foe
With evil thought approach, with cautions step, and slow.

3

The mule, with listening ear, and eyesight sharp and clear
Will quick detect the foe, if any ~~doth~~ should appear,
And then, with snort and bound, unless the guard be nigh,
The band will all stampede, and to the desert fly.

4

But all is quiet now, except the murmuring rill
That gently ripples near; all else is calm and still;
The stars with radiance pure, adorn the cloudless sky
While thoughts, with speed of light, to distant regions fly.

[page 169]

HEAR FROM HOME

June 3, 1858—

5

I think of home and friends—of wives and children dear,
And wish—if it were right—they might be with me here.
That I their voice might hear—their happy ~~voices~~ faces see,
And spend one hour at least, in their ~~blest~~ sweet company

6

I think of Childhoods scenes—of father and of mother
Who trained my youthful steps—of sisters and of brother;
Of friends who've passed the vail—of friends who yet may live;
And wonder if to me a single thought they give.

7

I think of future scenes through which the saints may pass,
And hope that I ~~ever~~ may be still faithful to the last.
That Error's gloomy reign on Earth may quickly cease—
That Truth may spread abroad and righteousness increase.

8

I think of that blest day when Zion shall be free:—
When all of Adam's race shall dwell in harmony.—
But see! the eastern sky begins to glow with light;—
~~Tis twilight~~ The dawn—appears and day, now ends my watch at night.

June 4 & 5, 1858—Worked on the farm.

June 6, 1858—At daylight br Twitchell came from Parowan, bringing me letters from both my wives, one from John Eager and one from Sixtus E. Johnson, who has just returned from a four years mission to the Sandwich Islands. No one can so well appreciate a letter as he who is far from home, and can only hear from there once in a great while.

June 7, 1858—Watered our land to day.

June 8, 1858—Plowed, and sowed ½ acre of wheat

Wednesday, June 9, 1858—To day Pres[t] Dame, Nephi, John Osborn and 9 others went to Parowan, exploring a new route, intending to bring out some cows. I wrote to my wives and to Sixtus. (Also sent my map to Pres[t] B. Young.)

June 10, 1858—Went for Cedar pickets to make a corral.

June 11 & 12, 1858—Plowed and planted corn, &c.

[page 170]

June 9, 1858—

Wrote the following lines:—

POOR UNCLE SAM

1

Oh Poor Uncle Sam has got into a muss
And with a few Mormons has kicked up a fuss,
For when men he sends over Mormons to rule
He cares not if they are all scandals or fools.

2

A governor he's sent us, A. Cumming by name
And he's always a coming—but cannot come in.
Last winter he started in hopes to come here,
But Brigham sent word that he'd better stay there.

3

The feed being poor where his cattle did graze,
A Mormon Steps up and unto him says:—
My dear friend, your cattle will all starve and die,
So I'll just drive 'em over to a valley near by*

4

Some Government wagons, corralled all around
Were found one bright morning all burned to the ground;†
But 'twas accidental ~~of~~ no doubt, for of course
No civilized people would take such a course.

5

This Gov'nor had with him a Colonel so great
Who swore he would conquer our free mountain state;‡
And into these vallies would speedily come,
And hang up that traitor—bold President Young.

6

But—"catch before hanging," is always the rule
And he that neglects it is surely a fool,
And this we have proven our Governor to be
For the Saints will escape and forever be free.

*The Mormons took several thousands of their mules and cattle.

†Supply trains were burnt by Maj. Lot Smith and his men.

‡Col. A. S. Johnson, who joined the rebellion. Killed at Shilo.

[page 171]

June 9, 1858—

7

Poor blind Uncle Sam may send on his troops
To conquer the Mormons—but tis of no use;
For the more we are conquered the faster we grow
And back to Missouri we surely will go.

A few days ago I wrote the following lines, suggested by the thoughts of Home,—earthly, and heavenly:—

THE SANCTUARY.

1

Dear wives, though for a time I'm called to roam
Among these deserts wild, so lone and drear,—
Denied the pleasures of my own dear home
That oft—so oft—my weary heart would cheer,—
Still all is right, and joy doth fill my heart
That I am counted to be worthy, one
Of Zion's pioneers, to take a part
In searching out a place where Saints may come.

2

In days of old, when Superstition reigned
And all in terror lived, in hate and strife.—
When human justice some poor victim claimed
To atone for some foul action with his life,
If to some church or altar he could flee,
Although pursued with unrelenting hate
And "Sanctuary" cry, then he was free,
And this was law in every Christian State.

3

And thus it has been often times with me
Since I my wives and children left behind,
To seek a place where Zion soon may flee
And leave her persecutors far behind

When up some mountain's steep and rugged height
I've toiled, in hope to see some pleasant place.

[page 172]

FINISH PLANTING. DRENCHED IN RAIN BY NIGHT.

June 9, 1858—

And naught beheld, to cheer my weary sight
But deserts, hills and dreary, trackless wastes,

4

Then Thought, with lightening speed doth quickly fly,
And refuge finds in that blest spot called home,
Where love, and peace and joys that never die
And endless years of happiness are known.
Hath Home such joys as these? methinks you say,
Is home so near akin to Paradise?
Yes, home hath joys that never will decay—
~~Love's sanctuary pure; that never dies~~.
A sanctuary pure, where Love ne'er dies.

Sunday, June 13, 1858—Attended meetings to day. J. Ward Christian, who presides in Br. Dame's absence, appointed myself, Lyman Curtis and Jabez Sowland overseers of the ditch.[47]

Tuesday, June 15, 1858—Rained a perfect deluge last night. I, and nearly all the men were sleeping on the ground, and were drenched with the rain. After the rain ceased, the camp was in an uproar with laughter, songs and jokes until morning.

June 16, 1858—Rained to day. Planting nearly finished.

June 17, 1858—Finished planting to day. Rained hard last night. We have wheat, corn, beans, peas, hemp, flax, cotton, melons, squashes, pumpkins, potatoes, and many kinds of small garden seeds nearly all which are up and growing nicely.

Friday, June 18, 1858—To day the herd stampeded, and were not brought back until noon. It was caused by the tormenting of horse flies. I went with James Duke, Isaac Turly[48] and George Bennett up the Cañon for wood. We found some ripe currants, then went up the perpendicular cliffs to the top. This was a very dangerous undertaking, and more than once as I was crawling on hands and knees on a narrow shelf of rock, with the jagged rocks hundreds of feet below me, where the slightest mishap would have sent me to the bottom, my flesh would creep upon my bones, almost. But I nevertheless always liked to be in such places—the more dangerous, and consequently the more exciting—the better. This has always been so with me since I could remember.

[page 173]

HEAR FROM HOME. AM TO STAY HERE ALL SUMMER.

June 18, 1858—When on top we had a grand view of the valley south and the long dry valley north. We felt an indescribable sense of freedom, and all the others wished me to be mouth in prayer, which I did, dedicating the country to the Lord, and consecrated this pass for the defense of the Saints. "Thus far shalt thou come—no farther." I named this Turley's cliff.

Saturday, June 19, 1858—Drew my map on a smaller scale—20 miles to an inch. About noon some indians reported that our express is coming in, at at 2 P.M. Brs. Sirrine and Carter came with considerable news. I recd 2 Deseret News, a letter from home, and

47 Lyman Curtis (1812–98) was a member of the vanguard company pioneers. He came west in 1847, served a mission in southern Utah to the Indians, and was a settler in Salem, Utah (Andrew Jenson, *Latter-day Saint Biographical Encyclopedia: A Compilation of Biographical Sketches of Prominent Men and Women in the Church of Jesus Christ of Latter-day Saints* [Salt Lake City: Andrew Jenson History Company, 1901–1936], 4:689).

48 This is likely Isaac Turley (1837–1908) (note spelling), the son of Theodore Turley (1801–1872), who presided on the ship *North America*, which brought over two hundred Saints from Liverpool to New York in 1840. Isaac was later instrumental in settling the Mexican colonies. Theodore died in Beaver, Utah, while Isaac died in the Mexican colonies (*Theodore Turley: A Journal* [Mesa, AZ: Milton Turley Family, 2006]; Arrington, *Brigham Young*, 80, 88).

also hear that one half of the company is to go home, the rest remain here. I am to remain.

I would like to go and see my family very much, but if I can do more good here than there, I am willing to stay. I am very glad to hear that my family is well, though they are disappointed that I am to stay here all summer. I read Presᵗ Buchanan's Proclamation of pardon to the Mormons—a tissue of lies—on condition of submission, and extermination for the contumacious.[49] I will stand for the truth, God being my helper, come life or death. If I fall—it is as a martyr; if I live, I hope to do good for our cause. This is all I live for—to do good, extend the Cause of righteousness, and so gain an exaltation in the celestial kingdom.

June 21, 1858—Went on a pleasure trip to Cave Spring Camp with James Duke, Silas Harris and James Mowry.[50] The mules had a runaway scrape down hill among the cedars but without doing any damage.

June 22, 1858—Went exploring Southward on foot a few miles, and Saw in the distance South, on a high mountain a fine grove of pine timber about 5 miles from Cave Springs. Good grass for stock all around. Went about 10 miles

[page 174]

ARRIVED AT HOME! PARTY.

June 23, 1858—Came home. Tried to get a shot at a wild cat.

June 25, 1858—Grubbed more land. To day J. N. Smith, M. Ensign and some others came from Parowan. Br. Dame sent for me to come home on a visit.[51] The Company brought 9 cows. The half of the company who are to stay, are to keep up the station, hunt for places to cache grain, explore, &c. Got a new shirt, a pair of old shoes, and letter from my wives.

June 26, 1858—Spent the time pleasantly with our friends. James McNight, an old fellow printer in Milwaukee, was here[52]

June 27, 1858—Started home, arriving there on the afternoon of the 30th

June 30, 1858—When about ¾ of a mile from home, we met my wives walking out that way.

No words can tell the joy I felt on meeting them again. We walked together home to Parowan, which to me seems the most beautiful place I ever saw, with its beautiful shade trees, neat picket fences and gardens.

Truly God has blessed me on this mission. My health has not been so good for many years, in fact, I am as rugged and rough as a bear. My hair long and Shaggy, and bleached to a sort of tow color by the sun, my face brown, almost, as an indian, and my clothes none of the cleanest.

In the evening there was a party, at which I enjoyed myself very much.

I found many faces unknown to me in Parowan—Saints who have emigrated south in the "Move." A family named Phister is living in the back part of my house. The Church machine shops are here in full operation, also a pail factory nearly ready for operation

Friday, July 2, 1858—Br. Dame and Nephi returned from S. L. City with word that the U. S. Army marched through that city on Sat. June 26. Bought a dragoon revolver price $36.⁰⁰ [$752] made at the Public Works by John Ash.[53]

[page 175]

NEARLY A MURDER BY INDIANS.

July 8, 1858—Traded my revolver with John L. Smith for an Adams (English) revolver.[54]

49 In trying to settle the Utah War, President James Buchanan sent Ben McCllullock and Issac Power to Utah with a pardon for the Latter-day Saints "if they would affirm their loyalty to the federal government." The Saints were not pleased at the accusation, claiming they had never been disloyal. Martineau's reaction is representative of this sentiment. *Contumacious* means stubbornly perverse or rebellious; willfully and obstinately disobedient; insubordinate.

50 Silas Harris was a private in the Mormon Battalion, Company B (Ricketts, *Arizona's Honeymoon Trail*, 23, 189). James Mowrey (note spelling) was a volunteer with the Mormon Battalion (Ricketts, *Arizona's Honeymoon Trail*, 266).

51 This is likely Jesse N. Smith and Marius Ensign.

52 James McKnight was listed as an assistant to President Brigham Young during the Mountain Meadows investigation (Brooks, *Mountain Meadows*, 165).

53 A dragoon is an armed soldier capable of fighting from horseback. He is armed with a short musket called a dragon.

54 An Adams revolver was considered a fine handgun designed by John Adams, a British designer and manufacturer. It was a double-action revolver.

July 10, 1858—General muster to day, which I took charge of.

July 19, 1858—Monday. Commenced haying

July 22, 1858—Heard G. A. Smith and S. Lyman preach to night they having just come from the north.[55] John Osborn was sent to Meadow Valley to bring in the Company.[56] Word has come that the crops at Meadow Valley are all killed by the black alkali.[57]

July 23, 1858—This morning Prest Dame gave me an honorable discharge from the Desert Mission, saying he was fully satisfied with my conduct and services on the mission. He also said Prest Young was much pleased with my map, it being the only intelligible one he had seen from there.

July 31, 1858—Three little boys today told the Pah-Eed chief that two of their squaws lay dead on the adobie yard. He got mad instantly, and wanted to kill some one to pay for it, without even trying to find out the truth of the report. Prest Dame had a hard time to keep him cool till the matter could be investigated. On sending to the adobie yard two squaws were found lying there—asleep!

[The following dates, Aug. 2, 5, 7 & 8, were not in the margin, as Martineau usually did, but within the paragraph margin with the text.]

Monday, August 2, 1858—Was elected County Surveyor.

August 5, 1858—Susan J. is quite unwell for a few days.

August 7, 1858—Susan J. still quite low. Got the Elders, who administered, and she immediately got better. She had a kind of bloody flux. Myself and Susan E. were also sick with the same disease at the same time.[58]

August 8, 1858—Susan J. improving Susan E. and myself no better.

Elders G. A. Smith and A. Lyman preached in the evening.

55 This is likely Amasa Lyman.

56 This is likely John W. Osborn (1833–95) of Beaver, Utah.

57 Black alkali is a deposit of sodium carbonate formed on the surface of the ground in semiarid climates.

58 Bloody flux is defined as an inflammation of the intestine. The symptoms are that the individual's excrement is mixed with blood.

[page 176]

TRIAL OF PRESt DAME WE GO TO BEAVER.

August 10, 11 & 12, 1858—For three days Elders G. A. Smith and A. Lyman have been examining and trying the case of Prest Dame who has been charged with a long list of misdemeanors, some charges running back for a time of five years. The list of Charges was signed by all the officers of this branch except C. C. Pendleton and myself. Br. Dame was much cast down when he showed me the charges against him, saying that although he was innocent, no one would believe it with so many names against him, there being one of his own counsellors, the Bishop and Council and all the High Council but myself. I told him I knew he was innocent, and would stick to him to the last—if he fell I would go with him. After a most searching investigation, Br. Dame came out unscathed, Br. G. A. Smith saying Br. Dame had not made half as many mistakes in the last five years as he himself had. And Br. Amasa Lyman said he had always thought well of Br. Dame but this had raised him 100 per cent in his estimation. A paper was drawn up certifying that the charges had no foundation in truth, and all were required to sign it, which they did, finally.

I was clerk at this trial taking down every man's testimony in full. I defended Br. Dame warmly during the whole trial; Br. Pendleton said but little as no one could tell how the decision would be pronounced. I hate a half-hearted policy—let a man be something or nothing.

Sunday, August ~~25~~ 15, 1858—Prest Smith preached. He also appointed Br J. N. Smith to go to the head waters of the Rio Virgin to start a new settlement for cotton growing.

August 18, 1858—Went to Beaver with the Brass Band. G. A. Smith, S. Lyman, E. Snow and C. C. Rich were present. E. Snow preached. After that a concert, lasting till about 4 A.M. I enjoyed myself much. Slept at the house of Wm. Willis.[59]

59 William W. Willis was a third lieutenant in the Mormon Battalion, Company A (Ricketts, *Arizona's Honeymoon Trail*, 21).

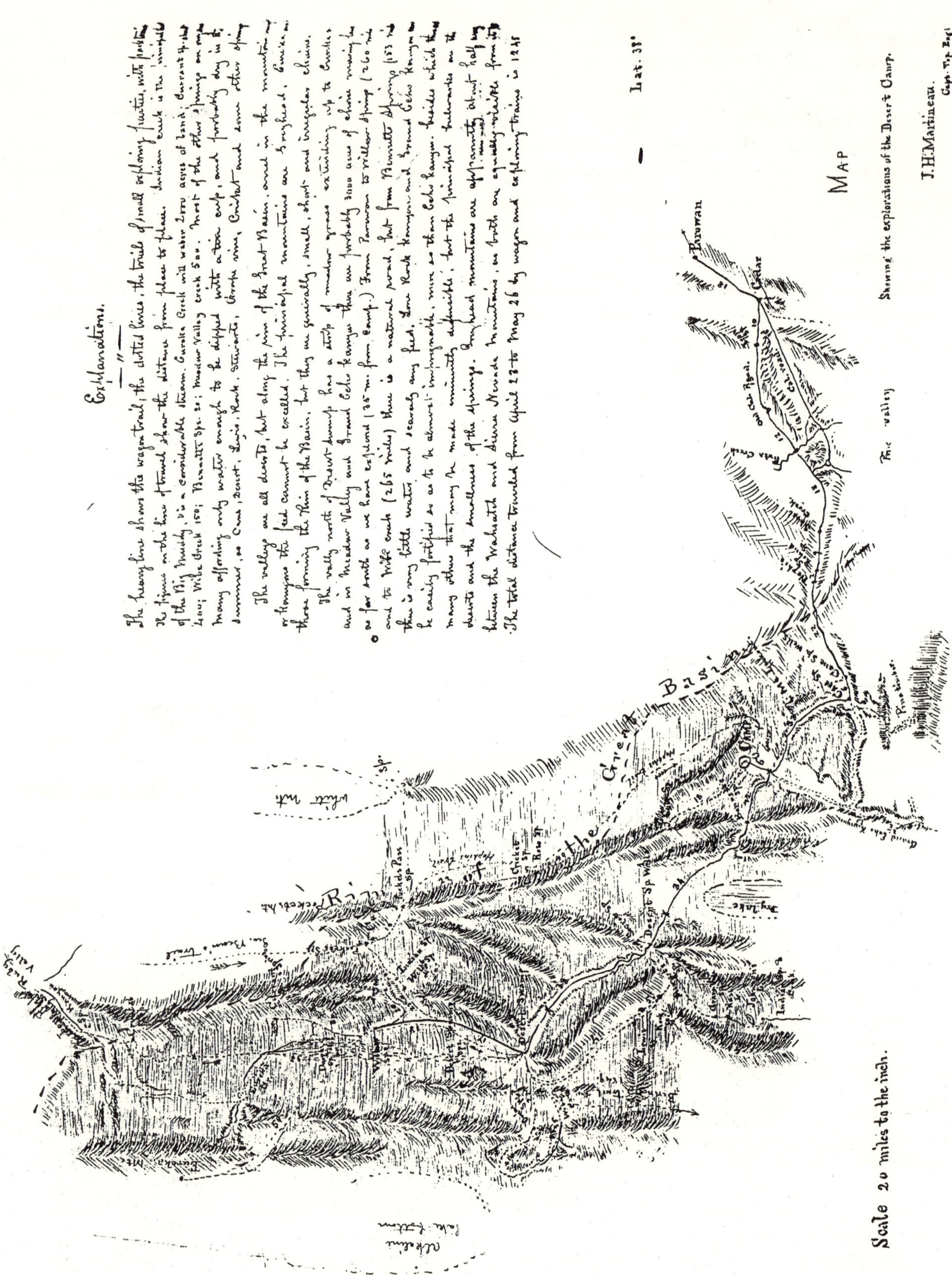

Fig. 3.5—Between sheets 176 and 177 is an exquisite map of the area west and north of Cedar City. With the map is an explanation. This is probably the map he gave to Brigham Young, who commented it was the most intelligible map he had ever seen.

[page 177]

MY FIRST SURVEYING AS COUNTY SURVEYOR.

August 19, 1858—Bought some works on Surveying, of Fred T. Perris, $7.50. [$157] to be paid for by a pig $4.00 [$84] two hens .50 [$10] and 3.00 [$63] on Br Thompson.[60] Got home at 9 P.M.

August 21, 1858—Went with my family up the Cañon and got some Choke Cherries.[61] Susan J. fell on the wagon and broke her croupper bone.[62]

August 24, 1858—To day I traded my oxen ($125.) [$2,611] Cow (40.$) [$835] two yearlings ($35.) [$731] (total $200.–) [$4,177] for a span of horses, the first horse team I ever had, of J. H. Rollins.

In the afternoon went to Summit Creek and laid out 8 5-acre lots for the brethren, using a chain, 3 fence poles. (and no Compass) This is my first surveying as County Surveyor.

August 27, 1858—I finished plastering my back rooms to day. Bought two cows of Paul Smith[63] for $35. [$731] and $45.00 [$940] and two calves ~~giving~~. I gave my back city lot for the calves; and gave a wagon box and rack and five acres of land for the Cows. I am to have the use of the wagon till the 1st of next April and 5 loads of wood besides. Truly the Lord has blessed me.

August 28, 1858—Went to Johnson Springs and surveyed 160 acres of grass land for Sixtus and the other boys. To day drove my horses for the first time, and Br. Dame's Carriage. Took my wives along.

August 30, 1858–Six wagon loads of Soldiers from Fort Crittenden went south to day. Think perhaps they are deserters.

August 31 & September 1, 1858—Worked at the pail factory, and engaged as a regular hand.

Sunday 5, 1858—At meeting to day to accept or reject Prest G. A. Smith's counsel lately given us to enclose a new field. Jas Lewis took up most of the time, going dead against Br. G. A. Smiths counsel. He questioned the propriety of obeying counsel, unless he could see why it was given. On vote being called, most of those present voted against Geo. A.'s Counsel, saying the frost would continue six (!) months longer in the new place as contemplated, than in the old field.

[page 178]

NEW FIELD REJECTED. FROST KILLS EVERYTHING.

September 5, 1858—On the opposite vote being called, the following persons voted to sustain Br. G. A. Smith's Counsel:—C. C. Pendleton, J. N. Smith, myself W. Talbot, Z B Decker, J. H. Henderson, W. Carter and Wm Adams.[64]

September 6, 1858—Frost to night killed almost everything, corn, wheat and other grain. So it seems after all the Lord can send frost into our old field if He wishes, even in the midst of summer!

September 18, 1858—Surveyed a small fort, 105 ft square, at Summit. Snowed to day.

September 14, 1858—Susan J. weaned Dellie to day, who has been quite sick for some time. She ought to have done so sooner.

September 21, 1858—Susan J.s sore eyes nearly well:—the baby's quite so, but she is still sick, with puking and purging. My eyes are also sore.

60 Frederick Thomas Perris (1837–1916) had a mixed history among the Saints. He was a professional engineer known for his work on the railroads of California. Born in England, he was naturalized as a U.S. citizen in Salt Lake City, in 1858. He was influential in laying out the plats for the Mormon settlement of Paris, Idaho. He laid out the city of San Bernardino while he was working for the California Southern Railway Company. He was also mentioned as an editor of the *Salt Lake Tribune* (Philip C. Serpico, *Santa Fe Route to the Pacific* [Santa Fe: Omni Publications, 1988]). Brother Thompson mentioned here is likely Edward Thompson, among the early Parowan settlers.

61 Chokecherries grow wild in the western states. They are a small dark red berry, about the size of a currant. They grow on shrubs four to five feet tall. The fruit can be dried or used for syrup and jelly.

62 Crupper usually refers to the rear of a horse. She may have broken her tailbone.

63 There are several Paul Smiths in familysearch.org, but none fit this time and reference.

64 There were numerous Talbots, but none matched this time frame. Zachariah B. Decker was among the first in the Iron Mission. At this writing he was forty-one years old and a Parowan farmer (Shirts and Shirts, *Trial Furnace*, 419). William Carter later lived in St. George and was part of the United Order in the settlement (Leonard J. Arrington, Feramorz Y. Fox, and Dean L. May, *Building the City of God: Community & Cooperation Among the Mormons* [Urbana: Univ. of Illinois Press, 1976], 164).

September 23, 1858—My eyes are very sore. I cannot work any more until they get better.

September 24, 1858—Sariah Eager went home to day, with Sixtus.

October 1, 1858—My eyes are about well. Was blind for some time, but after trying many remedies, cured them by raw onions, which wept all the inflammation out.

October 5, 1858—Made a map of the Rio Virgin Country for J N Smith for Prest Young.

October 23, 1858—Started for Salt Lake city with ~~Susan Julia~~ Samuel Gould, on horseback intending to go to Camp Floyd to trade my horse for some Government oxen and a wagon. There has been considerable rain and snow during this month.[65]

October 24, 1858—Leaving Paragoonah, this morning, we were joined by M. Ensign, who intends trying to sell his span of horses and wagon at Camp Floyd.

October 25, 1858—Left Beaver this morning in a severe snow storm, which beat in our faces all day. Camped at Pine Creek, in snow.

[page 179—see Appendix 3 for handwritten notes on genealogy and travels inserted here.]

START TO CAMP FLOYD.
MY FORTUNE TOLD.

October 26, 1858—Stopped this evening with Peter Boyce, at the Indian Farm at Corn Creek.

Thursday, October 28, 1858—Drove to Fillmore. I here went to see Mrs. Janvrin Dame a seeress, who derived her gift from an ordination by her father.[66]

She said Prosperity awaits you on this journey. You will have wealth in great abundance, and many wives and children Before long you will have two wives—as noble women as ever walked. One will be rather light favored; the other darker. Before long a dark favored girl will almost ask you to have her. You will hear of a murder soon. A heavy burden will soon be placed upon you before long, which will almost make you hang your head, but you will soon cheer up, and it will soon grow lighter. I do not think you will go on a mission, soon. You will have a chance to choose either a natural or a martyr's death. I think you will choose the latter, and be shot in the center of your breast, and will die quickly and easily. You will go into the midst of millions of beautiful women, and have your choice of them, as many as you wish. You are on a broad foundation and will never desert this Cause. You will always stand at the head of your family, though some of your wives will try to get ahead of you, but will not succeed, and will be sorry they had tried. You will get your wish (to do good) and will attain to honor by not pushing ahead.—you will be lucky in the long run.

She also told me many things I do not remember, I only insert the above out of curiosity, to see if it will be fulfilled. Some things she told me of the past were very true, which makes me think some of the future may be. She is thought to be almost infallible by the people of Fillmore.

November 2, 1858—Arrived at Santaquin. Heard of a murder a few days since at dry creek.

November 3, 1858—Camped within 8 miles of Camp Floyd.[67]

November 4, 1858—Went to Camp, but did not sell my horse. At night we went out into the prairie about 4 miles

[page 180—see Appendix 3 for Confederate money.]

CLOTHING GIVEN ME.
GO TO SALT LAKE CITY.

November 5, 1858—Sold my horse, saddle and bridle for $100 [$2,089].

November 6, 1858—Bought a yoke of oxen for $52.50 [$1,096]; also for $40.00 [$835] a large wagon, with a load of ox yokes, chains, &c and bows and a good cover.

Got acquainted with a Dragoon named Wilson Jones, who gave me a good blanket, blouse, new

65 J. H. M. "Iron County," *Deseret News*, October 23, 1858; Journal History.

66 The family lived in Nauvoo, Winter Quarters, and crossed the plains in 1848, settling in Fillmore. A seeress is a woman with the power to prophesy future events.

67 Camp Floyd was named after secretary of war John G. Floyd. It housed the U.S. troops moving into Utah (Thomas G. Alexander and Leonard J. Arrington, "Camp in the Sagebrush: Camp Floyd, Utah, 1858–61," *Utah Historical Quarterly* 34 [1966]: 3–21).

flannel shirt and a good overcoat, for which I pray our Father to bless him. I laid my hands upon his head and blessed him. I walked with him on his watch about two hours, and preached Mormonism to him, overcoming his many objections and prejudices, until finally he said when his time of service was out, he would be a Mormon and marry two wives! We would give me the clothing, though I refused for a time to take it, having nothing to pay for it.

This clothing soon afterwards saved my life, when going home, as will be seen further on.

November 8, 1858—Got to Santaquin.

November 9, 1858—Borrowed $65.—[$1,566] of Uncle Benjamin, and bought another yoke of oxen, intending to repay it in work. Found Sixtus, Editha and Jennette on their way home.

November 10, 1858—Sold wagon cover to Sixtus for $7.[00] [$146] and started to S. L. City with Uncle Benjamin.

November 12, 1858—Arrived in S. L. City. Bening [being] sent for to the Church Historian's office. I found Br. Geo. A. Smith had began a letter to me, which is herein inserted. I felt that to carry out this idea was quite a burden for one so inexperienced as myself. I will do the best I can, however. Rec[d] my commission as Captain of the Topographical Engineer Corps, and conversed with Pres[t] Young and D H Wells[68]

November 13 & 14, 1858—Attended Special Conference.[69]

November 15, 1858—Had a good long military conversation with Gen[l] Wells. Explaining to him my feelings about writing as requested by Br. G. A. Smith, he said he would bless me We accordingly went to the office, and he and Br. Wilford Woodruff laid hands on my head, and gave me a good blessing.

[page 181]

MY BLESSING AS A WRITER BY PRES[T] D. H. WELLS.

November 15, 1858—They said I should be greatly bless[d] in writing for the Church. My mind should be expanded and enlightened,—should be true to the faith—should be a ready writer, with wisdom and power to do good. I should have wisdom and power to elude my enemies when they should seek my life. And many other good things were promised me.

Sold my saddle and bridle to Uncle Benjamin for $20.—[$418] Wrote an article for the Desert News.[70]

November 16, 1858—Started home. Arrived at Santaquin on the 17th

November 17, 1858—And waited for Company home. Sent a copy of "Truth" to the Deseret News, and wrote the following lines for the Comfort of Mrs. Sarah Melissa Johnson:—[71]

LINES

Though life be filled with toils and cares—
Our pathway set with gins and snares,
And pitfalls deep:—
Though friends may fail in time of need
To lies and slander giving heed
And evil seek—
Yet what of that? Truth will prevail
And silence every evil tale,
And put to flight
The clouds of darkness ~~overhead~~ round us spread
That we may ~~droop~~ raise our drooping head
And dwell in light.

2

True friendship by the Truth will stand
And though opposed on every hand
Will still be true;
But friendship false, where storms shall rise
And darkness spreads along ~~the~~ our skies

68 This was likely Daniel Hammer Wells, second counselor to Brigham Young and a general in the Nauvoo Legion (Arrington, *Brigham Young*, 214).

69 For a conference report, see "Sunday," *Deseret News*, November 14, 1858; Journal History.

70 J. H. Martineau, "Truth," *Deseret News*, December 8, 1858; Utah Digital Newspapers. This is a poem Martineau authored.

71 Sarah Melissa Johnson was the daughter of Benjamin F. Johnson and Sarah Melissa Holman Johnson.

Will prove untrue.
If we for good have always sought
Nor cherished evil—e'en in thought
Then all is right;
For good will bring its own reward:—
Our ~~minds~~ souls with truth will be well stored—
And truth is light.

[page 182]

COLD WEATHER.

November 19, 1858—Started home, and drove to Nephi.

November 20, 1858—Started at midnight. Snowed all day. Camped at Chicken creek, and were overtaken by Sam[l] Gould and a deserter.

November 21, 1858—Crossing the Sevier Bridge, where there are two companies of Dragoons Camped to intercept deserters, our wagons were searched, but our deserter crossed over before us, walking so much unlike a soldier that they did not suspect him.

November 23, 1858—Still snowing. Traveling bad.

November 26, 1858—Snowed all day and night.

November 27, 1858—ditto

November 28, 1858—Traded my rifle for a pony. Started from Boyce's again.

December 1, 1858—Snowing hard

December 2, 1858—Left Beaver this morning. Snow deep, weather very cold. Wind blowed all day, drifting the snow in clouds. Camped at the entrance of Parowan valley. The night was intensely cold.

December 3, 1858—Rose early, being nearly frozen. Made a big fire, of cedar round which the cattle closed to warm themselves, so that they were singed by the flames sometime. My pony made himself room by the fire, by biting the oxen. Have about 20 miles to travel to day, with a heavy wagon and a poor team. The road is filled entirely full, with drifted snow, packed hard, no track broken, making it very hard to progress at all. Frost flew in the air all day, although the sun shone brightly all day—the cattle were white with frost all day. Towards night, I had had hard [. . .] work to keep warm by jumping about and thrashing myself, but as soon as the sun went down the cold became so intense I could scarcely keep from freezing, with all my clothing on and also all that the soldier had given me.

[page 183]

ALMOST FREEZE TO DEATH. HOME AGAIN.

December 3, 1858—For some time the cattle had been nearly given out, and about dusk they failed entirely. I unhitched them so they could take care of themselves, then got into the wagon, wrapped up in all my bedding, to wait for morning. While thus waiting two teams for California Came along, with 28 discharged teamsters of the U. S. Army. I saw that some of them were in danger of freezing, and told them to hurry up or they would freeze. One of them said he didn't care a damn—he was almost froze—and might as well freeze now as any time. After waiting awhile, I found myself freezing, so I left the wagon and things, mounted my pony, and started on the run to Paragoonah, distant two or three miles, arriving there in a few minutes so nearly frozen as to be unable to speak or stand, except with much difficulty. Silas S. Smith's wives soon brought me all right again with warm drinks. I told the Bishop of the men I had passed, freezing, and he sent out two wagons to help them in. They found five men lying in the snow, almost lifeless, besides many others badly frozen. Of the 28 men, 14 were frozen more or less,—some very badly.[72]

I should have frozen had it not been for the clothing given me by the soldier, and even then, but for my pony. I knew I was near death, and yet was in sight of the smoke curling from my own chimney at home.

December 4, 1858—Arrived at home, thankful for my safe arrival.

December 7, 1858—Traded my heifer for a stove—my first one. It is a half worn out one, but a blessing to us.

December 13, 1858—Sold my oxen to D. Ward for a heifer and 27½ bu wht.[73]

72 See "From Southern Utah," *Deseret News*, December 9, 1858; Journal History.

73 Daniel Ward was a member of the Utah Territorial Militia, Company C, Parowan. He was a Parowan sheepman (Shirts and Shirts, *Trial Furnace*, 494).

December 20, 1858—Recommenced work in the pail factory.

December 29, 1858—Quit work in the pail factory, having earned $49.50 [$1,034]

[page 184]

MY SON JOHN WILLIAM BORN

Saturday, January 1, 1859—At a party to day. A. Lyman preached two hours.

January 7, 1859—This morning, at 8 o'clock A.M. my wife Susan E. presented me with a fine boy weighing 9½ lbs. We blessed and named him John William, after my father John Martineau.[74]

January 11, 1859—Busy all day helping Elder A. Lyman to plan a house he proposes to build here, 91½' long, 31⅓' wide and one and a half stories high.

To day I was appointed Clerk of the County and Probate Courts; also am appointed Notary Public on the 13th of Dec. last by the Legislature.[75]

Saturday, February 12, 1859—Filed bonds as Notary Public before Judge James Lewis.

February 14, 1859—To day was elected Alderman for Parowan.[76]

February 20, 1859—This day all the Prayer circles were broken up, on account of there being so much disunion.

March 7, 1859—Attended County Court as clerk

March 14, 1859—Attended Probate Court as clerk

March 10, 1859—Surveyed Little Creek for Chas Hall, J. P. Hall and John Steele.

Saturday, March 6, 1859—Surveyed 20 acres of land for myself and E. Dolten.

March 30, 1859—Bought a saddle of Sixtus for $30.00 [$674]

April 1, 1859—Our Lamb "Nelly" died to day. She ate too much chopped grain. She was a great pet with us. Traded for a mare of William Hyde.[77]

April 4, 1859—Branded my mare with my brand

Fig. 3.6—James Henry Martineau brand.

April 5, 1859—This morning my mare had a fine colt

April 9, 1859—Went to Fort Johnson, and got my yoke of Steer two saddles, and some apple trees. Came home next day.

April 11, 1859—Began Surveying the new addition to our field Surveyed 480 acres into five acre lots, which at $1.~ [$22] pr lot amounts to $96.00 [$2,158]

April 16, 1859—We cast lots for the various new lots.

April 20, 1859—Traded cattle with Job P. Hall, giving him $45. [$1,012] boot.

[page 185]

THE AUTHORITIES HIDE UP IN THE MOUNTAINS. KEY.

April 21, 1859—To day Susan Julia was confined, having a fine fat boy, weighing 8¾ lbs. She suffered much for three days previously, but her delivery was safe and speedy.

April 22, 1859—To day we named our boy Lyman Royal, after his grand-father Lyman Royal Sherman. I also blessed him Received a letter from Prest G. A. Smith.

April 29, 1859—News came of the approach of ~~two~~ one compani~~es~~y of U. S. dragoons and one of Infantry, coming down here to make arrests of the authorities.

Monday, May 2, 1859—At noon about 75 Dragoons and 100 Infantry, with 47 baggage wagons, drawn by Six mules each, and a portable forge, passed through Parowan, accompanied by Judge Cradlebaugh.[78] They encamped ¾ of a mile from

74 See familysearch.org under "John William Martineau."

75 "Elections by Legislative Assembly," *Deseret News*, January 26, 1859; Journal History.

76 An alderman is a member of the local governing council.

77 William Hyde was a second sergeant in the Mormon Battalion, Company C (Ricketts, *Arizona's Honeymoon Trail*, 22).

78 John Cradlebaugh was a federal judge appointed by President Buchanan. The Saints were afraid the judge would gather the Church leaders and prosecute them without due process (Shirts and Shirts, *Trial Furnace*, 383; Arrington, *Brigham Young*, 276–280).

Fig. 3.7—Lyman Royal Martineau, son of James Henry and Susan Julia. Courtesy of James Henry Martineau Family Organization.

town, and many of them kept up a drunken row nearly all night, to the alarm of the citizens who are not used to such things. We kept up a strong guard all night.

On the approach of the troops the authorities of the place went into the mountains, to avoid being taken by them. Br. Dame thought some one had better go back into town, to watch for news, and try to find out the real object of their coming. We had been privately notified before, that they were coming to arrest leading Saints, but they gave out that they were merely coming to meet the Army paymaster, who was coming from California.

The night previous I dreamed I had found a Silver Key. So when Br. Dame wished some on[e] to go to pump and watch them, I volunteered, hoping I should be able to get the key to their movements. Br. Dame charged me to be careful of myself. So I spent the evening among them, and wormed from a Sergeant Healy the true object of their coming, which was not only to meet the paymaster, but to make the arrest of such leading mormons as they could, especially any concerned in the Mountain Meadow affair

[page 186]

I DISCOVER THE OBJECT OF CRADLEBAUGH'S EXPEDITION SOUTH.

May 2, 1859—Healy told me all their plans. After arresting the authorities, they will proceed to try them, having not only a Judge, but a Jury also, composed of Camp followers, teamsters &c Trial before such a tribunal, means condemnation, and I for one will not appear before any such a court, if I can help it. To night a soldier stole my dog.

May 3, 1859—The troops marched to Cedar City.

May 6, 1859—To day Prest Dame told me to send to the mountains: that it is the intention of the troops to take every man that is or has been in authority, and I, having been one of the presidency here, must flee or be in danger of my life.

I have broken no U. S. Laws, but must be hunted like a felon by U. S. Soldiers, apostates and indians. But after all, I am not the first one so treated, and will not, probably, be the last. I prepared for hiding up. I sealed up the public records and papers in a large stone Churn I have, and buried it in my garden.[79] At night I went out on the prairie, lay down by a sage bush in my blanket and slept till morning.

May 7, 1859—In the afternoon I went to the hidden camp, but after remaining awhile, it was thought best for me to remain in town, and help keep things right, and watch the Course of events.

We constantly hear of the threats the troops are making, south, They say they will hang all the principal men here, and confiscate their property. They say, "you have sown, but shall not reap your harvests."

They tried to arrest sundry persons south of here but could not catch them.

In the afternoon two men, sent by ~~Cradlebaugh~~ Genl. Johnson to ~~Genl Johnson~~ Cradlebaugh, at ~~Camp Floyd~~ as an express, passed through Parowan.

79 This was a container used to make butter from cream.

[page 187]

GO TO WASHINGTON TO SPEND THE 24TH

May 8, 1859—Traded my steers for a mare and harness. In the evening I rode over to Johnson Springs to learn the news from the Army.

Monday, May 9, 1859—Surveyed 17 City lots at Paragoonah outside the fort.

May 14, 1859—To day ~~Cradlebaugh's~~ Johnson's messengers returned to Camp Floyd

June 1, 1859—Finished sowing my crop today.

June 24, 1859—Surveyed the hay land into 105 lots, of half an acre each. Each head of family has one lot. My fees for Surveying them was $1.00 [$22] Each.

July 2, 1859—Surveyed 60 acres of Meadow below Parowan, on [Ceter] Creek bottoms

July 7, 1859—Traded my wild mare and colt for Henry Lunts Sheep (9 head) and 4 bu. Wheat.

All my children except Moroni have been very sick, one after the other, commencing with Lyman R, the youngest. The disease seemed to be inflammation of the bowels and lungs.

Saturday, July 16, 1859—S. Elvira still continues peevish, but the rest of the Children are well. Delcena now begins to say almost everything; John William can sit alone, and rise to his feet by a chair. My wives finished weaving their linsey to-day—16½ yds of good cloth.[80] I have been haying some. To day I surveyed 19 hay lots at Paragoonah, of 2½ acres each, and also bought a load of hay. Watered my wheat and oats. Felt quite unwell, with piles, headache, &c

Friday, July ~~24~~ 22, 1859—To day I started on a trip to Washington[81] to spend the 24th July. J. N. Smith & wife, myself and Susan J. and her two children accompanied Elders G. A. Smith and wife and A. Lyman and wife and others. We started from home at 2 P. M., took tea at sunset at Hamilton's and went on to Harmony, arriving there at 10.30 P. M. and stopped at the house of John D. Lee. Distance 36 miles.

July 23, 1859—Started at 9 A. M. and arrived at Washington[82] at 11 P. M. very much fatigued, wet with rain, and the wagon almost in pieces, owing to the rough and rocky road and our bad team of horses.

[page 188]

AT WASHINGTON.

July 23, 1859—Jesse's horse was balky, so we changed him at Cedar for another,—an unbroken on [one], who tried to run away several times over a very dangerous road—the black ridge. We had to lock the hind wheels and let him run, and the dragging of the wheels over the rocks shook out spokes and fellors.[83] We had to watch carefully along the road, and pick up every little stick to fix the wheels, wedge the tires &c For several hours before we got to Washington, it was so dark we could not follow the road, so I walked on ahead of our train to pilot it on, guiding the drivers by my voice. Sometimes I had to feel with my hand on the ground for the track. Never was a light much more welcome to us than the first we saw in Washington.

We put up at the house of Bishop Robt Covington[84]

Sunday, July 24, 1859—Breakfasted with Harrison Pearce.[85] Attended Meetings. Preaching by G. A. Smith and A. Lyman. In the evening I witnessed the death of a fine child of Wm Duggins, which choked to death on some grass. Took dinner with John D. Lee, who has a good house here, built of an extra quality of rock, which is abundant near by.

July 25, 1859—To day we celebrated the 24th In the evening there was a dance in John D. Lee's house. We took a look at the crops. Saw corn 12 or 15 feet high, and other vegetation in proportion. The weather intensely hot. Taken quite sick in the afternoon, but was better at night. We went to the river (Rio Virgin) and had a swim. We could not walk in the sand barefoot, without having a bush or something to stand

80 Linsey is a coarse fabric woven from linen or sometimes cotton warp and a coarse wool filling.

81 Washington, Utah, is located just northeast of St. George.

82 See "Saturday," *Deseret News,* July 23, 1859; Journal History.

83 Felloes are the rims or a section of the rim of a wheel supported by spokes.

84 Robert Covington was bishop of the Washington Ward from 1857 to 1869.

85 Harrison Pearce (1818–89) was the son of James Perry Pearce and Elizabeth Humphries Pearce. He was a resident of the Washington–St. George area.

on, every few moments. We feasted on melons, which grow extremely rich flavored and large.

[page 189]

TOQURVILLE.

July 26, 1859—Officiated as clerk at the marriage of Phebe Dart and And. S. Gibbons.[86]

July 27, 1859—Started home by way of Tokerville, where we arrived at 6 P. M. and were kindly received at the house of Willis Young.[87] At dusk F. D. Richards and J. A. Young arrived here from S. L. City.[88] Preaching in the city. Cotton grows well here, but corn is not so tall as at Washington. All this country is a vast bed of loose sand, filled with huge boulders, and carries a growth of many varieties of Cacti, prickely shrubs and in places stunted cedars. Lyman's eyes begin to be sore. Flies are terribly annoying.

July 28, 1859—Arrived at Harmony at 2 P. M. Our horses ran away twice. Dined with Br. Tinney. Continued on, and got to Hamilton's at 9 P. M. cold, wet, and our horses given out.

July 29, 1859—Went to Cedar. Dined with Henry Lunt. Attended preaching. In the afternoon there was a heavy storm and a furious flood in Coal Creek, which hindered us from crossing, until near sun set when we set out for Fort Johnson, but after going a half mile Jesse's horse again balked, and we had to stop all night with Elias Morris, near by.

Saturday, July 30, 1859—Started early, but my mare gave out, and Jesse N. Walked in from Summit to Parowan, 7 miles, and sent out a horse to meet us. We got home at noon, right glad to be there. Next time I travel I hope it will be with a better team and wagon.

Found all well, and a dance going on, in which we took part.[89]

August 1, 1859—Was clerk of election today.

August 4, 1859—With Pres^{s} Smith and Dame went and located some new city lots.

August 5, 1859—Wrote to Pres^{t} Young in the new Deseret Alphabet. Also sent returns of election to Sec. Hartnett, and sent money (\$1.$^{\underline{00}}$) [\$22] for my commission.

Pres^{t} Smith started home to day.

[page 190]

I BUY CORA, AN INDIAN GIRL.

Thursday, August 11, 1859—Began Surveying more city lots at Parowan. Plat B. These lots are on the north of the old plot, mostly.

August 13, 1859—Went to Paragoonah and surveyed some city lots 12 rods square. Finished on the 25 having laid out 28 lots.

August 27, 1859—Earthquake at 4 P. M.[90]

August 28, 1859—New field talked of. I am one of a committee appointed to locate it.

September 3, 1859—Started with Richd Benson for Tokerville with a load of starts for Job P. Hall. Drove to Harmony.

September 4, 1859—Arrived at Tokerville, which contains about fifteen families. Feasted on Melons.

September 5, 1859—Went 8 miles to Virgin City, a small place on the Rio Virgin river, where Nephi now lives. The road winds among rocks, so crooked, that sometimes we could not see our lead team.

September 6, 1859—Returned to Tokerville.

September 7, 1859—Started for home with a load of melons.

September 8, 1859—Got home and found John W. quite sick.

---

86 Martineau is preparing the paperwork in his official calling as clerk. The marriages of Andrew Smith Gibbons and Phebe Maria Dart would take place October 22, 1859, in Salt Lake City.

87 Toquerville, Utah, is northeast of St. George, between St. George and Cedar City. Located on Ash Creek, it was named after the Paiute Chief Toquer, whose village was on the creek. It was first settled in 1854 by the Southern Indian Mission group led by Rufus C. Allen, who was to learn the language and teach the natives. There was a Willis Smith Young (1829–1910) in Utah around this time.

88 J. A. Young could be Brigham Young's son, Joseph Angell Young (1834–75).

89 On July 30, 1859, Martineau reports a slight earthquake at Virgin City ("Saturday," *Deseret News*, July 30, 1859; Journal History).

90 J. H. Martineau, "From Southern Utah," *Deseret News*, 9:232, August 10, 1859; Journal History. Utah Digital Newspapers has the date of publication as September 21, 1859.

September 9, 1859—Cut up my corn, which is killed by the frost of last night. Had a letter from Bp. Hunter.

Saturday, September 10, 1859—To day I bought a little indian girl, about 2½ or 3 years old for a rifle. She was taken by the Pah–Eeds from the Colorado, and was around here for some time, sick. I pitied her, and got her to save her life. We named her Cora Colorado and intend to raise her as my daughter.[91]

October 9, 1859—During the past month I have been busy harvesting my crop some of which is badly hurt by the frost. My oats look well.

Having been appointed Chairman of a Committee to locate a new field, with Richd Benson and Ed^{d} Dolten, I drew up an article of agreement entirely annulling our old field. We located a new field of 1600 acres east of the present one.[92]

[page 191]

SUSAN E'S BLESSING BY I. MORLEY.

October 17, 1859—Patriarch Isaac Morley gave us the following blessings:—

My wife Susan E.s blessing:—

Sister Susan Ellen, we lay our hands upon your head in the name of Jesus, whose blood has atoned for thy sins, and we seal your father's blessings upon your head for your comfort and edification. Thou art entitled to all the blessings that have been extended to the daughters of Abraham. Thou art placed at the head of thy family as a mother in Israel. Much will be required of thee in bringing up thy offspring before the Lord, both in thy examples and counsels unto them. We bless thee with the blessings of prudence and wisdom, that thy mind may be stayed upon the Mighty God of Jacob. They are given thee for thy stewardship, for the occupancy of thy mind. Hearken to the voice of the Comforter, and the Lord will bless thee in rearing thy offspring before him. Suffer not thy counsels to be given in anger, and the Spirit of Peace will be thy Counselor. Thy Counsels will be in verity and truth before the Lord. The Lord has endued thy mind with the attributes of his own bosom, and the Lord will bless thee with all the blessings of the promised seed. Thy children will honor thee. They will preserve thy name and memory in honor from generation to generation. Thou art of Joseph. We seal the blessings of the Earth, the blessing of immortality, and eternal lives. We seal thee up by the keys of the holy Priesthood to enjoy all these blessings in time and throughout eternity. We ratify it in the name of Jesus Amen.

My Son Henry A's blessing

Brother Henry Augustus, in the name of the Lord and by virtue of the Priesthood, we lay our hands upon your head. We bless thee with thy father's Counsels and affection. Thou art blessed by birthright with thy father's blessing. Hearken ~~unto~~ the counsel of thy parents, and thy birthright shall never be taken from thee. and thou wilt realize through the keys of the holy priesthood, and the holy Anointing which will be sealed upon thee, the blessings and the gifts of these keys.

[page 192]

HENRY A'S BLESSING BY I. MORLEY. MORONI'S

October 17, 1859—Thou are entitled to all the blessings of Abraham by birthright, which will secure to thee, the blessing of flocks and herds. Thou wilt be honored with wives and children, for the extension of thy kingdom. Thou wilt have to proclaim the gospel, that thy garments may be cleansed from the blood of this generation. Thou wilt have to fill many missions, before thou art prepared to receive thy inheritance and to enjoy the fullness of the promised blessings yet thy heirship is secure to thee by Him who is faithful. We bless thee by promise with the keys of the holy anointing, with thy endowment, where thy mind will become illuminated with light. Thou art of Joseph, through the loins of Ephraim. Thou art blessed with the blood of the promised seed. Cherish in thy bosom

91 The Utes came with the child to Martineau's home in Parowan. They wanted to exchange the girl for a rifle and threatened to kill her if a trade could not be made. Martineau gave them his only rifle and took the girl. She was named Cora Colorado and was adopted into the James Henry and Susan Ellen Martineau family (Preston Nibley, *Stalwarts of Mormonism* [Salt Lake City: Deseret Book, 1954]).

92 This is likely Edward Dalton.

the attribute of faith, and thou wilt have power over disease. Thou wilt rebuke the winds and the waves. We seal thee up by the keys of the holy priesthood unto eternal lives in the name of Jesus, Amen.

My son Moroni's blessing:—

Brother Moroni Helaman, we lay our hands upon your head in the name of Jesus, and we seal the blessings of thy father upon your head. Hearken to his counsel, and to the counsel of thy mother and thou wilt live long upon the earth to do good—to build up Christ's kingdom: and thou wilt become like Moroni of old, a prophet, seer, and revelator. Like him thou wilt defend the cause of Zion. Many will be edified and instructed by thy counsel. The blessings of Abraham, Izaac and Jacob will attend thee in thy posterity. Thou wilt enjoy these blessings in flocks and herds. Thou will be numbered with the Sons of Zion in avenging the blood of the prophets. Thou wilt stand upon Mount Zion with the 144,000 having their robes washed and made white in the blood of the Lamb. Thou wilt be honored in redeeming the house of Jacob, for thou art of Joseph. Thou art entitled to all these blessings by birthright.

[page 193]

JOHN WILLIAMS BLESSING.
ELVIRA'S BLESSING.

October 17, 1859—Thou wilt plant vineyards, and eat the fruit of thy labor. Thou wilt see Zion redeemed, and the saints dwell there in peace under their own vines and fruit trees. The keys of the holy priesthood will continue with thee and thy posterity after thee. Be faithful, and thou wilt tarry until the coming of the Son of Man. By virtue of the holy priesthood we seal thee up to enjoy thrones and dominions with an eternal increase. We ratify it in the name of Jesus. Amen

My son John William's blessing:—

Brother John William, we lay our hands upon your head in the name of the Lord, and we seal your fathers blessings upon you by virtue of the keys of the holy priesthood. We seal all the blessings that have been extended upon the heads of Abraham, Isaac and Jacob. We seal upon this child by promise all the blessings of the holy anointing, that this child may be honored and blessed as the anointed of the Lord. We seal the attribute of faith upon the heart and memory of this little child, that through this attribute he may increase in knowledge—he may mature in wisdom. It shall be blessed in administering in anointing and in laying on of hands to rebuke disease The gifts of the gospel will illuminate the mind of this child. It will obtain the gift to discern between truth and error, between light and darkness. It will be blessed in its counsel in the midst of the sons of Zion. We bless it with every attribute, that it may be able to stand at the head of a numerous posterity. We seal the gift, by promise, that it may rebuke disease, that it may cause the lame to leap, the deaf to hear, Flocks and herds will be given it for the occupancy of its stewardship. Its name and priesthood will continue upon its posterity from generation to generation. We seal the blessings of health and life, with an eternal increase, in the name of Jesus. Amen.

My daughter Susan Elvira's blessing:—

Sister Susan Elvira, in the name of the Lord, and by virtue of the holy priesthood we lay our hands upon your head and we seal your father's blessings, with his counsels and his affections upon your memory.

[page 194]

ELVIRA'S AND DECENA'S BLESSINGS.

October 17, 1859—We bless thee in the morning of thy life, in the days of thy innocence, that thy life may be unspotted before thy creator. We bless thee with the attributes of love, fidelity and virtue, that these attributes may increase in thy bosom as thou art maturing in years. We bless thee with the daughters of Abraham with all the blessings of the promised seed. We bless thee with the attribute of faith that it may be a lamp in thy path—a key of knowledge to thy mind. We bless thee with the key of knowledge, that you may know truth from error—light from darkness. We seal the blessings of ~~thy~~ the earth for thy comfort and the comfort of thy posterity. We seal upon thee the blessings of life—the gift to rebuke disease, and we seal thee up to come forth in the morning of the first resurrection where thou wilt be clothed upon with the blessings of immortality and eternal lives. We ratify it in the name of Jesus. Amen.

My daughter Delcena Diadamie's blessing:—

Sister Delcena Diadamie, we place our hands upon your head in the name of the Lord Jesus, and we seal your father's blessings upon you, and we bless you in the morning of life, in the days of thy innocence, that thy days may be filled with usefulness, that thy life may be unspotted before thy Creator, and we Say this seal shall be a blessing unto this child. It will be quick to hearken to the counsel of its parents. We ~~heal~~ seal upon its heart and memory the attributes of love, fidelity and virtue. These attributes will be the governing influence upon the mind of this child. They will fill its mind with light. It will be a blessing in the midst of the daughters of Zion by its examples and by its precepts. It will be honored in its deportment in all its transactions in life. We bless sit with activity of mind—with activity of limb; we bless it in its gifts that have been bestowed upon it by the God of Nature. We bless it with a peaceful habitation, with its table [next line unreadable] gifts of mechanism and economy.

[page 195]

DELLIE'S AND LYMAN'S BLESSINGS.

October 17, 1859—Its garments will be decorated with the work of its own hands. It, will be blessed with the anointed of the Lord to rear sons and daughters to bear the keys of the everlasting priesthood. It is from Ephraim, and we seal the blessings of eternal lives. We ratify it in the name of Jesus. Amen.

My son Lyman Royal's blessing:—

Brother Lyman Royal. I lay my hands upon thy head in the name of Jesus, and I seal the blessings of your father upon you. I place the seals of Abraham, Isaac and Jacob upon thy head. I seal the attributes of faith, love and fidelity upon thy heart and upon thy memory. These attributes will continue with this child to illuminate its mind, and will be sealed upon the hearts of its posterity from generation to generation. I bless this child with the attributes of faith that it may be a key of knowledge—a lamp in its path to continue with it. I seal upon it the gift to rebuke disease, and to have power to cause the waves to be stayed and the winds to cease, through the keys of the everlasting Priesthood, which I seal upon the mind of this Child by promise. I bless it in its intellectual faculties, that they may expand upon the principles of salvation wide as eternity. I seal the blessing to proclaim the gospel to many people, that they may become stars in the crown of this child in the morning of the ressurrection. I bless it in the fruits of the earth; flocks and herds will be given this child for the occupancy of its stewardship. It shall stand at the head of a numerous posterity, and receive a kingdom, and become a king unto the Most High. It is of the blood of Ephraim. It is entitled to the blessings of immortality and eternal lives. I ratify this seal in the days of its innocence, that its heart may never be decayed by deceit, or led away by flattery, and I seal it up unto eternal life in the name of Jesus. Even so. Amen.

In giving these blessings, Br. Morley directed me to lay on hands with him, saying it is my privilege to bless my own posterity. He also told me to gather all my children together, at some time, and bless them.

[page 196]

MY BLESSING FROM BR. MORLEY.

October 17, 1859—In the evening, I received the following blessing from Father Morley:—

Brother James Henry, I lay my hands upon your head in the name of Jesus thy Redeemer, and I seal the blessings of the patriarchs upon you. I ratify all your former seals for their fulfillment and thy enjoyment. The Lord is thy friend for thy love of truth, for thy desires to honor the keys of the everlasting priesthood. The Lord will illuminate thy mind upon the principles pertaining to the holy priesthood. Thou shalt enjoy the blessings and realize the power and the keys pertaining to that priesthood. Thou wilt love her keys and her seals dearer than thy life. The time is near when thou wilt realize the blessings of these keys pertaining to the exaltation of man. Thou wilt obtain the knowledge of the Lord and of the exaltations of man by reason of this blessing. The Lord has endued thy mind with faculties to receive and retain the principles of Christs Kingdom. I seal the attribute of faith upon thy heart for its increase, for its power to be with thee, and to endue thee with power to heal the sick and to cause the lame to leap. Thou wilt be numbered with the anointed in redeeming Zion, and in the restoration of the house of Israel. It shall be thy gift and blessing by birthright, in redeeming thy father's household, that the paternal tie may be restored in the morn of the ressurrection. Through faith thou wilt obtain keys of power of priesthood, that will give thee victory over sin, where thy robes will be washed and made white in the blood of the Lamb. Let thy heart be Comforted. The Lord will bless thee with the fruit of the earth—with the increase of thy body, which will cause thee to sing the song of the Redeemer. I ratify this seal for thy comfort and edification. Thy descent is from the promised seed, and I seal thee up to enjoy the blessings of thrones and dominions with an eternal increase in the name of Jesus. Thou shalt have power given thee from on high to do much good. To have the discerning of spirits. Amen.

[page 197]

GO TO THE CITY WITH SUSAN JULIA

Tuesday, November 1, 1859—This day I started to Salt Lake city with Susan J. and her two children, taking my own wagon and horses. Went to Beaver, and stopped with Br. Thompson

November 2, 1859—Drove to Cove Creek. Rained in the evening, and we were very cold

November 3, 1859—Stopped with Peter Boyce, at Cove Creek and were very kindly treated.

November 4, 1859—Stopped at Cedar Fort, with David Savage.[93]

November 5, 1859—Camped 5 miles beyond the Sevier River.

November 6, 1859—Stopped at Br. Bryant's. Stormed all night. Susan and both the children were very sick all night.

Monday, November 7, 1859—Arrived at Santaquin. Found the folks all well. Saw Nephi the first time in more than a year.

November 8, 1859—Stopped at Provo with David Cluff Jr.[94]

November 9, 1859—Stopped at Lehi with Swen Jacobs.[95]

Thursday, November 10, 1859—Arrived in S. L. City. Stormed in the night. Very cold.

November 11, 1859—Sold 8 Buckskins @ \$1.[50] each, my beaver skins \$1.[00] [\$22] total amount \$26.[00] [\$585]

Sunday, November 13, 1859—Went to meeting. Saw Pres[ts] Wells and Smith, who said it was all right for me to move to S. L. City. I have examined several lots, with a view to purchase.

November 14, 1859—Started home, arriving at Santaquin the 15, and remained there two days. Wrote "Curiosities of the South" and "Rights of Citizenship" for the "Mountaineer."

November 18, 1859—Drove to Nephi, and stopped with David Cazier, and were kindly entertained.[96] Mrs. Bryant gave Susan three yds of Calico: Mrs. Cazier gave two yds domestic and a sun bonnet, and Mrs. Martha Spiner Heywood gave her Six agate (common) shirt buttons![97]

Saturday, November 19, 1859—Drove 42 very long miles to Manti. In crossing the dividing ridge between the vallies of Juab and San Pete, we passed through a snow storm.

We remained at Manti two days on account of Snow Storms. John Eager gave us 15 yds domestic,[98] 7½ yds of Calico, and 100 lbs saleratus (native) and 1¼ bu Oats.[99]

[page 198]

HORSES RAN AWAY DOWN SEVIER HILL.

Saturday November 19, 1859—While in S. L. City Mrs. Colebrook gave her a new velvet bonnet, cloth to make two hoods for the Children, and a cali-

93 Cedar Fort was a traveling stop between Salt Lake and southern Utah. It is located in southern Utah County. David Savage was likely the same who married Mary Ward of Parowan in 1858.

94 There are several David Cluffs in familysearch.org, but none fit the context of this entry.

95 Swen Jacobs was a one-time resident of Parowan. He was a second lieutenant in the Utah Territorial Militia, Company E, Cedar City, Fourth Platoon (Shirts and Shirts, *Trial Furnace*, 495).

96 David Crockett Cazier (1834–1929) was the son of William and Pleasant Cazier.

97 Calico is a cotton fabric.

98 In this context, *domestic* means towels, sheets, and blankets.

99 Saleratus is sodium bicarbonate, or baking soda.

co dress and mouselain-de-lasin skirt.[100] Truly we have been blessed thus far.

Tuesday, November 22, 1859—Started home, and had a narrow escape for our lives just before reaching the Sevier River near the bridge. ~~As~~ The road descends from the table lands by a narrow dry way, steep and winding down the sides of the hill for about half a mile. At the top of the hill my breast chain broke, letting the tongue point drop on the ground, and the wagon ran against the horses, which gave one furious kick—splitting the end board of the wagon box, and ran furiously down the narrow road—the tongue plowing the dirt by the horses feet. At one time it seemed as if the wagon would run off the dug-way and roll a hundred feet to the bottom: the horses would give a lucky jerk, and turn the wagon the other way towards the upper side, and threaten to turn us over that way. I held the horse as well as I could, and Susan behaved with the greatest coolness, not screaming once during that fearful ride. At length gaining the bottom of the valley the road turned short to the right down the river bank. The horses kept the road, but the wagon kept straight on to the river, stopping just on the edge of high perpendicular bank, not more than a rod from its brink. Down to the river was about 15 feet, with water over six feet deep. As the horses broke from the wagon I ran after them, and chased them about an hour, finally cornering them and catching them without the harness being much broken. As I started back, I met Susan, who had left the wagon to see what had become of me, leaving the children in the wagon. As we came back to the wagon I saw Dellie playing with my loaded revolver!

[page 199]

IF INNEN TUM, I SOOT 'EM.

November 22, 1859—As we came up she said, triumphantly "If innen tum, I soot 'em." (If the Indians come I'll shoot them.) I hardly knew what to thank the Lord for most:—our remarkable preservation coming down the hill, or that of my children, with the pistol. The Lord has truly blessed us bountifully.

November 23, 1859—Having fixed up things, I drove to Cedar Fort, and found Nephi and Mandana, his wife, detained by the sickness of their daughter Lovinna

November 24, 1859—Drove to Corn Creek, and waited one day there for Nephi to come up.

November 26, 1859—Started home this morning, and camped on the top of Pine Mountain pass in the cedars. Snow deep, and weather very cold. A Stranger Camped with us. It snowed all night.

November 27, 1859—Drove to the summit of the Beaver range and Camped in the road

November 28, 1859—Got home at 3 P.M. and found all well.

Friday, December 2, 1859—Traded my real estate here, consisting of my house and lot, 4 garden lots, 2½ acres hay land, and 20 acres of farm land, to Mrs. S. Ward for a house and lot in the 6th Ward S. L. City, with a pasture right for four cattle in the 6th Ward pasture.

December 6, 1859—Traded wagons with F. T. Whitney, giving him \$30.~ [\$674] boot, and next day sold W. Davenport \$25.00 [\$552] worth of books, and my clock to J. Fish for \$20.00 [\$450] and books \$10.00 [\$225].[101] Traded my horses, stove & 10 bu wheat to J. H. Rollins for a pair of mules

November 10, 1859—Bought a small Carriage of J. McGuffie for \$80.00 [\$1,799]

November 12, 1859—Went to Fort Johnson with Susan E. Home the 14th

November 21, 1859—Went to Cedar to Survey a new field, Surveyed 363 Acres.

November 24, 1859—Returned home, and went to a party in the evening.

November 31, 1859—Went with Susan E. to Beaver, we took two children Spent two days very pleasantly there.

100 Mousseline is a fine, sheer fabric resembling muslin.

101 William Davenport and Joseph Fish were among the first teachers in the pioneer schools of Parowan (Seegmiller, *History of Iron County*, 191).

PART

4

MOVING TO NORTHERN UTAH: SURVEYING BEGINS

[page 200]

BEGIN TO REMOVE TO SALT LAKE CITY. EARTHQUAKE.

January 3, 1860—We came home

January 7, 1860—Susan E. taken very ill this evening.

January 12, 1860—Bought Lot 3 Block 2 S. L. City of Mrs. Banks for $60.[00] [$1,300]

January 15, 1860—Experienced two shocks of Earthquake this morning at a quarter to 6 A.M. The first was quite severe, shaking things considerably, rattling dishes, swinging doors, and waking every one in town. The fowls were frightened squalling all over town, people shouting one to another and all excitement. The second shock was lighter. It occurred at 6.30 A.M.

Friday, February 17, 1860—Started to remove to Salt Lake City, taking Susan E. and her children and Cora. We had a wagon drawn by a yoke of oxen, and the Carriage and mules. Stopped at Paragoonah.

February 18, 1860—Traveled 18 miles and Camped

February 19, 1860—Drove to Beaver, and next day to Pine Creek. The weather is very cold.

February 21, 1860—Drove 5 miles to Cove Creek. Snowed all night.

February 22, 1860—Went to Corn Creek—a long drive, through snow arriving at Boyce's at about 10 o'clock at night.[1] The night was very dark, and the first I knew we were in the middle of an indian camp—Pahvants—and surrounded by indian dogs. I found that Boyce had moved away. But the indians treated us well. The Chief—Kanosh—sent an indian with us to show us the house, and directly two more came with wood for a fire, which they kindled for us. Other took the animals off to find grass for them, and then all left us alone for the night. I know if they wished to kill us they had us in their power, but the best we could do was to trust to their native honor, and as the event proved, this was best. In the morning they brought my teams, saying that they thought I should give them something for letting my animals eat their grass.

1 Corn Creek, Utah, is located in Garfield County at the confluence of the Corn and Birch creeks.

[page 201]

RETURN FOR SUSAN JULIA & FAMILY

February 22, 1860—This I gladly did. If I had tried to camp away by ourselves, they would have probably robbed us.

February 23, 1860—Drove to Fillmore and stopped with J. H. Dame

Friday, February 24, 1860—Went to the north end of Pauvan Valley and camped. Roads very bad,—snow—mud—water and ice.

Saturday, February 25, 1860—Camped near the Sevier with Geo. Day. Wrote to Susan J.[2]

Sunday, Friday 26, 1860—Camped 15 miles south of Nephi in soft, thin, deep mud. Winds very cold, and a most cheerless prospect. No fire, nor anything to make on of.

February 27, 1860—Got to Nephi, and stopped at Bryants. Very glad to have some shelter at last.

Tuesday, February 28, 1860—Arrived at Santaquin. Determined to leave my family for a while, and go to the city to prepare for them.[3]

Thursday, March 1, 1860—Started for the city alone, arriving there on Saturday the 3d and stopped with Uncle David T. LeBaron.[4] I spent three days inquiring about city lots. Visited Prest Young, who treated me very kindly, and talked about old times and scenes in Auburn, N.Y. where we both had lived. He offered me a house in the 19th ward for $1200.00 [$25,990] giving me my own time to pay for it. But I declined—not wishing to be in debt, if possible. I traded my lots in the 1st Ward to Orson Hyde for an acre in the 13th Ward, on Emigration Street, giving my carriage to boot.

I had previously bargained for a house and lot of Bradford Leonard (Blind Leonard, a notorious usurer) but he kindly released me from the trade, and gave me back my article of agreement, for which I feel very thankful.[5]

March 9, 1860—I returned to Santaquin on the 9th and Uncle Benjamin tried to persuade me to stop there and attend to his business, which I finally agreed to do. I started on my return to Parowan, to bring Susan J. and her family, arriving there on the

March 15, 1860—and proceeded to wind up my business there.

[page 202]

ACCUSED BY JAS LEWIS OF SWINDLING THE COUNTY.

March 15, 1860—While absent James Lewis stirred up an excitement against me, saying that I had cheated the county out of $40.00 [$866].[6] This was told all through the county, even Br. Dame, to whom I had been so true, not giving me any support. I heard of it while gone, and came home boiling with indignation, that I, who for years had been a complete servant to the people—a complete dog, almost—should be thus repaid. On arriving home I demanded an investigation of the County books, which Silas S. Smith, select man so warmly seconded that an investigation was had, resulting in the fact that my accounts were found correct, to a cent. The $40.00 [$866] item arose from the fact that Judge Lewis himself, who had received from me as clerk an order for $40.00 for official services for the year, had, on my resignation, and the appointment of a new clerk, received another $40.00 order for the same service. I believe he was dishonest, and tried to cover his extra $40.00 by bringing me into trouble. R. Benson helped the influence against me, desiring my

2 Martineau is complimented for his work in the Parowan Branch ("Saturday," *Deseret News*, February 25, 1860; Journal History).

3 Santaquin, Utah, originally known as Summit Creek, is located in Utah County approximately seventy miles south of Salt Lake. It was settled in 1851 by Benjamin F. Johnson (Richard Neitzel Holzapfel, *A History of Utah County* [Salt Lake City: Utah State Historical Society, 1999], 65–66).

4 David T. LeBaron lived in Spring Lake, Utah County. Prior to his immigrating to the Great Basin and just as the Mormons were driven from Illinois, LeBaron was a caretaker of the Nauvoo Temple. He purchased it for five thousand dollars just months before it was ransacked and set on fire by arsonists (Lisle G. Brown, comp., "Chronology of the Construction, Destruction, and Reconstruction of the Nauvoo Temple," February 2000; http://users.marshall.edu/~brown/nauvoo/chrono.html).

5 Several Bradford Leonards and Leonard Bradfords appear in Church history. None match this entry or context.

6 Martineau must have been significantly hurt by these accusations. Normally in his journals to date, when offended, he omits the name of the offender. Here it is included and denounced.

ruin and my place of County Surveyor. Any such spirit as that, unless repented of, will take a person out of this kingdom.

At the special session of the County Court, they all seemed very innocent—it was some one else who had said thus and so. I told them I knew all about it, who had done this, and what for. I told them I didn't care a d——n for the whole pile—if they wanted a fuss they could pitch in—I was ready. Lewis and Dame privately acknowledged their fault to me. I paid Ja[s] Lewis $35.[00] [$758] I did not owe him, at our settlement, so he might not lie about me after I had moved away, and $10.[00] [$217] to Rich[d] Benson on the same principle. In short, my going away seemed the signal for a general skimming process—(review of my doings in Iron County) the one who could get the most out of me, the best fellow. I escaped, however, with the loss of about $100 [$2,166]. and have some skin left, thank heaven.

[page 203]

REVIEW OF MY DOINGS IN IRON COUNTY

Thursday, April [no date] 1860—Left Parowan with my family, happy to leave behind us a set of hypocritical leeches and scandal mongers, of whom the Chief is James Lewis. He delights in carrion better than good meat. Nothing pleases him so much as the delinquencies of his brethren.—he has then something to talk about. Rich[d] Benson is a fitting match for him.

I have lived in Iron County nine years, 8 of which have been fully occupied by me in public business. I served as City Recorder 2 terms of two years each:—City Councillor and Alderman, one term each; was a school examiner, school teacher, County clerk under Judges Chapman Duncan, John Steele, C. C. Pendleton, and James Lewis for several years: Assessor & Collector of Fortification District No. 1.—Water Master, County Surveyor, Sheriff, Notary Public three terms of the Legislature.[7] Clerk in the Legislature one session, Stake historian, and recorder of Births, Marriages, and Deaths, of Baptisms and blessings, as drill master for the Militia, Adjutant of the Battalion, and of the 10th Infantry, with the rank of Lieut. Colonel: as a Captain in the Corps of Topographical Engineers, and as Tithing Clerk for many years. Besides this I spent much time other ways in the public service on exploring parties, Indian scouts etc. For almost all these offices there was no compensation, and I had to find stationery and office room for nothing and board myself. But I wanted to do good, and I trust for my reward for the future.

Although so busy, I found time to study much, in surveying, trigonometry, Astrology (a short time) and in the new alphabet. I took part in the Parowan Dramatic Association, copying off the parts, painting the scenery, and acting as treasurer.

[page 204]

ESTABLISHED IN 13TH WARD. TWO MEN KILLED.

April 1860—When I first went to Parowan, I was alone. When I went back to the north I had a family of ten, with a good wagon, carriage, yoke of oxen, span of mules, three cows, and household goods. Truly has the Lord blessed me, especially since entering into the order of Celestial marriage. I joined the Legion as a private and am now Reg[d] Adjutant. I joined the Church as a member—and am now a High Priest. May the Lord help me to be faithful to the end.

On arriving at Santaquin, Uncle Benjamin tried to get me to stay there, but I finally went on to the city arriving there May 5. with Susan J.

May 5, 1860—We occupied the house I bought of Elder Hyde. It is a small adobe room joined to a log room. The lot has three peach trees, two Black walnuts, and some currants.

While on my way here, we camped near Palmyra.[8] During the night it snowed and blowed very hard. My cattle strayed away, and I hunted them three days before I found them. During my search I went to a camp of U.S. troops camped at the mouth of Spanish Fork Cañon on their way to New Mexico, one of whom threatened to "bullet me." He did not do it, however.

The night we arrived at Salt Lake City, a little before going to bed, we heard two reports of fire arms not far

7 "Legislative Election," *Deseret News*, January 25, 1860; Utah Digital Newspapers.

8 Palmyra, Utah, is fifty-three miles south of Salt Lake City, in Utah County.

off, and said—"perhaps some one is shot." Snowed in the night—about 6 inches.

May 6, 1860—Very cold this morning. Frost killed many large peach trees all through the city. Found this morning that two men were killed by the guns we heard last night. One's name was [Brower the other Johnson.]

[page 205]

MOVE INTO THE GREER HOUSE. HAUNTED.

May ~~16~~ 11, 1860—On my way back from Santaquin, I stopped at Job's, the Astrologer's

Wednesday, May 16, 1860—Met another column of U.S. troops going to New Mexico, with about 25 wagons full of Apostates. There was quite a number of Mormon (!) women and girls among them—prostitutes.

May 17, 1860—Arrived in the city with Susan E. and family Found all well.

May 18, 1860—Henry began herding a small number of cows on the Bench and Ensign Peak[9]

May 23, 1860—Traded my mules, wagon and harness and Carriage to D. R. Greer for a house and lot in the 6th Ward, fronting on the Square (Old Fort) Greer is going back to Texas.

Also gave a cow, calf, and $10.00 [$217] in Molasses for a stove. Planted my garden.

June 9, 1860—Went to the West Mountain, Porter's Cañon with Susan J. and children to get out wood. 15 miles[10]

June 10, 1860—Borrowed a tent of Br. Porter to live in.

June 18, 1860—Returned home, having got out 3 cords of wood.

June 19, 1860—Rented 5 acres of Land of E. W. East, planted in corn. I am to cultivate it, and haul East 1/3 of the crop paying Bayles Sprouse $25 [$541]. for work he has done on it.

The house I have in the 6th Ward was not long since the headquarters of the Lot Huntington faction of Bill Hickman's Band.[11] Here Lott was guarded by his friends while he was recovering from his wound. When we moved in, I found a large bowie knife, a gold chain, and some other things. The house is also said to be haunted by a spirit who walks down stairs, through the kitchen and then disappears. I never saw any, however.

Saturday, June 30, 1860—Susan J. quite sick. Went to see S. M. Blair[12] about going to Cache County to survey for him and for the people at Franklin, which is now being settled.

[page 206]

GO TO CACHE COUNTY. FRANKLIN.

July 19, 1860—To day I start for Cache County, to survey for the Franklin people. Henry A. also goes with me. We have our wagon and oxen, and go along with S. M. Blair, who is moving up there. Br. J. W. Fox told me, he had spoken to Prest Young about my going up there to survey, and he had approved the idea. I went to see Br. Brigham, who comfirmed it, and said it would be good for me to locate one of my wives there, and be County surveyor. He invited me to attend the celebration of the 24th in Cottonwood Cañon. Went

9 Ensign Peak is in the Wasatch Range foothills just north of downtown Salt Lake City. Brigham Young hiked to the summit, 1,080 feet from the valley floor, after the Saints arrived in the Great Basin, and at the top he commented, "[this] was a proper place to raise an ensign to the nations" (*Contributor*, August 1880, 253).

10 West Mountain is north of Santaquin and northwest of Payson, Utah, approximately fifty miles south of Salt Lake.

11 Lott Huntington was a member of a prominent Utah family. His father Dimick Huntington was a member of the Mormon Battalion. The family immigrated to Massachusetts from England in 1635 and one reported descendant, Samuel Huntington, signed the U.S. Declaration of Independence (Donald G. Godfrey, "Zina Presindia Young Williams Card: Brigham's Daughter, Cardston's First Lady," *Journal of Mormon History* 23, no. 2 [Fall 1997]: 110). William Adam "Wild Bill" Hickman received his reputation due to his quick temper. He was a notorious outlaw of the time. Nevertheless, he was an aide to numerous Church Presidents and was instrumental in the western Mormon movement (Hope A. Hilton, *"Wild Bill" Hickman and the Mormon Frontier* [Salt Lake City: Signature Books, 1988]).

12 This could be S. M. Blair, who worked with Martineau in the early school educational developments in Cache Valley (Joel E. Ricks and Everett L. Cooley, *The History of a Valley: Cache Valley, Utah-Idaho* [Logan, UT: Cache Valley Centennial Commission, 1956], 323).

as far as Farmington and stopped with W. K. Rice, my old friend.

Monday, July 23, 1860—Went to ~~Paro~~ Brigham City, then went up the Cañon 4 miles and camped by a large spring creek.

July 24, 1860—We heard this morning the indian hostilities had broken out in Cache, and that two brethren had been killed at Smithfield and two wounded. Also two indians were killed. An Indian was confined for stealing horses, and some of his friends came to rescue him.

We lay by all day waiting for company. Spent the day in cleaning guns and pistols, and making bullets, and preparing for war.

July 25, 1860—Started through the pass, with men disposed as front and rear guards, and flankers. The women drove the teams and loose stock. Got to Wellsville before dark.

July 26, 1860—Drove to Providence, where Mr. Blair means to locate. He invited me to stop with him for a few days.

July 30, 1860—I started for Franklin, with Henry and got there at Sunset. all safe. Found the settlers at Franklin living in wagons and bowerys of brush and poles.

July 31, 1860—Began Surveying to day, and continued at it all week. I surveyed a farm of 2560 acres on the west side of Cub River.

[page 207]

ELECTED COUNTY SURVEYOR.

August 7, 1860—I was elected Co. Surveyor for Cache Co.

Thursday, August 9, 1860—Have been surveying hay land for some days. At this date I have earned $360.⁰⁰ [$7,797]. When I shall get my pay is another thing.

August 10, 1860—Returned to Providence, to Br. Blair's.

August 12, 1860—Began surveying for the Providence people's hay land.

August 12, 1860 [This date is in the journal twice.]—By invitation of Pres^t E. T. Benson I went to Wellsville and preached. Br. Benson told me he wished me to locate in Logan, and be County Surveyor, (to which office I was elected last Monday, while at Franklin). Also, to be chief clerk of the Cache County Tithing office. I hesitated to accept these offices, and next day Br. Benson and Bp. Maughan[13] told me also to act as County Clerk. Br. Benson said it would be well for me temporally and spiritually. Thus all my plans of living in S. L. City are knocked into "Pi."

August 13, 1860—Continued surveying hay land. Very disagreeable work, wading continually in water, in willows, and an intensely hot sun.

August 14, 1860—Began Surveying Logan island into ten-acre hay lots. The work is very difficult on account of the dense willows along the rivers.

August 15, 1860—Still surveying. Got a letter from my wives. Filed my bonds as County Surveyor.

August 16, 1860—Finished my surveying.

August 18, 1860—Went to Logan to calculate the yds cutting of a mill race being built by Benson & Thatcher. Br. Benson invited me to go with him on a trip to Franklin and I did no. I sent word to Henry, and went with Br. Benson to Hyde Park, and Dined. Br. Wm Hyde accompanied us from here.

August 19, 1860—Held a meeting at Franklin, then drove to Richmond, preached again, dined with Bp. Tidwell,[14] after which we went and visited Br. Saml Cozzens,[15] who was wounded in the fight at Smithfield about a month ago, being shot through the ~~Right~~ Left lung.

[page 208]

SUSAN J. RECEIVED HER ENDOWMENTS. WE ARE ALL SEALED

[heading continues on page 209]

August 19, 1860—We administered to him, and examined his wound. The breath passes in and out of

....

13 This is likely Peter Maughan, who founded Wellsville in 1856. Wellsville was the first permanent settlement of the Saints in Cache Valley. Maughan was later called as presiding bishop of the area (Donald G. Godfrey and Kenneth W. Godfrey, eds., *The Diaries of Charles Ora Card: The Utah Years, 1871–1886* [Provo, UT: Brigham Young University Religious Studies Center, 2006], 3–4; Ricks and Cooley, *History of Cache Valley*, 44).

14 Thomas Tidwell was bishop of the Richmond Ward (F. Ross Peterson, *A History of Cache County* [Salt Lake City: Utah State Historical Society, 1997], 36).

15 This is Samuel Cousins (Peterson, *History of Cache County*, 42).

the bullet hole at every breath. Sometimes a singular looking kind of worms crawl out of the hole. His life has thus far been preserved solely by the faith and power of the priesthood. He is very pale and weak. We then went to Smithfield and preached there, took supper at Hyde Park, and got to Logan an hour after dark. I remained at Br. Benson's all night.

August 20, 1860—Measured the mill race, which contains 757 4/27 yds.

Wednesday, August 22, 1860—Started home, arriving there on the 25th and found all well. The children had been sick, and so had Susan J.

August 27, 1860—Recd of W. H. Hooper my pay due for extra traveling expenses in 1856–7 (Legislative) $48.00–$4.80 [$1,040–$104].

August 29, 1860—Went to Coons Cañon and got Dolly and her calf.

Saturday, September 1, 1860—Sold my lot in the 1st Ward to Geo. Goddard for $75.00 [$1,624] in Gin and Guns.[16]

September 4, 1860—To day, John Eager went home again, after a weeks visit.

September 5, 1860—Sold my lot in the 13th Ward to W. S. Godbe[17] for $375.00 [$8,122] for medicines &c out of his dry store, at 25 % below retail price = $466.00 [$10,093]. $50.00 [$1,083] in Store pay.

Thursday, September 6, 1860—Sold the remaining ¼ acre of the Godbe lot to Walter Paul[18] for $100.00 [$2,166] in furniture, flour, & about $40. [$866] in Store pay.

September 8, 1860—Traded for goods to-day, about $185.00 [$4,007] I intend to start selling goods in Logan on a small scale.

September 9, 1860—Arranged for Susan J. to get her endowments.

Monday, September 10, 1860—Susan preparing for her endowments.

Wednesday, September 12, 1860—To day Susan J. received her endowment, myself and Susan E. also attended. After this was done we all went into another room, and were sealed at the alter by Presr Brigham Young. Susan E., Susan J. and her sister Mary Elvira Sherman, who died at Nauvoo. I told Br. Brigham that I believed the Prophet Joseph wanted Mary E., if <u>he</u> did, I did not wish to interfere in any way.

[page 209]

BY PRST B. YOUNG, ALSO M. E. SHERMAN, DECEASED

[heading continued from page 208]

September 12, 1860—Br. Brigham thought a few moments and said he would seal her to me, and when we get where Br. Joseph is, perhaps he may tell us something we have not yet known or thought of. Susan J. stood proxy.

Friday, September 14, 1860—Moved out of the 13th Ward house. Snow on the mountains this morning. Autumn has gone, I fear.

Saturday, September 15, 1860—To day I sold Cora to Brother A. B. Cherry,[19] who has no children at home now, and wants her for his own. As I thought he could do better by her than I, he being rich, I have concluded to let him have her. He gave me a rifle for her.

Tuesday, September 18, 1860—Sold my 6th Ward place to Joseph Asa[20] for $450.00 [$9,746]. I took three yoke of oxen, a new wagon, tent and buffalo robe. Sold my old oxen for $80.00 [$1,733] in goods. I gave a watch worth $12.00 [$260] and 25¢ [$5.41] in money (all I had) to help the missionaries just called to Europe. Br. G. A. Smith said I would have been sent, but for the fact that I am moving, and have no home anywhere for my family.

16 George Goddard was a prominent member of the Church who served extensively in the Sunday School organization of the Church (Godfrey and Godfrey, *Utah Years*, 65).

17 William S. Godbe led the Godbeites, who were excommunicated from the Church (Linda Sillitoe, *Welcoming the World: A History of Salt Lake County* [Salt Lake City: Salt Lake County, 1996], 67; Leonard J. Arrington, *Brigham Young: American Moses* [Urbana, IL: University of Illinois Press, 1986], 355–62, 374–75).

18 This could be Walter Paul, who was a resident of Mendon, Utah.

19 This could be Aaron B. Cherry, one of the first to serve in the Iron Mission (Morris A. Shirts and Kathryn H. Shirts, *A Trial Furnace: Southern Utah's Iron Mission* [Provo, UT: Brigham Young University Press, 1991], 428). Cora, as previously noted, is listed in FamilySearch as a Martineau. No reference could be found to Cora Colorado Cherry.

20 No Joseph Asa could be located fitting the context of this entry.

September 25, 1860—Sold two cows to day for $60.00 [$1,300] in goods. Also some furniture to Asa for $18.00 [$390] in goods. Gave him a transfer of my lot. Traded my wagon and $25.00 [$541] for a good carriage—the one Judge Eckles—the "bloody Judge" crossed the plains in with the army.[21]

Thursday, September 27, 1860—To day I started for Cache County, with Susan J. and her two children, leaving Susan E. until I can return for her. I took two wagons and teams, with a man named John Reese who agrees to drive one team to Logan for his passage there. Ran over my dog Watch—poor fellow—and hurt him somewhat. Got my gun at Cherry's and arrived at Rices after dark, being tired out.

September 28, 1860—Swapped my whiskey with Rice for Molasses. Drove to Weber and stopped with Mrs. Connel, a widow.

[page 210]

MOVING TO LOGAN, SUSAN J. IS RUN OVER. BREAK DOWN.

September 29, 1860—To day met some U. S. troops bringing in the remnant of a company of emigrants lately attacked by indians on the Northern route. Most of the Company had been massacred and tortured. Broke the tongue of my wagon in a mud hole; mended it, and went on until dark and stopped at the house of George Marsh, living about a mile south of Willard city.[22] After stopping there about two hours, they acted so coldly that we went on again, arriving at Willard city about 10 P.M. and being kindly entertained.

Sunday, September 30, 1860—Drove to Brigham City. Here John Reese, who had agreed to drive to Logan deserted us, and Susan J. had to drive one team.[23] I traded oxen with a man to get a gentler yoke, and we started. About 2 miles above Brigham city, Susan J. fell, being caught by her dress, and the loaded wagon passed over her. I administered to her, and helped her into the wagon, and then had both teams to drive up the cañon—a very rough, bad road. We only got 4 miles by the middle of the afternoon, to the Big Spring, eat, and went on about 1½ miles and broke down one wheel, by a man meeting us with a load of wood in a narrow place. We got the wagon a short distance further, where we could get it out of the road, and stopped, perforce.

In the night my new yoke of oxen went back to Brigham city, and I got up about 2 A.M. and followed them, finding them five miles below us. Susan J. did not know I had left her alone so long in the mountains, or she would have been very much afraid.

September 31, 1860—This morning I went two miles and got a long pole, and put under the ~~al~~ axle tree, and, started on again slowly. The road was full of grizzly bear tracks for about three miles,—quite recent ones.

[page 211]

BEAR TRACKS. LYMAN VERY SICK. BAD HAND.

1860—After a very toilsome march of 12 miles down the Cañons we arrived at Wellsville, thoroughly tired out.[24] For miles Susan J. had to walk along by the team, driving, the road being very bad, and lined with

21 D. R. Eckels (or Eckles) (1806–88) was a justice of the Utah Territorial Supreme Court from 1857 to 1860 (Robert E. Eckels, "Delana R. Eckels, 1806–1888: Chief Justice, Utah Territorial Supreme Court, 1857–60," typescript manuscript A 3293; Utah State Historical Society).

22 George Marsh was likely related to Elder Thomas Baldwin Marsh. Thomas Marsh was excommunicated for apostasy and later rebaptized; he died in 1866 in Ogden, Utah (Daniel H. Ludlow, ed., *Encyclopedia of Mormonism* [New York: Macmillan, 1992], 4:1641). Willard City is located just south of Brigham City, Utah.

23 This could be John Reese, who was a merchant in Salt Lake City.

24 Martineau is traveling north from Salt Lake to Brigham City. At Brigham City he turned east through Box Elder Canyon in the Wellsville Mountain range, which is the western border of Cache Valley. Wellsville is a small settlement southwest of Logan, at the foot of the Wellsville Mountains, and east of the Little Bear River. In 1856 the community was established by William H. Maughan. In 1863 it would be surveyed by Martineau, who would incorporate into the city what was called the Mormon community concept (LaRayne B. Christensen, Wilma J. Hall, and Ruth H. Maughan, *Windows of Wellsville: 1856–1984* [Wellsville, UT: Wellsville History Committee, 1985]; see also Ricks and Cooley, *History of Cache Valley*, "Maps and Illustrations," in back cover sleeve).

stumps, brush &c. Poor girl, it was quite an experience for her.

Wednesday, October 3, 1860—Arrived in Logan about noon, and camped on my city lots. In the night was a fearful storm and gale, lasting all night. Susan slept in one wagon, I in the other, and all night we lay holding on the wagon's covers, saying nothing for fear of waking the other. About morning, we found that each one had been awake all night, and had quite a laugh. Bp. Preston invited us to breakfast, which was very welcome indeed to us.[25]

Thursday, October 4, 1860—Engaged a house for 4 months of Geo. Peacock, at $3.00 [$65] per month.[26]

October 5, 1860—Moved into the house, and made shelves for the goods, of which I have nearly $1000. [$21,659] worth, in drugs, medicines, groceries, and some dry goods.[27]

October 6, 1860—Lyman R. is still very sick, having been for some weeks worn down by a constant diarrhea, which we have found it impossible to check thus far.

Sunday, October 7, 1860—Preached to day, in the old log meeting house. Our choir consisted of G. L. Farrell and his two sisters and N. W. Birdno, with an old fiddle. Sublime![28]

October 11, 1860—Lyman is better.

October 28, 1860—Have been to Franklin to collect some of my pay. I cut my finger a little, and caught cold in it, making finally a very bad hand of it. People thought for a time my finger would have to be amputated, if not my hand. I got some "black salve" of C. W. Card,[29] which healed it. It is made of olive oil, red precipitate and some other things which I do not remember now.

[page 212]

WENT TO S. L. CITY. LOGAN CONFERENCE.

October 30, 1860—Lyman is now about well. He was cured by washing in a warm bath, thoroughly, to open the pores, then bathing in burned liquor (Gin) and then anointing all over with oil. This stopped his disease, after all other remedies had failed of course. I had him administered to frequently.

Thursday November 1, 1860—Started to the city with 106 lbs butter to sell and arrived there without accident on the 3^d. Sold my butter at $.25 [$5.41] pr lbs and got some goods for it.

November 7, 1860—Started home, arriving in Logan on the 9th.

Saturday, November 17, 1860—Conference began at Logan today. I was appointed clerk. We had persons from all parts of the valley.

November 18, 1860—Pres^t Maughan having to day made the remark "The kingdom is ours, with its power and greatness" Suggested the following lines, which I wrote to day:—

THE KINGDOM IS OURS.

Air—Araby's daughter.

1

The kingdom is ours, with its power and glory
The kingdom is ours—then rejoice all ye saints:
Repeat to the world, the enlivening story
Rejoice all ye people and cease all complaints
Chorus.

25 William B. Preston was the first bishop in Logan, Utah. He was a California convert to the Church, and he became a prominent Utah businessman. He was later the fourth Presiding Bishop of the Church (Godfrey and Godfrey, *Utah Years*, 4; Peterson, *History of Cache County*, 91).

26 This could be George Peacock, a Logan farmer (Ray Somers, *History of Logan* [Logan, UT: Somers Historic Press, 1993], 67).

27 It appears Martineau is opening a drugstore ("Drug Store at Logan," *Deseret News,* September 26, 1860; Utah Digital Newspapers).

28 George L. Farrell was a prominent local businessman who had served in the Cache Valley Militia (Godfrey and Godfrey, *Utah Years*, 4; Ricks and Cooley, *History of Cache Valley*, 82). Nehemiah Wood Birdneau, often spelled *Birdno*, was a blacksmith and among the first settlers in Logan, Utah (Godfrey and Godfrey, *Utah Years*, 52; Ricks and Cooley, *History of Cache Valley*, 41).

29 This is likely Cyrus William Card, who had moved to Logan only nine months earlier. A New York native, Card's family joined the Church in 1843. He was a wheelwright and a millwright by trade (Godfrey and Godfrey, *Utah Years*, vi; A. James Hudson, *Charles Ora Card: Pioneer and Colonizer* [Cardston, Alberta: privately printed, 1963], 7–15).

The kingdom is ours—all our bonds have been broken.
There's nothing to hinder our serving the Lord
Fulfill all the words that the prophets have spoken
Be true to ourselves—to each other—and God.

2
Though long we have suffered oppression and sorrow
And nakedness, famine, and sickness and death
With faith we have looked for the bright coming morrow—
Though often of substance and comforts bereft.
Chorus.

3
Rejoice all ye Saints, the kingdom is ours
The victory is gained, though bloodless the strife:
The Lord for his people hath shown forth his pow'r
He hath blessed us with substance, with the blessings of life.
Chorus.

[page 213]

BUILD A LOG HOUSE AND MOVE INTO IT.

November 18, 1860—

4
Though often the time that the Saints have been driven
The ~~foes~~ strength of our foemen is broken and gone;
The bonds that have bound us, at last have been broken:—
Then lift up your hearts in thanksgiving and song.
Chorus

5
A new era has dawned—the kingdom of Zion
In splendor and brightness and glory shall shine;
The love and the power of God we'll rely on—
As in past, so in ~~future~~ present and all coming time.
Chorus.

Monday, November 19, 1860—Conference ended to-day. A good time.

November 20, 1860—Went to Franklin, to survey some city lots, and continued at it until the 29th when I started home, having collected 35 bushels of wheat.

At Richmond I found Susan J. who had got so lonesome she started to come to me. She was at the house of Br. W. H. Wright[30]—where we remained all night.

November 30, 1860—Home again.

December 6, 1860—Walked about 2 miles up Logan bottom with Della, and talked with Br. Fox,[31] who is leveling a canal from Logan river to Smithfield, which will require a ditch nearly ten miles long.

December 7, 1860—Attended a session of the County Court as clerk.

December 8, 1860—In the evening the court required me to stand treat. I accordingly brought some good liquor—gin—and some excellent cigars, all which Prest Benson, Maughan and the select men seemed to enjoy.[32] I began clerking with Blair & Farnsworth at $2.50 [$54] pr day

Monday, December 10, 1860—Sold my steers for logs to build a house, the logs to be laid up and roof on, composed of poles, grass and dirt. Joined the High Priests quorum, and was appointed clerk of the same. Susan J. has been quite sick for some time, but is now better.

30 This could be William H. Wright from Ogden (Richard C. Roberts and Richard W. Sadler, *A History of Weber County* [Salt Lake City: Utah State Historical Society, 1997], 136); or it could be William T. Wright, who was among the first Cache Valley settlers (Ricks and Cooley, *History of Cache Valley*, 46).

31 This is likely Jesse W. Fox, who was a government engineer. When Martineau became county surveyor, Fox was the territorial surveyor (Somers, *History of Logan*, 36; Peterson, *History of Cache County*, 49; Ricks and Cooley, *History of Cache Valley*, 57).

32 The Word of Wisdom was not a binding policy in the Church at this time. What is called the "Word of Wisdom," a health law, was revealed to the Prophet Joseph Smith on February 27, 1833. In future decades the prohibition movement would increase the Church's attention toward it, and several Church presidents suggested that following it become a requirement for entering the temple. Today the official Church policy requires abstinence from alcohol, tobacco, coffee, and tea.

December 28, 1860—Moved into our new house, and dedicated it to the Lord.

[page 214]

HELP SETTLE TITHING BOOKS

January 17, 1861—I received a certificate of election as Notary Public to day.[33] During the past month I have been clerking for Farnsworth & Co. having begun with them on Dec. 7th 1860, at $2.50 [$54] pr day. I have also been attending County business and my private business. I took a few lessons in French from Mrs. Elise Baliff, a French lady from Switzerland, who thinks I learn it well and easily. But I have not time to attend regular lessons.

January 26, 1861—Began teaching a military school.

January 27, 1861—Presᵗ. Benson, just returned from S. L. City, where the spirit of freedom burns brightly, went upon the hill just above his house and shouted "Hurrah for the United States of Deseret."

February 17, 1861—Since my last date nothing special has occurred. I bought a sleigh—my first—for $17.00 [$368]. It had no iron shoes, but has afforded much enjoyment. I have taken some lessons in French, and make good progress. About a week ago I made out some invitation tickets for a party, which were highly praised. They were ornamented with devices appropriate to the recipient, as for instance, Judge Maughan's represented a hand holding the scales of justice.

I hurt my finger a little, caught cold in it, and a very bad sore resulted, at one time endangering my whole hand. Br. Card made me some salve which healed it immediately. The following are the ingredients: 1 Lb. Red Lead, 4 oz. Gum Camphor, 1 qt olive oil, and 1 pt of vinegar, boiled together and stirred 4 hours. It is very good.

March 26, 1861—Have been very busy since my last entry. On the 19th of February I began to help settle the tithing books Continuing until March 18th without ceasing for Sunday evening meetings or anything else: beginning early in the morning and continuing until midnight. This is very severe labor, in connexion with computing figures all the time. My health, and that of the others engaged—G. L. Farrell, Frank Gunnell[34]—was visibly affected.

[page 215]

GO TO CONFERENCE. SUSAN GOES HOME. I GO TO SAN PETE.

March 26, 1861—Indeed Br. Gunnell became very sick. We have had a severe winter, but there now indications that spring will soon come. Br. S. M. Blair, just returned from S. L. City, informs me that Presᵗ Young is much pleased with my military school. Also, that he spoke well of me, and hoped surveying would recruit my health.

Susan J. has not been well for some time. She complains of a pain in her left side.

I have written frequently to Susan E. but do not hear often from her. I do not know the reason.

Tuesday, April 3, 1861—To day we start for Conference, leaving Louisa Ballif,[35] a daughter of Mrs. Ballif to take care of home. It was snowing heavily, and the roads almost impassible, the mud being almost hub deep. We had to walk much, through Snow, mud and water. Drove via Wellsville, 16 miles, and stopped with Br. A. Baker[36]

April 4, 1861—Arrived at Brigham city at dusk, after a very toilsome days travel. We did not know where to stop, and prayed the Lord to direct us to a welcome place. We felt to go to Br. Lorenzo Snow's, and were kindly welcomed, and felt at home. We found Sister Leonora Morley, an old friend.[37]

33 This was from the last month's elections ("Election of Territorial and Other Officers by the Legislative Assembly," *Deseret News*, December 26, 1860; Utah Digital Newspapers).

34 This is likely George L. Farrell. The other man, Francis Gunnell was with the first group who, in 1856, explored Cache Valley for possible settlement; in 1857 he was appointed the first recorder of Cache County. Gunnell was a schoolteacher and loved to sing (Ricks and Cooley, *History of Cache Valley*, 34, 35, 90).

35 Louisa Balliff was one of the first teachers in the area (Somers, *History of Logan*, 179).

36 This could be Albert Mowry Baker, a Mendon farmer who also served as justice of the peace. Mendon, Utah, is a western Cache Valley settlement just north of Wellsville (Godfrey and Godfrey, *Utah Years*, 270).

37 She is likely a member of the Isaac Morley family. Isaac Morley was instrumental in the settlement of Manti.

April 5, 1861—Drove to Weber River, stopping with Mrs. Cornwell.

April 6, 1861—Camped within Seven Miles of S. L. City, very tired.

April 7, 1861—Arrived in S. L. City about 9 A.M. Went to Conference in the afternoon.

Monday, April 8, 1861—Went to Chaffin's and got an Ambrotype of Susan and her two children. Stopped with Br. Heywood to night.

April 9, 1861—I started for Manti in a heavy storm (snow) leaving Susan J. to go home with G. L. Farrell and Birdno's team. I drove to Lehi, with B. F. Johnson, and stopped with Tho. Karren's[38]

April 11, 1861—Arrived at Santaquin, and found Aunt Melissa's Baby dead. Its mother died a few months ago. We buried the baby this evening.

[page 216]

MY BLESSING BY ISAAC MORLEY.

April 12, 1861—To day I arrived at Fountain Green, and found Albey L. Sherman and family all well.[39]

April 13, 1861—Arrived at Manti, and found Susan E. and all the children all well, as also John Eager and family.

Monday, April 15, 1861—To day I was requested by Orson Hyde to act as clerk at a trial beginning today, wherein Geo. Peacock and Warren Snow are to be tried before Orson Hyde, Isaac Morley, And^w^ S. Love and Wm Broadhed. myself, John Eager and—Robinson were clerks.

April 16, 1861—The trial closed this evening.

April 17, 1861—Spent all day in writing out my minutes of trial. In the evening I read them at a public meeting, the several charges being commented on by the judges. The affair finished at midnight.

Thursday, April 18, 1861—To day I received the following blessing from Br. Morley:—

Brother James Henry, in the name of Jesus I lay my hands upon thy head and I seal the blessing of comfort and consolation upon thy head for thy good; and I say unto thee this shall rest upon thy mind as a comfort and seal of fellowship between me and thyself, and between thee and thy brethren, for thy God is thy friend and will be thy monitor. Thou shalt be a blessing to thy brethren; they shall administer to thee of their substance. Thou shalt increase in knowledge and usefulness. Thou shalt dwell as a confidant in the midst of thy brethren. Thy fellowship will increase; responsibilities will be placed upon thee that will comfort thy heart. Because of thy usefulness thou wilt be a blessing to thy brethren. The fruit of the earth will crown thy labors; intelligence will be given to thee for the building up of thy kingdom. Thou shalt realize an increase of wealth, that thy time and thy talents may be spent for the building up of Christs kingdom. Thou shalt share in all the blessings of Abraham in thy priesthood,—in the fruit of thy body,—in thy everlasting inheritance. Thou shalt be honored through the keys of the holy anointing of redeeming thy progenitors and stand at the head of a numerous posterity. I place this seal for thy comfort, that you may realize the fulfilling of the seal.

[page 217]

GET HOME

April 18, 1861—Tis the voice of the Comforter, and I bless thee and seal thee up to the enjoyment of immortality and an eternal increase, in the name of Jesus, Amen. (John Eager, Scribe)

Friday, April 19, 1861—Started home, and went to Fountain Green yesterday To day arrived at Santaquin, and found Father Johnson with Nephi, Seth, Janette, Nephi's indian girl, and a boy—Tumpumb—now named Dan, just come up from Iron county. Sixtus and Seth are going to the states for some cotton machinery. We had a very pleasant meeting.

38 Thomas Karren (1810–76) was a Lehi, Utah, pioneer. He was called as a missionary to the Sandwich Islands from 1852 to 1866 and was also a private in Company E of the Mormon Battalion (Norma Baldwin Ricketts, ed., *Arizona's Honeymoon Trail and Mormon Wagon Roads* [Mesa, AZ: Cox, 2001], 29).

39 Fountain Green, Utah, was located in the northeastern part of Sanpete County, Utah. It was a small settlement approximately ninety miles south of Salt Lake. Albey L. Sherman was an inlaw via Martineau's marriage to Susan Julia Sherman Martineau.

Sunday, April 21, 1861—Started home, and encountered a severe storm. We stopped at Provo, with Mrs. Adaline Hugh Manning.[40]

April 22, 1861—Camped with the family, near the Point-of-the-mountain.

April 23, 1861—Arrived at D. T. LeBaron's in S. L. City.

Wednesday, April 24, 1861—Got daguerreotypes of all Susan's family and myself. Sent Susan J's likeness to Mary Julia Johnson, by Sixtus.

April 25, 1861—Again started for home,—the weather very cold.

April 30, 1861—Arrived at Logan, all well.

Saturday, May 4, 1861—Moved Susan E. into the house I got of Blair, in Lot 6 Block 14.

Saturday, May 11, 1861—Engaged as book keeper with the new firm of Box & Co at $75.00 [$1,624] pr month, receiving goods at 20% discount with the privilege of attending to surveying when needful.

Wednesday, May 22, 1861—Began Surveying at Smithfield.

May 23, 1861—Finished surveying this evening.

May 24, 1861—Got home, Drilled with the Minute Men,[41] and clerked in the afternoon.

May 28, 1861—Began Surveying the Logan hay lands to day, wading all day in water, and continued until Saturday June 1, having surveyed 1200 acres.

June 10, 1861—Box & Co having dissolved partnership, I continued keeping books for Thos. Box.[42]

June 30, 1861—Have been clerking, and also did some surveying at Millville.

[page 218]

SUSAN E'S VISION.

June 30, 1861—During the past month I have been improving my lot, putting up two log houses near the first one & digging a well,

Monday, July 15, 1861—This evening the minute men were ordered to camp on the Church farm, to watch the movements of a large Band—about 3000—of indians from Oregon, who are camped near Millville, and have made threats to clean out all the settlements. Fifty mounted men of whom I am one made our camp near the old Church farm house, and about a mile from the indians.

July 16, 1861—To day day we erected a bowery of poles, willows and grass to protect us from the scorching sun. Thos E. Ricks is our commander.[43]

July 17, 1861—I returned to Logan to get some things, and Susan E. informed me of a vision she had seen during the night of the 15th & 16th. Being soundly asleep, she suddenly awaked by a sound like a rushing wind, but there was no wind. She saw a light shining in the room, round, and as large as a wagon wheel; and while she looked at it wondering, a man's face appeared in it, and she gradually saw more and more of him until she could see his feet. He looked intently at her, with a kind, benevolent expression. All the rest of the room was in darkness. Then he began to vanish away, beginning at the feet, until finally the face disappeared, and then the light.

She lay awake for a good while wondering what it could mean, and wishing she had spoken to him. She finally fell asleep, and after a time awoke again, instantly as at first, and the same scene was repeated, only this time she saw him only to his waist. He was dressed in a suit of brown each time, was like a man 5 ft 8 middling stout. She raised herself, leaning on her elbow, and finally asked him what he wanted [. . .] ~~He~~ saying, "who are you, what do you want!" He smiled pleasantly upon her, and slowly disappeared.

She then became alarmed, and did not go to sleep any more that night. She could form no idea who he was, or what he wanted—nor can I.

[page 219]

HORSE THIEVES DISCOVERED AND KILLED. CHAS F. BORN.

Sunday, July 21, 1861—Had meeting at camp in the afternoon, at which Elders E. T. Benson, P. Maughan and S. M. Blair were present. During last

40 The L. S. Manning family was among the original Provo, Utah, pioneers (Holzapfel, *History of Utah County*, 21).

41 The original Minute Men were called by Brigham Young in 1856 to aid in the immigration of the Saints from Missouri to Salt Lake City (Arrington, *Brigham Young*, 250, 254–55, 260).

42 This could be Thomas Box of Salt Lake City.

43 Thomas E. Ricks was among the original settlers of Cache Valley. (Ricks and Cooley, *History of Cache Valley*, 41, 49–50).

week several scouting parties were sent out, resulting in the discovery of a retreat of horse thieves, four in number, which were pursued by our party about 35 miles, swimming Bear River and crossing a high mountain into S. L. Valley. They pursued them two days. Some of them were shot in the chase. One, Delos Gibson, escaped with another, and hid in some oak brush on the mountain side not far from Brigham City.[44] At one time their pursuers were close to them,—within a few steps,—and then turned back again. This was fortunate for them, for had they advanced a step or two further, they would have been shot, Gibson and his comrade having their pistols leveled on them, and cocked. Gibson was afterwards taken and hung, confessing the above.

July 23, 1861—Bought a wild horse of Henry W. Miller[45] for ten sheep. I want him for scouting service. The indians are still camped in their place, and we in ours watching their movements. In the settlements, the Infantry meet morning and evening for roll call, armed and equipped; and provisions are cooked, so that they may march any where at an hour's notice.

July 24, 1861—Came home this morning, and found Susan J. quite unwell. In the afternoon she was confined of a boy, weighing 8¼ lbs. at 6 o'clock P.M. We named him Charles Freeman Martineau. I named him Freeman in honor of the 24th inst.—the day of our deliverance from the mobs of Illinois and Missouri. He had a little gray hair on the crown of his head—the rest of his hair was black. He was marked by an indian who frightened Susan during the last winter.

Fig. 4.1—Charles Freeman Martineau, son of Susan Julia and James Henry. Courtesy of James Henry Martineau Family Organization.

[page 220]

GO TO S. L. CITY WITH SUSAN J. NARROW ESCAPE IN BOX ELDER CAÑON.

July 26, 1861—I brought news to Elder Benson that the indians were leaving the valley, having got frightened at our drilling the afternoon before.

The authorities had given them several thousand pounds of flour and about a dozen beef cattle.

I remained with Susan until the camp was broken up, which was on the 27th inst.

June 28, 1861—Have been helping to take care of Susan J. who is and has been quite poorly.

August 11, 1861—Made returns of our election of the 5th inst, and sent report to the Secretary of the Territory.

Monday, September 30, 1861—To day myself and Susan J. started for Salt Lake City, and in going down Box Elder Cañon had a very narrow escape. One of the tugs got unhooked going down the kanyon, the tongue dropped to the ground, the wagon ran against the team, and away they ran down the rocky, crooked, narrow road, I holding them as well as I could. Suddenly, after going thus about half a mile

44 Delos Gibson was a notorious criminal. In 1859 he shot James and Luke S. Johnson. He escaped from the Utah Penitentiary in 1862. He was recaptured and "while being returned to Salt Lake City, attempted escape by swimming the Weber River and was shot and killed" (James B. Hill, "History of Utah State Prison: 1850–1952" [master's thesis, Brigham Young University, 1952], quoted in Ray Hauter, "History of the Old Sugarhouse Prison—1850 to 1952," *Utah Peace Officer* 79, no. 1 [Spring 2002]).

45 Henry W. Miller was a sheep rancher and a resident of Farmington, Utah. He promoted the idea of "Fremont Island," in the middle of the Great Salt Lake, as an ideal place to raise sheep (Roberts and Sadler, *History of Weber County*, 21–22).

along a very dangerous road, and just as we came to the worst place of all, all the tugs unhooked at once, and the horses jerked me by the lines out of the wagon, which started backwards down a little hill to run off backwards into the creek below, the bank being several feet high, and the water dashing madly along. I just Caught the end of the tongue with the crook of my elbow and held the carriage until Susan got out and blocked the wheels.

We felt thankful to our Father for our deliverance for it was by his power we were saved. alone.

October 2, 1861—Arrived without further incident at S. L. City. We found that Uncle Jo[s] E. Johnson and family had arrived from the States: also Aunt Almira and her family, having run away from her husband, who is a Gentile and unwilling she should come here with her children.[46]

[page 221]

FOUNDED THE LOGAN DRAMATIC ASSOCIATION.[47]

October 1861—While in town we visited at Box's, Harriet Snyder's and Aunt Almira's. Did not feel welcome at Uncle D. T. LeBarron's. I had given him 80 lbs. flour and some pounds of butter. Sold my skins, and got some necessaries amounting to $22.[00] [$476]

At Conference, Pres[t] Young showed the only two ways in which husband and wife can be separated. The temple is to be built, 300 families are to be sent south to raise cotton, and 400 teams sent back for the poor.

Friday, October 11, 1861—Started for home, arriving there without incident, on the 13th and found all well at home.

Friday, October 17, 1861—Went with Susan E. to Richmond, and did some surveying, returning thence home on the 19th.

Monday, October 21, 1861—To day, myself, Benjamin Cluff and Jacob West[48] organized the Logan Dramatic Association. I was elected Secretary and Treasurer.

November 11, 1861—To day Miss Christina Rockingbeau—a Swiss German, began to live with us.

December 9, 1861—To day Jo[s] E. Hyde began to live with us.[49] He is to work 3 days a week for his board, washing and mending and I am to teach him surveying.

Thursday, December 12, 1861—I began this day to paint our scenery for theatre. We have already had two rehearsals of the "Jacobite" at Br. Benson's house who assisted us, his daughters Emma and Belle taking parts.

January 1, 1862—During the winter we have played once a week to pretty good houses, and have received considerable commendation. Our company consists of myself, J. E. Hyde, C. I Goodwin, W. Goodwin,[50] B. Cluff, J. West, and Rich[d] Evans.[51] Of ladies there were misses Emma and Belle Benson, Susan J. and Mrs. Cluff, besides some whom we called in to assist us as occasion required.

46 Joseph E. Johnson was a pioneer in the settlements of southern Utah and northern Arizona (Joseph Ellis Johnson Collection; Special Collections, J. Willard Marriott Library, University of Utah, Salt Lake City).

47 Mendon, Utah, was considered to have the first dramatic association, but this entry illustrates that Logan was not far behind. Drama was an important part of the pioneer social and recreational culture (Ricks and Cooley, *History of Cache Valley*, 425–27).

48 Jacob West was a Logan farmer. He apparently fell out of favor with the Church and "abandoned Mormonism" (Somers, *History of Logan*, 71; A. J. Simmonds, *The Gentile Comes to Cache Valley* [Logan, UT: Utah State University Press, 1976], 32).

49 Somers lists Joseph E. Hyde as a laborer (Somers, *History of Logan*, 62). There is also a J. W. Hyde who later served the as the *Logan Journal* city editor (Ricks and Cooley, *History of Cache Valley*, 402).

50 The Goodwins were described by Simmonds as "men of property and influence" (Simmonds, *The Gentile Comes to Cache Valley*, 33, 74). According to Somers, they were farmers and landowners who played a major role in settling the area west of the Bear River (Somers, *History of Logan*, 61; Peterson, *History of Cache County*, 145). C. I. Goodwin eventually left the Church over political differences with the leaders and moved to California at the time of the Edmunds-Tucker Act outlawing polygamy (Peterson, *History of Cache County*, 151). William Goodwin was the treasurer of the Logan Cooperative Mercantile and Manufacturing Institution in 1869, but he was later disfellowshipped (Ricks and Cooley, *History of Cache Valley*, 188; Simmonds, *The Gentile Comes to Cache Valley*, 11, 30.

51 Richard Evans was listed as a stationary engineer (Somers, *History of Logan*, 60).

Br. Benson gave us all the help and encouragement he could, but Br. P. Maughan always acted oddly towards us. I found the reason some ten years afterwards.

[page 222]

NEPHI BORN. GO TO S. L. CITY HORSEBACK. MARY MARRIED.

Tuesday, March 11, 1862—This morning at a quarter past 2 A. M. Susan E. presented me with a boy, whom we named Nephi. There was no one present except Susan J. and myself, but Susan got along very well, considering. We were taken by surprise, and had nothing ready for her—not even a bed. Mrs. Earl finally came when all was over.

The boy weighed 9 6/16 lbs.

March 16, 1862—Susan E. was up this morning and swept the room.

Last Monday, March 10th our Theatre was disorganized and J. F. Reed appointed President.[52]

On March 3, there was an election for officers to organize a state government, at which I was clerk.

I was also Secretary of a mass meeting called to choose delegates to a Constitutional Convention held in S. L. City last December.[53]

Tuesday, April 1, 1862—This morning I start with E. T. Benson on horseback to act as witness in a trial before the High Council in S. L. City, in which Thos Box appears against S. M. Blair. Difficulties have arisen in reference to the settlement of their business. The snow is still covering most of the valley, making traveling tedious. Stopped at Mendon.

April 2, 1862—Traveled all day in a driving snow storm. Stopped at Br. Reese's in Brigham city.

April 3, 1862—Stopped at Ogden, with Bp. Chauncey W. West.

April 4, 1862—Rode to Session Settlement, and stopped at Br. Carter's, the roads so far have been dreadful. Snow in some parts of the road knee deep.

52 John F. Reed was among the early settlers and a local merchant of the Cache Valley. He was later disfellowshipped from the Church (Somers, *History of Logan*, 68; Peterson, *History of Cache County*, 145; Simmonds, *The Gentile Comes to Cache Valley*, 101–2).

53 The Utah Constitutional Conventions were political meetings charged with moving the territory toward statehood.

April 5, 1862—Arrived in S. L. City, and stopped with Br. Box. Went to the theatre with Melissa Johnson.

April 9, 1862—Have attended Conference, which closed to day. In the evening Mary Johnson was married to Heber John Richards, son of Willard Richards, at the house of Uriah J. E. Johnson. John Eager was also there, together with about a dozen of the family connexion and friends. Elder F. D. Richards performed the ceremony.[54]

[page 223]

CROSS THE MOUNTAIN IN SNOW. START TO BEAR LAKE VALLEY, EXPLORING

April 10 & 11, 1862—Attended the trial before the High Council, which resulted in favor of Br. Box.

April 12, 1862—Started home alone, and arrived there on the 16th after a very hard time in the newly thawed mud. I stopped at Brigham City with Judge Samuel Smith,[55] who treated me very kindly. I thought I would try to cross the Mountains to Paradise, instead of by Mendon, thereby saving nearly a days travel, but had a very hard time. I was more than half a day going four miles down the mountain to Paradise, floundering along through deep snow, and at times hardly able to extricate myself and mare from its depths. When I arrived at Paradise I was completely exhausted, and so was my mare, but a comfortable rest with Bp. James family retored us.

Found all well at home.

54 Heber John Richards (1840–1919) is a son of F. D. Richards. The marriage was to Mary Julie Johnson.

55 Samuel Smith could be a cousin to the Prophet Joseph Smith. Paradise, Utah, was founded in 1860. It sits in the southern end of Cache Valley. In 1861, David James was called as bishop by Ezra T. Benson and Peter Maughan. Bishop James had an excellent relationship with the local Native Americans, believing it was better to feed them than to fight them. Each time Chief Washakie, a Shoshone, would call on Bishop James for beef, flour, and vegetables, the chief would look to the east and offer the bishop land in exchange for the food. Each time the chief came the same routine was followed: food was furnished, and the same land was sold over and over again to the bishop (Ricks and Cooley, *History of Cache Valley*, 54).

July 4, 1862—Had a good celebration. I was Marshall of the Day.[56]

July 8, 1862—This morning, having been notified last night, I started with an exploring party over the mountains into Bear Lake Country. In consequence of high water, we had to go by way of the Logan Ferry, at Rick's, by Mendon Wellsville, Hyrum, to Millville, about 30 miles. In crossing the river at Millville, the water went over our horses backs, wetting our provisions and blankets.

July 9, 1862—Started with 8 others up Blacksmith fork Cañon, Wm Garr being Captain of the Company,[57] myself the historian. There were T. E. Ricks, L. Vanluven, J. Bowen, L. Clifford, A. Bingham and two others from Hyrum. Went about 15 miles up the Cañon and camped. Road very dangerous to travel, winding along precipices where it was all we could do to squeeze along the face of the cliffs, the precipice being hundreds of feet high, and the path so narrow a horse could barely squeeze along. It made my flesh creep on my bones, as I led my horse, pulling and coaxing him along. We had no accident, however.

[page 224]

EXPLORING THE MOUNTAINS EAST OF CACHE

July 10, 1862—Continued up the Cañon, which grew wider as we went. The Cañon opens into a long narrow valley running north and south between the two paralell ranges of the Wahsatch Range. We crossed the eastern and higher range, traveling over much deep snow, into a large valley lying south of Bear Lake Valley. We camped on that side, by a large patch of snow. We suffered dreadfully, as did also our horses, with gnats in the daytime and large mosquitoes at night, which kept us from sleeping, except in a cloud of smoke. In the day time we had to fight the gnats without ceasing, and even then we swelled up badly about the head. Our horses were almost crazy with them.

July 11, 1862—Started home. Saw a grizzly bear, and myself and six others tried to capture him—unsuccessfully, however. He ran away, crashing through the brush. It was lucky he ran away, for if he had attacked us, some of us must have been killed. I had only a small five shooter pistol.

Soon after, we killed a large black tailed deer, which made a supper and breakfast for us. I and a few others went about five miles southward, and found a trail leading to Ogden Hole Cañon. The top of the mountains was covered with a heavy growth of quaking aspen and pine timber.

There was much sign of elk, deer, and bear, the ground being tracked up in places as if there had been a herd of two year old Cattle there.

July 12, 1862—Started down the Little Bear River Cañon towards Paradise, the road being exceedingly rough and dangerous. F. E. Ricks and L. Clifford picked up pieces of Iron ore. We arrived at the Logan River in the afternoon and determined to try and cross it though we knew it was a very dangerous undertaking, the river rushing by with a furious current. The river was ¼ of a mile wide, about breast deep, and swift.

[page 225]

YET. ANOTHER TRIP, EXPLORING NORTH.

July 12, 1862—We effected a crossing without accident, and got home at dusk. We considered that it is impracticable at this time to try to make a road over the mountains, on account of the great expense, and because for about six months in the year the snow is too deep.

I was notified to be ready for another trip north in three days, with two weeks provisions.

The following is a sketch of our last trip:—

Thursday, July 17, 1862—Today our company appointed to explore a feasible wagon route from this valley eastward, met at the bowery and were organized as follows:—T. E. Ricks, Captain, Wm Maughan and Wm Garr, Counsellors, J. H. Martineau Topographical Engineer, I J. Clark, Chaplain, G. L. Farrell clerk and Serg^t of the Guard, I. J. Clark Interpreter,[58]

56 J. H. Martineau, "Fourth of July Celebrations," *Deseret News*, July 16, 1862; Utah Digital Newspapers.

57 William Garr was among the early settlers in Cache Valley. He was appointed county sheriff when the county was organized (Peterson, *History of Cache County*, 28, 82; Ricks and Cooley, *History of Cache Valley*, 29–31, 90).

58 Israel J. Clark founded Clarkston, Utah. He was a Native American interpreter (Ricks and Cooley, *History of Cache*

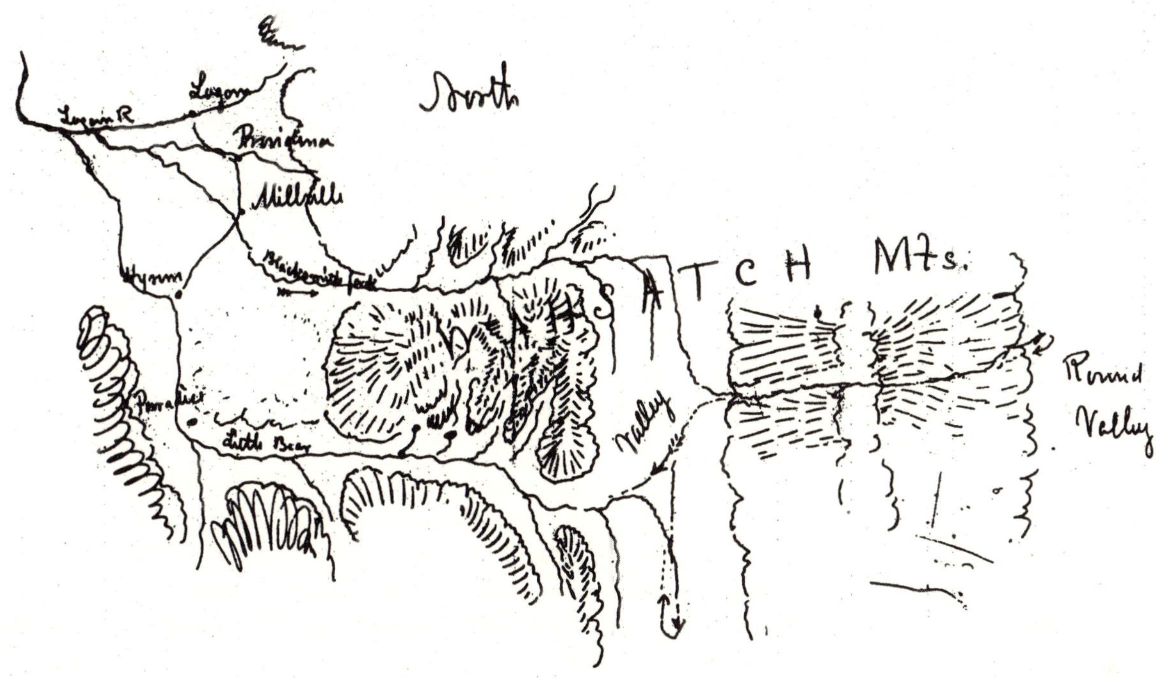

Fig. 4.2—Small map of Logan, Province, Millville, and Hyrum.

L. Collett[59] and J. P. Clifford,[60] assistants; besides the following persons:—Jo^{s} Baker,[61] Chas Bailey,[62] Evan Owens,[63] A. Bingham,[64] Jo^{s} Bowen, Wm Watterson,[65] J. H. Goodwin,[66] Chas A. Benson,[67] Isaac Woolf,[68] D. J. Merrill,[69] V. J. Cooper, W. H. Harris,[70] T. Tidwell, W. Head,[71] and J. S. Nelson,[72] 23 in all, with five pack animals, and a wagon, boat, and two span of mules.

We left Logan at 9 A.M. arriving at Cub River, 22 miles in the afternoon, and proceeded to cross, an operation very difficult and dangerous, the river being "up" and spread very wide—say ¼ of a mile. We final-

Valley, 40, 61, 79, 82, 277).

59 This Collett could be Sylvanus Collett, who settled south of Bear River and north of Mendon (Ricks and Cooley, *History of Cache Valley*, 82).

60 J. P. Clifford was a member of the high council for the first Cache Valley Stake (Ricks and Cooley, *History of Cache Valley*, 275).

61 Joseph Baker was among the original settlers in the valley (Somers, *History of Logan*, 30; Ricks and Cooley, *History of Cache Valley*, 29).

62 Charles R. Bailey was one of the original valley settlers and lived in Wellsville (Peterson, *History of Cache County*, 247; Ricks and Cooley, *History of Cache Valley*, 154).

63 Evan Owens was among the early settlers of Wellsville (Godfrey and Godfrey, *Utah Years*, 226).

64 Alonzo Bingham was among the original settlers who moved from Cedar City, Utah, to Wellsville (Ricks and Cooley, *History of Cache Valley*, 44–45).

65 William Watterson was a farmer living in Logan. He was among the first settlers of the valley (Ricks and Cooley, *History of Cache Valley*, 82; Simmonds, *The Gentile Comes to Cache Valley*, 71).

66 This could be James Goodwin, who was a store owner in Logan (Simmonds, *The Gentile Comes to Cache Valley*, 89–93).

67 Little is known about Charles Benson. He was the brother of Ezra T. Benson and accused of shooting a David Crockett on February 14, 1873. He was later hanged for the offense (Peterson, *History of Cache County*, 98–99; Somers, *History of Logan*, 323–24).

68 Isaac Woolf was a resident of Hyde Park, just south of Logan.

69 This could be Dudley Merrill, who was an 1858 settler in Smithfield, north of Logan (Ricks and Cooley, *History of Cache Valley*, 42).

70 This could be William Harris, a resident of Benson, Utah (Godfrey and Godfrey, *Utah Years*, 386).

71 This would likely be William Head, a resident of Preston, Idaho (Ricks and Cooley, *History of Cache Valley*, 71, 74; Godfrey and Godfrey, *Utah Years*, 454).

72 John Nelson was listed as a Logan farmer (Somers, *History of Logan*, 66).

ly all got across a little after dark, after much trouble, wet to the skin and tired out. I had my horse "Jack" on this trip as on the last,—no better animal can be found anywhere for such business.

[page 226]

EXPLORING IN BEAR LAKE VALLEY.

July 17, 1862—He is wise, brave, trusty, hardy, cool and not easily excited, and can climb rocks almost as well as a man—a splendid animal, which I got last fall of B. Cluff.

We camped on the other bank of the river, wet and cold, G. L. Farrell was taken sick, and we administered to him, and in the morning he was able to travel. In the night our horses stampeded, and after searching about an hour recovered about one third of them. We got the rest in the morning.

July 18, 1862—Traveled up Worm Creek Cañon about 15 miles to Mink Creek, which is about four or five feet deep, 45 or 50 wide, and very swift. Our crossing occupied a half day, nearly, and it was by great exertions we got over at all. Some men stripped, and, mounted on the largest horses, finally got across. We took our boat, with a strong lariat from the bow to each bank, got it across the stream with our provisions, guns, &c, and got the horses over by having a lariat fastened to them, and being pulled over by the men on the other side, which enabled them to keep up against the stream.

July 19, 1862—To day our route lay over the main ridge of the Mountains, and was very slow. Many times we held the wagon from tipping over, by main strength on the steep side hills, and let it down hills, by means of a rope held behind by the men. Near the summit we dined and found some good slate rock. We descended from the summit about 1½ miles, and camped. There is an immense amount of poles and timber on these mountains; the poles, especially are wonderfully tall and straight, and so thick one can hardly ride through them.

[page 227]

IN BEAR LAKE VALLEY.

Sunday, July 20, 1862—Went about 1½ miles down the Cañon and came out upon a high bench in the valley, which was clothed in a most luxuriant green. We traveled southward for some miles crossing several beautiful clear brooks, bordered with strawberries and full of fish, and at 2 P.M. we ~~camped~~ nooned on Bear River. We crossed the river, swimming the horses, and occupying four hours in the passage of the river which here was very deep, with a current of about five miles an hour. After crossing we proceeded about ten miles up the river and Camped on its banks, not far from the old camp of Peg Leg, a mountaineer, and near where the river enters the valley from the east. We camped in some tall Cottonwoods. The currants were just turning ripe a little. In Cache County they are ripe.

We found much travel to Oregon passing, and saw three Companies of Emigrants, one of which, consisting of about forty wagons and men, was much alarmed, thinking we would attack them, though of only half their force. We passed on, after asking them a few questions. We found next day that they started that night and traveled about 40 miles without stopping.

Monday, July 21, 1862—To day we sent two parties to explore two routes over the mountains, of which parties I was one. We went over the mountains east about 8 miles, and found a better place for a road than the present. About 3 P.M. Started homeward by way of Soda Springs and camped on a small Stream near the north end of the valley, where we had a feast of strawberries.

July 22, 1862—Nooned at Soda Springs. These are wonderful springs strongly impregnated with Soda, and with sugar and flavoring, as good as any soda water of the shops. We found remains of many wagons, and found the bones of a person buried last year, apparently. We thought it was a cache of goods, at first.

[page 228]

SODA SPRINGS.[73] HOME.

July 22, 1862—Here Bear River turns westward and passes southerly into Cache Valley. We crossed a dry open valley about ten or twelve miles, and passed thru ancient craters, the lava of which lay abundantly scattered around. The whole Country is volcanic. We

73 Soda Springs is located in southeast Idaho, Caribou County. Called Beer Springs by the early explorers, it was at the junction of the Oregon and California Trails.

saw many large Cracks in the earth, extending generally nearly north and south and of unknown depth. I named this Crater Valley. We entered another group of mountains on the west of this valley, and camped on beautiful creek, the waters of which flow northward into the Port Neuf, and then by Snake River into the Columbia and the Pacific.

Wednesday, July 23, 1862—This day we entered Marsh Valley, and turned Southeast, towards home. Camped on Marsh Creek, where Br. Tidwell[74] killed a deer, which was welcome to us for our provisions had just given out. We ate the deer for supper and breakfast.

July 24, 1862—Went about ten miles to Bear River, which is here much wider and larger than in Bear Lake valley. We spent some time trying to find a place where we could swim the horses across, the river being very wide, deep and swift, lined generally with thick willows, and marshy—quicksand banks. We finally found a place, and after about 6 hours hard labor, all got safely across and camped on the opposite bank.

July 25, 1862—Arrived at Franklin about noon and had a good dinner which our long fasting made doubly grateful We arrived home about 4 P.M. having traveled about 200 miles on this trip. We have been greatly blessed on the whole journey, for which I thank our Father in Heaven.

While on the trip, I had a large boil on my forehead, which was very painful, until "Jack" threw back his head, passing through the timber when a limb struck his face, and hit my boil with his head, bursting the boil, and almost making me faint with pain. It was a ridiculous accident.

[page 229]

GO TO SPRING LAKE AND SANTAQUIN, BUY A LEVEL. LEAVE SUSAN J.

July 26, 1862—Wrote out my minutes, and made a map of our travels for Pres[t] Young.

August 4, 1862—Was clerk of election to day, and was elected Surveyor for the next two years.

74 Thomas Tidwell was bishop of the Richmond Utah Ward (Ricks and Cooley, *History of Cache Valley*, 53, 277).

[**August 8, 1862**—]Went to Franklin to survey a town, which I did and returned on the 14th

Thursday, August 20, 1862—To day Susan J. and I started for S. L. City. In going down Box Elder Cañon we had a narrow escape: the breast strap broke, and let the tongue down, but the near horse held the wagon and the other horse until I got out and blocked the wheels and fixed the harness. We stopped at Brigham City with Elder L. Snow. We arrived at S. L. City on the 22, and next day drove to Battle Creek, next day to Spring Lake where Uncle J. E. Johnson lives and on the

August 25, 1862— arrived at Santaquin.

August 27, 1862—Here I traded for the level[75] I had come after, of a Mr. Wagner, an Engineer who had known and worked with my father. I gave him a horse, saddle and bridle worth about $100.[00] [$2,166] I started for home the same day at 11 A.M. leaving Susan J. who wishes to visit her relatives awhile. Drove to Provo.

August 28, 1862—Drove to S. L. City, and remained until noon of the 29th.

August 29, 1862—When I left for Logan, having bought a Jack for $100.[00] to be paid in Wheat

August 31, 1862—Arrived at home, and found all well.

September 3, 1862—Went with Susan E. after Choke Cherries, and budded some wild haw thorns with apple buds.

September 6, 1862—Today I received an appointment from Col. J. C. Little of Assistant Assessor of Internal revenue for Cache County—the 5th District.[76] I filed my bonds before Judge Maughan. Attended City Council in the afternoon.

September 7, 1862—Took Susan E. the two Mrs. Ballifs and Mrs. Montrose to Providence [and preached.]

75 This was a survey instrument used to measure differences in elevation.

76 This was likely Jesse C. Little, who was among the first Mormon explorers of the Cache Valley area. He was the second counselor to the Presiding Bishopric of the Church at this time (Godfrey and Godfrey, *Utah Years*, 309; Arrington, *Brigham Young*, 128; Somers, *History of Logan*, 17; "United States Internal Revenue Tax," *Deseret News,* September 24, 1862; Utah Digital Newspapers).

[page 230]

MY BLESSING BY JOHN YOUNG IN APRIL 11. 1862

September, 1862—The following is a copy of a Patriarchal blessing I received last spring, from John Young,[77] Patriarch: which, was given April 11. 1862. L. O. Littlefield,[78] scribe:—

(Br. John Young was then Patriarch to the Whole Church.)

Brother James, in the name of the Lord Jesus Christ our Savior, I lay my hand upon your head to bless you, and seal and ratify and confirm all former blessings, and feel to bless you in the name of the Lord, and say inasmuch as you endeavor to do right you shall be blessed from this time henceforth and forever, with those blessings that your heart desires in righteousness before your Heavenly Father. You have embraced the gospel of Salvation with an honest heart and full determination to live the life of the righteous and to do good in your day and generation, and help build up the kingdom on the Earth; therefore no good thing shall be witheld from you. You are a lawful heir to the blessings of the new and everlasting covenant, and inasmuch as you have gathered up with the Saints, willing rather to suffer affliction with the people of God than to enjoy the pleasures of the world for a season, you shall be a lawful heir to the priesthood, being a literal descendant of Joseph through the lineage of Ephraim, entitled to all the blessings which have been promised to the faithful sons of Abraham, which blessings shall rest upon you. You shall be a blessing to your father's house and hold a fullness of the holy priesthood, and be a blessing to your forefathers and to all you are associated with. You shall have wives and children and a numerous posterity upon the mountains of Israel, and they shall be blessed in their generations. You shall have power to govern and control yourself, and honor your holy priesthood, and your name shall be honorable in Israel. Your mind shall expand to comprehend the principles of the Kingdom. You shall be a mighty man in Israel. The spirit of wisdom and council and decision shall rest upon you. You shall become a bright and shining light. The gifts and graces of the Spirit shall rest upon your head. You shall have power to administer in holy things, and to the sick and afflicted, and they shall be healed and blessed under your administration.

[page 231]

1862—You never shall be tempted above what you are able to bear. Your pathway shall shine brighter and brighter even unto the perfect day. No power shall be able to turn you aside from the holy commandments delivered unto you. Your feet shall stand in sure places. What you put your hand to do shall prosper. You shall have houses and lands, fields and orchards, flocks and herds, for this is the heritage of the sons of Jacob. Truth and righteousness shall be the girdle of your loins. You shall have power to do much good in your day and generation, and be a minister of Salvation to those that sit in darkness and the shadow of death. I seal upon your head the blessings of health and life, and say you shall live on the earth 'till your hair becomes as white as the pure wool. You shall see the Salvation of the Lord and the overthrow of Babylon, and live to be gathered up to the center stake of Zion, and your eyes shall see the temples of the Lord, and your feet shall stand in his holy courts. You shall assist in gathering home Israel, and become a mighty hunter to look up the lost sheep of the House of Israel. You may have to pass through straightened circumstances, but there shall always be a way for your escape. Many may fall upon your right hand and upon your left, but put your trust in your Heavenly Father, and not a hair of your head shall fall. No enemy shall have power over you, but you shall have power over your enemies. All these blessings I seal upon your head, and all that your heart may desire in Righteousness before your Heavenly Father; therefore I say be of good cheer, for you shall have power to overcome, even to be a Savior upon Mount Zion: and have power to receive to yourself an everlasting inheritance in the new heavens and ~~the~~ new earth, and have power to gather your posterity around you, and rejoice with the great and the good. To this end I seal you up to a holy ressurrection, and say you shall come forth, clothed upon with your priestly garments, and have

77 John Willard Young (1844–1924) was the son of Brigham Young. He was known in Cache Valley for his role in the development of the Utah Northern Railroad.

78 Lyman O. Littlefield was a prominent Latter-day Saint writer of the nineteenth century (Godfrey and Godfrey, *Utah Years*, 168).

power to officiate in the holy ordinances for the restoration of your forefathers.

[page 232]

MY BLESSING. THATCHER'S HORSES STOLEN BY INDIANS.

1862—All these blessings are yours upon condition of your faithfulness and endurance to the end, and I can ~~say~~ seal you up to the day of redemption and say live forever. I do it according to the holy order and sealing power which binds on earth and for heaven, in the name of the Lord Jesus Christ, Amen.
[See Appendix 3 for letter from Ezra T. Benson inserted here.]

September 18, 1862—Lay in bed nearly all day, having had a chill the night previous. Towards night I took Susan E. down in the field, found some oats and gathered the peas.

September 20, 1862—Was sent to preach at Wellsville and Hyrum to preach on behalf of the Agricultural fair soon to be held. Had the good influence of the Holy Spirit and felt well.

Sunday, August 28, 1862—Today just about the close of the forenoon meeting word came that indians had stolen a band of 29 horses from the Church Farm.[79] Instantly all was bustle and excitement. Volunteers being called for to pursue. I was the first to volunteer. My horse was in the field over a mile distant and it took some little time to get him, so that by the time I got back the rest of the Company, about 20 in number, were starting. I had no time, therefore, to stop for dinner, but took one biscuit and hurried off. We followed their trail, which was made about midnight previously, and pressed on after them, being reinforced by men from Hyde Park, Smithfield, and Richmond as we passed along. Two miles north of Richmond they took to the mountains, and our route was very rough and hard to follow, but on we kept, stopping for nothing. As we passed to the east of Franklin J. E. Hyde ~~and N. W. Birdno~~ was detached to go there and get a pack horse load of provisions.

79 These are Church-owned farming co-ops.

[page 233]

WE PURSUE THE ROBBERS

September 28, 1862—Just at dark the advance came up with the indians who showed fight, and our boys waited for the rest to come up. By the time we got there it was pitch dark, and we could only cross the river (Cub River) with great difficulty. The night was very cold, cloudy, rainy, and dark, so that neither we nor the indians could travel. We accordingly camped (if it could be called so) within about 40 rods of each other, so that their guards and ours were close together. We lay down on the wet ground without fire or food, having had nothing since morning, wet and shivering with cold. I lay on the bare ground with my saddle and a small sheepskin for a cover, while the piercing wind and rain almost froze the blood in my veins, until near morning, when I got about an hour's sleep.

In the night Hyde passed close by us, but there being no fire and no noise, he went right past us, and so our supper went with him.

Monday, September 29, 1862—We started at dawn, but the enemy were as early as we, and had gone. We followed as fast as we could, and in about three hours found a horse they had left, belonging to Moses Thatcher:[80] he was glad to recover her. During the day we came across others that had given out, covered with foam, in this way we recovered eleven of them and sent them back, with some of our horses that had given out. We passed over high, steep mountains, clinging to our horses tails, and finally, about sun set came to where they had all separated, each one going away in a different direction to baffle our pursuit. This was in a body of thick timber several miles in extent. We found it useless to try to follow them any more, and on a vote being called of all the company, about 30 in number—it was decided to go back again, much to our disgust.

80 Moses Thatcher (1842–1909) moved to Cache Valley in 1859. He served a mission in Great Britain and was a prominent businessman in Cache Valley. He was an Apostle from 1879 to 1896, when he was dropped from the Quorum (Kenneth W. Godfrey, "Moses Thatcher in the Dock: His Trials, the Aftermath, and His Last Days," *Journal of Mormon History* 24 (Spring 1998): 54–88).

[page 234]

EAT. GET HOME THE THIRD DAY.

September 29, 1862—We hated to give up the chase, for we knew they were not far off, seeing very fresh sign, but there was no help for it. Passing down the Cañon we saw a black bear going up the steep hillside, but so fast we could not get a shot at him. He was fat and [sleek] and looked tempting, to men as hundry [hungry] as we were. During the day I ate about a handful of rose buds, and two dried Choke Cherries I found on a bush.

We had followed the Indians up Worm Creek Cañon, thence from its source northeasterly into the mountain

Last night three of our party, who could not find our camp because of our having no fire, stopped all night on a mountain, sitting up and holding their horses by their bridles—quite an uncomfortable way it was. In the morning they joined us. During the day we passed Bear Hunter's camp. He helped our enemies all he could to escape.

About 10 o'clock P.M. we met Hyde and four others with the provisions, and truly glad we were. We camped immediately and supped. It was by the merest chance we met at all, for it was pitchy dark. We were both following the same trail but in opposite directions. I did not eat much more than common, which surprised me. I made it up next day, however, my appetite having again become strong.

This night also was very cold, and I lay and shook all night.

September 30, 1862—We started before sun rise, having lost five of our horses. We traveled until near noon, and halted to rest our weary animals, sending men to hunt the missing ones. We all fell asleep in camp, and were awakened by the tramp of our recovered horses.

We took dinner in Franklin at 3 P.M. and got back to Logan in the evening. During these three days we had traveled about 100 miles.

[page 235]

GO TO S. L. CITY WITH SUSAN E. JACK FOUNDERS.

Wednesday, October 1, 1862—This afternoon word came that the Bannock indians, of Oregon were mustering at Soda Springs to sweep Cache Vally.[81] Preparations were made to defend ourselves, 25 men being sent to reinforce Franklin.

October 5, 1862—To day myself and 25 men went scouting as far as Franklin and returned the same night, seeing no signs of indians.

Tuesday, October 7, 1862—To day I took Susan E. with Elvira, John and Nephi starting to S. L. City, with a load of oats for the Contract filled by Br. Brigham. We left Henry and Moroni with Mrs. Painter.[82] We arrived at Wellsville at nearly night, but not feeling free to stop anywhere there, we kept on thinking to camp in the cañon, but kept traveling until we finally arrived at Brigham City late in the night, and stayed with John Rees.

October 10, 1862—We arrived in S. L. City to day, and found Sixtus and Editha. We stopped at Eugene Fulmer's[83]

October 11, 1862—This morning I found that my horse "Jack" had eaten ¾ bushel of wheat, and could not move an inch. I administered to him, and tried to bleed him, after which he got so he could walk a little. I spent most of the next two days trying to help him, as he was like to die, administering to him several times.

October 13, 1862—Started home and got as far as Farmington, where he was again much worse. We had to remain here with W. K. Rice four days. I sold

81 The Bannock tribe was a Native American tribe who lived in the area that is now southeastern Oregon and southern Idaho. They are related to the Paiutes. Their culture revolved around horses, and they were closely associated with the Northern Shoshone (Somers, *History of Logan*, 24).

82 This is likely Jane Herbert Painter, wife of George Painter, who was a resident of Logan (Donald G. Godfrey and Brigham Y. Card, eds., *The Diaries of Charles Ora Card: The Canadian Years, 1886–1903* [Salt Lake City: University of Utah Press, 1993], xxxvi; Hudson, *Charles Ora Card*, 180).

83 There were numerous Fulmers living in both Cache Valley and Salt Lake City. This is likely Eugene B. Fulmer of Salt Lake City, a relative of C. D. W. Fulmer of Logan (Ricks and Cooley, *History of Cache Valley*, 401–2).

my Jack to Rice for a barrel of molasses, a cow and five bushels of peaches.

October 17, 1862—We started again, arriving at Logan on the 19th.

October 21, 1862—Today Prest Young and company arrived here. Word came that several hundred troops had come near S. L. City from California.

October 22, 1862—Had a good meeting to day. The people voted to be willing to be classified in their labors; also to build a large Tabernacle. Pres. Young started home to day.

[page 236]

GO TO LOOK FOR TROOPS. BRING SUSAN J. HOME

Saturday, October 25, 1862—Br. Benson notified me to day, that he wished me to cross the Divide to Bear River Bridge to ascertain the truth of a report that a large body of troops were there. So myself, Bp. Preston, T. E. Ricks and two others went to see. Arriving at the ferry on Logan River, we found the boat was gone, but finally found a skiff sunk, which we raised and crossed in, swimming our horses. Tracks were found of a company going southward. We stopped all night—in Mendon.

October 26, 1862—Last night, at midnight, an express arrived at Mendon for that place to furnish 20 men to be ready to start at a minute's notice, to go and defend S. L. City from the troops. We started before sunrise and waded two miles, nearly, in the Mendon bottoms, through deep sloughs, frozen over almost hard enough to bear a man. Preston's and Ricks horses mired and they had to wade in the freezing water. We suffered much before the sun rose, our boots and legs being cased in ice. Got home a little after sun rise. Found men in Logan were under marching orders, as at Mendon.

November 7, 1862—Went to Franklin to survey. Preached and felt well.

November 11, 1862—Bought a second hand coat of W. Webster[84] for $25. [$541] for which I gave two sheep, one calf and four dollars in wheat. Also bought 7 grindstones for $30.00 [$650] of Packer.

November 13, 1862—Went to Wellsville, to assess Internal Revenue tax on some whiskey makers there. Came home.

November 16, 1862—Started to S. L. City to get Susan J. arriving there on the 18th, Tuesday. Found her at Uncle W. D. Johnsons. Spent two days there, and returned to Logan the 24th

Sunday, November 23, 1862—To day 70 U. S. Cavalry had a fight at Providence three miles from Logan, with Bear Hunter and his tribe.[85] They wished to rescue a white child they had. After a fight of 45 minutes, in which no one was hurt, the indians gave up the child, which had been taken at a massacre in Oregon.

[page 237]

BATTLE AT PROVIDENCE. BATTLE OF BEAR RIVER.

November 23, 1862—On the next day the soldiers returned to Camp Douglas, as the Camp of the newly arrived California troops is called, near S. L. City.

November 25, 1862—This morning, the indians having rallied strongly, near Providence, made such hostile demonstrations towards the brethren there, that a force of about 70 men rallied at Logan to go to their assistance. We had got about half way to Providence, when we saw the indians coming towards Logan; so we returned to await them. They soon arrived—about 40 warriors—and had a talk with Br. Benson and Bp. Maughan, demanding two Beeves from Providence, for having harbored the troops. Br. Benson sent to that place for one, but they did not send any, so we, of Logan furnished a beef and ten or twelve sacks of flour, and all was peace again.

December 1, 1862—Attended County Court again to day.

84 William I. Webster was a member of the Franklin Ward. He worked in the Sunday School for more than twenty-five years. His death was mentioned in Andrew Jenson, comp., *Church Chronology: A Record of Important Events Pertaining to the History of The Church of Jesus Christ of Latter-day Saints* [Salt Lake City: Deseret News, 1914], 214. See also Godfrey and Godfrey, *Utah Years*, 368.

85 Bear Hunter was a chief of the Shoshone. He was known for his raids, in which he stole horses and cattle (Ricks and Cooley, *History of Cache Valley*, 23; Peterson, *History of Cache County*, 42–43).

December 2, 1862—Went to Paradise to assess Internal Revenue Tax.

December 3, 1862—Surveyed for Hyrum people in the bottoms along the Little Bear River.

December 5, 1862—Bought a stove of Agrippa Cooper[86] for $30.⁰⁰ [$650] (the Gem)

December 9, 1862—Traded land with L. Mallory,[87] getting a loom & $10.⁻ [$217] boot.

December 11, 1862—Bought a carriage of H. Busembark[88] for $75. [$1,624] giving him a bull, $30.~ [$217] Sharp's Rifle $30.~and ten bushels of wheat.

December 12, 1862—Killed my beef cow—my first one since I am married.

January 1, 1863—During the last month I attended a dancing school, kept by A. Harris,[89] P. D. Griffiths[90] and P. Cranney.[91] Learned to waltz.[92]

February 1, 1863—In the latter part of January, Col. P. E. Connor with about 400 troops had a battle on Bear River, in which they totally defeated several hundred indians—shoshonies—under Bear Hunter, Sagwich, and Pocatello, and other chiefs.[93] The indians fought well, in a deep ravine, but the revolvers of the troops was too much for them, and they were [routed] with great slaughter.

[page 238]

BATTLE OF BEAR RIVER, CONTINUED.

February 1, 1863—The indians lost about 400 killed, including 90 squaws and children, many of whom were killed in cold blood. The soldiers ravished many squaws, among the dead and dying. The soldiers lost 14 killed on the field, 44 wounded, many of whom died, and had about 70 frosted, some quite badly. The weather was intensely cold, and Bear River, which the troops (cavalry) forded, was running full of ice. Connor had infantry and two howitzers which did not engage in the battle. The action was fought very badly, there being no organization or order among the troops, each one fighting independently. Col. Connor had no influence or sway during the battle, soldiers disobeying him to his face. At the close of the battle, four indians stole four horses of the Cavalry, and escaped with them, under a shower of bullets from the surrounding troops.[94]

Bear Hunter was shot while running more bullets, and fell forward with his breast in the fire, and so died.

The next morning after the battle, and after an intensely cold night, a dead squaw was found with a little baby trying to suck her icy breast. It was killed for pity, by the soldiers. About 100 indians escaped.

The dead and wounded soldiers were taken to S. L. City by the Mormons, in sleighs. On their return to Logan they quartered among the people. I kept about a dozen (14).

February 4, 1863—Started to S. L. City, arriving there on the 7th

---

86 Agrippa Cooper was among the first settlers of Richmond, Utah (Ricks and Cooley, *History of Cache Valley*, 42).

87 This may be Henry Mallory, who was among the first settlers in Logan (Ricks and Cooley, *History of Cache Valley*, 41).

88 This may be Isaac Busenback (note spelling), who was among the first settlers of Providence (Ricks and Cooley, *History of Cache Valley*, 39).

89 Alma Harris was a bishop of the Benson Ward, organized in 1877. His uncle was Martin Harris, one of the three witnesses to the Book of Mormon (Godfrey and Godfrey, *Utah Years*, 97).

90 Patterson D. Griffith was among the first settlers in the valley (Ricks and Cooley, *History of Cache Valley*, 46).

91 In the first Logan City elections of 1866, P. Cranney was elected to the city council and appointed city marshal (Ricks and Cooley, *History of Cache Valley*, 103).

92 In 1875 the waltz, also called *round dancing*, was halted in Latter-day Saint circles because the dance required close proximity and touching (Ricks and Cooley, *History of Cache Valley*, 299–300).

93 Colonel Patrick Connor led a corps of Third California Volunteers as a part of the Civil War. The corps never fought in that war, but they did help quell the Indian uprisings and keep the Saints stirred up in Utah. Connor established Camp Douglas (later Fort Douglas) in Salt Lake City, named in honor of Senator Stephen A. Douglas. Connor fought a continual war of words with the Mormon leadership. He entered the Battle of Bear River against the Native Americans in 1863, in which his corps massacred 215 Shoshone men, women, and children. Connor remained in Salt Lake after his military career and became involved in mining and the railroads. He began the Liberal Party in Utah as a force against the Mormon People's Party (Ricks and Cooley, *History of Cache Valley*, 51, 170; Sillitoe, *Welcoming the World*, 55–56; Brigham D. Madsen, *Glory Hunter: A Biography of Patrick Edward Connor* [Salt Lake City: Univ. of Utah Press, 1990]).

94 "Saturday," *Deseret News*, February, 7, 1863; Journal History.

February 9, 1863—Bought $31.⁰⁰ [$671] in goods. Went to Camp Douglas and collected $196.⁰⁰ [$4,245] for S. M. Blair. I arranged with Jacob Houtz,[95] to pay him 6000 lbs flour, to settle up a former debt I owe him on the Box business.

February 10, 1863—Started home, and got there on the 12th.

Sunday, March 1, 1863—Sent $20.⁰⁰ [$433] to Harris Bros Boston, for sewing machine.[96] We received word that Cache County is required this year to send back 53 teams and four guards for the poor emigration.

[page 239]

"JACK" RECOVERED. JESSE N. BORN. DELLA SEES A SPIRIT. JOHN W. SICK.

Wednesday, March 11, 1863—This evening Sam Pitch stole my horse "Jack" while I was at Franklin, out of Br. Alex. Stalker's correll [corral].[97] He is worth $150.⁰⁰ [$2,924]

March 12, 1863—Tracked my horse across Cub River, and saw by the course he had taken, that he had gone to Fort Hall. As there were no horses in Franklin that could overtake "Jack" I hired a sub-Chief to get him for me, promising him a good blanket, flour &c.

March 13, 1863—Returned home and heard report that a [cillission] between the saints and the troops at Camp Douglas is very imminent, and that the troops are entrenching

March 20, 1863—Went to Hyde Park with Br. Benson, and attended a party. Heard that my horse was got back.

March 21, 1863—"Jack" was brought home today by W. H. Packer. He had been re-stolen by Soy-aw-ger after he had tried in vain to induce the indian to give him up. He had a hard chase from Fort Hall, through deep snow. and was very badly used up. I paid $25.⁰⁰ [$487] for his recovery.

Monday, April 6, 1863—This morning, at a little after 3 o'clock A.M. Susan J. presented me with a fine boy, weighing 9¼ lbs. She was greatly blessed in her confinement, but had been quite unwell for some time previously. I named him Jesse Nathaniel, after my true friend Jesse N. Smith. We then blessed him and dedicated him to the Lord.

Fig. 4.3—Jesse Nathaniel Martineau, son of Susan Julia and James Henry. Courtesy of James Henry Martineau Family Organization.

Sunday, April 26, 1863—Today John William was taken with a pain and lameness in his ancle. It seems like rheumatism. About two weeks previously he sucked steam from the spout of a teakettle, and was badly burned in his mouth and throat. One night as

95 Jacob Houtz was a Springville, Utah, resident. He was instrumental in leading the immigrants across the plains. Settling in Springville, he worked with James Porter and Edward Hall in building and operating a flour mill.

96 The first sewing machine appeared in 1855 (Audrey M. Godfrey, "'The Queen of Inventions': The Sewing Machine Comes to Utah," *Journal of Mormon History* 32, no. 3 [Fall 2006]: 82–103; "Florence Sewing Machine," *Deseret News*, March 2, 1879; Journal History. In this advertisement Martineau, Budge, and Thatcher are listed as Cache Valley buyers).

97 Alexander Stalker was among the earliest settlers of Franklin, Idaho. In 1863 he constructed a gristmill along the Cub River (Ricks and Cooley, *History of Cache Valley*, 160).

Susan J. was undressing Dellie for bed, Dellie suddenly exclaimed, looking across the room to the top of the wall "Oh Ma! see that pretty woman—all dressed in white" Where? said Susan J. "Why right there—cant you see her—there she is—oh so beautiful."

[page 240]

DEATH OF JOHN WILLIAM AT 1.45 MAY 4, 1863.

April 26, 1863—Her mother was frightened, and hid her face, asking Dellie from time to time if she still saw her, Dellie answering yes, until she said "Now she's gone."

Sunday, May 4, 1863—Yesterday, John W. was taken worse in the morning. Up to this time, we did not think he was sick—only a kind of lameness of which he did not complain much. His mother made him a little quilt pallet on the floor, on which he would sometimes lie, talking to his mother, and sometimes he would crawl around on his hands and knees. But this morning, as soon as we awoke, we saw some kind of change in him. He seems to have much pain in his bowels and a high fever. In the evening Brs. Benson, Blair and D. B. Dille administered to him, but without much hope. He lay apparently insensible, with his eyes nearly closed, breathing quick and feverish. All the means we used, seemed to have no effect. Up to to day he often called me to pray for him saying, "Ma, I want Pa to bless me." "Ma, I want to be prayed." but to day he does not notice anyone. During the evening he had many spasms of pain, which ceased at about 11 P.M. From this until 1.45 this morning, he lay quiet, and peacefully unconscious until he died. When at last we felt to give him up, he expired while my hands were still upon his head.

He was four years three months and twenty three days old. He was much subject to affliction during his little life, from sickness, accidents &c He was of an affectionate disposition: and greatly attached to his mother, with whom he would stay instead of playing with the children. Dellie was his mate and they always delighted to play together. Many times in the day he would go to his mother, throw his arms around her neck and kiss her saying—"Ma, I love you."

[page 241]

SUSAN TEMPTED. BOUGHT AN AMBROTYPE APPARATUS OF E. COVINGTON.

1863—While he was lying in his burial robes. I took a profile sketch of his face, natural size, which is quite accurate, except in the lower lip. It is a hard trial to bury our children, but the will of the Lord be done. Why do our children die?

June 15, 1863—Since my last entry, I have been busy surveying in different places. I also, to day, leveled a canal for the Providence field, taking water from Logan river, 1½ miles along a steep bluff.

During the past week Susan J. has been much tempted by an evil spirit, who endeavored to get her to go with him, offering her great inducements to do so: showing her the ease and glories of his kingdom, contrasted with the poverty and hardships of life. He appeared in bodily form, but would flee away when Elders came to administer, returning after they went away.

She was almost tempted to go, but finally the Lord gave her power to overcome, for which, praised be His name forever. It is my faith that she will finally overcome, and receive her promised blessings.

Wednesday, July 1, 1863—To day I began to learn to take ambrotypes of Ed[d] Covington having bought an apparatus of him for $300.00 [$5,848]. He is to teach me the business, and have half the receipts while doing so. We went to Providence six days earning $96.00 [$1,872]

September 13, 1863—I have been haying, hauling adobies for a new house and have been to S. L. City. We have had pretty good health, and been prospered in business.

To day the teams sent from this valley last spring for the poor, returned in tolerably good condition. Elder C. C. Rich also arrived with a company, on their way north, to make a settlement in Bear Lake Valley

October 27, 1863—Began to Survey a city plat for Wellsville and worked two days.

[page 242]

SUSAN J.S RHEUMATISM. TOWN SITES SURVEYED.

October 29, 1863—Began surveying a town site for Mendon, laying out 9 blocks, including the public square, 64 lots in all.

October 30 & 31, 1863—Surveyed Hyrum city lots.

November 2, 1863—Began again at Wellsville, which I finished on the 5th having laid out 204 lots.

November 23, 1863—Began Surveying Richmond, and finished on the 26th Thursday.

Thursday, November 26, 1863—Got word from home that Susan J. is very ill with inflammatory rheumatism. I had a dream last night which warned me that there was trouble at home. I dreamed that my house was burning.

November 27, 1863—Got home and found Susan J. unable to move and suffering great pain continually, being unable to bear the slightest touch. She was taken sick on the 24th Tuesday in her feet and legs. Susan E. had been with her all the time, and was much worn down.

December 8, 1863—Br. Robt Murdock[98] today finished laying up my adobie house. It is 18' x 29' feet long, 12 high to the ceiling, with two rooms, adapted for a photographic gallery and office. I hauled the rock and laid the foundation myself; also hauled the adobies.

Susan J. is still very sick, requiring constant attention night and day. Nothing seems to do her any good. Hard times.

December 25, 1863—To day Susan J. was able for the first time to be brought to look out of the window. She took cold and got worse. I bought a sleigh for $50.00 [$975].

January 1, 1864—Susan J. is slowly recovering. She had to wean the Baby, Jesse N. in the beginning of her sickness and the poor little fellow has twice been very near death.

Susan E. and I have had to be with her night and day, constantly, having little or no assistance in waiting on her. I had a Danish girl for three weeks, but she was good for nothing. On the 28th December I hired Emma Durfee for $1.50 [$29] pr week commencing the 30th.[99]

[page 243]

ROUND VALLEY. INDIAN FUSS. FRANKLIN

Saturday, January 2, 1864—Today I took my wives sleighing, lifting Susan J. in and out carefully, in a bed, nice and warm.

January 5, 1864—Today Susan J. is able to sit at the table and walk a little, but still much rheumatism about her.

For many weeks Susan and I have not had our clothes off to sleep, but have lain down to sleep, when we could on a pallet on the floor and are almost worn out.

Twice during her sickness Susan J. has been near to the gates of death. At one time Prest Benson came and administered to her, but thought she would die. He said he had no feelings toward her but good. Wrote a long letter to B. F. Johnson.

Tuesday, March 22, 1864—To day at 2.30 A.M. Susan E. presented me with a boy, weighing 7 lbs. She was blessed in her illness, for which thank the Lord.

March 23, 1864—Named the baby George Albert, after Geo. A. Smith.

Thursday, September 15, 1864—Began Surveying some new settlements in Round Valley at the North end of Cache, and almost on the northern rim of the Great Basin. Up to this time, I have been very busy, but there has been nothing of much moment to record. Surveyed Stockton, town and farm lands. After this I laid out the town of Oxford, with farming and meadow lands adjoining, about three miles from Stockton. At daylight a messenger arrived with word that indians had made an outbreak on Franklin the previous day, and with orders for all to return to Franklin at once.

98 Robert Murdock opposed the 1872 petition for Utah statehood (Simmonds, *The Gentile Comes to Cache Valley*, 3).

99 Emma Durfee (1845–1907) was born in Nauvoo, Illinois, the daughter of Francillo Durfee and Mariam Jones Durfee. She was performing teenage labor at this entry. Ricks and Cooley cite a Francillo Durfey (note spelling) as among the early settlers of Providence, Utah (Ricks and Cooley, *History of Cache Valley*, 39).

We accordingly started back, there being 25 souls including the women and children. We expected to have to fight our way back, but met no hindrance. We had about 22 miles to travel. When we arrived at Franklin we found Br. P. Maughan with 300 minute men, and a large band of Indians from the north who had been having trouble with the people.

[page 244]

SURVEYED CLARKSTON, PETERSBURG AND PARADISE, PREVIOUSLY.

September 15, 1864—Wash-a-kee had about 300 warriors. A drunken indian had attempted to ride over a white woman, striking at her with a war club, so that she was obliged to get under his horse to avoid his blows. Some men were thrashing near by, and one ran up to rescue the woman and shot the indian with a small pistol, but not fattaly [fatally] wounding him. The indians prepared to avenge this and took a man coming from the Cañon, and for two hours threatened him with instant death, with knives hatches &c, drawing their knives almost across his throat, and thus tormenting him all they could.

During the night Br. Maughan arrived with help and <u>then</u> the indians were willing to <u>talk</u>. A final settlement was finally made, and the Indians went away. The two men who sold the indian the liquor—Sam[l] Parkinson and N. W. Packer had to pay a yoke of oxen each, to the indians, and a quantity of flour and potatoes.[100] During the three days negotiations I surveyed several miles of water ditches, and afterwards returned to Round Valley and finished my surveying there. My son Moroni was with me all the time. Had it not been for the instant arrival of the minute men, the indians would probably have done what they said and intended—destroyed the settlement.

I also spent some time with William Garner[101] in leveling for a canal from Bear River to irrigate the great body of land west of Cub River. We found it is practicable, but would be very expensive.

On the 22nd of July 1864 I had laid out a new Settlement on the west side of the valley, named Clarkston. And on the 20th of April last, I laid out a new settlement south of Hyrum, called Petersburg, also a city South of that place called Paradise; Also April 6, 1864 I laid out a city plot at Millville. These items were accidentally omitted in their proper place.

[page 245]

SWIM BEAR RIVER WITH A YOKE OF OXEN. JULIA H. BORN FEBRUARY 4, 1865.

1864—In July last, while coming from the survey of ~~Franklin~~ Clarkston, I had an adventure in Bear River, with I. J. Clarks team of oxen and wagon. Coming near the river, the oxen being very thirsty they ran with me to the river and plunged in to drink. The wagon crowded them into the deep river in a quick current, and away we went. After trying in vain to turn them to the shore, I gave whip liberally, and made them swim across the river with the wagon, our guns and bedding and Surveying instruments. Luckily they struck the only place on the opposite bank where they could make a landing, the banks generally being high and steep. The river there was about 600 feet wide.

During the fall, I leveled the Logan & Richmond Canal from Logan River to Richmond, some 16 miles, the canal to be 20 feet wide and 2 deep.

February 4, 1865—To-day Julia Henrietta Martineau was born at Logan, 9 P.M. At first Susan J. her mother got along very well, but she took cold and had an attack of puerperal fever[102] and nearly died. For six weeks life was a blank to her, for she remembered nothing that passed during that time. She was again attacked with rheumatism and for many weeks Susan

100 Samuel R. Parkinson was later president of the Franklin Cooperative. In 1886 he was sentenced to six months' imprisonment in the Boise Penitentiary and fined three hundred dollars for unlawful cohabitation (Ricks and Cooley, *History of Cache Valley*, 220). In the 1860s, Nathan Parker operated a ferry across the Bear River. Settlers used the ferry to transport supplies to Idaho and Montana (Ricks and Cooley, *History of Cache Valley*, 66).

101 This may be William Gardner (note spelling), who was a selectman in the first Cache County government (Peterson, *History of Cache County*, 82; Ricks and Cooley, *History of Cache Valley*, 90).

102 This fever sometimes occurs after the birth of a child and is often called childbed fever. It was commonly fatal.

E. and I had a very hard time with her, never being able to leave her for a moment. We did not go to bed, undressed, for weeks, Susan E. having to not only help her, but to take care also of all the children and family, all which duties she faithfully performed. May she never want for help in her time of need.

Fig. 4.4—Julia Henrietta Martineau, daughter of Susan Julia and James Henry Martineau. Courtesy of James Henry Martineau Family Organization.

During the winter I became convinced that nothing but a southern climate would help Susan J. and wrote to Pres^t Young to know if I could have his approbation to go south. He answered me, yes, and said I could go to either the Rio Virgin or the Colorado Country, as Elder E. Snow should wish me to do.

[page 246]

SURVEY WESTON. CONCLUDE TO GO SOUTH.

February 4, 1865—He wished me to go prepared to survey and level, and to perfect myself in those branches. Upon receipt of this I began to sell out. I paid $200.^00 [$2,490] for a share in building a new tabernacle in Logan, and gave about $60.^00 [$747] to help missionaries.

May 24, 1865—I surveyed Weston today. In crossing Cub River I experienced considerable danger, the river being very deep and swift. Many thought it impossible to do so, but my business being imperative I tried—and did cross it. We narrowly escaped being swept down the stream—had it been 10 feet wider than where the horses touched bottom on the other side we should have been lost. Henry A. was with me.

June 2, 1865—Leveled a long mill race for John Nielson on Logan River; also surveyed five acres there for his mill site.

In fording the Logan we narrowly escaped drowning.

Thursday, June 1, 1865—To day Susan J. was baptized for her health by B. M. Lewis[103] also at the same time Henry A., Moroni H, and S. Elvira were baptized into the Church. Dellie also wished to be baptized, but was not quite eight years old, and so she was not. I afterward wished she had been.

Susan J. had faith she would be healed. She has been getting better ever since.

August 6, 1865—Patriarch Charles Hyde[104] gave us the following blessings:—

My Blessing:—

James Henry, in the name of Jesus I place my hands upon thy head, and seal upon ~~thee~~ you a patriarchal

103 This may be Benjamin M. Lewis, who was bishop of the Logan First Ward and a farmer (Godfrey and Godfrey, *Utah Years*, 33; Somers, *History of Logan*, 64).

104 Charles W. Hyde was the brother of William and Rosel Hyde. Charles resided in Wellsville. Born in 1814, he was among the Saints who received their temple endowments in the Nauvoo Temple. As noted in Martineau's writing, multiple blessings at this time were common. Today an individual is given a single patriarchal blessing recorded and held by the individual.

blessing, for the eye of God has been upon thee from everlasting, and thou shalt be very useful in this kingdom in doing much business in writing and recording the council of heaven, and the angels of God shall rejoice over thee, for thou shalt be a patriarch to your family for ever and ever, a Savior on Mount Zion, with all the patriarchs, and shall converse with your Savior face to face, and many of the holy prophets since the world began. Thou art of Ephraim, and a lawful heir to the fulness of the priesthood and with wives and a great kingdom on the earth, and shall sit in council with the Ancient of Days, and with all the holy prophets since the world began, and you shall be the means of redeeming your father's family till you are satisfied, and be crowned with glory and eternal lives, with all your father's household for ever and ever. Amen.

[page 247]

August 6, 1865—

Susan E.'s blessing:—

Susan, I place my hands upon thy head and seal upon thee a father's blessing, for the eye of God has been upon thee from ever lasting, and thou shalt have the visions of God to comfort you while you remain on this earth, and you shall have visions and dreams and the revelations of God; and thou shalt ~~have~~ live until thou art 83 years old, and till the coming of the Messiah, and shall converse with him. Thou art of Joseph, and a lawful heir to the fulness of the priesthood and with thy companion and a great kingdom on the earth: and you shall be a prophetess on Mt. Zion, and shall be a Savior with thy companion, and shall be crowned with glory and eternal lives with God and the Lamb for ever and ever. Amen.

Nephi's Blessing:—

Nephi, beloved of the Father, I place my hands on thy head and seal upon thee a Patriarchal blessing, which shall be sealed in heaven: for thou shalt become a great and a mighty man, even like Nephi of old. No weapon formed against thee shall prosper. Thou shalt have power to raise the dead, and to do any miracle to forward this kingdom; and thou shalt proclaim this Gospel to many nations, kindreds, tongues and peoples, and thou shalt come upon Mt. Zion with the hundred and forty-four thousand in their robes of righteousness, and converse with many of the Holy Prophets face to face. You shall sit in Council with Joseph and Hyrum, and with your Redeemer. And thou art of Joseph and a lawful heir to the fulness of the priesthood, and with wives and great kingdom on the earth, Shall help to rear a temple in Jackson county, and you shall help ~~to~~ pave the streets around the temple in Jackson county with gold, and you shall hear the prophet Joseph talking unto you about the New Jerusalem.

[page 248]

August 6, 1865—These blessings I seal upon you with every desire of your heart, and with crowns of glory and eternal life, with all your father's household in the name of Jesus Christ. Amen.

George Albert's blessing:—

George Albert, in the name of Jesus I place my hands upon thy head and seal upon thee a father's blessing, for thou shalt become a great and mighty man in Zion, have power to do any miracle that was ever done on the earth to forward this kingdom; a lawful heir to the Patriarchal family, and shalt be a Patriarch on Mt. Zion. Thou art of Jacob, and a lawful heir to the fulness of the priesthood, even to the patriarchal family of Abraham, and a lawful heir to the fulness of the priesthood and with wives and a great kingdom on the earth, and a Savior on Mount Zion, and to set in council with the Ancient of Days, with all the holy patriarchs since the world began, with the blessings of eternal lives through God and the Lamb for ever and ever. Amen.

Susan J.'s Blessing:—

Susan, in the name of Jesus I place my hands on thy head and seal a father's blessing for the eye of God has been upon thee from everlasting and thou shalt have great wisdom and knowledge before the Lord thy God. Thou shalt have visions and revelations to comfort you, and your last days shall be your best days. I pray the Father that you may begin to amend from this very hour from your afflictions: that the Angels of God may be around about you and never forsake you.

[page 249]

August 6, 1865—Thou art a daughter of Ephraim and a lawful heir to the fulness of the Priesthood, and with thy companion shall have a great kingdom on the Earth, for your name shall be had in everlasting remembrance, and you shall teach many the way of life and salvation, for your table shall be spread with all the bounties of the earth, for no good thing shall be witheld from you. Thou shalt be the means of redeeming thy father's household, for I seal this blessing upon your head, with a crown of glory and eternal lives with all your father's household, forever and ever. Amen.

Charles' Blessing:—

Charles, in the name of Jesus I place my hands upon thy head and seal upon thee a patriarchal blessing, for the Father is well pleased with you, and thou shalt have great wisdom and knowledge with the Father on the Earth. Thou shalt be like Nephi of old, and the hidden treasures of the earth shall be unfolded to your mind, for no good thing shall be witheld from thee. Thou art of Joseph and a lawful heir to the fulness of the priesthood, and with wives and a kingdom on the Earth forever, and your table shall be spread with the bounties of the earth. For I ordain you an Elder, in the Church of Jesus Christ of Latter Day Saints that you may comprehend many things of the Father, and sit in council with the Ancient of Days, and receive the fulness of the priesthood by the hand of the Savior, and be crowned with eternal lives. Amen.

Jesse N's Blessing:—

Jesse Nathaniel in the name of Jesus I place my hands on thy head and seal upon thee a patriarchal blessing which shall be sealed in heaven for your good, and ordain you an Elder in the church of Jesus Christ of Latter Day Saints, that you may thwart every plan of the Destroyer, that you may live to the coming of the Messiah, for this is the mind and the will of the Father, for thou art one of the noble spirits come here to do his will upon this earth, and thou shall be like the brother of Jared.

[page 250]

August 6, 1865—Inasmuch as you will hearken to every council of thy parents, thou shalt have the heavens opened to your view, and comprehend many things of the kingdom of God on the earth. Thou art of Ephraim, and a lawful heir to the priesthood, and with wives and a great kingdom on the earth, and you shall have great treasures of the earth, and with every desire of thy heart upon Mount Zion, and thou shalt converse with your savior face to face, and shall be crowned with glory and eternal lives, with all your father's household, for ever and ever. Amen

Julia H.'s Blessing:—

Julia Henrietta, beloved of the father. I place my hands on thy head and seal upon you a father's blessing. Thou shalt be a natural prophetess on Mount Zion and the fulness of the priesthood in due time, and with a companion in a kingdom on the earth for ever and ever. It shall have a voice like a melodion to sing praises to God and the Lamb with the Savior: and the Savior will literally lay his hands upon this child when it grows up to womanhood; and it shall be a mother in Israel; and thy table shall be spread with all the bounties of the earth, for no good thing shall be witheld from this child. It shall have the revelations of God to comfort it, and shall teach many the way of life and Salvation, and shall stand on the earth at the coming of the Messiah, for I seal this blessing on this child, with eternal lives to God and the Lamb for ever and ever. Amen.

On May 6, 1854, E. H. Groves gave H. A. Martineau a blessing in Parowan, which was omitted in its proper place, and is now inserted here, as follows:—Recorded in Book A. Pages 439 and 440.

[page 251]

H. A. MARTINEAU'S BLESSING, GIVEN MAY 6, 1854

Henry Augustus in the name of Jesus of Nazareth, by virtue of the holy priesthood in me invested. I place my hands upon thy head to seal upon thee a patriarchal or father's blessing which shall rest upon thee and thou shalt realize the fulfillment thereof. Thou art in the days of thy childhood, yet a noble spirit inhabiteth thy tabernacle, and inasmuch as thy parents do their duty by thee, thou shalt grow up to mature age in invigoration of body and mind. The Holy Spirit will rest upon thee from thy infancy, and thou shalt become mighty in faith. The holy angels will be with thee, and in their hands they will bear thee up, and deliver thee from all thy enemies and from the power of him who hath the power of death. Thou art of the seed of Abraham of the loins of Joseph, and blood of Ephraim, which hath centered in thee, a lawful heir to the blessings and fulness of the holy priesthood which thou shalt receive in due time, that thou mayest be able to stand at the head of thy father's family, in the redemption of thy progenitors. Thou shalt become a father in Israel—thy posterity shall multiply and become numerous upon the earth. Thy name shall be perpetrated to the latest generation. Thou shalt obtain knowledge by dreams and visions and the administration of heavenly messengers. Thou shalt be delivered by the Holy Angels like unto Moroni in the day of battle. The Angel of Vengence shall be with thee—shall strengthen and nurse thy sinews that thou mayest be able to avenge the blood of innocence upon those that dwell upon the earth. Wisdom shall be given unto thee, that thou mayest be able to fill any mission or station that shall be given unto thee in thy day. I seal upon thy head the blessing of thy fathers Abraham Isaac and Jacob and thou shalt delight thyself in them. Peace and good order shall rest in thy habitations;—thou shalt receive the dews of heaven and the fruits of the earth. Wealth in great abundance shall flow into thy hands, and all things needful to render life happy and agreeable.

[page 252]
Thou shalt behold the winding up scene—the coming of thy Redeemer—the reign of peace upon the Earth, delight thyself in the blessing of the fruit of the vine and the olive yard—receive thy enduement and blessings in the temple in Zion, be anointed a king and a priest unto the most High God, receive thy crown, kingdom, power, dominion and eternal increase, be numbered with the hundred and forty-four thousand, reign with thy Redeemer upon the Earth. These blessings shall be sure unto thee. I seal them upon thy head in the name of Jesus of Nazareth, even so. Amen.

In June 1, 1857 Father Morley gave Susan J. and myself the following blessings, while Susan E. was at Manti. The copy which I had was gnawed by the mice, and some parts which I cannot now remember are here left blank. It was omitted in the time when it should have been inserted:—

My blessing:—

Brother James Henry I lay my hands upon thy head in the name of Jesus, and I ratify all thy former seals that they may become ~~seals~~ keys of priesthood to illuminate thy mind. I bless you with the blessings of Abraham that thou mayest enjoy all the blessings and powers of the everlasting priesthood, that this principle may become the rule of government in thy family. I seal upon thee by promise, the blessing of posterity, that thy seals may be extended upon them from generation to generation, that thy name may be preserved, thy [blank line]

Thou shalt enjoy all the blessings and seals of the holy ordinances which will be a lamp in thy path and a key of knowledge in thy mind, that thou mayest be honored in thy priesthood and administrations. Thou wilt be honored in preaching the gospel to many people.

[page 253]

SUSAN J'S BLESSING.
JUNE 1. 1857 BY I. MORLEY.

I bless thee with the blessing of becoming a restorer of thy father's household, that they may enjoy all the blessings of the promised seed, for thou hast the stewardship of this blessing. Thou wilt become a restorer to the house of Jacob, and stand at the head of a numerous posterity. I seal upon thee the gift to bless thy posterity, that thy seals may be extended upon them. I seal upon thee the gift of counsel, of wisdom and prudence, that thou mayest enjoy life and the blessings pertaining thereto; the fruits of the earth with flocks and herds will flow unto thee, for thou art blessed with the blood of the promised seed, and with an heirship to a celestial crown. I place these seals in the name of Jesus. Even so Amen and Amen.

Susan J,'s blessing:—

Sister Susan J. I lay my hands upon thy head by virtue of the holy priesthood, and I ratify thy former blessings by the keys of my office and by the authority of [blank] of priesthood, that thy seals may become a lamp in thy pathway and a guide unto thee. Thou shalt be blessed with the blessing of posterity for thy stewardship and which will require thy talent and gifts to be exercised for their good. I seal upon thee and upon thy memory the gift that thou mayest mature thy thoughts before they are expressed in words. Then shall thy faculties and gifts which have been given thee by the God of nature be brought into exercise for the good of the rising generation. Thou shalt be blessed with the attributes of love, thou shalt dwell as a confidant in the bosom of thy partner. I bless thee with powers and faculties of mind to overcome the follies of youth, that thou mayest become established in honor, in fidelity, and virtue. The Lord is thy Friend,—he is thy Benefactor, and thou shalt yet dwell with the mothers in Israel in Zion in peace. Thy children shall bless thee—they will revere thy counsel: the blessings of the holy ordinance will be enjoyed by thee. They will illuminate thy path.

[page 254]
They will invigorate thy mind and leave a lasting impress of responsibility upon thy memory. Thou art of Joseph and I seal these blessings by virtue of the priesthood, of endless lives in the mansions of thy Father, even so, Amen and Amen.

Abagail Leonora Morley[105] was scribe for both these blessings and now, April 1, 1874 Father Morley, Leonora and Susan are all gone. When will I follow?

Susan thought a great deal of this blessing because of the promise that she should "dwell as a confidant in the bosom of thy partner." She often referred to this promise in after years, and only a short time before she departed.

[Bottom half of page left empty.]

[page 255]
August 6, 1865—Today Pres[t] Brigham Young, Gen[l] D. H. Wells, Adj. Gen[l] Ross, and others from S. L. City organized Cache into a Military District and a Brigade consisting of three regiments, one Cavalry, under Col. T. E Ricks and two infantry, commanded by Col[s] Alvin Crockett and W. H. Maughan, respectively.

Col. Ezra T. Benson was elected Brig. General, W[m] Hyde Adjutant, myself Ass[t] Adjutant, Peter Maughan, Quartermaster, D. B. Lamoreaux Surgeon of Brigade[106] and W[m] K. Robinson[107] Color bearer. Tho[s] E. Ricks, Col. Cav. Reg[t] Alvin Crockett[108] and W[m] H. Maughan, Colonels of the 1st and 2[d] Regts of infantry.

[Last half of page left blank.]

[page 256]
August 9, 1865—Today Schwartz & Brother began boarding with us, and rented the store building at $10.[00] [$125] pr week.

During last month I have surveyed considerable. On July 12, the Providence Hay Land on Little Bear River.

On July 16 the Hyrum Hay Land on Little Bear River.

Also on the same time some land on the river bottom near Hyrum.

November 29, 1865—I surveyed a new field at Franklin, on the west of the State road

During the past summer I sold a part of my lot six rods square to D. B. Lamoreaux, with some fencing for $530.[00] [$6,598] of this he is to pay $150.[00] [$1,867] in work on the new Tabernacle, the balance in other pay at cash rates.

November 1865—I also surveyed an addition to the west field at Logan, extending to Logan River.

March 20, 1866—Surveyed the So-called "Minute Men's Pasture", Logan into city and farm lots, securing for my labor a five acre lot

105 Abigail Leonora Snow Morley (1801–72) was the daughter of Oliver Snow and the second wife of Isaac Morley. She passed away in Box Elder County, February 11, 1872.

106 David B. Lamoreaux was active in the politics of the valley and, during the construction of the temple, he was the superintendent of the sawmill (Nolan P. Olsen, *Logan Temple: The First 100 Years* [Providence, UT: Keith W. Watkins, 1978]; Simmonds, *The Gentile Comes to Cache Valley*, 28–29).

107 William K. Robinson was an alderman (member of the town council) for the city of Logan. He served with Martineau after the first elections (Ricks and Cooley, *History of Cache Valley*, 103; Simmonds, *The Gentile Comes to Cache Valley*, 38).

108 Alvin Crockett was among the leaders of Cache Valley. He was the first mayor of Logan in 1866 and was instrumental in educational development. He was appointed county game commissioner in 1878 (Ricks and Cooley, *History of Cache Valley*, 94, 103, 107; Simmonds, *The Gentile Comes to Cache Valley*, 27–29; Peterson, *History of Cache County*, 90, 96, 144, 191).

April 4, 1866—Surveyed a new water ditch for Providence 1¼ miles.

April 9, 1866—Surveyed a new water ditch for Hyrum.

April 10, 1866—Surveyed a new Mill race, for Hyrum

May 1, 1866—I surveyed for mill purposes for Geo. Thurston;[109] near Menden

May 2, 1866—Today, while at Mendon, indians stole Br. Thurston's child—Rosa—from home. She was a beautiful child about 2½ years old,—the pet of the family. All the people turned out to find her, but after days spent in hunting her, they gave her up. She was never seen again. From what we could learn, she was placed on a horse, between two indians, who wrapped a blanket round them all, and so took her off. The distress and grief of the parents was terrible.

I also Surveyed some additional farm land for Mendon, near Thurston's Mill.

June 11, 1866—Surveyed for a new Mill race at Logan for Benson & Thatcher, running through W. B. Rogers land near the upper mill.

[page 257]

START TO S. L. CITY WITH DELLIE, ELVIRA AND MORONI.

Friday, October 6, 1866—To day I started to conference with Moroni, Elvira and Dellie in the carriage. I had intended to take Susan J. but her baby Nettie, was taken sick just then, and so she did not dare to go. I concluded, as I had got ready, to take the children for a pleasure trip. They were all life and animation at the thought. We arrived at Brigham City near dark, and got some peaches of H. P. Jensen,[110] then drove to Willard, and stopped at Br. Zundel's.[111]

October 7, 1866—In the night Dellie was taken unwell, and Mrs. Zundel gave her some herb tea, so that she seemed well in the morning, when we started onward. The children enjoyed themselves very much here, playing with a goact [goat] and eating peaches. Br. Zundel is an old friend of Susan J.s mother, in Nauvoo.

When I arrived in sight of Ogden, Dellie complained of a severe head ache, which continued to increase. I made her a bed as good as I could in the carriage, and when I got to Ogden I tried to persuade her to let me take her home again, but she would not consent. She said "I want to go to the City." I drove to Rice's at Farmington, where Mrs. Rice did what she could for her. She thought it was worm fever.

October 8, 1866—Drove to the city about noon, and carried Dellie into Aunt Esther's. She was quite sick by this time, and I at once procured the service of an experienced nurse to take care of her. For a week we did all we could to break her fever, using herb tea &c. and administering frequently, but she steadily grew weaker.

Sunday, October 15, 1866—I got Dr. Clinton to see her. He at once said it was the Typhoid fever, and a desperate case.[112] Today I had her prayed for in the Prayer circle, also last night. Dr. C. applied blisters behind her ears, which seemed to rouse her from the lethargy into which she had fallen for some days.

October 18, 1866—She seems to be getting better—the fever is almost gone.

109 George Thurston was a leader of the Seventh Handcart Company, which arrived in the Salt Lake Valley in September 1857. He settled in Mendon, Utah, where he constructed a gristmill on Gardner's Creek. Mendon, Utah, is eight miles southwest of Logan in the Wellsville Mountains (*Isaac Sorensen's History of Mendon: A Pioneer Chronicle of a Mormon Settlement*, ed. Doran J. Baker, Charles S. Peterson, and Gene A. Ware [Salt Lake City: Publishers Press, 1988]).

110 H. P. Jensen is likely Hans P. Jensen who settled east of Brigham City, in Mantua, Utah. He was among the flax farmers (Frederick M. Huchel, *A History of Box Elder County* [Salt Lake City: Utah State Historical Society, 1999], 360–61).

111 This is Isaac David Eberhart Zundell (note spelling), one of the founders of Plymouth, Utah. He was appointed the first bishop of the Native Americans living east of Manila in Box Elder County. When the natives were moved to the Washakie Reservation, Zundell helped them dig a canal from Samaria to Washakie. He served as the presiding elder of the Portage Branch. He was also a member of the first Canadian exploration party in 1886 (Godfrey and Godfrey, *Utah Years*, 75; Godfrey and Card, *Canadian Years*, 10–12).

112 Typhoid fever is an infectious disease causing intestinal inflammation and ulcers.

[page 258]

DELLIE'S SICKNESS, AND

[heading continued on page 259]

October 18, 1866—She is quite weak, as she has eaten nothing since the 8th

October 19, 1866—Today she is apparently better. A few days ago I sent word to her mother to come to her immediately, and that I would pay any one who would bring her. She arrived today, having brought Jesse N. And Julia H., both unwell. A Mrs. Crane, a gentile, of Logan, sent a team and teamster to bring her down, after she had tried for a day or two among the Saints to get some one to take her to her dying child, without success.

When Susan J. Arrived, Dellie seemed to know her mother, who was much overcome to see her so sick, but thankful to be there in time.

October 20, 1866—This morning Dellie had her senses very well, and knew and kissed her mother, and played with her doll. About noon, Susan J. discovered something like black canker in her mouth. I went at once to Dr. J. L. Ormsby,[113] the partner of Dr. Clinton, who came at once to see about it. He pronounced it black canker, and a dangerous thing. He at once cauterized it with caustic.[114]

October 21, 1866—Dellie pulled out a tooth today—others are loose. She seemed not so well. All at once, about 11 A.M. she suddenly arose, almost dressed herself, and called for her new shoes and doll. She acted so strange, it filled us with fear and wonder. She also sat in a chair. We got her to bed again, and she sank away as before. About 2 P.M. she roused, sat up, and began to get out of bed. I took her on my lap. Her eyes were changed, and she appeared to be dying, continuing so for two hours; then she began to grow warmer and to revive again. We washed her in liquor, and gave her wine, and she finally became fully conscious again, and able to speak.

Sunday, October 22, 1866—She seemed better this morning. At noon, the Doctor cut out the black flesh in the top of her mouth. The caustic not having checked it. She bore this operation without a groan, pulled another tooth and again cauterized her mouth. In the afternoon she was much prostrated, and continued so all night, often screaming out as if in pain.

[page 259]

DEATH. OCT 23D, 1866

[heading continued from page 258]

Monday, October 23, 1866—Not so well this morning. She failed all day, and died at 9 o'clock P.M. For about two hours before she died, she lay with her eyes fixed on mine, never moving them, looking at me with such unutterable love. She constantly moved her arms, raising them up, touching her head and dropping them. A few moments before she departed, she suddenly looked up, as though at some bright presence, with a look of joy and happiness unspeakable, then again fixed her eyes on mine, and so continued till her departure, peacefully breathing her last.

[written in margin]

See p. 261

Who can tell my feelings! I had scarcely left her while she was sick—I had prayed for her continually, and had done all I could for her—and then to lose her at last. She always loved me intensely—never doing any thing she thought I would not like, and always trying to anticipate my wishes in every thing. Her greatest pleasure was to please me, always. But she is gone. I called on Sister Eliza R. Snow, a dear friend of Susan J.s in hope that she might be able to tell me what I could do for her. (This was before Susan came down) but she could not help me. But she gave me much comfort by her conversation.

October 24, 1866—The Lord gave,—He hath taken—blessed be His name. To day we buried my daughter. As she lay in her little coffin, I placed some beautiful flowers in her hand, saying "Dellie, this is Pa's last gift." Br. Jennings kindly sent his large carriage, also

113 This is most likely Oliver C. Ormsby, a graduate of the Rush Medical College who was the first person to enter into the drugstore business in Logan, founding the Pioneer Drug Company. He was also the school superintendent, a physician, a surgeon and the owner of one of the best-matched driving teams in the valley (Godfrey and Godfrey, *Utah Years*, 44; Somers, *History of Logan*, 55, 99, 321). Simmonds lists a Doctor J. S. Ormsby who was active in politics, but provides no further detail (Simmonds, *The Gentile Comes to Cache Valley*, 28).

114 A canker is an ulcerous sore of the mouth or lips. A caustic destroys the infected area by chemical action.

H. W. Lawrence, [115] and three others, and we laid her beside her mother's mother. where she had once before said she wished to be laid.

About three months before she died, as she lay in her bed one morning thinking, she suddenly said, "Ma, if I was to die, would you bury me by my grandmother?

[page 260]

October 24, 1866—The question startled her mother, who checked her and asked why she said that. She answered—"Oh, I didn't know if you would take so much trouble as that for me."

Susan J. told me, that she had been unwell for some days before I left for the city, but Dellie would not say anything about it for fear I would not "take her to the city."

After the funeral Susan and I went to H. W. Lawrence's by his invitation, as Aunt Esther's seemed so lonesome now. After stopping there two days, we returned home—one less in my family here—three now beyond the vail, to welcome me when I too shall go.

I afterwards wrote the following lines to the air of "Belle Brandon":—

1

Oh Dellie, my heart's sad and weary
With waiting and watching for thee:—
For thy sweet laugh so joyous and cheery.
That was ever like music to me.
But thou hast departed and left me
In sorrow lamenting thy loss.
Never more to my heart shall I press thee
Till my spirit is freed from its dross.

2

Oh Dellie if e'er tis permitted
For Spirits like thine to return
And revisit the scene they have quitted
Oh come to me, darling, oh come!
And bring with thee, Willie, thy brother
Thy playmate when you were both here
Let him visit his sorrowing mother
Her sad aching heart let him cheer

[page 261]

1866—

3

Oh dost thou remember that hour
When thy last lingering gaze dwelt on me,—
And my words, as I gave thee those flowers–
"Tis my last gift, my Della, to thee."
Thou hast passed from all weeping and sorrow,—
Thou hast entered that city so fair;
And when shall arrive my to-morrow
I'll join thee so joyfully there.

June 12, 1867—Today Joel Hills Martineau was born. His mother, S. E. was much blessed.

August 13, 1867—Today my daughter Elizabeth was born. Her mother Susan J. was blessed with a speedy recovery for which thanks be to His great name.

Fig. 4.5—Joel Hills Martineau, son of Susan Ellen and James Henry. Courtesy of James Henry Martineau Family Organization.

115 Henry W. Lawrence was a prominent Salt Lake City merchant involved in mining and real estate. He was later active in liberal politics (Sillitoe, *Welcoming the World*, 75).

Fig. 4.6—Elizabeth Martineau, daughter of Susan Julia and James Henry. Courtesy of James Henry Martineau Family Organization.

[written in margin]

From p. 259

Just before Della died she was lying as if asleep, when suddenly she began to sing "What is home without a mother—What are all the joys of earth." She sang these two lines very sweetly, then ceased. They were her last words. The last thing she ate was some beautiful grapes.

September 30, 1867—Have been at Malad City, Idaho[116] for some days, taking ambrotypes. I expect to survey out a city plot for the settlers here, but am waiting to see Bp. Daniels.

October 1, 1867—Began Surveying out a city plot for Malad city laying out 170 lots.

On the 22^d^ of September, last, I wrote the following:—

116 Malad City, Oneida County, Idaho, is located in southeast Idaho approximately forty-eight miles south of Pocatello, Idaho. The town, established in 1864, was a major stop-over point for wagons and supplies from Utah to the Idaho and Montana mines. It had the oldest department store in Idaho, the Evans Co-op Coast-to-Coast. It was the bishop's storehouse where Mormon pioneers brought and received supplies.

TWILIGHT MEMORIES

1

Tis eve, The Sunlight gilds with golden hue
The snowy, cloud-encircled mountain top,
And in the darkling, shadowy vale, the dew
On flower and leaflet gathers drop by drop.
The hour is silent, save the murmuring rill
That leaps along its steep and rocky bed:
Or save the distant-faintly tinkling bell.
Or soft-winged bat, that circles round my head.

[page 262]

AT MALAD CITY

September 22, 1867—

2

The visions of the past before me rise
And oft are happy—oft so sadly sweet
That tears unbidden, glisten in the eyes
At thought of those whom I no more shall meet.
I see again my Father's reverend form,
His grave demeaner and his stately air;
His sparkling eye, with love and friendship, warm
The forehead—crowned with silver-sprinkled hair.

3

My mother—ah! how sacred is that word!
The first that by the infant lip is spoken,
The last that on the battle plain is heard
From thousands, ere their thread of life is broken!
I see again her kind and loving face
That o'er me bent, in childhood's blissful slumber,—
Her gently beaming eye—her quiet grace—
Ah, who can e'er those happy memories number!

4

I hear again a spirit-whispered song
A sister used to sing, while at her feet
We nestled closely round. Her voice hath long
Been silent now. The cold white winding sheet
Enwraps our loved one's form, and on the Stone
Her name engraven is with moss o'ergrown,
A lily, pure and spotless, blooming, bright,

Life's spring awhile she graced—then passed from sight.

5

I had a brother once—a baby boy
Scarce two years old, with soft and ~~gentle~~ azure eye,
And wavy hair—his mother's latest joy
And happy as the bird that carolled nigh,
Years since have passed. I never saw him more
But have been told that on the battle plain
Where rushing armies trampled deep in gore
He rests among our country's valiant slain.
No purer patriotism than his was found—
No braver heart our banner gathered round.

[In margin, words pointing to the poem are unreadable.]

[page 263]

AT MALAD CITY.

6

How many tried and trusted friends are gone!—
How many times our aching hearts have bled!
How oft an old and half-remembered song,
Hath brought to mind those scenes forever fled!
And time is passing still. Today will be
Soon numbered with the shadowy, silent past
While rush we on towards eternity
That stretches out so broad—illimitable vast!

I also wrote the following lines in memory of my boyish days:—

BOYHOOD'S DAYS

How pleasant are the memories of the past–
The many scenes of wild and boyish glee,
When gathered we the ripe and falling mast
From walnut, hickory and chestnut tree:—
The pond, whose waters ~~still~~ clear we used to cleave
With strong and spreading arm—whose depth profound
We now explore—then up again to breathe.
While merry laughter echoes all around.
The skating pond—the coasting riding down the hill—
The winter-spelling school—the quilting bee!—
Our rambles round the old and mossy mill!—
Ah! we were happy as we well could be!
What tricks we played in school! How wrathful frowned
The master when some luckless, ill spent note
Directed to some giggling girl was found
By some great awkward, idle youngster wrote!
What punishment we sometimes used to suffer
From birch or ~~sitting twixt~~ placed between two ~~laughing~~ jeering misses.

[page 264]

September, 1867—
~~Who first would one side crowd and then the other~~
Who'd crowd us first one [on] one side then the other
Or cause our face to burn with ~~jeering~~ threatened kisses!
That punishment hath now its terror lost
As those may find, who try it to their cost.

At the time that it was contemplated in Congress to annex Utah to Nevada, I wrote the following:—

NEVADA. THE BANKRUPT.

Nevada the Bankrupt disconsolate sat
Perched up in her State-Sovreignity chair
Mourning money-bags empty, and worse than all that
Her credit all gone into thinnest of air.
The thought, too, oh! horror! of debts vast and swelling
And Bankruptcy staring her full in the face
The Pawnbroker ready to clear out her dwelling—
She seemed to have run to the end of her race.
While thus in the depth of her grief and despair
A friend came along—(a friend but in name)
And wishing to take the sad maid in a snare
With words soft and honied the Tempter began:—

2

Why sad and dejected? Why lovers that frown?
Tis always the darkest before the day-dawn.
Though your credits all gone, and empty your coffers,—
Tho' the jest of the clown and the butt of the scoffer—
Be watchful and crafty and never despair
And remember your danger makes anything fair.
There's Utah, your neighbor, has plenty of money,
And if you cant get it, twill be rather funny,
Petition to Congress that Utah shall aid
By taxing her cities, to see your debts paid
Annex her at once, and then it is done
And you may your course of extravagance run.

[page 265]

September 1867—

3

Tis true that the mormons have numerous wives
And lawless seducers must forfeit their lives.
That's rather unpleasant—tis horrible, sure—
Tis frightful to think of, but worse to endure.
But when they're annexed, you can rest at your ease
Abolish polygamy and sleep where you please
Repeal all their laws and make new ones at will,
Obliging the Mormons to foot all the bills
Become a great nation, with civilization
With taxes, corruption, and "regeneration"
And thus you will cover with honor and glory
The name of Nevada in all future story.

October 10, 1867—After finishing my Surveying at Malad City, I returned by way of Marsh Valley, and drove to Oxford where I remained three days taking ambrotypes.[117] I earned $96.00 [$1,276] and collected most of it, in sheep and produce and returned home in a few days.

117 Oxford, Franklin County, Idaho, is located east of Malad City. It is the northernmost community in Cache Valley. Jefferson Hunt is the Mormon pioneer most commonly associated with the history of the area. Hunt was a pioneer, soldier, and politician in Utah and California. Oxford was later where Harold B. Lee, a future Church President, taught school (Godfrey and Godfrey, *Utah Years*, 55).

My daughter Elizabeth (whom we call Lillie) has had several hard spells of sickness, but has been finally spared to us.

I wrote the following about this time:—

EVERY CLOUD IS STILL WITH SILVER LINED.

1

On Earth the bitter and the sweet are joined,—
The brightest skies are oft o'er spread with gloom;
The fairest flowers soon fade and strew the ground
And fondest love is shrouded in the tomb.
How oft the fairest hopes that cheer our morn
To disappointment ere the eve give way,
And like old Sampson when his locks were shorn
Our Strength gives place to weakness and decay.

[page 266]

1867—

2

But though on earth our path be strewn with thorns
And rough or smooth, leads ever to the tomb,
There is a clime where Love no more shall mourn
Where sweetest flowers in beauty ever bloom.
In that blest clime the skies are ever bright
And friends once met shall never ~~meet~~ part again,
But in the joy of Heaven's eternal light
Shall triumph o'er each earthly grief and pain.

3

Then let our hearts be filled with hope and joy,
With patience bear each keen but ~~passing~~ transient ill
In deed of love the passing hour employ—
Our fleeting ~~hours~~ time with acts of mercy fill
So shall our strength forever more increase
While heart to heart a kindred love shall bind,
Remembering this, in every passing grief,
That every cloud is still with silver lined.

March 28, 1868—Have been surveying a new town at Weston, for which I received $69.00 [$960] in payment and a balance of $71.00 [$988] due from Bp. John Maughan.

March 30, 1868—Surveyed an addition to the "West Field" at Logan.

April 6, 1868—Surveyed some city lots at Mendon: also some land on the bench, at the foot of the mountain for J. Baker and others.

April 7, 1868—Surveyed 120 acres at 3-Mile Creek[118] for Kidman and others, in ten acre lots. Also surveyed a tract 1½ miles square, at 4 Mile Creek for a herd ground.

April 8, 1868—Surveyed a herd ground for C. Bird[119] at 3-Mile Creek, of 760 acres. Also some land for J. Donaldson.

April 30, 1868—Surveyed Seven blocks of City Lots at Providence

May 28, 1868—Surveyed land up Logan bottoms on Logan Island.

During the latter part of this month I was engaged for some weeks in surveying the old U. S. Survey lines in Cache County so that the people may be able to pre-empt and enter their land, having began the work April 25 1868.

[page 267]

START ON THE UNION PACIFIC SURVEY.

Tuesday, July 7, 1868—I surveyed for Mendon, Wellsville, Paradise, Hyrum, Millville, Providence, and some for Logan. While in the field I received a telegram from Mr. S. B. Reed, Superintendent of Construction of the U.P.R.R. giving me an offer of employment as an engineer on that road.[120] Having consulted with Br. E. T. Benson, who gave me a blessing the day previous to my starting, I started on the for the Weber Cañon, with Br. S. B. Merrill.[121] We went to 3-Mile Creek, near Brigham city. Before leaving, I had let out my summer's work to Lew Herndon, a gentile.[122]

The evening before I started I blessed all my family, having been blessed myself by Br. Benson on the 5th (Sunday) W. H. Sherman also laid on hands with him.[123] I was promised wisdom, judgment and skill in my business, and that the power of the Holy Spirit should be with me, to give me power and influence with those I should be with: also every other necessary blessing. I should return honored by all as an Engineer and as a man.

July 8, 1868—Arrived at the mouth of Weber Cañon, and saw Mr. Tho Bates, the Engineer in charge, who informed me he had waited for me several days, but giving up all idea of my coming, had organized the party intended for me for another engineer. This was bad news for me. I had gone in debt at Logan for my outfit of some $80.00 [$1,113] and now had no way to work and pay for it. He could promise me nothing now, but he finally gave me a note to some of the Engineer parties up the river, that I might get a place as a common hand, if there should be any vacancies there. I was determined not to go home without getting something

118 This is an area northwest of Mendon. William Kidman and John Kidman were among the first settlers (Peterson, *History of Cache County*, 35–36).

119 Charles Bird (1803–1884) immigrated to Utah in 1850. He was a farmer, clothier, wool carder, Mendon's first merchant, and Mendon's second mayor (Sorensen, *History of Mendon*, 28).

120 The Union Pacific and Central Pacific Railroads produced employment for thousands of workers from Cache and Weber valley settlements (Ricks and Cooley, *History of Cache Valley*, 172–74). The Union Pacific Railroad became the first transcontinental railway when it joined the Central Pacific Railroad at Promontory Summit, Utah, in 1869. The UPRR would also eventually take over the Utah Central Railroad and the Utah & Northern Railroad. The Utah Central connected Ogden and Salt Lake. The Utah Southern connected south to Sandy, Lehi, Provo, Payson, and Juab; an extension of the Utah Southern went as far as Milford, north of Beaver. The Utah Northern connected Ogden to Brigham City, Logan, and Franklin, Idaho. The Utah and Northern connected Franklin, Idaho, to the Idaho and Montana mines, to Idaho Falls, and to Dillon, Montana. The Utah Eastern and the Summit County Railroads were spur lines dropping south from the Union Pacific line into Coalville and Park City, Utah (Leonard J. Arrington, *Great Basin Kingdom: An Economic History of the Latter-day Saints, 1830–1900* [Cambridge, MA: Harvard Univ. Press], 1958, 257–92).

121 Samuel B. Merrill served as first counselor to John G. Smith in the bishopric of the Smithfield Ward. In 1862 he was a counselor to Bishop Samuel Rockelley (Smithfield Historical Society, *Smithfield . . . as a City on a Hill* [Smithfield, UT: Smithfield Historical Society, 2001], 88).

122 The term *gentile* in this context simply means an individual who was not a member of the Church.

123 William H. Shearman was a director of the Logan Co-operative Mercantile and Manufacturing Institution, and in the 1860s he opened a store with the Thatchers. This store became the leading commercial house of the valley (Ricks and Cooley, *History of Cache Valley*, 189).

to pay my debts, even if I had to go as a common hand. Stopped at night with Br. Monteith.

[page 268]

ON THE WEBER

July 9, 1868—Started up Weber River on foot, and traveled about 20 miles to an Engineer camp, but found no opening

July 10, 1868—I went on next day still further, to near Lost Creek, and found Mr. Thos B. Morris & camp.[124] He ~~accepted me~~ also had a full company. I took dinner and then started down the river almost disheartened. While thus walking, Mr. Blickensderfer, Chief of the Utah Division overtook me, and promised to help me get a chance if possible.[125] I walked back to Monteith's—40 miles tried [tired] out. In the night Isaac Rogers[126] came down from Morris for me, so we started about midnight and got to his camp at sunrise, Sunday morning.

July 12, 1868—I have all the time trusted I would get along all right as Br. Benson had said, but the prospect seems very dark. Mr. Morris said I might Join his party as a Rodman, his being absent with another party. I had determined to keep on up the River till I could get employment, if I had to travel a month.

I was instructed in reading the Leveling Rod and in keeping the Level book. I felt very lonsome all day. Morris and his party are gentiles, just from the east, and full of bitterness against the Mormons. There is no congeniality of spirit between us. If it were not for the chance to become proficient as an Engineer I would not wish to stay an hour longer

Monday, July 13, 1868—Worked part of the day, and then moved camp.

July 14, 1868—Worked all day climbing along precipitous rocks, fifty feet high, where a misstep would have dashed me to pieces.

July 16, 1868—To day one of the men, Wykoff, would have drowned if I had not rescued him from his danger. The Weber river is at its highest point, and rushes madly and furiously on boiling and surging among the rocks, and very dangerous to cross in our skiff, "The Lady of the Lake." To day I got a letter from home, and found Elvira's picture in my coat pocket. I gave her a hearty kiss.

[page 269]

ON THE WEBER

July 21, 1868—We have to wade a part of the River today, very often. The water is up to our waists and runs so swiftly as to sometimes take us off our feet. It did me to day. The water is very deep below us.

July 24, 1868—Today Mr. Morris and seven others went up to Coalville[127] to spend the 24th, having been invited there. We had a pleasant dance in the evening and started back to Camp about 2 A.M. arriving at our camp about sunrise. I supped with my old friend W. W. Cluff, who is Bishop here.[128]

July 27, 1868—Having finished our work in this part, we moved down as far as Mountain Green. Two of the men went down in the boat, and found the body of a man who was killed a few days ago, while trying to escape from the sheriff who had arrested him for trying to force a woman. I had talked with the man a few days before, telling him he could get along well enough if he would let the women alone. He did not heed my advice and paid the penalty of his life. His body was on the point of a sand bar, half out of the water, and much decomposed.

July 28, 1868—Got three letters from home. The grasshoppers have nearly destroyed my crop. In the Weber Cañon, they cover rocks, shrubs and ground almost entirely, and some days we can hardly work they fly in our faces so.

124 Thomas B. Morris worked on the Union Pacific Railroad. On April 17, 1869, he reported to General Grenville Dodge at Promontory Summit that there was no strike of the workers and that they would be ready for more track in fifteen days. General Dodge was the chief engineer on the transcontinental railroad.

125 This is likely Robert Blickenderfer, a Union Pacific Railroad engineer.

126 This could be Isaac Rogers (1794–1880), who was a former resident of Kirtland, Ohio.

127 Coalville, Summit County, Utah, is located east of Salt Lake City. First called Chalk Creek, the town became Coalville when coal was discovered nearby.

128 W. W. Cluff was a member of the Summit Stake (Godfrey and Godfrey, *Utah Years*, 525).

July 30, 1868—We this day finished our work in the Cañon. I have, up to this date, done all kinds of work, almost: Carried Rod, chained, numbered stakes, cut brush &c Most of the time our work has been either climbing precipitous rocks, or wading in the water in the willows from our knees up sometimes to our chins. The days are intensely hot, and mosquitos fly in myriads. Our work has been full of hardships every day, but my health has been preserved for which I thank God.

I have got along quite well with the party thus far, although I defend Mormonism to the best of my ability.

[page 270]

IN S. L. CITY.

July 31, 1868—Today we start for S. L. City to have a week's holiday, arriving there on the same evening, 36 miles. We camped on a lot behind the theatre.[129]

~~July~~ **August 1, 1868**—Went to the theatre, and next day went to Aunt Esther's and found Julia and Nancy Babbitt and Della Barton; also Horace and Miles Johnson, all of them being my wives cousins.

August 3, 1868—Saw Pres[t] Young in his office

August 4, 1868—We all had our pictures taken, today, in a group in our ragged working Clothes.

August 5, 1868—Had an interview with Mr. Blickensderfer, who promised to use his influence for my advancement. To day I wrote the following lines for Aunt Esther with whom I had been talking of our departed ones:—

THE RESSURRECTION DAY.

1

When the day seems ~~long~~ lone and dreary
When dark clouds o'erspread the sky,—
When the soul is worn and weary
Almost willing, then, to die—
Oh how sweet and bright the vision
Of the near Millennial ray,
Changing earth into Elysium—
Hail the ressurrection day!

2

When the eye is red with weeping
And we breathe the heartfelt sigh:—
At the thought of loved ones sleeping,
Far away—and yet so nigh;—
Sweetly whispers then the spirit
"Mourner, wipe thy tears away!
Earth thy loved ones will revisit
In the ressurrection day.

[page 271]

July 5, 1868—

3

Oh how glad and sweet the meeting
On that bright, celestial morn!
Friends long severed, fondly greeting
Friends with hearts forever warm;
Infants then, like cherubs shining,
On their mother's bosoms ~~lay~~ lie,
Round their necks their arms entwining!
Joyful ressurrection day!

4

Wives and husbands reunited—
Never more asunder torn;—
Never more their fond love blighted
Never more their children mourn;—
Wait we then, in faith and meekness
While on Earth we longer stay,
Soon we'll taste Life's bliss and Sweetness
In the ressurrection day.

August 5, 1868—This evening Mr. Morris said we would start out again on Friday next. Sent $20 [$278] cash home to my family, in two letters.

Thursday, August 7, 1868—To day our party start out again, having provided new supplies. I am appointed topographer of our party the former incumbent being assigned to duty at the office in S. L. City. Instead of $45.00 [$626] pr month my salary is now $75.00 [$1,044] and not much to do on the line, only to take a topographical sketch of the line and country as we progress. I have also to make maps, profiles, plans, &c of the line. It just suits me. I think Mr.

129 According to Sillitoe, the Salt Lake Theatre was constructed at the location of First South and State Streets during 1861 and 1862. (Sillitoe, *Welcoming the World*, 63–65).

Morris does not want me to have the place, wishing to put a gentile friend of his there, but Mr. Blickensderfer has stood my friend.

I waited awhile at the Townsend House for some maps and overtook our camp at Sessions Settlement.

[page 272]

August 8, 1868—Arrived in Weber Cañon, where we have some little work to attend to. I went on ahead to select a camp ground and dined with Mr. Bratton, an Engineer at the mouth of Weber Cañon.

August 10, 1868—Ran a trial line from the mouth of the Cañon the bench towards Ogden. Found the bench 300 feet high and so gave up that line. We started the line down the river.

I began to take Topography, met Genl Dodge, the Chief Engineer, and was introduced to him.

August 11, 1868—Went back to Mountain Green, to change the line a little. Stopped at Enterprize,[130] at Jesse Harris.

August 13, 1868—Have been busy running a new line. Today I wrote the following:—

WHO WILL WELCOME FATHER HOME?

1

Who will welcome father home
When his work on earth is done;
When his hair is fleecy white —
A noble crown forever bright,—
When his home he shall regain
Who will welcome him again?

2

When the victory he hath won
Aided by the Holy One;
When his robes are pure and white
Shining with celestial light;
When the Priesthood calls him home
Who to greet him first will come?

3

Ah, I know who it will be
That will haste to welcome me;
~~And~~ Well I know those little feet
Whose patter sounds like music sweet
As they fly to welcome me
Back to heaven's eternity.

[page 273]

August 13, 1868—

4

And those little outstretched hands
Beckoning to brighter lands;
The love-lit eye—the smile so sweet—
Oh joy divine when we shall meet!
Dellie—Willie—ye will come
And sweetly welcome Father home.

5

And another will be there
With my cherub—children fair
One all spotless, pure and bright
Guardian Spirit, robed in white,
Thou, Elvira—wife—wilt come
And guide me to our blissful home.

Saturday, August 14, 1868—Today we finished this part of the line. This morning I wrote the following lines, descriptive of our labors as engineers, to the air "Red, White & Blue."

ENGINEER SONG

1

Come boys gather round and I'll sing you a song
About our proceedings as we move along,
Locating the Union Pacific Railway
Through deserts and mountains and plains far away.

Chorus.

Hurrah! hurrah! for the bold Engineer
Who tracks the wild desert without any fear,
Hurrah! hurrah! for the bold Engineer
Who tracks the wild desert without dread or fear.

130 This "Enterprize" is not what is now Enterprise, Utah. Mountain Green, Morgan County, Utah, is located up the Weber River from Ogden, whereas Enterprise, Washington County, Utah, is located in the southern end of the state.

2

We encounter a forest and cut our way through
With axes and bill hooks without more ado,
Through thickets of willows and brambles and thorns,
We steadily hew out a pathway along.
Chorus

[page 274]

August 14, 1868—

3

We came to a slough and we boldy wade in
Perchance to our middle, or up to the chin;
The water, tho muddy and noisome and black,
Shall not hinder or stop our locating the track.
Chorus.

4

On the side of a precipice, craggy and steep
The transit directs where the chainmen shall creep,
And clinging like bats to the steep mountain side,
They calmly look down on the fierce surging tide.
Chorus.

5

A ~~fierce~~ swift rushing river now crosses our path
Boiling and serging in furious wrath,
No matter—to cross it we boldly push in
Then blest is the fellow who knows how to swim.
Chorus

6

The winter's cold blast and the sun's burning ray,
Cannot hinder our progress, as day after day
We run to the westward, locating our line,
Till the Central Pacific we finally join.
Chorus.

7

The lone thirsty desert, so dreary and still
Spreads out from the Lake to the far distant hill;
Its vast bosom glitters ~~like~~ with salt, like the snow,
But "onward's" our motto, and onward we go.
Chorus

8

A beautiful lake now appears to our view,
Reflecting the mountains and heavens so blue;
With rapture we hasten to drink of the prize
But ah! tis a mirage, deceiving our eyes.
Chorus.

[page 275]

WESTWARD HO!

August 17, 1868—Began running our line down the river.

August 18, 1868—Conference at Ogden today, but I could not attend. Pres^{t} Young was there

August 20, 1868—Ran our line to the Hot Spring.

August 21, 1868—Made connection today with Maxwell's line near Willard City.[131] Our line ran for a distance of 2100 feet across an arm of Salt Lake.

August 25, 1868—Having finished our maps, &c of the line we have run, this afternoon we started on westward to begin again on the work of Location. Camped at a spring on Point Lookout Mountain, about 20 miles from Brigham City, with a man and his wife going to Idaho. We spent a very pleasant evening singing.

Thursday, August 27, 1868—To day we moved 17 miles to Genl Dodge's camp. He has an escort of 200 Dragoons.

August 28, 1868—We crossed the Promontory range today, obtaining a magnificent view of Spring and Bear River Bays, and the islands in the Lake. We passed Stephenson's C. P. Camp and Col. Hudnotts U. P. Camp. Traveled about 17 miles. I found a good sachel, which was handy.

August 29, 1868—Went 27 miles today to Locomotive Springs which, like all the springs, almost, of this part of the country, are salty. Here was a camp of C. P. engineers: also Hodges and Maxwell's U. P. parties making in all five engineer camps, making quite a city of tents. Here I found Victor Crockett of Logan,[132] a

131 Willard, Box Elder County, Utah, is just south of Brigham City on the northeastern shore of the Great Salt Lake.

132 Victor Crockett, a laborer, was an early settler in Logan (Somers, *History of Logan*, 59).

member of Hodges party. Was glad to see him. Wrote the following Lines on our Engineer Party.

THE MUSTER ROLL.

First, there's Mr. Morris, a shrewd engineer
And transitman Coons with eye quick and clear.
Bob Fulton, our leveler will see his way through
And Martineau all our topography do.

2

There's Corbus, or [our] Rodman and Wykoff,
Back Flag.
And Scurry and Brown with the chain never lag.

[page 276]

AT RED DOME PASS

August 29, 1868—
With Larkin our Stakeman, and Aleck to drive
And the cooks, Brown and Sabin, who cause us to
thrive.

3

The Teamsters come next, of our Engineer corps
Trowbridge, and Rogers, and also one more
Evernden, last but not least of the list,—
Either one absent, would sadly be missed.

4

Another there was—Rickseeker by name,
Who long ago into our company came;
Transferred to the office at Townsend Hotel
His presence we miss, but hope he is well.

5

If any one thinks we are spoony's or flats
Just tread on our coat tails, or knock off our hats.
They soon will find out the mistake they have
made
Where they find themselves lying some feet below
grade.

Monday, August 31, 1868—We started to day for Red Dome Pass, where our labors are to begin again. We traveled all day, along the N. W. end of the Great Salt Lake mud flats, covered with salt, which glistened so brightly in the bright sun, that it almost blinded us. We had to wear handkerchiefs over our faces. There is no road, at all and our teams travel slowly. We have one six-mule team, one 4-mule team, one 2-mule team, all loaded with supplies and camp equipage, and some horses, for riding. The men have to march. Myself and some others ascended to the top of Red Dome Mountain, and had a fine view of the country. Desolation reigns here supreme. To the Southward and as far as the eye can reach, extends a flat plain, as level as a floor, encrusted with salt, with here and there isolated peaks bounding the horizon. I think this mountain is about 2500 or 3000 feet above the lake.

[page 277]

1868—We traveled 30 miles and camped without water, but got some from a small stream 4 miles off.

Tuesday, September 1, 1868—Made our camp on Duff Creek. This water, though clear, is horrible, having an indescribable flavor. It almost made me think of carrion. We began to run a sixty-five foot grade line from the summit of the pass which has an elevation of 4780 above the sea,—about 560 feet above the Lake.

September 2, 1868—I went over the line and took slopes (angles of inclination of the ground) and made my notes.

September 4, 1868—Moved our camp back 9 miles.

September 5, 1868—Wrote home. Saw Lorin Farr, of Ogden,[133] who, with E. T. Benson and C. W. West,[134] has a contract to grade 100 miles for the Central Pacific R. R.

Went to Gen[l] Dodge's Camp, about 11 miles, to get a carpet bag of one of our party, just joined, from Philadelphia. Morris did not dare trust him to go, for fear he would get lost, not being used to mountains. Got back just as a fearful tempest of wind, rain, thunder and lightening began. The wind blew down

---

133 The family of Lorin Farr (1820–1908) immigrated to Utah in 1847. Brigham Young called Lorin to move to Ogden and preside over the Saints in that area. Lorin was the first mayor of Ogden, served as stake president, and was a member of the first territorial legislature (Godfrey and Godfrey, *Utah Years*, 107).

134 Chauncey W. West, a commander of the Weber Military District, was from Ogden. He organized the Cache Valley Militia (Peterson, *History of Cache County*, 39).

some of our tents, in spite of us. We flew around for a while in the rain, and just as we got all right, the storm ceased. It was a grand sight altogether.

September 7, 1868—Coons, our Transitman, being sick, I ran line today—We made connection eastward with Maxwell. Moved back to Red Dome Pass, at Duff Creek. Found Mr. Blickensderfer with orders to hurry up as fast as possible. Found a company of C. P. Engineers, camped there, who are locating their line on the same ground.

September 8, 1868—Was with Mr. B. all day. We climbed a mountain and triangulated all the peaks around. I saw Pilot Peak in Nevada, Desert Mountains, Raft River Mountains and other ranges. It was a grand view.[135] The Lake lay like a vast plate of silver in a setting of mountains whose desolate heads towered among the clouds.

[page 278]

September 8, 1868—I prayed, when alone, and dedicated all to the Lord. Mr. Morris hunted for us all day with lunch, but did not find us. He got to camp an hour after we did and seemed disgusted to find us there.

September 9, 1868—Sent our mail by Larkins to the nearest mail station—35 miles.

September 10, 1868—Moved camp, took topography of 12 miles line today.

September 11, 1868—Went with Morris today about 14 miles in advance, to find the place to connect with the party in advance. We found it. We also saw two mountain sheep. The Desert Mountain, rising from a flat plain fully 25 miles away to the south, seems to be only a mile or two.

September 13, 1868—Made a sketch of Desert Mountains for Mr. Blickensderfer

September 16, 1868—Sent maps to the mail line 60 miles by Larkins, having worked all night to finish them. Traveled 25 miles, and camped with Mr. Bates C. P. party. They are going to the Red Dome Pass to locate their line there. They are willing to bet their line will reach Ogden before ours. Went to bed without supper, being too tired, after being up all night and walking all day. I could have ridden by invitation of Morris, but would not, and see all the rest on foot.

September 17, 1868—Found Mr. Ives, C. P. Engineer party at Surprise or Grouse Creek.[136] Camped in a large meadow of several thousand acres of grass, with good water. Found a split stake holding a letter from Gen[l] Dodge to Morris.

September 18, 1868—Traveled 15 miles to [Tuano] Pass, and for the first time since we left Weber, had some good cold clear water. Threatens to snow. Felt unwell today and lay down to sleep. Followed the trail of our wagons after I got up, and met Clark with a horse Morris had sent back for me.

September 19, 1868—Crossed the pass today and met another C. P. party Camped at Peoguop Pass, from the summit of which I could see the Snowy range of Humbolt Mountains.

[page 279]

September 19, 1868—Found Gen[l] Dodge's party camped there, and soon Col. Hudnutt's[137] party arrived. Found Von Froben, Gen[l] Dodge's topographer here, and was glad to see him.

September 20, 1868—Ice this morning in our tin cups, 1/3 of an inch thick.

September 21, 1868—Began running our line east from the Summit of Peoguop Pass.

September 22, 1868—Made a map of Hudnotts line by request of Gen. Dodge.

Thursday, September 24, 1868—Thinking of my priestly robes,[138] I wrote these lines:—

135 Pilot Peak (9,182 feet) is in Elko County on the border of Utah and Nevada. The Desert Mountains are in Central Nevada; their highest peak would be Cleaver Peak (6,711 feet). The Raft River Mountains are in northern Utah; Dunn Benchmark (9,925 feet) is its highest peak. The Raft River flows from Utah to Idaho and is a tributary of the Snake River.

136 Grouse Creek, Box Elder County, Utah, is located west of the northern Great Salt Lake.

137 Hudnutt was apparently a railroad inspector (National Park Service, "Golden Spike: Cultural Landscape Report, Chapter 2: Site History," http://www.nps.gov/archive/gosp/clr /clr2d.htm).

138 Individuals participating in temple ordinances dress in white temple clothing. The temple endowment "is a series of symbols" relating to spirituality: "During the endowment, solemn covenants are made pertaining to honesty, purity, righteous service, and devotion" (Boyd K. Packer, *The Holy Temple* [Salt Lake City: Bookcraft, 1980], 71–72).

TO MY PRIESTLY ROBES.

1

Priestly Robes! so pure and white!
Type of that celestial light
That shines in heaven forever bright—
I sing of thee.

2

Priestly garments, white and clean!
When enrobed in thee, I seem
Almost of the bliss serene
Of heaven to taste.

3

When my feeble race is run
And my work on earth is done,
How sweet to rest me in the tomb
Enrobed in thee!

4

Death is Life—eternal Gain—
Glad release from Satan's reign,
Who no more can bring a stain
On thee, my robes.

5

When we meet our loved ones there—
Oh, so beautiful and fair!
Robes like thee they all will wear
In purity.

[page 280]

September 24, 1868—

6

Ye are pure and I must be
If I would be ~~enrobed~~ clothed in thee
And through all eternity
And enjoy eternally [appears erased]
Have ~~joy serene~~ a heavenly joy.

Friday, September 25, 1868—Cold nights and mornings, and we find the three stoves Larkins brought to us on horseback are very Comfortable indeed. He brought them nearly 80 miles. Yesterday Genl Dodge requested me to make a map of some 16 miles of Hudnutt's survey, to be sent to Mr. Reed. I did it to his satisfaction. While here, Mr. King of the U. S. Geological Survey passed along. They are on their way east with one wagon, and pack animals. Some U. P. contractors came looking for their contracts, to begin work. They wish to go to work at once.

September 27, 1868—Today Corbus left us to go on construction with Mr. Maxwell. Morris gave me an offer to take a party on Construction also. I finally consented and was so appointed.

September 28, 1868—Started east today. Recd letters from my wives, Elvira and Lyman.

September 30, 1868—Began to alter the line from Grouse Creek east. In the evening I assisted Mr. Blickensderfer to take observations with the Sextant, for variation of needle, taking observations on Jupiter and Polaris. I looked at the moons of Jupiter through his telescope—they were very beautiful, but the moon was gloriously beautiful.

October 4, 1868—Went with Scurry—an ex-confederate soldier, upon a high hill, where there was a beautiful view. I killed a rattlesnake there, and had a good talk about Mormonism.

October 5, 1868—Joined our line with Hodge's today, near the north end of the Ombe Mountains. Found some U. P. graders at work.

October 6, 1868—Ran a tangent line here of 24 miles, the C. P. lying close by and crossing ours.

[page 281]

COMING BACK. MEET BR. W. HYDE

October 7, 1868—Today Mr. Morris sent us all out, to see if we could kill any game, our provisions being almost gone. We have nothing to eat except about 50 lbs flour, as much of corn meal, a little molasses, and a few pickles for about 20 of us. It was all we could do to eat the cakes, heavy and coarse.

I started off alone for a mountain about ten miles away, walking through sandy and clayey wastes, but for miles not seeing even a Rabbit. When I came to the foot of the mountain, I saw fresh antelope tracks, made only about an hour before, but saw none of the timid creatures. I went to the top of the mountain, with great difficulty, there being only one narrow way to get up. As I walked I felt my leg strike something like a cord, and found it was a spider thread so large and strong as to cause me to feel it through my clothes. I brought it along. After doubling it, I could hardly break it.

I returned to camp at night, and found no one had killed anything.

October 9, 1868—We came to Some graders working on the C. P. from Ogden. Met Col. Wm Hyde and Arthur Stayner.[139] I was so glad I could have kissed them. Here we got a quarter of beef, and during the evening ate most of it up, being very hungry. I remained back several hours to visit Br. Hyde, and had to follow the line in the darkness of the night, by pacing the distance from one stake to another—100 feet—and by taking my course by the Stars. Once in a while I lit a match to verify the numbers on the stakes. Finally came upon our camp—on Terrace Point—all eating beef:—frying, roasting on sticks and on coals, while the cooks kept the stoves going. It was a strange scene. We did not put up our 5 tents.

[page 282]

BACK TO THE PROMONTORY

October 10, 1868—Went to Duff Creek, 18 miles. Found many camps of men from Cache County at work for the C.P.R.R. Saw Bps. Hughes,[140] Littlewood and Maughan.

October 12, 1868—Wrote home, and sent $20.00 [$278] to my folks.

Fig. 4.7–Martineau surveyed for the transcontinental and Utah railroads. These systems joined a nation and promoted economic development. On May 10, 1869, the completion of the transcontinental railroad was celebrated at Promontory, Utah. © Intellectual Reserve, Inc.

October 13, 1868—Saw today Bps. Hatch,[141] W. Hyde; S. Collett,[142] T. B. Cardon,[143] C. B. Robbins[144] and W. K. Robinson,[145] at Brr. Benson's camp. Had a good chat with Martha Robbins, and with Mrs. Mary Larsen Benson. Got some supplies of P. D. Griffeths.

October 14, 1868—Went to Locomotive Springs,[146] and were serenaded by the Ogden Brass Band, who are grading here.

October 15, 1868—Down to Salt Springs, and met our supplies. We had a 6-mule load of Sugar, Canned fruits, raisins, bottled pickles, dried fruit, fresh peaches, flour, bacon, mackerel, and other things. We have orders to locate a new line over the promontory, when we we get there.

October 16, 1868—We camped about 4 miles south of Parker's Springs on the U.P.R.R. line.

October 17, 1868—This evening Mr. Morris told me that Genl Dodge had sent orders for me to join Hudnutt's party, and help run a line from Locomotive Springs to Portland, Oregon.

I told him I would go for two months at $100.00 [$1,391] pr month, and my passage in the stage back.

139 Arthur Stayner was among the early Ogden, Utah, businessmen (Roberts and Sadler, *History of Weber County*, 86).

140 This was likely Henry Hughes. He served as the bishop of Mendon for thirty-one years (Sorensen, *History of Mendon*, 38).

141 This is likely Lorenzo Hatch, bishop of the Franklin Ward. He was on the board of directors for the Utah Northern Railroad Company (Peterson, *History of Cache County*, 71).

142 Sylvanus Collett was among the first settlers of Cache Junction, north of Mendon (Ricks and Cooley, *History of Cache Valley*, 82). Sylvanus and his brother Sylvester Collett were rumored to be members of the Danites (Simmonds, *The Gentile Comes to Cache Valley*, 10). According to Cornwall and Arrington, the Danites were a myth. As a result of violence and Mormon persecution in Missouri, a former Mormon dissident, Sampson Avard, accused the Church leaders of organizing a band of outlaws—the Danites—who would take revenge against the persecutors. Although no organization was ever documented in Utah, Missouri, or Illinois, the myth persisted (Ludlow, *Encyclopedia of Mormonism*, 356–57; Rebecca Coster Cornwall and Leonard J. Arrington, "Perpetuation of a Myth: Mormon Danites in Five Western Novels, 1840–90," *BYU Studies* 23, no. 2 (Spring 1983): 147–65).

143 T. B. Cardon was a Logan businessman. He was a photographer, a jeweler, and owned an art gallery (Somers, *History of Logan*, 55, 58, 110).

144 C. B. Robbins ran the first telegraph office in Cache Valley (Godfrey and Godfrey, *Utah Years*, 66).

145 W. K. Robinson was a Logan alderman and active in politics (Ricks and Cooley, *History of Cache Valley*, 103).

146 Locomotive Springs, located northwest of the Great Salt Lake, is very dry and inhospitable.

He said I could have those terms if I would stay until the line was completed. This I would not do.

October 30, 1868—At this date we have been running several lines over the Promontory seeking a better one than Hudnutt's if possible. Have been very busy at my business. Nephi Johnson came to see me today, having brought his family from Dixie. He looks very poorly in health.

October 31, 1868—Informed Morris of my intention to leave him and go home. He was very much opposed to it, and begged me to stay, which I finally concluded to do for a time. Moved to the east side of the promontory to a good spring.

Sunday, November 1, 1868—Went upon a high hill and prayed as usual. I could see Mount Nebo in the south, a 100 miles from S. L. City.

[page 283]

MIRED. GET HOME

November 7, 1868—Spent the week in taking cross section notes of Hudnutts two lines, one of 80 feet grade pr mile, the other of 90 feet. A comparative estimate of cost will be made of both those lines, to determine which shall be taken.

November 9, 1868—Went on the line, and made estimates of the culverts and masonry required, on both lines. Spent most of the night helping Morris make his estimates of cost of the two lines. We found that the 80 foot grade line would cost $596.000.[00] [$8,292,773] the 90 foot line $549,000.[00] [$7,638,812] The equation used on the U.P. is $50.[00] [$696] for each degree of (Central Angle) curvature; $15.[00] [$209] pr foot for length of line; 20 feet rise = 1 mile level road: $75.[00] [$1,044] pr lineal foot of arch culvert from 6 to 12 feet span, $4.50 [$63] pr lineal foot of Box culverts of 2 to 4 feet span. The actual cost of road bed for the 80-foot grade is $47.000 [$653,960] less than the 90-foot line, but the equation for length throws the balance the other way.

November 13, 1868—Started home to see my family, riding a mule. Passed through Mendon about 10 P.M. and started across the bottoms. After wandering around awhile, I found the bridge, but it was burned, and I could not ford the river, and I had to start back to Mendon. Going back I got lost, and got into a deep slough, half way up the mule's side. I could not get him to move an inch, and had to get off into the freezing water up to my breast. I had to work a long time to get him out. He was stubborn, and I could have shot him with a good grace if he had been mine. Got back to town about 11 P.M. nearly chilled through, and found a good warm fire at Cha[s] Bird's where I stopped for the night, thoroughly tired out having ridden about 70 miles.

November 14, 1868—Got home at 9 A.M. much rejoiced to meet my family again. Found my family as well as I had hoped to find them.

[page 284]

November 16, 1868—Paid some debts;—To Conrad $8.00 [could read $4] [$111 or $57], Mrs. Birdno $3.00 [$42]; L. Herndon (in full) $75.[00] [$1,044] Thatcher & Sons $40.[00] [$557].

November 17, 1868—Took some likenesses, amounting to $9.50 [$132].

November 18, 1868—Started back to camp. Tried to cross the Logan Bottoms, but could not, on account of water & ice, Hamptons.

November 19, 1868—Went back to Logan to see Br. Benson, about getting a contract at grading on the C.P.R.R. Got home and found Lillie quite sick. Susan E. drew a new quilt at a raffle of the Female Relief Society.

November 20, 1868—Waited all day to see Br. Benson.

Saturday, November 21, 1868—Started back to Camp not having made any arrangement with Br. Benson. Arrived at Camp at 9 P.M.[147]

November 27, 1868—Talked with Gov. L. Stanford, Pres[t] of C.P.R.R. Company, who wishes me to help them engineer.

Wednesday, December 2, 1868—Mr. Morris, myself and Teamster Evernden started south to triangulate from some high mountains. We camped about 7 miles south of the lines, on a small creek at the foot of a high mountain. We do this to connect the triangulations from the west, with that from the east, at Ogden, for the Smithsonian Institution.

147 For an interesting description of the railroad work, see "Our Local Correspondence," *Deseret News*, November 25, 1868; Utah Digital Newspapers.

Thursday, December 3, 1868—This morning Morris and Myself, started up the mountain. We hard hard work to reach the top, where we found it very cold. We took angles ~~ft~~ to the islands. & peaks all around us. Left the transit on the mountain and got back to camp quite late.

December ~~4~~ 3, 1868—Started up the mountain before sunrise, but as it began to be cloudy, we returned to camp. Morris thought best to leave me to do the work, while he went to Ogden, and accordingly he left us. We are well provided with provisions, bedding, stove and all things needful. Evemden went back to the main camp to take Morris and get some provisions.

December ~~5~~ 4, 1868—This morning still cloudy.

December ~~6~~ 5, 1868—Still unfavorable.

December ~~7~~ 6, 1868—This morning I started up the mountain alone while Evemden went to hunt the team, which had strayed away. After a very toilsome ascent, [continued on next page]

[page 285]

TRIANGULATING FROM MT. MARTINEAU.

December 6, 1868—I finally reached the Summit at 2 P.M. Just after getting my transit set and ready for work, clouds rolled up from the lake entirely enveloping me in the mist, so I could see nothing for about two hours. It is intensely cold, a piercing wind sweeping from the north. I went down a little way to escape the wind, and built a fire, by which I kept one side warm, while the other froze. At length the clouds settled below me, leaving me in bright sunshine, with the clouds below me like a vast illimitable ocean: the mountain peaks rising through them resembled Islands. At length a hole appeared in the cloud below through which I could see the earth. I seemed to be on another planet and had the strangest feelings until the clouds cleared away. Below me lay The lake—in fact—hundreds of square miles were spread out like a map. The mountains round S. L. City Tooele,[148] Ogden, Cache, The desert, Mt. Nebo,[149] nearly 200 miles south, Pilot Peak in Nevada, the Raft River Mountains, were all plainly visible. I took the necessary to all the prominent points and got through a little before the sun set. I started for camp, about ~~11~~ 8 miles, and toiled on the mountain with the transit for about 5 miles: then left the transit as it was quite dark and finally arrived in camp, tired out. In descending the mountain, in the dark, I slipped, fell rolled, and got to the bottom in all sorts of ways. Several times narrowly escaping going over precipices, which I could not see until just on the brink.

Evemden had walked 20 miles hunting for the mules, and found them finally within 500 yds of the camp, where they had been all day. He had seen Bp. Wm Hyde, who wished me to see him next day if I could so do, as he was going to leave there.

[page 286]

LEAVE THE COMPANY AT OGDEN. VISIT HENRY. HOME.

December 7, 1868—I started for Notch Peak.[150] I first went to my transit, and then had about 5 miles to go along the ridge of the mountains, which was in many places, quite dangerous, so that I had to lead my horse much of the time. Several times he slipped on the frozen earth and slid down the mountain side some distance. He presented a very comical appearance, sometimes. I finally reached the point desired, and took my angles. The wind was so piercing cold, I could hardly use the instrument, or write my figures in the book. Had a hard and dangerous time getting down the mountain.

December 8, 1868—Moved camp, intending to go to Hunsaker Mountain. Called at Benson's camp, and learned Br. Hyde had been dangerously kicked in the head by a horse, a few hours before (7th, 3 P.M.) and they had started home with him in a carriage. We drove quite fast for several miles, to overtake him but could not do it. We camped at the foot of Hunsaker Mountain. We were followed about a mile by a ~~lit~~ large

....

148 Tooele, Tooele County, Utah, is located west of Salt Lake City. The name of the town is thought to have been derived from a Native American word for *tumbleweed.*

149 Mount Nebo (11,928 feet) is the highest peak in Utah's Wasatch Mountain Range.

150 Notch Peak, located in Millard County, Utah, rises to an elevation of 9,654 feet with sheer cliffs.

grey wolf, who kept close behind the wagon, seemingly not at all afraid. We had no fire arms, and so could not kill him.

December 9, 1868—Ascended the mountain today. Took my angles arrived at Bear River ferry at 2.30 P.M. and at Brigham City at 7 P.M. very cold indeed. Went to Rosenbaums Hotel, and found it full and no room to sleep, so we slept in the stock yard, with about a dozen others.

December 10, 1868—Went on to Ogden to-day. Snowed all day.

December 15, 1868—Having determined to leave the party, I started up the Weber Cañon to Devil's gate to see my son, Henry who is working with Thos Stewart, grading. Walked there through deep snow. Very cold weather. Got to the camp and found Henry there, well, and grown much taller than when I saw him last.

December 16, 1868—Started home this morning, having directed Henry to come home in two or three days.

[page 287]

U.S. SURVEYING IN CACHE. UTAH CENTRAL R. R.

December 16, 1868—When I was going to Leave the Company, Mr. Morris tried hard to dissuade me, promising me permanent employment by the U.P.R.R. Company if I would stay. Said I was the best topographer on the whole U.P.R.R. line, which, as I am a Mormon, is considerable praise. He gave me a recommendation of the best kind, which was endorsed by the principal engineers of the Company, among the rest by Mr. Blickensdersfer, Coons, & others.

I arrived home on the 18th of December, truly glad to be once more with the Saints, in the bosom of my family.

April 24, 1869—Having been requested by Prest B. Young to assist Br. J. W. Fox in retracing the U.S. Survey lines in Cache Co. so that the people may enter their lands, I this day begin to do so, meeting Br. Fox and his party at Wellsville. Br. Fox began his survey for this valley at a spot in Levi Minnerly's garden,[151] where it was supposed a Stake once was. Br. Fox ran a line from Wellsville, through Hyrum, Church Farm, Providence, Logan, Hyde Park, Smithfield, Richmond and Franklin, So that those townsites may be entered. I proceeded with another party to survey the Quarter Section lines for Wellsville, Mendon, Hyrum, Paradise, Millville, Providence and Logan. I spent several weeks at this work, neglecting my photograph business, which was very good, being about $125.00 [$1,827] per month. I had no assurance of certainty for my pay, nor did I know if I would ever get any, but worked because it was necessary for it to be done for the benefit of the Saints, as I have already done, for many years past.

May 13, 1869—While surveying in the field, a telegram from Presr B. Young was handed me, requesting me to be in Ogden the next day, to assist in the work of engineering the Utah Central R.R. Br. J. W. Fox was chief Engineer, but had no knowledge of the business at all. I was the only one who had.

[page 288]

UTAH CENTRAL R. R.

May 14, 1869—Started for Ogden to day with a load of tithing grain. We slept in a stable in Brigham City. In the evening I saw the light of a passing train, the first since I was in Ohio in 1848.

May 15, 1869—Arrived in Ogden at noon. Br. Fox and Mr. Bates, an engineer of the C.P.R.R. had gone out to look out a place to cross the Weber River. Br. Fox had been anxiously waiting for me.

May 16, 1869—Went out on the ground with Br. Fox and Bates; also Missrs Jennings,[152] Sharp, Farr and others. Prest Young came to Ogden this evening.

May 17, 1869—Today a large assemblage met near the Weber R. to inaugurate the Utah Central. Prest. G. A. Smith the dedicating prayer and Prest. Young turned up the first earth. The ceremonies were very interesting. I telegraphed for Henry to Come and bring my level, and bedding.

151 Levi Minnerly was later arrested for polygamy (Godfrey and Godfrey, *Utah Years*, 559).

152 This is likely William Jennings, who was among the early industrial pioneers in Ogden (Roberts and Sadler, *History of Weber County*, 86). John Sharp and William Jennings were among the dignitaries invited to the dedication of the Utah Central Railroad Building in Ogden (Roberts and Sadler, *History of Weber County*, 113).

May 18, 1869—Today, I started with our party across the River, and camped on the opposite bank, near Wilson's settlement.

May 19, 1869—Began work today. I taught Jo^s^ West,[153] son of C. G. West, who wishes to learn engineering, how to read the leveling rod. Chas Hardy will use the line, myself the transit. Mr. Bates was also with us.

May 20, 1869—Today we ran 3 miles of preliminary line. Today a man here killed a large wild cat near our camp. It was about three feet long. Br. Fox placed me his 1st Assistant Engineer. Br. C. L. Ericson came to join us today.[154] He is a Sweede, just arrived in Utah, only about a year ago. Henry also came today.

May 24, 1869—John Fawsen Smith joined us today

May 26, 1869—I. F. Smith began helping us today, cross sectioning. Quite Stormy for several days.

May 27, 1869—On returning to camp to night. I found F. Little with a Mr. Lawrence, a U.P. Engineer, who had called to see us.

May 31, 1869—Received letters from each of my wives and one from Elvira.

[page 289]

FARMINGTON.

Tuesday, June 1, 1869—Wrote home, and sent papers to Moroni, Elvira & Lyman.

June 15, 1869—We have now got our line to Kay's Creek. We are restricted to a grade of not exceeding 40 feet rise per mile, and not more than 6° Curves, which makes it slow work for us, finding a good line fulfilling those conditions. The highest point of the line on the Land Ridge is 216 feet above the Weber River at Ogden. Our camp is well provided with tents, having five in all, three of which are wall tents 14' ×16'.

On Saturday last, I went to S. L. City and went to Uncle D. T. LeBaron's. I also saw John Steele, of Parowan, the first time for many years. We were glad to see each other, and talk over old times.

June 16, 1869—Ran the line to the Haight Bench, and had a good swim in a pond near our camp, which we moved there on the 17th.

June 21, 1869—Moved Camp to Farmington. Br. Fox's wife and two daughters have been camping with us for some time past. Sister Fox, who has long had poor health, is gaining fast. The presence of these ladies is a source of much pleasure to us all. Our company now consists of J. W. Fox, the Chief Engineer, myself, 1st assistant. J. F. Smith, Second Assistant, C. L. Erickson 3^d^ Assistant, Chas Hardy, Leveler; Jo^s^ A. West, Rodman, A. F. Doremus (who has just joined us) also Leveler, Jess Fox Jr. Rodman, Henry A. Martineau, Marker Oscar and Edward Hunter, sons of Bp. Hunter Chainman and Markers, Geo Day, Stake carrier, Hiram Young, a son of Brigham Young, Tapeman (with cross sectioners), two cooks and a teamster. Also O. F. Lyon, Leveler.

June 25, 1869—Our party had a dance and a play on the smooth green of the road where our camp is, in Farmington, in which many of the boys and girls of the place joined.

June 26, 1869—Moved camp to Session's, near Lyons place.

June 27, 1869—Wrote some playful verses for Miss Georgiana Fox as did Oscar Lyons, also, mine were as follows:—

[page 290]

June 27, 1869—

THE LITTLE FAIRY

1

In boyhoods days I often read
Of Faries, Elves and Goblins
And with a sigh had sometimes said
"Oh that I too might see one".

2

I older grew, and as I roamed
Among the wild wood flowers
I often sought to find their home
Beneath the leafy bowers.

153 Within the next two years, Joseph W. West would be a surveyor working in Weber County. The C. G. West referred to here is likely Chauncey W. West (Roberts and Sadler, *History of Weber County*, 71).

154 C. L. Ericson, also spelled Erickson, was a civil engineer for Salt Lake City. He also held a patent on a snowplow.

3

Thus often sought, but found them not
In flowery dell nor meadow,
Nor in the cool and darkling grot
Nor wild woods arching shadows

4

You know that faries, always kind,
And gentle, true and winning,
Will often ~~find~~ help, when one they find
Who needs their gentle blessing.

5

Well, there is one our camp attends
And as we move, she moveth
Whose presence joy and pleasure lends
Whose touch the sick one sootheth.

6

Sometimes she bringeth books to read
Sometime she bringeth flowers,
But always brings just what we need
To ~~soothe~~ cheer our lonely hours.

7

So now a fairy tis, tis plain
Because tis like the others
That in my youth but all in vain
I rambled to discover.

[page 291]

AT S. L. CITY

Thursday, July 1, 1869—We arrived with the Camp in S. L. City today, having run the line to the Hot Springs.

July 2, 1869—Spent the time examining the proposed route by the Hot Spring Lake, and in rowing upon it.

July 3, 1869—Brought the line to the edge of the City.

June [July] 4, 1869—Went to meeting and heard the new organ.[155] Received a long letter from Susan J.

July 5, 1869—Ran the line to ~~Union~~ Square (17th Ward) and then we went to the celebration, which was a grand one. There was about 3000 Children in the procession. I wrote to Susan J. and sent the following lines which I wrote on the line the other day:—

THE ~~TIES~~ BONDS OF LOVE.

1

Though one by one our friends are taken
To sleep awhile within the tomb,
Ere long each one with joy will waken
And burst forever from its gloom.

2

Oh happy thought! How sweet to waken
When loud the last great trump shall ring.
To meet the loved ones Death hath taken
And press them to our hearts again.

3

~~The ties~~ But bonds of Love, Death cannot sever,
E'en with his cold, relentless hand,
But stronger grows—and grows forever
That strong—unseen—yet mighty band.

Wednesday, July 7, 1869—Finished the location of the line today, terminating on South Temple, Babbit's Block, being 36+ miles from the Weber River.

July 8, 1869—Cross sectioned to day.

July 9, 1869—Got $38.80 [$555] worth of Clothing, also $40.00 [$585] cash. Called to see the Foxes.

[page 292]

Saturday, July 10, 1869—The line having been divided into three Divisions of Construction, A. F. Doremus[156] had the Ogden Division, extending to Kay's Creek. I took the Central, extending to Sessions, and J. F. Smith the third Division. Br. Fox wished me to take the Ogden, but I preferred the Central. I left the city for Farmington, to day with the following

155 Joseph H. Ridges installed the first tabernacle organ in 1867. Neils Johnson added to it in 1885.

156 Abraham Fairbanks Doremus was a Salt Lake City and Utah state engineer, noted for his work in water conservation and railroad construction.

party: C. L. Enizon, Henry A, Ed[d] Hunter, and Oscar F. Lyons.[157] My teamster, Calvin Richards, a son of Willard Richards—lives at Farmington. We stopped with Tho[s] Smith to night.

Got the following Recipe for Black Canker, which W. K. Rice had from John Sanderson:—[158]

"1 pt Strong garden sage tea
½ pt strong kinnekenick tea } each boiled separately
½ pt strong sumach tea
1 tea-spoonful Borax (not burned)
1 tea-spoonful Alum (not burned)
1 tea-spoonful Copperas (not burned)
1 tea-spoonful Goldenseal———

Strain the teas, then put in the other ingredients: boil and strain again. Sweeten with loaf sugar.

Use as a wash, with a new linen swab each time, not using the same swab or tea twice, have clean saucers each time. The ingredients must not be burned.

John Sanderson."

July 15, 1869—Tom Thumb, his wife, Commodore Nutt and Miss Minnie Warren came to our Hotel, Farmington; and exhibited themselves.[159] They had some beautiful ponies and carriage presented them by Queen Victoria.

July 24, 1869—Went to S. L. City, and saw cousin Nap. Van Slyke[160] just arrived from Madison, Wisconsin, with an excursion party, composed of 28, embracing the State offices of Wisconsin. I was waiting for him at the Townsend House, having seen a notice of their expected arrival today.

[page 293]

NAPOLEON VAN SLYKE

July 24, 1869—I tried to recognize him among the crowd—but could not. It is many years since I saw him. When he was shown me, I saw a man partly grey, with spectacles on nose. When I saw him last we were boys. How time rushes on! We spent two days very pleasantly together. He gave the address of my relatives:—

Mrs. Margaret Jackson, my foster nurse (a negress) is at Georgetown D. C.

Uncle Chauncey Mears, my mother's oldest brother, lives at Medina, Orleans Co, N. Y.

Almira Mears (his daughter, now Mrs. Dennis Scott) and Maria Mears, at the same place.

Mary Jane Mears (Mrs. T. E. Bottsford) Madison Wis.

James R. Mears (uncle) Pay Master U.S.A. and his son E. Russel Mears, Portland Oregon. His daughters Ellen and Caroline, are married.

Aunt Harriet Sherwin, lives with her daughters.

Mary Sherwin (Mrs. Norman Stewart) Baraboo, Wis.

Laura Starin (ne-Vanslyke) Fultonville N.Y.

Henrietta (Sherwin) is Mrs. C. W. Fillmore, Marengo, Ill.

Dewitt C. Poole (my cousin) Captain U.S.A. Whetstone Creek Sioux Reservation, Dakota

Peter and Mary Martineau, Milwaukee, Wis.

W. A. Mears, Cha[s] S. Mears, and N. B. Vanslyke, Madison, Wis.

Lois M. Martineau (Mrs. John P. W. Doerschlag)—nee—vos winkel) Chicago, Ill.

Vanslyke told me that last year he went to the city of Washington on business, and thought he would hunt up Margaret Jackson, the Negro Woman who was nurse to him and me in our infancy. She was a slave owned by my father in Alabama, whom my father brought to the North when he moved up, and gave her freedom.

[page 294]

MY OLD NURSE, MARGARET JACKSON.

July 25, 1869—She had not seen him since he was four years old, when I was two years of age. He spent some days tracing her up, and, at last found her residence in Georgetown D. C. He knocked, she came, and he said, "Does Mrs. Margaret Jackson live here!" She knew him instantly though forty three years old, and said "Yes, Is that you Master Napoleon?" The Negro nurses have a great memory and greater love for

157 Oscar L. Lyons was an experienced printer (Holzapfel, *History of Utah County*, 145).

158 John Sanderson was a friend from Parowan. He was among the first to serve in the Iron Mission (Shirts and Shirts, *Southern Utah's Iron Mission*, 438).

159 These were P. T. Barnum performers on tour.

160 Napoleon B. Van Slyke was born on December 21, 1822, in Syracuse, New York, and died on February 14, 1909, in Madison, Wisconsin.

their foster Children. She hugged and kissed him, and also inquired of me—her other son.

My cousin went on to California, and to Madison again.

I returned to Farmington and continued at work there, superintending the grading, and then disbanded our party, and came home, the work being so far advanced that two parties could oversee it all.

Spent the autumn as usual, surveying and photographing.

January 1, 1870—Still photographing, and continued doing so until Spring, when I surveyed considerable.

July 16, 1870—To-day Virginia Martineau, daughter of Susan J. was born.

My Mother-in-Law and Janette are here with James Johnson,[161] on a visit, having been here about a week. Mother-in-law and Susan E. & I were with Susan J. The babe was a fine one, and Susan got along very well.

September 28, 1870—To day Susan E. presented me with a fine daughter whom we named Gertrude. As was usual with her she was much blessed in her confinement.

Fig. 4.8—Virginia Martineau, daughter of Susan Julia and James Henry Martineau. Courtesy of James Henry Martineau Family Organization.

Fig. 4.9—Gertrude Martineau, daughter of Susan Ellen and James Henry Martineau. Courtesy of James Henry Martineau Family Organization.

[page 295]

UTAH NORTHERN R. R. STARTED

December 31, 1869[162]—During the past summer and autumn, I have been busy surveying ¼ sections in Cache County, but did not receive much pay for my work. But we have been preserved from accident and sickness to quite an extent, so much so, at least, that none of my family have been taken from me. For this I thank Our Father—the giver of all good.

August 14, 1871—Br. John W. Young, being in Logan, the proposition was made to build a Railroad from Logan to Ogden or from Ogden to Franklin, or Soda Springs. This was brought up in a meeting of the Priesthood of all the County, and unanimously received. A company was organized in a few days, but previous to this John W. Young and Bp. Preston requested me to make a preliminary examination of

161 James Johnson was among the first settlers of Winder, Idaho, six miles northwest of Preston (Ricks and Cooley, *History of Cache Valley*, 78).

162 It appears this date is incorrect, or the entry was added later.

the route over the Divide, so as to be able to report at the meeting of the company when it should organize. Accordingly myself and John Ash, as rodman, ran a line of levels to ascertain the height of the ridge &c, beginning on the 14th of August 1871.

In a few days the company organized, electing John W. Young, President, W. B. Preston, Vice President and a board of Directors, Secretary, &c No election was held for Chief Engineer, it afterwards appearing that J. W. Y. wished that office as well as President and General Superintendent. But Prest Young and V. Prest Preston wished me to take charge as an Engineer, promising me permanent employment on the line. I therefore dropped all other business and diverted my entire attention to the new Railroad. We named this the Utah Northern R.R. and the company decided to run a line from Ogden to Soda Springs and perhaps, eventually, to Montana, and connect with the Northern Pacific.

[page 296]

MAKE CITY DEEDS.

December 31, 1871—Up to this date I have been busy all the time with the railroad. I bought 4300 adobies of G. L. Farrell and built a room for Susan E. 16 X 20 one story high, but did not get it finished so as to move in until near spring. I also built a back room joining it for a kitchen.

The people of Cache turned out well, and did much labor, working, in fact, until winter set in. This was on the 1st of December, when, a deep snow came, which nearly buried up our tents, where we were camped on the divide. The snow fell nearly three feet deep on the level. We had no wood, and only a few green willow stakes, and most of them were covered up in the snow. After the storm cleared up, it was intensely cold, and we nearly froze. We finally got some sleighs from Mendon, who moved us in with our things. I stored them with Jasper Lemmon,[163] and we came home.

February 15, 1872—Up to this date I have been working constantly at city business, making out deeds, from the Mayor to the people, as they proved up their claims.

163 Jasper Lemmon (1835–1905) was a settler in Mendon, Utah, and was the first schoolteacher.

I now began making estimates of labor done in grading on the finished portions of the line, continuing at this until spring opened sufficiently to enable us to go out into the field again.

March 17, 1872—We started again out on the line, going to Mendon, and stopping with Jasper Lemmon again, hiring part of his house. My party consists of myself as Chief, Jos A. West, assistant, Tho. B. Cardon, Leveler, Henry A. Martineau, Rodman, Alfred and Edward Hanson,[164] Chainmen, Jasper Lemmon, Marker, N. V. Crockett[165] and David Steele and Robt Bain Cook.

During last fall, C. L. Enizon came to our camp having been sent, as he told us, by Prest B. Young. He put on a great air of authority and was determined to rule things if he could.

[page 297]

ENIZEN'S FIASCO. IN 1871.

1872—I had not been informed of being displaced, and would not give up the charge of things to him, and he finally went off in high dudgeon,[166] and endeavored to injure me all he could. I afterwards found he had not been sent by any authority whatever. Jos A. Young, with whom he was held in esteem had sent him, and Jos A. Young is not even so much as a shareholder in the company, much less an officer.

May 10, 1872—About this time we moved our camp over the divide to Bigler's Springs, where work was being very actively pushed, and remained there until June. By that time the construction train reached Biglers. We afterwards moved back to Mendon again.

During this time my business at home suffered considerably from my absence, so much so that I sold out my photographing apparatus and chemicals to Tho. B. Cardon.

December 31, 1872—We have been constantly engaged on the line up to this date, and the road

164 Edward Hanson is listed as a surveyor (Simmonds, *The Gentile Comes to Cache Valley*, 57).

165 N. V. Crockett (1831–1902) is likely Norman Victor Crockett, son of David and Lydia Young Crockett (Peterson, *History of Cache Valley*, 328).

166 "In high dudgeon" is to be in a state of intense indignation, feeling offense.

reached Logan in the winter, the cars arriving there on the [blank] day of [blank].[167]

It cost a great exertion to accomplish this. The ground froze solid for a foot in depth, and could not be plowed, until the top was taken off by picks, axes, &c. the men working during intensely cold weater, and carrying the frozen blocks of earth in their arms to build up the grade. Money would not have hired them to do it.

1873—I kept at work all winter, sometimes in the office, most of the time in the field until spring and then began running a line north of Logan to Franklin. I omitted to say in 1872 that Jo[s] A. West succeeded, by underhand work, in getting a separate party of his own, and ran a line from Brigham Junction to Ogden, 17 miles.

[page 298]

JOSEPH BORN,—AND DIED MAY 10, 1873.

March 1873—He was also sent to run a preliminary line from Logan to Soda Spring, a distance of 76.4 miles. He could not plot the line, nor take the topography, to make a map, and therefore, I had to go over and inspect it, and make a topographical map of it, which I did some time in August. But I found it impossible to make a correct plot of the line, his notes being so very inaccurate.

I had taught him engineering, as if he were a son of mine, and he repaid me by trying to get my position of Chief Engineer, to which I had been appointed in 1871. But as usual in such cases, he overreached himself, and disgusted the officers of the Company, so they would have nothing to do with him, except in case of urgent necessity.

April 23, 1873—To day my son Joseph was born, his mother being, as was usual with her, greatly blessed in her confinement. He was a very beautiful child but only weighed 3½ lbs. For some days he did very well, but took a cold which settled on his lungs and took him off in a few days.[168]

He was born at 4.55' A.M. and died May 10. 1873 at 6.40' A.M. and was buried the following day.

While he was sick, one of our neighbors recommended Winslow's Soothing Syrup to loosen his cough and phlegm and we gave him some, but did not help him any.[169] Susan J. thought perhaps it was detrimental to him and grieved very much over him. She was afraid his days were shortened by it. I do not think so. He was not strong enough to throw up the phlegm and would, I feel certain, have soon choked with it in his lungs and throat. Poor little fellow—he died peacefully, and sweetly. The funeral was held in

May 10, 1873—Susan E.s house, being larger. Bp. Preston was present.

[page 299]

[The top half of the page is blank.]

September 8, 1872—To day Susan E. was confined of a son, whom we named Theodore. She was much blessed in her confinement, for which I feel very thankful to our Father in Heaven.

Early in the spring, (or in February) I moved Susan J. to the south end of my first lot near the mill, having sold my small remaining piece of land near the meeting house, the fall previous, to Z.C.M.I. of Salt Lake city, who comtemplated putting up a large store there.[170] I sold the piece—about 11000 square feet—for $900.[00] [$14,621] cash. I paid $300.[00] [$4,874] for a strip of land facing the Benson & Thatcher Mill and paid $100 [$1,625] down toward building a brick house

167 Martineau apparently intended to fill in this date at a later time.

168 Martineau is preoccupied with family here and had not noted his involvement in developing the Salt Lake Free Library where "a small band of earnest women asked your co-operation, feeling inspired by the words of James Martineau, 'to individual faithfulness, and to the energy of private conscience, God has committed the history and purpose of mankind'" ("A Public Library for Salt Lake," *Deseret News*, March 19, 1873; Utah Digital Newspapers).

169 Winslow's Soothing Syrup was heavily advertised during this period. It was primarily recommended for soothing children who were teething. It contained morphine.

170 This is the Zion's Co-operative Mercantile Institution (ZCMI). It was a business cooperative to import wholesale goods and sell them at minimal profit to be divided "with the people at large." Branches of the ZCMI worked with home industries and distributed their goods through the ZCMI. (For a description of the Logan ZCMI, see Rick and Cooley, *History of Cache Valley*, 194, 195; see also Leonard J. Arrington, *Great Basin Kingdom* [Cambridge, MA: Harvard Univ. Press, 1958], 298–99).

there for Susan J. but did not get it started that fall. I also, that fall took Susan J. and Elvira to the fall conference going down with the Logan choir, which had been invited to join the Mass Choir in S. L. City, at Conference. Susan J. had at times pretty good health, but frequent and severe spells of sickness of several different kinds, such as dyspepsia, Leucorrhea,[171] Paralysis, Rheumatism and Heart disease which began to show itself about this time.

[page 300]

SUSAN J.'S FOREBODINGS

1873—I had grave forebodings that her time on earth would be short, but I could not fully make up my mind to give up to it either, but felt to contend against it all I could. For this cause I took her round, frequently, hoping a change of scene and air would help her. She, herself, seemed to feel the same forebodings, often saying she would not live long—would never live to see her house finished.

April—A few days after Joseph was born she took a bad cold, making her worse, until the baby sucked it from her and got very sick himself.

[Last half of page is blank.]

[page 301]

MILITARY JOURNAL[172]

1873—The following is a brief abstract of our military operations in Cache County:—

In 1860 the Militia of the valley were organized as a Regiment, of which Elder E. T. Benson was the Colonel, Wm Hyde Adjutant. In the year 1865 August 5th a Brigade was organized, on the high bench above Br. Benson's, and the following Brigade officers were elected: E. T. Benson, Brigadier General, William Hyde, Brigade Adjutant, Jas H. Martineau Assistant Adjutant, Peter Maughan Quartermaster, David B. Lamoreaux, Surgeon, William K. Robinson Color Bearer. There was one regiment of Cavalry, Col. T. E. Ricks, two Regiments of Infantry, the 1st Col. A. Crockett, the 2d Col. Wm Maughan. The total strength of the Brigade was 1094 men.

The first Brigade Muster was held on the 9th 10th and 11th of November 1865. The troops assembled at Logan and marched to Providence Bench and encamped.[173]

On June 23 1866 I was appointed Brigade Adjutant, Br. Hyde being appointed 1st Aid-de-Camp.

The Second Brigade Muster was held July 14, 1866

The third Brigade "Camp Deseret" was held—Oct. 24th, 25th, 26th 1866 on the Church Farm, near Millville. ~~At this Lt. Genl Wells and staff were present.~~

Nov. 10, 1866 a Brigade Court Martial convened at Logan, Composed as follows:—Col. Hyde, President. Adj. Martineau, Col T. E. Ricks, Col. A Crockett, Maj, W. Budge,[174] Judge Advocate, Col. Maughan was also appointed one of the Court, but did not attend, and was court martialed himself therefor.

A muster was held on the Church Reserve west of Millville on the 21, 22, & 23d of October 1867. At this muster Lt. Genl Wells, Brig. Genl B. Young Jr. Col. Jos S. Young, and Col. J. R. Winder[175] were present. Present 826 men. Camp Wells.

[page 302]

MILITARY JOURNAL.

A Brigade Court Martial convened at Logan on the 14th of Dec. 1867, composed of the following officers:—Col. W. Hyde, Adj. J H Martineau, Cols Ricks, Crockett and Maughan, and Maj. J. B. Roper Judge Advocate.[176]

---

171 *Dyspepsia* is acid indigestion, or heartburn. *Leukorrhea* is caused by vaginal inflammation.

172 See J. H. Martineau, "Military Movements in Cache County," *Deseret News*, June 12, 1867; Utah Digital Newspapers.

173 See "Muster and Drill in Cache Co.," *Deseret News*, November 7, 1866; Utah Digital Newspapers.

174 William Budge was superintendent of construction on the county buildings in Logan. He would later move to Bear Lake. He was president of the Logan Temple from 1906 to 1918 (Ricks and Cooley, *History of Cache Valley*, 94; Peterson, *History of Cache County*, 113).

175 This could be John Rex Winder, who was the second counselor to William B. Preston, Presiding Bishop of the Church.

176 This could be Joseph Roper, who farmed in Winder and lived in Preston, Idaho (Ricks and Cooley, *History of Cache Valley*, 78).

August 20. 1869, an order was issued for the adoption, in this Brigade, of Upton's Military Tactics, Gen[l] Wells having previously issued orders for its adoption by the Legion.

A Brigade Muster was held on the Church Reserve, nearly west of Logan, on the 20th 21st and 22[d] of September 1869. This we named "Camp Benson."

On Friday, Sept. 3. 1869 Gen[l] Benson fell dead at Ogden while on his way to S. L. City, in Company with Col. Alvin Crockett. He was 58 years of age.

On Sunday September 5, 1869 Gen[l] Benson was buried with Military honors.

An order was received by telegraph Sept. 18, 1869 assigning Col. Hyde to Command Cache Military District until further orders.[177]

Brigade Muster was held on Logan Island on the 28th 29th & 30 of September 1870. This was named "Camp Helaman."

Sept. 28. 1870 Col. William Hyde was elected Brigadier General on the parade ground. William B. Preston was elected 2nd Aid-de-camp

Dec. 4, 1871, Lt. Col. P. Maughan having died, W. B. Preston was appointed Brigade Quartermaster, and M. D. Hammond 2[d] Aid.

A Brigade Muster was held on Logan Island on the 16, 17, & 18th of October 1872. This was named "Camp Independence." The attendance was small, Gov. Schaffer having issued a proclamation forbidding all musters of any kind. Numbers took advantage of this to absent themselves from drill.

[page 303]

THE TITLE OF LIBERTY.

A brigade Muster was held on Logan Island and on the 14. 15 and 16th of October 1873, "Camp Independence." The attendance was small, but a good spirit prevailed. It snowed and stormed most of the time.

On Monday Morning at 3.30 A.M. of March 2, 1876 [or 74] Gen[l] Hyde died of "inability to swallow" after an illness of eight days, and was buried on the 4th with military honors.

The following lines were written two or three years ago, but the copy was mislaid:—

"THE TITLE OF LIBERTY."

"And now it came to pass that when Moroni, who was the chief commander of the armies of the Nephites, had heard of these dissensions, he was angry with Amlickiah. And it came to pass that he rent his coat and he took a piece thereof and he wrote upon it "In memory of our God, our Religion and our Freedom and our peace, our wives and our children." And he fastened it upon the end of a pole there of. * * * And he called it "The Title of Liberty." See Book of Alma, Chap. 21, Paragraph 7.

1

It was a time of grief and fear: and men
Grew stern, and fierce and hard of heart. As when
In battle joined the warrior seeks a foe
On whom to vent his rage, and blow for blow
Returns—resolved on victory or death.
So now, when strife and discard rent the earth,
And stormy passions shook the trembling land
Rebellion raised his evil, murderous hand.
And sought to over throw fair Freedom's throne
And Strew the plain with cities overthrown.

2

The mother to her heart her infant pressed
At many a sigh and many a hand caress:

[page 304]

THE TITLE OF LIBERTY

1873—
And breathed a prayer that Heaven would shield the form
Of her babes father, "mid the battle storm.
For lo! the proclamation had gone forth
From east to west—from South to chilly north!
By great Moroni sent the leader brave
Of Nephi's hosts, that all who wished to save
Their country's liberty's ~~foundation~~ great heaven's boon—

177 By 1871 the telegraph had been connected to hundreds of Mormon settlements. The first in Logan was in a store operated by C. B. Robbins behind the First National Bank Building (Ricks and Cooley, *History of Cache Valley*, 168).

Should to their ~~country's~~ leader's standard rally soon.

3

And now Moroni took his rended coat
And thereupon these godlike words he wrote:—
"In memory or our God, our Religion and our Freedom,"
And our peace, our wives and our children."
This, fixed upon a staff ~~he raised~~ on high he raised
And, cased in armor, knelt ~~to the Most High~~ him down and prayed;
And mightily ~~poured forth his~~ besought in earnest prayer
That Freedom's cause might prosper everywhere,
So long as in his country there should be
A Christian band, determined to be free:
Who ne'er should be down trodden by the foe
Unless their own transgressions brought them low.

4

He rose. The glorious light of freedom beamed
In his determined eye—and still it seemed
That eye,—whose glance might shake the bravest foe
Could yet, with gentleness and love o'erflow.
He issued grandly forth, and waved on high
His banner named—"The Title of Liberty,"
The host assembled there the words beheld
Upon the banner traced, and then there swelled
From myriad hearts a vast and ringing shout
As 'twere the voice of Freedom speaking out.—
Warning her ruthless enemies to flee
That Zion's lands forever might be free.

[page 305]

THE TITLE OF LIBERTY.

5

Then spoke the Warrior-Prince. "Let every hand
"That will maintain this Title in the land,
"Now draw the sword for Justice and for Right
"Clothed with the Lord's resistless power and might.
"A covenant make, forever to maintain
"Our rights and our religion,—thus to gain
"The blessings of the Lord upon our head
"Till we the victors be—our foemen fled."
Moroni ceased, and from that mighty throng
Again there rose a shout so loud and long
That heaven's eternal arches rang again
And listening angels echoed back the strain.

6

Then near his chief each warrior gathered round
And threw his rended coat upon the ground;
And this the covenant they made that day
While at Moroni's feet their garments lay:—
"If from the cause of Liberty we swerve
"May we receive the vengeance we deserve;
"And, like our rended garments at thy feet
"Prostrate before our foes their fury meet.
"And trodden under foot of Laman's host
"Their scorn became,—our ruin be their boast."

7

With joy Moroni heard the loyal sound
By thousands uttered, as they clustered round.
With words of burning eloquence he cheers
Each feeble soul, and dissipates his fears;
Points to the blessings past that have been given,
And teaches him to put his trust in heaven,
And now, from every part of Nephite land
There gathers up a true and valiant band,
With purpose firm their freedom to maintain,
Or pile their bodies on the battle plain.

[page 306]

THE TITLE OF LIBERTY

1873—

8

Meanwhile Rebellion's band—a motley crew
Where Amlickiah's craft together drew
Around his banners—trusting in their might
With boastful words and loud, prepared for fight.
But when Moroni with his host drew near
Their craven hearts began to quake with fear.
And to the north they took their secret flight
Screened by the misty shadows of the night;
In hope that, joined by Laman's dusky band
They might return and desolate the land.

9

Vain hope! Surrounded and cut off they yield
And sullen, ground their weapons on the field:—
All save a few, that to the northward fled
By Amlickiah, still their leader, led.
There, joined with Laman's tribes—the Nephites foes—
Conspired to overwhelm with future woes
The country they had left—no more their own—
From which—self exiled—they are forced to roam.

10

And now Moroni with his host returned;
Their country's freedom saved—their foemen bound—
And led as captives to that land again
Which they would rule, or give to blood and flame.
The traitors now must take a solemn oath
That they will all, until their latest breath
Their country's liberty Still shield from harm—
From secret foes within ~~and~~ or foreign arm,
Or else their worthless lives shall forfeit be—
A righteous sacrifice to Liberty.

11

Thus may each foe to Freedom's holy cause
Be ever vanquished, and her righteous laws
By valiant hearts be evermore sustained:
And Liberty—that born from heaven obtained—

[page 307]

1873—

Triumphant reign, from east to western shore
From north to south—till Tyrranny no more
Shall fetter Godlike man, and all shall be
True to our glorious "Title of Liberty."

May—During this month and the month of June the Branch line from the U.N.R.R. to Corinne was laid out and graded, a distance of about 4 miles.[178] During this time I had my party—some two weeks at Corinne, and the rest of the time at Brigham City, boarding at Col. C. Loveland's hotel. On this line, the bridge over Bear River is some 200 feet long, built of bents on piles, besides this there are two other bridges on Bear River bottoms of about 500 feet more, to allow the overflowed water to pass. The bridge is not built exactly as I designed it, the carpenters, in their ignorance, injuring its strength materially, by their alterations when I was absent.

June 8, 1873—On Sunday, the 8th while lying one soft and dreamy afternoon partly sleeping and partly waking, the Bell rang for church at Brigham City. It is the first time for twenty four years that I have been summoned to church by the voice of the bells, having all that time been in advance of them. The sound carried me back to the days of my boyhood, and for the time swept the past entirely away. I lived in the past, and a delicious yet half sad throng of memories came flooding over me, which I have tried, but very feebly, to express in the lines entitled "Sabbath Bells." And I thought, too, how infinitessimally insignificant we are in the great mass of life and humanity. I die, and the brook still flows on as it has for thousands of years past, and the flowers bloom and the trees, in their robes of emerald, still wave in the breezes of heaven as if I had never been. And my name, even, save in the memory of a very few, is soon forgotten.

[page 308]

Sunday, June 8, 1873—

SABBATH BELLS.

1

Sabbath Bells! Sabbath Bells!
What memories throng as your music swells!
How the shadows glide forth from the "long long ago"—
From the dim—distant past—that more distant still grows
As the years swiftly bear us, on time's silent tide
To that vast mystic ocean, eternity wide.

178 Corinne, Utah, is located just north of Brigham City. During the construction of the railroads, it was nicknamed Berg on the Bear, the City of the Ungodly, and Gentile City. The railroads attracted many to the area, most of whom were not members of the Church (Huchel, *History of Box Elder County*, 123–45; "Personal," *Corinne Daily Journal*, March 26, 1873; Utah Digital Newspapers).

2

Sabbath Bells! Sabbath Bells!
How sweetly are pealing your silvery knells!
While I list to your sound, from the Shadowy Clime
Comes the faint lingering voice of an echoing chime
That long ago rang in my childhoods bright hours
That were passed with the birds, 'mong the brooklets and flowers.

3

Sabbath Bells! Sabbath Bells!
Like a requiem soundeth that slow pealing knell!
For and e'en while I listen—a shadowy throng
With step slow and mournful, comes silent along;
And in that grim hearse, ~~with~~ neath its black waving plumes
Lies a mother's cold form, in her life's fairest bloom.

4

Sabbath Bells! Sabbath Bells!
Of scenes passing joyous that sounding note tells,
The funeral cortege hath vanished from sight
As the night giveth way to Aurora's pale light;
And the hours so happy still happier grow
But the dark ones are hid in the "Long Long Ago."

5

Sabbath Bells! Sabbath Bells!
How sad—yet how sweet are the memories that thrill!
Of songs that were sung,—words of love that were told—
Of kisses imprinted by lips that are ['now so' is written on top of these words] cold—
Of tresses of hair—hands waving adieu—
Now lying so still in the "long long ago."

[page 309]

JULY 4TH AT CORINNE. BEAR RIVER CAÑON.

June 8, 1873—

6

Sabbath Bells! Sabbath Bells!
Still to day, as of yore, your soft music swells,
The brook still is flowing, and flowers still bloom
Though friends dear and cherished pass into the tomb.
And we, too, the living, as years quickly go
Will be numbered, ere long, in the "Long, Long, Ago."

Friday, July 4, 1873—An excursion went to Corinne to day, by invitation of the Corinne people to celebrate, and have a rail road ride. There was about 200 persons on the train, which was nicely fitted up with evergreens and flags. I took Susan J. who has had very poor health for some time past—in fact, ever since Joseph died. She has frequent and severe fits of palpitation of the heart, which almost makes her drop to the floor, and sometimes prostrates her for a day or two, completely. We had a pleasant ride over, and were met by the Corinne Brass Band and marched to the Opera house, where the services were conducted. Dennis Tooky was orator of the day. After the speeches &c were over, a cold lunch was served, and then the hall was cleared for dancing. I was invited by a gentleman from Elbridge, N. Y. my old boyhood home to dine with him, so Susan and I went to Mrs. Stanley's where he boarded, and partook of a good dinner. Henry and Elvira also went to Corinne, and dined at Walsh's Hotel. As we were about to start home, at 4 P.M. while sitting in the car, Susan was suddenly seized with a very severe fainting spell, which continued more or less all the way home. I had to fan her constantly, and wet her face with water, spirits cologne or anything I could get. But she was over it by the next day, except that she was weak.

July 7, 1873—To day, by request of John W. Young I went with him to Bear River Cañon north, to examine the route of the U.N.R.R. through it, with the view of making a wagon road where the line will pass, so that it can be used as a rail road bed, if necessary.

[page 310]

BEAR RIVER CAÑON.

July 7, 1873—He told me to hire a conveyance which I did, having Bp. Preston's buggy, and N. Hanson's team.[179] I took Nephi along.

July 8, 1873—Drove to Station Creek and Mink Creek.

July 10, 1873—Went to Heads last night. To day I went to the Cañon and met Br. Young and Capt. Coddy and other. Explored around, and returned to Head's to night. We had been through the canon on foot 3 1/3 miles and back, and it took us from Sunrise to dark, of very severe toil. J. W. Young lost a valuable gold watch seal in Mink Creek near the mouth, worth, he said $100.$^{\underline{00}}$ [$1,625]. We decided to change the location from the South Side of the river—the shady side, to the north or sunny side, not only on account of sunshine there, but because the line can be built cheaper there. There were four of us J. W. Y myself, Bp L. H. Hatch and John Biggs of Franklin. When, after much consideration, John W. asked us to write on a slip of paper our individual judgment and decision as to which side of the River the line should be placed, we all thought, by the way Br. Young had talked all the while, that his feeling was to keep the line of the south, where it is now surveyed. So Bp. Hatch voted to keep it there, but he was chagrined to find that the others, including Br. Young, had voted to change it. The Bishop wished to vote the right way, but the wind happened to blow the wrong way. I, too, thought Br. Young, wished to keep the line as it was, but I voted according to my own judgment. I hate the principle of truckling[180] to anything contrary to our feelings just because some one higher does so.

July 11, 1873—Went to the Cañon again, with a party of graders, to set them at work and lay out the line. We went by way of Bridgeport, the river being too deep to ford. We camped on the brink of a deep gulch not far from the river which was impossible for us to cross, without a good deal of work.

[page 311]

BEAR R. CANON.
SUSAN E. GOES SOUTH

July 12, 1873—The company worked all day making a dug way down the side of the gulch, which is about 60 feet deep. Worked all day. The boys caught plenty of fish.

Sunday, July 13, 1873—The men finished the crossing to day. Yesterday, while the men were at work, I went up the cañon, and laid out the line for a considerable distance. We came home to day having been gone six days.

July 29, 1873—Went to Bear River Cañon again, with H. A. Martineau to assist in leveling. Had Henry's team and M. Thatcher's buggy. We arrived there next day.

July 31, 1873—We measured and laid out work to day, and returned home on the 1$^{\underline{st}}$ of August, having been gone four days.

August 11, 1873—Started again to the Cañon, with Henry and ~~his~~ my team and Thatcher's buggy, with Susan J. We drove to Wm Head's in the evening. who were much pleased to see us, especially Susan J. and Virginia.

August 12, 1873—Henry and I went on to the scene of labor, and returned home on the 14$^{\underline{th}}$ having measured and leveled for about half way through the Cañon. Got a bill of my time from John Biggs, which came to $112.^{00} [$1,820] including hire of horses and wagon, without anything for Henry, whom I paid myself, to the amount of $15.88 [$258].

When coming home, about 2 miles south of Richmond Susan had another bad spell, which lasted all night though we got home safely. It was palpitation, as usual with her. at times

September 18, 1873—Nothing of much moment at home up to date. I have been Surveying and Engineering as usual. In August I rented my old log house to H. J. Wallis, a mattress maker, for $1.$^{\underline{00}}$ [$16.25] pr week. On the 18th of September Susan E. with Henry, Joel, Albert, Gertrude and Theodore to visit her relations in the southern Country.

179 This is most likely Niels Hansen (note spelling), who operated and managed one of the gristmills grinding wheat for the settlers. He was also a bishop and acted as an alderman (Ricks and Cooley, *History of Cache Valley*, 160; Simmonds, *The Gentile Comes to Cache Valley*, 28; Somers, *History of Logan*, 77).

180 *Truckling* is to submit or yield to something, to be servile or submissive.

[page 312]

TAKE SUSAN J. TO S. L. CITY FOR THE LAST TIME.

September 18, 1873—She has not seen them for many years, and is afraid her father may die without her seeing him. Henry took his team and my ~~horses~~ wagon and away they went. I furnished Susan E. $15.00 [$244] in cash, besides some she had of Nephi, for traveling expenses. When they drove away, Susan J. said—"Susan has seen me for the last time—she will never see me again." She added, that she believed Susan E. thought so too, for said she "Susan had such a strange look as I bid her good bye."

Monday, October 6, 1873—To day I started to Conference with Susan J. Virginia and Charlie, to help take care of Virginia. We had intended to start earlier, but Lillie has been sick for about ten days with a fever, being at one time quite sick, but by the blessings of God she is now recovering. I leave her with Elvira, who will do well for her. and Sister Steele has promised to visit her every day, and nurse her if she should get a relapse. I would not go and leave her, if it were not that I feel I must get medical advice in S. L. City, and see if Susan J. has the heart disease or not, and if she has, what is best for her. Susan J. has been for some time quite weak, [illegible symbols], very much for nearly a month. She has taken considerable medicine for it, but to no good. We went by U.N.R.R. to Corinne, thence by C.P.R.R. to Ogden. When near Ogden, she was again taken, suddenly with [illegible symbols] very badly, but arrived safely at Ogden and went to a hotel near by, where we took dinner. Just after dinner, she had a miscarriage, of a little boy. I knew not what to do. To go home would occupy two days, including a night at Corinne, while to go to the city would occupy only two hours. As Susan seemed quite strong, we determined to go on. I borrowed a pair of blankets of the hotel keeper, got some cayenne pepper and nutmeg[181] and we went on.

181 Cayenne pepper is an herbal remedy for illnesses such as poor blood circulation, indigestion, and rheumatism. Nutmeg oil was used to treat digestive issues, nervous disorders, and rheumatic pain.

[page 313]

DR. BENEDICTS VERDICT FOR SUSAN J. HOME AGAIN.

October 6, 1873—Arriving at S. L. City I hired a carriage to convey her to Aunt Esthers, where we arrived all right.

October 7, 1873—I persuaded Susan to lie still All day, fearing the effects of moving around much.

October 8, 1873—To day Susan declared she felt quite well, and as if nothing had happened, not only to our great surprise but her own. She walked around the city all day, visiting her friends &c. We went to Alex. Pypers and staid all night there. We visited Dr. Benedict, who made an examination and said she had true heart disease. He said nothing could be done for it, only to keep calm, quiet, and take the world easy, as every excitement only made it worse. Susan said then she "must die, for she could not" fulfill those conditions. Benedict also said she should not take any medicine, for it would do no good, and only destroy her digestion and appetite. I felt, myself, as though it was her death warrant, for I know her ambitious and excitable disposition so well.

October 9, 1873—To day Susan walked all day from place to place until I was tired out. I wondered how she, in her weak condition is able to stand it. I think she felt as if she might as well enjoy herself all she could while she had a chance. We went last evening to the theatre.

October 10, 1873—We started home to day, at 5 a.m. and got there in the evening all right. We found Lillie still improving, but hardly able to walk around much. She gains very slowly.

Friday, November 14, 1873—The weather being pleasant I took Susan J. up to Richmond for her health. We stopped with Bp. Merrill's wife—Myra—

November 15, 1873—I took Susan and Mrs. Merrill this morning to High Creek where the graders are at work, and then to Merrill's Mill, to his wife Maria. Susan enjoyed herself very much. We came home at night. This is the last time but one Susan J. ever rode with me anywhere.

[page 314]

SUSAN J.S LAST SICKNESS

November 15, 1873—She was in high spirits all the time, laughing, talking and singing. Who could tell that her voice would so soon be hushed in death?

Thursday, November 27, 1873—To day Susan J. was sick abed. She has been for some time very poorly, but would not go to bed as long as she could help it.

November 28, 1873—To day I came home from the Railroad in a snow storm: found Susan in bed.

On the 16th of October last, she attended our Military Ball in Logan hall, at the conclusion of our Brigade muster. She looked bright and joyous, and enjoyed herself well, but felt the effects of it next day. She also went to our camp on the 15th and dined with us, or at least intended to, but did not.

November 29, 1873—To day she is some better.

November 30, 1873—The same. Still improving

December 1, 1873—To day she is up and around again, but not strong

December 2, 1873—I went to Providence to day, taking her with me in the Buggy. We traded some at the store, and when I went to get the team, they ran away—I fell out—and they broke the carriage all to pieces. Chas Johnson brought us home in his wagon.[182]

December 3, 1873—To day Susan is sick abed again.

Saturday, December 20, 1873—Up to this time Susan J. has been able to sit up some every day—perhaps from three to five hours. I have been constantly with her day and night, taking the best care I could of her, and watching nights so the room would not get cold, nor she want for anything. In the day time I worked much at my R.R. estimates, and sometimes played cards with her to pass away the time. She also played cards with the children for the same reason.

To day she is not able to sit up much, or to walk without help. She can eat nothing, much although I have got her everything I could that I thought she would like.

182 Charles Johnson was active in Logan drama (Somers, *History of Logan*, 129). Martineau was surveying in Providence ("Correspondence," *Deseret News*, December 3, 1873; Utah Digital Newspapers).

[page 315]

December 20, 1873—She determined to leave off the drinking of tea, although it seemed as if that was all that sustained her. She said, if she should die, she wished to do so, keeping the "Word of Wisdom." and if she lived, she would be better without it. She was one having an indomitable will, and she persevered and conquered. But it was a great struggle. How great, no one knows now, but myself, who saw the long struggle, for days and weeks to over come the old appetite—with nothing to take in place of it. I had wine for her, all the time, East India Bitters and Beer, but nothing filled the place of tea. She would think of it, and tears would dim her eyes, but she would not give up.

About this time she was attacked by a very severe pain across her stomach, which also aggravated her heart disease. This finally turned into inflammation of the stomach, causing her much severe pain, so much so, that she several times would faint from extreme pain, sometimes being insensible for ten or fifteen minutes at a time.

December 28, 1873—The inflammation has at last given way to our persistent efforts, and to day she is free from pain. She has had a hard time with [physic], poultices and injections, pour soul. Her limbs, abdomen and feet remain swollen, and we fear it is dropsy. She is sure it is.

December 29, 1873—To day Dr. O. C. Ormsby called to see her. He said it was dropsy, induced by heart disease, and that he could do nothing for her. He could give medicine to ease her pains—that is all. For about ten days she has required from two to four women to nurse her, with my aid. Mrs. Fanny Earl and her daughters have been very kind to us.[183] One of them has been with her every day, from morning until night, in fact, I do not know what I should have done without her, or her daughter Erminonda.

[page 316]

SUSAN J.S LAST SICKNESS.

December 29, 1873—During her severe pains, she prayed God to spare her, or take her from her sufferings—oh so pitifully. She has said all the time she

183 Mrs. F. Earl owned a local Logan confectionary (Somers, *History of Logan*, 59).

would die, but she wished to live for her children—what would become of them without a mother's care,—a father, however good—she thought—could not fill the deficiency. She read much in Gunn's Dispensatory, to see if there was anything that would help her.

I had bought her a garnet ring for a Christmas present, which pleased her very much.

About Christmas, she said she was satisfied with life, and desired to go. She conversed much about dying, and said it would be no worse for her to leave her children, than for the many others so left without a mother. She derived great comfort in the thought that I loved her children, and would do all I could for their good. She had no fear of death, but desired to be spared the pain.

On Sunday, 28th she wished me to bring the elders, and give her up, provided she could not be healed. J. E. Hyde came in, and he and I dedicated her to the Lord and gave her up—to His will. It was a hard thing for a husband to do—oh, so hard. When we had finished, she said—"oh I am so glad; so glad." "Good! Good! I am so glad."

About 2 P.M. she had another very severe spell. She could not be in one position a moment, but was like a woman in the fire, twisting, turning, now up, now down, her eyes staring with the extremity of her pain. and her unspeakable anguish.

She said she wished her children to be kept together, and to have and live in her house when done, and to have all her things, except a dress for Erminonda Earl, and a piece of new flannel (10 yds) for Fanny Earl.—also her black calico dress for Mrs. Steele.

[page 317]

She told Jesse N. to be true and faithful: not to swear, lie, drink liquor, &c, and to be a good boy. Being too weak to talk much, she said no more to the children then, but in the evening told Lyman the same, and said he had always been a good boy to her—and so had they all.

For several days she has had to be fanned almost constantly, in order to breathe, from the violence of her heart, and from the swelling of the dropsy. She passed a day of extreme anguish, and finally slept at 3 a.m.

December 30, 1873—The swelling still increases, also the 31st.

Thursday, January 1, 1874—The dropsical swelling still increases, with much pain at times. To night she told Lyman and Charles to stick to Mormonism, pay their tithing, not drink liquor, nor swear, gamble, lie, or do any mean thing.

January 2, 1874—No better

Saturday, January 3, 1874—Still no better. To day we killed the pig. While she was propped in her chair to day, as we have got her up every day—she asked for her cards. She said "I am going to tell my fortune, to see if I will live or die." She shuffled, cut and spread them out—all black—and threw them down wearily, saying "I am going to die."

January 4, 1874—No better to day.

January 5, 1874—Last night she had a good night's rest.

January 6, 1874—No better

January 7, 1874—This morning she said "Last night I prayed that if I was to live or die I might have some sign and in the night I thought a door opened in the side of the room, there, (pointing to the east side) and I saw my coffin standing up opposite,—a very large one. I thought I knew that it was the answer to my prayer. The coffin was so large—I thought—must I bloat so big as that before I die?"

[page 318]

S. JULIA'S LAST SICKNESS

January 8, 1874—Still slowly failing. Can eat nothing, without vomiting. Has been so for a long time. The idea of tapping was proposed, but not much said about it.

January 9, 1874—To day, she had a severe pain in the small of her back. I got a blister, but did not apply it thinking it would only cause pain, without doing any good.

Saturday, January 10, 1874—This morning she was weaker than usual, and unable to help herself at all, lying very lifeless. She said faintly "I shall die to day." She gave up taking any medicines. She talked much of her approaching death. In the evening all pain ceased, and she lay until midnight talking and looking more like an angel than a woman, talking of her death and looking so perfectly happy and resigned. It was a most lovely and glorious scene. She repeated to myself, Mrs. Steele and Mrs. Painter the lines she wrote on the death of her daughter, as follows:—

"LINES WRITTEN BY JULIA S. MARTINEAU ON THE DEATH OF OUR DAUGHTER DELCENA.

1

We are so lonely now my daughter dear
Since you have left us for a brighter sphere
Your absence causes us to mourn and weep
But that can not disturb your quiet sleep.

2

Sleep on in peace, for though thou'rt far away
Thy parents prayer shall be from day to day
To faithful, worthy and contented be
To meet their daughter in eternity.

[page 319]

3

Was it for some bad action I had done
That I was robbed of my sweet darling one?
If so, oh God, forgive the sin I pray
And take no more of my sweet babes away.

4

But teach me, Holy Father, how to be
A faithful servant unto them and Thee
And when at length our work on earth is done
Take us to Thee, in Thy celestial home.

She told me to tell Susan E. to be good to the children—saying she knew she would be, and was very sorry Susan E. did not answer her letter. At midnight she slept peacefully, and so continued for some time, then waked, and lay without pain, calmly talking of how she wanted things. She would like, if not too extravagant, her robe and clothes to be of linen. Nothing could exceed the peace and triumph that filled her soul. When I asked her testimony about Mormonism, she said "I would rather see every one of you dead to night, than for one of you to ~~apostatise~~ give up Mormonism."

At daylight she seemed dying. We brought all the children, and she kissed and took leave of them all including Elvira and Moroni who came to see her. She rallied a little after a while, having no pain only when she retched, which was often. She often wanted drink; and would immediately strain and vomit. In the evening we put a mustard plaster[184] on her stomach, and the vomiting ceased, and she had a pretty good nights rest.

A few days since she wished me to give her some paper and pencil. I did so and she wrote

TO MY CHILDREN

In memory of your mother, these, lines I pray you read
And in your album place them, and all their counsels heed.

[page 320]

SUSAN J.S LAST SICKNESS

January 10, 1874—She was too weak then to write any more, and rested.

Sunday, January 11, 1874—Was no better to day. About daylight we thought she was dying, and she kissed all good bye. We thought all day she was dying, but on the 12 she seemed a great deal better in the morning.

January 12, 1874—We got her into her chair as usual, and she had her work brought her. She tore the flannel into strips for the girls dresses. In the afternoon she was worse and passed a night of great pain.

January 13, 1874—No better. Susan has little hope.

January 14, 1874—Wrote to Eliza R. Snow,[185] about Susan, and asking how to make a proper apron by Susan's request.

Sunday, January 18, 1874—Our wedding day—17 years ago. Up to this time she has been gradually bloating with water and failing and this evening

184 A mustard plaster was thought to help with breathing and respiratory problems.

185 Eliza R. Snow (1804–87) was general president of the Relief Society and traveled the area encouraging local bishops to organize Relief Societies in each ward. Dubbed "Zion's poetess," she was a prolific writer revered by all (Maureen Ursenback Beecher, "The Eliza Enigma," *Dialogue: A Journal of Mormon Thought* 11 (Spring 1978): 30–43).

when Dr. Cranney and Leishman[186] came to administer to her, she suddenly desired to be tapped. She wished Dr. Cranney to perform the operation, and when he said it would be better for Dr. Ormsby to do it, she said she did not think he would come, because she would not submit to it when he came before. As Lamoreaux had the instruments, we sent for him. He came and tapped her, an inch and an eighth below the navel, cutting with the lance entirely through into the cavity. The water spouted as he withdrew the lance and inserted the tube. We took about 2½ gallons of water, and about as much more flowed during the night completely saturating every thing.

January 19, 1874—Ever since the operation there has been great pain at the opening. In the evening she vomited and strained so that a fleshy membrane protruded through the cut, about an inch. We tried in vain to get it back, but in the night it went back again.

January 20, 1874—Intense pain at the navel all day. She can only speak in a whisper. Water still continues to issue from the wound, keeping her and all the bed wet in spite of all the cloths we put around her. I got some morphine which served to still the pain.

[page 321]

CUT OFF AND SEWED UP. MISS E. R. SNOW'S LETTER.

Wednesday, January 21, 1874—This morning the membrane came out again, worse than before. I was much alarmed, and went to consult the Drs. Ormsby, who both said the puncture was too high—it should be not less than two or two and a half inches below the navel. Also that the lance (which should not have been used) had cut the omentum, or lining of the bowels, which had protruded. This must be got back and kept in or dangerous results might follow. We spent most of the day, trying to get it back, but could not, and Dr. Ormsby had finally to come and cut it off, and we put on a compress to keep it in. These operations she bore with the greatest fortitude.

January 22, 1874—This morning, about 5 A.M. it burst out again, and much worse than before. After trying nearly all day to get it back, the Doctor cut it off, and sewed up the hole in her belly. She thought it would be better, to cut the hole larger, put the membrane back, and then sew up the hole, but Ormsby thought it would not do, at all, for the hole was too large now. The water still flows copiously all the time. To day we had her in her chair, and she wanted to eat, and she ate ravenously wanting to taste of many things. At 3 P.M. she was seized with vomiting and continued until 5:30 P.M. after which she had a comfortable night until near morning, when she had another sinking spell, in which we thought she was dying. She was still anxious to have her burial clothes made, so she could see them, and see if they were made nicely. She still talked of her coming death with calmness and joy, longing for the time of her release. This evening I received a letter from Miss E. R. Snow giving her love to Susan with her blessing, also instructions about the apron &c.

[page 322]

SUSAN J.S LAST SICKNESS

[heading continues on page 323]

January 23, 1874—I had procured linen and other things for her burial robes, which the sisters round about made for her. Sister Betty Blair, who has been with us night and day for nearly three weeks having cut for them. I also got some fine white flannel for her petticoat and took the apron to Kate Irvin to make. She eats nothing, but is now free from pain. The water still issues.

January 24, 1874—No better

January 25, 1874—Much pain, and a very bad day. We thought several times she was dying.

Monday, January 26, 1874—Another very bad day. She suffers great pain on the left and lower side of the abdomen. Also in the neck and upper part of the chest.

January 27, 1874—Very bad this morning. She prayed to be released. Wanted to see her apron, but was much disappointed when she saw it. It was coarsely made, and not as I had showed ~~her~~ Mrs. Irvin to make it. She cried, and wanted another one. I promised her another, and got it. I then drew a pattern of the leaves

186 This could have been James A. Leishman, who was clerk of construction when the Logan Temple began and a local attorney (Peterson, *History of Cache County*, 114, 122; Somers, *History of Logan*, 64).

on the apron and Miss Erminonda Earl stitched it very nicely, but she never saw it, to enjoy it. She is very weak, and is hardly able to draw her breath.

About noon, when I was all alone she wished to get in her chair. Just then Mrs. Sarah Blair came in and we got her up. Immediately she was seized with the most excruciating pain I ever beheld in my life. She screamed dreadfully with the pain at her navel. She prayed for some one to kill her if they loved her, made us jerk her arms &c. The sweat stood all over me, from my agony of soul. After about 30 or 40 minutes the pain suddenly ceased for a few minutes, then recommenced as before. Aunt Betty heard her down to Susan E.'s and ran up. The pain soon ceased mostly, leaving her much exhausted. This was caused by inflammation. When mortification[187] set in the pain ceased.

[page 323]

HER DEATH. JAN. 28. 1874 AT 10.30 A.M.

[heading continues from page 322]

January 27, 1874—She was administered to frequently, and took morphine every half hour, which allayed her pain, much. She never suffered any more severe pain, but lay quiet only taking a little water in a spoon, one in a while.

Wednesday, January 28, 1874—About the same this morning. Very weak, scarcely able to speak. About 5.00 A.M. she wished me to "get up quick" for she was dying. She said "I would rather see Susan than any one on Earth." She was just able to speak. I supported her on my bosom, on a pillow from 5 a.m. until 9 a.m. and then lay her down again. At 6 a.m. she said to Lyman and Jesse to be good boys, and "tell everybody to forgive me if they have any thing against me"

She slept from 3 to 5 this last night of her ~~night~~ life. Her last words were to me when I asked her about 10 a.m. if I should hold her hands, she faintly answered "If you want to, or not,—I don't care."

At 10.30 A.M. as I sat at the table with Aunt Betty taking a cup of tea, she made a slight sound. I ran to her. She was dying. She only gasped once or twice. I asked her if she was going. She seemed to try to speak to me—could not. She passed away so calmly that for some moments we knew not if she were dead or living—but she had gone, leaving only the poor, pain-wracked tenement she had once dwelt in.[188]

Ah, who that has not had the experience, can know the agony of such a separation! I had looked for several weeks, for her departure, having no hope, but when it came—I was stunned. I seemed in a dream—I could not realize it. What, Susan gone—forever gone—I cannot believe it. But it must be so—that form, once so warm and full of life is colder than the stone. The ice itself seems not so cold. My tears flow as I write this after nearly three months have passed.

[page 324]

HER BURIAL.

Thursday, January 29, 1874—We buried her from the hall. Moroni and Nettie were sick at the time. Moroni with erysipelas[189] and Nettie with Scarlet fever, so they did not go to the funeral, nor Lillie and Virginia, it being cold and bad weather.

The choir sung "Milton" another piece "Sister thou wast mild and lovely." and "Greenville" We buried her beside her little Joseph.

I feel thankful that I was able to provide things to make her comfortable in her last sickness, but not those things, nor love itself, could keep her here. Now that she is gone, I would not have her back again. She is now free from the pain and sickness she has suffered so much from, especially the last eleven years of her life.

She had her weaknesses and failings, but she had many excellent virtues. She tried to live like a saint should in many respects; she taught her children to pray from their infancy up; to be truthful, honest, full of integrity, and to be true to Mormonism. What more could she do?

She promised to visit me, if she could be allowed so to do, and to watch over me, and keep me from evil. Oh, that it may be so!

187 Mortification in this context likely refers to the decay of body tissue.

188 The newspaper carried a small obituary ("Died," *Deseret News*, February 11, 1874; Utah Digital Newspapers).

189 Erysipelas is a fever resulting in a deep red inflammation of the skin.

As she lay, sweetly resting in her coffin, her face wore a peaceful expression, though the lines about the mouth gave token of her long years of pain.

Her coffin was large, as she dreamed, and was handsomely trimmed, and her robes were of fine linen. It was all I could do for her.

May I, also, depart in full faith and fellowship with the saints as she did, to receive a glorious ressurrection, & to meet those of my family who have gone before me. Amen.

[page 325]

January 29, 1874—Elvira attended the children faithfully during Susan's sickness the last month, and while they were sick after her death, and was kind and good to them, for which may God bless her forever and ever.

After Moroni and Nettie got well, Lillie and Virginia were taken down with the measels, but finally were restored to health through the blessings of the Father.

While at Bear River North last summer, I learned the following song, which pleased Susan J. very much, and she often sang it afterwards with me. The last that she ever sang at all was this song, the first verse and half the next, when her voice failed and she ceased. She never sang again, and that song—now following—has become a sacred one to me:—

LOVE, REST, AND HOME

1

Beyond the waking and the sleeping—
I shall be soon
Beyond the smiling and the weeping—
Beyond the sowing and the reaping—
I shall be soon

Chorus

Love, Rest and Home
Home sweet Home
Oh bliss to find when toil is over
Love, Rest and Home.

2

Beyond the blooming and the fading
I shall be soon
Beyond the shining and the shading
Beyond the hoping and the dreading
I shall be soon
(Here she ceased, her voice being weak & broken)
Chorus.

3

Beyond the parting and the meeting
I shall be soon.
Beyond the farewell and the greeting
Beyond the pulse's fever beating,
I shall be soon.
Chorus.

[note written in margin to explain the poem]
This tune I have written from memory, not having the notes at hand. The notes are correct but are perhaps written in the wrong key.

Fig. 4.10—"Love, Rest, and Home."

[page 326]

U.N.R.R. COMPLETED TO OGDEN & SMITHFIELD.

February 3 & 4, 1874—I went with Brs Preston and Hyde to Mendon to settle with the brethren there for the land taken by the U.N.R.R. and preached on the evening of the 3d with Br. Hyde—his last sermon there.

February 6, 1874—The U.N.R.R. having been finished to Ogden yesterday, a large number of leading men of Cache County went from Logan to Ogden on an excursion. We had a pleasant trip, the new road being pretty good, considering. As we came to the depot at Ogden we were welcomed by a Salute from the U.P.R.R. and the U.C.R.R. also by music from the Ogden Brass Band. In the evening there was a party at Brigham city, and the people there provided dinners for the visitors. I staid all night with H. P. Jensen, and was kindly treated by them.

February 9, 1874—We began laying track north of Smithfield. Laid about a mile and a quarter, and were stopped by the heavy snow

February 16, 1874—Went to Franklin to see how the bridge at Spring Creek, and the fill there, is getting along.

February 27, 1874—A party for Giles in the hall tonight.

Wednesday, April 1, 1874—During the past month I have been busy writing up my journal, which had to be entered from 1853, and was a labor of difficulty, on account of the items being contained in various books. But I am anxious to have it done, and then, should anything happen to me, my family and posterity may have a record of my life and actions. If I have not done much good I have endeavored to not do any evil;—at least, more than I can help. I have also done much writing for the U.N.R.R. Company, and have sent copies of my map of the country and line north of Ogden to Soda springs, and thence to Helena, to many places where they have been wanted—as to Government at Washington, New York, Chicago, Omaha, St. Louis and San Francisco.

[page 327]

LOCATE TERMINUS AT FRANKLIN. GO TO S. L. CITY

About a week ago I assisted in opening the snow blockade on the U.N.R.R. divide. The labor occupied 8 days, with about 200 men a day. The snow was in some places from 5 to 25 feet deep. I have also written and received many letters from my friends.

My family have all been well, but myself. I have not been well since Susan J. died, and have many times felt as if I might soon go too; but I desire to live, not only for my family's sake—but for the kingdom of God, now that there are so many enemies and apostates who are trying to destroy us. I wish to live to help fight them, and to see the victory of the Saints. I feel more than ever in my whole life the necessity of living the life of a Saint, and I hope to be able to do better than I have in time past, with the help of my Father in Heaven.

I go to day with Vice President W B Preston to locate the U.N.R.R. warehouse at Franklin. We went in his sleigh the snow being nearly two feet deep. Arrived there at dusk, twenty one miles.

Thursday, April 2, 1874—To day Preston, M. W. Merrill,[190] Bp. Hatch[191] and I located the site of our new warehouse near Franklin. Also the site of a new town,—the terminus of the U.N.R.R. I made arrangements for the morrow. Snow 2' deep.

April 3, 1874—Surveyed some city lots 40' x 150'. Walked on the snow.

April 4, 1874—Ditto. Came home.

Sunday, April 5, 1874—Started for S. L. City on R.R. and Logan city business. I also want relaxation, and rest for my eyes, which were made almost snow

190 Marriner Wood Merrill was called as a counselor in the Cache Valley Stake when Moses Thatcher was called to the Twelve Apostles. The stake president became William B. Preston with Merrill and Charles Ora Card as counselors. When Preston was called as Presiding Bishop of the Church, Card became the stake president. Merrill had served for eighteen years as bishop of the Richmond Ward. In 1884 he became the Logan Temple president, and in 1889 he was called to be a member of the Quorum of Twelve Apostles (Godfrey and Godfrey, *Utah Years*, 55).

191 This could be Lorenzo Hatch, who was a bishop in Franklin (Ricks and Cooley, *History of Cache Valley*, 54).

blind at Franklin. They pain me much, especially at night. Arrived in the city at 8 P.M. Found all well at Aunt E. M. LeBaron's.

[page 328]

TRIPS SOUTH OVER THE U.S.R.R. AND W & J.V.R.R.

April 6, 1874—Went to conference, which at noon adjourned to the 6th of May next. Elder O. Pratt spoke on the order of Enoch.[192] In the afternoon called to see Jesse W. Fox, Sur. Genl of Utah (Terl Sur. Genl) He gave me a certificate of the boundaries of Logan city on the South, as surveyed by him, as coming to and bounded by the north Branch of Logan River. Bought some large drawing paper for the U.N.R.R. and for Logan city; also tracing cloth, and other materials for my office. Br. Fox, who is Chief Engineer of the Utah Southern R.R. procured for me a pass to go over the line to Provo, as I desire to inspect it. Found Agnes LeBaron & Wm Hutchings[193] at Aunt E.s.

April 7, 1874—Went to Provo. Visited David Cluff Jr. also the office of the "Provo Times" and saw G. F. Lyons,[194] one of the editors and proprietors, who was formerly with me on the Utah Central R.R. as Leveler. Returned at 4 P.M.

Wednesday, April 8, 1874—Went to Sandy, and thence over the "Wahsatch and Jordan Valley R.R." up Little Cottonwood Cañon to its terminus, two miles above Granite—ten miles in all. This Road has a 3' Gauge, and an ascent, in places, of from 187 to 222 and above Granite, 280' feet per mile. Above Granite is located the Church quarries for the Temple. Several loads are brought down every day. The blocks average each about a ton. The trains are loaded down with Silver ore.

Near Sandy are several large Smelters, running out tons of lead and silver daily. A visit to the "Flagstaff" Smelter was quite interesting.

I also had a pass over this line, by the courtesy of Supt. Benson.

Br. Warwood, Engine driver on the U.S.R.R. also procured me a pass over the Bingham R.R. but I did not avail myself of it, not feeling very well, and returned to the city at 4 P.M. In our train was the [elder] "Bender" of Kansas murder notoriety.

[page 329]

Thursday, April 9, 1874—Started at 6 A.M. for home. Concluded to stop at Ogden to see J. A. West about his estimates in the Ogden Division of the U.N.R.R. Supt Moses Thatcher was also with me and stopped also. At noon we started north along the line. At Ogden River Bridge we spent some time fixing the pump there: then we walked to the construction train and partly riding and walking went about 8 miles north of Ogden inspecting the construction and section hands. The down train coming along, we came back to Ogden in the evening at about 6 P.M. I found Sister P. A. Benson on board our train, and assisted her on board the U.C.R.R. We (M.T. and I) stopped over night at Sam Farr's.[195] I called to see Penrose of the Ogden Junction.[196] Did not see West.

Friday, April 10, 1874—Came home, and found all well.

April 11, 1874—Wrote. Recd a letter from Henry A. also from Susan. She says she will soon start home.

Saturday, April 12, 1874—Start to Ogden to day to get the papers of West. Staid all night with Elder Franklin D. Richards.

Sunday, April 13, 1874—Went to Willard city, and stopped with Bp. G. W. Ward. I remained here making up the estimates on the Ogden Division, which West had not made.

Thursday, April 17, 1874—Went to Corinne on business. Paid $4.00 [$65] to the agent of Myers, of the Reporter. Returned to Willard.

Saturday, April 19, 1874—Came home. Found letters from my wife and Henrietta

192 Orson Pratt (1811–81) was an Apostle, voluminous writer, and theologian.

193 This could be William Willard Hutchings (1823–1904), who participated in the overland immigration of the Saints into Utah.

194 This is Oscar Lyons, who was a printer and associated with the *Provo Daily Times* (Holzapfel, *History of Utah County*, 145).

195 This could be Sarah Farr, one of the six wives of Lorin Farr. Lorin was a successful businessman, resident of Weber County, and a mayor of Ogden (Roberts and Sadler, *History of Weber County*, 173).

196 This is Charles W. Penrose, an associate editor of the *Ogden Junction*, a leading Weber County newspaper (Roberts and Sadler, *History of Weber County*, 220).

Sunday, April 20, 1874—Wrote to Henrietta.

April 21 & 22, 1874—Made estimates.

Saturday, April 26, 1874—Have been with the tracklayers several days. I also went up to Spring creek bridge to see how it is being finished. Found Gosland, the head carpenter, had made a botch of it, having built it out of line. I was much vexed at it. He was altering it the best he could.

[page 330]

GO TO CONFERENCE. ORDER OF ENOCH ADOPTED

April 26, 1874—The bridge is about 30 feet high and 170 long, built on piles with a bent on the top of them.

April 27, 1874—Began surveying a city plot at the terminus of the U.N.R.R. near Franklin. Lots 25'x130'. Continued until the 30th. The cars crossed the Spring Creek bridge the 30th

Saturday, May 2 & 3, 1874—The track was completed to the Warehouse today. And on the next day—Sunday—the people of Franklin turned out to finish it, put in the side tracks, & &c.

May 6, 1874—Finished at Franklin for the present.

May 7, 1874—This morning I start for the city to attend conference and bring Susan home. Arrived in S. L. City at 8 P.M. Found Susan and her family at Uncle David LeBaron's, all well, for which I thank our Father, who has thus far preserved them and us to meet in peace and safety.

Tuesday, May 12, 1874—Came home, with Susan, and Gertrude and Theodore. Henry, with Albert and Joel went home on Friday the 8th with the team.

We had a glorious Conference, most of the preaching being on the Order of Enoch. The church voted almost unanimously to unite in the New Order. I feel very thankful that it is now being instituted, and am determined to fully identify myself with it. I did not join the church to turn back at this late day. All that is of any worth to me is centered in Mormonism which grows dearer to me as I grow older. and with the help of God I hope to be able to continue faithful and true to the end. I gave in my name on Sunday April 26. 1874 to join the United Order, when John W. Young and B. Young Jr.[197] preached on the Subject at Logan.

There is a great opposition manifested by the Apostates and Gentiles, which I am glad to see

[page 331]

May 13, 1874—Made estimates, and next day surveyed a fence line for Prest Young on the Church Farm.

May 30, 1874—Since coming home from Conference, I have been very busy on the Railroad, scarcely being home more than one or two days at a time. About the 27th I spent several days at Richmond, surveying the city Townsite, and some work for individuals. I also went to Ogden and assisted J. A. West to copy his transit and Level notes, so they could be transferred to my office, he being no longer in the employ of the U.N.R.R. Company. Afterward Located another Water tank, near Richmond.

June 30, 1874—The past month has been much like the last,—very busy, most of the time surveying for private parties, without any startling event to break the peaceful current of our lives. About the first of the month I went to settle disputed lines of E. Van Orden[198] and Smith near Franklin.

On the 25th inst. I went to Corinne to survey a canal for irrigation for S. Howe and H. A. Jehu. Finished and came home on the 30th.

197 Brigham Young Jr. was the son of Brigham Young and Mary Ann Angell. He was ordained an Apostle in 1864, but he was not a member of the Quorum of the Twelve until 1868. Young owned a home in Logan and had business interests in the valley (Godfrey and Godfrey, *Utah Years*, 28). They are teaching the United Order. The United Order "refers to the cooperative establishment of business, community and church enterprises in an attempt to build Christian unity and economic self-sufficiency." President John Taylor would later teach that the order was a system of sharing of goods so as to alleviate poverty (Ludlow, *Encyclopedia of Mormonism*, 4:1493; also Leonard J. Arrington, Feramorz Y. Fox, and Dean L. May, *Building the City of God: Community & Cooperation Among the Mormons*, 2nd ed. [Urbana: Univ. of Illinois Press, 1976]).

198 Everett C. and Peter E. Van Orden were among the early settlers homesteading in Richmond (Ricks and Cooley, *History of Cache Valley*, 84).

July 1, 1874—Began Surveying on the Church Farm, in company with J. W. Fox and spent two days. The weather is intensely hot

July 4, 1874—Went on excursion to Ogden to spend the 4th. I met Elvira on the train, who was also going. She has been working for Mrs. B. Hampton for about 3 weeks. On the 24th of June I went to Franklin on an excursion of School and Sunday school Children. There were over 1000 persons in all.

The celebration at Ogden was a very tame affair, not worth going a mile to see. In the afternoon Elvira was taken sick and had to stay all night at the house of Thos Lewis, conductor.

[page 332]

ELVIRA ALMOST HOOKED BY A COW AT HAMPTON'S.

July 5, 1874—I remained all night to see to her. She soon got better and was able in the morning to come home, but got left, not being at the Depot on time. Weather still very hot. There were several hundred—probably 500 or 600 on the train.

July 6, 1874—Began to build a front picket fence. Hot.

July 7, 1874—Hot. A few days ago Elvira had a narrow escape from being gored to death by a wild Texan cow at Hamptons, which chased her and had nearly caught up to her when she dropped to the ground through fright, the brute almost upon her, when Br. Hampton[199] rushed to the rescue with a club and saved her.

Monday, July 13, 1874—Started this morning across the valley to survey for W. L. Williamson and others. Last week I spent most of the time fencing until Friday, when I went to Franklin on business. I also during the week made two copies of my map of the Utah Northern R.R. from Ogden to Helena, Montana. I located the line from Soda Springs northward by a map of the Territories, no line having been actually run north of Soda Springs, and only a preliminary from Franklin to that point, a distance of 56 miles.

The map had to be filed in the office of the Secretary of the Interior, Washington. I have previously made seven other copies for other Departments, there, map publishers &c.

The weather still continues extraordinarily hot.

July 16, 1874—Got home, having surveyed 1150 acres, and earned $47.00 [$764] most of which I got. Found Elvira just arrived.

This evening Moses Thatcher wished me to let him have one of my boys to do chores for him. I let Charlie go for him.

At this date Henry is working in the U.N.R.R. Warehouse at Franklin, at $75.00 [$1,218] pr month, half in U.N.R.R. stock

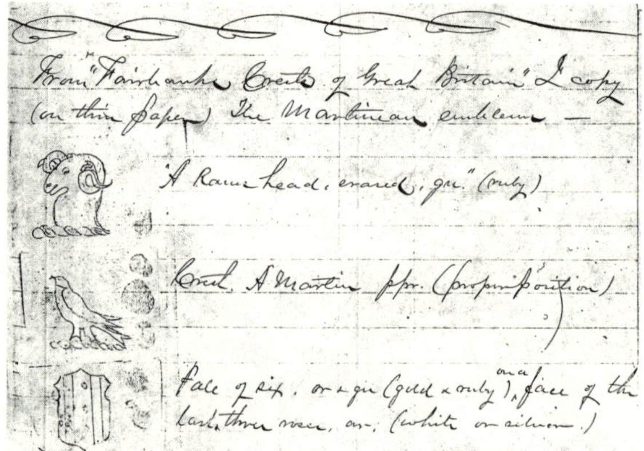

Fig. 4.11—Martineau emblems.

[page 333]

JUBILEE AT LOGAN

Friday, July 24, 1874—To day the Sunday school children throughout the Territory held a Jubilee, all the towns in Cache sending their children to Logan. There was about 3000 of them present who participated in the singing, which was very excellent. Br. William Knowles[200] led them. the Logan choir assisting. It was a beautiful sight to see the thousands of bright and happy faces and delightful to feel the peaceful and heavenly influence prevailing.

199 This could be Benjamin Y. Hampton, who operated the Berry River Ferry (Ricks and Cooley, *History of Cache Valley*, 176).

200 William Knowles was a chorister for the Sunday School in Logan (Ricks and Cooley, *History of Cache Valley*, 354). He later taught at Brigham Young College, which was established in 1877 (Ricks and Cooley, *History of Cache Valley*, 349–69).

Saturday, July 25, 1874—To day B. Samuel Johnson, son of Benjamin F. Johnson[201] came up from Spring Lake on a visit.

Friday, July 29, 1874—Sam asked me to day for Elvira and I gave my consent, counseling him to be a true and faithful Latter Day Saint. He returned home to day, borrowing $4.^{00} [$65] of me for his passage. Elvira, who had come home for a couple of days, also went back to Hampton's.

July 28, 1874—Last Monday I went over to Hampton's to bring home Elvira, and while there I went up Bear R. with Br. Hampton to the mouth of its Kanyon, and the first falls, which are about 8 ft high. The scenery is grand in the pass.

On Sat. July 31. B. Samuel Johnson, asked me for Elvira to which I assented.

August 2, 1874—To day the names of several persons were called to go on a mission to St. George, among them that of Henry.

Monday, August 3, 1874—Election for Delegate to day. Geo. Q. Cannon almost unanimously elected, this County giving a vote of only five for the gentile—Baskins.[202] I was clerk of election. Got the buggy repaired, costing $19.20 [$312]

Saturday, August 15, 1874—Pres^t Young held a two-days meeting in Logan beginning today. Several thousand present. He called considerable attention to the United Order.

Sunday, August 16, 1874—Meeting continued, and ended. Henry's name was called with others, for the St. George Mission. Haying for the last two weeks

[page 334]

August 14, 1874—To day I pulled down the old log cabin in which we at first lived on this city lot. It was one of the first built in Logan, and was erected by Bp. W. B. Preston.

August 16, 1874—To day a meeting was held and measures taken to organize the United Order in Logan.

Wednesday, September 9, 1874—Went to Corinne to level a long mill race for Howe & Co. taking Lyman with me. We boarded at the Central Hotel, spending two days on the work. I charged him $10.^{00} [$162] pr day for myself and $2.^{00} [$32] for Lyman.

I worked considerable on my house during this month, putting on rafters and sheeting, and also made considerable picket fence around my city lot.

Saturday, September 19, 1874—An officer drill having been appointed for the officers, to be held in Logan, a few assembled, and arrangements for the approaching annual three-days muster were made.

Thursday, September 24, 1874—To day is the beginning of the 3-days drill. The troops assembled at the old ground on Logan Island, about two miles from Logan city, and on the bank of Logan river. I went down the day before and arranged the Camp ground, in Company with Colonels Ricks and Crockett. The men continued to arrive from the various towns all day. There were three regiments on the ground: 1st Cavalry, Col. T. E. Ricks; 1st Inf. Col. Alvin Crockette 2nd Inf. Col. Wm H. Maughan, with the Wellsville Brass Band, and the Paradise and Smithfield bands of martial music.

Our mess consists of Brig. Genl Brigham Young Jr. myself, Brigade Adjutant General, Col. Moses Thatcher 1st Aid, Lt. Col. W. B. Preston Brigade Quartermaster, Surgeon, D B Lamoreaux, Ass^t Sur. O. C. Ormsby, Capt. M. D. Hammond, 2^d Aid;[203] Chaplain Saml Roskelly and color bearer Geo. T. Benson.[204]

201 Benjamin F. Johnson was from the Kirtland, Ohio, era of Church history. He participated in the construction of the Kirtland Temple.

202 R. N. Baskin was the Liberal Party candidate for congressional delegate. For a description of the election, see Ricks and Cooley, *History of Cache Valley*, 111. George Q. Cannon (1827–1901) was a businessman and editor. He launched the *Juvenile Instructor* in 1866, which was a children's magazine published until 1971. Cannon was an Apostle and counselor to several Church Presidents.

203 Milton D. Hammond was a counselor in the Cache Valley Stake presidency and later served as a member of the board of trustees for Brigham Young College (Ricks and Cooley, *History of Cache Valley*, 350, 380).

204 George T. Benson Jr. was the father of Ezra Taft Benson, thirteenth President of the Church.

[page 335]

GENERAL MUSTER. U. S. MARSHALS

1874—Mrs. M. A Maughan[205] and my daughter Elvira were cooks. Geo. Hibbard[206] acted as bugler for Head Quarters. The Camp presented a very lively appearance and to the unaccustomed eye, quite a novel and interesting one. Rumors were afloat, and had been for some time, that the Governor intended to put a stop to it, and was going to send up Deputy U.S. Marshals for that purpose, but we had no thought of abandoning it. As the event proved, Gov. Woods[207] was too wise to attempt it.

In the evening, at a meeting of officers, Genl Young proposed to do something in memory of the late Brig. Genl Wm Hyde, our former commander, and I proposed to change the name of our camp—"Independence", to "Camp Hyde", which was done.

September 25 & 26, 1874—The Muster continued three days, and was very interesting. There was a good feeling, only those attending who felt whole-souled in Mormonism, others taking advantage of Gentile influence to keep away.

October 31, 1874—During the past month I have been very busy Surveying at Paradise and Clarkston most of the time. Did not go to Conference.

On Sunday, the 25th B. Samuel Johnson came for the purpose of taking Elvira. I came home from Paradise and found him already come, and Henry also, who had come home from Franklin Depot, to prepare for his journey south.

Friday, October 30, 1874—Today Henry started south, having traded his buggy to Rollins for $90.00 [$1,462] and bought a wagon of the Co-op Store for $130.00 [$2,112]. B. Samuel also started south, taking Nephi with him, who is going to stay with Elvira all winter. Elvira will go with me on the cars. We gave her a new stove No 70, improved "charter oak" and quite a fit out of dishes and other small things, but not what I wished to give her, not being able to get anything from the stores.

[page 336]

ELVIRA MARRIED. I AM BAPTIZED FOR DEAD

1874—I let Henry have my compass, one of the best in Utah, a good Steel 4 rod Chain, and my Gravatt Level worth $110.00 [$1,787]. It cost me over $200.– [$3,249]. ~~I also furnished him about 500 lbs flour and some oats.~~ mistake

Saturday, October 31, 1874—Today Elvira and I started by railroad for Salt Lake City. We passed the boys about 4 P.M. about 10 miles north of Ogden, and arrived at Aunt Esther's at 8 P.M.

Sunday, November 1, 1874—The boys arrived there at midnight, having broken Sammy's axle point yesterday, and drove 30 miles to S. L. City dragging on a pole. I had been much troubled for fear they would not get to the city in time, as they must go through the Endowment House on Monday for their endowments and sealing.[208]

Monday, November 2, 1874—To day Henry, B. Samuel, and Elvira passed through the house. Sammuel [Samuel] and Elvira were sealed at 8 min after 3 o'clock P.M. by Pres. D. H. Wells, myself and Henry were present.[209]

~~Wed. 4~~ Tuesday, November 3, 1874—Today Samuel, Elvira and Henry and Nephi started south at 2 P. M.

Wednesday, November 4, 1874—This day I was baptized for the following dead relatives:—[210]

[It appears Martineau crossed people off the list as he completed their temple ordinances.]

My father John Martineau

his father ~~Ezekiel~~ Martineau (should be Stephen)

---

205 Mary Ann Weston Maughan was the wife of Peter Maughan. She was among the first Relief Society leaders in Cache Valley (Ricks and Cooley, *History of Cache Valley*, 296).

206 George Hibbard was a gardener (Somers, *History of Logan*, 62).

207 George L. Woods was territorial governor from 1871 to 1874. He did not care for the Mormons, and he was not reappointed.

208 The Endowment House was a building in Salt Lake City where members of the Church went for certain ordinances before the Salt Lake Temple was constructed. The *sealing* refers to the marriage of the young couple, "sealed for time and all eternity."

209 This was the marriage of Susan Elvira Martineau to Benjamin Samuel Johnson. Henry must have receieved his endowments at this time.

210 Martineau is being baptized as a proxy for family members who have passed on.

his father ~~William~~ Martineau (should be Stephen)

my uncle Peter Martineau, who died last month

my Mother's father James Mears

also his sons, (my uncles) Chauncey Mears and William Allen Mears

my mother's great uncle, Ethan Allen (of Fort Ticonderoga fame)

My brother Charles Augustus Martineau, who died in New York City, an infant, and

my brother (half) Charles Babcock, who died of measles in the U.S. Army near Murfreesborough Tenn. during the civil war.

[page 337]

I GO TO SPRING LAKE VILLA

November 1874—I could not think of the names of others of my relatives at the time, but hope to be baptized of more of them at a future time.

There were about 500 baptisms performed during the day.

Thursday, November 5, 1874—Started on the Utah Southern R.R. for Provo, arriving there at 10-15 A.M. Found the teams waiting there for me. We arrived at Spring Lake Villa at 6 P.M. and found Uncle Benjamin and his large family, consisting of 35 Children, and his wives and hired help, all well as usual.

Elvira received a cordial welcome from all and seemed well satisfied with her new home.

Friday, November 6, 1874—This morning B. Samuel and Elvira moved into Almon Babbitts house for the winter, he having been sent to St George to work on the temple this winter, also his brother Don C. Babbitt. To day came on a furious storm of rain and wind, which turned to snow, to the depth of about 3 inches. Weather cold and raw.

Saturday, November 7, 1874—Still stormy and cold. Uncle Benjamin had a dance in his house to night, the room being filled with his own family—wives, sons and daughters, and only three or four others present. Kemo, his indian boy, fiddled. It was a very pleasant party. Uncle B.'s boys and girls are a handsome, and intelligent set of Children, and would be a credit to any one. Danced to 12 P. M.

Sunday, November 8, 1874—Started home this morning, at 7 A.M. Nephi coming with me to drive the teams back. Road very bad in places. I got on the train just five minutes before it started, which was about 11 A.M. Got to S. L. City at 2 P.M. Found considerable snow there.

[page 338]

COAL DISCOVERY ON WEBER RIVER

November 1874—David T. LeBaron arrived home this evening, very tired, having walked over 30 miles from Tooele, through the mud.

Monday, November 9, 1874—Arrived at Logan at 2 P.M. having left S. L. City at 6 A.M. I found all well as usual at home.

Thursday, November 12, 1874—Went with Lorin Farr and Jo^{s} Richardson[211] to Franklin, on U.N.R.R. business.

Friday, November 13, 1874—Weather very stormy, so much so that we determined to come back to Logan, which we did, in a heavy rain and snow storm.

Saturday, November 14, 1874—Weather better this morning, but cold and wintry in appearance, the mountains being white to their bases.

Monday, November 23, 1874—Went to Ogden to day, not feeling able to do much labor about the place. Last week I spent in fixing my house, preparing for winter. Saw John Boulder in relation to our new coal mine near Evanston. About six weeks ago an indian showed a friend of mine, Edwin Crockett,[212] where there was coal near the U.P.R.R. beyond Evanston. He located me for a quarter Section with fifteen others, each having a quarter Section. There is more than forty feet of coal, in veins of from five to fifteen feet thick, one above another. The coal is said to be of good quality, and there are indications that it will coke. If so, it will be very valuable, for at present the whole Pacific slope is supplied with coke from Pennsylvania.

November 24, 1874—Returned home, and resumed work on my house.

November 25, 1874—Received a letter from my sister Henrietta, and one from Cousin Napoleon

---

211 Joseph and Benjamin Richardson were railroad contractors (Ricks and Cooley, *History of Cache Valley*, 174–75).

212 This is likely Alvin Crockett, and the location is Evanston, Wyoming.

B. Van Slyke who lives at Madison, Wisconsin. It was a very kind letter, and gave me much information in relation to my relatives on my mother's side which I here insert.

[Page 339]

MY MOTHERS RELATIVES, &C.

Wednesday, November 25, 1874—He says he knows nothing of my relations on father's side. He also wrote of Uncle Peter Martineau's death. Henrietta also wrote concerning it, giving date of death which was on the 15th September last. He fell dead of appoplexy, in a lawyers office. The following items Cousin Nap copied from my Grandmother Lois Mears' family bible, and some from other authentic sources:—

My mother's parents.
James Mears, born April 11. 1774 in
Died April 28. 1864, in Madison, Wisconsin.
aged 90 years and 17 days. He served in the war of 1812, in the State of New York.

Lois Sprague (Mears) born Feb. 26th 1779 in
Died May 23. 1861, in Madison Wis.
aged 82 y 2m 26d

Children	Born	Married	Died	Remarks
Eliza	Sept. 30. 1797	not	July 21. 1801	
Harry	July 31. 1799	"	Aug. 10. 1823	
John	Dec. 12. 1800	"	May 18. 1828	
Chauncey	Oct. 29. 1802	Dec. 25 1823	1873	Married Mary Dean
Laura	Feb. 15. 1804	March 10. 1822	Dec. 22. 1842	" Danl Van Slyke
Eliza	April 13. 1806	April 29. 1824	July 6. 1848 at Elbridge N.Y. and buried there	" John Martineau who died in 1838 buried in Elbridge On. Co. N. York
		Feb. 21. 1844 to Wm G. Babcock		
Harriet	March 31. 1808	June 23. 1825		Married John H. Pool
James Rockwell	July 26. 1810	March 22. 1836 about 1855		" Francis Russell " Lois Newton
Mary Ann	Apr. 12. 1812	July 31. 1834	Apr. 29. 1882 at Milwaukee Wisconsin	" Peter Martineau who died Sept. 15. 1874
William Allen	Apr. 2. 1814	Dec. 27. 1837 Aug. 11. 1846	Feb. 8. 1874	" Caroline Ferguson " Sarah Jane Maxwell

Fig. 4.12—Family record of James and Lois Mears.

[page 340]

Genealogy

Family Record of James and Lois Mears.

Children	Born	Married	Died	Remarks
Maria Louisa	April 5. 1816	April 13. 1837	Feb. 17. 1847	Married Harvey Abrahms who died in 1874
Chas. Sprague	Jan. 12. 1818	Nov. 12. 1840 Oct. 1848 to Harriet Anthony	1900	" Lucretia Martineau (my half sister.) who died in 18[illegible]
Henry	Aug. 31. 1826		Sept. 4. 1826	

Grand Children of James and Lois Mears.

Names	Born	Married	Died
Of Chauncey Mears			
Maria Louisa	Nov. 14. 1825		
Harriet Almira	Jan. 6. 1827	D. W. Scott Feb. 16 / 47	
John Henry	Apr. 20 1829	H B Hunt Nov. 21. 1850	
Mary Ann	March 9. 1832	— — — — — — —	April 7 1835
Mary Jane	March 26. 1836	J. C. Botsford	
Chauncey Dean	March 17. 1843	— — — — — — —	In the war, 1861
of Laura Vanslyke			
Napoleon Bonaparte	Dec. 21. 1822	Laura Sheldon Jan. 17. 1844 A. C. Corbett Mar. 30. 1859	
Of Eliza Martineau			
Emily Henrietta	Oct. 18. 1825	David C. Lyon	
James Henry	Mar. 13. 1828	Susan E. Johnson Jan. 8. 1852 Susan J. Sherman Jan. 18. 1857	Jan. 28. 1874, at Logan
Charles Augustus	Jan. 19. 1831	Jessie H. R. A. Grieve	Feb. 27. 1831, N. York city
Frances Eliza	Sept. 30. 1832	— — — — — — —	June 15. 1847, Victory N.Y.
Harriet	May 26. 1835	— — — — — — —	Oct. 16. 1837 Elbridge N.y.
Lois Elenor	Aug. 10. 1838	J. P. W. Voswinkel	
of — Babcock (Second husband's name = William Babcock)			
Caroline Mears	Jan. 7. 1845	— — — — — — —	Feb. 25. 1848 Victory N. York
Charles Sprague	Sept. 6. 1846	— — — — — — —	Died in the war, Murfreesboro March 1864 (measels)
Of Harriet Poole			
Laura Mears	July 31. 1826	J. H. Marsh Jan. 27. 1846	

Fig. 4.12 (cont.)

[page 341]

Genealogy

	Names	Born	Married	Died
of	Harriet Poole			
	De Witt Clinton	Sept. 25. 1828	Maria Pettis 1871	
	Mary Elizabeth	July 10. 1831	Norman Stewart Jan 5/52	
	Henrietta Lois	July 13. 1833	C. W. Fillmore Mar. 29/57	
of	—— Sherwin			
	William Henry	Nov. 5. 1838	Ellen	1872
of	James R. Mears			
	Emily	Mar. 8. 1837	----------	June 2. 1838
	Horace R	April 1839	----------	July 1840
	Ellen Stanley	Dec. 12. 1841	Edwin Ray Sep	
	Emery Russell	Mar. 26. 1843	in Ken.	
	Julia W.	Feb. 6. 1845	----------	Feb. 22. 1845
	Caroline E	Feb. 15. 1846	– McCormick	
	James R	Apr. 11. 1849	----------	March 12. 1850
	Norman Sprague	Aug. 5. 1851	----------	died
	Minnie	1857		
of	William A. Mears			
	George Ferguson	May 1. 1839	----------	July 31. 1841
	James Edward	Jan. 15. 1841	----------	June 2 1841
	Charles Henry	May 1. 1842	----------	July 25. 1845
	William Rockwell	Sept. 23. 1844	----------	Aug. 21. 1845
	William Allen Jr	Oct. 3. 1849		
-	W. A. & Maxwell			
	Annie Maxwell	1854		
	Samuel Maxwell	1855		
	Helen Louisa	1856		
of	Maria Louisa Abrahams			
	Mary Emily	March 27. 1839	_Sands	
	Alice Louisa	Jan. 7. 1841	Edward Kurtz	
	Laura Lucretia			
of	Charles Sprague			
	Alice	July 22. 1858		
	Florence	1863		

Fig. 4.12 (cont.)

[page 342]

Genealog (Continued)

Great Grand Children of James and Lois Mears. descended from

of Chauncey Mears:

Charles Henry, Son of John Henry

Frank Dewitt, Son of Harriet Almira Scott

of Eliza Martineau

John Martineau Lyon, Son of Emily Henrietta & David C. Lyon

Fannie Lyon, daughter of do " " " "

My own children = great grand children:-

	Born	Died	Married
Henry Augustus	Nov. 4. 1852. Parowan	—	M. Johnson
Moroni Helaman	Sept. 12. 1854 "	—	Dec. 17 1879 St George Temp
Susan Elvira	Aug. 14. 1856 "	—	Nov. 2. 1874 to B. S. Johnson
John William	Jan. 7. 1859 "	May 4. 1863. Logan	————
Nephi	March 11. 1862 Logan		E. P. Knowles
George Albert	March 22. 1864 "		Sept. 13. 1887 Emma Allred
Joel Hills	June 12. 1867 "		
Gertrude	Sept. 28. 1870 "		
Theodore	Sept. 8. 1872 "		
Anna Sariah			
James Edward	—	Oct. 17. 1880	————
Dora	Sept. 5. 1882		

The foregoing are children of Susan Ellen (Johnson) Martineau and the following are children of Susan Julia (Sherman) Martineau:-

	Born	Married	Died
Delcina Diadamie	Nov. 27. 1857 Parowan	————	Oct. 23 1865. Salt Lake City
Lyman Royal	April 21. 1859 "	Dec. 29. 1884	
Charles Freeman	July 24. 1861. Logan		
Jesse Nathaniel	April 6. 1863 "		
Julia Henrietta	Feb. 4. 1865 "		
Elizabeth	Aug. 13. 1867 "		
Virginia	July 16. 1870 "		
Joseph	April 23. 1873 "	————	May 10. 1873. Logan

Fig. 4.12 (cont.)

[page 343]

SALT LAKE CITY

November 28, 1874—During the past week I have been fixing up my house for winter, and on Sunday

November 29, 1874—went 13 miles to Paradise to do some surveying. Preached in the evenings. I spent two weeks, surveying and settling with the people, earning about $100.$^{\underline{00}}$ [$1,625] which was quite a help to us. I came home on Monday and found all well as usual.

December 14, 1874—Moroni and Charles were in the Cañon finishing a contract for 175 ties for the Utah Western R.R. The ties are red pine 5" X 5" X 6' @ 22¢ [$3.57] cash each. Remained at home this week and wrote to Henry and Elvira and Nephi.

Monday, December 21, 1874—By desire of Loren Farr, of Ogden, a Director of the U.N.R.R. I went to Ogden to assist in determining as to the arrangement of the grand depot at that place, of the Union Pacific, Central Pacific, Utah Central and Utah Northern Railroads.

December 22, 1874—We consulted with Br. Reeves, Agent U.C.R.R. and Mr. Pratt, Div. Supt. of C.P.R.R. about the grounds, and it was determined that I should go to S. L. City to copy the C. P. Map of the Depot grounds, Br. Farr going also. Arrived at dark at Aunt Esther's and found Uncle B. F. Johnson and Uncle D. T. LeBaron had arrived from Spring Lake, also cousin Vilate Johnson, who is helping Aunt Esther.

December 23, 1874—Copied the map in Mr. Marshall's office, the Attorney for the C.P.R.R. Came back to Ogden in the evening, and home next day, the 24th

December 24, 1874—Found Gertrude and Joel ailing with the Malignant Diptheria, which has already proved very fatal at Brigham city, the past season. Gertrude was taken on the 22nd and Joel on the 23^{d}. Spent a short time in a party and sat up with the children. In the night Theodore also, was taken with the same disease, and Virginia the next day.

[page 344]

LOCATE ROAD AT PARADISE

December 25, 1874—This morning Dr. O. C. Ormsby washed Joel's throat with nitrate of silver solution doing much good.

December 27, 1874—Children still sick. We sit up with them every night. To day I staid at home all day helping take care of the children. Yesterday, myself, C. O. Card and C. W. Card,[213] County Road officers, went to Paradise and located a country road through some disputed ground, returning the same day which was very cold.

December 28, 1874—Worked on map of Ogden Depot. Children are still about the same.

213 Charles Ora Card was Cyrus William Card's son. They owned the Card and Son Mill in Logan. Charles Ora Card would become the superintendent of construction for the Logan Tabernacle and the Logan Temple. He was primarily known for his exploration of the British territories and for leading a group of Cache Valley settlers into Alberta, Canada (Godfrey and Card, *Canadian Years*, ix–xl; Brigham Y. Card and others, *The Mormon Presence in Canada* [Edmonton: Univ. of Alberta Press, 1990]).

PART

5

THE SURVEYING CONTINUES, AND MARTINEAU PROSELYTIZES IN THE EASTERN STATES

[page 345]

LOCATE ROAD AT PARADISE

Friday, January 1, 1875—Went to day to Ogden to consult with Pres^{t} Lorin Farr and Mr. Pratt of the C.P.R.R. and Br. John Reeves of the Utah Central, in reference to the Depot grounds and buildings at Ogden. Saw them the same evening, and returned next day. Weather very pleasant,—streets dry and dusty.

The Same day (1st) Mr. Scupham, C.P.R.R. engineer, who had arrived here from San Francisco to explore for a route for a railroad from Logan or some point near it, across the mountains eastward to the Coal fields in the Bear River country, started up Blacksmith Fork Cañon in company with two men sent by Bp. O. N. Liljenquist, of Hyrum.[1] I spent several hours agreeably, in his company. Our children nearly well.

January 3, 1875—Last night was the last on which we sat up with the children, who are all well, I think, for which I thank our Father.

January 5, 1875—To day received a good letter from Henrietta, enclosing additional information in regard to my genealogy, which I insert on the page following. It gave me great joy to obtain this knowledge of my father and his relatives, and I hope to be able to obtain still more.

[page 345]

ADDITIONAL GENEALOGY.

GRANDPARENTS: MARRIED JUNE 5, 1785

Stephen Martineau born March 22nd 1761,

Ellenor Haughwout born Nov. 17th, 1764, his wife who died of cholera in N. York City in 1832.

THEIR CHILDREN:—

Stephen born Oct. 2nd 1785

Ellenor born March 14. 1787

1 Ola N. Liljenquist was president of a group of hundreds of Scandinavian Saints who immigrated to Utah in 1862. Liljenquist later became president of the Scandinavian Mission. While living in Hyrum, he served as bishop and was a member of the board of directors of the Utah Northern Railroad (Donald G. Godfrey and Kenneth W. Godfrey, eds., *The Diaries of Charles Ora Card: The Utah Years, 1871–1886* [Provo, UT: Religious Studies Center, Brigham Young Univ., 2006], 103).

Elizabeth born Nov. 3. 1788
Ann born May 14 1792
John born March 22, 1793 (my father, who died in Elbridge, Onondaga County, New York April 6, 1838.)
Egbert born Oct. 13. 1795
Abram born March 13. 1798
Maria born June 13, 1800 (Died 1832, of cholera)
Peter born Sept. 5, 1802 (Died in Milwaukee, Wis. On Septr 15th 1874, of appoplexy.)
Cornelius born April 7, 1805
Catherine born Dec. 14, 1808
[written in margin]
James Mears born April 11. 1774
Lois Sprague born Feb. 26. 1779

MY FATHER'S FAMILY:—

John Martineau, born on Staten Island, N.Y. March 22, 1793
Eliza Mears, (his wife) my mother, Born in Fabius, N. Y. April 13, 1806. Died in Elbridge Onondaga Co. N. York July 6. 1848. of child bed, a son, still born on July 5th
Married April 29th 1824, at Florida, New York

THEIR CHILDREN:—

Emily Henrietta Born Oct. 18. 1825
James Henry Born March 13. 1828, Port Jackson, Montgomery, N.Y.
Charles Augustus, born Jan. 19. 1831. Died Feb. 27, 1831, N. York city.
Frances Eliza born Sept. 31, 1831, Died June 15. 1847, Victory, N.Y.
Harriet born May 26, 1835—Died Oct. 16. 1837. Elbridge, N. York.
Lois Ellenor born Aug. 10. 1838
Caroline M. Babcock (half sister) born Jan. 9th 1845. Died Feb. 25 1848
Charles Sprague Babock, born Sept. 8, 1846, Victory N. York. Died in the (Union Army in camp near Stone River, in March 1864.
A brother, stillborn July 5. 1848, Victory, Cayuga Co. N. York.

[page 346]

MARRIED 24 YEARS. EXPLORE BEAR R. CAÑON.

January 5, 1875—Received a letter from Henry, who is still at Spring Lake, Utah County, getting ties for the Utah Southern R.R.

January 6, 1875—Yesterday and today I worked on my new city map of Logan, which is to be about 50 inches square. Answered Henry's letter. also Henrietta's

January 7, 1875—Worked on Logan City Map to day. Elvira came.

January 8 1875—To day is the 24th anniversary of our wedding, and Elvira's coming gives it éclat.[2] Where will we be 24 years hence? Quien Sabe! Rec^{d} and answered a letter from Aunt Mary A. Martineau, wife of my (late) Uncle Peter, who died Sept. 15th 1874. It also enclosed a letter to Uncle Peter from his cousin Isaac Haughwout—the son of my grandmother Martineau's brother. I wrote to him, asking for all the family information he could command. His present address is "Weston Lenawee Co. Michigan."[3]

Monday, January 11, 1875—To day I started to Hampton's Station on the Divide" to prospect for a new route of the U.N.R.R. to cross the ridge into Salt Lake valley. The ridge where the present line crosses it, has an elevation of 636 feet above Salt Lake valley, and the road has a gradient of 100 ft on the eastern side, and 90 feet pr mile on the western, and is much troubled with snow drifts in winter. I went to B. Hampton's and slept there.

January 12, 1875—To day I got a horse of Mrs. Hampton, and rode to the mouth of Bear River Cañon, to examine for a passable route. The weather very cold. Tied my horse at the mouth of the Cañon, and started up on foot.—the route being very dangerous on account of the steep hill sides and rocky precipices, lightly covered with a snow about a foot deep. I passed up about two miles to its upper entrance, to the "falls." This is a romantic place the whole river falling about twenty feet in one place, with smaller cascades above

2 *Éclat* is French for a "dazzling display."

3 Lenawee County, Michigan, is on the south-central Michigan border.

and below, with precipices of solid rock coming to the water's edge on each side.

[page 347]

1875—I had many very narrow escapes from falling, often saving myself from falling down the rocks by clutching at grass, rocks or bushes. I found the route practicable for a railroad, at a comparatively moderate expense, which I estimated at not more than $50.000 [$860,480] for the two miles. Got back at Hampton's at night, my clothes wet and frozen stiff. I got in the river four or five times.

Wednesday, January 13, 1875—Prospected along the line for a route up the Beaver Dam Hollow, with tunnel on summit but found this route more expensive than the other, with a grade of 80 and 90 feet pr. mile. At noon took the down train for Brigham city to make a map our line through that part of Box Elder county. Stopped with Judge S. Smith.

January 14, 1875—Worked at my map. Thawed, and blowed hard all night till near morning, then snowed heavily.

January 15, 1875—Started home, but was detained about 7 hours on the ridge by snow and ice on the track. Stopped at Mendon, with Chas Shumway[4] J Sen. Very cold.

Saturday, January 16, 1875—Came home, and found all about as usual.

Sunday, January 17, 1875—Still very cold. Began to rain Monday evening.

January 19, 1875—Rained all day and all night, taking off the snow very rapidly.

January 20, 1875—Several high embankments on the U.N.R.R. today were washed out. I was in bed all day trying to sweat.

January 21, 1875—Went over the Divide to Hampton's, to examine the first big break, in company with the Ass^{t} Sup^{r} and Master Mechanic T. Titenser.[5] We decided on a trestle bridge. Got home in the evening

January 22, 1875—To day I again went over to examine the next break, about ten miles beyond the other. At Hampton's myself and Merrill got on a hand car and started out in a driving storm, going down the long 90 feet grade of six miles at a rate of 25 miles per hour.

[page 348]

GO TO SPRING LAKE WITH ELVIRA AND VILATE JOHNSON

January 22, 1875—Made the necessary measurements and started back. The snow being deep, we found it very hard work to propel the car up the hill, so I got off and walked up to Hamptons—seven miles, facing the storm,—the path being very icy, so that I was very tired when I got back. Made draught[6] for another bridge 40 feet long and 20 high, with a proper bill of timbers.

Saturday, January 23, 1875—Worked on U.N. profile all day.

Monday, January 25, 26, & 27, 1875—Was on the divide, fighting snow with our trains.

Thursday, January 28, 1875—Elvira started home stopping a day or two at Mendon to visit her girl friends there. She started on Tuesday 26th instead of the 25th. I started on the 25th and she went on with me from Mendon. We got to S. L. city at 8^{20} P.M. and found Aunt Esther and family all well.

[written in margin]

Error, see paragraph

January 29, 1875—Saw W. H. Hooper relative to obtaining employment on the Utah Southern R.R. extension.

January 30, 1875—Started for Spring Lake with Elvira and Vilate Johnson, her husband's sister, who went by train as far as Provo, 48 miles. There Samuel met us with a team to take the party home. I kept out of his sight, to astonish him when he got, home, and went ~~on~~ up on the construction train, arriving there (Spring Lake some hours before they came. Samuel was quite astonished to find me there. I found Nephi,

4 The families of Charles and Alfred Shumway were among the first settlers in Mendon, Utah (Joel E. Ricks and Everett L. Cooley, eds., *The History of a Valley: Cache Valley, Utah-Idaho* [Logan, UT: Cache Valley Centennial Commission, 1956], 40).

5 This was Thomas Titensor (note spelling) from Cove, Utah. In January 1875, Titensor was the chief mechanic among four railroad mechanics (Ricks and Cooley, *History of a Valley*, 83, 186).

6 *Draught* is the British spelling of *draft.*

Henry and the Johnson family all as usual—Nephi quite hoarse. Danced in the evening.

Sunday, January 31, 1875—Went 8 miles to the South end of Utah Lake, where Uncle David T. LeBaron lives—fishing, and found him and his son David T. Jun. well. Uncle Benjamin and his wives Mary Ann (Samuel's mother) and Sarah Jane, also Nephi and two little boys. Came home at 6 P.M. a cold day.

[page 349]

Monday, February 1, 1875—Visited to day, and in the evening attended a good family dance.

February 2, 1875—Started home at noon, with Vilate. While at S. Lake I had a good visit with Henry and Nephi. Henry said he intended going on south in a few days, having been detained settling up the tie business. I hope he will go on and fill his mission. Uncle and cousin LeBarons came to Salt Lake city with us, where we arrived at 5.40 P.M. = $4.^{\underline{20}}$ h.

February 3, 1875—Tried to see my old friend W. H. Dame, now in prison charged with participation in the Mountain Meadow Massacre. Did not succeed in seeing him. Talked with John Sharp[7] relative to employment on the Utah Southern Extension, who gave me some encouragement. In the afternoon, went over the Utah ~~Northern~~ Western R.R. about 20 miles to Clinton's landing (in Salt Lake) Saw Dr. Clinton and other old friends there. Abram Doremus is Engineer of the line.[8] Got back at dark.

February 4, 1875—Had an interview with Sur. Gen[l] Kimball in relation to getting a contract for Surveying (U.S) in Cache County, who gave me some encouragement.

Friday, February 5, 1875—Came home, and found all well as usual. Found a letter from my second cousin Isaac Haughwout the substance of which is as follows:—

Said he thinks grandfather came from France, and that they (him and grandmother) lived and were buried at Richmond, County Seat of Staten Island—near which, about 2½ miles, grandfather owned a farm and a Stone house in which my father and his brother's and sisters were born. Thinks an Aunt—Nancy Deckir, is living in New York city with her daughter—Charlotte Moor.

I wrote to Haughwout also to Charlotte Moore to see if I can obtain further information.

[page 350]

SURVEY COUNTY ROADS. GO TO MEET M. THATCHER

February 6, 1875—Wrote several letters, and also in the Journal.

February 13, 1875—During the last week, have been working on my large map of Logan Townsite. To day (Saturday) I went to Clarkston to survey, and try to collect some of my dues there.

Sunday, February 14, 1875—Preached in the evening.

February 15, 1875—Began Surveying, for a cow and horse pasture. Weather clear and cold, and snow about a foot deep, on an average, with quite a crust, which holds one up part of the time—only, and makes walking very laborious.

February 16, 1875—Began Survey of County road from Idaho line to Box Elder County line, Surveyed 5½ miles.

February 17, 1875—Finished the road, and came home next day. Weather moderating, and sleighing disappearing.

Monday, February 22, 1875—Went with select man C. W. Card to locate the County road from Bear River Bridge to Logan.

February 23 & 24, 1875—Surveyed the road to Logan, 8^{m} 6^{r}

February 27, 1875—Surveyed the road from Logan south to Millville field fence

Monday, March 1, 1875—Went with several officers of the U.N.R.R. to Ogden to meet M. Thatcher and Cha[s] Nibley,[9] just returned from New York.

---

7 John Sharp was a bishop in Salt Lake City, and he was active in politics. Once a mob beat him severely, and he "might have been killed had a conductor from the Utah Central Railroad not intervened" (Linda Sillitoe, *Welcoming the World: A History of Salt Lake County* [Salt Lake: Salt Lake County, 1996], 66).

8 Doremus owned a ranch west of Salt Lake City, near Tooele.

9 Charles Wilson Nibley (1849–1931) emigrated from Scotland in 1860 and became a leading business leader in Cache County. While on his mission in the British Isles, 1877–78, he developed a deep friendship with Joseph F.

Met them as they alighted from the U.P.R.R. train. Transacted some R.R. business at the house of Hon. Lorin Farr, in connection with officers of the Ogden & Salt Lake R.R. Company.

March 2, 1875—Came home. It is desired that I should explore for a R.R. line up Blacksmith Fork and across the Wahsatch Mts. to the Bear River Valley, for coal. It will be a dangerous undertaking, the range being over thirty miles wide in an air line, and about 4000 feet above the valley, and 8000 above the sea, with snow from ten to thirty feet deep—no habitations on the route. It can only be done on snow shoes and is more dangerous than to be engaged in battle.

[page 351]

LETTER FROM J. BLICKENSDERFER JR,

March 4, 1875—Went to Hyrum to get men to go with me, but did not succeed. They were fearful of the hardship and risk. Snowed all day. Snowed hard all day.

March 6, 1875—Worked on my map of Logan Townsite, and on those of my county road surveys.

March 8, 1875—Attended County court, to assist in adjusting the difficulty between S. Obray and S. M^c^Murdie[10] about the road between them at Paradise. Also next day. Court allowed my bill of $119.⁰⁰ [$2,048] for surveying some County roads this winter, I paid it out in debts immediately, all but a little for my taxes.

March 13, 1875—Have spent the rest of this week on my city map. Received a long letter from J. Blickensderfer Jr. in reference to my making a series of triangulations on the Promontory and to Brigham city Court House. Had previously received one from him to Pres^t^ B. Young, which the latter sent me. J. B. Jr. was one of the principal engineers on the U.P.R.R. Survey—the most competent, in fact—and I became acquainted with him while I was engaged in that Survey. J. B. Jr. wishes me to complete a series of triangles for him, but only proposes to liquidate my expenses.

March 15, 1875—I wrote him I would do the work for about $100.⁰⁰ [$1,721] and would pay my own expenses. I attended city Council to day. Among other things done, Pres^t^ B. Young Jr. Hon. M. Thatcher and myself were appointed a committee, in conjunction with some from the County Court, to invite Gov. Axtell[11] to visit Logan, and to make necessary arrangements for his reception. At Tabernacle meeting tonight subscribed $100.⁰⁰ in addition to my former $200.⁰⁰ [$3,442] for that building. Last year $16.700 [$287,400] was expended on it, in bringing it up to the water-table, some twelve feet.

[page 352]

JUSTUS CLARK BURIED IN A SNOW-SLIDE.

March 16, 1875—Worked on map.

Saturday, March 20, 1875—To day the committee (myself and others) who were appointed by the City Council to invite Gov. Axtell to visit Logan, met and I wrote him a letter of invitation which we all signed, dating it the 22nd inst. as it can not go until then.

March 17, 1875—On Tuesday, word came that three men were just buried in a Snow slide in Providence Dry Cañon, about 4 miles from here. About 100 men quickly started up the mountain gorge to try to extricate & save them if possible. Arriving at the scene of the disaster, we found Br. I. J. Clark[12] and his son John had extricated themselves, but Justus, his son of 18 years age was not in sight. After we had dug in various

Smith. Nibley later served as the Presiding Bishop, replacing William B. Preston (Daniel H. Ludlow, ed., *Encyclopedia of Mormonism* [New York: Macmillian, 1992], 1643; Godfrey and Godfrey, *Utah Years*, 44).

10 Samuel Obray was a pioneer settling in Paradise. He and Samuel McMurdy were friends at one time (Godfrey and Godfrey, *Utah Years*, 376). McMurdy (note spelling) came to Wellsville after participating in the Mountain Meadows Massacre (Juanita Brooks, *The Mountain Meadows Massacre* [Norman, OK: Univ. of Oklahoma Press, 1991], 74, 83, 197, 241).

11 Appointed by President Ulysses S. Grant, Samuel Beach Axtell (1819–91) was territorial governor of Utah for only a few months during 1875. More moderate than his predecessor, he was criticized by the residents of the territory who were not members of the Church.

12 Israel J. Clark (1821–1905) founded Clarkston, Utah. Clark served a mission in the Idaho Salmon River areas where he learned the language of the Shoshone Indians (Ricks and Cooley, *History of a Valley*, 40, 61, 79, 82, 277).

places about ¾ of an hour, we found him within three feet of where I was digging, not more than two feet under the Surface, but Suffocated. He was lying on his face, tightly packed in the snow. He was a fine young man, of powerful frame and in robust health. The men were cutting railroad ties, when a gust of wind started a slide of snow, which carried him a short distance, when another came and buried him as we found him.

My old friend S. M. Blair also died to day. On the 15th inst. James Smith[13] was carried down the mountain nearly half a mile in a slide, passing over one cliff of rocks, and was left just on the verge of another about 40 feet high, the Snow going over the abyss.—a truly wonderful escape. He was not much hurt. Also a few days ago a snow slide entirely damd the Logan river for over an hour. It is now very dangerous to be in the mountains, snow slides occurring almost every day. The warm weather causes the snow to become heavy, and it breaks loose, gathering bulk as it descends, until they are sometimes immense.

[page 353]

CONFERENCE.[14]

March 27, 1875—This evening about dusk, Theodore fell into the well, which is about 15 feet deep, and narrowly escaped death. The trap door covering the well, (which is in the kitchen) was up, Charlie having just drawn a pail of water, and turned his back. Theodore fell head first, striking the edge of the floor, then, as we supposed, fell feet first to the water which is two feet deep. As soon as he was missed Moroni ran to the well, looked in and saw him, and got down to him as soon as possible, and got him out of the water. He was lying under the water, motionless, when rescued. As soon as he recovered he said "Ma, I fall in the well and get my new shoes all wet." It was a wonderful escaped truly, for which I thank the Lord.

Sunday, March 28, 1875—Theodore is all right to day.

April 3, 1875—To day the men finished my new well outside of the house. I shall fill the other up.

April 5, 1875—To day I started to Conference. Weather cold and snowy, as it has been most of last month.

April 6, 7, 8, 1875—Attended Conference, and called at the Surveyor General's office to see if I could get a contract of Surveying for government, but found the prospect quite uncertain, there being many gentile and apostate applicants for work. Mr. Froiseth promised to use his influence for me.

Thursday evening I was taken suddenly quite sick, having taken a violent cold and being quite billious.[15] Had several fainting spells in the night. Had David T. LeBaron, Benny Johnson and John Morrell,[16] my cousins by marriage administer to me. Started home on the morning of the 9th though feeling quite unwell. Arriving at Ogden I found that John W. Young had gone to S. L. City, and as I wished to see him I came back.

[page 354]

ANNA SARIAH BORN, MAY 4.TH 1875.

Friday, April 9, 1875—Found Br. Young, and saw him in reference to my Bear River Cañon Road business, which occupied me all day, so I returned to Aunt Esther's for the night, much surprising her. Ella has a new baby girl about 6 weeks old, of which she and all the family are very proud. It's name is Ella Bell.

Saturday, April 10, 1875—Came home, still feeling quite unwell. Found all at home well as usual.

May 1, 1875—Since conference I have been busy most of the time surveying, at Weston, Paradise and other places. Also surveyed County Roads, amounting in all to \$119.00 + 42.00 = \$161.00 which I received in County Scrip. Tuesday, April 13, Melissa Haws came to help.[17]

13 James Glover Smith was a bishop of Smithfield (Ricks and Cooley, *History of a Valley*, 53).

14 The conferences about which Martineau writes are general conferences of the Churchwide membership. A stake conference would be for a smaller area.

15 Biliousness is a disorder of the liver that causes nausea, abdominal pains, headache, and constipation.

16 This is likely Joseph Morrell, a Logan retailer who later served in the Cache Valley Stake presidency under George O. Pitkin (Ricks and Cooley, *History of a Valley*, 280–81).

17 Lucinda Melissa Haws (also spelled Hawes), was daughter of Lucinda Colehill Crockett Haws and Nathaniel Haws. Nathaniel was later active in construction of the temple. He sold a limekiln to the Church (Nolan Porter Olsen, *Logan*

Tuesday, May 4, 1875—This evening, at a quarter to eleven o'clock P.M. another spirit from heaven joined our family circle. She weighed 8½ lbs. We named her Anna Sariah, after Susan's mother's name, (the first name) and the latter name after her sister's. She was not named and blessed until the 7th.

On the 7th we had a snow storm, winding up a good rain. It was much needed. The rivers are all high and four bridges across Bear River have already been carried away.[18]

Wrote a letter to Br. Geo. L. Farrell, one of our choir, with whom I have sung and associated intimately for fifteen years. We have always been bosom friends, and have had many good times together, both at home and on many expeditions against indians, and for explorations—sometimes in very dangerous and trying circumstances.

In looking in one of the hymn books at meeting one day, I found some words written by him in farewell to the Choir, before his departure for England, and I wrote these lines in answer:—

[page 355]

LINES TO G. L. FARRELL[19] NOTTINGHAM ENGLAND.

1

Thou'rt far away, and plain and hill
And foaming billows sever,
But as of old, we claim thee still
And mean to claim thee, ever.

2

Though absent far, we'll not forget
Our joyous times together:
We loved thee then—we love thee yet
And hope to do so ever.

3

The time will come when thou'lt come home
And glad will be our greeting;
But some, perhaps, will then be gone
And in the grave be sleeping.

4

But there's a clime where we shall greet,
Where friends no more shall sever;
But as a choir again shall meet
And sing in heaven forever
May 1875.

Saturday, June 5, 1875—Since my last entry I have been busy surveying in various parts of the county, and have surveyed out several of our county roads. About three weeks ago one of our choir, Mrs. Arnott, a very sweet singer died suddenly, after an illness of only 24 hours, which was quite a shock to us. She was much beloved. This brings to mind the lines I wrote to Br. Farrell, though I little thought though would so soon be verified.

A few days ago Pres^t^ B. Young Jr. and I wrote to Gov. S. B. Axtell in reference to holding military musters in the county, asking an expression of his views.

[page 356]

S. L. CITY, VISIT W. H. DAME. COAL

June 5, 1875—To day we are looking for a visit from Prest. Young with several of the twelve. We had two meetings today, at which were present Elders E. Snow B. Young Jr. Geo. Q. Cannon, Phineas Young[20] and in the afternoon Pres^t^ Young.

Sunday, June 6, 1875—Good meetings today. Pres^t^ Young spoke with great power in reference to the United Order.

Monday, June 7, 1875—Pres^t^ Young and party returned home. I also went with his party, to S. L. City. Co. Court to day.

[written in margin]

Melissa H. quit work on 7th inst.

June 8, 1875—Called at Sur. General's Office to see if I could get a contract for Surveying, but could not. Paid Dwyer $10.00 [$172] for County Mapping

Temple: The First 100 Years [Providence, UT: Keith W. Watkins and Sons, 1978], 93).

18 Martineau often reports the weather to the newspaper ("From Thursday's Daily, May 4th," *Deseret News*, May 10, 1876; Utah Digital Newspapers).

19 Martineau and Farrell corresponded as illustrated in the journals and the newspaper ("Local and Other Matters," *Deseret News*, April 12, 1876; Utah Digital Newspapers).

20 Phineas Young was Brigham Young's brother.

paper I got at Conference; also $1.⁰⁰ [$17] for 3 months more of S. L. Herald.[21] Showed a specimen of my coal to T. W. Ellerbrek, Supt. of S. L. City Gas Co,[22] who was much pleased with its appearance. In the afternoon I went to the Penitentiary and saw Br. W. H. Dame, who has been confined 7 months on charge of murder, committed at the Mountain Meadows at the time of Buchanan's war on Utah. He is innocent, and I know it. It was a joyful meeting. We talked of old times, and of the crime of which he is charged. He wishes me to attend his trial as a witness, 12th July next at Beaver. I remained with him until 8 P.M.

June 9, 1875—Rained all night and some during the day. Aunt Esther and family are at Spring Lake, and Aunt Mary Ann Johnson and her daughter Mary are at the house in Salt Lake city. Called to see John W. Young, who starts for New York city again tomorrow.

Thursday, June 10, 1875—Started for Carter, on U.P.R.R. which is 127.4 miles east of Ogden in Company with Br. Young and his family, and a Mr. Owens, a coal expert who had come with Br. Young to examine coal in Utah.

[page 357]

CARTER STATION. COAL MINE

Thursday, June 10, 1875—Arrived at Ogden at 8 A.M. and at 9.30 Started on the U.P.R.R for Carter Station. As I passed up the Weber Cañon—the first time since I was surveying on the U.P. Railroad—the change seemed marvelous indeed; and as I whirled rapidly by so many familiar spots, where we had toiled so long in mud, water, thorny thickets, precipices and rocks, with a broiling sun, and legions of mosquitos I could hardly analyze my feelings. Near Evanston we entered Wyoming Territory. Evanston seems quite a flourishing little town.[23] Here machine shops of the R.R. are located, employing many hands, and disbursing about $20.000 [$344,192] pr month. Close to the town are the Evanston Coal mines, which supply most of the Coal used in Utah, and about 300 tons pr day to California. East of Evanston, the Country becomes very desolate and barren, and so continues for hundreds of miles. After passing about a dozen small villages and Stations, we arrived at Carter at 5 P.M, and were met by Judge Carter, of Fort Bridger, whom J. W. Y. had telegraphed to meet us, and his brother, R. H. Carter, who lives at the Station. I had come for the purpose of visiting our coal mine, and seeing for myself if it is worth anything. Br. Young went on to New York. I met Mr. & Mrs. Bevans, who were glad to see me. Stopped at Mr. Carter's.[24]

Friday, June 11, 1875—Mr. Carter having furnished us a wagon and team myself and Bevans started to the mine, arriving there at Sundown, a distance I think, of not less than 20 miles. (It had been represented to me as only 12 miles.) Found no one at the mine, but the tent was still standing, and we camped in it that night. Visited a new tunnel into the coal lately begun, in the South end of the coal mountain.

[page 358]

AT THE COAL MINE

Saturday, June 12, 1875—Went two miles north this morning to the main tunnel, and found a vast body of coal. The hill, lying north and south, faces very precipitously to the east, disclosing four or five veins of coal, varying from 15 to 40 feet thick with strata of gray and brown sandstone between them. The bottom vein is 40 feet thick, and extends for miles. The strata incline downwards to the west, at an angle of about 24° The following is a sketch of the place, looking north. I think there is fully 100 feet of good coal

21 American press at this time was known more for its colorful stories than for factual reporting. The Salt Lake papers followed that trend. The *Deseret News* reflected the Mormon view, while the *Salt Lake Tribune* reflected the non-Mormon view. Another paper, the *Salt Lake Herald*, was founded in 1872. Martineau was often given a byline as a reporter for several of these frontier newspapers (Sillitoe, *Welcoming the World*, 67).

22 In 1874, Thomas W. Ellerbeck was general bookkeeper for the Salt Lake City United Order (Leonard J. Arrington, Feramorz Y. Fox, and Dean L. May, *Building the City of God: Community & Cooperation Among the Mormons*, 2nd ed. [Urbana, IL: Univ. of Illinois Press, 1976], 406).

23 Evanston, Wyoming, was a major point in the Union Pacific Railroad. The railroad had reached Evanston in 1868 and, during the 1870s, the town was populated by Chinese workers who labored on the railroad and in nearby coal mines. Some nearby charcoal kilns are still a tourist attraction today.

24 At this writing no Carters seemed to match the context of these entries.

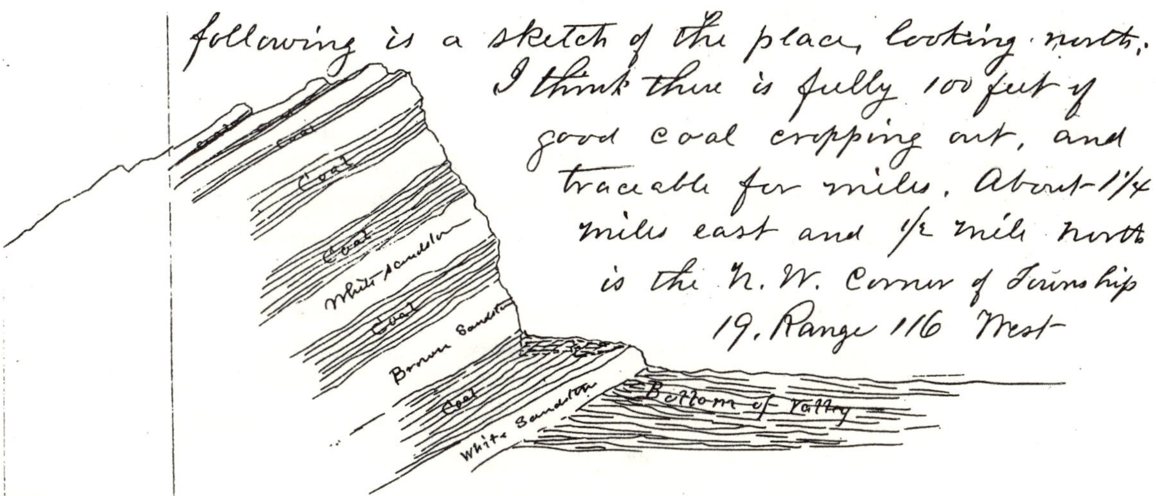

Fig. 5.1—Coal mine at Carter Station near Fort Bridger, Wyoming.

cropping out and traceable for miles. About 1¼ miles east and ½ mile north is the N.W. Corner of Township 19. Range 116 West

Carter Station is 18 miles in an air line from the mine being 9¼ miles east and 15¼ South. The following is a map copied by me from U. S. Survey Plats from the land office at Cheyenne, Wyoming Territory:—

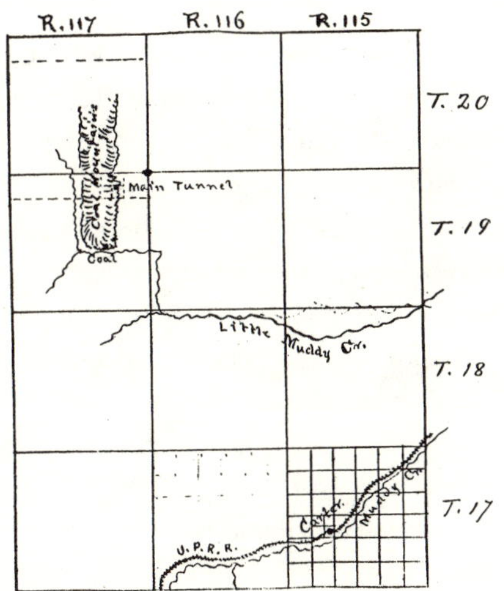

Fig. 5.2—Map of Carter Station.

[page 359]

GOV. AXTELL'S VISIT.

Saturday, June 12, 1875—Returned to Carter this evening with about 500 lbs coal. Saw several antelope and shot at one.

June 13, 1875—Sent a box of coal to John W. Young, N. Y. city, to have it analyzed for Coking qualities, and started home at 10.20 a.m. arriving at Ogden at 6 P.M. Stopped at Covington's tonight. Gave Mr. Pratt of the C.P.R.R.[25] some coal to send to his Company, at San Francisco.

June 14, 1875—Came home, and found all well as usual. City council afternoon and evening.

June 18, 1875—Recd my book on Bridge building (Whipple)[26] Planted beans.

Monday, June 21, 1875—Went to Mendon, to do surveying, and heard that Gov. S. B. Axtell is coming to Logan tomorrow. Attended a meeting in the evening and spoke.

June 22, 1875—Came home by morning train, Gov. Axtell came up in the afternoon on the freight train, having missed the regular.

Our Committee, Prest B. Young Jr Moses Thatcher and myself were scattered, the first being in San Pete Co., the second confined with a sick Child, leaving me only, and Bp. W. B. Preston to attend to every thing. Gov. Axtell took rooms at the Logan Hotel, kept by J. R. Blanchard,[27] where the city Corporation had

25 A William Jared Pratt was among the first settlers of Clifton, Idaho (Ricks and Cooley, *History of a Valley*, 63–64).

26 This is likely Squire Whipple, *An Essay on Bridge Building* (Utica, NY: H. H. Curtiss, 1847).

27 John R. Blanchard was among the first settlers of Logan. He owned a hotel, built and ran the Logan House and a livery stable, and carried mail (Ray Somers, *History of Logan* [Logan, UT: Somers Historic Press, 1993], 57, 303).

arranged for him. In the evening Bp. Preston, Hon. M. Thatcher, myself, Alderman H. K. Cranney,[28] City Marshall Alvin Crockett and County Clerk J. A. Leishman spent the evening with him, enjoying a very pleasant interview.

Wednesday, June 23, 1875—Myself, Bp. Preston and Judge M. D. Hammond accompanied the Governor to Providence where we remained an hour. While there I sent a boy on to Hyrum to inform them of our arrival there shortly. We got to Hyrum about noon, and took lunch at Br. James Unsworth's,[29]after which we proceeded to Paradise, and spent an hour there, returning to Hyrum about sunset. In the evening the Governor and Bp. Preston addressed a crowded Audience.

[page 360]

GOV. S. B. AXTELL'S VISIT[30]

June 23, 1875—The Gov[r] was much pleased with the place and the kind reception of the people, and they were very much pleased with him and with his good words, and his good, strong sense. The Bishop, H. C. Jackson,[31] and Brass Band of Paradise also attended in the evening.

June 24, 1875—Started at 10 A.M. and drove to Wellsville, four miles, having previously notified the people of our intended arrival. Found the Sunday School Children and many grown people, with flags and the Wellsville Brass Band ready to welcome him in a hearty manner, after which we proceeded to the house of Widow Howells. Here he made a very kind and good speech to the Children. Gov. Axtell addressed the people in the Hall in a very kind and excellent address, completely winning the people, as at other places. After dinner we returned to Logan, and he spoke very eloquently to a crowded house in the evening. The Bishop being detained, I Conducted him to the stand, and opened the proceedings until Bp. Preston Came.

June 25, 1875—Started in a special train to Franklin, with the Wellsville Band which I had invited, and quite a company of others, about forty in all. At Franklin we proceeded to the residence of Sister ~~Hezakiah~~ L. H. Hatch, visiting her an hour, and the Band playing some Airs. Here I found Mr. Jo[s] Richardson of New York City, who is starting work on the Utah Northern extension. Had some talk with him about it. He made me promise to come up again tomorrow. Br. Hatch is has been for several months hiding from U.S. officers from Idaho, who desire to arrest him on false charges.

[page 361]

CONTINUED

June 25, 1875—Returned and dined at Richmond, and after dinner attended another meeting, then proceeded to Smithfield, doing the Same, thence home, arriving about Seven P.M. Here I had supper for the Brass Band—some 18 in all, at the Hotel, and the Wellville Band returned home well pleased with their days trip.

During all these meetings, the general tenor of the Governor's remarks was for temperance, industry, beautifying and improving our beautiful valley and towns, kindness to our children and kindred subjects. Also upon our position as a Territory and the obedience we owe to the laws of the United States &c. He completely won the good feelings of the people by his pleasant and affable manner and his excellent remarks.

June 26, 1875—Being obliged to go to Franklin, I last evening took leave of Gov. Axtell, who leaves for Salt Lake City today. He will soon depart to New Mexico his future field of labor, having been removed to please the Carpet Bag Ring in Salt Lake city.[32]

28 H. K. Cranney was a prominent Cache County lawyer and farmer. He was the public prosecutor in 1867, the district attorney in 1869, and later a county attorney (Somers, *History of Logan*, 59; Ricks and Cooley, *History of a Valley*, 93).

29 James Unsworth was the postmaster in Hyrum, Utah. He was also a justice of the peace and served on the city council (Somers, *History of Logan*, 50).

30 "The Governor in Cache Valley," *Deseret News*, July 7, 1875; Utah Digital Newspapers.

31 Henry Clark Jackson was among the earliest settlers of Paradise, Utah (Ricks and Cooley, *History of a Valley*, 422).

32 *Carpet bag ring* is a derogatory term for politicians who take advantage of an unsettled situation and then quickly move on, traveling light with carpet handbags.

In a previous conversation upon the Proclamation of Gov. Schaffer, forbidding our citizens from carrying arms or mustering for drill, he said it was a most atrocious document, and he had thought of quietly revoking it, but finally thought it would not merit even so much notice as that.[33] He would treat it with the contempt of perfect silence, as it could never be enforced in any court of law. It was absurd, that any Governor, in time of peace, could affix the penalty of death for carrying arms or holding a militia muster, and call out U.S. Troops to enforce it. This was a disappointment, as I had hoped he would repeal that obnoxious document. In a conversation yesterday, I again introduced the subject, saying we wished all subjects of apparent opposition to even an alleged authority might be removed, and he told me he thought he would quietly revoke the thing as soon as he returned to S. L. City.

[page 362]

NOTE TO GOV. AXTELL, WHO RETURNS HOME.

June 26, 1875—At his request, I filled a sheet with statistical and other information concerning our valley, herding, irrigation, church government &c, and wrote the following note—postscript—to gently remind him of our hopes:—

"Logan, June 26, 1875

Gov. Axtell

Sir:—In reference to the Schaffer Proclamation forbidding musters, although it could not be ~~enforced~~ sustained in law, yet individuals might have to spend months in prison and expend much money to demonstrate the fact, and as we cannot with consistency give up this natural right and universal practice among americans, of annual musters, a revocation of that proclamation, thus preventing any opposition to an alleged authority, would be very gratefully received by the people of Utah.

Very Respectfully

James H. Martineau

Adj. of Cache Mil. Dist."

Having prepared a way for him to visit Logan Cañon with Br. J. A Leishman and Br. & Sister Penrose, I went to Franklin to see Richardson but accomplished nothing, and returned in the afternoon train.

Rec^d a telegram from John W. Young, N. York city, asking for another copy of my Article on Narrow gauge roads, published last spring in the "Helena Independent."[34]

[page 363]

OGDEN CELEBRATION, CALLED TO BEAVER. BAPTIZED

June 26, 1875—Wrote to Benna Johnson who desires to come up here to work, that he would probably find labor.

Saturday, July 3, 1875—During the past week I have been surveying the County roads in Mendon precinct.[35] I began work there on Wednesday June 30, and boarded with Br. Jo^s Richards:[36] On Friday July 2. 1875 I surveyed 160 acres for F. S. Reader.[37] I came home on Sunday morning, July 4.

Monday, July 5, 1875—Went to Ogden, in hope of receiving $5.00 [$86] from Br. Reader, but did not see him. Got my pay from his wife. Witnessed the torchlight procession of the Salt Lake city and the Ogden Fire Brigades, which was a very fine sight. Came home next day.

Wednesday, June 7, 1875—To day S. J. Steward, a Deputy U.S. Surveyor came to see me, in reference to helping him survey in this County.

June 8, 1875—Went with him To Wellsville, Hyrum and Millville. Found prospect of work to do.

June 10, 1875—Gave Stewart authority to procure field notes and plats of Cache County (U. S. Surveys) for the county, the Court having authorized

33 John Wilson Schaffer was another short-term Utah territorial governor; he was appointed by President Ulysses S. Grant in 1870. As reflected in this entry, Schaffer fought to crush the "Mormon rebellion" by restricting military drills and gatherings. He died in 1870 in Salt Lake City.

34 Helena is the state capital of Montana. The city's history involves the 1864 discovery of gold along the Last Chance Gulch. The *Independent Record* was the city's newspaper, founded in 1867.

35 Card and Martineau are working on the roads (see "Local and Other Matters," *Deseret News*, June 16, 1875; Utah Digital Newspapers).

36 This may be John Richards Jr., one of the first settlers of Mendon, Utah, or his relative.

37 There are many Reeders and Readers in Church history.

Fig. 5.3—James Henry Martineau and Susan Ellen Martineau with children; see journal entry, September 15, 1884. Courtesy of James Henry Martineau Family Organization.

me to procure them, and to pay $75.$^{\underline{00}}$ [$1,291] therefor.

Received a telegram from Sutherland & Bates, lawyers for my friend Col. W. H. Dame, of Iron Co. to go to Beaver shortly, as a witness for him. He is charged with Murder in the Mountain Meadow Massacre, but I know him to be innocent. As I have no money to pay my traveling expenses, I telegraphed them for $35.$^{\underline{00}}$ [$602] to be sent me for that purpose or I could not Come. This is not because I feel willing to leave him the lurch in time of need, but because I have no money nor any way to get it that I know of.

Sunday, July 11, 1875—To day is Susan's birthday. She is thirty nine years old to day, being not more than 15½ years old when we were married.

[page 364]

BAPTISMS INTO THE UNITED ORDER.

Sunday, July 11, 1875—We have therefore now been married 23 yrs 6$^{\underline{mo}}$ 3$^{\underline{days}}$ This seems, looking forward, quite a long time, but in retrospect it is short—only a dream. But in proof of its reality, we have with us at home, eleven children, viz:—Moroni, Albert, Joel, Theodore, Gertrude, and Anna, Susan E.'s children, with Charlie, Nettie, Jesse Lillie and Virginia of my deceased wife's family. Lyman R. eldest living of the latter brood, lives with Brigham Young Jr. and Henry, Elvira and Nephi are in the South, Henry at Johnson, Kane County, and Elvira and Nephi at Spring Lake Utah County. Besides these fifteen (15) three are gone before—Dellie, Willie and Joseph; also

Susan J. So there is in all quite a family of us—twenty-one. May God give us wisdom to train them aright and present them to Him in His Celestial Kingdom.

Susan has been a good, true and loving wife to me, kind to her own children, and a mother to the six motherless ones, for which may our Father bless her forever.

This afternoon myself, & Susan, with Nettie, Albert and Joel were baptized into the United Order. The three children last mentioned were baptized for the first time. B. M. Lewis baptized Susan, and I, Joel was baptized by B. M. Lewis—and confirmed by Bp. W. B. Preston, and I baptized Nettie and Albert, and they as well as we all, were confirmed by Bp. Preston. Susan was made quite sick for a day or two, the water was so cold. I baptized a swedish woman—my first baptism, before I did my children.

Saturday, July 17, 1875—During this week I have been busy at home, and have been two or three days to see Mr. Richardson principal owner of the Utah Northern, about the bridge across Cub River. He wished me to take a contract to build it.

[page 365]

LETTER FROM JOHN W. YOUNG ON COAL

July 17, 1875—I thought at first of doing so, but finally concluded to have nothing to do with it, because of my position as Chief Engineer of the Road. There is quite a disagreement between him and the Board of Directors of the Company.

Monday, July 19, 1875—To day I rec^{d} a letter from John W. Young, in reference to the assay of the coal I sent him from Carter Sta. some time since, together with the Report of Mr. Britton, who made the analysis. The following is a copy:—

Metropolitan Hotel New York City
July 12. 1875
J. H. Martineau Esq
Logan Utah
Dear Brother

Your favor of July 4th has just been received. In regard to ~~Mr.~~ Richardson, I mentioned you to him when he left, and supposed you would be employed.

Please find enclosed a copy of Britton's letter and analysis of the coal.

Communicate with me what you and the Brethren want to do about building a railroad to this coal.

Are you sure all your figures in your article on Narrow Gauge railroads are correct. I trust so, for I intend to republish your article in pamphlet form under your name.

We'll be glad to hear from you very soon, as to the condition of the coal mines, the parties owning it, &c.

In haste your Brother
Jno. W. Young.

Mr. Blodgett Britton's Letter:—
Philadelphia Pa. June 28 (1875)
Jno. W. Young Esq
Dear Sir. Herewith please
find Report of results of analysis of the sample of Utah Coal received from you.

The amount of water, perhaps, is understated but not much: it is very difficult to determine with any great accuracy the water in such coal.

[page 366]

ANALYSIS OF OUR COAL. BRITTON, PHIL.

July 1875—The coal cokes readily, and the quality of the coke you can see for yourself, for with this I mail a small box of it.

By drying at 500 Far. an excellent quality of fuel may be made.

Respectfully yours (signed) J.Bloget Britton.

Analysis.

Water expelled at 500 Far.	19.90
Volatile combustible matter	37.24
Fixed Carbon	41.67
Ash	1.19
	100.00

Am't of sulphur included in the above 0.36 100 of raw coal afforded of coke 41.96

(Sig) J. Bloget Britton

Charges for analysis	$16.00
Cost of trip to Phil. and return	7.20
Expressage on coal	3.40
	$26.60 [$458]

I here subjoin analysis of coal, made at Omaha by Charles Portiz, assayer of the U.P.R.R. copied by me from his Rep^{t}

		Rock Spring Coal.	
"Moisture	4.50	Moisture	4.050
Vol. Carbon	52.40	Vol. Car.	43.125
Fixed "	40.44	Fixed "	41.427
Ash	2.66	Sulpher	00.780
	100.00	Ash	10.618
Combustible	92.84		100.00
Incombustible	7.16	Combustible	84.552
	200.00	Incombustible	15.448
			100.000

The Rock Spring Coal is the best hitherto found in Utah. I answered the letter immediately, then went to Mendon to Survey land for C. Shumway Sen. Remained until Friday, and came home, being head of Committee to celebrate July 24th

Saturday, July 24, 1875—Celebrated as usual. Went with 22 of the choir and sat for photograph at T. B. Cardon's.

[page 367]

CHARLES F. AND JESSE N. BAPTIZED, SUN. JULY 18. 1875

July 1875—On Sunday the 18th inst Charlie and Jesse where baptized the former by Paul Cardon[38] and the latter by Eli Bell[39], and were confirmed by Thos Jones[40] who confirmed ~~C.F.~~ Jesse B. M. Lewis confirmed ~~J~~ Charlie.

July 25, 1875—Sent my article on Narrow Gauge R.R. to J. W. Young, having revised it somewhat. Went to Mendon this afternoon, and attended meeting.

July 27, 1875—Finished Surveying for B. C. Shumway, Mendon.

Sunday, August 8, 1875—Attended Meeting at Brigham City to day. D. H. Wells, W. Woodruff, G. Q. Cannon, L. Snow, R. Burton and others present. A good meeting. Preaching on the United Order. There are 1500 indians on Bear river, most of whom are baptized. Last Sunday over 300 Shoshones (of Washakie's Band) were baptized. This wonderful work is spreading rapidly among them.

August—During the past week have been drawing maps for the County. Recd a touching letter from Lois, detailing family afflictions, and asking for help. Also one from Henrietta. Answered the latter.

Monday, August 9, 1875—About noon, to day Br. Monteith of Paradise began work on my house.[41]

August 10, 1875—Excursion from S. L. City arrived today.

August 12, 1875—Prest B. Young Sen. arrived to day.

August 15, 1875—Prest B. Young Sen. preached to day. During the past week I have (with Br. Monteith) been working on my new house. Reports came of an indian fuss at Corinne, near which place are congregated many indians. On Friday and Saturday our city was full of them, they having been driven away by soldiers from Camp Douglas.

August 16, 1875—To day issued orders for a general muster to be held Sept. 16, 1875, to Continue 3 days. B. Young Jr. W. B. Preston M. Thatcher, T. E. Ricks and myself went and picked a camp ground which Genl Young named "Camp Axtell," after our late Governor, who had shown himself a gentleman to the people of Utah.

[page 368]

August 16, 1875—This afternoon A. J. Stewart, U.S. Deputy Surveyor,[42] arrived here, to begin Surveying.

38 Paul Cardon owned the Cache Valley House, a hotel constructed of adobe brick (Ricks and Cooley, *History of a Valley*, 146).

39 Eli Bell was a Logan carpenter (Somers, *History of Logan*, 57).

40 Thomas Jones was a "Block Teacher." The Church has long had a system of visiting local neighborhood members. Today's home teachers are assigned within a ward to visit families and attend to their needs and welfare (A. J. Simmonds, *The Gentile Comes to Cache Valley: A Study of the Logan Apostasies of 1874 and the Establishment of Non-Mormon Churches in Cache Valley, 1873–1913* [Logan, UT: Utah State Univ. Press, 1976], 20).

41 Alvin B. Montierth was one of the original settlers of Paradise, Utah (Ricks and Cooley, *History of a Valley*, 45).

42 Andrew J. Stewart was a surveyor who, with George Albert Smith, laid out the town of American Fork (Hubert Howe Bancroft, *History of Utah: 1540–1886* [San Francisco: History Company, 1889], 312n21).

Tuesday, August 17, 1875—To day Prest. Young returned home

Saturday, September 4, 1875—Started to S. L. City to day to go to funeral of Pres[t] Geo. A. Smith, who will be buried tomorrow.

Sunday, September 5, 1875—Br. G. A. Smith was buried to day from the new Tabernacle which was crowded. Met uncle B. F. Johnson, his sons Benny and Francis and his daughters Vilate, Hattie, Zina and Anna who had come from Spring Lake. Heard that Elvira and Nephi were well.

September 7, 1875—Came home with Salt Lake excursion to Logan, & found all well.

Thursday, September 9, 1875—Went with Stewart to Wellsville to Survey.

September 11, 1875—Came home, having nearly finished the townsite.

September 13, 1875—Devoted my time to preparing for the muster, the responsibility devolving mostly upon me as Adjutant General of Brigade.

September 15, 1875—Went down to the Camp ground, about 6 miles west of Logan, and staked out the ground for camping. Rained for several hours in the afternoon and evening. I went to bed early, cold and wet through, without having had any dinner or breakfast or supper, except 3 small cakes.

September 16, 1875—Many arrived on the ground today. Rained.

September 17, 1875—Still more troops came. Our exercises were spirited and well performed. Some trouble occurred in the evening with some drunken fools who had said they meant to "run the camp to night." But by some error in their calculations, the Camp "run" them, capturing one—Willard Jones, after a struggle.[43] We strengthened the guard, with orders to arrest every one trying to pass the lines without the countersign—Freedom." The rowdies kept the camp in an uproar till about 11 P.M.

[page 369]

MILITARY MUSTER, ON LOGAN R. CONFERENCE

September 18, 1875—To day another rough was arrested and also kept under guard. His name was Ugland, a bully. Our Muster ended to day, having been with the exception noted, very orderly and agreeable, with a very pleasant spirit prevailing. Sat. noon Susan came down to camp with several of the children which gave me much pleasure.

September 20, 1875—Settled our Camp Mess account, which was $11.09 [$191] to each of our eight. The names of our mess are as follows:—

1 Brigham Young Jr.	Brig. Gen[l]
2 Ja[s] H Martineau	Adj. Gen[l] of Brigade
3 Moses Thatcher	1st Aid (Col)
4 Wm B. Preston	Quartermaster (Lt. Col.)
5 O. C. Ormsby	Surgeon (Maj.)
6 M. D. Hammond	2nd Aid (Capt)
7 Sam[l] Roskelly	Chaplain (Capt)
8 Geo. T. Benson	Ensign bearer (Capt)

After the muster, I returned to Wellsville, and resumed the U.S. Survey of Township 10 N. Range 1 West, in which it is situated. On finishing there about the beginning of October, I came home and attended the General Conference in Salt Lake City, which continued five days. Previous to this, however, I went to the city, to the funeral of Prest. G. A. Smith, my old-time friend.

November 3, 1875—I went to Paradise to Survey T. 9 & 10 N—R. 1 E. and continued until the latter part of the month, working the last week in snow nearly a foot deep

[page 370]

SAMUEL & ELVIRA COME HOME. HENRY & MELISSA ARRIVE

Friday, November 5, 1875—To day B. Samuel Johnson, my son-in-law, and Elvira came from Spring Lake Villa, their home, to spend the winter with us. Moroni, who went with my team and wagon to help move them up, also came. It had been raining and snowing for many days and the roads were very bad indeed. The came home in a heavy snow storm.

43 William Jones was a bricklayer (Somers, *History of Logan*, 63).

Saturday, December 4, 1875—To day my son Henry A, and his wife Melissa arrived home on a visit from Kane County—over 400 miles south of here. They were married on the Monday previous—Monday Nov. 29, 1875—by Prest. D. H. Wells. His wife—Editha Melissa Johnson, is the daughter of Sixtus E. and Editha Johnson of Johnson, Kane Co. Utah, and niece to my wife. I was much pleased with her. Before they returned home, which was on Sat. Dec. 11. 1875, I was forced to return to Clarkston, to finish my U.S. Survey there. I went to Clarkston Monday Dec. 13, and began work next day, finishing on Mon. Dec. 20th 1875, and returned home on the 21st. Found our little Anna had been very sick—even to death—on the previous Sunday, but by the administration of Prest B. Young Jr. Moses Thatcher and Bp. T X Smith[44] she was healed, beginning to amend instantly, so that when I came home on Tuesday, she was apparently well. But by exposure that day, she had a relapse, with very dangerous symptoms, which caused us great uneasiness for a few days: but by the blessing of God she was restored in a few days.

December 24, 1875—Attended Christmas Eve Ball this evening. Rain and snow during the day and evening.

December 25, 1875—Christmas

December 31, 1875—Attended a select Ball in the Co-op building this evening, and had a pleasant time.

[page 371—See Appendix 3 for "Thoughts on Leaving Logan" article inserted here.]

SAMUEL & ELVIRA, & MORONI CALLED TO ARIZONA.

January 1, 1876—Today is the first day of the new year. The past year has on the whole, been a prosperous ~~for~~ one, for which we have to thank our Father in Heaven. We have especially been blessed with health in our numerous family—a blessing which many years of sickness in my family enables me to appreciate.

During December the City Council of Logan city had many sessions, revising old ordinances and passing new ones, which business engaged much of my time during that month. The labors of the Council terminated on Jan. 6. 1876, the duty of still further revising and codifying the ordinances being placed on the Committee on Revision, of which I am a member. Accordingly I continued at work on this business without cessation until Thursday the 20th when I was called on to do some Surveying at Hyrum for John Monson,[45] who had been called with 24 others from Cache County to go on a Mission into Arizona, to settle that Country. My son-in-law—Benjamin S. Johnson and my daughter Elvira were called, among the rest. The Call was made on Sunday Jan. 16. 1876.

January 27, 1876—Came home from Hyrum, having earned $78.00 [$1,382] during the week. I got a Colts pistol and Spencer rifle for Samuel, also ammunition and other things. Bought a cow and calf for $25.00 [$443].

February 3, 1876—Received about $20.00 [$354] worth of instruments &c from Gurley, Troy. N.Y. Among the rest, a protractor reading to one minute, price $4.50 [$80]

Sunday, February 6, 1876—To morrow Sammy and Elvira are to start to Arizona. I had to furnish many things they needed, because the Ward was so stingy, many persons subscribing $1.00 [$18] who ought to have put in $25.00 A few days ago Moroni, also, was notified to be ready to go in the spring, with another lot of missionaries, which makes three of my children called on missions within a year.

[page 372]

SAMMY & ELVIRA START TO ARIZONA. AUNT ESTHER'S DEATH.

Monday, February 7, 1876—To day my children Sammie and Elvira started for Arizona—a journey of nearly 900 miles in the dead of winter. They were pretty well fixed for the journey, having a good 2500 wagon, a middling span of ponies, two wagon covers, tools of various kinds, seeds, shotgun, Spencer rifle

44 Thomas X. Smith was bishop of the Logan Fourth Ward. He was a farmer and a city alderman serving with Martineau (Somers, *History of Logan*, 70; also Ricks and Cooley, *History of a Valley*, 103).

45 John Monson could be a member of the Hans Monson family in Hyrum, Utah (Ricks and Cooley, *History of a Valley*, 45).

and a revolver. I furnished cash and merchandise to the amount of $100.$^{\underline{00}}$ [$1,772] or more. They placed the wagon on a sleigh, another man and team going with them to assist them over the worst snow.

They departed in good spirits, but the parting was sad to us, not knowing when we shall see them again; but knowing that they are just as much in the care and keeping our Heavenly Father, and as safe, as if they were here with us. So we commended them to Our Father, and sent them away with our blessings. Moroni went with them the first day's journey across the Divide into Salt Lake Valley.

They reached Salt Lake City Friday, and remained there until the following Tuesday; Also spent a few days at Spring Lake, but received no help there, save a broom or so.

Monday, March 6, 1876—To day, at our Biennial City election I was re-elected to the City Council, together with most of the old members. Bp. W$^{\underline{m}}$. B. Preston being, as before our Mayor. Most of the past month, I have been revising and codifying our Municipal Ordinances.

Wednesday, March 15, 1876—To day received a telegram from Salt Lake City, that Aunt Esther M. LeBaron, my dearly loved sister in the Gospel, died this morning at 7 A.M. Had not heard she was sick. Answered that I would come to the city.

[page 373]

BURIAL.

Thursday, March 16, 1876—Started for Salt Lake City. On account of the U.N.R.R. being blockaded with snow, I had to travel 20 miles in an open sleigh. Arrived in the city 8.20 P.M.

Aunt Esther had been sick only a week, and was not considered at all dangerous by anyone, until the moment of her death. Talking with her son David F. she suddenly sat up, reached her hands to him, and expired, with a pleasant smile upon her countenance. Until the moment of her death, she thought she would soon be up and well. Truly, to her, Death had no sting. The last letters she wrote me, breathed the very essence of our holy religion, and was very precious to me. I am thankful to have been her friend here, and shall rejoice so much to meet her by-and-by. A pure and holy love existed between us, and had for years, because I knew she was true and faithful to Mormonism.

I found Uncle Benjamin, Uncle David LeBaron, and the rest of her family, and during the night Mrs. Ann Dunyon arrived, having traveled all night in a wagon through dreadful roads, to be here.

Friday, March 17, 1876—Friday we buried her, mourned and revered by all her friends and neighbors. Bp. Robt T. Burton (her Bishop) was absent, but Apostle Jo^{s} F. Smith preached her funeral sermon—one full of good instruction and comfort.

At the cemetery, I found the grave of my little Dellie. She lies beside her grandmother, Delcena Sherman, on the north side.

Saturday, March 18, 1876—Snowed hard all day

Sunday, March 19, 1876—Preached in the evening.

Monday, March 20, 1876—Came home, and found all well as usual.

[page 374]

APPOINTED NOTARY PUBLIC. TO BEAVER.

Monday, March 20, 1876—Attended City Council meeting in the evening, and was appointed Inspector of Buildings.

On the fourteenth of this month I was Commissioned a Notary Public for Cache County by the Governor, and qualified accordingly

Tuesday, March 28, 1876—For the past week I have been engaged on my County maps most of the time.

April 17, 1876—Went to Hyrum, to survey water ditches; and spent several days at it, and in dividing up a quarter section for Br. Jackson, also Lewis Howell. Bargained with Bp. O. N. Liljenquist for his spring carriage, to be paid for in surveying.

Tuesday, May 2, 1876—Received a subpoena from J. G. Sutherland,[46] on behalf of W$^{\underline{m}}$ H. Dame to attend the latter's trial at Beaver, on the 7th inst. Had only 25 minutes to take the train in. Arrived at S. L. City at 8.20

46 J. G. Sutherland was a lawyer for the Church's First Presidency (Bancroft, *History of Utah*, 565n46).

May 3 & 4, 1876—Spent the time trying to get means for the journey to Beaver. Got a pass over the U.S.R.R. and Dame arranged for my stage fare from York, 140$^{\underline{m}}$

Friday, May 5, 1876—Started for Beaver with J. G. Sutherland, also Elias Morris,[47] another witness. Reached York, 75$^{\underline{m}}$ at noon, then took stage (?) in company with eight others. Our conveyance was one of the littlest of the little "jerkies," and so tightly we were wedged in that once fixed, no one could move. All were gentiles except myself and Morris, and while they were not smoking they were drinking whiskey and telling obscene stories, and boasting of their achievements with women. Although all were professedly <u>gentlemen</u>, lawyers, bankers &c, their conversation was very disgusting. But they all condemned polygamy, saying it was the only thing against the Mormons.

The weather was very cold; snow and hail, with cold north winds, making it very uncomfortable indeed, and greatly aggravating my already severe cold.

[page 375]

BEAVER

At 9 P.M. we reached Chicken Creek, 30 miles, took supper, changed teams, went on, reaching Sevier river Bridge at 1 A.M. and Round Valley at daylight. Here we got a balky team, and we had to walk 3 miles to top of mountain. Passed through Holden and Fillmore, which are well built up, with fine orchards, arriving at Corn Creek at 2 P.M. where we breakfasted, having traveled 60$^{\underline{m}}$ from Chicken Creek. Here we had to hire an extra span of horses ourselves, to put with the stage (?) team, which was so poor it could hardly travel, even on a walk. About 9 P.M. we reached Cove,[48] and took supper. There being no relay of horses, we waited until 11 P.M. and then started on, reaching Pine Creek—6 miles—at 2½ A.M. Waited here till 5 A.M. and went on having a new team, and reached Beaver about 11 A.M. having had a very fatiguing journey of 140 miles by stage, the rest by rail, making in all about 320 miles from Logan.

May 7, 1876—Stopped at Mrs. Lee's for one day, the rest of the time I ate at Josiah Rogerson's,[49] sleeping at James Farrar's house, where Br. Dame was also stopping. He was in the custody of Rich$^{\underline{d}}$ Benson, of Parowan, who had been deputized a U.S. Marshal, for that purpose.

Saw many of my old friends, whom I had not met for 16 years. All had grown older, and were turning gray.

May 11, 1876—After many vain endeavors of [William H.] Dame and [John D.] Lee to get a trial, they were released on bail—$20.000 [$354,472] for Dame $15.000 [$265,854] for Lee, and $10,000 [$177,236] for Adair.[50] I went bail $1000 [$17,724]. on Dame's bond. In the evening a railroad meeting was held—mostly gentiles—presided over by Judge Boreman. They sent a Committee to invite me there. I went, therefore, and by request, spoke in relation to bringing a railroad down through that country. Dame not tried and he went home

[page 376—see Appendix 3 for letter from F. D. Richards, notes, a handwritten letter transcription, and a quote box inserted here.]

PAROWAN, GO TO BELLVUE.

Friday, May 12, 1876—Started with Dame and others to Parowan, to visit my old home and friends, arriving there about 5 P.M. I can not express how glad I was to see Parowan again, and the many old friends I found, all of whom were glad to see me. But all was changed. Houses pulled down, new ones built, and the trees grown so much larger. The little children I had left were now married, with families of their own.

---

47 Elias Morris was a Cedar City resident who was active in the Iron Mission at the time of the Mountain Meadows Massacre (Morris A. Shirts and Kathryn H. Shirts, *A Trial Furnace: Southern Utah's Iron Mission* [Provo, UT: Brigham Young Univ. Press, 1991], 348–50).

48 Cove Fort was a stopover point for the stages at that time. It has today been restored as a popular tourist attraction.

49 Josiah Rogerson was instrumental in establishing an education system in Parowan (Janet Burton Seegmiller, *A History of Iron County: Community above Self* [Salt Lake: Utah Historical Society,1998], 191).

50 Joseph Adair was among the original iron missionaries (Shirts and Shirts, *Trial Furnace*, 425; Brooks, *Mountain Meadows*, 194). Jacob S. Boreman was the judge presiding over the trial (Brooks, *Mountain Meadows*, 191, 194).

I stopped at Jesse N. Smith's with my sister-in-law Janet.[51]

Saturday, May 13, 1876—To day was Jesse's wedding anniversary—the 24th—and he gave a grand dinner in its honor, as well as for his two daughters, Adelaide and Hannah, who have just returned from being married. There was about 30 present, and a very pleasant time.

Saw Julia and Saml Orton, also Aunt Almera. Went upon a hill, where once I and my two wives had climbed before we left Parowan. It brought to mind things both pleasant and sad.

Sunday, May 14, 1876—Preached to day, afterwards visited Metta, our aforetime hired girl.

Monday, May 15, 1876—E. W. Dolten[52] lent me a little pony on which to ride to Bellvue, some 48 miles, and I started about noon, reaching cedar quite tired out. Stopped at Henry Lunt's, an old friend.

Tuesday, May 16, 1876—Went to Bellevue, 28 miles, facing a terrible storm of wind and sand. Was completely exhausted, and lay down with a hot fever. Father came home at night from Conference at St. George, and administered to me.

Here I lay sick a bed for several days, with my cough, which has now been bad for 6 weeks, very violent.

[page 377]

BLESSING, ON J. H. MARTINEAU.

May 16, 1876—Nothing has seemed to do it any good. It is a quick consumption, I am well aware, and will only be cured by the power of God. I have for many days been hoping to get to father's so that I may be healed, for I know he has great faith and power in healing the sick. I told him I should be healed if he had faith, for I had not yet performed my work, neither to the living or the dead. He blessed me with power and authority, and I began to amend immediately.

Saturday, May 20, 1876—To day was able to sit up some, and father gave me the following blessing; I acting as scribe:—

A Patriarchal Blessing given under the hands of Joel H. Johnson,[53] at Bellview, Utah, May 20, 1876, upon the head of James H. Martineau, son of John and Eliza Martineau, born in Port Jackson, Montgomery Co. N. Y. March 13, 1828.

James Henry Martineau, in the name of the Lord Jesus Christ of Nazareth I lay my hands upon thy head to give thee a father's or patriarchal blessing. Thou art of the seed of Ephraim, therefore entitled to all the blessings of the priesthood. I now seal upon thy head all the blessings and ordinations which have been conferred upon thee by the saints of the Lord. I now say unto thee as thou art now afflicted with disease, that it shall soon depart from thee, and thou shalt be restored to perfect health and soundness: for thou art or shall become a hunter to hunt thy brethren of the house of Ephraim and Israel from the dens and caves of the Earth and fish them from the islands of the sea, and gather them up to the lands that was given to their fathers for an everlasting possession. Thou shalt visit some of the nations of the earth, and they shall rejoice at the sound of thy voice, and shalt gather them up to the land of Zion.

[page 378]

J. H. MARTINEAU'S BLESSING, BY J. H. JOHNSON

May 20, 1876—Thou shalt go to the Center Stake of Zion, and shall assist in establishing the saints in that land, and do a great work in the temple which shall be reared there, for the redemption of thy dead; for they shall manifest themselves unto thee when the time comes for their redemption. I seal upon thy head all the blessings that were promised to Abraham, Isaac and Jacob, for thy seed shall become numerous and multiply and become a great and a mighty nation, clothed with the power of the holy priesthood. No enemy shall cross thy path to do thee any harm, for thou shalt have power to overcome all who shall lift their hands against thee. Thou shalt not come behind the chiefest of the saints of the Most High in the dispensation of the fullness of times. Thou shalt yet take more wives and raise up seed unto the Most High, who shall be great and mighty in their day and generation. Thou shalt live until thou art satisfied with life. When it is necessary for thee to accomplish thy work, the elements shall be subject to thy word, for thou shalt run and not be weary and walk and not

51 Janet Mauretta Johnson.

52 This may be Edward Dalton.

53 Joel Hills Johnson.

faint, and mount up on wings as eagles. Thou shalt be blessed of the Most High, and thy word shall be quick and powerful, causing the ears of them that hear them to tingle and their hearts to be penetrated; for many of the Nobles of the Earth shall receive counsel from thee and rejoice to hear the words of thy mouth; and thousands of the Lamanites shall lift up their heads and rejoice at the words from thy lips; for thou shalt be instrumental in bringing many of them to a knowledge of their fathers. All these blessings I seal upon thy head, with all that thy heart desirest, and seal thee up unto eternal lives, to come forth in the morning of the first Ressurrection, with all thy wives and offspring, to inherit glory, immortality and eternal lives, inasmuch as thou art faithful to hearken to the Words of Wisdom and Eternal life, in the name of Jesus Christ, Amen.

[page 379]

BARGAIN FOR LAND AT BELLVIEW, START HOME.

Sunday, May 21, 1876—Felt better to day. Talked with Father about buying part of his farm, with a view to moving my family there, so that if I am sent away from home for any long time, that they may be able to provide for themselves. This they could do, tending a vineyard, when they could not do much on a farm ~~here~~ in Logan.

Monday, May 22, 1876—Intended to start home to day, but such a cold wind from the north prevails, that I fear to undertake it.

Talked further about the proposed purchase, and finally made an offer to pay him $1000.~ [$17,724] for a certain part of his land beyond a big hollow, and one acre on this side the hollow, with one acre of water from South Ash Creek, and a building spot, with two years to pay it in, in stock or equivalent pay. He said he would think it over, and tell me in the morning. So I prayed that if it's best for me and this kingdom for me to make this purchase, that father may say "yes" in the morning; if not, that he may say "no," so that by this I may know if it is the will of the Lord.

Tuesday, May 23, 1876—This morning father said "yes," so I have now determined to buy the land. There is perhaps 8 or 9 acres, with an apple orchard, peach orchard, and about 3 acres choice grapes.

Started home, and reached Cedar, stopping with my old friend Bp. Henry Lunt, who were glad to see me. In the evening Br. Lunt and some of the brethren administered to me, so that I felt better, but was still weak and almost unable to travel.

[page 380]

BLESSING BY HENRY LUNT.

Wednesday, May 24, 1876—This morning Br. Lunt, who is a Patriarch, gave me the following blessing, I being scribe:—

Patriarch

A patriarchal blessing by Patriarch Henry Lunt, given at Cedar City, Utah, on May 24, 1876, on the head of James Henry Martineau, son of John and Eliza Martineau, born in Port Jackson, Montgomery County N.Y. March 13. 1828.

Brother James Henry Martineau in the name of Jesus Christ I lay my hands upon thy head to give thee a patriarchal blessing, inasmuch as thou desirest the same under my hands; and I can truly say in my heart that I feel to bless thee, and it is a pleasure so to do, for thou hast been true and faithful for many years, and being of the blood of Ephraim art entitled to all the blessings of Abraham, Isaac and Jacob. The Lord loveth thee for the integrity of thy heart, thy name is written in the Lamb's Book of Life. Thou wilt live to see the face of thy Savior, and the holy angels will administer unto thee, and will reveal to thee the genealogy of many of thy forefathers, which to thee are unknown. Thou shalt live until thou art satisfied with life, and inasmuch as thou wilt exercise faith thou shalt not taste of death, but be quickened and changed in the twinkling of an eye, and caught up to meet our Savior when he shall come in his glory. Thou shalt be crowned a King and a Priest to thy Most High God. Many are the blessings which are in store for thee, dear brother. The Lord hath a great work for thee to do. Thou shalt yet travel with thy family and assist in extending the borders of Zion.

[page 381]

REACH S. L. CITY.

May 24, 1876—Thou shalt be regarded as a wise Counsellor and a strong pillar in the Church. Thy last days shall be thy best. Thy posterity shall be great, and become great in the kingdom of God. I feel to say unto thee that thou shalt not lack for any good thing, for the Lord will bless thee with riches in abundance, and thou shalt have wherewith to administer to the poor. Thou shalt return home to thy family in peace and safety, and be blessed with good health and strength. Thy guardian angels have charge concerning thee. This is thy blessing, brother, not one word of which shall fail, for I seal it upon thy head in the name of Jesus Christ, even so, Amen.

Reached Parowan, completely tired out.

Thursday, May 25, 1876—To day I started home by mail wagon, leaving my friends all well as usual, but dreading the journey very much. Went to Beaver, 35 miles, completely covered with dust, and very tired.

Friday, May 26, 1876—Started in the stage, which, being covered, was much easier. Left Beaver at 1 P.M. having first had my portrait taken there, by J. Fennemore.[54] Went 20 miles to Pine Creek and supped, but coughed so I soon vomited it all up. Drove to Corn Creek about 11 P.M. Completely exhausted. Got a bed, and stopped until morning.

Saturday, May 27, 1876—Drove to Chicken Creek, 11 P.M. and stopped until morning, Still very unwell, and barely able to travel. Did not sleep until after 2 A.M.

Sunday, May 28, 1876—Reached terminus of U.S.R.R. at noon, but waited in vain for train for over an hour. Found that the track is washed out about 6 miles from here, So went to the break in a stage, and took train at Santaquin, reaching S. L. City at 5.40 P.M. Feel better today but coughed nearly all night.

[page 382]

HOME AGAIN.

May 29, 1876—Started home, arriving there at 5 P.M. being detained by a washout two hours. Found all well, for which I thank our Father. Susan had been sick a few days with toothache. No one can tell how glad I was to be at home once more, and feel that now I can get well.

At Parowan I wrote to Pres[t] Young in regard to my purchase at Bellview, saying if he disapproved in any way to let me know, and I would try to act in accordance with his wishes. I almost fear he may wish me to go to Arizona, while my children are so small, and not able to help much.

I found Charlie at work in the U.O. foundry and machine shop, and Nephi cutting stone for the Tabernacle,[55] with Lyman attending to things at home.

Saturday, June 3, 1876—To day I did some writing, being my first trial at work.

July 24, 1876—Went to Salt Lake City, but saw no one that I desired, everyone being out of town.

November & December 1876—Have been busy most of the time in laying out and overseeing a canal to be made to carry off the surplus waters of Honeyville, which now help to form Box Elder lake.[56] The Utah Northern runs through it about two miles, and in high water is much injured by the overflow and washing away of the grade. I boarded most of the time at Bishop Harper's, North String.[57] Lyman assisted me much of the time. I got about $250. [$4,431] in cloth and furniture of the Brigham Institution, which made us more comfortable. I also traded with M. D. Hammond for a span of horses & harness, at $320 [$5,672]. In Sept. I sent about $1100 [$19,496] worth of stock to dixie with Moroni and Nephi. I bought $1000 [$17,724]. worth of Pres[t] Young in exchange for part of my city lot—(Susan J's part.)

54 James Fennimore of Beaver, Utah, was a popular photographer at the time. He later photographed the execution of John D. Lee.

55 The early tabernacles were meant for large gatherings of Church members. Construction of the Logan Tabernacle, 1864–91, was stalled on numerous occasions, including during construction of the Logan Temple. It did, however, provide employment, as noted in this entry, and a place to worship (Ricks and Cooley, *History of a Valley*, 286–88).

56 See "Editor *Deseret News*," *Deseret News*, January 31, 1877; Utah Digital Newspapers.

57 Harper, Utah, was just five miles north of Brigham City. This town was also called Calls Fort, North Spring, North Ward, and Lake Side. Thomas Harper managed Anson Call's farm (Frederick M. Huchel, *A History of Box Elder County* [Salt Lake City: Utah State Historical Society, 1999], 347–51).

[page 383]

1877, RETROSPECT OF 1876.

Sunday, July 22, 1877—Since my last entry more than a year has intervened —one that has been a busy one for me. Some of the time I have been surveying for A. J. Stewart on his U.S. contract, at other times surveying on my own account in Cache County. Stewart has been trying to get his accounts and business closed, in which I have assisted him, with the hope I could get my pay from him. By our agreement, we were to share equally, the proceeds of the work done, which amounted to about $6200 [$109,886] besides about $1200 [$21,268] of work (resurveys) not allowed by the department. I am in his power, having no written agreement, and no witnesses except my own family.

July 1876—In the summer I went to Salt Lake city and saw the President relative to my projected trade with Father, which depended on Pres[t] Young's sanction for its completion. He told me it was all right—he felt very much gratified to have me go there. So I wrote as much to father, and told him I would consider our trade ratified.

September 1876—In September our regular 3 days autumnal muster, which was well attended, and was a pleasant time. As usual, I had the entire oversight of the matter, in its preparation and execution. Gen[l] B. Young Jr. not being very well posted in such matters.

October 1876—Went to Conference

January 26, 1877—Went to Salt Lake City to see if Stewarts business was near completion

January 27, 1877—Went to Sur. Gen[l] Kimball's office. I applied for a situation as draughtsman, and was accepted, subscribing an [. . .], and being sworn in as a regular U.S. employee.

[page 384]

ENTER SUR. GEN[L].S OFFICE AS DRAUGHTSMAN.

January 27, 1877—Rec[d] a letter from Moroni informing me that he had paid father over $500. [$9,136] worth of Stock on the land trade.

The cattle I bought of B. Young Jr. was mostly blooded stock,—Devon and Durham.[58] I bought a pure blood Bull and heifer, paying $150. [$2,741] and $125. [$2,284] respectively. The others were ½ & ¾ bloods, with a few common stock. The amount for which I sold the piece of lot was $1200 [$21,926], having on it a brick house partly Completed. Moroni and Nephi were about 6 weeks on the road to Johnson, and lost one cow and some calves.

March 4, 1877—Came home to be present at the County Court which was held the first Monday in March.

March 5, 1877—Attended Court, and returned to Salt Lake city next day

About this time I begun to board with Mrs. M. E. Jones, widow of N. V. Jones, having gone to her house on Sunday Feb. 26. 1877.

June 30, 1977—Up to this time I have been at work in the Sur. Gen[l].s office. But this terminates my term of engagement. I applied to the land office at Washington. J. A. Williamson, Commissioner[59] for permission to copy the plats and field notes of the U.S. Surveys in Cache County which was granted by letter from the Commissioner.

July 1, 1877—Went home to bring Susan to spend the 4th at Salt Lake City

July 2, 1877—We went to S. L. city.

July 3, 1877—Went to the circus

July 4, 1877—Went to Lake Point, about 22 miles, by Utah Western. There was quite a party of myself & Susan, with Charlie, Nettie and Anna, also Mrs. Jones, whom I knew 20 years ago at Babbitt's.

[page 385]

JAMES EDWARD BORN

1877—The wind blew a hurricane all day, and prevented the boat races that were to have come off, which was quite a disappointment.

58 Blooded stock means they were purebred, pedigreed, or of fine quality. Devon is a medium-size breed originating in Devon, England. Durham is a short-horned breed from Durham, England.

59 J. A. Williamson was a land agent and surveyor for the Union Pacific. He surveyed the town of Corinne, Utah, for the railroad. He was the first mayor of the town (Huchel, *History of Box Elder County*, 23, 127, 329).

We staid all day, returning at about 8 P.M. About 2000 persons were there.

July 6, 1877—Charlie went home.

July 8, 1877—We went home, and found the team for us at the depot. Found the Children all well.

July 10, 1877—I returned to the city to copy the field notes

July 16, 1877—Spent the day arranging with Gen[l] Kimball, the Sur. General the location of public lands I should survey under the Contract which he has promised me of about $7000 [$127,902]. My work will lie nearly all in the mountains, and will be extremely hard work to accomplish, but I am willing to do it, in order to mak [make] a start as a U.S. Deputy Surveyor.

Note. On Saturday May 5th 1877.

James Edward Martineau, my nineteenth child—my wife's eleventh) was born at 8.45 A.M. I was away from home at the time—the first time in all my experience. I was unable to be there, but arrived home the following day, and found Susan and her child doing well. Our friends—Sister R. Cranney and others had been very good and kind to her. Mother Lydia Y. Crockett was the midwife—an old friend of ours, who had previously officiated on many similar occasions for us. The baby was a fine child, & weighed 10 lbs.—our heaviest—the others had usually weighed from 8 to 9½ lbs. I felt very glad and thankful to find all so well with Susan, who felt it a trial that I was not present at the time to be a help and comfort to her in her time of trouble.

[page 386]

BIRTH & DEATH OF ELVIRA'S CHILD

1877—**Note.** My daughter Elvira's baby Bertha Elvira was born on March 4th 1877, Sunday, but lived only two days. She was a fine child, and my poor girl grieved much over the sad event. The baby was born at Johnson, Kane Co. Utah.

Note. My son Henry A.s Son, Charles Henry was born on Wednesday January ~~24~~ 27, 1877, at Hillsdale Iron County, Utah, and was also a fine child.

Grandfather and Grandmother Martineau! how that Sounds!

July 11, 1877—Today Gen[l] Kimball rec[d] notice of his suspension from office with instructions for the office to be closed.

July 13, 1877—Ceased work on the Cache Co. plats for the present.

July 17, 1877—Came home, and found Theodore, who had a slight attack of the Scarlet fever[60] last week, about well, for which I felt very thankful. All the rest of the family were well

NOTE.

May 15, 1877—Self and Lyman came home from S. L. City.

May 16, 1877—Surveyed for Jacobson, Pres[t]. B. Young & comp. arrived to locate site for temple. In the evening Pres[t] Young sent for me, and said he wished me to assist in laying out the temple, with Jesse W. Fox.

Thursday, May 17, 1877—Helped to lay out temple foundation.

May 18, 1877—At noon to day, the ground was dedicated, a cold, snowy, disagreeable day. Br. Fox laid the lines with var. 17° 20' E., the var. of local surveys, being 16° 20' E., the U. S. lines 18° 15' E. Pres[t]. Young said he wished it laid out true North and South, therefore I opposed his determination (Fox's) all I decently could.[61]

[page 387]

TEMPLE.

1877—I feel ashamed to be associated with such a foolish proceeding of Br. Fox's; as it is now located, the temple agrees neither with our city survey, being 3 feet out of line, nor within two feet of the true N. & S. line. I afterwards informed Pres[t] Thatcher and others about it.

Thursday [Saturday], May 19, 1877—Having informed Elder B. Young Jr. in regard to the laying out of the temple, we telegraphed to the President relative to it, asking what should be done. I did not see the answer.

Saturday, May 21, 1877 [the 21st was a Monday]—Fixed up the buggy.

....

60 Scarlet fever is a very contagious disease producing inflammation, headache, and a scarlet rash.

61 See George F. Gibbs, "Dedication of the Site for the Temple at Logan," *Deseret News*, March 23, 1877; Utah Digital Newspapers.

Sunday, May 22, 1877 [the 22nd was a Tuesday]—Wrote up my journal to date, leaving out much of interest, and getting things much mixed up, but it is better so, I think, than not to have any record at all. I leave a space for items I may hereafter think of, and continue on next page.

[Bottom half of page is blank.]

[page 388]

TEMPLE LETTER

July 23, 1877—At 3 P.M. the excursion from Salt Lake City arrived. Mrs. M. Eliza Jones, widow of N. V. Jones,[62] an old time friend, whom I first knew in the winter of 1856–7 at uncle A. W. Babbitt's came to spend a few days.

July 24, 1877—Attended the celebration to day. Sent a letter to Truman O. Angel Jr. Architect of Logan temple as follows:—

Logan July 22. 1877

Br. Angell, Architect for Logan temple.

I spoke to Pres^t^ M. Thatcher in regard to the fact that Br. Fox did not lay out the foundation of the temple "true north and south," as required by Pres^t^ Young, nor according to the survey of the city made by him; but with a variation of about 40' minutes from the Government survey, and of one degree from the local (city) survey. This variation in 171 feet, the length of the building, gives a variation of 2 feet from the Gov^t^ line, and of 3 feet from the local lines. Br. Thatcher says you told him the variation from true line was only 1⅛ inch, which is incorrect.

Br. Fox did this contrary to my urgent remonstrance, but finally said he would come up here before rock laying commenced, and rectify the lines.

Pres^t^ Young requested me to assist Br. Fox in setting the corners, and told me he wanted the line "true North and South." As they are not, and to escape responsibility of so needless a blunder, I hereby acquaint you, as Architect, with the facts in the case, before any more unnecessary expense is incurred.

When you come again, would it not be well to bring Br. Fox with you to rectify the lines?

Respectfully,

James H. Martineau."

The cause of the above letter is mostly found in the letter itself. I felt much perplexed that the work should have been so mismanaged, and so told Pres^t^ B. Young Jr, Pres^t^ M. Thatcher, also the architect, and Br. Chas. O. Card the Sup^t^ of construction, and finally Pres^t^ Preston, who saw at once the propriety of taking a course to clear myself of responsibility, and advised me to write the foregoing letter, which, when I read it to him, he said was just right.

[page 389]

July 26, 1877—Mrs. Jones went home to day taking my little daughter Elizabeth, who is now nearly ten years old. Susan and I accompanied them to Deweyville, 22 miles. Mrs. Jones has no small children, and is a very kind good woman whom I know will take the best and kindest care of her, otherwise I would not have allowed it. I know of no one living except Mrs. Jones, whom I would allow to take any of my children. Susan felt bad all the way home, and so did I. We all felt quite a vacancy in the family. But I believe all will be right with her.

My family is now quite scattered Henry A., Moroni H. and Nephi are at Hillsdale, Iron Co, Elvira and Sammy at Pahria, in southern Utah near the Arizona line, raising a crop preparatory to going back to Moencoppy, & Elizabeth in Salt Lake City. Lyman is now bookkeeping in the 2nd Ward Co-operative Institution, and Charles F. at work in the 1st Ward Co-op-Machine shop learning that trade. Geo. Albert is learning to make shoes at Nielson's. Jesse N. and the rest are at home. Last year Julia Henrietta learned to braid at Mrs. Cardon's. So I think my family is in a better situation than ever before, for which I humbly thank the Lord, the author of all good.

July 28, 1877—Saw Angell, the Architect, who informs me that Pres^t^ Young thinks best not to make any change, now that so much has been done. This I regret, for I believe Pres^t^ Young has not been fully informed in relation to it.

62 Nathaniel V. Jones was among those from the Iron Mission. The family was called by Brigham Young to found a lead industry (Shirts and Shirts, *Trial Furnace*, 279).

July 30, 1877—To day I was sent for to meet Mr. Washington Dunn, an Engineer just arrived from New York[63] [continued on next page]

[page 390]

TRIP TO BEAR RIVER CAÑON, EAST.

July 30, 1877—in relation to the Utah Northern R.R. Arrangements were made for Mr. Dunn, Sec[y] M. Thatcher and myself to go up to Bear River Cañon along the line of the proposed extension of the road, to examine the ground, to form some idea of the amount necessary to finish the 25 miles to Cottonwood.

July 31, 1877—We therefore went to Franklin to day, stopping at Lewis hotel.

August 1, 1877—Went about 14 miles along the line and returned to Franklin, where a special train was waiting to Convey us to Logan, arriving at home a little after 7 P.M. My estimate is that $80.000 [$146,739] will be enough to complete the 25 miles there being about ten miles already graded.

In November last, by request of Pres[t] John W. Young myself and A. F. Doremus traversed the line from Cottonwood down, making an estimate of work necessary, and expense req.[d] John Sherlock, Richardson's pretended engineer, finding we were going for that purpose, went up ahead of us and pulled up all his stakes, to prevent us from doing the work, but we did the best we could, estimating the distance station by station by they eye, also the probable amount of cut or fill and cost pr yd. for the work. After passing down about 14 miles we entered the "Narrows," a very narrow, deep & rocky Canon of about 3½ miles, endeavoring to lead our horses through, although it was said to be impossible to get horses through. We did get through, by the most arduous labor I ever performed, which, for one who has pioneered in the mountains so many years as I have, is saying a great deal, at times it seemed impossible to go any farther. Some times we had to go along in the edge of the foaming, surging rocky river, sometimes suddenly finding our horses swimming.

63 Washington Dunn was the superintendent of construction for the Utah and Northern Railroad by 1881.

[page 391]

DOREMUS POISONED (IN NOV. 1876)

August 1877—At other times our progress would be barred by a great rock projecting into the river, compelling an ascent up the almost inaccessible banks, a feat sometimes very difficult to accomplish. At dark we emerged at the lower end of the Cañon, utterly exausted, with nothing to eat, no bedding, a cold night, and in a wilderness miles from any house. Doremus ate a handful of berries, which the [he] thought were elderberries, but were very poisonous.[64] In a short time he was taken sick, rapidly growing worse and becoming very cold. I did all I could for him, but that was not much. The night was dark, and I went ahead trying to keep the trail, which we frequently lost, he being able to keep on his horse with great difficulty. His legs and arms became cold and numb, the numbness rapidly going to his vitals. About 9 P.M. I saw a camp fire, and we got Doremus to it, he being very far gone. We wrapped him in blankets with hot stones about him,[65] gave him hot tea &c. About 10 P.M. myself and the four boys camped there, administered to him. He immediately vomited some dark red and very acrid fluid, which skinned his throat and mouth, and he then gradually began to improve. I sat up all night with him, and by morning he was so much better he thought he could reach Franklin, about 15 miles distant, which we did that afternoon. It was a very narrow escape, and I am convinced he was only saved by the power of the priesthood. Some days afterwards, I made another trip to the tunnel to estimate some other work, for all which I rec[d] $50.[00] [$914] from Br. J. W. Young. My estimate for the total amount, exclusive of iron and ties was about $60,000 [$1,096,305].

[page 392]

August 2, 1877—Wrote to Lilly, at Mrs. M. E. Jones', Salt Lake City.

64 An elderberry is a berry used to make jelly and wine. This event was reported in the newspaper, but the dates are inconsistent ("Narrow Escape," *Deseret News*, October 25, 1876; Utah Digital Newspapers).

65 To keep warm while traveling, pioneers often heated rocks next to the campfire. They would then wrap the rocks and themselves in blankets.

August 7, 1877—To day Lieut. Geo. M. Wheeler,[66] U.S.A. Engineers, who is in charge of the Topographical and Geological Surveys in Utah, Called upon me, having been directed to me for information in regard to Northern Utah. He was accompanied by another of his party. I agreed to go with him to show him certain corners of the U.S. Surveys here.

August 8, 1877—Went to the corner to Tps. 11 1E. & 1W. and 12 1E. and 1W., also a corner 2 miles 60 lks east, on the township line. He will triangulate from these two points to various mountain peaks around. I called with him upon Moses Thatcher, W B Preston & M. H. Hammond.

The weather is still very hot, the thermometer for a month past, ranging from 90° to 107°

Saturday, August 18, 1877—Finished a report to Lieut. Geo. M. Wheeler U.S.A. of elevations of points along line of U.N.R.R. as follows

"Comparative elevations of points along line of Utah Northern R.R. from Ogden to Soda Springs, the waters of G. Salt Lake being assumed 0000.

These elevations are exact, being taken from levels of the survey of the U.N.R.R.

Elevations

0000 Great Salt Lake
88 C.P.R.R. track (old survey) about 400 feet east of the U.P.R.R. freight house
108 Brigham City Station
83 Warm Spring, Near Honeyville
115 Dewey's, at foot of dividing ridge between Cache and G. S. L. vallies
768 Summit of dividing ridge
245 Mendon
210 Bridge over Little Bear river (lowest part of Cache Valley

66 George M. Wheeler was with the United States Army Corp of Engineers. He and his party explored and mapped areas of Nevada, Arizona, and Utah. His party was the last of the military explorers in the Grand Canyon (University of Reno Library Special Collections; see also "Historic Maps by Wheeler, G.M." in the David Rumsey Map Collection, available online at http:// www.davidrumsey.com/directory/who/wheeler++G+m+/)

[page 393]

U. S. SURVEYING CONTRACT, CACHE CO. PLATS &C.

August 18, 1877—

294 Logan Station
330 Tabernacle square, Logan (Temple ground above the sea by Union Pacific levels 4648.49 feet)
350 Smithfield
322 Richmond
301 Franklin
817 Summit of tunnel ridge
394 Bear river, 1st bridge, surface of water
414 Bear river, Mouth of Narrows, surface of water
477 Bear river, surface of water, upper end of Narrows
687 Fellows creek
1307 Bear river, upper crossing, surface of water.
1336 Bear river, upper crossing, Bank of river
1564 Soda Springs (End of Preliminary line)
1582 Bear river, surface of water, (At point 5 miles above Soda Springs.)

I also gave him a map showing line from Ogden to Helena, Montana.

Tuesday, August 21, 1877—Went to Salt Lake city to complete copying the field notes and plats of U.S. Surveys for Cache County. Lyman will come tomorrow. Found Lillie and all the rest well.

August 30, 1877—To day signed my contract as U. S. Deputy Surveyor, for \$6500.[00] [\$118,766], my bonds being double the amount—\$13000. [\$237,533] W[m] Jennings and W[m] H. Hooper became my sureties.

Saturday, September 8, 1877—Rec[d] telegram from Washington, that my contract is approved.

Engaged John M. Odenheimer as Compassman at \$100 [\$1,827] pr. month, to be paid after I receive my pay from Government.

Got a solar compass from A. J. Stewart Sen at \$210.[00] [\$3,837] or \$25.00 [\$457] less than cost.

[page 394]

MR. GILBERT.

September 1877—Got it on account. This makes $710.00 [$12,973] I have received from him on my work Surveying. He owes me about $1300.00 [$23,753] yet on the same account.

September 14, 1877—Lyman went home to day, having assisted me in writing and platting.

Paid $20.00 [$365] for tent. Bought 2 pack saddles at $12.00 [$219] Also Gun. Revolver, ammunition, &c.

While Lyman was helping me in S. L. City, I made copies of 32 U.S. Survey plats (townships) for Judge Samuel Smith, of Box Elder County, at $5.00 [$91] each, half cash, half Co-operative Inst. (Brigham) products.[67]

September 17, 1877—Engaged Chas B. Jones[68] to assist in surveying, and got him some things.

Chas B. Jones went to Logan.

September 18, 1877—I went to Brigham City and stopped over night

September 19, 1877—Got some home made cloth and came home

September 24, 1877—Had a call from R.R. Gilbert, Geologist of Maj. Powell's[69] U.S. Geological Expedition, who came to obtain information relative to the county, irrigation &c He told me at parting, he had not spent such a profitable day, to him, at any one time. He said the highest water line through these vallies, is at an average height of about 1000 feet above the present level of Great Salt Lake, sometimes over and in one place less. Also that formerly, in the glacial epoch, when this was a great lake 500 X 350 miles in extent, and 1100 feet deep, it was fresh, having an outlet north, through Marsh valley, into Snake river and the Columbia.

Monday, October 1, 1877—Today John M. Odenheimer, my compassman arrived.

Tuesday, October 2, 1877—To day started on my U.S. Survey, with the following party:—Myself and Jesse N., J. M. Odenheimer, Compassman, Edd Hansen and Geo. Lewis Chainman; [. . .] McNeil [. . . man] & C. B. Jones, flag, and Chas Montrose[70] cook and packer.

[page 395]

U. S. SURVEY

October 2, 1877—We left home about 11 a.m. My outfit, including provisions, &c, amounts to nearly $1400.00:—[$25,580] tent, wagon and team, pack saddles, arms, &c. Each man provides his own revolvers, cups, plates, knives, and bedding. I also furnish a transit, $300.- [$5,482] and Solar Compass—$235.00 [$4,294].

Went about 25 miles and camped on South Fork of Little Bear river. Very cold night.

Wednesday, October 3, 1877—Found ice in my tin cup, this morning. Went about two miles, and most of the party went to a corner to begin running the Second Standard Parallel North, to the west, eight miles, through a high mountainous tract. I went round with the wagon, tent, &c. Montrose, whose horses had strayed off about 6 miles in the night, joined me about noon. We packed the bedding, provisions & on his two horses, and he struck into the hills to find the surveying party.

I went to Brigham City, and stopped with A. Nichols, the Bishop.[71] Had a very hard day's trip.

Thursday, October 4, 1877—Went to 3-mile creek, to see if my party had come through the mountains yet, but found no signs of them. Bought another frying pan, bread and butter, and went back to the place where my company started to work. Camped at dark, my team utterly exhausted. Cold.

67 Judge Samuel Smith was an influential Brigham City resident (Huchel, *History of Box Elder County*, 77, 307).

68 During the construction of the Logan Temple, Charles B. Jones was listed as a night watchman and was in charge of the lime, sand, and mortar that went into the building (Nolan Porter Olsen, *Logan Temple: The First 100 Years* [Providence, UT: Keith W. Watkins and Sons, 1978], 157).

69 Major John Wesley Powell directed the U.S. Geological Survey in 1881. Lake Powell, on the border of Utah and Arizona, bears his name.

70 Simmons mentions a Charles Montrose but provides no bibliographic information (Simmonds, *The Gentile Comes to Cache Valley*, 21).

71 Alvin Nicholas, along with William Godbe, Ben Hampton, and Mark Bigler, constructed a two-story hotel and restaurant called the Stage Coach Hotel (Huchel, *History of Box Elder County*, 320).

Friday, October 5, 1877—Waited all day to find my men, and went up on a high mountain to look for them. Can not guess where they are.

Saturday, October 6, 1877—Waited until near 3 P.M. and concluded they must have passed me unobserved. So I moved down the river about 2½ miles to the forks of the river, and Camped. The roads are covered with fresh bear tracks, but have not seen any yet. Jesse is very lonesome especially nights.

[page 396]

U.S. SURVEY

Sunday, October 7, 1877—Sent Jesse to Paradise for letters, but he got none. In the afternoon Montrose and the Chainmen came to camp, nearly starved. After eating we moved back to former camp and found the rest of the party. They had been since Wednesday noon running 8 miles! Rather unpromising beginning to my work!

Monday, October 8, 1877—Started over the ridge, 3 miles, East, while I and the packs went round. The party came up after sunset.

Tuesday, October 9, 1877—The party still continue east. They will have to cross a high ridge of the Wahsatch, having a general elevation of 10,000 feet above the sea. I, with Jesse and C. B. Jones, began running a Township line South between Ranges 1 & 2 East. We made 1½ miles and Camped on South East fork of Little Bear river at the Wellsville saw mill. About ½ mile above is the Twin Mills of Brigham City, where we went for supper. Threatens storm.

Wednesday, October 10,1877—Surveyed two miles to day. Br. H. P. Jensen came up, and told me to be at home while I remain here, at his place, for which I am very thankful.

Thursday, October 11, 1877—Stormy this morning, raining heavily. Went to Logan to get more supplies, being in the rain and hail all day. Got home at dark, and found, truly, "there is no place like home." Found family well.

Friday, October 12, 1877—Very busy fixing up for another start.

Saturday, October 13, 1877—Bought a wagon of M. D. Hammond, $147.50 [$2,695] paid $107.50 [$1,964] and gave note for $40. [$731]

Just before I started surveying I turned my buggy in to the temple fund, price $80.[00] I do not need it for several months, and when I do, I hope I may be able to get another. I also agreed to give in my lumber wagon (the old one) to the Tabernacle for $80.00 [$1,462]

[page 397]

U.S. SURVEY

October 15, 1877—Monday. Started for the mountains to resume survey. Stopped at night, at T. Obray's, Paradise, and got to the Brigham Co-op Twin mill next day.

Tuesday, October 16, 1877—Found Odenheimer & my men all there, having been there since Saturday morning. Odenheimer was sick.

I continue the survey, leaving Odenheimer sick in bed at the lodging house. Ran 1½ miles, over very rough ground.

Wednesday, October 17, 1877—Surveyed E. boundary of T. 8 N. R. 1 E. South to South boundary, and 1 mile W. the line crossing a very high mountain near its summit. The mt. is over 12000 ft high, and the ascent was very laborious.

Friday, October 19, 1877—To day nearly finished South boundary T. 8 N. R 1 E. At night Chas B. Jones did not come into camp. We searched for him, shouted, fired guns, and Jesse N. & I ascended a high mountain after dark and built a large bonfire to guide him to our camp, but to no avail. We camped that night in a cañon, leading from Cache to Ogden valleys, on a small brook.

Saturday, October 20, 1877—This morning found Jones about a mile from camp. He had wandered several miles last evening, and, finally found shelter with a man camping. I was very glad to find him all right, his mother being a widow. We returned to Twin Mills at dark.

Sunday, October 21, 1877—I came home, with Jesse N. & Jones, to see Henry & wife & Anna Hilton,[72] who arrived here from Hillsdale, Iron County, on Wed. 17th inst. Cha[s] Montrose, one of my party, whom I sent in to Logan on Thursday, the 18th saw them, and

72 There are numerous Anna and Annie Hiltons in Utah history.

brought me word. Montrose went in for medicine for Odenheimer. I got home at dark, & found all well.

I left Odenheimer orders to run the S. & E. boundaries of T. 8 N. R. 2 E. while I was away.

Thursday, October 25, 1877—I started back with the boys to continue survey. Got to Paradise. Snowed all night, covering our bed several inches deep. Snowed all day, so at 4 P.M. I started home, knowing I could not get up the Cañon with my load. I thought I would go back with the empty wagon for the party I left at the mills.

[page 398]

SETTLE ACCOUNTS WITH THE UTAH NORTHERN R.R.

Friday, October 26, 1877—Came home in face of a driving snow storm all the way.

Saturday, October 27, 1877—Determined to start to the mills this morning for my party, when in they came, having just arrived from Paradise, which place they reached last evening having found the snow in the mountains too deep to proceed with the work. Odenheimer was left at the mills.

Sunday—Sent Nephi & Jesse after Odenheimer, who all returned.

Monday, October 29, 1877—Settled my account with Odenheimer, as follows:—Time, 25 days, sick 5 days, leaving 20 days @ $4.00 [$73] pr day = $80.00 [$1,462]. Deducting $3.00 [$55] for shoes & $5.00 [$91] Cash advanced = $8.00 [$146] leaves $72.00 [$1,316] due. I got $12.00 [$219] Cash on

Tuesday, October 30, 1877—& paid him, and gave my note for the balance $60.00 [$1,096] payable on receipt of my pay from Washington. He went to Salt Lake City at 11 A.M. Good riddance. He ran only 31½ miles in the whole month.

November 3, 1877—Conference to day and next, 4th. Enjoyed a very good time. Had most excellent preaching from Prest. Taylor and others of the Twelve.

Sunday, November 11, 1877—During the last week, I have surveyed some, and written up my field notes, made plats, &c. of my work, and on Thursday and Friday Settled with the old Utah Northern R.R. Company.

My agreement with them is as follows:—

Chg^{d} to my a/c for supplies, sundries, &c	$4782.31
" " " for Tithing Office &c, balance	$216.00
total charged	$4998.31 [$91,328]
Credited on Ledger, for help, team, and for Supplies ch^{d} back	$1773.01
Cr. by 36 mo. time @ $100. cash & $50 vouchers pr. month	$5400.00
credits	$7173.01
Leaving a balance in my favor of	$2174.70
Besides this, a bill $170 (Canal)	170.00
vouchers due L. E. & others	511.62
" 282. & 35.	317.00
	$3173.32 [$57,982]

[page 399]
[quarter page left blank]

I find by reference to the books, that I have made estimates for work (grading) and given vouchers, to the amount of over $182.000 [$3,325,457], besides about as much more not done by the cubic yard.

Taking the whole amount of grading, I find that a man, team, and scraper, on an average, moved about 20 cubic yds of earth pr day, which is only about half of what first-rate men should do.

I now close my official connection with the Utah Northern R. R. Company, after being for over 6 years its Chief Engineer. Many things have been done in regard to the location and building of the road to which I was opposed but powerless to prevent. The ~~engi~~ Directors and officers of the Company were good men, but not engineers, not familiar with practical railroading, but would have their own way, often to the great detriment of the line. Their experience, while valuable to them, cost the company many thousands of dollars. But the worst of it is, to me, that their mistakes are sure to be credited the engineers, by those who do not know all the circumstances of each case. But I do not know that it will make any difference in the ressurrection. I know I have labored—and more faithfully than any one will ever know—with a view to the welfare of Zion all the time, and though I may not receive credit for it in this life, I will in the next.

The old Utah Northern R. R. Co. is now dead, and a new company formed—the Union Pacific Company having control. They have already commenced extending the road towards Montana.

[page 400]

CEREMONIES IN THE "HOUSE."

Sunday, Nov 18, 1877—During the last two weeks I have received several insolent letters from J. M. Odenheimer, my former Compassman, who demands more money pay and has not signed the affidavits (final oath) as he agreed to do. I have been detained from prosecution of my Surveys for several weeks, by stormy weather, only small pieces of work here and there. I hope soon to be able to go on.

December 5, 1877—Went to Mantua (formerly Copenhagan) to Survey the township in which it is situated, and stopped with Bp. P. C. Jensen[73]

Continued at this work until near Christmas, then came home on account of stormy weather, having finished most of my work there.

December 4, 1877—Bought the part lot and brick house I formerly owned, of Brigham Young Jr. for $1975.^{00} [$36,087] For this I give him $1000 [$18,272] in stock, now in Iron County $215 [$3,928] I paid for him at the 2nd Ward Co-op Institution, and my note due in 6 months, for $760.^{00} [$13,887] I have been negotiating for the purchase since August last.

There is still considerable work to be done on the house and lot to make it comfortable.

December 24, 1877—To day, moved into the new house, which has 5 rooms and cellar, and is much more roomy and comfortable.

December 25, 1877—Christmas. Worked surveying most of the day.

December 26, 1877—Wednesday, went to Salt Lake City to do certain work in the endowment house.

73 This is likely Hans P. Jensen of Mantua, Utah.

Thursday, December 27, 1877—Went through the "House,"[74] with Mary Eliza Jones, widow of N. V. Jones. Was sealed for "time" by Pres^t D. H. Wells, who said "Well, Sister Jones, you have got a mighty good man."

Friday, December 28, 1877—Transacted business in the Surveyor General's office, also for several following days.

January 1, 1878—New Years. Spent the day in Salt Lake City

January 2, 1878—Went to Payson to see Stewart, and try to get some of the pay due me. Walked about 3 miles to his house in the bottoms, and found him just starting out for S. L. city.

[page 401]

GO TO PAYSON TO SEE STEWART.

1878—So I went back with him on the return train, being just in time. I did not accomplish any thing by my trip, he refusing to pay $410.^{00} [$8,040] due.

January 4, 1878—Had a settlement with Stewart, by which, after deducting amounts I have received, he owes me $410.^{00} [$7,491] Of right he owes me about $1000 [$18,272] more, but having no written proof, I can not force the payment of it, and have to let it go.

He gave me an order for a certificate of deposit of $200 [$3,654] in favor of Mrs. Mary Salmon, also for her note of $300 [$5,482] (which is merely surety for the certificate). For this he charged me $225.^{00} [$4,111] I also tried to get him to give me a deed for the lot in Spring Lake that Sammy sold him for $150 [$2,741]. For this I offered him $185. [$3,380] to square the matter and have done with it. He partly promised to do so, but I place no trust in him.

Bought a Mason & Hamlin Organ of Calder & Careless[75] for $250.^{00}; [$4568] also bought a carpet and other things This I do to make home pl[e]asant and agreeable for my family, that they may not desire to roam.

74 This is the Endowment House where temple ordinances were performed.

75 The Mason & Hamlin Organ Company manufactured a reed pump organ that was distributed via the railroad throughout the West. The Calder & Careless Company were retailers in Salt Lake City.

January 6, 1878—Came home, bringing Lillie, who has been gone since July last, and was very glad to get home again. Found my family well as usual.

January 11, 1878—Went to Mendon, where they wish me to come and do some Surveying. There is prospect for considerable work there.

January 28, 1878—Went to Salt Lake City, in consequence of a telegram from Sur. Gen[l] Kimball, to see about my plats and notes I had put in. Found Eliza and family well. Going to the office, I found they had thrown out 4 miles of Standard Parallel, being $64.00 [$1,169] worth of line. I had been told to run that line, but they afterwards thought best to leave it out. While in Salt Lake City I heard of the appointment of a new Surveyor General for Utah.

[page 402]

IN SALT LAKE CITY

February 14, 1878—I concluded to stay and get the rest of my work in the office—about $500. [$9,136] more, and accordingly sent for my other plats and notes.

I remained in the city, working daily in the office on my maps and plats every day, and finally got all approved and my account made out on Thursday Feb. 14th

My work embraced the following plats.
2[d] Standard Parallel North,
in Ranges 1 & 2 W.
and 1. 2 & 3 E,
in all 19[m] 9[ch] 01[lks.] amounting to $302.80
Township boundaries
28[m] 76[ch] 58 lks. amounting to $380.90
Subdivision lines
91[m] 53[ch] 31[lks] amounting to $873.70
$1557.40 [$28,456]

{ Standard lines @ $16.[00] & $10.[00] pr mile
Township bound[s] $14.[00] & $7.[00] "
Subdivision lines $10.[00] & $6.[00] " }

February 15, 1878—Came home, and found all well as usual.

February 27, 1878—Attended city council to day. It was proposed that a system of water works be commenced for Logan city, and the matter was referred to Committee on Public improvements, to which I and Pres[t] M. Thatcher were added, and I instructed to make measurements and examination in reference to their location.

March 2, 1878—City Council met to night, at which I made my report, estimating the cost of bringing water in an 8 in. pipe at about $7.000. [$127,902]

The Mayor, W[m] B. Preston was authorized to take steps to begin the work, if it can be done for not to exceed $6500 [$118,766].

Br. F. Hurst has nearly finished graining our parlor.

Rec[d] from G. M. Ottinger[76] photographs of three large paintings of Montezuma and the ancient Aztecs.

Was elected to day, a Member of the "Utah Society of Civil and Mining Engineers" in Salt Lake City.

[page 403]

CONFERENCE

March 13, 1878—To day is my birth day, and I am now fifty years old. It seems impossible, yet, as I see my hairs beginning to whiten, and see so large a family round me, I can see that it may be true, easily enough. I am now the father of nineteen children, sixteen of whom are still alive with two grand children, Henry's and Elvira's. I have been much blessed and prospered by the Lord for the last four years, having but little sickness in my family, and with a fair share of prosperity.

This evening I had about eighteen persons invited to a birth day party, and we had a pleasant evening. Br. and Sister J. E. Hyde sent a cake with a watch seal enclosed within it, and a kind little note, which I here insert. Such mementos of affection are pleasant. Susan gave me a nice silk handkerchief, and Lyman a pair of gold sleeve buttons, so I find there some who love and esteem me, though I do not measure love by gifts.

[The Hydes' note is below:]

Logan Utah,

March 13th 1878

---

76 George M. Ottinger was an 1861 convert to the Church. Living in Salt Lake, he engaged in a number of occupations. His partner was photographer C. R. Savage. Active in the Utah Theatre, Ottinger painted scenery for various performances. He was director of the waterworks and president of the Deseret Academy, which is today the University of Utah. His paintings had a reputation for historical detail.

To our
Esteemed friend and brother
James H. Martineau
With the Compliments & Congratulations
of
Joseph E. and Annie L. Hyde
upon this
your Fiftieth Birth day—
Hoping
that you may live to enjoy very
many happy returns of the day,
And beg that you will accept the
enclosed token as a slight memento
of our good wishes for you and yours

On the 11th inst. I began Surveying at Mendon, but came home on the R.R. train to spend my birthday, returning to Mendon next day, and spent the week at work, earning about 140$ [$731]

March 17, 1878—Came home, and found a letter from Secretary Luckey[77] saying my application for Notorial Commission was granted, and enclosing bond, which I executed and returned by mail.

March 22, 1878—Have spent the week in putting in garden, and fixing walks, &c. The weather is very pleasant so far.

March 25, 1878—Went to Benson Surveying, and Continued there until Friday, the 29th and then came home. I found a note from L. S. Hills, cashier of Dest Natl Bank[78] saying my a/c had been paid

Thursday, April 4, 1878—Lyman and I went to Salt Lake City, to Conference. Found all well as usual.

Monday, April 8, 1878—Was presented to the new Surveyor General, F. Salomon.[79] Also settled my account at the Deseret National Bank.

[page 404]

April 8, 1878—Found a balance there due me of $845.40 [$15,447]. Sat for photographs, Lyman also.

April 9, 1878—Paid W. B. Preston $150.00 [$2,741] due him for carriage. Also paid some other accounts, and drew some money.

April 10, 1878—Lyman came home

April 11, 1878—I came home, and found all well as usual

April 13, 1878—Paid Z.C.M.I. in Logan $205.00 [$3,746] and took up my notes. Also paid M. D. Hammond 47.50, and J. F. Reed $43.00. Also paid C. Montrose $48.00 E. Hansen $49.90 C. McNiel 31$ and Geo Lewis[80] 47.80, all these last was for help surveying. The total my help cost was $308.00 [$5,628]. I feel like a free man, having paid in all nearly $1500.00 [$27,408] in debts.

April 15, 1878—Rented my other house to Br. [blank] Phillips for $6.00 [$108] pr month, to be paid $7.00 [$128] on J. H. Brown,[81] and the rest to be paid on Temple account. Bought watch for $55.00 [$1,005] ($27.50) [$502].

April 16, 1878—Br. Phillips and wife moved into my house. They have what garden spot I have not planted, also the fruit of the four apple trees nearest the house, but have nothing else, neither fruit nor lucern or clover.

April 20, 1878—To day found the following receipt for a salve which I know by experience to be very good!—

BLACK SALVE

Olive oil 3 qts; Rosin 3 ozs; Beeswax 3 ozs.

Melt together, heat almost to boiling, gradually add pulverized red lead 2¼ to 2½ lbs. Soon after all the lead is taken up by the oil, remove from the fire (the

77 Levi P. Luckey was the secretary of the Utah Territory, 1877–79. The Notorial Commission parallels today's notary public who certifies and attests to official documents.

78 The Deseret National Bank was organized in 1871 and immediately became the "Mormon bank." Lewis S. Hills was an original bookkeeper (Sillitoe, *Welcoming the World*, 56–57).

79 Fred Salomon of Missouri, was appointed by the U.S. President as surveyor general of Utah ("By Telegraph," *Deseret News,* February 6, 1878; Utah Digital Newspapers; also "Land Surveys," *Deseret News*, April 17, 1878; Utah Digital Newspapers).

80 George W. Lewis was a Logan farmer (Somers, *History of Logan*, 64).

81 This could be James H. Brown, who was an influential figure in Ogden. He was a captain in the Mormon Battalion (Norma Baldwin Ricketts, *The Mormon Battalion: U.S. Army of the West, 1846–1848* [Logan, UT: Utah State Univ. Press, 1996], 220; Richard C. Roberts and Richard W. Sadler, *A History of Weber County* [Salt Lake City: Utah State Historical Society, 1997], 132).

mixture will then be a brown or shining black.) When nearly cold, add pulverized camphor ½ oz.

Spread thinly on linen, twice a day.

Good for burns, fever sores, ulcers, &c.

April 25, 1878—Went to Wellsville to survey for W. H. Maughan. Stayed 3 days.

May 8, 1878—Surveyed on Church farm, for the Church, four days afterwards surveyed a canal to irrigate the land

May 13, 1878—Surveyed for P. M. Paulsen[82] and others and took a cow in payment $17.50 [$320].

[page 405]

LILLIE BAPTIZED.

May 15, 1878—Surveyed Canal, Church farm.

May 2, 1878—This day my daughter Elizabeth was baptized by Elder John Dahle,[83] and confirmed by Eli Bell. She is 10 yrs old

May 26, 1878—Went as missionary to Richmond, to preach to the High Priests. My 1st

May 29, 1878—Recd a letter from Lieut. G. M. Wheeler, U.S. Engs War Dept. with map of parts of Cache, Box Elder & Rich counties also part of Idaho, with request for me to lay thereon the U.N.R.R. line. I copied the map for my own use.

May 31, 1878—Surveyed new County road from Benson, Southward.

June 1, 1878—The boys finished the Croquet ground to day, and got the set of mallets &c required.

Sunday, June 2, 1878—Wrote letter to Elvira and Sammy, and sent photograph.

June 12, 1878—Went to the end of track, at Watson's, in Marsh Valley, Idaho, with some prominent men, as Gov. Emery, Sidney Dillon, Jay Gould and other railroad magnates.[84] Nearly ran off the track, running at a rapid rate, but got home safe. finished my map for the Engineer Dept. Washington, and sent it to Lieut. G. M. Wheeler.

June 17, 1878—Went to 3-mile creek to Survey for Muir and others Then to Mendon, to Gunnell's. Spent the week on U.S. work. On Thursday the 19th we came suddenly upon a bear, who, after growling savagely and showing fight, leisurely walked up the mountain gulch. We had gone down to the ravine to get some snow, the day being very hot, and we nearly famished for water. But we concluded that we did not care for any snow just then. It was a very hard days work; so steep and brushy that it took over four hours exhaustive labor to go about three-quarters of a mile: and this is a type of many others that I have spent in the mountains.

June 26, 1878—Thursday. Recd an official letter from Sur. Genl F. Salomon saying my Surveying contract is extended six months, viz: to Dec. 31, 1878: for this I am very thankful.

June 27, 1878—Began carpenter work on my barn

[page 406]

June 28, 1878— Went to Mantua, Box Elder Co. to Survey in Dry Lake Valley.

July 1, 1878—Came home having finished my surveys there

Engaged 6000 shingles for my barn from R. Jepson Found Susan still ill with a cold, as Jesse has been, ever since we went to Mantua, having caught cold at Maughan's Mill when he and Nephi went up there a few days ago for lumber.

Wednesday, July 3, 1878—Recd a letter from Lt. G. M. Wheeler, U.S.A. Washington, for additional particulars in reference to the Utah & Northern R.R. and promising me maps &c

Lyman and a party went up Logan Cañon to spend the fourth.

July 4, 1878—Spent the day as usual, working at maps & field notes

July 23, 1878—Finished my U.S. survey in Tp.12N. R.2W. and came home. Went to work on plats and field notes.

---

82 Paul M. Paulson was a Logan dentist (Somers, *History of Logan*, 81).

83 Johannes Dahle was one of the original settlers of Clarkston, Utah. Clarkston was laid out after the explorations of Elder Ezra T. Benson and James H. Martineau (Ricks and Cooley, *History of a Valley*, 60–61).

84 George W. Emery (1830–1909) was appointed governor of the Utah territory by President Ulysses S. Grant. Emery served from 1875 to 1880, and central Utah's Emery County is named in his honor. Sidney Dillon and Jay Gould were railroad investors (Ricks and Cooley, *History of a Valley*, 180).

Saturday, August 3, 1878—To day our quarterly Conference began, meetings being held in the upper room of our Tabernacle, which is nearly finished. It will seat nearly 4000 persons.

Sunday, August 4, 1878—Conference concluded today, having had a good time, and much good instruction.

Monday, August 5, 1878—I went to Salt Lake City with President John Taylor and company, reaching there at noon. I found all well as usual at Eliza's

August 14, 1878—Came home, having finished my business at the Surveyor General's office (Frd R. Salomon) I put in plats and field notes to the amount of $1412.92 [$25,817]. While I was in the city I went to Lake Point to bathe, I think it did me good.[85]

Just as we were leaving S. L. City, a battle took place at the depot, ten or twelve shots being fired, and several persons shot. I did not learn all the particulars. People flew around pretty lively to escape the bullets, fired by two gentiles from the west, who had run a foot race the day previous, wherein foul play was suspected and charged.

[page 407]

August 14, 1878—It was strange many others were not hit, there being quite a crowd around just then.

I found my family in Logan well as usual, only Anna was unwell and had sore eyes. I also found a letter from my sister Henrietta and a notice of election as County Surveyor for Cache County.

The hay was cut, but not hauled, having no wagon to haul it with.

Thursday, August 15, 1878—Spent the day writing in my new family record.

Thursday, September 5, 1878—To day I started into the mountains to work on my contract of U.S. land surveying, with my new wagon, and Nephi, Jesse, and three young men hired, at $1.50 [$27] pr day. We camped for the night in Blacksmith Fork Cañon.

September 6, 1878—Drove on, up to the head of East Fork of Little Bear River, where my work on the 2nd Standard Parallel North, begins.

Saturday, September 7, 1878—Begun work and ran 4 miles to the top of the main range of the Wahsatch Mountains. It was very laborious indeed, toiling mile after mile up the steep mountain side, through thickets of dense willows and other brush. We got back to camp after dark, thoroughly tired out. Nephi and Jesse had supper ready, consisting of Coffee, bread bacon and potatoes. As this days work is a type of many others, I shall not hereafter detail our daily labors.

September 8, 1878—Moved our camp today to the summit of the main range, and camped in an aspen forest Had a hard time ascending the mountains with our team, the ascent being very steep. In the night heard the cry of some wild animal

September 9, 1878—Continued our line east, while Nephi and Jesse went with the wagon.

[page 408]

U.S. SURVEY IN RICH COUNTY.

September 9, 1878—Ran about 5 miles nearly all the way through timber. At night we found our boys camped at Sugar Pine on a branch of Woodruff or Twelve-Mile Creek. Here we found two sheep herds of about 6000 sheep. We find the weather quite cold in this elevated region—about 7000 feet above the sea.

September 11, 1878—Finished the 2d Standard Today, connecting with a former survey. Yesterday we took my horses with packs, leaving the wagon at Sugar Pine, as we could take it no farther.

When on the return home to day, my horse Frank got scared, ran away, and scattered his pack about two miles. When we caught him he was entirely stripped. It delayed us several hours to find the things lost and scattered; we could not find the pack saddle, nor 8 links of the Chain; also two canteens. We camped after dark, feeling that things might have been worse.

---

85 Lake Point was a resort on the Great Salt Lake. Beaches, bathhouses, and a three-decked steamship were the major attractions (Sillitoe, *Welcoming the World*, 75–76).

September 14, 1878—Was nearly run over today by a magnificent buck but as I happened to have no fire arm with me he escaped. We afterwards saw many deer, in our daily travels through the timber and brush.

September 16, 1878—To-day Fred. Benson[86] quit and went home. Cause, too hard work for a lazy man. I went to Woodruff to get my horses reshod, after the runaway last week, and staid over night with a Mr. Putnam, returning to camp next day.

September 22, 1878—Returned to the summit, stopping at McMurdie's Mill, very tired and cold, working the remainder of the week on the west side of the mountains.[87]

Thursday, September 26, 1878—To day the boys were very late coming back to camp, not arriving until three or four hours after sun set. I was alarmed, fearing some accident had happened to some of them. I built and for hours kept up roaring fires in the willows, to guide them to camp, shouting at times to draw their attention.

[page 409]

U.S. SURVEY. RETURN HOME.

September 26, 1878—At last my call was answered by Nephi, over a mile away. and in half an hour the (they) came in, tired out completely. They had been in very rough country, which had delayed them, but no accident had occurred. I was very happy and thankful to see them again.

September 27, 1878—Started work to day, but after running a mile, a storm came on, and we quit and returned to Logan, our provisions being nearly gone.

Found my family all well.

Tuesday, October 1, 1878—Started to S. L. City to day. Found Eliza and her family well as usual

Monday, October 7, 1878—To day filed my bond in 3d District Court, in the Sum of $10.000 [$182,717] as a Deputy U.S. Mineral Surveyor, Brother C. W. Card and Judge M. D. Hammond being my Sureties.

Tuesday, October 8, 1878—Settled with Brigham Young, paying him $790.40 [$14,435] which was the amount, with interest, that I owed on my brick house. Started home in the afternoon. My time has been very busily occupied on this visit, in matters pertaining to land surveys, mining surveys and timber lands. I had discovered an intended raid about to be made by the U.S. officials on our people for cutting timber on public lands, and I set to work to Counteract, as far as possible, their evil intentions, consulting with Br. Preston, Hammond and others. At Ogden I staid all night with Joseph A. West, and

October 9, 1878—Came home today

October 29, 1878—To day the temple hands began to lay up my new adobe addition to my house, 25 X 36 ft. I am to pay cash for the work, which is the reason the temple committee do the work for me. The foundation was laid about two weeks ago.

[page 410—see Appendix 3 for handwritten letter inserted here.]

U.S. DEPUTY MINERAL SURVEYOR.

Thursday, October 31, 1878—To day I received official notice of my appointment as United States Deputy Mineral Surveyer, my oath and bond having been approved in Washington.

Saturday, November 2, 1878—Our quarterly conference begins to day. Weather very warm and pleasant. About two weeks ago I was surveying in the snow, up in the mountain for C. O. Card, [88] at what is called the temple mill and it looked very wintry, but the snow soon melted (much of it) making it more pleasant

86 Fred Collaher Benson was the son of Ezra T. Benson and Elizabeth Collaher.

87 Samuel McMurdy was on the first high council when the Cache Valley Stake was organized in 1860. He and his family settled in Wellsville in 1859 after coming from Cedar City, where Samuel had participated in the Mountain Meadows Massacre (Ricks and Cooley, *History of a Valley*, 38, 275; Juanita Brooks, *The Mountain Meadows Massacre* [Norman, OK: Univ. of Oklahoma Press, 1991], 83, 241; Shirts and Shirts, *Trial Furnace*, 484, 495).

88 Charles Ora Card was superintendent of the Logan Tabernacle and Logan Temple construction; thus the temple mill was within his charge. The construction of these buildings used the natural resources of the area. A wood camp was just down the canyon, and a limekiln was at the mouth of the canyon (Ricks and Cooley, *History of a Valley*, 284; Godfrey and Godfrey, *Utah Years*, 176–77).

Last week I rec^{d} a letter from B. T. Cummings Jr. [89] from Boston, saying he had traced my lineage back on my father's side, to 1716, and had got some 200 names, which gratifies me very much, as I greatly desire to do a work for the dead of my ancestors.

November 3, 1878—Conference closed to day—a good time.

November 6, 1878—The temple masons to day finished laying up the new house, which is added to the north side of the brick, and the addition is 25 ft N. X South by 37 ft east. It Contains on the ground floor, a hall and stairway, dining room 16 X 18 ft in clear, 9½ ft high, a kitchen 12 X 18 ft, a pantry 6 X 6 ft. with one porch 5 X 25 ft. and another 6½ by 13. There is, up stairs a large room 16 X 24 for Stairways and boys room. This makes us a comfortable home, with 9 rooms, cellar & 2 stairway, also 3 porches. Truly the Lord has greatly blessed us, and I thank Him sincerely, and give Him all the praise and honor for His mercies and blessings.

Friday, November 8, 1878—To day my trees and plants from Mallett's nursery Ohio, arrived. I give the following list:

9 varieties choice roses @	50¢ each
1 Marchal Neil rose	1.00
1 Tree rose	3.00
1 Snow ball	.50
1 Spira Billardi	1.25
2 White Lilacs	1.00
1 Magnolia	1.50

[page 411]

November 8, 1878—

1 variegated Althea	1.50
1 white paeony	.50
1 Kilmarnock Weeping Willow	3.00
6 Chestnut trees	2.50
6 golden raspberries	1.25
6 Blk. raspberries	1.25
6 Kittany blackberries	1.25
1 Brandywine raspberry	1.25
2 grapes	2.00 [or 2.95]
2 grapes	2.00
2 grapes	2.00
1 Downing Mulberry	.50
1 Hybrid Cherry	1.00
1 queen's crab	1.00
1 Weaver plum	.50
1 Souvenir do Congrew peach	.75
1 Foster peach	.75
1 Salway peach	.75
6 mountain gooseberries	1.00
6 White Dutch currants	1.25
1 clematis vine	1.00
1 Pewaukee apple	.50
1 Emperor Alexander	.50
1 Early Russian apple	.50
	Total $38.00 [$694]

These I heeled in for the winter, except the Marshal Niel rose, which we put in a box and took into the house.

November 19, 1878—Went to Rees's Ranch on Bear river to level for an irrigation canal for Rees, Farr & others. A cold day, with now and then some snow.

November 21, 1878—Laid in supplies for a surveying trip.

Since the adobie work was finished, Nov. 6, I have been very busy getting lumber, shingles, nails, lath, paints, oils &c for the house. The Carpenters and painters have been busy as bees; and during the time I sent off my returns of Some U.S. Surveys, about the 14th inst. I believe.

Monday, November 25, 1878—To day started on U.S. Survey, with E. Hanson, Geo. Lewis, Nephi, Charles and Jesse. We had a tent, stove, and other things needful for a cold time in the mountains. Traveled 16 miles, and camped in Blacksmith Fork Cañon. A very cold night.

November 26, 1878—Arrived at Hammond's ranch, & pitched camp.

November 28, 1878—Yesterday and today, fine weather, but cold.

November 29, 1878—Snowed last night, very cold today. Our altitude is about 7500 feet to 8000 above the sea.

89 This is likely Benjamin F. Cummings. He and his brother, Horace G. Cummings, later became newspaper businessmen in Logan (Ricks and Cooley, *History of a Valley*, 395).

[page 412]

U. S. SURVEY COMPLETED. FAMILY RECORD.

November 1878—Nephi cooks and I write up field notes &c. To day Nephi scared up three deer. I took my Winchester rifle and tried to find them, but did not.

Sunday, December 1, 1878—Moved camp about 8 miles North, to Mill creek. Here we continued the Survey all the week, finishing it ~~on~~ in a fearful mountain snow storm.

Saturday, December 7, 1878—Quit work and came home, after a long and tedious drive. The Change from the arctic climate and snow of the mountains, to the pleasant, dry valley was remarkable. I found all well at home, and many letters; among others, a letter from B. F. Cummings with over a hundred names of my ancestors, which he hunted up in New York state, mostly on Staten island. I insert a synopsis of his letter and report, as I deem it of great value, giving me opportunity to do a great work for my dead:

++++ "I herewith mail a list of all the names I could obtain in a several days search on Staten island, but the very oldest records of deeds and wills for Richmond County are kept at Albany

+++"and search the wills &c. of Richmond County. By so doing, I think I can learn who the first Martineau family were, who settled on the island.

"I am confident that I found the name of the first Haughwout as noted in the list of names. It was Peter, who with his wife Cornelia were members of the old Reformed Dutch Church, at Port Richmond.

Dr. Brownley, the present pastor, kindly searched an old record written in Dutch, and obtained the names of their children, as well as [thi. . .] for me.

+++"The names Haughwout and Martineau are spelled in the older records, in several different ways.

[page 413]

SUMMARY FOR 1878.

1878—Br. Cummings also states, that he found that the Martineau's first came from Dieppe France, [90] about the year 1682, one branch of the family going to England, the other to America.

December 22, 1878—Went to Salt Lake City to day, to help my office work through the Surveyor General's office.

During the last two weeks, I have been busy in hurrying the work on my house, carpenter work, plastering, painting and papering. The weather is Cold, and we have to keep fires all night.

I found all well in S. L. City, but my work in the office was "in statu quo."—Nothing had been done.

I therefore spent the time in copying my plats, field notes &c, and worked some in the office. I paid up on the organ, which has cost $265.$^{\underline{00}}$ [$4,842]

Bought a Bismark range—$87.00 [$1,589][91] & sent it home, also fixtures for the house.

The Lord has greatly blessed us during the past year. We have built a good barn, and quite an addition to the house which has cost about $1200 [$21,926]. Besides I paid B. Young $790.$^{\underline{00}}$ [$14,435] in full for the balance due on house and lot, which has now cost me about $3500 [$63,951]. I have also fenced in my 5 acre lot in the field, and sowed 3 acres of it to Lucerne.[92]

I also bought $38.$^{\underline{00}}$ [$694] worth of choice shrubs, flowers and fruit and shade trees, with which to help beautify Zion.

I desire to do what I can to help make Zion beautiful and lovely, and to surround my family with influences that will exalt and improve and make them happy, and in so doing to set a good example. May our Father continue to bless us and save us.

90 Dieppe, France, was located in the Haute-Normandy region of France. Historically, it was a small coastal fishing village. During the 1600s, numerous settlers moved from Dieppe to New France, which is now Quebec, Canada.

91 This is a flat-top cooking stove with an oven.

92 Lucerne is another name for alfalfa.

[page 414]

1879.

January 1, 1879—Spent to day in writing on my field notes. It snowed last night about a foot deep the first for the winter.

January 5, 1879—To day (Sunday) came home and found all afflicted with severe coughs and colds, which is now an epidemic.

January 12, 1879—Sunday. During last week we finished the dining room, and got the carpet down, Also moved in the organ, sideboard and desk. It now looks more comfortable and home like and I humbly thank our Father for His blessings and goodness.

A few days ago we heard of the decision of the U. S. Supreme Court in relation to polygamy,—condemning it.[93]

The U.S. government has now finally come out decidedly against God and His ordinances and we will see who shall prevail, God, or the wicked.

I think the nation will find they have pulled down a millstone upon their own heads, that will in the end grind them to powder.

January 22, 1879—To day went to S. L. City to attend to my Survey business. Found the family all well.

January 23, 1879—Went to the Sur. Gen[l] Office, and found nothing had been done while I was absent. I told Gen[l] Salomon I would go to work in the office on my notes and plats in order to help things along, and accordingly I did so, working about ten days. Amount of last return $3538.06 [$71,354].

In the mean time I got a scheme under way in reference to utilizing my coal prospect in Wyoming, Cranwell, Gen[l] Salomon, U.S. Marshals Shaughnessy and Dickert, U.S. Dep. Surveyor, are interested in it, and I hope to make something out of it.

[page 415]

START BACK TO NEW YORK WITH LYMAN.

1879—Gen[l] Salomon promised me a U.S. contract in Surveying, the present year, if possible. Says he likes my work very well.

Saturday, February 1, 1879—Came home, and found all well

Monday, February 3, 1879—Attended City Council, also next day, when I advocated the introduction of Water works. as Logan is uncommonly well situated for them. I was appointed on a Committee to examine and report at next meeting.

Wednesday, February 5, 1879—To day begun to make a map and profile of the U.N.R.R. for Mr. Clark, the owner.

February 6, 1879—Worked on profile

February 7, 1879—Went to Ogden to get map of Ogden Division of J. A. West. Attended a family gathering at F. D. Richards—his wife's birth day.

February 8, 1879—Came home

February 15, 1879—Worked all this week on profile of Utah Northern RR from Ogden to Franklin, about 82 miles. Had an evening party, of members of the choir, at which we enjoyed ourselves very much.

February 17, 1879—Was in bed all day with bad headache.

My contract of $6500 [$131,089] for U.S. Surveys is now all done. I am still a U.S. Deputy Mineral Surveryor, and have a recommendation from Sur. Gen[l] F. Salomon, of Utah, to the U.S. Sur. Gen[l] of Idaho, for appointment as a U.S. Mineral Surveyor for that Territory.

Sunday, February 23, 1879—Having made arrangements during the last two days to go back to the eastern states, together with Lyman R., I start today to Salt Lake City to procure money for the trip from the Deseret National Bank, arriving there 8.30 P.M. Before I started I called upon Elder J. F. Smith for

93 *Reynolds v. United States* was the first setback of a number of cases involving polygamy. The polygamy arguments escalated, resulting in the Edmunds Act in 1882, followed by the Edmunds-Tucker Act in 1887, and finally the Manifesto of 1890 ending the Church's practice of polygamy.

a blessing. He gave me a very good one. Said I should be preserved on my journey and should be blessed beyond my expectations.[94]

[page 416]

ON THE WAY TO THE EAST

Monday, February 24, 1879—Got Utah Northern R.R. bonds to the amount of $100.000 [$2,016,749] for M. Thatcher. Saw Sur. Gen. F. Salomon, who desired me to make a report in reference to the public lands of Utah, so far as I understand about them, to oppose Maj. Powell's schemes. This I did, today.

Got $550. [$11,092] at the bank for the journey, while Lyman has $100. [$2,017] more.

Tuesday, February 25, 1879—Started for the east. Arrived at Ogden and found Lyman awaiting me there, with M. Thatcher, who is also going east. Wm Jennings of S. L. City was also starting east. I had a pass to Omaha, a Saving of $77.50 [$1,563], but had to pay $8.00 [$161] for sleeper for myself and the same for Lyman. Left Ogden about 10 A.M. (9.50). Got a second hand ticket for Lyman, $63.00 [$1,271]. Took a lunch basket along. My feelings at finding myself on the way to the home of my Childhood, after an absence of so many years—35—were hard to analyze.

Wednesday, February 26, 1879—On waking found ourselves near Carbon. Saw a flock of antelopes bounding away from the train. Breakfasted at Rock Creek. But little snow on the ground—only in hollows and shady places. The weather is pleasant, but on account of our great altitude—about 7000 feet—is quite cold. When I left Utah, people were making gardens. Now in Wyoming Territory.

Thursday, February 27, 1878—Breakfast at Grand Island, on the Platte, Nebraska. Snow covers the ground, weather cold. Last night our train ran over and killed some cattle.

Arrived at Omaha at 3 P.M. and crossed the Missouri to Council Bluffs, and there changed our train, taking passage to Chicago via Chicago, Rock Island, & Pacific R.R. fare 16.00 sleeper 250, each = $18.50 [$373] Each

[page 417]

COUNCIL BLUFFS TO CHICAGO, MEET LOTIE.

February, 1879—The river is frozen solid—teams crossing constantly on the ice. Weather very cold, sleighing good. Left for Chicago 5 P.M. Found I had lost one hour in time by coming east from Ogden 1029 miles.

Friday, February 28, 1879—Reached Davenport, on the Mississippi at 9 A.M. a place of about 30,000 inhabitants. Here we cross the Mississippi on a very long bridge, passing the U.S. Arsenal on Rock island, Moline, on the east side, is a fine town. Considerable timber grows all along the road. Pass through Genesee, Atkinson, LaSalle & Joliet to Chicago, arriving there about 3 P.M. We stop at the Grand Pacific hotel, one of the best in the city. When I left this city in March 1849, its population was about 30.000—it is now nearly half a million.

Not knowing how to find my brother-in-law's house, (John P. Voswinkel) I sent him a note, saying a man from Utah, acquainted with her brother James would like to see his wife, if agreeable. He and his Son Fritz came to the hotel to see me, and having found me out, went with me to his house, and introduced me as an acquaintance of her brothers. Lois, my sister, was very glad to see me. After talking awhile, I could restrain myself no longer, and told her who I was. She could hardly believe her senses—threw her arms around my neck and kissed and cried and laughed a long time. She Could not remember me as she was so very young—only about 6 years—when I left home. I could not have known her, either, seeing a woman with gray hair—the mother of nine Children—five of them living. Their names—Fritz, Bertha, Carrie, Jennie and Lotie (or Nillie, as they call her. I too, have changed much in that long interval of time.

94 It is interesting that Martineau does not say much about the beginning of this mission. He must have been anxious to reconnect with his family in the East as well as feeling the emotions of leaving home. It was not uncommon in this era of Church history for members to return to their homelands to reconnect, teach, and establish good relations.

[page 418]

CHICAGO TO WASHINGTON. THE CAPITOL.

February 28, 1879—I remained until midnight, then returned to the Hotel, fearing Lyman would not rest, not knowing where I was. Lyman went to theatre with Brs. Thatcher and Jennings.

Saturday, March 1, 1879—Spent the day with my sisters family, with Lyman. We left Chicago at 5.15 P.M. on the Pittsburg, Fort Wayne & Chicago R.R. Cold, and snowed all night. Fare to Washington $17.50 Sleeper to Pittsburg 2.50 & to Washington $2.00 = $22.00 [$444]

Sunday, March 2, 1879—Arrived at Pittsburg at 12.15 noon. Still snowing and very disagreeable. Traveled about an hour along the Ohio River. Here Br. Thatcher left our party, continuing on to New York, while Lyman, Jennings and I waited till 8 P.M. for another train. Snowed all day. Did not see Pittsburg in all its glory of smoke, because it was Sunday, and many of its multitudinous furnaces and machine shops were idle.

Left at 8 P.M. on the Pennsylvania R.R. to Harrisburg: then by Northern Central R.R. to Baltimore; thence by Baltimore & Potomac to Washington. We got to Washington at 9 A.M.

Monday, March 3, 1879—Still snowing, but stopped about noon. Streets very wet and nasty.

We stopped at Willard's Hotel, because Br. Jennings wished to. This has long been a first class hotel.

After breakfast we started out to see the city. Went to the Capitol, and found Br. Geo. Q. Cannon, who procured us seats in the representatives hall gallery. We remained about an hour, listening to the speeches, then went all through the building looking at the pictures, statues, and the miracle of architecture presented on every side. From the dome we had a beautiful view of Maryland and Virginia, the Potomac river and the beautiful city.

[page 419]

AT THE CAPITOL AND NAVY YARD.

Tuesday, March 4, 1879—Went to the Capitol and witnessed the close of the Session. I thought the spirit of disorder ruled the hour, but was told it was the usual thing.

Thousands of ladies and gentlemen were in the corridors and galleries—pushing, panting and striving to get somewhere.

After the close of the session, at noon, Br. Cannon took up [us] all through the buildings and showed us the heating apparatus, the Library, attended a session of the Supreme Court, and heard the reading of decisions; and then, by invitation of Commander Evans of the Ship-of-War Saratoga, visited his ship, spent a pleasant half hour in his cabin, and then were shown over the ship, which is armed with 17 heavy guns 10^{in} caliber. We then went over the Monitor "Passaic." Her turret of solid iron, 11 inches thick, is deeply indented by the heavy shot of the rebels during the rebellion. We then went all through a torpedo boat. Returning, we saw some guns taken by Commodore Decatur from the Tripolitans in 1804, which had been taken by them from the Spaniards.

The Guns (2) of the Passaic carry 480 lbs shot, and require a charge of 50 to 100 lbs powder.

Found my Cousin Laura Starin (nee Poole) wife of John N. Starin, Representative from New York State, were staying at Willards also, with their daughter Carrie. Spent an hour with them in the evening, but they did not seem overjoyed to see us. Starin is a Millionaire, and seemed more cordial than she or her daughter, who is a pretty girl of about 16 or 17 years of age. They go to New York in the morning.

Wednesday, March ~~6~~ 5, 1879—To day Lyman and I went to Mount Vernon, 16 miles, by Steamer, the round trip one dollar.

[page 420]

MOUNT VERNON

March, 1879—Left Washington at 10 A.M. A delightful ride, passing Fort Wood. We found the Mansion looking as represented in pictures, and were shown through it by an attendant. Most of the furniture remains as it was when the family lived there. Among other things we saw the key of the Bastile, presented by LaFayette; also many personal mementos of Washington and his wife. I got some black walnuts from trees growing near the old tomb, also some oak leaves from within it, and a fragment of the tomb, which is small and unpretending. A new tomb has been erected by Congress in which repose the remains of General and Lady Washington, in two handsome Marble Sarcophagi. The South end is open and guarded by an iron gate through which the interior can be seen. I thought, as I gazed upon the coffins with a deep and indescribable emotion, that the United States—this great nation, is the true monument to his memory, the Constitution his true epitaph. His wife survived him only 18 months, never leaving his house nor receiving company. I also gathered some acorns and coffee beans to plant in Utah, which is now the only true home of Liberty. The estate, and its situations are most beautiful. Situated upon a high and commanding point, with the Potomac spread out before it, here about two miles wide, and with its beautiful Black Walnut, Sycamore, Magnolia, oaks, hickory and other trees, it is most lovely. Lovely it will always remain in my remembrance, as a pearl among days.

On our return we pass Fort Washington, a massive fortress, and the arsenal, with its rows of heavy Columbiads and piles of shot and shell.

In the evening went to the Theatre, and saw "Joshua Whitcomb"—a good play

Thursday, March 6, 1979—Br. Cannon took us to the President's house, and we had an introduction to him.

[page 421]

CORCORAN ART BUILDING.

March, 1879—The "East Room" is a magnificent apartment. We then visited the U.S. Treasury Building, and saw the 218 presses print greenbacks and Government bonds—the whole process. Saw also Gen[l] Twiggs[95] three swords, one presented by Congress, valued at $20.000 [$403,350], and two others $15000 [$302,512]. Visited the "Corcoran Art Building," with its beautiful paintings and statuary and medeaeval curiosities, such as bronzes, Armor and old plate. Of all the Statues, I admired most the "Apollo Belvidere," "Antinous of the Capitol," "Laocoon" "Dying Gladiator," "Endymion" "Venus victix (or Venus with the apple) "Venus di Medicis," "Venus rising from the Sea," "Clytie" (full life size) and the "Greek Slave"—a marvel of grace and beauty; also the "veiled men," and a "Bacchanti" (female) bust, very fine. There were also many others very beautiful and noble—especially the "Venus of Milo."

At 5 P.M. went by invitation of Br. Cannon to dine with him at the Riggs House. There were Brs. Cannon, Jennings, Rawlings, Stringfellow, Lyman and I. We had a fine dinner, a band playing for us, and the ~~forty~~ sixty tables each attended by Negro waiters in black broad cloth, white vests and gloves. We sat nearly two hours.

After dinner talked with General Coc. on the timber question.

Friday, March 7, 1879—Went with Br. Cannon to Mrs. Kitchums, and saw a bust she is making of Br. Cannon: thence to the Patent office and had an introduction to J. A. Williamson, Com[r] of the Gen[l] Land Office.[96]

Bought tickets to N. York $15.00 [$302]. Also set of Silver Tea Set, price $50.[00] [$1,008] got it for $26.00 [$524]. Left at 2 P.M. passing through Baltimore, Wilmington, Philadelphia, & Newark to N. York, arriving at Jersey

---

95 David Emanuel Twiggs (1790–1862) was a famous Civil War general.

96 J. A. Williamson was once a Union Pacific Railroad land agent, which is likely the commonality of this meeting. Now a federal land commissioner, he was stationed in Washington DC at this entry (William S. Greever, *Arid Domain: The Santa Fe Railway and Its Western Land Grant* [Palo Alto, CA: Stanford Univ. Press, 1954], 35).

[page 422]

NEW YORK CITY

March, 1879—Crossing Hudson river on ferry boat, and arriving at the Metropolitan hotel 10.30 P.M. Found Moses Thatcher there, and was glad to see him.

Saturday, March 8, 1879—Visited Anatomical Museum, [97] and walked about city.

Sunday, March 9, 1879—Went to Brooklyn and heard H. W. Beecher.[98] Returning, visited the "Battery," then took elevated railway to the "Central Park," drove around in a carriage about 6 miles for 25¢, then returned to hotel. In the evening Lyman went to Brooklyn and heard Talmage. I read and rested.

Monday, March 10, 1879—Posted letter to Susan, and to Geo. Q. Cannon. In the afternoon went to the Sea Side on Coney island, by Street Car, Ferry, Street car through Brooklyn and Railroad to the beach. Spent about two hours along the shore, gathering shells &c. Found a "Sea Spider" an ugly looking thing. Returned in the evening.

In the evening we went to "Union Park Theatre" and saw the "Bankers Daughter," on its 111th night. It was a good piece. Br. Thatcher got us tickets.

Tuesday, March 11, 1879—Went to Staten island, to Port Richmond, our old home. I could not find our old house. We lived there in 1835 & 36. Everything seems changed, and so much smaller than I remember. It makes me feel sad, as I see the changes, and all the dear old landmarks removed.

In the evening called on Jos Richardson with Br. Thatcher. He invited Lyman and I to go to Bridgeport, Conn. on the Steamer, and gave me tickets.

Wednesday, March 12, 1879—We started at 11 A.M. on steamer "Laura." The scenery is very interesting. We pass forts light houses &c, emerging into the open Sound; the shores of Long island very dim in the distance while that of Connecticut was only one or two miles away.

[page 423]

VISIT BRIDGEPORT, CONN.

March 12, 1879—The various vessels we passed and saw in the distance made the scene very picturesque and beautiful. We finally arrived at Bridgeport at 4.30 P.M. and found Mr. Geo. Richardson awaiting us with a carriage, which we entered and were driven all through the city and out to the Reservoir of the Water works. The day was very bleak and cold. We saw the works of the "Howe Sewing machines" and of the "Wheeler & Wilson Sewing Machines," each occupy many acres. Bridgeport is a pretty place. We then went to Mr. Richardson's house and dined about 8 P.M. then returned to the Steamer and started for New York, arriving there towards morning, 3 A.M. Altogether, it was a very pleasant trip.

March 13, 1879—Fort Schuyler frowns upon the passing traveler, its heavy guns sweeping and commanding the passage completely.[99] I think it would be difficult for any but a heavily armored fleet to go through the Sound and East river to attack New York.

Thursday, March 13, 1879—Lyman and I went around the city, visiting, among other places, A. T. Stewart's store—a magnificent place.[100] There are over 1000 Clerks employed there. I bought some ties, handkerchiefs &c for Susan there. In the evening Lyman went with Brs. Taylor and Teasdel to see O'Leary and his three competitors walk; afterwards to "Buckingham Palace Hotel" a habitus of "ladies of accommodating virtue, dances, &c. I went to Tony Pastor's Theatre[101] and saw a Burlesque on "H.M.S. Pinafore."

97 For a discussion about the historical anatomical museums in New York, see http://www.common-place.org/vol-04/no-02/sappol/.

98 This is likely Henry Ward Beecher, who was a famous preacher of the era. He applauded both science and religion for their contributions to God's plan. In 1883 he visited Salt Lake City on tour (Edward Wagenknecht, *Ambassadors for Christ: Seven American Preachers* [New York: Oxford Univ. Press, 1972]).

99 Fort Schuyler in the Bronx was a nineteenth-century fortification.

100 Called the "Marble Palace," the A. T. Stewart's Dry Goods Store opened in New York in 1846. Thriving particularly during the Civil War, the store made Stewart one of the richest people in New York.

101 Tony Pastor (1837–1908) was among the founders of American vaudeville, and his New York theatre was one of the original Broadway playhouses (Robert W. Synder, *Voice of the City: Vaudville and Popular Culture in New York* [New York: Oxford Univ. Press, 1989]).

Br. M. Thatcher said he could get a pass for Lyman over the Union Pacific R.R. and as this would save $77.50 [$1,563] passage money, I consented for him to go home with him, although I dread to have him go and leave me to go home alone another way. Saw Br. Jennings, who arrived this evening from Washington.

[page 424]

START HOMEWARD

Friday, March 14, 1879—This morning at 9 A.M. Lyman and Br. M. Thatcher started for home, via Pa. R.R. I started at 10.30 A.M. via Hudson River R.R. passing up the east bank of that river, which is frozen most of the distance. We arrived at Albany in 4½ hours, finding there all snow and ice. Here I turn westward and homeward to my earthy heaven. As we speed along the noble Mohawk, we seem to be in the midst of Winter. I passed Port Jackson, where I was born, but did not stop, also passing Fonda, where I wished to stop to visit Fultonville, my old home with Uncle William Mears. I left the train at Palatine Bridge, and then waited till 7 P.M. for an east bound train, when I went back 12 miles to Fonda, and there hired a sleigh to take me across the Mohawk to Fultonville to visit my Aunt Harriet Sherwin, who is keeping house for my cousin Laura Starin.

Lyman's passage, from N. York to Chicago is $18.00 [$363]; Mine, via N.Y. Central, Great Western (Canada) and Michigan Central, to Chicago, is $22.00 [$444].

At Port Jackson the house is still standing in which I was born. It is a large one, now used as a hotel. This my Aunt Harriet told me.

I arrived at Cousin John H. Starin's house at 8½ P.M. found there my Aunt Harriet and her granddaughter, Alice Fillmore, a daughter of my cousin Nettie Fillmore. She is a pretty girl of about 22 years age.

Saturday, March 15, 1879—Here I am in Fultonville, after an absence of 35 years. All is changed. The Mohawk, which I remember as a river about as wide as the Mississippi, is a small, narrow stream, only a pistol shot across. The valley, too, seems so narrow, the hills so low, and all seems dwarfed.

[page 425]

FULTONVILLE, AT COUSIN STARINS.

1879—I was much disappointed. J. H. Starin and my cousin Laura, his wife, are at Washington, he being a Representative from this State, but they insisted on my visiting their home.

Their house and grounds are magnificent—worth several hundred thousand dollars. They have 500 Acres, laid out as parks, gardens, lawns, deer park, race course, farms &c, with fountains, green houses, aviaries, &c while the house itself is magnificently finished and furnished. There are two beautiful groups of Statuary in the parlor;—Columbus before Queen Isabella, and a Greek Slave.

Aunt Harriet is 71 years, but is still handsome and hale.[102] She gave me her photograph. She was a favorite Aunt of mine, when a boy, and I love her still. From her I learned many things of interest relative to our family. I was also much pleased with my cousin Alice.

We drove around in the sleigh, visiting Uncle William's old house—my former home—also round the grounds, I saw his horses, thoroughbreds—some 30 in number; also about 30 Choice Aldernay cows (some Durhams), some 18 Carriages of various kinds; two 12 pr guns for 4th of July occasions, and the conservatory, which contains thousands of rare and beautiful plants. Among others, a tree fern once owned by Geo. Washington, Orange trees in bloom and with fruit ripening, an Agave Americana, and very many others not to be enumerated.

The day was very cold, Snow drifting, and like the dead of winter. Angeline Sherwin, my cousin, lives at "Woman's Ranch" John Days River Idaho.

Sunday, March 16, 1879—Snowing heavily this morning. At 2.20 left, arriving at Jordan at 7.35 P.M. and stopped over night. The snow, along by Rome & Utica is very deep. Here in Jordan no one talks of spring yet—all is winter. I made a mistake on last page. Did not leave Fultonville until today.

102 *Hale* means healthy and of sound mind.

[page 426]

ELBRIDGE.

Tuesday, March 18, 1879—This morning hired a sleigh and drove over to Elbridge As I drove down the long street, all seemed changed. Even the old "Munro Academy" was gone, and a handsome church erected in its place. I saw a fine building on the other side of the street, and asked a man what building that was. He said it was the Academy. I said "it used to be on the other side of the street, didn't it?" He said, "Oh no, it was always where it is now." He was a man grown, and had never remembered it as being anywhere else. This incident made me realize more than anything else, how the years had flown since I lived there.

I halted opposite the place where we used to live, but the house was gone, and even the tall locusts, other trees growing in their place. Grandfather Mears' house was also so changed as to be almost unrecognizable: the old toll gate removed, the orchards cut down, and even the old red school house removed—a nice white one in its place. I drove along, quite melancholy, to the old grave yard, and hunted round till I found our family graves among the drifts of snow. There they were—father, mother, Sisters Lucretia, Fannie, & Harriet, and Aunt Louisa Mears Abrahams and her husband Harvey. On father's stone was this verse

"Sweet peace and heavenly peace and humble joy
Divinely beam on his exalted Soul
Distruction gild and crown him for the skies
With incommunicable luster bright."
His age "45 yrs and 15 days."
On sister Harriets stone, this verse & inscription
Died Oct, 16, 1837, aged 2 yrs 4[mo] 21 days.

[page 427]

ELBRIDGE CEMETERY.

March 18, 1879—
"Thy days, my little one, were few
An angel's morning visit,
That came and vanished like the dew,
Twas here—tis gone—where is it."

On Mother's stone is only the simple line
"Our Mother."

On sister Lucretia's Stone after her name &c
"Died May 26, 1841, age 23 yrs and 27 days
23
1818

On Uncle Harvey Abrahms' stone, "died Dec. 18, 1873 age 66 years.
66
1807

On ~~sister Lucretia's~~ Aunt Louisa's
Maria Louisa Abrahms, Died Feb. 17. 1847, age 30 yrs, 10[mo], 12 days.

My sister Fanny has no tomb stone. She lies next to my father, I believe. My Mother's Uncle Dan[l] Sprague, (I believe that was his first name, Daniel) is buried near by, but there is no stone.

No one can tell my feelings as I thus stood by the couches,—the frozen, snowy couches of the dead. I knelt by my mothers and with the tears flowing said "And is it thus we meet, my mother."

There is one inestimable consolation: I can do a work for them, by which the family bonds may be reunited, and they made partakers of the blessing of the gospel in a world to come, and this, with the help of my Father in Heaven, I intend to do.

The grave yard was the first place where I felt at home. All round me I saw the names of friends long since dead, whose names came to me so fresh and natural, after having been forgotten by me for nearly forty years.

[page 428]

ELBRIDGE—ROCHESTER

March 18, 1879—From the cemetery I went to the old "Carpenter's brook, where Uncle Chauncey and I used to fish for the beautiful speckled trout, thence on to see the old "Cucumber tree" and to other places, then returned to Elbridge, and stopped at Rice's old place. Here I found his son, David Rice, who, when he found who I was, gave me a very very cordial greeting. I took dinner there, and soon met his brother William, my old school mate. They pressed me to stay over night, but I could not, and bade them a reluctant good bye, returning to Jordan in time to take the evening train to Rochester.

I wrote the following lines, suggested by the changes I found, and illustrative of my feelings:

TIME CHANGES ALL.

Oh swift rushing Time, how rapid thy flight!
How wondrous thy power for change or decay!
The morn's radiant glow thou shroudest ere night
While youth's airy castles thou meltest away.

I stand on the soil that my boyish feet pressed,
But changed are the faces and altered the scene;
The friends of my youth now silently rest—
Their couches are earthy, their cov'ring is green.

Old buildings are gone—~~once~~ my childish hearts pride
And old trees have yielded to ~~Time~~ Thy mighty sway;
The hills, too, have dwindled, the streams not so wide
The distances shorter—e'en changed is the day.

Then a day seemed a week,—now a week seems a day
A month, slowly speeding—seemed never to end;
Now years swiftly speeding, pass quickly away
And nearer and nearer approaches the End.

[page 429]

NIAGARA FALLS, DETROIT, FORT WAYNE.

March 19, 1879—
The End, did I say? No, beginning of Life
For Death's but the portal of Life's joyous Court,
The haven of rest, where husband and wife
And Children and loved ones shall never more part.

March 19, 1879—This morning I find myself in Rochester at the Waverly House. Weather still very cold. Visited the Genesse Falls—about 100 ft high.[103] Left at 7 A.M. and reached Niagara Suspension Bridge at 10 A.M. and Niagara falls, two miles distant a few minutes later. I visited the falls about two hours, and then returned to the Suspension bridge.

All that I have read in praise of the falls, is true. Crossing the bridge, we enter British territory; and I go westward via the Great Western R.R. Pass Hamilton at the west end of Lake Ontario, and many smaller towns, arriving at Windsor opposite Detroit at 10 P.M. and cross (the train) on a ferry boat. I put up at the Russell House opposite the City Hall Distance from Suspension Bridge, Niagara, to Windsor, 230 miles. Across Detroit river one mile.

Thursday, March 20, 1879—This morning took street car to Fort Wayne, 3½ miles from Detroit, to see my cousin Dewitt C. Poole, Capt. 22^{d} Inf, U.S.A. On arriving there I saw a group of officers, among them, Dewitt. We were glad to see each other after so many years. We went to his quarters, and there I met his wife, a charming lady, quite pretty and very pleasant. They have a daughter, Helen Louisa, 6 years old, and a little boy—John Hudson, after Dewitts father, five months old. His wife's name is Maria W. and she treated me very cordially.

They live very comfortably, their house of five rooms handsomely furnished. The Fort and officers quarters are situated on the bank of Detroit river, and are very pleasantly situated.

[page 430]

DETROIT TO CHICAGO.

March 20, 1879—Dewitt took me all about and through the fort, which is a regular, permanent fortress, cost about $1.500.000 [$30,251,231], Walls of masonry, with casemate and barbette guns, bomb proofs, glacis covered-ways, magazines &c with two story stone fireproof barracks for the men. Weather cold and snowy. I was introduced to a number of officers, and found them very pleasant fellows. They were Maj. Hoff, Capt. Bush Lieuts Sharp and Mosher, and Mrs. Mosher, a nice lady, Maj. Brooks, and others.

103 The town of Genesee Falls is located in the southeastern corner of Wyoming County, New York. The Genesee River borders the eastern edge of the town.

Friday, March 21, 1879—In the evening Dewitt took Molly (his wife) & I to the Opera, to see "H.M.S. Pinafore" and spent a very pleasant evening. Dewitt gave me his photograph, and his wife promised me hers.

Saturday, March 22, 1879—Start this morning at 10 A.M. for Chicago by Michigan Central, distance 284 miles. We pass through a fine country and many nice towns, and gain our first view of Lake Michigan at Michigan City, reaching Chicago 7.4 P.M. Snowed hard when we left Detroit. At Depot met Lyman, John & Fritz and found Sister Lotie and family well, and very glad to meet again.

Sunday, March 23, 1879—Went with Lotie and Lyman to hear Rev. Dr. Colyer preach at the Unitarian Church, and afterwards attended Sunday School there. His preaching is like thin air—nothing of it, and I am astonished that intelligent people can be satisfied with such teachers.

Monday, March 24, 1879—Went with Lotie through furniture, dry goods, Bric-a-brac, crockery, and other stores, to see what they had.

[page 431]

FURNITURE, LOTIE SICK & HEALED

March 25, 1879—Rained all day. In the evening went to see "Pinafore" with Lotie, Lyman, Fritz and Bertha. Good play, & a fine orchestra, led by Max Maretzek, McVickers theatre.[104] Chorus of forty voices on stage.

Wednesday, March 26, 1879—Went through town with John, and chose a suite of furniture price $85.00 [$1,714].

Thursday, March 27, 1879—Lotie gave me a beautiful ivory type of herself,[105] also some old letters of father to mother before they were married; also letters written by Sister Lucretia, Mother;—Mother's Morocco pocket, and keepsakes of grandmother Mears.

Friday, March 28, 1879—Bought a suite furniture of Holton & Hildreth for $75.00 [$1,513], boxing 6.50 [$131] stand 1.50 [$30], Pier glass, boxed $32.50 [$655] and priced $25.00 [$504] Cash on it.

Bought of S. Hyman 1 Doz spoons 6.00 [$121]; pie knife 4.00 [$81] Soup ladle $3.00 [$61]: Gold pen and pencil 6.50 [$131]:

Bought of Burrell & Tyrrell China ware tea set 84 pieces $24.24 [$489];

In the evening Lyman went to the rolling mills.

~~Sat. 29~~—About 2 A.M. this morning John called me into his room hurriedly & I found Lotie just alive. I could only hear her faint whisper by holding my ear close to her mouth. She was nearly gone. It was a sudden attack about the heart. I asked John if I should administer to her. He said "Yes." I did so & she shortly began to revive, and passed into a peaceful sleep, from which she rose in the morning apparently well. God blessed her for which praise be to his holy name.

Saturday, March 29, 1879—Around town. Got spoons marked.

[page 432]

STOCK YARDS. ROLLING MILLS.

March 30, 1879—Went to see the stock yards, where 20000 hogs are killed daily. It is a vast concern. Hogs are killed, cleaned and hung up, four in a minute. Everything but shoulders, sides and hams are put in immense steam vats, steamed to a pulp, all grease extracted, the balance sold for manure.

I saw millions of pounds of hams, shoulders and sides stacked up, salting; and thousands of barrels packed.

In afternoon walked with John, Lotie, Lyman and Carrie in Lincoln Park[106] and on the Lake Shore; and had a pleasant time. In the Park are bears, wolves, wild cats, opossums, Raccoons, Owls, Swans, and rare ducks and other birds. Also two monstrous grizzly bears.

Monday, March 30, 1879 [Monday was the 31st]—This morning Lyman started home via C.B. & Q.R.R., leaving here 10.30 A.M. I was sorry to part with him. We all went to the Depot to see him off. Got a letter from Nettie, with ten dollars to help me come

104 Max Maretzek (1821–97) was a famous conductor and composer. The McVickers Theater is part of Chicago history. It was burned to the ground in the Chicago Fire of 1871 and was reconstructed the next year.

105 According to *The British Journal of Photography*, August 5, 1860, an *ivorytype* is a "colored photograph, finished so as to resemble a miniature or portrait on ivory."

106 Lincoln Park is located in Chicago's north end.

to St. Paul to see them. Also a letter from Nettie Poole Tillmon, Marengo, with invitation to visit her.

Tuesday, April 1, 1879—Election in Chicago, to day. Communists have made fearful threats against the rich, if they cannot elect their candidates. They elect Several of the Aldermen and Councillors. Many of the better classes fear for the future.

I visited the rolling works, where iron ore is first converted into Bessemer steel, [107] then into huge bars or blocks, about 6 ft long, weighing over 600 lbs.; then rolled into rails for railroads. The works are very extensive, and are well worth visiting.

Wednesday, April 2, 1879—This morning Lotie, Nelly and I started for Madison via Chicago & N.W. Railway.

[page 433]

MADISON, WISCONSIN

Wednesday, April 2, 1879—It soon began to snow furiously, continuing all day. We arrived at our destination at 4 P.M. and received a hearty welcome from Aunt Jenny Mears and her daughter Helen, my cousin, whom I now saw for the first time: Aunt Jenny is the widow of my uncle William with whom I lived when a boy, and who was always very kind to me.

Thursday, April 3, 1879—Helen took me through the State House, which is a very fine building, standing in a beautiful park. There are many field pieces, 12 pdrs, which passed through the war; among them are some taken from the rebels. There is also a collection of many standards, which were torn and rent in many a hard fought field, both Union and rebel flags. To me a very interesting collection.

I met Uncle Charles Mears, my old boyhood companion,—only ten years my senior. He is white haired, but has the same odd ways he had when a young man. He invited me to stay at his house. We arranged that I should sleep there, and dine at Aunt Jenny's. I like his wife Harriet—or Hattie—very much; Also my cousin, her daughter Flora, age 16, a very pretty, modest girl. She has a sister, Alice married and a mother, also a nice girl.

Friday, April 4, 1879—Uncle Charles took me through Science Hall, an adjunct of the State University.[108] It is a large and costly building, of cut stone, with rooms devoted to Minerology, Geology, Botany, Chemistry & all the various sciences and arts. The Observatory and University buildings are in the same grounds. Also the U.S. Magnetic Observatory. The stone used is a cream Dolomite.

[page 434]

MADISON

Saturday, April 5, 1879—Walked round town, and rode with Lotie & Helen.

Sunday, April 6, 1879—Attended Episcopal Church with Aunt Jenny and L. A fine building, but with only a <u>form</u> of religion for its worshippers. Afterwards took a long walk with Lotie, who is quite feeble, but ambitious.

Monday, April 7, 1879—Went through the U.S. Magnetic Underground Observatory, the only one in the United States.[109] It was erected by Cousin N. B. Vanslyke under direction of the U.S. Coast Survey. You enter by a long covered archway, under ground, provided with doors at different places, so as to keep out all external influence of heat, light and sound. The room itself is a brick vault, in which stand very delicate apparatus for noting and recording the changes in the direction and dip of the needle. The apparatus is wonderfully Sensitive. All the observations are taken in the dark. Even a candle moved about the room, disturbs the instruments instantly. All pocket knives, keys &c and all iron or steel we had about us had to be left outside, Even a tin button, moved about in the room produced a disturbance of the instruments. All observations are self recording.

In the evening I took Aunt Jenny and Lotie to see John M^c^Culloch in "Richard Third," His power and ability in depicting the passions are wonderful.

107 Henry Bessemer (1813–98) was an inventor and engineer known for developing the first inexpensive industrial mass production of steel.

108 This was the University of Wisconsin at Madison.

109 The U.S. Coast and Geodetic Survey (now defunct), inspired by the research of John E. Davis, established the magnetic observatory at the University of Wisconsin campus in 1868. The U.S. Coast and Geodetic Survey was dismantled in 1888, and the observatory was emptied of equipment. The building now houses a museum.

Tuesday, April 8, 1879—Started for St Paul, Minnesota, to see my sister Nettie Lyon, leaving Madison at 4 P.M. the distance is, from Chicago to Madison, 138 miles from Madison to St. Paul 272 miles; from Chicago to St. Paul 410 miles.

I found some old books of fathers at Uncle Chas Mears, which he kindly gave me.

[page 435]

TO ST. PAUL, MINN. NETTIE & LEO.

Tuesday, April 8, 1879—The fare from Madison to St Paul is $10.65 [$215], sleeper $2.00 [$40] additional. Fare from Chicago to Madison is $4.95 [$100].

The Scenery from Madison, northward, becomes quite beautiful, with hills, rocks and woods. In the neighborhood of Baraboo, Merrimac (where we cross the Wisconsin river, a large stream, the Scenery is beautiful. We Sup at Baraboo. Here my cousin Mary (Poole) Stewart resides. Night.

Wednesday, April 9, 1879—Arrive at St Paul about 7 A.M. in a rain. I took hack and drove to Nettie's. Saw Leo, my brother in law. His first looks pleased me, & I liked him better as I knew him longer. He is a Presbyterian Minister, over 71, but still hale and hearty, and an indefatigable worker in the cause of religion as he understands it. My sister Nettie 2½ years older than I, is quite deaf, and also quite gray, but still her good lovable self. I did not know her, nor she me. Her son John Martineau, a young man of about 20, is a fine fellow, and her daughter Fanny, is a dear little girl, petite and graceful, and with winning ways.

I had telegraphed my coming, but the message had not been delivered, so all were much Surprised as well as delighted to see me. My Sister—I had not seen her since the year 1847, when at midnight we parted on an Erie Canal boat, she going to her Uncle Chauncey's and I on to Milwaukee Wis.—she a gay, beautiful girl—I, a green awkward boy, too fond of books and seclusions and study to be fit for Society. Since then, what changes!

We had so much to talk about, while Leo sat by delighted. He said we took up our old acquaintance just where we broke it off then—just like Children. In fact, we lived our childhood over again.

[page 436]

ST PAUL, MINNEAPOLIS, MINNEHAHA.

Wednesday, April 9, 1879—In the afternoon I walked about the city, which is a fine one, of some 40000 inhabitants, with many fine residences and Churches. It is built on high bluffs of the Mississippi, about 100 to 300 feet high, in terraces. There are two bridges across the river, one of which is over 100 feet high, and a favorite place for suicides.

Thursday, April 10, 1879—Leo took me to Minneapolis, built at the falls of St Anthony, distance 15 miles. It is a place of some 35 or 40000 people, and will be a larger place by virtue of its situation at the head of navigation of the Missippi. We crossed the river (going up) about a mile above St. Paul, passing by the falls of Minnehaha, a romantic place. The falls are about 60 feet high.

~~St Paul~~ Minneapolis has some of the largest flour mills in the world. One that I visited, has 40 run of large Stone in operation, grinding about 1500 bushels of wheat daily. I saw the ruins of the mills that exploded last year, killing all in them, some 18 men. I visited a paper mill, also the falls of St Anthony, now become a mere water power. Was introduced to Dr. Presbyterian Minister, also to Leo's son Alexander and his wife, with whom we dined. He is baggage master on the Chicago, Milwaukee & St. Paul R.R.

Leo had just returned from a trip to Winnipeg in the British possessions, also Pembima & the Red River of the North.

We returned home by another route. On the way up, we crossed the Minnesota river, at the mouth of which stands Fort Snelling, with a garrison of U.S. troops.

[page 437]

ST PAUL

Thursday, April 10, 1879—It stands on a high point between the two rivers, Mississippi & Minnesota, commanding both. They are building a bridge across the Missippi here, the piers of which will be, I judge, about 100 feet high.

Nettie gave me mother's pin cushion, also a lace cap she (Mother) used to wear, my old bible I had in the Mexican War; my daguerreotype, taken the day I enlisted last in the U.S. army, in Milwaukee, [110] and last and best, my mothers silhouette, taken when she was about 32. It seemed so natural to me.

Friday, April 11, 1879—Good Friday. Nettie and I went to see the shops and stores. She bought for Susan & I, a silver-plated pickle dish, $3.00 [$61] as a present from Her and Leo. I bought her a set silver plated tea knives $2.75 [$55] and breast pin $2.50 [$50], as a present from Susan & I. I also bought a handsome silver plated cake plate for Susan, $6.00 [$121].

Saturday, April 12, 1879—Leo got a horse and carriage for Nett and I to go riding. We drove all through the city. He went somewhere—60 miles—to preach. Nettie showed me some of father's old drawings, plats of surveys on Staten island at Port Richmond Estimate for the Croton Water Works, New York. Wrote home and sent the silver ware by express.

Sunday, April 13, 1879—Went to Presbyterian Church. It was Easter Sunday, a great day with Sectarians. Mr. Breed, a big gun, preached a grand discourse—they said, I could only perceive an essay, without any gospel in it. I told Fanny so, raising her ire a little.

[page 438]

DISTANCES TRAVELED. LETTER FROM I. N. SPRAGUE

April 13, 1879—The following are some of the distances I have traveled since leaving home:—

Logan to S.L. City	97 miles
S. L. City to Ogden Utah	37
Ogden to Omaha Neb.	1029
Omaha to Chicago Ill.	502
Chicago to Pittsburg Pa.	
Pittsburg to Washington D.C. via Harrisburg P.A.	
Washington to New York via Balt[r] & Phil[a]	
Washington to Mt Vernon Va. (and returns)	32
New York to Port Richmond (and returns)	20
New York to Bridgeport Conn. (return, Steamer)	140
New York to Coney island (return)	20
New York to Albany N.york	148
Albany to Niagara falls (Canada)	
Niagara falls to Detroit, Mich (via Great Westn Canada)	230
Detroit to Chicago Ill.	284
Chicago to Minneapolis Minn.	425
Minneapolis to Madison, Wis	233
Madison, Wis to Milwaukee	81
Milwaukee to Chicago	85
Madison to Baraboo & returns	75
Chicago to Ogden	1531
Ogden to S. L. City	37
S. L. City to Logan	97

In the evening Nettie gave me her and Leo's pictures, grandmother's old snuff box, Uncle William's "Seasons" and some other little keepsakes.

The following items I got from a letter from Rev. Dr. Isaac N. Sprague, of Detroit, my mother's cousin:—

"Direct descent, backward, from my father Daniel, sister (?) of Lois Mears, your grandmother,

Daniel, my father
William, his father, 1760
William, his father, 1740

[page 439]

LETTER FROM I. N. SPRAGUE

April 13, 1879—

Jeremiah, his father,			1700
Anthony,	"	"	1660
William	"	"	1620
Edward	"	"	1600

I send you all the line from which your and my family have sprung. There is another line which branches off about 1720, and which reaches down to Rev. Dan[l] G. Sprague, deceased, of South Orange, and to Edward Payson S. of Salem, N.Y. now living.

Glad to hear from you at any time. Yours &c.

I. N. Sprague

110 A daguerreotype was a photograph.

I also copied from my mother's album, the following record of deaths of my uncles ~~and aunts:~~—

Daniel Vanslyke,	died	Dec. 4. 1831
John H. Poole	"	Sept. 10. 1835
John Martineau	"	April 6. 1838
Peter Martineau	"	Sept. 15. 1874

Marriages

Laura	married	May 10. 1832
Chauncey	"	Dec. 23. 1823
Eliza	"	April 29. 1824
Harriet	"	June 23. 1825
Mary Ann	"	July 31st 1834
James Russell	"	April 1836
Maria Louisa	"	April 13, 1837
William Allen	"	December 1837
Charles Sprague	"	1849 (second time)

Also copied from Mother's Album:—
"Started for Alabama Sept. 21, 1824
Returned in July 1826
Started for Washington Nov. 1828
Returned to Elbridge in May 1832
Went to New York in the fall of 1834
Returned to Elbridge May 1837
Went to Victory, Cayuga Co. N.Y. in 1844"

[page 440]

April 13, 1879—

Copied from David C. Lyon's journal:—

David C. Lyon was born Nov. 7. 1809 in the town of Oswegatchie St. Lawrence Co. N.york, and married Eliza Shiland Jan. 1. 1847 who died June 2, 1851 at Mineral Point, Wisconsin.

David C. Lyon Married Emily H. Martineau at Milwaukee Oct. 30. 1855.

Children of David & Eliza Lyon:—

Mary L. Lyon, born Nov. 17. 1847, at Cambridge, N.Y.

Alexander B. Lyon, born Apr. 3. 1851 at Mineral Point, Wis.

(Both now, April 13. 1879, Alive.)

Children of David C. & Nettie Lyon:—

Fannie M. Lyon, born Nov. 13. 1856, at Bedford, N.Y.

John Martineau Lyon, born Aug. 18. 1860 at Winona, Minn.

Monday, April 14, 1879—This morning I copied many items from mothers album. She was of refined taste, as shown by her selections of poetry, and her beautiful paintings of flowers &c.

Wrote to my grandmother's brother Rev. Isaac N. Sprague, Detroit, Michigan, relative to his ancestors.

LINES WRITTEN BY FATHER TO MY MOTHER (FROM HER ALBUM)

With what a feverish mind do I behold
These scenes, which witnessed oft as pure a love
As ever dwelt within a mortal breast
When, she, the dear companion of my walks
At whose appearance Nature Seemed to breathe
New fragrance round, and wear her sweetest smiles
Would point each beauty to my raptured view
Would bid me mark how white the hawthorn flower
What verdure[111] decked the lawn beneath our feet
How gay the poplars, and, amid their green
How pensive did the cedars hues appear,
With what a majesty the setting sun
Cast his mild radiance on the winding stream,
Whose scarcely ruffled breast, inverted showed
The various tree which on its borders grew,

[page 441]

April 14, 1879—

And each light cloud that high in ether sailed,
How sweet the robin trilled his amorous lay
How soft the wood dove cooed unto his mate
And then when she had caught my wandering eye
Turned from the charms which nature spread around
To gaze on those a thousand times more dear.
How has she hid her face upon my breast
And said she ne'er could make me Nature's lover,
Oh, who could see her and not Nature love!
Oh! She could bend me to her very will

111 *Verdure* means green, flourishing vegetation.

My Soul's emotions all were in her power
And yet, (so gently did she bear the sway)
She never found a wish but what was mine.
I have seen many
Whom the thoughtless world would call more fair
More beautiful than she, but never have my eyes
Beheld the face which more expressed that evenness of soul
That meek sweet temper which is ever pleased
When it can give delight, that mind informed
By reason's precepts, candid and sincere:
That breast by every gentle passion swayed.
The throne of virtue, innocence and truth
And all the mental charms by which the sex
Can make this world a paradise to man.
Oft have I looked upon her angel eyes to see
Sweet fancy sporting in their beams; have looked
Until unutterable love has swelled the tear
Of transport in my own. I could not help it.
I ne'er can think of her, but what my eyes
Are tenants to my will and play the infant.
Here we strayed,
How strongly memory paints upon my heart
That dear, dear glance, which first betrayed her love.
How widely different from her love was mine;
For though with such a warmth her passion glowed
That she has often told me she would die
And thought the simple blossom of the thorn place there
More lovely than the garden rose; and sweeter
Than the violet of the vale. Yet why I knew not
But I would sometimes feel as tho these flowers
Should not be suffered there; they might
From her loved bosom steal its snows, or rob
Her balmy breath of half its sweetness. I have
Unawares, taken them, and torn their leaves
And strewed them in her walks; and once,
(Such fancies fill a lover's brain—alas that e'er
Their warning should be true) I thought I heard
A dying flowret say "beware, rash youth,
These gusts of passion rule; torn from her breast
My fate may yet be thine."

J. Martineau

The following lines, also from mother's album were written by father on the death of my baby brother Charles Augustus:—

"Poor little one! Most bitterly did pain
And life's worst ills assail thine early age.
And quickly tired with this life's rough pilgrimage
Thy wearied spirit did its heaven regain.
Now, far from the low star
Of this dim spot, in Heaven then dost repose
And look'st and smilest on this world's transient woes.

May 27. 1832."

[page 442]

FATHER'S LINES TO MY MOTHER BEFORE MARRIAGE.

Monday, April 14, 1879—
If that would but secure my happiness,
Yet it was mild as is the Solar ray
In that soft season when the plastic hand of nature
Moulds for Amathea's horn her embrio fruits.
And scatters wild her flowers. Mine was the
Ardor of the mid day blaze, when on the torrid regions
Phoebus pours his fervid beams! And nature beams around
Here I have plucked the wild flower for her breast

[page 443]

LEAVE ST PAUL. REUNITED, AT LAST.

Monday, April 14, 1879—I spent the forenoon writing, intending to return to Madison by the night train, with Henrietta, who will go with me, so that once more she, I, and Lotie may be all together.

I have had a very pleasant visit here. I love Leo, for he is a true, noble, and good man, in every sense of the word. I love his children, Fannie and John, and I love my sister Nettie, who is still the same good, lovable, gentle and intelligent one she always was.

We were to leave by the 7 P.M. train, and as the time drew near, I dreaded to say good bye. My niece has twined herself closely round my heart, and it is hard to part, but it must be. Leo said we should probably never meet on earth again. He is 70 and very broken down. I told him if I outlive him, my home should be the home of his family—they should come to me. This seemed to please him very much.

Br. Leo went with us to the Depot, and on parting gave me a loving kiss, which I returned. After starting, our train continued along the bank of the Mississippi for many miles, through very beautiful scenery, the moon gilding the broad expanse of the noble river with its silvery light. Nettie and I retired to our sleeping berths, and in the morning found ourselves near Portage, where we took breakfast. Here we took another train to Madison, 39 miles distant. On our way down from St Paul, we cross the river at Hastings, to the west side, then down that side to LaCrosse, where we cross to the east side again.

April 15, 1879—We found all well at Madison, but Aunt Jennie and Loty away. So Nett & I went to see our cousin Alice, Uncle Charles' daughter, married to Mr. Palmer. The folks soon came home, and then, for the first time in thirty five years we three were all together again.

[page 444]

MADISON, AGAIN, THEN TO BARABOO TO SEE COZ. MARY.

Tuesday, April 15, 1879—Today cousin Napoleon B. Vanslyke returned from the White Sulphur Springs, Arkansas, where he has been for a month for the benefit of his health. He called to see me. We were very glad to meet again.

Wednesday, April 16, 1879—Visited Cousin Minnie (Mears) Hobbies, daughter of my Uncle James Mears and Lois Mears.

Thursday, April 17, 1879—Supped at Napoleon's and had a very pleasant evening. I like his wife, Anna, very much. She has a daughter, May, 18 years of age, a nice brunette, and a son James, about 16.

Thursday, April 17, 1879—Called to see Aunt Lois, widow of Uncle James. Rec^{d} a letter from Lois, informing me of ~~his~~ Lyman's call to a mission in England.[112] My sisters thought it was awful to take a man away from his business, for years, to preach in a foreign land without salary.

Friday, April 18, 1879—Went this afternoon to Baraboo, 36 miles, to see my cousin Mary (Poole) Stuart. Arrived at 7 P.M. found all well, with a family of five young men, sons, no daughters. Glad to meet again. Mary used to be a favorite of mine. She told me grandfather James Mears had a brother—Roswell, and a sister Lucy, who married Mr. Rockwell. She said James & Lois Mears were married in Rutland, Vt.

Mary's father John Hudson Poole, was son of John Hudson Poole Sen. Mary was born at Oriskany, N.Y.

Spent a very pleasant evening with Mary, whom I used to love very much. Her husband, Norman Stuart, is a fine looking man of 52. No religionist, but seems an honest hearted man.

Saturday, April 19, 1879—Left Baraboo at 8 A.M., reached Madison 9.38 A.M. Lotie was at the Depot, taking same train that I left, going home to Chicago. Found all well at Chicago. At 5 P.M. dined at Aunt Lois', with Aunt Jenny, Netty, Aunt Harriet & Cousin Flora, and spent a pleasant evening.

[page 445]

ARRIVE AT MILWAUKEE AUNT MARY MARTINEAU

April 19 & 20, 1879—Visited Nap [Napoleon]. Rowed on Fourth, or Monona Lake with Uncle Charles in his boat, rode with Nap around the city and out to the cemetery. Here I found the graves of grandfather and Grandmother Mears. The cemetery is beautifully located. An interesting part of it was that occupied by Confederate dead. Long rows of graves, all just of a length, of the rebel prisoners, struck me very forcibly. Poor fellows! They came a long way from their homes in Georgia, Alabama, and other states, to die here. In the evening took tea with Napoleon's family.

Monday, April 21, 1879—To day start for Chicago on my way home, leaving at 8.30 A.M. I took an affectionate farewell of Nettie & all my relatives, who all seemed to regret my departure very much. Before leaving, I blessed Nettie for her deafness, in the name of

112 See "General Conference," *Deseret News*, April 9, 1879; Utah Digital Newspapers.

Jesus. I pray she may be healed, as I told her she should be. It was very hard to part from her, my true, noble and loving sister.

I went via Milwaukee, (85 miles distant) fare 4.90 to Chicago, so as to see Aunt Mary Martineau. Napoleon went with me to the depot, and lent me $25.00 [$504] to come home with.

Arrived at Milwaukee 12.30, noon, and put up at the hotel. Did not find Aunt M. till about 5 P.M. She had sold her house to Mr. Kurtz, husband of my cousin Alice Abrahms, and now lives with them. She received me kindly, and told me many things relative to father and our family affairs. She told me grandfather Mears was born in Mass. He was son of John Mears, who was a Major in Washington's army.

Grandmother Mears was born in Lebanon, Connecticut, 20 miles from Norwich. Was married at 17 years of age, in Vermont.

[page 446]

MILWAUKEE

Monday, April 21, 1879—Simeon Mears, brother of grandfather, has the family records of the Mears family, and has been living in Chicago until lately, and may now be. Besides Simeon, there were Isaac, John & Joseph Mears. Grandfather James Mears served in the War of 1812 against the British. His father, John Mears, a Major in Washington's army in the French and indian War was taken prisoner at Oswego & sent to Quebec, thence in a French ship to France, but was retaken by an English Frigate and taken to England with others, arriving there literally naked and covered with vermin. He got a license to beg, and received £.5 from a lady "for his good looks.*

[written in margin]

**Arrived home after absence of 5 years and found his family had erected a grave stone for him, supposing him dead.*

Simeon Mears (who has the family bible) was son of Joseph Mears, my great uncle.

Aunt Mary gave me letters, drawings &c of fathers. Also a mat made by grandmother, a pin cushion of mother's, and her silver door plate with the family name "Martineau" upon it. She says I look and act like father and Uncle Peter. We talked and cried together. She tried hard to make me leave Utah,—she would help me with her property &c. I could not think of such a thing, of course. She tried to convert me from Mormonism, being a zealous Presbyterian. I slept and ate at the "Kirby House." I walked through the city, but all is so changed I can remember nothing but the bluffs and Lake Michigan. The city is full of fine residences, costing from $40.000 [$806,699] to $400.000 [$8,066,995] and is a very beautiful city.

Tuesday, April 22, 1879—Went to Forest Hill cemetery with Aunt M. in a carriage, which was quite a treat to her. We visited Uncle Peter's grave, which is, as yet, without any tombstone, but she hopes to have one before a year is gone by. Slept at the house to night.

Wednesday, April 23, 1879—Left at 1 P.M. arriving at Chicago at 4 P.M. 85 miles. Found all well. Talked until late with a Dr. Hobart, about Utah and the Mormons.

[page 447]

CHICAGO AGAIN. START HOME.

Thursday, April 24, 1879—Went down town with Lotie. Saw a fine lot of Italian Statuary, the pieces ranging from 100$ [$2,017] to $600 [$12,100] Each. Bought a military dictionary.

Friday, April 25, 1879—Wrote to friends, Uncle Charley, Nettie, Aunt Mary and Crocheron. Saw my old friend and flame Julia Buchanan—but how changed! Once beautiful now "fat, fair, and fifty five," and anything but neat and tidy. To day Lotie sat for her picture.

Saturday, April 26, 1879—Arranged about my furniture, then went with Lotie and Carrie to Lincoln Park, and rowed an hour on the lake.

Sunday, April 27, 1879—We all went and visited Julia Buchanan Grubb! returning in the evening.

Monday, April 28, 1879—Left at 10.30 A.M. on C.B. & Q. road for home. Lotie and Carrie went 30 minutes previous to a place 7 miles out to see a friend. We passed through without stopping, and I saw them waving their hands on the platform as they passed.

I found W. W. Riter, of S. L. City[113] on the train, going home. Crossed the Mississippi at dusk, at Burlington.

Tuesday, April 29, 1879—Arrived at Omaha 10 A.M. Got my pass from S. H. Clark, Supt. U.P.R.R.[114] and left Omaha 12.15 noon. Supped at Grand Island

Wednesday, April 30, 1879—Passed Sherman, elevation 8200 ft above the sea. The wind was very cold, and snow lay all around us. The grass had not yet started. Train stops to dine at Cheyenne, and sup at Rock Creek. Mr. S. Foster of San Francisco gave me his card, and wished me to call on him in that city

[page 448]

SALT LAKE CITY. PRES^T J. TAYLOR. HOME AGAIN.

Thursday, May 1, 1879—Awoke this morning in the Bitter Creek country. very cold, dreary and desolate country. Dine at Evanston, and reach Ogden at 6.15 P.M. As I could not go North from here until tomorrow, I went on to S. L. City, and found Eliza quite unwell, and father Chamberlin dead. Met G. W. Crocheron at the depot. He had sent word to me at Ogden to see him in S. L. City, in reference to a mining prospect.

Friday, May 2, 1879[115]—By appointment, met Pres^t John Taylor, Crocheron, and Mr. Corbitt [blank] at the Presidents house to talk about our mining prospect. He discouraged our doing anything with it just now.

Br. Taylor had me meet him in his office, to talk about my being sealed to some one—my father, for instance. He also took me in his carriage through the temple grounds. He wished me to stay until tomorrow, as he thought Supt. John Sharp wanted me on the Utah Southern R.R. to help locate the new road.

Saturday, May 3, 1879—Saw Br. Sharp, but he had procured assistance he needed on the road. He gave me a pass over U.C.R.R.

Sunday, May 4, 1879—Came home. My family hardly knew me because I had partially shaved. They were all well, for which, and for my safe return, I thank our Father in Heaven.

I have been able to do much good with my relations in removing prejudice in their minds, and in gathering much information relative to my progenitors, for whom I desire to do a work. As I have the stewardship of that blessing, even to be a restorer to our family, and to do a good work for the dead.

[page 449]

LYMAN'S CALL & SETTING APART. WATER WORKS.

May, 1879—I find that Lyman R. was called on his mission to Europe, on Monday April 7. 1879. He was set apart for his mission by Apostles F. D. Richards and Moses Thatcher on May 7th in S. L. City. Received his endowments on Thursday May 8. 1879, and started on his mission on Monday May 19. 1879.

While absent, several of the children were very sick with something like croup, but by the blessing of the Lord, through administration, they were all healed.

113 W. W. Riter was a wealthy, influential Salt Lake City businessman.

114 In 1877, S. H. Clark purchased the Utah Northern Railroad when it defaulted on bonds and interest due.

115 Martineau filed survey reports on this day ("Land Surveys," *Deseret News,* May 7, 1879; Utah Digital Newspapers).

PART

6

TRAVELS SEARCHING FOR A "CITY OF REFUGE," LOGAN TEMPLE DEDICATION

[page 449]

LYMAN'S CALL & SETTING APART. WATER WORKS.

May 1879—On April 7. A. O. Lamoreaux rented & moved into our other house.[1]

May 5, 1879—Went to S. L. City, to welcome D. H. Wells home from prison. Grand.

May 16, 1879—We had a party for Lyman this evening—girls & boys. All seemed to enjoy themselves very much.

May 8, 1879—By request of Mayor W. B. Preston we made an examination of ground, to locate Water Works for our city.

May 17 or 18 Bought span of horses $250.^{00}$ [$5,042]. Paid cash 200$ [$4,034].

May 9, 1879—To day I spent in leveling and surveying the line where we will lay the pipe. After this, the Mayor appointed Watermaster T. X. Smith and myself to take charge of the work. This we did, Br. Smith letting out the contracts for digging the pipe trenches. We continued thus about two weeks, but the work not being pushed as the Mayor desired, he told me on Saturday to

May 24, 1879—take sole charge of the work, releasing Br. Smith, who has much other business to attend to. Since that time I have been very busy, letting out jobs of excavation, filling, hauling iron pipe &c and paying men for their work. Our pipe (6^{in}) required a trench 4½ feet deep, 2 ft wide at top and 15 in. at bottom, for digging which, we paid 40¢ pr cubic yd. in hard cement gravel, 25¢ in sandy soil & 45¢ for [some]. The reservoir, 24 x 70 x 6 x to 12 feet in gravel, 35¢ pr cubic yd.

[page 450]

May 21, 1879—Paid E. Hansen[2] $71.00 [$1,432] in full of his a/c for help on my Survey Contract. Previous payment $11.50 [$232]

Settled with E. Curtis in full. Paid $5.^{50}$ [$111]

1 A. O. Lamoreaux was a farmer and carpenter in Logan (Ray Somers, *History of Logan* [Logan, UT: Somers Historic Press, 1993], 64).

2 Edward Hanson and Ed Holden were later instrumental in the construction of a power plant at the mouth of Logan Canyon (Somers, *History of Logan*, 259).

[written in margin]

Inserted in the wrong place. Should be on previous page.

Note When Lyman went on his mission the Bishop, B. M. Lewis gave him $48.00! [$968] Some others gave him something, and I gave him $161.00 [$3,247] cash for his journey, besides purchasing clothing &c.

Susan and I went with him as far as Ogden & stayed at the house of Br. F. D. Richards. It seemed hard to take leave of him, to be gone so long and so far away as England. Seth Langton[3] & Frank Benson[4] accompanied them as far as Omaha, going to the Southern states. Joseph Goddard[5] goes with him to England.

Lyman carries with him the good will of all the Saints, being universally respected by all.[6]

Wednesday, June 11, 1879—To day our chairs & crockery came from Chicago.[7]

Thursday, June 12, 1879—The freight was $74.76 [$1,508] + 45¢ = $75.21 All in good order. Mrs. Cranney has been helping Susan Sew for about 3 weeks, making up clothing &c.

I insert here a blessing given by Patriarch Joseph L. Heywood to my son Moroni:—

Hillsdale Iron Co. Jan. 30. 1879

A blessing by J. L. Heywood on the head of M. H. Martineau, son of Jas H. Martineau and Susan Ellen Johnson born at Parowan Iron Co. Utah Sept. 12. 1854

Br. M. H. I place my hands on thy head in the name of the Lord Jesus and by virtue of the authority which has been conferred upon me by the servants of the Lord seal upon thee a father's blessing.

3 Seth Langton settled Smithfield, Utah (Joel E. Ricks and Everett L. Cooley, eds., *The History of a Valley: Cache Valley, Utah-Idaho* [Logan, UT: Cache Valley Centennial Commission, 1956], 41–42).

4 This is likely F. G. Benson, a farmer, who resided in Logan (Somers, *History of Logan*, 57).

5 Joseph Goddard was the first telegraph operator (Donald G. Godfrey and Kenneth W. Godfrey, eds., *The Diaries of Charles Ora Card: The Utah Years, 1871–1886* [Provo, UT: Religious Studies Center, Brigham Young Univ., 2006], 93).

6 "Departing Missionaries," *Deseret News*, May 26, 1879; Utah Digital Newspapers

7 "Arrivals, Releases, Appointments," *Deseret News*, July 2, 1879; Utah Digital Newspapers.

[page 451]

MORONI'S BLESSING BY J L HEYWOOD

1879—Thou art a legal heir to the priesthood, I bless thee with all the blessings of Abraham, Isaac and Jacob that pertain to the elders of Israel in the dispensation of the fullness of times. Thou shalt be blessed with wives and children with all things needful for their comfort and convenience, and in all the labors of thy hands inasmuch as they are performed with an eye single to the Glory of God. Thou art of the blood of Israel and thine inheritance shall be upon the land of Zion in connection with thy father's house. I seal thee up unto eternal life with the blessing of eternal lives to come forth in the morning of the first ressurrection in the name of Jesus of Nazareth. Amen.

July 20, 1879—Up to this time I have been busy with the water-works. Last Sunday Susan and I went to Mendon. I was sent, with Prest G. L. Farrell, to preach to the High Priests. Also the 2d Sunday of June we went to Smithfield on the same mission. About the first of July I went to S. L. City on business, to see if I could obtain another Surveying Contract from Govr but I found no chance this season. I also called to see Crocheron, about the mine.

I have received several letters from Lyman. He is traveling in the Liverpool Conference. He feels well in his work, though he finds deep distress and poverty among the people; also much wickedness and degradation. Also hear from Moroni & Henry that they think of going to Arizona this fall, with Father and several of the family. Also heard from Elvira, who is now in Arizona. We sent her a box of goods & things by a brother Taylor, who is now on his way there.

[page 452]

WATER TURNED INTO LOGAN WATER WORKS. BREAK.

July 20, 1879—To day Br. Flamm, just returned from Switzerland brought me a letter from Lyman. Apostle Moses Thatcher said to day, he is called to a mission to Mexico, to open that country to the Gospel.

July 24, 1879—Our Logan Choir to day gave a Concert in the Tabernacle, to a good house. We realized over $117.[00] [$2,360] which is to go towards buying a good organ for the building.

Sunday, August 3, 1879—To day Pres[t] Thatcher appointed me to take the initiative in organizing rifle clubs throughout the County. It is hoped they will exert a good moral effect upon our enemies.

Br. W. H. Wright and wife, of Ogden took dinner with us. They are old friends.

Monday, August 4, 1879—Began today, to get up a rifle club in Logan. Had very good success in obtaining names.

Thursday, August 28, 1879—To day turned water into the tank by Mayor Preston's wish, though the bottom is not yet quite ready, nor the sluice gates in, only temporary ones. Telegraphed to paper.

Friday, August 29, 1879—At 11 A.M. turned water into pipes at tank, and tried the hose on the fire hydrants. All worked well.

August 31, 1879—Sunday at 10 A.M. I was notified the tank was leaking. Went up and found water had gone down somewhere, and burst out below, filling the Logan & Hyde Park canal and bursting its banks. Before the water of the canal could be stopped at the head, two great breaks washed in the banks, and the ground below flooded. I quickly turned off the water from coming into the tank, and tried to find out where the leak was, finally succeeding. It was somewhat discouraging, at the end of so long a labor, but the fault was not mine.

[page 453]

August 31, 1879— Pres[t] John Taylor and several of the Twelve were here and held a very good meeting. Geo Q. Cannon, just released from prison by habeas corpus, was also here. Pres[t] Taylor said "it is no wonder if the toes of Nebuchadnezzar's image kick us now and then, when they are smote by the stone cut out without hands. They naturally would kick back."

I asked Pres[t] Taylor if my children, born after being sealed by Apostle Geo. A. Smith in Parowan, but not in the Endowment house or temple, must be sealed or adopted to me in the Temple, as our first sealing was only to answer until a temple can be built. We were sealed by Geo. A. Smith, May 13, 1852, I believe. The date is in the first part of this record. Br. Taylor said they should be adopted to us.

Wednesday, September 3, 1879—Surveyed some for D. Stoddard, Wellsville[8]

September 5, 1879—Surveyed some for Thatcher estate, Logan

September 16, 1879—Surveyed canal for Providence and Millville people, one canal, being about 9 miles

September 17, 1879—Surveyed canal about 7 miles

September 18, 1879—Surveyed another canal of about 5 miles. After dinner, my chainmen suddenly shouted "Bears! Bears!" and started after two cubs about 5 mo. old. The boys had no weapons, but the sportman's instinct naturally led them on. Being very hot and tired, I lay still waiting for the boys to come back. Hearing a noise after about half an hour, I saw one of the bears pursued by two of the boys, making directly for me. This roused me. I seized a small willow and attacked Bruin, who never minded my blows at all, but made for a stockyard in the edge of Millville, we in full pursuit. A woman seeing the fracas, joined in pursuit with a pitchfork and rendered valuable assistance in Bruin's capture, which we finally effected after a serious struggle.

[page 454]

CAPTURE TWO BEARS. FAIR. MAJ. POWELL'S WORKS REC[D]

September 18, 1879—We got a rope round his neck, and heard a shout from the other fellow who had the other bear in hand, but was nearly exhausted by the struggle. We hurried there and finally secured him, also. They were of the grizzly kind, and very savage—bit and scratched furiously. The boys conducted them home in triumph. It was quite an exciting episode.

September 14, 1879—To day I was sent to Franklin with J. A. Leishman to preach to the High Priests. Susan and Mrs. Leishman had a good time, and came home next day. I have been sent every month, but one, since I came home from the east, to preach to

8 David Stoddard was among the first settlers of Wellsville (Ricks and Cooley, *History of a Valley*, 38).

the High Priests. I have always felt well, and enjoyed a good spirit in doing so.

September 30, 1879—To night Moroni arrived from his home in Iron County—some 360 miles away, about 10 P.M. but did not Come in the house till next morning, to surprise us. He has been gone three years, and we were very glad to see him again. He left all well at home. Henry & he think of moving to Arizona this fall.

Friday, October 3, 1879—To day Charley, Jesse and Albert went to S. L. city to see the fair and Conference.

[written in margin]

Note ~~

I forgot to note our Cache County Fair, which came off on the 23. 24, & 25th September. It was a very fine display. I drew a diploma for Best Topographical Maps, and also for best plan for 50 ft span wooden bridge

Also received a communication from Dept. of the Interior, relative to my views in connexion with proposed changes in land, timber and mineral laws and regulations.

Also received Govt reports from Maj. Powell's exploring & geological expeditions.

[page 455]

SURVEY AT EAGLE ROCK, IDAHO. BLESSING BY JOHN SMITH

October 1879—Went to Eagle Rock, Idaho,[9] to survey for the "Idaho Snake river Gold Mining Company." Left Log [Logan] at 11 P.M. arriving at Snake river (Eagle Rock) at 9 A.M. next day. Surveyed a gold placer claim 246 feet wide and 13000 feet long, along the north bank of the Snake river.

I returned home the 17th, traveling by the Utah & Northern R.R.

October 5, 1879—Went to Conference, S. L. City. Found E. & family well. While in Salt Lake City I received the following blessing, by Patriarch John Smith, given Oct. 8, 1879.

Brother James, as thou desirest it, I place my hands upon thy head to pronounce and seal a blessing upon thee, as the Spirit shall indite. Thou art of the house of Israel and have yielded obedience to the gospel with an honest heart, notwithstanding thy pathway hath been fraught with trials and ~~afflictions~~ difficulties, the Lord hath been mindful of thee from thy birth. He hath given thine angels charge concerning thee, who hath watched over thee in the past, delivered thee from among thine enemies, and preserved thy life, that you might perform a mission on the earth which would exalt thee among the fathers in Israel, and give unto thee an inheritance among the Saints. Reflect upon the past, and thou shalt realize that the hand of the Lord hath been over thee for good. Look forward to the future and thou shalt comprehend the blessings which it is the will of the Lord to bestow upon thee, that you may secure unto thyself the blessing of eternal life. Thou art of the lineage of Ephraim, and entitled to the blessings of Abraham, Isaac and Jacob, with the gift of the priesthood. Therefore slacken not in thine endeavors to do good, and the blessings of the Lord shall attend thee, give thee peace of mind, strength of body, and make thee equal unto every task; for thy guardian angel shall not ~~not~~ forsake thee, but will whisper in thine ear, warn thee of danger, give thee strength in time of trial, and power over evil and unclean spirits, and if necessary in the future as in the past thou shalt prophesy. Thou shalt also have power over the Adversary and banish him from thy habitations, that health and peace may reign wheresoever thou shalt dwell. For the God of Israel has heard thy petition.

[page 456]

BLESSING BY JOHN SMITH.

October 8, 1879—He knows the secrets of thy heart, and is pleased with thine integrity. Thy days and years shall be prolonged until thou art satisfied. Thy name shall be handed down with thy posterity from generation to generation, and had in honorable remembrance among the Saints. It is thy right, through the priesthood which you bear, to sit in council with thy brethren. It is also thy duty to exhort the saints to faithfulness, and assist in gathering scattered Israel, do a work for many of thy kindred who are now in darkness, who are numbered with the honest in heart among the living and the dead, and also to be a savior of thy father's house. Be guided continually by the prompting of the Monitor within thee, and thou shalt

9 Eagle Rock, Idaho, is today Idaho Falls.

have power over thine enemies. The Spirit of the Lord shall direct thy course, and thy mind shall be opened, and thou shalt comprehend things past, present, and to come, and it shall be well with thee, temporally and spiritually, both here and hereafter. Therefore be at rest in thy mind, and look forward to the future with pleasure. This, with all thy former blessings and promises which have been conferred upon thee heretofore by any of the Servants of God, I seal upon thee in the name of Jesus Christ and by virtue and authority of the holy priesthood, and I seal thee up unto Eternal life, with power to come forth in the morning of the first ressurrection, with many of thy friends and kindred, even so. Amen. (J. H. M. scribe)

This blessing gives me much pleasure and Comfort, and strengthens me in striving to do good. I hope I may be faithful to the end, and have power and influence with my family for good; that they may all be true and faithful, also

October 23, 1879—Went to Mendon, and Surveyed for I. Sorenson[10] and J. Lemon. Preached in the evening, and felt well. On the second Sunday of this month I was sent, with J. A. Leishman, to Lewiston, to preach to the High Priests, which I did, and was much blessed of the Lord. I take a delight in exhorting, in my weak way, the Saints in places where I go.

[page 457]

October 23, 1879—I know there is nothing outside of Mormonism, that is worth thinking of, much less practicing.

October 27, 1879—Went to Wellsville to survey a long irrigation canal. Spent five days on this work, laying out a canal 14½ miles long, with a fall of 5.3 ft pr mile. Came home in time to attend our usual Quarterly Conference, and to assist at a Concert given by the Logan Choir. The Conference was a very good one, and the Spirit of the Lord was with us. Br. O. Pratt gave a very grand description of the New Jerusalem (Zion), its temple, and about our stewardship and inheritances. Bp. L. D. Hardy,[11] 1st Counsellor to Presiding Bp. Edd Hunter, and Br. C. W. Penrose dined with us; also Bp. H. Hughes of Mendon.

Monday, November 3, 1879—Began to day to level a large Canal from the Logan river northward, along the foot of the mountains. It will be expensive work, costing many thousand dollars per mile.[12] I spent three days in making a commencement,—two miles—

November 6, 1879—Went to Wellsville to locate another canal from Little Bear river, for Williamson[13] and others, coming home on Saturday, in a cold snow storm—the first, this year. I brought with me Miss Emma Lindley—a hired girl to help Susan.

Received a letter from John C. Anderson, of Eagle Rock, Idaho,[14] who wishes me to do the engineering of a large Canal to issue from Snake river, about 25 miles above the bridge. He agrees to my terms, $200.00 [$4,034] pr month and board.

November 11, 1879—Left Logan with Jesse at 11 P.M. on U.&N. R.R. Got to Eagle Rock next morning, the 12th and started in wagons, with Br. M. D. Hammond, the contractor, to go up the river. Weather very cold. Camped in a vacant house of Jas Marker's.

Thursday, November 13, 1879—This morning went to place for canal, and camped on the bank of Snake river, in a grove of Cottonwoods and tall willows. Our tent contains besides Jesse & I, a Mr. King, my assistant and Mr. E. T. Gleason, my cook.

10 Isaac Sorensen (note spelling) was among the original settlers of Mendon, Utah. He served a mission in Denmark after which he worked on the temple earning $3–4 ($61–82) per day to pay off his debts (Somers, *History of Logan*, 33–34; Ross F. Peterson, *A History of Cache County* [Salt Lake City: Utah State Historical Society, 1997], 117).

11 Leonard W. Hardy was first counselor to the Presiding Bishop Edward Hunter (Daniel H. Ludlow, ed., *Encyclopedia of Mormonism* [New York: Macmillan, 1992], 4:1638).

12 "Cache Valley Canals," *Deseret News*, November 2, 1879; Utah Digital Newspapers.

13 This is likely James Williamson, who was a road supervisor from Wellsville, Utah (Ricks and Cooley, *History of a Valley*, 92).

14 John C. Anderson and his brother Robert Anderson operated a general store in Eagle Rock, which grew to become the Anderson Brothers Banking Company (Utah State University Libraries: Manuscripts, "John C. Anderson Diary [1866]"; Glen Barrett, *Mackinaws Down the Missouri* [Logan, UT: Utah State Univ. Press, 1973]).

[page 458]

SNAKE RIVER CANAL. CAMP ON RIVER

November 13, 1879—We have a small sheet iron stove, and necessary cooking utensils. In the afternoon, began leveling for head of Canal. This will be a large and costly one, many miles long, and heavy work for a mile and a half.

November 14, 1879—Snowed to day. Very cold.

November 15, 1879—Leveled and looked out a route.

November 16, 1879—Snowed. Very cold

November 17, 1879—Altered line of Canal, from 20 feet wide in bottom to ten feet wide

December 3, 1879—Went down to Eagle Rock. Got letters from home & Elvira

Sunday, December 7, 1879—Snowed all day, and next day, 8th

Sunday, December 14, 1879—Snowing many days. Have been very sick for about a week, with burning fever & constipation, and finally turning to a bad flux. Got Jesse to administer to me, after which I began to get better.

Sunday, December 21, 1879—Terribly blustery and Snowy. Bruce killed 4 deer to day close to camp. Still troubled with piles[15] and want of appetite.

Thursday, December 25, 1879—This morning a herd of nine deer passed close by our camp. Bruce and I ran out to get a shot, but did not kill any, they being on the run. Bruce froze one of his fingers while we were out—only about 15 minutes. Thermometer about 30° below zero. At dusk we saw a herd of 20 Elk across the river. Intensely cold. The steam from the river forms a vast Cloud hovering above it, while the ice goes crushing and grinding down the river very swiftly. The river is about 600 feet wide and 20 deep. When full it is here about 1500 feet wide—in other places where it does not run so fast, nearly half a mile wide.

December 26, 1879—Last night mercury froze in thermometer. Today the men killed 9 elk and 5 deer.

December 30, 1879—Went to Eagle Rock and sent Jesse home. Also sent home a hind quarter of elk.

December 31, 1879—Came back to camp.

15 Piles are hemorrhoids.

[page 459]

January 1, 1880—Worked all day. Next day made me a bed tick and filled it with hay.

January 3, 1880—Wrote letters to Lyman and Elvira.

January 6, 1880—Started home. Was called on by Bankers in Ogden to pay a note of $100.$\underline{^{00}}$ [$2,088] which I endorsed for A. C. Brown last summer. Arrived at Logan 7th.

Thursday, January 8, 1880—Went to Ogden, and got Brown to settle his note himself, instead of myself. He seemed sorry that I had taken so long a journey—some 480 miles going and returning,—in the winter, on account of his negligence.

January 9, 1880—Went to S. L. City. Found all well as usual.

January 13, 1880—Returned home yesterday. Today began survey of Logan & Smithfield canal,[16] with E. Hanson and Jesse assistants. Continued to Jan. 22^{d}. Weather cold, Snow deep, and work along the rocky cliffs and precipices very dangerous. Several times nearly lost my life, by almost falling down the precipices, where I should have been dashed to pieces. But God preserved me.

Saturday, January 24, 1880—Started again for Eagle Rock, alone. Have left Jesse going to school, with Charly, Nephi, and others.

January 29, 1880—Broke up my housekeeping, having discharged King, and there being only Gleason and I. I board at Hammond's camp, still sleeping in my tent and using it for an office.

February 3, 1880—Sent letters to Susan, Henry, Lyman, Lotie, & Anderson.

Monday, February 9, 1880—Began building crib for head gate. The cribs are 20 feet square, built of heavy Red pine logs, notched and pinned at corners, and tied at centers with logs dove-tailed and pinned. The Cribs are to be filled with rock.

16 The various canyon creeks and the four river systems of Cache Valley were appropriated for irrigation. Delivering water to the expanding settlements was a challenging task. The Logan and Smithfield Canal was one of the 118 cooperative canal systems in Cache Valley by 1900 (Ricks and Cooley, *History of a Valley*, 148–50, 208–10; see also Ricks and Cooley, *History of a Valley*, "Major Irrigation Canals Constructed in Cache Valley, 1856–1956," map inside back cover).

February 15, 1880—It has been snowing every day for a week. To day I shaved myself—the first time in over 20 years.

February 21, 1880—Rec^d^ letters from home. Next day sent ¼ beef home, with letters.

[page 460]

PRES^T^ JOHN TAYLOR BLESSES ME.

March 1, 1880—Went to Logan on Friday Feb. 27, 3^d^ Went to S. L. City, home 7th.

March 10, 1880—Surveyed at Mendon for J. Lemmon and others, 11th cold.

March 9, 1880—Laid out alterations of Logan Mill race, for Garff & L.

March 15, 1880—Attended a grand party at Ormsby's with Susan.

March 19, 1880—Gave a party and supper to about 30 persons.

March 22, 1880—Started to Eagle Rock to day. After having made a Survey for C. W. Card in West field. Snow still quite deep.

March 23, 1880—Arrived at camp.

April 1, 1880—Began building wall in side of cribs, with cement.

April 4, 1880—Started home and to Conference in S. L. City

April 17, 1880—Called to S. L. City to Survey mining claims of Crocheron.

April 18, 1880—Went to S. L. City.

April 20 & 21, 1880—Surveyed Mining Claims up city Creek for self, G. W. Crocheron, and three others. An assay shows value of ore to be $131.26 [$2,740] pr ton, Silver.

April 22, 1880—Called to see Mrs. James Russell who has a fine crystal.

Monday, April 26, 1880—I Asked Pres^t^ Taylor to bless me. I desired that I may not be conquered by advancing years, but that my bodily and mental health and strength may be preserved, also my eyesight and hearing, and other bodily powers; so that I may be able to do much work for the Kingdom of God in the future; for I feel that there is a great work for me to do yet. Pres^t^ Taylor called in Apostles Rich and Richards, and gave me a good blessing,[17] for which I thank My Father—the giver of all good gifts and blessings.

Recorded two mining claims—the "Rising Sun" and "Sherman," in Hot Springs Mining District.

April 27, 1880—Came home.

April 29, 1880—Surveyed for John Irvine,[18] at Logan.

Went to Red Rock, with Pres^t^ S. Dillon & U.P.R.R. officials by invitation of J. Blickensderfer Chf. Eng.

Sunday, May 9, 1880—Snowed hard to day.

May 10, 1880—Surveyed for G. L. Farrell, & next day at Mendon

May 12, 1880—Got home

May 13, 1880—Started at 11 P.M. with Jesse to go to Market Lake, Idaho.

[page 461]

RUN INTO TEAM AND SCRAPERS ON R.R.

1880—The Union Pacific R.R. officials desired me to go there to see what can be done to preserve the U.&N.R.R. track from the waters of Snake river, which overflows the country for about ten miles along the track. Different Union Pacific engineers differed in their plans, and Supt. J. T. Clark desired me to go and settle the matter,—see what should be done, and do it.

May 14, 1880—Arrived at Market Lake[19] at 10 A.M. in a heavy driving Snow Storm. There is but one house here—the section house, and poor accommodations.

Sunday, May 16, 1880—Went to Logan to see Supt. G. W. Thatcher[20]

17 It is interesting to note that Martineau dutifully transcribes, in beautiful penmanship, the many blessings given upon the heads of himself and his family, but he did not record this one. Martineau was fifty-two and was apparently beginning to feel his age.

18 John Irvine was a farmer who was active in opposition politics (Somers, *History of Logan*, 62; A. J. Simmonds, *The Gentile Comes to Cache Valley: A Study of Logan Apostates of 1874 and the Establishment of Non-Mormon Churches in Cache Valley, 1873–1913* [Logan, UT: Utah State Univ. Press, 1976], 28).

19 Market Lake, Idaho, was just outside of Idaho Falls. Today it is Roberts, Idaho.

20 George W. Thatcher was the brother of Apostle Moses Thatcher. George was part of the Thatcher Brothers business

May 17, 1880—Returned 18th at camp.

May 21, 1880—Went to Logan on business.

May 24, 1800—Started back to Market Lake. Have 43 teams and Scrapers at work building levee to keep Snake river away from the R.R. track.

May 28, 1880—Supt. Thatcher and U.P. Director Ames visited the levee and seemed satisfied with the work.

I forgot to say that in March last I was again appointed Notary Public, by the new Governor, my former appointment having expired.[21]

June 9, 1880—Narrowly escaped death. I ran into a span of horses with scraper, on the R.R. track. I was in front of hand car, traveling about 16 miles pr hour, and we thought the team would get out of the way before we got to it, but we got there too quickly. There was a regular melee—horses struggling and kicking, and we all in a pile. How I got out of the scrape I don't know, but I did. I do know, however, that it was only by the hand of God that my life was preserved, and to Him be all praise.

June 17, 1880—Return to Logan and back again next day.

June 24, 1880—Finished work at Market Lake, having built two miles of levee from 2 to 15 feet high and from 6 to 10 feet wide on top—25 to 60 feet wide at bottom.

[page 462]

FINISH AT MARKET LAKE. BREAK. GO TO CANAL.

June 24, 1880—Also nearly six miles of widening the R.R. track so it would stand the river; and filled up Some eleven bridges. Also riprapped[22] about 1000 feet of embankment. The whole work comes to some $5000. [$104,387] (and over) The river is now very high, and a solid sheet of water lies against the levee, from 2 to 10 feet deep.

At six P.M. all being well, we started to go to the Canal. Arrived at Eagle Rock at 7 P.M. and in a few minutes the engine of the work train came tearing up, bringing word that the levee had broken, and the water had carried away one of the R.R. bridges.

Jesse & I got on the engine and hurried back,—went to the bridge in question, where a furious torrent was passing through. The R.R. hands worked all night, with the train hauling rock which we thru in to preserve the ends of the embankment from washing away. Next day another train with hands arrived from the north, so there was about 100 men at work fixing up things. At night Jesse and I again left, and went to Eagle Rock, and thence on 26th to the Camp on Canal.

July 1, 1880—Started home, leaving Jesse to see to things.

July 2, 1880—Went to S. L. City with Nephi, leaving Susan and Charles to come next day. Eddie was quite unwell.

July 4, 1880—Witnessed the Gentile celebration of the 4th L. D. Saints did not join in with them. Until we can celebrate like other citizens of the U.S. we do not feel like doing anything. As a sample of gentile-ism—in the procession, just behind the orator of the day and other U.S. officials, came a carriage with noted prostitutes in it—there by favor of their particular friends, the U.S. officials above referred to. A nice spectacle! If it had been the Mormons' what a howl of virtuous indignation would have sounded through the land!

[page 463]

JULY 4TH CELEBRATION.

July 7, 1880—We returned home, and found all well.

I find the following lines, composed by me some time ago:—

IN GOD DO WE TRUST.

In God do we trust
Tho' creatures of dust.
He hath sustained us in days that are past—
Great is His love and His goodness how vast
Saving us always from hate's deadly blast
In Him do we trust

---

operations in Cache Valley (Ricks and Cooley, *History of Cache Valley*, 190; Somers, *History of Logan*, 70, 83).

21 "Notaries Public," *Deseret News*, February 25, 1880; Utah Digital Newspapers.

22 This term refers to creating a foundation or wall using broken stones. For information on the levees, see "Correspondence from the North, Market Lake," *Deseret News*, June 23, 1880; Utah Digital Newspapers.

Tho' creatures of dust.

The wicked in pride
May rage and may chide
Fight against Zion, in wickedness bold
Plunder and slay as ~~in days of old~~ prophets foretold—
*The ending will be as the prophets have told: [written in margin]
Purging from evil like refining of gold
Tho' foes may assail
The truth will prevail.

The Kingdom of God
Shall spread all abroad;
Hunters and fishers shall search the world o'er
Gath'ring the honest from each foreign shore:—
Zion will be the down-trodden no more,
But triumph again
And evermore reign.

And Zion shall shine
With splendor divine
Enlivening Earth with its glorious ray—
Chasing the shadows of darkness away—
Ushering in the Millennial day,
To end nevermore
Till Time shall be o'er.

[page 464]

July 10, 1880—Went to Brigham City to level for a R.R. tank.

July 12, 1880—Attended meeting of City Council, after which started at 10.30 P.M. for my canal work near Eagle Rock, Idaho, arriving there 9 A.M. next day.

Friday, July 17, 1880—Came home, found all well

August 28, 1880—Went back to Eagle Rock—146 miles. Took Jesse.

September 5, 1880—Came home on business. Found all well.

September 13, 1880—Went back.

September 24, 1880—Finished 1st Section of Canal, moved to the Forks. Another canal.

October 14, 1880—A telegram from Susan, saying James Edward is very dangerously sick with erysipelas.[23] He was taken ill Wed. Oct. 6th 1880 with great pain in his ancle [ankle], and inflammation. Constant care and medicines were given, but he continued to grow worse constantly, and teased for me to come home. He said I had been gone long enough, and wanted me to come home and pray for him.

I took the freight train at 9 A.M. and got home about 10 P.M. Found him very bad indeed,—in great pain, his ancle and leg swollen very much indeed. His mother and I sat up with him all night,—as she had done from the first. I found that Charles had been very attentive and kind all the time, and had quit work in the Utah & Northern R.R. machine shop to help her.

Friday, October 15, 1880—No better. Suffers great pain.

Saturday, October 16, 1880—Worse. To day he saw Nephi come with a load of potatoes. He wished to be carried so he could see him at the window. When he saw Nephi, whom he loved very much, he smiled and said "Hello" so sweetly.

[page 465]

He had a little bag of dimes and nickels—some 90¢, given him by various ones. These he asked for, looked at, then turned away his head and said "When I get well I'm do'in to dive [give] them to the Temple."[24] These were almost his last words. As the disease progressed upward, he suffered greatly in his body and head. He was in dreadful pain, screaming for long times at once. Praying for him would alleviate for the time, but had no power to cure him. The night was so distressing to him, his mother finally could not bear it any longer, and at about 5 A.M. prayed the Lord if he was not to be healed—to take him from his pain. He then sank into a peaceful sleep, never waking. He died at 5.15 A.M. Sunday Oct. 17, 1880. His last breath passed so softly none knew when it ceased until he was gone. Charles was the first to discover it, Susan sitting by overcome with so many days and nights of watching.

23 James Edward was Martineau's eleventh child with Susan Ellen Johnson Martineau. He was born in 1877 and passed away in 1880. Erysipelas is related to streptococcus.

24 Children were invited to contribute to the building of the Logan Temple by saving and donating their nickels. This is what the Martineau boys were doing with their "bag of dimes."

He was a very beautiful child, with large & very beautiful, mild and expressive eyes; and of a very noble, intelligent spirit, and a most lovely disposition. I feel satisfied from some circumstances that took place before, that he staid his time on earth. We had the elders frequently, and exerted great faith for him. But as he could not live, he died in the Lord, to rise in the dawn of the ressurrection, and to be with the first to welcome us when we come. "The Lord gave, hath taken away, and blessed be His name forever, for all His ways are just and righteous.

We had the earnest sympathy of many dear friends; among the first were Br. & Sister Moses Thatcher, Sisters Benson and Farr. They and others did all that true friendship could prompt.

[page 466]

EDDIE'S BURIAL. MOVE JOHN WILLIAM

October 17, 1880—The funeral was at our house. Apostle Thatcher, President W. B. Preston, Dr. Ormsby, Councillor Holt, Patriarch Joel Ricks and others spoke, and the Logan choir sung. He was buried next my wife Susan J. on Monday Oct. 18th 1880 at P.M.

October 19, 1880—To day myself, Susan, Nephi and Jesse and Anna went to the old burying ground and took up John W. who has now been buried 17 years. We found the coffin pretty good, and opened it. His mother knew him at once, and said "That is my little boy."

His hair was unchanged in appearance. We laid him beside James Edward.

October 20, 1880—Went to Salt Lake City with my chain and Solar compass, per instructions from Washington, to have them tested by the government standard. Arrived 8.20 P.M. and found E. and family well.

October 22, 1880—Went on Arsenal Hill[25] with several U.S. deputies and tested our instruments. I found my chain 3 in. too long; my solar was in good adjustment, but the reading of the needle was. Var. 17°E., while, by the Meridian established by the U.S. Coast Survey, it is 16° 32', difference 28' excess of true reading. The other other instruments—transits—all varied. Got my Chain shortened to 66.06 feet, the U.S. Standard.

Saturday, October 23, 1880—Came home. While in S.L. City, saw Mrs. S. J. Russell, who lold [told] me various things.

Before I went to S. L. City, sitting after breakfast with Susan, she saw many things. She said,—

"I see people—women, mostly—coming on foot from the east—hurriedly, with little bundles & I see over their heads an angel going towards the East, to the states. It is an angel of peace. Oh! they won't receive it.

[page 467]

SUSAN'S VISION. SHOT AT

It comes back, sorrowfully. I see soldiers and indians—the soldiers fall before them. I see many of our people rising up, like flocks of birds, and going Southward—southeast—They go a few at a time—their removal makes no excitement or notice of those who remain. It is the true saints who go. I see a temple in a far country being built. It is not now begun. I see the towers rising up. It is in a country of old ruins, and seems a tropical land. I think you will go there." This is in short the substance of what she saw, looking in my cup, the leaves of which seemed to move about and to become magnified as to numbers—one leaf appearing many.

I think it is a true picture of what will soon come to pass. It agrees very much with what Mrs. R. told me some months ago.

Monday, October 25, 1880—Went to Eagle Rock. Next morning saw Mr. Carter [finishes in next entry]

October 26, 1880—who wishes me to Survey two townships for him. Laid out canal work for Geo. Heath.

October 28, 1880—Came to the house at noon for dinner, and I found two "cow boys" at Anderson's store, shooting around and threatening peoples lives. These "Cow boys' are cattle herders, and are desperadoes. They have for months terrorized all this section of country. While I was at a window of Anderson's house, shaving, one of them saw me and shot at me, the ball coming through the glass just over my head.

25 Arsenal Hill was a popular shooting range in Salt Lake City (Linda Sillitoe, *Welcoming the World: A History of Salt Lake County* [Salt Lake City: Salt Lake County, 1996], 77).

I did not see him till he fired. I therefore moved my glass from the window and finished shaving. The fellow showed another the hole he had made and said "I'd have killed the G—d d—d Son of a b—h shaving up there if I'd had my own pistol," They continued shooting till almost 2-30 P.M. when two or [. . .] men started for them with guns.

[page 468]

October 28, 1880—In the fight following, both desperadoes were killed. I saw them killed, but had no hand in it. Many shots were fired—about 40 in all. Many had narrow escapes from stray bullets. The verdict of the coroner's jury was—justifiable homicide," which met public sentiment fully.[26] I thank the Lord for preserving my life, and pray I may be able to spend it in doing good.

October 29, 1880—Returned to Logan.

On Sunday Oct. 3. 1880 I wrote the following lines to Susan:—

TO MY LOVED AND LOVING WIFE.

Oh, wife of my bosom, how blest was the hour
When, youthful, we yielded to Love's gentle power;
But of seasons since then—Oh! how many have sped!
How memory turns to the scenes that are fled!

I think of the trials through which we have passed—
Together we shivered in Sorrow's keen blast—
In storm or in sunshine together have trod—
Together rejoiced in the goodness of God.

Oh, thankful I am, that our Father above
Gave your heart to my trust—that He gave me your love:–
That me you have loved, in my weakness and pride—
That me you still love, and still cling to my side.
No, not to my side—enshrined in my heart—
Forever thy haven—thence ne'er to depart.
And joyous or grieving—exalted or low
Unchanging forever, in weal or in woe.

[page 469]

BIRTHS OF HENRY'S, MORONI'S & ELVIRA'S CHILDREN &C

October 1880—
Unchanging, I said—ah, there I was wrong:
Forever and ever, as time rolls along
Our love shall increase, and grow perfect and pure,
While ~~eternity lasts~~, ~~and the heavens or we shall~~
heaven shall last our being endure.
James

Camp on Willow Creek, Oneida County Idaho, Oct. 3^{d}. 1880.

October 31, 1880—Attended meeting. Have a bad cold.

November 2, 1880—Elections for Delegate to Congress. Voted for G. Q. Cannon with Susan. Paid school tax $27.00 [$564]

Wednesday, November 3, 1880—Attended City Council.

November 7, 1880—Paid D. James $100.00 [$2,088] on water pipe account, and arranged for hot water pipes, bath &c. to the amount of $100. more

November 9, 1880—Went to Franklin to Subdivide land for Holland.[27]

November 13, 1880—Finished, and came home. Cold, snowy & stormy.

November 15, 1880—Surveyed extension of canal leading to water tank.

Received letter from Moroni. He says he was married Dec. 17. 1879 by J. D. T. McAllister, in the St. George temple. His wife's name was Sarah S. Johnson, daughter of Sixtus Johnson. my wife's brother. She was born April 13. 1863, at Virgin City Kane Co. Utah

26 "The Eagle Rock Shooting," *Deseret News*, November 10, 1880; Utah Digital Newspapers.

27 Three Hollands lived in Logan. James Holland was a railroad clerk. Jonathan and Thomas Holland were laborers (Somers, *History of Logan*, 62).

Henry's wife Melissa Editha Johnson, was born May 16. 1859, at Fort Johnson, Iron Co, Utah.

Their son, Charles Henry, was born Jan. 27. 1876 at Hillsdale, Iron Co.

Daughter, Susan Edith, born Nov. 16. 1878 at Hillsdale, died May 28. 1880, at St John, Apache Co. Arizona

Daughter, Bertha Mandana, born May 7th 1880, at St. John, Apache Co. Arizona

B. S. and Elvira Johnson's girl was born at Lone Pine, Apache Co, Arizona, Sept. 22, 1880.

A son of Moroni & Sarah, born at St John, Ari. Oct. 17. 1880

[page 470]

NEW CONTRACT FOR U.S. SURVEY. — CONTRACT NO 100.

Thursday, November 18, 1880—Met Mr. Carter, and arranged to Survey 2 townships for him.

Friday, November 19, 1880—Went to S. L. City, to make arrangements for the survey, and get contract to do the work. The amount deposited to make the survey is $2095.00 [$43,738]

November 22, 1880—Filed my bonds—$4040.00 [$84,344] W. Jennings & L. S. Hills my bondsmen. The work is T.10N.R.43 & T.14N.R.4E. also part of 3d Standard Parcl N.

Also recd telegram from J. W. Young to go to him on Atlantic & Pacific R.R. in New Mexico.

November 25, 1880—Returned to Logan. Found all well.

November 26, 1880—Sent for Galvanic belt.[28]

November 28, 1880—Was today elected Prest of the Cach [Cache] Co. Branch of American Bible Society, R. S. Watson LDS Vice Prest Wm Goodwin Treas & Rev. Dr. Park Sec.[29]

Also sent T. C. Bailey 2 Cer. of Deposit $380. [$7,933]

Also bought new stove for parlor $29.00 [$605]

Wednesday, December 1, 1880—City Council met. Recd telegram that my contract for U.S. Survey was approved.

December 6, 1880—Settled with Logan City. My credit is $70.15 [$1,465]

December 11, 1880—Recd letter from Elvira, & wrote to J. Blickensderfer

Paid Co. taxes $32.72 [$683]; Total taxes for year $76.00 [$1,588]

December 20, 1880—Went to Eagle Rock, to see about canal &c

December 24, 1880—Returned home. Paid $225.00 [$4,697] for 300 bu wheat. Made arrangements for new Bay window—

March 19, 1881—My former contract for U.S. Survey having been cancelled, to allow an addition, a new one, No 100, was approved to day, amounting to $3980. [$80,104] (about) This includes the survey of four townships and 24 miles of 3d Standard Parallel and Guide Meridian.

During the past winter I had a bay window put in, also a chimney, grate and mantel in the parlor, which was refurnished with a new velvet carpet, chandelier &c amounting to over $250. [$5,038]

[page 471]

WE GO TO KANAB.

April 12, 1881—To day Susan and I, with Jesse N. and Anna started to go to Iron County to do some surveying. Susan and Anna will go to Kanab and Johnson to see her father and other relatives.

April 20, 1881—After staying in S. L. City 8 days, we start south by Utah Southern this morning at 7 A.M. Dined at Juab, and took the Utah Southern Extension, passing down the Sevier river and through the Great desert to Milford, arriving there at 10 P.M. 228 miles from S. L. City.

April 21, 1881—Started by stage for Cedar City, about 56 miles, at 8 A.M. After a toilsome journey, over rough roads, arrived at H. Lunts at 9 P.M.

---

28 Newspapers of the time advertised the Galvanic Belt as a "Life Renewer . . . a wonderful invention. Disease in male or female cured without medicine" (http://theoldentimes.com/life_renewer.html). It was available by mail order via San Francisco. Modern medicine describes it as quackery.

29 The American Bible Society, founded 1816, was organized to "make the Bible available to every person in a language and format each can understand and afford." Rev. Calvin M. Parks opened the Presbyterian Church in Logan in 1878 (Simmonds, *The Gentile Comes to Cache Valley*, 41; Peterson, *History of Cache County*, 146; Ricks and Cooley, *History of a Valley*, 315–16).

April 22, 1881—Went 18 miles to Parowan, and had a good visit with WH Dame's family. Aunt Almera and Ortons; also saw many old friends. Came back, and hired Lunt's carriage and horses to go to St. George, paying him $4.00 [$81] pr day for them.

Monday, April 25, 1881—Started to St. George, with Lunts Covered carriage and a good span of horses. Took dinner at Bellvue, and got to Silver Reef, 38 miles about sundown. The road is very rough in most places, and deep sand where it is not rocky. The change of climate was very sudden and remarkable, Silver Reef being more than 2000 feet lower than Cedar City, is surrounded by a totally different kind of vegetation, Cacti of many varieties growing everywhere, with many new & beautiful kinds of flowers. We found Uncle Jo[s] E. Johnson's wife, Eliza and family living there, and staid with her. Got acquainted with her daughter Muriel, who is engaged to be married.

April 26, 1881—Visited The Christy Silver Mill, and saw the whole process of milling ore, from the grinding of the ore to the casting of the silver bricks, which weigh about 150 lbs, and are worth about $1600. [$32,243] The silver is taken up by quicksilver.

[page 472]

TO ST. GEORGE. ANNA SICK. VIRGIN CITY.

April 26, 1881—About noon we started again, for St. George, pasing [passing] by several other silver mines and mills. I saw a large petrified log laying beside the road, and broke off a piece, which is rich in silver. We passed through Harrisburg, and at night, nearly, took dinner at Uncle J. E. Johnson's wife's Hannah, at Washington. Here Anna seemed unwell, as from a heavy cold. We arrived at Uncle J. E. J's in St George a little before Sunset, & were very kindly received by him and his daughter Rosemary who were living there alone, tending the bees & fruit.

Wednesday, April 27, 1881—Anna today is quite sick—symptoms of measles. So we staid about the house, to attend to her.

Thursday, April 28, 1881—Anna worse. Had a pleasant time with Aunt Sally and Uncle John Tuttle,[30] of Manti. Saw Apostle Erastus Snow about making survey near Kanab.

30 John Tuttle was a Manti, Utah, pioneer.

Friday, April 29, 1881—Anna better. She has had a very severe attack of measles, but is doing well. Uncle Joseph E. & Rose do all they can for us, and I like them very much.

Saturday, April 30, 1881—Anna nearly well. We rode around the city & saw the Temple. St George is a city of gardens & vineyards, with many good, and tasteful residences.

Sunday, May 1, 1881—Called to see Br. John L. Smith, brother of Pres[t]. G. A Smith—He is one of our old-time friends, & I was glad to see him again & so was Susan.

Monday, May 2, 1881—We think Anna can bear the journey now, and so today we start for Virgin City—about 35 miles distant. We leave Uncle Joseph and Cousin Rose his lovely daughter, with regret. Did not stop in Washington, having a long, rough road before us. We passed through Leeds and Toker, where we stopped to visit Br. John Steel and wife—old Parowan friends. We lunched there, then drove on 8 miles to Virgin City, To our Sister—Sariah Workman & her husband. Found them in bed, but had a happy meeting—the first for many years.

[page 473]

SUSAN & ANNA GO TO KANAB, I TO CEDAR, & SURVEYING.

May 2, 1881—The scenery is strange, wonderfully wild and desolate,—like nothing else to be seen north of this section of country. Virgin City, a small village, nestles between precipitous ranges, on the right bank of the Rio Virgin river, an affluent of the Colorado.

Visited until about noon, then sorrowfully I and Jesse left Susan and Anna, to return to Cedar. I prayed God to bless & preserve them. Susan expects her brother Nephi's team and his son Joel to take her and Anna to Kanab, some 60 miles distant, through a wild sandy desert. She left virgin city May 3[d] and drove 40 miles to Windsor Castle, (or Pipe Springs)[31] and stopped

31 Pipe Springs, Arizona, is just southeast of Kanab, Utah. It was an important watering stopover for pioneers trekking between Kanab and St. George and traveling from Arizona to the north. It was also called Winsor, or Windsor, Castle (Martha Sonntag Bradley, *A History of Kane County* [Salt Lake City: Utah State Historical Society, 1999], 73–74).

all night, sleeping on the floor, and next day drove 20 miles to Kanab, to her brother Nephi's house, very tired and worn out. And was taken worse, and was very sick for some days. After a visit of a week, Susan went to Johnson, 12 miles farther east, situated in a cañon, draining south into the Colorado. Here she was taken very sick for some days, and remained till I and Jesse came for her, June 1st. Now for my movements.

Tuesday, May 3, 1881—I drove from Virgin to Toker, took supper, and thence 8 miles to Bellvue, where we stopped with Br. Sylvester.

May 4, 1881—Drove to Cedar City, at 3 P.M.

Thursday, May 5, 1881—Settled with H. Lunt today:—Board, team &c—[42 or] $112.00 [$2,257] Started up Cedar Canon today, with my party & begun work on my contract, to Survey Tp.36S.R.10W. a high & mountainous, full of precipices, steep mountains, and deep gorges, almost impassible. I had much difficulty in finding any starting corner, and spent several days in making a beginning. I continued on this work until May 27. 1881, Friday, having had a very arduous, trying and perilous experience.

[page 474]

TO VIRGIN CITY, KANAB, AND JOHNSON

May 27, 1881—Several times I narrowly escaped death among its precipices, some of which were hundreds of feet high, but by the blessing of our Father, Jesse & I were preserved, and to Him be all the praise and honor. My expenses on this Survey were very heavy, and cost me as much as it was worth.

Rec[d] a letter from A. F. Doremus, Chf. Eng. of the Utah & Nevada R.R. desiring my service as Engineer, at once, with permanent employment.

May 28, 1881—Finished contract of this Township.

May 30, 1881—We started today with Lunt's team for Johnson & drove to Virgin city 44 miles, & found all well.

May 31, 1881—Left Virgin city for Kanab, 60 miles, 8 A.M. Watered at Workman's Ranch, 7 miles—miserable water—alkaline, also at Short creek, 20 miles, one horse was nearly given out. Roads sandy & hard to travel. Arrived at Pipe Springs, (or Windsor Castle) about 8 P.M. team tired clear out. Got feed for horses and lunch for selves, and a few old quilts to sleep on the porch floor. The road today has been a dreary wilderness & sandy waste, with cedars in places. Windsor Castle was built for defense against the indians, of Stone. The walls are two stories high enclosing a court, entred [entered] by a gateway, closed at night—by heavy doors. No windows open to the outside, but on the second stories are rows of narrow loop holes for shooting rifles from the upper rooms. Two sides of the square are occupied by stone two story buildings. A large and good spring rises in the fort and running out, serves to irrigate ten acres of land. It is a lone and cheerless spot to live, but a welcome sight for the lonely and weary traveler.

June 1, 1881—Paid $2.00 [$40] for horse feed & our lunches, & started at 7 ½ a.m. for Kanab, 20 miles dist.

[page 475]

AT JOHNSON. OUR BLESSINGS.

June 1, 1881—Arrived at Kanab at noon, and took dinner with Nephi's daughter, the family being at Johnson, where we arrived at 5 P.M. and found all well. I was glad.

Found the relatives assembled in honor of the 50th anniversary of father-in-law Joel H. Johnson's baptism into the church. I was not in time for the meeting, which broke up as I came Father Johnson's posterity number to day 29 children, 146 grand children, and 45 great-grand children, all of whome are in the church, except those not living. Saw cousins by the dozen, also Nephi, and Seth, Susan's brothers, and their wives, Uncle W. D. Johnson & family and many others. Father-in-law Johnson is 79 years old, but is hale and hearty, and able to work every day, with his wives Janett and Margaret. Susan, his wife, is in Arizona. Johnson is situated in a beautiful cañon, whose sides are bounded by perpendicular walls of sandstone, through which the water oozes and is collected in trenches. It is cool and clear. There are only a few families living here.

Found Susan and Anna well, and was very glad to meet them again. Both had been sick, Susan quite so. They had spent a week at Kanab, and had a pleasant visit there.

June 2, 1881—Spent the day visiting our friends, very happily. This evening Father gave us our Patriarchal blessings, as follows:—

A Patriarchal Blessing by J. H. Johnson on the head of Susan E. Martineau, J daughter of Joel H. Johnson, born in Kirtland, Ohio, July 11. 1836. Given June 2. 1881.

Susan Johnson my daughter, I lay my hands upon thy head to give thee a father's or patriarchal blessing, and in the name of the Lord Jesus Christ I bless thee with all the blessings of thy fathers Abraham, Isaac and Jacob. Thou art an Ephraimite in whom there is no guile, therefore thou art entitled to all the blessings of the daughters of Ephraim, and inasmuch as thou hast been and ~~art~~ shall be faithful thou shalt live long upon the earth, and to share in the priesthood with thy companion, power to drive the Destroyer from thy household.

[page 476]

BLESSINGS OF SUSAN, AND JESSE N.

Thursday, June 2, 1881—The Spirit of God shall abide in thy bosom like a well of water springing up unto everlasting life. Thou shalt know and understand the things that appertain to thy glory and exaltation far beyond what thou hast ever comprehended before in thy life. Thy friends from behind the vail, some of them, shall visit thee in thy vision in the night time, and instruct thee in all things that appertain to thy exaltation and glory. Thou shalt comprehend the things of God far beyond what thou hast experienced, and thou shalt have power to overcome thine enemies, and every thing that is uncongenial with the principles of life and salvation. Thine offspring shall become a great and a mighty people in the midst of the earth, clothed with the power of the holy priesthood, and mighty men of God with honor and renown shall spring from thee. And inasmuch as thou art faithful to hearken to the words of wisdom and eternal life, I seal thee up unto eternal lives with thy companion and thy children, to come forth in the morning of the first ressurrection, clothed with glory, immortality and eternal lives. All these blessings I seal upon thy head in the name of Jesus Christ. Even so. Amen.

A Patriarchal blessing by Joel H. Johnson upon the head of Jesse N. Martineau, son of James H. and Susan J. Martineau born April 6. 1863, in Logan Cache Co. Utah.

Jesse Nathaniel Martineau in the name of the Lord Jesus Christ of Nazareth I lay my hands upon thy head to give thee a patriarchal or father's blessing. Thou art an Israelite through the loins of Ephraim, and art entitled to all the blessings that God has promised to the faithful, inasmuch as thou art faithful to do His will upon the earth. Thou shalt be clothed with the power of the priesthood in due time, to lay hands upon the sick and they shall recover, and to become a hunter and a fisher to hunt thy brethren of the house of Israel from the dens and caves of the earth, and to fish them from the islands of the sea.

[page 477]

JESSE'S BLESSING

Thursday, June 2, 1881—Thou shalt be clothed with wisdom and knowledge and understanding, for the Holy Ghost shall visit thee at times and cause thee to understand the things of God, and clothe thee with wisdom, to thy great astonishment. Thou shalt have power to bring thousands into the Kingdom of God, and many of the great men of the earth shall come to thee for ~~wisdom~~ counsel and for wisdom in the calamities that shall fall upon the earth. Thou shalt have power to escape the power of the Destroyer, and to cast Satan's yoke upon his own neck, and be free from the power of sin and death; and heavenly messengers shall visit thee and instruct thee in all thy duties of life and shall touch thee even as Jesus Christ touched the three Nephites, that thou mayest live long upon the earth and not taste death. No enemy shall cross thy path and prosper while thou art faithful to promulgate the principles of righteousness, and build up the children of Zion. Thy wisdom shall be great and known among all men. The power of the Holy Ghost shall overshadow thee, and thou shalt become a mighty man of God, and I seal thee up unto eternal lives, for thy offspring shall become great and mighty upon the earth, and thou shalt come forth in the morning of the first ressurrection, clothed with glory, immortality and eternal lives. All these blessings I seal upon thy head, inasmuch as thou art faithful to fulfill thy covenant upon the earth, and hearken to the Words of Wisdom and eternal life, in the name of Jesus, Even So. Amen

Seth's wife, Lydia, also received a blessing at the same time, I being scribe for all three. By desire of Brother Seth, I determined to go home by way of Hillsdale and the Sevier river, so as to visit him at his home, though by so doing I miss Kanab.

[page 478]

LINES TO AUNT JANE. HILLSDALE

Friday, June 3, 1881—Visited Uncle W. D. Johnson's and took dinner. Met Col. Worth, Engineer on the Denver & Rio Grande R.R. who wished my help as an Engineer.[32] By request of Aunt Jane, I wrote a few lines in her album, as follows:—

TO AN OLD AND DEAR FRIEND.

Dear Friend, the years have swiftly sped
    Since first we met.
For some,—now resting with the dead
Our eyes their briny drops have shed:—
    Some with us yet
Remain, to lighten up our way
With Love's benignant, heavenly ray.
We'll make the most of every hour
Draw sweetness from each lovely flower
    But let its thorns alone:
Do right and trust our Father's love,
And at the last, in Heaven above
    Meet round His glorious throne.
            Johnson June 3[d] 1881

June 3, 1881—At 2.25 P.M. we started homeward, having enjoyed our visit much, and taken leave of friends we may never see again. For about 20 miles our way lies up a level cañon, bounded on each side by cliffs, red, white, or grey—most beautiful and in places grand. About 9 P.M. we arrived at Cousin Julia Pulsipher's ranch in the midst of Cedar covered hills, where we stayed all night

June 4, 1881—Got to Hillsdale about 4 P.M. situated on the Sevier river. Only 5 or 8 families here. Took supper with Seth wife Martha; then drove about two miles up to the mouth of a canon where Seth's farm is, and stayed all night with Seth and Lydia. Seth has quite a good farm here of 30 or 40 acres, with pines growing all around. Spent a very pleasant evening.

June 5, 1881—Drove to Panguich 10 miles, thence 10 miles to mouth of Bear Creek cañon, and eat a lunch: then went up the Cañon into Bear Valley, some 6 miles; thence, up and over the high mountain pass near Little Creek Peak upon which snow was lying in patches, thence descending by Little Creek Cañon about 10 miles to Paragoonah, and thence 5 miles to Parowan, arriving there at 9 P.M. after a drive of 50 miles.

[page 479]

PAROWAN, CEDAR. HOMEWARD ON STAGE, MILFORD AND

[continues with heading on next page]

Sunday, June 5, 1881—Bear & Dog vallies have many thousands of Prairie Dogs, who live in large villages, & are quite amusing in their actions. Were very glad to get to Br. W. H. Dame's—our dear old friends, where we felt at home. Had a pleasant visit with them.

Monday, June 6, 1881—Called on Aunt Almera, and took dinner with her. Also called to see Sam[l] Orton & family, and at 2 P.M. started for Cedar, arriving there about sunset. Our team and selves pretty well jaded. Anna enjoyed the journey very much, noticing everything that we passed.

~~**Tuesday, June 7, 1881**~~—Settled store a/c. find I owe $207.25 [$4,176], besides some $300 [$6,046] paid help, and other expenses. Have paid H. Lunt for board, help, and team ($4.00 [$81] pr. day) about $142.00 [$2,862]. He knows how to Charge friends as well as strangers.

Tuesday, June 7, 1881—Started at midnight to day, on coach for Milford, 56 miles. The coach was crowded, but we squeezed in, Jesse riding outside with the driver. It seemed as if the long, cold, rough ride would never bring us to the morning, for one could neither sleep nor keep awake. We got to Minersville about 10.30 A.M. and waited there till about 1 P.M.

32 The Denver & Rio Grande Western Railroad was part of the transcontinental railway connecting Denver and Salt Lake City.

Here I met A. D. Ferron,[33] who was on his way to Cedar to inspect my survey. I wrote M^c^Farlane to assist him in every way. We got to Milford 3 P.M.—Anna quite unwell. Glad to see a railroad once more, and exchange the dust, jolts and tedium of a "jerky" for the cars.

Wednesday, June 8, 1881—Started at 3 A.M. on Utah Southern Ex. R.R. & arrived at S.L. City at 6 P.M., 232 miles, very glad to be so near home again. Found Eliza and family all well.

[page 480]
[continued from previous page header]

SALT LAKE CITY. HOME. SURVEY 3^D^ STANDARD. S.L. CITY

June 9, 1881—Was busy all day in the city.

Friday, June 10, 1881—Went home. Found all the family well, for which I thank our Heavenly Father. Found Biddle renting our other house. Went into it June 3^d^, rent $5.00 [$101] pr month.

Friday, June 17, 1881—Begun Survey of 3° Standard Parallel North. The line runs across high, rugged, snowy mountains, 10000 ft above the Sea, very hard, rough and dangerous to cross. We kept on this work till the 24th, having run 12^m*^ Standard Parallel and 8 miles Guide Meridian North.

Wednesday, June 29, 1881—Started to Salt Lake City. Got there 8 P.M. Next day, the 30th borrowed money of Deseret Nat^l^ Bank

July 1, 1881—Paid $65.00 [$1,310] to Z.C.M.I & other places.

July 2, 1881—Got my new transit tested and find the needle is true within 4' of true Va. The variation on the Meridian at S.L. City, established by U.S. Survey, is 16° 32' E. My transit reads 16° 28'. Rec^d^ a printed commission as U.S. Mineral Surveyor and U.S. Land Surveyor.

July 4, 1881—Went with Eliza to Lake Point. Saw Miss Phister.

July 5, 1881—Prest Taylor[34] wishes me to go to Cedar and survey his (the Church's) Coal claim.

July 8, 1881—Paid D. James $65.00 [$1310] on a/c, Little and Roundy $22.10 [$445] Put my notes & plat of Surveys North in Sur. Genl office. The amount of this work is $1304.37 [$265,278]. Sent a bonnet home to Susan.

July 9, 1881—Started South to Cedar.

July 10, 1881—Arrived at Cedar 9 P.M.

July 12 & 13, 1881—Made surveys in mountains and returned to Cedar. Visited three of Uncle J. E. Johnson's daughters.—Josetta, Julia and Amanda (Clark).

July 14, 1881—Started home, Reached Milford ~~m~~ 3 P.M.

July 15, 1881—Reached S. L. City.

July 20, 1881—Delivered my plat and notes of Survey of Tp.36 S. R.10 W. into Sur. Genl offices value $900.^00^ [$18,137]

[page 481]

July 20, 1881—Gave plat of coal survey to Pres^t^ Taylor.

July 22, 1881—Start home. Arrived 10.15 P.M.

August 8, 1881—Today start on Survey of T.14 N. R.4 E. and R.3 E.

August 9, 1881—Arrived on ground and camped at Badger Springs, about 2 miles west of Garden City, Rich Co. Utah. This little town of about 50 families lies on the west shore of Bear Lake, here about ten miles wide. The beach is sandy and pebbly, the water clear and good.

August 13, 1881—Near Cook's Mills, Swan Creek gushes forth in an immense volume from the solid rock, and makes quite a large stream. Moved over the mountains to Canteen Springs.

August 17, 1881—Finished this township and moved over to the one west

August 31, 1881—Finished these two Townships and started home. Camped on Logan River.

September 21, 1881—Came home. Found all well, but our cow dead.

Started up Blacksmith Fork to Survey Tp. 10N.R.4E.

September 22, 1881—Noon, arrived on the ground and begun work.

September 23, 1881—Rained, Did not work.

33 Augustus D. Ferron was an eastern Utah rancher and pioneer. His survey work opened the area to homesteading. Ferron, Utah, carries his name.

34 John Taylor was ordained President of the Church on October 10, 1880, after the death of Brigham Young in 1877.

September 24, 1881—I came to Logan. My party worked on survey.

September 26, 1881—Some of the boys got lost and were out til near 10 P.M. We built huge bonfires, shouted, and fired guns to attract their attention, and finally were glad to hear an answering pistol shot. My boys Charley and Jesse were of the number. They came in utterly exhausted.

Once before, Hansen's party got lost, and were out all night without coats or food, surrounded by bears and patches of snow. We built bonfires and fired guns, but without avail. They came into camp about Sunrise next morning. I was glad, having been fearful they might have fallen down some of the numerous precipices, some of which are 500 to 800 feet high. They crawled along in the dark where they would not have dared to go in daylight

[page 482]

FINISH MY CONTRACT. FAIR & CONFERENCE.

Friday, September 29, 1881—Snowed hard all day, with piercing wind. We were very uncomfortable, camped in the snow and wind. I lay in bed all day trying to keep warm.

Saturday, September 30, 1881—Finished work today, Snow knee deep. Moved our camp. The Change from deep snow and cold winter to warm weather and dry grassy ground, was very remarkable. We left the snow, when moving, in traveling down the cañon about two miles. A fine buck bounded across our path, but I could not get a good shot, and he escaped.

October 1, 1881—Came home. This finishes all my fieldwork of my contract no. 100 for $3,906.00 [$78,713]. It has been very arduous. I lost flesh—from 170 lbs to 163, my weight when I finished. I had several narrow escapes from death, among the precipices and cliff, many of which were from 200 to 800 ft in depth, but was preserved by the goodness of God, to whom be all praise and honor.

Charles run the transit in the survey of the last township, and afforded me much needed rest.

October 3, 1881—Susan and I went to S. L. City, to see the Ter[l] [Territorial] Fair and attend Conference, which each gave us great pleasure, meeting many old time friends.

October 12, 1881—Returned home, and found all well. Nettie took charge of the housework and family while we were absent,—her first experience of the kind, and she had done very well.

Saturday, October 22, 1881—Rec[d] telegram from Sur. Gen[l] Office, S.L. City last night, and start this morning at 4 A.M. Arrive at noon. Spent two weeks working up my notes & plats. Finished my office work Nov 4th

Friday, November 4, 1881—Return home, find all well.

November 5, 1881—Quarterly Conference today and Sunday 6th I was elected Alternate for High Council Lyman Supt. M.I.A.[35]

[page 483]

LYMAN GETS HOME. & IS MADE SUPT. Y.M.M.I.A. FOR STAKE

Thursday, November 10, 1881—Went with Charley to Ogden to meet Lyman. He did not come until 1.30 A.M. of Friday 11th. We were very glad to meet again. I found him somewhat changed in the 2½ years passed, more manly and cultivated. He was in charge of the Company of emigrants—396—and had had a pretty hard time taking care of so many, most of whom had never been 20 miles from home in their lives before. He was sick all the way across the ocean, and unwell when he boarded the Steamship, having been much overworked in the Liverpool office.

Part of the Saints went north, and most of them to S. L. City. We went with them to see all done. Lyman went to the Pres[t] Office, and reported. He was complimented by Pres[t] Jo[s] F. Smith for having well filled his mission. I called with him to see numerous friends in the city, and returned to Logan arriving 11 P.M.

Saturday, November 12, 1881—It was truly a joyful time with us all. Br. Preston's folks would not be denied, so we all took him up there to see them. After coming back, we sat up till 2 P.M. [A.M.] talking, and looking at our presents,—such as album, books, razors, shells, dolls &c. which were all very nice.

35 Lyman Martineau's return from his mission to Great Britain and Europe was reported in "Coming Home," *Deseret News*, October 19, 1881, and November 16, 1881; Utah Digital Newspapers.

Sunday, November 13, 1881—Today Lyman preached—was much affected at first, seeing so many friends at once; but Br. Moses Thatcher kindly assisted him to start.

November 20, 1881—Lyman started today, with Apostle Thatcher Prest Preston, and B. F. Cummings, on a tour through our Stake. Lyman goes to visit and organize Young Men's M. I. Assns[36] He was put in Supt. for the whole County and Stake at last Quar. Conference in Logan. During last week he had to go to S. L. City, to see to some emigration business.

[page 484]

Friday, November 25, 1881—Self and Susan attended Presbyterian Church Reception and had a pleasant time.

Tuesday, November 29, 1881—~~In~~ Wrote to Aunt Mary Martineau. Nettie sent me a letter she had recd from Aunt Mary, full of bitterness towards her and especially towards me—"the Mormonite," as she termed me. So I thought I would write her. to try to make her feel better towards me. I pray I may have an influence with her for good. The following is a copy of my letter to her, which I insert, to show I hold no bitterness towards her.

Logan Nov. 29, 1881

My dear Aunt Mary

It has been a long time since I have heard from you, except indirectly, and so I seat myself to write a few lines. Having mentioned, previously, in my letters to Nettie, that I never hear from you, she very kindly sent me one you had written her. It did me good to see your writing again, it seemed so familiar. I think it very much resembles my mother's, and to some extent, my father's, though, as I seem to remember his, it was a smaller hand and not so plain. I do not remember my uncle Peter's writing. In fact, I never saw much of his writing. As I write this, how vividly comes to mind the short but very pleasant visit I had with you and cousin Alice. I only wish I could have spent a longer time, though, as you were then moving, it would probably have put you to too much bother. I remember, too, that you would make me occupy a bed, while you lay on the floor. But I did not like it, at all. I felt ashamed to do so, only you seemed bent upon it. But I thank you very much for your kindness to me while there, and for the pleasant little ride we had to the cemetery, and to my dear Uncle's grave. Have you erected a stone yet, to mark his last resting place? I hope so. For if you should suddenly depart, who should know the grave?

[page 485]

MY LETTER TO AUNT MARY MARTINEAU.

I am afraid I should not be able to find it, Though perhaps I would. If you should need a little help to put up a nice stone, I would cheerfully contribute to that end, and so would, no doubt, Alice. I always think of uncle Peter with love, for his goodness to me while I lived with you (and the same for you, too, dear Aunt,) After I came away from your house, (on my visit) I thought of so many things I wanted to talk to you about. When with you, I could think of hardly anything. It all seemed so strange. When I left, in 1849, Alice was just a little girl; when I saw her again she was a woman—a matron with a nice family of children. I could not realize it. You, although a little older, seemed just the same as in years long before—just the same industrious, busy, energetic Aunt Mary that I knew long—long—before.

I believe my dear Aunt, that in the next existence, one source of pleasure and of happiness will be the remembrance of former love and friendship here on earth. Earthly things will have no place there, but love, charity, forgiveness, kindness, and kindred attributes are not earthly, but heavenly, and will endure throughout eternity. You know, "God is Love." How much there is to encourage us to live virtuous and holy lives, and how much of true happiness there is in so living. I live in peace with all. I think the world is big enough for all—even for heathens and unbelievers.—God blesses all, and sends "the rain upon the just and the unjust." All these things teach me the necessity of cultivating charity; for the apostle says, without charity all the other gifts are nothing.

When I say I feel at peace with all, I do not include the really, knowingly wicked—such as Guitteau

36 The Mutual Improvement Association (MIA) was an organization of the young men and young women of the Church until the 1970s.

[Guiteau].[37] I can only wish to see him executed for his unprovoked and cowardly murder of the President. I think to murder any one is a crime not to be forgiven (the Bible says "No murderer hath eternal life" &c) but can only be atoned by his life; but to kill a ruler of a country is much worse, for it has an influence upon a whole nation, or even more than one. Guitteau's trial seems to me a disgusting farce and a disgrace to our nation.

[page 486]

MY LETTER TO AUNT MARY MARTINEAU

Tuesday, November 29, 1881—Does it not seem so to you? As soon as the telegraph announced the death of the President, the Mayor and city council of Logan—in which I am an Alderman[38]—telegraphed to Mrs. Garfield the sympathy and condolences of our entire community as a body: memorial services were held in our Tabernacle, which holds 4000 people, and was crowded. Rev. Dr. Park, Presbyterian minister here—joined with our elders in the service. The Episcopal minister did not participate—he may have been absent. Stores and all public buildings were draped in mourning for a month, and flags at half mast signified our grief for the President and his family. It seemed so hard, after so long a struggle, ~~with~~ that Death should finally overcome. But he, no doubt, is with the blest in that land which, ere long, will receive us.

I am President of the Cache County Branch of the American Bible Society: Dr. Parks is Secretary—also one of the directors. The Presbyterians had a sociable or reception in their church a few evenings ago, which my wife—Susan—and I attended. It was pleasant, and we enjoyed ourselves very well. Dr. Parks came here from Washington, D.C. He and family are cultivated people, and very pleasant. We visit each other, and have a very pleasant intercourse together. His daughter, Mrs. Shirley—is our Post Mistress for Logan.

Some things in your letter to Nettie I do not understand, but seemed to indicate unpleasant feeling about something. But I hope such feelings will not exist among us, for it is not in accordance with Christ's teachings and example. And it seems to me, we are too few—too many have gone—for us who remain to harbor any unkind feelings towards each other. I, for one, do not and will not.

I am very glad to hear so good an account of yourse [yourself] good health, income, freedom from care, and ability, as you say, to take long journeys.

[page 487]

LYMAN AND ALLEY MARRIED.[39]

November 29, 1881—I hope you will come here and make me a visit—a good long one. You would enjoy yourself very much, I know. Here, everything is so different from what you have seen before. Our grand old mountains 10000 to 12000 feet high, are alone worth a visit, and the climate is so fine. Do come. You can come so easy now. Only about four days in a Pullman car,—it is almost like being at home. I would do all I could to make your visit pleasant, and so would Susan. Will you? But my paper (and your patience, too, I fear) is done and I close with love to you and Alice, and all, Write soon to

Your Old Nephew

J. H. Martineau."

P.S. My Son, while in London, made the acquaintance with Rev. Dr. James Martineau, Also David Martineau, and Solicitor Basil Martineau, who all treated him royally. We obtained Martineau genealogy back to 1682, and have many hundred names of our progenitors. J.H.M.

Tuesday, November 29, 1881—Heavy Snow last night. It is about a foot deep this morning.

December 13, 1881—Tho[s] Biddle left my house which he has had 6⅓ months at $4.00 [$81] pr mo. Has paid nothing.

Thursday, December 29, 1881—To day, about 11 A.M. my Son Lyman R. Martineau and Alley Preston were sealed in the Endowment House, Salt

37 Charles Guiteau assassinated President James A. Garfield in July 1881. He is known as the second person in history to assassinate a president of the United States.

38 Martineau was elected alderman in February 1880 ("Cache County Elections," *Deseret News*, March 3, 1880; Utah Digital Newspapers).

39 "Joined in Wedlock," *Deseret News*, January 4, 1882; Utah Digital Newspapers.

Lake City, by Joseph F. Smith. W. B. Preston & Angus M. Cannon were witnesses. They went down the day previous, accompanied by Alley's father Prest Wm B. Preston. Alley is all I can desire in a daughter, and I thank our Father for thus blessing us. They returned the same day they were married. May all needful blessings attend them.

December 30, 1881—This evening a family party was held at Prest Preston's, at which Collins and Ella (Thatcher) Fullmer (who were married at the same time as Lyman) were also present. We had a pleasant time.

[page 488]

OUR 30TH WEDDING DAY AND PARTY.

December 30, 1881—It brought vividly to my mind the marriages of Henry. Elvira and Moroni, in the days of our poverty. No costly wedding gifts adorned their tables,—no fine dinners, costly dresses or nice furniture and dwelling awaited their union; neither did they my own; but I hope they were equally fortunate in their choice of companions, and that they may be equally happy through life. Their experience gained while poor will be invaluable to them when rich, and God can as easily bless them as any others. And this I pray He will do.

[written in margin]

1882.

Friday, January 8, 1882—This evening we celebrated our 30th anniversary of our wedding, by a nice party and supper. There were over 20 invited guests, which, with our own family, made a nice company. Our parlor was beautifully lighted by a chandelier and other lamps, the grate glowed warmly with its coal fire, and everything was pleasant. How thankful Susan and I are that God has enabled us to thus entertain our friends. This it is that makes these things pleasant for us—not for a vain display. Everything passed off well, and all were pleased. We had some nice wedding presents too.

January 10, 1881—Today I finished my "Military History of Cache County." This I was induced to write, by E. W. Tullidge, editor of "Tullidge's Quarterly Magazine." He also desires me to write my autobiography for publication in the same Quarterly.[40]

Saturday, January 21, 1882—Started for S.L. City at noon, arriving 8 P.M. Found all reasonably well.

Monday, January 23, 1882—Attended to business at Sur. Genl office & other places.

[page 489]

January 24, 1882—Saw Tullidge about the city business connected with his magazine. He highly praises my article. Paid Jennings a/c $58.85 [$1,186], and borrowed $200 [$4,030] of bank to pay debts. Bought some chairs for Eliza. Paid J. A. West $34.00 [$685] in full of all accounts. Paid Dest News for paper to Henrietta 6 months 2.00$ [$40] Bought Small alarm clock $4.00 and suit for self $24.00 [$484] Before I went to S.L. City our water had been frozen off—pipes—mains—froze. Found my U.S. Survey accounts had not yet been sent off.

Tuesday, January 31, 1882—Returned home. Found Susan at a grand Co-op party. I went at 11 P.M. and enjoyed myself.

The day before I came home I met Mrs. Oliver Walker—my first mistress on arriving in Utah. I first hired out to her husband in July 1850. Was glad to see her after a lapse of 31 years.

Wednesday, ~~March~~ February 1, 1882—Attended City Council, and got appropriations of $200 [$4,030] for Tullidge's magazine, against quite an opposition.

February 3 & 4, 1882—Quarterly Conference. Br. Edd Dolten of Parowan an old friend, also Br. L. J. Nuttall staid two days with us. Had a pleasant time. Let Br. Nuttall take my T. O.[41] order for $62.00 [$1,249] to have it rectified.

40 James H. Martineau, "The Military History of Cache County," *Tullidge's Quarterly Magazine* (1882): 123–131. Edward W. Tullidge published the magazine beginning in 1880 and also wrote *The History of Salt Lake City and Its Founders*, which was reprinted from the magazine "and relates the leading incidents of Mormon history between 1845 and 1865" (Ronald W. Walker, "Edward Tullidge: Historian of the Mormon Commonwealth," *Journal of Mormon History* 3 [1976]: 55–72).

41 Martineau is paying his "tithes and offerings" here.

February 16, 1882—Sent my "final oaths" to Sur. Gen[l] office.

February 12, 1882—Sunday. Was re-elected Pres[t] Cache County Branch of Amer. Bible Society. Do not like it.

February 16, 1882—Arranged with Fred. Turner to take ½ interest with him in Iron mine, near Paradise.

February 22, 1882—Heard today that Congress (the Senate) has passed the "Edmunds Bill," disfranchising us as a people on account of polygamy. I think God understands His business, and will bring good out of it in the end.

March 1, 1882—This evening attended City Council, the last time the old council will sit. I have been a member ever since Logan City was organized in 1866—16 years, and I am willing to retire.

[page 490]

CHARLES CALLED ON MISSION—'54— EDMUNDS BILL

March 1, 1882—I know if God wants me in any position He will place me there; and I do not wish to be anywhere that I do not think is according to His mind and will.

March 5, 1882—This morning Charley received notice from Pres[t] John Taylor that he is called to go on mission to the Southern States April 11th proximo. Charley answered same day that he would go at the time appointed. He has been going to B.Y. College[42] for some months. Susan is getting better of her nervous prostration and will, I hope, soon be well.

March 13, 1882—Monday. This is my 54th birthday. It seems hard to believe I was only 32 years old when I came to Logan, but then, Henry, my oldest, was only 8 years old! In the evening Alley came to see us also Br. & Sister Jo[s] Goddard, and had a pleasant time. Lyman was in Ogden. Nephi was 20 years old on the Saturday previous. Susan had a bad head ache all day.

March 14, 1882—News came by telegraph that the "Edmunds Bill" has passed. All right. God rules, this work is His, and He will control it to his glory, and all men—saints and sinners are alike in His hand. Our enemies can do nothing more than He permits, and He will permit nothing which is not for our good. All we can do is to still serve God and trust Him fully. All will be well, and may I, with all my family be true to the end, no matter how or when the end shall come. I have once dedicated my home and possessions to the flames, and would rather do so again than have our enemies enjoy the fruits of our toils and labors. I think we shall have a tight place for 3 or 4 years, and then emerge as a people immensely strengthened in political power, wealth and influence.[43]

[page 491]

GENEALOGICAL INFORMATION FROM HENRIETTA

March 1882—Should persecution drive from Utah any leading men or polygamists, they will simply become so many missionaries abroad, whereas at home their influence is not felt.

March 16, 1882—This evening the old city Council held their last Session, and the new one their first. I did not attend, on account of a furious snowstorm that raged until late. We we [were] also invited to Goddard's.

March 18, 1882—Lyman appointed City Councillor, Logan. Also Ass[r] & Coll[r] Cache Co.

March 20, 1882—To day received a letter from Sister Nettie, in which she gives the following genealogical information:—

42 Brigham Young College began in 1877, meeting in the basement of the Logan Tabernacle. The Board of Trustees was appointed by Brigham Young and included Brigham Young Jr., William B. Preston, Milton D. Hammond, Moses Thatcher, Charles Ora Card, and G. W. Thatcher. Ida Ione Cook was the first principal of the college (Ricks and Cooley, *History of a Valley*, 348–69; Peterson, *History of Cache County*, 110, 151). This was a different institution than the Utah State Agricultural College, today's Utah State University. Brigham Young College held its last graduation ceremonies on May 22, 1926 (Ricks and Cooley, *History of a Valley*, 369).

43 During the growing persecution against polygamists, Church leaders, fathers, and husbands went into hiding; others migrated north to Canada or south to Mexico. They adopted pseudonyms in correspondence to avoid identification by the U.S. marshals.

James Mears (my mother's father) was born in Sharon Conn. April 11. 1774

Lois Sprague (Mears) his wife, born Lebanon Conn. Feb. 22. 1779.

James R. Mears (uncle) was born [blank]

died at Madison Wis. April 26. 1878

William Babcock (my stepfather) was born at Poultney, Vt. 1806. He died near Racine, Wisconsin abt 1864 [added later in shaky handwriting]

Aunt Laura (Mears) Vanslyke died at Jordan, NY in 1847

James and Lois Mears had two sons named Henry:

the first died at Amsterdam N.Y. aged 24 yrs The other Henry died a young babe.

My grandmother, Lois Sprague Mears, was the grand-daughter of a son of Lord Hutchinson, Eng. which son, an officer of the English army, was killed at the Fort Edwards massacre, by the indians in Montcalm's army, in the "French and indian War." His name was Stephen Hutchinson.

My sister Henrietta was married to ~~Jo[s]~~ David C. Lyon at Milwaukee, Wis. Oct. 30. 1855.

[page 492]

GENEALOGICAL INFORMATION FROM HENRIETTA

March 1882—David C. Lyon was born at Ogdensburg, N.Y. Nov. 7. 1809 His father was named John, also his grandfather, who with others came from Morristown, N.J. traveling by canoes, except where a portage was necessary, and settled where Ogdensburg now is. David C. Lyon's mother's name was Elizabeth Blanchard, who died when he was 6 months old (May 1810) He has three half brothers (Blanchards)—Harvey, Charles and George. D. C. Lyons' first wife was named Eliza Shiland, of Cambridge N.Y. who died at Mineral Point, Wis.

[written in margin]

Error. Father's first wife was the widow of Capt Hawkins & dau. of Earl Stanhope who had disinherited her

Of my father's first wife and family:—~~Jane Varley~~, Sarah Hawkins (widow of Capt Hawk[ins]) my father's first wife, whom he married in England, was daughter of ~~Jane C. Varley~~: she was an artist; and ~~gran~~daughter of the Earl of Stanhope. ~~Her mother, Jane C~~. She married Capt. Hawkins, Royal Navy, for which she was disinherited by the Earl, her grandfather. ~~Jane~~ had two children Samuel and Elizabeth Hawkins. She herself died soon after landing in (Baltimore?) Phila[a] of yellow fever.

Samuel Hawkins was a warrant officer in the U. S. Navy, was with the U. S. exploring expedition of Com. Wilkes to the Antarctic continent, thus disavowed and subsequently died. Do not know if Elizabeth is still alive at this time or not. These two children were my father's step children. His own, by ~~Jane Varley~~, Sarah Stanhope Hawkins, were Julia and Lucretia Martineau, of whom Lucretia died in 1838–9 and Julia, who married a man named Winslow, a printer, of Boston Mass. who I do not know is dead or alive now. Henrietta thinks Elizabeth ~~Varley~~ Hawkins is still living in Brooklyn N. Y.

Rudolph Walker was cousin (on father's side) of Coz. N. B. Van Slyke, of Madison Wis.

My father was in England 6 or 7 years, having left America when he was 18 or 19 years old.

[page 493]

CHARLES STARTS ON HIS MISSION. I GO TO S. L. CITY.

March 19, 1882—Snowed again.

April 1, 1882—Met as a delegate from Logan 1st Ward, in a county convention to choose delegates to Territorial convention to be held in S. L. city to adopt a constitution for a state government. I was temporary chairman. Lyman was appointed alternate, though not by my wish.

Wednesday, April 5, 1882—Started to S. L. city, with Charles F. who now starts on his mission to the southern states. Arrived in S. L. city at noon, and called with Charles at President's office to report for duty.

April 6 & 7, 1882—Snowed all the time.

Saturday, April 8, 1882—Took Charles and Eliza to Theatre. Got his provisions.

Monday, April 10, 1882—Charles rec[d] his endowments. I went through with him, and assisted in setting him and others apart for their missions. Introduced him to and talked with Sisters E. R. Snow

Smith and Bathsheba Smith.[44] Jo^s F. Smith was mouth, with myself and Patriarch John Smith in setting him apart.

Tuesday, April 11, 1882—This morning Charles started on train for the East, I going with him as far as Ogden, where he obtained tickets at half rates, $36.75 [$741] to St. Louis, and also paying $4.00 [$81] for his share of a sleeping berth—Pullman car. Nathaniel Haws was his comrade, many others went with him. It was sorrowful to part with him, at the last. I blessed him, and gave him the best council I could. When the train took him away I went by myself and cried, though I am willing he should go, and feel thankful I have sons counted worthy to go as missionaries. I trust in God, and hope my sons may return in due time, having gained experience and perhaps brought some one into the church.

[page 494]

SOLD PIECE OF GROUND. AUNT MARY MARTINEAU'S DEATH.

Tuesday, April 11, 1882—Returned home about 11 P. M. Found all well.

April 12, 1882—Ordered Artesian well[45] machinery from St Louis $375. [$7,557]

April 15, 1882—Wrote again to same parties, also to J. W. Young, for pass.

April 18, 1882—Still more snow, and again on 24th and 20th 4 inches.

April 24, 1882—Sent again for Artesian outfit. Rec^d a letter from my nephew F. W. Voswinkel on 22^d from Montana.

April 29, 1882—Rec^d word my Survey of last year for U.S. is allowed. Paid debts to amount of about $1300. [$26,197]

May 6 & 7, 1882—Quarterly Conference held here. Br. G. F. Gibbs and Pres^t Taylor's son stopped with us.[46] Sunday afternoon Apostle F. D. Richards invited me to attend a meeting of the Pres^t and Council at Pres^t Preston's. The business was in relation to the Temple:—as to procuring a water supply &c. Also some other things.

May 8, 1882—Sold David Lewis[47] part of my lot, 35 x 100 feet, for $700. [$14,106]

May 9, 1882—Surveyed on the College lands for Holt & Fletcher.

May 10, 1882—Paid Nielsen (H. L.) $10.00 [$202] Hammond $20.50 [$413] for books. To temple (donation) $50.00 [$1,008].

May 11, 1882—Paid Curtis $5.65 [$114] E. Hansen $20.00 [$403], 12th ord bees.

May 13, 1882—Wrote again for Augur, also to F. D. Richards and other Paid J. G. Charles[48] $10.50 [$212]. Bought clock $10.50 [or $18.50]

May 16, 1882—Rec^d letter from Henrietta, enclosing one from my Cousin Alice L. Kurtz, of Milwaukee 91 Prospect St. with information of Aunt Mary A. Martineau's death, which occurred on Sat. Apr. 29th 1882 at 11 P.M. of old age. Her death was peaceful and painless, after an illness of 3 weeks. She was a little over 70 years when she died. But two of my uncles and aunts are left, Uncle Charles Sprague Mears and Aunt Harriett Mears (Sherwin). None of the Martineau name are left but myself. I hope to be a restorer to my family—those who are dead—and to found a numerous stock of living ones.

[page 495]

May 18, 1882—Rec^d answer from Apostle F. D. Richards. He says my letter to him is full of valuable suggestions in reference to furnishing the Temple with water.

May 19, 1882—Rec^d letter from J. E. Johnson. He says some of the family are called to go into Mexico. He is going and wants us.

May 18, 1882—On the 18 the Female Relief Societies of Logan held a grand Picnic, at which over 500 sat down. They had a good time. Susan was the President of the Committee of 18 Ladies. All went off well. The Committee presented Mrs. E. G. Benson, the Prest. of the Stake, a silver cake basket and goblet.

May 20, 1882—Rec^d letter from Elvira and Moroni. Moroni has another child born, but he did not give the date of birth. Wrote to Uncle J. E J. & said

44 Bathsheba Wilson Bigler Smith (1822–1910) was the wife of George A. Smith.

45 An artesian well flows naturally without the aid of pumps.

46 George F. Gibbs was a clerk in President John Taylor's office.

47 Davis Lewis was a photographer and artist.

48 John Charles was a Logan grocer.

I would like to go into Mexico, too. We have no longer any country, and no rights,—not even so much as Southern slaves had years ago. I would rather wander in other lands, a free man, than stay here, a slave. I come from too many generations of freemen and patriots to be willing to submit to any such thing.[49] Wrote to Elvira and J. E. J.

Monday, May 22, 1882—Went to Ogden as Witness in case of Griffiths vs Rees. Staid at night with Wm Stowell.[50]

May 23, 1882—Was relieved from court. at 6.15 Went to S. L. City found all well there.

May 25, 1882—Paid D. James $45.00 [$907] in full, on my water pipes.

May 27, 1882—Sat for photograph. at Savage's.

Thursday, June 1, 1882—Today went through the "House" to refresh my memory.[51] Enjoyed myself very well.

[Bottom line of page is unreadable.]

[page 496]

GERTRUDE GOES TO LIVE WITH LYMAN.

June 3, 1882—Wrote in Miss Nelly Hardy's album, these lines agreeable to her request for a memento:—

Nelly, happiness and pleasure,
Joy and love and peace be thine:
Every blessing without measure—
(I dont know how to end this line.)

Monday, June 5, 1882—Wrote to J. E. Johnson & Charles. Gertrude is sick—measles.

June 6, 1882—Nephi went into Cañon to work in timber

June 7, 1882—Recd letter from P. J. Barratt, Ogden, who wants me to Survey his mining claim. Wrote him ~~next~~ same day. Paid

C. B. Robbins, for 4th Ward store. $100.00 [$2015] on a/c (check)

Also to L. Angel[52] for help surveying $28.00 [$564] (check).

June 12, 1882—Rcd. letter and photo from Coz. Rose Johnson. Made plat for Br. J. U. Stucki, Paris Bear Lake Co. Idaho.

Presented my daughter Alley Martineau a sett of China, value $19.00 [$383]

June 14, 1882—Bought a new wringer, $6.75 [$136]

June 17, 1882—Anna is getting sick with chicken pox

June 18, 1882—Gave my photograph to Lyman

June 21, 1882—Anna is about well. Today Gertrude[53] went to Lyman's to live. He and Alley want to keep her, till she grows up, and as I think it will be for her welfare, I consented.

June 23, 1882—Seth and Charles Jones came up from city.

June 27, 1882—Dug some new potatoes today.

July 14, 1882—Order well-boring augur,[54] price $475.00 [$9,572].

July 6, 1882—Sold ½ acre of land in field for $150.00 [$3,023].

July 11, 1882—Surveyed for John Nelson. Susan's birthday today. She is 46 years old, and dearer than ever.

July 15, 1882—Insured my house and barn for $3500.00 [$70,531]

July 16, 1882—Virginia's birthday. She is 12 years old. [the 1 in 12 is crossed through]

July 24, 1882—Charles birthday. He is 21 years old.

July 28, 1882—My well augur came today. Weighs 5290 lbs The freight was $217.04 [$4,374]

49 Persecution builds once again for the Church because of polygamy. Several congressional actions eventually lead to an underground Mormon culture.

50 William Stowell was an Ogden businessman who dealt in real estate ("Supreme Court," *Ogden Standard Examiner*, January 19, 1895; Utah Digital Newspapers).

51 The Endowment House.

52 This could have been either Leonard Angell (1863–1908) or Lewis Angell (1868–1910), both teenage sons of Truman O. Angell (note spelling).

53 Gertrude Martineau was born in 1870 to James and Susan Ellen. Gertrude would be twelve years old at this entry.

54 This is well-drilling equipment. The augur channels the residue from the hole to the surface.

[page 497]

DANGER ON G. S. LAKE

August 8, 1882—Borrowed $100.⁰⁰ [$2,015] of Mrs. Torgeson[55] @ 1½ pr cent. Also $100.⁰⁰ from J. Irvine at same rate.

August 16, 1882—Went to take Netta to S. L. City, to attend the Deseret University, as a Normal Scholar.[56] She was recommended as such by the teachers of the Brigham Young College of Logan.

August 19, 1882—Took Netta to Lake Point. Hired a sail boat & sailor and went out about 5 miles in the G. S. Lake, and were caught in a furious squall. We were forced to run before the wind, the waves very rough, & had hard work to save our lives. When the squall passed over, we had a hard time in getting ashore. We finally got ashore about a mile from the R.R. Station, being carried by the boatman, after which we reached the train by great exertion, just as it started. During our danger on the lake, tossing about on the waves, Netta was perfectly calm and cool. She said she prayed for safety, and then felt all right. So did I. but we had a narrow escape.

August 21, 1882—Went with Netta to the University today and on [continued in next entry]

August 22, 1882—Came home

September 6, 1882—Moved machine to Church farm to bore a well.[57]

September 7, 1882—Today Theodore was baptized, by Br. Larsen, and confirmed by myself and Joseph Goddard. Began to bore, after asking God's blessing upon our labors.

September 9, 1882—Joel began to do chores for Geo. W. Thatcher.

September 15, 1882—Borrowed $100.⁰⁰ [$2,015] of J. Irvine @ 1½ pr cent pr mo.

September 18, 1882—Rained last night, & snow on mountains.

September 23, 1882—Geo. Albert came home today from Arizona.

September 25, 1882—By telegram from Nephi and Seth Johnson, we learn of the death of father Joel H. Johnson, which had just occurred at Johnson, Kane Co, Utah, after a short illness.

October 3, 1882—Rented my house to Isaac Smith @ $6.⁰⁰ [$121] pr mo.[58] Still trying to bore, but hard work.

[page 498]

NEPHEW JOHN LYON'S DEATH, BY RAILROAD. DORA

October 10, 1882—Settled with Deseret Nat[l] Bank, and find my total transactions amount to $7319.19 [$14,495]

October 11, 1882—A letter from my sister tells me of my nephew John Lyon's death by being killed on a railway. He was 23 years & 43 days old, a most exemplary young man, and as a son all that any one could ask.

Rec[d] a letter from Brig. Gen[l] Young to get the case of Surgical instruments from Lamoreaux.

October 14, 1882—Snowed all day.

This morning Sister G. W. Thatcher sent over to see if we wanted to take a foundling baby girl, which they found on their doorstep this morning We accordingly took the poor little girl, which was about five weeks old, and nearly dead with cold and exposure, having been exposed to cold rain and snow during the night. It took till almost night to get her warmed again. We named her "Dora" (a gift) and by the help of God intend to be father and mother to her. Many people called in to see her. We think she was left by some woman from S. L. City, but do not know. She is a pretty little girl, but quite poor. But in Susan she has found a mother indeed, one who will not only love her, but who knows how to take care of her. We fix the 5th of September as her birth day, from the best indications.

October 24, 1882—Surveyed for College.

55 This is likely the widow of Canute Torgensen (note spelling); Canute was among the first telegraph operators in Logan (Ricks and Cooley, *History of a Valley*, 168).

56 Deseret University, or the University of Deseret, functioned between 1850 and 1882, at which time it became the University of Utah. John R. Park is credited with leading it from a struggling school into a stable institution (Sillitoe, *Welcoming the World*, 40, 66, 75, 89, 119).

57 "Artesian Wells," *Deseret News*, September 20, 1882; Utah Digital Newspapers.

58 There were two Isaac Smiths in Logan at this time. One was a dentist, and the other owned a produce company (Somers, *History of Logan*, 82).

October 27, 1882—Moved machine home, and abandoned well, having bored about 65 feet deep. The sand kept running in fast as we could get it out, and we could not force the tubing down. The water had risen to the surface, and ran out a little. I think troughs may be fixed, so as to water stock. I intend to bore in another place. The work has been full of vexations delays and accidents, from the first, and has caused me a heavy expense at the machine shop.

[page 499]

November 7, 1882—We start to Oxford, to bore a well for A. Duddenhausen.[59] My terms are $1.00 [$20] pr foot, for a depth of 100 feet, in good soil. Rock, to be higher. He sent a team to help move the machinery to Oxford, 40 miles. Went to Richmond, and stopped at Prest M. W. Merrill's.

November 8, 1882—Went on, and reached Oxford after dark.

November 9, 1882—Rain this morning, changing into snow. Set up machine in heavy storm, and put up tent.

November 10, 1882—Snowing still, with cold wind,—drifting snow.

November 11, 1882—Stormed all forenoon. Began work in afternoon.

November 15, 1882—Went home by train today, and left Nephi and Jesse at work

November 16, 1882—Bought a ton of coal $8.50 [$171] Br. Moses Thatcher invited me to accompany him and Erastus Snow on their proposed trip or missions to Mexico & Arizona,[60] and I determined to go, if possible. Lyman gave me $20.00 [$403] to help my expense a/c

November 21, 1882—Started north to try and sell the machine to Duddenhausen. Found the boys had been boring & had reached a depth of 75 feet

November 22, 1882—Sold machine to Duddenhausen & J. Sant for $700.00 [$14,106] and for work &c $785.00 [$15,819] Came home, and fixed to go to Mexico tomorrow. Took 2 notes, for $425.00 [$8,565] and $360.00 [$7,255]

November 23, 1882—Recd word from Apostle E. Snow he could not go till Friday.

November 24, 1882—Friday. Started this morning at 4.50 A. M. with Apostle Moses Thatcher. Each had a lunch basket, to save meals along railroad, $1.00 [$20] each. Met Br. Snow on his arrival from S. L. City, and, having a missionary certificate from Prest John Taylor, I obtained a ticket to San Francisco, Cal, 883 miles, at $26.50 [$534] and sleeping car ticket for same place $6.00 [$121]. Left Ogden at 6.45 P. M.

Saturday, November 25, 1882—Awake this morning at Halleck, Nevada. Got a poor breakfast at Elko, dined at noon at Battle Mountain, 348 miles from Ogden, and supped at Humbolt Station. Hewe [here] we were detained several hours, while a temporary track was built around a wrecked train about 20 miles ahead.

[page 500]

GO TO SAN FRANCISCO.

November 25, 1882—We saw 23 freight cars splintered and broken, piled one above the other, a chaotic mas 30 ft high, while a dead breakman lay under the ruins. At 8.50 P.M. we reached Reno, a lively little town, & near the eastern foot of the Sierra Nevadas. We began to ascend the mountains about 9 P.M. The journey through Nevada is <u>very</u> dreary. passing for the whole distance through a desert.

Sunday, November 26, 1882—About 1 A.M. we were detained near the summit of the Sierra Nevadas for 2 hours by a burning snow shed before us, and at daylight we found ourselves in California, among its foot hills, pine and oak trees, and green grass. As we near Sacramento the country becomes level, and very beautiful. We reached Sacramento at 7 A.M. and took breakfast. The Sacramento river is about 600 or 800 feet wide, muddy, and deep enough for steamboats. Here we met a dense fog rolling in from the Pacific, and continued so until we reached San Francisco at noon. At Benicia our train was ferried across an arm of the Bay; thence skirting along the shore about 40 miles we reach Oakland and leave our train. Entering a steamer, we cross the Bay 6 miles, to San Francisco. The sight was very interesting to me;

59 The Duddenhausen family appears to be among the German Saints who settled Oxford, Idaho, at the north end of Cache Valley.

60 James H. McClintock, *Mormon Settlement in Arizona: A Record of Peaceful Conquest of a Desert* (Phoenix: Manufacturing Stationers, 1921), 236–37.

vessels of all kinds at anchor or moving about, with the great city, crowning its high and steep hills before us. At the wharf we entered a coach and were taken to the "Palace Hotel," the largest and finest one in the world. It cost over $8.000.000 [$161,214,800] and has 1100 magnificently furnished rooms. We had three rooms on 3^d floor opening into each other, with Bathroom, washroom and cupboard, all handsomely furnished in Brussels carpets, marble mantles, and fine furniture, with gass in four rooms. For this and our meals, we paid altogether, $10.^00 [$202] pr day, a rate far less in proportion than in S. L. City or places east.

[page 501]

AT THE PACIFIC SHORE.

November 1882—At last I have reached the place I started for 34 years ago, but in a manner quite different than at first. Then I traveled with an ox team, taking 3 months for a journey now requiring only 2¼!

The Palace Hotel is built round a court, handsomly paved with marble, and glassed overhead forming a delightful resort for guests.

Monday, November 27, 1882—Today got tickets to Deming, New Mexico, about 1200 miles, $50.^00 [$1,008] and a rate to go home from Deming to Ogden, over 2000 miles, for $90.^00 [$1,189], with stop over privileges. both ways. Afterwards called on Gilb^t Clements and J. Linforth, formerly Mormons in S. L. City.[61] In evening Saw "Uncle Tom's Cabin"—a poor play.[62]

Tuesday, November 28, 1882—Visited the Mint, which has capacity to coin $80.000.000 [$1,612,148,004] coin per month, and saw the whole process. Afterwards Brs. Snow & Thatcher sat for Photographs. I did not—cash too scarce. In the afternoon went 7 miles to the Pacific shore, near the Cliff House. Here hundreds of seals were swimming and disporting in the sea, or climbing the rocks. Also visited a Life-saving station, and examined the boats, line-gun and other things, returning through the Park. We traveled by Street railway 4 miles for 5 cents. We had previously visited Woodward's gardens on Sunday. Here are to be found almost all kinds of animals, birds, fish and reptiles: also most beautiful flowers, blooming in open air, palms and other rare trees. On the ocean shore I picked up a few shells.

Wednesday, November 29, 1882—Left the city at 9.30, crossing again to Oakland, and thence turning southward, and passing through central California. We took supper at Madera, 185^m. Saw many teams, of 6 to 8 horses and 6 plows, plowing. At about midnight passed the "Loop" in the mountains,

[page 502]

AT THURSTON'S, AND ON THE OCEAN.

Thursday, November 30, 1882—Arrived at Los Angeles at 8.55 A.M. Here we took train for Santa Ana, on the coast, 34 miles: then hired a carriage and driver, to go to Geo. Thurston's Br. Snow's Son in law, about 26 miles beyond. We reached his place about 7 P.M. after having lost our road and wandered 6 miles over the hills in the dark. We were put right by a Mr. H. G. Rosenbaum, who piloted us several miles, and would take no compensation.[63] We found Thurston living about ½ a mile from the ocean, with olives, oranges, lemons, figs, grapes, English walnuts, apples and other fruit in abundance, and were kindly received by the family.

Friday, December 1, 1882—I went to the sea shore directly from breakfast, and cannot express in words the joy, delight, and awe with which I watched the breakers roll in and break upon the shore. The sea has an immense and indescribable Charm for me. I found a place where rocks somewhat broke the fury of the waves, and had a good bath in the Pacific, thus realizing a dream of my youth. Br. Thatcher afterwards came with another young man, a son of Thurston's, who went in, and would have drowned but for assistance from Br. Thatcher, who saved him at the last moment. Afterwards I and a young man got a skiff launched with

61 Gilbert Clements was a British convert who came to Salt Lake City in 1854. In the 1870s a James Linforth was a financial agent for the Church. He had worked in London and San Francisco (Leonard J. Arrington, *Great Basin Kingdom: An Economic History of the Saints, 1830–1950* [Urbana, IL: Univ. of Illinois Press, 1986], 311).

62 *Uncle Tom's Cabin*, by Harriet Beecher Stowe, was first published as a serial and appeared as a book in 1852. Here it was adapted into a theatrical play.

63 Familysearch.org lists an H. G. Rosenbaum family who were farmers in San Juan, Los Angeles County.

some difficulty and danger, and I rowed out for about a mile, and tried to catch some fish, shoals of which I could see in the clear water beneath me. Rolling on the billows was very very delightful for me, but the boy got sea sick and I had to bring him ashore, landing with difficulty. Brs. Thatcher & Snow watched us uneasily from the shore. I picked up some beautiful Abelone shells from which mother of pearl is made. I spent the day, until night, reluctantly coming away although I had nothing to eat all day. The island of Santa Catalina was dimly visible many miles from shore.

[page 503]

YUMA, MARICOPA, AND TEMPE.

Saturday, December 2, 1882—Return to Los Angeles to day, and put up at Grand Central hotel, Did not like it, and changed to the Cosmopolitan, a very good place. Found R. Hughes, who formerly lived in Cache County, and took a bath,[64] Russian, Electric, which nearly boiled and shocked the life out of me for a while.

Sunday, December 3, 1882— This city has 16.000 inhabitants, and the American part is well built. The Mexican part is crowded, with low, flat roofed houses, and anything but beautiful. Walked through the cemetery, which was full of flowers, Roses, geraniums &c, in full bloom. The city has many orange groves, which with their rich, dark glossy green leaves and bright oranges, are very beautiful. The weather was warm, 72° in shade.

Monday, December 4, 1882—Started east and 9 A.M. passing through a lovely country, grassy hills, green and beautiful and orange groves right and left, with Pepper trees, cyprus, and eucalyptus all around. Passing over the San Gorgonio pass, we descend into a veritable desert, a large part of which is 260 feet lower than the ocean, and in Summer intensely hot. We got to Yuma, on the Colorado river, at dark, and had a good meal there. Could not see much of the place on account of darkness.

Tuesday, December 5, 1882—Arrived at Maricopa Station at 1.45 A.M. and found Pres[t] M[c]Donald waiting for us, with his carriage & Uncle Benjamin's, to take us to Tempe, 28 miles distant. Started before daylight, as there was no chance to sleep, and at 8 A.M. crossed the Gila about 12[m] from the R.R. and eat breakfast. The Gila is here a muddy stream, not very wide & about 2 feet deep. A village of the Pima Indians is on the river—they are all farmers. Arrived at Tempe about 3 P.M. and found uncle Joseph E. very sick, having taken a very severe cold while planting cabbages after a shower.

[page 504]

UNCLE JOSEPH VERY SICK. AT MESA & JONESVILLE.

Tuesday, December 5, 1882—He was very low, and I had no hope for him. Br. Thatcher and I administered to Benja's wife Bell, who was also quite sick. Found many of the family living in poor mexican houses, adobe, with flat dirt roofs, and not very well satisfied.

Wednesday, December 6, 1882—Went and visited among the family. Dined at Mr. Haydens,[65] with Snow, Thatcher & Uncle Benjamin. After which they went to Phoenix, 9 miles N. W. on the Salt River, which is quite a river.

Thursday, December 7, 1882—Administered again to Belle, and to Uncle Jos E. with Brs. Snow & Thatcher. Poor Rose felt very bad at the thought of losing her father, to whom she was most tenderly attached. The weather is quite warm in the sun,—uncomfortable for me, thickly clothed as I am. Left in the afternoon for Mesa city, reaching there, 7 miles, after dark, & stopped with Pres[t] A. F. Macdonald.

Friday, December 8, 1882—Went to Jonesville, three miles, with the brethren, to hold meeting. On the way passed near an ancient Nephite canal of huge dimensions, which branches into four others of large size. Our people now use one as a canal. Jonesville

64 This could be a relative of the Henry Hughes family of Mendon, Utah.

65 Charles T. Hayden was a Tempe pioneer who was kind to the Mormon settlers. He established Hayden's Ferry at today's location of the Mill Avenue Bridge, which crossed the Salt River from Phoenix to Tempe, a distance of approximately eight miles. Carl Hayden, his son, was a ferryman, merchant, and miller. The Hayden Mill still stands as a Tempe landmark (James H. McClintock, *Mormon Settlements in Arizona* [Phoenix: Manufacturing Stationers, 1921], 219).

consists of a few families. About 50 were present at the meeting, when Brs. Thatcher, Snow and I spoke. Returned to Mesa at dusk. About a mile off from the road were some ancient ruins of a city, the walls several feet high, stone.

Saturday, December 9, 1882—Meetings in forenoon, afternoon, and evening. I spoke in the afternoon, and feel much blessed. In the evening there was priesthood meeting. Dined with Mrs. Sarah Ricks Turman.

Sunday, December 10, 1882—3 Meetings again to day. I spoke ¾ of an hour in the forenoon, and felt well. In the afternoon officers were elected for a Stake organization, complete, and several Bishops and Councillors were appointed, and all voted in and ordained. The stake was named "Maricopa" stake

[page 505]

LEAVE MESA. TUCSON.

Monday, December 11, 1882—We leave here today. I find many friends here whom I know and like. Pres^t Macdonald and family have treated us very kindly, also Br. & Sister Bush & many others. By request I wrote for Sister MacDonald, in her album:—To Mrs. Elizabeth G. Macdonald:—

As thou, dear sister, hast been proved
  A kind and thoughtful friend,
So may thy joys, thy peace and love
  Grow brighter, to the end.

I like Mesa very much, but fear it is too warm here in summer. But for those who like warm weather, it is a good and rich country. As we left at 11.30 A. M. and drove through the plains, I saw much ancient crockery scattered over the earth, while many gigantic Sequoias rise like pillars all over the plain, generally having a height of 15 to 30 feet, and a diameter of a foot or more. They look very strange, being destitute of leaves or any regular branches.

This morning Uncle Benj. F. was present from Tempé, and says yesterday 16 more wagons of the family came in. Uncle Jos. E. is failing, and cannot live. Poor Rose, no one will feel his loss as she will. In his sleep he often calls for her, and she rarely leaves him day or night

We reached the Gila about Sunset, and lunched, arriving at Maricopa Sta. at 7.30 P.M. As we did not wish to enter the filthy "hotel" there, crowded with low, debased looking ruffians, we lay down in the Corral among the mules, and slept until train time—about 1.50 A. M.—then took train.

Tuesday, December 12, 1882—Reached Tucson for breakfast—nearly the oldest city in America, being about 350 years old. The American part is thriving, and much business is done there. The Mexican portion is a collection of poor hovels and sheds.

[page 506]

START TO SONORA. CONTENTION. CHARLESTON. HEREFORD.

Tuesday, December 12, 1882—Arrived at Benson, our terminus, 8.35 A. M. & found D. P. Kimball[66] and J. Hill there with carriages for us. We proceeded thence to Br. Kimballs, 6 miles, and were hospitably welcomed by his family. So here we are, after a journey of about 2000 miles, in Southern Arizona After supper, with br. C. Layton[67] I went to A. Bingham's[68] to stay. Administered to his daughter, who was quite sick. Very cold night, thermometer at freezing point.

Wednesday, December 13, 1882—Found letter from home, and Charles. Went to Benson and while there I weighed—171½ lbs. a gain of 8 lbs. since I left home. From Benson I went to J. Hill's to stay, with Br. Layton, some 15 miles, & about 10 miles below Tombstone,[69] the county seat, a place of about 6000

66 In 1871, David P. Kimball was president of the Paris Idaho Stake (Leonard J. Arrington, *Brigham Young: American Moses* [Urbana, IL: Univ. of Illinois Press, 1986], 336).

67 In 1883, Christopher Layton was living in St. David, just north of the Mexican border; he had come from Kaysville, Utah. He was the organizer of many of the southeastern Gila Valley wards. When he served as a branch president, one of his counselors was David P. Kimball (McClintock, *Mormon Settlement in Arizona*, 262–63).

68 This could be Alonzo Bingham, who was among the first settlers of Hyrum, Utah (Ricks and Cooley, *History of a Valley*, 45).

69 This is part of the scattering of the Mormons as a result of the approaching wave of persecution. Note the population of Tombstone.

people and several mills (quartz) in a rich mining district.

Thursday, December 14, 1882—Went to St Davids to meeting. I spoke, also Br. Thatcher. In the afternoon Pres[t] Snow spoke. After meeting went to D P Kimball's, and wrote letters.

Friday, December 15, 1882—Started for Sonora to day with three carriages, 1 four-horse team and one horseman; we had in all 14 men, viz:—Brs. E. Snow, M. Thatcher, C. Layton, Self, D. P. Kimball, Hill, Bebec, Horne, Merrill, Curtis & others From St Davids we drove through Contention, 10 m. where there are two Quartz mills: thence to Charleston & hired a room to cook and sleep in at a feed corral. Charleston is 27 m. South of Benson, and on the San Pedro river. Here, also, are quartz mills. After supper Br. Snow was elected Pres[t] of the company and chaplain, M. Thatcher clerk & correspondent, D P Kimball Camp master & officer of the Guard, and myself Chief Steward, Br. Trejo interpreter

Saturday, December 16, 1882—Started 9 A.M. Passed up the San Pedro,[70] past Hereford and Ochoeville, while Br. Trejo[71] went on to Tombstone, to see the Mexican Consul there about our getting over the line into Mexico. Charleston to Hereford 15 miles.

[page 507]

SAN PEDRO RANCH, SONORA

Saturday, December 16, 1882—Towards evening crossed the boundary line, and stood on Mexican soil. The line is marked by a stone monument, on the top of a mesa, east of the road. At sunset reached the ancient Presidio de San Pedro, built in 1530, 7 miles South of the Line, and here found Señor Jose Maria Elias, the owner of the San Pedro Ranch. We also found the Mexican custom house and guards here, who examined our wagons, valises, &c, took account of our animals with their brands, ourselves, and all pertaining to us, and required payment of several hundred ($275.) [$5,542] dollars, as duty on wagons & horses. Camped near the fort, and hired a Mexican to herd our horses, so they would not be stolen. Br. Trejo came up at dusk, having rode 52 miles. Cold night. A mouse crawled over my feet in the night, and I thought it was a scorpion till I found it. From Benson to the Customs House is about 60 miles, over a beautiful country, the foot hills and mountains covered with live oak (evergreen)

Sunday, December 17, 1882—Went with Señor Elias to look over his ranch, and traveled up the San Pedro to its head, 1 ½ miles, lunched, and returned. The Ranch is 40 leagues square, and he asks $165.000.00 [$3,325,055] for it, or $55,000 [$1,108,352] for his 1/3 interest.[72] Its elevation is 5400 feet. At our return to the fort, Señor Elias gave us a room in the fort to sleep in, and was very courteous. The accompanying is a plan of the old fort, built of adobes, and a strong place of defense in its time. The Custom House (Aduana) is near by on the other side of the road. The custom house officer was Castilian[73] with very fair complexion—pink and white, blue eyes and light hair: but the Soldiers were a dark and villainous looking set, who looked as if it would be a pleasure to cut a man's throat.

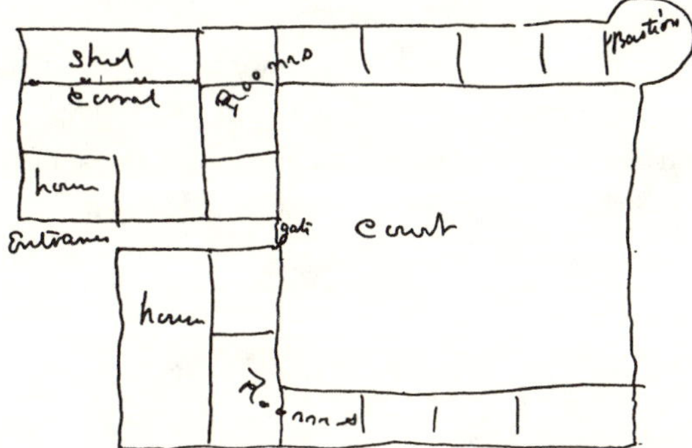

Fig. 6.1—Presidio de San Pedro.

70 The San Pedro River flows from Arizona into Mexico. Early Mormon colonies dot the river (McClintock, *Mormon Settlement in Arizona*, x).

71 Meliton Gonzales Trejo was a member of the original 1875 party sent to explore Sonora. He was a translator and would later assist in the translation of the Book of Mormon and other Church literature into Spanish (F. LaMond Tullis, *Mormons In Mexico: The Dynamics of Faith and Culture* [Logan: Utah State Univ. Press, 1987] 18, 33, 45).

72 This is a large ranch that the exploration party is apparently interested in purchasing. A league is an old land measure in Mexico. One league equals approximately 4,400 acres.

73 Castile is a region of central Spain.

[page 508]

BISBEE COPPER MINE.[74]

Sunday, December 17, 1882—In deed, only a few days ago two travelers were found murdered not far from here, supposed by indians, but there is good reason to believe they were killed by these very fellows for plunder. Br. Snow could make no satisfactory trade for the place, and to me it seems unsuited for a place for a "city of refuge"[75] which we were sent out to find.

Monday, December 18, 1882—Started back at 8.25 a.m. to go to the San Bernardino Ranch, on the head of the Yaqui river, & near the Chihuahua line. Received back the money first deposited, and started for Bisbee, passing Ochoeville and Hereford. Near Sunset we entered a pass (Mule Pass) in the Mule Mts. & camped at a rancher's place at dark. Paid 10¢ a head for watering animals, About a mile from the famous Bisbee Copper mine. Got a good joke on Br. Layton. He saw a dark, dirty fellow come to the well for water with his donkey and water kegs, and supposing him a Mexican, and wishing to know what he would ask for his "Burro" or donkey, said in Spanish, "Señor, Quantos valle la esta Burro." The supposed Mexican answered in regular American twang, "What's the matter with you, now?" The dialogue was overheard, and afterwards afforded much fun for the party, as Br. Layton rather prides himself on his Spanish.

Tuesday, December 19, 1882—Started east, and soon entered Sulphur Spring valley, about 140 miles long, and 25 to 40 wide, which we crossed, ascended a sloping bench a few miles, and came to Mud Springs & nooned. Then gave new name to the springs. I proposed the name "Pedrogoso Sps" as it lies in a pass of the Pedrogoso Mts.

74 Gold, copper, and silver were found in the southeast Arizona desert. Bisbee, Arizona, became the center of that mining development. It was a mining town, not a Mormon settlement, named after DeWitt Bisbee, who was among the original financiers of the Copper Queen Mine. The city is west of Douglas, Arizona, and approximately fifteen miles from the Sonora, Mexico, border.

75 "City of refuge" is a common phrase in Mormon history. As members of the church sought to avoid persecution they were driven to seek a land where they could live in peace.

[page 509]

PEDROGOSO SPRINGS. SILVER CREEK. SAN BERNARDINO.

December 1882—Other names were proposed, but mine was adopted by unanimous vote. Thence drove 8m. to Silver Creek Spring and camped. Good clear water, & rich Soil around. Drove to day 38 miles, yesterday 37. The country abounds in many beautiful kinds of cactus, some, the Mescal—growing 25 to 30 feet high, with great clusters of flowers. The natives make a liquor like whiskey from its root. It has a smoky taste.

Wednesday, December 20, 1882—Pleasant morning, drove 15 miles—descending—and came to the Presidio of San Bernardino, 350 years old, built of adobes, and now in ruins.[76] It has been a strong fortress, sufficient for several thousand men, but long ago its inhabitants were killed by indians. The walls of the buildings still stand about 10 or 12 feet high, and seem as if they may stand a century or more, yet. I examined the ground around, and found the soil poor, and in my opinion the place is very unfit for the settlement of our people, having very little water, and no timber but mesquite. A square monument about 4½ feet high, and 4 square at the base, marks the boundary line. After looking around for some hours and exploring several miles, we suddenly felt best to return to our last camp and started about sun down, arriving about 8½. Stormed in the night, with a flurry of snow. (We afterwards found there were indians who would have been troublesome, as they killed some men there a few days after, but we did not thus know it.) The Lord moved us away by His spirit, and so saved us from danger. To Him be the praise.

Thursday, December 21, 1882—Drove back to Pedrogoso Sps. & thence 9 miles to forks of the road, where several (4) left us here to return to St Davids,[77] while the rest go to Smithville and the Gila river country. After dinner, went on to a cattle ranch on White

76 This was an ancient Spanish fortress in Sonora, Mexico, just south of Douglas, Arizona. The ruins are still visible today.

77 Saint David, Arizona, was a small Mormon settlement founded in 1877. Not far from Tombstone, Arizona, it was named after David W. Patten who was an apostle from 1835–1838. He was killed in the Battle of Crooked River, Missouri.

river and camped with some cattle thieves, as we had good reason to believe, but they treated us well. The scenery today is very lovely, grass waving everywhere, and the hills of a beautiful form. Very cold night. 35 miles.

[page 510]

WM. FIFE'S. HELEN'S DOME. BOWIE. MOODY'S

Friday, December 22, 1882—Very cold morning, ice ¾ inch thick. Sent a man up to Campbell's, 15m. to ask him to meet us at Wm Fife's tomorrow, and we reached that place at noon, and were kindly welcomed by Br. Fife and his two wives and family. Were very glad to meet a woman and girls again—wanted to kiss them. They were also very glad to see us. They live in a most beautiful grove of evergreen oats, broad and spreading, with Manzanita & Cactus growing around.

~~Friday~~ Saturday, December 23, 1882—This forenoon Br. Layton and I, with Hill & Fife, drove over the country all the forenoon, and found a good place for a small settlement on a spring. After dinner we started on our journey, but lost our proper road, taking one which led us several miles out of our course. Towards evening we crossed the Dos Cabezas range,[78] and camped at a spring near Camp Bowie, above which rises the perpendicular peak of a Mountain called "Helen's Dome" from the wife of Capt. Stone, commander of the Post. She was thrown over the precipice by the indians, in full view of the garrison, some years ago. This is a very romantic part of the country, and very beautiful.

Sunday, December 24, 1882—About 16 miles brings us to Bowie Sta. on the S.P.R.R. Here is an artesian well 300 feet deep, with water quite warm—almost hot. We watered and drove on a mile and nooned, after which drove 17 miles to another deep well, bought water, supped and drove 10 miles and camped about 8 P.M. Drove 44 miles today. Br. Snow feels quite ill.

Monday, December 25, 1882—Drove 18 miles to Safford, county seat of Graham county:[79] thence 7 miles to John Moody's[80] where we found, at 11 A.M. a long table plentifully spread with everything nice, and to which we were pressed to sit down.

[page 511]

SMITHVILLE, CURTIS, STAKE PROPOSED.

December 1882—Br. Moody's folks had put up the dinner as a Christmas dinner, and to welcome Br. J. Pace[81] and other settlers just arrived from Utah. After dinner we came to Smithville,[82] about 2 P.M. and found the children engaged in a dance. We were hospitably met. I went to Jo^s^ Foster's[83] to stop—an old Loganite. In the evening there was a dance for grown people, but I went to bed, being quite tired.

Tuesday, December 26, 1882—This morning we went ~~6~~ 8 miles down the Gila to Curtis, and held meeting at 10 A.M. I spoke and felt well. Brs. Snow, Layton, & Thatcher also spoke. We had a good meeting, and after dinner returned to Smithville, and had meeting at 2 P.M. at which I, and Brs. Snow, Kimball & Thatcher spoke, & I dismissed. In the evening the Y.M. & Y.L. Society's[84] presented their reports, at which I spoke, also, Brs. Thatcher and Snow. Smithville has about 100 families, living in poor habitations, but the farm land is rich, with plenty of Gila water. Also

78 The Dos Cabezas Mountain Wilderness is found in Cochise County, Arizona, approximately twenty miles east of Wilcox, Arizona.

79 Safford, Arizona, was another Mormon settlement of 1873–74. The town is named after the Pacely Killen Safford, the Arizona territorial governor.

80 John M. Moody was among the first settlers in Thatcher, Arizona. He arrived in the summer of 1881 (McClintock, *Mormon Settlement in Arizona*, 248).

81 James Pace was a resident of Thatcher, Arizona, and a former member of the Mormon Battalion (Norma Baldwin Ricketts, ed., *Arizona's Honeymoon Trail and Mormon Wagon Roads* [Mesa, AZ: Cox, 2001], 171, 174, 176, 178, 180–81, 321, 328; McClintock, *Mormon Settlement in Arizona*, 28–29, 36).

82 Smithville, Arizona, today called Pima, was a Mormon settlement in the Gila Valley. It was the only one settled out of necessity rather than under the direction of Church leadership (McClintock, *Mormon Settlement in Arizona*, 244–45).

83 Joseph Foster was one of the first Cache Valley settlers in Whitney, Utah (Ricks and Cooley, *History of a Valley*, 74).

84 These are the Young Men's and Young Ladies' Mutual Improvement Associations.

abundance of mesquite for firewood and big cottonwoods for building. The Gila is quite a stream—about 400 or 500 feet wide, and 2 ft deep, muddy, but not brackish—excellent for irrigation. At the meeting to day the name of St Curtis was changed to "Curtis."[85] Another small settlement is just started a little up the river on the north side, and another at Moody's, five miles above. A few miles below, are the ruins of a city 5 miles long by 3 wide, still in tolerable preservation. The Cottonwood trees have mistletoe growing upon them—a beautiful evergreen vine, with small, pearly berries.

Wednesday, December 27, 1882—Meeting again to day, fore noon and afternoon. Before the afternoon meeting it was proposed to Brs. Layton, Kimball and myself, that we should be appointed a Presidency of a Stake to be organized here, by Elders Snow & Thatcher, and wishing to know how we felt about the matter.

[page 512]

A SURPRISE, & 70$. EUREKA. WILCOX. ST DAVIDS.

Wednesday, December 27, 1882—It took us by surprise, but after thinking a little while, I said I did not feel competent for such a position, but would like to be where I thought the Lord would like to have me. Br. Kimball had Similar feelings, but Br. Layton did not wish to accept—would like to see Pres^t Taylor about it. So it was decided not to organize a stake now, but simply set apart officers for a ward. Accordingly Jo^s H. Rogers[86] was put in as Bishop of Smithville, with two counsellors, and presiding officers for the other places, which was done. Another dance this evening, but I did not attend.

[written in margin in shaky writing]

At this time the name Smithville was changed to Pima.

Thursday, December 28, 1882—Drove 20 miles and nooned. Here we found quite a surprise in the shape of a nice picnic already spread for us, by parties who had gone ahead of us, unknow to us. After dinner they gave us some $70.^{00} [$1,411] to help us on our way. The people of Mesa had made a similar donation of $13.^{00} [$262] before. We crossed a spur of Mt Graham, and arrived at Eureka Springs about 8 P.M, having driven 43 miles. At first, and until Mr. Leatsch found we were Mormons, we could get no permission to stop, but when he found who we were, he received us very hospitably—a great blessing to us, for the weather was very cold, and the next Ranch was 18^m farther on. Here I met Major McCrary, U.S. Paymaster, who knows my cousin Dewitt C. Poole, who is also Paymaster in the U. S. Army.

Friday, December 29, 1882—Drove 36 miles to Wilcox Sta. S.P.R.R. in 6 hours. Here M. Thatcher, Snow, Kimball, and I took train for St Davids, 47 miles, arriving there near sundown. At Wilcox Br. Snow and I bought return tickets to Ogden $90.^{00} [$1,814] each, and here Br. Snow learned by Tel. of the death of his wife, Artemisia, whom he left very sick, and not expecting to live. She was the wife of his youth and her loss stirred him deeply.

[page 513]

BRS. SNOW AND LAYTON RETURN HOME. LYMAN A FATHER

December 29, 1882—He controlled his feelings very well, but I could see how he suffered secretly. 83^m today by carriage and train.

December 30, 1882—Wrote letters today. Also wrote letters for Br. Snow, and compared notes of our trip with Br. Thatcher.

Sunday, December 31, 1882—Went to Sunday School, and spoke, also Layton & Br. Thatcher. Dined at Frank Campbell, and Br. Layton and I proposed to buy his gristmill for $1000^{00} [$20,152] In the afternoon, Brs. Snow and Thatcher spoke splendidly, I never heard Br. Snow speak so well in my life before. Br. D. P. Kimball was set apart as Bishop, with Brs. Horne and A. Bingham counsel. I dismissed and staid that night at Mrs. Hubbard's.

Monday, January 1, 1883—Attended a wedding of Bingham's daughter, at which a Mr. Howard,

85 Moses Curtis was the first settler, in 1881, of St. Curtis, Arizona. Today it is called Eden (McClintock, *Mormon Settlement in Arizona*, 248).

86 Joseph H. Rogers, not to be confused with Josephine W. Rogers, was a leader in the Gila Valley settlements (McClintock, *Mormon Settlement in Arizona*, 246).

claimant of the lands above St Davids on an old Mexican grant—appeared uninvited, but was sent away in high dudgeon by Br. Snow.[87] In the evening attended a good party at St Davids and enjoyed myself well. The music was made by two Mexicans from Tombstone, with a fiddle and guitar. Also wrote letters home. Br. Thatcher wishes me to go with him on his next trip into Mexico, while Brs. Snow and Layton will return home. Br. Snow suffering severely with Brights disease[88] and other derangements.

Tuesday, January 2, 1883—Meeting at St Davids at 10 A.M. Br. Snow gave me his photograph, taken in ~~S. L. City~~ San Francisco, on our way here, and seemed to feel very well towards me. In the afternoon Brs. Snow & Layton started home. I heard today of the death of Uncle Jos. E. Johnson. Poor Rose! She fainted on her father's coffin. I also heard from Br. Thatcher that Lyman is a father Rained all night, a very unusual thing for this time of the year here.

[page 514]

2ND TRIP INTO SONORA. LA NORIA, SONOITA, SAN RAFAEL

January 3, 1883—Snow on mountains this morning. Rained all day, nearly. Read and wrote.

Thursday, January 4, 1883—Started again for Sonora with Brs. Thatcher, D. P. Kimball, and five others, with two carriages. We drove to Contention, got some few things there, and started up the Babacomiré valley, intending to cross into Mexico at La Noria, and passing the Ranch of San Rafael, which has been recommended to us, to purchase. Camped at a lone cabin 20 miles. Heard that indians are killing people in Sonora. Bought hay.

Friday, January 5, 1883—Drove 14 miles and nooned at a pool of water, after which ascended, and crossed a spur of the Huachuca Mts. at 3 P.M. passing through a most lovely country, grassy, and covered with Live Oaks, & some white oaks and cedars, also Sycamores. We came down into the San Rafael valley & Ranch, and camped at the Ranch house. This ranch is a very fine one for stock, but no water for irrigation. The house is 5 miles from the U. S. line. Here we learn there is no Mexican house at La Noria, and to enter the country without the proper papers, subjects our property to confiscation and ourselves to be taken as prisoners to Ures. So we decide to go back and around to Los Nogales where there is a custom house.

Saturday, January 6, 1883—Drove 17 miles through a beautiful country, to the valley of Sonoita, and dined. While eating, a man came up, nearly starved, and wanted something to eat, which we gave, and also a quantity to take with him. He disappeared as suddenly as he came, and was doubtless an escaped convict from Tucson, who had escaped some time before, after nearly killing his keeper. We passed down the Sonoita, a beautiful little stream, bordered with timber of various kinds, such as Cottonwood, Ash, Sycamore &c

[page 515]

CINCO ALAMOS. CALABASAS.

January 6, 1883—The Sonoita valley is wonderfully rich, but the houses and farms have long been unoccupied, their owners having been killed many years ago by Apaches. The Sonora R.R. passes down this valley, and is a well built road.[89] We camped at a deserted and ruinous ranch, where the sunflowers stood 18 to 20 ft high and very thick, and this without irrigation. At 8 P.M. a kind of fear suddenly came over us, and we moved into the houses, not feeling safe from indians outside. A strange and melancholy feeling came over us, as I thought of the cruel scenes of blood and murder enacted here long years ago, and the air seemed full of the spirits of the dead. Near the house stands an immense cottonwood, full 30 feet circumference, spreading into five large ones a few feet from the ground, each 10 or 12 feet circumference. This place I call Cinco Alamos (5 Cottonwoods). As this place is a type of many others, I here give a rough sketch of it:—

87 "In high dudgeon" is to be in a state of indignation.

88 Bright's disease is the inflammation of a kidney.

89 The Sonora Railroad was an important part of Mexican modernization. Just as in other countries, the railroad was important to transportation and national economies. The Sonora rails were meant to connect eastern and western Mexico.

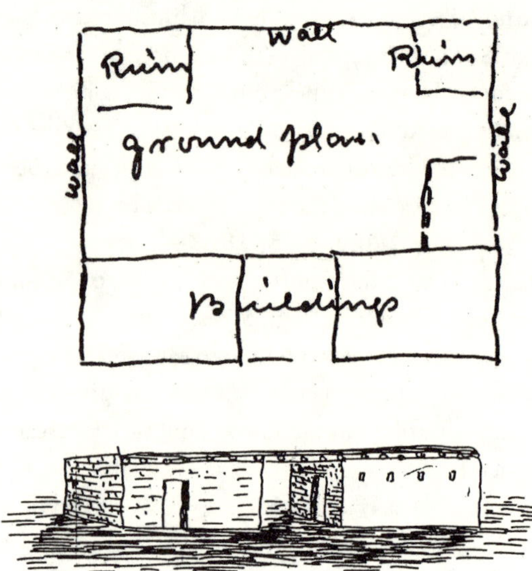

Fig. 6.2—Cinco Alamos.

The houses have no windows, and are provided with loopholes for musketry, located near the flat dirt roofs. They are built of adobes, generally mixed with straw.

Sunday, January 7, 1883—7 miles over a rocky country to Calabases, once a flourishing Mexican town, but exterminated by indians about 150 years ago, nothing remains of the old town but the name, which signifies squashes. There is a fine brick hotel here, and the railroad men are trying to build up a new town here. They would like to have our people settle there. The Sonoita here joins the Santa Cruz, and both sink and disappear, to come again to the surface about 70 or 80 miles north near the Gila.

[page 516]

LOS NOGALES, BUENA VISTA, MEZCAL, LA PAZ.

January 7, 1883—We here turn up the valley, ascending a small brook called the Potrero, and thence from Calabasas 11 miles to Los Nogales, a Mexican town built on the Boundary line, one half Mexican and the south part American.[90] A Mexican flag was flying from their custom house, and the American flag from ours. The town is small, and only important from its position. The name "Nogales" signifies walnuts, but we did not see any trees there. It is about on the summit of a chain of wooded hills, and beautifully situated. Here our teams, wagons, luggage &c was inspected and a list thereof taken; also a deposit of $127.^{00}$ [$2,559] was made on account of our horses and wagons. We left thus at 3.25 P.M. and followed along the Sonora R.R. some 2 miles and then turned off to the east among some beautifully wooded and grassy hills, and soon began to descend towards the Santa Cruz. Before reaching it, one of Kimball's horses got sick, and we camped at a small spring. Many walnut trees grow along the hollow, and we gathered plenty of them (Black Walnuts) to eat. Distance 32 miles.

Monday, January 8, 1883—Today is the 31st anniversary of my marriage. Who would have thought one year ago that to day I should be in Mexico. Two miles brought us to the Santa Cruz and Ranch of Buena Vista, where we found a few families, but the owner was absent. His name is Emanuel Martinez and Buena Vista is about 14^{m} from Los Nogales. Martinez also owns the next ranch above—the Mescal. At Buena Vista they were distilling Mezcal, a national whiskey, from the Mezcal cactus.[91] It is clear as water and colorless, and very strong. It cannot be adulterated with water, as it will not mix. We passed up the Santa Cruz vally, one of the most beautiful I ever saw, passing through the "Mez-cal" Santa Barbara & La Paz Ranches. The country is rich, and the climate delightful. This would be the very place, in my opinion, for the proposed city of Refuge being easy of access by rail and a very desirable place to live in.

90 Calabasas or Calabazas was a post office settlement, "a Papago Indian village, a Mexican garrison, a U.S. military base, a mining camp, and a farming community before becoming a railroad stop that was determined to become the gateway to Mexico." It was abandoned in 1913 (http://ghosttowns.com/states/az/calabasas.html). Nogales, Arizona, and Nogales, Mexico, are immediately across the border from one another. The term *Los dos Nogales* refers to the twin cities (Byrd Granger, ed., *Arizona's Names: X Marks the Place* [Tucson: Treasure Chest Publication, 1983], 437).

91 The Mezcal cactus was used for food, drink, and fiber by the native tribes.

[page 517]

LA PAZ. SAN LAZARO. COCOSPERA.

January 8, 1883— La Paz is only one house of which the following is a sketch:

Fig. 6.3—La Paz.

Here we saw a novel way of bringing water: A horse was carrier. He had a canvas sack hung across the horse, with a large pocket on each side to hold the water, and in the bottom of each pocket was a cows horn hanging point down. I was wondering how the water was to come out, as there was no hole through the horn, but a woman soon solved my difficulty. She set a pail beneath, pushed <u>up</u> the horn, allowing the water to flow <u>around</u> it. When the pail was full, she pulled the horn down, which closed the hole in the pocket tightly, the weight of the water pressing it to its place. Left La Paz at 2.30 and reached the ruined and ancient town of San Lazaro, of which nothing remains but the church. A few families now live there, in wretched huts. Here we bought some beef & corn, paying about 5¢ pr lb. for the corn & about 8¢ for the beef. Two miles farther brought us to the top of a low divide, and we then descend a beautiful open cañon towards Cocospera, to see which, with the Santa Cruz valley, is the object of this journey. We camped in a most beautiful place, surrounded by Live Oaks and Black Walnuts. At San Lazaro a road turns up Easterly to Santa Cruz, 8 miles distant.

Tuesday, January 9, 1883—A few miles lower down, we come into Cocospera valley,—lovely in the extreme—but not now cultivated, as the water seems to have disappeared. Many ancient canals are still visible.[92] Formerly a city stood here, the ruins of which still remain, surrounding a large and once beautiful church, standing on a mesa about 100 feet above the valley. In the valley below are trees belonging to the old monks or priests: among them I saw quinces, dates, pomegranates, and other choice trees.

[page 518]

COCOSPERA CHURCH

January 9, 1883—This place was founded about 300 years ago, and was a place of note, but the inhabitants were killed by indians long ago—about 100 years. We stopped to examine the church about ¾ hour. It had been surrounded by a wall and buildings forming a square of about 500 feet, the Church fronting the South, built of bricks, with massive walls and roof arched inside and covered outside with tiles. Inside, we found part of the roof fallen in, but intact at each end. The walls and ceiling, formed of plaster of paris, was covered with flowers, heads of cherubs &c painted—not very artistically, while niches for the images of saints, pilasters and other ornamental work, made it very beautiful. We went up a winding stairway into the choir, which was paved with square flat brick, and overhead, in a circle, were inscribed "Honor et gloria ad Deus solé."—"<u>Honor and glory to God alone</u>," as I translate it. From the open tower the view was lovely in the extreme. How much more so must it have been in the time of its prosperity! We were filled with very sad feelings, and as at Cinco Alamos, on the Sonoita, the air seemed peopled with myriads of spirits of the dead—those who had once lived, loved, intrigued, bought and sold, hated, married, aggrandized themselves and pulled down others. The church had evidently been the last refuge of the miserable victims. The doors and windows had been bricked up, except a small opening in the main entrance, just large enough for one person to squeeze through, and two holes left to fire through. I almost seemed to hear the cries of despair from shrieking women and children, as they fell beneath the merciless knife and tomahawk of their slayers. I took an imperfect sketch of the South front, but did not have time to finish the view of the side. <u>In</u> the church, two rude crosses marked the graves of two children, buried among the fallen debris from the roof, and near the foot of the altar.

92 The Hohokam people occupied Arizona for hundreds of years before the Saints arrived. This is a reference to the canal system these original people constructed to water their crops. Today's Salt River Valley canal system follows these same lines.

Fig. 6.4—South front of Cocospera Church, Sonora.

[page 519]

COCOSPERA. BABAZAQUE

January 9, 1883—The whole building was built of ~~wood~~ masonry, no wood being visible.

We left the place with saddened hearts, and went down the beautiful valley, now deserted except one large farm. We passed through beautiful groves of large Black Walnut trees, while the mesquite, cottonwood, sycamore and hackberry, grew unusually large. A few miles farther brought us to the entrance of a Cañon, down which flows a fine stream of pure water, shaded for miles by a thick mass of timber, while on the mountain sides immense cacti grew in wonderful profusion. Especially noticeable was the Sequoia gigantea. I give here a sketch of various kinds of Cacti growing in different places, according to attitude and climate. There are many other very strange and beautiful varieties, which I cannot here show.

The cañon we descended is about 10 miles in length, and then opens out into a broad valley for about 6 miles to the farm of Babazaque, which is owned by Col. Hilario S. Gabilondo and his mother, and comprises several hundred acres of choice land well fenced and well cultivated, with plenty of good water. We camped here, the owner being known to Br. Trejo. Gabilondo offered to rent us his farm for half products, or $1500 pr year cash, and to furnish 4 teams, plows & buildings, for 4 years.

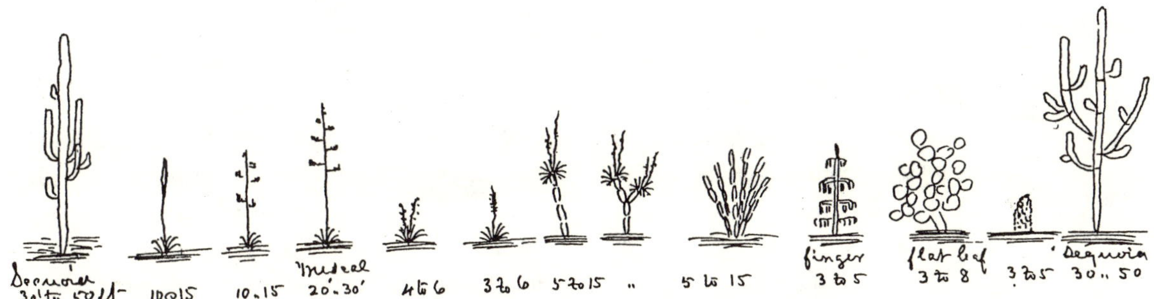

Fig. 6.5—Various kinds of cacti.

[page 520]

VEQUITA, LA FLORES.

January 9, 1883—Kimball's horse was very sick, and we abandoned the idea of going any further south, although we had intended to go to Magdalena, some 6 leagues distant. A Mexican league = 5000 varas, of 33_ in. each, = 2.61 miles English.

Wednesday, January 10, 1883—Br. Kimball's horse still sick, and we lay by until 1.20 P.M. This forenoon Br. Teeples shot a crow, which much displeased Gabilondo, who said the crows always gave them notice of the approach of hostile Indians a day or so ahead of their raids, & they regard them as friends. We crossed a bench about 5 miles, to the Vanbuto river valley, down which passes the Sonora R.R. and at Vequita inquired our way, to La Flores, about 5 miles up the river, which we reached and camped at, 5 P.M.

This is a small Mexican hamlet, with rich farms well fenced, and here we bought some corn @ 5¢ Br. Thatcher and I went upon the bench; some 80 ft high, and were enchanted with the lovely view. It brought to mind Gray's Elegy—"The curfew tolls—the knell of parting day." It was a scene of perfect repose, content, and peace, and I felt as if I would like to live there, and help to evangelize the people, who, though ignorant, seem honest & kind, and are of the royal blood of Joseph. The men were plowing with oxen, having a straight stick tied to their horns, and drawing a wooden plow, like this:—

Fig. 6.6—Mexican plow.

The plow, handle and all, is of one crooked stick, with a small plate of iron on the end to keep it from wearing; the end of the tongue being tied to the yoke. American plows are scarce, because of the extremely high import duty.

Thursday, January 11, 1883—Started early—a delightful balmy morning. I went on ahead, on foot, at times leaving the road, & wandering among the noble trees that crowd much of the valley.

[page 521]

AGUA ZAREA, LOS NOGALES, ST DAVIDS

January 11, 1883—At noon, 11 miles we stopped near the upper end of the vally, after which we passed through a cañon for 2 or 3 miles, coming out in a fine open grassy valley, at the Cascosa Ranch. Camped at 5 at Agua Zarca R.R. Station, in some beautiful live oaks. Distance 28^{m}. The climate here is perceptibly cooler, as we must have risen, coming up the river, some 2000 or 2500 feet

Friday, January, 12, 1883—Started at 8.20, and reached Los Nogales at 10.40 distance 11 miles. Got back our deposit money, bought supplies and went on at noon. Here I bought 6 1-pound cakes of brown sugar, made by Mexicans, and called "Panoche" for 50¢; also ½ pint of "Mezcal," a liquor like Scotch Whiskey, made from the mezcal root, for 50¢ also. From Los Nogales to Benson, by rail, is 88^{m} to Guaymas 265^{m}

or 426 Kilometers. The R.R. fare in Mexico is by law 3¢ pr. kilometer; in Arizona 10¢ pr mile,—more than double. The regular fare from Benson to Guaymas, is $8.30 [$167] to Nogales & thence $12.75 [$257] total $21.05, [$424] for 353 miles of R.R. At Los Nogales we learn that yesterday Indians killed 15 Mexicans just in the section of country we desired to visit, had not our horse got sick, and caused us to turn northward. We reached Calabasas at 3.10 and went on, up the Sonoita about 12 m. and camped. Distance 35 miles.

Saturday, January 13, 1883—This morning four of us took train, at 5 A.M. for St Davids, leaving the teams to follow. We reached St. Davids at about 8.30. On the train we met a Mr. Block, who had kindly assisted us to enter Sonora at San Pedro, just returning from Sonora, where the Indians had taken all he had, except his scalp and life. But he felt well satisfied to get so easy as that.

Sunday, January 14, 1883—Put on clean clothes, and bathed in the San Pedro. Went to meeting and spoke. Wrote to Henrietta & Charles—also [word missing]. Had letters [words missing]

[page 522]

LOS ANGELES. SACRAMENTO. HOME AGAIN.

Monday, January 15, 1883—To day Br. Thatcher baptized about 20 persons, which I took down an account from Orrin D. Merrill of his trip some years ago, after thieves with stolen horses, a wonderful instance of courage and perseverance.[93]

Tuesday, January 16, 1883—At 3.55 (San Fran. time) Br. Thatcher & I started home! What magic in that word! Took sleeper & arrived at Los Angeles about 4.30 P.M. and then met James Mack, of Smithfield.[94] At Yuma I got a few photos of Scenery there, and bought some 3 articles of indian pottery as curiosities. Left Los Angeles at 5 P.M. and reached Lathrop at 10.35 A.M. Here Br. Thatcher left me, to go on to San Francisco, while I proceed to Sacramento, which city I reached at about 2 P.M. I took a bath, cleaned up, and then walked all around the town, visited the State Capitol, and C. P. Machine shops, and saw iron rolled into bars, rods, rails &c. Put up at the Western Hotel, a good and cheap place. Meals 25^{c} bed 50^{c}.

Wednesday & Thursday, January 17 & 18, 1883—Waited all day for Br. Thatcher to arrive, & bought a valise, oranges &c. A terribly long day. In the evening Br. T. arrived, and at 8 P.M. we started east. In Sacramento the lawns were green, flowers were blooming in open air, and it did not seem winter.

~~Thursday January 18,~~ Friday, January 19, 1883—Awoke this morning in Nevada; thermometer 37° below zero! What a change! We could hardly believe the instrument. Had to put overcoats on to keep comfortable in the sleeper.

~~Friday January 19,~~ Saturday, January 20, 1883—Near home, but very cold weather. Reached Ogden 8.35 & took U. & N. R. R. for Logan, reaching there 9.30 P.M.—58^{m}. Found all well, and intensely cold weather. Truly the Lord has blessed me on this journey. We have been preserved from Indians, railroad wrecks and train robbers, and sickness, and I have gained a knowledge of the south which I have long desired. My family have been sick with mumps and other ailments, but have been preserved from Small pox, of which many cases exist in Logan now.

[page 523]

CALLED TO ARIZONA. ALLEY, MY GRANDCHILD. KAYSVILLE.

Sunday, January 21, 1883—Went to see Lyman's family, and my new granddaughter Alley, who was born Dec. 22. 1882 at 9.30 P.M. Found them all well, with Virginia, who is still with them. Have taken a bad cold.

Monday, January 22, 1883—Thermometer 32° below Zero! Bad cold. Kept in bed a day or two, to ease my cough.

Saturday, January 27, 1883—This morning Br. Thatcher sent me word, that I am called to move to Southern Arizona, and have been appointed 2nd Counsellor to C. Layton, who is appointed President of that new Stake. Br. Thatcher afterwards told me that we, (as a Presidency of the Stake) have also the responsibility of colonizing Mexico. I told him I thought that a great responsibility. He said it was, but he should assist us all he could, as Pres^{t} of the Mexican Mission.

93 Orrin D. Merrill was a pioneer who was instrumental in the settling of the San Pedro River Valley.

94 James Mack was among the first settlers of Hyde Park, Utah (Ricks and Cooley, *History of a Valley*, 46).

I do not see how I can go, very well, unless I can sell out here, so as to get means to go with, but if God requires the move, He can & will open the way for me to go.

Tuesday, January 30, 1883—Sold 20 feet land, on 3^{d} Street, to T. W. R. Nelson, for \$400.$^{\underline{00}}$ [\$8,061] Next day paid it nearly all away on debts.

February 2, 1883—This evening we were invited to a party in honor of Br. M. Thatcher's 41st birth day, A nice time.

February 3, 1883—Sold Duddenhausen's note at Bank \$365.10 [\$7,355] & paid \$300.$^{\underline{00}}$ [\$6,046] in Store a/cs., besides \$18.50 [\$373] city tax &c.

February 5, 1883—Sold 20 ft of lot to Ostlund for \$350.$^{\underline{00}}$ [\$7,053] and paid Store (Robbins) \$153.80 [\$3,099] in full. Also p^{d} other debts.

Tuesday, February 6, 1883—Went to Kaysville, to see Pres^{t} Layton, & staid all night with him. We talked over matters pertaining to our move south. We have special rates by rail, viz. Car freights to Bowie \$350.^{00} [\$7,053] Passenger rates \$90.$^{\underline{00}}$ [\$1,814] \$65. [\$1,310] & \$55.$^{\underline{00}}$ [\$1,108] and can take 6 horses on a car with our loading. These are very low rates, for \$ 2000 miles travel.

[page 524]

SET APART AS COUNCILLOR

Wednesday, February 7, 1883—When I was invited to Br. Thatcher's birth day party, I wrote the following lines as a memento: copying the first verse from a former poem:——

HOME—THE SANCTUARY

In days of old, when Superstition reigned
And all in terror lived and hate and strife,
When human justice some poor victim claimed
T'atone for some foul action with his life
If to some church or altar he could flee
Altho' pursued with unrelenting hate,
And "Sanctuary" cry, then he was free
And this was law in every Christian state.

Those days are past;—~~thy~~ our sanctuary safe
Is Home—blest refuge from the wicked world,
From all its cares and strifes—its hate and rage—
And from the shafts by spite and malice hurled,
We Here safely rest, and then, when Duty calls,
Again go forth, and with resistless might
And ponderous blows, assail old Babylon's walls,
Maintaining still the fierce and stubborn fight.

When far from home, engaged in duties high
~~Thy~~ Our thoughts may refuge find in that blest home—
That Sanctuary pure, where Love and Joy,
And endless years of happiness are known.
Hath home such joys as these? Methinks you say,
Is Home so near akin to Paradise?
Yes. Home hath joys that never will decay—
A Sanctuary safe, where Love ne'er dies.

Wednesday, February 7, 1883—Br. Layton and I dined with Pres^{t} Taylor in the Gardo House,[95] after which we went to the Council of the Presidency and Twelve, and were set apart for our new calling, under the hands of Pres^{t} Taylor, J. F. Smith, Apostles Woodruff, Richards & Carrington, D. H. Wells and Patriarch John Smith.[96]

[page 525]

BR. PRESTON'S SILVER WEDDING.

February 7, 1883—Br. J. F. Smith was mouth when I was set apart, and he pronounced a good

95 Constructed in 1873 by Brigham Young, the Gardo House was located in Salt Lake on South Temple Street across from the Beehive House. President John Taylor made it his office home in 1881. This mansion—often called Amelia's Palace because it was named after Brigham Young's youngest wife, Amelia Folsom Young—rivaled the finest homes in the city.

96 See "Correspondence: St. David, Cochise County, A.T., March 3, 1883," *Deseret News*, March 21, 1883; Utah Digital Newspapers.

blessing upon me. Considerable discussion was had in regard to the name of the new Stake to be organized in Southern Arizona and Northern Mexico. Several names suggested, did not suit Pres^{t} Taylor, who said he wanted it distinctly understood, that this organization was with special reference to Mexico, and a work there. He wanted a name that would relate to both Arizona and Mexico. This was an important organization—the first stake ever organized extending into a foreign country. He gave us much good council, in reference to starting the work in Mexico, and in colonizing that land. By a vote, we were finally directed not to settle at Smithville, as first intended, but at St Davids as being nearer Mexico. After meeting, I went to Eliza's and found all well,—and Nettie very glad to see me, the first time since August last.

February 8 & 9, 1883—Visited and wrote letters. Ordered map of Mexico.

February 10, 1883—Called to see H. J. Richards & family

Sunday, February 11, 1883—Went to Kaysville to see Br. Layton again, and came on home, at 11.20 P.M. All well.

Monday, February 12, 1883—Visited.

Tuesday, February 13, 1883—Destroyed numerous receipts, notes, &c, first taking a memorandum of them. Sold 4 32/160 acres land in the field, for \$600.^{00} [\$12,091] half in cash, half in note

February ~~15~~ 14, 1883—Sold 2 feet x ~~100~~ 113 to Ostlund, for \$40.^{00} [\$806] Settled with W B Preston for the well on Church farm, \$58.^{50} [\$1,169] We attended Br. & Sister Preston's Silver Wedding, with members of their family, and had a pleasant time. We gave them a new pie knife, \$5.^{00} [\$101]

February 16, 1883—Paid Mrs. Torgeson on note 100.^{00} [\$2,015] & interest \$9.00 [\$181] \$109.^{00} [\$2,197]

Paid H J Grant,[97] in full \$20.50 [\$413] for insurance,

February 15, 1883—Went to Br. Thatcher's this evening, who gave a good blessing, of which the following is a synopsis:—

[page 526]

MY BLESSING BY BR. THATCHER. TO S. L. CITY

Thursday, February 15, 1883—He said:—"You are called to a great mission and shall do a great work. You shall have great wisdom, and power to do much good. You shall have great influence among that people (Mexicans) even surpassing your most sanguine expectations. They will be willing to defend you and even to die for you if necessary. You shall be strong, and live many years, and assist in planting many colonies in that land, until they shall all run together. You shall have great joy in your labors, and shall never lack for food or clothing. You shall never be alone, and when you are alone you shall have company. You shall be quick to hear and to understand, and shall be a great blessing to that people. You shall have every righteous desire of your heart Thousands shall come to you for council, and you shall be able to counsel them as they shall need. Live humble and prayerful and all needful blessings shall be yours.

February 19, 1883—Sold a heifer for \$25.^{00} [\$504] Rec^{d} cash from J. Lemon & H. Hughes \$12.50 [\$251.90]

On the 15th Sent my bill for surveying Logan & Smithfield canal to R. Smith, as follows:—

Work Jan 11th to 14th, 4 days, and from 19th to 26th, same month, 8 days, 12 days in all \$96.00 [\$1,935]

On the 17th destroyed many receipts &c for bills and notes paid, keeping a copy of dates, am't &c

February 20, 1883—Jesse and Albert had their photos taken

Leveled for Thatcher's new mill

Friday, March 2, 1883—Went to Kaysville to see about Arizona trip. Then called to see Mrs. Lamb at Farmington, and then went to S. L. city

March 5, 1883—Called on Mrs. Russell, who encouraged me much in regard to the future.

97 This could be Heber J. Grant (1856–1945), who at this entry would have been a member of the Quorum of Twelve Apostles for just a few months. He was called from his position as Tooele Stake president to serve with the Twelve on October 16, 1882. He later became the President of the Church. Note the entry dates are off, probably because Martineau was in a hurry. The entries are less personal because he entered Arizona knowing only a few people, but he continued to record the simple daily events.

[page 527—see Appendix 3 for letter from Christopher Layton and newspaper clipping inserted here.]

LAST MEETING IN LOGAN. NETTA GOES. WE START TO ARIZONA.

March 6, 1883—Started home, calling at Kaysville on my way. At Ogden got prices for grain, potatoes &c of Farr Bro^s^.

March 7, 1883—Got home & found Dora quite sick, but better.

March 9, 1883—Netta came home to day from S. L. City.

March 11, 1883—Nephi's birthday—21 years old. May he have many.[98] Attended meeting in Logan for the last time. How that sounds, after having been a constant attendant for 23 years. Pres^t^ Thatcher called on me to speak, which I did, followed by the celebrated Phil Robinson, the great English War correspondent.[99] Lyman & Alley spent the day with us; also some others. In the evening quite a number of young folks came in to see Jesse & Albert, previous to their departure tomorrow. Our things are packed and loaded into the wagon. This afternoon my best mare, was badly kicked on the stifle joint, so I cannot take her.[100] Tried in several places to buy another. Nephi finally bought another horse for $150.^00^ [$3,023] I blessed the mare and hope she may get well, though many think she must be killed.

Monday, March 12, 1883—Nett started for S. L. city at 4 A.M. Jesse & Albert started with the team and wagon at 6 A.M. In the afternoon went by invitation to O. C. Ormsby's, & spent a few hours pleasantly with Apostle M. Thatcher and wife. Have determined to take Lilly with me, so we were up late, packing trunks and valises. Sold 5 acres of hay land to Lyman for $250.^00^ [$5,038] Lilly sat up all night, fearing she might oversleep herself.

Tuesday, March 13, 1883—My 55th Birth day. Got up at 2 A.M. and we started from the pleasant and beautiful home God has blessed me with, and which Apostle M. Thatcher said he wished I could move bodily to Arizona. I do not know how long it will be before I get another one so pleasant: that will be as God wills, and will be just right.[101]

[page 528]

LEAVE OGDEN. IDAHO, SACRAMENTO. LATHROP.

Tuesday, March 13, 1883—It is hard to leave so many dear friends as I do in Logan, but I hope not only to keep my old ones but make so many new ones. Hardest of all to leave my dear, true and loving wife—Susan, for so long a time: for not having sold out the place, she and the rest must stay here a while. May God bless them all forever!

We reached Ogden at 9 A.M. and in the afternoon I sent Lilly down to S. L. city to stay until we should be ready to leave Ogden. I paid M. Thatcher the $12.50 [$252] I owed him, at Ogden.

Wednesday, March 14, 1883—Bought 1000 lbs flour, 1000 lbs Barly, 200 lbs. Lucern seed, 23 bu. Potatoes & garden seed, and also 8 kegs nails and some garden tools. Began to load the car. The boys did not arrive with the wagon until this morning.

Thursday, March 15, 1883—Finished loading the car, with Groesbeck and Jesse with Groesbeck's team and mine in the car, for which I paid $350.^00^ [$7,053] to Benson, my part, $600. [$12,091] in all for the car. Also paid for our passage $52.50 [$1,058] for Adults. Our fares came to $236.25 [$4,761] including Seth, who came up with Lilly on this mornings train. At 2.40 P.M. we left Ogden, 25 souls in all.

[written in margin]
Leave Logan

98 The Nephi Martineau family history has been published (Anita Martineau Schwendiman, *Family History of Nephi Martineau and Emmeline Knowles Martineau* [Rexburg, ID: Ricks College Press, 1987]). A hard copy of this history can be located at the Mesa Arizona Family History Center.

99 Phil Robinson (1847–1902) was a British author. His notoriety came from his war correspondence for the *London Daily Telegraph*. At this appearance he was on a special assignment correspondent's tour for the *New York World* (Phil Robinson, *Sinners and Saints: A Tour Across the States, and Round Them with Three Months Among the Mormons* [Boston: Roberts Brothers, 1883]).

100 The stifle joint is a kneelike joint on the hind leg of the horse.

101 Somers lists the Martineau home address as between First and Second Streets in Logan (Ray Somers, *History of Logan* [Logan, UT: Somers Historic Press, 1993], 65).

March 16 & 17, 1883—In Idaho. Nothing worthy of note.

Sunday, March 18, 1883—Wake on the Sierra Nevada. Pass through many miles of snow sheds. Scenery beautiful and in some places sublime. Begin to see flowers, and trees in bloom. Reached Sacramento at 2.30 P.M. and changed Cars. Seth and Jesse went away and neglected to get their bedding out of the car, and so lost it, which was quite a serious matter to us afterward. Left Sacramento about 5 P.M. and reached Lathrop at 9.30 P.M.—56 miles, where we changed cars again, waiting until 3 A.M. next morning.

Monday, March 19, 1883—Left Lathrop at 3 A.M. Cold and foggy. Telegraphed to the Supt. about my bedding We pass through a poor country. Bought some shoes for Lilly, and a looking glass

[page 529]

LOS ANGELES. YUMA. BENSON. ST DAVID. SUR^y. CANAL.

March 20, 1883—Reached Los Angeles 2.30 P.M. having passed through a dreary desert for hundreds of miles. Bought parasol and a mattress, also about 100 oranges @ 1¢ each. Left at 6.10 P.M.

March 21, 1883—Wake at Indio, 260 feet below the level of the sea. Passed, and visited Volcano Springs, where hot mud boils up constantly. Reached Yuma about 2 P.M. and learned there are 40 cases of Small pox here. Saw indians, men and women, nearly naked. weather quite warm, and the Colorado rising. Left about 5 P.M. passing along the Gila.[102]

Thursday, March 22, 1883—Stopped 2 hours in Tucson. Thermometer 84° Reached Benson at 5 P.M. and found Br. Layton's team waiting for us and his daughter's family. Reached St David at 8 P.M. and stopped with Br. Wild's family. Groesbeck's and Jones families remained at Benson all night.

March 23, 1883—Got teams to bring up the others at Benson. They were much discouraged to find so poorly built up a place, after living so long in Logan—the garden.

Saturday, March 24, 1883—Looked over the city plat, and found a block to build on. Afterwards went to Benson to see if our car had arrived. Found it had, and gone up the Sonora R. R. to Contention, 8 miles above St David. Got back home, and found Albert had arrived with the horses, and word we must unload tomorrow.

Sunday, March 25, 1883—Sent the boys to Contention to unload the car. They got back after dark, with everything. I went to meeting and preached, and felt well.

Monday, March 26, 1883—Unpacked our things, and found two bowls and a picture broken, also a glass jar. Other things all right.

March 27, 28, & 29, 1883—Surveyed on St David Canal, with Jesse and Seth Jones, a distance of about 6 miles. Grade 5 feet pr mile.

[page 530]

SET APART H. W. BRIZZIE ON MISSION TO SONORA.

Friday, March 30, 1883—To day Brs. Layton, Kimball and I blessed and set apart Henry W. Brizzee and his son Arthur, aged 14, as missionaries to Sonora. Br. Brizzee understands the Spanish well.[103]

After coming here we boarded a week with Wilds' family, and began to keep house ourselves on Monday Mch. 26th I let Wilds have 100 lbs of Potatoes, $5.00 [$101] and half sack flour $250, [$50] also 2 lb butter 85¢ [$17]

[written in margin]
Board ourselves on 26th

Saturday, March 31, 1833—Surveyed land for D P Kimball and myself.

Sunday, April 1, 1883—Brs. Layton and Kimball went to Tucson to enter land, for themselves and for me (160 A.)

April 3, 1883—Finished planting about an acre of potatoes. Got a good letter from Charles. Went out north & picked out some good land for our family.

102 The smallpox scare did not miss St. David, Arizona ("The Small Pox Scare," *Deseret News*, April 11, 1883; Utah Digital Newspapers).

103 Henry W. Brizzee was one of the original settlers sent by Brigham Young in 1874 to explore the Mexico Territory.

Wednesday, April 4, 1883—Went to Tombstone to make filing for land. Was introduced to Gen. Wardwell, Judge Peel & others.[104]

April 5, 1883—Returned at noon. The whole country is up on account of so many indian massacres round us during the last two weeks. Men are volunteering to go against them, and they call on us at St David to furnish some horses to help mount the men. We held meeting in the evening, and decided to send 8 or 10 horses to help them. We think best to do this, as the indians richly deserve death, and otherwise we would be looked upon as favoring the indians. Paid $2.00 [$40] for entry D. P. Kimballs.

Friday, April 6, 1883—To day is Jesse's birth day—20 years old. May he have many more to come. Albert's was on the [blank] of [blank]. The boys have been clearing land, & Albert plowing.

April 7, 1883—Wrote to W. D. Johnson, informing him he is called to be a bishop over St David.[105]

Sunday, April 8, 1883—Lilly was taken very sick in meeting,—a hot fever. A man came from Tombstone to get horses to help fit out the Rangers.

April ~~7~~ 9, 1883—Got some poor hay. Lilly still sick, and I cannot get any woman or girl to help. Jesse cooks

[page 531]

LILLY SICK. PLANT CORN, PEAS, ONIONS &C

April 10, 1883—Got another load hay to day. Rec^{d} some grape and Bamboo cuttings from Cal^{a} to day.

April 11, 1883—Bought two loads hay & sold one to Groesbeck, $5.00 [$101].

April 12, 1883—Lilly still sick. Every one tells me to give her quinine. Both she and I have more faith in administration. Br. Reed fixed some drops for her. To day bought a house of 3 rooms, and lot of C. Bingham, for $250.$^{\underline{00}}$ [$5,038] down and $150. [$3,023] more in 2 months. Also. I paid J. McRae $20. [$403] of the $60. [$1,209] I owe him for a city lot under the canal. I buy it so as to have some garden this Summer.[106]

April 13, 1883—Lilly seems a little better.

April 14, 1883—Seth and the ~~boys~~ Jesse leveled on ~~upper~~ lower canal. Albert plowed, and I set out the 150 grapes and 11 Bamboos.

April 15, 1883—Lilly up and dressed to day.

April 16, 1883—Went to Benson and bo't garden seeds.[107] I was to day elected Pres^{t} of the St David Irrigation Company.[108] I did not wish the office, but Pres^{t} Layton & Kimball wished me to take it.

Rec^{d} a letter from home, & one from Henry, who is called to a mission among the Navajoes.

Tuesday, April 17, 1883—Wrote home and to the Utah Journal. Planted peas. Lilly worse again. Planted corn.

April 18, 1883—Surveyed for Br. Kimball

April 19, 1883—Paid Cash to Mrs. Wild, $3.00 [$60]. Also flour $2.50 [$50] and potatoes $4.^{50} [$91], on room rent.

Saturday, April 21, 1883—Planted 10 lbs onion setts. also 3 qts peas. Grosbeck's baby died to day.

Sunday, April 22, 1883—Spoke at funeral. Lilly about well again.

April 23, 1883—Got 683 lbs potatoes, on credit, of C. Layton, to plant.

April 24, 1883—Let out some work on Canal.

April 25, 1883—Leveled on upper canal

April 26, 1883—Planted ½ acre of potatoes yesterday. Leveled on lower canal to day.

---

104 This could be William Lauterman Wardwell (1857–86). His letters describe Arizona much as Martineau sees it. These letters are part of the Arizona State Library, Archives and Public Records. Judge Peel could be B. L. Peel of Tombstone.

105 This is could be D. W. Johnson, who would later work to facilitate good relations with Mexican president Porfirio Díaz (F. LaMond Tullis, *Mormons in Mexico: The Dynamics of Faith and Culture* [Logan, UT: Utah State Univ. Press, 1987], 75).

106 C. Bingham is likely Calvin Bingham (1827–91). "Brother Reed" could have been Calvin (1821–95) or Heber Reed (1847–1902). There were numerous McRaes listed at the St. David Cemetery, but none matched this entry.

107 Benson, Arizona, was named after William B. Benson. It was a railroad town just a few miles north of St. David. Founded in 1880, Benson was along the transcontinental Southern Pacific Railroad line. The railroad provided transportation to the new mining communities of the South.

108 Settlers and the earlier Native Americans took their water from the San Pedro River running through the areas. The St. David Irrigation Company was tapping those resources for farming.

April 27, 1883—Lilly and I went to Tombstone, & I bought a plow, price $19.^{00} [$405] and 4 chairs ~~$4.00~~ $8.00 [$363].

[page 532]

HORSE THIEVES CHASED.

April 28, 1883—Finished planting garden, 2 acres in all.

Sunday, April 29, 1883—Some horse thieves passed here at 2 A.M. with 9 horses. I got men on their trail in about an hour, who followed them and in two days recovered the horses.

April 30, 1883—Resigned my office of U.S. Land and Min^{l} Surveyor.

Tuesday, May 1, 1883—May day. Seth, King consort. A nice exhibition

Saturday, May 5, 1883—Went to Benson & paid $80.^{00} [$1,612] to enter 320 acres Desert land

Sunday, May 6, 1883—Went as far as Layton's this evening, on our way to the Settlements on the Gila. Br. J. Hill goes to take me, Brs. Layton and Kimball, in another buggy.

May 7, 1883—Start at 6 A.M. and drove 67 m. to Hooker's Ranch.

May 8, 1883—Drove to Smithville, ~~67~~ 43 miles, arriving at 7 P.M.

May 9, 1883—Drove up the Gila on N. Side, visiting settlers, then to Safford, and looked at Grist Mill, which we had some thought of buying. Dined at J. Moody's. In evening held a council meeting.

Thursday, May 10, 1883—Went to Curtis, 8^{m} below, and held meeting. Called a Bishop and two councillors, for Curtis. Held a priesthood meeting at Smithville in the evening.

Friday, May 11, 1883—Spent the day in Council. Dined at E. W. Easts.[109]

Saturday, May 12, 1883—Meeting to day, at 10 & 2 p.m. Well attended. We named the following places:—Graham, Curtis, Thatcher and changed the name of Smithville to Pima, as the Government will recognize no other.

Sunday, May 13, 1883—Meetings today. I spoke and felt well.

May 14, 1883—Started home, drove 67^{m} to Hudson's ranch. Br. Layton quite unwell, with cold.

May 15, 1883—Reached home at evening. Br. Layton's mule nearly died on the way, which delayed us.

May 16, 1883—Rained hard to day.

May 17, 1883—Planted Squashes and melons. Plowed in field N.

May 18, 1883—Wrote letters.

May 19, 1883—Surveyed on town site.

Sunday, May 20, 1883—Meetings at St. David.

May 21, 1883—Seth went to Benson to get work

May 22, 1883—Seth went to Contention to get work. He did.[110]

[page 533]

May 23, 1883—Watered garden, and planted Sorghum.

May 24, 1883—Moved into our own house. It seems nice to be in our own home again, even if it be a humble one. Br. Kimball lent me a stove and a load of hay. I hoed corn and peas.

Friday, May 25, 1883—Got a new wagon of Br. Layton, and sent team to Benson for some freight for Tombstone. Jesse got back at dark

May 26, 1883—Albert went with freight. Quite hot, 92° in house.

Sunday, May 27, 1883—Very hot. 95° in house. Albert got back at noon. $12.^{00} [$242]

Monday, May 28, 1883—Went to Benson with Lilly. Bought tub & washboard also a ham, and 2 sack feed, and lumber to make a kitchen table. Hauled some things for Groesbeck. Saw a wreck of freight train on S.P.R.R. near Benson. One man killed. Begun to haul adobes for back ad^{n} [addition]

Tuesday, May 29, 1883—Heard that Br. Bingham was killed Sunday last, while freighting.[111] Laid foundation and a few adobes.

Wednesday, May 30, 1883—Br. Bingham's funeral today.

---

109 This would be Edward W. East, a former Texas missionary.

110 Contention, Arizona, established in 1880, was just east of Tombstone. It thrived during the 1880s with three silver mills. It was abandoned in 1888. The name comes from two competing miners who both claimed ownership of the same mine.

111 "Deplorable Accident," *Deseret News*, June 13, 1883; Utah Digital Newspapers.

Thursday, May 31, 1883—Worked on house. Jesse helped Widow Bingham 1 day.

Friday, June 1, 1883—Jesse helped repair canal.

[Note: Dates are out of order. Martineau has noted this in the original to correct the order.]

Thursday, May 31, 1883—Sold my wagon to T. Jones for 40 acres land. Arranged for wire (10 bales) with D. P. K. and got 2 loads of hay of him. Wrote home and to Charly & Journal.

Saturday, June 2, 1883—Conference today.[112] Well attended from the Gila, 110^{m}

Sunday, June 3, 1883—Conference today. Spoke and felt well. We organized another new ward—McDonald, 4 miles above here, with H. J. Home as Bishop.[113]

June 4, 1883—Worked on house. Got 2 sacks feed at Benson. Ther^{r} 95° Rec^{d} letters from home.

June 5, 1883—Settled with Layton for 2 wagons $120.$^{\underline{00}}$ [$2,418] each (exact cost), one of which I turn to Kimball to pay for wire, and gave Layton note for $277.50 [$5,592]

June 6, 1883—Bought spring wagon of D. P. K. for 100$ 9$^{\underline{mo}}$ time. Also borrowed 403 feet lumber of T. Office. Work on house. Ther. 98°

June 7, 1883—Paid 11.20 [$226] for adobes.

June 8, 1883—Bought 1166 lbs fence wire of D. P. Kimball for $157.41 [$3,172] & gave note to C. Layton, in all $277.50 [$5,592], interest 10 o/c from date.

[page 534]

June 8, 1883—This am't covered pay due C. Layton on a wagon I bought from him at 120^{\underline{00}}$ [$2,418]

Surveyed for D P Kimball. Finished wall of house.

June 9, 1883—Gave note to D P Kimball for $100.$^{\underline{00}}$ [$2,015] for wagon, 9 mo.

June 13, 1883—Got lumber for Stable $52.$^{\underline{00}}$ [$1,048] Began shingling.

June 14, 1883—Finished this evening.

June 15, 1883—Attended Luke Hill's funeral today.

June 16, 1883—Seth came back to live.

June 18, 1883—Seth got team to plow his land. He and Albert camp out at Layton's. Thermometer 104°

June 19, 1883—Finished Stable. Cost $50.$^{\underline{00}}$ + 15= $65.$^{\underline{00}}$ [$1,310]

June 20 & 21, 1883—Worked in garden. 104°

June 22, 1883—Made bedstead.

June 25, 1883—Irrigated. 106°

June 26, 1883—Planted corn. 107°

June 27, 1883—Funeral of Br. Newel, kicked by a mule at Chiricahua.[114] Sent my papers for filing on land to Tucson.

June 28, 1883—Sowed 180 lbs lucern seed, on 6½ acres. Rain. 102°

June 29, 1883—A little rain. Considerable on Whetstone & Dragoon Mts. Planted sweet corn & fought potato bugs. 80°

June 30, 1883—Shingled for A. Cluff.

July 2, 1883—Rec^{d} certificate of deposit of $80.$^{\underline{00}}$ [$1,612] for entry of 320 Acres desert land. Wrote letters. Boys in field.

July 3, 1883—Went to Benson and got $300.$^{\underline{00}}$ [$6,046] Sent by Lyman for land I had sold. Paid debts

July 4, 1883—Celebrated, & danced.

July 5, 1883—Paid Mrs. Bingham $120.$^{\underline{00}}$ [$2,418] on house, also p^{d} for lumber and some smaller debts.

July 6, 1883—Went to Tombstone, and gave County deed for road through my land.

July 10, 1883—Began to build a section house of adobes.

Seth went to Benson to get work.

July 12, 1883—Rec^{d} letter from M. Thatcher. Planted 50 lbs beans.

July 14, 1883—Hired 3 Mexicans to clean out my well, at $8.$^{\underline{00}}$ [$161]

July 16, 1883—Got letters from G. Clements & others. Made me a bedstead.

---

112 "St. Joseph Stake Conference," *Deseret News,* June 27, 1883; Utah Digital Newspapers.

113 This could be Henry Holmes (note spelling), who was with the first Mexican exploration party in 1874 (McClintock, *Mormon Settlement in Arizona*, 135–36).

114 At this writing no "Brother Newel" could be located matching this entry. It is probable that Martineau, being new to the area, was trying to learn the names of those who would become associates; thus many first names were omitted.

July 17, 1883—For some time thermometer ranged from 82° to 88°. Surveyed on town plat ½ day, with Jesse and Albert.

[page 535]

July 18, 1883—Surveyed ½ day on town plat, with Jesse & Albert.

July 20, 1883—Built privy.

July 22, 1883—I came to Utah 33 years ago today. Pres^t Layton got home from Utah. Lilly & I went to meet him.[115]

July 27, 1883—Made me a stand. Considerable rain for some days.

July 28, 1883—Seth returned home again, having quit work. Rain.

August 2, 1883—Jesse & Albert began work on upper canal.

August 4, 1883—Began fencing my 80 near Layton's. Rain.

August 7, 1883—Traded wagons with F. Campbell

August 11, 1883—Finished setting 1 mile of posts, (351 in No.)

Fig. 6.7—Charles Freeman Martineau served in the Southern States Mission. This is the mission home in Chattanooga, Tennessee. Courtesy of James Henry Martineau Family Organization.

August 13, 1883—Letter from Moroni. His son Howard died Aug. 3. Netta still sick with rheumatism, began in July. Also learned that Charles is sick in Tennessee, very.[116]

August 15, 1883—Began to stretch wire on fencing

August 16, 1883—Brs. Layton, Kimball & I visited the Whetstone Mts, 12^m

The boys finished wiring the fence—1 mile.

August 17, 1883—Rec^d check for $75.^00 [$1,511] Next day went to Tombstone to get it cased [cashed]. Lyman sent it to me to come home with, Netta being very sick.

August 23, 1883—Started back to Utah today, taking some large Cacti for Lyman and Pres^t Preston, weighing 140 lbs. Went by Emigrant Cars. In San Francisco took a severe cold and was sick all the way to Logan, arrived there Sept. 1. 18843.

September 1, 1883—Found all well but Netta, who is very weak and ill, though somewhat better. From this time till Conference was busy settling up with people and working around home.

October 2, 1883—Started to Conference.

October 5, 1883—Conference. Pres^t Taylor said "Each stake is a perfect organization in itself, just as the Church is." H J Grant said "Those who do not pay their tithing cannot go to the Temple."

Pres^t Taylor:—Stake presidents should encourage Quorums, and see that people join them. Each stake is a perfect facsimile of the Church. Stake Presidents must be careful not to assume responsibilities of other peoples sins. They must get right after wrong doers.

[page 536]

CONFERENCE

October 5, 1883—They must wake up to the duties of their callings. When you administer to the sick always say "if not appointed unto death."

October 7, 1883—"The Spirit of God is not a part of the Gospel. It is in all people of intelligence."

October 8 & 9, 10, 1883—Attended a special meeting of First Presidency, Apostles, Stake Presidencies, Pres^ts of Seventies & the Presiding Bishopric. Many things taught, and a glorious time.

115 During Layton's absence, he and Martineau had been in correspondence ("Better Than Gold," *Deseret News*, July 18, 1883; Utah Digital Newspapers).

116 For a report on Charles's success, see "Local and Other Matters: Just Forty Years ago," *Deseret News*, July 18, 1883; Utah Digital News.

October 11, 1883—Visited flowing well & inspected the Brockett Augur.

October 12, 1883—Came home. Took Dora, she is about 5 weeks old—a waif.[117]

October 17, 1883—Snow storm today. Dora sick and feeble—hardly alive.

October 18, 1883—Went with Theodore to S. L. City to see about augur. While in S. L. City attended Bishop Hunter's funeral. Also inspected the working of the Brockett Augur.

October 26, 1883—Wrote to Pres[t] J. Morgan relative to releasing Charles, who is quite sick with chills and fever.[118]

October 27, 1883—Came home.

November 2, 1883—Br. Moses Thatcher and I administered to Netta. He gave her a very good blessing.

November 4 & 5, 1883—Quarterly Conference. Cold & rainy.

November 14, 1883—Went to Provo to see And. J. Stewart, and if I could collect what he owes. He would not pay me—he owes me over $410.[00] [$8,061] for work I did for him, Surveying in Cache Co. 1875

November 16, 1883—Returned to S. L. City.

November 18, 1883—Attended Tabernacle. Was called to the stand & prayed. Preached in evening in 15th Ward.

November 19, 1883—Snowy.

November 20, 1883—This morning Charles arrived by Denver & R.G.RR feeling pretty well. Had one chill on train. I am very thankful he has returned safe & sound.[119]

November 21, 1883—Went to Logan. Heard of D P Kimball's death yester day.

November 23, 1883—Charles began work at U.N.R.R. shop, his old place.

November 29, 1883—Susan & I had thanksgiving dinner with M. Thatcher's family, & had a pleasant time.

December 8, 1883—Netta much worse today, coughed hard and spit blood. We called in Dr. Ormsby. Joel came home from the cañon with his foot cut.

[page 537]

NETTA'S SICKNESS 1884.

December 10, 1883—Netta much worse, dropy [dropsy] having set in. Her feet and legs begin to swell. Sat up all night in her chair and coughed very hard. Failing rapidly, and is seems as if nothing but the power of the Lord can save her.

December 11, 1883—I sat up all night with Netta, who passed a very bad night. Dropsy increasing. She slept not more than 5 minutes at a time.

December 12, 1883—The doctor says the water is accumulating round Netta's heart, and that she cannot possibly live. I pray for and administer to her often. I know God is able to heal her, if it is his will.

December 21, 1883—Up to this time Netta has been in a very precarious situation. We have had the Elders many times to administer to her, and for a few days she has improved. Last night is the first night for a long time I have not been up with her. For weeks she has not been able to lie in a bed, but has sat day and night in a chair. Poor girl, she has suffered much.

December 22, 1883—Netta much worse again, the swelling ascending into her body. Dora very fretful and weak. Was almost dead when we took her.

Tuesday, January 1, 1884—Nett looks better, the swelling is nearly all gone. Susan sick last night and sick abed all day. Very cold.

January 2, 1884—Susan still quite sick. Alley came down to help.

January 3, 1884—Gertrude has a very bad Cough. Susan can sit up.

January 5, 1884—By letter we learn that Jesse is called to learn Spanish, with others, with view to future mission in Mexico. Netta's dropsy nearly all gone.

[written in margin]

Jan. 6. 1884

Charles was ord[d] a Seventy by Sylvester Lowe

Tuesday, January 8, 1884—Have been married 32 years. Got a gold ring for S.

117 *Waif* means she was a homeless child.

118 This could have been John Morgan (1842–94), who served as a seventy between 1884 and 1894. While today the First Quorum of Seventy is a governing body of the Church, functioning to assist the Quorum of the Twelve Apostles and the First Presidency, in Martineau's time the seventy never met as an official body but were scattered geographically throughout the settlements.

119 "Missionaries from South," *Deseret News*, November 28, 1883; Utah Digital Newspapers.

January 10, 1884—Began work in T. Office today

January 17, 1884—Lyman got me a suit of clothes—$34.00 [$709]

January 21, 1884—Joel began in the Journal office, asst Book keeper. Did not sit up with Nett last night for first time.

January 24, 1884—Nett not so well. Dora has been sick for a week with Canker.

[page 538]

LAY OUT TEMPLE GROUNDS.

January 24, 1884—Truly I have had my hands full, but the Lord has thus far preserved all our lives, for which all praise to His name.

February 24, 1884—Was called to sit in the high council, and was chosen to Speak, in case of Brown vs. Hopkins.[120] Settled with T. O. [Tithing Office] for my labor in setting the Stake accounts, & recd $100.00 [$2,086] work.[121]

March 18, 1884—Dora walked today across the room! Paid Kimball's note ($100.00) by Lyman's help. I gave Lyman my note for $185.00 [$3,859] due in 6mo at 1 o/c per month interest

March 20, 1884—Snowing still.

April 1, 1884—Went to Conference

April 4, 5, & 6, 1884—Conference. At priesthood meeting strong preaching on plurality. All presiding officers must accept the law or resign. Br. W. B. Preston was appointed Presiding Bishop.

April 7, 1884—Special meeting of Presidency, Apostles & Stake Presidents. Prest Taylor explained Sec. 132 (on Plural Marriage) very fully, section by section; and it was voted unanimously that all presiding officers must obey it, or resign.

Tuesday, April 8, 1884—Attended Central Board of Trade, and was added, a member. Also Prest Layton.

April 9, 1884—Another meeting at the Grand Council. Much good teaching,

April 10, 1884—Came home to Logan.

April 25, 1884—Sold desk to T B Cardon for $45.00 [$939] in goods.

April 26, 1884—Snowy and cold.

May 1, 1884—Began collecting statistics of the Temple for the Utah Journal today.

Monday, May 5, 1884—Last night Nephi had a son born to him at 1h 50' a.m. (Standard time—28min fast of true local time.) Began to lay out the ornamental walks and drives around the Temple, according to plan furnished by Don C. Young.[122]

May 10, 1884—Nett rode out in carriage for the first time to day. was to day appointed by the Logan Temple Committee (per F. D. Richards)[123] to make out a full report of the work from the first, for the Temple Committee, for record in the Church history and for the Temple record.

May 15, 1884—Henry Lunt & wife arrived from Cedar city to be at the dedication of the Temple. Mrs. Lucy B. Young, & her daughter Susa Y. Gates & child also stop with us.

[page 539]

DEDICATION OF LOGAN TEMPLE.

May 16, 1884—Quarterly Conference began today. Visited temple.

May 17, 1884—Myself, Susan and Netta attended the dedication of the Temple. About 2000 present, all having cards of invitation. My seat was in the stand, left side, assigned Presidents of Stakes. The ceremonies were simple but impressive. After the prayer of dedication was read by Prest J. Taylor, and singing and addresses by G. Q. Cannon, Jos F. Smith, W. Woodruff, L. Snow, Prest Taylor asked all to rise and shout "Hosanna! hosanna! hosanna to God and the Lamb! Amen! Amen! Amen!"[124]

---

120 At this writing there were no case histories located relative to *Brown v. Hopkins* in the Online News Archives for the Cache Valley Court History.

121 In February 1884, Martineau advertised his Logan home for sale (see advertisement, "For Sale," *Deseret News*, February 13, 1884, and May 7, 1884; Utah Digital Newspapers.

122 Don Carlos Young was one of the Church architects.

123 This is likely Franklin D. Richards.

124 This is the dedication of the Logan Temple, a momentous occasion in Cache Valley history and Martineau's life. The temple was the centerpiece of the city, pioneering efforts, and expectations. For a comparative primary account of the dedication day and activities, see Charles Ora Card's writings on these same dates (Godfrey and Godfrey, eds.,

Fig. 6.8—Martineau's Logan home. Courtesy of James Henry Martineau Family Organization.

After this Pres[t] Taylor led all the people through the building from Top to bottom.

May 18 & 19, 1884—Similar ceremonies were held the two following days so that other might be gratified. I went all three days by invitation.

We have with us, besides Br. & Sister Lunt and L. B. Young[125] and daughter, Br. & Sister Russell, and Seth Johnson, who came unexpectedly, and was very welcome indeed. Besides this, quite a number from places around, stayed with us, making our house pretty full,—over twenty sleeping and eating with us.

Utah Years, 517–23; see also Ricks and Cooley, *History of a Valley*, 282–86; "The Logan Temple," *Deseret News*, June 4, 1884; Utah Digital Newspapers; "The Logan Temple," *Ogden Standard Examiner*, August 7, 1884; Utah Digital Newspapers). Martineau's excitement is illustrated in the following entries when he is vicariously conducting the sacred ordinances of baptism, confirmation, the endowment, and sealings (weddings) for his deceased ancestors. These entries are full of Martineau family genealogy.

125 This could be Lucy B. Young, wife of Brigham Young, or Lorenzo Dow Young, his brother.

May 20, 1884—To day Pat[h] H. Lunt blessed Susan, Netta & Joel Susan, Nett and I got a recommend to do work in the Temple. Sister Young gave me a name to be sealed to me—Marie St Pierre, who died in 1872, born 1833 also Clara St Vincent, died 1872, born 1854. Afterwards, Susa Young gave me four more.[126]

TEMPLE WORK.

May 21, 1884—Began work for the dead, with Susan and Netta. I was endowed for my father, being ordained for him an Elder by Erastus Snow. Susan acted for Marie St Pierre, who was sealed to me by Pres[t] Geo. Q. Cannon, E. Snow and Orson Smith witnesses. Netta acted for herself, though very weak.

126 It was common in early Church history for men to have deceased women sealed to them to form family units in the world to come. The practice was discontinued and replaced with the sealing of known families.

May 23, 1884—Susan and I in the Temple. I acted for my father Susan for Clara St Vincent. As all this work is specified in full in my genealogical record, I only give the names we worked for each day.

May 24, 1884—Worked laying out Temple grounds.

May 26, 1884—Gave list of names for baptism & worked on grounds.

[page 540]

TEMPLE WORK. DORA ADOPTED

May 1884—Sister Young gave me three more names—five in all—of women to be endowed and sealed to me. They are

Sophia Gilmier, born 1818 died 1872

Mary Essebrous, born 1820 died 1872

Mary Gertrude, born 1840 died 1872

May 27, 1884—To day I was baptized to renew my covenant & for 26 dead Netta for her health and for 7 dead Sister Young was very kind to Netta—took her into a private room & prayed with her

May 28, 1884—I acted for my mother's father, James Mears, & Susan for Sophia Gilmier, who was sealed to me. Netta acted for my mother, and was proxy for her in sealing my father and mother, I acting for father. What a blessed privilege to reunite my father & mother.

May 29, 1884—I endowed for my uncle Peter Martineau, Susan for Mary Essebrous and Netta for gr. mother Ellenor Haughout. Mary Essebrous was sealed to me, Susan being proxy.

May 30, 1884—I endowed for Chauncey Mears, my uncle; & Susan for Mary Gertrude (sealed to me) Nett went on pic nic to day.

June 3, 1884—Was baptized with Nephi for 55, Nett & Virginia for 55 = 110

June 4, 1884—I endowed for my stepfather W[m] G. Babcock, Susan for Jane Varley, Father's 1st wife, & to whom she was sealed. Nett for gr. mother Lois Sprague, who was sealed to Gr. Father Ja[s] Mears.

June 5, 1884—I ~~ordained~~ endowed for Stephen Martineau, Nett for his wife & Susan for Mary E. Sherman, her cousin—my wife. Sealed

June 6, 1884—I end[d] for Uncle W[m] A. Mears, Nephi for my brother Cha[s] Sprague Babcock, Susan for Aunt Mary Dean, Nett for my sister Julia.

Dora was sealed to me as my daughter & Susan's[127] The ceremony was witnessed by many with interest some with tears of joy. All thought she was fortunate, and Susan and I felt very thankful—felt as if a child was just born to us. We each had a powerful testimony that the matter was right with the Lord.

This was the first adoption of the kind perform[d] in the Temple. Dora acted very well all through the ceremony.

[page 541]

TEMPLE WORK

June 10, 1884—I was baptized for 55, Nephi for 28, Joel 27 Theodore 28 Gertrude 10 Emma for 15. Finished 8.45 P.M.

June 11, 1884—I endowed for Elie Martineau, ancestor, Susan for Aunt Caroline Ferguson Mears, Nephi for Gaston Martineau.

June 12, 1884—I end[d] for Francis Martineau, Susan for Susan Macon, who was sealed to me. Nett too ill to go to Temple.

June 13, 1884—I end[d] for Uncle James R. Mears, Susan for his wife Francis Russell.

June [15 or 17], 1884—Emmeline was bap[d] for 15, Anna for 10, Jene 43.

June 18, 1884—I end[d] for Ethan Allen, Susan for Mrs. W. G. Babcock, my step father's 1st wife.

Eliza came today, with Harry Chamberlin
& Mary Lamb, to visit the temple.

June 19, 1884—I end[d] for Uncle John Mears, Susan for Marguerite Barbesson (ancestor) Elie & Marguerite sealed.

June 20, 1884—I for Stephen Martineau, S. for Charity Christopher (my Aunt)

June 23, 1884—Wrote the following lines in Mrs. Rhoda Y. M[c]Alister's Album, using some "Maya" indian words:— taught me by Br. O. V. Aoy of Merida, Yucatan:—

I think I'll write a little "Maya",
So here I scribble—Kottain gwayah?
(come here)
"No sir, I wont," perhaps you'll say.

---

127 Records of this sealing are found at familysearch.org. Dora is listed as the thirteenth child of James Henry and Susan Ellen Martineau.

My footsteps point another way."
If that's the case, then "Bash—ah—kattah"
(where go you)
(This, too, is Maya—not Mahratta)
If to answer this you do not wish
I'll cease, and say "Yos—bottick—tich."
(good luck to you)
Query.
You've read good authors by the score
Byron, Shakspeare, Scott and Moore
And other poets:
Now don't you think these lines of mine
Than theirs more soulful—more sublime?
I'm sure they show it.

[page 542]

TEMPLE WORK

June 23, 1884—In the Maya language kottain gwayah means "Come here:" "Bash—ah—kattah" = Where are you going:" Yos bottick tich = Good luck go with you.

Wednesday, June 25, 1884—End[d] for Abram Martineau, Susan, Mrs. Abram M. Susan Smith for aunt Laura Mears, Eliza A Benson for Aunt Mary A. Mears (Martineau) Emma for Ellenor Martineau;

Pres[t] McAllister and Bp. D H Cannon dined with us.

June 26, 1884—End[d] for John Mears, Susan, Mrs. John Mears, E. A. Benson for Aunt Maria Louisa Mears

June 27, 1884—End[d] for Henry Mears; Susan, Huldah Hutchinson (Sealed to me) Elizabeth G. Benson for Maria Martineau, Eliza A. Benson for Elizabeth Martineau. Anna Crockett for Ann Martineau

June 29, 1884—Susan took an overdose of Iodine for rheumatism, and was poisoned, almost fatally. She took mustard, egg, & other things to vomit, which saved her, together with administration, but was very sick.[128]

June 30, 1884—Better, but still very weak

July 1, 1884—Nephi baptized for 10, Anna for 17.

July 2, 1884—End[d] for Uncle Daniel Van Slyke, Nephi for Harvey Abrahms, John Laird for Abraham Merrill; Susan for Susannah Martineau. The following were sealed to me Susannah Martineau, Mary Martineau, Hannah Martineau, Sarah Columbine, Elizabeth Brewer, Beatrice Sumner. My four Uncles & wives were sealed.

July 3, 1884—Endowed for Abraham Decker, Susan for my sister Lucretia Martineau (Mears), Lucy B. Young for Judith E. Blake, E. A. Benson for Eliza Martineau; Prescinda Smith (~~Young~~) for Catherine Martineau; Susan J. Smith for Sarah Martineau; Lucy Cardon for Ann Martineau; E. G. Benson for Emily Martineau.

The six last named were sealed to me.

July 4, 1884—End[d] for Jo[s] Christopher, Susan for my sister Francis E. Martineau Prescinda Smith for Ellen Martineau Lucy Cardon for Lucy Martineau; E. G. Benson for Lois Hutchinson & Elizabeth Townsend for Marianne Martineau; all of them were sealed to me.

[page 543]

OUR SECOND A.

July 4, 1884—Wrote to Pres[t] Jo[s] F. Smith & offered him my two sisters Lucretia and Francis, which offer he gratefully accepted.

July 6, 1884—He also said Self and wives might (Pres[t] Taylor said) have our Second Anointings. For this, Father, I thank Thee, and pray we may prove worthy so great blessings.

Fig. 6.9—Diamond drawing appears in margin next to July 6 entry.

July 9, 1884—End[d] for Stephen Hutchinson, Nephi for Benj. Martineau, Susan for Miss Rand; Emma for Margaret Haughout, Mrs. Liljenquist for Elizabeth Haughout; E. A. Benson for Catherine Haughout; Anna Crockett for Cath[e] Keteltas, Mrs. M[c]Neil for Cornelia Haughout, Mrs. Morrell for Ann Haughout; & E. Crowther for Elenor Haughout; all these 8 were sealed to me

Thursday, July 10, 1884—End[d] for Isaac Haughout; Susan for my cousin Mary Poole. Mrs. M.

128 Iodine was used as an antiseptic.

A. S. R. Smith for Rachel Haughout. Lucy B. Young for Allatta Cozine, Mrs. Crowther, Alujay Webb; Mrs. McNiel, Elizth Martineau, Anna Crockett, Charity Martineau; E. A. P. Benson, Margaret Martineau, Mrs. Morrell, Miss Rand; Mrs. Liljenquist, Gertrude Martineau. of these last, ~~eight~~ four were sealed to me. (on the 11th)

[written in margin in shaky writing]

2nd A

2ND A

Myself, Susan E. and Susan J. recd our 2d A, from Prest Mariner W. Merrill; Witnesses Tho. X. Smith & Samuel Roskelly, about 4.30 P.M. Father, I thank Thee. Help us to be true and faithful to the end I ask Thee, in the name of Jesus, our Redeemer. Amen.[129]

July 11, 1884—Endd for Wm Sprague, Susan for Margarette Haughout; Margaret & Elizth Martineau, Allatta Cozine & Alujay Webb were sealed to me. After this, Mrs. Robbins recd her 2d A. and I acted for her dead husband. (?)

[written in margin]

2nd Anointing

July 14, 1884—Virginia and Anna were baptized for 37 persons. Mrs. S. J. Russell and Nils L. Hagberg and Sarah Westwood arrived from S. L. City: The latter to be married, and all stopped with us.

Mrs. Russell gave me the name of Sophia Billott, her aunt, to be endowed and sealed to me. Also Br. Hagberg gave me his mother—Anna Maria Hagberg, to be endowed and sealed to me.

[page 544]

TEMPLE WORK. MARY E. JOHNSON. LYMAN & DELLA SEALED

July 16, 1884—Endd for Egbert Martineau, Susan for Harriet Martineau, the English Authoress.

July 17, 1884—Endd for Uncle John Hudson Poole; Lyman for Uncle Cornelius Martineau; Susan for Mrs. Wm Sprague, E. A. Benson for Mary Martineau;

Recd a letter from Margaret Johnson, giving me her daughter Mary Elizabeth to me (Susan's ½ sister). Also a letter from Sixtus E. Johnson giving me permission to be adopted to father Joel H. Johnson.

[written in margin in very shaky writing]

This was an error [and it points to being adopted by father Joel H. Johnson.]

This evening Susan looked in a crystal for the first time, and could see clearly in it—saw many things of much interest.

July 18, 1884—Endd for Wm Sprague, Lyman for Wm Sherwin, Susan for Mary Elizabeth Johnson; E. A. Benson for Anna Maria Hagberg, who with Mary E. Johnson were sealed to me.

July 23, 1884—Endd for Nels Hagberg, Susan for Martha Monson, Nett for Mrs. Wm Sprague, Mrs. Maughan for Margaret Williment, Mrs. Burnham for Mrs. Ethan Allen, E. A. Benson for Rachel Martineau,

Lyman Royal and Delcena Diadamie, Susan J's children, born before she had her endowments but after she was sealed to me, were this day sealed to me, Netta acting for her mother, and Virginia for Delcena, and Lyman for himself. Thankful.

[written in margin]

Note. This sealing of children was needless, as afterwards decided.

July 24, 1884—Endd for Saml Hawkins, Susan for Mrs. Wm Sprague, M. A. Maughan for Margaret Martineau; E. A. Benson for Mrs. Gaston Martineau. Mrs. Poppleton for Margaret Jardine; E. Townsend for Mary Alice Martineau. (These three last were sealed to me.)

July 25, 1884—Endd for Seth Sprague, Susan for Elizabeth Marriott Martineau, M. A. Maughan for Amelia Columbine; Mrs. Burgess for Mary [g] Martineau; E. A. Benson for Mary Martineau, Mrs. Poppleton for Jane Martineau, All these were sealed to [word missing].

Susan was then sealed to her father, Nephi proxy for his grandfather Joel H Johnson (Susan's father), and Sister Zina D. H. Smith (Young) acting for her

129 The washing and anointings are part of the temple endowment. The ritual symbolizes "the cleansing of the soul from sins and iniquities" (Ludlow, *Encyclopedia of Mormonism*, 4:1551). "Second anointing" refers to a ceremony reserved for those who were called to receive them by the President of the Church (John David Buerger, *The Mysteries of Godliness: a History of Mormon Temple Worship* [San Francisco: Smith Research Associates, 1994]).

mother Anna Pixley Johnson Johnson, Pres[t] M. W. Merrill sealed them. (needless)

[The last word is in shaky hand writing, apparently added at a later date.]

[page 545]

SUSAN SEALED TO HER FATHER. LYMAN'S CHILD BORN

July 25, 1884—This morning Lyman and Alley had a little girl born to them, at 4.30 A.M. (Standard time, 4 A.M. local time) She was afterwards named Harriet Ann after Sister H. A. Preston.)

July 30, 1884—End[d] for Cornelius Martineau, G. W. Cummings for John Sprague; Susan for Mrs. Seth Sprague; Mrs. E. F. Sweet for Esther Sprague; Mrs. Hughes for Hannah Maxon; M. A. Maughan for Eunice Sprague;

Monday, July 28, 1884—To day I was blessed by W[m] J. Smith, Patriarch, in substance as follows:—

Br. Martineau, I place my hands upon your head and confirm the anointing with which you have just been anointed, and seal and confirm upon you all your former blessings. The Lord loveth thee for thine integrity, & has given his holy angel charge over thee, who shall never leave nor forsake thee, and who shall preserve thee from the power of the wicked, and deliver thee from thy enemies in time of danger. Thou shalt have health and strength, and vigor of body and of mind; thou shalt run like a deer and be strong as a lion. No enemy shall prosper against thee, but thou shalt have power over all thy enemies. Thou shalt be blessed in all you put your hand in righteousness to do, and have power to fill any mission or station appointed to you. You shall be mighty in the priesthood, and have mighty faith, even like to the Brother of Jared, even to perform any miracle that ever was done on the earth—to cause the sun & moon to stand still, and to move mountains if necessary for the prosperity of the work of the Lord; and thou shalt have power to heal the sick and afflicted, the dumb, ~~and~~ the blind, the deaf and the lame, to cause the drooping head to look up and comfort those who mourn, and shall be a great blessing to all you may be associated with. I seal upon you the Second Comforter. You shall live to be full of years, and shall be full of life and vigor to the end, and shall see and converse with the Savior face to face.

[page 546]

BLESSSINGS BY W[M] J SMITH. SUSAN'S

July 28, 1884—You shall do a great work in bringing souls to Christ, and shall do a mighty work among the Lamanites, and shall have power to learn tongues and languages, and shall be preserved from every evil. The Lord will open your way before you that you may move your family to Arizona, therefore be of good cheer, for when the time comes for you to go your way shall open, and you shall be greatly prospered in that land. You shall do a mighty work in Mexico, and the Angel of the Lord will be with thee, to deliver thee in time of danger, and from prison walls, that shall not be able to hold thee; and thousands of the Seed of Lehi shall rejoice to hear thee and see thee, and to comfort and bless thee, And thou shalt be faithful to the end of thy life, and be exalted to a throne in the celestial glory. Therefore rejoice and trust in God thy Friend.

This blessing and Susan's was given in our parlor.

SUSAN'S BLESSINGS.

Sister Martineau, We lay our hands upon your head and seal the anointing which has now been administered to you and confirm it upon you, together with all your former confirmations and blessings, and say they shall be sure unto you. The Lord loveth thee, and will bless thee all you desire in righteousness, for no good thing or blessing shall he withheld from thee. Thou shalt have great faith, and great power to heal the sick. You shall be sent for far and near, and many shall bless thee and rejoice because of thee, for you shall cause the drooping head to rise, and comfort those who mourn, and shall be filled with wisdom, that your counsels shall be full of life and salvation to those to whom you shall speak. You shall have visions and dreams, and be a prophetess and seeress, and shalt be taught great and mighty principles by heavenly messengers, and shall see and converse with the Savior face to face. Sickness and disease and death shall flee from before you, and you shall truly be a mother in Israel, and a comfort and help to your husband, and a blessing to your family.

[page 547]

SUSAN'S BLESSINGS (CONT^D^)

July 28, 1884—(Susan's cont^d^) Your name shall be honorable in Israel. You shall do a great work in the Temples of the Lord, and be a Savior to many of the dead, in acting for them in the ordinances of the Gospel. You shall have health, and strength of body and mind, and shall live to be old and full of days. and your last days shall be your best. Rejoice therefore in the blessings which God has and will bestow upon you, for no good thing shall be withheld from thee. You shall have a numerous posterity, who shall be mighty in the priesthood, Your children and all your father's house shall be saved. You shall be a wise counselor and a comfort to your husband, and shall help him to fulfill his mission in the lands to which you are sent, and shall have wisdom to govern and control all your family affairs in wisdom and in righteousness.

J. H. Martineau Scribe

In giving these blessings Pat^h^ Smith said he felt impelled by the Spirit to bless us, and said when he was done that he saw great and mighty things which he had not specified, and said he felt the Lord would greatly bless us. For all this I feel very thankful to our Father, and hope I may be faithful to the end.

Thursday, July 31, 1884—Endowed for Wm Sprague, Geo. W. Cummings for James Sprague, Susan for Mrs. John Sprague, Sister Hughes for Mrs. James Sprague, Mrs. Maughan for Mrs. Jesse Sprague, Mrs. Burgess for Rebecca Martineau, Anna Johnson Henstrom for Rebeca Johnson Henstrom, Mrs. Cummings for Elizabeth Martineau, Mrs. Maria F. Smith for Mary Martineau.

August 1, 1884—End^d^ for Danl Sprague, Susan for Mrs. John Martineau, Mrs. Maughan for Mrs. Stephen Martineau, Mrs. Hughes for Caroline Martineau, Mrs. Hewett for Hannah Martineau, Mrs. Burgess for Elizabeth Martineau.

In the evening assisted Lyman to name and bless his baby—Harriett Ann—named for Sister Preston.

Wednesday, August 6, 1884—End^d^ for Stephen Keteltas, Susan for Mrs. Stephen Keteltas, M. F. Smith for Sarah Neave, M. A. Maughan for Margaret Martineau. Sarah Neave & Margaret Martineau sealed to me.

[page 548]

LYMAN BAP^D^ FOR THE DEAD, ALSO ANNA.

August 7, 1884—End^d^ for Abraham Egbert, Susan for Mrs. Ann Egbert, M. F. Smith for Harriet Sprague, Mrs. Cummings for Mary Ann Sprague.

August 8, 1884—End^d^ for Peter Haughout, M. F. Smith for Emeline Martineau, E. A. Benson for Mrs. Addra Perrine.

Susan was too ill to go to the temple today—the only time. We both regretted it very much, for it's like being in heaven to work in the temple for the dead.

Sunday, August 10, 1884—Joel was today ordained Priest by Bp. B. M. Lewis and on

August 11, 1884—began his duty as a Teacher in the ward.

August 13, 1884—End^d^ for Ichabod Babcock, Susan for Alley Haughout Miss Mary Ellen Wright for Margaret Haughout, Mrs. E. Hughes for Caroline Martineau (sealed to me), Eliz^h^ Martineau (sealed to me)

August 14, 1884—End^d^ for James Cozine, Susan for Mrs. Jane Haughout Emeline Martineau was sealed to me.

August 15, 1884—End^d^ for Nicholas Haughout, Susan for Mrs. Nicholas H E. A. Benson for Mrs. Hannah H.

August 18, 1884—Settled with Temple Supt. Card[130] for my labor laying out the ornamental grounds around the temple, and for making the temple report—$54.^00^ [$1,127]

August 19, 1884—Paid the U. O. Co. $41.30 [$862] in full

Lyman was baptized for 17 and Anna for 14 persons.

August 20, 1884—To day Niels Larsen Hagberg came to Logan to be sealed to me as my son, his mother having already been sealed as my wife.[131] He was accordingly sealed.

I was Endowed for Peter E. Haughout, Neils for Benj. Martineau, Lyman for Peter Haughout, Susan

130 This is Charles Ora Card, superintendent of the temple construction. See Godfrey and Godfrey, *Utah Years*, for a transcript of Card's diaries.

131 Familysearch.org simply lists Nils Larsen Hagberg (note spelling) as a Swedish immigrant.

for Mrs. Beryl Martineau, M. A. Maughan for Mrs. John Martineau, Netta for Mrs. Elenor Haughout, Mrs. Smith for Elizabeth Hawkins, Mrs. Maughan for Sophia Billott; The last two were sealed to me.

When N. L. Hagberg was sealed to me, Susan acted for his mother at the altar. Hagberg gave me $60. [$1,250] to get him some of my land in Arizona.

August 21, 1884—Went to S. L. City to sell part of my lot. Paid Mrs. Teeples 24$ [$501] in full.

August 22, 1884—Saw Asmussen about my lot. The body of John H. Gibbs, the martyr, arrived from Tennessee. A great demonstration in the city in his honor.[132]

[page 549]

IN S. L. CITY. BR. J H. GIBBS BODY BROUGHT HOME. SETH MARRIED.

August 23, 1884—Sold part of my city lot to Asmussen for $1645 [$34,317] cash and a gold watch and chain at cost price ($85.⁰⁰) [$1,173] for Susan.

Sunday, August 24, 1884—Memorial service in the Tabernacle in honor of the Martyrs.

August 25, 1884—Bought Iron bedstead & mattress $15.⁰⁰ [$313] + 3.75 [$78].

August 26, 1884—Eliza and Seth went to Kaysville. I saw Pres^t^ J. F. Smith who said my two dead wives Mary Elvira Sherman and Mary Elizabeth Johnson should receive the 2^d^ A. Said he would have my two sisters, Lucretia and Francis, sealed to his father Hyrum Smith or to himself. Went to the Lake and bathed.

August 27, 1884—Went to Logan.

Thursday, August 28, 1884—I end^d^ for Stephen Martineau, Lyman for John Martineau John R. Barnes for Jesse Sprague, Susan for Charity Beatty, Mrs. Lufkin for Frances Haughout, M. A. Maughan for Mrs. Alley Haughout, Mrs. Layton for Mrs. Wm Sherwin, Mrs. Andrews for Mrs. J. H. Poole, Eliza Jones Martineau for Mrs. Cornelia Haughout.

132 John H. Gibbs died at Cane Creek, Tennessee, during his mission to the southern states. The story of the Tennessee murders is found in the *Autobiography of B. H. Roberts*, ed. Gary James Bergera (Salt Lake City: Signature Books, 1990), chapter 17.

Seth C. Jones and Anna Layton married today. Charity Beatty was sealed to me.

August 30, 1884—Sold mirror to Lyman for his, ($15.⁰⁰) [$313] and $60. [$1,252] to be applied on my note for $185. [$3,859] which he holds.

Tuesday, September 2, 1884—Susan was baptized by R. Bain[133] for her health and to R. cov.^t^

September 3, 1884—Nett came from the city with a bad cough. Made deed to Asmussen for the land

September 4, 1884—Went to Ogden & Stopped at Layton's, in Kaysville.

September 5, 1884—Arr^d^ at S. L. City. Got recommend for my two dead wives Mary E. Sherman & Mary E. Johnson to have their 2^d^ A. Had talk with Pres^t^ Taylor about Arizona and Mexican mission. He dont want people to leave their posts. Quite cold.

Saturday, September 6, 1884—Got my pay from Asmussen.

Sunday, September 7, 1884—Cold & rainy. Saw Uncle David LeBaron and Don.

September 9, 1884—Got home.

September 10, 1884—Paid debts—$300.25 [$6,266]—Mrs. Palmer $4.95 [$103] S. Langton $8.⁰⁰ [$167] J Irvine (notes & int) $273.⁰⁰ [$5,695] Goods $14.30 [$298]

[page 550]

2ND A. FOR TWO. LEAVE LOGAN

Thursday, September 11, 1884—Susan and I went to the Temple and rec^d^ 2^d^ for Mary E. Sherman Martineau and Mary Elizabeth Johnson Martineau from Pres^t^ M. W. Merrill

September 12, 1884—Paid Z.C.M.I. $84.⁶⁰ [$1,765] Gave them note for balance $100.⁰⁰ [$2,086] 1 o/c pr. mo. Paid 4th Ward Store $464.⁰⁰ [$9,680] & gave note for balance due ($170.⁰⁰) [$3,546] 1 o/c pr. mo. Lyman gave Susan & me each a nice ring. I gave him my Utah Garnet.

September 13, 1884—Went to Church farm & spent the day with Nephi & Emma

133 Robert A. Bains was one of the original settlers of Smithfield.

Sunday, September 14, 1884—Lyman & Alley, Nephi & Emma, spent the day with us, I gave them my parting counsels.

September 15, 1884—We all sat for a family picture at D. Lewis', at Lyman's expense. He also got rings for Nett & Lilly. I sent a silver teapot each to my sister Netta and Lotie by Exp.

Tuesday, September 16, 1884—Began packing up, Lyman and Charles helped. Sold them my parlor chairs for $60.$^{\underline{00}}$ [$1,252] and the Carpet to Lyman for $60.$^{\underline{00}}$ Gave Lyman the Sofa ($40.) [$834] & to Charles the Rocker, $20.$^{\underline{00}}$ [$417] and the Parlor stove $25.^{00} [$522]. To Nephi our Bismark Range for his small stove & gave him chairs, tables, and many other things. Gave Charles the Bedstead & mattress.

September 17, 1884—Finished packing, & Sent things to depot. In the evening went to Lyman's to sleep. (and to Br. Preston's)

Thursday, September 18, 1884—Rose at 3.30 and left Logan at 4.30 A.M. Lyman going with us to Ogden. Our parting with our family and Br. Preston's was sad—the sundering of ties that have been binding us together for so many years. But these are stirring times, and no one can say where we may <u>all</u> be in five or ten years. We have lived here over 24 years, and have formed close friendships with many dear friends: but at the call of duty we should be ready always to respond, without regrets or unwillingness, for the Lord loves a willing heart. I was 32 when I came here and am now over 56—getting on the silvery side of life; and I can say truthfully, that in all this time I have not knowingly injured or defrauded a single soul, nor at any time oppressed the poor. My conscience is clear and void of all offense to <u>all</u>. In all things and at all times I have ever sought the public good in preference to my own,—have always placed <u>my</u> affairs second to the public welfare and good. I have never been found opposing the priesthood and ruling authorities, but have always been in unison with them. I do not boast in this, but render thanks to God, that <u>he</u> has caused me to be willing to do this, and has helped me to be faithful thus far: and I pray He may help me to the end.

We arrived at Ogden at 8 A.M. and stopped at the "Central Hotel." Our baggage consists of 5 trunks & 2100 lbs freight. I got a shot gun at Ogden, with ammunition &c. for $30.$^{\underline{00}}$ [$626] also some clothing for Susan. Lyman Got some also for the girls and Lilla. Paid $300.$^{\underline{00}}$ [$6,258] for our fare (3^{d} class)—6 full tickets, and left Ogden at 6.15 P.M. (Pacific time) 7.25 Ogden time. Lyman was with us till the train started.

September 19, 1884—Awoke at Terrace, Elko about 10 P.M. Cool.

September 20, 1884—Sunrise at Battle Mountain. Paid 25¢ [$5] for a potato at the "Capital Hotel," Winnemucka at noon, and Rye Patch at dark.

Sunday, September 21, 1884—Reno at 5 A.M. Waited till 9 A.M. on account of a R. R. wreck ahead, by which a man or two was killed. Begin to ascend the Sierra Nevada's snowy range. At Truckee 2 P.M. Left there with three engines. Passed Donner Lake, and reached the Summit at 4 P.M. reaching Auburn 9 P.M. We passed through over 40 miles of Snow sheds, most of it continuous, and very disagreeable to us, as it hid from us much of the grand scenery we passed.

September 22, 1884—Wake near San Francisco Bay. Reach Oakland at 9.40 A.M. and San F. at 11.30 A.M. Went to the "American Exchange"—a pretty good "cheap" place, $1.25 [$26] per day—board and room. Good tables, but poor rooms.

Bought hats for Susan, Lilla & Virginia also Theodore; coats for the Girls. Foggy and cold.

PART

ARIZONA AND MEXICO

[page 552]

LOS ANGELES. TUCSON. HOME.

September 22, 1884—Bought hats for Susan, Lilla & Virginia also Theodore; coats for the girls. Foggy and cold.

September 23, 1884—Foggy this morning. We all went to the Cliff house by Cable road and Carriage, saw hundreds of Seals, also the head bones of a whale, played on the shore with the waves and returned by train to the city; then visited "Woodward's Gardens," and returned to the Hotel. Then I went to C.P.R.R. general offices, saw Mr. R. Gray, Genl Ft. Agt, and got a reduction on household movables, boxed, from $6.70 [$140] to $3.80 [$79.40] per hund. [hundred] for our people moving to Arizona, from Ogden to Benson. Left San F. at 7 P.M. and at the Oakland Pier met Eli and Harry Dennison—old schoolmates of Elbridge. Left Oakland 10.30 P.M.

Wednesday, September 24, 1884—Woke at Lathrop, 82$^{\underline{m}}$ at 5 A.M. Met Uncle D. T. LeBaron and Don, on their way to Mesa, Arizona. Tulare, at dark. Plenty of melons, and grapes 2½¢ [$0.03 = $0.63] pr lb.

Thursday, September 25, 1884—Tehatchapi Loop about sun rise. Los Angeles 2 P.M. being attached to the Express train at Tehatchapi. Left Los Angeles 10 P.M. Here we bought sugar, C. oil & other provisions, also grapes @ 2½¢ lb, apples &c.

September 26, 1884—Wake on San Gorgonio Pass in a cloud & rain storm: Indio ~~8:30 A.M.~~ noon 350 feet lower than the sea; very hot. Yuma 3 P.M. The new R.R. bridge nearly finished. Left Yuma 4 P.M.

Saturday, September 27, 1884—Uncle D. T. & Don got off at Maricopa Sta. at 2 A.M. to go to Tempe, reached Tucson at 9 A.M. & were hitched on to Express train, reaching Benson at noon. After we had tried in vain to get a team to St. David, Seth and Lilla appeared with W$^{\underline{m}}$ Layton's team and wagon, and we reached St. David at 4 P.M. Our new home.

Sunday, September 28, 1884—Went to meeting, and next day. Jesse at hay field.

September 29, 1884—Went to Benson & got map $1.15 [$24] Expr. Charges. Our baggage not yet arrived. Thermometer 90°.

September 30, 1884—Went for my freight. Paid $5.00 [$104] storage & $88.^{40} [$1,844] frt.

Wednesday, October 1 & 2, 1884—Unpacked our things. Our house is too little to hold them all.

[page 553]

SURVEY THATCHER. BLESSED BY PAT^H MCBRIDE

October 4, 1884—Started for Pima, to attend our Conference, by S.P.R.R.; reached Bowie 4 P.M. 64 miles & found no way to go on.

Sunday, October 5, 1884—Hired team to take me to Solomonville[1]—38 miles—$8.^00 [$167] Staid there all night, and hired team to go to Safford, 5 miles for $2.^00 [$43] Reached there at 9 A.M. and met Pres^t Layton.

October 12, 1884—Preached at Layton; also Bp. Roundy, on "Emigre."[2]

October 13, 1884—Began to Survey a city plat at Thatcher. (Moody's)

October 14, 1884—Finished survey for the present. Var. by U.S. Sur. 12°34'E.

October 15, 1884—Went to Pima, and met Aunt Harriett Johnson, her two daughters Diadamie and Blanch, also their husbands James H. Carlton & Geo. Aikin, who live 6 miles below here.[3] Saw Co. Sur. J. D. Holladay, who made me his Deputy. Patriarch W^m McBride told me I should be prospered & blessed from this day forth, being constrained to do so by the Holy Spirit. This comforted me very much, for I was very low spirited, having a large family and no means of support for them—no team, cow, chickens, buggy, plow, nor provisions. He invited me to dinner, after which he gave me the following blessing:—

Patriarchal Blessing by W^m McBride, given in Pima, A. T. [Arizona Territory] Oct. 15. 1884, upon the head of James, son of John Martineau and Eliza Mears Martineau, born March 13, 1828 in Port Jackson, Montgomery Co. N.Y.

Br. James, in the name of the Lord Jesus I lay my hands upon thy head, and by the authority of the Holy Priesthood I seal upon thee a Patriarchal blessing, and also seal and confirm upon thee all thy former blessings & ordinations, and I say unto thee, be thou comforted, for thou art of the blood of the House of Israel and lineage of Ephraim, and called, chosen, ordained and set apart before the foundations of this world were laid to come forth in the dispensation in which we now live, to bear thy part in the redemption of Zion and the restoration of the House of Israel, and to lay the foundation for the Salvation and exaltation of thy father's house for many generations, back, both for the living and for the dead, and to teach them how to save themselves with their dead;

[page 554]

SURVEYED GRAHAM, PIMA & CURTIS, MEETINGS AT PIMA.

and to perform this work thou mayest yet have to travel and hunt up the sons and daughters of Jacob, teach them the plan of Salvation, and to build temples, that they may administer ordinances therein, that will produce their salvation, both living and dead; and the Lord requires that thou should teach thy children to build upon the foundation that thou hast laid, that thy work may be complete, for unto this end wast thou born, and by obedience to the new and everlasting covenant thou shalt secure to thyself, thy wives, thy children, relatives and friends an everlasting inheritance; for I seal upon thee the blessings of life and health and Strength, and thou shalt receive a crown of eternal lives, and thy part in the morning of the first ressurrection with all that are near and dear unto thee in the name of Jesus. Amen.

I was scribe for him.

Thursday, October 16, 1884—Went to Graham to survey a town plat. Saw peanuts growing, also Sweet potatoes: and the 2^d crop potatoes.

October 17, 1884—Surveyed Graham today and the next.

1 Today's Solomon, Arizona, is located just east of Safford.

2 The Roundys were influential in the Arizona Mormon settlements. Lorenzo Roundy was among the first explorers in the San Francisco Mountains and Little Colorado River areas of Arizona. He, however, drowned while crossing the Colorado River during a spring flood in 1876. *Émigré* denotes someone who was forced to flee his or her country as opposed to an emigrant who leaves on his or her own will (Daniel H. Ludlow, ed., *Encyclopedia of Mormonism* [New York: Macmillan, 1992], 1:66; James H. McClintock, *Mormon Settlement in Arizona* [Tucson: Univ. of Arizona Press, 1921], 87).

3 James H. Carlton became one of the founders of the Oaxaca colonies in Mexico (Thomas Cottam Romney, *The Mormon Colonies in Mexico* [Salt Lake City: Univ. of Utah Press, 2005], 100, 115).

October 18, 1884—Letter from Sur. Genl of Arizona, saying he would appoint me Deputy U.S. Surveyor.

Sunday, October 19, 1884—Pres^{t} Layton and I went to Pima & held meeting.

October 20, 1884—Began to Survey Pima, and finished.

October 24, 1884—Rainy for several days.

October 25, 1884—Priesthood meeting at Central.

Sunday, October 26, 1884—Preached at Central.

October 27, 1884—Wrote to Des. News. Went to Carlton's to Survey his land. Went across the Gila in a skiff.[4]

October 28, 1884—A light frost (the first) last night. Surveyed.

October 29, 1884—Went to Curtis, & began Survey of town plat.

October 30, 1884—Finished the Survey

October 31, 1884—Went to Pima. Rec^{d} letters from home. Wrote letters.

Saturday, November 1, 1884—Apostles Young & Grant arrived at Pima[5]

Sunday, November 2, 1884—Meetings today. At evening meeting several members of the High Council were ordained by Apostles Young & Grant, Pres^{t} Layton and myself. I ordained Hiram Weech a High Priest and set him apart as a High Councillor. Attended a party at Bush's in the evening.

[page 555]

November 3, 1884—Went to Curtis and held meetings in forenoon, then went to Central and held another. ~~then returned to Pima~~ After meeting at Central, I ordained Jacob. G. Bigler a High Councillor and High Priest, after which Pres^{t} Layton and I returned to Safford, while Apostles Young and Grant held meeting at Thatcher.[6]

November 4, 1884—Tues. Went to Graham and held meeting. and met there Brs Young & Grant. I preached, followed by Brs. Young & Grant. Meeting at Layton at 3 P.M. In the evening a Council was held, after which I went to Central, arriving there at 11 P.M.

November 5, 1884—Walked 5 m. to Pima. In afternoon went back to Layton.

November 6, 1884—Walked to Alred's and examined the Canal, 6 miles.

November 7, 1884—Borrowed Bp. Welker's horse, and rode over the Country.

November 8, 1884—Went to Central to a Canal meeting, after meeting Pres^{t} Layton and I ordained Alfred Cluff a High Priest and set set him apart as a High Councillor; Pres^{t} Layton officiating.[7]

Sunday, November 9, 1884—Meeting at Layton. Blessed a baby. After meeting went with Pres^{t} Layton to his land, and rented [40 or 60] acres, with water for ¼ the crop (for him).

Monday, November 10, 1884—Pres^{t} Layton and family moved away this morning before daylight to avoid arrest for polygamy. I went to Layton to resurvey their canal, but abandoned it. Earned \$6.$^{\underline{00}}$ [\$125] Hear many rumors of impending trouble.

November 11, 1884—Went to Fonda's Ranch, 10 miles, to survey for some stock men. (Bert. E. Veatch)

November 12, 1884—Surveyed, running 4 miles through thick mesquite.

November 13, 1884—Surveyed all day. Earned \$21.^{00} [\$438]

November 14, 1884—Surved for Mr. Dowdle. Earned \$10.$^{\underline{00}}$ [\$209].

November 15, 1884—Returned to Safford. Found the mill closed and Joseph Layton gone to Tucson, by subpoena before Grand Jury. Hear that Roundy, Rogers, Fuller, Loving & others have fled, to avoid arrest for polygamy.[8] By letter from home learn that nearly all the family are sick. Wrote to Henry.

---

4 Jas. H. Martineau, "Correspondence: A Prolific Region," *Deseret News*, November 4, 1885; Journal History.

5 These are Apostles Brigham Young Jr. and Heber J. Grant.

6 There are numerous Bigelows in Arizona Mormon history; at this writing no match was found correlating with this entry.

7 Alfred Cluff was among the original settlers in Forestdale, Arizona, near Show Low (Norma Baldwin Ricketts, *Arizona's Honeymoon Trail and Mormon Wagon Roads* [Mesa, AZ: Cox Printing, 2001], 137).

8 There were several Fullers who could match this description. This could be John Loving, a resident of Pima (Ricketts, *Arizona's Honeymoon Trail*, 69, 134–35).

Sunday, November 16, 1884—Walked to Thatcher and held meeting.

November 17, 1884—Walked to Pima, and heard that U.S. officials had been there, acting very suspiciously. Attended a party in the evening, given to the Sonora missionaries.

[page 556]

RETURN FROM SAFFORD. MISSIONARIES START TO SONORA

November 19, 1884—Started for St David with our two teams and missionaries for Sonora. The Gila Settlements furnish 2 4-mule teams and wagons, four extra riding horses, and 7 men. The Salt-River brethren at Mesa are to furnish others. At noon met J. Layton returning from Tucson.[9]

November 18, 1884—Last evening Br. Montierth and family, with Pr. Layton's 4 sons, arrived from Utah at dark, having left home in Utah Sept 3^{d} 1884.

November 20, 1884—Drove to Wilcox and nooned, then 12^{m} further=32$^{\underline{m}}$

November 21, 1884—Reached home 2 P.M. having ridden 5 hours in rain. Found my family better—most of them well. Found Apostles Young & Grant at St David. Went to a party at Bp. Johnson's in the evening. Rainy.

November 22, 1884—Rain all last night. We set apart Wm D. Johnson as st Councillor in place of D. P. Kimball, Br. Brigham being mouth. Br. B. Young said I had better move to the Gila valley, to obtain a living, as I had no chance here. And then if I should be called into Mexico would have something to go with.[10]

Sunday, November 23, 1884—Netta thinks she is threatened with dropsy. Had good meetings today, Br. Brigham speaking with power. In the evening Apostles Young & Grant administered to Netta, and promised her life and health.

November 24, 1884—The apostles ~~and missionaries~~ started to day, the teams having gone previously. I wrote letters to Utah.

Monday, December 1, 1884—Went to Tombstone with Mother, Netta & Jesse. Netta stood the trip pretty well, but was worse in the night. Paid my Co. Taxes, of \$19.$^{\underline{00}}$ [\$396] Bought rocking chair.

December 2, 1884—Went for wood, with Susan and Netta. She got tired.

December 3, 1884—Party. Susan & I went a little while. At bed time Nett found dropsy in her ancles, and she coughs very much.

December 4, 1884—Went to Benson to get medicine for Nett, & walked home 8 miles. Quite tired.

December 5 ~~6~~, 1884—Wrote answer to J. R. Rogers from Casas Grandes Mex. for Pres^{t} Layton.[11]

December 6, 1884—Water meeting this evening. St David canal, at which the canal was voted to extend to our land.

[page 557]

MISSIONARIES RETURN FROM SONORA. I GO HOME.

Sunday, December 7, 1884—Went to meeting, after which Pres$^{\underline{t}}$. Layton called on me and Br. Johnson to go with him to Safford, to try and settle the difficulty between him and Dr. Groesbeek. Slept at Laytons.

December 8, 1884—Started at 7 in a rain storm, and drove to Frisk's 46 miles, through rain most of the time.

December 9, 1884—Crossed Chiricahua Mts. via Stockton Pass, going for ten miles in a dense cloud, with rain and hail. Reached Safford at dark, 40 miles. Cold & stormy journey. In the evening Johnson & I went to see Groesbeek.

December 10, 1884—Attempted to compromise, but poor success. Rainy.

December 11, 1884—Pres^{t} Layton and J. Hill started back before daylight. Johnson & I settled with Groesbeek, so far as to get the case out of court.[12]

---

9 This is likely Christopher Layton (Helen R. Cole, *One Hundred Years in Thatcher, 1883–1983* [Thatcher, AZ: Town of Thatcher, 1983], 11, 15; Myron W. McIntyre and Noel R. Barton, eds., *Christopher Layton* [Thatcher, AZ: Christopher Layton Family Organization, 1966]).

10 William Dydamous Johnson later became the first bishop in Colonia Díaz, Mexico. He was among the prominent early pioneers in the Gila Valley (Romney, *The Mormon Colonies in Mexico*, 76; Cole, *One Hundred Years in Thatcher*, 250).

11 There are numerous Rogers in eastern Arizona Mormon history. At this writing none matched this entry.

12 On this date Martineau wrote another letter to the newspaper encouraging settlers to come south (J. H. Martineau, "A Prolific Country of Which This Is a Compendious

December 12, 1884—Settled in full with Groesbeek. Heavy rains & snow.

December 13, 1884—Still cold and rainy. Also a little snow—melts.

December 14, 1884—Preached at Layton. Storm over, clear and cold.

December 15, 1884—Br. Montierth and I run trial line for canal.[13]

December 16, 1884—Surveyed for Anderson

December 19, 1884—Surveyed for D. Groesbeek. Met my old friend, the daughter of Sam[l] West, formerly Nancy West, now Mrs. J H Rollins.

Sunday, December 21, 1884—Wrote to Lotie. Preached in Layton, and ordained Geo. Morris a High Priest and set him apart as 2[d] Counselor to Bp. John Welker.[14] Hear[d] that Netta is worse yesterday.

December 22, 1884—Started home with Br. A. M. Montierth, and young Roundy. Drove 30 m. and camped.

December 23, 1884—Drove 34 m. and camped.

December 24, 1884—Reached home about noon, having driven 22[m] total 88[m] Found Netta's dropsy much worse, her swelling having reached her body. Found Jesse just going for some freight sent us by Lyman, some 350 lbs, for which the charges were $39.50 [$824]. We got the sewing machine, 14 jars of fruit, and some goods sent by Lyman & Charles as a Christmas gift, for which we were very thankful, as it came in good time.

December 25, 1884—Brother Montierth went home today. Storm at night.

Description," *Deseret Evening News*, December 20, 1884; Journal History).

13 Alvin B. Montierth was one of the Cache Valley settlers who had moved to Arizona. He was among the first in Paradise, Utah (Joel E. Ricks and Everett L. Cooley, *The History of a Valley: Cache Valley, Utah-Idaho* [Logan, UT: Cache Valley Centennial Commission, 1956], 45).

14 John Welker was the first bishop of the Layton Ward in Graham County, Arizona (Hubert H. Bancroft, *The Works of Hubert Howe Bancroft, XVII, History of Arizona and New Mexico, 1530–1888* [San Francisco: History Company Publishers, 1889], 533n36). Interestingly, this footnote appears to have come from a manuscript of James H. Martineau, "Settlements in Arizona." Geo. Morris could be George L. Morris of Safford.

December 26, 1884—Stormy all day. Conference commenced. Yesterday the expedition arrived from Sonora all right.

[page 558]

1885. JOEL & THEODORE ORDAINED

December 26, 1884—H. M. Merrill was voted to be sustained as Presiding Elder here.[15]

Saturday & Sunday, December 27 & 28, 1884—Conference two days. We set apart M H Merrill as Presiding Elder over St David today. I let Br. Layton have my revolver, scabbard, and about 40 cartridges on my debt, at $24.[00] [$501] I also spent 8 days in his service, helping him to compromise with Groesbeek, for which I charge him $26.[00] [$542] Rains day & night.

Monday, December 29, 1884—Storm all night. Cold this morning. Netta not so well, and I sat up with her all night.

December 30, 1884—Netta seems a little better, but the swelling increases. Settled, partially, with Mrs. Kimball, who claims $12.[00] [$250].

December 31, 1884—Netta had a bad night. Held council at Laytons with Brs. Layton, Johnson & Macdonald.[16]

[written in margin]

1885

Thursday, January 1, 1885—Br. Layton & Macdonald went away today. Netta about the same. The storm is over for the present, but nights are cold, and the ground freezes a little at night. Telegram from J. Taylor

Friday, January 2, 1885—Netta seems a little easier this morning, but at times she seems smothering. She has more faith in administration than last winter. Her appetite is almost gone, and she cannot turn or raise in bed, nor help herself in the least. Her

15 This could be Morgan Henry Merrill, son of Philemon C. Merrill of Safford. He would have been eighteen years of age at this sustaining (Cole, *One Hundred Years in Thatcher*, 288–89).

16 On this date the *Deseret News* published an article written by Martineau encouraging people from Utah to come to Arizona (J. H. Martineau, "A Prolific Country," *Deseret News*, December 31, 1884; Utah Digital Newspapers).

stomach is so weak as to reject almost everything she swallows. Wrote to Br. Layton

Saturday, January 3, 1885—Netta about the same, but growing weaker. Has no rest, but is in constant distress, wishing all the time to be moved into some easier position, but each move hurting her much. Snowed about an inch in the night—a remarkable thing for this climate. It all melted at sunrise. Wrote to Henry about Netta, and to see if they can help me to a team in any way.

Sunday, January 4, 1885—At meeting today I presented the name of Joel H. for ordination as Elder and Theodore for Deacon. After meeting they were ordained, I mouth in each case. In the evening Joel assisted in laying on hands for the first time, on Netta, who seems better today.

January 5, 1885—Netta had a very bad night and is worse to day. The swelling increased and water oozed from her feet and legs, which are swelled almost to bursting.

[page 559]

January 1885—Met with Br. P. C. Merrill, and other refugees on the river bank, and appointed P. C. Merrill Pres[t] John S. Merrill Capt, and Geo. W Lake Recorder of their party.[17] Also told them not to start till we hear from Pres[t] Taylor, but be ready to start any time and keep out of danger in the mean time.

Tuesday, January 6, 1885—Netta still worse, she coughs and spits blood. We held her for some time in a blanket to give her rest.

Wednesday, January 7, 1885—No improvement, but weaker. Wrote to Lizzie Smith for Netta. Last night she took a change and became easier, sleeping much of the time; and all day she has lain, free from pain, and sleeping most of the time, raising now and then for a drink or to vomit or cough. I fear this is a change heralding her departure. I went up into the hills, and dedicated her to the Lord, asking that if she is to go that she may do so quickly and without any pain or suffering, for she has suffered so long. She can eat nothing or keep anything on her stomach, and can speak but little above a whisper. She does not realize her low state, till I talked to her about it, and told her to give my love to her mother if she should see her before I do. She said she would, but said she would not do so yet awhile—she was all right—far better than she had been; "Why," said she, "I don't have any pain now." I played on the organ for her, as she loves to have me do. The last tune was "Sweet home," which she noticed and spoke about.

The day was so warm, we kept both doors open. We all feel that our darling is nearly gone. She has always been lovely in character, and now, when she asks for anything does so with such a heavenly smile on her poor weak face. When I said to her "My poor girl," she said, "No Pa, not <u>poor</u>—I'm quite a size" with a lovely smile (and referring to her dropsical swelling).

[page 560]

NETTA'S DEATH[18]

Wednesday, January 7, 1885—This evening Pres[t] Johnson returned from the Gila, and rec[d] a letter from Pres[t] Taylor saying he and a party of nine will be here in a day or so, on their way to Mexico.

Pres[t] Johnson, Bp. H. Merrill and I laid our hands upon her and dedicated her to the Lord about 10 P.M. This evening she spoke to Susan, saying what a good mother she has been to her always. She wished her to sit where she could see her. She sleeps or dozes most of the time, rousing occasionally to ask for something, and when she does, her face is lighted up with a lovely and heavenly smile.

Thursday, January 8, 1885—She seems stronger, and sat up a long time, sleeping most of the time. She drinks often, but vomits directly. She eats nothing but a little broth. Her general condition is like yesterday's. I went to Benson & back.

17 Philemon C. Merrill was an early pioneer in St. David. His notoriety stems from his leadership in the Mormon Battalion, in which he was a third lieutenant in Company B. John S. Merrill was Henry Morgan Merrill's older brother (Ricketts, *The Mormon Battalion*, 22; McClintock, *Mormon Settlement in Arizona*, 235; Ricketts, *Arizona's Honeymoon Trail*, 213). George W. Lake was among the pioneers settling originally along the Little Colorado River where they attempted to live the United Order (Ricketts, *Arizona's Honeymoon Trail*, 8; McClintock, *Mormon Settlement in Arizona*, 136, 146, 147, 188).

18 "A Lamentable Death," *Deseret News*, January 21, 1885; Utah Digital Newspapers.

Friday, January 9, 1885—This morning at 6.15 She passed peacefully away without a struggle. She had been sleeping when all at once she said, "Oh Huldah," and raised her hands to be raised up. She was raised up and expired in a few moments.

It all seems a dream. Netta was almost 20, and in all her life never gave me cause for trouble or grief. She was most lovely in character, and was loved by all who knew her. She has made her exaltation sure, and last summer did a good work in the temple for the dead. In her temple robes she looked more like an angel than a mortal, and many noticed it. I can only Say "The Lord gave, the Lord hath taken away. Blessed be the name of the Lord." For many days before her death I prayed that if it be the will of God to heal her, that he would do so soon. If it is His will for her to be taken, that He would do so speedily, that she might not linger in pain and distress.

Our neighbors have been very kind & good. For several nights they have set up with us, and especially Alex. McRae and Huldah Hubbard and Esther Walmsley, Also Sister Beebee, whom may the Lord bless.[19]

[page 561]

[NETTA'S DEATH.] AND BURIAL. PRES^T TAYLOR ARRIVES. SONORA TRIP.

Saturday, January 10, 1885—Funeral today at 11 A.M. The choir sung "Sister thou wast mild and lovely," which was sung at her mother's funeral also. Pat^h P. C. Merrill spoke, also Pres^t Johnson and Bp. M. H. Merrill. The day was warm and very delightful.

Sunday, January 11, 1885—Good meeting today. I ordained Jos Alex. McRae an Elder, and we set him apart as Pres^t Y.M.M.I.A. of St David. Took Supper at McRae's by invitation.

Tuesday, January 13, 1885—Pres^t J. Taylor and party arrived this afternoon, as follows:— J. F. Smith, M. Thatcher, E. Snow, John Sharp, Geo. Reynolds, H. J. Grant, Jesse N. Smith, Lot Smith & others. Bro. Thatcher & J. N. Smith came to our house. Lyman sent me a check for \$50.^{00} [\$1,082] rec^d today. Held meeting in the evening, when Pres^t Taylor & Smith and J. N. Smith spoke.

January 14, 1885—Meeting at 10 A.M. Remarks by Pres^t Taylor, E. Snow, M. Thatcher, John Q. Cannon & Geo. Reynolds.[20] Pres^t J. F. Smith dined with us. By invitation I joined Pres^t Taylor's party for the trip to Sonora. We started at 4.20 P.M. We travel in the Utah Central Director's Car, arranged for Cooking, dining, and sleeping—everything nice and comfortable. We reached Los Nogales, a R.R. Station on the boundary line at 10 P.M. The Mexican officials were very courteous, not examining our baggage at all, and offering money &c if we needed. It was decided in Council that M. Thatcher, myself, J. N. Smith & Lot Smith[21] ~~& I~~ should be a committee to examine lands &c for Sale, with view to buying if satisfactory, with M. G. Trejo as interpreter. We took leave of Pres^t Taylor & the others at bed time, as we are to leave the train in the night. At 2 A.M. we reached Magdalena & left the train, stopping at the "French Hotel." "Hotel Francis"

[page 562]

MAGDELENA. IMURIS

Thursday, January 15, 1885—Walked around Magdalena, admiring the orange trees loaded with fruit. Saw also lemon trees, palms, pomegranates &c. Cactus (flat-leaved kind) grows 25 feet high, with a regular trunk 6 to 8 inches in diameter. Visited a fine church. About 11.30 we saw some 6 or 7 armed police, running down the street, and immediately heard heavy firing near by, which continued till about 40 shots were fired. Heard that the police were trying to arrest a man & did so, after shooting him in the side of

19 Alexander McRae was reported to be among the men imprisoned in the Liberty Jail with the Prophet Joseph Smith (Ricketts, *Arizona's Honeymoon Trail*, 58–59). There are several Hubbards in the history of the Arizona settlements. Elisha F. Hubbard Sr. was the first bishop of the Hubbard settlement (McClintock, *Mormon Settlement in Arizona*, 249).

20 George Reynolds (1842–1909) was traveling with the General Authorities. He later became a seventy. At this entry John Q. Cannon was second counselor to the Presiding Bishop William B. Preston. Later excommunicated in 1886, he was rebaptized in 1888.

21 Lot Smith was a member of the Mormon Battalion. He was in the first exploration party in Sonora. Living in Yuba City, Arizona, he later lost his life in a fight with the Indians (Ricketts, *The Mormon Battalion*, 15, 265–66; McClintock, *Mormon Settlement in Arizona*, 159–60).

his head. Magdalena has about 3000 pop[n] Streets are narrow and all houses, nearly, built in Mexican Style. Got some oranges and lemons from trees, for 2¢ each. Learned of ranches for sale near Imuris.

January 16, 1885—Started at 8 A.M. with a hired carriage for Imuris, 12 miles up the Magdalena river. Our team was a poor, little, scrawny team, and balky as we found to our sorrow. Went 5 m. and came to a ford of the Magdalena R. but were detained there two hours or more, by our horses balking & in trying to get another animal. We finally hired a horse which the Mexican said was "bueno" but when we got into the river he, too, balked, and we were there a long time. Br. Thatcher got on a horse and crossed, and I finally took off my pants and waded the river—about up to my waist. Finally myself, Jesse N. & Trejo started to walk the rest of the way to Imuris—7 miles, leaving M. Thatcher & Lot Smith with the team & baggage. We got to Imuris about half an hour before the team—pretty tired. Staid at R.R. Sta. and had to sleep on a dirty floor, Br. Thatcher & I being, as we always are on such trips, mates. After supper I visited Senor Col. Hilario Gabilondo.[22] His daughter speaks good English, and explained about her father's ranch which he has for sale. One, "Rancho de San Nicolas" South of Frontera, has four sq. leagues = ~~about~~ 17305.6 acres.

[page 563]

PREST TAYLOR & PARTY RETURN HOME. NETTA

Price $8,000.[00] [$173,121] Also a ranch 3 m. from Imuris, price $12,000 [$259,682], va. 12° 8' E. which has about 700 & 800 acres. It is called the "Rancho de la Galera, de Gavilondo, and is mostly under fence. It is a good piece of land. He lives in a pretty good house, with flat dirt roof and brick floor. We also visited during the day several other ranches.

January 17, 1885—At 2 A.M. boarded the return train, and got home about noon. We were immediately summoned to Council meeting which continued until night. At the meeting were Pres[t] Taylor and party, & Pres[t] Layton, Johnson & myself. Discussed our present situation, and necessary moves for us to make. In the evening held meeting in the school house.

Sunday, January 18, 1885—Council meeting in the morning, and public meeting at 10 A.M. Pres[t] Taylor preached, after dinner the party went in Carriages to Benson & took train for San Francisco & Ogden. On the way down Bp. J. Q. Cannon proposed I should be appointed Bps. Agent for this Stake, which would require me to move to the Gila. I was appointed, subject to the approval of Bp. Preston. Bp. Cannon gave me considerable instruction in regard to my duties. At the station I offered to give Pres[t] J. F. Smith my Netta. He eagerly assented and said he had wished for it, but hesitated to ask me for her, but as he already has two of my sisters would be very glad to have her also. Hoped he would be worthy of her. and thankful for my confidence in him. They left at 2.15 P.M. Pres[t] Layton with them. We decided unanimously in the council, to locate in Chihuahua and a committee was appointed to purchase land there.

I sent by Br. Thatcher, Netta's napkin ring to Nephi and Emma; a ring of hers to Charlie, and a beautiful locket to Lyman & Alley as mementos of our dear girl—now gone to rest. She is well worthy, I think, of the exaltation in store for her.

[page 564]

ALBERT STARTS FOR SPRINGERVILLE. WITH J. N. SMITH & LOT

January 19, 1885—I procured horses and Saddles for Lot Smith & Jesse N. to go over the mountains to warn their people. I and Susan went to Tombstone and cashed Lyman's check. Jesse went to haul for Allred. Had a surprise party in the evening.

January 20, 1885—This morning Lot and Jesse N. Smith, Albrt [Albert] and some others, started with pack animals for St. Johns. I got some blanks from Goodman, needful for me as Bps. Agent.

Wednesday, January 21, 1885—This morning Pres[t] Johnson and I started for the Gila valley to warn polygamists to escape from their enemies, and to instruct the Bishops. Stopped for the night at Wilcox at Eureka Hotel.

---

22 Commander Hilario Gabilondo was a leader in the Mexican Army. His influence was particularly noted in the northern Mexican states of Sonora and Chihuahua where the Mormon colonies existed (Thomas Edwin Farish, *History of Arizona, Vol. 1* [San Francisco: Filmer Brothers, 1915], 327–43).

January 22, 1885—Arrived at Safford, and visited Bp. Welker.

January 23, 1885—Went to Thatcher and Central & talked to the Bishops, thence to Pima, to Bp. J. Taylor's

Saturday, January 24, 1885—Went to Curtis—found three in danger there and advised them to go immediately, Returned to Pima. Learned that U.S. marshals are about—hunting.

Sunday, January 25, 1885—Went to Sunday School & spoke, meeting in the afternoon. Sent a messenger to Curtis to notify them about the marshals. At dark drove to Safford. Think of getting some land and city lot at Central.

January 26, 1885—Went to Graham with Pres[t] Johnson. Found the Bishop and his counsellors gone to Mexico, having left P. O. Peterson in charge.[23] We appointed him acting bishop, until Bp. Yorgensen returns. Returned to Safford and went to Layton and held meeting in the evening.

January 27, 1885—Br. Johnson returned to St David, and I began settling tithing at Layton, and finished next day.

January 29, 1885—Went to Thatcher Ward to settle tithing. Finished.

January 30, 1885—Went to Central on same business.

January 31, 1885—Went to Pima to attend priesthood meeting, and then returned to ~~Central~~ Graham.

[page 565]

BOUGHT HOUSE. SETTLING TITHING. JESSE & LOT SMITH CAME.

February 1, 1885—Held meeting at Graham, and set apart Br. P. O. Peterson as Acting Bishop. After meeting returned to Central to finish there.

Monday, February 2, 1885—Finished settling at Central, and got a city lot of Bp. Jo[s] Cluff for $22.50 [$487]. Returned to Pima in the evening. Br. P. K. M[c]Bride returned from Mexico this evening.[24]

February 3, 1885—Worked on tithing books.

Wednesday, February 4, 1885—Bought a house and lot and a half share of water for $425.[00] [$9,197] of S. F. Wilson. Am to pay him ~~$150.00~~ $100.[00] [$2,164] down, & gave him my note for $275.[00] [$5,951] payable Jan. 10. 1886. Also a note for $50.00 [$1,082] in 3 mo. Went to Curtis in the afternoon, after paying Wilson $50.[00] which I borrowed from the T. office

February 5, 1885—Attended fast meeting in Curtis, after which I settled tithing and returned to Pima. At meeting, blessed and named Septemma Layton's baby

February 6, 1885—Wrote home and to W. E. Basset. Worked on books.

February 7, 1885—Went to Solomonville to get a desk. Got one for $9.25 [$200] On my return to Safford, found Jesse,—just arrived.

Sunday, February 8, 1885—Attended meeting, after which went to Sister Rogers, by her invitation, to board. Before this, I staid at Bp. J. Taylor's, who were very kind to me.

February 9, 1885—Got clay to plaster my house. Seth Jones moved in.

Tuesday, February 10, 1885—Began work on house. My letter of credentials as Bishops Agent for St Joseph Stake, arrived

February 11 & 12, 1885—Began plastering to day at 15¢ pr yd.

February 13 & 14, 1885—Went to Graham to settle tithing

February 15, 1885—Meeting at Graham, and returned to Pima.

February 17, 1885—Finished plastering house

23 Peter O. Peterson was in St. George working on the temple when he received his call and moved to Arizona (Ricketts, *Arizona's Honeymoon Trail*, 122).

24 Joseph Cluff was among the first settlers of Center, between Thatcher and Pima. The family moved in the early spring of 1884 (Allen Bertell and Cherrel B. Weech, *A History of Mount Graham* [Safford, AZ: Authors, 2000], 90, 98, 122). P. K. McBride could be Peter Howard McBride. The latter was a talented musician living in Ogden, Utah, when he was called to help promote music throughout the Church. In Arizona he lived along the Little Colorado River and later in the Gila Valley (Clarence F. Turley and Anna Tenney Turley, *History of the Mormon Colonies in Mexico [The Juarez Stake], 1885–1980* [Salt Lake City: Publishers Press, 1996], 37; Nelle S. Hatch, *Colonia Juarez: An Intimate Account of a Mormon Village* [Salt Lake City: Deseret Book, 1954]; Susan Arrington Madsen, *I Walked to Zion: True Stories of Young Pioneers on the Mormon Trail* [Salt Lake City: Deseret Book, 1994]).

February 19, 1885—Went to Graham and Layton

February 20, 1885—Got Bp. Yorgensen's Spring wagon to bring my family from St David. Sent $15.00 [$325] to Deseret News. This evening Jesse N. Smith and Lot Smith arrived, to meet Br. Moses Thatcher, Prest McDonald and the Presidency of this Stake in council. They left a large company on the road to Chihuahua. Br. Thatcher not being here, they determined not to wait here, but return to their company.

[page 566]

ARRIVE AT PIMA MCH. 1. GERTRUDE TAKEN SICK.

February 21, 1885—Started for St David for my family, with Webb's and Norton's teams and Nuttall's horses. Drove 40 miles and stopped at Williamson's ranch in the Graham Mts. Stockton Pass, one of my horses being sick all the afternoon.[25]

Sunday, February 22, 1885—Near Croton Spring met Prst Layton and Johnson, who said I was needed in council at Pima, but excused me. Began to Storm heavily, but Jesse and I determined to go clear through to St David if we drove all night. After a few miles we got lost in the drenching, driving rain, and camped about 11 P.M. cold, wet and hungry.

February 23, 1885—This morning the storm had ceased, and we found ourselves about half a mile from Dragoon Station. At 10 A.M. met Brs. M. Thatcher, and McDonald. Got home at noon. Sold my corral to Tho. Jones for $12.00 [$260] to be paid in tithing.

February 24, 1885—Rained all night and most of to day.

Wednesday, February 25, 1885—Sold my house and lot for $300.00 [$6,492] tithing—mostly, to Peter A Lofgreen, 5$ [$108] store pay & 85.00 [$1,839] in a cow. Began packing up. The two teams arrived that are to help me move.[26]

Thursday, February 26, 1885—Started at 1 P.M. Sold stable to J. Christiansen for $15.00 [$325] Went about 12 m. and camped without water.

February 27, 1885—Four horses gone this morning, but found them by 9 A.M. Stopped for the night at Wilcox

February 28, 1885—Started at 8 A.M. by the Cienega road, and camped at Mays well, 20 miles.

March ~~29~~ 1, 1885—Arrived at Pima 7.35 P.M.—50 miles. Found Henry and Albert at the house, having arrived about an hour before, from the Little Colorado, Eastern Arizona. They had been nearly two weeks on the road, & had traveled through much Snow in Crossing the Mogolton Mts.

March 2, 1885—Began to unload, and fix things. Breakfasted at Sister Rogers, who was very kind to us.

March 3, 1885—Got some lumber to make a cupboard. Gertrude was taken with a chill in the afternoon, which soon resulted in a violent fever

March 6, 1885—Plowed some in Garden.

March 7, 1885—Went to Layton and Got a desk for the office $35.00 [$757].

[page 567]

GERTRUDE'S BLESSING

March 9, 1885—David T. LeBaron—a skipper arrived. Got some trees of him.

March 10, 1885—Set out my peach trees and grape roots. Peach trees here are now in bloom.

March 11, 1885—Have paid Wilson to date, $150.00 [$3,246] Cash and order to Frank Thurston for grain $64.00 [$1,385] total $214.00 [$4,631].[27]

March 12, 1885—Went to Layton and Safford. Got 111 lbs potatoes for seed at $5.55 [$120].

March 13, 1885—My birthday—57 years old. Planted potatoes.

March 14, 1885—Planted peas

March 15, 1885—Patriarch McBride administered to Gertrude and gave her the following blessing:–

25 Mount Graham is a prominent mountain peak in eastern Arizona reaching almost eleven thousand feet. It had a profound influence on the Mormon settlements and industry (Allen Bertell and Cherrel B. Weech, *A History of Mount Graham* [Safford, AZ, 2000]).

26 Peter Andrew Lofgreen (1847–1922) was the bishop of the St. David Ward for twenty years and later the patriarch. He moved to Arizona from Huntsville, Utah, in 1883. At one time he was a reporter for the St. Louis, Missouri, *Globe Democrat* and had studied medicine (McIntyre and Barton, *Christopher Layton*, 154).

27 This could be Frank Thurston of Pima, Arizona. He had a lime kiln not far from town and was killed by Apaches who were passing through the area stealing horses (McClintock, *Mormon Settlement in Arizona*, 254).

A patriarchal blessing by Wm McBride, given in Pima, Graham Co. Arizona, March 15. 1885, upon the head of Gertrude Martineau, daughter of James Henry & Susan Ellen Johnson Martineau, born Sept. 28.1870 in Logan Cache Co. Utah.

Sister Gertude, in the name of the Lord Jesus I lay my hands upon thy head, and by the authority of the holy priesthood I seal upon thee a patriarchal blessing: and I seal upon thee all thy former blessings. and I confirm and seal upon thee the blessings life and health and strength, and of wisdom and understanding, that thou mayest know how to take care of thy body that thy life may be prolonged: for thou wast called, chosen, and set apart before the foundations of this Earth were laid to bear thy part in the redemption of Zion, and in the restoration of the daughters of Israel, for thou art of the house of Joseph that was sold into Egypt, and of the blood of Manassah. Thou shalt become an instrument in the hands of the Lord in doing much for the restoration of the daughters of Manassah, in teaching them the gospel in languages that thou dost not now understand, and administer ordinances unto them in the temples of the Lord that will produce their salvation. Thou shalt teach them and learn them how to save themselves with their dead; and thou shalt do a great work for thy father's house, for the living, and the dead for many generations back. And thou shalt have visions and dreams & manifestations of the Holy Spirit, and shall learn to ~~understand~~ read the whisperings of the still small voice that Shall make known unto the [thee] the mind and will of the Lord.

[page 568]

QUAR. CONFERENCE. SURVEY SOLOMONVILLE. ALEX. McRAY ASKS.

March 15, 1885—And the Lord will give thee a companion if thou desirest it with all thy heart, that will be true and faithful, and will assist thee in thy mission upon the earth, and will secure unto thee an everlasting inheritance and a crown of Eternal Lives, and a part in the morning of the First Ressurrection, with all that is near and dear unto thee, for I seal the words of this blessing upon thee in the name of the Lord Jesus. Amen.

Thursday, March 19, 1885—Finished my settlement of tithing for the Stake, after a very arduous labor, the accounts being in very bad shape. The total of accounts, notes, and means received was $10.605.00 [$229,494] Planted melons and other seeds.

March 20, 1885—Planted garden corn.

March 23, 1885—Went to Safford, and Surveyed for Mr. Anderson, $10.00 [$215] Got a bale of fence wire, 97 lbs = $9.70 [$210].

March 25, 1885—Got 2000 lbs of flour from C. Layton to sell, and another bale of wire, 119 lbs. to fence N. Side of tithing lot.

March 26, 1885—Fenced north and South sides of my lot with wire. Sunday School Jubilee today, and Female Relief [Society] Conference next day.

March 28, 1885—Conference (Quarterly) to day and tomorrow. Wrote to Baldwin about my debt, and arranged to send him the money due him by Alex. McRae. Set apart Hiram Weech Prest H. Priests Quorum, with J. G. Bigler 1st & Tho. Jones 2d Counsellors. I set apart Br. Jones. Also Jas Duke Prest and Wm J. Ranson 1st & Levi Curtis 2d Counr to Prest of Elders Quo. I set apart Br. Curtis. Also Seth C. Jones was ordained a High Priest, to act as prest Y.M.M.I.A. Prest C. Layton did not attend meeting, not deeming it wise.[28]

March 20, 1885—Conference. Prest Layton at meeting. Left for St David in the afternoon. I sold a horse to Tho. Jones for 50$ [$1,082] tithing, to be paid in one year

March 30, 1885—Shingled the new kitchen. Sent for letter press to San F.

March 31, 1885—Alex. McRae asked me for Elizabeth.[29] I gave consent. Went with Jesse to Solomonville to survey a Mexican town plat. Agreed to do it for $120.00 [$2,597].

April 2 & 3 & 4, 1885—Surveyed town plat.

[page 569]

April 5, 1885—Came home with Br. Weech. On the way we met Br. Lines, and bought his farm—35 acres—for ten cows or $500.00 [$10,820], half to be paid down, the rest in 6 months. Bo't cow of H. Weech

28 Joseph East, "Arizona Conference," *Deseret News*, April 15, 1885; Utah Digital Newspapers.

29 There are several Alexander McRaes throughout history; however, none matched this entry.

for $50.00 [$1,082] and cow & calf of Mrs. Gale $55.00 [$1,190]: also one from T. office.

April 6, 1885—Bo't cow of D. Norton[30] for $45.00 [$974] Went back to Solomonville. Jesse surveyed for Jesus Aros, $5.00 [$108] I worked on map.

April 7, 1885—Attended Session of Supervisors, and applied for books for Surveyor's office. Mapped in afternoon.

April 8, 1885—Finished my 2 plats for Judge Hyatt

April 9, 1885—Settled with Rejino Chavarria for survey of town.[31] Donated $3.00 [$65] to the Mexicans to help them build a church. Surveyed a section for I. E. Solomon, $20.00 [$433].[32] Our board bill, 8 days, $25.00 [$541]. My trees arrived from Los Angeles, 2 orange, 2 pepper, 2 Eucalyptus. Freight chgs. (Express) $16.25 [$352].

April 10, 1885—Surveyed for Jesus Aros. Settled with Solomon & came home.

April 13, 1885—Wrote to all the Bishops in regard to Defense fund, and gave them their several apportionments. Went to Solomonville with B. Weech to see about entering our Town Site and our land, which we accomplished. Br. Weech entered the Quar. Sec, in which is my land and his, under Desert Land Act.

April 15, 1885—Set out 120 tomato plants.

April 18, 1885—Went to ~~Layton~~ Safford and settled with C. Layton. Paid him note and interest $180.77 [$3,912] Potatoes & meat 21.69 [$469]. Horses & harness $275.00 [$5,951], Total $477.46 [$10,332]. He owed me on a/c $27.00 [$584] Bal. due him $450.00 [$9,738] which I paid him. Took his order on the mill for $128.49 [$2,780].

Sunday, April 19, 1885—Recd the horses and harness

April 20, 1885—Letter press came. Total cost, $35.70 [$773], with letter books &c

April 21, 1885—Went to Safford for medicine for Gertrude, who still lies helpless in bed.

30 This could be D. E. Norton, who was a resident of Pima.

31 At this writing no match could be found for this name.

32 This is likely Isador E. Solomon, who was a leader in the Safford area for many years (McClintock, *Mormon Settlement in Arizona*, 242).

April 22, 1885—Surveyed our (Weech) Quar. Sec. Very cold wind from North, which killed wheat in fields, melons &c in gardens

April 23, 1885—Made plats of Pima, and sent plats to Solomon of his sur.

April 24, 1885—Boys hauled rock for well. I worked in field. Got mower.

April 25, 1885—Started mower, cutting Alfalfa for East & others. Storm.

April 27, 1885—Went to Central and held meeting

April 28, 1885—Delivered three cows to Lines, for his land. Owe 7 still

April 29, 1885—Plowed, and sowed some Lucerne—1 acre

[page 570]

APACHES BREAK OUT. FORTS THOMAS & GRANT

May 1, 1885—May day celebration. I went to Solomonville & bought a grindstone

May 2, 1885—Heavy rain today.

May 3, 1885—Went to Thatcher with Prest Johnson, and held meeting.

May 4, 1885—Heavy rain. We all worked in field.

May 6, 1885—To day the Sisters (East, Ransom, McBride & Moody) washed and anointed Gertrude, and blessed her. She was immediately made much better, and became free from pain, which for many weeks has been agonizing.

My two orange trees begin to bud. They have cost me $26.00 [$563]. Figs and grapes are growing.

May 12, 1885—Potatoes, peas, & some melons in bloom; peanuts growing nicely.

May 13, 1885—Wrote historical letter to Historian F. D. Richards relative to St Joseph Stake. Recd wedding cake from Wm B. Preston & Kate Pyper.

Thursday, May 14, 1885—To day Henry started home to bring his family accompanied by Albert. We ordained Albert an Elder, he having been accepted by vote last Sunday, at which time my family were admitted into 2 ward.

Friday, May 15, 1885—Surveyed M. Cluff's ranch.

Saturday, May 16, 1885—Planted Corn.

Sunday, May 17, 1885—Went to Safford and held meeting with Pres^{ts} Layton & Johnson. Apaches broke out again.

Monday, May 18, 1885—Paid Germain Co. 1.15 in full on trees.

Wednesday, May 20, 1885—Bought a Carriage of J D Holladay for $150.00 [$3,246] and paid $100.00 [$2,164] down.

Thursday, May 21, 1885—Jesse & I started for near Fort Grant to survey Camped at the Cienega.

Friday, May 22, 1885—Reached Fort Grant 2 P.M having crossed the mountains by Stockton pass. Arrived at Wicks at 3 P.M. Tested lines.

Saturday, May 23, 1885—Surveyed for H. Wicks ¼ sec. of land. 40.00 and started for Fort Thomas. Camped in the Cedar Springs Pass.

Sunday, May 24, 1885—Reached Fort Thomas at noon. a Hole

[page 571]

SURVEYED TOWN AT FORT THOMAS.

May 25, 1885—Surveyed For Thompson. 20$ [$433]. and returned home.

June 1, 2, 3, 1885—Built stable and Carriage shed. Lumber cost $85.00 [$1,839]

Sunday, June 7, 1885—Went to meeting in Pima. Pres^{t} Layton present.

June 8, 1885—Rec^{d} letter form Lyman. "Clarion" arrives.

June 10, 1885—Went to Safford to consult with Pres^{t} Layton in regard to our policy in indian matters.

June 11, 1885—Held mass meeting in Pima.

June 13, 1885—Went to the county mass meeting in Solomonville.

June 14, 1885—Went to Graham with ~~Presy~~ Susan & held meeting.

June 15, 1885—To day we cut our lucern 2nd time

June 19, 1885—Sent my two mares to the top of Graham Mt. to herd.

Sunday, June 21, 1885—Attended meeting in Pima. Very warm weather

June 22, 1885—A little rain this morning. Paid Holladay in full for my carriage, $25.00 [$541]—total $150.00 [$3,246]

June 23, 1885—More rain. Planted beans yesterday & today—1½ acres.

June 25, 1885—Watered my Lucern in garden for the first time.

Friday, June 26, 1885—Went to Central to attend Ladies Quarterly conference. Had a very good meeting in a bowery. Susan went.

Saturday, June 27, 1885—Regular Quarterly Conference at Central. Present the Stake Presidency and Patriarchs and Bishops of all the wards but McDonald. Had a very good meeting.[33]

Sunday, June 28, 1885—Conference again today. I spoke several times during the two days, and felt well.

July 1, 1885—Watered land in field. Got word to survey a town plat at Fort Thomas, 13 miles below here, on the Gila.

July 2, 1885—Began survey of Thomas, & finished next day. 3^{d} Rec^{d} $75.00 [$1,623] for the work. Returned home. 3^{d} inst.

Saturday, July 4, 1885—Gave Crockett my order on him for a cow, bought of W. M. Clifford. Attended celebration, and was orator of the day. Lizzie and Virginia sang "Far away," After meeting went with Susan to a pic-nic on the banks of the Gila, and there met the Johnson family.

Monday, July 6, 1885—Attended priesthood meeting in Pima.[34] It was determined to make a large canal from Layton to Pima and myself, W. D. Johnson & R. A. Allred were appointed a committee to draft articles of incorporation for the company. Still planting corn. 100°

[page 572]

Saturday, July 11, 1885—Susan's birthday,—49—may she have more until she has enough, and would rather go home, but I don't want her to go before I do. I bought boots.

Sunday, July 12, 1885—Went with ~~Susan~~ Lizzie to Curtis, and preached. Hot

July 13, 1885—Wrote to all the bishops relative to tithing &c. 102°

....

33 Jas. East, "Minutes of Quarterly Conference," *Deseret News*, July 22, 1885; Utah Digital Newspapers.

34 J. H. Martineau, "Arizona Items," *Deseret News*, July 22, 1885; Utah Digital Newspapers.

July 14, 1885—Sent east for some liquid glue. Put in a large head gate in Smithville canal. Thermometer 102° The rainy season is at hand, with showers on the mountains around us. We need rain very much.

July 15, 1885—Still at work on head gate. Jesse cut lucern 3d time.

July 16, 1885—Boys hauled hay. Showery all around. Virginia had a sewing bee in honor of her birth day—her 15th In the evening had singing and guitar music.

July 17, 1885—Finished hauling our hay.

July 21, 1885—The hardest rain I ever saw for an hour.

Thursday, July 23, 1885—Last night about midnight, Henry and family, & Albert arrived from Apache Co. having been 16 days on the road. They expect to settle here.

Last Sunday (19th) went to Layton with Prest W. D. Johnson to hold meeting. Prest Layton quite sick.

Saturday, July 25, 1885—Took Gertrude riding for the first time, lifting her carefully in & out of the carriage.—the first time Since March 1,st

Sunday, July 26, 1885—Went to Thatcher, & held meeting. Afterwards went to Safford to see Prest Layton who is still sick. In the evening attended High Priests meeting in Pima.

July 27, 1885—Wrote to Bp. Preston. Planted potatoes in field.

Wednesday, July 29, 1885—Jesse started to day to help drive stock from near Camp Thomas to Apache Co., to be absent 4 to 6 weeks, in company with several others.

Saturday, August 1, 1885—Susan and I, with several of the children went fishing. They caught 70 fish.

Sunday, August 2, 1885—Meeting at Pima. Wrote to Charles & others.

Monday, August 3, 1885—Went to Safford to survey a new canal, with Joel.

[page 573]

B. YOUNG ARRIVES FROM MEXICO.

August 4 & 5, 1885—Surveyed on canal. Returned to Pima on 5th as Br. B. Young came at 6 P.M. of the 5th on his way from Sonora to join some of the Apostles at El Paso.

Thursday, August 6, 1885—Two meetings were held at Pima today. Br. Brigham gave an account of his journeys in Mexico, and the good prospects of our work there. He also made a demand for $200.00 [$4,328] Cash tithing from this stake, which I collected from the various wards. Br. B. spent considerable time with us, and enjoyed himself.

August 7, 1885—Went with Susan to Safford to see Br. B. away, and to pay him the money.

August 8, 1885—Sent to Tucson for wagon bow

August 11, 1885—Finished my well, 28 ft deep—good water. Bought 5 bales of wire for fencing, $48.00 [$1,039].

August 14, 1885—David Johnson and family, also Alley his brother, arrived from Apache County, to settle.[35]

August 21, 1885—Heavy rain last night. Went with Susan to the Hot Springs to see about taking Gertrude there for her health.

August 22, 1885—To day a Mr. John Stiger arrived from Texas.[36] He says he has come to investigate Mormonism in consequence of reading some of my articles in the Deseret News.

August 23, 1885—Attended meeting in Pima.

August 27, 1885—Went to Solomonville. Susan is very sick with a hot fever.

August 28, 1885—Jesse returned from St John's, Apache County, well.

August 29, 1885—Attended priesthood meeting at Pima.

August 30, 1885—Attended meeting at Pima.

September 5, 1885—To day Dora is three years old. She had some gifts.

September 6, 1885—Prest Layton, Johnson & self held meeting in Pima. In council decided to visit St David soon.

September 7, 1885—Susan's fever has gone, and now she has what seems erysipelas in her finger and arm. I took her to Safford for medical examination.

Tuesday, September 8, 1885—Started to St David. Stopped at Layton's.

35 David Johnson was the brother to the Benjamin F. Johnson noted earlier.

36 At this writing no match could be found for this name.

[page 574]

VISIT ST DAVID AND RETURN. SUSAN SICK.

September 9, 1885—Left Layton's at 5.30 A.M. Drove to Wilcox, 55 miles

September 10, 1885—Arrived at St David, 4 P.M., 40 miles. Heavy storm. I took Jesse as far as Wilcox, there to take train for Logan where he is to go to school for a time. Felt very sad to part with him. For many years he has been with me in all my journeys surveying, and together we have passed through many hardships, as well as good times. At Benson he had to lay over for a day, because of a washout near Pantana.

September 11, 1885—Held council meeting at Pres^{t} Layton's, and attended a trial in the evening of H. Blair & Huldah Hubbard.[37]

September 12, 1885—Went to Benson to see Jesse, but he had gone on. Saw in the paper the notice of death of my daughter-in-law Sarah Westwood Hagberg, who was married last summer. In the evening attended a trial of 4 young men for sacrilege.

Sunday, September 13, 1885—Held two meetings in St David.

September 14, 1885—Went to Tombstone to see about well-pipe. Got a new lamp shade for our lamp.

Wednesday, September 16, 1885—Started home, Drove to Wilcox.

September 17, 1885—Reached Safford, and staid at Pres^{t} Layton's

September 18, 1885—Home, and found Susan some better, but her arm still quite swollen and inflamed.

Saturday, September 19, 1885—Took Susan to Safford and had her arm lanced.

Sunday, September 20, 1885—Meeting in Pima. Weather very warm yet. Got letter from Lyman, with offer to take his sisters if I feel willing. I ordained Robt Ferrin an Elder.[38]

Monday, September 21, 1885—Went to Central to consult with Pres^{t} Johnson. We appointed 3 new High Councillors, one of whom is Henry.

Tuesday, September 22, 1885—Wrote to Egan, at Clifton, about surveying for him. David T. LeBaron goes from Pima back, to meet his wife, who is on her way to Mexico.

September 25, 1885—Attended meeting of the High Council, the first regular one in this stake. No business was done, no quorum present.

Monday, September 28, 1885—High Council organized. Tried O. D. Merrill, also Morgan, Lot and Rialdo Merrill, & cut all from the church.[39]

September 30, 1885—Attended a canal meeting at Safford, & engaged to survey the new Canal

[page 575]

Sunday, October 3, 1885—Went to Safford to survey. Found Pres^{ts} Layton and Johnson had gone last night to Mexico, to avoid arrest.

Monday, October 4, 1885—Began Survey of Canal, surveyed all the week. Soon after Pres^{t} Layton left, a U.S. marshall came for him. Took Mrs. H. Groesbeck to Tucson.

October 12, 1885—Ordered a Sulky plow, & paid $35.00 [$757] on it.

October 15, 1885—Finished survey to Pima Canal, about 14 miles. Pres^{t} Layton returned.

Friday, October 16, 1885—Bought 160 acres of Pres^{t} Layton for $1000.00 [$21,640] to be paid in two years, from the crops raised. Interest, 10 o/c.

October 18, 1885—Held meeting at Thatcher, Susan went with me.

October 19, 1885—Went to Thatcher to help locate a new town site.

October 20, 1885—Surveyed for Mr. L. Frye

October 22, 1885—Heavy rain—first for many weeks. Gathered beans in.

37 J. H. Blair and Huldah Hubbard were married July 11, 1886, in St. David (Pat Bennett, "1880–1890 Marriages in Cochise County," http://www.mycochise.com/marriages1880.php).

38 Robert Ferrin was eighteen when he moved to Pima, Arizona, with his family on January 2, 1882. His father, Jacob Samuel Ferrin, was later killed by Indians while he was hauling freight from Bowie and Globe, Arizona. After the death of his father, Samuel took over the freight business. He married Zobedia Abelia Crockett, October 29, 1995 (McClintock, *Mormon Settlement in Arizona*, 253, 292).

39 This could be Rialdo Merrill, son of D. J. Merrill, from the Pima, Arizona, area. All the Merrills were farmers and laborers.

Fig. 7.1—Drawing of hand pointing to October 12.

[dates out of order in journal]

October 12, 1885—Henry and Albert started to cut hay near Bowie Sta. taking my mower, rake and span of mares.

October 22, 1885—Rec^{d} a long letter from Moses Thatcher relative to disfellowshipping, cutting off and restoring.

October 28, 1885—Beebe wrote me saying I can have his machine for boring artesian wells for $175 [$3,787].

November 2, 1885—Surveyed additional lots at Thatcher.

November 3, 1885—Started to Duncan, to Survey that place. Staid all night at Solomonville

November 4, 1885—Drove in mail wagon to Sheldon 36 miles. The train having gone I hired a passage 8 miles further to Duncan by private wagon. Stopped with Mr. G. W. Parks

November 5, 1885—Surveyed in forenoon in rain. Quit at noon and went by Arizona & New Mexico R.R. to Clifton, 32 miles. Very expensive road, passing for miles through rocky gorges, over high bridges 60 to 90 ft high. Clifton lies on San Francisco river, deep in towering cliffs & hills. It is a mining town—mostly Mexican, of some 500 people. Full of low gambling places, brothels, and saloons. It is the center of a great copper mining works. Called at Clifton Clarion office.

[page 576]

MEN KILLED BY APACHES.

November 7, 1885—Returned to Duncan, & surveyed in afternoon.

November 9, 1885—Still Surveying. A great indian scare, caused by recent murders near Deming. Reports of Indians at Ash Springs, which is on my road home. Do not think it safe to travel that way home.

November 12, 1885—Have earned about $100.^{00} [$2,164] and rec^{d} $55 [$1,190]. of it. Still due me from Parks $45.00 [$974]. Started home by A.& N.M.R.R. to Lordsburg. Found on arrival there the S.P.R.R. train had gone West, & I had to stay all night. Lordsburg is 4700 feet above the sea. Duncan is about 3800 ft. From Duncan to L. is 39 miles.

November 13, 1885—At ~~noon~~ 9.30 took train for Bowie. Got there 11.30 50 miles, and have to remain all night. Bargained with Wickersham for his boring outfit, at $380.^{00} [$8,223]

November 14, 1885—Started at daylight by mail for home, & reached there 5 P.M.—55 miles. Found all well. Paid 20$ [$433] J. D. H.

Susan had gone to get her arm lanced again, and did not get home till after dark.

November 15, 1885—Meeting at Pima.

November 17, 1885—Surveyed lots in Thatcher.

Wednesday, November 18, 1885—Sent Joel with team to Bowie to get Sulky plow Hired W. Owens for a few days while Joel is gone.

November 20, 1885—Rainy today.

Saturday, November 21, 1885—Rec^{d} $75.^{00} [$1,623] from Lyman and Charles for Lilla's passage money to Logan. Got my buggy home fixed all right, and paid $3.00 [$65] on it. Owe 3$ more

November 22, 1885—Joel got home in the night with plow. Held meeting at Safford, Pres^{t} Layton having got home last night.

November 23, 1885—Went to visit Carlton's

November 24, 1885—Met Pres^{ts} Layton & Johnson at Thatcher, to select lots for public buildings and for ourselves. At night Theodore got home from the hay camp with three of the horses. Wrote to Jesse.

November 25, 1885—Surveyed more lots at Thatcher. Gertrude went, and drove team, threw out stakes &c.

[page 577]

MEETINGS OF THE APOSTLES. LILLA GOES TO UTAH.

November 26, 1885—Went to Solomonville & paid taxes $17.70 + 2.00 = 19.70 [$426] Gertrude went also. Heard of two men being killed by Apaches.

November 27, 1885—Wrote to Sur. Genl for appointment as Deputy, also for field notes & plat of Tp. 8 S. R. 26 E.

November 28, 1885—Priesthood meeting in Pima. Dismissed at noon, as we expect Apostles E. Snow, Young & Lyman.

November 29, 1885—Meeting at Pima, at 10 A.M. Apostles not present. Large attendance both forenoon and afternoon. Jacob Hamblin spoke very interestingly.

November 30, 1885—Another man killed 10 miles from here and one about 7 miles. Set corners for meeting house in Pima.

Tuesday, December 1, 1885—Went to meeting at Thatcher & Central, and met Elders E. Snow & wife, F. M. Lyman, and our old friend Emma Smith.[40] Heard at noon of the killing of two of our Layton boys—the Wright brothers, by indians this morning, about 12 miles from Solomonville, while in pursuit of stolen horses.[41] In the evening Elder B. Young arrived. Held Council at Br. Snows place.

December 2, 1885—Went to Layton to funeral of Wright brothers, with Susan, and took B. Young and Emma Smith. In the evening took B. Young & F. M. Lyman to Curtis, and held meeting there.

December 3, 1885—Returned with them to Pima, and held meetings at 4 P.M. Elders Snow & wife, Young, Lyman & Layton dined with us. About 6.30 P.M. I started with Lilla to Safford, to start from there in the morning to Utah. Held Council till near midnight.

December 4, 1885—Left Safford about 7 A.M. I took F. M. Lyman & Lilla, Reached May's well at noon, 25 miles. Here our Escort of Six mounted men returned, We reached Wilcox about sun set.

December 5, 1885—Drove to St David by Sunset. Took leave of Lilla this morning, and again at Dragon pass where the train overtook us. She went with Aunt Harriett Johnson and Leslie Webb.[42]

[page 578]

CHARLES MARRIED JAN. 20. 1886

December 6 & 7, 1885—Meetings held in St David each day. Held council meetings each day with the Apostles. B. Young started to Hermosillo[43] on the 7th Arranged for a small party to go by wagons into Sonora, with B. Y. & F. M. L.

December 8, 1885—Went to Hill's with Br. Lyman. Wrote letter to the "Star" by request of Br. Snow to correct false statements of Dr. Groesbeck.[44] Returned after night to Br. Layton's place. Very cold weather.

December 9, 1885—Went to Wilcox. Contracted to deliver D. H. Smith & Co 5000 lbs chop feed at 2¢ Got some goods on credit that we needed very much, $27.58 [$597].

December 10, 1885—Reached Pima about 6 P.M.—55 miles.

December 11, 1885—Attended Women's Conference.

December 12 & 13, 1885—Quarterly Conference.[45] Traded Carriages with Br. C. Layton. Ordained J. A. Burns a High Priest and set him apart as Bp. Taylor's 2d Counr

December 25, 1885—To day we had a family dinner—about 30 present.

December 26, 1885—Albert went to Wilcox for the well-borer outfit.

January 1, 1886—Rain to day turning to snow at night. Cold. Albert came.

Friday, January 8, 1886—Our 34th Wedding anniversary. Had company & dinner.

January 9, 1886—Albert & Theodore started to St David for the mares.

Today I was elected one of the Directors of the Z.C.M.I. store.

January 11, 1886—Qualified as Director. Recd letter from Charles who is going to be married soon to Miss Eva Rice.

---

40 Francis M. Lyman (1840–1916) was an Apostle. Emma Smith could be Emma Smoot Smith-Woodruff, plural wife of Elder Wilford Woodruff.

41 Those killed were Lorenzo and Seth Wright (McClintock, *Mormon Settlement in Arizona*, 254). Note McClintock's reference to Martineau's later assessment of the Indian military capabilities.

42 This could be Leslie Webb of Graham, Arizona.

43 Hermosillo, Sonora, Mexico.

44 Dr. Groesbeck was one of the postmasters who distributed mail from his place of business.

45 Joseph East, "St. Joseph Stake Conference," *Deseret News*, January 13, 1886; Utah Digital Newspapers.

Fig. 7.2—Eva Rice Martineau, wife of Charles Freeman Martineau.

January 12, 1886—Applied to Gov. Zulick to be Notary Public.[46]

Tuesday, January 19, 1886—Wrote to Pres^{t} Taylor about Tithing paid to M. Curtis. Also sent receipt of B. Young for $200. [$4,328] cash paid him in July last.

Tuesday, January 26, 1886—The boys went to Thatcher to begin plowing.[47]

January 21, 1886—Today Charles was married to Miss Eva Rice[48]

February 4, 1886—In crossing the Gila, was nearly carried down strem. Got my books and papers wet.

Saturday, February ~~7~~ 6, 1886—Got home. Letter from Charles & Eva, also Lilla

Sunday, February 7, 1886—Wrote to Chas & Eva. also to Lilla.

[page 579]

ALBERT & JOEL ORDAINED SEVENTIES AT CONFERENCE.

February 9, 1886—Set out grape cuttings

Saturday, February 27, 1886—Finished tithing settlement today. Have had all the work to do myself

Sunday, February 28, 1886—At meeting at Central I ordained J. P. Johnson High Priest and set him apart as 2^{d} Coun^{r} to Bp. G. M. Haws.[49]

March 2, 1886—Acted to day as Notary—first time in Arizona. I was appointed by Gov. Zulick Jany 20$^{\underline{th}}$

March 12, 1886—Rec^{d} word that land has been bought in Mexico by Br. Teasdale

Saturday, March 13, 1886—I am 58 years old today! How the years fly! Joel sick yesterday and today

Friday, March 19, 1886—Conference of Female Relief Societies.

Saturday, March 20, 1886—Our Quarterly Conference begun today.[50] At noon Pres^{t} S. B. Young, from S. L. City came, to organize the 89th Quo. of Seventies.

March 21, 1886—The 89th Quo. organized today. Joel and Albert were voted to be members. Joel was ordained a Seventy by Pres^{t} James R. Welker: Albert by Pres^{t} Joseph East.[51]

Henry was voted a Home Missionary.

Y.M.M.I.A. & Y.L.M.I.A. Conference in evening.

March 22, 1886—Took Br. Young and wife and Susan riding: and in the evening to Safford.

---

46 Conrad Meyer Zulick (1839–1910) was the Arizona territorial governor from 1885 to 1889. He is known for moving the capital of Arizona from Prescott to Phoenix and restoring the franchise vote to the Mormons of the territory.

47 Martineau defends the Church and encourages settlers (J. H. Martineau, "A Libel Refuted," *Deseret News*, February 17, 1886; Utah Digital Newspapers).

48 This is Charles Freeman Martineau (1861–1935), the son of James Henry Martineau and Susan Julia Sherman. His new wife was Eva Rosetta Rice. They raised their family in Logan, Utah.

49 George M. Haws later became the first bishop of the Chuichupa, Mexico, settlement with Benjamin J. Johnson and Samuel J. Brown as counselors (Romney, *The Mormon Colonies in Mexico*, 113).

50 Joseph East, "St. Joseph Stake Conference, *Deseret News*, April 21, 1886; Utah Digital Newspapers.

51 James R. Welker arrived in Safford in 1883. His home today is on the registry of historic places. Joseph East could be Joseph Fielding East, who lived in Brigham City, Apache County, Arizona.

March 23, 1886—Meeting at Safford today (evening).

March 24, 1886—Ordered a washing machine for Br. Layton. Came home. Found offer from Grant, Odell & Co, of farm machinery, wagons &c to start that business here.[52]

March 26, 1886—Put our cows in herd. Declined Grant & Co's offer.

Ordered a "Binder" by J. D. Holladay. I am to pay freight when it comes, $50.$\underline{^{00}}$ [$1,082] on tithing, and the balance in 6 & 18 months, equal payments. The first payment to be in next Nov., the second one year after.

March 27, 1886—Priesthood meeting at Central.

March 28, 1886—Meeting at Layton. Three Mexicans baptized.

March 30, 1886—Letter came addressed to Mr. Bowker. Got an arm chair $4.00 [$87].

March 31, 1886—Got 5 gall. oil:

[page 580]

Temple Memoranda.

April 3, 1886—Answered letter from John Q. Cannon.

April 4, 1886—Meeting at Safford. Grape vines opened their leaves.

Monday, April 5, 1886—Began to lower my dry well. Got 2 feet water

April 8, 1886—Rec^{d} notice I am appointed to examine for site for a Bridge across Gila river, and report probable expense for building (By the County). Got a petition started to get a Money Order Office in Pima.

Saturday, April 10, 1886—In looking through my records of Temple Work I find the following items:—[53]

May 21, 1884—Began work in the temple, as one of the first company—Self, wife, and Netta.

September 11, 1884—Finished temple work.

Thursday, July 10, 1884—Self and Susan rec^{d} our 2nd A.[54] Also for Susan J.

September 11, 1884—Rec^{d} 2^{d} A. by Susan for Mary Elvira Sherman Martineau and Mary Elizabeth Johnson Martineau. Finished Work

[written in margin in shaky writing]

(2 A)

July 11, 1884—I rec^{d} 2^{d} A. for John Robbins

September 2, 1884—Susan was baptized for her health, & to renew Covenant.

[written in margin]

Netta

Netta began work in the temple may 21st, but was very weak. She worked a few days from time to time, until Aug. 20th which was her last work in the temple.

[written in margin]

August 20

The temple workers were very kind to her, especially Sisters Prescinda Kimball, Lucy B. Young, Minirva Snow, Zina D. H. Young, Young Zina Williams, E. G. Benson and others, whom may our Father ever Bless.[55]

[written in margin]

Baptisms for dead

52 This business, known as Grant, Odell & Company, became the Cooperative Wagon Machine Company (Mary Jane Fritzen, "Consolidated Wagon and Machine Company," http://www.bonnevilleheritage.org/resources/historytext/CWandM.htm).

53 Martineau is recording his Logan Temple work from previous records.

54 These are second anointings. Martineau is using several abbreviations—second A., 2d A, 2 A, and so forth—to reference this ordinance in respect for its sacredness and the fear of persecution during these times.

55 Prescindia L. H. B. Kimball was the wife of Heber C. Kimball (Donald G. Godfrey and Kenneth W. Godfrey, *The Diaries of Charles Ora Card: The Utah Years, 1871–1886* [Provo, UT: Religious Studies Center, Brigham Young Univ., 2006], 511). Zina D. H. Young was the wife of Brigham Young and the first counselor of the general Church Relief Society to President Eliza R. Snow (Martha Sonntag Bradley and Mary Brown Firmage Woodward, *Four Zinas: A Story of Mothers and Daughters on the Mormon Frontier* [Salt Lake City: Signature Books, 2000], 174–214). Young Zina Williams is Zina Presindia Young Williams Card. She was the daughter of Zina D. H. and Brigham Young. She was the wife of Charles Ora Card, of Logan, and was the "First Lady" of the Canadian settlements (Donald G. Godfrey, "Zina Presindia Young Williams Card: Brigham's Daughter, Cardston's First Lady," *Journal of Mormon History* 23, no. 2 [Fall 1997]: 107–27). There are several Minerva Snows and E. G. Bensons in Logan history. At this writing none matched this entry.

Myself, Netta, Gean (Virginia), Gertrude, Anna, Joel, Charles, Theodore, Lyman, Nephi & Emmeline performed baptisms for 470 dead.

[written in margin]

Endowments

Of this number about 200 were endowed, and nearly all of them Sealed; most of them to former companions, and quite a number to me, who had no husbands to be united to. The names of those sealed to me are on next page.

[written in margin]

Dora

June 6, 1884—Today Dora was sealed to Self and Susan by J. T. D. McAllister, the first of the kind in the temple.

[page 581]

TEMPLE MEMORANDA, CON[D]

Sealed [. . . written in shaky hand]

1. Susan Ellen Johnson Martineau May 13, 1852
   Sept. 12. 1860
2. Susan Julia Sherman Jan. 18, 1857
   Sept. 12. 1860
3. Mary Elvira Sherman 2A Sept. 12. 1860

[2A, meaning second annointings, was written in the margin parallel to these first three entries]

4. Marie St. Pierre May 21. 1884
5. Clara St. Vincent May 23. 1884
6. Sophia Gilmier May 28. 1884
7. Mary Essebrous May 29. 1884
8. Mary Gertrude May 30. 1884
9. Susan Macon June 12. 1884
10. Huldah Hutchinson June 27. 1884
11. Susannah Martineau July 2. 1884
12. Mary Martineau July 2. 1884
13. Hannah Martineau July 2. 1884
14. Sarah Columbine July 2. 1884
15. Elizabeth Brewer July 2. 1884
16. Beatrice Sumner July 2. 1884
17. Judith Elizabeth Blake July 3 1884
18. Catherine Martineau July 3 1884
19. Sarah Martineau July 3 1884
20. Ann Martineau July 3 1884
21. Emily Martineau July 3 1884
22. Ellen Martineau July 4 1884
23. Lucy Martineau July 4 1884
24. Marianne Martineau July 4 1884
25. Miss Rand July 9 1884
26. Margaret Haughout July 9 1884
27. Elizabeth Haughout July 9 1884
28. Catherine Haughout July 9 1884
29. Cornelia Haughout July 9 1884
30. Ann Haughout July 9 1884
31. Elenor Haughout July 9 1884
32. Catherine Keteltas July 9 1884
33. Gertrude Haughout July 10 1884
34. Miss Rand July 10 1884
35. Margaret Martineau July 10 1884
36. Charity Martineau July 10 1884

[page 582]

TEMPLE MEMORANDA, CONT[D]

37. Alujay Webb July 11. 1884
38. Allatta Cozine July 11. 1884
39. Elizabeth Martineau July 11. 1884
40. Rachel Haughout July 11. 1884
41. Margarette Haughout July 11. 1884
42. Mary Elizabeth Johnson July 18 1884

[*2d* added in shaky handwriting]

43. Anna Maria Hagberg July 18 1884
44. Rachel Martineau July 23 1884
45. Mary Alice Martineau July 24 1884
46. Margaret Jardine July 24 1884
47. Margaret Martineau July 24 1884
48. Elizabeth Marriott Martineau July 25 1884
49. Amelia Columbine July 25 1884
50. Mary Martineau July 25 1884
51. Jane Martineau July 25 1884
52. Mary Martineau July 25 1884
53. Sarah Neave Aug. 6 1884
54. Margaret Martineau Aug. 6 1884
55. Caroline Martineau Aug. 13th 1884
56. Elizabeth Martineau Aug. 13th 1884
57. Emeline Martineau Aug. 14 1884
58. Elizabeth Hawkins Aug. 20 1884
59. Sophia Billott (Billow) Aug. 20 1884
60. Charity Beatty Aug. 28th 1884
61. Harriett Martineau July 16. 1884
62. Mary Martineau July 17 1884
63. Margaret Williment July 23 1884

Nelly Benson, 2d [added in shaky handwriting]

[page 583]

April 15, 1886—Sent recommends to Jesse N. and Elizabeth, so they may join the Logan Ward, and be able to labor in the temple.[56]

April 16, 1886—Several of my grape vines are in blossom.

Saturday, April 17, 1886—Rec^{d} letter from W. B. Preston, who wished to meet me at St David. ~~In half an hour myself and Br. Layton were on our way to Safford.~~

Monday, April 19, 1886—Br.^{s} Thurber and Bean of Br. Preston's company came. Got a new washing machine, cost about $13.50 [$292]. Sent back the blank bonds to Sur. Genl office, as I cannot find any one to sign such high bonds $10.^{000} [$226,402]. Sent a conveyance for Br. W. B. P. at Bowie, but he was not there.

April 23, 1886—Letter from W. B. P. to meet him and R. J. Burton at St David tomorrow. Started in 10 minutes to Safford.

Saturday, April 24, 1886—Started from Safford at 5 A.M. Arrived at Wilcox, 50 miles at 3 P.M. Stopped two hours and camped out at Croton Sps. 60 miles.

Sunday, April 25, 1886—Started at 5 A.M. Reached St David 10 A.M. 40 miles. Found the brethren had not yet arrived, but they did in two hours, and had meeting at 2 P.M.

April 26, 1886—We all went to John Hill's and staid all night.

April 27, 1886—Went to Tombstone. Got my watch cleaned. Bought a suit of clothes $20.$^{\underline{00}}$ [$433] the first for almost 3 years.

Wednesday, April 28, 1886—Back to St D. found Br. Thurber had arrived from the Gila.[57] Advised Bp. Merrill to let Jo^{s} G. Allred have the church stock to herd, at $2.$^{\underline{00}}$ [$43] pr year, he to be responsible. Hear reports of hostile indians near by in the Whetstone Mts.

56 Martineau is sending temple recommends to his children. In the temple recommend interview, the applicant responds to questions about living health laws, supporting the Church authorities, living a moral lifestyle, and serving others.

57 This could be Bishop A. D. Thurber, who played a significant part in the defense of the Mexican colonies (Romney, *Mormon Colonies in Mexico*, 192–93).

April 29, 1886—We start for home at 7 A.M. with Mrs. Allred & son. Sleep at Wilcox. At Dragoon Station found the agent barricaded and much alarmed, on account of Apaches nearby. Some troops had passed a little before in chase.

April 30, 1886—Start at 5.30—May's well, 20$^{\underline{m}}$ 9.15 Safford 2.15 P.M. 50 miles. I got home in the evening. Theatre.

Saturday, May 1, 1886—Forwarded letters to Bp. Preston, La Ascencion Mexico

May 6, 1886—Read that U.S. Atty Genl Maury said "it would have been infinitely better if the Mormons had all been put to the sword long ago."[58]

[page 584]

ST DAVID
HENRY'S SON JESSE DIED.[59]

May 6, 1886—Susan prophesied that his hair should fall from his head, his teeth fall out, & his flesh rot upon his bones." I believe it. She also said, "Edmunds shall die a beggar in the street." and be esteemed most infamous forever." They are worthy.[60]

58 Statements such as this made life difficult for the Mormons. Maury could have been an assistant in the offices of the attorney general. The U.S. attorney general at the time was Augustus Hill Garland, who served from 1885 to 1889.

59 "Deaths," *Deseret News*, June 16, 1886; Utah Digital Newspapers.

60 This is a reference to the author of the Edmunds Act of 1882 and Edmunds–Tucker Act of 1887. The primary author, Senator George Franklin Edmunds, sought to destroy the Mormon Church in its continued practice of polygamy. The act began proceedings that would disincorporate the Church; create the forfeitures of property; dissolve the Perpetual Emigrating Fund Company (controlling funds used to provide loans to immigrants to help establish themselves); empower the federal authorities to demand Church leaders produce books, records, and papers documenting property; and abolish woman suffrage in Utah. The results cost the Church significantly. It scattered the Saints throughout the West and sent many into a "Mormon underground," basically hiding to keep away from the marshals. It divided families by disinheriting children of plural marriages and, in general, created fear and chaos (Leonard J. Arrington, *Great Basin Kingdom: An Economic History of the Latter-day Saints, 1830–1900* [Cambridge, MA: Harvard Univ. Press, 1958], 360–79).

May 7, 1886—Albert arrived from Wilcox with 3887 lbs chopd grain I had there. To day I was assessed for taxes, personal 690.00 [$14,932] Real 900.00 [$19,476] = $1590 [$34,408].

May 13, 1886—Finished planting my garden in Pima,—peanuts, corn, squashes, melons & big sunflowers. Tomatoes

May 15, 1886—High Council met to try W. Hawkins[61] for profanity & drunkenness. Recd my new carriage spring ~~$7.00~~ $6.72 [$145].

May 19, 1886—Got my carriage fixed.

May 20, 1886—Started for St David with Susan. Staid at Layton's Heard reports of late indian murders, but I must go on

May 21, 1886—Susan felt impressed to return, but did not tell me then. Arrived at Wilcox. Heard of men being killed yesterday close to our intended route.

May 22, 1886—At Dragoon pass were told that indians crossed the road just ahead of us, and soldirs had gone in chase. Arrived at St D. at 5 P.M, the horses much jaded and lame. Staid at Bebee's. Folks much astonished to see us come alone amid so many murders.

Sunday, May 23, 1886—Meeting. We learn by letter Jesse died yesterday of croup.

Monday, May 24, 1886—Transacted business with Bp. Merrill. Heard of eight more murders committed yesterday, all around us.

May 25, 1886—Start home much against the wish of the people who all think it very dangerous. I offered to send Susan by train and mail to Pima, so she might go safe, but she would not leave me. Went to Wilcox.

May 26, 1886—We are told by Genl Miles and citizens not to go without company, but I know of no company, and I must go to meet Bp. Preston.[62] When we turned off into the "cienega road," which lies many miles among hills, ravines, rocks and brush, and therefore very dangerous, I felt the danger fully but said nothing to alarm Susan.

[page 585]

[A note appears to have been written many years later, in shaky handwriting, added as a title.]

IN DRASTIC DANGER OF DEATH BY IND. [. . .]

May 1886—At May's well we both felt a sense of great danger. The place was deserted, the cattle gone and many horse tracks at the troughs. We only watered and drove quickly away for six miles to a place out the hills, and there fed the team and ate lunch; then drove on reaching Laytons at 5. Br. Layton was greatly pleased to see us. He had greatly feared for us, and had tried to have an escort go to meet us, along with Albert. We heard while at St David, Monday, that our dear little grandson Jesse B. died Sat. morning. He was taken with croup the night we left, and soon died. This was why Susan felt impressed to stay.

We found at Br. Layton's Bps. Preston & Burton, E. Snow, wife, girl and boy, and spent 2 hours resting, then went on and got home at 8 P.M. after a very dangerous journey. Susan explained why she sat so much of the time with her head close to mine—she wished the same ball that should strike me to kill her too.

We also learn that our neighbor on the same block, Frank Thurston. was killed by Apaches on Sunday evening about 6 miles from Pima, and they also took horses from Curtis the same night. Troops had gone in pursuit.

We (Susan & I) gave thanks to God for our preservation, for it was only by His power we were preserved.

May ~~26~~ 27, 1886—Worked on my accounts with Bp. Preston. We heard some indians were seen near Pima, and a party of men went out to see. They found them to be indian scouts, and nearly had a fight.

May 28, 1886—Bps. Preston and Burton start home today. Also Brs. Thurber and Bean. Wrote to Bp. J. Q. Cannon.

May 29, 1886—Priesthood meeting at Layton.

May 31, 1886—Started my new Binder today. Henry manager. It cost 200$ [$4,328] + 60$ [$1,298] + 9.60 [$208] = $269.60 [$5,834]

[page 586]

June 2, 1886—This evening B. Young and Brs. Perkins & Rogers came and stop with us.

61 At this writing no match was found for this name.

62 This was Major-General Nelson A. Miles, who, at this entry, was commander of the troops in the Department of Arizona. He was noted for his wars with Sitting Bull, Crazy Horse, Spotted Eagle, and Geronimo. On November 8, 1887, in Tucson, the citizens of Arizona presented him with a sword of honor for his services.

June 3, 1886—Br. Young left this afternoon, after a pleasant visit.

June 5, 1886—Examined the Gila for locations of Bridge, having been appointed Chairman of that committee by [Suprv. . .]

Sunday, June 6, 1886—Meeting at Pima.

June 7, 1886—Leveled and Surveyed for bridge.

June 10, 1886—Have been estimating cost of bridge till now.

Friday, June 11, 1886—Relief Society Conference. I attended.

Saturday, June 12, 1886—Quarterly Conference, also Sun. 13.[63] A good time.

June 14, 15, 16, 17, 1886—Estimated for bridge

June 18, 1886—Made plan for Sun dial

June 19, 1886—High Council at Central. Bp. Welker vs Campbell

Sunday, June 20, 1886—Meeting at Mathews Branch. Br. Layton sick. We located spot for new town.

Tuesday, June 22, 1886—I married Benj. Willard Johnson and Sarah May Weller[64] today at 2 P.M. at Carlton's.

Saturday, June 26, 1886—Worked on my accounts all the week. Found some lines composed long ago, and not recorded:—(Also, priesthood meeting.)

MY LOVED ONES ARE GONE

The Missing Ones

Some of my loved ones—my
children—are gone!—
Where, where are they?
I miss their sweet prattle—their jubilant song
That day after day so joyously rang—
Where, where are they?

With hearts light and happy they played
round my door,
Day after day;
Or tumbling and frisking about on the floor—
How with playthings and toys they
littered it o'er—
Gone, now, are they.

How often in sport have they climbed on
my knee!
Not there, are they;
With arms soft and loving encircling me—
With kisses so sweet and so tender—ah me!
Where, now, are they?

[page 587]

1886—

Shall I seek for the little ones missing,
tonight,
Gone from my fold?
Will they ever—or never more gladden my sight
With their bright winsome ways, and
their eyes tender light,
Precious as Gold?

Not here shall I search—twere futile and vain—
Not here are they:
But fled from this region of ~~sorrow~~
trouble and pain
Where they shall see sorrow—oh never again—
Safe—safe are they.

To the heavens above—to the mansions of light
There have they gone:
No grief will enshroud like a shadow of night,
Nor sorrow nor parting their happiness blight
Safe, now, at home.
S. L. City. Jan. 29. 1882.

June 27, 1886—Sunday. Went to Curtis, with Susan. Good meeting. Coming home, was overtaken by a Cavalry soldier with orders to warn settlers of another band of indians.

Monday, June 28, 1886—Wrote certificate of Willard Johnson's marriage. This evening, at 9.40 P.M. Henry had another daughter born to him. She weighed 9lbs.

Tuesday, June 29, 1886—Wrote in Tithing books.

63 "Quarterly Conference," *Deseret News*, July 14, 1886; Utah Digital Newspapers.

64 Martineau is performing the wedding ceremony for Benjamin Willard Johnson (1865–1939) and Sarah May Weller (1871–1939). They moved about the Southwest, from Safford to Mesa, Globe, and Pima, then to San Bernardino and Los Angeles. They had eleven children.

Friday, July 2—Settled with Henry about our land. He has paid hay 57.33 cow 40.00 = $97.33 [$2,106] I sell him 10 acres land for $225.00 [$4,869] with $35.00 [$757] in canal stock included), he to have two years to pay it in.

Monday, July 5, 1886—Celebration in Pima. I worked at my books all day.

July 6, 1886—Went to Solomonville, and presented Report on Bridge. Also presented bill for service, $58.00 [$1,255]

July 7, 1886—Wrote to Forbes, C.R.R.R. agent, Ogden, about special rate.

[page 588]

July 7, 1886—Wrote to Bp. Merrill about Church Cattle. Heavy rain—the first since last January.

Thursday, July 8, 1886—Henry started the binder again,—has been broken.

Saturday, July 10, 1886—The boys bring word that the heading machines cannot cut our grain.[65] It will be a great loss—our year's labor, and many debts to be paid, for which I had depended upon this crop. But I think all will be right in the end, though now it seems dark—very.

Sunday, July 11, 1886—To day Susan in 50 years old. It seems but a little while since I married her, a young, slim girl of 15. It seems so strange, that only 50 years ago she lived in Heaven, associating with God, the Savior, and the spirits of light, as brother and sister. I wrote the following lines in honor of her birthday:—

TO MY DEAR WIFE ON HER FIFTIETH BIRTHDAY.

1

Fifty years! As future, the time seems immense.
But fifty years past—how speedy ~~its~~ their flight!
And doubtless, when we shall be called to go hence
Our life here will seem as a dream of the night.

2

How strangely it seems that so lately you dwelt
In the Heaven of Heavens—with the Father and Son,
And ~~the~~ with Spirits of Light, who kept their estate
When Lucifer fell, with the spirits ~~he'd~~ he had won!

3

You kept your Estate, and a promise received
In the Second Estate that you should come forth:—
Should there be anointed a Priestess and Queen—
Be mother of Spirits—be Eve to an Earth.

4

How wondrous the love of Our Father in Heaven!
How wondrous His mercy—how wondrous His grace!
That we, after all the offense we have given
May again be permitted to look on His face!

[page 589]

VIRGINIA RETURNS TO LOGAN.

July, 1886—

5

How trivial and worthless this world's honors seem:—
[The second word "trivial" is written above "transient," but neither is crossed out.]
How transient our sorrows when once they ~~shall be~~ are past:!
'Twill seem like the ills of a night's troubled dream
When through this Estate we safely have passed.
Pima July 11, 1886

July 12, 1886—Began cutting our grain with the mower. Finished 15th

Monday, July 19, 1886—B. Young arrived from Mexico today, and staid with us till 4 P.P. and then went on to Apache Co.

Tuesday, July 20, 1886—Henry finished work with the binder. Has cut 79 ½ acres @ $2.00 [$43] = $159.00 [$3,441]

July 23, 1886—Threshed grain. Had 52 sacks, expected 600.

65 The heading machine superseded the first threshing machine used in the grain harvest.

Wednesday, July 28, 1886—Rec[d] my tithing schedules and went to work on my amended report. Cut Lucern again yesterday.

July 29, 1886—Began boring for water with my Augur. Next day broke shaft, and left augur in well 26 feet deep. Dug it out. Have been quite lame for a week, caused by cutting brush on my farm.

Wednesday, August 4, 1886—Went to Thatcher and chose site for Tithing Office.

August 7, 1886—Laid out the foundation for it.

Sunday, August 8, 1886—Went with Stake Presidency and held meetings in Curtis and Mathews

Tuesday, August 18, 1886—Started with Jean to Wilcox, to put her on train for Utah. Camped at the Cienega. Heavy storm at evening.

August ~~18~~ 19, 1886—Arrived at Wilcox. Heard that the R. R. is blockaded by washouts for the last four days.

Thursday, August 29, 1886—Jean started on train at 9 P.M. in company with the two widows Wright, whose husbands were killed by Indians last fall. I felt sad to part with her, but think it is for her best good to go to her brothers in Utah—Logan. Anna went with us. Started for home next morning, and got there about 8 P.M.

[page 590]

LYMAN AND MORONI'S CHILDREN BORN.

August 23, 1886—Sent to J B Alden for book. From this time on worked Continually on my report to G. T. office to date of

September 4, 1886—and then waited for a few days.

September 7, 1886—To day Henry, Albert & Joel went haying.

September 9, 1886—A good rain.

September 14, 1886—I cut my Lucern.

September 17, 1886—Today Lyman and Alley had a son born, 12:20 [... M.] weighed 11 lbs. named him [blank]

Today the Presidency located place for a new town in Mathews ward. Attended F. Relief Conf. in afternoon.

September 18 & 19, 1886—Quarterly Conference.[66]

Monday, September 20, 1886—Began auditing my tithing report with Pres[t] Layton and W. D. Johnson, which he approved and signed.

A girl was born to Moroni and Sarah to-day.

September 30, 1886—Finished auditing my tithing reports with Br. Layton.

October 4, 1886—Sent my T.O. [Tithing Office] returns to S. L. City. Plowed weeds.

October 5, 1886—Plowed weeds, & did not quit till after sunset & quit work wet through with sweat. Got chilled in coming home.

October 6, 1886—Taken with rheumatism, and took to bed.

October 23, 1886—Up to this time I have been confined to bed with a severe season of Sciatica, unable to sit up and suffering greatly[67]

Today R. A. Allred visited me on behalf of others to see if I would run for Legislature.[68] I said no. He said I would have the full vote of the gentile towns. Judge Hyatt also sent to me for the same purpose.

October 21, 1886—Today Susan was set apart as Pres[t] of the R. S. of Pima, by Bp. Taylor.

October 26, 1886—Henry and Albert came home from haying today. Yesterday rec[d] letter from Bp. Preston acknowledging receipt of my returns. O.K.

[page 591]

ELVIRA'S BOY BORN, AT MESA. ALSO CHARLIE'S

October 29, 1886—Cut my Lucern for the last time this year.

November 4, 1886—Was carried to the Hot Springs today. Susan went with me, and Henry.

November 6, 1886—Begin to feel better from the hot baths

November 9, 1886—Gertrude came today to try the baths for her lameness.

66 Joseph East, "Pima Stake Conference," *Deseret News*, October 6, 1886; Utah Digital Newspapers.

67 The sciatica is a long nerve on the back side of the thigh. It can cause a painful condition in the thigh and the hip area as Martineau is experiencing here.

68 R. A. Allred is listed as a carpenter from the Teviston District, Cochise County.

November 12, 1886—Joel got home from haying ~~Nov.~~ today.

[dates out of order in journal]

November 1, 1886—Today Elvira presented another grandchild. Born at Mesa, Maricopa Co. A. T. at 1.30

November 17, 1886—I walked about 6 rods today.

November 22, 1886—Cold. Snowed a few minutes.

November 27, 1886—Much worse last night and today.

November 29, 1886—Last night slept from 9 P.M. to 4 A.M., the first sleep since October 6th of more than one or two hours in the twenty four. Have had no sleep, for months, only from one to two hours each 24 hours. I have taken laudanum and morphine, but it only lulls the pain—does not make me sleep.

Wednesday, December 1, 1886—Went home by Presᵗ Layton's advice, to be nearer the help of the priesthood.

December 4, 1886—Gertrude came home from the springs.

December 10, 1886—Female Relief [Society] Conference. I did not attend.

December 11 & 12, 1886—Quarterly Conference. I went in carriage. Spoke once.

Wednesday, December 22, 1886—Having been appointed by Probate Court one of appraisers in Collins estate. Went to Thomas to Survey the place to set off the widow's portion.

Thursday, December 23, 1886—Surveyed

Friday, December 24, 1886—Ditto. Came home in afternoon for Christmas.

December 27, 1886—High Council at Central.

December 20, 1886—Today Charles and Eva had a son born to them at Logan at 1.30 P.M.

December 28, 1886—Returned to Collins to finish up

December 29, 1886—finished & returned home. My bill $35.00 [$757]. Henry got his hand hurt blasting. He came home.

[page 592]

1887.

December 31, 1886—Recᵈ box of C. gifts from Lyman and Allie. Wrote them.

January 1, 1887—Today F. Gunnell, W. Maughan, Baxter and Poppleton came. Exiles.[69] Moroni admitted Jan 2ᵈ a member of Pima ward, with his family.

January 5, 1887—Resurveyed part of Union Canal.

January 7, 1887—Attended justices court as witness in A. M. M. case.

January 8, 1887—Our 35th wedding day. Had a house full of family & friends.

January 10, 1887—To day attended City Council as Mayor of Pima.

January 11, 1887—Self & F. Gunnell start for St David, on tithing business. Drove to Layton and stopped with Packer's.

January 12, 1887—Drove to Wilcox, next day to St David, F. 13th

January 14, 1887—To Tucson. Saw Sur. Genˡ Hise, in relation to making copies of U.S. surveys in Graham Co.[70]

January 15, 1887—Made plats all day. Next day, very lonesome.

January 17, 1887—Copied plats, also next day 18th. Went to a fire.

January 19, 1887—Finished. Got my watch fixed

January 20, 1887—Returned to St David. Found M. Thatcher there, just from Mexico. Glad to meet each other, also to see Br. Gunnell. Held meeting in the evening.

[written in margin]

Dead.

January 21, 1887—Start home. John Hill came to bring Br. M. T. to the Gila. While riding with Br. Thatcher, talking with him, and without any premonition or ill feeling of any kind, I was suddenly struck dead, to all appearance. Br. T. hastily called the others up and they all thought I was dead for a time. After a

69 Francis Gunnell, William Maughan, Robert or John Baxter, and William Poppleton are all Martineau's associates from Logan, Utah. They are exiles from the Edmunds–Tucker Act, fleeing persecution and prosecution for polygamy. From Logan some Saints fled north to Canada with Charles Ora Card, others south to Mexico with Moses Thatcher (Godfrey and Godfrey, *The Utah Years*, 565–70; F. LaMond Tullis, *Mormons in Mexico: The Dynamics of Faith and Culture* [Logan, UT: Utah State Univ. Press, 1996], 57).

70 John Hise was the Arizona surveyor general.

lapse of 30 minutes I came too, but was weak. They hurriedly drove on to Wilcox, 16 miles, Br. T. having first administered to me. He asked if I would call a doctor. I said no, I wanted nothing but the administrations of the priesthood,—had no faith in any thing else. The brethren were all as kind as could be, to me, especially Br. T. He said I must quit work for a time and go to Utah to recuperate. In this they all joined. Next day drove home. Br. T. staying at Thatcher Ward.

[page 593]

January 1887—Br. Thatcher thinks my attack was apoplectic, or else exhaustion caused by over work.[71]

January 22, 1887—Br. T. came in to day and stopped with me. He says I must give up the Bishop's Agency. and take a rest of two or three months in Utah. I said I had no means for the trip, but he said he would give me $50.⁰⁰ [$1,082] for that purpose.

Sunday, January 23, 1887—Meeting in Pima. Br. Thatcher preached, and was filled with the Holy Spirit. Pres[t] Layton also spoke.

Tuesday, January 25, 1887—Br. T. held meeting again this evening.

Wednesday, January 26, 1887—Br. T. Started for St Louis this morning, with John Campbell, to buy saw and gristmills &c for Juarez in Chihuahua.[72] He left me a check for $50.⁰⁰ [$1,082] and told me to go to Utah and rest. May God ever bless him, and repay him a hundred fold. He approves my moving to Mexico, if Bp. Preston releases me from the Bps. Agency. Br. T. wrote to him to recommend it.

I feel drawn to Mexico, although I understand well the great amount of heavy labor required in a new country, and my own lack of physical strength. But I think a great work awaits me there, in helping to save the seed of Abraham in that land, who must have the gospel brought to them; and I am willing, if it be the Lord's will, to labor in that cause. My past blessings by various patriarchs, all point to this work in that land.

January 29, 1887—Priesthood meeting and High Council meeting to day. I read Pres[t] Taylor's instructions to me in letter just received, relative to ordination of High Priests. I was appointed to make a plan of our proposed Tabernacle and send it to Pres[t] Taylor for approval. I bought today of Pres[t] Layton a large ditch plow for use in Mexico. I paid 100.⁰⁰ [$2,164] for it. Also arranged for Albert to go with Br. Gunnell, drive team, and take up a place for me there.

Sunday, January 30, 1887—Meeting in Pima.

[page 594]

GO TO UTAH, SNOW BLOCKADE IN SIERRA NEVADA.

February 8, 1887—To day went to Solomonville to file affidavit for my pension for service in the Mexican War.

February 10, 1887—This evening attended City Council, as Mayor. As I intend to Start for Utah tomorrow, and Susan feels apprehensive about my traveling alone in my poor health, I went to Patriarch W[m] M[c]Bride for a blessing He gave me a good one, saying I should go and come in peace and safety. After he sat down again, he suddenly said, "He that is unjustly accusing you to injure you shall Serve you." I said—"Why no one would do that against me." He repeated his former words, and I said again "I am sure no one would try to injure me—I injure no one." He said, "Someone is doing this. I am not deceived by the Spirit." I said, "Even if any one is trying to injure me, I don't wish him to serve me." He said, "Why, what would you do," I said, "Why, I would forgive him, and let him go."

Friday, February 11, 1887—Started this morning, Moroni going with me to Wilcox. Staid all night with a stock man, W[m] Fonda.[73]

February 12, 1887—Took train this evening at 7.30 P.M. in a sleeper as I did not feel able to go such a way in a 3[d] Class.

February 13, 1887—Breakfast at Yuma, Dine at Indio, sup at Los Angeles

Monday, February 14, 1887—Breakfast at Tulare, Dine at Lathrop, San F. at 4.40 P.M.

71 It would appear Martineau had suffered a stroke. *Apoplectic* means to strike down. It is a paralysis caused by a stroke.

72 John Campbell was a former Congressman and rancher in St. John's, Arizona (Mark E. Miller, "St. John's Saints Interethnic Conflict in Northeastern Arizona, 1880–1885," *Journal of Mormon History* 23, no. 1 [Spring 1997]: 87).

73 This could be William Bridendoll Fonda, who married Leah Louis Robins, 1886, of Safford, Arizona.

Tuesday, February 15, 1887—Left San Francisco at 3 P.M. and reached Colfax 11 P.M. Here we found several trains blockaded by Snow.

Thursday, February 17, 1887—Many trains and hundreds of passengers here. Start at 2.15 P.M, with 3 engines and 12 cars. At Blue Cañon met two trains going west, Snow 8 to 10 feet deep. Sup at Truckee.

February 18, 1887—Breakfast at Elko, Nevada. Reach Ogden 10:45 P.M.

Saturday, February 19, 1887—Got to Logan 2 P.M. and found all well. The girls did not expect me.

Monday, February 21, 1887—Visited Nephi's family, and next day visited Eva.

Wednesday, February 23, 1887—Went to S. L. City and found Eliza well.

Friday, February 25, 1887—Found charges against me, sent by Br. Layton, who had been fair to my face.

[page 595]

CHARGES MADE BY LAYTON.

February 25, 1887—Bp. Preston said he did not believe them, and told me to write a full refutation of them which I did, on 26th

February 26, 1887—I copied Layton's letter, and sent reply to Prest Taylor.[74]

Tuesday, March 1, 1887—Saw Sister Grieve to day—a pleasant visit.

Thursday, March 3, 1887—To day we got positive assurance of the passage of the new Edmunds-Tucker bill. I then determined to fulfill the law of God so soon as He will open my way to do so. This evening I saw for the first time Jessie Grieve—a pleasant companion. Great rejoicing among the Gentiles. They say Mormonism is doomed now. A momentous question propounded Jessie.[75]

Friday, March 4, 1887—Wrote to our Bishops on tithing matters, especially stock.

March 5, 1887—At priesthood meeting, it was said that points relating to doctrine must be submitted to the High Council.

Friday, March 11, 1887—Hunted names of ancestors in Historian's Office, about ~~100~~ 105.

Saturday, March 12, 1887—Lyman came last evening. To a question of mine—Si senor [señor]

Sunday, March 13, 1887—Lyman took Eliza and I riding to day, before meeting.

March 14, 1887—Attended practice of the Choral Union this evening.

Tuesday, March 15, 1887—Went to top of Ensign Peak today—a hard jaunt for me. In the evening got word that deputies were watching me, so I left Eliza's and went to Bp. Preston's to stay.[76]

Saturday, March 19, 1887—Got my recommend from Prest Taylor, O.K. for temple work. Jesse came this evening with Church team. Arranged to do some baptizing for Bp. Whitney on Monday next. viz:—Miss Jessie Grieve, who desires to do some work in the Logan temple.

Sunday, March 20, 1887—Jesse is engaged for the church for the summer by Bp. P.

Monday, March 21, 1887—Got tickets for self and May Preston, to Logan. Baptized Jessie Grieve by request of O. T. W. in the Bath House.

Tuesday, March 22, 1887—Went to Logan, found all well. Visited Zina Young.[77]

March 23, 1887—Charles came from Pocatello to see us and "young Zina", and had a pleasant visit.[78]

---

74 Little is known of this conflict. Christopher Layton was president of the St. Joseph Stake, and Martineau was his counselor in that stake presidency. As will be seen in later entries, it appears Layton was concerned about the way Martineau was keeping the tithing books. Martineau was cleared of any wrongdoing, and Layton would later ask Martineau for instructions as to how the books were to be kept. Histories of both men reflect continued dedication to the gospel (McIntyre and Barton, *Christopher Layton*, 145–46, 243; Cole, *One Hundred Years in Thatcher*, 9–15).

75 There are a number of Jessie Grieves, but at this writing none matched the context of this entry.

76 Following the passage of the Edmunds–Tucker Act, U.S. marshals scoured the area using spotters and former Church members to help them capture Church leaders and polygamists.

77 This is Zina Young Williams Card, who was also in hiding in the Mormon underground at this time (Godfrey, "Zina Presindia Young Williams Card," 118–21).

78 This is Zina Young Card Brown, who was the daughter of Zina Young Williams Card and Charles Ora Card. She migrated to Canada with her mother and father and later became the wife of Hugh B. Brown (Bradley, *Four Zinas*, 405–66).

March 24, 1887—Wrote letters to Susan and Anna, visited with Charles.

March 26, 1887—Attended choir practice, but was disappointed—so many faces gone—so many new ones. Not like my old choir, of which I was a member 24 years.

Sunday, March 27, 1887—I preached, to day. Weather Cold and Snowy.

March 29, 1887—Arrival ~~of~~ at Sister Zina's of Jessie H. R. A. Grieves.

[page 596]

JESSIE H. ENDOWED

March 30, 1887—Jessie Helen R. A. Grieves endowed to day for herself. Not sealed. Began in temple. I was endowed for Abraham Martineau, Margaret Martineau, endowed by S. M. Benson; Marie Martineau, by E. Nankevin; Sarah Martineau by E. Lundberg, Elizabeth Finch, by M. R. Henderson; Catherine Martineau, by J. C. Christianson. Marg[t] Martineau was sealed to me, Mary T. Richards, proxy, saw Jesse G

March 31, 1887—I endowed for Daniel Corson, Susan Columbine was endowed by M. R. Henderson; Marriott Marg[t] Bunny by S. M. Benson, Fanny Martineau, by S. B. More; Eliz[th] Rankin by J. C. Christiansen; Caroline B. Parry by Lavina Parry. To day Marie Martineau and Susan Columbine were sealed to me. Jessie H. returned home. Sealing could not be done in the Temple, so Jessie returned home.

[written in margin]

Mrs. M. P. W. Young sealing proxy

April 1, 1887—I endowed for David Martineau, Ann Columbine, by Mrs. Benson, Mary Columbine by J. C. Christiansen, Susan Martineau by E. Lundberg, Elizabeth Brewer by E. Nankevin, Mrs. Gaston Hogle by M. R. Henderson.

To day I wrote to Pres[t] Taylor relative to doing a work for Jeanne d'Arc and Charlotte Corday. Zina showed me the arrow found in the skeleton by Jo[s] Smith when on the road to redeem Zion. He gave it to Brigham, and he to his daughter Zina. The one slain was Zelph, a Lamanite general.[79] [added later in shaky handwriting]

April 2, 1887—Wrote to Susan, Professor J. W. Mears and Joel

April 4, 1887—Went to S. L. City, on way to Conference, in [. . .]

April 5, 1887—In the evening went with Jessie H. G. to Pat[h] Hyde for a blessing. He then blessed me (See p. 601) and then wanted me to bless him, which I did, giving him great pleasure. He said I told him just what Jos. Smith had said to him before and gave him the same blessings. It was a very good time.

April 6, 1887—Went to Provo, to Conference, met Jesse N. Smith there, & we both went to Bp. Ja[s] R. Johnson's who was very good to us.

April 7 & 8, 1887—Meeting again, Lyman at afternoon meeting. and went back same day. At evening Jessie Grieves came with several others supposing Conference would last till Sunday.

April 9, 1887—Returned to S. L. City.

April 10, 1887—Visited Della's grave. Very cold and Stormy.

April 11, 1887—Still cold and Stormy.

[page 597]

While going to S. L. City April 4th I wrote the following lines, to the tune and song "I'll remember you, love in my prayers"—a beautiful tune.

I'LL REMEMBER YOU, LOVE, IN MY PRAYERS.

[added in shaky handwriting] Jessie Helen Grieve

1

In the heaven of heavens, together we dwelt
With our Father and Mother in love,
And often together in unison knelt
As we worshipped with spirits above.
Then first were we parted, when came we to earth
To dwell on this planet below

79 During the travels of Zion's Camp, Joseph Smith and others unearthed the bones of ancient skeletons. From revelation, Joseph declared they were the bones of ancient Lamanites. For more information, see Wilford Woodruff, *Wilford Woodruff's Journal*, ed. Scott G. Kenney (Midvale, UT: Signature Books, 1983), 1:10.

To forget all we knew—e'en our heavenly birth
To suffer affliction and woe.

Chorus

Be where we may—at home or away—
We'll share all our joys and our cares.
And at morn or at eve, when to Father I pray
I'll remember you, love, in my prayers.

2

But all is not sorrow, nor is it all pain
That we are here Called to endure;
What we fancy a loss is an infinite gain—
A glory, eternal and sure.
Then let us be happy, whate'er may betide,
If sunshine, or clouds round us spread,
Up the [pathway] of Life we together will glide—
Together life's pathway we'll tread.
[written in the margin]
pathway [Price]

Chorus.

3

Should Sorrows assail us—should faults ones forsake—
Our footsteps grow feeble and sore,—
We'll trust in our Father, and fresh Courage take—
To each other be true evermore.
In joy or in sorrow together be one,
Cheered by an unchangeable love;
And when Exaltations and ~~thrones we have~~ won
[written above "~~thrones~~"] heaven is
We'll reign with Our Father above.

Chorus

[page 598]

[written at the top of the page at a later date, in shaky handwriting.]

April 18, 1887

x Jessie H. sealed to me in Endowment House by Apostle F. D. Richards, very secretly. John Lyon Witness holding a lighted candle. Richards hidden from my view.[80]

April 12, 1887—Wrote to Albey Sherman, about doing work for his father and mother. Also to Susan.

Wednesday, April 13, 1887—Bought a gold watch Case for my watch—$32.^{00}$ [$692] Went to Church farm with Lyman.

April 14, 1887—Visited M. Sloan.[81] Lyman went home.

April 15, 1887—Went to theatre with Alley, saw E. Booth in Shylock [&]

April 16, 1887—Saw him in Othello.[82]

Sunday, April 17, 1887—Rainy and cold. Went to 17th Ward, also to tabernacle.

Monday, April 18, 1887—Today C. Fullmer and Ella went home.[83] x Dos Sunt ein.

[written in margin]

Jessie sealed to me [Martineau draws a small five-point star with a circle in the middle, next to "sealed."]

quite Cold. At about 8:30 P.M. [added later] I and J. H. R. A. Grieve [then continued with] went to endowment house, each one alone, and entering by a different gate. Sealed at 9 P.M. one witness, [added later] to Jessie Helen Russell Anderson Grieves.

Tuesday, April 19, 1887—Wrote letters home, Walked. Also visited, at house of Jessie's mother. Jessie born November 23, 1864 near Edinburg Scotland.

Wednesday, April 20, 1887—Had a narrow chance for escape this morning—team

April 21, 1887—Snow, cold and muddy.

April 22, 1887—W B Preston went away today, may follow tomorrow.

[written in margin]

*Jessie 2^{d} A** [included a star here]

80 The Saints worked to fulfill their religious convictions while hiding from the U.S. marshals. Martineau, here and in the next several pages of his journal, is performing temple ordinances for his deceased family. John Lyon was an engineer living in Logan (Ray Somers, *History of Logan* [Logan, UT: Somers Historic Press, 1993], 65).

81 This is likely R. W. Sloan, instrumental in developing the Logan Power, Light, and Heating Company in 1890 and later influential in the newspapers (Ricks and Cooley, *History of a Valley*, 228, 399–401).

82 Edwin Booth (1833–93) was a renowned actor of the nineteenth century noted for his performance of Shakespeare's plays. His career was interrupted in April 1865, when his brother, John Wilkes Booth, assassinated Abraham Lincoln.

83 C. D. W. Fullmer was vice president of the Logan Utah Journal Publishing Company (Ricks and Cooley, *History of a Valley*, 401–2).

This evening at about 8.30, the 2[d] A. was administered in the historian's office to Jessie H. R. A. G. Martineau by F. D. Richards and myself laying on hands with him.

Friday, April 29, 1887—Returned to Logan, with Allie and Harriett. At Ogden we met the Queen of the Sandwich islands on her way east.

April 30, 1887—Quarterly Conference in Logan. In the evening we went to hear the opera "Chunks," in which Jesse, Lilla and Virginia have part. It went off very well.

Sunday, May 1, 1887—Snow on ground this morning, and quite cold. Wrote to Pres[t] Taylor relative to Joan d'Arc and Charlotte Corday.

May 4, 1887—I was endowed for Paul Columbine today.

I was endowed for Gaston Martineau, Mrs. E. B. Smith for Catherine Skottowe, M. R. Henderson for Margaret Martineau, M. H. Anderson for Elizabeth Martineau, E. B. M[c]Neil for Sarah Martineau, J. M. Thomassen for Marion Martineau, M. P. W. Young for Ann O'Brien.

[written in margin]

M P W. Young S. proxy

Read in Times and Seasons page 746 vol. 5 that Shem was Melchisedec.[84]

May 6, 1887—I endowed for Mr. Haughout, E. B. M[c]Neil for Nelly Haughout,

[page 599]

May 1887—M R Henderson for Eliz[th] Francis Beatty, M. H. Anderson for Jane Taylor.

May 6, 1887—Also Cha[s] Blackwell for Francis Columbine

May 7, 1887—Writing my biography for publication by E. W. Tullidge in his "History of Northern Utah." finished it next day. Have some thoughts of going on a trip to England, Lyman wishes it. But there will not be enough time for me before I must return to meet some of the 12 in Pima on important business relative to myself and Pres[t] Layton.

Wednesday, May 11, 1887—I was endowed for Peter Martineau, Sarah Moffat for Marriott Martineau, M R Henderson for Margaret Martineau, M H. Anderson for Catherine Martineau Foss, B. B. Hoth for Eliza Barnard. E B M[c]Neil for Margaret Ronalds.

Today were sealed Peter Martineau and Margaret Ronalds: Mr. Haughout and M. Martineau, Francis Haughout & Mrs. Francis Haughout, and Paul Columbine & Elizabeth Brewer and Catherine Skittowe.

Nephi was endowed for Joseph Martineau and M. M. Burris for Sarah Meadows, and C. A. Henderson for Melia Hardingham.

May 12, 1887—I was endowed for John Martineau, M H Anderson for Theodora Martha Dyball, E. B. M[c]Neil for Catherine Harris, M. M. Burris for Margaret Williment, B. B. Hoth for Susan Macon.

[written in margin]

Mrs. J. T. Richards Sealing proxy

May 13, 1887—To day were sealed Joseph Martineau & Caroline B. Parry, Peter Columbine & Marie Martineau, John Martineau & Marriott Marg[t] Bunny, Rich[d] Williment & May Martineau.

I endowed for Peter Columbine. Nephi for Rich[d] Williment. E. B. M[c]Niel for Elizabeth Humphrey. M. M. Burris for Ann Dorothy Clark, M R Henderson for Catherine Marsh, M. H. Anderson for Susanne Scott, B B Hoth for Elizabeth Bromton.

Tuesday, May 17, 1887—To day Lyman was baptized of 65 and Lilla for 37.

[page 600]

May 18, 1887—I endowed for Philip Meadows Martineau, M R Henderson for Mrs. Ann Haughout, M. H. Anderson for Mrs. Peter Haughout, M M. Burris for Eliz.[th] Haughout, M. B Kent for Mary Haughout

There were sealed Philip M. Martineau & Eliz.[th] Humphreys and Ann Dorothy Clark.

May 19, 1887—I endowed for Hewett Rand, Nephi for Peter F. Martineau, M R Henderson for Mary Davis Guild, M H Anderson for Elizabeth Mears, M M. Burris for Harmeh Mears, M B Kent for Mary Mears, M. A. Kent for Ann Bogart. Sealed to me M.D. Guild, E. Mears, H. Mears, & Mary Mears.

[written in margin]

Mrs. Jane T. Richards Sealing proxy.

May 20, 1887—I endowed for David Columbine, Nephi for Peter Columbine, M H Anderson for Allette

84 The *Times and Seasons* was published between 1839 and 1846. First printed in Nauvoo, it was the official voice of the Church at the time.

Haughout, M. M. Burris for Elizabeth Martineau, M. B. Kent for Mrs. Elizabeth Blackburn. M. A. Kent for Theodora Martha Blake, M R Henderson for Elizabeth Mears.

There were sealed Peter Columbine & Melia Hardingham, David Columbine & Theodora Martha Dyball (per J. T. Richards) and myself and Elizabeth Mears, also myself and Nellie Benson (per A. B. Benson)

May 21, 1887—Wrote to prest J. Taylor for 2[d] A for Nellie Benson.

May 24, 1887—Finished reading proofs of my biography.

May 25, 1887—I endowed for David Martineau, Nephi for Francis Columbine, M. M. Burris for Mary Mears, M H Anderson for Winnifred Sprague.

There were sealed David Martineau & Sarah Meadows, and Francis Columbine & Susan Macon.

May 26, 1887—I endowed for Jaques d'Arc (Father of Jeanne) Nephi for Mr. Egbert, M R Henderson for Mrs. Sarah Dexter, M. H. Anderson for Catherine Mears, M M. Burris for Sarah Mears, M B Kent for Isabeau de Vouthon (mother of Joan of Arc) E B M[c]Neil for Eliz[th] Mears.

There were sealed Hewett Rand & Mary Columbine, Jaques d'Arc and Isabeau de Vouthon, Mr. Egbert & Eliz[th] Martineau.

I acted as proxy for Peter Stubbs, dead, sealed to two wives, (dead

[written in margin]

M. P. W. Young—S. proxy this week.

[page 601]

May 27, 1887—I endowed for John Dexter, Nephi for Thomas Vernon, M R Henderson for Elizabeth Johnson, M H Anderson for Mary Mudge, M M Burris for Catherine Mears, E. B. M[c]Neil for Mary Catherine Mears, M B Kent for Marg[t] Keteltas.

There were sealed John Dexter & Winnifred Sprague, Thomas Vernon & Mary Mears.

Received permission for 2 A. for Nellie Benson, Also a letter from F. M. Lyman. Settled with those who have assisted in the temple, by Nephi's liberality, to amount of $33.[00] [$714] besides some other I paid myself.

[written in margin]

M. P. W. Young. sealing proxy this week

May 28, 1887—Charles went to Pocatello to day, after two days visit, which I much enjoyed. He feels well in the gospel.

Memoranda. He was born 24 July 1861, married Eva Rosetta Rice 21 Jan. 1886, Their son Cha[s] Freeman Jr. born 20 Dec. 1886. Was ordained Elder by C. W. Hyde, Aug. 6. 1865

April 5, 1887—The following blessing was given me in S. L. City by Patriarch Charles W. Hyde, April 5. 1887.

Beloved Brother, I place my hands upon thy head and seal upon you a patriarchal blessing. And thou shalt yet be called to proclaim this gospel from land to land and from sea to sea, and no power shall stay thy hand; and you shall proclaim the gospel from city to city, even to the house of Israel, and they will call thee blessed of the Father. And you shall see Zion redeemed, and stand with your Redeemer and with the prophet Joseph when the Saints will be free. And be comforted, for Zion shall be redeemed: for they shall bind up the law and seal up the testimony. For you know not the blessings which the Lord thy God has for you. For thou art of Ephraim and a lawful heir to the fullness of the priesthood, And if thou desirest it thou shalt converse with the three Nephites, and they shall unlock to you things that shall not enter the heart of man. And I seal upon your head eternal life, with all thy father's household. Even so. Amen and amen.

(Recorded in Book J. folio 178.) See p. 596

[page 602]

May 30, 1887—Jessie H. R. A. Grieve received her blessing at same time, I being scribe.

To day our family and the Thatchers decorated the graves of our dead. Sister Preston had a large box of flowers brought from her garden in S. L City. for the purpose. Very warm.

Wednesday, June 1, 1887—Br. [blank]

To day I was endowed for Peter Columbine, and Nephi for David Martineau. There were sealed today Gaston Martineau & Mrs. Gaston Hoyle Martineau: Peter Columbine & Eliz[th] Brunton; David Martineau & Catherine Harris. I acted for the males, and Sister May T. Richards for the females, in sealing.

I also acted as proxy for W[m] Lea, dead, in sealing two wives to him, by Mrs. Stubbs.

I wrote to Bp. C. Pulsipher, Huntington, Emery Co. Utah relative to Albey's standing in the Church, as what he will do about working for the dead (his father &c) so that if he will not do anything for them my children may. Lyman Sherman has waited long for his blessings, having died in full faith and fellowship, in 1838, in Far West, Mo. a martyr, as I have been told by H. C. Kimball and Geo. A. Smith. He was one of the first Seven Presidents of Seventies, and shortly before his death was called to be an Apostle, but died before he was ordained. He was father to my wife Susan Julia Sherman.[85]

June 2, 1887—I endowed Arthur Martineau and Nephi, Philip Martineau; Sister Adaline B. Benson endowed for Mary Mears. There were sealed Arthur Martineau and Ann O'Brien, also Philip Martineau & Eliz[th] Frances Beatty. After which I was proxy, in sealing two wives to John Stubbs. At 2.30 P.M. Nellie Benson Martineau received her 2[d] A. Sister Adaline B. A. Benson being proxy. This is the first case of the kind in this dispensation, I am told, of a Lamanite woman receiving this ordinance. I rejoice to be one of those counted worthy to save and exalt one of the daughters of Lehi, and I believe that Lehi and Moroni and other holy ones will also rejoice, and will bless and aid me in my labors for the salvation of the living children of Lehi, whose redemption is very near at hand, and to whom I am to be a messenger & a hunter, if I forfeit not my blessings.

[page 603]

June 2, 1887—I feel as if my great life labor is just about to commence; although, in one sense, I have labored faithfully for 36 years, striving to build up Zion in my humble capacity.

Friday, June 3, 1887—I endowed Mr. Neave by Nephi, and I endowed John Martineau Lyon, my nephew. Emmeline was endowed for Ruth Mears and Mary A. B. Freeze for Mrs. Thomas Vernon. Sister Frieze is my dear friend, and helped me today for friendship's sake. There were sealed, Mr. Neave & Catherine Martineau, M. A. B. Frieze being proxy.

I have been quite feeble all this week, having at times strange sensations. I know I stand very near the vail.—So near I can almost see beyond it, and I can see so many principles of truth—oh, so plainly. Oh Father, I thank Thee for the work I have been permitted to do for my dead—even to be a savior to so many. Help me, my Father, to continue, and to be true to the end:—help me, Father, to become pure in heart, that I may not forfeit my kingdom and exaltation in Thy presence. In my last letter to my dear wife Susan I made a covenant with her and me, to be a ~~such~~ covenant forever between us:—that no woman shall ever come between her and me—no one shall ever take her place in my love:—for she is the wife of my youth, and has always been true and faithful—has always been a help. Help me, my Father, to keep my covenant, and to be a blessing to her. And not only to her, but to all whom Thou dost give unto me, for thou hast said, my Father, that I shall be blessed in every gift that is given unto me. Oh, help me to be worthy.

Saturday, June 4, 1887—Sister Preston returned to S. L. City to day, and her son Will started for Chicago to meet his father and May.

Monday, June 6, 1887—I went to S. L. City, stopping at Bp. Preston's, not feeling safe to go elsewhere.

June 7, 1887—Took Sister P. to hear "Belshazzar" in the big Tabernacle.

[page 604]

June 13, 1887—I obtained some names for baptism from the "Encyclopedia Britannica," of Martini's (from Italy) back to the year 1256

June 14, 1887—Went bathing at Garfield, on Salt Lake.

Thursday, June 16, 1887—Went to closing exercises of the University with Sister Preston.

Saturday, June 18, 1887—Went driving with Sister P. and Nett & Lutie Thatcher. Also to Garfield, & bathed, which does me good.

....

85 Martineau is trying to see that the temple ordinances are being conducted for his wife's family. Charles, John, and William Pulsipher were brothers with a southern-Utah connection to Martineau (Janet Burton Seegmiller, *A History of Iron County: Community above Self* [Salt Lake City: Utah Historical Society, 1998], 366). Albey Lyman Sherman is Martineau's brother-in-law, the brother to Susan Julia Sherman, Martineau's second wife.

June 20, 1887—Rec[d] letters from Susan and Albert, and answered. Commenced writing my collection of "Pearls."[86]

June 21, 1887—Ordered 1000 tithing receipts for Pima T. [Tithing] office. Wrote

June 23, 1887—Went to Garfield & bathed. Wrote in "Pearls."

June 24 & 25, 1887—Wrote in my "Pearls."

June 27, 1887—Letters from Susan and Henry. C. Layton still devilish. Attended Teacher's Institute at University.

June 28, 1887—With Mrs. P. drove Mr. & Mrs. Rouse around town, and then went to Garfield with them, at opening of that Resort, a large number present. Wrote to Susan.

Friday, July 1, 1887—Went to Garfield with Teacher's Institute Excursion. Had a good dinner for 10¢ Bathed twice & had a good time. On return visited Br. Norman with my friend. He gave me a good blessing and Comforted me much. Also the same for my friend. In the evening Bp. P. got home, with May W. &

Saturday, July 1, 1887—I returned to Logan. At Ogden ordered shoe for Trudie. Found Charlie & wife living in my house for which I am glad. He has quit the R. R. service.

July 4, 1887—Spent to day at home (Lyman's) Nephi & Emma there. In the evening a big fire near to Stores, in Logan.[87]

Wednesday, July 6, 1887—Temple Work. I endowed ~~John Mears~~, Oliver Burt, I find some temple work done, while I was away, as follows:—

June 8	Nephi	endowed	John Mears
	Emma	"	Tirza Colly
June 9	Nephi	"	Oliver King
	Emma	"	Lucinda Cooley
June 10	Nephi	"	W[m] Hancock
	Emma	"	Jerusha Cooley

86 It appears Martineau is creating a special file for his "pearls"—letters and writings close to his heart.

87 See the report on the Logan fire at "Logan Fire," *Deseret News,* April 27, 1887; Utah Digital Newspapers.

Also the following work done by Sister Elizabeth Pyper Angell:—

[page 605]

July 6, 1887—June 22[d] Catherine Stevens; 23[d] Mary Haughout, 24th Mary Langton.

July 7, 1887—I endowed Oliver Collins. Sealings to day:— Oliver Burt & ~~Lucina~~ Jerusha Cooley; Oliver Collins & Lucinda Cooley, Zina D. H. Smith was proxy both times in sealing.

July 8, 1887—I endowed Peter Terry, & had him sealed to Tirza Cooley, Marg[t] W. Young, her proxy in sealing.

Saturday, July 9, 1887—Sent Pension Papers to Gelston & Co. Washington D. C. To day Lyman & Alley & kids went to S. L. City.

Sunday, July 10, 1887—Rain last night. A man in the girls bed room at 3 A.M. I could find no one. Believe it was Jesse.

Rain all day. Letter from Susan.

July 11, 1887—Sent her & girls some things from Allie. Also wrote to her.

July 12, 1887—Wrote in "Pearls." Letter from Susan.

July 13, 1887—I endowed James Mears and had his wife Elizabeth sealed to him. Letters from Tullidge and others. Rain.

July 14, 1887—I endowed Samuel Mears. Sent pay for T. O. book, $6.50 [$141] Rec[d] a letter from Annie W. Mears, my cousin, Albion. Neb.

July 15, 1887—I endowed Levi Woodsun for Sister Lufkin.

July 16, 1887—Wrote to Albert & to Susan—particular—and to J. W. Young. To day is Virginia's ~~16~~ 17th birth day. May she have very many happy ones, and much happiness in this life, and life eternal. Copied two of my poems for Sister H. A. Preston, by her request. "Bells" & "Memories."

Monday, July 18, 1887—Lyman returned from S. L. City.

Tuesday, July 19, 1887—Wrote in "Pearls." Sent a cork shoe to Trudie.

Wednesday, July 20, 1887—I endowed for "Thomas Vernon, b. 1740

Thursday, July 21, 1887—Jessie came. I sent T. O. Blank book to Pima $6.85 [$148].

Friday, July 22, 1887—I endowed John Dexter, b. 1639, Jessie G. endowed Mary Mears, B. 1699. I had sealed to day, Sam[l] Mears & Mary Mears, also John Dexter & Mrs. Sarah Dexter.

Wrote for my new recommend to temple, the old one having expired July 31st proximo.

July 25, 1887—Wrote to A. M. Cannon for renewed rec[d] for Jessie.[88]

Tuesday, July 26, 1887—I was baptized to day for Seven persons, some of them as Simone di Martino, Lippo Memmo, and Guglielmo Memmo, being born as early as 1256 to 1283. Jessie was baptized for four of my dead, and also for 84 or [of] her own dead.

[page 606]

ELIZABETH FIRST ENDOWED.

Wednesday, July 27, 1887—I endowed Samuel May. Lilla was endowed for herself. To day I sealed Samuel May, & Catherine Mears, also Tho[s] Vernon & Mary Mears, Jessie for J. Thompson.

July 28, 1887—I endowed (another) Tho[s] Vernon, Lilla, Ruth Cooley Eva, for Margaret Cooley; Jessie for Marg[t] Thompson.

I had sealed to day, Tho[s] Vernon & Mrs. Tho[s] Vernon, Oliver King & Ruth Cooley, W[m] Hancock & Marg[t] Cooley, I acted Proxy at the Altar for Edw[d] Taylor, in sealing.

Friday, July 29, 1887—Memorial service in the temple in honor of Pres[t] Taylor, who died July 25. I was one of the speakers appointed.[89]

I endowed John Mears, b. 1790, Jessie, Susanna Story Lilla, Antie Boelen, Eva, Sarah Pierce; and had Sealed John Mears & Susannah Story.

Yesterday, Jessie had her eyes anointed by Pres[t] Merrill, and was blessed by him, Br. Edlefson & myself, and her eyes (nearly blind) immediately healed, so that she removed her glasses, and could see to read well. Several others were healed of deafness in the temple. The Lord has not forgotten His promises and his people.

Monday, August 1, 1887—Election to day. I had the honor of being a witness in the marriage of Bell Harris, who was in prison so long for her former husband's sake.[90] In throwing off such a woman, he threw away a pearl, and showed himself unworthy,

Tuesday, August 2, 1887—Jessie was baptized for 308, all at one time, the greatest number ever done at any one time by one person.

Wednesday, August 3, 1887—I endowed Abraham Keteltas, Jessie, Helen Anderson

August 4, 1887—I endowed Pierce Pool, There were sealed, Abraham Keteltas & Antie Boelen, Pierce Pool & Sarah Pierce.

August 5, 1887—Eva endowed for Cornelia Haughout. Jessie went home.

Saturday, August 6, 1887—Conference to day and tomorrow, H. J. Grant present & on Sunday forenoon M. Thatcher spoke powerfully. Rec[d] directions from Bp. Preston, relative to cattle, and I wrote to our Bishops in Arizona accordingly. Nettie Thatcher gave me her Photo.

[written in margin]

Note

I fasted from Tuesday, 2, to Sat. 6th hoping for a blessing from the Lord.

[page 607]

August 8, 1887—Sent orders to the Bishops of St Joseph Stake, relative to the Church cattle. Also to Joel. Nettie Thatcher gave me her photo.[91]

August 9, 1887—To day Alley and Sister Preston came home. The baby, Royal, has been very sick, but is better. Rec[d] Trudie's shoe, again, to be fixt.

Wednesday, August 10, 1887—I endowed Stephen Martineau (over again) and had him again sealed to his wife Elenor,—an error in first sealing.

88 This is likely Abraham H. Cannon (note middle initial). Abraham H. Cannon (1859–96) was a seventy at the time of this entry and became an Apostle in 1889.

89 Thousands crowded the Salt Lake City Tabernacle for the funeral of John Taylor, but many were unable to attend. President Taylor passed away while in hiding. Apostles and other leaders of the Church were unable to attend for fear of being arrested by U.S. marshals (Leonard J. Arrington, ed., *The Presidents of the Church: Biographical Essays* [Salt Lake City: Deseret Book, 1986], 75–114).

90 This is likely Isabelle M. Harris, who married Nels Lars Nelson.

91 This could be Nettie Thatcher, wife of R. W. Sloan, daughter of George Washington Thatcher of Logan, Utah.

August 10, 1887—Letter from Tullidge—says he has given order on me to G. Q. Cannon & Co. for $100.[00] [$2,164].

Thursday, August 11, 1887—I endowed Rob[t] Mears

Friday, August 12, 1887—I endowed Lucas Covert. Had sealings—Rob[t] Mears and Elizabeth Johnson, also Lucas Covert & Cornelia Haughout. I was proxy at the altar in sealing, for W[m] Little dead and Eliza Little alive, Also W[m] Philtpot, John Allen Jr. and John Pingriff dead and Martha Ann Chandler. I began to fast this evening, hoping God will bless me.

Saturday, August 13 & 14, 1887—Still fasting.

Monday, August 15, 1887—Still fasting all day. Gave in names for baptism.

Tuesday, August 16, 1887—Ended my fast this morning, having eaten nothing since last Friday—3 days & 5 nights. I was baptized for 56 persons: and Miss Josephine Johanna Riser baptized 13 for me—may God reward her.

Wednesday, August 17, 1887—I endowed Cajeme, a great Yaqui chief, of Sonora. I was proxy at the altar in sealing, for James Lindsay dead & Agnes L. Scroggie; also for Isaac Williams, Tho[s] Bowen, & Benj. Evans, with Mary Evans Jeremy:—also William Worvill, Tho[s] Worvill, and Rob[t] Plumb, with Mrs. Harriet Worvill.

August 18, 1887—I endowed Benito Juarez, Pres[t] of Mex. (full blood indian) Mrs. Henderson for Hilena Haughout, M. H. Anderson, for Mehetabel Davenport, Hilena Haughout was sealed to me, Mrs. Jane T. Richards, Proxy.

August 19, 1887—I endowed Montezuma, Mex, Emperor, Mrs. Henderson for Mehetabel Dawes, M H Anderson for Catherine Bloomfield.

August 20, 1887—Went to Nephi's.

Sunday, August 21, 1887— Returned to Logan. Lilla, Charles & Eva returned from a week in Logan Cañon, Coming home, Eva & baby were thrown from the wagon and somewhat hurt—not seriously.

[page 608]

Tuesday, August 23, 1887—Charles was baptized for [blank] dead, Mrs. Preston went home. Susan writes that C. Layton still tries to injure me, & has called in all the tithing books to find something against me. The Lord judge.

Wednesday, August 24, 1887—I endowed Simone di Martino, born 1283, Italy, Mrs. Henderson for Jane Smith.

August 25, 1887—I endowed Canonicus, indian chief, Mrs. Henderson for Giovanna Memmo, wife of Simone di Martino. Had them sealed to day.

Friday, August 26, 1887—I endowed W[m] Maycock, Mrs Henderson for Mrs. Roswell Mears, Mrs. Morrell Benson for Mrs. Joseph Mears, Josephine J. Riser for Helen Bourne, & M. B. Kent for Louisa Day,

Saturday, August 27, 1887—Wrote all day, in my Temple Books. Charles sick to day.

Sunday, August 28, 1887—Charles sick—Cholera Morbus—administered.[92] Last evening saw Moses Thatcher and J. W. Taylor. Rec[d] letters from St George saying I can have 2[d] A for Emmeline Drake, wife of my father-in-law Joel H. Johnson, for which I rejoice much. I had applied some time previously, to Pres[t] Taylor for the privilege, which he gave conditionally, (if the other wives had rec[d] their 2[d] A.

Tuesday, August 30, 1887—To day Josephine J. Riser was baptized for 51 names for me, Among them, Lady Hester Stanhope who lived and died in Syria, at Jun, June 23. 1839, eldest child of Charles, 3[d] Earl of Stanhope, and granddaughter of Earl of Chatham & of Lord Chesterfield.[93] Jessie came today.

August 31, 1887—I endowed Aaron Cooley, Jessie Virginia Johnson, Mrs. Staines, Cora Rice, J. Farraday Henry Stanley, M R Henderson Ahunatie, C. Henderson, Magus, S. M. Benson, Cacica. All five later were sealed to me, by M. P. W. Y.

September 1, 1887—I endowed Thayendanegea (Brant) G. A. Godfrey for Benj. Withwell, F. Lundberg for Isaac Haughout; Jessie for Lady Hester Stanhope, M R Henderson for Mary Blackburn, C. Henderson for Fanny Ann Clark, S. M. Benson for Mary Martineau, Mrs. P. Staines for Jane Martineau.

I had sealed, Henry Stanley & Harriet Sprague; Benj. Withwell & Mary Ann Sprague.

September 2, 1887—I endowed Pontiac; G. A Godfrey Peter Haughout John M. Lewis for Roswell Mears,

92 *Cholera Morbus* is the era name for gastroenteritis, an inflammation of the stomach and intestines.

93 This is likely Josephine Johanna Reiser of Providence, Utah.

[page 609]

September 2, 1887—John Farraday for Jacob Johnson; Jessie for Weetamoo, M. H. Henderson for Mary Fisher; C. Henderson for Mary Wright; S. M. Benson for Patience Scott; P. M. Staines for Mrs. Hester Stanhope; M. A. Bingham for Ann Burrows; Ida Lewis for Caroline Martineau, S. E. D. Hanks Isabella Wilde, Josephine J Riser for Marie Jourdain Sealed Roswell Mears and Mrs. Roswell Mears.

September 4, 1887—D H Wells staid at Lyman's to day.

September 5, 1887—Wrote to Bp. Preston, relative to T. Office cattle, Also home. Gave in names for Baptism.

Tuesday, September 6, 1887—Was baptized for 308 of Jessie's relatives. She was baptized for four of mine and 106 of her relatives. 7th ~~Jessie retd~~

Wednesday, September ~~8~~ 7, 1887—I endowed Wamsutta, J. Faraday for Chas Stanhope (3d Earl), W. C. Lewis for Anthony Housman, G. A. Godfrey for Wm Bodine, Eva for Louise La Vallier, M. H. Henderson for Dorothy Waugh. Sealed Peter Haughout and Mrs. Peter Haughout, Isaac Haughout & Mrs. Ann Haughout, Jacob Johnson & Elizabeth Haughout, Anthony Housman & Mary Haughout. Sealed to me, Ann Burrows. Also G. M. Thompson for Mr. Holland.

September 8, 1887—Nephi endowed Joseph Mears, Eva for Elizabeth Mary Jillard, W. J. McCulloch for Mr. Cunningham,

[written in margin]

Jessie'd retd S. L. City

Jessie retd to S. L. city. Wrote home to Susan & childn. Recd. letter from Prest Woodruff, giving consent to my adoption to Joel H. Johnson which I desired, as it was agreed upon between J. H. J. and myself many years ago. Also in relation to 2 A. for Emmeline W. C. Johnson. Wrote to him in reply, asking that Sister Adaline B. A. Benson receive the ordinance for E. W. C. Johnson in place of my wife, who is in Arizona.

Friday, September 9, 1887—Recd letter from W. B. Preston, relative to cattle. I endowed Guilliaume Pierre, Nephi, Charles Martineau, Alley P. Martineau for Mary Martineau. Sealed, W. Bodine & Aletta Haughout, C. Stanhope & Mrs. Hester Stanhope, Mr. Holland & Fanny Martineau, Mr. Cunningham & Susan Martineau, Joseph Mears & Mrs. Jos Mears, G. Pierre & Marie Jourdain, Charles Martineau & E. M. Jillard.

[page 610]

ALBERT MARRIED TO EMMA ALLRED.

September 9, 1887—Wrote to J. N. Smith about cattle.

Monday, September 12, 1887—Very cold, Snow on mountains. Saw Bp. W. B. Preston & got permission to build a tithing office in Pima.

Tuesday, September 13, 1887—I was baptized for 240 for Jessie and 4 for myself. Wrote to Joel and appointed Weech and Webb to assist in trading Church cattle with Layton.

Wednesday, September 14, 1887—I endowed John Blackburn. Sealed him and his wife Elizth Blackburn. Wrote to Prest Woodruff about 2d A. for E. W. C. Johnson.

September 15, 1887—I endowed Samuel Dexter & had him sealed to Catharina Martineau.

Friday, September 16, 1887—I endowed John Martineau, and Sealed to M. Mudge. Sealed to me Mary Fisher.

Monday, September 19, 1887—Continued copying my "Pearls" for Alley.

Wednesday, September 21, 1887—I endowed Edwd Haughout and sealed him to A. Bogart Recd permission for E. W. C. J.s 2d A.

September 22, 1887—I endd J. Hilyard and had him sealed to A. Columbine. Had sealed to me Patience Scott and Mary Wright.

Friday, September 23, 1887—I endd Saml Mears, & sealed to his wife Mary C. Mears. Had sealed to me Dorothy Waugh & Mary Martineau.

Saturday, September 24, 1887—Saw W. Webb today, from Pima. He tells me Geo. Albert[94] was married on Tuesday Sept. 13. 1887, to Emma Alred.

Lyman got me a suit of clothing, shirts &c. for which Our Father will bless him, as I do.

This morning before light I had a vision:—

I was sleeping soundly, and was suddenly waked by several distinct taps like a pencil striking a table, and

94 George Albert Martineau was a son through Susan Ellen Johnson. George Albert's marriage to Emma Pauline Allred was his third marriage.

was instantly wide awake. I saw with my eyes a procession of people or spirits, walking two and two, towards a cloud on my left, wherein were some personages in authority, but veiled by the cloud so that I could not see their faces. Each person carried in his hand, elevated, something like a leafy [~~or a~~] branch or bough, seemingly as a symbol of joy or triumph, and the procession extended far away into the distance. Over their heads was a scroll on which was written "Come to me all ye weary and heavy laden, and I will give you rest."

[page 611]

September 1887—There seemed to be a thin, silvery veil between them and me, making them a little dim or not quite plain. I saw on my right, faces peering from a cloud, oh, how full of malice and hatred and wickedness, gazing at those who were walking towards the place of rest: but they were powerless to do harm, and this made them look so hideous and evil. The scene was lighted with an indescribable silvery or pale light, although it was a dark, moonless night. I saw this for quite a while. This was given for my comfort, and to teach me to whom to go for help and rest in time of trial or anxiety and care. If we go to God in the right way, in humility, repentance and faith, He will give us rest, and the spirits of evil cannot prevent. Oh, what comfort to know we have a true Friend. And oh, may I be worthy, like Abraham, to be called the Friend of God.

Monday, September 26, 1887—Letter from Susan. Albert had started for St George temple with Emma, to be sealed. He went on 14th.[95]

Tuesday, September 27, 1887—Eva was baptized for 8 persons for me.

September 28, 1887—I endowed James Mears, Sarah Burns for Mary Mears. I had sealed J. Mears & M. Davenport. I was also proxy for Sister Berry in sealing two wives to her husband. Saw W. Webb and S. Burns married. Isabella Wilde was sealed to me.

Thursday, September 29, 1887—I Endowed John Mears; W. Webb, Wm Dawes; S. B. Webb, Mercy Mears, Adaline B. A. Benson, Mary Mears. Had the following sealed:— John Mears & Mary Mears, Tho. Blake & Theodora M. Blake, Wm Dawes & Mehit^{l} Dawes, Francis Fletcher & Marriett Martineau, Tho. Martineau & Elizth Rankin, Wm Henry Blake & Louisa Day, Thos Martineau & Helen Bourne, Robt R. Martineau & Jane Smith.

[written in the margin in shaky handwriting]
2^{d} A
Sep. 29 1887

2^{D} A. [SECOND ANOINTING]

September 29, 1887—To day my father's wife, Emeline Wise Cranney Johnson, born June 1. 1815. Ohio, wife of Joel Hills Johnson was anointed to him by M. W. Merrill, Adaline Brooks Andrus Benson sitting for her.

[page 612]

September 29, 1887—I for him, Samuel Roskelly witness and recorder. How I thank Thee, Oh Father, for this privilege to me, blessing to Emmeline, and added glory to my Father-in-law Johnson. They have both passed behind the vail, they are both safe, and both have now entered into their glory as King and Priestess—Priest and Queen. Help me, my Father, also to be true to the end, that I may gain my exaltation. She died Aug. 11. 1887 Logan.

Friday, September 30, 1887—I endowed John Mears; Lyman, Thos Mears; Nephi, Cornelius Martineau; Alley, Mrs. Mary Mears; Emma, Mrs. Marg^{t} Martineau. Sealed, To J. H. M. Louise La Valliere; other sealings. Cornelius Martineau and Mrs. Marg^{t} Martineau, Thos Martineau & Mary Martineau John Mears & Mary Mears, Wm Mason & Elizth Brewer Columbine, David Jardine & Sarah Martineau, James Lee & Margaret Martineau, Edwd Foss & Catharine Martineau.

In this sealing Lyman & Alley officiated for Thos Mears & wife, Nephi & Emma for Cornelius & wife. myself & Emme for the other dead.

After temple hours, we all went through the temple.

October 1, 1887—In the morning I went to Nephi's, returning on the next day.

95 This wagon road became known as the Arizona Honeymoon Trail. Couples desiring marriage were joined by a local civil authority and later "sealed" in a temple by a religious authority. The closest temple at the time was St. George, Utah (Ricketts, *Arizona's Honeymoon Trail*).

Sunday, October 2, 1887—All the children and grandchildren assembled at Lyman's today. At dinner there were 16 besides me. A very pleasant day.

October 5, 1887—Went to S. L. City with Gene. Lyman and the 2 chil^n stopped at Bp. Preston's. Conference lasted 4 days, and Pres^t Woodruff came on the stand and spoke having been a long time hidden. Very cold weather

October 12, 1887—Had a very pleasant visit at Br. Norman's. He is 87, but is full of the Holy Spirit and the gift of prophecy. Sister Grieve and Jessie Helen were there also. Br. Norman gave me a good blessing, after which we blessed all the others, and were happy.

[page 613]

October 13, 1887—Visited J. H. Smith and had a pleasant visit. in relation to affairs in Pima, in connexion with Pres^t Layton. Russells.

October 14, 1887—Staid this evening at Bp. P's house with Jean.

October 15, 1887—Came home. Found all well.

October 16, 1887—Began fasting this evening, for 3½ days.

October 17 & 18, 1887—Writing names in my temple record—1048.

October 19, 1887—I endowed Benjamin Martineau.[68] Full temple.

October 20, 1887—I endowed Gerritt Keteltas. Wrote to Joel, Gertrude, Henry and mother (Susan). Rec^d letter from Shearman relative to business in Engineering on S.P.R.R.

While in S. L. City, the hand of the Lord was upon me for good in a remarkable manner. in two cases. the first. on the 12th when a teacher was engaged for a school: and on the same day when I received authority to do temple work for certain dead. For all these blessings, I thank our Father in heaven. On Wed. evening I finished my three and ½ days fast. I fasted that God would open the way for me to go speedily to my home & with means to pay all my debts. The testimony of the spirit came to me like this, "Be patient, for in the Lord's own time you will go in peace, and all will be well." I believe this, but it is hard to wait; may I be patient and trust in my Father who is in heaven, who doeth all things well. Jesse N. came home.

Friday, October 21, 1887—I endowed Samuel Mears & Wrote to Jessie. I was proxy at the altar, for John Buckerfield and Joseph Wallett. I had sealed Gerritt Keteltas & Catherine Stevens.

Saturday, October 22, 1887—Got additional names for baptism, among which are the Earls Chatham, Chesterfield, Bedford and Stanhope, all related to my father by marriage, Also five Popes of Rome, my ancestors, viz:—Martinus 1st, 2^d, 3^d, 4th & 5. the first being born in the year 600. Also St Martin, who was born about 316 Died 400. Also an ancestor, Martina, a young girl, a martyr, killed in 235 for her christianity.

[page 614]

October 23, 1887—Lyman's baby, Royal, begins walking to day, for himself.

Monday, October 24, 1887—Still very cold weather. Rec^d letter (farewell) from Jes Charles and Nephi start for Star valley, Wyoming Ter.

October 25, 1887—Snowing this morning. I was baptized for 36 and Mary T. Richards for 9 of my relations, including Martina. I felt happy in having this privilege to help the dead. my friend departed to day.

Wednesday, October 26, 1887—I endowed Samuel Guild, Lilla, Martina.

October 27, 1887—I endowed James Pool. Had sealed to me, Mercy Mears and Martina; also sealed the dead:—Samuel Guild and Sarah Mears; also James Pool & Mary Langdon. Wrote to D. P. Anderson;—told him I had been baptized for his dead—543. Wrote to Sixtus Johnson:—told him of my work for his father's wife Emeline W. Cranny Johnson. Yesterday wrote to my friend, who started from Ogden on Tues. the 25th having heard from the day before.

Friday, October 28, 1887—Wrote to Susan. Last eve saw M. T. on eve of departure and told him he should not be molested. This I felt to say by the spirit of prophecy, and may our Father grant it. Bought a fountain pen. I endowed Leffert Haughout, and sealed to his wife Mary Haughout. Rec^d letter from Pres^t Woodruff, with permission to do temple Work for some of the early martyrs.

Saturday, October 29, 1887—A dull day for me—nothing much to do.

Sunday, October 30, 1887—Dined at G. W. Thatcher's with Lyman's and Preston's families.

Tuesday, November 1, 1887—Was baptized today for 17 persons, for some sisters who needed male help, and was glad to help so many more of the dead. Sister Eliz[th] Russell Hamblin was baptized for five persons for me, martyrs of the 3[d] century in Rome. Yesterday I wrote to Jessie. Also to W. Woodruff, in regard to the five martyrs, I desire them as wives.

Wednesday, November 2, 1887—I endowed Judge Crittenden.

November 3, 1887—I endowed Peter Haughout, and had him sealed to his wife Cornelia. Also had sealed two indians, a chief and his wife, who lived some 200 years ago in Mass.[s] Wamsutta & Weetamoo. I believe they are the first dead Lamanites endowed and sealed in this dispensation.

[page 615]

November 3, 1887—I feel honored in doing this work for the dead, of the house of Lehi. and I greatly desire to do much more.

Also sealed Judge Crittenden & Eunice Sprague. Rec[d] a letter from Vallejo, Cal. Nephi and Charles returned from their trip to Star Valley. Wyoming. Rec[d] letter from Susan. Joel & one from my son Neils, from Sweeden. Spent the afternoon and evening at Moses Thatcher's, with Lyman's folks, and Sister W. B. Preston, also Langton's and Jeppeson's families. A pleasant time.

Friday, November 4, 1887—I endowed Tho[s] Michael Greenhow. We all went to H. E. Hatch's and spent the afternoon and evening.

Saturday, November 5, 1887—Sister Preston and Grandma Thatcher went home to day.

Sunday, November 6, 1887—Wrote to Susan and Vallejo. Rec[d] letter from A. M. Montirth.

November 7, 1887—Also wrote to Annie S. Mears, of Albion. Neb. and to Nettie and Lois. After noon, went to Nephi's.

Tuesday, November 8, 1887—Lyman, Bassett and others on U. G.

Wednesday, November 9, 1887—I endowed John Martineau, Marg[t] A. Kent, Rufina M. and Sariah Moffett, Secunda [E.]

Thursday, November 10, 1887—I endowed James Lee; Nephi. J. Alison. S. Moffett. Denisa [R]; Mrs. Thomassen, Apollonia [R] Emma, Julia [S]. These five were christian, virgin martyrs, slain ~~from~~ in 238, ~~to~~ 250, 257, 257, & 457. They were sealed to me by authority of Pres[t] Woodruff. I also had sealed:—

John Martineau Lyon and Caroline Martineau
Tho[s] Michael Greenhow and Elizabeth Martineau
James Lee and Sarah Martineau
John Martineau and Jane Taylor———

Monday, November 14, 1887—Borrowed $500.[00] [$10,820] of Logan Bank at 1 o/c pr mo. Lyman sec[ty]

Tuesday, November 15, 1887—Went to S. L. City, Charles went also, to work in D&R.G. shops

November 16, 1887—Returned, having visited Eliza, Prestons and others in S. L. city.

November 17, 1887—Got things for Susan and children.

November 18, 1887—A family meeting to day—sad to me. In the evening I gave Alley a patriarchal blessing, by her request, which is on record in my "Temple record."

Saturday, November 19, 1887—Left Logan, with Lyman at 4 A.M. parting from him at Ogden. I took C. P. fast train at 8:30 A.M. I secured a ½ 1st class rate to Deming for $37.50 [$812], as a clergyman, by virtue of my certificate as such, and an appointment as missionary in Arizona, New Mexico and Old Mexico.

[page 616]

LEAVE LOGAN FOR PIMA.

November 19, 1887—While I have been in Logan, my children have done all they could for my comfort, and on coming away, they sent many things for Susan and the children, for which may God forever bless and prosper them.

The last nine or ten months have been important to me in many ways. In the temple, I have had baptisms for about 600 men, and for about as many women: have procured Endowment and sealing for nearly 200 Souls; have had 36 wives (dead) sealed to me & endowed; and obtained the 2[d] A. for two of them—one living and one dead—an indian girl—the first Lamanite who rec[d] that holy ordinance in this dispensation—Nellie Benson. I also procured the 2[d] A. for a wife we sealed to father Joel H. Johnson—Emmeline Wire Cranney Johnson—. The Lord also blessed me in the gift of a companion, who received the 2[d] A. mentioned above. I spent much time searching after truth, gleaning from many church publications precious truths—keys of intelligence—which I compiled into a book which I named "Pearls." This I copied for Nephi, also for Alley. In attending to all these, and my temple duties, I worked almost without intermission, day and night, and so accomplished a great work, for which all praise be to our Father for His goodness and blessing. I spent no time in traveling around, never going to any other town, although often invited to do so. In the Temple Pres[t] M. W. Merrill told me I had done a mighty work—none excelling me.

I dined at Terrace, supped at Elko, and there telegraphed to Jessie, to meet me at Sacramento tomorrow afternoon.

Sunday, November 20, 1887—Breakfast at Reno. Arrived Sacramento 3.20 P.M. No Jessie. Took room at Western Hotel, and waited there all next day.

Tuesday, November 22 & 23, 1887—Telegraphed J. Started for Vallejo & arr[d] 6.30 P.M. Found Mrs. Lizzie Russell, Jessie's aunt, but Jessie was absent in San F. since the last ten days. Next day telegraphed for Calmer's address in San F. Visited the Mare Island Navy Yard, and saw the French ship-of-war "Duchesne," armored with huge steel breech-loading guns, and Gattings, and 600 crew.

[page 617]

November 24, 1887—Wrote to Mrs. Grieve, and telegraphed by Mrs. Russell in answer to mine. Spent the evening at Mrs. Russell's, who was once a L.D.S.

November 25, 1887—Went to San F. this morning at 8.10 reaching there at 9.45. Put up at American Exchange. Immediately started out to find Calmer's friend, at Elgin Park, and did so, but no Jessie to be heard of, as she has not been there. Where, in this great and wicked city, is she? No one can tell my agony of mind when I went to bed—and only when I cried unto the Lord—"thy will, not mine, be done"—only then did peace come to me, and my agony assuage.

November 26, 1887—Hunted the streets and cars all day—unsuccessfully—and at 3.30 P.M. started on my homeward way, feeling that I was leaving hope behind—some one who might become a prey to wolves—worse than dead. Oh Father preserve and shield her from evil.

November 27, 1887—At 6 A.M. this morning, I was awakened by a violent shock, and found we had collided with another train, ascending the mountains near Caliente. Our engine—the front one—was used up, the tender smashing entirely through the next car, and several of them being splintered into small kindling wood. It was a miracle our sleeper was not thrown off the high trestle on which we stopped; had we fallen, many must have been killed, and burned alive. For this deliverance I thank thee, my Father. We were detained half a day, arriving at Los Angeles at 2 A.M. (the 28th)

November 28, 1887—At 9.15 A.M. Started again for Pima. Arrived at Colton 11.45 and stopped off to try for employment on the S.P.R.R., having had some encouragement. Found there is no opening for me. All right.

Tuesday, November 29, 1887—Took train at noon: dined at Indio, Supped at Yuma 7 P.M.

Wednesday, November 30, 1887—Tucson at 5.0 A.M. Benson 7.00, Wilcox 8.30 & Bowie 9.15 A.M. Took room in R.R. Hotel, waiting for conveyance home.

Friday, December 2, 1887—Started home in stage, as my team did not come. Met Joel about 18 miles coming for me. Reached home at 6 P.M. in a cold rain storm, and found all well as usual. No place like home.

Sunday, December 4, 1887—Meeting in Pima, and spoke. People glad to see me.

December 5, 1887—Visited some today.

Tuesday, December 6, 1887—Saw B. Young to day. He went to St John, Albert went with him.

[page 618]

December 11, 1887—Wrote to Alley and Lyman. Cold and windy.

December 12, 1887—Went to Solomonville, surveying. Surveyed, also next day

December 14, 1887—Rain all day—did not work

Friday, December 16, 1887—Paid $30.15 [$652] taxes. Returned home next day—Saturday 17th

December 18, 1887—Meeting in Pima. Bp. Seavy of Juarez, Mex. spoke. Wrote to J and to Nephi.

December 19, 1887—Went again to Solomonville, surveying.

Wednesday, December 21, 1887—Finished the Canal, and farm land surveys. Came home. Weather very cold, with Snow enough to whiten the ground.

Thursday, December 22, 1887—Attended Y.M.M.I. Conference in Pima.[96]

December 23, 1887—Attended F. Relief Conference in Central

Saturday, December 24, 1887—Quarterly Conference to day and next. Good meetings. Albert and Joel were voted to be home missionaries for stake.

December 26, 1887—Worked on my county survey maps.

December 27 to 29, 1887—Surveyed for A. Baker 500 acres. Letter from Alley.

Friday, December 30, 1887—Worked on my plats. Elvira and her four children came from Mesa. Have not seen her for 13 years before.

December 31, 1887—Priesthood meeting in Thatcher. Had settlement of some difficulty with Pres[t] Layton.

January 1, 1888—Sunday meeting. Also had a family gathering, 24 present.

January 2, 1888—Surveyed. Letter from Jessie Helen, from Oakland. Cal.

January 3, 1888—Went to Solomonvill to sell my plats to the county.

January 4, 1888—Sold them—31—for $155.[00] [$3,354] Co. warrants & returned home.

Sunday, January 8, 1888—Today Susan and I have been married 36 years. From 2 my family, with grand children and sons wives = 60: viz:—21, children; 27 Gr. children, with 100 wives, living or dead. Truly has God blessed me most bountifully.

Monday, January 9, 1888—Had our annual wedding dinner, and a full house.

January 10, 1888—Surveyed for O. Elmer. Cold and windy.

January 11, 1888—Surveyed canal for Jerry Taylor & others.

Thursday, January 12, 1888—Made out deeds for Baker.

January 13, 1888—Wrote to Nephi to come and visit us soon.

January 16, 1888—Letter from W. B. P. Next day Sent resignation as Bps. Agt.

January 17, 1888—Began the mason work for T. Office in Pima.

January 21, 1888—Sent to Gurley for Mex. Vara chain, also for paper at Boston worked on my plans for the tithing office.

[page 619]

January 24, 1888—Went to Fort Thomas, surveying; returned 26th

Sunday, January 29, 1888—This evening Ada Johnson, Susan's niece, was married to Tom East, by Pres[t] W. D. Johnson. I fear, a very poor match.

January 30, 1888—Went to Safford, surveying.

January 31, 1888—Sent $150.[00] [$3,246] Cash to G. T. O. and next day $100.[00] [$2,164] more

February 1 ~~&2~~, 1888—Went to Thatcher, to settle tithing, Returned 3[d] Gave to Pres[t] C. Layton my Defense fund Book, together with $145.[10] [$3,240] in full settlement. Check for 108.50 [$2,348], cash $36.60 [$792]. Susan very sick, with sinking spells.

February 4, 1888—Surveyed Pima Canal. Was subpoenaed to go to Tucson as witness in trial, Voelkel vs Mrs. Collins.

February 5, 1888—Wrote to Jessie. Meeting in Pima.

February 6, 1888—Surveyed new Canal, at Pima.

February 7, 1888—Started to Tucson, as witness in Mrs. Collins' land trial. By stage to Bowie, reached Tucson 2 A.M. 110[m] from Bowie.

February 15, 1888—Finished my business as witness and started home 5 P.M. Stopped at Benson, and next day went to St David, to settle tithing.

February 17, 1888—Finished at St David, went to Benson, took train & reached Bowie 11 P.M.

February 18, 1888—Home again, and glad. Have still a very bad cold.

February 20, 1888—Went and settled tithing at Curtis and Graham.

February 21, 1888—At Layton, same business. Home next day.

February 23, 1888—Went to Solomonville to survey a canal. Home next day.

March 3, 1888—Rec[d] letter from John W. Young, Washington. Wishes me to go to Gila Bend and examine as to location &c for a big dam and canal. In order to telegraph to him, had to go to Fort Thomas.

March 4, 1888—Finished my Tithing Reports today.

96 Joel H. Martineau, "Young Men's Conference," *Deseret News*, January 1, 1888; Utah Digital Newspapers.

March 5, 1888—Surveyed for L. Voelkel and returned next day.

March 10, 1888—Went to Safford to settle with Bp. Merrill

March 11, 1888—Attended funeral of little Coz. Damie Carlton. Charlie & family and Virginia moved to S. L. City to day.

Thursday, March 13, 1888—I am 60 years old today. Had a family dinner.

March 16, 1888—Susan taken very sick, from night exposure at Mathews.

March 17, 1888—Letters from Lyman and Lilla. Ans[d] next day.

Sunday, March 25, 1888—To day I drop my calling as Pres[ts] counsellor, having resigned on the 15th inst. to remove into Mexico. I rec[d] permission from Pres[t] Taylor to do so in March 1887. I have always felt out of place, and as if not wanted by Br. Layton.

[page 620]

April 1, 1888—Relinquished my entry of land at St. David. Also wrote to Br. Seth Johnson, to Jesse, and others. About this time finished my Tithing reports.

April 5 to 7, 1888—Surveyed at Solomonville. Got home and found Dora sick. Gertrude was also taken quite sick with fever. In evening she was administered to, and healed: Dora also. Letters from Lilla and Gean.

Sunday, April 8, 1888—Not feeling well myself.

April 10, 1888—Unable to sit up, with lame back.

April 16, 1888—Up to this date, I have been confined to house, but better now. Rec[d] choice roses and other plants from the east and set them out. Rec[d] letter from S. E. Johnson, Juarez Mex.; gives good report of things.

April 19, 1888—Sent part of my Tithing report to Bp. Preston, also letter to him.

April 24, 1888—Took my tithing reports to Pres[t] Layton for his examination & signature, but he did not take time to attend to it. This is now the fourth time I have gone to Thatcher to see him for that business. It seems to me he delays on purpose to bring me into disrepute with the general authorities.

May 2, 1888—Bought a new Wood Mower $90.[00] [$1,948].

May 3, 1888—Began cutting our Lucern hay. Quite lame in my back.

May 9, 1888—Delivered tithing keys and books to Bp. J. Taylor. Good riddance.

Sunday, May 13, 1888—My Brother in law, David C. Lyon died in St. Paul. Min.

May 15, 1888—Rec[d] 2 no[s] of Western Galaxy from E. W. Tullidge, with request to write for the magazine.

May 16, 1888—Wrote article for Galaxy, "Visit to Sonora, Mexico."

May 21, 1888—Rec[d] blank deed to fill out, for sale of my house and lot in Logan, $3000.[00] [$64,921].

May 22, 1888—Got the deed acknowledged and returned it on 24th

May 25, 1888—Narrowly escaped a bite from a "Gila Monster" while surveying today. It is more fatal than a rattlesnake. It is a kind of lizard.

June 1, 1888—Bought a carriage of C. Layton today, $175.[00] [$3,787] Sold one to him about a month ago, for $180.[00] [$3,895] Again tried to get him to examine the Tithing & church papers.

June 5, 1888—Sold my plow (Sulky) and binder, $150.[00] [$3,246].

Since my return from Utah I have had much surveying to do, for gentiles, mostly, which has brought me several hundred dollars, so I have not needed to draw any of that resulting from Sale of the old home.

Again took my church papers to turn them to Layton, but he had no time to attend to them.

[page 621]

June 8, 1888—I turned over 27 head of stock to C. Layton, per Albret [Albert].

June 25, 1888—Bp. W. B. Preston came to Pima. Appointed to meet tomorrow.

June 26, 1888—He examined my Tithing reports for 1887 and found them all right.

Wednesday, June 27, 1888—Examined my personal account, and accepted it. I turned G. T. Office orders &c to him, also delivered some stock by his verbal order. Dined with us. He Left next day. He said we could change Susan's cows from Kanab to Pima

July 8, 1888—Settled tithing business (stock a/c) with Crockett and Albert, and finished up all my tithing business. Thankful. Bp. John Taylor, of Pima, having unjustly withheld from me water in the Canal

Co. to am't of $42.00 [$909] which I had bought and paid for last year. I thought best not to contend about it, but my garden and trees are dying for want of the water.

July 11, 1888—Susan's Birth day. Had a family dinner & house full. May she have many more such anniversaries. I let Henry have H. Blair's note (due me) for $33.70 [$729], he to pay me when he can.

At our family party today Patriarch Wm McBride & wife were present, and in the afternoon gave the following blessings, which I took down as clerk:—

Susan's Blessing:

Sister Susan, in the name of the Lord Jesus I place my hands upon thy head and by the authority of the holy priesthood I seal upon you a patriarchal blessing, and I say unto thee, dear Susan, lift up thy head and rejoice, for thy name is recorded in the Lamb's Book of Life never to be blotted out, for the Lord is well pleased with thee, and thy sins are forgiven. For thou has had many troubles, trials, and afflictions; but they have been brought upon thee for thy exaltation and glory, and for thine own faith thou shalt be exalted very high, & thou shalt preside over queens: for thou art of the leading blood of Israel, of the lineage of Ephraim: but thy lineage is so closely connected with that of Manasseh that it cannot be separated, for they cannot be made perfect without thee, neither canst thou be made perfect without them.

[page 622]

July 11, 1888—The Lord will grant thee life, health and Strength, wisdom and understanding. For thou shalt begin to have joy and pleasure in thy last days: for thy last days shall be thy best days: for thou shalt live to see knowledge cover the earth, and see thy household redeemed: and all things shall appear before thee for thy honor and thy glory and thou shalt extend blessings to thy household, and to thy friends and to thy Relatives, and to thy Father's house in general. Thou shalt be blessed with wisdom and understanding that none shall excel: and in connexion with thy companion, thou shalt fulfill thy mission upon the earth, both for the living and for the dead, and receive an exaltation, inheritance and crown of eternal lives, and thy part in the morning of the first ressurrection, with all that are near and dear unto thee: and I seal and confirm upon thee all thy former blessings, in the name of Jesus. Amen.

George Albert's Blessing:—

Brother George Albert, in the name of the Lord Jesus and by Authority of the holy priesthood I lay my hands upon thy head and I seal upon thee a patriarchal blessing: and I say unto thee, be thou faithful unto the end of thy days; for thou wast called, chosen and set apart to bear thy part in the redemption of Zion, and the bringing about the restoration of the House of Israel, and to lay the foundation for the Salvation and exaltation of thy father's house for many generations back: for thou art of the holy priesthood after order of Enoch: for thy lineage is in Ephraim, who is the firstborn of Israel, holding the keys of the blessings of the gospel in every land: and thou shalt be a mighty instrument in the hands of the Almighty in restoring peace to the earth and turning the government into the hands of the just; for unto this end wast thou born, and in performing this great work thou shalt travel much for the gospel's sake, and bringing the Sons and daughters of Jacob from their long dispersion, which the Lord made known to them by their forefathers, and the land shall be blessed for their sake. Thou shalt assist them in building temples, and shalt administer ordinances unto them therein that will produce their salvation: and thou shalt teach them how to be saved, and how to save themselves for many generations back, both for the living and the dead.

[page 623]

And by obedience to the new and everlasting covenant thou shalt secure unto thyself and unto thy wives and children, friends and relatives, an everlasting inheritance and crowns of eternal lives, with all that are near and dear unto thee: for I seal these words upon thee in the name of Jesus. Amen.

Anna Sariah's Blessing:—

Sister Anna Sariah, in the name of the Lord Jesus I lay my hands upon thy head, and by virtue and authority of the Holy Priesthood I seal upon thee a patriarchal blessing: and I say unto thee, honor thy father and thy mother, and thy days shall be many upon the earth; and if they wilt give heed unto this blessing it shall be a comfort unto thee in time and a guide unto thee through thy future life. For thou art of the house of Jacob through the loins of Ephraim: and thou shalt be a blessing and a comfort to thy father's house, and shall be an instrument in the hands of the Lord in doing much for their Salvation and exaltation: And thou shalt be a blessing to the daughters of Jacob, for thou shalt become a teacher and a counsellor unto them, and shall administer ordinances in the temple of the Lord that shall be the means of their salvation and exaltation: and thou shalt administer ordinances in languages that thou dost not now understand and teach them to save themselves with their dead for many generations back: and when thou shalt commence this work, the Lord will give thee dreams and visions and manifestations of his holy spirit: and thou shalt learn to read the whisperings of the still small voice that shall make known unto thee the mind and will of the Father; and will teach thee how to choose a true and faithful companion that will assist thee in thy mission upon the earth and make thy journey through life easy and comfortable: and thou shalt labor upon the foundation that has already been laid for the salvation and exaltation of thy father's house for many generations back; for thy children shall be as numerous as the sands upon the sea shore and thou shalt be blessed in thy labors from this time forth with health and strength: and the blessings of the heavens shall be thine and the blessings of the earth shall not be withheld from thee; for I seal this upon thee with all that is near and dear unto thee, in the name of Jesus. Amen.

[page 624]
July 11, 1888—

Joel H's Blessing:—

Br. Joel, in the name of the Lord Jesus Christ I lay my hands upon thy head and by virtue and authority of the holy priesthood I seal upon thee a patriarchal blessing: for thou was called, chosen, ordained and set apart before the foundations of this earth were laid, and did there covenant and agree that thou wouldst come forth in the dispensation in which we now live, and bear thy part in the redemption of Zion, and the restoration of the House of Israel: for thou art of the lineage of the house of Israel through the loins of Ephraim: and this was all recorded in the heavens and in the law before thou left the eternal worlds. I say unto thee that thou shalt fill thy mission with honor to thy Father in heaven and to thy father on earth, and to thy exaltation. And in so doing the Lord will bless thee with every blessing that is necessary to thy exaltation, and will give thee wives and children to suit thy circumstances. And thou shalt become an instrument in the hands of the Lord in doing much for the redemption of thy father's house: and shall build upon the foundations already laid for their salvation and exaltation. For thou shalt have wisdom and understanding in all thy movements: and thy brethren shall seek unto thee for counsel: and through obedience to thy counsel they shall be exalted: for the Lord will give thee mighty wisdom in the counsels thou shalt bear to the house of Israel. For thou shalt become a savior on Mt. Zion, and thou shalt judge the house of Esau; and they will acknowledge thy kingdom to be the Lord's: And thou shalt hunt up Israel from the ends of the Earth and bring them to the Zion of the last days; And among the house of Israel thou shalt be called the Wonderful Counsellor: and thy heart shall be filled with wisdom and thy tongue shall be loosed; and thou shalt speak with understanding and to the comfort of all the subjects of Israel.

[page 625]
July 11, 1888—And thy faith shall increase, and thou shalt have power over all evil spirits; and by obedience to the Everlasting covenant thou shalt receive an everlasting inheritance for thyself, thy children and friends, and be crowned with eternal lives, and come forth in the morning of the first ressurrection and receive thy exaltation: for I seal these words upon thee with all thy former blessings and ordinations, in the name of Jesus. Amen.

Theodore's Blessing:—

Brother Theodore, in the name of the Lord Jesus I put my hands upon thy head and by the authority of the holy priesthood I seal upon thee a patriarchal blessing. I say unto thee, be thou faithful and true, and the spirit of the gospel shall follow thee in all thy ups and downs in life. I say unto thee, prepare thyself, for thou hast a mighty mission given unto thee on Earth; for thy calling is to labor for Zion; and for the restoration of the house of Israel and to carry the gospel to those that sit in darkness. For thy lineage is of the house of

Israel, through the loins of Ephraim. And to perform this work thou wilt have to travel much for the Gospel's sake, from land to land and from Sea to sea, and bring them in from their long dispersion to their own land that has been bequeathed to them by their fathers of old; And I say unto thee, prepare thyself, for thou shalt have many difficulties to pass through. Thou shalt see thy fellow man fall upon thy right and upon thy left. Pestilence and famine shall stalk through the land, and thou shalt see great distress among the nations; but through faith thy life shall be preserved. Thou shalt gather in the house of Israel, and the Angel of the Lord shall go before thee: and when it is necessary he will give thee power over the elements. Evil spirits shall flee from before thee, and thou shalt cause springs to break forth from the desert if it be necessary to quench the thirst of the house of Israel; and rivers shall be turned out of their courses an [and] will lead them over dry shod. For the Lord will give thee a faithful companion that ~~will~~ shall labor with thee for the salvation of the living and the dead, and bring about the salvation and redemption of thy father's house; and their exaltation for many generations back.

[page 626]

July 11, 1888—For thou shalt administer ordinances for them in the temple in the order of the holy priesthood, through blood of Ephraim who is appointed to preside, and a king upon the earth in the latter days. And thy posterity shall be numerous, and thou shalt be blessed above thy fellow men. For thou wilt be true, because thou art faithful, and angels shall meet with thee and converse with thee, and tell thee what to do: for I seal these words upon thee in the name of Jesus. Amen.

Dora's Blessing:—

Sister Dora in the name of the Lord Jesus I lay my hands upon thy head and by authority of the holy priesthood I seal upon thee a father's blessing which is after the patriarchal order. And I say unto thee, thou art of the loins and blood of Ephraim. And be faithful and true to thy father and mother and learn to honor them. For the Lord will hold them accountable for all that they may teach thee in relation to the Gospel in preparing thy mind to receive the same, until thy mind shall become matured, and then the Lord will begin to hold thee accountable for thyself. I seal upon thee the blessing of life, of health and of strength, that thou mayest be able to enjoy life while thou hast the privilege of sojourning here upon the earth. I seal upon thee knowledge, that thou mayest know how to take care of thy body, that thy life may be prolonged and preserved. For there is much for thee to do in bringing about the restoration of the daughters of Jacob in teaching them the gospel of life and salvation, in administering the ordinances that will produce it. And in this labor thou shalt be blessed and strengthened in body and mind: for thou art of the blood of the house of Ephraim, who is the first born, according to the priesthood which belongeth to thee according to thy sex. Thou shalt do much in blessing and comforting thy father's house, in bringing about the salvation and exaltation of the same. For God will give thee wisdom and understanding in all things pertaining to thy mission: for I seal these words upon thee, and leave room for a greater blessing to follow, in the name of Jesus. Amen.

[page 627]

START TO VISIT MEXICO WITH JOEL

Thursday, July 12, 1888—Today Joel and I started to Mexico, to look for a place in which to settle my family. We drove 10 miles and camped. Next day we drove 30 miles, having a heavy thunderstorm in the afternoon. We reached the S.P.R.R. next evening, and were in a tremendous storm which beat into the wagon, and wet our bed and things. Going east along the railroad track, we passed Stein's Pass at noon, & camped within 8 m. of Lordsburg. We passed through Lordsburg on the 16th where we got some spoons, bread &c On the 17th we passed Sopar, where we bought water from a well 750 ft deep. We passed Gage next day, and reached Deming, 170^{m} from Pima, on the 18th Here I spent about 20$ [$433] for provisions, ammunition, skillet, & and other things.

July 18, 1888—I here met Br. Eaton and traded my horse Bob to him for a mule, as horses have to pay 40$ [$866] duty entering Mexico. Camped 12^{m} from Deming. Up to this time we have had storms almost every day. At Deming I got a pass from the Custom House officer to enable me to return free of duty.

July 19, 1888—Tonight we camped on Mexican Soil, and next day, 20th, got to Boca Grande at 10 A.M. and arrived opposite Diaz at noon of Saturday, 21st

Saturday, July 21, 1888—Called to see Coz. W. D. Johnson, then went on to La Ascencion, where is the Mex. Custom House. but did not get all papers fixed, so had to return to Diaz.

July 22, 1888—At meeting spoke, and felt well, and as if in presence of a Select company of Saints.

July 23, 1888—Finished at the custom house. I had to pay $34.00 [$736] for my wagon and harness, as duty, and for my papers. Today Br. M. Thatcher passed Ascencion, returning to Utah.

July 24, 1888—Attended celebration dance this evening. Br. Thatcher & others spoke eloquently. O. F. Whitney and ladies were also there.[97] Felt a slight earthquake this morning. To day my animals strayed away, not being hobbled. Rains heavily, every day.

July 25, 1888—This afternoon the Administrador, Plutarcho Enriquez, with other Mexican gentlemen, came and remained till late, then staid all night, on account of the storm. We had a very pleasant time, and a good feeling prevailed. All the Mexicans wrote in Spanish, sentiments in Br. Thatcher's album.

July 26, 1888—Today Brs. Thatcher and Whitney, with their ladies, returned to Utah. Have hunted my team, unsuccessfully.

[page 628]

IN MEXICO

July 30, 1888—Up to this time we have had heavy daily rains, and have sought for my team, but without avail. To day Coz. David Wilson & family came.[98]

August 1, 1888—Sent letter to Susan. Cannot find my horses. Must buy a team.

Sunday, August 5, 1888—This evening we started south at 5.30 P.M. having bought a team of A. Peterson for $300.00 [$6,492] on credit (to be paid in 10 cows and calves).

August 6, 1888—Obtained pass to south, at La Ascencion. Passed the inner, or State guards at noon, at "Ojo del Paraje." Reached Casas Grande river at evening & camped.

August 7, 1888—Passed Coralitios in forenoon. Casas Grande 5 P.M. and reached Juarez 9 P.M. = 46m Distance from Diaz 70 m. and from home 340m. Stopped with my brother Sixtus E. Johnson. Glad.

August 8, 1888—Wrote home to day, & looked round next day seeing what is best to do, &c also the 10th

August 11, 1888—Started for Corallis. Saw some antelope on the San Diego Ranch. Camped high up in the Sierra Madre, in the "Park," & among pines.

Sunday, August 12, 1888—Reached Lower Corallis, or Cave Vally, and saw mill, at noon. Visited the ancient caves. An Olla 11 ft high 15 ft diameter.

August 13, 1888—Went 7m to Corallis, and stopped with J. N. Smith Jun, A lovely place miles of green grass, flowers and pines. Cool atmosphere, cold night. An altitude of about 6800 feet—almost on the Summit of Sierra Madre. I felt a spirit of freedom and liberty here—more than in the vallies below. I felt this to be a refuge for Liberty, whence she should never be driven, and embody my feelings, in a limited degree, in the following lines, addressed to Sierra Madre—the "Mother Mountain."

LINES TO THE SIERRA MADRE MOUNTAINS.

I am here, in thy heart, oh "Mother of
Mountains."
I am tired and weary—oh here let me rest!
Let me lave my hot brow in thy cool sparkling
fountains,
And rest my worn head on thy motherly breast!

2

I have fled from a land full of sorrow and
sadness:—
From a land filled with turmoil, disunion and
strife;
Where the leaders of men seem stricken with
madness
And where Anarchy threatens fair Liberty's life.

---

97 Orson F. Whitney (1855–1931) was the traveling companion of Elder Moses Thatcher. Whitney became an Apostle in 1903 and served until his death in 1931.

98 Several families were headed by a David Wilson living in the Díaz, Dublán, and Juárez colonies of Mexico (Turley and Turley, *History of the Mormon Colonies in Mexico*, 59, 289).

[page 629]

August, 1888—

3

Oh Madre! be thou unto Freedom a haven!—
A strong place of refuge no foe dare assail!
Whence Liberty fair shall never be driven,
Nor longer her children's misfortunes bewail!

4

May thy crags give defiance—each gorge be a fortress—
Each valley a stronghold that none may invade:
Thy foe's boasted power be turned into weakness!—
Be scattered their legions, and broken each blade!

5

Oh Madre! as children we seek thy protection!
Oh be thou our refuge!—we cling to thy breast!
And while the world rages and seeks our destruction
'Mid thy vallies and peaks—'mid thy clouds will we rest.

Bought a house & 2 lots in Juarez of F. Spencer for $210.00 (Mexican).

August 15, 1888—Start home this morning, having spent yesterday in looking around. Reach Juarez at 9 P.M. in a heavy rain. Distance 33 miles, and the road over the mountains very rocky, and steep in places.

August 16, 1888—Recd a letter from Susan, start home next day, the [17th]

August 17, 1888—after buying a house and lot of Br. F. Spencer for $210.00

August 20, 1888—Arrive at Ascension about noon. Applied for papers to re-enter Mexico 3 mo. from date.

August 21, 1888—Passed through Diaz, and reached Deming on 24th

August 24, 1888—Traded my team with J. Eaton for a pair of mules. Had 2 heavy storms, lately, and once I nearly had my left hand shot off, while taking my gun from the wagon. A spirit whispered me to change the position of my hand, and the gun discharged the next instant, burning my wrist and shirt cuffs. Reached home Wed. Aug. 29th having been absent just 7 ~~months~~ weeks & traveled 750m Heavy rain at home.

Wednesday, August 29, 1888—I made application, directed to Henry Eyring[99] 1a Calle De Soto no. 2 City of Mexico, for papers as Colonists, for myself, Joel, and Moroni, and asked for ~~exp~~ exemption from Custom house duties for the following articles:—

[page 630]

August 29, 1888—For myself: 2 wagons, with covers, harness for 4 animals, 1 stove, furniture and pipe, 1 table, 1 stand, 4 chairs. 1 Cabinet organ, 1 Iron bedstead, bedding for family, 1 spring mattress, ~~for fc~~ 1 saddle, 2 mirrors, Books and instruments, map paper and d. instruments, Scales, food. (100 kilos flour 25 k. bacon) arms and ammunition.

For Joe [Joel]

2 wagons & 2 setts harness & 2 wagon covers, 100 k. flour, 25 k. bacon, 2 plows, shovels & tools. 1 mower, & Ag. implements, 2 chairs, Box of books & photos in frames, Arms and Ammunition. China & glassware, 4 silver ware, knives, forks & spoons.

For Moroni.

1 wagon, cover, 2 s. harness, 1 stove & furniture & pipe, household furniture, Ag. implements & tools, bedding 100 k. flour 25 k, bacon, Books, Saddle, Lamp & oil, arms and ammunition.

September 2, 1888—Have been busy at my correspondence. I wrote to Lilla, Jesse (who is called to a mission in Germany), Mrs. S. J. Russell, H. Eyring, Mexico, and others.

September 5 & 6, 1888—To day Dora is 6 years old. She had a little party. I went to Solomonville and prepared my pension papers, which I sent off to Washington. I hope my pension may be granted.

September 6, 1888—I find in Webster's Unabd Dictionary, the following in reference to my family name:—Martineau—:

In Latin, Martinus, male, Martina, female
In Italian, Martino, also Martini (plural)
In Spanish, Martino, ~~also derivative Martinez~~
In French, Martineau, sometimes Martin
In Portuguese, Martinho

99 At this writing Henry Eyring was the Mexico City Mission president. He was released in December 1888 and returned to Colonia Juárez (Tullis, *Mormons in Mexico*, 70).

In German, Martin

In English, Martin

This is important, as an aid in tracing our genealogy.

September 11 & 12, 1888—Rec[d] letter from F. Gunnell offering to sell me 500$ [$10,820] stock in the Juarez (Mex.) Sawmill Co, which I directed on that Lyman should pay him for from my funds.

[page 631—see Appendix 3 for note on pension and grandparents inserted here.]

September 15, 1888—Had an interview with Apostle J. H. Smith and Bp. R. T. Burton, relative to false accusations made against me by Pres[t] C. Layton. After meeting (Quar. Conf.) in the afternoon met with the High Council

Sunday, September 16, 1888—Was rebaptized this evening & confirmed next morning by Apostle Smith and R. Burton, having confirmed upon me all former blessings, gifts, ordinances, sealings and keys.

Monday, September 17, 1888—Pres[t]. Layton said in afternoon meeting yesterday that Bp. Preston had fully exhonerated me from anything wrong in my tithing business as Bps. Agent, my accounts being found all right.[100]

Tuesday, September 18, 1888—This morning at 7.45, Albert had a son born to him. To his increase may there be no end. Brs. Smith and Burton leave the valley today. Wrote to Mexico by Henry's request for apapers [papers] to admit him as a colonist to Mexico. Asked for the following to be exempted:—

4 chairs, 1 old Bureau, 2 pr horses, 2 S. harness double, 2 wagons 4 log chains 1 sewing maching, 1 Chest Carpenters tools, 1 Small mirror & dishes, 1 Stove, furniture & pipe, Beds and Bedding, 1 Small stand, a few photos, framed Arms and Ammunition, plow and Ag. tools 100 kilos flour 20 kilos Bacon, 1 wash. machine 200 pounds nails & a few groceries for present use.

September 19, 1888—Sent $6.80 [$147] to Dr. G. A. Scott for magnetic articles: 1 flesh Brush, 1 no. 3 hair Brush, 1 Sciatic appliance, & 30[¢] for postage.

September 21, 1888—Wrote to Patriarch H. Norman & Virginia. Delivered Petersen 3 cows on team acc't. Rec[d] letter from Gelston.

September 25, 1888—Wrote Gelston and sent him $1.[00] [$22] more: also to M. E. J.

September 27, 1888—Laid out new Co. Road, also next day.

September 30, 1888—Rec[d] letter from City of Mexico, as to what I may bring into Mexico free of duty, also the same for Joel and Moroni, and letter explaining same from Henry Eyring.

[page 632]

September 30, 1888—We may enter, free of duty, as follows:—

for Myself: 2 wagons and covers, 2 pr harness, 2 tables 4 chairs, iron bedstead and mattress, 1 sett scales, 100 kilos flour 25 kilos meat, Bedding, agricultural tools. Books

Joel: 2 wagons and covers, 2 setts harness, 2 chairs 100 kilos flour 25 kilos bacon, 1 sett crockery and glassware, 1 set nickel platewares, books &c

Moroni: 1 wagon and cover, 2 setts harness, furniture for the use of family, 100 kilos flour 25 k. bacon, 1 Lamp and oil, Books &c

Upon all other articles duty must be paid.

Monday, October 1, 1888—Rec[d] long letter from Lyman, also 2 from Nephi.

October 3, 1888—Wrote to Lyman, telling him again, to buy Gunnell's $500.[00] [$10,820] interest in the Juarez Saw Mill Co. Paid Petersen 3 cows and 1 Calf on horse team a/c. Sick

October 4, 1888—Surveyed for J. Blake, at Safford: home next day.

October 5, 1888—Sent Scott $7.58 [$164] for 1 M. Belt 1W. Belt 1 k. Cap. 2 no. 1 Brushes 2 pr insoles & .58¢ [$13] postage.

October 7, 1888—Joel has hot fever. I am still unwell.

October 8, 1888—Rec[d] first goods ordered form Scott.

Note [October] 2

By letter from Nephi, I learn he had a narrow escape from a fearful death, on Tues. Oct. 2. His horse jumped, the saddle turned, his foot hung in the stirrup and he was furiously dragged a 100 yds. He had given himself up to death, when his foot came loose. He was

100 Here we see the conclusion of a misunderstanding between Christopher Layton and Martineau.

badly bruised, but broke no bones. Thank God for his mercy.

October 11, 1888—Sent to J. B. Alden, No. 393 Pearl St N. Y. $7.89 [$171] for books; also for Life of Jos Smith and History of Mexico = total $17.39 [$376].[101] Also wrote to Lyman for $300.00 [$6,492].

October 13, 1888—Wrote to Bps. Preston & Burton, and Ap.l John H. Smith.

Sunday, October 21, 1888—Susan and I dined with Patriarch Wm McBride. As I entered, he said he felt as if he must give me a blessing, and asked if I wanted one. I said yes, and he then gave me the following: which is very much like others I have had before:—

[page 633]

MORONI'S BOY BORN

Br. Martineau, I feel a desire to bless you, although I am in pain all through my body with rheumatism. But my heart is free, and it is full of blessings for you. I say unto you that you shall be greatly blessed, with Susan and all your wives and children, and shall be blessed and prospered in all you undertake in humility. You shall be great and mighty in the priesthood. You and your sons shall reign and rule over Kings and Princes and Nobles, and Susan shall preside over Queens, and you, over kingdoms and over a great posterity. Your word shall be strong and powerful, even to cause the hypocrite to tremble, and the wicked to flee away from before you. Your daughters shall be filled with the spirit of the Lord, and your sons become mighty in the priesthood, and shall be mighty rulers in the land. Your wives and children shall increase like a fruitful vine, and your children shall become great people. And I say unto you in the name of the Lord, that if any shall interfere or meddle with your family, to cause disunion, without your consent, they shall burn their fingers. I seal upon you every blessing you desire in humility that is for your good, and I seal you up to eternal life in the name of Jesus. Amen.

Br. McBride seemed full of the Holy Spirit, and spoke with much power. His blessing was a great comfort to me and to Susan.

Note: By letter from Lyman I learn that Jesse N. Started on Oct 10th for his mission in Germany. May God preserve and bless him always. He arrived at N. Y. city Oct 16th and sailed in the Alaska.

October 26, 1888—Moroni had a son born to him this morning at 3–10 A.M. He weighed 10 lbs. I ordered $70.00 [$1,515] worth of fruit trees, vines and plants of Cluff, and paid him $31.00 [$671] down. Bought a plow, $14.00 [$303] and recd my books from Alden, N. Y.

October 28, 1888—Recd my magnetic goods from Dr. G. A. Scott, 842 Pearl St. N. Y.

[page 634]

PENSION PAPERS

November 6, 1888—Election to day. I voted for the first time in Arizona. There is too much trickery and ring work in politics to suit me, and it is very nauseous to me. I recd ~~my~~ transfer from F. Gunnell for $500.00 [$10,820] in stock in Juarez Saw Mill Co. by letter from Lyman. Also recd my certificate no. 17226 for Mexican War Pension, which is $8.00 [$173] pr month, from Jany 29, 1887, which, to Sept. 4, 1888 is $153.33 [$3,318]. From this is to be deducted $25.00 [$541] to Gelston & Co. Attys

November 7, 1888—Joel started to Mexico this afternoon, with load. I wrote to Lyman. Weather quite cold.

November 8, 1888—I sold my transit, level, 2 chains, and protractor to C. Brown, the new Co. Surveyor for $400.00 [$8,656] taking his mules, harness and wagon in payment. Yesterday morning the plants were killed in the garden, for the first. Wrote to E. H. Gelston & Co, to Lyman, and to T. H. Allen.

November 9, 1888—Finished Survey of Pima Canal.

[written in margin in shaky handwriting]
1st payment of Pension [. . .]

---

101 Martineau is learning about his newly adopted country. As the Saints fled to Mexico and Canada, they were counseled to learn of the lands and the local customs, observe the laws, and work with the native peoples.

November 10, 1888—Paid Weech $100.[00] [$2,164] for my land. Executed vouchers for my first payment of pension, at Solomonville. Cold.

November 13, 1888—Sent For Froissarts Chronicles[102] $1.34 [$29] Des. News $3.00 [$65] Herald $8.50 [184] Yesterday sent for my pension check of 153.33 [$3,318]. also for Mexican Laws $5.[00] [$108], to Gurley .70¢ [$15]. Wrote again to Bp Preston about cows, T. O. orders &c

November 14, 1888—Sent $30.[00] [$649] to Montgomery Ward & Co. for goods

November 15, 1888—Wrote article for Tucson Star, defending Pres[t] Layton from certain unjust charges

November 16, 1888—Sent a lot of old notes to Lyman, Sum, $743.50 [$16,089], some of it paid

November 17, 1888—Sent for Cloak for Anna and suit for Theodore, to California

November 18, 1888—Moroni and Albert got home. Rainy.

November 19, 1888—Wrote to Lilla. Killed a beef steer

November 22, 1888—Sent $31.45 [$681] to W. & L. Cal. for goods

November 23, 1888—Sent 3.93 for lasts, shoe nails &c Also 12.[00] for Electric goods from Dr. Scott, and on [26th]

November 26, 1888—Bought wagon of Bp. Taylor & sold my old one.

November 27, 1888—Gave my level to Brown (sold him). Rec[d] my Froissart.

November 28, 1888—Rec[d] suit of clothes for Theodore:—too small. Sent for another

[page 635]

LYMAN'S BABY BORN, MY 30TH GRAND CHILD

November 29, 1888—Sold my house and lot to H. Lines, for $600.[00] [$12,984] in horses, cattle, goods &c It is less than it has cost me. But I want to sell every thing I have in this place.

November 30, 1888—Sent 6.17 [$134] to Vickery and 6.50 to W. L. & Co. for mdse. Also sent old level to Gurley to be repaired, with 15.[00] [$134] cash.

Finished my index to "Pearls."

December 2, 1888—Special conference held by John Morgan

December 3, 1888—Alley and Lyman's baby born at 5 P.M.

December 4, 1888—Rec[d] $39.[00] [$844] mdse from W. L. & Co. and $30.[00] [$649] from Chicago with a beautiful ring for Susan, emrald and diamond.

December 5, 1888—Wrote to Jesse, who is now in Berne, Switzerland.[103] He arrived in Liverpool Oct. 29, by the "Alaska," spent a little time in London, also in Paris. Paid $27.03 [$585] tax

December 8, 1888—We measured height, with shoes &c on, as follows:—

myself	6' 11½" [5' 11½"]
Susan	5' 5"
Gertrude	5'6"
Dora	3' 9"
Anna	5' 3"
Theodore	5' 9½"

Yesterday drew my first cash on pension, to Sept. 4. 1888 = $128.33 [$2,777]. I resigned for Joel, his post as Secretary & Treasurer of 89th Quo. of 70[s] and as ditto for Stake Y.M.M.I.A. He and David Johnson arrived from Juarez, Mex, 370[m] in 12 days, and brought the mule we lost near Diaz last summer.

December 10, 1888—Got my iron lasts & shoe nails from the post. Traded wagons with Moroni.

December 12, 1888—Bought of N. P. Wordin, a mare of his in Mexico, for $55.[00] [$1,190]. Sent $10.[00] [$216] to W. L. & Co. Cal. for goods: also for shoe findings. Sold my stove to Moroni for $10.[00] and traded cow with him.

Got the following Ague Cure from R. Silva, a mexican.

Into 2 oz vinegar put white of 1 Egg, beaten up. add tablespoonful sugar and add half teacup of water. Drink once a day. It will cure the Chills and Fever in 2 to 4 days.

The boys started to Globe today, with 3 span each.

December 13, 1888—Rec[d] letter from Lyman, telling of the birth of his little girl, Dec. 3[d] at 5 P.M.

102 Tracing the rivalry between ancient England and France, Froissart's *Chronicles* describe the years 1322 until 1400.

103 "Missionaries," *Deseret News*, December 5, 1888; Utah Digital Newspapers.

Also sent checks for $400.[00] [$8,656] I rec[d] letter from J. T. Wells, editor of "Contributor" asking me to write for that magazine.[104]

December 14, 1888—Heavy rain. Wrote Lyman.

Mem.

While in Utah, last year, I rec[d] the following blessing from Pat. C. W. Hyde, April 5. 1887:—

[page 636]

MEMORANDUM—OF APRIL 5. 1887

Beloved Brother, I place my hands upon thy head, and seal upon you a patriarchal blessing. And thou shalt yet be called to proclaim this gospel from land to land and from sea to sea, and no power shall stay thy hand. And you shall proclaim the gospel from city to city, even to the house of Israel, and they will call thee Blessed of the Father. And you shall see Zion redeemed, and stand with your Redeemer and with the prophet Joseph when the Saints will be free. And be comforted, for Zion shall be redeemed: for they shall bind up the law and seal up the testimony. For you know not the blessings which the Lord thy God has for you. For thou art of Ephraim, and a lawful heir to the fullness of the priesthood; and if thou desirest it thou shalt converse with the Three Nephites, and they shall unlock to you things that shall not enter the heart of man. And I seal upon your head eternal life, with all thy father's household. Even so, Amen and amen.

At the same time he gave the following blessing to Miss Jessie Helen Anderson Grieves, I being scribe:—

[Last half of page is blank. Blessing not recorded in this journal.]

[page 637]

December 15, 1888—Rec[d] letter from J W Young, requesting me to go and see Gila Canal Subscribed for the books published for a course of reading for the Y.M.M.I.A. as prescribed by the Gen[l] Sup[t]

December 16 & 17, 1888—Quar. Conference. On 17th I went to Ft Thomas and telegraphed M R Locke, El Paso, Texas, relative to going to visit the Gila Bend Canal, below Phoenix A.T.

December 18, 1888—Rec[d] goods from Vickery

December 20, 1888—Wrote to J W Young. Joel arrived from Mexico on Sunday night, Dec. ~~16th~~ 9th David Johnson, his cousin, also. (Note. Error. They arrived Dec. 9th) Sent to S. Ward & Co Boston, for Writing case & rubbers. Wrote to M. Thatcher

December 21, 1888—Sent essay—Arizona—to "Contributor." Rec[d] letters from Mr. Locke, El Paso, relative to taking charge of his canal (the construction) near Gila Bend. ~~An~~ Rainy, still.

December 26, 1888—Started this morning for El Paso, Texas, to see Mr. Locke.

December 27, 1888—At El Paso. Mr. Locke engaged me as engineer in charge of St. Louis canal, near Gila Bend. Ariz. with salary of $200.[00] [$4,328] pr month and all necessary expenses. Started ~~home at~~ noon for Mesa.

December 29, 1888—Arr.[d] at Mesa & saw C. T. Robson on canal business[105]

December 30, 1888—Went to Nephi, and saw Sam and Elvira the first time for years.

1889

January 1, 1889—Took dinner at Don LeBaron's[106]

January 2, 1889—Went to Phoenix to see C. S. Masten, canal business

January 8, 1889—Went to Gila Bend with Masten & Robson. Started up river 40[m.]

104 The *Contributor* was published from 1879 to 1896 by Junius F. Wells (note middle initial). It was the forerunner of the *Improvement Era*, published from 1897 to 1970. Junius F. Wells was the son of Daniel H. Wells. Junius was among the organizers of the Young Men's Mutual Improvement Organization. He was a noted businessman and intellectual. Martineau wrote numerous articles over the next few years for this publication. At times he utilized his own name and other times wrote under the pen name "Santiago." We have footnoted his contributions as mentioned in the diaries and listed additional references in the bibliography.

105 This could be Charles I. Robson (note different middle initial), who was among the first immigrants in Mesa, Arizona. He was later president of the Maricopa Stake (McClintock, *Mormon Settlement in Arizona*, 212, 220).

106 This could be David T. LeBaron from Tempe, Arizona (McClintock, *Mormon Settlement in Arizona*, 219).

January 9, 1889—Reached head of canal. Quite cold nights. Did some leveling. Started home, & stopped at Benson, to visit St David.

January 10, 1889—At St David, agreed with Calvin Reid for him to build a fence around Netta's grave. for $8.^{00}$ [$173] returned to Bowie

January 11, 1889—Reached home. All well.

January 16, 1889—Got recommends for Juarez Ward for self and family.

January 18, 1889—Pres^t^ Layton came to me for information as to making out Tithing settlement for 1888. Showed him how to do it.[107]

January 19, 1889—Our house filled with a surprise party—a pleasant time. Gave accounts due me of $136.^{00} [$2,943] to Albert & Moroni to collect. Sold my carriage for $150.^{00} [$3,246] Pres^t^ Layton owes me for the survey of Thatcher about $200.^{00} [$4,328] which he will not pay

[page 638]

January 22, 1889—Gertrude and I start in stage. for Bowie, She is going to Utah, I to Gila Bend, to take charge of Canal work. The stage was robbed the day before, but we got to Bowie all right, after dark. Took train 8 P.M. and reached Maricopa next morning 5 A.M. Thence to Tempe & Mesa, reaching last place on 24th

January 24, 1889—Went to Phoenix to see Masten, returning next day to Mesa. Visited David Johnson, and found the following verses in Julia's Album (once her mother's)

To Aunt Julia.

Dark night has now her mantle cast
    On mountain peak and vale serene,
While softly sighs the passing blast
    And glimmering stars are faintly seen.

But soon the sun's enlivening ray
    Will tinge with gold the mountain height,—
Will chase the gloom of night away
    And storm clouds banish from our sight.

Thus oft our souls are plunged in grief,—
    Afflictions, too, our steps attend,
Our hours of joy so few and brief
    That Death appears our truest friend.

But soon will dawn a brighter day
    Than this, which now upon us lowers,
For brightest are the sun's warm rays
    That follow soon a chilling shower.

Then let us still in hope look up
    And make the most of each bright hour
And strive to fill life's crystal cup
    With honey gathered from each flower.

S. L. City, April 11, 1855.

January 27, 1889—Went to Sam's & Elvira's camp, 7 miles distant. They are clearing land for someone.

[page 639]

1880—Rec^d^ word from Joel. Mother and family left Pima on the 25th with five wagons. Henry & family and J. Carlton and family also went with them, driving cows & horses.

I had sold my house and lot in Pima for about $550.^{00} [$11,902] much less than it cost me, and failed to get five head of cows and steers I had bought of the Church. My move makes me lose several hundred dollars, but I am glad to get away from Pima, and move into Mexico.

February 1, 1889—Arrived at Gila Bend, leaving Gertrude at Elvira's, 6 A.M.

February 4, 1889—W. C. Masten came & went again. I began to take inventory of Company tools, carts, scrapers, &c. at Gila Bend.

February 6, 1889—Finished inventory. Started to El Paso. Fare $21.80 [$472].

February 7, 1889—Arrived in Deming 6 A.M. and at El Paso 9.30 A.M, 80^m^ farther Saw Locke but got no money. Returned to Deming next day.

February 9, 1889—Hired carriage and went 5 miles to meet Susan & family.

February 11, 1889—Left Deming 3 P.M. with teams, for Mexico.

February 12, 1889—Lost 3 horses last night. Joel went to look for them

107 Christopher Layton, who earlier questioned Martineau's handling of the tithing books, now returned to him for instructions on how entries were to be recorded.

Febuary 13, 1889—Joel returned with horses this afternoon, having had nothing to eat since he left yesterday. Traveled a few miles.

February 14, 1889—Rain this morning, & cold wind. Camped near Las Palomas.

February 15, 1889—Theodore and David joined us with the cattle this morning. Met [Mr. and Br. written on top of each other] Taylor, merchant, and paid him \$50.00 Mexican money for Spencer, due on the house and lot in Juarez. Arr[d] in Palomas, and got our wagons all inspected by 5 P.M. very cold and windy. Duties were about \$95.00 [\$2,056].

February 16, 1889—I here left my family, they to go on into Mexico, I to return to Gila Bend. But I hated the parting. I leave the family in the care of our Father. Went by stage from Palomas to Deming—44 miles—in one day. Ticket to Gila Bend \$22.15 [\$479].

February 17, 1889—Arrived in Gila Bend 6 A.M.

February 21, 1889—Began journey to head of canal, with party of surveyors. Spent a few days leveling and examining river fall and returned to Gila Bend on 24th

March 5, 1889—Started again on Survey, and began at junction of Salt and Gila Rivers. Exposed to heavy rain, and slept in wet bedding. No fire.

March 10, 1889—Examined top of Robbins Butte, an ancient wall still fortifies its summit. Indian hyeroglyphics mark the rocks on the summit.

[page 640]

March 11, 1889—Leveled in the pass. Very hot & suffered for water

March 12, 1889—Returned to Gila Bend, to prepare notes and report.

March 13, 1889—My 61st Birth day.

March 14, 1889—Lon Hall proposed to me to leave employment of Locke & Co., saying I could make \$200.000 [\$200 = \$4,328] by the change I told them I was bound in honor to Locke & Co. and did not agree to abandon them for another company.

March 15, 1889—Locke, Masten, Barnes & I held consultation on Canal matters, after which they returned east.

March 18, 1889—Went up the river 40 miles to locate another head of canal.

March 20, 1889—Returned to Gila Bend, thence to Phoenix. Examined records.

March 30, 1889—Started out with full survey party to Locate a line for canal, the previous line being abandoned on my recommendation, as being a very poor one.

April 28, 1889—Finished 60 miles of location, and quit for the present.

April 30, 1889—Went to Elvira's at Nephi, & to Mesa.

May 3, 1889—Went to Phoenix. Hall made his propositions to me again.

May 4, 1889—At Nephi, Sam & Elvira had an ice cream party. Nice.

While camping on the Gila in March (2d), I wrote the following lines

TO MY DARLING NETTA.

Oh darling Netta! mournful was the hour
When from thy loving father thou didst part!
He dearly loved thee, but he had not power
To keep thee longer near his aching heart.

He loved thee, darling, more than tongue can tell!
And more! much more than thou coulds't even guess.
In life he loved thee, and he loves thee still
Though now beyond all reach of fond caress.

But dearly as he loved, he would not call
Thee back to dwell in mortal form again!
Exposed to grief and sorrow, and to all
That tends to disappointment fear and pain.

[page 641]

No! Thou has safely passed those trials dread
That all <u>must</u> pass who dwell in this estate,
Thy griefs are o'er—thy pains forever fled,
And safe from Snares and pitfalls are thy feet.

Oh that mine eye the silvery veil might pierce—
That hides from mortal thy radiant light!
That I again might see thee face to face—
Might see thee now, So beautiful and bright!

But tis not so ordained, and all must wait
Their own appointed time, with patience meek;
And in this life so live, that at the gate
Of Paradise, our loved ones we may meet.

May 8, 1889—Returned to Gila Bend. Began work on survey notes of canal and profile.

May 10, 1889—Today Elvira's baby girl was born, weighed 11½ lbs. They named her Anna Gertrude.

May 19, 1889—Sent $20.^{00} [$433] to Susan by mail. She never got it.

May 21, 1889—Rec^d letter from L. H. Poole, U.S. Agent at Tucson He says 3 Poole brothers came from England years ago. One settled in Delaware, one in Maryland. The other, I believe, is ancestor of my cousin D. C. Poole, U. S. A.

May 22, 1889—Went to Nephi, for Gertrude.

May 25, 1889—We left Sam's and Elvira's. Patriarch B. F. Johnson gave her and Samuel the following blessings:—

Note These two blessings are recorded in my temple and blessing record, which is now in Mexico. (See page 660.) Gertrude and I went to Maricopa, Staid over night. gave her much fatherly counsel.

May 26, 1889—Arrived at Gila Bend. Gertrude staid at Rowley's.

May 17, 1889—Gertrude started for Logan, Utah, to day. I had felt worried about her going 2000 miles alone, but after I blessed her I felt that all would be well with her. Mrs. Rowley went with her as far as Lathrop, Cal.

[page 642]

GERTRUDE GOES TO LOGAN. I NEARLY DIED IN THE DESERT OF THIRST.

May 27, 1889—She went to Logan safely, except that on 28th she was very sick—pain in her side. Gov. Waterman & wife and daughter were very good to her, and did all they could to help her. May God reward them.

May 29, 1889—Sent claims for loss of tithing stock to Washington and informed Bp. Preston.

June 6, 1889—Sent essay to "Contributor" for publication.

June 23, 1889—Sent 2 articles to Contributor.

June 29, 1889—Was judge at School election

July 8, 1889—Went to Phoenix, and next day to Sam's.

July 12, 1889—Returned to Gila Bend.

July 14, 1889—To day Jose Manuel, a Yaqui indian, was killed a few yards from me, while resisting arrest. I was foreman of the Coroner's jury. He was about 28 years old. I must do temple work for him, or have it done.

July 15, 1889—People much alarmed. It is reported indians from Mexico are coming to revenge Manuel's death.

July 17, 1889—Sent final claim for indian depredation in 1886 to amount of $235.^{00} [$5,058] (cow $50 [$1,082] Loss on horse $185.^{00} [$4,003]).

July 21, 1889—Another scare about indians coming.

July 25, 1889—To day narrowly escaped death from thirst. I went about 35 miles away on horseback, with no water, and had a hard time crossing a high rocky ridge, which much exhausted me. I dug in bottom of dry gulch for water but found none. Then rode a few miles until I could hardly keep the saddle, then dismounted and lay on the sand about two hours to gain strength. I then crawled to my saddle and rode a few more miles, then had to lie down again for a long time. But I grew weaker all the time instead of stronger, and lay in a hazy, dreamy state, with no inclination to move. I thought I would let the horse go, but I knew when he arrived at home without me, all the people would be alarmed and might hunt all night for me. Then I thought of the work I still had to do, according to my blessings, and prayed God to strengthen me, so I could get home.

[page 643]

I NEARLY DIED IN THE DESERT OF THIRST. UP THE RIVER AGAIN

July—Before this I felt too weak to rise; but after prayer I felt stronger, so that I got upon my feet and stood awhile by my horse, holding by the saddle. Then I prayed again, and was strengthened so I could climb to his back. Then, holding by both hands to the saddle, my horse took his own way to Gila Bend. Who can imagine my joy when I first saw the trees at the Station. Arrived there, the people were very kind to me, helping restore me, but they said I was crazy all night. It was only the blessing of God I was saved & to Him be all the glory and praise. I had eaten three cactus fruits, which helped me somewhat, and was careful to keep my mouth shut and breathe through my nose. This prevented me from suffering such an agony of thirst as otherwise I should have done—learned in my former experiences in the deserts. A hot wind was blowing all day, which seemed to dry out all the moisture of my body, even to my very blood, and to dry up the kidneys. I had not thought the desert winds so deadly, though I had known of men before now, perishing on the deserts. Those who use spirits cannot stand it as well as those who do not. This I know.

July 26 & 27, 1889—Still quite weak and feeble, otherwise all right. I had received a letter from Susan, in Mexico, just a day or two before I went into the desert, warning me to take care of myself. The Spirit had warned her, but I was not careful enough, thinking myself too tough and hardy to fear anything.

July 28, 1889—Wrote to Lyman to send Jesse $75.[00] [$1,623] so he could go to the Paris Exposition

July 31, 1889—To day Locke, Masten, myself, Hodnett & L. W. Locke, with tent & camp outfit went up to the head of canal, to inspect line. In the afternoon Masten was overcome by the heat, and we camped early.

[page 644]

August 1, 1889—Reached Gila river about noon. Masten again overcome with heat. We laid him down and poured water all over his body all the afternoon to keep him alive. I walked up the river a mile or more, to examine river at the head of line, and concluded to change its location. I was nearly overcome, at one time by the heat. At evening, moved camp two miles down.

August 2, 1889—The directors accepted my last location, as best. Started home in the morning. At noon stopped under a Cottonwood for dinner, and Masten was again overcome by heat. We doused him continually with water until night to keep him alive. One of our horses while standing under the tree, also fell. We poured water over him, and I secretly laid hands upon and blessed him. This restored him. At night we started for our long march, while the darkness should make it cool, traveling until midnight, and camped at a deserted house and well.

August 3, 1889—Reached Gila Bend 10 A.M. Heard that two other men had been prostrated on the 2[d] and a horse died from heat. So this shows the intense heat we endured.

August 6, 1889—Read that in Guatemala is a lake ~~Amitlan~~ Amatitlan, in the bottom of which lies a city sunk. No doubt this is one of those which sunk when the Savior was crucified. See Book of Mormon.

August 7, 1889—Received word from Masten to go to Tucson to stay. Went.

August 8, 1889—By Judge W. H. Barne's request I wrote a description of our canal line, the land & general particulars for presentation to capitalists in New York. Judge Barnes complimented the article very highly. From this time, I was very busy making estimates of canal, working on profile, copying U.S. Survey plats, and making map of the Gila Bend Country.

August 27, 1889—Today the Great Feast of St. Augustine begins celebrated by the Catholics for a month. They have bull fights by day by Mexican Matadors Mexican Circus, horse racing &c. And at night thousands gather at the fairgrounds.

[page 645]

August, 1889—Here are many Booths for sale of liquors, fruits, suppers, fancy work, shooting galleries, and about 18 gambling tables. These are surrounded constantly by crowds of men and women, betting on roulette, rouge et noir, faro, keno and other games whose names I did not know. There was also an excellent Mexican band and a band composed of Papago indians, who presided at a dancing floor, which was occupied by Mexicans or indians dancing. Sunday is the greatest day of all for these things. While looking upon these people, Sundays, thus desecrating the Lord's day without thought of wrong, I thought of Jonah and the people of Nineveh, of whom the Lord said there were 120.000 besides many cattle, who knew not their right hand from their left. So with these—in dense darkness—and God will, I believe, be merciful to them because of it.

September 2, 1889—Sent a map to M. R. Locke in N. Y. for his use.

September 5, 1889—The Senatorial Committee on Irrigation visited Tucson one day and took testimony. I was invited by the Committee to speak for Graham Co. but declined. Afterwards, by invitation, I rode with them all around Tucson.

September 10, 1889—Was requested to help temporarily in the Sur. Gen[l] office, Tucson, the chief clerk being about to go away for a while on account of sickness. I Continued at this work until Oct. 12th at $5.[00] [$108] pr. day. Gen. R. A. Johnson seemed satisfied with me.

September 13, 1889—Received a letter from Lyman with $75.[00] He wrote that Allie had had a dream that Susan was away from home in a strange town and destitute of money. She gave Lyman no peace till he sent me the $75.[00] [$1,623] for her use. I suppose she is safe at home in Juarez Mex. as I told her lately not to start from home for Utah until I could send her money needful, and she had answered me she was not so green as to start on a 2000 mile journey without money.

[page 646]

September 13, 1889—In a few minutes a telegram came from her, from Deming N. M. asking for money to come on with. I was utterly astonished, but sent her the money just received from Lyman, which the Lord had caused him to send, (by Allie's dream) just in time for her use. Our Father is very good and watchful over those whom He loves as He does Susan, whom He has styled "Beloved of the Lord." I telegraphed her to come on at once.

September 14, 1889—Got telegram from Susan. She has started.

September 15, 1889—Susan came with Dora this morning at 2 A.M. I had been up all night, waiting for her, and walked miles upon the track in my impatience. We talked until morning. I had not seen her since in January 1889.

September 16, 1889—We attended the Mexican Celebration of Independence. A fine affair. Thousands of Mexicans present, not one drunk, noisy, or ungentlemanly in any way. Not so an equal number of Americans. The Mexican ladies were dressed with exquisite taste as to colors in dress. Fireworks at night. I felt one with them.

September 17, 1889—Susan must go on, so as to have her visit in Logan before cold weather. I dread the parting. I blessed her, got her a ticket to Ogden $71.15 [$1,540], also sleeping berth $13.00 [$281], and got for her $25.[00] [$541] pocket money. Truly has God opened my way and hers. She suddenly determined, in Juarez, to Start north. Borrowed $20.[00] [$433] of Cardon Saw a covered wagon in the street, asked for a ride to Carlton's, 15 miles, Seized Satchel & Dora and went to Carlton's. Found him just going on the next day to Deming, N. M. and he gave her passage to that place. There my money met her, and so the Lord prospered her at every moment and turn. She safely reached Logan on the 21st all well, and met Lyman at Ogden, where he went to meet her.

[page 647]

September 18, 1889—Susan and Dora start to Logan at 2.50 A.M. Sad. Continued work in the Sur. Gen[l] Office. He offers me a contract of Surveying 120 miles of the west boundary of the San Carlos Reservation, at $22 [$476] pr mile.

September 25, 1889—To night I felt impelled to make the same covenant relative to tithing that Joseph Smith and Oliver Cowdery did, as recorded in the life of Joseph. This covenant of theirs seems a more particular covenant than it is usually thought, and I desire to be in the same bonds as Br. Joseph. This covenant I have written in the back part of my Temple Record in full. God help me to keep it.

October 3, 1889—To day I felt impelled to bless the Gila Bend canal enterprise, that it may be completed, and be for the final benefit of the Saints when they shall possess the land, that the land may be made fruitful and productive. This I did, & asked the Father to ratify it.

By Judge Barnes request. I wrote a description of the Gila Bend Canal line, the land, productions &c &c to Mr. Murphy, of Phoenix, who desired to answer New York letters.

October 7, 1889—Sent an article for publication in Young Woman's Journal, in answer to Susa Young Gates request. Sent $10.[00] [$216] tithing to S. L. T. Office.

October 12, 1889—Finished my work in Sur. Gen[l] office.

October 15, 1889—Paid $15.[00] [$323] more tithing, which is all I owe. Wrote to my adopted son Neils L. Hagberg, S. L. City.

October 18, 1889—By letter I learn Moroni and family start to Mexico to day, having sent the cattle two days before.

October 19, 1889—Judge Barnes told me he would see that I should have a share in the canal, as a "promoter."

October 20, 1889—Wrote a frontier Ball in 1851 for Y. W. Journal.

October 25, 1889—Received a letter from Pres[t] Woodruff, asking me to do some Surveying for the Papago indian mission. I answered that I would, with pleasure.

October 30, 1889—Heard of the death of my old friend Francis Gunnell. who died Oct. 20, of heart trouble. A good man.

[page 648]

November 2, 1889—Sent to Gurley for a new Survey chain.

November 24, 1889—Rec[d] a letter from Virginia with the following lines:—

TO NETTA'S MEMORY.

by Virginia

In a lonely spot some miles away
We laid our darling Sister.
Oh yes! She was as fair as day
And oh! how much we miss her!

She was but young—a budding flow'r
When she was called away,
We waited for the fearful hour—
She could no longer Stay.

We left the home we loved so well
And to the southward went.
We thought 'twould thus her health improve
And give her life and strength.

But 'twas not long before Death came
And took her soul away,
But in the other world again
We hope to meet some day.

S. L. City Nov. 18. 1889

November 27, 1889—Rec[d] Tullidges History of Northern Utah, containing my biography, in garbled form.

Hearing Lt. Donaldson and wife sing a hymn called "Flee As A Bird," and liking very much the soft plaintive air, this evening I hastily wrote some other lines of my own to the same tune, entitled "Hark to the voice of the Shepherd."

[page 649]

HARK TO THE VOICE OF THE SHEPHERD. AIR, "FLEE AS A BIRD."

Hark, 'tis the voice of the Shepherd
Calling His flock as of old;
List to His voice and be gathered
Safely and sure in His fold!
Haste! For the wolves are about thee:—
Raging and fierce to destroy thee.—
Fly, for the arms that await thee
Would thee so gladly enfold,
Oh! would thee so gladly enfold!

Why will ye wander in danger,
Sorrow and darkness and pain,
Come! be no longer a ranger!
Come to thy Father again!
He in His love will enfold thee!
He with His might will defend thee!
He to a throne will exalt thee!
Ever with Him thou shalt reign.
In glory with Him thou shalt reign!
forever to reign

[note: "forever to reign" was added years later in shaky hand]

[written in margin]

Forever in glory shalt reign.

December 1, 1889—Letter from Susan and Gertrude. They wish to return home. I wrote in answer—Come!

Elvira wrote to me, and sent this little verse expressive of her love to me:—

When you are sitting all alone
Reflecting on the past,
Remember that you have my love,

Which will forever last.

During this month the celebrated trial of men suspected of complicity in the Wham robbery was being conducted in Tucson. About 200 witnesses were present from Graham County, on the two sides, among them Cousin Melissa Johnson and daughter-in-law Emma, Albert's wife, who were witnesses for the prosecution.

December 8, 1889—I walked with Melissa to see the old Catholic Convent ruin, about 300 years old.

[page 650]

December 9, 1889—Emma testified in Court to day. Complimented highly.

December 10, 1889—Paid Weech $10.<u>00</u> [$216] for share of taxes on land, Pima. Gave Emma a nice dress and Albert a book.

December 15, 1889—To day the Pima witnesses all returned, the Wham trial being over, and accused acquitted.

This trial was called the "Mormon robbery trial," the accused being ostensible members of the Church, but only one of them in fellowship. It was part of a crusade against the Mormons.

December 18, 1889—Susan writes she will be at Gila Bend New years. Glad.

December 22, 1889—Began to fast for 24 hours, pursuant to request of Pres[t] Taylor sent to all the Saints.

December 23, 1889—Fasted until night.

December 26, 1889—Copied names in Temple Record still unworked for, into a smaller book, so I can send the Temple Record home.

December 30, 1889—Left Tucson for Gila Bend. Have been in Tucson 5 months, nearly, and have been very busy, mapping and other work. I have written many letters to my family in Mexico, Logan, Pima, and to Jesse N. who is in Switzerland on mission. I have constantly taught them principles of life in my letters, and stimulated them to be Saints indeed. I have prayed much, and fasted; and have sought to gain a victory over all my sins, and to be filled with the Holy Spirit. Many times I have had precious answers to my prayers, & many principles of truth have been unfolded to my mind in answer to prayer. I have tried all I could to exert a good influence for Mormonism, and think I have done some good. I have become acquainted with many prominent men, and in that, I have labored for Zion the best I cold. By request, I have been a constant writer for the "Contributor," as a general thing writing of early days in Utah, so that the youth of Zion may have some idea as to the labors and trials of the early settlers of Utah.

[page 651]

December 1889—May the Father bless all these, my labors, for my heart's greatest desire in this life is to help build up and establish Zion, to do good to all, and to bring Souls to God. That I may do this, I ask Him constantly to give me health and strength and every other blessing needful, spiritually, and to bless my labors temporally, that my hands and time and labors may be free and untrammeled, so I can the more effectually help to establish Zion and labor for the salvation of Souls, especially the Lamanites, so long driven, oppressed, robbed and slain. Oh! Father! hasten the time for their redemption, and the time when Zion shall be free! Grant that I may stand among my children as a patriarch and father indeed, to teach and help in the way of life, that not one may be lost, but all saved in the Celestial Glory: and that all my family may be one with me in this great work. Amen.

December 31, 1889—Was today arrested by Noonan for a debt due him by the Canal Company. Found security. Wrote to Lock, also Judge Barnes Concerning it.

1890

January 1, 1890—Telegram from Susan. She started Dec. 31st glad!

January 2, 1890—Letter from Locke & Co. My hotel bill at the San Havier, Tucson, is $270.<u>40</u> [$5,852] Copied my blessings and Susan's in small book which I can have with me.

January 3, 1890—Rec[d] Letter from Susan. She, Trudie and Dora came at 7 P.M. All well. How thankful I am to see them. She came on the only through train from Sacramento that has come for a month, all railroad travel through California having been interrupted by washouts. At Sacramento the officials recommended her to go by sea from San Francisco to Los Angeles, as she could not go through by rail.

[page 652]

January 3, 1890—Susan and Gertrude consulted, and finally decided to stick to the train, and try it by land. She succeeded, though sometimes in much danger. On one occasion the train was all night going ten miles, over washed out and hastily fixed road, creeping slowly and carefully along. But they came right through to Gila Bend, the only through train for a month previous and for two weeks after; for the very day they reached Gila Bend the track was all washed out behind them near Colton, Cal. Truly the blessing and hand of God has been over them, for good. Had they left Logan a day sooner or a day later, they could not have come through, except with vexatious delays and expense. I Thank the Father for His goodness. My joy at meeting my family was great.

January 4, 1890—To day Noonan was glad to withdraw his suit.

January 5, 1890—This morning we left Gila Bend at 2 P.M. the train being many hours late. Reached Maricopa at 4 A.M. and Tempe at 6 A.M. Sam met us there. Found Uncle Benja quite sick. I blessed him, and cheered him up, and he felt better. Rained on us as we went to Nephi. Found Elvira and children well, and very glad to see us after so long separation.

January 6, 1890—Went to Mesa, dined at Pres[t] Robison's. Saw ~~Gr~~ Mother Susan Johnson, Susan's step mother, lately come from Apache Co. Saw many of our relatives.

January 8, 1890—Our Wedding anniversary. Elvira had a nice dinner. Gertrude taken quite sick. Wrote article for "Contributor," "A journey in 1854 in Utah."

January 9, 1890—Gertrude better. Visited C. T. Robson, 10th on Canal matters.

January 14, 1890—Gertrude well of La Grippe, but Elvira takes it.

January 17, 1890—Bought a sewing machine for Elvira. Gave note, 90 days for $50.[00] [$1,082] to Stewart. Interest 1½ o/c from maturity.

January 19, 1890—Letter from Joel, with size of our house as follows:—

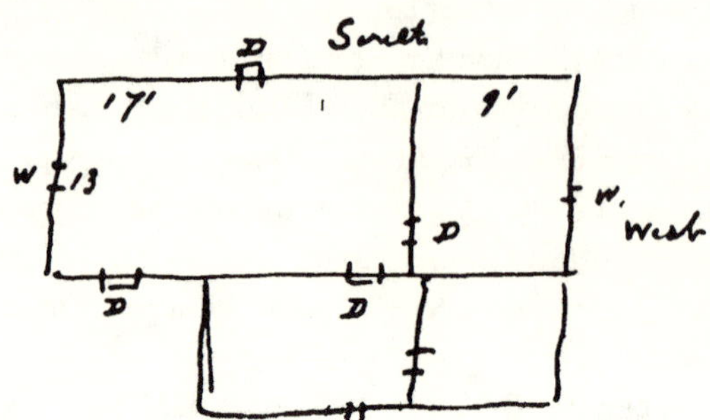

Fig. 7.3—Floor plan of Colonia Juárez house.

I wish to build a good house in front and joining to the old one, and for this reason I have sent for dimensions of the old house I bought in Juarez.

[page 653]

January 21, 1890—Susan down with La Grippe, quite bad. In the evening she asked me to administer to her, which I did. The Lord gave each of us strong faith, and she was healed almost immediately. Thanks be to the Father for His mercy.

January 23, 1890—Wrote to Charlie and advised him to come to Gila Bend and set up blacksmith shop. This I did, to get him into a warmer and better climate than where he is now, in S. L. City, threatened with consumption.

January 28, 1890—Took Susan to Phoenix, and bought some dress patterns.

January 31, 1890—I went to Phoenix to meet Murphy. To no purpose.

February 3, 1890—Wrote to Murphy I would not be a party to any plan that would injure Locke & Co. If he can sell his franchise as he thinks and make $5000 [$108,200] each, for us, without hurting Locke & Co, all right. If not, I will not join in with him, as, to me, honor is worth more than gold, just as when the Hall's offered me $200.000 to kill Locke & Co's scheme. Locke & Co. have employed me, and they trust me: so I must not forfeit the confidence they place in me.

February 9, 1890—Wrote for "Contributor" A Mystery of the desert," and of Walker's (Indian Chief) Nephite money.

February 16, 1890—Wrote for "Contributor" Elvira's story of the indian outbreak of 1882, and killing of Robinson near Show low.

February 21, 1890—Sent to Lyman for $200.[00] [$4,328] so Mother can get home.

February 27, 1890—Renewed my subscription to N. Y. World

March 4, 1890—Bought goods for Susan at Mesa, credit, $27.60 [$597] of which $7.00 [$151] was for Sam.

March 6, 1890—

Bought additional goods at Mesa credit

$27.60 [$597]
11.35 [$246]
$38.95 [$843]

March 11, 1890—Susan and I sat for photos at Mesa.

Ordered 3 doz. cards @ $9.00 [$195] and 1 doz Of Gertrude & Viva 6$ [$130] = $15.00 [$325] Went to Tempe to negotiate loan by mortgage of Sam's 160 acres. Did so, for $1000.00 [$21,640] Previous to this we went to Uncle Benjamin's—patriarch—and got patriarchal blessings for her and me; and again we (Uncle B. and I) ordained and set her apart as a nurse and comforter to the sick and the troubled, and as a midwife, as follows:—

Blessing by Benj. F. Johnson, Patriarch, upon Jas H. Martineau given in Tempe, Arizona, Jan 30, 1890.

Brother James, in the name of the Lord Jesus and by virtue of the priesthood of the fathers I place my hands upon thy head to say such things unto thee relating to the past and the future as the Lord shall give to me by the inspiration of His Spirit. I say unto thee, lift up thy head and let thy heart rejoice before the Lord, for He hath thee in His remembrance, even to fulfill unto thee every desire of thy heart, and bestow upon thee every blessing that His servants have pronounced upon thy head. For He hath a great purpose in thee, even from before the foundation of the Earth, and for the accomplishment of His purpose He hath gathered thee out, and in blessing raised thee above thy fellows. And from the days of thy birth His angel had charge concerning thee, the arm of His power hath been around thee, and the hand of the Lord hath led thee, even in ways that thou knewest not, and for a purpose plainly known unto Himself which thou didst not understand. In all the circumstances of thy life He hath been near unto thee to strengthen thee; and the arm of His power and the Spirit of His might shall never be withdrawn from thee. For thou shalt raise up and go forward, and no power shall turn thee backward from fulfilling the purposes of the Almighty. The spirit of wisdom and council hath been sealed upon thy head, and it shall be more fully developed within thee; and thou shalt lead forth in the redemption of the covenant people of the Lord, to assist mightily in the re-establishment of Jacob upon the land given them by the Father. Unto them thou shalt become a Prince and a Patriarch, a Prophet and a Seer: and thou and thy Sons shall be an arm of power, even to be as the horns of Ephraim in assisting to push together the people, and to establish them upon the land of their inheritance. And when the cities of the Gentiles are waste, behold thou shalt go forth with thy children and thy children's children to redeem the waste places, and to inhabit the cities that are made desolate. Thy years shall be many upon the earth, even according to the fullness of the desire of thy heart. The Lord hath given thee wisdom to lead thy family in the ways of the just, to honor Him, and they shall rise up and call thee blessed all the days of thy life, and carry thy name and thy fame in honor throughout all generations of Time.

[page 655]

Susan's Blessing

1890—The treasures of the earth shall be unto thee in great fullness, whereby thou shalt be able to assist in bringing to pass the redemption of Zion, the rearing of His holy temple, the gathering and sustaining of the meek of the earth, whereby the blessing of the poor shall ever be upon thy head. All the blessings that have been conferred upon thee in priesthood thou shalt hold forever, and shall lack in no good thing, to prepare thee to fulfill every degree of usefulness and to attain to every greatness that is according to the desires of thy heart. Thou shalt stand as a Savior in thy father's house, and be numbered among those who are Saviors upon Mount Zion, even to the accomplishment of a mighty work among the living and the dead. For it is even thy privilege to live to see the holy temple reared in Zion, and the glory of the Lord resting upon its towers, and to minister therein, when His glory shall fill its courts. Now all these blessings I seal upon thy head, and I seal thee up unto eternal lives, to come forth in the morning of the First Ressurrection, clothed in glory, immortality and eternal lives, in the name of Jesus. Amen.

Patriarchal Blessing by B. F. Johnson, upon Susan E. J. Martineau, given in Tempe, Arizona, Jan 30, 1890.

Sister Susan, in the name of the Lord Jesus and by virtue of the patriarchal priesthood, I place my hands upon thy head in blessing, that the Lord may speak through me to the joy and comfort of thy heart, or to admonish and strengthen thee in the path that leadeth back into His presence. Thou art one of the Beloved of the Lord; thou was valiant for the truth, and before the earth was thou didst shout hosanna that it would be thy privilege to come forth in this dispensation to assist in bringing forth and establishing Zion preparatory to a reign of peace upon the earth. To this end the Father blessed thee and sent thee as with a crown of glory upon thy head, that through thee mighty men and women should live upon the earth to be prophets, seers and mighty men, to lead forth in establishing righteousness and truth, to the rebuke of iniquity and sin, whose arm shall be strong against oppression, and in avenging innocent blood.

[page 656]

Blessing upon Susan

1890—Thou has earnestly sought to fulfill the Law of Sarah and to lead thy children to honor the Lord thy God. Because of this He shall honor thee, and all thy children shall remain steadfast before Him. They shall rise up and bless thee all thy days, and carry thy name in honor through all generations of time. The Lord shall bestow upon thee more fully the spirit of wisdom and Council, and of the mothers and matrons of Zion thou shalt stand among those who are the most honored, because of the words of wisdom and comfort that as rubies shall fall from thy lips. The spirit and power of blessing and consolation shall rest upon thee in mighty power, even that all whom thou shalt bless shall be blessed indeed. The blessings of the earth shall be unto thee, and when the meek shall flee unto Zion in the great day of tribulation, thou shalt feed the hungry, clothe the naked and give shelter to the homeless, and thy words of consolation will bind up the sorrowful and the broken-hearted. And when because of wickedness the cities of the land shall become desolate, thou, together with thy husband and all thy family shall go forth to inhabit the cities that are desolate, and to inhabit the waste places. The Lord knoweth the integrity of thy heart and all thy sacrifice, and He will never leave thee alone that thy Spirit shall droop before Him, for his angels shall camp around thee, to be as thy companions. His arms shall sustain thee, his hand shall lead thee. His spirit shall fill thy heart with consolation and joy continually, while the visions of heaven shall be opened unto thee, to rebuke affiction [affliction], to command the Destroyer that no power shall invade thy habitation to destroy thy peace or take away thy loved ones. Years shall be multiplied upon thy head, and thou shalt live even to the fullness of thy desires; and it is thy privilege to assist in the work both for the living and the dead, in the holy temple that shall be reared in Zion; to strike hands with the Son of Man when He shall descend to his holy temple, and to associate with those loved ones whom He will bring with Him. And in blessings thou shalt lack in no good thing. Thy inheritance shall be forever in Zion, which thou shalt receive with thy companion and family when the Ancient of Days shall sit. I rebuke from thy heart and mind every principle of doubt that might trouble thee, or any principle of fear that might spring up in thy heart, and say unto thee that thy way shall ever be open before thee.

[page 657]

Susan's Ordination Blessing

1890—Now all these blessings I seal upon thy head, and seal thee up unto eternal lives, to come forth in the morning of the first ressurrection clothed upon with glory, immortality and eternal lives in the name of Jesus. Amen. (See page 660 for Elvira's

Blessing and ordination by Patriarchs B. F. Johnson and James H. Martineau upon Susan E. J. Martineau, given in Tempe Arizona, Feb 25. 1890. (B. F. J. mouth)

Susan, we lay our hands upon thee and ask God to give unto us His Spirit, that our words may be dictated by it. Thou art of the Seed of the Blessed; thou art a Princess and a Priestess and a Queen; and thou hast by inheritance a right to all the blessings of the daughters of Abraham. In these thy rights are unlimited, even to all the rights and blessings of Sarah. Thou shalt be filled with great wisdom as a Nurse, and be a great comfort, a help and a blessing to the sick, the afflicted, and to those who are bowed down and distressed, of the poor of the earth. Many shall seek unto thee of the poor and also the rich; and health and peace shall drop from the ends of thy fingers, and consolation and Comfort from thy lips. We ordain thee and set thee apart as a Nurse and as a Midwife, and thou shalt administer peace and comfort to the afflicted. The sick shall rise up at thy touch, and sickness and death shall flee away from thy presence. No blessing thou shalt desire, that pertains to the daughters of Abraham, shall be denied thee. Thou shalt be filled with words of peace and comfort to those whose hearts are bowed down in grief or trouble, and they shall rejoice greatly at thy presence, And all that is good and womanly and pure shall be with thee and in thee continually, even to the fullness of thy desires. All these blessings, and all that you desire we seal and confirm upon thee in the name of the Lord Jesus Christ. Amen.

Father, I thank thee for these blessings

[page 658]

Elvira's Blessing.

1890—The following blessing was given to Elvira by Pat^{h} Joel H. Johnson, at Johnson. Kane Co. Utah, Jan 19th 1879. Born in Parowan, Utah Aug. 14. 1856. She was then wife of B. S. Johnson.

Susan Martineau Johnson, in the name of the Lord Jesus Christ of Nazareth, I lay my hands upon thy head to give thee a fathers or patriarchal blessing, and to confirm all the blessings thou hast received from the Elders of Israel. Thou art of the seed of Ephraim, and, entitled to all the blessings of the holy men and women of old; therefore I bless ~~thee~~ you with the Spirit of the living God to abide in your bosom forever like a well of water springing up unto everlasting life. Thou shalt be an assistant with thy companion in teaching the daughters of Ephraim the principles of eternal life, civilization and economy. Thou shalt have many children, and thy seed shall be great in the earth. Inasmuch as thou wilt bring them up in righteousness, thou shalt have power to drive the Destroyer from their midst when thy companion is absent. Messengers from behind the vail shall visit thee in times of sorrow and trial, and give thee counsel and comfort. No enemy shall cross thy path and prosper while thou art faithful to do the will of God. Thou shalt be beloved by all faithful saints, and thy name shall be had in honorable remembrance by all the pure in heart. Thou shalt live long upon the earth and when the ressurrection are given thou shalt be quickened. I seal ~~all~~ upon thy head all the blessings that thy heart can conceive or desire, and seal thee up unto eternal lives with thy companion, to inherit thrones, powers and dominions, and come forth in the morning of the first resurrection shouldst thou fall asleep, with glory, immortality and eternal lives. All these blessings are thine, if thou art faithful to hearken to the words of wisdom and eternal life, in the name of Jesus Christ. Amen.

Note: The foregoing was not recorded in Joel H. Johnson's record through inadvertence. I therefore send it to B. F. Johnson, Patriarch, to be recorded in his Record of Blessings. Copied from the original, Nephi, A. T. March 6, 1890

[page 659]

FAMILY LEAVE DEMING FOR HOME.

March 12, 1890—Left Samuel's for Tempe, on our way to Mexico. Got $1000 [$21,640]. at Tempe Nat^{l} Bank, less bank charges $48.90 [$1,058] which includes 3 mo. interest @ 1½ o/c = $15.^{00} [$325] pr month. Gave Sam $7.00 [$151], Elvira $15.^{00} paid D. T. LeBaron's family, by Sam $35.^{00} [$757] p^{d} Armstrong for goods $16.80 [$364]. 3 tickets to Maricopa 7.50

March 13, 1890—Left Tempe 5 A.M, Arr. Maricopa 6.15 A.M. Took S.P.R.R. at 11.00 A.M. 3 tickets to Deming $45.90 [$993] & .65 extra for excess of 40 lbs baggage.

March 14, 1890—Arrived at Deming N. M. at 2 A.M. Staid at R. R. hotel. Met Joel and Anna. All were overjoyed to meet again. After breakfast moved to St. James hotel, Our bill at R. R. hotel for 2 rooms and breakfast was, $6.75 [$146]

March 15, 1890—Deposited $700.^{00} [$15,148] in First National Bank, Deming.

March 17, 1890—Met Peterson, of Diaz, whom I owed $15.^{00} [$325], horse trade, in full.

I find I still owe in Juarez, for house and Lot, Mex. money, $135.^{00}

I owe Clough for trees (U.S. money) balance old a/c, $39.00

I owe Clough for Joel's trees <u>$31.30</u>

[total] $70.30 [$1,521]

Susan also owes P. Cardon, cash $20.00 + 1.40 = $21.40 [$463]. I gave her the money to pay it him.

Also gave her $400.00 Mexican money and to Joel $13.00 Mexi. cash.

In Deming we traded over $410.00 [$8,872] including a wagon $120.00 [$2,597] Also bought harness $48.00 [$1,039] on time, of H. Nordhaus. In settling up, I gave checks for $304.00 [$6,579] (for the $400.00 Mexi. money @ 76¢) and $300.00 for use. Also deposited $200.00 [$4,228] Thatcher Bank and drew $50.00 [$1,082]. Paid St James Hotel bill for 6 ⅓ days, $35.75 [$774]. Our expenses have been heavy, but the family needed much clothing and household goods. We waited 6 days for Company, and I enjoyed myself very much with my family together, and it was a dread to part from them. Joel hired a span of mules of Hainey to haul the new wagon and load as far as Diaz. The folks made up considerable clothing in Deming, and were busy as bees.

Thursday, March 20, 1890—The family at last left Deming in the afternoon—4 P.M.—a dreadful windy day with clouds of sand filling the air. My Consul papers cost $6.25 [$135].

[page 660]

March 20, 1890—I went a little distance with Susan, she driving the mules with Gertrude, and Joel and Anna driving the other team. At last I alighted with tearful kisses, and stood and watched the teams as long as I could see them, then sorrowfully returned to my desolate room. It will be very good in the next estate, that there will no more be sorrowful partings from loved ones. I took train for Gila Bend at 9 P.M. and arrived there at 9 A.M. next morning, the 21st on Friday.

March 21, 1890—I found plenty of letters and papers, and spent next day in answering letters &c.

March 22, 1890—I also sent to "Contributor" some poems, "Title of Liberty," "Boyhood's Days" and "Missing Ones." Also to Y. W. Journal, "Lines to my wife" and "Truth." Also sent for pension.

March 24, 1890—Got photos of Susan, Gertrude and Dora from Logan, and sent some to Elvira and Albert. Wrote to Genl Raum, U. S. Pension Commissioner, about my pension.

March 25, 1890—Sent two articles to Contributor, Seeking a refuge in the desert, including the lost company, Snake dinner &c &c I have spent all spare time in writing up my journal from my pocket notes. copying blessings into it, &c to date of 26th

Patriarchal Blessing upon S. Elvira M. Johnson by B. F. Johnson, Tempe A. T. Jan. 30. 1890. Born 14 Aug. 1856

Elvira, my daughter, in the name of Jesus, by virtue of the patriarchal priesthood, I place my hands upon thy head in blessing, praying that the Lord may give me through the inspiration of His Spirit, words of counsel, admonition and blessing, to be keys of knowledge and principles of faith to govern thee all thy life. Thou art one of those born in Zion in the new Covenant, entitled to all the blessings, dominion, increase and exaltation pertaining to the daughters of Abraham. Because of thy love for the truth and the integrity of thy heart, Thou art one of the most loved of the ~~Lord~~ Father. He sent thee to the earth with a crown of joy upon thy head that thou mightest become a medium of Salvation and restoration upon the earth. To this end He gave His angels charge concerning thee, to hedge thee round about from evil, and to open the pathway of they feet, to protect thy life to the fulfillment of the mission for which thou hast come to the earth: for which purpose He hath given thee a companion, and shalt multiply unto thee children until they shall be around thee as thick clusters of grapes upon a fruitful vine, whom thou shalt lead in the way of the Lord to honor Him, and they shall honor and bless thee all thy days, and carry thy name in honor throughout all generations of time.

[page 661]

Thou dost delight in the way of the Lord, and because of thy love for the truth, the Lord shall make thee great. For thou shalt stand as a counsellor among the honored of thy sex, and by thy example thou shalt teach them to honor the law of Sarah. Thy husband shall love and honor thee, and thy house shall be a house of joy and peace, and all who dwell therein shall rise up to bless thee. The blessings of the earth shall be multiplied unto thee, even in the fruits of flocks and herds, orchards and gardens, and thou shalt dwell in costly habitations; and when the meek shall flee to Zion, through the abundance that shall be around thee, thou shalt feed, clothe and comfort the poor and the needy, and give habitations to the homeless; and the blessings of the poor shall ever rest upon thee; and with thy husband thou shalt do thy full part in all the works of righteousness pertaining to the building up of Zion, gathering her children, rearing her holy temples, and laboring therein, both for the living and the dead; for thou shalt see the holy temple reared in Zion, shall strike hands with the Son of Man when He shall descend to the earth, and shall minister therein when His glory shall fill its courts. Thy days shall be many upon the earth, and thy power for usefulness shall be great. For the spirit of blessing and consolation shall rest upon thee and faith shall spring up in thy heart, to rebuke affliction, to command the Destroyer that no power shall invade thy habitations to destroy thy peace or take away thy loved ones. The angels shall camp around thee, if thou wilt be admonished to call upon the name of the Lord thy God and to forget not to call upon His name.

[page 662]

1890—For thou art among the most favored of the daughters of Abraham, and entitled to every privilege that belongs to the wives, the mothers and the matrons ~~of~~ in Zion, to stand in thy place as a counsellor to admonish, to teach, and to cultivate the younger of thy sex; and all who hear thy voice shall cleave unto thee and love thee; and all thy kindred shall rejoice in thee because of the wisdom and spirit of consolation and blessing which shall drop as pearls from thy lips. Associated with thy husband thou shalt stand in thy place and officiate for thy sex in the great day of Israel's crowning under the hands of the children of Ephraim. And thy inheritance shall be forever in Zion, which, with thy companion thou shalt receive when the Ancient of Days does sit. All these blessings I seal upon thy head, together with all thy former blessings, and I seal thee up unto eternal lives, to come forth in the morning of the first ressurrection, to inherit thrones and dominions, in the name of the Lord Jesus Christ. Amen.

Patriarchal Blessing by B. F. Johnson, given in Tempe A. T. May 25, 1889, upon Benjamin Samuel Johnson, son of Benjamin F. and Mary Ann Johnson, born in Santaquin, Utah Co. Utah, April 20th, 1853

Benjamin Samuel, in the name of the Lord Jesus and through the priesthood of the Fathers, I lay my hands upon thy head to give thee a father's blessing. Thou art one of those who were valiant for the truth and didst shout hosanna to the Most High before the foundations of the earth were laid, that it would be thy privilege to come forth to assist in bringing forth Zion and in gathering her children from the four corners of the earth. Thy blessing is in Ephraim, and the Lord has a mighty work for thee to do in assisting to bring to pass His purposes. He has given thee a companion & He will continue to multiply blessings unto thee, according to the fullness of thy desires to serve and obey Him; and inasmuch as thou wilt accept it, thou shalt become a minister of salvation and one of the mightiest among the sons of Zion, & thy voice shall make the wicked to tremble in nations afar off.

[page 663]

1890—And the meek of the earth shall rejoice in thee, and gather around thee as flocks unto their shepherds. The winds and the waves shall obey thee, Devils shall flee before thee, while the sick and the lame, the blind and the halt, shall be healed by thy command. The Spirit of the Lord shall be within thee, and His wisdom shall be as a well of water springing up unto eternal life. Thy arm shall be strong to resist oppression and to avenge the blood of the innocent. The poor shall ever rejoice in thee, for the Lord will open unto thee the treasures of the earth, & thou shalt feed the hungry, clothe the naked, and be mighty in assisting to rear the temples, cities and bulwarks in Zion and in gathering her children. Wives and children shall be multiplied unto thee, and thou shalt lead them in the way of the Lord, and they shall honor thee, & they shall carry thy name and fame in honor to all generations of time. Thy days and thy years shall be multiplied unto thee. Thou shalt assist in rearing the holy temple in Zion, and thou shalt minister therein with thy companion, when the glory of the Lord shall rest upon its towers and fill its courts: and when Israel returns from the north country to receive their crowning in Zion, thou and thy companion shalt minister unto them. Thy habitations shall ever be in peace, and abundance of the earth shall ever be unto thee. Faith shall increase with thee; wisdom and the treasures of knowledge shall ~~shall~~ fill thee. The Lord shall loose thy tongue, and thou shalt become a mighty councillor in Zion: and every blessing that thy heart shall desire the Lord will bestow upon thee. All these blessings I seal upon thee with power to accomplish every good purpose of thy heart; and I seal thee up unto eternal life, to come forth in the morning of the first ressurrection, to be crowned with glory, immortality and eternal lives, in the name of Jesus. Amen.

J. H. Martineau, Scribe

[page 664]

March 27, 1890—Went to Nephi. Found Elvira and family well, but Susan was not there and it seemed very lonesome to me, although Elvira was as good to me as she could be, and so were they all. I spent several days in copying keys of principle from the "Times and Seasons," of 1884, into my book of "Pearls." Among other things a description of the city of Zion, as it will be laid out, and its twelve temples.

April 3, 1890—Started back to Gila Bend, Pres[t] Robson having declined to do anything with the canal work. At Gila Bend I found letters from Susan, Joel, and others. My duties in the Mexican Custom House at La Ascencion amounted to $145.[00] [$3,138], of which $32.67 [$707] was on new wagon, $39.49 [$703] on new harness, $11.80 [$255] on Side saddle (worth about $8.00 [$173]) on 100 lbs sugar $6.81 [$147]. Aduana papers $20.45 [$443]. So you see it costs something to go into Mexico.

April 6, 1890—Letter from Locke to go to Tucson. He sent $10.[00] [$216] for expenses. Arrived in Tucson 2.15 P.M. Began to make estimates (canal)

April 8, 1890—Changed from Palace Hotel to the Russ House.

April 9, 1890—Made Canal report to Col. Snead, our N. Y. broker and agent. Also began to board (day) at Cosmopolitan hotel and sleeping on a cot in Barnes' office.

April 10, 1890—Sent report and map of Canal lands, to Locke.

April 11, 1890—Letter from Jesse N. who is traveling in Germany.

April 12, 1890—Good news about canal from Locke. On strength of it bought 2 collars and 20[¢] worth (6) of oranges.

April 15, 1890—Letter from Virginia, who is in S. L. City alone, in debt, trying to earn her own living. Sent her $15.00 [$325].

April 16, 1890—Engaged by Barnes and Capt. A. E. Miltimore U.S.A. as Engineer to bring out water from the Rillito creek 10 miles from here, near Fort Lowell. Went with Miltimore to look at it. Began making estimates and surveys on the work (Rillito).

April 19, 1890—Locke expects to begin work right away on our canal. Wants me ready

April 20, 1890—Woke suddenly and thought I heard Susan cry out, "Oh James," as if sick. I prayed for her—which is all I can do for her now.

April 22, 1890—Caught bad cold on the Rillito, by sitting in Shade with coat off. From this time continued canal work and making plan and estimates for reservoir &c.

[page 665]

May 5, 1890—Today the Mexicans celebrate their victory over Maximilian—the Cinco de Mayo—(5th of May). Receive and write many letters.

May 12, 1890—Wrote a kind, good letter to Jessie, enclosed under cover to Ja[s] Sharp, where she is teaching his children. The letter and money I sent Virginia returned to me. Sent it her again, care of Charlie. Sent my article to Contributor, "A Leap for life or death." I send monthly articles to it for publication.

May 21, 1890—Sent $48.00 [$1,089] to Nordhaus, Deming, to pay for the harness.

May 23, 1890—Sent articles to Young Woman's Journal, "Woman's Power," also poetry, "I'll remember you love in my prayers."

May 25, 1890—Wrote article for Phoenix "Gazette," in defense of Mormonism.

May 26, 1890—Wrote article for Tucson "Star," in defense of Mormonism.

May 31, 1890—Wrote article for Tucson "Star," on our religious belief. by request.

June 6, 1890—Sent $50. [$1,082] to pay for Elvira's Sewing machine & $20.[00] [$433] to store.

June 10, 1890—Went to Gila Bend and returned Tucson 12th

June 13, 1890—Sent $60.[00] [$1,298] to Susan. Attended Capt. Miltimore's court martial.

June 19, 1890—Got a letter from Jessie's mother. Forbids me to write again.[108] All my enemies shall finally fall away, and God will give me the victory. Gen[l] R. A. Johnson offered me a small survey of part of township near Yuma. Accepted it.

June 21, 1890—Executed Bond, as U. S. Dep. Surveyor, $1200.[00] [$25,968]

June 22, 1890—Sent plan of house to Susan.

June 24, 1890—~~Recd a check from "Contributor" for $20.00 my first pay as an Author. Also~~ A letter from Adaline Benson, of Logan.[109]

June 29, 1890—My friend J. A. Heatley was very sad. No work, no money. I felt impressed & told him he should have his way opened from this time. He said he believed my words.

July 1, 1890—Rec[d] a letter from F. K. Nebecker.[110] He wants to marry Lilla.

July 5, 1890—Sent articles to Contributor: "Scout," and "Wonderful Ride."

July 7, 1890—Sent Theodore $3.00 [$65] at Deming, a little bit, but nearly all I had.

July 5, 1890—Wrote a blessing letter to Susan. Received a letter from her next day. She dreamed she wanted to come to me, but a swift river intervened. She went into a room, went to the door, saw she was near the shore, jumped about five feet, and found me not expecting her.

July 9, 1890—I had a singular dream, which I believe will at some future time be fulfilled. (see next page)

[page 666]

July 9, 1890—

Scene 1.

I seemed to be in a large room with three or four men whom I knew but do not now recollect. One of them told me I was to move a large flock of sheep—700.000—from where we were to the South, It seemed to me an immense undertaking, so great a number, and I spoke of it, when one said quickly, "Why, there are 500.000 of them already there." (in the South) I felt relieved as the labor seemed so much less, now.

Scene 2nd Got ready to travel, with teams &c. Found the well dipped almost dry—so many getting water. Then started out with a team of 7 or 8 spans of mules & big wagon.

Scene 3. I was in the South, and saw a tall palm tree, with a large fruit hanging just under its leaves, Looking closer, I saw a braided basket hanging there—the fruit inside, and the object of the basket was to protect the fruit until it should come to maturity. The basket was much in shape of a thimble 18 or 20 inches long, mouth upward.

My interpretation. I believe the 700.000 sheep was to show that a great many sheep—indians, or seed of Joseph—are to be gathered into the fold of Christ in the land South, and that I may be called at some time, to help gather them. And it is not generally known there are so many sheep now there.

The draining of the well, seems to show the fullness of our preparations for the work, and using all our resources for it.

The fruit growing on the palm, hidden and protected by the basket, shows God has good fruit ripening there, hidden from the world for the present, but quietly growing and ripening, and will be preserved from evil. The palm shows a warm southern climate, perhaps, Mexico, Central or South America.

When I went to bed, I was anxious about my debts, and prayed for a comforting dream. This dream was given, not in answer to my temporal anxieties, but in relation to our spiritual labors, as more important.—the salvation of Souls.

July 16, 1890—Received $450.[00] [$9,738] from Logan, being the remainder that I had in Bank there—the last of my $3000.[00] [$64,921] All right. My Father will provide.

[page 667]

1890—A Wonder. Contributor sent me $20.[00] [$433] for my writing. This is the first I ever received so.

---

108 This could be a reference to Martineau's third wife, Jesse Helen Russell Anderson Grieve. They were married in the Salt Lake City Endowment House on April 18, 1887.

109 There are Adeline Bensons (note spelling) in Logan, Utah; none match this entry.

110 Frank K. Nebeker (note spelling difference here and in the October 30th entry) was an instructor at Brigham Young College. He taught "English, rhetoric, history and theology." Ricks and Cooley defined him as a "dapper gentleman" (Ricks and Cooley, *History of a Valley*, 355).

July 17, 1890—Deposited $450.^{00} [$9,738] in Consolidated National Bank of Tucson. Paid Des. News $6.00 [$130] for 2 copies of paper

July 21, 1890—Rec^{d} my written instructions as U.S. Dep. Surveyor, from Johnson.

July 22, 1890—Thermometer 109°, hottest day thus far.

July 31, 1890—Began to Copy my Book of "Pearls," so Henry can have a copy.

August 3, 1890—Began surveying Rillito canal. Very hot, 107° Caught in a cloud burst and flood. Worked on canal from day to day to [blank]

August 9, 1890—Sent Bank of Tempe $400.^{00} [$8,656] to apply on Sam's note. ($1000. [$21,640]) Also sent interest for the month—$9.^{00} [$195] which continued every month until April 1891. I constantly receive and write letters, 10 to 15 a week, which, with other work, keeps me very busy.

August 11, 1890—Spent today in regulating the Solar transit I will survey with.

August 13, 1890—Rec^{d} a letter from the Bank of Tempe giving me more time in which to pay Sam's note of $1000 [$21,640]. This was in answer to my prayer for help from the Lord. The note was given due in 6 mo. and secured by mortgage on Sam's entry of 160 acres, containing the homes of himself and six brothers. I feared lest the bank foreclose, and take their homes, & such a disgrace to me, robbing them of their homes seemed to me worse than death. After I prayed, the voice of the Spirit whispered that I should not come to any disgrace or evil but should pay all my debts in due time to the full satisfaction of all concerned; that no one should suffer any loss by me, and that God would bless me and give me my desires. Also other precious promises, which greatly cheered me.

August 17, 1890—Sunday. Fasted all day till night, and prayed much.

August 18 , 1890—A letter from my sister Netta (Mrs. D. C. Lyon) She says our father's first wife was a Mrs. Hawkins, widow of Captain Hawkins of the British Navy, who had two children, Samuel & Elizabeth, both dead many years ago. Mrs. Hawkins was daughter to Earl Stanhope, who at his death willed her £8.000 and £1000 each to ~~Samuel & Elizabeth, her children~~. Julia and Lucretia, her children by my father—my half sisters.

[page 668]

August 18, 1890—I believe Mrs. Hawkins was originally [several words erased] daughter to Earl Stanhope, who is related closely to the Earls of Bedford,

Rec^{d} letter from nephi. He had endowed No. 8 George Hows on May 15.1890. Ord^{d} by Robt Henderson & S. Roskelly. Emma endowed Mrs. Maria Margaret Hows, his wife & was proxy in sealing by Pres^{t} M. W. Merrill, May 15/90

On May 16, 1890 Nephi Endowed David Elwin, ord^{d} by M. W. Merrill. Emma endowed Mary Clementine Stuart. Sealed by N. C. Edlefsen. Witnesses R. Henderson, J. A. McAlister.

August 23, 1890—To day Lyman had a boy born to him, who weighed 10 lbs. He was named Preston Martineau. after Bp. Preston.

August 25, 1890—Copied into "Pearls" from Pres^{t} Woodruff's sermon.

August 29, 1890—Letter from Susan. She says Gertrude, Anna & Dora were poisoned and nearly died, by eating toadstools in a mistake for mushrooms. They were only saved by prompt emetics, and especially by the power of the priesthood. Gertrude was very sick a week or ten days. The others got well sooner. Susan had been warned in a dream the previous night, but forgot all about it until they were poisoned. I thank thee, my Father, for thy goodness.

September 2, 1890—A good letter from M. Thatcher. He says Lyman has a new boy. Have not heard from Lyman yet about it.

September 5, 1890—Letter from Lyman, who says his boy was born Sat. 23^{d} Aug. & weighed 10 lbs.

September 11, 1890—Finished my surveys, estimates and plans of the Rillito dam and canal

September 13, 1890—Borrowed $175.^{00} [$3,787] from Bank for my survey, in addition to my $50.^{00} [$1,082] in bank. Wrote an article for the "Star" by request, condemning the Fiesta de San Augustin. Also finished copying my "Pearls." By letter from Charles I learn his new baby boy was born Aug. 11th at 12 P.M. His is Bryant Sherman Martineau

September 14, 1890—My bill for engineering &c on Rillito creek, amounts to $217.05 [$4,707], against Pima Land and Water Company.

[page 669]

September 15, 1890—Started to day for Yuma, to Survey U. S. public land.

September 16, 1890—Arrived at Yuma, 240 miles, And arranged for Mexicans. Was detained at Yuma by rain and washout until the [18th]

September 18, 1890—I went to Blaisdell, 10 miles with my party of four men to begin work on Survey. Found beginning point, & Surv^{d} ½ mile.

September 19, 1890—Very hot. Ran 4^{m} and thus had to walk 5 miles to camp arrived late, tired out. Almost stepped a big coiled rattle snake, but saw him in time to miss stepping on him. He was coiled up in thick grass and weeds.

September 20, 1890—Not so hot today—only 120° in shade.

September 28, 1890—Have been surveying all last week, & suffered much from intense heat, thirst and fatigue, climbing steep rocky hills & mountains, or going through dense thickets of thorns. One day I was toiling up a high mountain, almost exhausted with heat & thirst, and in my distress prayed for a little cool wind to revive me. Immediately a gentle, cooling breeze came, unspeakably refreshing to me. I was so glad tears of joy flowed as I thanked the Holy Father for his mercies. He also heard and answered my prayers for aid at other times. The Lord is very merciful.

September 29, 1890—Went from Blaisdell to Gila City, 6 miles, to finish the rest of the Township on North Side of the Gila river, which is high, broad and deep. Crossed in a Mexican's boat.

October 2, 1890—Finished my survey, and returned to Blaisdell. I also had meandered both banks of the Gila—over 17 miles—all of which was in dense thickets of thorns or river mud, & suffered greatly from heat and thirst. Often had to creep on hands and knees under the brush to get through, my clothing wet through with sweat. It was the hardest job I ever had to do in my life.

October 7, 1890—Detained by another washout since ~~last~~ 4th inst. My expenses of survey are $250.^{00} [$5,410] Went to Gila Bend.

October 8, 1890—To Tucson.

October 11, 1890—To day Judge Barnes said he would no longer pay for my board on behalf of the Gila Bend Canal Co. I have only $5 [$108] or $6.^{00} [$130] money. What I shall do I do not know, but I believe God will open my way for me, though it seems very dark, naturally speaking.

[page 670]

October 11, 1890—I can get no employment of any kind, to pay for food, much less to pay any thing on the debt I owe or the monthly interest of $12.^{00} [$260] which must be paid or I be disgraced, the note and mortgage foreclosed. my kindred lose their homes—all by my act. A gloomy picture—a failure would be worse than death to me, because of the shame, grief and dishonor. I can get nothing from the Canal Company, which owes me nearly $5000 [$108,201]. But God has made precious promises to me—and says I will be able to pay all honorably;—I shall not be disgraced; and my time of payment on the note will be extended for me.

Rec^{d} a note from the Bank saying the note had been extended (for payment) a year longer. Oh what a joy to me! How thankful I am to the Father that He has granted this to me, and that He had promised it & fulfilled His promise; thus greatly increasing my faith, & knowledge of the influence and voice of the Holy Spirit. I have fasted and prayed much, and sought to put away all evil and to draw near to God, who has said, "Draw near unto me and I will draw near unto you." I have claimed his promises, in humility and as much faith as I could exercise, and in answer to prayers have received precious promises. But I have doubted, and thought perhaps I was deceived by my own anxiety, mistaking it for the voice of the Holy Spirit. This caused me to pray more, and to ask for light. The answer came in plainness, just as I would reason with my son. The Spirit said, "There are but two powers, that of God and of Satan. Satan does not incite to do any good, but only evil, but the heavenly influence incites to do good, put away all sin, keep all the commandments of the Lord, & to live a holy, pure life. Hath not the voice unto you taught you to do all this? Yes, verily. Was it not good? Yes, verily. As no good comes from Satan, but only from God, this was the voice of God unto thee. Dost thou not see it?" Oh, the mercy and goodness of the Father to condescend to reason thus with me, so full of doubts and unbelief, and yet striving by all means in my power to gain faith and holiness and put away all my evils and my unbelief.

[page 671]

October 11, 1890—So I knew it was the voice of the Lord unto me by the Holy Spirit. And the Lord says in a revelation "I will tell thee in thy heart and in they mind" (See Doc & Cov Sec. 8 v. 2) "Now behold this is the Spirit of revelation; behold this is the spirit by which Moses brought the children of Israel through the Red Sea on dry ground."

Thus I learned the voice of the Holy Spirit—the spirit of revelation, but only in weakness and trembling. But I prayed and fasted much, asking for the spirit of revelation, that I might know the voice of the Holy Spirit, even as plainly as did Moses, and that I might not be deceived by any other spirit. And the Father, in His mercy, and for His own purposes, has greatly blessed me in this, and hath many times answered my questions and instructed me in regard to principles I did not understand, as plainly as one talking with another. All honor, and glory be to the Father for His mercy forever.

October 19, 1890—Went with Mr. Thomas, Engineer of the Royal Albert docks, London, to look at my proposed work on the Rillito. He greatly approved what I had done, and my plans. Prayed, and was told the Lord was going to prosper me soon. So I went and bought me a hat, out of my little money. I was told to wear good clothes, and not to doubt. So I also bought a shirt and some collars and necktie, believing the intimation of the Spirit.

October 20, 1890—Wrote to Susan, and blessed her. She deserves it all. She prays for me and comforts me, prophesying good for me.

October 22, 1890—Presented my field notes of Survey to Sur. Gen[l] Johnson. Sent article for "Contributor," and article for "Star" on the "Manifesto" of last Conference.[111]

October 30, 1890—Rec[d] a letter from F. K. Nebeker, who asks me for Lilla.

October 31, 1890—Told Nebeker "yes"—if he would be good always to Lilla and be a true L. D. Saint.[112] Rec[d] a letter from Don LeBaron, who is distressed about the mortgage, so he wants to sell.

[page 672]

October 31, 1890—I felt very badly about it, and asked for help. I was greatly comforted. Told I should be able to pay every debt and no one should lose by me, but be benefited, for they should sell for a better price than they could obtain now. So I was comforted; for I believe it, though I cannot see any way for it to come true, naturally speaking. Samuel & Elvira are also much distressed. for their kindred are very angry with them, and treat them shamefully, which adds much to my grief. Wrote to comfort them, and prophesied good for them.

November 2, 1890—Wrote article for "Star" and "Gazette." Fasted and prayed, and had precious principles explained to me by the Spirit. I fast now each Sunday and Thursday—all day, striving to gain power favor ["favor" written over the top of "power"] with the Lord, faith, and spirit of revelation. I also pray regularly morning noon and night, besides other times. We are so counseled to do by Apostle Lyman, and I find the more I pray, the more I gain in faith and the Holy Spirit, which testifies to me when I pray that my prayer is heard and will be answered. But I am told that although what I ask for is right, it is not expedient to have everything at once, but a little at a time, lest the top of the tree outgrow the root; and thus grow more steadily, slowly and safely. I can see this is best. So if I do not get what I desire now, it is because it is not for my best good; therefore I am content, knowing that the Lord doeth all things well.[113]

111 The Manifesto of 1890 issued by President Wilford Woodruff discontinued the practice of plural marriage. This pivotal proclamation sparked rumors, leading to dissenting splinter groups, and ushered the primary body of the Church into the mainstream of American society. For the Official Declaration 1 and related excerpts of "Wilford Woodruff Regarding the Manifesto," see "Official Declaration 1," Doctrine and Covenants; Ludlow, *Encyclopedia of Mormonism*, 2:852–53. For a Logan perspective, see Ricks and Cooley, *History of a Valley*, 116–17; for a Mexican perspective, see Tullis, *Mormons in Mexico*, 69–70.

112 Compare with entry and related footnote regarding July 1 of this same year.

113 Martineau describes not only his financial struggles but also spiritual challenges and feelings in this time of transition within the Church. Thursday was a "fast day" in the Church. The purpose of fasting was a renewal of the spirit. Today's fast day practice suggests that the members of the Church

November 5, 1890—Letter from "Contributor." Praise for my articles & wish me to Continue writing. Wrote "A Stolen Child."[114]

November 6, 1890—fasted,

November 7, 1890—Revised my article for publication.

November 8, 1890—A good comforting letter from Br. M. Thatcher. Hear good news about our canal. Am desired to make profile and report, for parties in New York. This took me several days, but only in the end for disappointment and double discouragement.

November 13, 1890—Had a letter from Mr. Blaisdell.[115] I had given him a check for $22.00 [$476], and it was found I had no funds in the bank.

[page 673]

1890—His letter was a scorcher. I was very much distressed. Disgrace was before me, and I had no money to pay it. nor any way to earn any. I had eaten nothing from Tuesday to ~~Thursday~~ Saturday evening for want of money for meals, keeping 50¢ [$11]—all I had—for an emergency. I fasted and prayed "Oh Father help me in my distress and help me that I may not be disgraced." He comforted me, and said my way should be opened. To ask Judge Barnes (who had told me he would not advance another cent upon any consideration) for money: that he would let me have it, and be a friend to me. So I felt comforted, though it was hard to believe I could get any money from Barnes, knowing his cold, greedy Spirit for wealth, and his inordinate selfishness. I prayed earnestly for faith.

November 14, 1890—I asked Barnes for $30.00 [$649] to pay Blaisdell and for a week's board at the restaurant. He would not, but when I said I had not eaten for so many days. he let me have it without a word. I will remember him for it. It was the answer to prayer, and fulfilled the promise of the Father to me, in every particular. Oh my Father, I thank thee and praise and adore thy holy name for all thy goodness to me a sinner! Oh that I may be able to spend the rest of my life in doing the will of my Father, who is so good to me in thus teaching me faith in Him, and how to know the voice of the spirit by so many testimonies—promises & fulfillments.

I feel that surely God is preparing me for something great—that I may yet do a great work for Zion, and [. . .] thus preparing me for it. I paid Blaisdell, and got a week's meal ticket—$5.00 [$108] with $3.00 [$65] left.

[written in margin]

Henry's baby girl was born November 14. 1890 of Melissa.

November 16, 1890—Sunday. Fasted as usual, and climbed Sentinel Hill. It was shown me that Moroni stood on this hill and viewed the camp beneath his retreating host of Nephites, who marched past this point on their way from [the] south, coming by where Nogales now stands, the only natural pass west of the Sierra Madres. So I call it Moroni's hill. Prayed and had a blessed time.

[page 674]

November 20, 1890—Wrote—"Utah in 1850" for "Contributor."[116]

November 23, 1890—Sunday. Fasted and prayed. Was told I should begin to prosper from this very hour; my way will open; friends will be raised up to me, and I shall be blessed.

November 26, 1890—Was engaged to work as special draughtsman in office of Surveyor General, to make a map of the west boundary of the White Mountain Indian reservation, 92 1/5 miles long, at $125.00 [$2,705] per month. Thus hath the father begun to fulfill His promise in blessing me. Father, I thank thee.

December 4, 1890—Recd letter from Col. R. J. Hinton, Interior Dept, Washington, requesting me to send statistics about canals &c. &c

December 10, 1890—Henry says in his letter Melissa's baby was born November 14/90 Susan says we now have 38 grand children, as follows:—Henry 7 [children], Moroni 7 Elvira 7 Nephi 4 Albert 1 Lyman 5 Charly 3, Hagberg 4 = 38. The promise to me is that

abstain from two meals on the first Sunday of the month and give the money saved to the poor through fast offerings.

114 Santiago, "A Stolen Child," *Contributor*, December 1890, 75–78.

115 This is likely from one of the Blaisdell family of Yuma, Arizona, where Martineau was working for a short period. Blaisdell was also the name given a farm area just west of Yuma.

116 James Henry Martineau, "Pioneer Sketches, Utah in 1850," *Contributor*, January 1891, 93–96.

my children shall become a great nation, and it will be fulfilled.

December 11, 1890—A letter from Susan. She has had a hard time and has done nobly. Her brother Almon went to Deming, took smallpox came home and died. Then his wife and two children died in a week or two, and his three remaining children were quarantined 1½ miles in a house all alone, no one daring to go to them, only to bring them provisions. Susan and her niece Anna Hilton, went one day to see them and determined to stay with the poor little stricken flock of 15, 11 and 8 years of age, although neither of them had had the disease, and were therefore almost certain to take it, and there was no physician or medicine in the country. So they staid several days, until some one was sent as nurse who had had the disease, and they returned home. But God wonderfully blessed them, so that neither of them took the disease, nor infected any of their families by their clothing. It was a true miracle, or exhibition of the power and blessings of the Lord, and of faith and heroism in Susan and Anna. May the Father bless them forever. I blessed her in letter.

[page 675]

1890–1891

December 13, 1890—Was in great need of money to pay tax on my land in Pima, to prevent it being sold by the sheriff, and to day got $60.[00] [$1,298] sent me by Susan, who sold our new wagon to Henry for $150.[00] [$3,246] So I sent money for taxes to Pima.

December 14, 1890—Sat. Fasted 24 hours. A letter from Susan telling of her danger. Does not know yet if she will have smallpox or not. Prayed much for her. Elvira and Sam write that Uncle Benjamin, Don LeBaron and others had to flee to Mexico on a few hours notice to escape arrest for polygamy. I had just written uncle Ben that his place was in Mexico, and he skipped while my letter was on the way to him, & reached him in Mexico. So I was led aright.

December 17, 1890—Nephi writes he has bought a lot of church cattle on credit, of Bp. Preston.

December 21, 1890—Sunday. Fasted as usual, all day

December 25, 1890—Thursday. Fasted as usual, all day

December 27, 1890—Wrote for Contributor "Athirst in the desert."—my own experience near Gila bend some months ago.[117]

December 28, 1890—Fasted.

December 29, 1890—Sent $4.[00] [$87] for Juvenile Instructor for Susan & Henry.

December 31, 1890—Rec[d] ~~$131~~ $126.40 [$2,735] for this month's work, also $20.84 [$451] for November.

JANUARY 1891 THURSDAY

Thursday, January 1, 1891—Fasted, to begin the year humbly and faithfully, in hopes I may do better this year than ever before.

Wrote article for Contributor, "Legends of the Deluge."

January 2, 1891—Believing that the Lord is going to bless me and open my way more fully, I bought an overcoat—$10.50 [$227]—which I much needed in this cold weather.

January 4, 1891—Fasted, as this is Sunday. Took a five mile walk. Wrote as usual to Susan.

January 7, 1891—Sent $2.48 [$54] to Montgomery Ward & Co. for chess men and bible.

January 12, 1891—Very cold. Was obliged to buy a mattress for my cot, $3.00 [$65]

To day Joel started with three others across the Sierra Madre Mts, into Sonora to see a tract of land offered for sale. This I learned from letters from Susan.

January 18, 1891—Fasted, being Thursday. I fast Sundays and Thursdays.

[page 676]

January 19, 1891—Subscribed for Sunday Republican for Susan. By request of Agricultural Dept. Washington, I made them a report of canals &c of Arizona.

January 20, 1891—By letter from Jesse N. I find he has been traveling through Germany, Switzerland, and Italy. Lyman having sent him money for that pur-

117 James Henry Martineau, "A Thirst in the Desert," *Contributor*, February 1891, 155–58. See also J. H. Martineau, "A Mild Climate," *Deseret News*, December 27, 1890; Utah Digital Newspapers.

pose. Lyman is a good son and a good brother, and he has done much for his mothers children.

January 21, 1891—Had fun with a phonograph this evening at Gen[l] R. A. Johnson's house for the first time in my life.[118]

January 22, 1891—To day I was greatly frightened. The Sur. Gen[l] (Johnson) told me he expected my survey would be rejected. The Gov. Inspector had reported to him that a certain corner was not as represented in my notes, &c &c If my survey be rejected I will have no means to repay my loan at the Tucson bank ($200.$^{\underline{00}}$) [$4,328] nor redeem Sam's mortgage, and disgrace and shame will cover me. I walked in the public square until late in the night, and besought the Father to avert such great disaster. I prayed that He would take me, rather than have it happen me. The Holy Spirit comforted me and said I should <u>not</u> be disgraced; all will be well; to see Bussey (Gov[t] Inspector of surveys) and he will be my friend, and will help me.

~~**January 23 , 1891**~~—I saw Bussey, and explained about the Corner to Bussey's satisfaction. He said he will do all he can for me.

I have continually extraordinary trials and contradictions (spiritual) but I believe they are to test my faith, and to prepare me for something better and greater, that I may do a greater work. Also to teach me to know and trust the voice and teachings of the Holy Spirit, that it may be a guide to me. The promise, "Come unto me all ye weary and heavy laden and I will give you rest," is a great comfort to me, and I do strive with all my might to come unto Him.

Sent another article to Contributor "Traditions of the Deluge."[119]

January 27, 1891—Bad word again about my survey. It seems sure to be rejected. No hope, naturally speaking. Prayed, and the Lord comforted me, just as He did before, repeating the same promises. It gave me faith, though I can not see how it can come about.

[page 677]

January 31, 1891—Rec[d] my pay for this month, $129.60 [$2,805]

FEBRUARY 1891 SUNDAY

February 1, 1891—Sunday. Walked upon the mountain west of Tucson and prayed. I found beautiful flowers growing there among the rocks. I Sent Albert $10.$^{\underline{00}}$ [$216] to help him pay his taxes. Fasted.

February 8, 1891—Fasted all day as usual. being Thursday. Paid my note in bank for $175.^{00} [$3,787] & $13.^{00} [$281] interest = $188.$^{\underline{00}}$ [$4,068]. I thank thee, my Father, that one big debt is thus paid.

February 11, 1891—To day Albert's baby was born (learned subsequently)

February 14, 1891—Letter from Virginia. Says she is going to marry Ed[d] Sudbury in a few months, and desires my approbation.[120]

February 15, 1891—Sunday. Fasted as usual and wrote to Virginia.

February 16, 1891—Sent 38[¢] for book on chess, also for a book for Dora. Letter from Elvira. Says her baby had been very sick, saved only by faith and the priesthood. She feels very thankful, continually, she was taught by her parents to pray to God while a child. Her prayers have often been answered.

February 17, 1891—Albert writes me of the birth of their baby-girl, born Feb. 11$^{\underline{th}}$ She is named Emma. He had sold his place and will move into Mexico next fall.

February 18, 1891—Last Monday morning about 2 A.M. I awoke & prayed, & asked how I might know positively the voice and teaching of the Holy Spirit, and how did Moses know it, being taught, as the revelation tells us—"I will tell you in your heart and in your mind" &c (See Chap. 8 of Doc. & Cov.) which is called the spirit of revelation.[121] I was shown how Moses was taught and he proved it by his obedience, which brings not only faith but <u>knowledge</u>.

118 This is likely one of Thomas A. Edison's inventions, the Edison Cylinder or the Edison Standard Phonograph.

119 James Henry Martineau, "Traditions of the Deluge, I. The Chaldean Story," *Contributor*, March 1891, 167–71; see also James Henry Martineau, "Traditions of the Deluge, II. Greek and Other Traditions," *Contributor*, April 1891, 213–17.

120 Virginia Martineau (1870–1904) was the fifth child of James Henry and Susan Julia Sherman Martineau. Virginia and Edward Sudbury were married September 16, 1891.

121 Martineau is finding strength from the scriptures. He references Doctrine and Covenants 8:2–3; 9:7–9, which talk about answers to prayer.

Also, it is right to anoint my own body or members when diseased to bless it, and rebuke disease from it as from the body of anyone else. I asked this because of my rheumatism, catarrh and injured voice & lungs.[122] So I arose, lit a candle, and anointed and blessed various parts, & rebuked disease.

[page 678]

February 18, 1891—The pain all left every part. I was told I should be healed by so doing, and not to buy drugs and medicines. I had been thinking to buy some catarrh medicine and liniment. I felt a strong faith in this ordinance and in the promises, and will not buy drugs any more. I felt overflowing with joy to think the Lord would so teach one so sinful as I am. But He is full of mercy.

February 19, 1891—Rec[d] a letter from Edward Sudbury, asking for Genie. I told him in reply—yes, if he would love and cherish her, and so live as a Saint as to gain his celestial glory. Not knowing him myself, I wrote to Lyman & sent him Sudbury's letter, if he could say nothing against him.

February 20, 1891—Wrote to F. F. Hintze, late a missionary in Armenia, asking for date &c on monument of an ancestor—a Roman officer, whose ancient tomb he saw in Armenia.[123] Erected in memory of one Martinus. The Encyclopedia Britannica says my name—Martineau—was Martinus in Latin, Martino in Italian, Martinho in Portuguese, Martino in Spanish, & Martin in German and English. I have ascertained my ancestors were of ancient Roman stock. Besides this ancient Roman Soldier—Martinus, in the year 235 A.D. another relative—a young girl 15 years old was burned as a christian martyr. Her name was Martina—feminine form of Martinus. I have had her baptized, endowed, and sealed to me as a wife. Poor girl! She waited a long time for her redemption—over 1600 years. She was burned because she would not abjure her religion, only 15 years old.[124] How many L. D. Saints would do that to day? Would I be able to do it. I would not like to be tested.

February 22, 1891—As I was going to my room to night about 12.30 (midnight), a fellow wanted to rob me as I was returning from playing chess, but he did not make it out.

[page 679]

February 26, 1891—Word came from Washington that my survey is approved! Words are feeble to express my joy and thankfulness. The amount—$518.14 [$11,213] was almost like a gift, for the Sur.[r] General had said the survey would be rejected; though I tried, as much as possible, to have faith in the promise made me by the Holy Spirit that ~~I~~ my survey would be approved and I would get my pay.—a promise made me when in anguish of soul I cried unto God for help, almost wishing for death. The Father gave me peace and comfort, but when I began to think about it naturally, it seemed so unlikely that I feared lest I had been deceived, and that some other—some evil spirit—had deceived me. But when I prayed to know about this, the answer was always the same—I should not be disgraced but should get my pay, and this would be another testimony to me that the voice which had spoken to me was the voice of the Holy Spirit—the same that spoke to and led Moses in the wilderness. This, then, was my greatest joy—to know that the Lord hears and answers my prayers, weak and sinful as I am, in His wonderful mercy and goodness. How merciful should we be to those who injure us, when the Lord is so merciful to us. I pray thee, oh Father, to forgive my weakness and doubts! Help me to put away all doubt, and have full trust in Thee, and help me that I may know the voice of the Spirit as plainly as did Moses thy servant!

February 28, 1891—Rec[d] my month's pay, $92.40 [$2,000].

MARCH 1891

March 1, 1891—Fasted, Sunday. Wrote to Susan as usual. All this winter I have written many letters each week, to Susan and the children, teaching them principles of truth and holiness to the best of my ability, that I may be clear, and that they may be one with me in the building up of the work of the Lord, and that the promises made me may all be fulfilled, as I believe they will be, for I have faith that the Lord will help me.

122 *Catarrh* is inflammation of mucous membranes, especially of the nose and throat.

123 Ferdinand F. Hintze was the Turkish Mission president.

124 *Abjure* is to renounce or recant solemnly.

[page 680]

March 4, 1891—Took a very bad cold—like Lagrippe.

March 4 7, 1891—This morning after prayer I received instructions about my house I shall build in Mexico, and a room in it dedicated to prayer &c, And of blessings I shall receive in it. Also that I shall receive all my canal pay in due time: also great and glorious promises of blessings and prosperity & usefulness in Mexico, which I believed but will not write now, lest it seem like boasting. It is not boasting in me, but a wish to show the goodness of the Lord to me, and how He fulfills his promises—that I write these things for an example to my family.

March 8, 1891—Sunday. Fasted as usual.

March 10, 1891—Finished my Maps to day and cease work in the office. I have received in all, there, $402.63 [$8,713] and $5.00 [$108] besides, making $407.63 [$8,871]. This has enabled me to pay much of my debts, but I still owe at Tempe $600.00 [$12,984] and $110.00 [$2,380] at Deming, both at 1½ o/c pr. month interest, which I do not know how to pay, having now no more work. But I have a promise from the Lord that I will soon be able to pay all honorably, and I believe it. My pay is $34.65 [$750] making as before stated $402.65 [$8,713].

March 13, 1891—My Birthday—63 years old! I, who always used to think I would not pass 40. At first I thought I would have a treat today—a good 50¢ dinner (as I usually eat but twice a day, often only once a day for several days together). Then I thought best to begin my 64th year in humility—fasting and prayer, that I may do better this year than the last. So I fasted all day, and had many precious keys given me to understand why I was led to leave my beautiful home in Logan for the south with a miserable house and poverty: why I had been afflicted and tried as I have been—all of which have been for my experience and good. Also received precious promises, which will all be so many additional testimonies when fulfilled. Recd loving letters from Susan and Henry. Also a call from J. W. Young, to go to Deming and be Engineer on his new Railroad which he is to build through Mexico to the Pacific. Answered Him, Said I would come.

[page 681]

March 15, 1891—Sunday. fasted. Recd telegram from Ex.-Gov. Wolfley to meet him and moneyed men from Illinois at Gila Bend and with them visit the site of his proposed dam across the Gila River and see, as an Expert, what damage, if any, the late tremendous flood had caused to the site. Previous to this, by Wolfley's request, I had given him a plan for a timber dam at that point, which he much approved. I prayed about it, and was told to go—I should be blessed.[125]

Recd letter from F. F. Hintze, the returned missionary. He says the the tomb of Martinus, the Roman Solder, is in the province of Aleppo, Syria. The inscription was much defaced by time, and the dates illegible. Says Br. Lucander was the one who saw it.

March 16, 1891—Letter from Edd Sudbury, thanking me for my consent.

March 17, 1891—Went to Gila Bend, arrived at 8.30, breakfasted, then went with Wolfly, and William and Samuel Jack of Peoria Ill. up the river 24 miles to the site for dam.

March 18, 1891—Made some measurements of river bed. Dam will be 1800 ft long, and about 20 or 24 ft high. Returned to Gila Bend.

March 19, 1891—Made calculations for my report. Recd $45.00 [$974] fees.

March 20, 1891—Returned to Tucson.

March 23, 1891—Sent $100.00 [$2,164] to Bank of Tempe to apply on Benja's note. Wolfley wants me to copy my map for him—4 copies.

March 24, 1891—Recd draft from Washington for $518.14 [$11,213] of which I sent to Tempe $500.00 [$10,820] to finish payment of Benja's note. Oh how thankful I am it is all paid, just as I was promised, when all seemed so dark, and no earthly way to pay it. But the Lord fulfilled his promise to me, thanks and honor be unto Him forever. Wrote to Benja & Elvira to tell them the good news, that they and I are free!

March 26, 1891—Sent my report to Wm Jack, Peoria Ill. To day Judge Barnes proposed to give to

125 Lewis Wolfley served as Arizona governor from 1889 to 1890 but was not popular. In 1893 he surveyed for the Atlantic and Pacific Railroad Company. In 1889 he started his own newspaper named the *Arizona Republican*, today known as the *Arizona Republic*. For the politics of the era, see John S. Goff, *Arizona Territory 1863–1920: A Political History* (Tucson: University of Arizona Press, 1970).

me and Geo. J. Roskruge a 1/12 share in the Tucson Land and Water Company in return for preliminary surveys we should make to bring water from the Santa Catalina Mts. to Tucson, 12 or 15 miles, in pipes. I believe I will be blessed in it and so accepted the offer. My share would be 2000 shares.

[page 682]

March 25, 1891—The Company own a 1000 acres of good land near Ft Lowell—10 miles from town, and a canal franchise.[126]

March 28, 1891—Got my receipt from Bank of Tempe for payment in full of Samuel's note and mortgage. Finished my 4 maps for Wolfley & received for them $20.00 [$433] Wolfley wants me to make full plans and estimates for his dam and canal, and says I can be Engineer of the work. Also Sur. Genl R. A. Johnson offered to give me another U. S. contract for a land survey of several townships. "When it rains, it pours."

March 29, 1891—Fasted. (Sunday) Went on the hills to pray & be alone.

March 30 , 1891—Began estimates etc for the Dam. Sent my monthly Gila Bend Canal Co. account. The company owe me at the date $6000.00 [$129,841] which I hope to get some time.

March 31, 1891—This morning had a joyful time and precious promises.

Recd 2 volumes (bound) of Contributor, and one sent to Netta.

APRIL—1891.

April 1, 1891—Had a precious season of prayer this morning. Went to Santa Catalina Mts. this morning to see if we can bring water thence in pipes to Tucson.[127] Returned on [3rd]

April 3, 1891—The plan is feasible and good.

April 4, 1891—Recd my trunk from Gila Bend

April 5, 1891—Sunday, fasted as usual. Albert says they named their last baby girl—Elzadie, after Emma's mother.

April 6, 1891—Wrote again to J. W. Young to know if he wants me still on his Mex. Pacific R.R. Survey. I would rather be there, on less salary, than work here among gentiles And Mexico is to be my home for a time, and I would rather build up that land. Sent Spencer's mex. map to him. Started out again to survey water route to Tucson from the mountains. We spent some days in this work, returning to Tucson on Friday 10th

April 10, 1891—Found many letters, as usual. Also letter from J. W. Young to Come to Deming as Engineer on R.R. @ $150.00 [$3,246] pr mo. I prayed for guidance whether to go, or stay here and take the U.S. Surveying offered me, by which I can make much better wages, but be away from my family

[page 683]

April 10, 1891—My desire is to be nearer my family, and I decide to go to the new R. Road, and this the spirit teaches me.

April 11, 1891—Wrote to Albert about my farm—to sell it. Wrote J.W.Y. I will come and assist on his work. Made plans and estimates for Wolfley, for his dam and Canal.

April 12, 1891—Sunday. Fast & pray. Wrote some in my journal.

Recd letters from Home as usual, also from W. D. Johnson Manager North Mex. Pacific Proj, saying he would send a pass for me.

April 13, 1891—Made plan of dam for Wolfley, & recd $10.00 [$216] for it.

April 14, 1891—Estimated on Sabina Cañon water works.[128]

---

126 George L. Ruskruge was a surveyor and supporter of public education in Tucson. He was instrumental in creating the Tucson Unified School District. His survey papers, maps, and correspondence relating to his work in southern Arizona are at the University of Arizona Library Special Collections. Today the Fort Lowell Public Park and Museum attracts tourists to northeast Tucson. The camp, established in 1866, was then on the outskirts of Tucson. The purpose of the fort was to protect the settlers (see Caroline M. Mughston, *Old Fort Lowell* [Tucson: State Consolidate Publishing, 1911]).

127 These mountains are immediately north of Tucson. Mount Lemmon is the prominent peak at just over nine thousand feet. Today it is the only ski resort in southern Arizona.

128 This is a reference to Sabino Canyon (note spelling).

April 15, 1891—Estimated on Sabina Cañon water works. Sent $4.50 [$97] to Desert News for 1 yr. semi Some to Susan & 6 mo. Weekly for me.

April 16, 1891—Sent $5.00 [$108] for books on Hyd. Engineering to Gurly, Troy N. Y.

Worked on Sabina Cañon water works as usual. Up to date I have spent this season all my time since Mch, 1st 1891 and previous to that time 3 months in 1890.

Saturday, April 18, 1891—The Baron von Wendt started to N.Y. city to day to sell his placer gold mine or get money to work it. He made me promise to go and survey for a storage dam and pipe line, to work his placer, and promises to help my interests. I felt impelled to tell him he should be prospered & blessed in his trip and business, which pleased him much.

Recd Letter from the Genl Manager of the N. Mex P. Ry, saying I am engaged as Engineer on that road.

April 19, 1891—Sunday, fasted as usual

April 21, 1891—Prest Harrison visited Tucson. I saw him. Great doings.

April 23, 1891—Sent article to Contributor "Trials and tribulations of a Surveyor."[129] Directed Contributor and Journal to be sent to me here. I had a heavenly time this morning in prayer, and received great promises from the Father.

April 26, 1891—Sunday, and fasted. Next day sent pay roll for Aps.

April 27, 1891—Started with J. C. Scrivener for the placer gold mine at foot of Sante Rita mts. Camped 33 miles away.

April 28, 1891—At destination 58 m. from Tucson.

April 29 & 30, 1891—Worked on Survey of dam and pipe line.

MAY 1. 1891

May 1, 1891—Finished survey and started back to Tucson at 1 P.M.

[page 684]

May 2, 1891—Reached Tucson 1 P.M. tired, hot and dusty.

May 5, 1891—Editor L. C. Hughes of "Star" said Miss I. C. De Velling, a lady organizer of W. C. T. union, who had read my poem "Twilight Memories," in the paper, wished me to call on her. I did so, and spent a pleasant evening. She is a talented & good lady.[130]

May 6, 1891—Wrote an article for "Star" in reply to attack in "Republian" ["Republican"] entitled "no polygamy in the Mormon Church now."

May 8, 1891—Finished estimates, maps and report on the Santa Rita gold placer, and sent to Baron von Wendt. Also worked on Sabina Cañon water supply.

May 10, 1891—Sunday: fasted as usual. Have been very busy on maps estimates and family correspondence all the time. I am still trying to gain the victory over all my sins, and trying to draw nearer to God. I am very happy, except that I so greatly desire to be with my dear family, but I feel that the Lord is leading me, and I desire to be fully subject to his will.

May 11, 1891—This morning after prayer, the Lord gave me precious promises relative to priesthood and its calling, and in regard to temporal and spiritual prosperity—that from this time I shall proper. Help me, my Father, to draw near to Thee.

May 12, 1891—Election day for members to Constitutional Convention.

May 13, 1891—Still working on my plans and estimates for Sabina water.

May 14, 1891—Letter from Jesse N. in Berlin, Germany. He has been honorably released, and expects to leave England May 9th He had been to Munich, Nuremberg, Leipsic, Dresden and other places. He had gained a testimony for himself of this Gospel, and had baptized 12 persons into the Church. Father I think thee for all thy Goodness.

May 15, 1891—Felt sad to day. Prayed and was much comforted & blessed.

May 17, 1891—Sunday. Fasted as usual, and was blessed.

129 James Henry Martineau, "An Engineer's Tribulations," *Contributor*, June 1891, 317–20.

130 Louis C. Hughes pioneered the newspaper known as the *Tucson Star*. He later served as governor from 1893 to 1896 (Jay Wagoner, *Arizona Territory, 1863–1912; A Political History* [Tucson: University of Arizona Press, 1970]). Isabelle C. De Velling could be a temperance lecturer in the area, but at this writing no match could be located.

May 18, 1891—The Baron Alex. von Vendt wrote me from New York, saying he wants me to do his Engineering for his placer mines. I asked the Father, who gave me a testimony in regard to it. So I wrote him favorably.

May 20, 1891—W. D. Johnson wrote me to come to Deming as Engineer on the new North Mex. Pacific R. Y.

[page 685—see Appendix 3 for letter inserted here.]

May 21, 1891—Went to Nephi to visit B. S. & Elvira.

May 23, 1891—I went to Phoenix to see about Sam's mortgage. On our return Elvira and I crossed the Salt River on the ties, the river being dangerous to ford.[131]

May 27, 1891—To day D. T. LeBaron and family, Vilate Johnson and Aunt Susan Johnson and daughter went to Mexico. Surveyed Samuel's 160 land entry, subdividing it. Rec[d] pass R.R.

May 29, 1891—Started for Deming, and arrived there June 2 at 2 A.M. Stopped one day in Tucson to get my things. Read that Gen. B. B. Eggleston, gr. nephew of Ethan Allen, died 27 May 1891 at Wichita, Kansas. My relative.

JUNE 1891

June 2, 1891—Find I must go to Chihuahua city to locate line to Gurrero, instead of being near my family. Disappointed.

June 3, 1891—Met Henry, first time in more than two years.

June 7, 1891—Sunday, meeting at W. D. Johnson's. I spoke first time in a year.

June 10, 1891—Lilla was married to day to Frank K. Nebeker.

June 12, 1891—Went to El Paso 6 A.M. at 6.15 P.M. left Juarez on Mex. Central R.R. and arrived at Chihuahua on [continued in next entry]

June 13, 1891—at 6.30 A.M. on Saturday.

June 14, 1891—Wrote letters to my family and others. Visited places.

June 15, 1891—In company with Chf. Eng. Smith examined surveyed route for 16 miles on horseback.

June 16, 1891—Examined other possible routes.

June 17, 1891—Made alteration in completed line ¾ mile. Broke inst.

June 19, 1891—Began locating line from completed portion (8[m]) and continued at this work until Aug. 14.th

June 20, 1891—Moved into Camp at Las Escobas ravine, 8[m] away.

June 25, 1891—A. J. Stewart came as my transitman. It was unfortunate for me, causing my subsequent departure from the work.

JULY 1891

July 4, 1891—Went to Chihuahua in the evening to the celebration.

July 19, 1891—Discharged Stewart for incompetency.

July 25, 1891—Turned over the party to Mr. Mathews son, and began duty as topographer.

[page 686]

HOME AGAIN IN JUAREZ.

August 12, 1891—Was transferred to the office in Deming, and will quit work. Was promised by J. Fewson Smith, Chf Eng.[132] that my pay should be continued to end of the month at full rate of $150.[00] [$3,246] which promise he broke in settling, in Deming. I am glad to leave the Company, and go to my home.

August 14, 1891—Joel and I left camp, and in the evening left for Deming. Joel Joined me in camp on June 19, having left home on the 15th Rec[d] a little money from Smith to pay our way home, $40.[00] Mex. Equal to $32.20 [$699] U. S. cash.

131 The Salt River provides primary irrigation for the Phoenix area even today. However, the river no longer flows except in heavy storm weather. The irrigation canals developed by the native people and the pioneers continue providing water today.

132 John Fewson Smith was at one time a surveyor in Weber County (Lora Crouch, "The Utah Central Railroad," in *Daughters of Utah Pioneers, Our Pioneer Heritage* [Salt Lake City: Utah State Historical Society Library, 1967], 10:137–92.

August 15, 1891—Arrived at El Paso 7.30 A.M. Joel left train at Gallego. At Las Escobas we left some good Mexican friends—Luis Anchendo & wife, and daughters Tomasa, Catarina, Maria and Jesus. Also a little boy José. Arr[d] Deming at 8.30 P.M. Sunday 16th, and fasted all day. Blessed.

August 17, 1891—Wrote Susan to come for me. Wrote Genie, and sent her names for temple work, Said names are noted in pencil in my temple record. Taken very sick.

August 18 & 19, 1891—Sick. Fasted all day. Better to night (19th)

August 21, 1891—Saw Albert and his little George, first time in 3 yrs.

August 22, 1891—Settled with R.R. Co. They only pay me $362.14 [$7,837] instead of 450. [$9,738] as agreed before in Chihuahua. John Fewson Smith, the engineer, has deliberately lied to me about my dues.

August 24, 1891—Am tired of waiting for Susan to come for me and so take advantage of my R.R. pass to go to Los Angeles and Santa Monica, Cal. Was absent 5 days in all; bathed in the sea, and bought some clothing &c. Also passed near the new lake in Southern Colorado desert.—Found no one is coming for me and got a chance to ride as far as Diaz, paying $6.[00] [$130] to Mrs. Black. Left Deming at ~~noon~~ ~~5.~~1.00 P.M. 29th Reached Diaz

September 1, 1891—Sept. 1. having had heavy rains all the way. Mrs. Black was very good to me on the journey for which may the Lord reward her. As I passed Boca Grande I saw Br. Gil[t] Webb, who has been a friend to me, and blessed him.

September 3, 1891—Started for home, hiring Mrs. Black's son to take me for $5.[00] [$108].

September 4, 1891—Reached home at sunset, and met Theodore the first time in three years, it being a year and a half since I had seen any others of the family. I thank the Lord

[page 687]

OCTOBER

September 5 & 6, 1891—Conference (the first) in the Mexican Mission at Juarez. Apostle Teasdel presiding.[133] A very good time. Manager A. F. Macdonald engaged me to Survey the boundaries of the Caralles Purchase, 5 ¾ miles wide 23[m] long, all in the summits of the Sierra Madre Mts.[134]

September 16, 1891—To day we held a celebration of Mexican Independence.

September 20, 1891—Sunday. A boy was born this morning to Henry by Mary A. Thurston, at 12.10 A.M.

September 30, 1891—To day Moroni's wife come to us much alarmed because her husband did not come home, and she feared he was dead. Susan told her all was well with him, and I afterwards said the same to her, having asked God about it, and having received an answer that all is well with him.

Last Sunday I felt impressed to say by the same spirit of prophecy to Bp. J. N. Smith Jr. when he was in very low spirits because of charges brought against him, that he would be fully vindicated and come out all right. He was greatly comforted, and I was glad to comfort him. Three days after, he came and said my words had proven true to the letter, and he rejoiced. I thank Thee, Father, for thy blessing to me, in giving me a portion of the spirit of prophecy, for which I have fasted and prayed much.[135]

OCTOBER

October 1, 1891—Thursday. Fasted as usual. To day Hernandes, wife & child were baptized into the church, Mexicans.

October 3, 1891—Sat. Started this evening with Theodore and J. M. Macfarlan Surveying Corrales Boundary line.[136] Drove to Pratt's, 12 miles, and

133 George Teasdale (1831–1907) was ordained an Apostle in 1882.

134 Alexander F. MacDonald, once president of the Maricopa Stake, was transferred to lead the northern Mexico area. He had been among the first in Chihuahua, Mexico (McClintock, *Mormon Settlement in Arizona*, 220–21; Romney, *Mormon Colonies in Mexico*, 58–59).

135 On this day Martineau writes a descriptive letter of the Mexican colonies (J. H. Martineau, "Letter from Mexico," *Deseret News*, October 24, 1891; Utah Digital Newspapers).

136 John M. Macfarlane was a surveyor and at one time worked in St. George, Utah (Lowell B. Bennion, "A Bird's-Eye View of Erastus Snow's St. George, Utah," *Utah Historical Quarterly* 45 [Spring 1979]: 311–27).

camped, remaining all next day. Sunday. Before I left I bought a stove of H. Shumway for $56.50 [$1,223]. Henry took us with his team and wagon. Theo. killed a wild turkey.

October 5, 1891—Started up the cañon, and had heavy rains all day. Camped at O. Allen's dairy, and waited there all next day for men from Pacheco to help on our survey.

October 8, 1891—four men came from Pacheco, and we went to the place of beginning in Strawberry vally and camped, in a cañon of grand precipices and cliffs.

[page 688]

October 9, 1891—Started on survey of east boundary, running South. Had to climb a high mountain with our pack animals, Henry going round into Hop valley another way. Theo. killed a fine deer to day. Heard the cry of a mountain lion or Jaguar last night.

October 10, 1891—Hard work crossing deep Cañons and precipices. Reached Hop creek at sunset, and found Henry camped there. Henry had killed 5 wild turkeys.

October 10, 1891 [this date is written twice]—Spent the day in triangulating across Hop valley, wide and deep. Henry shot a bear, but did not kill him.

October ~~12~~ 11, 1891—Sunday. Henry and Theo. looked for the wounded bear, found him and killed him, and four men brought it to camp. I did not eat any of him. It was a large brown one. Henry went home for supplies I went up to a cave once dwelt in by Cliff dwellers, high up the side of a cliff, on the wall was traced a picture like this, some 20 feet long:—

Fig. 7.4—Cave picture.

I was very tired, and under its influence wrote the following lines:—

THE SAINTS' REST.

Rest for the weary hands
Folded across the breast!
Now that are sundered Life's silver strands—
Rest ~~for the weary~~ from thy labors—rest!

2

Rest for the weary feet
Treading on stones and thorns!
Bruised and torn at every step—
Rest in the coming morn!

3

Rest for the weary eye
Tired with piercing the night!
Shineth now brightly the light on high—
Darkness hath taken its flight.

4

[written beside verse 4 in shaky handwriting is "weary"]
Rest for the silent tongue!
Long hath it plead for right!
[written in shaky hand above "right" is "light"]
[this next line added in shaky handwriting]
Oft praying [& hanging on] tight
~~Soon will~~ Now shall its song of triumph be sung—
Truth hath put Error to flight—!

[page 689]

1891—

5

Rest for the weary heart
[Next line added in shaky handwriting]
Walking for other in pain
Throbbing so oft in pain!
Never again shall the tear drop start—
Never, oh never again!

6

Thou who wast weary and faint
Rest ~~thy~~ for Earths labor is done!
Open to thee is the heavenly gate!
Now is thy glory won!

October ~~13~~ 12, 1891—Some more men came from Pacheco, making 11 in all. I took the latitude by solar compass 30° 3' N. We moved camp, climbing difficult steeps with our 5 pack horses. & not knowing where we would find water. Camped at dark in a deep cañon, at ruins of ancients, but Theo. and W. Porter were not in camp.[137] We fired guns, shouted, and I went up on hill side and kept a large fire buring for hours, shouting every few minutes. Other men went up on a high peak and built a fire. At last in answer to my shout we heard a faint answer a mile away, and heard a distant gun fired; and knew they were coming down the cañon. I had prayed much, and was answered that the young men were safe, but the sound of the answering voice was sweet indeed to my ears, and the dew dimmed my eyes. The boys got in all right. The shot we heard was one from Theo. which killed a fine deer. Oh, how good the Father is to hear my prayers! The Spirit also told me that Gertrude and Anna shall both have mates who will love and cherish them always, and gain a celestial exaltation. I received also many other precious promises.

October 13, 1891—I started two deer today but did not shoot, as we have meat enough, and we must not shed blood unnecessarily. One of the men killed a deer to day, and one next day.

Established a Stone monument for S.E. Corner of the Survey, 8700 metres from place of beginning

[page 690]

AT THE RIO DE GABILANAS.

October 20, 1891—We have steadily cut our way through heavy pines and across steep and high mountains and tremendous cañons, until to day, when we descended the precipitous sides of a deep gorge of the Rio de Gabilanas, (River of Hawks) 1000 ft deep, and only wide enough at the bottom for the rushing torrent. Strangely enough, we found our camp by an old Stone ruin—Toltec—and enjoyed much the clear, cool water. I lay down early while the boys sung songs round our fire, and thought of the littleness of man compared with the works of nature. which suggested the following lines:—

SONG OF THE TORRENT.

My couch is spread
In the rocky bed
　　Of a Cañon dark and wild
Whose craggy steeps
Full a thousand feet
　　Are cliffs and boulders piled

2

The oak and pine
And clinging vine
　　And rocks that arch o'erhead
Safe covert make
For Bear and Snake
　　And Jaguar, fierce and dread.

3

There's a stealthy tread
About my bed,
　　And the panther's wailing cry
Is borne on the breeze
As it stirs the trees,
　　With ~~a~~ its solemn, eerie sigh.

4

The Torrent's song
As it leaps along
　　Its rocky, devious way
Hath now a tongue
As it rushes on
　　And this I hear it say!—

[page 691]

CORRALES BOUNDARY SURVEY.

[This appears to be a topical reminder written at the top of the page]

5

"Vain man! Who art so proud and strong
In self conceit so wise,
What is thy life? And infant's span!
What see'st thou with thine eyes?
[added later] Behold then ope thine eyes!
That grand old oak was strong and firm
Five hundred years ago!
What is thy life! A passing gleam—
A flake of melting snow!

137 These are likely sons of Sanford Porter.

6

That huge gray rock, ~~that~~ which thee o'ertowers
Counts ~~centuries~~ 1000 years by scores;
Its years pass quick as summer showers—
Compare its age with yours!
And I, the Brook, that speak to thee,
Through centuries untold
thousands of years [written above "centuries" but neither one crossed out]
Have sung my song unceasingly—
Cans't thou be called old?

7

~~And~~ Here mighty nations have been born—
Grown haughty in their pride;
Have waged great wars—been overthrown—
Decreased—decayed—and died!
And generations, too, have passed,
A countless, misty throng,
Have lived and died, until at last
Their names are e'en [now] unknown.

8

Here, by thy couch old ruins lie
Of a race now lost and dead;
Unseen, their spirits hover nigh
And cluster round thy head.
For centuries they dwelt—increased—
And roamed these mountains grand,
Now, even Memory hath ceased
Of those who held this land.

[page 692]

CORRALES BOUNDARY SURVEY

October 1891—

9

Then what is man!—A passing sigh—
A mote that floats in air,
Like clouds, a moment seen on high
That quickly disappear.
Then art thou old, thou passing Breath?
Dost thou lay claim to age?
A moment here—and then comes Death
To close thy earthly page."

10

For a moment dumb
Is the Torrent's tongue
And ceased is its sermon grand;
Our camp fire bright
~~Bathe~~ with ruddy light
~~The cliffs on either hand~~
Brightens the cliffs aroun [added text at a later date in shaky writing and crossed out the above]

11

Then again begins
The Brook to sing
Its interrupted song
And Stars Shine bright
With silvery light
As I lie and ponder long.

October 23, 1891—Friday. Macfarlane, my aid, was unwilling to stay any longer on the survey, and decided, against my protest, to go home, when we were within five miles of the end of South boundary. Our position was indeed difficult. We were on the brink of an immense gorge 2000 feet deep, down which it was almost impossible for our pack animals to go; but I had triangulated across it—1¼ mile—and got a point located on the farther ridge. So we turned back.

October 24, 1891—Sat. Descended to Gabilanas river 8 miles, thence up and over the Main summit of the Sierra Madres to Pacheco, reaching there at Sun set, tired and hungry.

[page 693]

October 25, 1891—Sunday. Attended meeting in Pacheco, then went to Br. Henry Lunt's to stay until we can get to Juarez.

October 31, 1891—Arrived at home, having staid last night at Br. H. Pratt's ranch 12 miles from Juarez.[138] Apostle Teasdel was there. Took Lat. of Juarez with my Solar Compass and John M. Macfarlane's transit. It is 30° 20' N. Long. 108° W. Found my family well, for which I thank thee, my Father. During this trip

138 Helaman Pratt, the son of Parley P. Pratt, was among the first settlers in Colonia Juárez. He was one of the presidents of the Mexican Mission. Elder George Teasdale was also a president of the Mexican Mission.

He has strengthened me most wonderfully to endure the hardships entailed by high, steep mountains and almost impassible gorges; and He has blessed me in answer to prayer, with many precious promises. He also heard and Answered the prayers of Theodore, on several occasions.

NOVEMBER

November 5, 1891—Attended fast meeting and blessed Henry's last baby Frank Thurston, by Mary A. Thurston, his wife for time.

November 12, 1891—Sowed Lucerne seed on city lot & in field.

November 16, 1891—Began my map of the Corrales Survey.

November 22, 1891—Quarterly Conference of the Mex. Mission, G. Teasdel, presiding

November 23, 1891—To day Joel H. Martineau and Mary Ann Thurston were sealed for time by Apostle Teasdel in my house.

November 25, 1891—While laying up adobes I was taken with lame back so as to be almost helpless. Continued Several days.

DECEMBER

December 5, 1891—Settled my herd bill with Moroni & paid him $67.$^{\underline{00}}$ [$1,450] I find we have 28 Cattle, and 8 belonging to Susan, and 29 horses including four of Gertrudes and 4 of Anna's.

December 17, 1891—Killed a steer for beef.

December 25, 1891—Christmas. Worked all day laying adobes.

December 26, 1891—My ranch account, for am't due the Colonization Co. for 1891 amounts to $30.$^{\underline{00}}$ [$649] being due on wood $2.00 [$43] on 29 horses $11.00 [$238] & 32 cattle $11.50 [$249] also for rent of 5 acres land $2.50 [$54], and two city lots $3.00 [$65].

On Christmas I was able to buy only a pair of cotton Stockings for Susan's Christmas gift. Quite cold, 15°

December 29, 1891—fell from Scaffold while laying adobes, Somewhat jarred

December 30, 1891—finished the adobe house. Blizzard & Snow on 31st

December 31, 1891—just enough to whiten the ground.

[page 694]

January 5, 1892—Wrote these lines for a song to the tune "Sounds from the shore"

It breathes of scenes forever fled—
Of happy hours to come:—
Of loved ones resting with the dead
Gone to their glorious home
It breathes of childhood happy hours
And scenes of youthful glee
Of meadows green and wildwood flowers—
That sweet sound from the sea.

January 24, 1892—Was put into office as one of the field and fence committee.

January 25, 1892—Helped lay off fence for the field.

FEBRUARY

February 4, 1892—Started up the mountains to meet Col. Kosterlitzky, Mexican Manager of public lands of Sonora.[139] Camped.

February 5, 1892—Reached G. C. Williams' house.[140] The colonel came in afternoon with his escorts. Drew article of agreement for sale of his land to G. C. Williams and others for $35.000 [$35,000 = $757,406]

February 6, 1892—The estate is called "Los Horcones," (the forks) and has about 118000 acres, lying on the Bavispe river, in Sonora. We have three years in which to pay for the land. I believe God has brought this about, that we may get a foothold in Sonora. Br. Williams promises me the Surveying of the land, and Col. Emilio Kosterlitzky will make me

---

139 This is likely General Emilio Kosterlitzky, who owned a large tract of land in the area (Romney, *Mormon Colonies in Mexico*, 67; Turley and Turley, *History of Mormon Colonies in Mexico*, 284).

140 As the colonies in Mexico began to expand, George C. Williams was a member of that group (Turley and Turley, *History of Mormon Colonies in Mexico*, 34; Romney, *Mormon Colonies in Mexico*, 60).

State or Gov[t] Surveyor for public lands in Sonora. I like the appearance of the Colonel much.[141]

February 7, 1892—Started home, weather very cold. Heavy snow storm from noon until 9 P.M. with cold piercing wind. Got home at 8.30 P.M. Glad. Found letters from North. Lyman's little girl Reita has died in Logan, age 3 yrs. Also got a letter from Gov. Wolfley, offering me charge of construction of a Canal 30 miles long, near Gila Bend. with good salary of $200 [$4,328] pr month. I prayed for light and was told not to go there to labor for the wicked gentiles, but labor in Mexico, and God will bless me.

February 9, 1892—Wrote Wolfley, declining, with thanks, also to Br. M. Thatcher, telling him what we have done. I decline Wolfley's offer because I wish to be with the saints and help build up Zion: and not to help build up that Gentile nation, for this was shown by the spirit to be my duty in answer to my prayer.

[page 695]

GO TO SONORA.

February 16, 1892—Started to day with Theodore and Anna, also Moroni, Eddie. Br. Sixtus & others, to go over the Sierra Madre Mts. to the new purchase on the Bavispe or Yaqui river, Sonora. Camped near some old Aztec ruins, the walls being yet about 30 ft high and 4 ft thick, built of adobes. It was once a large and important place, surrounded by outworks and walls.

February 17, 1892—Camped near Ramus, 25[m] Moroni joined us this evening, with our band of 22 horses.

February 18, 1892—Drove to Casa de Janos, 20[m] thence 4 m. and camped.

February 19, 1892—Moved near Punta de Aqua, and camped near Caritas.

February 20, 1892—Laid by all day for rest of Company to arrive.

February 21, 1892—Sunday. Br. G. C. Williams, our leader, came. Sixtus & David Johnson and Gruwell also came. Moved 3 miles.

February 22, 1892—Mon. Began work on road over mountain, cutting oak and making dug ways. I was appointed president of camp. Col. Kosterlitzky and his party camped with us on lost cr.

February 25, 1892—Working every day on road. Rained heavily

February 26, 1892—Still raining, till noon. Some of the company moved on.

February 29, 1892—We moved over the Summit, about 2½ miles, & camped in deep ravine. Cold weather.

MARCH 1892

March 1, 1892—Anna climbed a high mountain peak, alone.

March 2, 1892—Heavy winds and rain, turned to snow in the night.

March 4, 1892—Still snowing and blowing, & very cold, until 5th

March 6, 1892—Moved 2½ miles to top of high peak. Moved again 1 m. on 8th

March 9, 1892—Reached Bavispe River (Yaqui) and camped. Met here a company of Mexicans from Bavispe to welcome us. They brought a beef Steer and keg of mescal. Had songs &c.

March 10, 1892—Began to cross a rough hilly country, towards purchase. Very rough and bad roads 10 miles. It took us till the [15th]

March 15, 1892—Arrived at Los Horcones, and settled for work.

March 16, 1892—Began to Survey the canal

March 20, 1892—Sunday. To day held meeting. How many centuries have elapsed since any saints have had a meeting in this land! Probably 1500 years. I presided. My thoughts were difficult to analyze.

[page 696]

AT CAMP FENOCHIO 1892 DORA BAPTIZED MAY APRIL

March 25, 1892—Constantly working on canal, cool nights. Ice in wash dish. Took latitude of camp,—Fenochio—30° 27' N.[142]

141 J. H. Martineau, "A New Mexican Colony," *Deseret News*, April 16, 1892; Utah Digital Newspapers.

142 This is likely Ferrichio named after General Juan Ferrichio of Hermosillo ("A New Mexican Colony," *Deseret Evening News*, April 12, 1892; Journal History).

APRIL 1

April 1, 1892—Friday. Ice this morning on still water.

April 5, 1892—Snow on mountain peaks around, & cold nights. Dora Baptized.

April 6, 1892—Water in Canal at last, but dam is not yet finished.

April 7, 1892—Fast day. I fasted. Sixtus & David went to Juarez.

April 17, 1892—Got letters. Elvira had a new baby girl, born March 5th Her name is Emma Vilate, Nephi is called to go on a Mission to Europe next fall. Got letter from Ex. Gov. Powers relative to Canal near Gila Bend.

April 20, 1892—Col Kosterlitzky, wife, and escort came to visit us. Had a pleasant party in the evening, songs &c &c

April 28, 1892—The water in the canal got to the field, for the first time. I planted squashes, corn &c Set out our fruit trees.

MAY 1

May 1, 1892—Sunday. Up to this date I have presided over the camp, by vote of the colony, but Br. Williams, lately returned from Chihuahua says Bp. J. N. Smith had appointed P. A. Dillman to act as Presiding Priest over the Colony.[143] So today at meetings I stated this, and resigned to him.

May 2, 1892—Surveyed our field, and find we have only 25 acres in it,—about an acre to each family. Our Canal and dam has cost us nearly $2000.00 [$43,280] making cost of our water $80.00 [$1,731] and more, per acre. This is owing to the bad management of Br. G. C. Williams, who will have everything his own way, as he is the purchaser of this Ranch of Los Horcones, which consists of 26½ Sitios of 4428 acres each, making about 118000 acres in all. Theodore and I have constantly worked on the road and canal, most of the time living on dry graham bread and water, having no groceries, meat, butter nor milk. I dip a piece of dry coarse bread in water, and am very thankful for it. The Lord has caused the Mexicans to be very good to us, bringing us meal, beans and sometimes beef, which we got on credit, and have told us not to go hungry. They think we have done a great work. Col. Kosterlitzky said to me in March

[page 697]

May, 1892—"We have 3800 men in this District, and the whole of them would not have done as much work in 3 months as you people have done in two weeks." There never was a road from Sonora to Chihuahua, until we made it.—a small party of 22 men. There was a burro trail, but that was a very steep and difficult one

May 4, 1892—Today Anna is 17. She is bright, cheerful, strong and healthy, a favorite with all in camp, and a great blessing to me on this trip.—never complaining at any hardship or discomfort. And the same with Theodore.

May 11, 1892—Planted potatoes, and cane, also squashes and melons.

May 16, 1892—We started home today, but not being able to get up the steep hills, had to return. Yesterday, 11 P.M. Col. Kosterlitzky and his troops passed our camp in pursuit of hostile Apaches who had stolen some horses. He return on the 24th having killed the indians and got the horses.

May 24, 1892—I went to Bavispe, 21 miles, to rent land for corn. On the way I asked the Father, to open my way to do so if it was best, and to close it up if it is not for the best. The Col. Said he had got a good farm for me, and I went to see it. The land belongs to Donaciano Parra, the Guide.[144]

May 25, 1892—Accepted the offer. I take his field of about 15 acres, for three years, to pay no rent, but bring it into cultivation by ditches, plowing &c Got all the papers made out and returned to Fenochio. This old place—Bavispe—was destroyed by earthquake 5 years ago, and many people killed. Altitude of the place, by U. S. barometer = 3600 feet.

May 30, 1892—Finished up our field fence and Moroni's.

143 Jessie N. Smith and Peter A. Dillman were among the first settlers of Colonia Pacheco (Turley and Turley, *History of Mormon Colonies in Mexico*, 17, 26–27; Romney, *Mormon Colonies in Mexico*, 108–9).

144 The Parra family was among the first generation of Mexican Mormons. They were merchants and landowners (Tullis, *Mormons in Mexico*, 110).

To day Patriarch Lunt gave Gertrude a blessing:—[145]

A blessing by Henry Lunt, Patriarch, upon the head of Gertrude, daughter of James Henry & Susan Ellen Johnson Martineau, born Sept. 28th 1870, Logan Cache Co. Utah.

Beloved sister Gertrude inasmuch as thou hast desired a blessing at my hands I feel to comply with thy wishes as thou art worthy through obedience to the Gospel, also by lineage, being of the blood of Ephraim, and a daughter of Zion born under the new and everlasting covenant, and being pure in heart and meek in Spirit.

[page 698]

GERTRUDE'S BLESSING.

May 30, 1892—The Lord loveth thee for thine integrity, and for seeking after the imperishable riches of heaven. Thou shalt realize every desire of thy heart in righteousness, and shalt be blessed in the own due time of the Lord with a husband, by whom thou shalt raise up a numerous posterity, that shall become great in goodness and virtue and righteousness, and in connection with thy husband thou shalt reign as a Queen in heaven in celestial glory. Thy name is written in the Lamb's Book of Life, and thy guardian Angel watcheth over thee. Thou shalt be healed up of all thine infirmities and injuries that thou hast received to thy body. I seal upon thee a renewal of health and strength, and reconfirm upon thee all thy former blessings, ministering angels shall visit thee & converse with thee in a familiar manner as one friend with another, and shall reveal unto thee many important things that shall fill thy soul with joy and gladness unspeakable. Give thy heart unto the Lord in thy young and tender years and great wisdom shall be given unto thee, and thou shalt become a bright and shining light amongst the daughters of Zion. Keep the Word of Wisdom and thou shalt have a healthy body, and live until thou art satisfied with life, shall sleep but for a little season, and come forth in the morning of the ressurrection, crowned with glory, immortality and eternal lives in connection with thy husband, all of which blessings I seal upon thy head in the name of the Lord Jesus Christ, Even So, Amen.

Monday, May 31, 1892—Theo. and I went to our farm near Bavispe, to begin planting

JUNE 1

Tuesday. June 1, 1892—Leveled a ditch for our land to bring water upon it, over half a mile long. Watered land, plowed, and planted corn and cane.

June 4, 1892—Returned to Fenochio (our camp, named in honor of Genl Juan Fenochio.)

Monday, June 6, 1892—Paid G. C. Williams on provision a/c, or land, $10.00 cash, and a store, $15.00 = $25.00 [$541] Sold my farm in Pima to John Kartchner for $600.00 [$12,984] Amer. money, to be paid for in cash $30.00 [$6,491] and good American cows and heifers at $25.00 and $12.50 [$271] respectively.

[page 699]

JUNE. RETURN TO JUAREZ

June, 1892—Then started home to Juarez, with Theo, Anna, Self, and Dick Bloomfield.[146] Went 8m and camped. Reached home on Friday June 10th tired and hungry, and our team given out.

June 10, 1892—Theo. walked 5 miles into town and got Joel's horses to help us in. Found all well but Gertrude, but she is much better, and can walk around now, having been blessed by Apostle Teasdale.

Monday, June 13, 1892—Wrote to Lyman and Geo. Roskruge.[147] Also to M. Thatcher to get him to buy my mill shares, as we are so destitute. Susan had eaten her last corn meal, and knew not where to get any more in this time of famine, when lo! a letter from Lyman with $40.00 [$866] sent by him ($25.00) [$541] Nephi $10.00 [$216] and Jesse ($5.00) [$108] She said tears of joy ran down her cheeks. With this she got flour, $10.00 Sent me $10.00 and got some things in the store she needed very badly. Truly God is good to us,

145 This is Patriarch Henry Lunt of Colonia Juárez (Romney, *Mormon Colonies in Mexico*, 140).

146 Dick Bloomfield is likely a part of the John Bloomfield family, who were among the first settlers in Colonia Juárez (Romney, *Mormon Colonies in Mexico*, 85).

147 This could be George James Roskruge, who was a Logan associate. His papers are at the Arizona Historical Society, Library and Archives, Southern Arizona Division.

and hears our prayers, and fulfils his promises; for He has sealed upon me that I shall not want for food nor clothing, neither my family. Once before Lyman Sent Susan money when she needed it, being impelled by a dream his wife Alley had.

June 16, 1892—Sent my pension papers to B. Y. M^c^Keyes, Deming, a notary, by Benja Johnson.[148] Visited Pres^t^ Teasdale, and told him of my habit of asking God to direct me, and of his goodness in answering me, but as I had heard he was opposed to our Los Horcones Colony I feared I might have been deceived by a lying spirit that had told me God had opened up that land to us and that I should be blessed by Him. It is thing I cannot afford to be deceived in, and so came to him. He said I had <u>not</u> been deceived. "No! no! no! no!" said he. Said it was a good thing for one of experience, like me, to be there, and gave me much comfort. I had asked the Father the night previous, and He told me by His Spirit, to see Br. Teasdale, and he would be friend to me and bless me, as he <u>did.</u>

A glorious and blessed privilege it is, to ask the Father and receive an answer, just as one answereth another. For over two years has God thus blessed, led, and taught me, praised be His holy name, for such goodness to me So poor and weak as I am. Help me, Oh Father, to grow and increase in the gifts & knowledge of the Spirit.

[page 700]

JUNE. WENT TO GALEANA.

June 17, 1892—Planted beans and squashes, next day

June 21, 1892—Theodore and Moroni started back to Sonora. Lost horses same night.

Wednesday, June 22, 1892—Boys started again. Rain next day. Cucumbers on 28th

Wednesday, June 29, 1892—Started to Galeana with letter from Macdonald, to try and get the surveying of Galeana. Joel & his wife and Gertrude also went. Camped 17 miles in Chocolate Pass, famous for indian atrocities.

Thursday, June 30, 1892—Galeana at noon. Saw the Presidente Salomí C. Garcia, who said I could do the work if I would obtain proper license from the Governor. I sent my application for license by him, and started home at 2 P.M. camping again in Chocolate Pass, where a large company of Mexicans were killed by Apaches. At sunset a big thunder storm came on. Joel & I who had tried to lie on the ground, got into the wagon with the Girls at 1.30 A.M. wet to the skin, and sat up all the rest of the night, wrapped in wet quilts. Prayed that none of us be taken ill in any way.

JULY 1892

July 1, 1892—Got home at 2 P.M. no one being hurt by the storm. Thankful.

July 2, 1892—Planted corn. Got letter from W. D. Johnson Jr. asking me to go south into Mexico to examine an estate a Syndicate think of buying, and report as to farm land, water for irrigation &c.[149]

July 6, 1892—Letter from Sam and Elvira. Also letter from Genie, who has a new baby, born 25 June 1892, weighs 8½ lbs. named Sheridan Edward. Sam's letter gave me much comfort, and I insert part of it:—

"Am sorry times are so hard there with you, and I feel as if the hand of the Lord is in it, for if there was plenty to eat and drink there and a land of plenty, it would be just as bad there as here; it would soon be run over with devils and wicked men, and you would soon have to move on or be persecuted. The Lord is trying you to see if you can stand that kind of trouble, and my faith is, after He has proven you in that, then He will open the door to plenty again to you: for as sure as the Sun Shines, the Lord has got His eye upon you, and He loves you, and He is not going to see you go hungry nor destitute of anything that you and Mother needs. So the Spirit said to me, when it spoke to me that you was in destitute circumstances, and for me to write to the boys in Logan; and so we did. And it also said you was doing a good work, and out of your

148 This is likely Benjamin F. Johnson, among the first to explore the area for colonization (Tullis, *Mormons in Mexico*, 53; see also Turley and Turley, *History of the Mormon Colonies in Mexico*, 48).

149 William D. Johnson was a superintendent of the school system in Juárez (Turley and Turley, *History of the Mormon Colonies in Mexico*, 40; Romney, *Mormon Colonies in Mexico*, 130).

work would spring a great work for us as a family to go on with."

Much more, in the same spirit. It comforted me much.

July 11, 1892—Susan's birthday, 56 years old. Had a family dinner.

[page 701]

JOEL'S BABY BORN & DIED

July 11, 1892— By letter from Moroni I learn he traded my Pima farm to Br. Kartchener for 14 Amer. Cows, 9 Calves 1 heifer, 1 horse & tent &c to amount of $79.30 [$1,716][150]

July 23, 1892—Up to this time I have been busy in the garden, hoeing, planting corn and lucern seed. To day Joel's wife, Annie, was confined with a 7 mo. baby girl, at 10 A.M. which lived only 5 hours. I blessed and named her Mary Ann, after her mother. Annie is quite low, having suffered much the last 6 days. The midwife finally had to take the placenta by force.

July 24, 1892—Buried the baby today, Sunday.

July 25, 1892—Celebrated the 24th, I was Chaplain, games & dance in after part of the day. Wrote to Lyman, Nephi, Morris Murphy and others.

July 27, 1892—Sent blank deed to John Kartchener for the farm I sold him in Pima for $600.00 [$12,984] (37 3/10 acres) taking cows &c for pay. Also sent order to Welch to make the deed to him.

AUGUST

August 2, 1892—Letter from Theodore, who is alone on farm, near Bavispe. He is lonesome, poor fellow, all alone. He sent us the following verses:—(his first attempt at poetry)

TO THE LOVED ONES AT HOME.

While sitting here thinking of home, mother
My thoughts turn insensibly to thee
I seemed to see you a sitting
'Neath the spreading cottonwood tree.

You appeared to be reading, dear mother
For you held a book in your hand,
But I believe you were thinking of me, mother,
Alone in this far distant land.

Whenever I let my thoughts stray, mother,
I begin thinking of father and you,
Which makes me feel so lonesome & friendless
That I dont know what on earth to do.

I've oft wondered since leaving home, mother
If I've one friend on the earth that is true;
But though all the world hate me, dear mother,
I still have dear father and you.

[page 702]

GERTRUDE GOES TO ARIZONA.

August 2, 1892—
Do any brothers and sisters at home, mother
Ever think of the one far away:
Who is living alone among strangers
In solitude, day after day.

But things will change sometime, dear mother
When we will be parted no more;
Our family will be gathered together
In union and peace evermore.

I pray for you day after day mother,
That you may become well and strong,
For I know that our Father can heal you
From the pains you have suffered so long.

I hope that you'll not think me foolish, mother,
For sending these verses to you;
They express my thoughts, feebly, dear mother
But every word written is true.

Thursday, August 4, 1892—Fast day.

Friday, August 5, 1892—To day Gertrude starts for Arizona, to visit awhile with Samuel &

150 John Kartchner was among the first settlers in Cave Valley, Mexico (Turley and Turley, *History of the Mormon Colonies in Mexico*, 64; Romney, *Mormon Colonies in Mexico*, 65, 103–4). The hardships of the Mexican colonies are illustrated here as many settlers were transients moving from Utah and Arizona to Mexico and back.

Elvira, Gathered 10 qts grapes from our vine, our first vintage.

August 21, 1892—Theodore got home from Sonora. He says cattle had eaten all his corn and cane. Anna went to San Diego ranch to work for a few weeks.

August 22, 1892—Joel got home with goods from Gallego for store, 135[m] I am still planting corn in garden.

August 29, 1892—Moroni got back from Sonora. Has come for his family.

August 30, 1892—To day Theodore went to work in Saw Mill. We had a family reunion in honor of Mother Susan Johnson's 80th birthday

SEPTEMBER

September 5, 1892—Dora is 10 yrs old to day. Had a little party.[151]

September 10, 1892—Henry's baby was born this morning at 3.35 weighed 10 lbs.

[page 703]

September 12, 1892—I began work in grist mill as a helper, and to help reweigh 32000[#] wheat for the Corralitos Co. about which there is some dispute as to weight.

September 16, 1892—We celebrated Mexican Independence day.

September 17, 1892—To day Apaches took a horse from C. Whipple, a few miles from here, but he escaped unhurt. They have also stolen others from San Pedro ranch. Pursued by mounted men.

For some time I have been in much doubt as to what is best for me to do or where live, having no means of support here, as an Engineer or otherwise. I asked the Father in prayer and received this answer:—

That I should not go back to live in Utah or Arizona. That He had led me to Mexico for a purpose of His own, and here I shall make my home; build a good house of brick and make it nice & beautiful, for in it shall be entertained some of the leading men of this State and Nation. After I have lived here a few years, and am called to go farther South I shall sell out at no loss, and go to a place or land where there will be room for me and my family and friends to gather about me; and begin to grow into a nation as has been promised me. Also that I shall prosper spiritually and temporally from this day forth. Also many other precious promises. For all this I am thankful to the Father, who heareth our prayers.

Monday, September 19, 1892—This morning Apaches killed Sister Thompson and her son and shot another boy through the body. He and a little girl about 6 years old started through the woods 2 miles for help, but the boy fainted on the way. A party went from here after the indians but did not find them in a weeks hunt. Another party went out, found their trail, and followed it for days. We hear no word from them.

OCTOBER

Saturday, October 1, 1892—I quit the mill today, 12 days time. Another alarm today Some Mexicans from Corallitos at the mill said indians had stolen 16 mules. We sent a party out at dusk and another at 3 A.M. Sunday, who found the mules and think they may only have strayed away.

October 2, 1892—We have made a military organization here, of a Company of five [tens] each. Miles P. Romney Cap[t] J. Harper Lieutenant.[152]

[page 704]

ANNA MARRIED

October 2, 1892—Theodore quit the mill & came home to go to school. Also Anna quit work at San Diego—6 weeks. Yesterday I sent an article, "The Cross" to Contributor.

October 5, 1892—Wrote to John Wedderburn, Washington D.C. relative to my claim for Indian dep-

151 September 2, 1892, Martineau encourages incoming settlers (J. H. Martineau, "Letter from Mexico," *Deseret News*, September 24, 1892; Utah Digital Newspapers. See also "Letter from Mexico," *Deseret Evening News*, September 2, 1892; Journal History).

152 Miles P. Romney was among the first settlers in Colonia Juárez; his wife taught school there (Romney, *Mormon Colonies in Mexico*, 85; Tullis, *Mormons in Mexico*, 55–58; Turley and Turley, *History of the Mormon Colonies in Mexico*, 37).

redations (for the church) filed 1890 amounting to $225.$^{\underline{00}}$ [$4,869]

October 6, 1892—Went to San Diego Rancho to survey a canal. Gone 2 days and earned $10.$^{\underline{00}}$ [$216] Was very thankful to earn something.

October 10, 1892—Began taking lessons in Spanish, Henry Eyring, teacher.

October 26, 1892—Learn by letter from Lyman, that Jesse has gone to Chicago, to attend a business college.

NOVEMBER

November 1, 1892—Moroni came from Sonora, to hunt his cattle & horses. Susan and I are going to start to Deming tomorrow.

November 2, 1892—Rained and Snowed all day and last night

November 3, 1892—The same. We gave up our journey.

November 11, 1892—Wrote to John W. Young, 85 Londen Well E. C. London.

November 14, 1892—Wrote to President Porforio Diaz, Mex, relative to what I can do in engineering, and what I would like to do.[153] Blessed the letter, that a good influence may go with it. If not, it will all be right, for God knows best what is good for us.

Friday, November 18, 1892—To day at 3 P.M. Anna S. married Henry Samuel Walser at my house.[154] The ceremony was by Apostle Geoge Teasdel, who sealed them for time and eternity, and gave them a good blessing. We had a house full, and a good dinner. I had been suffering two days with an attack of pleurisy in my left side, suffering severely. Pres^{t} Teasdel, Sixtus E. Johnson & J. J. Walser administered to me, Br. Teasdel being mouth. He also blessed me in other particulars, saying I had been led here by the Lord and should be able to do what I had been appointed to do, and that wealth and prosperity should flow unto me to enable me to do my work.

November 19, 1892—By letter from Gertrude she says she had had a bad fall from a horse that ran with her under a low shed and scraped her off, She falling on top of his head, and narrowly escaping a broken neck. But she had now recovered from the fall.

[page 705]

November 26, 1892—Quarterly conference begins to day, lasting 3 days

November 27, 1892—Was at priesthood meeting chosen an alternate in the High Council.

DECEMBER

December 1, 1892—Finished article for "Contributor," a table of dates of births and deaths of ancient patriarchs.

Learn by letter Lyman's baby was born on Nov. 24, 1892, at 9 A.M. Her name Martha Claytor

December 7, 1892—Started to Mesa, Arizona, with Br. Spillsbury at noon. We hear that Gertrude is very sick and needs me. Cold weather. Drove to Dublan and stayed with Br. F. G. Williams.[155] Br. Williams at first said he could not take me, his team was so poor. But the answer of the Spirit was that I <u>should</u> go, and with Br. Williams. So next day Br. W. said I <u>could</u> go with him, and I did.

December 8, 1892—Drove 25$^{\underline{m}}$ and camped. Very cold weather

December 9, 1892—Arrived at Diaz, and went on next day, reaching Las Palomas, the custom house in the evening.

December 12, 1892—In the Territory of New Mexico. Snow on mountains and bitterly cold.

December 13, 1892—Reached Deming at noon. Paid Williams $5.00 [$108] passage money, got a hat and a few little things, and R.R. ticket to Tempe $16.90 [$366], and left Deming 8 P.M.

153 Porfirio Díaz (note spelling) was the president of Mexico. He welcomed the Mormon colonies but was a dictator and ruled Mexico with a strong hand (Romney, *Mormon Colonies in Mexico*, 13–19; Tullis, *Mormons in Mexico*, 56–59, 75).

154 This was the first marriage of Annie Sariah Martineau (note spelling), daughter of James Henry and Susan Ellen Johnson Martineau. Annie married Henry Samuel Walser in Colonia Juárez on this date. They had two children before her husband's death in 1897.

155 Frederick G. Williams was a member of the bishopric in Colonia Dublán, Mexico (Romney, *Mormon Colonies in Mexico*, 100; Turley and Turley, *History of the Mormon Colonies in Mexico*, 210).

December 14, 1892—reaching Tucson 5 A.M. next day, Maricopa Sta^n 8 A.M. Tempe 10.45, and son-in-law B. S. Johnson's 12.30 P.M. Found Gertrude very ill with agonizing pain behind her eyes. For weeks she has been unable to see, or have her eyes unbound. All the rest of Sam's family were well.

December 15, 1892—I wrote to Susan to come, and to bring Dora.

December 18, 1892—Quarterly conference at Mesa. I spoke & felt well. I spent some days in copying items from an old copy of "Times and Seasons" of 1844/

December 25, 1892—Christmas, but not as if at home. Preached in Nephi.

December 27, 1892—Gertrude improves daily, but is very feeble still.

December 28, 1892—Went to Franklin Johnson's wedding at Mesa. He is eldest son of Joseph, Sam's brother.

[page 706]

1893

December 28, 1892—Br. John Reidhead, an old friend of Sam's came to stay.

I received a letter from Sur. Genl Royal Johnson to go to Tucson and work in his office as draughtsman

December 30, 1892—Sent my account for indian depredations to Washington, and made plats for Br. Cosby, of Mesa. Made out a bill for Sam of indian depredations he suffered in Apache Co. some years ago, in being driven from their home, farm, and all they had, narrowly escaping with life.

December 31, 1892—Went 6 miles to Tempe. Gertrude went with me, the first time she has been out in 6 weeks.

1893

January 1893—Took dinner at James Turman's in Mesa, and had a pleasant time with them, who are my true friends.

Lyman's baby is named Martha Claytor, after Bp. W. B. Preston's mother.

January 3, 1893—I blessed Gertrude, and started to Tucson, reaching there 3.15 A.M.

January 4, 1893—Began work in Sur.^r Genl office at $4.00 [$87] per day. Took a room with board at $7.50 [$162] per week.

January 6, 1893—Recd a letter from Susan at Nephi, where she arrived on the fifth, being 9 days on the road from Juarez to Deming, in cold weather and poor food & bedding. At Deming her cousins David T. and Harriet LeBaron did not even invite her into their house, which was adjoining the corral in which Susan camped all night, in cold winter weather and nothing but a crust of dry bread and some water for supper and breakfast. I was very angry when I heard of it.

January 8, 1893—Our 41st anniversary of our marriage. I sat for photo.

January 11, 1893—Moved to the "Cosmopolitan Hotel," at $25.^00 [$541] per month.

January 15, 1893—The Baron Alex. Von Wendt called to see me, with Mr. Lavagnino, a Rothschild mining expert. Gave him my opinion of the Santa Rita gold placers belonging to von Wendt.

January 19, 1893—I am tempted to take a contract for U.S. land survey, but the answer I received is not to do so. The Lord hath other work for me,—I shall have a place in Mexico where I may gather my family, kindred and friends about me and grow into a great people—a nation—which shall not go into captivity as ancient Israel because this is the last dispensation.

[page 707]

1893—Also, my brethren shall receive a testimony in my favor, and shall lift me up among them and make me mighty in Israel. Help me, Father, to receive all promised me.

I have now been a member of the Church 42 years, and in that time how many changes,—ups and downs—lights and shadows—joy and sadness,—health and sickness and death—plenty and poverty!

January 21, 1893—Spent my last dime, but today my pension came of $24.^00 [$519] so I did not go hungry.

January 25, 1893—Moved to Gibbons' room, $10.^00 [$216] per month.

January 28, 1893—Bought 3 opals of a traveler, because of their beauty.

FEBRUARY

February 4, 1893—I asked the Father if I should take a survey contract offered me by Gen[l] Johnson. The answer was "Yes," and shall be blessed in it from beginning to end thereof.

February 6, 1893—Sent $40.00 [$866] to Sam and Susan, Sam having sent Susan $20.00 [$433] to help her on her way from Mexico.

February 11, 1893—Br. Spillsbury came along on his way home to Colonia Juarez. I sent some things to Anna, and arranged with him to take a can of honey to Juarez for me, giving him $3.00 [$65] to pay duties on things sent Anna.

February 12, 1893—Sent for "Lives and times of the Roman Pontiffs." in the hope to learn something of my Roman or Italian ancestry.

I know my ancestry was [...] notable in Italy, mostly in the church, as Popes (Martin 1.2. 3. 4 & 5th also as eminent painters and scholars, and hope to learn enough about them to do temple work for them.

February 14, 1893—Wrote again to my wife Jessie Helen, who utterly and without any reason known to me, refuses to correspond with me. I am satisfied it is because of her mothers influence, though I have never, to my knowledge, done anything to incur her dislike nor can I guess at the cause of her enmity.

[page 708]

1893

February 1893—As she is a member of the Salt Lake Choir I sent her letter to Even Stephens, the leader, to deliver to her.

MARCH

March 8, 1893—Sent $20.00 [$433] to Susan

March 13, 1893—To day I am 65 years old, but I cannot realize it, only as I see how old some of my children are.

On Thursday morning, the 9th as I prayed, a voice said to me "I ordain thee a patriarch in my church." This is spiritual, and I may now exercise the gift of prophecy when moved upon by the Holy Spirit. And the time will come when I shall be ordained by my brethren.

I celebrated by birthday by an oyster stew, 50¢ doing without one regular meal, to make up for it. I eat out two meals a day, 25¢ each, to save money and get ahead a little. Two meals a day is all I ever have eaten in Tucson for some years, and for weeks at a time only one meal a day, when I had but little means to live on. Upon one occasion I went from Monday afternoon until Saturday without eating anything at all, having but 50¢ in the world and no way to get any more. So I kept the 50¢ in reserve in case of emergency, but it was not pleasant.

March 14, 1893—Received my "Lives of Roman Pontiffs" &c but was much disappointed, as it does not supply the items I want.

March 15, 1893—I received $150.00 [$3,246] by letter from Lyman. He sent me $90.00 [$1,948] and Nephi and Charles $30.00 [$649] each, so I could come to the dedication of the Salt Lake temple. Sent Susan $15.00 [$325] to help her to get ready for the journey.

March 28, 1893—Susan and Gertrude started for S. L. City

March 29, 1893—I joined them on train at 3 A.M. going via Deming N.M.

Left Deming 11.30 A.M, and went north by Atchison. T & Santa Fe R.R. Our fare from Deming to S.L. City was $36.40 [$788] each, and from Tucson to Deming $11.00 [$238]

March 30, 1893—At Colorado Springs 3.30 and summit of mountains 4.35 P.M.

March 31, 1893—At Aspen Junction 5.30 A.M. and Grand Junction at 10.00 A.M. Lay by until 2.00 P.M. We passed through Leadville about midnight, altitude 11.000 feet. Cold, with Snow all about us, and Pike's Peak rising high to the South east many miles distant.

[page 709]

March 1893—Grand Junction is on the west side of the Rocky mountains. We have passed through grand mountain scenery, pine clad, cold and snowy. In the afternoon we cross Green river (the upper Colorado) and soon enter Utah, and begin the ascent of the Wahsatch Mts, descending through Spanish Fork Cañon and arriving at Ogden [continues in next entry]

April 1, 1893—about 9 P.M. arriving at S. L. City 12.40 A.M. and stopped with Eliza

April 4, 5 & 6, 1893—Conference was held 4th and 5th So the temple can be dedicated April 6th just 40 years from its commencement. Lyman took us to the theatre.

April 7, 1893—The 7th was the time set for people from Mexico to attend the dedication services, which were very impressive. But there was not such manifestations of holy influences as when the Manti Temple was dedicated, owing, I believe, to the fact that now all are permitted to enter who have any standing at all in the church, good or poor standing: so that many attended who were utterly unworthy to do any temple work. About 1000 gentiles and apostates were permitted to go through the building before it was dedicated, who were filled with amazement at its beauty, grandeur and magnificence. The "Tribune" our deadliest foe, described it as "dream of supernatural beauty."

When my son Nephi, a member of the famed Logan Choir went through a few days after, he heard heavenly music that entirely overcame him. He is one of the pure in heart, if there be any such living.

In the evening we attended a grand concert of over 600 children, dressed in the costumes of many countries, and who sang songs in various languages.

April 8 & 9, 1893—Cold, and snow 4 inches deep.

April 10, 1893—We went to Logan and found all well, and all glad to see us, as also Gean and Eliza in S. L. City when we arrived there. Gean's husband Edward Sudbury, is absent on a mission on the Society islands.

[page 710]

1893—Gean lives near his parents, and has a fine boy. A snow storm the evening we got to Lyman's place in Logan. It seems so strange and Logan seems strange also, after an absence of 5 ½ years. The streets seem narrow and the trees appear stunted, compared with those in Arizona.

April 12, 1893—Yesterday was cold and snowy. Saw Nephi and his family, and had a joyful time

April 15, 1893—Spent the day at Nephi's, who gave a family dinner.

April 16, 1893—Administered again to Apostle M. Thatcher, who is very low—not able to sit up, with dyspepsia, and is in much danger. Bp. & Mrs. W. B. Preston came from S. L. City to be with him.

April 17, 1893—Returned to Lyman's, as Nephi is going off to his farm to sow wheat.

April 18, 1893—Snow this morning, and quite cold.

April 20, 1893—Began work in the temple, myself, Susan & Gertrude.

I endowed David Martineau, born in Eng. 25 Jan. 1788, Died June 1836. Bap. 10 June 1884

His wife Caroline Elizabeth Hyde, born 1796, Eng. —Bap. Sept. 1887 Gertrude was endowed for her, and my wife Susan proxy in sealing April 21st.

April 20, 1893 [second entry of same date]—Mrs. Benj Martineau born in N. York 1770 died—Bap 19 Aug. 1887. Her husband was previously endowed, Susan proxy in Endowment and sealing, April 20, 1893

J. Alison, Born 1770 Eng. Bap. 10 June 1884, Endowed Nov. 10 1887, and his wife Margaret Martineau, born Eng. 1778. Bap. 15 July 1884, Endowed 5 May 1887, were sealed, I and Susan officiating for them.

April 21, 1893—I endowed George Martineau, b. 5 Apr. 1792, Eng. Bap. 10th June 1884, and his wife Sarah Greenhow, Endowed by Susan, born 1797, Eng. Bap. 19 Aug. 1884, Sealed today, by Susan and me.

Gertrude was ~~ordained~~ Endowed for Caroline E. Hyde. All above Sealings were by Br. N. C. Edlefsen, who also blessed Gertrude to heal her eyes, which pain her very much, assisted by me and Cousin W. D. Johnson Jr. In the evening we went to the Theatre.

[page 711]

April 21, 1893—I presented to the Logan Temple Library 4 volumes of "Lives and Times of the Roman Pontiffs," cost $8.70 [$188]

April 22, 1893—Snow again to day.

April 23, 1893—We all went to Nephi's and had a good time,—we, Lyman's & Allie, Genie, Frank Nebeker and Lilla. Had songs and a very pleasant time.

April 25, 1893—All met at Lyman's and had a good time with a family supper in the evening.

April 26, 1893—I went to the Temple. Lyman gave us considerable dry goods, for which may God bless him with plenty.

April 30, 1893—Attended Conference and had a good meeting, also May 1st

MAY

May 2, 1893—Went to S. L. City, Virginia went also. Susan and Gertrude remained at Logan.

May 3, 1893—Talked with Mrs. Jane C. Young, about getting an interview with my wife Jessie, whose mother prevents her from coming to me. She said she would do all to help me she can.

May 4, 1893—Lyman came to see about having an examination of Gertrude.

May 5, 1893—Saw Sister Young. She had visited Jessie, but can not say if Jessie will see me or not. Susan and Gertrude came to day. We all stay with Virginia.

May 7, 1893—We went in Street cars to Camp Douglass, very cold.

May 8, 1893—I determined to see Jessie, and went to the house, but her mother shut the door in my face and forbade me entrance. I went away out of sight and waited until I saw her mother go away, and then went again to the door and had a talk with Jessie, but she said I must not enter, as her mother had forbidden it. She looked sick and bad, and seemed to feel very badly, but did not dare to let me come in, and told me I must not even write to her, only I might send her a fig leaf, but no writing in the letter. Poor girl. I know she longed to come to me, and she will sometime.

May 9, 1893—Went to Bp. Prestons and spent the day, and staid all night. They were very kind indeed.

May 10, 1893—Started 11 P.M. to Station and had to wait there until [11th] [continued in next entry]

May 11, 1893—3 A.M. before we could start via Denver & [R...]

[page 712]

1893—Gertrude remained in S. L.City, hoping it would be better for her. Crossed the Wahsatch Mts. amid snow & ice, also, the Rocky Mts, arriving at Colorado Springs at 7 A.M. [continued in next entry]

May 12, 1893—and waited there until 4.40 P.M. reached Pueblo 5.50 P.M. and LaJunta 8.30 P.M. and lay over until next day

May 13, 1893—at 9.50 A.M. Reached Trinidad 1.15 P.M. Socorro

May 14, 1893—7.15 A.M. and arrived at Deming 12.40, noon, From Logan to Deming is 1149 miles. Stopped at a hotel

May 15, 1893—found some L. D. Saints here,—Br. & Sis. Farnsworth, who made Susan welcome at their house.[156] I am anxious to return to Tucson to work in the Sur. Genl office, & so I left Susan here, she to return to Colonia Juarez with Br. Macdonald's company.[157] I hated to leave her here, for her to make such a long journey—5 or 6 days—with wagon, camping out at night, but I knew there was no work there for me to do, and I could best show my love by earning means for her comfort. So at 2.20 P.M. I took train for Tucson, reaching there at 10.45 P.M. Susan was obliged to wait in Deming ten days for a chance to get home, finally returning in company with Apostle Teasdale and others, and found all well in Juarez.

May 16, 1893—Saw Sur. Genl Johnson, who said there was no work for me in the office, as his time of office was nearly expired. This is a great disappointment to me: here a long distance from home, and with money enough to keep me 3 or 4 days, and no means to leave Tucson. What shall I do? It is all so dark.

May 17, 1893—This morning I prayed for help, and received answer that all will be well with me, and my way shall be opened for me. I will trust in the promise of the Spirit. My room (the cheapest I can get) is 20¢ pr day, and I eat but one meal a day, 25¢, trying to make my few dollars hold out as long as possible.

May 20, 1893—Still looks very dark, and as if I must beg or starve. Prayed and received a comforting answer.

May 21, 1893—Wrote to Jessie Helen and sent the fig leaf as she wished me, but nothing in words, as she told me. Fasted 24 hours and prayed and was comforted.

[page 713]

May 22, 1893—A letter from Susan, full of comfort and prophecy, of good to me, saying my way will be opened and all will be well with me.

---

156 Alonzo L. Farnsworth was among the first settlers in Round Valley, Mexico. He was the first branch president in Colonia García (Turley and Turley, *History of the Mormon Colonies in Mexico*, 251; Tullis, *Mormons in Mexico*, 110).

157 This could be A. F. Macdonald, who lived in Colonia García (Turley and Turley, *History of the Mormon Colonies in Mexico*, 28; Tullis, *Mormons in Mexico*, 144–45; McClintock, *Mormon Settlement in Arizona*, 267).

In the afternoon Genl Johnson promised me work in the office, to continue until he should resign. Oh how thankful I am—rescued from apparent starvation, and still more thankful because I see the voice which promised me blessing was truly the voice of the Holy Spirit. I am striving hard to learn to know his voice, and thus my faith strengthens.

May 23, 1893—Began work in the office as draughtsman, at $4. [$87] per day. I thank thee, my Father, for thy goodness.

May 24, 1893—I prayed and asked concerning Anna M. Hagberg—dead many years ago—and sealed to me as wife. She was the mother of my sealed son Niels M. Hagberg. I received answer that she had joyfully received all my temple work for her—endowments and sealing to me. So Niels is truly my own son as any from my loins, and I must cultivate him as such.

MAY

May 2, 1893—Made a map for Howe and got $4.[00] [$87] for it

Sunday, May 4, 1893—At about 2 A.M. I dreamed about Jessie Helen. I was at a Sunday meeting and was called to lead the singing. As I went to take my place, Jessie also came to take her seat near by on my left hand, but just as she was about to sit down two women slipped into the two chairs before she could sit, and she had to sit partly on their laps, and seemed annoyed at them. We sang some hymns, and as she turned away she spoke of taking to her notes again.

I awoke, and the meaning of the dream, and if it had any meaning, I was told it had, to have comfort in it, have faith in it and write it down so that I may remember it more perfectly when I see the fulfillment of it. The full interpretation will not be made known to me now, but will be in the future. And the dream is for my comfort.

[page 714]

JUNE 1893 JULY

June 4, 1893—Even now she desires in her heart to correspond with me, and will in due time when opposing influences are removed. as they will be, and she will come to me as a true and loving wife.

And the Spirit said to me "I seal upon thee at this time the gift of dreams and interpretation that thou mayest be comforted, instructed or warned, and if thou wilt receive this in faith and do according as thou art shown thy gift shall grow and increase, & prepare thee for the blessing of heavenly messengers, even of angels & the Three Nephites, and this because thou hast long sought these gifts because my servant the Prophet counseled my Saints to seek for them. Thou shalt write thy dream, and in due time thou shalt know concerning the two women who sat where Jessie expected to sit, more fully."

I was instructed more fully, and referred to Joseph when he was warned to flee into Egypt, with the infant Savior: how he at once awoke, told Mary, arose and prepared his beasts for the journey, while Mary prepared the child for the for the journey, and took food and water. And so, if I am instructed in a dream, and do as I am told, I shall be blessed. Oh my Father, I thank thee for thy goodness to me in this, and in giving me money for my needful food and lodging.

June 19, 1893—Sur. Gen[l] Manning offers me a contract to Survey 5 townships. I asked the Father, and was told I shall be blessed in doing the work and in receiving my pay.

June 24, 1893—Filed my bonds of $4500.[00] [$97,381]. Contract no. 30

June 27, 1893—Have 2 more townships to Survey, contract no. 32; bonds $2000. [$43,280] I thank thee oh Father, for giving me work.

June 28, 1893—Got my second bond (contract no. 32) fixed today. This evening ex-Gov. Wolfley engaged me to survey for the Gila Bend Canal & Irr[n] Company along the line of their canal, and to pay me $10.[00] [$216] per day and board.[158] I felt as if this was a great blessing to me, and that my way is opening wonderfully. Sent money to Susan.

158 Gila Bend, Arizona, is southwest of Phoenix, a distance of several hundred miles from his home in Colonia Juárez, Mexico. The western Arizona desert canals had no Native American patterns for these pioneers to follow as in the Salt River Valley of Phoenix, so construction was a significant challenge.

JULY

July 3, 1893—Received my commission as Deputy M. S. Surveyor, also was appointed Chief Engineer of the Gila Bend Canal and Irrigation Company.

[page 715]

July 3, 1893—I got trunk, bedding &c, and started to Gila Bend at 9.45 P.M. arriving next morning at [continued in next entry]

July 4, 1893—2.25 A.M. Before accepting this work Ja^{s} McMillan Superintendent of the Canal, agreed in writing to pay me the sum agreed upon at the completion of my work, and paid me $20.^{00} [$433] in advance. At 8 A.M. the same day I and McMillan started in a carriage up the river to the dam 20 miles. The canal and dam has cost up to this time over $700.000.^{00} [$15,148,122] and they are still unfinished. My work is to connect the line of canal with the U.S. public land Survey Section corners, and make a map of the same for the whole length of the canal, 38 miles. The weather is very hot, but I am glad to have employment, to earn means for my family.

July 5, 1893—Got my help and began work, continuing from day to day until Sunday the 9th when I went to Gila Bend for letters.

July 9, 1893—Last night I had a dream, and awoke and thought about it. I thought I was in some public meeting, standing just at the entrance and some one at the other end of the room said "Let three men come forward." Without knowing why, I at once stepped forward and then stopped, ashamed at my own forwardness, but was in a moment at the far end of the room. I then heard read the ~~notes~~ minutes of the meeting, which said I was ordained 1st counsellor to the President of the Stake and also President or to act as President because the President would be absent so much of the time that I might act as such more properly, and hence was ordained President as well. Also that I would have $1200. [$25,968] a year, also $200. [$4,328] which would be enough to sustain my family in comfort.

The dream was so vivid and strange. I asked that if it had no real meaning for me it might all pass from my mind. x [in margin by next sentence] If it has a meaning, that it may remain in my memory.

July 11, 1893—Worked all day in intense heat—124° in shade, without a breath of air. At one time was nearly overcome by the heat and all became dark and I felt like death was upon me, but I had sufficient thought and life to rebuke the Evil One that my life might be spared.

[page 716]

July 11, 1893—As soon as I prayed and rebuked the evil powers, it passed away & I continued my work. Day after day my instrument became so hot I could not touch it without burning my hands severely, and we drank enormous quantities of water, which immediately came out through the skin like as through a sieve, and our clothes from head to foot wet as though I had been in the river. Had I not thus perspired I would have died.

July 19, 1893—Reached Gila Bend—20 miles—with my survey

July 25, 1893—Finished the field work of my survey, and will now have easier time, as I will be at work in the office, making my maps. in Gila Bend. Have received and written many letters from my family and Sent Gertrude and Eliza a little money.

July 26, 1893—Received my "instructions" for the surveys I am to make.

AUGUST

August 1, 1893—Got $40.^{00} [$866] from McMillan, which, with $20.^{00} [$433] before makes $60 [$1,298] in all. Went to Tucson to finish my work.

Sunday, August 6, 1893—Took a long walk, and wished I could see the family.

August 13, 1893—Recei'd my pay for the month of June, $104.^{00} [$2,251] and wrote to Theodore to come and help on my survey.

August 22, 1893—Finished my maps of the Gila Bend Canal Survey My time has been 44 days in all, hard work. and the balance due me is $304.^{75} [$6,595] which is promised me in a few days.

August 26, 1893—I lent von Wendt $10.^{00} [$216] He was in great need and was about discouraged. Settled my accounts in Tucson and started to Mesa about midnight.

August 27, 1893—Reached my son-in-law Samuel Johnson about 10 A.M. and went to Conference in the afternoon, and preached.

SEPTEMBER 2ND

September 2, 1893—I went to High Priests meeting to day at Mesa. At the place of meeting I found Br. Charles Allen in horrible agony He was bitten on the toe this morning by a small black spider, with a ~~bu~~ round, black and shining, about the size of a buck shot.

[page 717]

September, 1893—He could not have suffered more had he been in the fire. I learned afterwards he suffered two or three days and nights before his pain left him.

September 6, 1893—Have tried to borrow money to commence my survey, but the panic in business is still so great that I have not been able to raise a cent. I went to Tempe to see if I could borrow there. The Cashier said they were not making loans to any body—times were to dangerous.

September 8, 1893—I went to Phoenix to see if I could get money there. I must have money to buy a transit, get supplies, teams &c for my party. I went to several banks, but got the same answer from all—"We are not making loans now." What to do I did not know. Phoenix was my last hope and without I get money my contract must forfeit. I had had a promise that I would be blessed in it, But it seemed now impossible, and I began to wonder "have I been deceived—was it an evil spirit, and not the Holy Spirit which promised me a blessing upon my contract? If I have been deceived, what have I to cling to! In this sad state of mind I stood on a street corner and saw a bank sign I had never seen before, and thinking, "they can only refuse, like the others" I went there and made known my business. Mr. W. K. James said his bank was not making any loans, but he had some money to loan on good security. In the end I borrowed of him $600.00 [$12,984] giving him power of attorney to collect my survey pay when it should be due me. For this I must pay him $250.00, [$5,410] or $850.00 [$18,304] in all in return—pretty big interest. But it was my only chance, and I felt that God had opened my way, getting the money from a Stranger as I did, and best of all—I knew that I had not been deceived and that the voice which had promised me a blessing was not a lying spirit, but the Holy Spirit. For this I am very thankful, more than words can tell.

I am diligently trying to learn the voice of the Holy Spirit, and could not bear the thought that I may be deceived in it. I am thankful I am not deceived, am gaining faith in God's promises, and gaining knowledge of the principle of revelation and prophecy, as Prest Woodruff has said it is our duty to do.

[page 718]

September 8, 1893—I returned to Sam's and found letters saying the Genl Land Dept, Washn, had approved my contract, and sent me all necessary blank books, field notes and instructions.

September 14, 1893—Went to Phoenix again and concluded my deal with Mr. James, for the $600.00 [$12,984] I sent $100.00 [$2,164] to W. & L. E. Gurley, Troy N.Y. in part payment for a transit, to cost about $300.00 [$6,492] also for Survey chain and steel rule. This to me is a day to be remembered, for God's blessing to me. I sent more names to Gertrude, in Logan, to be endowed for in the temple.

During all these months I have spent much time in writing to Susan and my children, as well as to many others. I receive my pension every 3 months, of $24.00 [$519] which is quite a help to us, although but a small amount. I send von Wendt money from time to time, dividing with him, as he sorely needs it, and some way I feel very much drawn to him, as well as he to me. He is a Russian Baron of ancient lineage (of the Knights of Malta) who conquered east Prussia many hundred years ago, the country of the Wends, whence his family name of von Wendt. He is a mine operator and expert, who has lost his means and is about discouraged. I have cheered him up all I can, and he seems to think me his only trusted friend in Tucson, having no confidence in any other person here. It is, I believe, from the Lord.

September 23, 1893—Albert writes me their last baby is named Ernest.

September 27, 1893—Nephi has another baby, don't know the name yet. Sent 25$ [$541] for Susan to come to Mesa. Got a letter from Joel Saying my solar compass and other things had been sent from Juarez and were now at Bisbee A. T. my boys are not coming from Mexico, as they think they are too late, all but Theodore, who I think will come.

October 4, 1893—My new transit is come to Tucson, and my solar has been sent me from Bisbee.

[page 719]

This finishes the first volume—a book so large that I never expected to fill it, and yet the story of my life is not all told. In this volume are noted many things not worth record, while I find, on looking back, that I have omitted many that should have been noted. In part, this has been because some things appeared at the time of some importance, which time subsequently disproved; and some things, of apparently little moment afterwards proved to be important as time unfolded the future.

I now leave this volume and begin again in volume two, a book of 500 pages. How many of them my remaining years may require I know not, neither is it important. I wish to remain here only so long as I can do good and help to advance the work of the Lord. When the time comes that I can no longer do so, then it will be much better to go on to the next and higher life. I have received promises which entitle me to get many years in this, my second estate, and if I do not fail too grievously in my duty and so forfeit them, or forfeit them by want of faith—doubt and unbelief,—fruitful source of loss of blessings—I may continue, until I may assist in building the city of Zion and her twelve temples, and do a work therein for many of the dead, which I greatly desire to do, if it be the will of the Father, in company with my dear Susan—the wife of my youth, the companion and sharer of my toils, my trials, my sorrows and my joys—always my help and comfort—always filled with hope, comfort and consolation, whom may our Father forever bless with his choice blessings.[159]

[See Appendix 3 for letters, note, certificates, and newspaper clippings inserted in the back of Journal 1.]

159 The reader feels a glimpse of Martineau's mind here as he is organizing his journal from his life's writings. He is sixty-five years old at this juncture in his writing and wants to leave something of significance for his family. In so doing, he left a record of the challenges of a western pioneer.

◁ PART ▷

TESTIMONY AND TRIALS

My Life

James H. Martineau

Vol. 2

Fig. 8.1—Heading to Volume 2.

[Starts on page 3. There are no pages 1 or 2. See Appendix 4 for newspaper articles inserted in the original. Personal letters are transcribed as they were inserted here before his journal entries. Martineau, in organizing his history, wrote in two large legal size copybooks, as noted in the preface. "Vol. 2" refers to the second book.]

[page 3]

October 5, 1893—I went to Phoenix and got some goods, and on the 6th got my solar compass, chain and a few other things I had sent for to Mexico.

October 8, 1893—Sent money to Theodore at Wilcox so he could come to Tucson.

October 14, 1893—Started to Tucson, arriving at 2.15 A.M. Got my transit and new chain, and had them tested by Chief Clk. Geo. J. Roskringe. They were found in good condition.

October 17, 1893—By letter from Nephi I learn his last baby was born in September, and named Elva. Theodore came.

October 19, 1893—My party of surveyors came from mesa to day having been 5 days on the journey.

October 20, 1893—Bought supplies for our survey party.

October 21, 1893—Started for my field of work about 20 miles away, my party consists of Saml Johnson and Arthur Openshaw,[1] chainmen, Theodore, flagman, J. W. Johnson, Cook, Aloneson Reidhead, teamster, John J. Tucker, axeman & self, 7 in all, with tent, one wagon, and two ~~deans.~~ teams. Camped at Crane's place.

October 22, 1893—Sunday, rested

October 23, 1893—Began the Survey of the 4th Standard Parallel South Ranges 16 & 17 East

October 25, 1893—Last night I dreamed of the Savior and of being with him. It gave me much comfort.

1 Arthur Openshaw was a Tempe, Arizona, bishop (James H. McClintock, *Mormon Settlement in Arizona: A Record of Peaceful Conquest of the Desert* [Phoenix: Manufacturing Stationers, 1921], 210).

November 4, 1893—To day I finished the Survey of Tp. 17 E. and tomorrow begin on Tp. 16 East.

November 17, 1893—Finished my Survey of Contract No. 32 and started to Tucson. This work has been very hard, being in a very rough, mountainous and rocky country, full of cactus and prickly shrubs. Some days it was all we could do to run a survey of 1 ½ miles, starting at Sunrise and not getting into camp until late at night, tired out completely. Our shoes soon were off our feet, and I bought two raw hides with which to tie up our feet, but which were soon cut through by the sharp rocks. We had to haul all our water for miles, and, all in all, it was a hard trip, quite cold at the end. Spent the night in Tucson of 18th

[page 4]

November 18, 1893—We arrived in Tucson at 2 P.M. and all went on towards home but ~~Theo and I~~ me. Cold, with prospect of rain.

November 20, 1893—I began work on my plats and field notes.

November 23, 1893—Still working on my field notes. Received telegram from Susan, who is at Bowie Station with Dora, & will be at Tucson to night at midnight. I borrowed $5.00 [$108] to help me to Mesa, and met Susan on the train. I had not seen her since May, nor Dora since 18 months, when I left Colonia Juarez. We arrived at Tempe at 3 A.M. and lodged at a hotel, going then to Sams by Stage, reaching him at 10 A.M.

Susan had stopped off at Bowie Sta. on her way to Arizona to visit Albert and Emma at Thatcher. She had an uneventful journey from home to Deming, and was blessed in all her journeys.

Anna's baby girl, Phyllis, was born Nov. 13/93 10.45 P.M. and weighed 9 lbs.

Was very glad to see my family after so long separation, and was warmly welcomed by Samuel and Elvira. From this time I continued work on my field notes and plats

December 9, 1893—I went to Phoenix today to see R. C. Powers,[2] in order to have him give me the knowledge of where to begin my Survey, Contract No. 32, he having surveyed near. Theodore was rebaptized today by Bp. Openshaw.

Sunday, December 10, 1893—At meeting today I was mouth in confirming Theodore. He is trying to live a pure and holy life.

December 12, 1893—To day I finished my field notes, plats &c & sent to Tucson

December 13, 1893—Got supplies for my survey north of Phoenix, and on

December 14, 1893—Started out with my party, the same as before, except I had one more in party than before. Camped in Nevada Corral at Phoenix

December 15, 1893—Bought additional supplies

December 16, 1893—Left Phoenix, and drove 10 miles to my work near ~~Hardin's place~~ mail Station 18m from town

[page 5]

December 18, 1893—Began survey, but was quite unwell all day, with a burning fever.

December 22, 1893—Again began work, and ran line 6 miles & returned.

December 23, 1893—Heavy rain all last night and today. Could not work.

December 24, 1893—Still very sick, with much cough. All thought best to quit and take me home. We reached home at 10 P.M. I having lain on a bed all the way. Samuel also was quite unwell. From this time on I got worse, having with my fever an incessant cough, and my friends thought my condition dangerous.

December 28, 1893—When I prayed early this morning I received a promise by the voice of the spirit, that my faith shall increase from this hour, until it shall become like that of Abraham, Noah and the brother of Jared, also that I shall soon be restored to health and finish my survey in the time appointed, and shall

2 Ridgely C. Powers was engaged in early Arizona mining, surveying, and engineering. He was a promoter and had an extensive interest in real estate (*A Historical and Bibliographical Record of the Territory of Arizona* [Chicago: McFarland and Poole, 1896], 492–93).

be blessed in it from beginning to end. Lilla & Gertie wrote me from Logan, and sent me Pres[t] Woodruff's remedy for kidney complaints, as follows:—

1 oz hops, 1 oz senna, 1 oz celery seed, 1 oz Buchu leaves all steeped in a quart of water.[3] When done, strain into a pint of holland gin. Dose, a table spoonful 3 times a day. But the teaching of the spirit to me was, not to trust to medicines, but rather to consecrated oil and administration.

December 31, 1893—Still very sick with fever, incessant cough, sore throat and headache. But I believe in the promise that I shall be healed soon. We received a letter from Mexico, stating that Joel and Anna had a pair of twins born, boys, who lived only a few hours—long enough to be named and blessed.

[written in margin]

Twins born Dec. 8, named Joel and Joseph Franklin.

JANUARY 1894.

January 1, 1894—Still sick, threatened with pneumonia. Slept last night.

January 8, 1894—Over 42 years of marriage. I feel much better today, and so are Elvira and Wilmirth, both having la grippe. The Father has been very good to me and mine all these 42 years, and I thank and praise him.

Still sick, distressing cough, headache and fever. I use consecrated oil as my medicine. I prayed to the Father to know if I ought to have a doctor as my friends recommended me.

[page 6]

January 8, 1894—The answer, by the voice of the Spirit was, not to depend upon doctors, but use holy oil with prayer, faith and administration by the Elders, and I should be healed. And so I follow it out the best I can knowing God is abundantly able to heal me if he will.

January 13, 1894—To day Theodore split his foot with an axe, and bled so much he became very faint. I am now able to walk out but am very weak. I was hoping soon to be able to go back to my surveys, but Theodore's accident will hinder.

January 16, 1894—To day we counted up our family, as follows: Self and 4 wives = 5[;] children, 21, Grandchildren, 55, sons wives (mine) 10, total, 91. Forty two years ago I stood alone. But god has given a promise that I shall become a great people,—a nation, and I hope I may not forfeit it.

January 20, 1894—To day I surveyed a piece of Sam's land for him, and hope soon to go to work again. The Father has verified his promise, and healed me without a doctor.

January 21, 1894—To day I again attended meeting and spoke.

January 22, 1894—At 2 P.M. I again set out with my party to finish my U. S. land Survey and went to Phoenix, 18 miles.

January 23, 1894—I borrowed $150.[00] [$3,246] at the bank to obtain supplies, and sent $80.[00] [$1,731] to Gertrude, so she may come to us. We went on to where we had left our tent and supplies when we came home in December, and found about $10.—[$216] worth of provisions had been stolen.

January 24, 1894—Began to survey again, and lost a screw from my transit which disabled it, until I thought, and made one out of a leaden bullet, which enables me to go on until I can send to the factory in Troy, N. Y. for another.

January 29, 1894—This morning Alanson went home, very ill with pain in his ear, which was almost unbearable, and Sam volunteered to cook in his place, besides his duty as Chainman. Theodore drives team, being able only to hobble about a little. His foot has healed remarkably and from the time he was administered to at first, has had no pain to speak of although the bone was cut.

It is by the blessing of the Lord.

February 1, 1894—To day Sam's boy—Joseph—came from home to help in Alanson's place. I went to Phoenix on business.

February 6, 1894—Moved camp, having finished T.3 N. R. 3. East

February 8, 1894—Have sold my old Solar Compass, which cost me $460[00] [$9,954] to the factory, for a Barometer worth $50.00 [$1,082]. My solar compass had a history. In 1877 I did the field work for

3 Hops are the dried, ripe cones of the humulus flower used in brewing and medicine. Senna is a medicinal plant with leaflets or pods and yellow flowers. Buchu is a southern African shrub whose leaves are used as a mild diuretic and urinary antiseptic.

A. J. Stewart, who had a U. S. land survey, and earned between $800.[00] [$17,312] and $900.[00] [$19,476] Stewart paid me the Compass, worth about $150.[00] [$3,246] charging me $400.[00] [$8,656] for it, and afterwards cheated me out of the balance due me—$440.[00] [$9,522] But with this instrument I afterwards [did] considerable government surveying, which I could not have done without it.

February 9, 1894—To night at about 11 P.M. I prayed, and received an answer, in which, among other great promises, I was promised the Apostleship "whether in the Quorum of the Twelve or not, it mattereth not to thee." This seemed too great, almost, for one like me, but it was repeated twice, once before, a month or so, this was said to me, "Behold I have chosen thee to be mine apostle to the Lamanites." This was in connexion with other great blessings: but I felt as if it might probably be that I would be one "sent" to them, as the word apostle means "sent." but not ordained as an Apostle, and I was told this should be an incentive to live a holy life; also, that He will not suffer me to be tempted more than I can bear, that I may do the work to which I have been appointed from before the foundation of the world. I was again promised a land of promise, where I and my people may rest in safety, while judgement shall go forth upon the earth; and it shall be among the Lamanites, who shall be a bulwark of defense to us. And they shall have mighty faith, even as when Jesus appeared to them, so that even their dead shall be raised, some of the elder ones become white through faith, and their children be born white, for so shall the curse be removed, and also many other glorious promises. Help me, oh God to so live that I may not forfeit these blessings.

[page 8]

February 10, 1894—We got caught some miles from camp in a heavy rain storm, wetting and chilling us as it turned to icy sleet. Got to camp nearly chilled and frozen.

February 13, 1894—Alanson returned, nearly well, and Jodie went home.

February 19, 1894—I went to Phoenix and thence to Mesa and found all well. Got my new aneroid Surveying Barometer, the best of its kind.

February 25, 1894—I find the elevation of our camp, 15[m] north of Phoenix is 2358 ft.

MARCH 1894.

March 6, 1894—Finished T. 5 N. R. 2 E.

March 13, 1894—Finished all my survey contract to day, five townships in this contract, Started home at noon. Truly God has blessed us very much, according to his promise.

March 14, 1894—Got home to Nephi,[4] and found all well, and Gertrude came from Logan, Utah. Immediately commenced to make my plats and write my field notes, which I finished on the 30th [**March, 1894**] and sent them to Tucson,—the Sur. Gen[ls] office.

[written in margin]

Recipe for Blk. ink.

I found the following recipe to make black ink:—

½ oz Extract of Logwood, 10 grains Bichromate of potash,[5] dissolve in 1 qt. hot rain water, When cold, pour into glass bottle and leave uncorked a week or two.

Baking Powder. 5 oz tartaric acid, 8 oz Bi-carb. of Soda, 16 ozs potato starch, all dried in cool oven, mix by a sieve. Dose ½ teaspoonful for a pint of flour. Mix with cold water and bake at once in hot oven.

APRIL 1894

April 11, 1894—Br. and Sister Truman Sent for Susan to help with their sick baby. We both went, and remained with them.

April 13, 1894—Borrowed $50.[00] [$1,082] of W. K. James, paid some debts in Phoenix, [continued in next entry]

April 20, 1894—and Saw J. M. Rice, attorney for the Peoria Canal Co.[6] He wants me to do some more work on the canal. Left Phoenix 9 P.M. on my way to Tucson, where I went to expedite my Survey business. Arrived there at 3 A.M. on the 21st

4 The settlement of Nephi, Arizona, was organized in 1887. It was just west of Mesa in what is today Tempe. Patriarch Benjamin F. Johnson was among the families living in Nephi (McClintock, *Mormon Settlement in Arizona*, 220).

5 Potash is a crude, impure form of potassium carbonate obtained from wood ashes.

6 Peoria, Arizona, is located northwest of Phoenix. Many of these towns Martineau mentions are now part of the Phoenix metropolitan area.

MAY 4

May 4, 1894—Went to the university to compare and test my barometer with that at the university, a mercurial one. Mine agrees nearly in reading, being 0.07 of an inch higher.

[page 9]

May 4, 1894—Mr. D. T. Horton of New York city sent von Wendt $100.[00] [$2,164] which is a great blessing to us. he and I living together and doing our own cooking on a small coal oil lamp—stove. He is a first class cook.[7]

May 23, 1894—Sent a dress each to Susan, Gertie, and Dora. Von Wendt, my friend and chum, gave me $5.00 [$108] for the purpose.

May 30, 1894—To day von Wendt and I, with teamster, started for the Santa Rita Mt. about 45 or 50 miles distant, to look at a silver and lead mine we have thoughts of bonding, to work it or sell it. Watered at Davis' Ranch, which is 1300 ft. higher than Tucson. We camped a few miles below Greaterville, among beautiful oaks and grassy hills. Night cold.

May 31, 1894—Rose at 4 A.M. and at 9. A.M. reached Greaterville, a small village at the foot of Santa Rita Peak, which is 10000 ft high.

JUNE 1894

June 1, 1894—We examined three mining claims owned by Mr. John Anderson.[8] and filed location notice on an old abandoned gold mine. The elevations are as follow:—Greaterville 5114 ft, the mines, on a high ridge 5390 ft. on pass of the ridge 5500 ft.

June 2, 1894—I obtained a bond on Anderson's 3 mines, good for 3 mo. If they turn out well and we desire to keep them, I must pay him $1500.[00] [$32,460] for them. Started home at 4 P.M. and Camped near a well. Night quite cool.

June 3, 1894—Arrived at Tucson at 7 P.M.

June 12, 1894—Made out my account against the U. S. for my 2 contracts as follows:—Contract No. 32 $838.93, [$18,155] Con[t] no. 32 $2441.72 [$52,839] total, $3280.65 [$70,994]. I gave Alex. von Wendt a power of attorney, so he may sell the mines I have bonded. I rec[d] a telegram from Gila Bend saying I need not come to work on the canal, which somewhat disappointed me, but I know all will be for the best.

June 21, 1894—Rec[d] word from Horton, who reports against our mines and cannot use them. Having finished my business here I start

June 22, 1894—for Mesa, arriving there next day, 10. A.M. Found Susan still at Br. Furman's, ~~helping with the sick baby~~.

June 24, 1894—Went to meeting, and spoke. After, I went with Susan to Sam's, and in the evening Theodore[9] and Celia Johnson came to me and announced their engagement, asking my blessing, which I cordially gave. with my consent, in which Susan coincided.

Fig. 8.2—Theodore and Celia Johnson Martineau Family. Courtesy of James Henry Martineau Family Organization.

7 At this writing no match could be found for the names D. T. Horton and Alex von Wendt.

8 John B. Anderson held mining interests in the area (John B. Anderson, "Mining and Personal Papers," Arizona Historical Society, Southern Arizona Division, Libraries and Archives).

9 Theodore is the son of James Henry and Susan Ellen Martineau.

[page 10]

June 24, 1894—Susan made a good liniment for rheumatism, as follows:—1 oz each of oil cinnamon and chloroform, 2 oz alcohol.

JULY 3

July 3, 1894—To day Gertrude was severely ill all day. We administered often. The next day she was better and free from pain.

July 7, 1894—This morning Susan, Theodore, Gertrude and Dora started with Celia and Joseph Johnson and family, for the hills. I remain at Mesa to write up Uncle Benjamin's journal in his book. The family went on and I spent a week in writing up his journal.

Saturday, July 14, 1894—At noon all returned from the hills, having had quite a pleasant outing, But Gertrude had not improved any and in the night was taken with severe pain in her side. We administered often, but she obtained but temporary help.

Sunday, July 15, 1894—Gertrude is in extreme pain in her side—it seems like some internal inflammation. Administration helps her for the moment only, giving her a five minute sleep.

July 16, 1894—Gertrude still worse, and wants a physician, as she

July 17, 1894—thinks something is wrong internally. I walked to Mesa 4 miles and return, and Dr. Sabin, who thinks her in great danger, through inflammation caused by a stoppage in her small intestines—peronitis [peritonitis[10]]—and gave her opiates to relieve her agony, and took means to remove the obstruction by means of a fountain syringe.

July 18, 1894—She is still the same, but indications are better.

July 19 & 20, 1894—Improving a little, and fever decreasing. The obstruction is removed, mostly, and her pain less.

July 21, 1894—Sat up a few minutes while her bed was made. Fever gone, but she is very weak

July 23 & 24, 1894—We remained by her bedside, to fan her and help her all we can.

July 26, 1894—Dr. Sabin will not call any more unless we send for him, as he thinks she will not need him, if she will continue with the medicine he left her.

[page 11]

July 27, 1894—Gertie not so well today. but I hope nothing serious.

July 28, 1894—Uncle Benj. F. Johnson's birthday, celebrated by many of his family gathering at Don M LeBaron's[11] place, where a fine dinner was prepared in a grove of fig trees, Songs sung, and kind speeches by myself and his sons and friends. There were several hundred present at this, his 76th birth day.

July 31, 1894—Gertrude slowly improving, but not able to stand on her feet, nor to eat anything, more than 2 or 3 oysters at a time. She has very severe pain behind the eyeballs.

AUGUST

August 2, 1894—Gertrude wishes to be moved to Mesa, where Br. and Sister James Furman invite her to come to their house. We carried her to a carriage and took her there, receiving a kindly welcome from the family who gave up a room for her, and a place at the table for us all, Susan, Dora & me. May God bless them, they may never want friends in time of need. I board at Uncle Ben's, and am writing up his journal

August 7, 1894—Gertie walked a few steps today. Theodore received a patriarchal blessing from uncle Benjamin to day:—

[page 12—Martineau left half of pages 11–12 blank, likely to return and reinsert the record of the blessing.]

[page 13]

August 21, 1894—Received instructions from the Sur. Genl L. H. Manning[12] in regard to resurvey-

10 Peritonitis is an inflammation of the peritoneal cavity, where the intestines lie.

11 Don M. LeBaron came to Mesa, Arizona, in 1879. He established a bakery and general store before moving to the Mexican colonies (J. H. Martineau, "Birthday Reunion," *Deseret News*, August 11, 1894; Utah Digital Newspapers).

12 L. H. Manning was the survey general for the territory of Arizona. He homesteaded in the Rincon Mountains east of Tucson. He was active in Tucson's politics (he was the mayor in 1905) as well as in educational development (Ross

ing the line between my line and Powers', to see which is correct, as they vary somewhat. I quit writing for Uncle Benjamin for the present.

Susan has fears that she has dropsy, but I hope it is not so.

August 22, 1894—Borrowed $60.[00] [$1,298] from the Mesa Bank at 2 o/c pr month. Administered to Susan, and she is better in health.

August 23, 1894—I went to Phoenix to meet Powers, who will assist me in making the resurvey. We started to work on the next day.

August 25, 1894—Very tired to day, also raw and so lame I could hardly get back to our camp. Glad tomorrow is Sunday.

August 29, 1894—Have finished all I have to do, and leave Powers to make a resurvey of part of his contract.

August 30, 1894—Started home by stage, arriving at 7 P.M. and found Gertie pretty well, also Susan and Dora. We have my tent pitched under the trees at Furman's place, and Gertie and Dora sleep in the house, Susan and I in the tent. We have a small folding table, a few dishes and an oil stove to cook on, and Sister Furman and Jim are as good and kind as can be. I pray that they may never want for anything needful while they live. No blood-relation could be kinder than they have always been.

SEPTEMBER 1895 [1894]

[Martineau inadvertently wrote the wrong year]

September 1, 1894—must go to Tucson on my Survey business, and von Wendt writes he has something good in view—gold mines.

September 3, 1894—Started to Tucson. Found von Wendt well and glad to see me. Thinks he has a good mine in view through Mr. Horton of N. Y. City. Am working up our last notes of joint survey and making plat of the same.

September 24, 1894—Sam and Elvira have a new baby, born Sept. 24 They named her Rita (Margarite)

OCTOBER 1894

October 1, 1894—As I am doing Powers work in the making of all our survey notes &c, also in rewriting his old field notes, he sent me 25$ [$541] on my application, which will keep us on a while longer. I sent Susan $5.00 [$108].

October 24, 1894—By letter from Jesse N. I learn he is in Streator, Ill. working as a hotel clerk there.

[page 14]

NOVEMBER 1894

November 4, 1894—Saw James F. Johnson on his way to Mexico. he wants me to go to Mesa, keep the store books until his return home, and write for his father, Uncle Ben, and says he will pay me a little wages for it. So I return home, having filed the notes in the Sur. Gen[l] Office of our new Survey (Powers & mine). Left at 12 midnight.

November 5, 1894—Got home. All is excitement about the election.

November 6, 1894—Election day, but I did not vote. I began writing again for Uncle Benjamin

November 19, 1894—Surveyed a small piece of land for Sam.

November 23, 1894—I moved my family into two rooms, instead of the one Susan had hired while I was in Tucson. I pay $6.00 [$130] pr month for the new place. Susan has a swelling and sore in her breast, which all think a cancer. Dr. Bailey also declared it a cancer. We prayed, and both received the same testimony—that it is <u>not</u> a cancer, but an ulcer, and she shall be healed of it.

DECEMBER 1894

December 1, 1894—The swelling in her breast is increasing and more painful. We anoint and rebuke it.

December 7, 1894—Theodore is anxious to go to Utah to school, and has saved money enough for his passage there. I got some clothing in the store for him, gave him my new overcoat and some shirts &c, to help fit him out and gave him a blessing. He starts tomorrow

F. Holland, "Manning Cabin," Nomination to the National Registry of Historical Places; on file in Pima County Cultural Resources Program Office, Tucson, 1972).

December 8, 1894—Theo. started at 9 P.M. accompanied to Tempe by quite a number of relatives besides my own family. Many tears were shed, and many hearty good byes. He goes to enter the U. S. Agricultural College, Logan, Utah, and fit himself for a higher usefulness in Zion. He had worked hard all the fall and summer, helping at farm work, in order to get the money necessary for the journey. As I have not received my pay for my U. S. land survey I am unable to help him much, but wish I could, as he is a good son and one every way worthy.

[page 15]

December 8, 1894—I am still busy every day writing for Uncle Benjamin. Frank credited me the munificent sum of $25.00 [$130] on my Store account for over a months services. Gertie is able to go to parties now and then, but suffers very much nearly all the time. She says that when she goes to a dance, it only puts her usual pain in another part of her body, for she is never without pain.

December 20, 1894—I am invited to go to Tucson by Sur. Genl Manning to do mapping, to begin Jan. 1st—one months employment. I answered I would come Jan. 2nd 1895.

I am very thankful to have even a month's work, to earn something for my loved ones, and for this, O Father I thank thee.

December 25, 1894—By invitation we had our Christmas dinner at Furman's and had a pleasant time together.

JANUARY 1895

January 1, 1895—To day we had dinner at Uncle Benjamin's; but I had to hurry away from the table to take the coach to Tempe. I blessed my family before departure, and reached Tempe in time to see a balloon ascension by a woman, who came down in a parachute safely. Reached Tucson next day, at 3 A.M.

January 2, 1894—Began mapping in the office.

January 7, 1894—Bought a nice brooch for Susan, for our wedding day.

January 8, 1894—Our 43^{d} wedding anniversary. Greatly has God blessed us in our married life. We have had sorrow, sickness and death, plenty and poverty, pleasure and pain; but only enough for our good, to perfect us in faith, patience and knowledge,—knowledge gained only by experience. And in no other way can we become perfected. If we have sorrows we know how to sympathise with others who are sad, for we can understand their troubles.

But I have been blessed as have been but few men, in my beloved Companion—one among ten thousand; and in my Children, who thus far have all proved honorable and true to the truth. One other there is, who holds aloof, but why I know not, unless it be by the verity of her mother, whom I never injured in the smallest particular.

[page 16]

January 8, 1895—But I have a testimony that she will yet return to me as a true and loving companion.

To day poor Gertie is sick in bed with la grippe. as I learn by letter.

January 9, 1895—I am lodging again with Baron Alex. von Wendt. We do our own cooking, and although forced to be economical and eat but twice a day, we get along very well. I bought a quilt, as nights are cold.

January 14, 1895—I bought a silk dress pattern for Susan, the first she has ever had. The cost was $8.35 [$188]. She deserves one, if any one does.

January 28, 1895—I felt quite anxious, as my month draws to a close, hoping I may have one or two more months employment. I prayed for this, and received testimony that I shall have two or three month's work. At noon, the Chief Clerk told me I could continue on, next month and perhaps two months; thus verifying the whisperings of the Holy Spirit to me. In the evening one of the draughtsmen resigned his position and told me I could have his place, as he had something else he could do. Truly God is very good to me, in giving me words of comfort by the voice of his Holy Spirit when I ask him, unworthy as I am.

January 29, 1895—To day my survey papers were sent to Washington.

FEBRUARY 1895

February 1, 1895—To day Manning told me I could have 3 or 4 month's work. Truly the promise of the Father is being fulfilled. And I am learning more and more to know the voice of the Spirit when he whispers to me.

February 2, 1895—Br. and Sister Pierce called to see me, on their home to Mexico. I Sent a few little things to Anna, by them.

February 4, 1895—By letter from Susan I learn Wilmirth was married to Alanson Reidhead on January 31, 1895 This is the first marriage of any of my grand-children. Wilmirth was about 14 or 15 yrs old I think.

[page 17]

February 4, 1895—To day the U. S. inspector examined my Survey of the two townships near Tucson. I naturally felt a trifle anxious, as upon his report would depend the acceptance of my survey. So I asked the Father to cause him to accept it,—to see nothing that might be imperfect, or that would keep him from accepting the work; and I received a clear testimony he would receive the survey.

February 6, 1895—The inspector returned to Tucson, and reports my Survey excellent,—the most perfect he has ever seen; and said the Authorities in Washington might suspect him of putting up a job &c. As I know all land surveys are very imperfect, through errors in chaining and courses, I was very much astonished, and could plainly see that God had led him to go over only such portions as were exact: or if not, the inspector had made just the same errors I had (if any there were) so it all appeared right to him. I do not mean that God caused him to accept work that should not be, for my work was really much better than average surveys, and therefore should be accepted. The Father fulfilled the promises of the Spirit to me; and for this I praise his holy name, and am thankful I am learning more and more the voice of the Spirit, which said to me not long since in Mesa, to "do nothing except thou shalt ask the Father, and if the Spirit saith unto thee "do it," thou shalt do it; and if he saith "do it not," then thou shalt not do it, and so thou shalt be blessed in all thou shalt do."

But for a year or more it has been my custom to ask for guidance, and many times—always—has an answer come in words spoken to me by the Holy Spirit, and it is the same with my dear wife Susan. Notably, on one occasion in Juarez when my old friend John Macfarlane was sick she prayed for him, and an answer came in words "He shall depart; it is the will of the Father."

[page 18]

February 6, 1895—At this time he was apparently nearly well and went to Utah, but suddenly died. This blessing is to me above all price—to know God actually hears and answers me, weak and sinful as I am. How wondrous is his mercy and goodness, and how little I can do in return! But it is the great desire of my soul to do all I possibly can to help redeem Zion, and redeem the Souls of men and bring them to God. This I desire more than all earth can give could I have it all.

February 7, 1895—I have thought much of moving my family here from Mesa, so I can provide better for their comfort, but have feared evil influences here. This morning I asked if it is best to bring them here,—shall it be well for them! The answer of the Spirit to me, in answer to my prayer was,—"Bring thy family here unto thee; they shall be blessed, and no evil shall come to any of them nor to thee, and all shall be well with thee."

I had some fear that Gertrude might be led to love my friend Alex. von Wendt, who is social and attractive, but not a member of the Church. He and I have "bached" together many months and like each other very well; but I do not want any daughter to marry one not a member of the Church. I understood from the answer given, that no evil should come to Gertrude through him. And so I at once announced to him I would bring my family to Tucson, as he had often urged, and I wrote my family to get ready at once and I would come for them. Engaged a house of 6 rooms conditionally.

February 14, 1895—Bought wood and family supplies, and stored them.

February 15, 1895—von Wendt started to day to visit some mines, and in the evening I started to Mesa.

February 16, 1895—Settled some bills in Mesa, and we all went to Sam's, and remained all night.

February 17, 1895—Started from Tempe at 9 A.M. Sam and quite a number of the relatives going there with us.

[page 19]

February 18, 1895—Got to Tucson at 3 A.M, and resumed work in office.

February 20, 1895—Wrote to Joel to buy 1/6 interest in a threshing machine.

February 23, 1895—To day von Wendt got back and called to see us. He reported well of the mines he had secured, as being rich in silver, with some copper and gold.

My sons in Mexico wish we may buy land in the new Chuichupe country, situated in the mountains about 50 miles south of Pacheco. A Lot is 5000 meters square, equal to 6175 acres. Price $1.^{00} [$22] per hectare,[13] equals 40¢ [$9] per acre. The payment to be made in 3, 6 and 9 yrs after 1st payment, colonists to have many concessions for a term of ten years. Br. Macdonald gave me all these particulars, and I will buy land there if I can. Being in the tops of the mountains the climate is delightful and salubrious, with plenty of timber, grass and wild game. Each colonist over 12 years old will receive 50.^{00} [$1,124] which will apply in part payment for the land.

MARCH 1895

March 13, 1895—My 67th birthday. We had a nice Supper which von Wendt shared with us. Got word that Aunt Sally Tuttle, the only sister of my dear wife's mother, died Feb. 11th quite suddenly. She had been for years a temple worker, and was an excellent woman. Her exaltation is gained, for she has been true to the end.

March 16, 1895—Got word from Washington my Rincon Survey is approved.[14] The value is 839.93 [$18,875] I believe. I am very thankful, not only for the money but because I see that God has heard and blessed me, and that the voice which promised it was the voice of the Holy Spirit,—not that of any lying spirit. And this increases my faith.

March 22, 1895—My sister Henrietta says my niece Bertha is the matron of the Children's Hospital, Columbus, Ohio, and her sister Jenny is teacher in the U. S. indian school at Fort Felton. Joel has sold my sawmill for Lumber. $500.00 [$11,875].

March 26, 1895—Received word that my other survey is approved, value $2349.93 [$52,807] This is as the Spirit had said to me would be, and I am thankful.

[page 20]

APRIL 1895

April 2, 1895—Mr. von Went came to us, having badly burned his foot, scalding it badly. We fixed him a cot in the front room and made him as comfortable as possible. Messrs. Horton, Barney and another, who came from New York to examine a so-called placer gold claim,[15] have returned from visiting it, much disgusted. They found nothing of value, and this is as I told von Wendt it would be.

April 14, 1895—This evening Mr. von Wendt surprised me very much by asking me for Gertrude as a wife. I had not thought of such a thing. I had given him a home in his illness from his burn, and I knew he liked our family, but I did not think of any wish on his part to marry my daughter. I felt much disturbed at the thought of my daughter marrying one not of the faith, and told him it was contrary to our principles to so permit. He plead his love, and said that although he did not believe in any of the churches or religions of the day, he did believe the Mormons were nearer right than any of them, and his religion consisted in doing good—doing all the good he could, and no harm or evil to any. I told him I would consider, and tell him in the morning. I wanted an opportunity to ask the Lord for guidance. I asked the Father concerning the matter, and the answer of the Spirit was "Be of good cheer and fear not, for no evil shall come to thy daughter Gertrude through him or any other man. He is one who is honest in heart, and will receive the gospel, and do a mighty work in Zion." Therefore I felt to trust in God, and that it would be right to give my consent to Gertrude's marriage to him, relying upon the promises given me. But it was quite a trial to my faith, seeming to me such a serious matter—thus I had always firmly

13 A hectare is a metric unit of surface area equal to 10,000 square meters (equivalent to 2.47 acres).

14 The Rincon Mountains are east of Tucson. Today the range constitutes the eastern boundary for the city of Tucson and is the location of the Saguaro National Park.

15 Placer mining is separating valuable minerals from sand or small gravel.

set myself against, especially in case of covenants made in holy places.

[page 21]

April 1895—So it was with fear and anxiety I determined to give my consent, which nothing would have induced me to do, except the promise of the Spirit.

April 15, 1895—This morning I told von Wendt he had my consent provided he and Gertrude continue of the same mind when he returns from New York City a few months hence, as he intends soon to go east to sell mining property.

This morning before daylight the voice of the Spirit came to me, repeating what I have previously written, and saying also God had brought von W. and me together, for a purpose of his own; that von W. would bless me in temporal things and I should be a blessing to him in spiritual things; that noble spirits should be sent to them who will never turn away from God, but be exalted with Gertrude and von Wendt in the celestial glory, and this was said to me three times, giving me great comfort.

And Susan, praying also, received the same testimony; for she, too, had the same anxiety about the matter, and the same fears, that I had, especially as Gertrude said she would leave it all to us, although she loves him with her whole heart. This responsibility on our heads makes Susan and me more anxious to be guided by the Holy Spirit in this important matter.

All we can do is to receive and believe the word of the Spirit, and trust our Father in Heaven. Gertrude says he is the first and the only one who ever attracted her and she loves him, but does not wish to violate any covenant she has made, nor do anything wrong.

April 16, 1895—I wrote to Lochrin, Pension Commissioner, withdrawing my application for increase of pension as a Mexican War veteran 8$ [$180] per month to 12$ [$270] agreeable to the late law, because I would have to swear in as "in indigent circumstances—a beggar—which I decline to do, although I am poor, with nothing but my daily labor to sustain us.

[page 22]

April 17, 1895—This morning when I prayed, I received precious promises by the whisperings of the Holy Spirit. I was told von Wendt was appointed before this world was, to be Gertie's husband, and he shall become a man after God's own heart and do a mighty work in Zion. Gertie will not be obliged to violate her covenants in marrying him. When he is ready to go to New York he shall have money to go with for his way to obtain it will open to him; and he shall be prospered there in his business to the fullness of his expectations, and even more so. He shall love and be true to Gertie all his life, and wealth shall in abundance flow to him and to me. Also that I shall be mighty in Israel, a leader, a mighty prophet, with power to do mighty miracles and a mighty work in bringing souls to God; besides other great promises. I thank thee, oh my Father, and ask thee to help me to live so as to attain all these great blessings, which have been already sealed upon me by patriarchs.

MAY.

May 1, 1894—Up to this date von Wendt has been slowly improving, but has been mostly confined to his cot. My wife and I, not withstanding the testimonies we have received, feel anxious about Gertie's union with one out of the Church, and have frequently prayed about it, but we both have always the same comforting answer, that "no evil shall come to thy daughter through von Wendt," and so we comfort ourselves, and feel to trust in God that all will be well, although we cannot see how it will come about. But we know God is fully able to do his own will in all things.

I borrowed $300.00 [$6,741] in the bank to day, and sent $40.00 [$899] to Sam, who is in great need, and gave $200.00 [$4,494] to von Wendt, he having obtained $150.00 [$3,371] more from a Mr. S. Franklin, his lawyer. It was with difficulty I could borrow the money having no property in this country.

[page 23]

May 1, 1895—But in this way the promise was fulfilled that von W. would have money necessary for his journey when the time for it arrives.

May 2, 1895—To day von Wend started for New York city to sell his mining property, which we hope he may do.

May 5, 1895—I received a letter from Sam in which he says I shall be greatly blessed. He says "I do know you will have the privilege to pay all you owe; and that yours and mother's last days will be the best days of your lives, and the happiest days; for you are going to have plenty, and you will live to see your children and your grand children all around you, and they will rise up and bless you; and you will both be a blessing to others." He testified that he knew this by the testimony of the holy Spirit. I feel thankful and happy, for I believe his words.

May 6, 1895—Got word that my second survey contract has been ordered paid me, amount, $2349.93 [$52,807] being $143.31 [$3,220] less that what I applied for.

I thank Thee, my Father, for this fulfillment of thy promise to me!

May 14, 1895—Rec^{d} a treasury draft for the amount, and at once Commenced paying my debts. I had borrowed of W K James, of Phoenix $650.^{00} [$14,607] for which I paid $930.^{00} [$20,899] I borrowed 150. [$3,371] of Hickey and paid him $210.^{00} [$4,719] I paid my note to the bank here and $3.60 [$81] interest, also many other debts which reduces my money almost to 0, but I am glad to be able to pay all honorably. At this time I had not told Susan I had received my money, wishing to be able to say I had rec^{d} it and had paid my debts, which we had worried over, and was free. I had sent the draft to Phoenix to pay Mr. James and it did not come back till the 18th.

May 18, 1895—This morning before I received my draft from the post office, Susan was awaked in the early hours about daylight by the sound of clinking money, as if I was counting it, like silver dollars.

[page 24]

May 18, 1895—She heard it so loud and plain she feared a burglar was in the room, robbing me of money. And because I made no sound feared I had been made insensible until she heard me breathe, as usual. As soon as I awoke she told me of it. When I went to the post I found my draft for $1416.93 [$31,841] waiting me. So she was enlightened by the Holy Spirit.

May 19, 1895—This morning I had a vivid dream, relative to the power and might of the United States. I saw a tall liberty pole, about 250 or 300 ft high, and much admired it height and straightness. As I looked again I saw it was bent over at the lower one of its three splices, the upper 2/3 part being almost horizontal. But I saw the pole was not broken at the bottom splice, although it seemed at first to be. I knew this pole represented the United States. I awoke, and the interpretation came, that thus would be humbled the glory of this nation, and seem to be broken and destroyed, but not entirely, the bottom part being firm, sustaining still the upper part. So the great hurt may be healed.

May 24, 1895—By letter from my nephew Fritz Voswinkel I learn he is visiting Logan, likes the country, and will bring his wife and two children from Omaha. He was married Dec. 15, 1889 to Emma Phillips, has Emma and Lois. His sister Bertha was born June 9. 1864. Fritz was born Jan. 27. 1862

May 29, 1895—Got word my Rincon survey is ordered paid.

May 30, 1895—Rec^{d} a telegram from Anna S. at Deming. Sent her $20.^{00} [$449] to Come to Tucson

May 31, 1895—Anna came with her baby girl Phyllis. We were very glad indeed.

This finishes my engagement at the office, as there is no money to pay me for June. The Sur. General informed me if I would work next month and wait for my pay, he would insure it to me, which I agree to do.

[page 25]

June 1, 1895—I continue work in the office. I had been told by the Chief Clerk I could work no more, but the voice of the Spirit had said I should work as long as I desire. I feared some lying spirit had promised me this, but now I found it was true, and that it was the voice of the holy Spirit which had told me. It makes me very happy to know God hears and answers me, when I know I am so weak, doubting and unworthy. He is very good to me.

June 2, 1895—Subscribed for Cosmopolitan for 6 months.[16]

June 7, 1895—Subscribed for "Chronicles" for 6 months.

16 *Cosmopolitan* magazine began in 1886. Its founder was Paul Schlicht. It was advertised at the time as a "first-class family magazine" and would have cost approximately fifteen cents (Edwin Emery and Henry Ladd Smith, *The Press and America*, 2nd ed. [New York: Prentice-Hall, 1954], 352).

June 15, 1895—Sent von Wendt $100.$^{\underline{00}}$ [$2,247] I still continue to receive the same good testimonies concerning him by the Spirit.

June 16, 1895—Received my pay for the Rincon Survey,—$838.93 [$18,852] a total for both surveys of $3188.86 [$71,659]. Thus has the Father verified his promise that I should "be blessed and prospered in my survey from beginning to end," although for a time it seemed as if my work would be disallowed by the inspector.

June 20, 1895—At this date I have paid all borrowed money; store debts and all my survey hands, besides sending $10.^{00} [$225] to $20.^{00} [$449] per month to Theodore, and buying many dresses for Anna and my family besides other goods. I still owe about $350.$^{\underline{00}}$ [$7,865] which I hope to be able to pay when von Wend repays me. I am very thankful indeed to be so nearly free of debt once more, and pray that I may no more be brought so deeply in debt. For 6 years I have earned nothing to speak of—say $500.$^{\underline{00}}$—[$11,236] and by sickness of my family my expenses have been constant and increasing. But I am now free from nearly all debt and I am very glad indeed. At many times it has seemed dark as Egypt, and had it not been for the promises I received from the Spirit I should have despaired. For many months at a time I had only 2 meals a day, and for some months only one meal a day but still I was able to keep up very well.

[page 26]

June 20, 1895—If I got very hungry I asked the Father to remove it, and then I forgot all about being hungry for hours at a time. And sometimes I got to my last 50 cents and had no idea where the next would come from. So God has given me a chance to trust Him and to grow in faith, and in the knowledge of the voice and influence of the Holy Spirit,—blessings of far greater worth than millions of money.

Surveyor General Manning offered me a small contract of a few hundred dollars, to survey the west boundary of the Pia indian reservation, but as I found I would be able to clear very little I declined it especially as both Susan and Gertrude opposed it.

JULY 1895

July 11, 1895—To day Susan is 59 years old, more than 43 years of which she has been my wife, a comfort & a blessing.

July 16, 1895—I telegraphed $180.$^{\underline{00}}$ [$4,045] to J. F. Johnson, in part payment for 2500 acres of land in the Chuhuachupe purchase, in the Sierra Madre Mts, Mexico, as my sons in Mexico are desirous to settle there in the new settlement. The land is rich, timber and grass abundant, and enough rain to produce good crops. Also sent $20.$^{\underline{00}}$ [$449] to Theodore as usual, in college, Logan, Utah.

July 25, 1895—The money I telegraphed J. F. Johnson returned to me uncalled for. I then sent $100.$^{\underline{00}}$ [$2,247] to Alex. von Wendt in New York city.

AUGUST 1895

August 1, 1895—Sent $15.$^{\underline{00}}$ [$337] to Theodore. Telegraphed to my grand-dau. Bertha Martineau, daughter of Henry A. and who is arrived at Deming on her way to visit us, money for her fare to Tucson.

August 2, 1895—Bertha came this evening on the train. She is 15, full grown and comely, and we were glad to meet her.

August 7, 1895—Sent a pale Sea green crystal to New York, to find out if it is of value. Henry found it in Mexico. Rec^{d} first weekly Leslie.

[page 27—see Appendix 5 for letter from Susan E. inserted here.]

August 13, 1895—Mr. Lavaginino, an Italian mine expert, called to see me. Sent for medicine for Susan, to reduce flesh, as she is quite fleshy, weighing nearly 250 lbs, which makes it hard for her to go about much.

August 17, 1895—Sent $1.30 [$29] to Chicago for a blank book in which to continue my journal. (It is this book.)

August 20, 1895—Sent $8.50 [$191] to Juv. Instructor, Salt Lake city, for Moroni.[17]

17 The *Juvenile Instructor* was the first children's magazine published by the Church, beginning in 1866 (Doyle L. Green,

SEPTEMBER

September 9, 1895—To day Elvira, my eldest daughter, came by wagon from Nephi, 5 days journey, with Joseph, Emma & Gertrude to visit us, we not expecting them. It was a very pleasant surprise to us.

Gertrude has now been in bed for about two weeks. While her mother was rubbing her hip as usual, she felt the head of the hip bone move from its place, which rendered her unable to walk without great pain, which she bears, as she always has, with the greatest patience.

September 12, 1895—We went to the circus, but Elvira did not go.

September 13, 1895—She started home this morning—a long journey—and to Camp out every night in the wilderness. But she is a true pioneer, brave and self reliant.

September 15, 1895—Susan was very sick all day, but was healed by faith, in a speedy and remarkable manner, by the blessing of the Father, to whom be all honor and praise.

September 17, 1895—Dora began going to School. She is 12 years old, but has had no schooling, as she seemed almost unable to learn or remember anything heretofore. I blessed her, that her memory might become good, and she be able to learn and become wise and useful, & I believe she will.

September 18, 1895—Letter from Alex. von Wendt, who is very sick in New York. He says he has willed all he has to Gertie if he dies. Susan and I each prayed for him, and we both received the same answer—that he should recover, and yet do a great work in Zion.

September 19, 1895—We wrote words of comfort and promise to him. Gertie was very sick during the night, but is better in the morning. She has great faith in administrations.

[page 28]

October 2, 1895—von Wendt writes he has been very sick, and did not expect to live, but is better now, and not in danger. It was pulmonary illness.

"The Church and Its Magazines," *Ensign*, January 1971, 12–15).

October 3, 1895—Sent Joel's level to Troy to be repaired.

October 5, 1895—Gertrude is slowly improving, but still keeps her bed. Theo. writes that he has been put in charge of a squad of 12 men at the U. S. Agricultural College, Utah, and is making good progress in study. Also, that he will soon be put in charge of the Class in wood turning.

October 14, 1895—Received my Deseret Semi News, as correspondent.

October 15, 1895—Got telegram from Deming that a team is waiting there to take her home to Colonia Juarez, Mexico. She began to pack up at once; also Bertha.

October 16, 1895—Anna and Bertha started at 9 A.M. for home. We were very sorry to have them go, but they had made us a long and pleasant visit and so we must feel resigned. We will greatly miss little Phyllis with her cute, winsome ways which made her so dear us.

October 18, 1895—Joel's level came, repaired. The expenses in all are nearly $20.$^{\underline{00}}$ [$449]

October 20, 1895—To day I took Gertie and the rest for an hour's ride in a carriage, but it tired her considerably.

October 27, 1895—Took a walk early this morning and found the body of a man murdered but a short time before, lying in a ravine, soaked from head to feet in blood. He proved to be a miner, killed by two Mexicans.

NOVEMBER 1895

November 13, 1895—Sent $10.$^{\underline{00}}$ [$225] to von W. Sent article to Deseret News.

November 14, 1895—Sent $10.$^{\underline{00}}$ [$225] to Theodore.

November 16, 1895—I am offered another survey contract of $2000.^{00} [$44,943] adjoining the Apache indian reservation; but as it will not pay much, if properly done, I do not accept.

November 18, 1895—Ceased work in the Sur. General's Office.

When I came from Mesa I had assurance of only one month's work. I prayed, asking that I might have 3 or 4 months additional. (In January last when I first came here) and received answer that I should have, and even more, and so this has been abundantly fulfilled.

This causes my faith to greatly increase.

[page 29]

November 19, 1895—By letter from Nephi, today, we learn he has another Son born, on Nov 12th—weight 11 lbs.

November 23, 1895—I am still lame with rheumatism in my back & legs. This morning before daylight I prayed and received a glorious testimony, which I hardly dare to write;—I am to do a mighty work in Zion—be like Seth a perfect man,—walk with God like Enoch;— be mighty in priesthood and calling among the saints, and a mighty pillar in the Church;—see my Savior in the flesh and remain until He, comes, to bring souls to him,—Susan to remain with me—to assist me and to do a mighty work in the temple in Zion—in the Center Stake—for the redemption of our dead, and to receive great blessings therein.

Great blessings also were promised Gertie;—health and a perfect healing of her lameness,—a husband who shall be one after God's own heart and attain an exaltation in the celestial glory with her and their children & grandchildren who shall do a mighty work in Zion.

Also many other great and comforting promises. To the natural mind such things may seem impossible, but we know if we do the works of Enoch we will receive the same reward as he, and attain the same glory. I believe I shall receive these blessings; if I do not, it will be because I do not do my part, for our Father fails not.

November 26, 1895—Sent an article for publication to the Salt Lake Herald.[18]

November 28, 1895—Thanksgiving day, and a chicken. We have had much to be thankful for up to the present time. We have been blessed greatly here in Tucson, with much better health, and I with employment, by which to sustain my family.

November 29, 1895—A letter from Virginia. She writes that her last child named for her, Virginia, was born Oct. 7th 1895, and was blessed by her father Edward Sudbury, Oct. 15. 1895.

DECEMBER 1895

December 2, 1895—Received last months salary, $97.80 [$2,198] and paid it nearly all away for our monthly accounts and to Theodore, to whom I send monthly $10. [$225] to $20.00 [$449] To day Dora started to the public school

[page 30]

December 4, 1895—Mr. Alex von Wendt returned to us from New York. He had made a partial sale, to a small amount, and gave me $100 [$2,247], on account the money I had sent him.

December 11, 1895—I sent a nice dress to Emma, Albert's wife. While von Wendt was in New York I sent him $410.00 [$9,213], money which I needed badly for my family, but which I thought he needed worse.

December 14, 1895—Sent for the N. Y. World for Joel and Anna, having also sent the San Francisco Chronicle to Henry A.[19]

December 15, 1895—I received my quarterly pension of $24.00 [$539].

December 16, 1895—By letter from Joel we learn he had a fine son born on Dec. 7th 1895, weighing 10 lbs. His name is Leland.

December 17, 1895—I sent Theodore $15.00 [$337] I ceased work in the office.

December 18, 1895—Letter from Nephi informs me he will start on his mission on Feb. 15th He seems full of the Spirit of his calling, as the following extracts from his letter indicates:—

"Logan Dec. 8, 1895

Dear father, mother and all

x x x I received my letter from "Box 13" [or Box B] which informed me that my mission would be to the Southern States, and I am well satisfied to go there, on

18 The *Salt Lake Herald* began in 1872 and echoed the political voice of the Church (Linda Sillitoe, *Welcoming the World: A History of Salt Lake County* [Salt Lake City: Salt Lake County, 1996], 67).

19 The *New York World* was established in 1860. It came as a part of the Penny Press Era and was a paper with religious overtones. In 1883 it was sold to Pulitzer and would participate in the infamous Pulitzer crusades. The *San Francisco Chronicle* was founded in 1865 by Michael H. de Young and his brother Charles de Young. The paper was active in civic and political campaigns of the era (Emery and Smith, *The Press and America*, 299, 359, 376, 381).

account of being a cheaper place to go. Now I will sell a piece of my land and get entirely out of debt, and will still have 120 acres left, which will be enough for the present. I had to mortgage my land for $450.00 [$10,112] to pay for the land, and lawyers fees, and now by selling 40 acres I will be out of debt and have no interest to pay every month. The way is being opened up for me to dispose of every thing so that I can go at the appointed time. The words are true which say the Lord will ask nothing only as he will open the way to accomplish it, and it has been so in my case. I have partly learned one thing—I say partly, because I can not always discern the right spirit—but can see that as I follow ~~the~~ its influences that I am nearly always right.

[page 31]

December 1895—[letter continues] I try to give place to that Spirit continually in all my temporal affairs, and find it every ready to lead me aright; and the more I watch and study it the better satisfied I am. It is good to pray always, or have a humble spirit, and then that spirit will abide in us continually, to lead us in the ways of truth. How beautiful!

A person who would be happy should be possessed of pure thoughts, humble spirit,—a clean tabernacle, and then the Spirit of God could abide therein. How beautiful will be those who fought the good fight and are worthy of the blessings of the faithful. I can see no peace, only as is found in the gospel. My ambition is to be a good man in the Church, in preference to being a governor, or Senator, which was plainly shown when the Savior chose the fishermen to follow him. We should honor the priesthood we have, and do our duty in that, and then there would be harmony in all the Church. How nice it would be to see you and talk about these things that are of so much value to us. I am thankful for my parents, who have taught me truth. We as children, owe a debt we can never repay. May God bless you both, and prosper you, and ever give you his spirit to comfort you, and may your last days be your best days, that you may live long to counsel your children in righteousness is my prayer continually." x x x

Your loving son Nephi.

I have inserted this letter to show the pure, humble and holy spirit which—as always—possesses him.

[page 32]

December 18, 1895—In answering Nephi's[20] letter, I wrote the following as a promised blessing to him:—

Nephi, you shall go and return in peace and safety, be blessed and prospered in your absence and do a good work, and no power shall hurt you. Your family, also, shall be blessed and prospered while you are away, and none shall be taken while you are away but all of them shall greet you on your return with great joy and pleasure. Your mission shall be a great blessing to you, causing you to grow and increase in spiritual gifts and blessings, in prophesy and revelations, in visions and dreams and interpretation of the same: in the gift of healing, and in faith, and in the knowledge of the influence and power of the Holy Spirit, who will be your constant companion, and fill you with great wisdom and power to do good. You shall be blessed more than your greatest anticipations, and the power of God will be manifested in your behalf. The heavens are full of blessings for you and for your family, therefore do not have any fears nor doubts, but believe, and trust in God, and you shall see the fulfillment of every word of this prophecy and blessing, for I pronounce and seal it upon you by my authority as patriarch to my family in the name of Jesus the Redeemer, Amen.

In writing this, I felt it was by the influence of the holy spirit. It was not so much a <u>blessing</u> as a prophecy, for I do not understand that we have authority to <u>seal</u> a blessing without at the same time laying on hands. I also wrote that he should "strive to be like Enoch that God may love you, and that you may walk with him. till the coming of the Savior in his power and glory."

[page 33]

December 18, 1895—I asked the Father if what I have written to him is right, and the answer came—"<u>it is right, write it down</u>." and so I sent him (Nephi) the letter, and record it here. [blank space] our first cold weather to day.

December 20, 1895—Von Wendt started to examine the Cababi mines he has, and to start work on them.

20 Nephi Martineau would have been thirty-three years of age at this time.

December 24, 1895—Sent a box of things to our children in Mexico, Henry being at Deming, N. M. with his team.

December 25, 1895—Christmas, and a turkey, our first own turkey for years.

December 28, 1895—Von Wendt returned, having had a very cold time. He brought a dozen chickens, and a Spaniel pup—Molly.

JANUARY 1896

January 3, 1896—Had another turkey dinner to day.

Sent to Hall Chemical Co, St. Louis, for 80 days treatment obesity pills for Susan, as they seem to reduce her weight.

January 4, 1896—Letter from Joel. Says they have named baby Leland Knowlton. They say it is a very nice baby. Of course it is.

Mr. von Wendt and I, with a teamster started for Graterville, 48 miles, at foot of Mount Santa Rita, to look at a new gold placer. Arrived at Ensenbergs at 5 P.M.

January 5, 1896—Looked over the ground some.

January 6, 1896—Went up the mountain, and took levels for a dam. In the afternoon witnessed the operation of a dry washer (or winnower) which blows away the dirt and leaves the gold. The ground seems quite rich, say $1.00 [$23] to the cub. yard.

January 7, 1896—Very cold and windy. Prospected in the mountains for a water supply, for hydraulic purposes in mining.

January 8, 1896—Started home at 9 A.M. arrived at 4 P.M. and found all well.

This is our 44th anniversary of our marriage, and is always our most enjoyable occasion or holiday.

January 9, 1896—The Surveyor General again gave me work in the office for a short time. And thus is fulfilled the word I received in answer to my prayer that my way may be opened. The answer to me was, my way shall be open before me from this time forth, and that I shall not any more be brought into such poverty and want as in Colonia Juarez and Mesa, and that I shall be prospered in all I do, and abundant wealth will flow unto me, that I may do good, I have had this promise several times in answer to my prayers. Truly the Father is very merciful and good to us.

[page 34]

January 25, 1896—Ceased work again, there being no funds on hand for me, an extra employee. I believe still, it is all right.

FEBRUARY 1896

February 1, 1896—Today von W. and I went with Mr. Charloe to survey a copper mine, which we did, returning at night, pretty tired.

February 5, 1896—Sent Theodore $20.00 [$467] This morning Erxleben, a draughtsman in the office, came to ask me to go to work in the office in his place for a week or ten days, as he wished to be absent for a while. I was very glad for the chance to earn something for my family, as our expenses are nearly $3.00 [$70] a day, And so my way opens again, if only for a short time.

February 9, 1896—von W. went to see the Silver bell mine. Susan and I wrote a comforting letter to Nephi.

February 10, 1896—von W. returned, bringing a very good report of the mine, which he says is very valuable.

February 13, 1896—Sent for a galvanic or Electric Battery, also some electric belts &c, and applied for an agency.

von W. Started to his Cababi mines.

February 16, 1896—I feel impressed to take Mary Harris, a girl of 16, who lately in a fit of despondency killed herself in California, caused by ill treatment and cruelty. I know suicide is a grievous sin, but I think she will be forgiven, because she was driven wild. But this will be as the priesthood shall rule.

February 18, 1896—von W. returned. He found that the men he was employing at his mines had "jumped" them to deprive him of them, they all the time eating his bread. But he made them undo what they had done. He went in good time, surely.

[page 35]

February 21, 1896—Susan and I sat for our photos today.

February 24, 1896—Received a letter from Apostle F. D. Richards, to whom I had written, asking instruction in regard to the letter I had written to Nephi, promising him blessings, Dec. 18th

February 25, 1896—He said it was right to promise blessings by the spirit of prophecy to persons absent, but to seal a blessing upon one it was necessary for that one to be present, so that he who would seal the blessing might lay his hands upon the one to be blessed. And this is just as I understand it. In looking over the blessing I sent to Nephi I see that I wrote it in that way,—by promise. Apostle Richards said:—"I see no objection to a man writing a blessing if it be revealed to him by the Holy Spirit, and sending it to the one for whom it is intended; but, the sealing it upon that person is a quite another thing, while such a blessing dictated by revelation will just as surely come to a fulfillment as if it had been sealed upon a person.

His letter is very kind, and I will try to profit by it.

February 28, 1896—Received our Photos, which friends say look natural.

MARCH 1896

March 7, 1896—This evening Benj. Samuel & his boy James, Cousin James F. and his little boy, and Vaughan Guthrie came, on their way to Mexico. They remained next day, Sunday.

March 9, 1896—The boys went on their way. We sent a box of things to the children in Mexico, also our photos.

March 13, 1896—This is my 68th birth day. I cannot realize it. Is it possible I am almost 70 years old? It must be so.

SUSAN.

I think it right to insert in this record something concerning my dear wife Susan Ellen. She was born in Kirtland, our first temple city, Geagua Co, Ohio, July 11, 1836, being a daughter of Patriarch Joel H. Johnson and Anna Pixley Johnson. Her mother dying when Susan E. was only 4 years old, she was reared by her step-mother, Susan Bryant, whom her father married some years after his first wife's death.

[page 36]

February 13, 1896—She spent some years also with her grandmother. By reason of the persecutions of the saints she was reared in poverty among mobs, who repeatedly drove the family from place to place, keeping them in poverty and distress, and at times threatening their lives. At one period, when living on Crooked Creek, two miles from Ramus in Illinois, a mob one day came to the house, about 30 in number, mounted and armed, their faces blackened, and halted in front of the door. Susan and her brother Seth came to the door in obedience to their call, and stood there hand in hand, trembling with fear,—two little tots, only 8 and 6 years old respectively. Well might they fear and tremble, for mobs had already pillaged and burned scores of houses, shot or whipped men to death, ravished women and committed other horrible atrocities, until, in the minds of the children, the name "mob" meant all that was fearful and horrid. The mob asked for father Johnson. The children said he was not at home. The mob told them to tell their father to take his family in two weeks, or they would come and burn their house and kill them all. Then they rode away to harass other families in like manner.

What could the family do? They had no means for travel—no means to make a new home if robbed of this one. They could only resign themselves to any fate that might overtake them.

In a few weeks the mob came again, about midnight, and with fearful oaths demanded why the family were not gone. Father Johnson told them that all the family were sick and could not go, some of the mob swore they would burn them out now; others said that would be too bad, as the family was sick; and the discussion terminated in a quarrel between the two factions. In the end they said the family could have just ten days longer in which to leave; if not gone by that time, sick or well, they might look for death.

[page 37]

There seemed no hope for escape. All the family were sick, they had neither team, wagon nor money with which to move and make a new home. But just a day or two before the ten days were out, a forlorn party of four families came along, seeking refuge in Nauvoo. They had but one old, rickety little wagon and two poor little scrubs of horses. Susan's father obtained permission to go with this party to Nauvoo, and did so, leaving home, farm, cows, pigs, poultry and household goods to the spoilers. Think of it! Five families, with but one poor little team and wagon which could carry only a few quilts for each family, with perhaps a bag of corn meal,—the men, women and children trudging painfully along through rain and mud on foot. But, as "a man will give all that he hath for his life"—they were glad to go, even in so sad a plight.

After most of the saints had been driven from Nauvoo, Susan remained there with her grandmother, and witnessed the burning of the Temple, set on fire and destroyed by the mob. Her father, with most of his family having gone to Utah in 1848, she followed in 1850, traveling in the care of her Uncle Geo. Johnston [Johnson] and his family. The Cholera, which killed so many thousands of emigrants upon the plains in that year, attacked the little company in which she journeyed. Day after day Death claimed his victims, for every one attacked in the party died except Susan. She, too, lay desperately ill with the scourge alone in her wagon. Stephen Markham, Captain of the Company, in his rounds found her near unto death. He spoke cheerfully, said she must not die, and asked if she believed she could be healed by the laying on of hands. She answered "Yes." "Well then," said he, "we'll have you out of this right away." He brought some elders, she was administered to and healed immediately, by the power of God, and soon was well as ever. Of this little company of 28 families, 15 persons were stricken, of whom 14 died, she, of them all, being the only one who recovered; and this, that she might fulfill the work appointed her.

[page 38]

1896—Slowly journeying with their ox teams for some weeks they at length came to the country of the Cheyennes, and met a party of these indians on a hunting tour. The company remained encamped two nights and one day in one place on account of stormy weather, during which time an Indian became enamored with Susan, then 14 years of age, and comely to look upon, with a lovely complexion and well formed figure. He wanted her for a wife. A young man, Andy Kelly, an irishman who had deserted from the army at Fort Kearney, and had joined the Company hoping to get to the gold fields of California told the indian he could have her for 5 ponies, some buffalo robes and some other things, just for a joke. But the indian was in earnest, not understanding such jokes, and next day came to camp bringing the five horses and the other things specified in the bargain. Of course he was told it was all in fun—that the whites never sould their girls for wives to any one. But the indian could not be made to understand this; he had made a fair bargain, had fulfilled his part of it and now wanted the whites to fulfill theirs. When he finally found he could not have Susan he was furious, and departed, muttering revenge.

No indians came around afterwards and the company were glad, supposing their visitors had gone entirely away, and had much fun over the poor fellow's disappointment. At night a terrible tempest came on, such as the Platte valley is famous for—tempest, deluging rain, vivid lightning and tremendous thunder. It seemed as though the tent would be blown away, so Susan and some others went out into the driving storm to help hold the tent ropes and keep it in place. While thus engaged in holding the tent, which stood close to the bank of the river, which was fringed beneath by a dense growth of willows, she felt herself suddenly seized and placed upon a horse, the pitchy blackness of the night preventing her from seeing who it was, but not for a moment thinking of an indian.

[page 39]

Just then a bright glare of the lightning revealed an indian in the act of springing upon the horse behind her, ready to dash away with her. Her screams instantly brought her help, as she leaped from the horse, while her dusky lover—disappointed and baffled in his daring scheme—dashed away down the bank into the thicket and was instantly lost to sight. She was thus providentially saved from a fate worse than death, and did not soon venture again outside the camp. The morning light showed how the indian had approached the camp along the river bank and waited till the night became dark as Egypt, then brought his horse up near the tent, and waited for a favorable moment to seize and carry her off. Poor fellow! With him, as with so many others, "the course of true love never does run smooth." That night the indians revenged themselves by creeping into camp and stealing every kettle, frying pan, dish, axe or tool of any kind not put into the wagons but left around the camp fire as they usually were. But the hunting party never came in sight of the company again.

Kelly, the young man who had caused all the trouble, went with the company as far as Great Salt Lake, then stole all the clothing and blankets from the man who had given him food and passage, and soon got into the city chain gang. What finally became of him Susan knows not.

One day while journeying up the Platte River she and a girl named Ann Howard strayed away from the road gathering choke cherries. After a pleasant time they mounted a ridge and looked for the wagon train, but in vain. Far as the eye could reach not a wagon was to be seen. Somewhat alarmed at being thus left alone in the vast prairies of the roaming Cheyenne indians, who might at any moment appear, swoop down upon them and carry them away into an eternal captivity, they regained the wagon trail as soon as possible, and pressed forward to overtake the Company. Thus they went on, mile after mile, still hoping but never coming in sight of the wagons. Night came on, while now and then the distant cry of the prairie wolves could be heard, but fortunately always in the distance.

[page 40]

1896—And so hour after hour in the darkness of the vast and lonely plains, tired out and wearied, these two girls went on until at length the figure of a man suddenly appeared before them in the darkness. They supposed him to be an indian, but the welcome voice of Andy Kelly disippated all their not baseless fears. Knowing they had not arrived in camp, he had come out to meet them at a place where the trail forked, and placing them both upon his horse he conducted them to the camp, where they arrived after ten o'clock at night. Truly a lonesome and a hazardous walk for two lone girls in an indian country.—one which they never repeated.

Susan remained in Salt Lake City until the fall of 1851, when she, in company with Susan West who afterwards became a wife of Pres[t] Geo. A. Smith, and a few families, went to Parowan, Iron Co. Utah. When Patriarch Joel H. Johnson, her father, founded Fort Johnson, she went there and remained until I married her there, on Jan. 8, 1852. John L. Smith, now patriarch, united us in wedlock—his first experience in that line, and John D. Lee, who met so tragic an end, was one of the wedding guests. Our nuptial couch consisted of a few quilts spread upon the floor,—afterwards in a wagon box; and when I took her to Parowan, our future home, our bedstead was only a few boards laid across some trestles. At length I became rich enough to buy a regular bedstead, but this, being unpainted, was not stylish—far from it. To remedy this we bought some red face paint from an indian, (a Pah Eed) Susan mixed it with some sour milk, and with it we painted our bedstead and a table. We had no varnish, but took the fat of a prairie dog I had killed, and rubbed it over the paint with a rag until it resembled a French polish. Many were the glances of pride be bestowed upon these articles of furniture. I do not believe that Queen Victoria feels as proud to day of any article of furniture She has in her house, as we did when we looked at our brilliant scarlet tinted bedstead and table.

[page 41]

Since then Susan has passed with me through many trying scenes of poverty, sickness, trouble and danger—things that would try one to the center—but never has she murmured nor complained, and "because she has not, she shall be exalted very high," for so saith the Lord. She spent a night moulding bullets by the fireside, while I, with the other men guarded the approaches to our fort, while the long night was made hideous by the yells of the Utes, as they danced their war and scalp dances not far away. They had told us the previous day that they would kill every soul in the fort. They were 400 warriors, well armed; we, a hundred men, poorly armed, encumbered with women and children and 300 miles from help. And so, at other times, was our little settlement threatened, but never, in any such scenes did she ever show cowardice. She was always at such times calm and cool, trusting always in God. Of such mothers are born heroes.

And when in 1886 the Apaches filled Arizona with blood and torture—slaying hundreds of settlers—Susan and I had to travel with a team from St. David to Pima—a 110 miles—to reach our home in Pima, right through a section where they were murdering people every day—a route which Gen[l] Miles had forbidden any settlers to traverse because he could furnish them no aid—even then she would not leave me. I wished her to go by rail to Bowie Station, thence by stage home, a route comparatively safe, while I would come on alone with my horses and carriage. If she came with me she could be of no help if attacked; and if Death was waiting for a victim on our trail it was far better for but one to die instead of both. It is bad enough for a man to be in danger of torture and death, but ten times worse to have a loved and helpless one with him at such a time. But all such arguments fell upon deaf ears. She would stay and go with me, and my fate should be hers. When we started, our friends as they bid us good bye (and said afterwards) believed they would never again behold us alive.

[page 42]

March 13, 1896—We traveled for miles through canons and hills, the roadside lined with rocks and bushes, any one of which might hide a lurking Apache; but we prayed our Father to protect us, and not let the Apaches see us, and he heard our prayer. Once we came so near the indians, who were lurking just over a low ridge near by, that we saw one of their dogs prowling about. We crossed their trails freshly made, and at a watering place, where I intended to rest and lunch, the ground was covered with fresh pony tracks recently made. Pausing only to water our tired but splendid animals, we drove swiftly on, and by sunset were safe. But while passing near the foe Susan forced from me a dreadful promise—the most fearful a man can make who loves his wife. She said "James, make me one promise:—If the indians come upon us, and you are not yet killed, promise me that you will kill me yourself." Said I, "How can I promise such a thing—I would rather die myself." Said she, "Would you rather have me fall into their hands alive, to be tortured?" "No, but how could I kill you my dear wife!" But she was firm in her request, and nothing could move her. And I knew, too, that a quick death at my hand would be a thousand times more merciful than such tortures as the Apaches had already inflicted upon many women and children. But oh! what a dreadful thing it is to be obliged to make so fearful a promise! No one can begin to realize it until he faces the dread alternative. At last I gave the promise she desired, inwardly resolving that if one bullet of mine should make her free another should do for me.

But the Father heard our prayers, and though we passed near the Savages they saw us not. In all this days journey, threatened with a fearful death, Susan never once lost her calmness and peace of mind, nor showed any fear. She was a true heroine and I rejoice to be able to chronicle these facts, that her children to the latest generation may honor her forever.

[page 43]

March 13, 1896—But I pray we may never again be in such a straight, if it be according to the will of the Father. What may yet befall us I know not, but my constant prayer is that we may never be parted—neither in life nor in death.

SUSAN JULIA SHERMAN (DECEASED)

I think I have mentioned in the course of this journal all items of interest relating to my wife Susan Julia Sherman and therefore will add nothing more, until I shall find out items of interest of which I am now ignorant, except to say I believe no mother taught her children true and holy principles more carefully than she, and she died firm in the faith and in full fellowship with the saints. She now rests from her labors, having attained, through ordinances in her behalf in the Logan Temple, all the exaltation pertaining to a fullness of the priesthood, even to be a priestess and queen in the highest degree of the celestial glory by obedience to the law of celestial marriage as revealed by Joseph the Prophet and Seer. Peace to her memory until we shall meet again.

March 20, 1896—Last night I dreamed of having a handsome service of Gold upon my table, I may yet see this fulfilled; if not, it will be all right. Have dreamed several times of having gold in plenty. I believe the Father will give me all I need.

March 29, 1896—B. Samuel and party returned from Deming, having been unable to enter Mexico, owing to increased stringency of regulations:

APRIL. 4.

April 4, 1896—This evening I felt impressed to visit Gov. L. C. Hughes, who has been removed from Office as Governor. He has been a true friend to the saints and to me, giving me space in his paper for replies to attacks upon the Saints, when in our darkest hour. For this I pray God to bless him, and I was told to visit and give him words of comfort, for they shall be fulfilled. I went and did so. He much appreciated this, and said he believed what I told him, for he knew I believed in prayer, and he also did. I told him he should gain the victory over his enemies, and some of them should yet come to him bending, and asking him for favors. He was affected to dimness in the eyes, and said he could not tell me how much good I had done him.

I am thankful I was able to comfort him.

[page 44]

April 11, 1896—Ceased work in the Sur. Genl Office—no more work. I know not how we will get along here, without money of employment, but I believe the Father will open up my way.

April 21, 1896—Filed a bill against the U. S. Land Office for $71.72 [$1,675] which is righteously due me on last Survey.

April 22, 1896—This morning, after secret prayer, I had a very comforting answer, and received many great and glorious promises. Truly the Father is very merciful and good to me.

April 24, 1896—I sent an article to the Des[t] News in support of the last "Manifesto" in relation to political and other matters.[21]

April 28, 1896—This afternoon about 2 P.M., after secret prayer I had a greatly comforting answer thereto, by the voice of the Holy Spirit. and things were made plain about which I had been in doubt. For instance, whether it was right for me to be in Tucson with my family—away from the Saints. Also, if I had been deceived by any lying spirit, or that what I had received as from the Holy Spirit had been from an evil source. I was told to reflect and consider whether I had been taught by that spirit ~~to~~ good or evil; that the Evil One never incites any one to do Good, because there is no good whatever in him; if there were, he would not be the Son of Perdition that he is, but after having atoned for his sins the good in him would receive its reward.

But the Holy Spirit does always incite to do good, and thus I may know to judge between them. And I was told that the Spirit which had promised me blessings, and that spirit which now speaks to me is the voice of the Holy Spirit, and therefore to fear not, nor doubt nor be troubled, for the Father loveth me because of my desires to do right, and He saith, "Behold I know the secret desires of thy heart, to overcome sin, to work righteousness, to honor and glorify thy Father in heaven, and when thou desirest a blessing, shall I turn thee away with a curse?

[page 45]

April 28, 1896—Wouldst thou do so to a son who desired to do thy will? And shall I be less just than thou? Verily no. Therefore rejoice and be glad, for the spirit that speaketh unto thee is the voice of the Holy Spirit, and if thou shalt believe and obey it thou shalt be blessed indeed, and no power shall hinder, and be not troubled because thou art here with thy family, for I have brought thee here for a purpose of mine own, which thou shalt more fully know in due time; but in part it is that thou shall grow to be mighty in faith; for when troubles make it seem dark unto thee, and my Spirit speaketh words of comfort unto thee, and they are afterwards fulfilled, then thy faith shall grow and become mighty,—thy wisdom also. And the time is near, Even very near, when thy friend shall sell a part of his mines and give thee money in plenty, and thou shalt be able to go to my saints and thy family, and be free from thy present life. And although thou art out of work and thy money nearly gone, fear not, for I will open thy way, and thou shalt have means for thy food and raiment, and for shelter and other purposes, and be not again destitute as in Mexico and Mesa, for thou shalt have wealth in abundance, even mighty wealth, that thou mayest do a great and a mightier work in the temporal building up and redemption of Zion, in buying lands, building mills and machinery for the good of my saints, and for doing good in general. For thy friend shall sell his mining property and receive great wealth, and impart freely unto thee, that thou mayest do these things. And fear not for thy daughter Gertrude, for she shall not be led to do evil by him, but shall be true and faithful, and shall suffer no loss by him nor any other man. And he shall have his eyes opened, for he is honest in heart, and when he knoweth the truth he will receive it and do a mighty work in Zion, for he shall open the doors of salvation to his kindred, for some of them are honest in heart and will receive the truth.

21 J. H. Martineau, "More of that Manifesto," *Deseret Evening News*, April 29, 1896; Journal History; see also *Deseret News*, May 5, 1896; Utah Digital Newspapers.

[page 46]

April 28, 1896—And thou shalt assist him in this, for he shall desire it; and some of the great and mighty shall receive thy testimony, and thus it shall be fulfilled that was sealed upon thee, that "the great and the wise shall submit themselves unto thee, they shall consecrate their gain to the Lord and their substance to the God of the whole earth; thou shalt lead them to Zion with their riches." And he shall do a mighty work in Zion, and thou, my son, shall do a mighty work in Zion. For this cause I have gathered thee out from among thy kindred, and given thee power to receive the truth and to be firm and unshaken unto the present time. And thou shalt declare my word, and thy voice shall be as the voice of an angel and as the voice of a lion; for the righteous shall rejoice to hear thee, but the wicked shall flee away and tremble. And I will show forth my power through thee, and give thee power to do mighty miracles among the House of Joseph, even to raise the dead to life if needful, to cause the earth to shake and the rivers to turn their course."

And other great and mighty blessings were given me, and I pray I may live so as to obtain them. And I have a sure testimony these sayings are true, and if they be not fulfilled, the fault will be mine; not of the Father. Praise and glory be unto him forever, Amen.

After writing this down on a memorandum, I asked if what I have written is all as it should be, and if any thing is not right that it may be made known to me. Also, shall I record it in my record? The answer to me is—"it is all true and right and pleasing to the Father and to write it, that my children after me may read it and be blessed and strengthened in their faith. I have therefore recorded it in this book.

[page 47]

April 29, 1896—Spent considerable time in writing up my journal.

In ~~Feb~~. March 4 last Susan's Aunt, her father's sister Almera died in Parowan Iron Co. Utah, of old age, at the age of [blank] She was a wife of the Prophet Joseph Smith, being sealed to him in Nauvoo. After his death she married a Mr. Barton, who afterwards apostatized, by whom she had five children, who all died before she did, two of them in Parowan. She was a true saint to the end of her life.

In April, 1896 Susan's step mother, Susan Bryant Johnson second wife of her father, died in Diaz, State of Chihuahua, Mex. in her 84th year of asthma.[22] She married Joel H. Johnson in October 1840, he being a widower with five Children, Sixtus, Sariah, Nephi, Susan and Seth, Susan being then 4 yrs of age. She received her 2nd A. in the St. George temple, and lived many years in Utah—from 184~~7~~8 and in Mexico as a pioneer, sharing all its hardships bravely. She was the mother of 8 children, only two of whom, David and Joel, survive her.

Two or three days after her death occurred that of her Uncle, William D. Johnson, also in Diaz, Mexico, after a short illness. He was one of the younger brother of Susan's father.

Thus do the old veterans of early Mormonism pass away, and soon, if we do not also pass, will we; too be left almost alone. But if we can be true to the end it will all be right.

MAY 1896

May 1, 1896—Yesterday I received $39.53 [$923] for my office work in April, which is not enough to pay last month's living expenses, which are over $2.00 [$47] per day. Our rent is $20.00 [$467]; Ice $2.30 [$54], milk $3.00 [$30], with wood and grocery bills, not counting what we need for clothing &c. Naturally speaking, with nothing in sight before me, by which to get any means, it looks very dark indeed. The only thing I have upon which to depend is the promise of the Lord through the voice of the Spirit that we shall not want. But sometimes the thought comes to me "Was it the voice of the holy spirit, or was it a lying spirit, to deceive me?"

[page 48]

MORONI'S DEATH

May 1, 1896—Then when I ask the Father concerning this, I always receive the same comforting answer, that the voice which speaks to me is the voice of the Holy Spirit, and reminds me that the Evil spirit never incites any one to do good, but always to evil,

22 "Susan Bryant Johnson," *Deseret News*, May 9, 1896; Utah Digital Newspapers.

because there is no good in him. If there were, he could not be the Son of Perdition, for the good that would be in him must be saved. And I do know that the voice which guides me does always incite me to good, and comforts me,—gives me strength and courage and faith in God, and hence I know it is the voice of the Holy Spirit. And I believe the Father thus causes me to be in close places is that I may grow in faith,—seeing the promises of God fulfilled when it seems almost impossible that they can be.

And I know that by this experience, which in some cases has been marvelous, and by the blessing of the Father, I have increased in the gift of faith. And so all these things which seem to me trials are right and for my good. Blessed be the name of the Father. And so I try all I can to exercise faith that we shall not come to want, but that we shall have means for our support, and I believe we will.

May 4, 1896—Received a letter from my grdaughter Alley Martineau daughter of Lyman and Alley. Her first to me. I had previously received one from her little sister Harriet; both are precious mementos to me.

[written in margin]

Lilla's girl

May 7, 1896—By letter from Lilla I learn she has a new baby girl, born April 10, 1896, ~~not yet~~ named. Marjorie

[written in margin]

Moroni's death

May 8, 1896—We also received a letter from Melissa, dated April 27 which conveys the terribly sudden tidings of the death of our dear son Moroni which occurred April 22, 1896 in Mariana (or Chuichupe) the new settlement in the tops of the Sierra Madre Mts. Sonora, Mexico. He was taken ill Thursday night April 16th with a chill and a stiff neck, but did not complain of being sick or of any pain until he died. On Monday, 20th he began to labor in his breathing, but no one thought him seriously ill, nor did he himself, refusing to take any strong medicine, and desiring only the nursing of his beloved wife Sarah Sophia.

[page 49]

They had three elders to administer to him, Henry being absent,—leaving home on a prospecting trip with some brethren on the 21st He had no thought that Moroni was seriously ill, or he would not have gone away.

During the night Moroni's breast and ears turned dark—visible in the morning. He told his son Eddie how to plow a piece of land near by, and Eddie went to do it, but had only plowed two furrows before his father was dead. These are all the particulars I could glean from the letter. but Henry will soon give us a full detail I hope.

Moroni was born Sept. 12, 1854 in Parowan, Utah. In 1860 removed to Salt Lake City, and thence to Logan, where he lived many years and was a great help to me in Surveying and other work. He was called, with Henry and Elvira and her husband B. Samuel Johnson to a mission in the south,—Arizona—and in September 1876 went there, never again returning to Logan. Henry and Samuel had gone the previous spring, on Feb 7th 1876. In Dec. 17. 1879 he married his cousin Sarah Sophia Johnson, daughter of Sixtus E. and Editha Johnson, being sealed in the St George temple. He immediately proceeded to Apache Co. Arizona with Henry and Samuel and their families, and for several years endured much hardship and privation, in settling the country, infested with Mexicans, Indians and renegades. who stole many horses and other stock, year after year.

After we removed to Pia, Graham Co. Ariz. he and Henry removed there to join us, and when we moved into Mexico they determined to go with us. Moroni removed to Colonia Juarez in the fall of 1889, and afterwards to Pacheco in 1890, thence returning to Juarez.

[page 50]

MORONI'S DEATH

1896—Being a raiser of cattle, and there being poor range about Juarez, he and I went to over the Sierra into Sonora and helped found Oaxaca, on the head of the Yaqui river (there called the Bavispe). We left Juarez on the 6th of Feb. 1892 and arrived at the place of destination on the 15th of March 1892, we had to build a road across the mountains, and had to make many miles of heavy dugway,[23] and do much

23 A dugway is a path or road dug through a hillside or sunk below the surface of the land.

blasting of rock. Theodore and Anna also went with me, Moroni leaving his family behind. We also moved most of our cattle and horses with us.

As we could not get along with our leader "Parson" Williams (who soon apostatised) I returned to Juarez in the summer, and Moroni came back in 1894. While he resided in Oaxaca, he was appointed constable in the municipal organization there, and was teacher in the Sunday School, and a most efficient worker. In March 1895 he with Sixtus and others settled at Chuichupe on the western slope of the Sierra Madre Mts, (since named Mariano) where he died. He had laid a foundation there for a good home, but died while all was yet in embryo.

His was a character of the truest integrity and of unselfish devotion to the work of the Lord, in which he was always a most energetic laborer. He was always full of fun and good humor, and full of bright natural wit and good sound sense. He was a Seventy, and he honored his priesthood to the best of his ability, keeping strictly the laws of tithing and Word of Wisdom, and receiving in his heart sincerely every law, regulation, and doctrine of the Church, never in opposition thereto, nor to his presiding leaders in the priesthood.

[page 51]

1896—Few have left a better or more unsullied record, and his exaltation is sure, dying in full faith and fellowship in the Church. He had nine children—7 living—and another soon to be born, and died nearly 42 years of age, in his prime. He lived in great happiness with his beloved wife and family, and taught them principles of righteousness all his days. He has "fought the good fight" and has gone to his sure reward.

May 9, 1896—This morning about daylight, I asked why it was that Moroni had been taken, seeing that his patriarchal blessing had not yet been fulfilled. I inquired if it was because of Sin in me, or in him, or why it was. I received a very comforting answer, of which this is the spirit:—It was not because of sin in me nor in him, but because he had stayed here his full appointed time. Spirits come to earth according to law and order, in their appointed times and seasons and return to the spirit world, and enter into their Third Estate at the time appointed to do so. And so it was with him: he had finished all his labors here, and gone to do other and greater labors in the spirit world. His work there is to preach the gospel to our ancient fathers who died without it,—the ancient ones of our own family or lineage, that they may be prepared to receive temple ordinances when they shall be performed for them. He has passed all danger from the power of the Evil One, and has made his calling and election Sure, to attain a throne as one of the Kings of Eternity—one of the Gods. For although he had not received <u>all</u> the Temple Ordinances (the 2nd A. and others) yet, as he has never rejected or opposed any one of the laws of heaven, he is entitled to a full and a complete exaltation, and his anointings and other ordinances can be administered to him by proxy in a day to come. And his early death shall cause him no loss; For his works shall follow him.

[page 52]

May 9, 1896—All this was comforting to me, and especially that referring to the work he is now to do for the ancients of my lineage; and I wondered much, when it was all shown to me so plainly I had never thought of it before. As we do temple work for our dead relatives—each for his own family—so we should, in the spirit world naturally preach to our own family and prepare them to receive the temple work some time to be performed for them. It is as plain as the Sun to me—why did I never think of it before.

But after all, our hearts are sore. Moroni was always good and obedient at home, kind and loving to his mother and sisters and to me. He was always punctual in attendance to Sunday schools, Y. M. M. I. A. meetings, his Elders and Seventies Quorum meetings, his Sunday meetings; and active in discharge of all his duties. Blessed are the dead who die in the Lord; and their works shall follow him.

Yesterday I telegraphed the sad news to Lyman, and sent an obituary notice to the Deseret News. Also sent many letters, and words of comfort for poor Sadie and her fatherless children.

To day (9th) I have spent in recording all these things. Also prayed and received a comforting answer.

May 11, 1896—Sent an article to Des. News on the first discovery of lead and silver in Utah, also about Viroqua's escape from Squash head.[24]

---

24 James H. Martineau, "Indian Reminiscences," *Deseret Evening News*, May 15, 1896; Journal History.

May 16, 1896—Sent an article in defense of the last "Manifesto" of the Authorities, relative to acting in accordance with the priesthood.

May 18, 1896—Received word my claim against the U. S. is just, and to make out an account in due form. which I at once did.

May 20, 1896—Filed my account to amount of $127.72 [$2,983], the same being approved by Suv. Genl Geo. J. Roskruge. He also offers me a contract to survey a township, at rates $20 [$467] to $23 [$537] pr mile.

[page 53]

May 23, 1896—Sent article on early settlement of Utah, and its difficulties.[25]

May 31, 1896—Sarah sent me the following particulars of Moroni's death[26] dated Mariano May 21. 1896:—

My dear Father and Mother and sisters, I will try and write a few lines. It is a month tomorrow since my dear Moroni died. Oh dear! it is terrible to think about; I never get it off from my mind when I am around home. He commenced Thursday (16th April) night with a head ache that lasted Friday. Saturday he had a pain in his shoulder; the pain left his shoulder and went under his left arm. I got that stopped and he seemed to be getting better. He sat up ~~in bed~~ part of the time and walked around. He went down to Henry's on Monday night. (20th) I did not want him to go—he said he felt well enough. I put my big coat around him. In the night he woke me up breathing so hard and such a rattling in his throat. Anything we done for him did him no good. He never wanted any body to do any thing but me. I tried my best to get him to let me go and get somebody to come. He said "You are doing all you can, I don't want anybody else." At last he gave his consent for me to send for Dama (Didame Carlton)[27] She came and asked him how he felt. He said "I am better." Inside of a half an hour he was dead. He was sitting up in bed, his head fell over one side, and he died without a struggle. He said he was in no pain after I got it stopped under his arm. He has tried to do better since he came here than he ever did before. He paid a full tithing and took such interest in the Sunday School and anything to teach the young, and he felt so anxious about the children; he wanted them to be better than other children. He has worked so hard since we have been here; when he was sick he would talk about his work so much. But the Lord's will be done, and not ours, but it is a great trial for me. x x x I hope you are all well. From your loving daughter

Sarah Martineau"

[page 54]

June 4, 1896—Sent article to Desret News, concerning the indian raid at Ogden in 1850.[28]

June 10, 1896—Von Wendt to day received an offer of $30000.00 [$700,778] per year besides all expenses to go to South Africa to manage mines for an English mining company;—about $40,000 [$934,371] in all. He to contract for 3 years service. I hope he will not accept.

June 5, 1896—On the 5th inst. Sur. Genl Roskruge offered me a Contract to survey a township, mountainous, at four times the usual price, the work amounting to over $1500.00 [$35,039] I asked concerning it; the answer was—not to take it. So I informed him I would not. It was a temptation for I could probably clear over $1000.00 [$2,336] on it, in a month time.

June 13, 1896—This morning I was greatly blessed in prayer, and in the answers I received—great promises. It was also said to me "I ordain thee by promise, a patriarch in the church, to bless the saints, and those whom thou shalt bless shall be blessed, and whom thou shalt curse shall be cursed. Thou shalt have all the rights and powers and privileges pertaining to this office." But I understood, that no one must curse to avenge a personal wrong, but only when needful to advance the work of the Lord, as in the case of Zeezrom.[29] I will not here record the great promis-

25 James H. Martineau, "Indian Reminiscences," *Deseret News*, May 23, 1896; Utah Digital Newspapers.

26 Moroni H. Martineau, *Deseret Evening News*, May 16, 1896; Journal History; see also *Deseret News*, January 23, 1896; Utah Digital Newspapers.

27 This is likely Diadamia Wheeler Johnson Carlton (note spelling; 1856–99). The Carltons lived in the colony of Chuichupe, Mexico.

28 J. H. Martineau, "Plundered by Indians," *Deseret News*, July 25, 1896; Utah Digital Newspapers.

29 Zeezrom is a Book of Mormon character, an antagonist of the prophet Alma.

es made me, but it was shown me that the dreams or visions I had over 40 years ago should be fulfilled as I saw them, and I should do the work therein manifested to me. One I will mention: that in which I stood with a multitude on the bank of a mighty river. They were being baptized and as each man stepped forward, I, as a recorder, took down a list of all his property, and then he was baptized. The interpretation to this is,—the time will come when people will be required to consecrate all property when they join the church, each receiving a portion back as his stewardship. And I believe it will be so.

How merciful is our Father, to hear and answer our feeble prayers—and we so weak, doubting and evil!

[page 55]

June 15, 1896—The weather is very hot—108° in the shade. No sunstrokes

June 16, 1896—I have been greatly troubled in mind because of the deep darkness of my friend A. von W. He desires to marry Gertrude, but he believes not in God nor His Son Jesus, the Redeemer. Why do I have him about my family, if this be so, and I know the result of such a thing? It is because in some things he has a noble spirit—a desire to do all the good he possibly can; and especially, because, when I asked concerning him and the attachment between him and Gertrude, the answer came—"Fear not, no evil shall come to thy daughter because of him; he shall receive the gospel and do a mighty work in Israel. I have brought him and thee together, that thou mayest be a blessing to him in spiritual things, and he be a blessing unto thee in temporal things." Believing this, I have suffered this intimacy to go on, though to my natural sense very obnoxious.

To day, feeling very sad about this, I prayed again, and received the same answers, and much more to comfort me and my dear wife.

June 14, 1896—Today Albert and Emma had another son born to them.

June 18, 1896—Received my pension of \$24.^{00} [\$561] and paid my rent \$20.^{00} [\$467] retaining \$4.^{00} [\$93] for expenses. Naturally speaking, it looks very dark to me, being without money in a land like this, but I hope and trust in our Father's word.

June 23, 1896—Was today appointed U. S. Deputy Mineral Surveyor for Arizona, by Sur. Genl Geo. J. Roskruge. As I know no one here to whom I would care to go to be bondsmen for me in this to the amount of \$10.000.^{00} [\$233,593] I sent blanks to Lyman, hoping he may be able to get them subscribed in Utah. If I can get this office I may earn something for my family.

June 24, 1896—Wrote an article for Deseret News—early history of Parowan; guarding, and the daily life of Settlers, with their toils and dangers.

[page 56]

June 28, 1896—Sunday. This morning, in answer to prayer, I received many great promises, most of which I do not think best to write now; but refer to some.

I was told not to purchase a home in the north, (Utah) though I might dwell there at times and labor in the Temples. I must make my home in Mexico, for in that land I am to labor, and there I shall be greatly blessed and honored, even to be as was Joseph in Egypt. Then I may do a mighty work among the Lamanites, among whom the power of God shall be shown mightily, even to the raising of the dead, and the causing of the earth to shake. And it was shown to me how the earth shall be desolated by great and bloody wars, causing the death of millions of men, women and children; also tempests, earthquakes, tidal waves, pestilence, famine, wild beasts, reptiles, and insects, that shall breed worms in people until they shall die. And many also among the Saints shall fall, because of lack of faith and because they keep not the laws of God. I also received a renewal of promises concerning Von W. and of prosperity for my family,—even that from this time forth I shall be prospered, and shall very soon receive the money still due me from Government on my survey.

JULY 1896

July 7, 1896—By letter from Lilla we learn she has named her baby girl Marjorie.

July 11, 1896—Susan's 60th Birthday! And yet it seems but a little time since I saw her first, a slim, rosy pretty young girl not yet ~~fifteen~~ sixteen! [This last word appears to be added in shaky hand when Martineau was older.] The Father has been very good to me in giving me such a wife—a help mate in very deed. I pray that she may have many more birthdays, each happier than the other, and that she may have the desires of her heart. Wrote the following lines:—

[page 57—see Appendix 5 for a letter from Martineau to Susan E. inserted here.]

[It appears Martineau added some words which are unreadable and later scribbled out in a very shaky handwriting]

1

Dear wife tis sixty years since first thine eyes
In thy last birth,
Opened, to view with wonder and surprise
[this line was erased and is unreadable]
So dim, so dark, so dreary—S[tart of] gloom—
"Twas like an entrance, almost, to a tomb!

2

Was thy first home so glorious? so bright?
Did Earth seem drear
Because of change from that celestial light
When thy obedient spirit took its flight
And nestled here?

3

Ah yes! No darkness there! no strife! no fear!—
No grief!—no pain!
But all of these assail thee quickly here,
And cause the sigh, the moan, the frequent tear—
That falls as rain!

4

But through the clouds the light of heaven appears—
A glorious light!
Dispelling gloom and doubt,—all griefs and fears;
With promise, too, of joy in future years;—
An end to night!

5

Let us be faithful, while on Earth we dwell
And patient be;
Trusting in Him who doeth all things well—
In hope of joys no mortal tongue can tell—
From Satan free!

6

As we with Father and with Mother dwelt
Through ages vast,—
As Brother and as Sister walked, and knelt
Together in praise,—sweet union felt,—
Again at last

[page 58]

July 11, 1896—

7

We will to Father and to Mother come,
Our trials o'er;
And hear with joyful hearts the words "Well done
~~Reign ye upon your glorious throne—~~
Forever more"!

This was all the gift I could offer, having no means to buy her a better one.

July 14, 1896—Sent my new blank bonds as U. S. Deputy Mineral Surveyor to Lyman, for him to find me Sureties [securities] in the amount of $10.000.$^{\underline{00}}$ [$233,593] He is now absent in Chicago as an Alternate delegate to the Convention which the Democrats have called.

July 24, 1896—To day Samuel and Elvira had a son (Seth Guernsey) born to them at 12 o'clock, healthy and plump,—weighed 12½ lbs.

Susan and I had written them previously, to anoint and bless Elvira and all should be well with her and her babe, whom we felt impressed would be a boy.

On the 26$^{\underline{th}}$ Sam's sister Mary Park died in childbirth.

Sent article on early settlement of Parowan, the fort, drouth [drought], &c

Sent a letter to inquire why I do not receive the $127.72 [$2,983] due from the Government.

July 24, 1896—Sur. Genl Roskruge offers me a contract to run 45 miles of line to cut off the Coal lands in Indian reservation, at $30.$^{\underline{00}}$ [$701] a mile. It would probably take 3 or 4 weeks time. I am now sadly in need of money,—in debt for our living expenses since April, and $40.[00] [$934] rent, with no visible means to continue here, nor to go away, and it looks very dark, naturally speaking. But I have the promise, by the voice of the Spirit, that all shall be well with me and my family, and I try to have faith in the promises and goodness of God.

July 29, 1896—I asked concerning the Contract which is offered me, and which I had desired much to obtain, but was told "touch it not—take it not."

[page 59]

July ~~29~~ 31, 1896—Being in doubt, fearing I might have been deceived, and that what I had taken as the voice of the Spirit might have been something else, I inquired again of the Lord concerning the Contract offer[ed] me, by which I could clear over a thousand dollars, and which in my present poverty seems so desirable, and received an answer, a part of which I insert, as a testimony to help my children in a future time. I was again told "touch it not—take it not, for it is not needful for thee, for I will bless thee abundantly in other ways, and thou shalt know it is from the hand of thy Father in Heaven. Thou shalt not be brought into poverty and want, neither shalt thou be brought into shame because of thy debts, for thou shalt be able to pay them to the full satisfaction of all. Thou hast been brought into trouble and difficulty in order that thy faith may become mighty, and thou hast been brought to this place for a purpose of mine own, which thou shalt know hereafter, but in mine own time thou shalt return to the Saints and to thy family. Thou shalt not labor to build up this nation, for vengeance must overtake it. My saints have been slain and many hundreds have laid down their lives because of persecution, they have been robbed & plundered and driven, and not one has been punished for these things, but the nation has winked at it all, and as a people have rejected the gospel. Therefore they must suffer what my servant Joseph has declared concerning them. But they shall not be utterly destroyed, for my Saints shall be as the Salt to preserve them.

Thou art called to labor in Mexico and in the lands south, and there thou shalt be mightily blessed, for thou shalt be in that land as was Joseph in the house of Pharoah. They shall seek unto thee, for thou shalt be filled with wisdom from on high.

[page 60]

July 31, 1896—Thou shalt do a great work in that land, for there are millions there who are of the blood of Joseph, heirs to all the promises made to Abraham, Isaac, and Jacob."

Other great and glorious promises were made to me, and the Spirit saith that this is the voice of the Holy Ghost, and not that of a lying Spirit, nor of my own desires and anxiety. I praise thee, my Father, for thy wonderful goodness, and pray thee to so live as to attain to all that is promised. I will not take the Contract offered me, but trust in the Lord for my blessing. Help me, my Father.

AUGUST 1896.

August 1896—I feel impelled to insert here a letter recently received from Nephi, now on a mission in Kentucky,[30] which, shows a lovely spirit, and a soul devoted to the work of the Father; and I am thankful indeed that I have a representative who is laboring so energetically.

Campellvill, Taylor Co. Ky.
July 23. 1896

My dear parents

Your ever welcome letter came and found me after I returned from Conference, having been about 4 weeks without any mail of any kind and then I received a letter that Leigh had been very sick. I fasted and prayed for him and got the assurance that he would be all right again.

Of course you are interested in your son, and he reads your good letters over and over. Don't be afraid to ask questions. I went to Conference and we were there told that the Lord required of us to travel without purse or scrip in the future, (read Doc. & Cov. 84 Sec.) I sent my money to the office at Chattanooga to pay for books and tracts, and went forth on our journey of 125 miles to Taylor Co. being on the road about 10 days, we leaving without money, trusting in the Lord. I did not feel justified in laying in a supply of writing material, but we go out to prove the word of the Lord when he says he will raise up friends to administer to our wants.

30 "In Kentucky Conference," *Deseret News*, July 11, 1896; Utah Digital Newspapers.

[page 61]

August 1896—Just as soon as I quit traveling with money I was more humble and put all my trust in the Lord. The first thing I received was a nice handkerchief, which I was needing, also some soap, which was handed me by a lady in a store, after hearing a gospel conversation. If I had told her what I needed it was those things. We were out of blacking and stayed at a house where we used theirs. I prayed for blacking and on going to the post office got a letter with sufficient stamps to get every thing we needed. These things came just as they were needed, and if they were small things it shows that the Lord is able to help us. People ask to do our washing, so you see we are better off than if we were worrying about money to pay our way with. I have been very busy of late. I wrote home and told Emma that if she got any money for me to send it to Chattanooga to pay for books and tracts which we distribute. Now if any money comes to me I will use what I need and send the rest to the office, and consider any that might come sent me of the Lord. As President Kimball says, "The bridge is cut, brethren, go forth in this way and you will become mighty in the sight of the Lord." I was humbled several times in tears, and it seemed that it was necessary, to bring me in the right position. I have had the Spirit of the Lord resting upon me until my frame just shook, and the Lord has shown me just what is required to fill an honorable mission. We can not work in this work without being humble and prayerful, and at times I was not in that way. I repented of my nonsense and fasted and prayed, and my prayers were answered and I have felt good ever since and am very thankful that I was able to see the error of my ways.

[page 62]

August 1896—I prayed to the Lord mightily and asked him to bring me into subjection. I don't tell you these things to scare you and to make you think I hav'nt enjoyed my labors some of the time, but just as soon as I laid my money away, got rid of it by sending it away and fasting and praying, having a partner who is strict in prayer, I have the assurance that my labors have been accepted of the Lord, and it is an experience I would not like to do without. I have been able to meet men and look them in the face. You know I used to be very bashful, but the fear is fast leaving me. It is a tough ordeal to pass through for about 3 or 4 months until we get acquainted with the people and the way of preaching the gospel. Now all of that has vanished away.

I guess I better tell you what was the matter with me. My companion was younger than me ~~and~~ and it was his right to preside over me, he being out 16 months. I did not want to be dictated to all the time and was somewhat rebellious, I suppose, like Laman and Lemuel. We went along several days trying to hold meetings under such conditions. He is a young man from Tooele Co. and a good young man, but I could not stand to be under some one else. One night we retired to the woods to have prayer. We kneeled together asking the Lord to soften our hearts so that we could work in peace and love. We then separated to have secret prayer. I asked the Lord to bring me under subjection and to unite us together in love and union. I finished first and set down on a log. He came near & set down by me. I said we were talking about being out here preaching, and our hearts were softened.

[page 63]

August 1896—That feeling of love came upon us both at the same time; we embraced each other—tears ~~came~~ flowed from our eyes—we were both melted and asked each other's forgiveness. Such is the feelings the gospel brings to the penitent, and there is a love existing between us which only the gospel brings. That is the same spirit which great men have possessed, and it was necessary, thanks for it. We hav'nt felt the same since, but have a love for each other which unites us together in all our labors. We Could not go along in any other way.

The time has passed by quickly and we are doing a good work which is as follows; Since 3^d of July;—Meetings held 20, Miles walked 110, visits 3, revisits 38, tracts distributed 65, gospel conversations 45, which last from 10 minutes to an hour. So you can see that is twice the amount of work we were able to do before. People everywhere kill spring Chickens—have them nearly every meal, but we generally go without our meal when we hold meeting so as to be able to speak better. They are after us on all sides, saying "<u>Come and stay with me</u>," "<u>Ain't you coming to my house before you leave</u>?" "<u>Will you be coming to preach in our district</u>?" And it is becoming unpopular to speak against us in any way—men ready to defend us on every hand. The work is progressing rapidly and the people are following us from one place to another, some coming for miles through the timber to hear the gospel. We are magnified in their eyes, and they think we have been to College for years. Zion is coming to the front and thousands will be found who are seeking the truth and waiting for a chance. We have a branch organized in the next county, a membership of 34 and more getting ready. We are the first elders that have ever preached in this county, and it seems as though the Lord has his spirit striving with them.

[page 64]

August 1896—Think of the people that are visited every day in the South. We have 365 Elders; just think what a grand work we are engaged in, gathering out the honest in heart from the nations of the earth. I have many dear friends here, and would hate to see them destroyed with the judgements which will come. Pres[t] Kimball said in Conference "Some of you Elders will be called to come out here to preside." Just think of it! being called to come out here ~~to preside~~ and live and teach the people day after day in the meetings; think of the thousands of children growing up here, and all of them can't be wicked, but they need the Gospel to be preached to them that they may have a chance to grow up in it as our children do. My heart is reaching out after the people, and there are a great many of them waiting for the gospel who will receive it with open arms. Our elders are getting among the bankers and lawyers & doctors; They are all studying it. I don't want to go home. I prefer to stay and enjoy the mission and try to do my part, that I may stand on Mt. Zion worthy of the blessings. I am 5 years younger, only my hair is coming out on top of my head. I could write you as much again if I only had time, but I must get myself ready to speak, not having time to study much. God bless you all

From your loving Son

P.S. I will write you as often as I can. Dear parents I know how to appreciate you more every day, and my heart is full of blessings for you. And don't be afraid to ask me any questions. I am your son just the same, and just let Gertie kiss you both for me, and may our hearts be ever bound together in love. Don't think I have forgotten you, we live too far apart, but our hearts can be bound together with the Spirit of the Lord, and I hope to meet you when I come home, and I will be a better man in every way.

[page 65]

August 1896—May you have the peace of heaven to be with you.

Nephi.

I sent extracts from this letter to the Deseret News for publication. (Forgot to insert)

August 4, 1896—To day Von Wendt told us he had played his last card and had failed. All his efforts to get means had come to naught, and he did not know what would become of us all. He has no money, and I have been living on credit since April. To the natural eye it looks black as night.

Susan and I prayed in secret, and each had a very comforting answer,—that all shall be well with us, & we shall have means from source unexpected to us, also much more that was very comforting to us and strengthening to our faith and trust in God. We are surely passing through an experience calculated for our good and to give us a great increase in faith. For now we have to live by faith, having nothing to look to but the help of our Father in Heaven.

August 14, 1896—I have been quite unwell for some days, but am now much better. It was kidney trouble, to which I am subject.

August 18, 1896—Susan is very sick. A cold settled on her lungs, and she has a heavy rattling in her throat at every breath. I anoint her and rebuke the disease and bless her frequently, and I have promise she shall be healed. Much better next day.

August 20, 1896—Susan sat up a little while

August 21, 1896—Von Wendt feels very blue,—says he dont see how we are to exist. I prayed and received a comforting answer, as I always do, and was told that all shall be well with us. To the natural eye it is black as night. Heavily in debt for rent, grocery account, ice, milk, and washing, with no means to pay my debts, and nothing in sight for us—not even means to move away. But we trust in God.

[page 66]

August 31, 1896—My account for pay still due me for Surveys came to day, reduced about $50.00 [$1,168] It is very discouraging.

SEPTEMBER.

September 3, 1896—My bonds, executed in Utah, for commission as U. S. Mineral Surveyor, came, but were found incorrect. So I sent new papers to Lyman to be filled anew. My bond is to the amount of $20,000 [$467,186], my sureties, Lyman, Bishop W. B. Preston and Judge C. H. Hart.

September 6, 1896—Susan's rheumatism is still very painful. For 2 weeks she has not been able to dress or undress herself nor to turn in bed without help. She took a hot air bath which seemed to help her.

September 9&10, 1896—Susan had another Turkish bath, but was worse afterwards. There is much rain, which is probably the cause.

September 13, 1896—Von Wendt received a letter from Barney, in New York, which has entirely discouraged him. He says he has done all he can—can do nothing more; he has no more hope. Says he will go to Colorado if he can get means to go with, and see if he can do anything there. I asked concerning the matter, and was told all shall be well with us; he shall receive the money he needs to hold the mine and work it, and it shall be to his astonishment. He shall be blessed and prospered, his eyes shall be opened, he shall know that God lives and that Jesus is the Christ, and shall do a great work in Zion. He shall have great wealth and shall be a blessing to us, to help us. I was told to trust in the Lord and fear not, for all shall be well. This was repeated three times.

So I went to his rooms to comfort him, but he could not believe what I said—that he should come out all right. But I had a testimony that what I had told him was true.

How wonderfully good is the Father, to hear and answer the prayers of one so weak and sinful as I am, and to give Susan the same comforting testimonies as he has so many times given me! Praise and honor be to him, forever and ever.

[page 67]

September 13 & 14, 1896—Received a letter from Lyman, who is discouraged about the bonds. I wrote him in answer, to do nothing more about them, but let it go. I believe God will bless me in some other way, for I receive great promises from him. I know if I do not attain them the fault will be with me and not with the Father.

For a considerable time I have been subject to great and contradictory influences—Evil and Good,—from the darkness of night to the glory of the noon-day Sun. I know the Evil One is determined to prevent me from gaining my exaltation, but the voice of the Holy Spirit tells me I shall, for I shall never be tempted more than I can bear. And this gives me great comfort, realizing how weak I am, and how great is the power of the Evil One. But the Father is infinitely more powerful, and I know if I take a course to make and keep Him my friend and helper, no power can hinder me from gaining my exaltation. This is a great comfort. I am passing through an experience fearful to the natural man, but I believe it is to perfect me, and for an increase in faith, patience, humility and in all good gifts.

In all these troubles Susan and Gertrude are great helps; they do not lose their faith no matter how dark things appear; and strengthen my faith greatly.

Dora again began to attend the public school, to day. She is hard to learn and remember, or understand, but since I have blessed her in her intellect she has greatly improved, and can now work in the simple rules of arithmetic, and reads in easy lessons. She has gifts in music and drawing, which I hope I may be able to cultivate.

September 17, 1896—Received word that my account against the Government for balance due me for Surveys, of $71.61 [$1,673] is allowed. Thankful.[31]

September 18, 1896—To day in aswer to prayer I received many comforting promises, and among others, this, spoken in reference to my desires to do a great work in bringing the Lamanites, or House of Joseph—to the fold of Christ, according to that which has been sealed upon me by authority of the priesthood;—"I ordain thee a Prince and a Patriarch, a Prophet and a Seer,"—to the house of Joseph.

[page 68]

September 18, 1896—I desired to know if this is a complete ordination or one by promise, and the

31 This week Martineau writes a description on Mexico's independence celebrations (J. H. Martineau, "Mexican Celebration," *Deseret News*, September 26, 1896; Utah Digital Newspapers).

answer was very clear and plain, and I write it for instruction of my family;—Although the Lord hath all power both on earth and in heaven, he hath given authority to men on Earth to regulate and rule in the authority of the priesthood all things pertaining to the Church on earth; and He honors each man holding authority in the priesthood in his particular calling. Hence, when Saul was stricken down by the power of God while persecuting the saints, and asked what he should do, the Lord, instead of telling him (Saul) himself, told him to go to a certain town, & find a certain man, who would tell him what to do, Thus God honored the man who held the authority on earth to govern the church. And so, though I am ordained to certain callings by the Lord, I may not officiate in them until properly authorized also by the church authorities. And this that there may be order in the Church. A man may hold a fullness of the priesthood, and by it have power to officiate in any office in the church, but he cannot act in any office in a Ward or Stake until he is properly called and appointed to do so by proper authority. A High Priest's office is to officiate as a President, but not until he is appointed specially to do so. A Seventy is to preach as a traveling missionary, but not until he is sent. A man may hold all the priesthood there is, and yet may not act as a Ward Teacher or a Deacon, Even, until properly appointed so to act. If it were not so, all the men in a ward might be Deacons—or none at all—and all would be confusion.

September 18, 1896—Received my pension for last quarter,—$24.00 [$561] Welcome.

OCTOBER 1

October 1, 1896—To day Von Wendt received 400.00 [$9,344] from Mr. Barney to apply on the mine he has bonded, and the time of which would expire to morrow. This would be ruin to him, and what he had greatly feared, as Barney had said there was no chance to raise any money in New York on account of the Silver-money panic in the east.

[page 69]
I had been anxious too, because Von Wendt had given up all hope. Susan and I both prayed concerning the matter, and each received a plain, comforting answer. The voice of the Spirit said He surely should get the money he needed, and should be greatly prospered.

So the greatest joy to me in this (and to Susan) was the knowledge that we had not been deceived by any Evil spirit, but had been taught by the Holy Spirit, which is a great encouragement in our faith, for its increase.

October 3, 1896—This morning in answer to my prayer I received a Testimony it was accepted, also myself and family were accepted. And I received a great promise—the same that is recorded in the "Compendium," in the "Gems from Joseph's teachings, where he speaks of "The Other Comforter," saying that when the Father sees fit he will say to one "Son, thou shalt be exalted, &c." Even so came the promise to me, "My son, thou shalt be exalted. Thou art not all free from sin and weaknesses, but because thou dost hunger to become pure and holy, and to do a mighty work in Zion for her redemption, and to do a mighty work in bringing souls unto me, thou shalt become mighty in priesthood and calling, and be a mighty leader among thy brethren." And other words very comforting, and great promises, which I pray I may be able to attain unto. And if I fail, I know it will be my fault, not that of the Father.

October 14, 1896—For some time my prospects have been very dark, being in debt in Tucson for rent, provisions &c to the amount of $200.00 [$4,672] and the debt increasing $2.00 [$47] a day, with no apparent means to pay it or to leave the town (as I could not endure to do in debt) In answer to my prayer that I might have employment in the Sur. General's Office the answer came that I surely shall have employment there while I need it. Also, that I shall be prospered from this time forth in all I undertake. And that no hand or voice raised against me shall prosper.

[page 70]
October 14, 1896—And my life, age and strength shall be renewed, that I may yet do a great work for the redemption of the dead, as well as the living, especially among the House of Joseph. Also many other great promises.

It makes me very thankful and full of wonder at the mercy and goodness of the Almighty to thus hear and answer one so unworthy as me, and the great desire of my heart is to become pure in heart and holy—to be like Enoch, and other holy men of old.

October 15, 1896—Sent another article to the Deseret News, on early scenes in Parowan and the death of Walker, the Utah Chief.[32]

October 20, 1896—This morning before day light I was reflecting upon the explanation given by Joseph the Prophet upon this quotation from John the Revelator:—"Four destroying Angels having power over the four quarters of the earth until the Servants of God are sealed in their foreheads,"—"Which signifies," Joseph says, "sealing the blessing upon their heads, meaning the everlasting covenant, thereby making their calling and election sure. When a seal is put upon the father and mother it secures their posterity, so they cannot be lost, but will be saved by virtue of the covenant of their father and mother."

The part I have written at the last in sloping hand was what I could not clearly understand, as to me it seemed to deprive some children of their agency, and saving them whether they seek for or desire it or not. But by the blessing of the Father it was made plain to me in answer to prayer, and I write it for the benefit of my children: not as instruction or teaching to the Church, which is not my right, but as words of wisdom and instruction to my own family. It is this:—

When a spirit leaves his first estate where he dwelt for ages with the Father and the Holy ones, and filled with the wisdom of the heavens, and comes on earth, entering his second estate, he forgets all he formerly knew; but Satan has authority to tempt him, to cause him to do evil if he can, Satan being learned in the wisdom of the heavens and having forgotten nothing.

[page 71]

October 20, 1896—Therefore, the man could not of his own power stand against the knowledge and power of the Evil One; he can only stand by the aid given him from the Heavens. What is this aid? First, it is a portion of the inspiration of the Holy Spirit which is given to all to help them distinguish between right and wrong, evil and good; and secondly, the aid given by our guardian angels, as is written in "Paracletes," published in the "Times and Seasons," vol. 6 page 891, as follows:—That none of the work of the hands of the "Son" might be lost, or any of the souls which his Father had given Him might be left in prison, angels were commissioned to watch over Idumea, and act as spiritual guides to every soul, "lest they should fall and dash their feet against a stone." They were denominated "The Angels of Our Presence."

As all <u>must</u> be aided thus from the Heavens to enable them to withstand the Powers of Darkness, their free agency is not destroyed or infringed by the help they receive from above: and when the "<u>blessing</u>" first referred to in the words of Joseph is sealed upon the parents, it is a covenant that this aid shall be given their posterity in time of need.

The blessing sealed upon my head by Patriarch John Young that—"You shall never be tempted above what you are able to bear."—is in full agreement with the foregoing, because my sincere <u>desire</u> and my <u>will</u> is to serve God and live a holy life; therefore if I am aided in this, it does not infringe my agency in the least but is in full accord with it. If I should knowingly and with full purpose choose evil and reject good I could not claim this help and blessing, because all blessing can only be obtained through perfect obedience to the "Head."

I have not made this so clear and plain as it was shown to me: but if my posterity will seek to know more fully than I have shown, let them ask God in humility, faith and prayer and it shall be shown unto them and made plain.

[page 72]

October 20, 1896—But one may say,—suppose parents who have been thus sealed and blessed have a son—and there are many such—who has no religious feeling or desire; who cares for nothing but worldly things and has no desire to gain any knowledge of heavenly things:—one who barely has a Standing in the church but is dead and lifeless:—Shall such a one be saved without any effort on his part? Is not that saving him without his agency?

I answer—No. There is a vast difference between <u>salvation</u> and <u>exaltation</u>; a man may be <u>saved</u> and not <u>exalted</u>. Every soul will be saved in some degree of glory except such as commit the sin against the Holy Ghost—the unpardonable sin—and become "sons of Perdition." And as every one must reap that which he

32 J. H. Martineau, "Buried Alive by Indians," *Deseret News,* November 31, 1896; Utah Digital Newspapers.

sows, he will receive all that his works entitle him to. So, such a son will be saved in some glory, even if it be not the celestial, though I do not say he may not attain to a glory, even, in that. For "in the celestial glory there are three heavens or degrees," and only those who attain to the highest may become Kings of Kings and Lords of Lords—the Gods of Eternity. And a man who, as described above, lives as a drone in the Church can not become a Son of Perdition—become lost—because he does not know enough. For to entitle a man to become a Son of Perdition he must be far enough advanced to become a God; and the prophet has said that the number of those who will attain to the highest exaltation will be very few, because they are not willing, in this life, to make the sacrifice necessary to attain to it. What must a man sacrifice? He must sacrifice all things, or be willing to,—the dearest things to his heart—even life itself. just as Jesus had to do to gain his exaltation. For it is said—"& it had been agreed by the Gods and the Grand Council of Heaven, that all the family of the "Head" that would do as He or his eldest Son did, should be exalted to the same glory."

[page 73]

October 20, 1896—And as Jesus follows in the path of his Father, so we must follow Jesus if we would attain an exaltation with Him.

October 25, 1896—This morning I received word from the Treasury Department, Washington, that my "account" for balance due me on my Survey was disallowed. This account was for $71.62 [$1,673], and had been declared just by the General Land Office Dep[t] and ordered paid. This news was a great disappointment to me, as I had depended upon it to help pay my debts here.

For some time I felt much discouraged; but after I had prayed, I felt comforted. I received answer that no shame or contempt shall come upon me because of my debts here, for I shall have power to pay them all, and shall be blessed and prospered all I need. I believe in the promise I have received, although everything looks to the natural eye as black as ink.

October 26, 1896—Wrote to the Commissioner of Interior about my claim just rejected after its approval at the General Land Office, and sent him original papers and instructions received, to show my claim is just.

October 30, 1896—Hired an organ at $2.50 [$58] pr. month, for the comfort of our family in our lonely condition. We visit no one, and no one visits us, nor do we wish it, for there is nothing which is congenial with the wicked people of Tucson.

NOVEMBER.

November 3, 1896—Election day. McKinley elected President. Wrote to Locke.

November 4, 1896—By letter from Netta, learn the names of two of family of Martineau in France, which my niece Fanny found in the Historical Library in Paris:—

Pierre Martineau, Seigneur du Perron, Elector du Beauvais, Picardy, who was declared noble in the council of Deuce in June 1667: also

—Martineau, Baroness de Thuré, (Dates not given by Fanny.)

The family arms of Pierre Martineau, are azure Field with 3 towers, silver, with cross of Jerusalem, (Like this)

Fig. 8.3—Pierre Martineau family coat of arms. See Appendix 1 for current family coat of arms.

[page 74]

November 7, 1896—Letter from Sarah, Moroni's widow. A son was born to her on Oct. 4th, weighed 10 lbs. She was blessed in her confinement, her sister Anna being with her. She thinks of calling her boy Helaman, after his father. I am very thankful all was well with her. Both Susan and I had testimony that all would be, and that it would be a boy.

November 9, 1896—A feeling of great darkness and dread came over me this evening, because all looks so dark before me in regard to our means to pay debts, and in regard to going away from Tucson, to be with the saints and with my family. My way seemed hedged up on all sides, with no way of escape, for all things seem to fail me, and nothing but disappointment remaining. I cannot bear to think of leaving here in debt—so disgraceful—and yet my debts, now about $230.00 [$5,373] here increase day by day, with no way in sight in which to pay them. At no time in my life have I felt in so bad a straight. We have been in depth of poverty before, deeper than now, but we were among our brethren, and knew they would not suffer us to starve. But here, there are no brothers nor sisters, and we are alone.

But I prayed, and received a comforting answer—a promise that all shall be well with us. Susan read some of my patriarchal blessings to me, and had faith all would be well. I felt ashamed and repented of my doubts and fears, asked God to forgive me, and received testimony that he did forgive me. He is wonderfully merciful to me.

November 10, 1896—This morning before day light I had a good season of prayer, and received many glorious promises and instruction, some of which I was told to write for the benefit of my children, and I now do so.

I was told to fear not, all shall be well with us; to be filled with joy and peace, for my Father has set his hand to bless me.

[page 75]

November 10, 1896—He will lift me up and make me mighty among my brethren in priesthood and calling. The Father had led me to Tucson for his own purpose and I have not sinned in coming here, nor in bringing my family here; and when the time comes for us to leave, our way shall open abundantly before us. I shall have Employment, and means to pay my debts, and not be turned out of our house, nor be brought into any shame or trouble because of debts. The trials, (as we think them) we now pass through, are for the purpose of giving us experience and an increase in faith, to fit and prepare us for far greater work to come, which has been appointed me before I came to earth, and for which I was gathered out from among my kindred. Jesus had to suffer more than any other man could, and live, to gain the experience necessary for him, even as His Father had done before him, and as all Gods have done and must forever do, for there is but one path leading to a celestial exaltation, and all must walk in it who would gain that exaltation. My faith shall increase from this hour, and I shall increase in all heavenly gifts, all of which I have a right to, except those which pertain especially to the Presidency of the Church [insert in shaky handwriting cannot be read] by virtue of holding the fullness of the holy priesthood which has been conferred upon me. I may bless my family with full faith and power, for my words shall be sealed and ratified in the heavens and shall be fulfilled. I must seek continually to the Lord in humility and faith, and be filled continually with the Holy Ghost, and know his voice, that it may be a constant help and guide. It was by understanding this "still small voice" of the Spirit that Moses led the hebrews through the Red Sea, and not by the audible voice of God as a usual thing. And von Wendt shall be greatly prospered in his business, and his eyes shall be opened, and he shall receive the gospel and do a mighty work in Zion, especially in the redemption of his father's family and kindred, in which I may assist him.

[page 76]

November 10, 1896—Many other comforting promises were made me, and instruction given, for which I thank the Father.

How great is His mercy, to notice one so small and so full of evil as I am. He, who has created all the worlds in the starry heavens, and how I ought to strive to gain the victory over all my sins, and become pure in heart—and this is my great desire to do.

November 24, 1896—Moved to day to a house of three rooms, being cheaper, and $16.00 [$374] a month instead of $25.00 [$584] as formerly.

November 27, 1896—Sworn as a juror to day for the first time in my life.

November 28, 1896—Sat as juror to day in a burglary case—Luis Naranja.

November 29, 1896—Today Susan found Moroni's certificate as a Seventy. He was ordained a Seventy by Joseph W. Smith on November 30th 1885, in Arizona, county of [blank]

The certificate is numbered 145, and countersigned by Jacob Gates of the Pres. of Seventies and John M. Whittaker, clk. on May 23d 1890. (Book 1, No. 145.)

DECEMBER 1

December 1, 1896—Received pay as Juror 3 days, my first experience: $5.35 [$125] I also lettered a map for the County Surveyor, price $5.00 [$117] I feel very thankful for this chance to earn something, the first, except $5.00 during the Summer, since April of this year. I have been all this time steadily running into debt for rent, Groceries and provisions, milk and ice, and if it were not for the promises I receive, in answer to prayer, I should feel almost to despair. I cannot honorably go away so heavily in debt, and to remain only increases the trouble. But when I pray concerning it, the answer is always the same—that I shall be blessed, my way opened before me so I shall be able to pay all my debts honorably, and when the time comes for me to go from here I shall have means to go in comfort. I confess it is hard to keep my faith from faltering. And yet I know God is all powerful to do what he wills to perform.

December 3, 1896—To day is the first general fast day of the Church, ~~it~~ it having been changed from the first Thursday in each month to the first Sunday in the month. Mother and I fasted until night—twenty four hours.

[page 77]

December 9, 1896—Finished lettering another map, price $5.00 [$117]. Very thankful. Sent article to the Des. News, on "Walker, the Utah Chief."[33]

December 10, 1896—Today I weigh 182lbs, Susan 226lbs and Gertie 130lbs

Today on looking for a stamp in my pocket book I found to my astonishment a silver half dollar. I had been without a nickel, having spent my last nickel for postage stamps. I asked Susan and Gertie if they had placed the money there, & they declared they had not, having none they could give me. I felt as this must have been placed there by an angel, as it could have come there in no other way. I asked, and was told it was brought by a heavenly messenger; and it made me rejoice greatly, not because of the value, which is small, but because it fulfills the promise sealed upon me, of the ministering of angels. And this shows me I am still in the favor of the Lord to a certain degree, and that I have not forfeited the blessing sealed upon me by several patriarchs as well as by the voice of the Holy Spirit to me. Truly, the mercy and loving kindness of the Lord to me are great!

And in the summer of 1888 my life was saved from instant death when my guardian angel spoke, as with an audible voice—"turn your hand." I did so, and at the instant my gun was discharged, just missing my body but burning my wrist and sleeve.

December 11, 1896—To be more certain, and not to record something. which might be a mistake, I inquired again, and was told the same as before, and that the money was given me, not as something of value, but to show me that the eye of the Father is upon me, that he knows my needs, and will not desert me, even in my present deep financial troubles. And for this I thank my Father in heaven.

December 12, 1896—Samuel and Elvira write Wilmirth has been quite sick for a week or more, vomiting continually, day and night.

December 24, 1896—This morning we received a fine turkey from Samuel and Elvira, which was very acceptable indeed. Wilmirth no better. I received a testimony concerning her, for thus said the voice of the Spirit to me,—"Thy granddaughter hath lived her appointed time, and shall depart in peace, and shall suffer no loss, for so hath her time been appointed from before the foundation of the earth.

[page 78]

December 24, 1896—And she shall receive an exaltation in the celestial glory with the Father, and all is well with her." And I write this, that my children may realize more fully that the Father hears and answers us when we seek unto him in humility and faith, teaching us by the voice of the Spirit when it is expedient, but sometimes I have been told I should understand at some future time, but not now, the thing I wished to know.

December 25, 1896—Christmas, and a happier one than I expected, for I had only $2.00 [$47] to spend, and the shops were filled with beautiful Christmas presents. Baron von Wendt dined with us and brought a bottle of Champagne, the first we ever had at any meal. We did not care for it very much, however.

33 James H. Martineau, "Chief Walker's Methods," *Deseret News*, December 26, 1896; Utah Digital Newspapers.

December 26, 1896—This morning about 3 o'clock, after a season of prayer, I had a joyful season, receiving many great and glorious promises, and having principles of truth made plain to me. I was told, among other things, that my sins are forgiven, and that I am accepted by the Father, with all my family, although I I and they are not all pure and clean, but the Father knows that in my heart I truly desire to put away all sin, to become pure in heart and to live a holy life; to do good and bring many souls to Him; and for this cause He is merciful to us. Also that I nor any of my family shall be never tempted more than we can bear, and shall all be saved together in the Celestial Glory. I was told that I shall do a mighty work for the redemption of the house of Joseph upon this land and be a restorer to the house of Jacob,—I should be a Prince and a Patriarch, a Prophet and a Seer unto them, as has already been sealed upon me by the Patriarch. Great and glorious were also other promises made me. And now, I know how weak and sinful I am, and how easily led astray; and if I fail to receive any of these blessings it will not be because God has failed, but because of failure in me. But I pray that I may not forfeit these blessings.

December 27, 1896—This morning these things were all shown me again, also I was told that my son Moroni shall suffer no loss being called away in his prime, For he was needed there to do a work in connexion with that performed for our dead which could not be done here.

[page 79]

December 27, 1896—Also, that although he had not obeyed the law of plural marriage yet he had never opposed it, but had received it in his heart, and should receive his exaltation accordingly; and that I should have wives sealed to him, and receive the 2nd A. for him. Also that he will visit me, yet in this life, for which I am very thankful, having asked that he may be permitted to do so.

December 31, 1896—To day we had a roast goose, the first in our married life. It was furnished by von Wendt, who, with us, watched the old year out and the new one in.

JANUARY 1897.

January 1, 1897—To day was rainy and cold.[34]

January 7, 1897—Received a letter from Jesse N.—Chicago. He sent me $12.00 [$280] for which I was very thankful indeed, as I found that unless I could pay something on my debt due our grocer, he would not let us have anything more on credit, and as I had no money, we would be brought to beggary or almost starvation. I was glad to be able to pay $10.00 [$234] on the account.

I know God put it into Jesse's heart to send it me. Early in December last, Charly sent me $10.00 which I paid on my rent, and thus was able to keep my word given, that I would pay it. And for this I was very thankful, for I would rather be dead than dishonored.

I thank our Father for his care and goodness.

January 8, 1897—To day is the 45th anniversary of our marriage. I can scarcely realize it can be so. Forty five years, as a future, seems a very long time; but as past—it is all as a dream. Susan and I recalled the names of those who lived in Parowan at that time, and of all the men and women who then lived there, and of many young people—all have passed away except a few, probably eight or ten in all. It seems so strange that Susan and I have been thus left behind, lingering almost alone, while so many strong, robust people have passed away.

And while life, for itself, has no great attraction for me, I am thankful we have been thus preserved, and have been enabled to do the work for the dead we have done, to the number of about 2000, and that we have received all the temple ordinances given this side of the veil.

[page 80]

January 8, 1897—And I have a hope and desire to still, in this life, do a much greater work, and for this I have the promise of the Lord. If I fail to realize its fulfillment, it will be my fault, not that of the Father.

I have had a strange and hard experience for a long time past; every thing I touched turned to ashes, and

34 Martineau writes an article describing Christmas in Tucson and the "oldest City in the United States" (J. H. Martineau, "Flowers in Bloom," *Deseret Evening News*, January 13, 1897; Journal History).

every hope and every plan, apparently sure, has failed. I had strong hopes of appointment as City Engineer, but on Jan. 4th that hope also failed, and I am left here, in debt here $250.00 [$5,840],—debt increasing daily, with no visible or probable way to pay it, and unable to leave here. Even if I could go to Elvira's, as they urge us to do, I could not feel satisfied to go leaving my debts unpaid. And yet, every time I ask the Father concerning these things, I always get the same comforting answer:—that I shall be able to pay all my debts honorably and have means to go to the saints and to my family in due time, and that all shall be well with us. And Susan always has the same answer to her prayers. Sometimes a fear arises in my mind that perhaps I have been deceived, and that my comforting answer has not come from the Holy Spirit but from an evil source. And then I have been plainly shown how to judge the spirits;—that a spirit which incites to good, tells us to cleave to God and to righteousness, to do good and to bless is from above and not from beneath; for no good whatever cometh from the Evil One because there is no good in him. I there were, he could not be Perdition, for the good in him must be saved in some glory, even if it be as one of the faintest and smallest stars. Therefore, nothing good can come from Lucifer but only darkness, fear, doubt and trouble of mind.

[page 81]

January 8, 1897—And by this I know the answers received have been from the Lord by the voice of the Holy Ghost, and so I am better able to bear up against what would otherwise crush my life out.

And I know all this is for my good; to teach me to trust fully in God no matter how impossible his word seems of fulfillment;—to seek more unto him; for He will have all the glory of our salvation. "Without faith we cannot please God," and difficulties,—met and overcome—are necessary to give an increase in faith. If there be no opposition or difficulty we have no need of faith. If the sea had been as solid ground Peter would not have had need of faith to walk upon it; and it is he whose flour bin is empty who must ask in faith "give us this day our daily bread," not he whose bin is full. And I believe this schooling is to prepare me for a work still greater than any in my past; and I only pray "Father, not my will, but thine be done," and that I may not at any time murmur or sin in thought word or deed because of disappointments.

Von Wendt came in despondent, saying he had lost his gold placers, which had cost him many thousand dollars, and he feels as if all is gone. I prayed, and the answer is—he shall yet be blessed and prospered abundantly; his eyes shall be opened, and he shall receive and obey the truth, and do a great work for Zion, and for his progenitors. And so I endeavored to comfort him, and he felt better. The Father is wonderfully good to hear and answer one so unworthy as I am.

I had no means to get any present for my dear Susan on this wedding anniversary, as I have always done, and so, for a present, and token of my love I composed the following, as I walked out in the evening in the outskirts of town among the brushy chaparal. They seem a little sad, but it is because of our sad surroundings, and of the memory of times and friends long since passed away.

[page 82]

[written at top of page in shaky hand]

See p. 57

January 8, 1897—

TO MY DEAR SUSAN, ON OUR 45TH WEDDING DAY.

1

Five and forty years have sped
Since the hour that saw us wed.
Years of pleasure mixed with pain,—
Songs of gladness,—tears like rain,—
Happy moments—hours of woe—
So they come and so they go!

2

Friends have vanished from our sight
Entering heav'ns refulgent light;
Souls to us from heaven came—
Some have gone—some still remain.
Not to us is given to know
Who shall stay and who shall go.

3

Tears in torrents we have shed

While with grief our hearts have bled.
Hopes ~~we~~ once cherish'd baseless seem
As bubbles floating on the stream;
And we are tossed—tossed to and fro
As whirl in storm, the flakes of snow.

4

But not all somber—not all drear,—
Not all sigh or blinding tear!
Many ~~hours~~ years, like glimpse of heav'n
To us have been in mercy giv'n;—
A foretaste of that peace and love
That reigns forever in heav'n above.

5

Many of our friends are gone—
Those of our youth; almost alone
We linger now—among new friends
Until our earthly work shall end
When again with joy we'll greet
Those whom here no more shall meet.

[page 83]

[written at top of page]

See page 57

January 8, 1897—

6

Soon the clouds shall break away!
Soon shall shine the glorious day!
Heaven's blessings on thee rest—
My Queen!—my princess!—be thou blessed!
Thou, with me, shalt vict'ry gain!—
Enthroned Thou.—A Mother Queen.

January 8, 1897—To day a letter from David Booth, of Brigham City, gives me information relative to Cora Colorado, the indian girl I bought of the Utes in Parowan about the year 1856 to save her life, and whom, when we lived in Salt Lake City in 1860, we allowed Br. Cherry, of what is now called Centerville, Davis Co, Utah, to take as his own child. He said his children were all married and gone, and he and his wife were lonely in their big house. And so we let him have her, he being well off and able to do better by her than we could, who had so large a family and were so poor.

He says Cora went and lived in Mound Fort with Wells Chase and wife for some years, until she died of quick consumption, and is buried in Ogden cemetery. She had a child—a boy, Joseph Hyrum—having been betrayed under promise of marriage by one Joseph Johnson. Before she died she requested Mrs. Booth to care for her boy, which she did until he died, aged 3 years 3 months 18 days, and was buried in Plain City. I was very thankful for this information, for I did not know what had become of her. I want a work done for her in the temple, and I want her sealed to me with her son. I consider her as much married in reality as are all who are married by the gentile law, which has no real authority to join man and wife. And her sin was one of ignorance and of her surroundings, which a merciful Father above has forgiven. And let him who is without sin cast the first stone. The Spirit approves this, and saith unto me—take her to wife and it shall be approved of God.

[page 84]

January 8, 1897—To day von Wendt says he has lost his placers, through not having done his assessment work upon them. We hoped to sell them or gain much from them, but that hope is gone and it seems darker than ever. All that enables me to keep up at all is the faith I have in the answers which I receive in prayer, and even then my fears are great, although I pray continually for an increase in faith. I feel that nothing except the overruling blessing of the Lord will lift me out of my troubles. I prayed for help and had a good, comforting answer.

January 10, 1897—Received a letter from Jesse N. Chicago, Ill. He wrote a kind letter and sent me $12.<u>00</u> for which I am very thankful indeed, as it will enable me to pay my month's rent, and keep me from being turned out.

[written in margin]

Note

[This entry is an error, as Jesse's gift is noted January 7th.]

January 16, 1897—Received an invitation to become a member of the Arizona Association of Civil Engineers, at Phoenix, which I accepted.

January 19, 1897—Sent an article to the Deseret News relative to Walker, the Utah Chief—"King of the

Mountains."[35] Received a letter from Gean, Eureka, Juab Co. Utah, enclosing $15.00 [$350], ten from her and Edward, and $5.00 [$117] from Charley. Father I thank thee, for it enables me to keep my credit in the provision store by making a payment.

January 23, 1897—Received a letter from Albert and Emma, inviting us to come and stay awhile with them,—a very kind letter. I answered that we would do so, if we could get R. R. fare as I did not feel it safe for Susan and Gertrude to make so long a journey by wagon in their weak condition. Susan has been unable to dress or undress herself now for over four months, on account of rheumatism in her arms and shoulders, and Gertie's hip is very weak and painful. Paid rent $16.^{00} [$374].

[written in margin]

Lyman's boy

To day at 12, noon, a fine boy was born to Lyman and Alley, weighing ten pounds. I learned this a few days later. He sent me ~~$10.00~~ ten, and wrote very kindly.

January 25, 1897—Applied to Com^{r} of Genl Land Office, Washington, for employment in the Sur. Genl Office here.

[page 85]

January 28, 1897—By Sam's request I made out a deed from him and Elvira for 6 acres land to Saml Openshaw. Wilmirth, their eldest daughter, is still very sick, dangerously so, and has been for about two months. But they think she is improving.

FEBRUARY.

February 4, 1897—Rec^{d} word from Washington there is no vacancy for me in the Sur. Genl Office here.

February 6, 1897—To day Jesse N. Smith and C. R. Hakes spent the evening with us, very pleasantly. Jesse was my wedding guest over 45 years ago at Fort Johnson, and Br. Hakes lived with us in Parowan in 1858—both old friends. We had a happy time indeed.

February 7, 1897—Attended the Consecration of the new Catholic Cathedral here, at which there was an Archbishop, three or four Bishops in their gorgeous gold embroidered robes, with many lesser dignitaries—all of them in official robes and insignia. They were all in woman's dress and all wore a short white night gown, (apparently) made either of lawn or of lace. It was one continued scene of senseless mummery and show-bowing, kneeling, signing of the cross, scattering holy water &c. Gertrude also went, although she had a headache.

February 16, 1897—Sent another article to the Des.^{t} News, relative to early times in Parowan—a plot to take the fort by the Pah.eeds[36]

February 17, 1897—This morning after awakening I went again to sleep and dreamed the two following dreams. As they seem significant I now record them.

I thought I happened to look at my right foot and was surprised to see a hole worn through the top by my big toe. As I was wondering that I had never seen it before, I saw it growing larger, and was as large as a silver dollar, exposing all my toes, which I did not like. While still looking and wondering, the whole shoe suddenly split apart from the toe upwards, and the sides fell down flat on each side. After a momentary dismay I said to myself, laughing, "Well, now I wont have to spend any money for mending it." And the dream ceased. Then I thought I was traveling along a road, and saw one or two hawks sailing over my head; one sailed lower and finally settled upon my head, its long straight tail projecting in front of me.

[page 86]

February 17, 1897—I siezed the tail with my right hand while with the other I tried to secure his legs or head, as he struggled to get away. Having secured him, he spoke as a man, saying, "Come in the house and have something to eat." I said "Why, how can you give me anything to eat?" He answered "Oh, thats all right, come in; my wife will fix up something for you." I looked, and there beside the road stood his house, his wife and his boys and girls standing by. and the hawk now appeared as a man. I saw that my boys were getting out of my wagon, having part of my survey instruments in their hands, ready to accept the man's

35 J. H. Martineau, "Chief Walker's Doings," *Deseret News*, February 6, 1897; Utah Digital Newspapers.

36 J. H. Martineau, "In Early Utah," *Deseret News*, March 13, 1897; Utah Digital Newspapers.

invitation, so I was getting out also when I found it all a dream.

It struck me so forcibly that I felt it meant something, and I inquired concerning it, asking if it was a dream given for a purpose, or only a vision of the night without meaning. I was told it was (both of them) a significant dream, which I should understand after a while, when they will both of them be fulfilled; but I did not get the full interpretation, except this,—that there is to be some kind of a change for me, of which these dreams are significant. I was instructed to write them, as I have now done.

February 19, 1897—A letter from Joel, saying if we will come home he will send money to carry us to Deming and meet us there with team to bring us to Colonia Juarez. I believe he is led to do this by a good spirit, and wrote accepting his offer. As it will require about \$50.[00] [\$1,168] to pay sundry small debts here, I wrote to Lyman, Lilla, Charley and Virginia, asking them to send me each a part of that sum, so I can go honorably, and not as one running away from his creditors. Even then I will have to make some arrangement with regard to the remaining \$200.[00] [\$4,672] I owe, which I hope I can do. I have several hundred dollars (\$650.[00]) [\$15,184] due me, but cannot collect it at present.

[page 87]

February 19, 1897—My rent (\$16.[00]) [\$374] falls due on the 23[d], with not a dollar to pay it. But I have a testimony that all will be well with us. If it were not for the help and comfort I receive through prayer, it seems to me I could not endure such anxiety.

February 24, 1897—In looking through my journal, I find I have failed to note many incidents which would be of interest, now that so many years have passed, but which at the time seemed of little interest; and I think best to record some of them.

About the year 1852 the people of Parowan, where we then lived, thought best to give the Pah-eed indians a feast, to make them feel more friendly. A long table was improvised of boards and trestles, which by the contributions of the people was covered with a bountiful supply of food, nearly all of which was of vegetables, beef being an article of which we had only a very little—say a small piece once in 6 or 8 months. Cows were more valued than gold, and nearly all the team work of the colony was done by oxen; so no one could afford to kill his team. The indians ate all they could—which is saying a good deal—and were told to take away all that was not eaten. Most of what was left was stewed summer squash, they had no vessels or dishes in which to carry it away. But "where there's a will there's a way," and they soon found a way. Each buck took off his leggings, (made of deer skin,) tied a string around the bottom of the leg, and lo!—a sack big enough to contain nearly a half bushel, all the remnants were scraped into these sacks, cemented into a solid mass by the stewed squash; and away all marched—the men, especially, in a costume very light and airy.

Before they went, however, Pres[t] John C. L. Smith, thought it a good time to advise them how to live, so as to increase and not die out. He made them a long speech, the burden of which was—cease laziness, learn to work like the Mormons. If they would do this they would increase and multiply; if not they would all die off until none would be left.

[page 88]

February 24, 1897—We thought they were all convinced, until Kanarra, the wise old chief asked a question which entirely upset Pres[t] Smith's whole argument. Pointing to our cemetery not far away he quietly asked "Who lie up there?" That was all he said but that was enough. All who were buried there were Mormons—not one indian among them. All the tribe appreciated the force of Kanarra's question, and expressed their satisfaction at such a knock-down reply, by sighns and grunts of pleasure. It was some time before any of us could think of any answer, or explain why so many of our people lay dead and no indians when they had been told they must imitate the Mormons or all die off.

At another time the tribe congregated near our house and gambled until some had lost all they owned, among them one indian, who, having lost everything else, gambled off his wife. But the squaw did not wish to go with her new husband, and unseen by them slipped hurriedly into our house, without speaking; hid first behind the door, then went and got under some clothing, then under the bed, But not feeling safe yet, she passed out of the back door and down into a small out-door cellar, where she stood behind the open door. Not more than ten minutes had passed when suddenly an indian entered armed with a big butcher knife in his hand. Without saying a word he began looking for the squaw all through the room and examined every place where the squaw had hid, knife in hand ready to kill her on sight. We looked on in dismay, knowing we could do nothing to save the poor woman, with the whole tribe ready to condemn her. The indian then went out the back door, went down into the cellar and looked in, as it had nothing in it he went away without entering, while the squaw stood within a foot of him behind the door. He then went to our corral and looked all through it and then to other corrals. When he had gone the squaw followed on his track, knowing that he would not look again in any place he had once inspected.

[page 89]

February 24, 1897—And so she escaped, and finally rejoined her original husband, as we understood.

One morning old Kanarra came to Pres[t] W[m] H. Dame and asked him if there was any Mormon in Parowan whom he did not love much. A peculiar feeling struck Pres[t] Dame and he answered that he loved all in the fort. "But," said Kanarra, "is'nt there some you love only a very little," me-a-pooch,"—showing about a half inch of his finger. "No," said Pres[t] Dame, "I love them all, heap,—shaunt," opening his arms wide as he said so. After a time he found the reason of all these inquiries. The night previous, around their campfire, an indian told how his brother had been killed five years before for stealing cattle, and he said his blood had never been revenged, his spirit was lamenting because no white person had been slain to atone for it. So the tribe said they would go immediately to the fort, kill some one, and after the excitement had blown over they could go and explain all about it. But Kanarra said "No, if we kill some one to night in the dark, it may be some one that the Mormons love very much, and they will make a big fuss about it. I will go tomorrow and find out if there is any one they don't like much; we will kill that one. It will pay the debt and the Mormons will not be so mad." The tribe thought this was wise, and this was why Kanarra came to ask Pres[t] Dame if there was any one he didn't love much. It took all day before the Chief could be induced to give up his scheme.

In the summer of 1851 I was boarding with Gilbert Moss.[37] One Sunday morning I had discharged my long-loaded rifle in order to clean it; had washed it out and had placed a cap on the tube to dry that part when I was called in to eat breakfast. I set the gun down and went in. While eating, word came that the indians had taken our herd of loose cattle running on the range about 14 miles distant, near Buckhorn Springs, and calling for volunteers to go and recover them.

[page 90]

February 24, 1897—I jumped up, hurried out to get a horse, and as soon as mounted I siezed my rifle as it stood outside the house and hurried to overtake the rest of the company. Arriving on the cattle range we found where the cattle had been rounded up in a bunch, but could not find any tracks of indians or horses driving any of them away. The ground was soft, sandy and without any grass, so that I could track a rabbit anywhere, and we wondered greatly that we could find no indian signs. At length we adopted a course which was successful. We formed a line of men about ten steps apart, one end of which was at the place of the round up, and circled slowly round and round, scanning every foot of the ground between each man, and gradually widening our circle farther and farther from the center. When we had thus examined every foot of ground for a distance of about half a mile from the center, we suddenly found tracks of indians driving cattle away towards the mountains, and found trails leading to the west, north and east, where the stolen cattle had been driven away. We afterwards learned how the indians had accomplished this. Each indian carried the hoof of an ox, and as he drove away the stolen cattle placed the ox foot over the tracks, pointing it towards the round up, thus making it appear that every track led that way and none from it, thus entirely

37 Gilbert Moss is likely a southern Utah associate. At this writing the only reference to Gilbert Moss was located in a subpoena for him in relation to the Mountain Meadows trial.

obliterating all their own tracks for a long distance from the round-up. They knew this would delay us a long time in finding their tracks and give them ample time to get away with the booty. And they succeeded, for we never recovered any of our cattle.

I found where two indians mounted on ponies had driven away an ox, making for the mouth of the Little Creek Cañon some nine or ten miles away, and I thought I would do something very smart.

[page 91]
So without saying anything to the others, I rode off, trailing my two indians, hoping to get back the ox, much to my individual renown. I trailed them until I entered the cañon, and then went forward, scanning every bush or rock to prevent being fired on from ambush, my gun cocked and ready to fire on the instant. I thought if I fired and missed I would wheel and run until out of range, so I could reload, then return to the attack. I followed the trail thus about two miles up the cañon, and then, as it was near sunset, and I was many miles from home and alone, I started home, Arriving there after dark. All this time I had forgotten my gun was empty, for I could see the cap in place, and because we always kept our guns loaded night or day. After eating something, I thought I would shoot off my gun and load it afresh, so stepped out and fired, aiming for fun at the nearly-full moon. To my surprise only the cap exploded—but no gun fire. "Mighty lucky I didn't see any indians, or I would have been killed," thought I. I put on another cap; still my gun did not fire. I then pricked powder into the tube, put on another cap and pulled trigger. Still my gun would not fire, and I wondered greatly that my gun, always so sure, failed to explode. I then spent quite a time in pricking powder into the tube, until I knew there was enough to at least force the ball out of the gun, and then with another cap, fired again. Same result. I was nonplussed; then I cocked the gun and blew down the muzzle with my mouth, and to my astonishment heard my breath whistle out of the tube! The gun was entirely empty! Then I remembered, all at once, how I had washed out the rifle and how I had left it standing empty beside the door, and had finally seized it and carried it all day, supposing it was loaded as usual. I was more thankful than ever that I had found no indians, or I would not be writing this now. I did not tell anybody of this for many years, knowing I would be made a laughing stock.

[page 92]
[written in margin]
1851

February 24, 1897—In the summer of 1851 Walker, the famous Chief of the Utahs came to Parowan one Sunday, with his tribe. Walker and Ammon were invited to the stand, and they both spoke a little while. Walker said he had been told the Mormons were good dancers, and he wanted to see us dance, and as he was going away soon he wanted us to dance <u>now</u>. It was thought best to humor him; so meeting was dismissed, and we all went outside to a level place, got a fiddler, and danced several cotillions. The day was hot, clouds of dust nearly hid the dancers and begrimed their faces with mingled sweat and dirt. But Walker said "Stop! you don't know how to dance! I will show you how!" Crestfallen, we stood aside, while about 60 warriors took our places, forming an exact circle, facing inward. Then two others began to clap their hand singing "a-ya! a-ya! a-yah! a-yah! and all circled to the left, keeping perfect time. At the signal all circled the other way; and so on alternately for half an hour. Walker then said "I have showed you how men dance. Don't dance like little children any more!" Their perfect unity of time and motion was wonderful; I have never seen anything equal to it in all my life. It was like the motions of a machine—not that of 60 individuals.

[written in margin]
1851

I will now narrate an incident which occurred in the spring of 1851 while on my way to Iron County with W[m] K. Rice. We laid over a few days at American Fork, Utah Co. and hearing there were mountain sheep upon a high mountain east of the settlement I started alone to capture some of them. A few miles brought me to the foot of the mountain which rose above me very steep and apparently quite inaccessible. I clambered up a steep slope of small loose stones which slid down hill as I tried to ascend, so that it was only with the greatest labor and effort that I could advance at all.

[page 93]
But at last I reached the foot of the steep precipitous mountain, the top of which seemed about 500 feet

above me, almost perpendicular. I saw a large crack which I thought might aid my ascent, and began to work my way up, clinging with hands and toes to rough projections of the rock, my gun slung to my back. In this way I reached to about 20 feet of the top, when a fierce gust of wind almost blew me away from the face of the rock, so that for several minutes I only saved myself by clinging desperately to the rock I hugged. Every few minutes the gusts came again; and looking up, I could see nothing above my head to enable me to get any higher,—absolutely nothing to cling to,—and so almost at the top, I was obliged to give it up, and descend.

But how was I to descend? As I looked down during a slight lull in the tempest the giddy height—about 475 ft—made me so weak that I almost lost my hold to the cliff; so I could only descend by carefully feeling with my foot for a place to rest on a little lower, then find something to take hold of a little lower, and carefully change my position to one a little lower down. And so, slowly and with the most imminent danger of a fall to certain death, I worked my way down the cliff side to its foot, thankful indeed to be on safe footing once more. It was truly a marvelous escape from death. Had I fallen and not been instantly killed, I would have died there, for no one would have known where to have looked for me. Only the ravens and wolves would have known. I got back to my wagon late that night completely exhausted.

[written in margin]

1851

But I was in a far worse scrape in the summer of 1851, at Parowan. One Sunday I ascended a high peak south of Parowan to view the country, ascending by a long easy ridge, a distance of about 5 miles. I had no water, and on arrival at the top was almost famished for water.

[page 94]

February 24, 1897—I looked for something green and juicy to chew, for moisture to my mouth, but could see nothing except a species of cactus. I peeled a piece of one, and chewed and ate. At length it made me gag, and I attempted to spit it out, but could not, for it joined some that I had already swallowed, and all clung together in a glutinous mass. So I seized it with my fingers to pull it out. But I was like a necronancer,[38] who pulls out a hundred yards of ribbon from his mouth; for as I pulled the stuff out, that in my stomach clung to it and it all came out in one long slimy string which made me gag fearfully as it came out. When it was all out I sat and laughed until the tears ran down my cheeks, thinking how I must have appeared in the operation.

I took a view—a sketch—of the fort and all the surrounding mountains to the north west, including the Little Salt Lake about 8 miles distant, then, as the afternoon was waning, started down the mountain. To reach to bottom sooner, I did not return the way I came, but went directly down the steep side; and to avoid brush and cactus, got into the bed of a small hollow, descending rapidly as I jumped down from one rock to another, and thought I would soon be at the bottom. I finally jumped down some eight or ten feet to a rocky platform, and found to my dismay that my next jump would be at least 150 feet. Of course I immediately attempted to retrace my last jump, but but I could not climb up again. The rock, though not high, was smooth and had no projections on which to place my feet or cling to with my hands. I struggled desperately to ascend the rock, knowing starvation would be my fate if I remained there. But all in vain. I took off my shoes, and tried to cling with my bare toes and hands to the rock. But I could only ascend two or three feet, and then slip to the bottom again. After an hours struggle I sat down to consider what to do.

[page 95]

I lay on my stomach and crawled to the edge of the precipice and looked over. Below me, 150 feet, were jagged rocks, and a tall pine tree stood below and some little distance from the foot of the cliff.

To more perfectly calm my mind, I made a sketch of the opposite side of the cañon, which was formed of tall pillars of stone over a hundred feet in height, each having a broad cap stone of another kind of rock. These pillars seemed to have been formed by a process of erosion and reminded me of giants guarding the domains of the mountain elves or spirits. By the time my sketch was finished, my mind was perfectly calm and clear. I knew if I could not get back the way I came, I must either remain there and perish of thirst

38 Necromancy is the practice of magic.

and starvation, or I must jump down a shear descent of 150 feet, with a chance to alight safely in the top of the pine beneath, or, failing this, be torn to pieces by its limbs or be dashed to death on the rocks below. These were my only alternatives. I crawled again to the edge and looked. The tree top was full 30 or 40 feet below me, and stood so far out that it was doubtful if I could jump out far enough to land in its top. The view below made me shudder, and my limbs grew weak.

I made another desperate attempt to scale the rock, but could not, and I knew I must die there slowly or risk a violent death by a leap into that awful abyss. It is a fearful thing to be compelled to make choice between two such deaths, with no one to advise with, and the knowledge that no one would even know what had become of me;—for I was in a place to which no person would ever come. At last I made up my mind to leap for life or death. I had room to take three steps from the wall to the edge, and I ran, to leap, But as I neared the edge and saw into the abyss below all strength left my knees and I could hardly stand. I tottered back to the rock and panted until I became calm again.

[page 96]

February 24, 1897—And then I again essayed to leap, but as before all strength left my knees, so I could hardly stand on my feet. Third attempt was the same. I knew if I tried to jump in that state I could not leap out far enough to alight in the tree, and even if I should, what would prevent me from being torn by the branches, falling from so great a height?

I reflected on the promises made by Patriarch John Smith (uncle to the Prophet Joseph) in his blessing upon my head. I could not see that I had done anything bad enough to forfeit them, consequently I must live to fulfill them. And so I gained faith enough to pray for strength and for safety in the leap I must now make. I arose, determined to do, or die and end it all. I rushed again at the brink. And now, instead of weakness my sinews and limbs were as steel; I shot far out into the air, and in a moment found myself clinging to two limbs—one in each hand—with a grip like that of death, but safe and unharmed; not a shred of my clothing torn or disarranged, not a scratch or a mark upon me. How this came about I had no knowledge, for I knew nothing as I fell swiftly through the air, and had no knowledge of grasping at or clutching a branch of the tree. But there I was, safe and unharmed. I know now that I was saved by the power of God. He it was who guided my hands to the limbs by which I hung and enabled me to retain my hold when falling with so great speed, and that, too, without tearing my hands as such a strain would naturally do; he it was He who gave me strength to leap out so far,—who steeled my muscles and strengthened my limbs, for no other power could have preserved me.

I climbed down from one limb to another until the last one, and then hung and dropped from that about 20 feet to the ground—safe and unharmed!

[page 97]

I examined the tree carefully. It was about four feet in diameter, and judging by other trees of similar size I cut down afterwards, was fully 125 or 130 feet high.

[The marginal notes are showing Martineau's age as they are written with a shaky hand. These comments are organizational notes written as he progresses in this writing.]

[written in margin]

1851

I know that nothing but the power of God preserved my life, and to him be all the praise and honor. I reached the fort in due time, but did not tell any one of my scrape, knowing I would be laughed at for getting into such a predicament.

[written in margin]

1851

In February 1851, while living at Farmington with William K Rice I went one day upon the high mountain east of the village climbing a sharp ridge from which the snow had been blown off. Arriving at the summit I started down the north slope of the mountain, walking [on] a hard frozen crust which was covered with four inches of light, new fallen snow. I slipped down and began sliding down the steep declivity, striving vainly to stop my progress by clenching at the hard frozen crust, while quite a big heap of loose snow piled up in front of me—making me a sort of avalanche. I slid swiftly down the slope a quarter of a mile before I could catch hold of any brush or tree top, but at length did so, and holding on with all my strength I stopped while my snow pile went on. What was my surprise and horror to see it slide only a few yards and disappear as it went over a precipice 100 feet in depth, while I remained alive almost upon its very brink! I quickly got upon all fours and by hard work and the blessing of the Father reached a place of safety.

[written in margin]
1850

On a previous date I went up on the mountain side to get a view of the lake and scenery, and noticing a big object in a Cedar tree, went to see what it was. I found it was the body of a dead indian, wrapped up in buffalo robes and placed there for sepulture[39] to be secure from the wolves as was the custom of the indians of the plains in general. Upon his body lay his gun, which he needed to enter the spirit world in respectable style as a hunter and warrior. I found it had no lock, and the barrel was tied to the stock with a string, and so I thought it would be rather a disgrace to him in the spirit world rather than an honor, and took it away, as it might be of some little use to me in this.

[page 98]

February 24, 1897—I afterwards sold it in S. L. City to Peck & McBride, blacksmiths for a small value in gun percussion tubes. It was while in their shop to sell it, I inquired of Hezekiah Peck if he had any book to prove the Book of Mormon true.[40] He said he had, and brought out Winchester's Evidences of the Book of Mormon. I sat down and read it through, was convinced by it, and asked him (Peck) to baptize me. He being very busy just then called his partner, William McBride, to go and baptize me. We went to the temple block, then not enclosed, through which the west branch of City Creek flowed toward the Jordan river, and hunted up and down it until we found a place, near the center of the block, where he baptized and confirmed me at the water's edge. The day was bitterly raw, windy and cold, but I did not care. I was filled with a joy beyond words and could only say to myself with exultation "Now I am a Mormon! Now I'm a Mormon!" When I asked for baptism I did not believe Joseph Smith was a prophet. I thought all such things, and miracles, were long past. But when I was confirmed I received the Holy Ghost, and by his testimony knew for myself that <u>all</u> Mormonism was true, as I had been told I <u>should</u> know if I would be baptized with an honest heart to know the truth. I knew I <u>was</u> honest in the matter, and hence went forward in the holy ordinance of baptism.

[written in margin]
Bap^{d} Jany 19, 1851

And now, (March 1, 1897) my testimony to all who may ever know of me is still firm and unshaken, but on the contrary strengthened by a thousand proofs, that the principles of truth as revealed by God through Joseph Smith the Prophet are the gospel of salvation to us and are verily true and holy; and I charge and command my children after me, to the latest generation to sustain honor, obey and practice this all their lives.

[page 99]

February 24, 1897—So obeying they shall attain not only salvation but an exaltation in the celestial glory; and without obedience unto this gospel they will lose all, which I pray may never be.

I acknowledge the hand of the Lord in bringing me to a knowledge of the truth, for he gave me the desire to investigate the doctrines of the church, when as a gentile emigrant among the saints no one cared enough for me to teach me anything except two widow women; one of whom lived in a small house near the temple block on South Temple street, whose name I never knew, (but hope to, by-and-bye) and the other, Sister Picket, once the wife of Don Carlos Smith. These two women converted me to the truth of the gospel. I never heard a sermon from an elder until after I was baptized a member of the church. At this time Widow Pickett and her two grown daughters lived with William Walker, at Farmington, Utah. She lent me the "Voice of Warning."

[written in margin]
July 2nd, 1850

I well remember the day I entered S. L. City. The east "bench" or sloping foothills was covered with a dense growth of sunflowers about four feet high and indian women went through, beating the ripe seeds into their baskets for food.

39 *Sepulture* is the act of placing for burial.

40 Hezekiah Peck was a Logan associate (Donald G. Godfrey and Kenneth W. Godfrey, *The Diaries of Charles Ora Card: The Utah Years, 1871–1886* [Provo, UT: Religious Studies Center, Brigham Young Univ., 2006], 144, 362).

As we passed along Emigration street, I saw a city lot a little way ahead which was enclosed with a fence made of raw hide strips stretched from post to post. The cow herd was just ahead of us, and an old bull who saw the fence seemed to take offense at it. He walked deliberately to it and with his horns tore it all down and then walked on. In all the city I saw not a sign upon any building to indicate a trade or business. There was not a store or shop of any kind on what is now the main business street—East Temple St.—The street was fenced on each side with a pole fence of two or three poles high, and on each block stood a little house of one story, built generally of adobe, with a dirt roof; not a tree planted, and all new and crude. The "Council House" was but a few feet high, and against its walls I sat leaning when William Walker came along and hired me to work for him at Farmington.

[page 100]

February 24, 1897—At this time (just before harvest) wheat was worth $10.^{00} [$234] a bushel in gold, but after harvest the price fell to $3.00 [$70] at which price it remained several years. Being a printer by trade, my first thought was to enter the Deseret News Office which had just started to publish that paper, but as a harvest hand could earn a bushel of wheat a day—$10.^{00}—I thought best not to go into the office at the wages offered, and so I did not. How small are the things which turn the whole current of our lives! Had I went to printing, I would have had an entirely different life from that I have led, and would probably have been dead long ere this, as printers are short lived, owing to the composition of the type metal.

After I went to live with Walker I worked 6 weeks cutting wheat with a sickle,—my first experience— Also made ditch fence and dug and stoned up a well thirty feet deep. Mary Walker, his second wife, taught me to tell fortunes with cards, and I became noted far and near. All the girls round about came to me with their love troubles, seeming to have implicit confidence in me, though I never tried to pry into their affairs, and never betrayed any of their secrets. I knew pretty well who they kept company with, and as I told their fortunes watched their eyes. I could tell if I was anywhere near the truth by looking at them. I had much enjoyment for a while until I tired of it and told them I could not really know or tell anything by cards. They said they knew better; I had told so and so, and it had all come true, &c. &c. And so I had, but not by the cards.

[written in margin]
1851
While Rice and I were waiting at Peteetneet (now Payson) I determined to remain there, and went and selected a farm. There were about seven families just starting a settlement there, who had commenced two or three log houses. I told them I was going to settle there.

[page 101]

They said all right; I could have all the land I wanted, but no water for irrigation—the seven families claimed it all. And it was small in quantity. The whole stream when taken out ran in a single plow furrow. Now the who [whole] country round about is a meadow, farm, garden or orchard, with water enough for all. And this brings to mind a prophecy I heard Pres[t] H. C. Kimball make on May 12th 1851 at Parowan. He said as the needs of the people for water increased so should the waters increase; and said "write it down." I wrote it at the time, and have seen it fulfilled from that day to this. I have seen a little spring so small that I could only get a drink by taking a spoonful at a time until I got a cup full; and some years later I found at that same place five families living, with farms, gardens and orchards—so had the waters of that spring increased. At my first visit I was in company with Geo. A. Smith and Amasa Lyman, Apostles, and other brethren and sisters, on our way to Washington, in southern Utah.

I here relate an incident that occurred in the first settlement of Iron County. Sep. 1851 [date written in shaky hand]

In the summer of 1852 word came to Parowan that indians had stolen cattle from Fort Johnson the previous night and help was asked to recover them, as that settlement was too weak retake them and at the same time leave men enough to protect the families. Accordingly about a dozen men went to their assistance from Parowan, the writer among the number. The party left Fort Johnson some 15 or 16 in number, found the trail of the indians and the stolen ox and followed as fast as possible, our progress retarded at times where the indians, taking advantage of hard ground, concealed their trail as is their custom, causing much loss of time in recovering it. It would be a waste of time to try to follow a thieving band or a war party except as guided by their trail, as they use every stratagem to elude their pursuers.

To recover the trail when lost we scattered a little distance apart so as to scan every inch between, watching for signs which would be without significance to an unpracticed eye—a twig freshly broken—a spear of grass broken or bent aside, or a pebble lately displaced.

[page 102]

[written in margin]

1851

Sometimes the ground was so hard for a considerable distance that even an ox track was only very faintly discernible; and the course of the thieves was surmised by supposing the course <u>we</u> would take if we were ourselves the guilty party.

After many miles we found that the ox, driven most of the time on the run had tired, and his captors to hasten his movements had shot him repeatedly with their small arrows but not so as to seriously wound him, and occasionally we found them on the way as they had dropped out of his skin.

At length we saw some ravens circling high above a small rocky hill and were satisfied the beast had been killed there or that his flesh had been there hidden. Hastening to the spot we found we were right, and after a search discovered the meat cut up and hidden in a cavity and so neatly covered by rocks that had we not been told by the ravens we would never have suspected such a thing, or thought of looking there for any thing.

As the Indians had here scattered we divided into two parties, one to scout the country north of the Iron Mountain and the other south of it. Each man took a big piece of the meat and tied it to his saddle for supper as we had no other food with us, and then away to find the indians. Our party scouted on the south of Iron Mountain and at night camped at the Iron Springs—the scene of many a bloody deed of the natives—and next day returned to Fort Johnson. Here we found the remainder of our party, who had had a more exciting experience.

They had suddenly come upon two indians and a boy of about 7 or 8 years hidden in a bunch of willows, had captured them and had taken away their bows and arrows and butcher knives, and then started for Fort Johnson driving the two men before them and one of the horsemen carrying the boy behind him.

[page 103]

Coming to a small stream with banks four or five feet perpendicular, with soft miry bottom, consequently impassible for horses, the indians saw their chance, cleared the stream and fled like frightened deer. By the time our boys had found a crossing the indians were far away. A hard chase brought their pursuers within gun shot and brisk fire was opened upon them, but apparently with out effect, although all were excellent marksmen. As soon as a gun was pointed the indians sprung sideways right and left, so no one could take sure aim with their rifles—their only arms—and many times as soon as a man had fired at an indian, the latter would rush up to him and try to pull him from his horse, and a man had all he could do to get away and load again, and by this time the indian would be far in advance.

At length Samuel Hamilton determined to overtake and seize by main force the one he was after, but the latter seizing Sam by the leg nearly pulled him from his horse before Hamilton fired a shot that stretched the indian on the ground.[41] During the melee the other indian escaped wounded, and the party brought the boy to the Fort where he was adopted in the family of Joel H. Johnson, after whom the place was named—a veteran of Kirtland days. The boy was renamed Sam, was kindly treated, and grew up to manhood.

Kanarra the chief said it was all right; he had often told the man not to steal or he would get killed, and it was all right. But there was a sequel to all this.

Five years later, as the tribe sat about their camp fire one night the brother of the slain indian said the spirit of his brother was crying for revenge,—some white person must be killed to pay the debt.

41 Samuel L. Hamilton was a southern Utah associate. A member of the Utah Territorial Militia, Company F. Cedar City, Fifth Platoon (Morris A. Shirts and Kathryn H. Shirts, *A Trial Furnace: Southern Utah's Iron Mission* [Provo, UT: Brigham Young University Press, 2001], 496).

[page 104][42]

[written in margin in shaky hand]

1851

According to indian ideas this was perfectly correct, and they were about to go to Parowan that night to kill some one; but Kanarra said "No, if we go tonight we may kill some one the Mormons love very much, and they will be very mad. I will go in the morning and find out if there is any one they don't like much. We will kill him, and then the people wont be mad or make war." This was approved. Next morning Kanarra came to President Wm H. Dame and asked if there was any one in Parowan whom he did not love much. The question seemed suspicious to Pres^t Dame and he said, "No, I love them all." "But," said Kanarra, "isn't there some one you love only me-a-poots"—a very little, measuring about half an inch on his finger. "No," said Pres^t Dame, "I love them all–shaunt!–shaunt!"—very much. At last he found the cause of Kanarra's visit as explained above, and had to labor for hours before he prevailed on the chief to forego his purposed revenge; and the chief in his turn had a hard task to convert his men to sustain his agreement with Pres^t Dame. He was only able to do this by showing that the settlers were aware of their purpose, and there would be war; and then they could no longer beg bread nor procure guns and ammunition. And so this danger was averted through the blessing of the Lord.

42 Compare story versions with Martineau Journal, original pages 88–89.

PART

9

RESUMING THE DIARY AND GOING HOME

I NOW RESUME MY DIARY.

February 19, 1897—Wrote to my children in Utah for help to return home.

MARCH

March 2, 1897—Lyman sent me $10.[00] [$234] Paid $8.[00] [$187] to store on a/c. having previously got means to pay my rent.

March 5, 1897—Theo. sent me $5.[00] [$117] from his scanty means. I had not asked him for help, knowing he needed it very much himself.

[page 105]

March 8, 1897—Bot pants, $2.50 [$58]—the first for a year.

March 12, 1897—Albert writes he is unable to send us any money. I know he would if he could. I have written three times to Pres[t] Christopher Layton who owes me nearly $300 [$7,008] dollars, to send me something, if only 40 or 50$ [$1,168], but he does not respond nor answer me. He is wealthy. God judge between us.

March 11, 1897—Wrote again to Joel, asking him to send me help at once, and we would come home.

March 13, 1897—My 69th birth day. Getting old. As a great treat I got a chicken for dinner, cost 75¢ [$18].

March 15, 1897—Susan had a dangerous attack of heart failure. I believe she would have died but for the blessing of God and administration. She seemed to see strange things, said she saw Turkey all devoured save the head and legs—typical of that country.

March 16, 1897—Susan has recovered. Rec[d] a letter from Geannie, who writes lovingly and promises help soon.

March 18, 1897—Sent article to Des. News,—Indian feast in Parowan.[1]

March 19, 1897—Letter from Charles and Virginia with $25.00 [$584], ten of which was from Virginia, $15 [$350] from Charley.

March 20, 1897—Letter from Jesse N. Says he can get no money now, will send some later.

1 J. H. Martineau, "Gave an Indian Dinner," *Deseret Evening News*, March 27, 1897; "In Early Utah," March 6, 1897; Journal History; see also "An Indian Dinner," April 3, 1897; Utah Digital Newspapers.

March 21, 1897—Last night Mr. von Wendt had a dream, of climbing up a very high, steep and difficult hill, we following with him. I felt this was a dream from the Lord for his and our comfort, as we all finally reached the top. We are truly in a very difficult way now, and have no hope except in the help of the Lord, which I believe he will give us. This is the testimony to me.

March 22, 1897—To day our married granddaughter Wilmirth died after an illness of about 5 months. She died at 11 a.m.

March 24, 1897—visited Several of my creditors, to whom I owe sums for the paper, ice, milk, rent, &c, and told them I was unable to pay them now, but would as soon as I could. They were very good and told me not to worry, for they knew I would pay when I could.

[page 106]

March 24, 1897—I know that God softened their hearts, and to him be all the praise.

March 29, 1897—Wrote to a famous surgeon in New York City, Dr. W. T. Bull, No. 35 West 36th St. (residence) or No. 33 East 33d St. (hospital) detailing particulars of Gertrude's lameness, and asking if he thinks he can cure her.

March 31, 1897—I owe store at this date $123.55 [$2,886]. I wish I could pay.

APRIL.

April 3, 1897—Recd a letter from Elvira, giving particulars of Wilmirth's last illness and death, which I here record;—(Extracts)

Nephi April 1, 1897

"Sam left for California on March 30th Baby was quite sick, but is all right now. He is cutting teeth, so I expect a hard time all alone, but we are all in the hands of the Lord. x x On March 14th Wilmirth was feeling better and wanted to go for a ride. x x We made a bed in our carriage for her and she was so happy she cried for joy. Father B. F. Johnson came at one o'clock and gave her a patriarchal blessing. She slept then for hours but seemed very weak. Monday she did not eat anything, but drank a little rice water and an egg beat up in milk, and that was all nourishment she ever took afterwards. Tuesday (16) she asked me to put her in her chair. She wanted to fix things in her chest so she could find them when she would want them. She took every thing out, folded them and put them all back. She said "I will give this to Gertie when she gets big," and so on, presents to all the children. The 19th was Jodie's birth day. She was much weaker than the day before. Her stomach hurt her so bad she cried "Oh ma! can't you do something for me! My stomach is on fire! I am almost wild! I anointed her and asked the Lord to take away that awful pain, that she might not suffer any more with it.

[page 107]

WILMIRTH'S LAST MOMENTS

April 3, 1897—It left her at once and she was quite easy for an hour. At one o'clock she asked for water. I raised her up and she sank away as if dead. Celia and Mabel were with me. They began rubbing her, but her heart did not move. I said "I think she will never breathe again." Just then she came to, and said "Oh ma! I want Martin Allred." I knew she wanted him to administer to her. He came and administered to her, and in the mean time Ben had gone for Pa and Alanson. When they came she was much better, but from that time had a deathly expression and could not talk only by the greatest effort, but gradually declined. She knew the end was near, but had faith to the last. She called the children to her and kissed them. She called Jodie. He came with little Gurnie in his arms. She said "Oh I love you so!" and kissed them both, and said "Ma has such good boys." She hugged Alanson and told him she loved him and he must be good. Then he went out and did not see her alive again. I had her head on my arm, Pa was kneeling beside her. She said "Oh you blessed, good pa!" She then seemed in much pain, but could not tell us anything. She opened her eyes and saw me and said "Oh Ma!" and breathed a few times, and her spirit passed away (Mch 22) I said "Oh I thank Thee, Heavenly Father, for this release."

Not long before she and Alanson were sealed by one of the Apostles (Young or Grant) which made her very happy. She had been married a little over two years. She was always a good girl, and a great comfort to her parents and brothers and sisters. All is well with her, and her exaltation is sure.

When I first heard of her sickness I asked concerning her, and the answer came "She will pass away. She has remained her appointed time and shall suffer no loss, but shall receive an exaltation in the celestial glory." And I had the same testimony several times afterward.

[page 108]

April 3, 1897—Sent article to Des. News, on taking of Sam in 1851 &c.[2]

April 7, 1897—John Angus Johnson came, canvassing for a cabinet.

April 8, 1897—Received a letter from Henry, saying he will soon come to Deming for us. We were very thankful, and began packing.

April 12, 1897—Received R. R. tickets from Henry, who is in Deming.

April 13, 1897—Started this morning at 1 o'clock P.M. Von W. and Angus saw us off on train. We were very ill provided with clothes &c, as we had only $5.00 [$117] for all expenses, but were very glad to be able to go at all. I left in debt about $335.00 [$7,825] but arranged with my creditors to pay when I could. I made a not [note] for Ivancovich, our grocer, for $125.55 [$2,933] and one to Drachman, for rent, about $25.00 [$584]

Reached Deming at 9:30 A.M. and was glad to meet Henry after so long an absence. We left Deming at 3.30 P.M, our goods in a lumber wagon and Susan, Dora Gertrude and I in a covered carriage. Drove 10 miles and camped.

April 14, 1897—Camped just across the line in Mexico. I felt happy to be in Mexico again.

April 15, 1897—Reached Palomas at 8 A.M. and were detained 3 hours while our trunks and boxes were inspected. We paid $3.48 [$81] duty on our sewing machine and clothes wringer, and camped in the hills. A heavy wind came up, and a great storm threatened, which was bad, as we had no tent, and would have to lie on the ground, wet or dry. But the Lord overruled, and the storm passed one side. The elevation at Palomas is about 4000 feet.

April 16, 1897—About noon came to the Boca Grande of the Casas Grande river, and about 5 P.M. came to the guard station at the Espia, where we were again inspected.

April 17, 1897—Arrived at Diaz about 10 A.M. and stopped with our niece Anna [blank space]. Elevation of Diaz 4380 ft.

April 18, 1897—Being unable to get feed for our horses we had to go on. Drove 12 miles and camped near Ascension Lake.

April 19, 1897—Passed through Corallitos, a mining town, and camped near Barrancos, a deserted mining town.

[page 109]

April 20, 1897—At noon came to Dublan, and took dinner with Sister Dora Pratt, wife of Heleman Pratt, and at sunset came to our home in Colonia Juarez. Very glad and thankful to be at home after so long an absence,—over four years. The village, of 700 inhabitants, seemed beautiful with its forest of fruit trees and tasteful brick buildings. Our home is small, and, in fact, a hovel, but it is home, and I thank our Father who has finally brought us home again, when it seemed so difficult to attain, and could not, had it not been for our dear children—especially Henry A—in Juarez. Elevation of Dublan, by 2 observations, is 5230 feet.

Tuesday— Colonia Juarez again.

We found Joel and family living in our house, and all our family in Mexico well and prospering

April 21, 1897—I began pruning fruit trees and fixing up things.

April 23, 1897—Joel and family moved into another house, ours being too small for so many of us. I took an observation with Solar transit, and find the Latitude 30° 15' 30", var. of needle 11° 8' E.

April 25, 1897—Sunday. Was called upon to speak to day. From this time I continued at work in my orchard and garden until

MAY 1ST 1897

May 1, 1897—Plowed part of my lot (Joel did) having watered it. Up to this time we could not procure any meat or butter, but got some milk at times from Joel or Anna (Annita.)

2 An article on pursuing the natives appeared close to this date (J. H. Martineau, "Trailing Indian Thieves," *Deseret Evening News*, April 17, 1897; Journal History).

May 3, 1897—Bought a ham of fresh pork, for $2.50 [$58] on credit. Planted seeds.

May 4, 1897—Watered city lots to day, and got some beef.[3]

May 5, 1897—Attended the celebration of Cinco de Mayo (5th of May)—a national anniversary of the defeat of the French by Mexicans during Maximillian's attempt to rule Mexico. The girls joined in as a may day celebration. I met Elder Locander, who told me of seeing, between Antioch and Laodicea, on the site of an ancient intrenched Roman Camp, an ancient monument of marble erected by a Roman Officer to the memory of his beloved daughter—Lucilla Martinus—our ancestor. The monument was like this. Br Locander says, and of a date about the year A.D. ninety. I shall be glad to do a work for her in the temple of the Lord.

Fig. 9.1—Lucilla Martinus monument.

[page 110]

May 5, 1897—To day attended the celebration of the Fifth of May, a great Mexican holiday in honor of a victory of Mexico over Marshal Bazaimes French Army, in Maximilian's time.

May 18, 1897—Dr. W. T. Bull, of N. Y. City, 35 West 35th Street gives little encouragement in regard to Gertrude's lameness, but refers me to good surgeons nearer than N. Y. City, viz: Prof. J. D. Griffiths, Kansas City, Mo

Charles A. Powers Denver, Col. and Prof. N. Senn, Chicago, Ill. as being reliable.

May 20, 1897—By invitation I started to Colonia Diaz, 70 miles dist. to attend conference, with Pat.h W. R. R. Stowell, Sister Eyring and Miss ~~Burrows~~ Burrull. Went 40 m. and camped.

May 21, 1897—Arrived at Diaz at evening. Attended a conjoint of the young men and young women.

May 22, 1897—Regular Quary Conference met, continuing next day (Sunday) 23d and finished Mon. 24th

[written in margin]

Anna's boy born.

May 23, 1897—This morning at 5.45 Anna Walser gave birth to a fine boy, weighing 9 lbs. She was much blessed in her time of trial, having previously been anointed and blessed for this event by Sister Fife and my dear wife. I had prayed regarding her, and received testimony she would be greatly blessed in her confinement, and that her child would be a boy, one of the noble spirits held in reserve to do a great work for Zion.

May 26, 1897—Returned home and found all well. I was much benefited in my health by the trip, as I was almost too unwell to be about my work before I went.

May 27, 1897—Patriarch Henry Lunt and his wife Ellen, friends of 46 years, came to see us. He blessed us after dinner saying we should not from this time forth want for food or comforts of life, for our way shall be wonderfully opened and I shall build my house and have plenty within it

I gave him a cane, and in return he gave me his whittled stick, saying that as long as I keep it I shall be prospered in all things with the desire of my heart. I will keep it, trusting his words may prove true, as I believe they will.

[page 111]

~~June~~ 31 May 31, 1897—Wrote to Des. News an account of finding the dead body of Francis Schlatter, "the Healer," in the cañon about 12 miles above here. I saw his things, which were being taken to Casas Grandes. Among others was his famous copper healing

3 On this date Martineau wrote about the value of the Mexican dollar (J. H. Martineau, "No Loafers There," *Deseret Evening News*, May 14, 1897, 12; Journal History).

rod, 3 feet long, 2 to 2 ½ in thick, weighing 28 ½ lbs. Also sent my pension papers.[4]

JUNE.

[written in margin]
Death of von Wendt.

Wednesday, June 2, 1897—By newspaper learn of the death of my dear friend, Baron Alexander Wenden, or, as he styled himself, Alex. von Wendt. which occurred in St. Joseph's Hospital, Tucson, Arizona, on the afternoon of May 26th 1897. He had been sick about six weeks, being taken down soon after we left Tucson on April 13th For two weeks our cousin John Angus Johnson lived with him in his rooms and tenderly waited upon him, for which von W. was very thankful. von W. rallied from his first attack and wrote me he would soon go to his bonded silver-lead mine and commence shipping ore from it. Soon after this we received word from Dr. W. F. Smith that he was worse and had gone to the hospital, where he could be made perfectly comfortable. But he steadily grew worse, and soon we learned of his death, which came as a great shock to us all. as he seemed to possess a wonderfully strong constitution, and, excepting some lung trouble, seemed in perfect physical condition. He was just on the eve of great financial success. An eastern syndicate was about to commence working his placer mines, from which he expected an income of $500 or $600 [$11,680–$14,016] a day; and also expected a revenue from his silver mine of about $250 to 300$ [$5,840—$7,008] per day, in all which I would have had a fair share. But this was not to so be.

He was a descendant of one of the noblest families of Russia, his ancestral home being in the Baltic Provinces, a few miles from Stettin on the Duna or Divina river. He was a descendant of the Knights of Malta a branch of whom about a thousand years ago, had conquered the Wends, a nation of north eastern Germany Hence his family name—Wenden—or von Wendt.

[page 112]

June 2, 1897—He had been an officer in the Russian household "Guards," but came to america about 20 years ago and engaged in Mining in Colorado, where he gained and lost several fortunes. He came to Arizona for the benefit of his lungs, which were somewhat affected.

He was not a member of any church, but his religion consisted in doing all the good he could, and in making others happy. He thought that the Mormon religion was the nearest right of any, so far as he understood it. He was very jovial, social and genial, a polished, well educated gentleman and the soul of honor in his business dealings.—emphatically an honest hearted man.—one who will receive the gospel and its blessings in a time to come, when I can do a work for him in the Temple of the Lord.

I think proper to record his last letter to me:— as it shows his indomitable will and energy:—

Tucson Arizona May 2, 1897
P. O. Box 373

My dear Brother

Your letter of April the 21st at hand. but it was not in my power to answer as I have been for the last two weeks and more on my back with gastric fever and general debility, Oh my! I now know for the first time what sickness is! Oh my! I never want any more of it—never! never! I am just out of bed and am very weak. For nine long days nothing passed my lips but water and a little buttermilk. I have lost 14 lbs and I look just like a yellow wax figure but it seems Providence don't want me yet. I am gaining strength every hour, and expect in a few days to start for the P. W. mine to work.

I must tell you a curious thing. When I fell sick I had not a cent, but enough provisions, so that your cousin had plenty to eat.

[page 113]

1897—[letter continues] Well, I was sick, got sicker and sicker. Your cousin attended to me kindly; then he failed entirely with his enterprise. Poor fellow! He took it terrible to heart that he could not make a success of it and besides, he was very short in cash, and I had none. I was laying and thinking—thinking, my head as big as a barrel! burning, throbbing, aching, but I was thinking delirious impossibilities and wishing I

4 J. H. Martineau, "Schlatter's Death," *Deseret Evening News*, June 11, 1897, 9; Journal History.

had some lemons, some fruit,—something to quench my fearful thirst, when there comes a knock at a door and a telegram telling me he will send me shortly tomorrow the necessary money to see if we cannot make some money by shipping the ore from the P. W. mine. Imagine my relief! I borrowed from Dr. Smith a few Doll[s] and got medicine and fruit at once. Is not there a Providence? I will start out in a few days to see what I can do in the mountains. I need a little more strength. Your cousin stayed with me two weeks and left Tucson in disgust; he could do nothing here. Poor fellow! Well, he is a kind and good fellow and I think a great deal of him.

I finally have found out Underwood. He is doing everything for Underwood, and is an absolute selfish and designing man! I never was more mistaken in my life than in him. Some time I will tell you all.

I have seen all your creditors, and they all had a kind word for you, and behaved like gentlemen. They all said they were perfectly sure that you would pay them whenever you can. You know very well that as soon as I can scrape the money together that I will pay every sent you owe.

Write me as often as you can and tell me how Gertie is getting on.

[page 114]

June 2, 1897—[letter continues] I got a letter very short from your friend Dr. Bull I enclose the same; it seems he has written to you before this letter. You never told me about it. You must have forgotten it. He gives but little encouragement for poor Gertie,—it almost breaks my heart to think that there should be no help; but I don't believe it! She will yet get well and no mistake, Don't, please, show her this letter, or she may lose courage! Be careful! Give my love to the Duchess and ask her if she takes the exercise still? I cannot write more: I am played out. My love to all!

And I remain always yours,

Alex

The man Underwood referred to was his man of business. The "Duchess" is my dear wife, whom he always so addressed, calling Gertie "Princess."

I afterwards received a letter from his friend Dr. T. M. Smith, saying (date of May 14) that von W. had been very sick for 3 weeks, but was in the St Joseph's hospital, in good care, and was in hopes he would recover.

Saturday, June 5, 1897—Wrote a biographical sketch of Solomon Chamberlain, one of the earliest numbers of the Church, at the request of his daughter, Mrs Sariah L. Redd and sent it to the Deseret news.[5]

June 5, 1897—Gertrude received the following letter from Dr. T. M. Smith, relative to the last illness of her dear friend Alex. von Wendt, which I insert:—

Tucson, Arizona May 27th 1897

Miss Gertrude Martineau

Dear Miss;

It is with feelings of great sorrow that I inform you of the death of a good friend, namely, the Baron. He passed away on the evening of the 25th at 5.35.

[page 115]

June 5, 1897—[letter continues] Poor fellow had a hard struggle, and the trip over the mountain was more than he could stand. I insisted on waiting until he was stronger, but he had made up his mind to go, and it was foolish to be complaining all the time, and that he would go if he died on the way. You know when he made up his mind to do anything he generally carried it out. The next day after getting to camp he wanted to go to Reitz' camp, a distance of 4 miles, and I told him he was not able to stand the trip, and asked if he would put it off, as it might prove a very expensive trip, and he was not accustomed to riding horseback or to the rays of the sun. But he would go, and before we got through looking at the property, he became prostrated and would have fallen had I not been with him. After resting for a time he managed to get back to camp, and that evening was a very sick man. His fingers to the knuckles were very cold, and he became frightened and thought he was going to die, and wished he were in Tucson. Fortunately I went prepared to administer to his wants, and in a little while he was free from pain and spent rather a good night; and early next morning we left for Tucson. When he came home I wanted him to go where he could have good nursing and plenty of fresh air, which would be very necessary for him to have to ever recover. But he seemed to think differently, so I waited on him day and night, and I had the

5 James H. Martineau, "Colonia Juarez, Chihuahua," *Deseret News*, June 15, 1897; Journal History.

doctors go see him, and they diagnosed his disease as I had and said that they knew of nothing better to give him than what I had prescribed, but as I am not practicing I ~~am~~ was only consulting physician. But I will state that I do not believe any Dr. could have saved his life, for in the early stages of his disease he would not take any medicines, and his temperature used to go to 105°, and while it got down to normal, and he might have gotten through all right, had not his case become complicated.

[page 116]

June 5, 1897—He had typhoid-pneumonial fever in its worst form. Mr. Johnson was so kind to him, and he insisted on the Baron doing something, but he would not take what he needed. He wanted for nothing, and I seen that he was well cared for while sick, and when he died I seen that he was given a respectable burial. And it is my earnest prayer that he has gone to a happier world than this. He was conscious up to a short time before he died, and he was brave to the last and did not fear death. One of the sisters asked him if he would like to see any of his spiritual friends. He said no, his religion was the "Golden Rule." I have not been well for a some time nor do I feel like writing now, so please excuse all imperfections. I herewith enclose your letter addressed to the Baron which was received this morning. With best wishes I remain most respectfully Dr. T. M. Smith. (Hurriedly.)

This letter gave Gertie much comfort, as she had feared he might have wanted for proper care, needs and burial

June 6, 1897—Today Patriarch Wm R. R. Stowell gave Gertie the following blessing, I being scribe:—(omitted by accident)

June 16, 1897—We were weighed on the mill scales to day: I weigh 163 lbs Susan 215 lbs and Gertie 121 lbs I have lost 10 lbs Susan 11 lbs and Gertie 5 lbs. I guess it is on account of our poor fare—mostly bread and milk with occasional meat. We got our cow home two days ago. Her milk is a great help to us. On the 15th we bought a tub and other things. Also flour 50 #

June 17, 1897—Attended the funeral of Geo. Hawes' child & Spoke.

June 19, 1897—Henry, Sadi and Bertha went home. Brother Sixtus E. Johnson also went home to Chuichupe.

[page 117]

June 19, 1897—Gertie to day received a very kind, sympathetic letter from Dr. T. M. Smith, giving full particulars of the last illness and death of von Wendt. I pray God to bless him forever.

CEMENT

I insert 2 recipes which I think valuable;—

To make a good cement;—8 parts furnace ashes, slag or coke, 4 of slacked lime and 1 of clay: mix dry, then moisten with water, varied proportions for aerial or hydraulic cement.

MUSHROOM BED.

A box 3 ft sq and 20 ins deep. In the bottom place a compost four ins. deep composed of 3 parts cow-dung & 1 pt. soil, Then a layer 2 ins deep of compost & broken spawn brick; upon this 8 ins. of compost, pat gently and water well. Mushrooms will appear in 2 weeks and furnish regular supply for 2 years, with one brick of spawn. Must be kept in the shade.

JULY

July 2, 1897—Up to this time I have been very busy, working in my garden, trimming the fruit and other trees; and putting things in good order.

To day the Stake Presidency, (A. W. Ivins, H. Eyring and H. Pratt) engaged me to finish the surveys of the Juarez Colony purchase; I am to have ten dollars a day, half in cash and store pay and half in other good pay. This is only half the rate I ought to have, to be in proportion to the labor and pay given others, but I am thankful indeed for this, having earned nothing to speak of in the last year or two.[6]

July 3, 1897—To day, a Mr. Mundy, of El Paso and Mexico City came for me to go over the mountains and survey some land for him in Sonora. Prest Ivins kindly permitted me to do so, and I left home at 5 P.M, going 16 miles to Dublan where I found Mr.

6 Anthony W. Ivins was the first president of the Juárez Stake; Henry Eyring and Helaman Pratt were his counselors (Thomas Cottam Romney, *The Mormon Colonies in Mexico* [Salt Lake City: Univ. of Utah Press, 2005], 130–39).

Mundy ready to start out. As soon as we had supper, about 10 P.M. we left Dublan with a team and wagon of Emanuel Cardon's.[7]

[page 118]

July 3, 1897—After crossing the Casas Grandes river we lost our way and wandered about until near midnight, and then camped.

July 4, 1897—Arose and started at 4.30; found the road, reached Ramus at 10 a.m. and breakfasted; then proceeded to Casa de Janos, arriving there about 11 P.M. The night was dark and rainy, and we had quite a time crossing the San Pedro. Finally camped in the mud about midnight, wet & hungry.

July 5, 1897—Started at 4 A.M. passing Ojetos at 3 P.M. Rain. Camped on the bare wet and muddy ground at 7 P.M.

July 6, 1897—Arrived at Carretas at 10 A.M. and remained the rest of the day. Mr. Boyd, the owner of the estate was very kind.

July 7, 1897—As this is the end of the wagon road we (Mr. Mundy, his son and myself) proceed over the crest of the Sierra Madres on horseback, my transit & bedding on a pack mule. Our trail was a very bad one; up and down steeps, winding along Steep rocky mountains sides where a misstep of a horse might send him and his rider tumbling down the jagged rocks. Two or three times I thought best to dismount and go afoot. We reached Bavispe about 2 P.M. This place is still much in ruins caused by an earthquake some years ago, in which 46 persons were killed and many wounded by falling walls and buildings. We finally reached Galerita, our stopping place, about night

July 8, 1897—Surveyed the farm partially

July 9, 1897—Finished the survey of about 170 acres, and at 1 P.M. Started back to Carritas. Going up the cañon Mr. Mundy & I took the wrong trail, but found a Mexican who said he would show us a trail to Carritos. He took us to a disused trail and left us. The trail soon became very bad, and was very difficult to follow, leading us among rock which were almost impassible for our horses, and finally over a high rocky, steep crest of the mountain. Here a thunder storm overtook us, and night came on, dark as Egypt. We lost our way, wandering about until 9 P.M. when we finally got to Carritos.

[page 119]

July 9, 1897—I think Mundy was much frightened, because Indians had not long before killed a mule near the ranch, and many mountain lions abounded. I was not afraid, because of the promises made me from above.

July 10, 1897—Worked up my field notes for Mr. Mundy. Heavy rain. Received my pay $100.[00] [$2,336] Rained hard next day.

July 13, 1897—Started home on horseback, with a Mexican packer, my things on a pack mule. Rode to Ojetos, 24 miles.

July 14, 1897—Went to Ramus, 35 m.

July 15, 1897—To Dublan. Got conveyance home, arriving 7 P.M. very much worn with my tedious journey, but happy with $100.[00] [$2,336]

July 16, 1897—Paid $11.[00] cash tithing. Heavy rain.

July 24, 1897—The 24th July—celebrated in good style. Houses broken into.

July 27, 1897—Began my survey of Colonia Juarez, also next 3 days = 4

AUGUST.

August 1, 1897—Received word from Stockslager & Heard, Washington D.C. that they had collected my claim of $72.52 [$1,694] against U. S. for land surveys, their fees being $20.[00] [$467] of it.

Another proof of the goodness of our Father. This account had been allowed in full by the Genal Land Office, & disallowed by the Auditor of the Treasury Dept,[n] as being just, but that it could not be paid me because the books for 1896 had been closed. I felt sad, for the amount, tho' small, was much to me in my straightened circumstances. I asked concerning it, and was told I should receive it. And yet it seemed to be impossible, because the Treasury Dep[t] utterly refused to pay. After putting it in the hands of Attorneys in Washington and waiting almost a year, I find the

7 The Cardons were influential in Logan and in the Mexican colonies. Emanuel Philip Cardon was the son of Joseph S. Cardon (Norma Baldwin Ricketts, *Arizona's Honeymoon Trail and Mormon Wagon Roads* [Mesa, AZ: Cox, 2001], 62).

word of the Spirit true & faithful. And so my faith is strengthened.

August 2 & 3, 1897—Surveyed in very rough mountains, Exhausted and wet through with rain on the 3d. Too tired for supper.

August 5, 1897—Leveled 1300 feet of Canal for Prest Ivins.

August 6, 1897—Surveyed West from Muscal Cor. through rough mountains for about 3 miles. I shouted to the chainmen in front a distance of two miles, and they heard plainly and obeyed my directions as to locating a monument of stones on the line. Very tired at night.

[page 120]

August 7, 1897—Surveyed part of the boundaries of Macdonald's, Davis and Eyring's pastures, in very high, rough mountains, and was very tired at night.[8] Much of the time it was almost impossible for me to get along the steep, rocky slopes with my instrument without falling.[9]

August 12, 1897—Surveyed ½ day in the field and spent the rest of the day platting. Heavy rain.

August 13, 1897—One day draughting and calculating areas. Much rain.

August 31, 1897—Up to this time have spent some time on my map and in Surveying. In the latter part of the month Albert telegraphed me from the Mexican Custom house at Las Palomas, that he was there and could not cross the line into Mexico. Joel started to help him in, but found on arrival at Palomas that Albert and family had returned home, much to our and his disappointment.

[written in margin]
I go to El Paso, and got von. W. Trunk
Theo. came home.

I omitted to say that on Aug. 16th I started to El Paso, and on arriving at Dublan met Theodore, just returning home from his three years in the Agricultural College, Utah.

8 This is likely Alexander F. MacDonald, who pioneered the land purchase with Mexico for the colonies. Joseph C. Davis was on the high council in the Juárez Stake (Romney, *The Mormon Colonies*, 85, 139).

9 A letter appears on this date describing old-fashioned parties (J. H. Martineau, "An Old Time Dancing Party," *Deseret News*, August 7, 1897; Utah Digital Newspapers).

At El Paso I got Baron von Wendt's trunk, which had been sent me by Dr. T. M. Smith of Tucson. It contained his two canes, jewelry and many little trinkets he used to have on his table. I ask God to bless Dr. Smith for his kindness in the matter. I returned home on the 21st in time for our Quar. Conference. It was on the 22nd we got the telegram from Albert, who wished to visit us with his family, and on the 23d that Joel started to go and bring him in.

Henry and Melissa and family also made us a visit in the latter part of August, returning home Sept. 2nd

SEPTEMBER 1897.

September 1, 1897—Theodore went away with Guy Taylor to help him buy cattle, to be gone ten or fifteen days. They went South.

September 11, 1897—Up to this time I have surveyed some and worked on my map some, but at noon I had to give up, being taken violently ill with diarrhea.

September 17, 1897—Have got worse all the time, having very copious watery stools 12 to 15 times a day, which nothing seems to check, and my flesh seems all turning to water and is all running away.

[page 121]

September 17, 1897—I am aware I am in a precarious position, for at my age such a condition is very dangerous. I am not afraid of death, for as I look back upon my life since I received the gospel 50 years ago I find causes of comfort, in this, That I have always held my private interests secondary to duty to the Church; I have never at any time been in opposition to the Holy priesthood, either in word, deed or influence; I have always labored with my might to help build up Zion; and have done all I could for our dead, having done a work, more or less complete for about 2000 souls, and what is still better, have received a testimony that our temple work for them has all been received joyfully. So I know I shall meet many friends in the next estate.

But I do not like to leave my family, especially in such poor circumstances, living as we do, in a mere hovel, and with no permanent means of support. And I hate the thought of being buried in such a horrible place as our burial ground is—nothing but a mass of stones and gravel. I would rather choose a soft loamy soil, near some murmuring mountain stream, and where at times the sweet whispering breath of the pines might float above me. But after all, it does not matter. The will of the Father is always best, and I truly say in my heart—"Not my will, Father, but thine be done."

September 27, 1897—Still very sick and weak—my case still doubtful.

September 28, 1897—It seems impossible to keep warm, especially my feet and legs up to my knees, even with hot irons in bed. This afternoon, after I prayed, asking the Father to make known to me if I had committed a sin sufficient to cause me to forfeit my promised blessings, or if I am still entitled to them, I received a very comforting answer:—that although not clear from sin I have not forfeited my blessings. I prayed again that I might be healed. Immediately I felt a warm sensation flow down from my body through my legs to my feet, which at once became warm again, and filled with the spirit of life. It was something which I cannot describe. I felt it was an answer to my prayer—a testimony my work is not completed, and that I shall live. From this time began gradually to improve, but very slowly, as I have had no appetite from the beginning.

To day 6 young men started on missions, among them our dear friend L. Guy Taylor, who has been very kind to us.

[page 122]

September 28, 1897—Able to sit up a little, and wrote letters of introduction for Guy to Lyman and Jesse N.

September 29, 1897—Better this morning, and with an appetite—the first for weeks. Henry Walser and Anita went to Guy's house to stay until his wife, Minnie, comes home from S. L. City.

September 30, 1897—Received a telegram from Lyman, who wants to know if I am better, or shall he come to me. Guy T. said he would answer from El Paso.

OCTOBER 1897

October 1, 1897—Measured one of our apples: = 12 1/8 ins one way and 12 3/4ins the other way. Have had some larger than this; all excellent in flavor.

October 2, 1897—Knowing I have narrowly escaped death, I feel it important to here record certain things pertaining to our genealogy, which would be liable to be lost should I suddenly pass away. I felt best to write to Lyman in relation to it, and here record the letter I sent:—

October 3, 1897—

Colonia Juarez, Mex. Oct. 3. 1897

My dear Lyman

My recent sickness, from which I had slight expectation of recovery for some days, caused me to remember some things which I wish my children to know, and which, had I passed away, would have been lost to them. Among these are certain things pertaining to our family genealogy, and which are of much importance in our work for our dead; and which. if I myself cannot attend to it, owing to my distance from a temple, may eventually be of use to my descendants. But I hope I may yet be able to do much in the temple myself.

I have spent a great deal of research to trace back our lineage as far as possible, and have ascertained many facts which will greatly aid in our work for the dead.

The British Encyclopedia shows that first we came of ancient Roman stock, in the days of the Roman Empire, saying that the Latin name of Martineau was <u>Martinus</u>. Also, that <u>Martinus</u>, translated into English, French and German is <u>Martin</u>; in Italian and Spanish, <u>Martino</u>; in Portuguese <u>Martinho</u>, (pronounced Martinyo) You wonder then why in French it is now <u>Martineau</u> instead of <u>Martin</u> or <u>Martino</u>. I will explain. During the Middle ages, and since, there was much communication and emigration between France and Italy; and Italians, removing to France had to change the spelling of their name, changing the final O in the name to <u>eau</u> in order to get the proper sound in French; just as I have to do here in Mexico, for here, <u>Martineau</u> does not give our name at all.

[page 123]

October 3, 1897—In Spanish each vowel makes a syllable, so that our name—<u>Martineau</u>—they would pronounced <u>Mar–tin-á-ah-oo</u>; but <u>Martino</u> gives them the correct name at once.

The Encyclopedia also says that Martino and Marino are identically the same, the t being sometimes omitted. So Martineau, Martinus, Martin, Martino, Marino, Martinho, are all of the same ancient stock. In Latin, where a masculine name ends in us or o, the corresponding feminine will end in a;—thus Augustus, Augusta; Julius, Julia; Octavius and Octavia; Claudio, Virgilio &c become Claudia, Virgilia in feminine, So in our family in Latin, Martinus, male, becomes Martina, female, of which there is an illustrious example in Saint Martina, who was burned alive in the year 235 A. D. aged 15 years, during one of the early persecutions against the Christians. She sympathised with an old man about to be burned, and had to so suffer herself or deny her religion. So she died. Bro. Locander of this place, while on mission in Syria, found near the ruins of an old Roman entrenched camp near Antioch, an old marble tomb erected by Martinus, the commander of the Roman army to the memory of his "dearly beloved daughter Lucilla" The date was about the time of the destruction of Jerusalem by Titus,—about A. D. 70.

For generations the family lived in Rome, Sienna and. Bologna, and as a rule were eminent as Churchmen, artists and physicians. Seven of the Roman Pontiffs were of the family, as follows:—

Pope Eutychiames, son of Pope Martinus, died Dec. 8 283 A. D.

St Martin, Pope, son of Fabricius, Italy, died Sept 16. 655 A. D.

Marinus 1st, Pope, of Montefiascone, Italy, died 24 Feb 884 A. D.

Marinus 2nd, Pope, of Montefiascone, Italy, died June 946 A. D.

[page 124]

October 3, 1897—

Martin 4th, Pope, died in Perugia, Italy, in A.D. 1285

Martin 5th, Pope, died in Perugia, Italy, in A.D. 1417

Besides these were many others very eminent in the Roman Church, as Marinus, Duke of Rome in A.D. 720; and Marinus, Papal Legate to Paris in A.D. 948. I have been baptized for all these Popes except Martin V. To obtain these records I searched the "Lives of the ~~Ropes~~ "Roman Pontiffs." and Rankes "History of the Popes" and other works.

The Duke of Veragua, who represented Columbus at the World's Fair in 1894, had Martineau blood, his ancestor, the grandson of Columbus having married a Martino of Spain whence he descended.

The Martino's of Italy who went to France adopted the French spelling, and thence to England and America. My father spelled his name Martino at first, when I was a boy. He was connected by his first marriage with some of the noblest blood of England, as the Earl of Chesterfield, Earl of Bedford, Earl of Mints, Lord Russell and Earl Stanhope. He married as his first wife the gr. daughter of Earl Stanhope, who willed to my father's wife £18000 and £1000 to each of her two Children by my father, Julia and Lucretia; but these bequests have long since reverted to the Crown of England.

On mother's side, her mother was a descendant of Lord Hutchinson, whose son, an officer in the English army, was killed in the Massacre at the Capture of Fort William Henry in 1757 by French and indians under Montcalm. My gr. mother was gr. niece of Ethan Allen of Ticonderoga fame, and was mixed with the blood of the Spragues. My mother's father, James Mears, was of English blood. He fought in the war of 1812; his father was a Commissary under Washington; in the revolution; and his father was captured in the French war of 1754–9 at the taking of Oswego by French troops under Gen. Montcalm. All our ancestors have been defenders of liberty of Conscience from the days of the Huguenots. My only brother laid down his life for the Union in 1863; and I, myself, volunteered for the whole war with Mexico, and since then have many times put my life in peril in the cause of the L. D. S.

[page 125]

October 3, 1897—Your grandfather Lyman R. Sherman was appointed an apostle, but died of exposure before he could be ordained. Presᵗ H. C. Kimball and Geo. A. Smith each told me he died as a Martyr, and would receive the glory of a Martyr. And of the Johnsons—Joseph Smith had four of the Johnson women—your gr. aunts sealed to him, your gr. mother being one: she was sealed to him for time only. She and Eliza Snow lived together as his wives, and your mother often sat on Joseph's lap. He made himself at home often in the house of my father-in-law, Joel H. Johnson, in Macedonia.

So far as what the world call "good blood," we stand with the best, but of course that is all nonsense; it is folly to try to bank upon what somebody else has done generations ago. The only truly "good blood" is that of the man or woman, who, consecrating his all to the service of his Father, remains true to the end, and who finally gains an exaltation to a crown which will never fall from his head, as all human crowns are sure, sooner or later, to do. We are <u>ancestors</u> ourselves, and if we remain true and faithful will attain to a far higher glory than any earthly ruler who ever lived. Keep these things that I have written always in view, that you may be able to add a link to the chain from time to time; and if you do not care to labor for the dead, your children or gr-children may, in time to come.

I am able to sit up and work a little and hope soon to be well again. Aunt S's ulcer is slowly healing, and Gertie and Dora and Theo. are as usual. Give my love to all and my blessing,

Your loving father James H. Martineau }
Santiago Enrique Martino }
Please excuse blunders.

Monday, October 4, 1897—Received a telegram from Lyman, saying he would be here to day, and at 10' o'clock P.M. he arrived. He came because of my illness, and brought medicines which he thought would be needful.

[page 126]

HENRY WALSER'S DEATH.

October 4, 1897—This is the first day I have been up nearly all of the day, and he was greatly pleased to see me so well. We were <u>very</u>, <u>very</u>, pleased to see him after four years and a half absence. Lyman has always been very good to us, and I pray God he may never want friends.

October 8, 1897—Lyman's visit is now ended, much to our regret, as he cannot be spared from his duties in Utah, especially in connexion with tithing business. He advised to build a good house at once, and offered aid to amount of \$100.00 [\$2,336] He gave me the plan of May Preston Moyle's new house as a guide. He gave Joel much good business advice, and says we have a nice place here. Says he can see great possibilities for us in Mexico, and that he will advise Jesse N. to come here from Chicago instead of to Logan. Br. Bentley showed him some of the country in his carriage and spent much time trying to get him a conveyance to the railroad at Dublan, but did not succeed until midnight.

Saturday, October 9, 1897—Lyman started home at 4:30 A.M. My bowels became very loose again, but I accepted Br. Jo^s C. Bentley's invitation to go with him to visit the mountain settlements.[10] We started at 8. A.M, traveled 12 miles to the mouth of San Diego cañon, then 4 miles up the mountain dug way to the top, thence up hill and down to Pacheco, in all 33 miles. All the road except the first 12 miles is through timber, and road very rough and bad. Stopped at Bishop Hardy's.

Sunday, October 10, 1897—Held two meetings to day. I spoke in both and had much liberty of the Spirit. Br. Bentley re-organized the Y. M. M. I. Association

Yesterday at 5 P.M. my son-in-law Henry S. Walser was terribly mangled by a circular saw in the Thatcher Steam Saw mill. His right leg was almost entirely severed near the hip and the flesh fearfully mangled. He then fell forward upon the saw which cut through six ribs and into his lung, making an awful wound. Word was sent home to his father, who at 9 P.M. started to see him followed by Anna and the two children, with others. They arrived about 1 A.M.

[page 127]

October 10, 1897—Henry was so weak he could hardly speak, and wished to be released from his sufferings: but after being administered to he rallied. Anna and children arrived a little later, to his great joy. He was placed upon a stretcher and willing hands carried him many miles over the rough roads—about 12 miles—and when at the bottom and on smooth roads he was placed in a carriage and taken to his own home. A messenger to Dublan telegraphed to Corralitos, 35 miles for a surgeon, and the R. R. company sent an engine to bring him to Dublan, and in a few hours he reached this place.

He amutated [amputated] the leg and dressed the wound in his side, using 26 stitches, being assisted by

10 Joseph C. Bentley was a bishop of the Juárez Ward and later president of the stake (Romney, *The Mormon Colonies*, 93, 98, 140, 155, 258).

Dr. Mrs. Saville, our local doctor who did all she could to give aid, and was very efficient.

October 12, 1897—Tues. This morning Henry suddenly passed away at 5 A.M. in full faith and fellowship with the saints. During his brief stay everybody did all in their power to aid, causing him to say "It is good to have plenty of friends." His funeral was very largely attended. Br. James of Dublan, paid for the run of the engine for Surgeon Stovall, and the young men paid the surgeon's bill of $100.00 [$2,336], also the coffin was made gratis by [left blank]

Henry was universally beloved; always cheerful, loving and tender as husband and father, very industrious and helpful, prominent in the Choir and Band, and in all good works. He and Anna have had five years of very happy married life and has now gone to his reward, for his exaltation is sure. Poor Anna has been very brave all through these trying scenes, and has borne up wonderfully well.

I NOW RETURN TO MY JOURNEY.

October 11, 1897—Monday. We went 8 miles to Garcia, and held meeting; also re-organized to Y.M.M.I.Association there. I here took a very severe cold and hoarseness, the altitude of Garcia being reported at 7100 feet, nearly 2000 feet higher than Colonia Juarez. My diarrhea also became much worse, making me quite uneasy.

October 12, 1897—Drove 35 miles over the continental divide to Chuichupe arriving about sunset. Found Bertha and Charlie sick with measels, and some of Sadie's children sick with the same

[page 128]

October 12, 1897—Henry was at home because of their sickness. Br. Bentley here re-organized the Y.M.M.I.Asso[n] but I visited with Henry's folks. This place has altitude of about 7000 feet, and at 12 miles, on the South west foot of the range you will see palms growing. Had to leave early next morning, being only a passenger.

October 13, 1897—Drove homeward as far as Garcia and held meeting, in which I spoke, with great liberty of the Spirit.

October 14, 1897—Thurs. Got home at Sunset. Two hours ago we heard for the first time of the terrible accident which has left Anna a widow and her children fatherless. Found all well as usual but much depressed in spirit. For myself, I feel that the trip has done me good, as the Spirit intimated to me before I left home, or I would not have started away.

Saturday, October 16, 1897—Surveyed all day, the first work for many days.

Sunday, October 17, 1897—Spoke in meeting to day.

October 22, 1897—To day Gertrude began clerking in the "Tienda de la Colonia,"—Seavy's store.

October 23, 1897—I surveyed again today, but was hardly able to do so, my diarrhea having returned, and having quite a fever.

October 24, 1897—Sunday. This morning, in answer to prayer, I enjoyed the manifestation of the Holy Spirit, much to my comfort. I received many good promises—renewals of those formally promised. Among other things I was told not to fear to ask guidance even for small matters, for God delights to bless his children who seek unto him. To not fear to lay on hands to bless my family and to rebuke disease and unholy spirits for God would seal my words in the heavens and ratify them. Also, He has called me to this land to assist in a great work, and I shall be prospered from this time forth and greatly blessed. Also many other great and glorious promises, which will all be sure unto me, unless I lose them by my own fault. I thank thee, oh Father, for thy goodness, and pray that I may so live as to have thy favor and blessing always

NOVEMBER

November 2, 1897—To day Anna moved to her own house, as she would be more comfortable there. Theodore boards with her, and will help about the chores, &c.

[page 129]

DEATH OF JESSIE HELEN RUSSELL ANDERSON GRIEVE MAR[R]

November 5, 1897—To day I learned for the first time of the death of my wife Jessie Helen R. A. Grieve, which occurred nearly a year ago, as I am now informed. I had never heard she was sick, as her mother would not allow any correspondence between us, and Jessie, a gentle girl, was much under her mother's influence. I do not know why her mother disliked me, and there was never a ill word between Jessie and me. It is said she died of consumption. I have great pleasure in the knowledge that I have been the means of great good to her. I caused her to receive her Endowments, and her 2nd A, which last is more than we can conceive. She is past all trials, and her exaltation is sure, as a Princess and one of the Queens of heaven. She did some temple work in Logan in 1887, and may have done more since then. While a young girl in Scotland, living a few miles from Edinburg, she spent much time in making a record of her ancestry from the Records in that city; and obtained over a thousand names, which I have recorded in my temple record, having been baptized for many hundreds of the males of her family. This last came about in a curious manner. Her mother wished me to do the temple work for the family, as neither her husband nor brothers would do it, and accordingly I was baptized for several hundred—nearly a thousand—of her male names. After this, a written authorization from the head of the family was required, for filing in the temple record, and Mrs. Greaves was afraid to tell her husband or brothers that I had already done the work, without their orders, and hardly knew what to do. She finally urged her brother John C. Anderson, to do it. He replied "I am too busy building and making money and cannot take the time. Get some one in Logan to do it. Get Br. Martineau to do it—he lives in Logan." She inwardly rejoiced at this, and told him to write the request and authority for me to do it, which he at once did. So I filed the proper authorization for what I had already done. I could see the hand of the Lord in all this and have since received a testimony that all I so labored for have joyfully received the work done by me.

[page 130]

November 5, 1897—I thank the Lord for giving me this opportunity to work for the dead,—a work which to me is most delightful.

I married her at the time of the passage of the last and most stringent anti-polygamy law of congress, considering that to be the best way to show where I stood, just as I married Susan J. Sherman in 1857, when the U. S. government was about to exterminate all polygamists by aid of the army.

When Jessie and I were sealed, each of us had to go to the endowment house alone, enter by a different gate and at a different time of the night, so no one might suspect. With only two witnesses, and the person officiating concealed from our view that we might not know who it was, and by the light of a single candle, the ceremony was performed.

But I knew who sealed us, by the voice—that of apostle F. D. R. We left the building as we came—each one going our ways alone in the darkness to our homes. When I asked consent of Prest John Taylor for her to receive her 2nd A. he at once gave it. We met at the upper room of the Historians Office, coming there, as before, singly in the night. Apostle F. D. Richards performed the ceremony, asking me to assist by laying on my hands, which I did, and thus she received the highest ordinance possible for mortality to receive.

I did not inform any of my family in Utah of my marriage, in order that they might not be compelled to testify against me in court, should I be arrested, which they could not do, if they did not know of it. I rode with her in a carriage around S. L. City a number of times, in Bishop Preston's carriage, but was not troubled by any U.S. Officers.

At one time I received an intimation from the President's Office that U. S. Marshals were watching me, and so I left the house of my wife, Mary E. Jones, and went to stay at Bishop Preston's, and at my son Lyman R.'s place in Logan.

In November of 1887 Jessie Helen started for Arizona, to meet me there, but when she arrived at Vallejo, where an apostate aunt of hers lived, she was persuaded to return to Utah, which she did, and thus never came to me in Arizona, as she first intended to do.

[page 131]

November 5, 1897—In 1893, when Susan and I went to the dedication of the Salt Lake Temple, Susan went to see Jessie at the house of a mutual friend,—one of Brigham Young's wives—and tried to persuade her to go to us in Mexico, which she said she would do; but her mother again intervened, and prevented this. I saw her once during this time for a little while, and this was the last I saw of her on earth.

Praise and blessing to Susan, for doing what she did, for it was a great—a noble act,—one that will exalt her in the heavens. She thus proved the integrity of her heart beyond all doubt.

After hearing to day of Jessie's death, I received a good and comforting answer concerning her, and I know all is well with her, and she will reign with me—one of the Queens of Heaven.

November 6, 1897—Saturday. Theodore came over to day, and we laid out the foundation for our new dwelling. I laid a little of the foundation wall. Although possessing little means to build such a house, I believe God will open my way to erect it, for such is the testimony to me.

November 10, 1897—Wed. This morning, as I lay awake about 3 o'clock, I prayed, as I often do in the night, and received a glorious and comforting answer, with promise of many blessings from the heavens and from the earth. I will record some of these things, that my family may profit thereby, and learn to look to the Lord in faith, knowing that if our Father, in his goodness, will hear and answer one of his children, he is equally willing to bless another in the same manner.

I was told, among many other things, to look forward to the future with joy and gladness, for it is full of blessings to me and mine. That I shall be blessed and prospered from this time forth; blessed and prospered in building and furnishing my house beyond my expectations; to build it according to my present plan and Lyman's; for it shall be a house in which not only my brethren but natives of this land may sojourn, and will not be too large as I have thought it would be. That I have been brought to this land to do a great work, and shall perform it, for I shall be strengthened in body and in mind, and my age renewed for that purpose.

[page 132]

Wednesday, November 10th, 1897—That I shall become mighty among my brethren in priesthood and in calling that I may be able to do a greater work; and that the people of this land will love, trust, honor, and defend me if necessary, with their lives; that my faith shall become like that of the brother of Jared, and I shall have power to mighty works—even to raise the dead to life if necessary and to cause the earth to shake, and that I shall never be tempted more than I can bear, nor be turned aside from the commandments I shall receive. Many other promises were given which I do not feel to write. I do not write these things in a boasting spirit. I know if I receive them it will be by the help of our Father: and if I do not, it will be because of my own shortcomings and lack of faith, which at times becomes very weak.

November 28, 1897—A few days ago I received a check for $51.72 [$1,208] which was due me from the U.S. Government as a balance for my surveys made in 1893–4. This amount, though justly due me, had been disallowed by the Treasury Department because, as they said, my account had been closed. In answer to prayer three years ago I was told I should receive my pay, not withstanding I had been told it would not be paid me; and thus it seemed as if it was useless for me to hope for it. But thus has the promise of the Spirit been fulfilled; and I record it as a testimony, to assist the faith of my family and posterity.

To day I wrote to Lorenzo Snow, President of the temple in S. L. City, in regard to the principle of sealing men and women in marriage a number of times,—as to why it was necessary. For instance Susan and I were first sealed by apostle Geo. A. Smith in Parowan, Utah, in May 1852, and were afterwards sealed by Prest B. Young in 1860. We were endowed in March, 11th 1852, and our first child born Nov. 4. 1852. The question with me is,—if the first sealing is valid and of use, why must it be repeated? And if it must be repeated, as ours was, and others, is not the first sealing without value and force?

[page 133]

November 28, 1897—Also, will it not be necessary for our first born to be sealed to us, seeing that he was begotten before our endowments.

DECEMBER 1
HENRY, MELISSA AND 2 CHILDREN CAME

December 6, 1898—Took advantage of excursion rates to El Paso, and started for that place, having business there making it necessary to go. Stayed at the R. R. Station near Dublan

December 7, 1897—In El Paso, 140m about 4 P.M. Got a bed and room for 25¢

December 8, 1897—Attended to my business and bought some goods for my family, remaining also the next day, as no train went south until

December 10, 1897—the tenth, Oct, (Friday) on which day I reached Dublan. Cold.

December 11, 1897—Sat. Arrived home and found all well as usual, except that Melissa had been very near death, from a miscarriage, but is now rapidly improving in health and strength. I omitted to mention that on Dec. 2 the wind demolished a part of Joel's new brick and adobe house he is building.

December 22, 1897—Snowed all day but melted as it fell, also next day.

December 24, 1897—Snow 2 in. deep this morning. Dora had a bas [bad] fit of some kind Administered, and she soon got better, but was quite ill all day.[11]

December 26, 1897—To day Dora had a very bad fit

December 29, 1897—To day Henry and family went home. The same evening we were invited to a social party at Br. John J. Walser's. A good time.

December 31, 1897—Attended a social party at Mrs. Dv. Saville's, and enjoyed it.

JANUARY 1898

January 1, 1898—Worked all day, and the next, lining our board room with brown sheeting, and so made it warmer and pleasanter.

January 8, 1898—Got a new bedstead for Gertie and Dora, for \$16.[00] [\$374].

This is our 46th anniversary of our wedding, but we did not try, as we usually do, to have a celebration, having so little means to procure eatables, and so did not expect anything. But at evening we were visited by all our children in Juarez, also by Sister Saville and daughter, and our friend John Telford, whom Theodore had caused to come from Richmond, Utah. We had a very pleasant evening. and a good supper, much of which was contributed by our visitors. I cannot realize we have been so long united, but so it it, the Father be praised.

[page 134]

January 12, 1898—To day received the following in answer to the letter I sent to Pres[t] Lorenzo Snow in November, and which he had submitted for consideration to the First Presidency and Twelve:

"Salt Lake City, Utah 24th Dec. 1897

Elder James H. Martineau

Dear Brother. In replying to the questions submitted by you in your letter of Nov. 28th 1897, it is not necessary to repeat them here, as you will find them covered by a decision made on Thursday, December 16th 1897, by the Council of the First Presidency and the Twelve Apostles, which was as follows:

(1st) That the sealing of a couple outside of a temple, as husband and wife for time and eternity by one holding the requisite authority (The President of the Church, or any one deputed by him) is as valid as when performed in the House of the Lord, even when either or both of the parties have not been previously endowed.

(2nd) That children born after such sealing are legal heirs, even if begotten before the sealing occurred, and it is therefore unnecessary to seal them to their parents.

(3[d]) No measures are at present afoot looking to the erection of a temple in Mexico.

Your Brother in the Gospel

Lorenzo Snow."

This decision of the General Church Authorities sets at rest a question which has for many years been undecided in the church. For example, Susan and I were sealed for time and eternity as husband and wife in Parowan, Utah, in May 1852, by Apostle Geo. A. Smith; and sealed again by Pres[t] B. Young in S. L. City, Endowment House, in 1860, in order to be sealed "over the alter." And Susan Sherman was sealed to me, first, in the President's office, S. L. City, in 1857 and again in the Endowment House by Pres[t] Young in 1860. So this question has now been settled authoritatively.

[page 135]

January 12, 1898—The contention has been that a sealing was invalid if done before one or both of the parties had been endowed; also that it must be performed over an altar, to be legal and binding. This sets at rest all doubts relative to the Sealing of Annie S. to Henry S. Walser, neither of whom had had their endowments.

January 14, 1898—Two inches of snow this morning. Soon melted away.

11 As the "fits" progress, they sound much like epilepsy.

January 15, 1898—Col. Miguel Ahumada, Governor of Chihuahua, together with 50 or 60 leading Mexicans, officers of the State, Military officers and others paid us a visit. We had a good program lasting over an hour, of speeches, songs and music by the Band and Choir, after which tables were spread with a fine dinner, which was eaten by more than 200 souls. Our visitors were much pleased with our town and with their reception, and praised our people highly, returning to the R. R. Station at Casas Grandes in the afternoon. I was introduced to the Governor, also to State Surveyor Senor de Bergue.[12]

January 28, 1898—Have been very ill with Lagrippe for almost 2 week.[13] But in the last 3 or 4 days copied a map for Alex F. Macdonald, receiving $12.$^{\underline{00}}$ [$280] for it. Am recovering slowly.

January 31, 1898—To day Pres[t] A. W. Ivins started to the City of Mexico, and took my map of the Colonia Juarez survey, which is almost completed. I also sent with him a petition for appointment as official Surveyor and Engineer in the republic, hoping it may increase my power for good.

And today occurred three funerals, 2 little babies and a dear friend—Leroy Cluff, who died suddenly of pneumonia, leaving an almost helpless wife, who is a cousin of ours, formerly Maisie

FEBRUARY 1898

February 4, 1898—Two funerals to day, in our little town of 600 people

Saturday, February 5, 1898—To day Albert unexpectedly came to us. We had not had opportunity to visit with him for many years.

February 11, 1898—Henry came to day from Chuichupe & brought Bertha to go to the academy.

Sunday, February 13, 1898—To day Gertrude was taken very sick,—great pain in her spine and head, fever &c.

[page 136]

February 13th, 1898—I have been most of the time in bed for about a month, with the Grippe and also a stricture of the prostrate gland, which incapacitates me almost entirely from labor, on account of intense pain. I have labored at clearing my city lot of brush and trees which have covered much of it for an hour or so at a time, then resting on a bed for most of the day, in this time and manner doing some work.

February 15th ~~17th~~, 1898—To night Gertrude was so much worse, with such a difficulty of breathing that Dr. Saville thought she was dying. I had her administered to many times and sat up with her all night, my hand on her head all the time, praying for and blessing her. Better next morning.

February 18, 1898—Susan taken very sick with grippe, as also Theodore and Albert; so we are all sick in the house, including Dora. There are also many in the town who are also sick with the same complaint—la grippe. Gertrude very low.

February 20, 1898—Gertrude very low still, We deny all visitors, as she cannot endure the least noise, even of talking in a low tone in the next room. This morning she sleeps by aid of morphine. Susan is better, but unable to sit up longer than a few minutes at a time. I do not know what we would do if Anita was not our good ministering angel. She has been with us night and day since Gertrude's first sickness. Albert is still suffering with cough and his lungs, but is able to get around, as are Dora and myself.

February 22, 1898—Gertrude begins to improve, which is because of administrations of the priesthood. Albert went up to Chuichupe to day, to see the country. Went with Henry.

February 23, 1898—Gertie sat up in a chair for the first time, about an hour. For some days Susan has been very sick also, with La grippe but she is now nearly well.

February 25, 1898—By invitation of Mrs. Saville Gertrude went today to her house to remain a few days, it being more quiet and comfortable for her.

[page 137]

MARCH.

March 1, 1898—At the priesthood meeting to day I was appointed one of a committee of five to examine for a site for a wagon bridge over the river, and report probable cost of one.

12 James H. Martineau, "Gubernatorial Visit," *Deseret Evening News*, January 24, 1898; Journal History.

13 *La gripe* is the Spanish term for influenza.

March 4, 1898—Examined for site for bridge, with Committee. Apostles J. H. Smith and John W. Taylor came.[14]

March 5, 1898—Special Conference to day. Good time; also next day, Sun^{y}.

March 7, 1898—Susan and I visited the Apostles and had a pleasant time.

March 8, 1898—I made measurements for a truss bridge over the river at a point 200 feet wide, and commenced plan for bridge.

March 11, 1898—Showed my plan for a bridge to the Apostles, who approved.

Susan and Gertie and all are well now as usual, except that Gertie is too weak to walk much. I also, am troubled with a stricture, or something, in my left groin, which prevents me from doing much work or even walking, and at times is extremely painful. But I hope I may be healed. I know that He who formed my body is able to renovale [renovate] and Strengthen it.

Our orchard is in bloom, and is beautiful indeed. I have done much work in our garden, putting it in better shape. Theodore has done much to improve the lot I let him have, and I hope to be able to build a pleasant home.

March 13, 1898—Sunday. This is my 70$^{\underline{th}}$ birthday! It seems almost impossible that I have attained the full age allotted to man but so it is. As I look back upon my past, it all seems as a dream;—a dream sometimes happy,—sometimes like a nightmare of sorrow and trouble. But I acknowledge the hand of the Lord in all, and say all is right. No doubt I have needed every sharp lesson I have had. I know it was necessary, for my experience and perfection, as no one can profit much by another's experience.

As I review my past life, I see I have many things to be thankful for, and with all my failings, I can say I have never given any of my family evil counsel to my knowledge. I have always taught them to honor the holy priesthood, to be faithful and obedient, to be diligent in all duties of L. D. Saints

[page 138]

March 13, 1898—I have never upheld any in wrong doing, I myself though coming far short of what I should be, have never at any time put my own private interests before the public good or the work of the Lord. I have never raised my voice or influence against any of my leaders or authorities in Ward, Stake, or the Church. I have never brought any one before a teacher or a Bishop or High Council, but have suffered wrong rather than help to cause division among the saints,—have paid debts twice over rather than contend. God has been wonderfully good to me. He gathered me from my kindred, who were good people according to their light; gave the Gospel, with the holy Melchisedek priesthood, and the fullness of the priesthood; gave me my first and second anointings and all the blessings pertaining thereto; he has given me keys of power to act as a Savior on Mount Zion for many of the dead—about 2000 in number, with a testimony that all have received the temple ordinances in their behalf with joy and rejoicing, confirming this by an open vision in 1887 in Logan; He has given me a hundred wives, living and dead, sealed and endowed, of whom six have received their Second Anointing; He has given me twenty one sons and daughters, with nearly seventy grand children, and one great-grandchild, from my daughter Elvira. He has sent me noble spirits, who, thus far, have all been true and faithful as L. D. Saints, honored and respected by all, four of whom, Lyman, Charles, Jesse, and Nephi have filled foreign missions honorably, and Henry, Moroni and Elvira, called in Conference as missionaries to extend the borders of Zion. All this, and much more he has done for me, besides preserving my life by his special power, when nothing else would have saved it. Once, in 1850, when thousands died of cholera on the great plains, and I was given up to die, the angel of the Lord healed me instantaneously in the night time, telling me in an audible voice three times "You will not die," to which I answered "If I do not die I will take it as a sign the Lord has got a work for me to do," at other times miraculously preserved from death, and once actually raised from the dead—(being dead) by the

14 J. H. Martineau, "Colonia Juarez, Mexico," *Deseret News*, March 7, 1898; Journal History; see also "A Dreadful Crime," *Deseret News*, March 12, 1898; Utah Digital Newspapers. These stories authored by Martineau concerned the murder of Agnes McDonald. Follow-up stories of revenge are denied (J. H. Martineau, "Black Jack Story Denied," *Deseret News*, April 30, 1898; Utah Digital Newspapers).

power of God through the ministration of Apostle Thatcher and other brethren.

[page 139]

March 13, 1898—At another time preserved from death by obeying the audible voice of a guardian angel in July or August 1888, when a heavily loaded gun discharged.

Should I not be thankful!—humble, and very obedient to all the laws of heaven! Verily—yes!

And now I pray our Father, if it is his will, to help me to live so that I may gain all that has been sealed upon me by the holy priesthood, and that all my family may be exalted with me in the celestial Glory. Amen.

Yesterday I received a letter from Lyman, which I here insert:—

Logan March 7, 1898

Mr. James H. Martineau

Colonia Juarez Mexico

My dear father,

Your good letter came some time ago, but press of tithing ofcs [offices] and sickness have prevented me from writing, and am still under the pressure, and can only write you briefly so as to reach you by the time your birthday comes. I and we congratulate you on reaching 3 score and 10 years, and on a fair prospect for living several years—say 20—yet. I wish you many happy returns of the day, and that during the unfoldment of the years to come, you may take greater pleasure in life, and that your large family may be willing & able to cheer your heart, and strew flowers along your pathway, and you be able to reap the harvest from your good example, sown through many years of storms & Sunshine in the past. We honor you for your integrity to the truth, for your loyalty to the cause of Christ which you espoused as a youth, and for the many virtues & good councils you have shown forth in your eventful career.

[page 140]

March 13, 1898—[letter continues] I am sorry your health is bad again, and sorry, too, to hear that Aunt Susan, Gertrude, and others have been sick with the grippe. I hope you are all better by now. [blank] I was shocked to read in to day's Herald that Sister Macdonald had been strangled to death by those black fiends who surround you on all sides. It almost makes me feel like removing my objections to your staying in such a place, but I fear, as in the past, my objections would not count for much. Still, it does seem as though you were almost out of the world.

For about two months we here in Logan have had trouble, and it is not all over yet. Lilla was confined day before yes'day, Mch. 5th but the little child, a large, beautiful boy. only lived a few moments. He was well formed and perfect in every way except there was a sort of tumor about his throat which had so enveloped his windpipe, that he could not breathe. No medical skill could do any good, though Sis G. C. & G. S. Ormsby's were both there. Lilla stood it pretty bravely, and to day is as well as we could expect. They gave the baby the name Dwight, and we buried him yesterday in the N. E. corner of the grave lot where mother and the other three of your dead are laid.

Charlie's baby, James Miller, is still very sick. The pneumonia left him very ~~sick~~ weak, and before he was strong, his lung became filled with water, which if a few days treatment does not carry off, will have to be tapped. I believe he will pull through, but it is a tight place for the little fellow.

Alley's right hand is still very bad, too lame to write or do much with. & the doctor is giving her electric treatment, which is the only thing that has done her any good yet.

[page 141]

March 13, 1898—[letter continues] It is a sort of muscular rheumatism. I must close. All join in love to all and pray the Lord may bless & preserve you all from harm and evil. Write soon.

Your aff[t] son L. R. Martineau.

Our children gathered in the evening, and we had a good time—a very pleasant time. I hope we may have more. Counted, living and dead, 118 in our family, one being a Gr.-grandchild.

March 15, 1898—Having been appointed, with others, to examine and find a place to build a wagon bridge across the river, we spent the day in so doing, and finally decided on a proper site; looking also at other proposed sites, taking levels, &c.

March 16, 1898—Made a plat of the Chuichupe purchase. which is 5000 meters square.

March 18, 1898—Henry and family, also Sadie and Sixtus returned home. Perfected and finished my plan for a 2-span bridge, 66 ft each span, with approaches.

March 19, 1898—Bought a saddle of J. O. Davis and two poles ($47.^{00}) for $45.$^{\underline{00}}$ [$1,098–$1,051] cash order on Col$^{\underline{n}}$ Company and a pair of leggins, ($5.$^{\underline{00}}$) [$117].

March 20, 1898—Pres^{t} Ivins returned from Mexico yesterday, & preached to day. After meeting I was appointed Chair$^{\underline{n}}$ of Committee to locate and superintend construction of an irrigation Canal for Tenaja field.

March 21, 1898—With Pres^{t} Ivins located the dividing line between Scott and Stowell. Scott gave up all claim to the land, and Pres^{t} Ivins located Stowell's N. E. line, saying that as Scott had given up all claim to the land in dispute, it should revert to the Colonization company, for public use.

Joel laid out my garden for planting, and hauled me some lumber for a new cow shed, barn and corral.

At the land meeting a few days ago Theo. and I drew our lots contiguous, mine 14.15 Acres and his 16.+ acres. Both pieces are excellent land.

Albert started home at 3.30 P.M. We were very sorry to have him go. His visit has been very pleasant.

[page 142]

March 23, 1898—Set out a lot of Blackberry plants.

March 24, 1898—At a meeting to consider the building of a wagon bridge over the river, I made my report as Engineer, which was accepted. and it was decided to build the bridge at the crossing we had selected. I and two others were appointed a Committee to receive and pass upon all plans for a bridge which might be presented by any person.

March 25, 1898—Surveyed for a canal for the lower Tenaja field. Very windy.

March 26,1898—Worked on plan for bridge part of the day. High Priests meeting, and had an enjoyable time.

Have just learned from Sister Henrietta, of the recent death of my nephew, Fritz Voswinkel, of softening of the brain. He left a wife and two little girls. He was Lois' only son, and was a good young man.

Thursday, March 31, 1898—According to previous appointment met with the two others of the Bridge Committee to examine and receive a plan for a bridge across the Piedras Verdes river in Juarez. Three plans were presented, one by me, one by R. Scott and one by F. G. Wall. With us were Pres^{t} A. W. Ivins ands Bishop J. C. Bentley. My plan was accepted. It provides for a bridge of two spans of 66 feet each, timber, constructed on the Whipple truss system, and will cost probably from $2000 to $3000 [$46,719 to $70,078] dollars. The Committee adjourned before finally deciding what to do

Friday, April 1, 1898—Surveyed all day on the Tenaja field canal.

April 2, 1898—Bought a saddle for $47.$^{\underline{00}}$ [$1,098] of J. O. Davis

Sunday, April 3, 1898—The bridge committee formally adopted my plan of bridge.

April 4, 1898—Started to El Paso with Gertrude, and went to Dublan.

April 5, 1898—Very cold. Took train 8.30 A.M., third class, to save expense, $3.60 [$84] each. Car was full to overflowing of Mexicans all going to El Paso or Ciudad Juarez to spend Holy week. very uncomfortable all day. Arrived Juarez 5 P.M.

April 6 & 7, 1898—Attended to my business, and next day

April 8, 1898—returned home and found all well. Found a letter from Charlie informing me of the death of his little boy James Miller, which occurred March 23$^{\underline{d}}$—1898. at 1 o'clock P.M.

[page 143]

April 8, 1898—On Tues. April 5$^{\underline{th}}$ Joel's baby boy was born. A hard time for all. A letter from Lilla says she has almost recovered from her attack of Paralysis; can talk, but cannot sing a note. She was a fine singer before. Her left hand is also unusable, from the paralysis. I hope she will soon entirely recover.

Saturday, April 9, 1898—Worked on bridge plans. The Committee wish to advertise for bids on contract to build it. The following is a sketch of the proposed bridge:—[a space was left in the journal, but no sketch was included]

Sunday, April 10$^{\underline{th}}$, 1898—Very warm and threatens rain.

Thursday, April 7, 1898—[note that this date is out of order] Last Thursday, at priesthood meeting, my plan for a bridge across the Piedras Verdes river in Juarez, was formally adopted. to be built. It will be of 2 spans, each 67½ feet, with approaches 65 feet, total length 200 feet.

April 13, 1898—Counting up my family, living and dead, including those who have married my sons and daughters, I find the number as follows:—self and 3 wives = 4 Children 40, Gr. children 71, Gr.Gr. child 1, total 115. Besides these, my son Neils L. Hagberg has had 2 or three born of which I have no account at present. Truly, God has greatly blessed and added unto me, praise be to his holy name, for to him is due all the honor and glory of our salvation. In addition to the above number, I have had sealed to me, for time and eternity 96 wives, and have had a testimony that all have received the temple ordinances with Joy and rejoicing. (211 in all) Help me so to live oh my Father, that I may receive all in the end which thou hast committed into my hands. Amen.

April 18, 1898—Have spent several days working up my plans for the bridge, specifications &c. Leveled to day across river

April 19, 1898—Arranged about my pay for Survey of the Chuichupe purchase with Petersen the owner:—I am to receive $500. [$11,680] payable in Land $350.00 [$8,176] (100 acres) and cash $150.00 [$3,504]

April 20, 1898—Just one year since we returned home from Arizona, and in that time we have been much blessed.

[page 144]

April 21, 1898—Patriarch Henry Lunt, whom we have known since the spring of 1851 visited us to day. When departing, he said that having heard us talk and feeling our spirit he felt to prophecy upon my head, uncovering his own head he said "I prophecy that from this day and this very hour you shall be blessed and prospered more than you have since you have been in Mexico, both spiritually and temporally; in all things. You shall see it fulfilled. Amen." I felt a testimony within me that his words will be verified, and felt very thankful for the promise.[15]

April 28, 1898—Started to day to go to Chuichupe, to survey the lands of that settlement, with J. C. Petersen, arriving there on the

April 30th, 1898—30th chilled completely through. Found Henry's family and Moroni's, all well

MAY 1, 1898 SUNDAY

May 1, 1898—Found Pres[t] Ivins here, and made mining map for him, as he must start for Juarez early tomorrow. Spoke in meeting and felt well.

May 2, 1898—Took Latitude, 29° 23' 30" Altitude 7505 feet. All vegetation here is only just starting, with frosty nights.

May 3, 1898—This morning at 4:42 A.M. made an observation on Polaris, and found variation of needle 11° 27' E, very cold. To day I began the survey, which will cover 5000 meters square,—a little over nine square miles. Much of today's work was in pine timber with tall grass among the trees. Sent to Susan for under clothing. Suffered in my groin, as climbing steep and rocky hills and deep gulches, with my heavy transit inflamed my already much inflamed and swollen prostrate gland, which for weeks past has caused me at times excruciating pain, and has almost totally incapacitated me from all labor. Henry now carried my transit so I could lie down. I prayed for relief, and God heard my prayer and removed all the pain. Before I left Juarez I asked the Father if I would be able to do the work. The answer came, that I would be, that I should be strengthened for we work, and that I should not suffer much pain in my groin, but it should be healed through anointing, prayer & faith, and that I should go and return in peace and safty [safety] and be greatly blessed. And I already find this blessing is being verified.

[page 145]

May 6, 1898—To day Petersen returned home. Paid me $25.00 [$584].

15 J. H. Martineau, "No Vengeance Wreaked Upon the Gang as Reported—Prosperity in the Colonies," *Deseret Evening News*, April 23, 1898; Journal History.

May 10, 1898—Still surveying. In the night received glorious promises. I shall be healed of the stricture, not by Surgeon's aid or Gentile physicians but by the power of God through anointing, prayer and faith. Many blessings and promises were made for my family.

This morning a prospector went hunting and has not returned. His partners fear he is lost. Great forest fires rage in the west, filling the heavens with dense smoke.

May 11, 1898—Men hunted for the lost man. Unsuccessful.

May 12, 1898—Two parties of miners came in whose camps and all they contained had been burned, with heavy loss of clothing bedding, provisions, ammunition, currency & assaying outfit. Still hunting the lost man. Found where he had killed and eaten a skunk. Every man who could get a horse was hunting for him.[16]

May 13, 1898—Wrote to Deseret News.[17] My party also searching for lost man, so could not work. Same on the 14th

May 15, 1898—Preached and felt well. In the evening a meeting was held to devise means to build some kind of a fort or protection against possible trouble, according to the counsel of Apostles Smith and Taylor recently given at Garcia. It was decided to build a house of adobe or brick 27 x 40 ft and surround it with a timber palisade large enough to hold stock and other property in case of necessity. Some of the men hunting the lost man returned, with his burro and blankets, but did not find him. The Land Company engaged me to resurvey the town site, at $10. [$234] per day.

May 16, 1898—Began the town Survey, also 17th, 18, & 19th and finished it.

May 18, 1898—Theodore arrived on the 18th Weather still very cold and windy, frost every night.

[page 146]

May 18, 1898—The lost man was found by Mexican cattle herders about 30 miles distant, still crawling away from the settlement. He was nearly demented and must soon have died. He felt very grateful that our people had hunted for him so long.

May 21, 1898—Finished the survey to day, except a little here & there. The heavy wind ceased for the first, since my arrival.[18]

May 26, 1898—Rode over the surrounding country with Henry, & families. Theodore went on a hunt with 8 others, to be gone some days. He went on the 25th Theo. Sent in 2 deer he killed

May 27, 1898—Chose my land, of which I am to have 100 acres besides $150.00 [$3,504] cash. I took 40 Acres (16 Hektares)[19] of good timber the rest in open land, all of it good. I feel that I have been greatly blessed in this, and the promise made me in the beginning has been fulfilled in a manner very wonderful to me.

I have been full of life and strength and vigor. I who for so many months have been weak, feeble and filled with pain, unable to walk half a mile without having to go to bed. And I have labored hard without pain in my groin, which has for months been impossible. I know it has been only through the special blessing of the Lord in answer to my prayers. I have anointed the diseased place night and morning, in the name of Jesus, and the swelling and stricture has constantly decreased. And thus, through pains and troubles our faith is increased, therefore these so-called evils are actually blessings.

May 28, 1898—As I lay awake this morning I prayed and received most glorious promises, mostly a reiteration of those given before.

May 29, 1898—Theo. got back, having killed more deer than all the rest of the 8, who had chaffed him as a "tenderfoot."[20] He also killed 2 Bears, with Geo. Johnson

May 30, 1898—I find, by average of 63 observations of my aneroid, that the elevation of this place is 7505 feet by instrument scale and 7468 by published elevation table.

16 On May 12, 1898, Martineau wrote a letter for the *Deseret News* describing Colonia Chuichupa; Journal History.

17 Martineau wrote on May 14, 1898, under the pen name "Salamander." Here he described the dedication of the Juárez Stake Academy ("Juarez Stake Academy," *Deseret News*, June 4, 1898; Utah Digital Newspapers).

18 J. H. Martineau, "Missing Prosecutor—Items from a Mormon Town in Mexico," *Deseret Evening News*, May 24, 1898; Journal History. This is somewhat of a recruiting article encouraging people to come to the Mexican settlement.

19 One hektare [hectare] is equivalent to 2.47 acres.

20 To chaff is to tease in a good-natured way.

May 31, 1898—Rec[d] $40.[00] [$934] cash on survey. Started home at 1 P.M. with a deer which Theo killed for me yesterday.[21]

[page 147]

June 2, 1898—I arrived (with Henry) at home on Thurs. June 2nd all well, but quite tired. On our way home we passed for 40 miles through forest fires and smoke at times very dense. Found all at home well. Dora had had a severe fit while I was absent, and had been found senseless on the ground, by administering, she came to all right, and now is well.

June 3, 1898—Paid $20.[00] [$467] cash tithing.

June 4, 1898—Wrote letters and rested.

Sunday, June 5, 1898—A slight thunder shower to day.

June 15, 1898—Went to Casas Grandes and filed application for citizenship with the Presidente. Paid 5.50$ [$128].

June 29, 1898—To day Joel, Gertrude and Dora, also Anna Walser went with others by wagon into the mountains to Chuichupa for an outing, to be gone 2 or 3 weeks.

JULY

Sunday, July 3, 1898—I blessed Theodore Stanley, the new born child of Joel and Mary Ann Martineau, in fast meeting.

July 11, 1898—Susan's birthday. We were alone, and I too poor to make her any birthday present, which I regret.

Heard that Aunt Harriet, my last living aunt had recently died, aged 91 years. Died June 24, Fultonville.

July 24, 1898—There was celebration of Pioneer Day, but neither I nor Susan went, both being unwell, Susan real sick.

[word written in margin]

Note

Aunt Harriet's first husband's name was John E. Poole. He was one of the Engineers on the Erie Canal.

AUGUST.

August 17, 1898—Theodore went to the R. R. Station at Dublan to work for the R. R. Company. He believed he would do well and have permanent employment.

August 24, 1898—Henry A. also went there to work in shops.

SEPTEMBER

September 7, 1898—A big flood in our river, the Piedras Verdas, which did considerable damage, but no lives (of people) lost.

September 18, 1898—To day Theodore and I signed fresh applications for citizenship. He was at home on a visit.[22]

For a long time I have been very unwell and scarcely able to be around, on account, mostly, of swelling in my left groin, which the least work causes extreme pain.

[page 148]

September 18, 1898—Also, my general health is very poor, and I seem to be failing fast. Susan and I have decided it best for me to go to Logan and work in the temple for awhile, if the way will open. I do not know how long my stay on earth will be, and there is much important temple work for me to do or have done and I am anxious to do it.

September 20, 1898—Received a letter from Jessie N. and his lately wedded wife. I record the letter of his wife, because of its genealogical value, as follows:—

Chicago, Sept. 11. 1898

Dear Father

In answer to your request will give you such information as I possess in regard to my people. Have not

---

21 In this article Martineau reports on the events of Chuichupa, Mexico (J. H. Martineau, "A Hunter Found in a Pitiful Condition—Items of Interest About Chuichupa, Chihuahua," *Deseret Evening News*, June 20, 1898; Journal History; see also "From Mexico," June 25, 1898; Utah Digital Newspapers).

22 On the next day Martineau writes the newspaper describing the Mexican independence celebrations (J. H. Martineau, "Mexican Independence," *Deseret News*, September 24, 1898; Journal History).

exact date of father's birth, but will write to my mother. I was born in Sharon, Wis. Dec. 21st 1861. My name was Eliza Belle Johnson. My father, William Warren Johnson, was a private in the 13th Wis., died of typhoid fever when I was six months old. (1862) Mother's maiden name was Mariette Leavitt; Grandfather, Peter Leavitt. Grand mother's maiden name was Sarah Spaulding.—her mother's name was Baker; all New England people of English descent,

Great Grandfather Johnson's name was William W., born Dec. 2. 1785; his wife Nancy.—have not her maiden name, born June 28, 1788. My grandfather and the rest of their children in the following order:—

William E.,	Jan. 24. 1812
Dewitt C.,	Feb. 9. 1813
Ansil L.	Aug. 14, 1814
Daniel B.	Feb. 14. 1816
Welcome W.	Oct. 26. 1817
Harty J.	May 16. 1819
David M.	Oct. 7 1821

[page 149]

September 20, 1898—

John L. H.	Feb. 3. 1826
Warren	March 5. 1830

My father had two Sisters and one brother. One sister, Eliza, died young; the other Caroline H. Bell, is living in Hadley, Mass. The brother, Edward Eaton Johnson is now living in Los Angeles. He has the family record back to—I think—1626, when William Johnson married Nancy Eaton in London, Eng. I have one brother, Willis E. Johnson, born Dec. 8. 1859,—is now living in Myrtle, Cal.

My mother married Alexander Hyatt when I was five years old. He was killed by lightening in Syracuse, Neb. April 1883. My mother is now living in Oregon City, Oregon, with my younger brothers Willard and George Hyatt. They are both good men and very dear to me.

There has never been, so far as we know, a drunkard, a pauper, a criminal, or a disreputable person of either sex in my father's or mother's family. [blank] Enclose obituary. Please return, as it is the only one I have. Will leave news for Jess to write. We have not much of this world's goods, but are very happy together and see no reason why we shall not continue to be so. With much love to yourself, "Aunt Susan" and the rest of the family, I am yours affectionately

Belle M.

September 22, 1898—Answered Jesse's and Belle's letter.

September 24, 1898—Sold my wagon, 2 horses and harness for $400.00, $100 [$9,344–$2,336] to be cash, so I can go to Utah, hoping to renew my health. I have been quite feeble all the season, with a swelling in my left groin, which was very painful from doing any labor.[23]

Note September 16, 1898—On Sept 16th a daughter, Nola—was born to Albert & Emma Martineau, in Thatcher, Graham Co. Arizona.

[page 150]

September 28, 1898—To day Gertrude is 28 years of age. I gave her a carbuncle pin, which had belonged to Von Wendt.[24] We are still putting up peaches, trying to save all we can, but many bushels go to waste. An extraordinary yield of fruit this year.

September 29, 1898—Delivered 2 maps of my Chuichupa Surveys to Prest Ivins. My bill for work against the Colonization Co. is $455.00 [$10,628].

September 30, 1898—Started to go to S. L. City, Utah. In the last ten days I have two very severe attacks of pain in my left side lasting a half hour each, causing exquisite pain. I fear it is my kidneys that are affected. Stayed all night at the R. R. Station.

~~November~~ October 1, 1898—Went by rail to El Paso, Texas, 150 miles. During the night I had another severe attack of kidney pains.

October 2, 1898—Left El Paso at 10 A.M. by A. T. & S. F. R. R.

October 3, 1898—Awoke this morning not far from Trinidad, Colorado.

October 4, 1898—Awoke a few miles west of Green river. Arrived in S. L. City about noon. Went to Bp. Preston's to stop, not being able to find Eliza.

23 J. H. Martineau, "Mexican Independence," *Deseret Evening News*, September 24, 1898; Journal History.

24 A carbuncle is a gemstone, like a garnet, which is cut with a convex back and polished but not cut into facets.

October 6, 1898—General Semi Annual Conference. During the two previous days the great Welsh Eistedfodd was held, a great musical treat.[25]

October 7, 1898—Br. & Sister David Booth of Brigham City called to tell me about Cora, an indian girl, who died some years before in Plain City, or near there. She was the girl Wm Rice bought of the Utes in the spring of 1851 at Parowan, Iron Co. She had been endowed and sealed to me as a wife some years previously.

[written in margin]

Sunday Oct. 8. 1898.—Solemn Assembly held Each quorum of Priesthood voted separately in confirming nominations of Presidency.

October 10, 1898—Went to Logan, and found all my family well and glad to see me. Found many warm friends, but many have departed this life, which makes it seem lonely to me.

October 14, 1898—By letter from David Booth I learn that Cora died, March 2, 1867. She had a son, named Joseph Hyrum, begotten by a gentile named Johnson, who betrayed and then deserted her. The boy died ~~Mch. 24~~, ~~22~~ May 20 1869 aged ~~one~~ 3 years 2 months years. He was blessed in Plain City. His mother gave him to Br. Robinson, and he took his name—Robinson. On Robinson's death, his wife took him till he died. She gave him up to me, as the child of my wife. May God ever bless her for her kindness to the poor motherless child.

[written in margin]

Cora died March 2/67 The boy Joseph was born Mch. 22 1866 Died May 20 1869

[page 151—see Appendix 5 for newspaper clippings inserted here.]

October 1898—At the Conference attended the great Solemn Assembly.

October 16, 1898—Sunday. Went with Lyman and Alley to Riverdale to visit Nephi and family. Found them all well. Went over his farm of 180 acres. Attended church, and preached. Came home in the evening. Cold weather.

October 17, 1898—To day Lyman got clothing for me:—shoes, 2 shirts, 2 pr drawers, necktie, gloves, stockings, silk handkerchief & two pair Union knit garments. May our Father ever bless him.

October 19, 1898—Wednesday. Went to the temple. Was endowed for Thos Corlett

October 20, 1898—At the temple, I endowed Chas H. Sumner. He and Corlett's wives having previously been endowed I had them each sealed to their wives, I, proxy for the men, and Mary Thompson Richards for the women.

October 21, 1898—Went to Richmond to visit the family of John Telford.[26]

October 22, 1898—After a good visit I returned to Logan.

October 23, 1898—Visited at Charley's, with Lyman and Alley.

October 25, 1898—Taken violently sick, with attack of excruciating pain in my left side, as before. After some hours had a little rest

October 26, 1898—Severe pain continues. No sleep at night. Dr. Ormsby called.

October 27, 1898—Still great pain, and bloody urine, which is also very muddy. Dr. Ormsby says it is stone in the kidney, passing and tearing its way to the bladder, Gave me morphine every 2 hours until pains abated. He made an examination of my groin and said it was a rupture, which at my age can not be healed, and I must wear a trus [truss] hereafter, to prevent an enlargement of the opening. Rec^{d} a letter from Wells Chase, in whose house Cora died, telling of her death.

October 28, 1898—Still in bed but improving. Lilla brought me fruit & oysters.

October 29, 1898—Arose and dressed and went down stairs, but am very weak. In the afternoon Lyman, Charley & Frank bought me an overcoat and Lilla bought me gum overshoes.

October 30 & 31 1898—Attended Quarterly Conference.

---

25 Eisteddfod (note spelling) is a Welsh festival or competition among poets and musicians.

26 Martineau is visiting old friends (Joel E. Ricks and Everett L. Cooley, eds., *The History of a Valley: Cache Valley, Utah–Idaho* [Logan, UT: Cache Valley Centennial Commission, 1956], 92).

NOVEMBER

November 3, 1898—I endowed ~~Anthony~~ Jeremiah Sprage [Sprague], and Wm Fawcet endowed for me Anthony Sprague.

[page 152]

November 2, 1898—I ordained John Mears, and sealed him & his wife.

November 3, 1898—Andena Nelson ~~endowed for me Margaret Martineau Wilde and~~ acted in sealing but not in endowing any one. Ada Elizabeth Bott Peterson endowed for me [left blank]

November 4, 1898—I endowed Elijah Mears, and sealed him and his wife Margaret Martineau (Wilde). Ada E. B. Petersen being proxy for his wife. William Fawcett endowed for me William Sprague. Andena Nelson endowed for me Margaret Martineau. Ada E. B. Petersen endowed for me Mrs. Daniel G. Sprague. I had all four couples sealed.

November 8, 1898—I was baptized for 121 persons, most of them Lamanite chiefs. Of the few whites, I acted for Alex. von Wendt and his father Herman von Wendt. Also for Martinus, a Roman general who lived about the year A. D. 90 My daughter Elizabeth was baptized for his "beloved daughter Lucilla" as named upon an ancient marble tomb, between Damascus and Alleppo, in Syria, which tomb was discovered some years ago by Elder Locander, a Greek missionary laboring in that land. He gave me all these particulars. Elizabeth was baptized for 5 women, and Mrs. Katy Pyper Preston for four.

November 9, 1898—I endowed Martinus, Eva endowed his daughter Lucilla, and the following sisters of the Relief Society endowed for me as follows:—Caroline W. Affleck, for Alicia Ann Murphy, Ada Parkinson England for Harriet Mears; Nettie T. Sloan for Pocahontas; Jean C. Thatcher for Na-do-wa-qua; Annie [left blank] for Ali-quip–pa; Catherine C. Bronchly for Mrs. Henry Schoolcraft; Susan E. Terry for Sanoga, Lissetto C. Cummings for O-me-shug. I was very thankful for their aid, and they shall never lose by it. Their help was procured through the aid of Sister Affleck, Relief Socy President.

The indian names are those of Chieftainesses of various American tribes.

November 10, 1898—I endowed my uncle John Hudson Poole, and sealed him and Aunt Harriett Mears, his wife, Sister Mary T. Richards (wife of Apostle Richards) being her proxy.

[page 153]

November 10, 1898—Lyman's wife Alley Preston, has now been very sick two days, with severe attack of kidney disease. She has been in poor health a long time.

November 11, 1898—I endowed F. T. Wilde and sealed to him Margaret Martineau, M. T. Richards her proxy.

Lyman sent my R. R. ticket to S. L. City to get an extension of time on it.

November 12, 1898—Worked all day making out a list of names of Children to be sealed to parents,—my parents, grandparents, uncles, aunts, &c.

November 13, 1898—Alley still very sick. Her Father, Bp. Wm B. Preston came to see her.

November 14, 1898—Went to the temple and gave in my list of names. for sealing, as children to parents.

November 15, 1898—To day, myself. Lyman, Nephi, Lilla and Emma acted in the sealings, men for men, women for women.

I was sealed to my father and mother, also all my brothers and sisters.

My father was sealed to his father, also all his brothers & sisters (my uncles and aunts). I did not go back any farther, because I did not know the names of any other of my gr-gr. father's children. but will wait until I know them

I also sealed my maternal grand parents all their children—the Mears family, but went no farther back for the same reason as in the case of paternal ancestors.

How thankful I am, that I now have a father and a mother. having been all these years an orphan; and they, now, have their children—before childless and alone. I thank the Father that he has permitted me to do such a glorious work! Now I can meet my father and mother without shame and confusion.

November 16, 1898—I endowed Alfred Higginson and Eva, Ellen Martineau, Nephi Endowed Daniel G. Sprague and Emma, Mrs. Danl G. Sprague.

I sealed both couples, Emma being proxy for both women.

[page 154]

November 16, 1898—William Fawcett end[d] for me Thomas Martineau.

I had sealed to me as wives, Lucilla, Aliquippa, and Nadowagua, Emma being proxy for them.

To day I was talking with Apostle Merrill about the various gifts and offices of the church, and I remarked that I had never desired any office in the church of authority and power to sit and rule or judge the saints, but only one. He said, you have desired power and authority to bless. I said yes, I had always desired the power to bless people. He said "You ought to be a Patriarch. Pres[t] Woodruff told me to search for just such men as you, and ordain them Patriarchs. But it must be done in order. Write to President Snow, tell him your desire, and tell him I consider you worthy, and that I would take great pleasure in ordaining you to that office." I said I hated to write about such a thing. He said "Write, just as I have told you. It will be all right."

In the afternoon I wrote according to his direction, and before sealing the letter spread it before me, asked the Lord to dictate the matter and inspire Pres[t] Snow to decide as the Father wishes, to say "yes" or "no," as the will of God will be right in either case. Then folded & sealed and sent the letter.

I had previously (a few days) been told by the Spirit I would be ordained a Patriarch very soon. And now I prayed, to know if I had done right in the matter. I received a plain answer, in words, by the Holy Spirit, that I had done exactly right and had been led by the Holy Spirit. That I had been held in reserve, and gathered out from all my numerous connections For this very purpose, to take the lead in their redemption: That I had been ordained a Patriarch before I came to this Earth, and that all was according to the will of the Father. All this was a great comfort to me, and I believed all would be as I desired.

[page 155]

November 17, 1898—I endowed William Henry Martineau. Received my R. R. ticket, extended to Dec. 31. 1898, for which I am thankful.

November 18, 1898—I endowed Paul Larsen for Christina Larsen, she not having any male to help her in the temple. She helped me in return by endowing for me Lucy Martin, and her friend endowed for me Abagail Mears (by Catherine L. Keller)

November 20, 1898—Snow storm. Snow 14 inches deep. Very cold.

November 21, 1898—Very cold. Zero.

November 24, 1898—Thanksgiving Day. Dined at Charley's, supped Lyman's

November 25, 2898—Rec[d] a letter from the First Presidency, saying they had written to Apostle Merrill to ordain me to that priesthood, (Patriarchal) and praying that I might magnify that high and holy calling.

November 30, 1898—This day I was ordained a Patriarch in the Church of Jesus Christ of Latter Day Saints in the Logan Temple, by Apostle Marriner W. Merrill, Samuel Roskelly, witness. The following is my certificate of ordination:—[27]

Office of the Logan Temple
Logan, Utah, 30th Nov. 1898

To All Concerned:

This certifies that Elder James Henry Martineau has this day been Ordained and set Apart, a Patriarch[28] in the Church of Jesus Christ of Latter Day Saints, by Apostle M. W. Merrill in the Logan Temple.

Samuel Roskelly
Recorder Logan Temple
Witness

[In margin]
Gean's baby born

27 Marriner Wood Merrill (1835–1906) was a bishop in Richmond, Utah, for eighteen years and later president of the Logan Stake. In 1884 he became president of the Logan Temple and was ordained an Apostle in 1889 (Donald G. Godfrey and Kenneth W. Godfrey, *The Diaries of Charles Ora Card: The Utah Years, 1871–1886* [Provo, UT: Religious Studies Center, Brigham Young Univ., 2006], 53–55).

28 This is a significant calling of great honor in the life of Martineau. A patriarch confers blessings on members of the Church. These important blessings are recorded and give the individual "admonitions, promises and assurances" (Daniel H. Ludlow, ed., *Encyclopedia of Mormonism* [New York: Macmillan, 1992], 3:1064). Today, each stake organization has a patriarch for the blessing of the members.

Got letter from Edward Sudbury saying a daughter was born to them on 27th November, at 7.30 P.M.

I endowed Thomas Preston Gentlee.

DECEMBER

December 1, 1898—Alley very sick all night.

I endowed John May. Sealed T. P. Gentlee & Abagail Mears;—John May and Mrs. John May;—Wm H. Martineau and Lucy Martin.

[page 156]

December 1, 1898—While the company (about 50) were passing through the vail, I and about a dozen others heard singing,—male and female voices—in the temple. It was a concert of Angels, and sounded as if in another room. I rejoice at being counted worthy of so great a blessing & honor.

December 2, 1898—I endowed Mr. Webb, and sealed him to Alujay Haughout. Fanny Earl endowed for me Harriet Columbine. In all sealings Sister Mary T. Richards was my assistant, except when otherwise noted.

This finishes my temple work for this time. I missed very much the presence with me in the Temple of my dear wife Susan, whose absence takes away much of my pleasure.

December 4, 1898—Sunday. Alley is still very dangerously ill. She has been unable to lie down for a long time, because of smothering, being much bloated with dropsical water. Her heart also troubles her very much at times, and she coughs up blood. Her father, Bp. W. B. Preston says she can only be saved by the power of God, and this is my belief too.

December 5, 1898—Nephi came for me in a sleigh, to visit his family.

December 6, 1898—Very cold, –6° below zero. Blessed Nephi and Emma but had not time to bless the children.

December 7, 1898—Returned to Lyman's. Very cold weather. Found Alley scarcely able to speak or move herself.

December 8, 1898—Received 6$ [$140] in letter from Sudbury, for passage to visit him and Gean in Eureka, Juab Co. Utah. Could not have visited them without it, being without money.

This morning I felt very sad. A consultation of doctors decided it necessary, in order to save Alley's life, to take her unborn child instrumentally—8th month. In such case, she would have only one chance in ten for life;—without that operation, she must die. We all felt very bad about it. This morning I asked the Father about her, and received a comforting answer,—"That she is not to pass away now, not having finished her work on Earth. Her child shall be born in due time, naturally, and she shall amend from this hour.

[page 157]

December 8, 1898—I must go and seal these blessings upon her. I arose at once, and on the way to Lyman's prayed again, fearing I might have been deceived, as it seemed impossible almost, that this could be fulfilled, but received again the same answer. Once more, at the house, I prayed again, and received the same. I blessed her. She believed and wept with joy. In 12 hours, on Dec. 9th

December 9, 1898—Alley's baby girl was born, 3.40 A.M. perfect in form,—weighed 5 lbs. It was a natural but unexpected birth, and was by the direct power and blessing of the Lord. The Doctor told me, in answer to my question—"It was just by good luck that it happened." It was not "luck", but the power of God in her behalf, as had been manifested to me. By request I blessed the baby, but she was not named.

In the evening I gave patriarchal blessings to Lyman and Alley, Katy Preston, Eva, and the nurse, Miss [blank]

I SAT UP ALL NIGHT.

December 10, 1898—Alley is wonderfully improved this morning. Lyman took me to photographer's to sit for a likeness, after which took sorrowful leave of all the dear ones, including Sister Harriet Preston, and at 3.30 started to S. L. City. There at 7.30 and stopped at Oscar Moyle's (Preston's son-in-law)

December 11, 1898—Sunday. Meeting in tabernacle. Went to Presiding Patriarch John Smith for instruction in my duty as a patriarch, and wrote a blessing for a young man who came in.[29]

29 Martineau is recording the blessing being given under the hand of Patriarch John Smith.

December 14, 1898—Visited the last two days, and today start 7:30 A.M. to Eureka to visit Sudbury and children, three of whom I have not yet seen. Arrived there about10.30 A.M. Was glad to see them all—Jeannie cried when she met me.

December 16, 1898—Blessed Edward, Geannie, Sherman, Lyman, Virginia and the baby, whom we named Florence, Also blessed Miss Frances G. Hovey, the hired girl.

December 17, 1898—At 3.30 P.M. started to S. L. City, arrived 7.30 P.M.

December 19, 1898—Blessed Moyle's 2 children, Harriet and Elizabeth. May put up for me a nice lunch basket, by Sister Preston's direction. They all treated me very kindly, both in Logan and S. L. City, also every one I met.

[page 158]

December 19, 1898—I found Eliza in very poor health, completely broken down. By her request I blessed her before I left.

December 20, 1898—Started for home at 8.30 A.M. in a heavy snow storm. Our train killed a man on the track near Provo. Noon at Helper, night on the state line, Grand Junction 6 P.M.

December 21, 1898—Pueblo 5 A.M. Change Cars. Arrive Trinidad 10.40 A.M. Change Cars. Arrive Raton Summit at noon in heavy snow storm, Ribera 5 P.M. Albuquerque 9.20 P.M.

December 22, 1898—El Paso at 10 A.M. Sent $1.45 [$34] for Ainslee's and McClure's Magazines.

December 23, 1898—Paid $5.85 [$137] duty on two dress patterns given Susan & Gertrude by Sister Preston, and by Alley and Lilla. Start 8.30 A.M. and arrive at Dublan near Sunset. Came home in mail wagon at 8.15 P.M. very cold. Found all well. Rejoiced. The many presents sent by our loved ones caused all at home much joy & thankfulness. Truly I have been greatly blessed in going & returning, just as I was told (Susan also) before I left home. I have greatly improved in health, and though ruptured, I am far stronger, though wearing a truss. I weigh 169 lbs, a gain of 30 lbs. Since I left home. I found Theodore, Anna and her children domiciled at home, making us crowded somewhat, but it is for the best, I think. Anna can rent her house, and can work in the store while mother tends her children.

December 24, 1898—Concert and tableaus in the evening. Theo. as Santa Claus.

December 25, 1898—Christmas. Spoke in meeting. Very cold weather

December 26, 1898—More pleasant this morning.

December 27 & 28, 1898—Worked on my temple record, inserting work recently done.

December 29, 1898—Settled my tithing, amounting to about $60.00 [$1,402].

December 30, 1898—Recording blessings I gave in Utah. almost sick with a cold.

December 31, 1898—Attended a Christmas festival—a very pleasant one.

JANUARY 1899.

January 1, 1899—Finished recording blessings, all but two of them.

January 2, 1899—Completed recording. My cold somewhat better.

January 3, 1899—Very windy & threatens rain. Letter from Lyman says Alley is still very weak.

[page 159— see Appendix 5 for newspaper clippings inserted here.]

January 3, 1899—While in Utah I copied a letter from Sister Henrietta to Lyman, giving all she knew relative to our ancestors, part of which I now record here;— She says:—

"My father (John Martineau) was born on Staten Island & brought up on his father's farm, until about 18 years of age, to avoid being apprenticed to a cabinet maker (I believe it was to a hatter) he ran away to England, found a home in London, studied medicine (and surgery) and married a widow ten years his senior, with two children. Her name was Mrs. Hawkins, widow of Capt. Hawkins, British Royal Navy. Her two children were Samuel and Elizabeth, whom I remember as a boy. Samuel was a Warrant Officer in the U. S. Navy, and was with Commodore Wilkes[30] in his 3 year

30 Charles Wilkes (1798–1877) was the first person to explore the Antarctic from 1832 to 1842. He brought back a wealth of scientific knowledge (Alan Gurney, *Below the Convergence: Voyages toward Antarctica, 1699–1839* [Rutherford, NJ: Penguin USA, 1998]).

exploring expedition in 1840 when he discovered the Antarctic Continent. Mrs. Hawkins was of noble family, and had offended her family by marrying beneath her rank. (note) She was the second daughter of Lord Charles Stanhope, 3[d] Earl of Chesterfield, was born 1778. When her father died he willed her 2 children (Sam[l] & Eliz[h]) £18000 each (=$90000) [$2,102,335] but they never got it.

Father lived in England 6 years & returned to America, landed in Baltimore, where his wife soon died of yellow fever. He gave up Medicine, studied engineering, had several Gov[t] jobs, among them, the Muscle Shoals Canal, Tennessee, the Delaware Breakwater while he lived in Georgetown D. C. and the Croton Water Works, N. Y. City, which he surveyed, & was appointed to oversee its construction; but after six months was obliged to give up work, from consumption, & soon died in Elbridge, Onondaga. Co, N. Y. April 6, 1838. He had a splendid physique—6' 2" tall, broad in proportion, not handsome, but of sweet disposition, gentle, kindly and unassuming,—too confiding for his own good, believing every one as good & true as himself. His name was engraved on the great granite reservoir, N. Y. City, 42 St. He seemed born to command. There was nothing low, common or vulgar about him,—a nobleman by nature and by descent.

Go to Staten Island by ferry to Port Richmond, thence to "New Dorp" past the "Old Black Horse" inn, so on to the old church (Moravian) and past the Martineau and Vanderbilt farm which join each other.

[page 160]

January 3, 1899—Our mother, Eliza Mears, was daughter of James Mears & Lois Sprague, who were married Jan. 1. 1796. She and Gr-father Mears started on horseback (she sitting behind him) to a village to find a minister to marry them. Near the village, a small stream was swollen by rains and unfordable. They shouted until a man came to see, whom they told to bring a minister, which he did. Gr-father and gr-mother got off the horse and stoon [stood] upon one bank of the stream whiled the minister stood on the other side, shouted the ceremony to them; they shouting back "yes" in return, were pronounced husband and wife, remounted, and went home to a little log cabin in the woods, their future home.

My gr-gr. father, John Mears, was soldier in the French & Indian War of 1756, and when Montcalm captured Fort Oswego, he and other prisoners were sent by ship to France, but on the way were taken by an English ship, taken to England penniless and naked, given license to beg, & after five years begging got enough to take him home.[31] One lady gave him £.1 "because he was so handsome". At home he found a fine tombstone erected to his memory. He afterward married & had a large family. One branch—Simeon Mears, lumber merchant, lives in Chicago. He is my mother's cousin.

The Hutchinsons were the maternal ancestors of my Gr. Mother Mears, her mother being Lois (or Eunice) daughter of Stephen Hutchinson, younger son of Lord Hutchinson, Eng. When his elder brother assumed the title, he said he would go to America and found a family of his own. He settled in Newburyport, Mass. & had a family. One son, Stephen, was killed in the massacre of Fort William Henry, at the head of Lake George N. Y. by the indians under Montcalm. His daughter Lois (or Eunice) married W[m] Sprague my g.g.g.gr.father. All the Hutchinsons were fond of music, and all could sing. Grandmother herself was a famous singer and had a splendid voice.

[page 161]

THE SPRAGUES, MY MATERNAL ANCESTORS.

January 3, 1899—They were from Dorsetshire Eng. Samuel Sprague was one of the "Boston Tea Party," and his son Charles, was a poet. 50 years ago. Major William Sprague, son of William, married Lois (or Eunice) Hutchinson of Newburyport, Mass. my gr-grandmother. Major Sprague was a small man, active and alert and quite fearless. William Sprague was in the revolutionary Army, an Armorer. He died

31 The French and Indian War was fought in the Appalachian region of what is currently Canada and the United States. It was a war primarily between the British and the French with Native Americans fighting on both sides.

before the war closed, leaving a wife & nine children, six sons & 3 daughters, and a farm in Mass. His widow married Maj. Noah Allen, brother of Ethan Allen. My grandmother, Lois Sprague Mears, was the youngest of the flock, and it when she was 15 that her mother married Maj. Noah Allen. He was detailed with 30 others, to witness the execution of Major Andre. His sons were William (died young) Seth, James, John, Jesse, Daniel. The Spragues were all men of means. Grandmother Mears' Aunt Sprague, married Commodore Tuttle of the Navy (English or American) Rev. Wm B. Sprague D. D. was a famous minister 50 years ago in Albany, N. Y. was gr. ma's Cousin.

From British Encyclopedia I gathered items pertaining to the family connections of father's first wife, the mother of my sisters Julia and Lucretia:—

She was the second daughter of Lord Charles Stanhope, 3^{d} Earl of Chesterfield and was born 1778. her mother being Lady Hester Pitt, the sister of William Pitt, 1st Earl of Chatham. The first daughter was Lady Hester Lucy Stanhope; the third daughter was Lady Lucy Rachel Stanhope, who married Thomas Taylor, an Apothecary. The first wife was married Dec. 19. 1774. Died July 20, 1780.

Lord Stanhope's first wife died and he married as his second wife Louisa Grenville, daughter of Hon. Henry Grenville. She was married Mch. 17. 1781. Her father was a younger brother of Earl Temple and George Grenville. She died in March, 1829. She was mother of three sons by Lord Chas Stanhope.

Philip Dormer Stanhope, 4th Earl Chesterfield, was a son of Philip Stanhope and Elizabeth Saville, dau. of Marquis of Halifax. He was born in London 1694. Died 24th Mch 1773.

[page 162]

January 3, 1899—He had an illegitimate son, Philip Stanhope, by Madame du Bouchet, born in 1732. This son died 1768.

The wife of the Earl was Melusina von Schulemberg, an illegitimate daughter of George 1st King of England. He married her 1733, but had no children by her, & adopted his illegitimate son as his heir.

William Pitt, (uncle of my wife Lady Hester Lucy Stanhope) and Earl of Chatham, was born London Nov. 15 1708. Died May 11. 1778. He was younger son of Robt Pitt of Boconnock, and grandson of Thomas Pitt, of Madras, India.

Robt Pitt (father Earl Chatham) died 1727. His elder brother was Thomas Pitt.

I am tempted to insert a letter from Lyman to Joel, not because of his praise, which I know I do not deserve, for no one on earth knows so well as I do the many imperfections I have and the many ways in which I come short; but because it shows his love, which hides or covers many failings in me, and because I think my other children feel towards me as he does; and therefore it is precious to me:—

[written in margin]

Letter to Joel by Lyman

Logan, Dec. 15, 1898

Dear Joel, I have not answered before because of much to do and because father was here & kept all of you fully posted as to himself and us. But he has left us after two months visit, much to our regret, for his stay has been too brief entirely. We all enjoyed him so much; and the way he has improved in health is glorious; He is the best preserved man of 71 years that I know in the country. He was sick for about a week, but got medical advice that helped him much, & he soon ~~regained his~~ recovered. I have but one regret, and that is the fact that he has moved away from here. For he would live years longer if he were here in this bracing, healthful locality and so would your mother in my opinion. Besides he—they—deserve to stay here and partake of some of the fruits of the civilization they helped to plant here.

[page 163—see Appendix 5 for photo of Brigham Young and newspaper clipping on the death of Henrietta inserted here.]

January 3, 1899—The temple work is father's natural sphere, during the remainder of his life, and he ought to be able to do it. But I presume all will end well.

Of course from my stand point you boys as well as father, made a great mistake when you left Cache. for others who remained are comfortable, happy, possessors of abundance and their families near, to pluck spiritual and intellectual fruits abounding in our temples of God & temples of learning. In fact Theo. knows I told him to stay here & with me try to get you all back. But I must not dwell upon this one of my hobbies, & I only mention it because father's recent visit and departure arouses anew all the old longings for you all to be here. Father is a grand man and I must confess that a long separation of fourteen years, since he moved from Logan had made us almost strangers until this two months again brought us together, and I must say, Joel, that we boys have much to thank God for that we have such a noble father; honorable, refined, intelligent, always full of hope & charity & faith. He blends that great trinity Faith, Hope, Charity more perfectly than any man I know in the Church. He has gone to visit Gean at Eureka for a few days, and I believe expects to leave S. L. City for El Paso about 19th.

Alley has been very sick for 6 weeks, and for ten days we almost despaired of her life. But the Lord heard our prayers, and she has been spared to us to one inexpressible joy. Father has no doubt kept you informed so I will refrain from repeating it. She is gaining slowly, & though I do not expect her to be strong enough to do much or get out of doors till the warm weather of April bids a friendly good bye to March winds and frosts, yet I hope that in 3 or 4 weeks she can get out of bed. Well Joel my boy, press on with hope and courage, to get out of debt, as you express a desire, & may the Lord ever be near to aid you in all things. Love to Annie and Aunt Susan, Annie W., Gertie, Dora, Theo & all Henry's and Moroni's folks, and a merry christmas to you all. Write soon. L. R. Martineau

[page 164]

January 5, 1899—During this day surveyed some in Lower Tenaja field

January 6, 1899—Blessed Joel, Mary Ann, and their two children.

January 7, 1899—Johnny's birth day. He would be 40 years of age now. Recorded blessings in my Temple Record.

January 8, 1899—To day is our 47th wedding day, and now, at noon, I think of my position just 47 years ago, when I stood solitary and alone, like a Robinson Crusoe, only I had no domain I could call my own. Now, what a change! Now, with wives, children and their companions and one great-grand child, Elbert Johnson, Elvira's gr. son, we number 115; and thus far, none have in any manner brought any shame or disgrace or sorrow upon our heads. Of the 115 total 6 of our children have passed away, 17 grand-children and 2 wives also, making 25 who have left us, & 90 who remain, exclusive of the children my son Nels L. Hagberg has by his last wife during the last 5 or 6 years.

In addition, there have been sealed to me as wives in the temple one hundred wives for eternity and one, Mary Eliza Jones, for time only. Of the 102 wives sealed to me of whom I have received a testimony that all have accepted the work done for them with joy and gladness—six have received their 2nd A.—the last and highest ordinance that can be bestowed upon Earth. Among them, Nelly Benson, an indian girl raised by Apostle Ezra T. Benson and wife Adaline, and who died aged about 25 years, received her 2nd A. and I was told at the time, this was the first time in this dispensation that any Lamanite woman had received this ordinance, which I consider a great honor to me, as her husband. I myself having previously (July 10 1884) received the same in connection with my two wives Susan E. J. and Susan J. S. in the Logan Temple. In the priesthood, I was ordained a Seventy by J. M. Grant in February 1851 in S. L. City, Utah, and a High Priest by Geo. A. Smith in May, 1854 in Parowan, at the time I was appointed 2nd Counsellor to Prest. of Stake John C. L. Smith.

[page 165]

January 8, 1899—On Nov. 30th 1898 I was ordained to the high and holy priesthood of a Patriarch in the Church by Apostle Marriner W. Merrill, Saml Roskelly, Temple Recorder, as a Witness, in the Logan Temple, by direction of the First Presidency of the Church.

In temple work I and my family, have done a work more or less complete, for over 2000 of the dead, and I have had a testimony that our work has been accepted by them all. In 1887, I saw them in open vision, passing in a triumphal and joyful procession before me, a Scrolle written above their heads saying "Come unto me all ye who are weary and heavy laden, and I will give you rest." While the maticious [malicious] faces of a multitude of devils glared upon them as they passed, but unable to harm them.

This temple work has been the greatest joy of my life—the thought that so many have been released from their prison house, placed beyond the power of Satan, and put on their way to an exaltation in the

Celestial Glory. To me, in comparison, the wealth of a million worlds like this would be as nothing, and my soul is filled with joy and thankfulness to our Father that I have been thus permitted, in connection with my family, to be Saviors on Mt. Zion. In this work, while we lived in Logan, where the temple stands, my beloved wife Susan E. J. was very energetic, missing only one day (and that from sickness) while we remained in Logan, and considerable work at intervals, since then. Susan J. Sherman died before the temple was completed—10 years—and therefore has no record for work in its holy precincts. Truly few men have been so blessed as I,—not with temporal wealth, for we are poor in this world's good, but have a riches that will last through all the eternities, providing I and mine do <u>our</u> part. Father help us so to do, I ask in the name of Jesus. Amen.

January 11, 1899—Heard that Theodore, who is on the farm he leased in Dublan, is quite sick, pleurisy & threatened with pneumonia.

[page 166]

January 12, 1899—Tried to get him home, but Dr. Keat said he must not be moved. He finally came home in a few days, recovering fast.

January 28, 1899—Henry as Secretary of Chuichupa Land Comp. Settled with me as follows on my Land Survey account:—

Total cash due me for survey $150.00 and $40.00 = $190.00

" amt to be paid in land $350.00

[$12,614] $540.00

I have received land $280.00 * $75.00 = $355.00 [$7,825]

" " " Cash $164.00, now due me to settle a/c $21.00

To day I made some mining plats for A. W. Ivins $5.00

January 30, 1899—This evening I blessed Henry and Gertrude, whose blessings will be found in my temple record, also those of Joel and family.

January 31, 1899—Gave Sadie S. Martineau (Moroni's widow) her blessing. Henry et.al. also Theodore, went to Chuichupa. Theo. went for his health, being still feeling miserable.

FEBRUARY.

February 23, 1899—Dora very sick to day. Had a hard fit before arising.

February 24, 1899—Still very sick. Theo. came from Chuichupa

February 28, 1899—Theo. and Gertie went to Chuichupa. Gertie has had miserable health for a long time and we hope the change may do her good. Dora is better, but not well.

Bargained my horses to Theo, conditionally.

MARCH

March 1, 1899—Planted peas.

March 2, 1899—At Priesthood meeting it was decided to build a bridge across the Piedras Verdes river here, upon my plan. I & two others were appointed to be a building committee.

March 6, 1899—Began as correspondent for El Paso Herald.

March 13, 1899—My 71st Birth day. In the evening I was surprised by arrival to supper of Br. J. J. Walser and his wives, Bp. J. C. Bentley's wife, Mrs. Dr. Saville and daughter and Joel and family. My folks had planned it, and we had a pleasant evening.

I cannot realize I am so aged, only I find myself tiring more quickly when I work, and my bodily strength less.

[page 167]

****LYMAN'S BABE MAY P. DIED.***

March 23, 1899—Gertrude came home from Chuichupa, much improved. Henry and Charles came at Same time with Lois and Edith

March 25 & 26, 1899—Sunday school conference. A good time. Brs. Maeser and L. J. Nutall came from S. L. City to attend it.

March 27, 1899—Surveyed in the hills for McDonald and E. Taylor

March 28, 1899—Made map of Survey.

APRIL

April 4, 1899—Henry and family went home. Before they went I gave Patriarchal blessings to Charles, Lois and Edith, on April 3d—

April 12, 1899—Theodore came for me to go to Chuichupa and help him survey some mining claims.

April 14, 1899—Started with him, got caught in rain and wet through. Camped on mountain in old shanty, elevation about 7000 ft.

April 15, 1899—Rained all forenoon. Camped near Garcia

April 16, 1899—Sunday. Passed over the Continental divide 7400 ft. elevation.

April 17, 1899—Reached Chuichupa 9.30 A.M. Found all well as usual.

April 18, 1899—Went to a party in the evening, after giving blessings to the families of Henry and Moroni, such as had not already received them.

April 19, 1899—I started home with Cal. Allred, having left my instruments with Theodore to do the surveys spoken of. Got home on

April 22, 1899—Saturday and found all well.

***April 21st, 1899**—On Friday April 21st Lyman's little babe, May Preston, died suddenly, at 4.30 P.M. She weighted only 5 lbs 9 oz at her death, having gained scarcely any in weight since her birth. She was born prematurely, and caused almost the sacrifice of her mother's life.

April 25, 1899—Albert, Emma and their 5 children came, having left Thatcher, Arizona, Mch. 31st and traveled with 2 wagons about 400 miles. All were well, and his horses were in good condition

April 23, 1899—On Sunday morning I had a very delightful dream. I was in a large building, new to me, and was told some one wished to see me in the next room. I entered and saw a man lying in a bed, aged, with white hair and long beard. I knew him as an old friend whom I had not seen for a long time, and was exceeding glad to meet him again, as he was also, to see me, reaching up his arms and embracing me.

[page 168]

April 23, 1899—I cannot describe our exquisite joy in thus meeting again; words cannot express it. As I looked I saw another man lying beside him, aged and white haired like the first, & one whom also I knew as an old, long absent friend. He and I also embraced, with the same unutterable joy, & then I saw another lying by his side, with whom I had the same joyful embrace and greeting. I knew them all, and knew they were Patriarchs, and they welcomed me as a fellow patriarch—one of that Quorum. I awoke, thrilled with exquisite joy, it all seemed so real, but could not now remember who they were, nor where I had known them. It seemed to me that they had died before I saw them.

I do not know if this means that I shall soon go to them or not, but it gives me joy to know how I shall be received when I do go, either soon or late. Like Abraham, I praise the Father with exceeding thankfulness and rejoicing, for the bestowal upon me of this high and holy calling and priesthood,—as Patriarch,—promised me so many years ago; and pray that I may be able to fulfill all its duties in a manner pleasing to our Father in Heaven, who has been so wonderfully good to me.

April 29, 1899—Helped haul my adobes for additional house room.

MAY

May 2, 1899—Began to make a map of Colonia Juarez for the Colonization company. Worked on it all day.

[written in margin]

Note April 25th

On April 25th Albert and his family of wife and five children arrived from Arizona. He said he had dreaded to pull up and make another home, but an influence had continually drawn him to Mexico, and he had to come. I hope he will not regret coming, although he left a good home in Thatcher, Arizona.

May 5, 1899—To day was the Cinco de Mayo celebration—the Mexican day of rejoicing over the victory achieved over the French in Peuebla. Our town celebrated, also, we being now all counted Mexicans.

[page 169]

May 5, 1899—I began to lay up the adobes of my new house, but it is slow work, as I have to mix the mortar and carry it and the adobes and then lay them; but slow work is better than nothing. I have tried to get a mason to do it, but have been unable, they being engaged months ahead. I am glad to know how to do such work myself.

May 6, 1899—Continued laying adobes. Theodore and Bertha came.

May 7, 1899—Blessed Albert and Emma, also their children George A. & Elzadie. Also blessed Avelina E. Mills and her daughter Carolina M. Saville

May 8, 1899—Blessed Albert's children Leland A., Ernest and Nola the baby girl. In the evening D [Dora] had a very severe fit & fell from her chair and hurt herself, wrenching her back. We administered at once and she soon went to sleep and rested sweetly, through the blessing of the Lord. For the first time in administering to her I blessed her that she should be entirely healed of her fits in due time, and I pray that she may be. For three years we have not felt easy to have her absent from us any length of time, as she is taken at any unexpected moment, and it is a constant worry for us. I made two maps for Theodore of a mining survey he made lately, and he took them in the evening and went to Guerrero to have them recorded. I also copied Albert's family blessings into the Blessing record, and unloaded 400 adobes. So I have had a very busy day. Got $1.[00] [$23] worth of strawberries.

May 9, 1899—Finished recording Albert's blessings, Albert and family Started for Chuichupa, where he thinks of making a home if he feels satisfied there. We have had a pleasant visit of about two weeks, and I pray that they may be blessed as they need.

May 10, 1899—Blessed Dora. Laid 800 adobes today with Charlie's help, who came here on the 8th

May 11, 1899—Still laying adobes. Our school term closes to day.

May 12, 1899—Blessed Anna's children, Phyllis and Frederick Wenden Walser while their mother was at the school dance.

May 13, 1899—Changed the foundation of front room, making it larger.

[page 170]

May 28, 1899—Gave a blessing to Sister Hannah Ballinger.

June 5, 1899—While upon my scaffold to day, with Susan and Dora handing adobes from a pile of lumber the scaffold fell to the ground with a crash. I clung to the wall until everything below had settled, and then dropped upon the debris without injury, thanks to the Lord. Had I fallen with the adobes &c I would have been badly hurt, as the timbers were broken into long splinters.

June 16, 1899—This morning I dreamed a very vivid dream of an ancient fortification of cut stone of the Nephites. I looked at it with much interest. Its name was At lán qui At lá ya.

July 1, 1899—To day Joel and Theodore began helping me put the roof on my new house, the outside walls being done, raised 12 feet above top of foundation. I began laying the walls in April, and for three months have labored far beyond my strength, laying foundations, hauling clay, mixing mortar, helping haul and unload adobes, then carrying them and laying in wall, carrying, too, the mortar, thus doing ten minutes work to lay adobes in the wall one minute. Sometimes Dora helped carry mortar and bring adobes, being anxious to help, as also Susan and Gertrude, but none of them were able to do much, all of them being crippled invalids. I could not get any mason or other help, having no money, scarcely, and so had to undertake the work myself, or else the rainy season would flood our poor cabin through the sieve-like roof. The Lord gave me strength, or I could not have accomplished the work. As it was, many times I was so exhausted that I could not eat. But the walls are up, all but the inside ones.

There is still a great labor;—the old walls to take down, the debris to take care of and the roof and inside wood work to make. I got my adobes little by little, and must get lumber and shingles and nails in the same way. But I hope to succeed at last.

[page 171]

July 3, 1899—Began shingling, having a few to begin with, and threatening of rains.

July 6, 1899—A heavy rain, the beginning of the rainy season. The South end is covered—about one third the roof—and so much is dry.

July 7, 1899—Dora had a severe fit, or it would have been, had she not been instantly administered to, and obtained relief at once. Poor girl! She has had many, fearful to behold. I pray she may be healed of them.

July 8, 1899—Theodore and Joel quit work, to work for themselves, leaving me to plod on alone the best I can.

July 11, 1899—Susan's 63[d] birth day. I pray that she may has as many more, or as many as she shall desire. As I look back more than 47 years, when first we came together and wed, it all seems a dream. She was then not quite 16, plump, fair to see,—a bright, active girl; now, getting somewhat gray and quite lame with rheumatism in her knees, making it difficult for her to walk much. In all these years, in sickness and health, poverty or plenty, joy or sorrow, calm or tempest, sunshine or clouded skies, she has always been the same true, sympathetic, faithful companion, wife and mother—a helpmate indeed, and not to us alone, but to the sick or sad around her, who have many times been made to rejoice through her administrations to the sick and words of comfort to the sad. May her last days be her brightest and best. They <u>will</u>.

July 17, 1899—Finished shingling the house, except a few along the comb.

July 20, 1899—Have two floors laid, but have no material for the other.

To day Moses Thatcher, Lucien Farr and J. D. Haines walked in having just come from Utah. I was very glad to see them again. I cannot help feeling sad for Br. Thatcher's present situation, losing his position as Apostle, even if he was rightly dealt with, which I do not doubt. All are weak,—all liable to be overcome by evil influences, for Satan will not suffer us to gain an exaltation if he can prevent it. I do hope may come out all right in the end. He has done much good, and shall not lose his reward.[32]

[page 172]

Thursday, July 20, 1899—Our Quarterly conference begins this evening. Apostle B. Young being present, at meeting of Relief Society Conf^{e}

Friday, July 21, 1899—Meeting again today. Instructed in regard to the necessity of paying a full tithing, in accordance with instructions of Pres^{t} Lorenzo Snow at the Solemn Assembly, held July 2$^{\underline{nd}}$ in S. L. City. Priesthood meeting in the evening.

July 24, 1899—Elders B. Young and Bp Farr dined with us after celebration of the 24$^{\underline{th}}$

July 31, 1899—Moses Thatcher, Lucien Farr and J. D. Haines dined with us, also Henry. On <u>25$^{\underline{th}}$</u> Theo. returned to Chuichupa.

July 27$^{\underline{th}}$, 1899—Dora had a bad fit to day: fell and injured collar bone.

32 Moses Thatcher was released from the Quorum of Twelve Apostles because of his opposition to the Manifesto of 1890 (Kenneth W. Godfrey, "Moses Thatcher in the Dock: His Trials, the Aftermath, and His Last Days," *Journal of Mormon History* [Spring 1998]: 54–88).

Tuesday, August 1, 1899—Moses Thatcher and friends breakfasted with us, just before their starting home to Utah

August 7, 1899—Dora had a very hard fit:—fell full length upon the floor and hurt herself badly. After administration, she soon seemed all right.

August 10, 1899—Henry came last night from R. R. station shop

August 11, 1899—He began to work on my house, inside. To day I was taken very suddenly with a flux.[33]

August 12, 1899—Very ill,—constant, copious discharges. Took much Cholera medicine—"Sun Cholera cure."

August 13, 1899—Better to day, but much worse next day.

August 15, 1899—Able to work a little.

Friday, August 18, 1899—Went to Casas Grandes and paid my first tax, of $1.80 [$42] for 1899, as tax on irrigation water for one city lot.

August 21, 1899—Albert bought my stock;—21 cows., 2 3 yr. olds, 6 yearlings and 6 horses, for $900 [$21,023]. The stamps on bill of sale were $5.40 [$126]. The State levies tax of 2o/c, = $18.$^{\underline{00}}$ [$420] and Republic a tax of 30o/c of $18.$^{\underline{00}}$, = $5.40, total $23.40 [$547].

August 29, 1899—Dora had another fit to day.

September 1, 1899—Hired conveyance and went with Susan and Dora to Dublan to visit Tenney's folks, and had a pleasant time.

September 9, 1899—Anna and her children went to Williams' ranch—an out. We bought a nice dress for Bertha McClellan, who has been very good to us, in [letting] us have milk and in other ways.

[page 173]

September 11, 1899—Gertrude also went to Williams' ranch in the mountains with Bentley and wife.

September 12, 1899—Theo. sent my transit from Chuichupa, but no key to it.

September 16, 1899—Grand celebration of Mexican independence. By letter from Lyman I learn

33 Flux is a watery discharge from the bowels, as with diarrhea.

of Sister Henrietta's death some weeks ago, exact date not mentioned. He sent me Fanny's explanatory letter, which I here insert:—

Chemainus B.C.[34]

Vancouver's Island Aug. 22. 1899

My dear Cousin Lyman

Your letter reached me yesterday and I hasten to reply now to your kind inquiries about my dear mother. I have had many letters from relatives and friends, and you can imagine how very hard it has been to write of Mama, as it brings my terrible bereavement so before me, and I have only written necessary letters.

On the steamer, coming out here between Seattle and Victoria, she fell and broke her wrist, which, with other bruises, gave a severe shock to her nervous system, from which, though she seemed to rally for a time, was hastened her death, but the failing was so gradual, and her spirits so wonderful when at all free from pain, one could not realize in the least—that is—that death was near. As she seemed so weak, the doctor advised me to take her to the hospital for more complete care than I could give her; as rheumatism had settled in her weak arm and shoulder, and she suffered most intensely,—especially during the night. So I went there with her. The next day she had a sudden sinking spell, and the following morning passed from earth to heaven,—one of the sweetest saints that ever lived. The few people we here met were all ~~attached~~ attracted to her by her cheerful spirit, bright intellect and loveable ways, and seemed to love her. All were kind to her, and to me in my desolation which I realize more every day,—over 2000 miles away from our old home and friends. Mamma had been very anxious for a change to a milder climate and was so delighted to come out here, and never regretted it.

[page 174]

September 16, 1899—It will always be a grief to me that you did not know her. She had the Martineau courage, spirit and brightness, which were with her to the last, as well as her christian faith, and her patience during those years of misfortune have been remarked by all who knew her. I should have sent word at once to your father but did not know his address, so I shall depend upon you to let him know. According to Mama's wish I shall remain here in this family to fulfill my engagement, which closes next year. I have as pupil, the only daughter, a young girl of 18, and this is her last year of study.

I hope cousin Allie and the children are well, and that you will send me the photograph you were about to send to Mama. I have none of Mama which I can spare at present, but the negative of the one I like best is in St. Paul, and I hope before long to have some more taken. With kindest regards to you all, Affectionately

Your cousin Fannie M. Lyon

Will you not write to me once in a while? Remember, I am a stranger in a strange land."

My dear sister was born 18th Oct. 1825, and was thus in her 74th year when she died. Although not a member of the Church of Christ, she loved righteousness, had a practical faith in prayer, and will, no doubt, receive the truth in the estate to which she has gone, and receive the ordinances of the temple which I shall have performed for her.

Only Lois and I now remain of our mother's family, and Uncle Charles Sprague Mears alone of my grandparent (on my mother's side) Our Father only knows when my time will arrive to pass away from this mortal life and some one write of me "He was" &c &c. It matters not to me—the Father doeth all things well. I do not wish to live any longer than I am able to do good and help the work of the Lord in my weak way.

[page 175]

September 16, 1899—When no longer able to do this I pray that I may not linger in this vale of tears.

To day we celebrated Mexican Independence.

September 23, 1899—Dora had a bad fit this evening and we had hard work to get her into the house. Anna and her children came home from Williams' place in the mountains.

September 24, 1899—Dora had another fit this morning—a severe one. She fell heavily to the floor and mangled her tongue badly.

September 28, 1899—To day is Gertie's 29th birth day. We had a pleasant company and supper in the evening.

34 Chemainus, British Columbia, Canada, is just north of the city of Victoria, on Vancouver Island.

OCTOBER 1899

October 10, 1899—Joel and Gertrude went to the mountains, Gertie for her health and Joel to Chuichupa on business.

I wrote to Ass[t] U. S. Treasurer at New York to ~~stp~~ stop payment of check No. 388.860 dated Mch. 17. 1899 in my favor. Mex. War pension, $24.[00] [$561] I had sold same to Bentley & Harris for $50.40 [$1,177] Mex. currency.

For about ten days I have been glazing my windows and painting, but it is slow work for an amateur.

October 14, 1899—Theodore came from Chuichupa to attend conference.

October 20, 1899—Dora had a severe fit to day. Administered, and she soon recovered.

October 21 & 22, 1899—Quarterly Conference in Juarez.

NOVEMBER

November 13, 1899—Dora had a fit again to day.

November 15, 1899—Br. David Spillsbury brought a cow which had been lost three years. I paid him $10.[00] [$234] for it. I am thankful.

November 16, 1899—Jo[s] Turley began plastering my house.[35]

November 17, 1899—Henry and Albert, and Sarah came from Chuichupa for family supplies.

November 24, 1899—Rec[d] an appointment (unsolicited) as mineral Surveyor in Sabinal mineral District. Gertrude came home from Williams' mountain ranch, after absence of six weeks. She seems much improved in health.

November 25, 1899—We moved into our new rooms, and thank the Lord for his blessing, enabling me, amid many difficulties, to build them.

[page 176]

November 26, 1899—Sunday. Apostle A. O. Woodruff and Mrs. McCune present in meeting.[36] A happy time. In the afternoon was organized a political club, of which I am one of five executive Committe. We drafted a memorial to Pres[t] Diaz, praing [praising] him to serve another term as President of Mexico.

November 27, 1899—Gave Mrs McCune a patriarchal blessing.

DECEMBER

December 2, 1899—Went to Dublan to attend their ward Conference. Apostle Woodruff and Mrs. McCune gave much good instruction. A change was made in the Bishopric of Dublan, Bp. Winslow Farr, retiring for age, and a new Bishop,—Sam[l] J. Robinson ordained instead. There being some disunion in relation to Counsellors. br. Woodruff called a special Council of himself, the Stake Presidency,—Patriarchs and High Council: There still being a lack of unanimity, another council was called—Elder Woodruff, Stake Presidents Pratt and Eyring, and Pat[h] Stowell, and myself, who finally decided the matter. Accordingly, Br. S. J. Robinson was chosen Bishop, with Jos. L. Cardon 1st and Anson V. Call 2nd Counsellors. All were unanimously sustained by vote of the Conference. It was a surprise to the people, but satisfactory.[37]

December 3, 1899—Gave a blessing to Coun[r] Call's wife,—Dora Pratt Call and came home, refreshed with my outing. Found all well at home.

December 7, 1899—Made mining map for Duthie and Vance. $10.00 [$234].

December 9, 1899—A heavy wind to day, and quite cold.

Learn by Logan Journal that Lilla has a son.

Rec[d] 500 lbs flour from Jarvis, the most at one time for many years.

December 10, 1899—Gave a blessing to Jo[s] A. Woolley, and he gave me $2.[00] [$47].

December 12, 1899—Surveyed the "El Pajarito Grande" mine for Croff = $30.[00] [$701].

---

35 Joseph Hartley Turley was the son of Isaac and Sarah Greenwood Turley (Ricketts, *Arizona's Honeymoon Trail*, 33).

36 Abraham O. Woodruff (1872–1904) served as an Apostle from 1897 until his death.

37 These gentlemen were all active members in the Mexican colonies (Romney, *The Mormon Colonies*, 98–100).

December 15, 1899—Laid our new rag carpet. It gave us great pleasure, as we begin to grow more homelike and comfortable, as in days past. I thank our Father for His blessings this year, in enabling to build our comfortable home without any visible means, scarcely, to build with.

[page 177]

December 15, 1899—It has been almost entirely the work of my own hands and labor from the very foundation up, my sons having done very little towards it. And one great satisfaction is that it is paid for. I have been engaged upon it ever since last April, and it lacks much even now, of completion, as I have another room and hall and porch to erect. I hope I shall be prospered in doing so.

December 16, 1899—Made maps of the mining survey and signed them as "El Perito Practico, J. H. Martineau," with my official scrawl below my name, as above, which the law of Mexico requires.

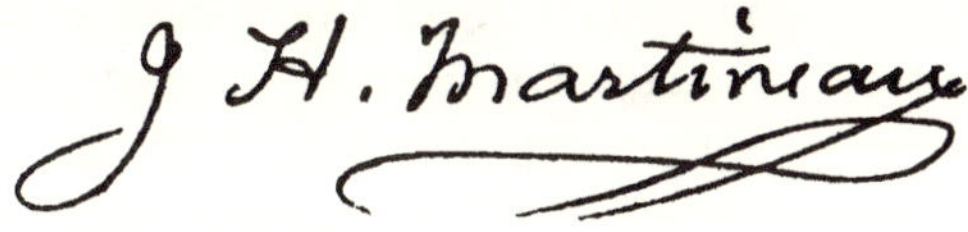

Fig. 9.2—Signature.

Also made a pair of gates and hung them.

December 17, 1899—Received a letter from Theodore, who has recently been called as a Missionary, from which I insert the following paragraphs:—

"My school work keeps me very busy in connection with my work in the M. I. A, though I am still trying to find time to study the Bible, Book of M. Doc. & Cov, Preaching and Public Speaking, The Youth's Companion, Draper's Intellectual development of Europe, the Almanac, and a few other books, in the desperate hope of being able to catch a few Noble ideas; but alas! how meager are the results! Perhaps you can imagine the chaotic condition of my mind since I received the fateful missive!

Of course I wrote and told them I should be pleased to go at some future time, but oh dear! when will it be? With debts to pay and money for the trip, who can tell how long it will be before I shall be in condition to go? Not I, I am sure.

It almost makes me "wave and go wild" when I think how poorly I am prepared to go out into the world to carry a message which I myself so imperfectly understand. I suppose, however, that it is one of the ways the Lord has of punishing His careless children, so I shall try to make the best of my situation and improve it as much as possible in the short time at my disposal.

[page 178]

December 17, 1899—I know the Lord will bless me with means, if I will only put my trust in Him and do my own duty, so I have no fears as to the results."

For several months Theodore has felt a desire to go on a mission, feeling he could do so better now than when he might be called and have to leave a family, deprived of his help, though always diffident as to his ability as a missionary. I pray he may go and honorably fill his mission.

December 31, 1899—I have paid $50.00 [$1,168] tithing this year, nearly all cash. It was a full tithing and something over, as all my increase this year has not been $500.00 [$11,680]. But I would rather be over than under in my payments.

JANUARY 1900.

January 2, 1900—To day Guy C. Taylor asked my consent to his marriage with Gertrude. Knowing his integrity and worthiness I gave my consent. But I do not see just now, how it can be effected, as Pres^t L. Snow has closed the door of plural marriage.[38]

January 4, 1900—Went to El Paso on business, returning on the 6th

January 8, 1900—We celebrated this, the 48th anniversary of our wedding. Had a nice supper and a company of friends, and had a very enjoyable time

January 10, 1900—Surveyed fence line of Lower Tenaja field, 1 day $10 [$234].

January 15 & 16, 1900—Surveyed a canal for Lower Tenaja field,—2 days 20$ [$467].

January 18, 1900—To day, in company with Pres^t A. W. Ivins I started to the new purchase of land

38 There was resistence to the Manifesto within the Church as evidenced in this entry. This is likely Guy Taylor of Colonia Juárez. He was married to Minnie Cardon at the time. Gertrude would be a plural wife.

in Sonora—the Batifilto ranch—We stayed over night at 2nd Counr H. Pratt. Very cold.

January 19, 1900—Started by starlight for Diaz. Very cold weather. Got to Diaz, 55 m about sunset. I stayed at Br. Thayn's. Went to Relief Society meeting in the evening.

January 20 & 21, 1900—Attended Quarterly Conference, a very enjoyable one. On the 21st I gave blessings to Elizabeth, Thayn and Nephi Tenney. I caused Elizabeth (Sun) to be ordained or blessed as a Midwife and nurse, which she had so earnestly desired might be done.

[page 179]

January 21, 1900—I also administered to young Elizabeth Thayn, who has long been greatly afflicted.

January 22, 1900—Left Diaz at 9.30 A.M. Our Company consists of Prests Ivins and Pratt, myself, as Engineer, and High Councillor Orson P. Brown and wife, Also Bishop Geo. C. Negley. Drove 25 miles and camped. Night very cold.[39]

January 23, 1900—Started early and drove to near the summit of Sierra Madre pass. Night cold and windy.

January 24, 1900—Drove 30 miles to Colonia Oaxaca. The descent from the Summit, for about 3½ miles was steep and sometimes very rough, the descent being about 3000 feet in that distance.

January 25, 1900—Reached Batipito (pronounced Bat-i-pé-to.) about 2½ hours after dark, a distance of 25 miles. The night was pitch dark, so I could hardly see our horses. We lost our road, and wandered until finally we heard dogs barking in the distance, and reached a Small Mexican hamlet of Mescal distillers, who directed us to the camp, about 1 mile distant, and glad indeed we were to see the bright camp fire, and to have a nice warm Supper of fresh venison. We found 8 men, from S. L. City and Payson, Utah, who had been waiting for us about a week.

The Mescal liquor referred to is made from the century plant, or [blank space] as it is known in Mexico. A piece is cut from the head of the plant, about as large as a good Sized Cabbage, which is roasted 24 hours, which makes it sweet, as if steeped in molasses. Being crushed, the juice is distilled into Mescal, much like whiskey in appearance,—a strong, pure liquor, but having a smoky flavor which is disagreeable to my palate.

January 26, 1900—Commenced running trial canal lines to get water from the river, which has but little fall—about 8 or 9 feet per mile. Spent several days at this work & finally found a suitable line for an irrigation Canal. After this I surveyed a city plat of about 40 or 50 blocks each 100 meter square, 4 lots in a block. After this was done I laid out some hectare lots, 2 hectare and 4 hectare lots in the field finishing our labors on the 16th for the present, and leaving camp near Sunset. Went 4 miles and camped.

[page 180]

January 28, 1900—Sunday. To day was held a regular Sunday meeting on this ground,—the first, probably, since the destruction of the Nephites 1500 years ago. I opened, by prayer, and Prests Ivins and Pratt spoke, myself also. Two women, wives of Robt L. McCall, named Christina Smith & Christina Southeimer McCall were present, the first Colonist women in the Settlement.[40] We met in a shanty belonging to Samuel Lewis

February 4, 1900—Meeting again to day. I spoke again

February 11, 1900—Meeting to day, Prest Ivins organized a Branch of the Oaxaca Ward, Bishop Naegle being present. L. S. Huish was appointed Presiding Elder, E. Huish Clerk, also Brs S. J. Jarvis, Snarr and Hunsaker an Executive committee.[41]

The bottom lands are covered with a coarse grass 4 to 8 feet high and so close and thick it is hard to survey through it. This grass is called Sacatón.

Sunday, February 18, 1900—Meeting to day. I spoke and felt the Spirit of prophecy predicting that the rains shall increase, falling in what are now the dry seasons, new springs shall break forth and the streams shall increase in volume.

39 Orson P. Brown became bishop of the Oaxaca Ward in 1901. The reference to Geo. C. Negley could be John C. Naegle, who was on the high council in Colonia Juárez. See the entry for February 11 (Romney, *The Mormon Colonies*, 114, 122, 140).

40 Robert Lindsay McCall was a resident of Colonia Juárez.

41 The Huish and Snarr families were among the first to settle Colonia Morelos (Romney, *The Mormon Colonies*, 121).

I will say, that while in Colonia Batipito I blessed E. Huish & Son, J J Huber and brother, R. L. McCall & his two wives. At Oaxaca I blessed Anna Naegle, Geo. W. and Phebe Scott by their request. I stayed with Conrad Naegle's family in Oaxaca. Well treated.

February 19, 1900—Started for home in a heavy gale, which broke limbs from the trees. Drove over the mountain pass and camped after dark. Night very windy and cold

February 20, 1900—Drove about 50 miles. Camp cold and windy.

February 21, 1900—Started by daylight, Drove 48 miles, reaching home at 7 P.M. Very glad to be at home again. Found all well.

On this trip my labor has been very arduous, but the Father blessed and sustained me, so that I had no cause to complain.

February 22, 1900—Dora had a fit at the table to day, the first in 2 mon [months]

[page 181]

February 24 & 25, 1900—Apostles Grant and Clawson,[42] Mrs. Grant, Karl G. Maeser and J. Golden Kimball spoke by the power of the holy Spirit, and we had a glorious Conference. The Sunday schools have an enrollment of 1591, average attendance 80 o/c [%]. Our stake has paid \$37000$^{\underline{00}}$ [\$864,293] tithing this year, an average of about \$75.$^{\underline{00}}$ [\$1,752] pr tithe payer. We were highly complimented, but told not to become vain glorious, for we will have all the opposition we want, in Mexico.

February 26, 1900—Theodore Came. He is thus far on his way to his mission in the United States.

February 28, 1900—Surveyed Upper Teneja Canal, also next day, 2 days

MARCH 1900

March 2, 1900—Surveyed Lower (Canal,) Tenaja field, 2 days in all.

March 3, 1900—To day George Orrin Jacoby, a little boy 9 years old came to live with us. He came last fall from Ohio, with missionary E. McClellan, but they did not wish to keep him, so we take him. His family are still in the States, too poor to come to Mexico just now.

March 9, 1900—Visited Orson Brown's family. Blessed him and his wife.

March 10 & 11, 1900—Susan quite unwell, and in much pain, with cough. [line dittoed for March 11]

March 12, 1900—Susan is recovering. It was quite severe while it lasted.

March 13, 1900—My 72nd birth day. Worked hard, surveying land and at other work.

In my younger days I never expected to live to be more than 45 or 50, and now I am 72. Truly the Lord has been very kind and merciful to me. I still feel full of life and ambition, but find I tire much [more] quickly than in years past, and my rupture incapacitates me from hard manual labor. If my faith does not fail I hope to go back to the center stake of Zion, according to the promise made me. I know that He who formed my body has power to renew and strengthen it if it is His will, and if it is <u>not</u> His will, of course I do not desire it.

March 16, 1900—I have been greatly in doubt whether to go to Conference in April or not, on account of taking so much means that is needed at home.

[page 182]

March 16, 1900—I prayed and received answer that it would be <u>right</u>, and that I should be blessed in so doing, and should suffer no loss. Last night Susan asked about it, and had an answer similar to mine. So now I feel to go and to trust in the Lord that it may not be injurious for my family.

March 17, 1900—Attended an annual meeting of the Relief Society in honor of the organization of the society by Joseph Smith. We had a very pleasant time.

March 18, 1900—Blessed Bp. Jo^{s} C. Bentley, also Ethel and Orrin

March 19, 1900—Rented my 15 acres of land to John Allen for 1/5th, delivered to me at my home.

March 21, 1900—Have finally determined to go to Conference. I have been undecided, because it seems selfish to use so much money for the trip, that my family ~~de~~ needs at home. I asked the Father this morning and was told in answer to "go, you shall be blessed, your family shall be blessed in your absence,

42 This is Rudger Clawson (1857–1943). He was called as an Apostle in 1898 and later served as a counselor to President Lorenzo Snow.

and Dora shall have no fit while you are gone, and she shall be healed entirely." I also had other glorious promises, which I hope will be fulfilled.

In the evening the girls had a party in honor of Theodore, who will soon go upon his mission.

March 29, 1900—Blessed Sister Gladys Bentley and her 3 children

APRIL 1900

April 1, 1899—Blessed Manrique Gonzales, a young Mexican man who has joined the church. He has a great work. Also Blessed Mabel Allen.

April 2, 1900—Started at 5 A.M. to go to S. L. City, with Theodore. Arr[d] at El Paso 4.30 P.M. Left El Paso at 8.30 P.M.

April 4, 1900—Left Pueblo at noon in heavy rain, which turned to snow as we ascend the mountains along the Arkansas river.

April 5, 1900—Arrived at S. L. City about noon and stopped with Bp. Preston's family.

April 6, 7, & 8, 1900—Attended conference. Smoot Reed [the numbers 2 & 1 are penned above the name, meaning Reed Smoot] ord[d] apostle

April 9, 1900—Theodore was ordained a Seventy by Apostle Reed Smoot, in the mission assigned him in the Southern States.[43]

[page 183]

April 10, 1900—Still snowing. Theo. and I went to Logan. Arr[d] 11.40 A.M. Found all the family well. Went to Lyman's to stay.

April 12, 1900—Began temple work. I endowed David Columbine. Theodore was endowed for himself. I had Dav[d] Columbine and Ann Elwyn Sealed as husband and wife.

April 13, 1900—I end[d] Mr. Webb, and sealed him and Norjay Haughout.

April 15, 1900—Sunday. Spoke in the Tabernacle this afternoon. Also in the Sunday School. Blessed Charles F. Martineau Jun and Bp. B. M. Lewis.

April 17, 1900—Theo. started on his mission

April 18, 1900—By letter from Virginia learn she has small pox in Eureka Her husband has got well of it, and she is quarantined, alone with her children. She feels pretty bad.

I end[d] Mr. Cozine & Sealed him and Nelly Haughout.

April 19, 1900—I end[d] Mr. Stillwell. Theo. left S. L. City. Sister Preston and May made him a nice lunch for journey. Charlie came home from sheep herd, sick with La Grippe

April 18, 1900—I blessed Harriet A. and L. Royal Jr. Martineau

April 20, 1900—I end[d] Mr. Perrine, & Sealed him and wife, also Sealed Stillwell and wife.

April 21, 1900—Blessed my Son Charles F. Martineau

April 25, 1900—Wed. I end[d] Rob[t] T. Elwyn

April 26, 1900—I end[d] John Rand

April 27, 1900—I end[d] Mr. Barlow, Sealed him & Miss Bloomfield. Also sealed Mr. & Mrs. John Rand.

Letter from Theo. His field is South Alabama. Conf[c]

April 29 & 30, 1900—Apostles Grant, Teasdale and Lyman present. They dropped some Bishop, and ordained 3 Patriarchs. F. M. Lyman gave instructions to Patriarchs. Must set dates of events to happen:—should not give too long blessings. Must obey the Word of Wisdom and set a good and holy example to all. Saw Nephi, just from his new farm.

MAY 1900

May 2, 1900—Nephi went back to Blue Creek farm.

I end[d] Paul Maurice

May 3, 1900—Unwell and did not go to the temple. Snowy.

May 4, 1900—Charlie's boy Freeman quite sick.

I end[d] Mr. Dyer, Mrs. Affleck End[d] Mrs. Sarah Allen

[page 184]

May 4, 1900—Mrs. ~~M. A. Maughand~~—Hibbard end[d] Maria M. Wheelock.

Mrs. M. A. Maughan End[d] Mrs. Headly

This morning I awoke very deaf, my right ear entirely

43 Reed Smoot (1862–1941) was ordained an Apostle on April 8, 1900, and served as a U.S. senator from 1903 to 1932.

May 7, 1900—Got the valise and clothes Theo. Sent home.

May 9, 1900—Lyman and Alley helped me in the temple.

I Endowed Francis Columbine

Lyman endowed Henry H. Mears

Alley endowed Theodora Martineau (Elwin)

Mrs. Maughan endowed Catherine Barlow

Katy Preston endowed Mrs. John Dexter

Mrs. Hurst endowed Miss Bloomfield

I had sealed—H. H. Mears & wife, Paul Maurice and Margaret Keteltas, Mrs. Maughan prox. in Sealing.

May 10, 1900—I endowed Alex. Stanhope

Lyman endowed William Martineau

Alley endowed Mrs. Joseph May

Mrs. Hurst endowed Mrs. Robt Greenhow

Mrs. Affleck endowed Ana Maria Gallega

May 11, 1900—I endowed James Stanhope

Lyman endowed Mr. Hutchinson

Alley endowed Mary Clementine Stuart

Mrs. Hurst endowed Lillie Dean

I blessed Booker, Verne and Claytor Preston.

Charlie's boys Freeman and Bryant still quite sick.

May 12, 1900—Blessed Alley, Preston, Martha, Allen and C. M. Hurst

May 13, 1900—Blessed Lyman R. Sen. and wife Alley P.

May 14, 1900—Lyman bought me a new suit of clothes, 2 shirts. hat, pair shoes, collars, neck tie, and socks. He shall never want for comfortable clothing, nor friends in time of need. My best pantaloons were broken out in the rear, displaying a flag of truce.

May 15, 1900—To day Lyman Royal Jun. was baptized for 6 persons:—James Martineau, Stephen Hutchinson, Charles Stanhope (Earl) ~~Giovanni Battista Martini~~, (Earl) Philip Stanhope and ~~Simone Martini~~

Alley Martineau was baptized for my sister Emily H. Martineau, Melusina von Schulemberg, Lois Hutchinson Madame du Bouchet, all rel. by blood or marriage

[page 185]

May 15, 1900—Harriet A. was baptized for [left blank] Lady Louisa Grenville, dau. of Earl of Halifax, Lady Hester Pitt, sister of famous William Pitt, Lady Elizabeth Saville, Countess of Stanhope, and Lady Lucy Rachel Stanhope, dau. of Earl of Stanhope, all being relatives-in-law. All the males bap. for by my grandson Royal were all relatives by blood or by marriage.

My father's first wife was daughter of ~~Philip Durnes~~ Charles Stanhope, ~~4th~~ 3^{d} Earl, and his two daughters by her, Julia and Lucretia, my half sisters, were grand daughters of the Earl. My father's wife had first married Captain Hawkins, British Royal Navy, and was disowned by her father for the so-called misalliance. She had two children by him, Samuel Hawkins and Elizabeth Hawkins, whom I well remember. Samuel was a Warrant Officer in the U.S. Navy, and was with Com. Wilkes in the Antarctic Exploring chuise [cruise], 1840, when he discovered the Antarctic continent. He used to bring us beautiful shells, which I used to admire. Julia married a Mr. Winslow, a printer, of Boston. I never knew their later lives.

When Earl Stanhope died, he willed to his daughter—my father's wife £18000 (about $90,000) [$2,102,335] and to each of the two children, Samuel and Elizabeth, £2000 ($10,000) [$233,593] By some mischance these legacies were never received, and I suppose can never be recovered by any of father's family by his second wife—my own mother.

May 16, 1900—I Endowed James Martineau (Revd Unitarian)

Mrs. Hymus Endowed Mrs. Thomas T. Allen

Mrs. M. A. Maughan Endowed Mrs. William Allen

Mrs. Brenchly Endowed Mrs. James Johnson

Mrs. Hymus Endowed Mrs. Juana Pavon

May 17, 1900—I endowed ~~Mr.~~ John Hutchinson

Blessed Mr. Hibbard, and Mrs. Brenchly, who had worked for me in the temple, and Blessed Lillian Gardner, whose grandmother, Mrs. Affleck, had worked for me in the temple also.

[page 186]

May 18, 1900—I endowed (Earl) Philip Dormer Stanhope

My dau. Lilla endowed my sister Netta

Mrs. Hurst endowed Mad^{e} von Schulemberg

Mrs. Cath^{e} Preston endowed Mad. du Bouchet

Mrs. Hymus endowed Ana Maria Huarte

There were also sealed nine couples:—

Mr. Dyer & Mary Dyer, Mrs. Cath[e] Preston proxy
Rob[t] T. Elwin & Theodora Martineau, Lilla proxy
Alex. Stanhope & Mrs. Alex. Stanhope, Lilla proxy
James Stanhope & Mrs. James Stanhope, Lilla proxy
Mr. Hutchinson & Ann Hutchinson, Lilla proxy
James Martineau & Helen Higginson, Lilla proxy
John Hutchinson & Lucy Apsley, Lilla proxy
Philip [Dornier or Dormer] Stanhope & Mrs. P. D. Stanhope, Lilla proxy
David C. Lyon & Emily H. Martineau, Lilla proxy

This finishes my temple work for the present. I thank, Thee, my Father in Heaven, that I have been permitted to do this holy work, and pray I may be permitted to do much more, for the redemption of the dead. Could I have my wish, it would be to spend my remaining days in the Temple.

May 21, 1900—Went to Nephi's home in Riverside, King P. Office. He was still absent, but I blessed his six children, as follows:—Aurelia, Mabel, Susan Elizabeth, Elva, and William Knowles Martineau.

May 18, 1900—I omitted to note above, that on May 18th I blessed my daughter Elizabeth Martineau Nebeker, her children, Frank Knowlton, Marjorie and Lyman Martineau Nebeker, and her hired girl, Mary Nuffer.

May 23, 1900—Howard Nephi, Nephi's oldest son, came to Logan and I blessed him. All Nephi's family are now blessed except his second son, Lee Edward, who is at the Blue creek farm with his father. Visited the agricultural College.

At 4 P.M. I left Logan for home. Lyman gave me \$10.[00] [\$234] for expense money, Cath[e] P. Preston \$2.[00] [\$47] and Booker \$1.[00] [\$23] Also Lilla gave me \$1.[00]—all she had.

It was sorrowful parting from my dear ones.

[page 187]

May 23, 1900—Lyman and Alley invited to dinner Lilla & family, also Eva and family, also Simpson Molen, a very dear friend, and after dinner made a snap shot with her Kodak of me and my three little grand daughters—Martha, Marjorie and Clare, with little Allen between my knees.

I arrived in S. L. City about 8 P.M. and was warmly received by Br. & Sister Preston, also by May Preston Moyle.

May 24, 1900—Visited several old friends.

May 25, 1900—Went to Virginia M. Sudbury, my daughter, to stay.

May 26, 1900—Visited Mrs. Emily Hill Woodmansee. Dined at Thatchers Was introduced by Frank Nebeker to Lawyer Geo. Q Rich.[44] He said he had long known of me, was glad to meet me, and began blessing me, with much fervor, prophecying great blessings for me. Spoke of the great and good work I had performed for the church, said it was accepted by the Lord, and that I should yet do much more, and become a mighty man in Israel. I was astonished.

May 27, 1900—May Preston Moyle had a company to dinner to day. Br. & Sis. Preston, Moses Thatcher and Lettie, also their dau.-in-law Caddie and myself.

May 28, 1900—Again visited Eliza

May 29, 1900—Virginia's sister in law—Anna Sudbury has a very sick baby, ill with pneumonia, which was thought must die. I administered, and promised life, which I pray God may grant, but the doctor and friends have no hope at all & said nothing more can be done for the child, all, save Lavina Sudbury, who is helping take care of the child. She has faith for little Raymond. I gave her a comforting blessing. Took leave of Genie & children, and at 8.05 P.M. left S. L. City for home! home! and my loved ones in Mexico. Moses Thatcher, and Sarah Farr and her two sons also go to Mexico at same time.

Sister Preston has been as good to me as possible, and so have all in the North. May God ever bless them

May 30, 1900—At Helper, 12.25 A.M. Green River 4.45 A.M. Grand Junction, Colorado, 6 A.M. Glenwood Sps. 8.47 A.M. Tennessee Pass Tunnel (Rocky Mountain range) noon Pueblo, 5.30 P.M. Lay by all night.

[page 188]

May 31, 1900—Leave Pueblo 7.30 A.M. Change cars Trinidad 11 A.M Raton tunnel 12.30 (noon) Raton town 12.50 P.M. Los Vegas 4.30 P.M.

44 George Q. Rich was the son of Elder Charles C. Rich, who was from Logan and would have known Martineau (Godfrey and Godfrey, *The Utah Years, 1871–1886*, 224; Leonard J. Arrington, *Charles C. Rich: Mormon General and Western Frontiersman* [Provo, UT: Brigham Young University Press, 1974], 296–97).

Albuquerque 9 P.M. and lay by 3 hours. Here 18 or 20 young indian girls entered the car, going home from some school. They were from 15 to 18 years of age, bright, pretty and full of talk and fun as could be—just as boys let out of school always are.

JUNE, 1900

June 1, 1900—Daylight at San Marcial, New Mexico. Sunrise at Crocker. At 8 A.M. one of our engines ran off the track which delayed us some time, but no one was hurt. At 10 A.M. at Fort Bliss, were examined by quarantine officers. Arr[d] at El Paso 10.25 A.M. Stay all night at Zieger Hotel.

June 2, 1900—Leave Cuidad Juarez at 8.35 A.M. Dublan 5 P.M. Home 9 P.M. Found all well as usual, and Dora has had no fit since I left home, just as I was promised before I went away. Thanks be to thee, Oh Lord!

Learned particulars of Joel's injuries:—teeth broken out on one side of face, lower lip cut entirely through, large gash under chin, bruised all over and two ribs broken off spine, and spine badly hurt. Had watchers for weeks & has lately gone up to Chuichupa, being able to walk & do a little work. His escape from death was a miracle, as he fell 24 feet to solid ground, with the frame and timbers of the barn. The other man was hurt, but not seriously.

June 8, 1900—Settled my survey a/c for Sonora Survey, amounting to $275.00 [$6,424]. of which I have had, and paid on debts, $242.50 [$5,665], leaving bal. due me $32.50 [$759].

While absent Albert had paid me 75$ [$1,752] on note and $12[00] [$289] interest for 3 months on same note for $400.[00] [$9,344].

On June 4th a Mr. John M[c]Comb, agent for Smith, Davis, & Hartmann of California who have bought 500000 acres of timber land in the mountains near our settlements, engaged me to survey the lands purchased, at $10. [$234]—per day and board. I fear I shall not be able to do the work, unless the Lord shall strengthen me as I hope He will.

[page 189]

June 13, 1900—Rec[d] 390 [lbs] flour $25.00 [$584] on order from Col[n] Company ($25.00) I owing them $1.00 [$23] on same. Paid Haws for hauling same $1.50 [$35].

Have been busy, up to this date, in recording the 35 blessings and bringing up my journal to date.

June 23, 1900—A Mr. John M[c]Comb, agent for Smith, Davis & Hartmann, of Cal. a timber Company, came and engaged me to survey the boundaries of a tract of timber lately bought by them joining our mountain settlements of 200,000 hectares (about 500000 acres,—nearly 740 Sq. miles) He to pay me $10.[00] [$234] pr day and also furnish me horse to ride and man to carry transit for me.

June 25, 1900—Made a small map for him, $5.00 [$117]. We start on Survey to day, reaching Garcia next day, and camped at old mill site.

June 27, 1900—Took variation of magnetic needle by observation on Polaris & found it 10° 30' East, add Azimuth 1° 25, = total var. 11° 55' E. and Lat. 29° 59' N.

June 28, 1900—Our men arrived from Chuichupa, with pack animals.

June 29, 1900—Benan [began] work, by starting out to find the N. E. Corner of the land to be surveyed. We traveled all day over high ridges and deep cañons full thirty miles, without food, but with plenty of rain. Did not find the corner.

June 30, 1900—Went to an old Stone monument on high mountain, and from it ran east, on Lat. 30°

JULY 1. 1900.

Sunday, July 1, 1900—Went to Garcia and spoke in the meeting on invitation of Bp. Whetton.

July 2, 1900—Continued survey east, over tremendous gorges and high ridges and in heavy timber, and on the

July 5, 1900—5th found the old Corner sought for, which is the N. W. Corner of Zone 6;—N. E. Cor. Zone 1, = the N. E. Cor. of our tract to be Sur[d].

July 6, 1900—Went to beginning point on Mountain and ran West, Camping at night near Rio de Gavilana, (River of Hawks.)

July 7, 1900—Reached the brink of the Gorge of the Rio Gavilana, but could not cross to day, as the defile is over 1000 ft deep, precipitous sides, difficult to cross either way. Thus far we have had rain every day.

Fig. 9.3—Ancient Paquime ruins not far from Colonia Juárez. Courtesy of James Henry Martineau Family Organization.

July 8, 1900—Rained all day, and we did not work.

July 9, 1900—Triangulated across the Gorge, which took all day.

[page 190]

July 9, 1900—The distance across, from brink to brink, diagonally, was 820 meters,= about half a mile.

July 10, 1900—About half a mile above where the line crossed the cañon, and on top of a steep conical hill in the bottom of the gorge, are the ruins of an ancient stone fortification, with walls about 10 or 12 feet high. It is accessible by one path only, which is only wide enough for one man to pass at a time, and so was almost impregnable to ancient foes, armed only with bows, arrows, swords and spears. Oh that those gray stones could tell the scenes that have transpired in and about those walls.

Passing through the pines westward, we find many old stone ruins of dwellings, and many places where the land has been terraced (and still is) to make level spots for cultivation. Every little hollow even, often not more than 10 or 15 feet wide between rocky ridges, have still those ancient Stone wall terraces, usually 2 to 4 feet high, to retain the earth from washing away, the Terrace walls being one or two rods apart. Also, all the more level spots of ground now covered with pine and oak timber, was cultivated also in ancient Nephite times. An immense population once inhabited the land, who raised their crops by rain, which must have been, in ancient times, much more frequent and abundant than now.[45]

What has been will be again, and from this time on the rains will increase in frequency and volume, new

45 J. H. Martineau, "Millions Surely Lived There Once," *Deseret News*, July 28, 1900, 4; Journal History.

springs will break forth where water has never yet run, streams will flow in gulches now dry, and the streams now flowing will become larger. And so the thirsty desert shall become a garden, and the wilderness shall blossom as the rose.

And so we continued the survey west about 19 miles then southward, much of the way so broken and precipitous it could not be measured with a chain, and the distance calculable only by triangulation. I remember one space, less than two miles wide, which took two of our men nearly a whole day to cross on foot. Sometimes, to go from one point to another only a mile or two distant, would require nearly a whole day of most toilsome exertion to accomplish.

[page 191]

July 13, 1900—This day I narrowly escaped death. I had to ascend a high & exceedingly steep mountain, and as my horse would not be led, but must be pulled along by main force, I found I must ride. I slowly zigzagged my way up over loose sliding stones, large or small, going only a few steps at a time, the mountain so steep that it made me dizzy to look down to its foot 2000 feet below. I desired to pass a small oak 8 inches diameter by going on its lower side, but my horse suddenly veered to the left, passing under a large horizontal limb which was just high enough to miss the saddle. This brought the limb against my lower abdomen, I all the time doing my best to stop the horse and to back him, but without avail. The horse was afraid he would fall, and I could do nothing with him to stop him as he still pressed slowly forward, squeezing my abdomen harder and harder against the limb, until it seemed as if it would break my back short off. But Orson M[c]Clellan saw my situation, rushed to my rescue, seized the bridle bitts and pounded the horse over the head with a big stone until he thus forced the horse back and released me. Had the animal taken one single step farther, I would have been killed. And so the Lord has once more spared and preserved my life. It must surely be because my earthly work is not yet finished,—not because of any special worthiness in me. Many other times I rode along steep mountain sides where a misstep would have sent horse and rider tumbling down tremendous depts. It reminds me of one of the men, who, in describing his own experience in such perilous riding, when shame prevented him from getting off his horse, and walking. Says he "I just said up all my back prayers and held my breath." But God has been very good to me, and it must have been for a purpose.

The rains finally hindered us so much we abandon the survey until the rainy season is over, and return to Colonia Juarez on Sunday, July 22nd 1900, finding my family about as well as usual, though Dora had had some fits while I was absent.

When riding through the forest and grass covered earth with its flowers,—strange to me, but beautiful, I had many seasons of delightful, heavenly communion, and glorious and comforting promises from the heavens, and at times instruction where I desired it from the voice & inspiration of the Holy Ghost. I pray that God will help me to so live as to be counted worthy to receive the blessings promised me and mine.

[page 192]

July 24, 1900—A fine celebration to day

July 25, 1900—Rec[d] part of my pay—$80.[00] [$1,869] leaving still due me $170 [$3,971] for field work, and not including $60. [1,402] due me for mapping and estimates to date of July 31.st

AUGUST

August 29, 1900—First day of our Colony Fair. I drew 1st Prize for pomegranates, mine being the first raised in the Colony. Gertrude had prize for gentleman's neck tie. Fair ended next day.

Gov. Ahumeda and suite, also many Mexicans were here and highly pleased.

SEPTEMBER

September 3, 1900—Deposited check rec[d] of timber Company for $170.[00] [$3,971] with Bently & Harris. It is No. 1199, on Banco Minero, of Chihuahua.

Sent the names and records of birth, death & endowment of my Sisters Francis Eliza and my daughter Julia Henrietta to Joseph F. Smith, who has desired them, Julia H. to be his wife & Francis E. to be sealed to his father, Hyrum Smith.

September 8, 1900—This evening we had a party in honor of Theodore's birthday about 22 guests.

I wrote a few lines in an address & blessing to him, which all present signed. We thought it would please him.[46]

September 19, 1900—Rec[d] a letter from Pres[t] J. F. Smith, thanking me, and saying he would have the sealings of my sister and daughter performed soon, and would send me all particulars when done. I know of no one in the church to whom I would sooner give them, than to him and his father.

Both of my wives—Susans—were connected to the Smith family. Their Grandmother was sealed by the prophet Joseph to his uncle John Smith, and all her children sealed to him as a father. Br. John Smith became Patriarch to the Church after William Smith, and died in S. L. City in 1854. The blessings he gave Susan E. and Henry A. were about the last he ever gave

[page 193]

October 19, 1900—Blessed Susan's niece Anna S. Eager-Tenney, who has been with us about two weeks, and who returns home tomorrow. She has been a great help to us in taking care of our fruit and in nursing Gertrude, who has been very sick for about ten days, with a spinal trouble, which has been very painful all the time.[47]

NOVEMBER 1900.

November 1, 1900—Dora had two fits today. I have prayed for her, and have been answered that she shall be fully healed.

November 13, 1900—Rec[d] letter, (pasted at end of this book) saying he had sealed my sister Frances Eliza to his father Hyrum Smith, and my daughter Julia Henrietta to himself, in Salt Lake Temple, on Wed. Oct. 31, 1900, John R. Winder officiating in both cases, Br. Smith's wife Edna L. Smith acting proxy in each case, and Geo. Romney and W[m] W. Riter being witnesses for each sealing. I know no man now living to whom I would sooner have given them. In January, 1885, when Pres[t] Smith accompanied Pres[t] Taylor & party to Guaymas, Mexico, he took breakfast with us, and looked at the photos in our Album until he came to Netta's. Here he stopped turning the leaves, looking at her until breakfast. A week after, as about to leave us for his home I asked him if he would like her sealed to him. He answered, "That was what I was wishing as I looked at her picture." I said "You may have her sealed to you." He said earnestly "Oh yes, if you think I would be worthy of her." He spoke very humbly, and I know he is worthy, and will remain so all his days.

It has been revealed to me that she accepts him gladly as her husband, her king and her priest through all the eternities. And now I am satisfied, as to both of them.

November 20, 1900—An important event this evening at about 9 P.M. in the union, as I understand of Gertrude to Guy Taylor

This morning Br. J. F. Smith and party started home, holding meeting to night in Dublan. Before they departed they (Br. Smith and Woodruff, Bp Geo Negley and I administered to Dora, Br. Smith being mouth. Dora said she believed she would be healed if Br. Smith would bless her, and I believe she will be. Br. Smith thanked me warmly for Netta and my sister Frances Eliza. We also administered to 2 others before they went away, and Br. Smith gave me some important instructions in relation to the patriarchal priesthood.

[page 194]

November 20, 1900—Have heard that on Sunday, 11th inst. two of our people killed three apaches about 10 miles from Pacheco, being attacked by 6 renegade Apaches. Pres[t] Ivins and Apostle Woodruff helped bury the indians. The brethren had to kill or be killed, and Br. Woodruff and Br. Smith said they were justified in defending themselves.

November 22, 1900—I was engaged today to survey a mining claim in the Guaynopeta District in Sonora. I believe we will not be attacked by the indians.[48]

December 31, 1900—I find I have paid the following tithing this year:—Cash $56.00 [$1,308],

46 J. H. Martineau, "The Mexican Colonies," *Deseret Evening News*, September 10, 1900; Journal History.

47 J. H. Martineau, "Divine Healer, An Impostor," *Deseret Evening News*, October 22, 1900; Journal History.

48 Letter from J. H. Martineau to the *Deseret Evening News*, November 24, 1900; Journal History; see also *Deseret News*, November 30, 1900; Journal History.

stock, chickens, eggs, fruit &c $22.00 [$514],= $78.00 [$1,822]. So God has greatly blessed me in the past year in temporal things as well as spiritually. During the last 4 months I have devoted much time to visiting the sick and administering to them and comforting and strengthening them as much as I have been able, and God has blessed me in this, very greatly. It has been delightful to me, in thus helping those who need help.

1901

January 6, 1901—This evening, about 8.30 P.M. Anna S. Walser, my dear daughter so early widowed in Oct. 1897, was united to Edward Turley.

January 8, 1901—Our 49th Wedding anniversary. Did not celebrate to day because of the absence of Henry A. and Anna S; both are absent in El Paso. They both returned on the evening of the 9th

January 9, 1901—Had a family dinner this evening. Present Guy and Edward, Henry A. our own family at home and Bp. J. C. Bentley, his wives Maggie and Gladys, and Mrs. A. E. Saville, sister of Gladys. Spent a pleasant evening and had a good dinner—2 Chickens etc. Ada J East went home.

January 12, 1901—Surveyed cow pasture of about 1400 acres. I was very ill and in much pain all the afternoon.

January 15, 1901—Blessed Miss Mary Richardson of Diaz. Red letter from "Improvement Era" requesting me to write for it.[49]

[page 195]
Also from "El Progresso" to act as correspondent. I am already correspondent for the Deseret News, Utah, and the "El Paso Daily Herald". I was blessed and set apart in the "50"s by direction of President Geo. A. Smith, under the hands of Prest. Danl H. Wells, F. D. Richards and another apostle whose name I do not at this moment remember, to write for the "News," and I write for the El Paso Herald that I may give "our side" a public hearing when necessity demands. It is for the same cause I write for "El Progreso." though it is all work I would like to shun, if possible. I have not the time nor inclination for it all, but I have been able, many times, to present a public refutation of many malignant attacks upon our people, and none of my efforts have ever been refused publication by any gentile paper. Thus I have done some good with my pen, for which Our Father be praised.

MY YEAR OF JUBILEE

January 19, 1901—To day is 50 years since I was made free through baptism into the Church, by Elder William McBride, on the Temple block where now stands the temple, in the West Branch of City Creek, which then ran west into the Jordan.

As ancient Israel celebrated each 50th year as one of Jubilee, wherein all slaves and bond servants became free, and where the nation could enjoy a year's rest, so I also regard this date at the era of my deliverance from the bonds of Satan, in that I am a partaker in the freedom the gospel gives.

As such, I desire that all my posterity after me shall forever remember and honor this anniversary, until it will no longer be best to do so.

I thank Our Father that He has preserved me thus long in the truth, and that with all my sins of Commission and omission, and many mistakes, He has been so kind and merciful to me, and has bestowed so many and so great blessings upon me. I pray that I may be true to the end. Amen.

January 25, 1901—Have done several days surveying, some of it mountain work, though still feeble from continued la grippe.

[page 196]
January 29, 1901—Helped a carpenter to place lumber on my barn, which is still unfinished.

FEBRUARY

February 5, 1901—Today Anna moved to her new home, about a block distant. It made quite a vacancy, for she and her children had been with us so long—over two years.

I hope she may be as happy as is consistent with weak humanity. Edward Turley, her husband for time, is a good man, and desired her years ago, also his wife

49 The *Improvement Era* was one of several publications created by the Church between 1866 and 1902. The young men of the Church were the target audience.

Ida Eyring Turley, desired her as a sister-wife all these years. May our Father bless them all.

February 11, 1901—To day Dora had three bad fits. I think they are caused by foul stomach. She will be healed of them.

February 12, 1901—Rec[d] a letter from Atty. F. W. Lake, San Francisco. He thinks he can recover $80.[00] [$1,869] from the U. S. Gov[t] I signed agreement to give him half he collects,—nothing if he gains nothing. "A half loaf is better than none."

February 19, 1901—A letter from Virginia, my daughter, tells me she lost her daughter Virginia, age 5 years, by pneumonia, on Sat. Feb. 9th inst. The little girl was a bright and good child. She, at least, is safe from Satan's power.

***February 15, 1901**—I learn my son Albert has a new daughter, born on Friday Feb. 15th inst. in Chuichupa.

MARCH

March 4, 1901—Fruit trees, viz:—almonds, peaches, plums, apricots all in bloom. Apples, pears, cherries and small fruit will soon come also.

March 7, 1901—Dora had two slight attacks,—prevented by administration.

March 9, 1901—Susan and I, went to E. Turley's and had a family dinner.

BLESSING TO NEPHI

February 5, 1901—I find a slip overlooked at the time, which I here insert:—

"Prayed for Nephi in his present distressd mind, and his financial troubles, at about 4 A.M. and was told by the voice of the Spirit to write to him as follows:—

"Write unto thy son Nephi and say unto him he shall be blessed from this time forth far more than in years past. He shall be blessed with an increase in wisdom in his business, in faith, and in all temporal blessings, and shall be greatly prospered in all he shall put his hands to do.—he and his family.

[page 197]

March 1901—It is my will that he shall remain upon his farm for the present, and shall be prospered in his labors until it is my will for him to move to Mexico, and when that time shall come he shall sell his property and home to good advantage, and shall be blessed in Mexico in a still greater degree, he and his family, seal these blessings upon him in thy letter to him, and they shall be sealed and ratified in the heavens. Even So. Amen.

[See Appendix 5 for two letters from family inserted here.]

I immediately arose, lighted a lamp, and wrote as I had been instructed by the voice of the Spirit. I afterwards got a letter from him in which he expressed his great joy in what I had written to him. I pray that he may be blessed in this,—he is worthy.

He has been in debt ever since he returned from his mission in Kentucky, owing nearly $3000.[00] [$70,078] and his crops scarcely pay interest and taxes on the land. He has about 180 acres about 9 miles from Logan, on Bear river,—a good farm, but with wheat at 35¢ [$8] pr bushel, farmers can hardly live.

March 16, 1901—Albert came from Chuichupa. Returned 20th Today we got a cow & calf, which will help us considerably.

March 19, 1901—A letter from Theo, who expects soon to be released as a Conference president, and to be called to Chattanooga office.

March 25, 1901—This morning I start for the mountains to finish the timber Survey I began last summer in company with Mr. John M[c]Comb, agent of the timber company.

During the last six months I have been constantly going among the sick and administering to them, and the Lord has greatly blessed me and the sick in all this, which has greatly increased my faith, and has given me a more perfect knowledge of the voice and inspiration of the Holy Spirit. For before going to the house of the sick person I always asked the Father, to know if the sick would be blessed or healed under my ministration. When the reply was affirmative, of course I could administer "in faith believing," and so my desire was granted in behalf of the sick ones; they were blessed and so was I.

[page 198]

March 25, 1901—We reached Garcia next day, made our camp, and waited for our men to join us. On the 26' made an observation on Polaris to find the variation of the magnetic needle, which was 11° 15' E. On the 27th took the Lat. N. 29° 53' 30", our camp being about 4400 meters South of the North boundary of the land to be surveyed, which is about N. 30° 0' or N. 29° 54'. On the 28th our men all arrived and on the [continued with next entry]

March 29, 1901—29th we moved camp, to begin the Survey of the east bound^{y}

March 30, 1901—Began our survey of east boundary running south, over high ridges and deep Cañons. I triangulated from point to point to ascertain distances, chaining being impracticable, covering to day 10914^{m}

March 31, 1901—Moved Camp about 12 ^{miles}. In the afternoon it began to snow with a driving, wind, piercingly cold, which by

APRIL 1, 1901

April 1, 1901—night became a terrible blizzard. We suffered with cold each one revoling [revolving] before the fire—freezing one side and roasting the other. I went to bed with all my clothes on, but was cold all night. The snow all melted in a few days, but nights and mornings were very cold, and ice formed every nights about half an inch thick, or more. And So we continued slowly southward, over high mountains at an altitude of full 10000 feet, and crossing deep Cañons, the whole distance being through pine timber.

April 6, 1901—Camped on the Las Pumas stream, which runs north into the Rio Chico.

April 8, 1901—Reached the brow of south side of Rio Chico cañon or gorge and built monument of stone 6 ft. high about noon. We could not cross it. From brink to brink was over a mile & about 3000 feet in depth, with sides very precipitous.

April 9, 1901—Sent two men to find a way to reach the South bank and put up a flag to be triangulated to. Edward, my grandson, was one of them. It took them all day to cross and return.

April 10, 1901—Triangulated, and found distance across—1976$^{met.}$ about 1¼ miles. There being a deep, impassible gorge also on our right, we took all day to go around its head, crossing it where the Rio Dolores joins it, and killing a deer on our way. We went south until we came to a point west of the flag we set the day before, and triangulated to it across the Chasm,—over two miles.

[page 199]

April 1901—The country south being impracticable we ran an offset line west from our flag over a very broken & mountainous country a distance of 10394^{met} and built a stone monument on a ridge, ten ran South 11182 ^{met} to the boundary of our tract to be surveyed, then along the South line westward to the summit of the Candelaria Mts. some 10000 or 11000 feet high. Here we were all day in another snow storm, and we made

April 17, 1901—camp between patches of old snow. Arrived here April 17th

April 21, 1901—Took latitude on South boundary; N. 29° 25'

April 22, 1901—Moved camp about 7 miles to the Rio Guaynopa and camped in an ancient, ruinous old Spanish building, near an old Spanish Mine. The Change from Snow to palms in so short a distance was very remarkable. Our way was up and down high, steep and rocky mountains, in some places dangerous to ride on horse back, but I rode all the way. As I came to the bottom of the gorge I heard one—a regular rough-rider, dare devil—who had led his horse down, say to McComb "Why, Martineau rode all the way to the bottom." I was the only one who did so, and in some places it made my flesh creep a little on my bones. But I was not really afraid, for I asked God to bless my horse, that he might not fall stumble, or slip, and that I might ride safely, and I had a testimony that all would be well with me. I trusted it it, and all was well with me, thanks to our Father. What a blessing it is that God—the Omnipotent—will hear and answer the prayers of so weak and sinful ones as I am and others! What could we do without His goodness and mercy in our behalf!

April 23, 1901—Ascended a high and very steep mountain several thousand feet, then down again, and "up hill and down dale" hour after hour, stopping from time to time to fix the packs on our eight mules. We passed a little pile of stones with a rude cross in its top—the resting place of some poor fellow. We follow the trail that leads over into Sonora. Camped on a small rivulet, near which lay the remains of a man—his bones only. Unknown he lies—till the ressurrection shall call him to life again.

April 24, 1901—This morning all our animals are gone. Yesterday we sent men to top of a high ridge back of us, to erect a monument of stone with a tall post, to which I can triangulate to day.

[page 200]

April 24, 1901—I took my party some distance west to find a place suitable for triangulation, while others hunted the animals. They were found high up the mountain side were they could get no farther. One of my men and horse rolled a distance down the mountain, breaking his rifle to pieces, otherwise with no harm.

April 25, 1901—Moved camp three miles while I surveyed onward through thick white oaks. Set a flag on West side of a deep Cañon for triangulation, after which chained onward and quit on brow of another great gorge, after placing a flag on line on its other side.

April 26, 1901—Went to flags and triangulated back to last nights quitting point. Distance, nearly 2 miles. The country west being almost impassible by reason of gorges and cliffs, we concluded not to go any farther west on South boundary, and turned to the north, placing a monument of stones and tall post with flag on South brow of a tremendous and impassible gorge, about 2 miles wide and 3000 feet deep.

We have come thus far on the South boundary 37722 meters nearly 25 miles. Most of the distance was over country impossible to chain, and was only crossed by triangulating from one ridge to another—sometimes over 10000 meter—6 or 7 miles.

April 27, 1901—As it was impossible to chain or even triangulate north, we moved camp towards the main range in order to get round the head of these deep gorges, passing through a very difficult country of rocks, defiles and steep ascents and descents, & camped among rocks where we could hardly find place for our beds.

April 28, 1901—Sent men to explore and find, if possible, a point where we could get on our western boundary line. Men came back at night unsuccessful.

April 29, 1901—Ascended a high mountain ridge and went miles north along its crest, and at night camped as usual.

April 30, 1901—Men hunted all day for a chance to get on line. Could not find any way to do so—so many chasms & cliffs. Camp on Ryan's Creek.

MAY 1.

May 1, 1901—Ascended mountain ridge again and followed it some miles northward, to a point so steep we could follow it no longer, and we were obliged to return to camp again.

[page 201]

May 2, 1901—Moved camp a few miles into another cañon, but had great difficulty in getting out again to another place, climbing hills so steep our pack animals could not carry their light loads up them—men having to carry the packages up one by one. Sent men hunting for a camp ground near our west boundary line. Unsuccessful.

May 3, 1901—Ascended a very high, steep ridge, and after going some miles found a place for triangulating to a monument we set last summer. Moved camp near to this point.

May 4, 1901—Moved camp again. Triangulated east to point on high peat, nearly 11000 meters.

May 5, 1901—Triangulated west to flag set on ridge west, 1½ miles. This took us all day to do.

May 6, 1901—Triangulated back to last night's position on ridge east. This was a tremendously hard day's work, and sometimes dangerous. It was all I could do to get along, at much danger to life or limb. My shoes were all in rages, and the nails in the soles cut and hurt me terribly as I walked—as I had to, much of the time, as it was all I could do to get along afoot.

This finishes up our entire survey, connecting with the point where we quit last year. The entire boundary is 196486 meter about 123 miles, enclosing nearly 800 sq. miles of mountain, timber land—nearly 500000 acres.

This has been without exception the hardest and worst work I have ever had in all my 48 years experience as a surveyor. Many, many times my life was in imminent danger, but God was merciful, and preserved me through it all. To Him be all the honor and glory of my salvation.

May 7, 1901—Started homward, and camped in Bacon's Cañon.

May 8, 1901—Arrived at Chuichupa about 1 P.M. hungry, tired and worn out. During the last four days we had no bread. I soon had a dish of bread and milk! A luxury indeed. Found Mary A. Joel's wife has a new baby girl, also Alberts wife the latter some 3 month's old.

May 9 & 10, 1901—Made a connection of Chuichupa with the eastern boundary, which finishes the field work of this survey. And on the 11th and 12th reached home—and oh! how glad!

[page 202]

May 10, 1901—On the 10th all our family met at Joel's and had a family dinner. About 29 or 30 being represented in this place. It was a very enjoyable time.

May 12, 1901—Sunday. At home again. I am thankful indeed.

May 25, 1901—To date I have been working up my field notes and map.

My time, field work, 44 days, amounts to $440.00
My time 14 day office work 140.00
[$13,548] $580.00

May 23, 1901—Paid cash, on tithing o/c $50.00 [$1,168].

May 26, 1901—Received $300.00 [$7,008] on account, also blankets $17.00 [$397].

The same amount of time, on U. S. Land Survey would have brought me 5000$, [$116,796]—or about $3000.00 [$70,078] clear.

May 26, 1901—Finished a map for McComb. He wants another.

May 31, 1901—Have been very busy working in garden, planting corn &c.

JUNE

June 6, 1901—Anna returned from Chuichupa

June 8, 1901—Theodore came unexpectedly, having been honorably released by Prest Ben. E. Rich from his mission. He has been gone a little over a year. Was some month a traveling elder, then appointed President of the Alabama & Florida Conference, then called to the General Office in Chattanooga. He has been highly praised by Prest Rich.

Yesterday received word from Jesse N. and Belle. They were both to be baptized on May 30th—She for the first time; he, to renew his covenant. He wrote a very good letter.

June 15, 1901—By letter from Elvira I learn she has a new baby boy, name is Don Charles Johnson. Born April 24, 1901.

JULY 1901

July 2, 1901—Anna moved to her new home, a house of two rooms, barn with abundant fruit trees, strawberries &c

Got my new chiffonier,[50] cost $50.00 [$1,168] Very heavy rain in the night,—the first of the coming rainy season.

July 11, 1901—Susan's birthday, her 65th. We had a good dinner. may she have many more, some, even, in New Jerusalem—Zion.

July 14, 1901—Dora had another epileptic fit. I believe she will be finally healed of them.

July 15, 1901—She had another, fell and was badly bruised.

[page 203]

EVA AILEEN MARTINEAU BORN TO CHARLES & EVA. AUG. 8

July 15, 1901—Paid $20.00 [$467] cash on tithing—$70.00 [$1,635] this year. I am glad I can pay it—it is no trial to me.

AUGUST

August 6, 1901—Cut my ~~second~~ third crop of lucerne,[51] and carried it all to the barn, a pitchfork full at a time, which caused rupture to pain me much. Very hot weather

August 8, 1901—Charles' wife Eva gave birth to a baby girl—Eva Aileen

August 13, 1901—Finished my lucerne cutting. I used a scythe.

August 20, 1901—Received a letter from grandson Knowlton Nebeker, saying his mother (Lilla, or Elizabeth) has a new baby girl. She (his mother) is very

50 A chiffonier is a high chest of drawers or bureau, often having a mirror on top.

51 Lucerne is alfalfa.

ill,—paralyzed, deaf and can hardly frame sentences of more than 6 or 8 words. This is a very dreadful condition, and I pray She may be healed.

August 21, 1901—Planted beans, as an experiment as to proper time.

August 23, 1901—Surveyed for B. Stowell, his pasture land.

August 24, 1901—Made observation last night on Polaris, to get variation of the magnetic needle, which I find to be 11° 25' East.

August 25, 1901—Gertrude was taken very sick today, It seems to be meningenetis. She suffered dreadfully. She could not sit nor lie down, but was obliged to stand on her feet to breathe at all. Finally, we had to hold her up, and she seemed as if about to die. I believe she was saved through the ordinance of administration and prayer of faith. But she still has a severe pain through her body at pit of her stomach, so bad that she can hardly breathe. Were up with her all night. I note here, that these pains continued nearly a week, gradually growing less and finally ceased, leaving her very weak. We administer frequently, and she is benifited.

August 31, 1901—In absence of A F. Macdonald, Pres[t] of High Priests Quo. I presided, by his direction and that of Pres[t] A. W. Ivins.

SEPTEMBER

September 2, 1901—Surveyed for Stowell. For about a week I have been very unwell with severe dysentery, very difficult to chech [check], but am now much better—getting well again.

September 3, 1901—Gertrud walked a little to day—a few steps only. Dora almost had a fit, twice, and would have, but for prayer and administration. She became unconscious, but did not fall, being noticed in time.

[page 204]

SEPTEMBER CONT[D]

September 3, 1901—Oh, how thankful I would be could she be entirely healed. I believe she will be, finally

September 5, 1901—Dora's 19th Birthday. Made her a nice dinner. I gave her a nice mirror as birthday present. She had a slight fit in the evening but we rebuked it in time. Gertie sat at the table, first time in many weeks.

September 13, 1901—Gertrude had convulsions, and soon we thought her dying. Sister A. E. Saville came at 10 P.M. also several Elders, who administered. Mrs. S. remained all night, doing what she could for her.

September 14–17, 1901—Very low, almost lifeless. Too weak to speak aloud.

September 18, 1901—May pass away any moment.

September 19, 1901—She can speak, faintly, a little

September 20, 1901—Apostle Cowley administered to her.[52] All these days we can admit no visitors, and we speak only in low whispers, in any part of the house.

September 23, 1901—She can now speak a little—very little, but cannot endure conversation around her. Some days ago we telegraphed for her husband, Guy, to hurry home. He came this evening, home from Pavral, Mex.

September 27, 1901—This evening Gertie had a sinking spell, very bad one. We thought her dying for some hours. We could hardly perceive her breathe, or feel any pulse for full half an hour, but she finally revived.

September 28, 1901—Had another, also a frightful one.

OCT. 1901.

October 1, 1901—Gertie sat up a few minutes, but was worse next day.

October 3, 1901—She talked some to day and laughed a little. Also 6th 7th & 8th.

October 9, 1901—I went to Dublan & got some goods. Blessed Irena and Verde Pratt

October 19, 1901—Gertie wose [worse] again

October 20, 1901—Great hail storm. Broke shingles and glass; killed many small animals, birds &c,

52 This is Matthias F. Cowley (1858–1940). He was ordained an Apostle in 1897 but resigned in 1905, with his priesthood suspended in 1911. He was restored to full membership in 1936.

destroyed fruit and crops still unharvested. Hail piled 2 ft deep in places.

NOVEMBER

November 15, 1901—Dora had a fit & fell severely to the floor.

[page 205]

November 17, 1901—Let Theo. take my transit to Survey for O. P. Brown, in the mountains.

November 20, 1901—Pres[t] Ivins engaged me to subdivide the new purchase of land—78000 acres—at Dublan. Blessed Roxey and Myrtle Stowell. Made mining maps for Theodore's surveys.

November 22, 1901—Blessed Lettie Stowell Anna was blessed today with a nice baby girl at 8–15 A.M. and was much blessed in delivery.

November 26, 1901—Tuesday, went to Dublan and began Survey.

[written in margin]

note Nov. 5th

Learn by letter that Geannie had a baby born on Nov. 5th—a son.

DECEMBER 1901.

December 11, 1901—Blessed Flossie E. Ossmen

December 12, 1901—Sent a nice wire mattress cot for Dora, who is not well. Heavy gale all day. Could not work

December 13, 1901—Storm continues, with Snow 2 inches deep. No working.

December 16, 17, 18, 1901—Surveyed part of city plat. Heard Dora is very sick. Dismissed my helpers, started home almost sunset. Arrived home 7.45 P.M. and found Dora had died half an hour before, of lung fever.[53] Susan had written to me to come, but I had received no letters. It was an awful shock to me, especially, that I was absent, and could not be with her to comfort her by my presence, for she loved me with intensity, as I did her.

She had been sick twelve days, being taken ill in the 6th of the month, with pain in side. All that tenderest love could dictate was done for her, but without avail, for she steadily failed, day by day, until the end.

On the day she died she sat up while her hair was combed, and retained consciousness until the last. An hour before she passed away, she whispered a prayer, asking forgiveness for all her sins. She had asked Gertie to forgive if she had anything against her, and she "wished Papa would come." She suffered greatly all the time till about an hour before her death, when all pain ceased, and she passed peacefully to her rest, and to go on to her exaltation in the Celestial glory.

[page 206]

December 18, 1901 con[d]—[continued] Oh how my heart and Susan's and Gertrude's grieved. Dora was pure in heart, if any upon earth can be, and received gladly every truth and law of the gospel. She never talked ill of any one, nor could she bear to hear it. She delighted to do all she could to help her mother, me, or Gertie, even when weak and unwell. She was very neat and tasteful in her attire, and in her hair, and delighted in all things beautiful. She was a very sweet singer, with clear, pure voice, and played the organ uncommonly well and with exceeding delicacy of touch and time; and she had a passion for music, also drew very nicely, having natural genius for music and drawing. In short, she was by nature refined, but much of the time wore an expression somewhat sad,—inherited, no doubt. What is our life here but meetings and partings! The latter almost always so sad! But to know and appreciate the sweet one must know the bitter; how else can we be qualified to sit as a King or Queen—as a judge? Thus Christ had to suffer, to enable Him to understand and to sympathise with the sorrows and troubles of a world. And it is all right and absolutely necessary to our advancement and perfection. Father! Thy will not ours be done!

December 20th, 1901—At her funeral a large number of young ladies came to our house and walked in procession behind the coffin to the school house, and covered it with rare and beautiful flowers.

She used to say "Mama, I'm going to live with you and papa always; if I ever get married I will still live always with you." Dear girl! We will meet by-and-bye, to part no more, to mingle in love with others of our family who have gone before.

53 Lung fever is pneumonia.

December 24, 1901—This is Christmas eve, but it is no Christmas for me, or my dear Susan or Gertrude. We feel too sad,—our house seems to lonely. Always before for many, many years, we have had children about us, all anxious and full of expectation as to what the morrow would bring them.

[page 207]

December 24, 1901—It is so no longer, and our souls are sad.

And yet we should rejoice, seeing God has so greatly blessed us, notwithstanding our many transgressions. Help us, Oh Father, to become pure in heart, that we may finally come and dwell with Thee!

December 28, 1901—Finished papering two rooms, and put down our new tapestry bed room carpet—the first we ever had. About 25 metres cost $40.^00^ [$934]. Our home looks much improved now.

1902

January 8, 1902—To day is the 50th Anniversary of our marriage, but our fond anticipation of a family reunion were not fulfilled. No one came from the north, and of our family in Mexico, outside of Juarez, only Albert & his son and Theodore were present. Anna and Gertrude were with us. Well, it makes no difference. What is the 50th Anniversary, compared with the fifty thousandth—or the 50 millionth, or a still greater number than that? for eternity is still beyond all such figures, and is truly incomprehensible to us, yet so long shall our union continue—worlds without end; and that, too, without sorrow, pain or sad partings! Oh! how happy and glorious is the the thought! And what is this short span of life here on this "dark and dreary world."[54]

January 13, 1902—Returned to Colonia Dublan to finish survey there, the city plat to be a little over 2 miles in length and breadth. I continued this work until Jan. 30th when I finished. I gave blessings to several while in Dublan, and received one myself from Patriarch Winslow Farr. Returned home

January 31, 1902—Jan. 31st having labored in cold, disagreeable weather.

54 "Still Others," *Deseret Evening News*, June 16, 1902; Journal History. The article focuses on fiftieth anniversaries.

The following is my blessing from Bro. Farr:—

Brother James Martineau, by virtue of my office and calling I place my hands on thy head and give thee a patriarchal blessing, and desire that the spirit of the Lord may direct the words that may be used in this blessing. Thou wast with the Father when the foundations of this earth were laid and the morning stars sang together and the sons of God shouted for joy.

[page 208]

January 19, 1902—Thou art one of the noble sons of God selected by our Father in heaven to come forth on the earth in the dispensation of the fullness of times. Thou didst keep thy first estate with the Father, and have chosen thy parentage and the dispensation to come forth on the earth, and the eye of the Lord has been over thee from the hour of thy birth, and the Lord has seen thy integrity, and witnessed many of thy trials and tribulations and sacrifices for the gospel's sake, and great is thy reward in heaven. Thou shalt be blessed with the gift of wisdom and the spirit of discernment to comprehend the mysteries of God, and the Lord is well pleased with thee, for thou hast filled an honorable mission on the Earth. Thou shalt have faith like unto the brother of Jared. Thou shalt have power to cast evil influences from those that are afflicted, the dumb shall speak, the deaf shall hear, the blind shall see, and the lame shall walk at thy command. Thou art of the seed of Joseph that was sold into Egypt by his brethren through the loins of Ephraim, and thou shalt receive thine inheritance with that seed. For thy name is written in the Lamb's Book of Life, and thou shalt be numbered with the 144.000, and thou shalt stand as a Savior on Mt. Zion and become a mighty man in Israel. and thy name shall be handed down in honorable remembrance through future generations, and shall meet with those who have been true and faithful to the Lord. The Lord has accepted thy labors in redeeming the dead and will continue to do so until thou art satisfied. Thou shalt live as long as life is desirable, and when thou hast finished thy work on the Earth thou shalt wear the crown of eternal life. And I bless thee with the blessings of Abraham Isaac and Jacob, with power to come forth in the morning of the first ressurrection, and I seal thee up unto eternal life in the name of Jesus Christ. Amen.

Recorded on page 116 Book "A"[55]

[page 209]

January 30, 1902—I was thankful for the promises in this blessing. They agree fully with all my previous blessings, which is of itself, a testimony that it was given by the same spirit and power as the others,—the dictation of the Holy Spirit.

January 31st, 1902—Returned home, having finished my work for the present.

FEBRUARY 1902

February 3, 1902—Began on maps of Dublan Survey.

February 7, 1902—Bertha's boy was born today about noon. This is another Gr. Gr. Child for us.

February 20, 1902—Up to this time I have been mostly busy on maps. I now commence on Canal note calculations.

Gertrude has been very sick and still is, not being able to turn in bed, unless moved by some one.

February 23, 1902—She is better to day, but not able to sit up.

MARCH

March 6, 1902—Was examined to day by Dr. Keate, as I am about to apply for an increase in pension. Found my lungs tolerably good, kidneys not first class condition, & my rupture in left groin, ample cause for increase.

March 11, 1902—Went to El Paso to file application for increase pension. Remained in El Paso until 14th

March 13, 1902—My 74th Birth day

March 15, 1902—Found Gertrude still very weak, with frequent sinking spells, when she seems as if dying until we can administer to her, rebuking those spells.

March 16, 1902—Settled with Presᵗ Ivins for my Dublan surveys

Total from beginning in Nov. last, field work $380.00

Office work 42.50

I am to receive pay for this $422.50

from the tithing office–no money add– 2.50

$425.00

[$9,928]

March 27, 1902—Sent small record of my narrow escape to Lyman by Bp. J. C. Bentley, going to Conference.

[page 210]

April 18, 1902—My grand daughter, Editha Martineau, eldest daughter of Moroni & Sarah Martineau, died to day aged about 16 years, after an illness of 16 days. She had some internal female disorder.

She was a lovely girl in form, feature & character, foremost as a Sunday School Secretary,—in Y. L. M. I. Assn and in all religious duties. I believe she has gone to assist in the work already commenced here on earth for the dead, to carry it on on the other side of the vail. She was one worthy, I think, for this work, in the highest degree.

[written in margin]

Theo's marriage Mch. 23d

Learn that Theodore and Josephine Thurston were married (Sealed for time and eternity) by Path A. F. Macdonald, in Garcia, on the 23d day of Mch. 1902

April 24, 1902—Gertrude had 6 bad sinking spells to day. We must watch her every moment

April 25, 1902—Blessed William and Dayer LeBaron and Adelbert Taylor.

April 27, 1902—Recd letter from Fred. W. Lake, Land Atty in Washington, D.C. who says he can recover $80.00 [$1,869] I paid some years ago for U. S. land I did not hold, he to receive half, if he secures the claim.

Mrs. M. A. Thurston & boy came; also Theo. & wife Josephine, who are on the way to a place called Matachic, about 200m South.

On the day previous I was engaged by Alonzo Farnsworth, acting for a Dr. Robert Nichol, of Matachic, to go there and survey a canal line for him, about 9 miles in length.[56] My terms, as usual, $10.00 [$234] pr day & all necessary expenses.

55 Here is another indication of the many writings Martineau is using to organize his journal.

56 Matachic, Mexico, is a mountain settlement in the province of Chihuahua.

April 28, 1902—Started to Matachic, riding 16^{m} to Dublan with Theo. Raymond A. Farnsworth, husband of my gr.-daughter Bertha M. Martineau, who is going to Matachic, not being ready to start, had to lay over all next day.

[page 211]

April 30, 1902—To day started on our journey south, with Raymond & wife and my Gr. Gr. son, born Feb. 7th, also Theodore & wife. My place to ride was on a heavily laden freight wagon, and was not at all comfortable. Camped after dark. Cold.

May 1 & 2, 1902—Passed through Galeana, on the Santa Maria river, and on next day came to El Valle, a nice place with beautiful plaza, blooming with roses and flowering shrubs.

May 3, 1902—Pass to day through high, broken ground

May 4, 1902—Reach the Rio Sta Maria again at noon. Had a little rain.

May 5, 1902—Continue over high hills; camp in cold, bleak place having passed through Cruces

May 6, 1902—Pass Maniquipa, the last place near head of Sta Maria Then cross the Hacienda del Toro, and camp in pass of mountains, leading west into the valley of Rio Aros

Near our camp was a huge monument or pile of Stones about 6 or feet diameter at base and same height surmounted by a rough cross made of two sticks tied together. This was to commemorate many dead Mexicans slain here some years ago by Apaches. This same pass, in 1893 or 4 was the scene of another tragedy, when Mexican troops surrounded and killed some 40 or more men whom they styled rebels. Those who surrendered were all hanged upon trees near by.

May 7, 1902—At noon came to Mátachic, our destination. This hamlet is several hundred years old, having been an indian village when the Spaniards first came, as its name, ending in "chic"—a common Aztec termination.

Ten miles below is Temosochic, about 8 miles above is Tejolocachic, both of them once indian villages.

Dr. Robert Nichol, whose canal I am to survey, received us kindly, and let Raymond and Theodore each have a room, until they can build for themselves. He gave me a nice room. The house is built in Mexican Style (I like the style, too), like this:—

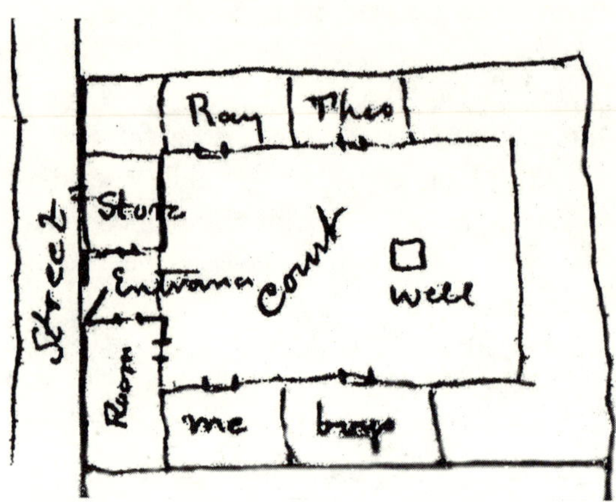

Fig. 9.4—Nichols' Mexican-style home.

a wide entrance from street, large enough for a wagon to drive through, leads into a court, into which all rooms open, they having no openings outwardly.

[page 212]

May 7, 1902—Wealthy Mexicans make these inner courts places of fairy-like beauty, with fountains, flowers, beautiful plants and shrubs and vines, the court paved and surrounded on its four sides by a broad paved court or cloister sustained by massive columns and arches.

In Chihuahua I have glanced through open entrances and beheld courts that seemed like paradise, so wonderfully beautiful were they, while the outside of the house might resemble a barn. This style has many advantages. Children need not play in the streets with undesirable companions, but each family can be by itself, and when the one outer entrance is closed, everything about the place is safe and secure.

May 8, 1902—Measured 1000 metres of a canal, to see how much fall in that distance, and took the levels.

May 9, 1902—Went to point where canal is to be taken out, and did some preparatory leveling. Was quite unwell, having been ill with a flux some days on the journey, so I was quite weak, and besides had a burning fever. Very tired at night.

Saturday, May 10, 1902—In bed all day. Prayed God to heal me.

Sunday, May 11, 1902—In bed all day but my fever is gone and bowels better.

Monday, May 12 & 13, 1902—Worked on Canal Survey. Bothered by rain. In the evening Dr. Nichol knocked my transit over, and it was so badly injured it must be sent to New York to be repaired.

May 13, 1902—Tried to fix and use transit, but could not do so. Dr. Nichol agrees to pay expense of repairs in full

May 15, 1902—Gave Patriarchal Blessing to Josephine, as follows:

Blessing upon Josephine Thurston Martineau, daughter of Peter Franklin & Mary Ann Spendlove Thurston Martineau, born in Pima, Arizona, March 26, 1886.

Dear daughter Josephine, in the name of the Lord Jesus Christ and in the authority of the Holy priesthood I seal upon you the blessing of your father, which shall be a comfort to you in time to come, and be fulfilled according to your faith and faithfulness.

[page 213]

You are in the days of your youth, but the Lord hath appointed unto you power to perform a great and good work in helping to bring to pass His holy purposes. You are of noble lineage, being one of the daughters of Joseph through the lineage of Ephraim, therefore entitled by birth, being of lineal descent. to all the blessings pertaining to the daughters of Joseph. The Lord has appointed a great work for you to do, and inasmuch as you will seek unto Him in faith and humility the visions of the heavens shall be opened to your view. You shall be instructed in visions and dreams, and it is your privilege to know and understand the voice and inspiration of the Holy Ghost, that when you are in doubt or uncertainty in matters appertaining to your own affairs you may ask for instruction from the Holy Spirit and receive it. I seal upon you great faith and charity, with power to heal the sick and afflicted, I seal upon you wisdom and understanding sufficient for every time and necessity. And now, my daughter, inasmuch as you have been afflicted with weakness and debility I rebuke it in the authority of the Holy priesthood and in the name of the Lord Jesus Christ and say unto you that you shall become well, healthy and strong, and filled with renewed life, spirit and vigor, You shall be a help and comfort to your husband and a wise counsellor, and dwell in his bosom as a confidant. Strive to keep all the commandments of the Lord, strive to live a holy life, and nothing that is for your good shall be denied you. I seal you up to come forth in the morning of the first ressurrection, and seal you up unto eternal lives, to reign as a priestess and Queen forever in the celestial glory, upon condition of your faithfulness and endurance unto the end in the name of the Lord, Jesus Christ. Amen.

Matachic, May 15, 1902

May 16, 1902—Am told this morning that Mr. Nichol will send me in his carriage to Guerrero—30 miles, for which I am very glad, as I expected to have to go on a freight wagon laden with ore, taking two days, a very unpleasant way of travel.

[page 214]

May 16, 1902—Before going I sealed the following blessing upon my Gr-Gr.-son Raymond Alonzo Farnsworth,—Bertha's son.

This is notable as the first of any of my Gr.-Grand children to be blessed:—

Patriarchal Blessing upon Raymond Alonzo Farnsworth, son of Raymond Alonzo & Bertha Mandana Martineau Farnsworth, born in Dublan, Mex, Feb. 7. 1902. Given in ~~Cola Dubl~~ Mátachic, Mex. May 16. 1902

Raymond Alonzo, in the name of the Lord Jesus Christ and in the authority of the holy priesthood I seal upon you a blessing which shall rest upon you and be a blessing indeed. You are of the blood of Joseph through the lineage of Ephraim, a lawful heir to all the blessings priesthood and powers sealed upon Abraham, Isaac and Jacob. A great work is appointed unto you in the redemption of Zion, and it is your privilege to live to assist in the redemption of Zion and in the building up of the holy city Zion,—the New Jerusalem. You shall labor there in the holy temple of the Lord and receive mighty blessings therein, even a fulness of the holy priesthood, with all the powers appertaining thereto. I seal upon you all the spiritual gifts that shall be needful for you, with blessings upon your labors. You shall never be tempted more than you are able to bear, and no power of evil shall prevail against you. The blessings that await you are great and mighty and shall be revealed to you more fully hereafter. I seal you up unto eternal lives, to reign as a King and a Priest with God through all the eternities, in the name of the Lord Jesus Christ. Amen.

About 9 A.M. I started on my return home and came to Guerrero a little before sunset, 30 miles. There being no hotel. I slept in an old deserted building, awakened in the morning by the bugle calls of the troops stationed there.

[page 215]

May 16, 1902—It is a small city though an old one, and has an elevation of nearly 7000 feet. While in Matachic I took the Latitude on the 11th inst,—N. 27° 57' 30"

May 17, 1902—Started at 7.30 A.M. in stage for Miñaca, arriving there, 8 miles—about 9. A.M. Miñaca is the western terminus of the Chihuahua & Pacific R. R. but it will soon be extended farther to the west. I took passage here—3d class, $3.00 [$70] to Chihuahua, about 150m and reached Chihuahua about 5 P.M.

May 18, 1902—Started for C. Juarez 10.30 A.M. arriving there 6.40 P.M.

May 19, 1902—Came home 9 P.M. having to face a cold wind from the R. R. Station, by which I took a severe cold. Found my family in good condition as I hoped for, Gertrude somewhat better, but still confined to her bed.

I have had a fatiguing trip of over 700 miles, over 200 of which was by wagon, camping out at night, and did not accomplish that I went for, through the breaking of my transit, but was nevertheless blessed while away & my family were also. I found Mrs. M. A. Thurston, the 2nd wife of Henry, with her 10-yr old son Frank, installed at home, to assist in taking care of Gertrude and helping my dear wife, who had been quite ill while I was away.

May 21, 1902—To day blessed Mary Amy Johnson, also M. A. S. T. Martineau and Frank, her son. My cold is still quite bad.

Patriarchal Blessing upon Frank Thurston Martineau Son of Henry A. and Mary Ann Spendlove Thurston Martineau, born in Cola Juarez. Mexico, Sept. 19. 1891

Frank, in the name of the L. J. Christ and in the authority of the holy priesthood I seal a patriarchal blessing upon you, which shall be fulfilled upon condition of your faithfulness and endurance unto the end. You are one of those who were faithful & valiant when Lucifer fell, and for this cause you have been permitted to take part in the work of the last days. You are of Ephraim by lineal descent, a natural born heir to the fulness of the priesthood with all its blessings & powers.

[page 216]

May 21, 1902— The Angel of the Lord will watch over you & preserve you in the hour of temptation and danger. No hand or voice raised against you shall prosper and no power of evil shall prevail against you, so long as you keep the commandments of the Lord. In due time you shall receive your endowments and all the holy ordinances of the temple. You shall do a great work in the redemption of the living and the dead. You shall speak with power and authority, causing the righteous to rejoice, and the wicked to tremble. You shall have great faith, like unto that of Enoch, and like him the heavens shall be unfolded to your vision, and you shall receive instruction from the heavens, The gift of healing is yours, and many of the sick and afflicted shall be made whole under your administrations. You shall understand the voice and inspiration of the Holy Ghost, and be instructed as to your duty when in doubt or uncertainty, if you will seek unto the Lord for it in faith and humility. You shall be blessed in your labors and have the comforts of life, and there is no blessing to which you may not aspire if you will ask for it in faith and humility, inasmuch as it is for your good. I seal you up unto eternal lives, to enjoy all the blessings and glories of the heavens, in the name of Jesus Christ. Amen.

May 27, 1902—Hired team and took Susan to Dublan.

JUNE 1902

June 2, 1902—Theodore and Josephine removed from us to the house they rented of B. Stowell.

I paid cash tithing to day $15.00 [$350].

June 3, 1902—The old folk Party came off today, Guy took Gertie in her invalid chair, and she remained until after dinner, though faint and fatigued, by the blessing she received. She did not feel able to go, but Guy persuaded her. She seemed to take no harm, though she previously could not sit up longer than half an hour.

[page 217]

June 6, 1902—Elvira came to see us from St David, Arizona, bringing three children with her. We had not seen her for about seven years, and her visit was a treat, though Gertie is still very sick and cannot endure much noise

May 31, 1902—On last Saturday, May 31st, I took charge of the High Priests meeting, in the Absence of Presᵗ Counʳ Redd, having been appointed to do so in the Priesthood meeting.

JUNE 1902

June 7, 1902—A slight sprinkling today—the first for seven months.

June 17, 1902—Sold 50 lbs Apricots for $4.00 [$93], the first fruit we ever sold.

June 18, 1902—Hired team and took Susan & Elvira and children riding.

June 19, 1902—Blessed Elvira, Gertrude, Guernsey and Don Charles.

June 20, 1902—Elvira returned home at 10 A.M. today, her baby being quite sick with bowel complaint and sore eyes.

[written in margin]

Gertie ill—very. convulsions.

At 11 A.M. Gertie had a fearful convulsion, and one at 6 P.M. both being very dreadful. She lay As one dead between them, and for several days was very low indeed, the slight appetite she previously had being gone.

June 27, 1902—Last night Gertie dreamed of being in the next world with Bp. G. W. Seavy, who died a few days ago.[57] He was very busy and happy. She told him how his family was grieving for him. He said they would cease after a while. Some one showed her two beautiful crowns, one of which was for her in her own reward, the other was hers because of the work she had done in the temple for the Baron Alex. von Wendt (von Wenden, true name) to whom she was at one time Engaged to be married. She tried them on, and they both fitted her beautifully. They were circlets of Gold, narrow at the back, becoming wider in front, with a magnificent stone in the front-center. She desired to have them now, but was told she must wait awhile until she had finished her work on earth.

[written in margin]

Baron Alex. von Wenden was enowed [endowed] Oct. 4. 1897. Guy Taylor proxy. in Salt Lake temple.

Before this, when she heard of the death of Bishop Sevy, she cried much, saying, "why cannot I̲ die or get well, and not have to suffer the agonizing pain I do."

I fear her dream indicates her speedy departure. If she cannot be healed, it would be a mercy to her, for she suffers intense pain continually. She says she cannot endure it much longer. She is too weak.

[page 218]

PATRIARCHAL BLESSING UPON SUSAN ELVIRA MARTINEAU JOHNSON. GIVEN JUNE 19. 1902

June 19, 1902–Susan Elvira, in the name of the Lord Jesus Christ and by authority of the holy priesthood I seal upon you a patriarchal blessing. You are one of the noble spirits held in reserve from before the foundation of the Earth because you was true and faithful to our Father in Heaven when Lucifer led away many after him. You have been true and faithful these many years, sometimes in sorrow & privation, in poverty and danger, in helping to establish Zion. The Lord has accepted your labors in the past and will reward you in time to come beyond the power of any mortal mind to conceive; therefore let your mind be filled with joy and peace. The blessing of the Lord will continue upon you in a much greater degree than in times that are past, You may ask the Father for any blessing that you may desire, and if it is for your good you shall receive it. You shall never be tempted more than you can bear, and no power shall turn you aside from the truth. I reconfirm upon you all the blessings that have hitherto been sealed upon you, I seal upon you an increase of faith, an increase of wisdom and intelligence, with power to heal the sick and afflicted, to comfort the sad and broken-hearted, and to be a blessing unto all with whom you associated. You shall do a great work in the temples of the Lord and redeem from prison a Multitude of the dead, that they may attain unto to blessings pertaining to the holy priesthood, In this work you shall have great joy, and receive a testimony that your work for the dead is accepted by them, and by your Father in

57 This is Bishop George W. Sevey (note spelling) of Colonia Juárez (Romney, *The Mormon Colonies*, 99).

heaven. You shall have power to know and understand the inspiration of the Holy Ghost, that you may ask the Father for instruction if it is needful and receive it.

[page 219]

And you shall walk in Light and not in darkness. And now I say unto you for your comfort, as you are about to return to your home, you shall be blessed and prospered in your journey, and all shall be well with you and your children. You and your husband and family shall be prospered and blessed from this time henceforth with all that is needful for your comfort and happiness. Your table shall be filled with abundance: health and peace shall reign in your habitations, and you shall have plenty, to help the poor and needy. Accept every law of the Gospel and strive to live a holy life and no power shall prevent you from receiving the blessings sealed upon you. I seal you up unto eternal lives, to reign as a Priestess and Queen forever in the celestial glory, in the name of the Lord Jesus Christ. Amen.

Patriarchal Blessing upon Anna Gertrude Johnson, Born May 10th 1889, in Nephi, Arizona.

Anna Gertrude, in the name of the Lord Jesus Christ and by authority of the Holy Priesthood I seal the blessing of your father upon you. You are one of the daughters of Joseph who was sold into Egypt. of the lineage of Ephraim by lineal descent, entitled to all the blessings, powers, and priesthood that appertains to the daughters of Sarah. You have been held in reserve to do your part in the work of the last days, For this purpose your life shall be preserved through every danger, for your Guardian Angel will never desert you, but will warn you in time to escape evil. I bless you with health and strength, with vigor of body and of mind, with great faith and charity; with wisdom and understanding, that you may do good in your day and generation, I seal upon you power to heal the sick and afflicted, and to comfort those who are sad and troubled in mind. You shall be taught by visions and dreams and shall understand the voice and inspiration of the Holy Spirit, that you may be directed in your labors and be comforted & strengthened in the hour of trial,

[page 220]

June 19, 1902—You shall be united with a man of God, and rear a posterity that shall be mighty in Israel. No power shall turn you aside from the path of righteousness, and you shall have power to do great good, not only to the living but in the redemption of the dead. Some of them will make themselves known to you that you may do a work for their redemption. Peace and plenty shall be in your habitations and the blessings of the earth shall be yours in abundance. These are but a few of the blessings in store for you, for the Lord loves you and will make you to be a prophetess in Israel. It is your privilege to assist in building up Zion—the New Jerusalem—and to do a great work in the temple which shall be reared there for the redemption of the dead, and to enjoy for a time the safety, peace and glory of the Holy City. All these blessings and many more are yours upon condition of faithfulness and endurance unto the end, for I seal them upon you in the name of Jesus, and seal you up unto eternal lives, even to an exaltation as a Pristess and Queen in the heavens forever, in the name of the Lord Jesus Christ. Amen.

Patriarchal Blessing upon Seth Guernsey Johnson Born 24 July 1897 in Nephi Arizona.

Seth Guernsey, in the name of the Lord Jesus Christ and by authority of the Holy Priesthood I seal upon you your father's blessing, which shall be a help and comfort to you in days to come. You are of Ephraim, entitled to all the blessings that were sealed upon Abraham, Isaac and Jacob. It is your privilege to have a posterity that shall be like that of Abraham,—even like unto the sands of the sea for multitudes. I seal upon you the gift of healing, that you may heal the sick and afflicted, and help and comfort those who are sad and troubled in mind. I seal upon you wisdom and intelligence sufficient for every time and duty, that you may assist mightily in the building up and redemption of Zion and in bringing to pass the purposes of the Almighty.

[page 221]

June 19, 1902—You shall carry the words of life and salvation to those who are now in darkness, and many shall receive the truth through your instrumentality. I seal upon you health and strength in every faculty of your mind & body. You shall be preserved in the hour of danger, and no weapon formed against you shall prosper. You shall be blessed in your labors in the building up of Zion, and it is your privilege to assist in the building up of the New Jerusalem and to labor therein for the redemption of the dead. Others shall seal blessings upon you in addition to these, even all you desire that are for your good. I now seal you up unto eternal lives, to reign & rule in the celestial glory, and to enjoy all the blessings and glories of the heavens in the name of the Lord Jesus Christ. Amen.

Patriarchal Blessing upon Don Charles Johnson, born 24th April 1901 in St David, Arizona.

Don Charles, in the name of the Lord Jesus Christ and by authority of the holy priesthood I seal the blessing of your father upon you, that it shall rest upon you & enable you to fulfill every duty that shall be placed upon you. You are of the royal blood of Ephraim by natural descent, entitled to all the power, blessings & priesthood of Abraham, Isaac and Jacob. Your feet shall stand upon a sure foundation, and no power shall turn you away from the truth, for you never shall be tempted more than you are able to bear. A holy being has charge concerning you, who will preserve you in the hour of temptation and danger, that you may do your part in the work of the Lord. And now, inasmuch as you are sick and afflicted, I rebuke all disease from your body and your eyes, that you shall be perfectly healed and made whole; & I seal upon you health and strength, with vigor of body and of mind and every needful blessing.

[page 222]

June 19, 1902—It is your privilege to do a great work for the living and the dead, whereby you may gain to yourself an exaltation in the celestial glory. You are in the days of your youth but a great and a holy work is appointed unto you, and no power of evil shall prevent your fulfilling it. You are entitled to all the blessings pertaining to the priesthood, even to be a patriarch in the Church of J. C. of L. D. Saints, and to fulfill this holy office and calling I seal upon you revelation and prophecy & discernment, with every other blessing necessary to magnify this high and holy calling in the priesthood.

These are but a few of the blessings in store for you, for many others shall be sealed upon you in due time, even all that your heart shall desire, inasmuch as they are expedient for you. I seal you up unto eternal lives, to reign as a King and a Priest in the heavens forever in the celestial glory in the name of the Lord Jesus Christ. Amen.

June 26, 1902—A heavy rain today, the first for over 7 months. The drouth has caused the death of many cattle, for lack of food and water. Also, there is only a fourth of usual wheat.

GERTRUDES DREAM.

June 27, 1902—She dreamed she had passed to the next world, and was with Bp. G. W. Seavy, who died a few day previously: he was happy and very busy. Some one showed her two beautiful crowns for her, one for her self and the other given her for the temple work she had done for her friend the Baron Alex. von Wendt (true name "Von Wenden) a Russian nobleman who had loved her and wished to marry her. These golden circlets were narrow behind, becoming broad and high in front, with a magnificent. (See page 217 where this is written.)

JULY 1, 1902

July 1, 1902—Having business in El Paso I went there today, and returned home on the 4th While in El Paso I enrolled as Correspondent for the El Paso Daily News.

On my return found Gertrude very much worse.

[page 223]

July 2, 1902—On Wednesday she was all day in extreme agony, and it was feared she could not survive the day, nor would she, had it not been for the Administration of the Elders. She has been very weak ever since, though pain not so severe. She could only speak in a faint whisper to me, and could not bear any talking in usual tone of voice in the room. She sent a note to Bp. Bentley asking him to request all the people to pray for all the week and to pray and fast for her on the next fast day, that she might be healed and freed from her intolerable pains.

During the week the young Ladies Ass$^{\underline{n}}$ fasted and prayed for her, also other organizations.

July 6, 1902—Sunday, 6$^{\underline{th}}$ Fast day. At meeting today special prayer was offered for Gertrude, and one speaker said she was one of the noblest spirits among us. After meeting Pres^{t} Ivins, Bp. Bentley & Harris, with 6 others, came to her and administered. Pres^{t} Ivins as mouth and J. J. Waler anointing.[58] She felt better, and not so full of pain afterwards. She is so weak she can only speak in a faint whisper, and lies as one dead, save her gentle breathing. Oh Father, if it be thy will, I pray thee heal her!

July 7, 1902—Gertrude a little better, but still very weak

July 13, 1902—Gertrude Still improving, but very slowly, better one day, worse next.

July 28, 1902—Went to Casas Grandes on water tax business,

Joel went to El Paso to hunt employment, with several others.

July 31, 1902—Gov. Col. Miguel Ahumada and a company of 13 others, with Gen. Angel Martinez paid us a visit.[59] Had a fine meeting, speeches, songs, choir and instrumental music and they were all much pleased.

AUGUST 1902

August 1, 1902—Henry went on his way to Miñaca, for employment. He is still very weak and feeble. Hopes to get tie contract on the new railroad. Theodore went next day, hoping to get some employment near Henry

August 9, 1902—Gertrude improving; hopes soon to be able to sit up.

August 3, 1902—On the 3^{d} inst,—fast day, the people prayed & fasted for her, and a dozen Elders administered to her at bedtime, and the power of the Lord was in her behalf

[page 224]

August 9, 1902—To day I was employed by Mr. Booker to survey land for him—boundaries only—a tract 360 sq. miles = 230400 Acres, salary as usual—$10.$^{\underline{00}}$ [$234] per day and my expenses.

August 10, 1902—Very heavy rains ~~all~~ to day. Much needed. Gertie went out of doors a little while in her wheel chair, & enjoyed it much before the rain. In the afternoon, Guy became quite sick, and very much so by evening. Josephine is getting better, but cannot sit up yet. I have been quite feeble for some days past, so I could hardly go to administer to the sick around us, but feel a little better now.

August 11, 1902—Still raining. Guy some better.

August 12, 1902—The suspension foot bridge across the river gave way today, and three boys narrowly escaped death in the high waters. It was put up in a few days, again, in a narrower place. River unfordable still

I appointed W. C. McClellan to preside at next meeting of high priests, as I expect to be absent.[60]

August 13, 1902—Guy still quite sick

August 15, 1902—Friday. I started to Casas Grandes to go on my survey. Found Booker not quite ready.

August 16, 1902—Spent day getting ready for a start

August 17, 1902—Left Casas Grandes, Crossed the river at Coralitos, Very dangerous. Nearly 2 hours getting both wagons over. Waters just at top of horses' backs, & running swiftly.

August 18, 1902—Found no one in Janos who could show me any of the corner monuments of proposed survey. Camped 12 miles farther, on Palitada Springs creek.

August 19, 1902—Took Latitude, and prepared Stakes. Lat. 30° 55' N.

August 20, 1902—Señor Ascanio Azcarate came and showed me one Monument on the line, and I began Survey

August 21, 1902—Sr. Zapata came, to show me corner monuments.[61] I continued the Survey, finishing

58 This is likely John J. Walser (note spelling), who was a member of the Juárez Stake high council (Romney, *The Mormon Colonies*, 139).

59 These would be provincial dignitaries of Chihuahua.

60 William C. McClellan was a member of the Juárez Stake high council (Romney, *The Mormon Colonies*, 139).

61 This could be Emiliano Zapata, who later played a part in the Mexican Revolution. He was described as both a

on Sept. 3. The lines passed in places among high and steep mountains, in other places for miles together in shallow lakes and swamps formed by the almost constant rains. Mosquitoes! No end to the clouds of them—almost unbearable. Having to move camp often, and making my bed on wet ground my bedding became wet, and for weeks I slept in wet bedding, but by the blessing of the Lord I was strengthened for the toilsome work, and the wet bed did not seem to hurt me.

[page 225]

September 3, 1902—One day I sent my teamster to Diaz for provisions. He returned empty, and said he passed through 5 miles of water before reaching Diaz, the river having overflowed to a width—both sides of 7 or 8 miles.

On our return, we expected to camp at the same place as before when we crossed the river at Coralitos, but found it impossible, as the water was all around us, and still pouring out from the river in a vast sheet. In the next morning our tent stood on the only dry ground for a long distance around, the water still rising. I left the men and with one team started alone for home, as I lived on same side of the river, The rest of the party all lived on the other side. A Cowboy and his horse were drowned the day before we came to the crossing. Leaving the camp I traveled miles through water before reaching higher land.

September 6, 1902—Found Gertrude still in bed, the rest of the family as usual, and our peach trees, many of them broken down by weight of fruit,

September 11, 1902—Went to see Booker to get my pay for my work. He was away, so on next day I started home with Ray Pratt and carriage.

September 12, 1902—Before we reached the river, our horses got stuck in a deep mud hole, caused by overflow of the river. They went in half way up their sides, and then fell down in it. We had a hard time to get out, by help of Mexicans who came along. When we reached the river, we dared not try to ford it, as the water was higher than our carriage and would have washed it away. We did not know how to get back to Dublan, through that deep mud hole, but a Mexican came along and piloted us around it through his field. May our Father ever bless him.

September 13, 1902—Crossed the river in another place, not so deep but very swift and somewhat dangerous. A man's team was drowned there two days previously. A Mexican on horseback hitched a lariat to the end of our wagon tongue and to the horn of his saddle, and so, with difficulty we crossed safely, and thanked our Father sincerely. Got home late at night.

"southern bandit" and a "southern savior" (F. LaMond Tullis, *Mormons in Mexico: The Dynamics of Faith and Culture* [Logan, UT: Utah State Univ. Press, 1987], 97).

PART

10

"BACK TO THAT COLD CLIMATE": SERVING IN THE TEMPLE AND BLESSING THE SAINTS

[page 226]

September 17, 1902—To day Elvira's son James H. Johnson, of St David, Cochise Co. Arizona, came, to go to the Academy this term of school. He is 20 years old, and 6 ft 4^{in} tall.

September 21, 1902—To day it seems as if our long continued rains are about over. The sun Shines. Much fruit, spread out to dry has spoiled, owing to the damp atmosphere.

September 22, 1902—Sold some apples, pears and peaches, to day $12.84 [$300] We have given away several wagon loads rather than have them spoil, as many bushels have, on the ground.

September 27, 1902—Rec^{d} check from Booker for my pay, $259.00 Mex. equal to $105.^{00} [$2,453] in gold. This for nearly a months work. but glad indeed to get it.

September 28, 1902—In looking through my papers I found the following letter from my wife Jesse Helen, explaining why she did not come home to me in Arizona, but stopped in Alameda, Cal.:—

"1860 Central Avenue

Alameda, Cal. Nov. 30. 1887.

My dear friend

You surely have not received two letters which I sent to you. One addressed Great Western Hotel, Sacramento, and the other to Vallejo. In my last I wanted to see you and tell you fully why I thought it safer not to go South with you. D. P. A. Sent to Vallejo a long letter telling everything. How they found it out I know not, and they sent to know if I was there and my Aunt telegraphed back to him that I was not there, that I had been and gone again, and that she knew nothing about me. They say if they find you they will make you suffer, you know in what way, I presume. That was the motive for me acting as I have done since I knew of that D. P. A's letter. My Aunt thought also it was better for me to go away, so that she would feel free, should anything serious take place. I have been expecting to see you all week, but my friend did not come. I have felt very impatient at times, almost forget what I was about, I would be so very absent minded.

[page 227]

Will you, my friend, send me Bp. W. Bassett's address, so that I can write to Ma without sending it to the house. Did you see Ma, or Mrs. Russell last time you were in the city? I have sent to Bowie for my freight, 2 boxes, both weighing 525 pounds, marked J. H.

Fig. 10.1—Colonia Juárez Academy. Courtesy of James Henry Martineau Family Organization.

Grieve, Smithville, Arizona via Bowie Station S.P.R.R. via C.P.R.R. They were prepaid before I left. I sent for them on the 9th inst,. but I have not received any word from the freight agent. You might make inquiry about them and confer a favor upon me by so doing. When you write again sign as formerly. I was surprised that morning when I was asked about you, and they wished to know if it was so, so that she might know what was best to be done. It was immediate action, for we knew not the hour that some one might enter in to intercept me. We went to S. F. C. (San Francisco) spent the day there, it being Thursday. On Saturday I started for Alameda, and here I am still. I do feel so lonely at times with no one to talk to about things that are nearest and dearest to me. You know what it is, having been in the same position yourself. Yet I can always find a refuge in prayer. Oh! Never forget me at any time, even though we are separated by distance. I think the old adage is true "Absence makes the heart grow fonder." Don't you think that California is a great Sabbath breaking State? I think it is really worse than the European Continent; hardly any one here observes the Sabbath. Last Sunday I rode on the train to Alameda Wharf. I had my book and writing tablet with me. I did feel so refreshed while sitting on the end of the pier with the sea breeze blowing upon my temples. It finally drove all my headache away. Each one seems to go to the most places of amusement on Sunday. All week it has been raining off & on. My written address is Miss Jessie Russell c/o Mrs. Wertheimer, 1860, Central Avenue, Alameda, Cal. You may guess why I take this name. I am having a little experience just now, which I think may do me good in after life.

[page 228]

1902—I hope you will find every one well in the South, also Gertrude; leg improving. Write me a long letter as soon as you can. Tonight I felt I could not go to sleep without writing you a few lines. If we taste the bitter beforehand we shall appreciate the sweet when it comes along. I am well, hoping you and the others are the same.

I am your a. b. c.

P. S. Address all letters to the following address until I tell you to change a. b. c.

Miss Jessie Russell o/c Mrs. Wertheimer

1860 Central Avenue. Alameda Cal."

[written in margin]

Letter of Jessie's

This letter from my dear wife explained to me what I could not before understand, of her doings in California. She did what she considered was for the best, though it parted us forever in this life—but not in the next. There I shall meet her again—and oh, what joy! Wicked men and women can have no power there to hurt or trouble: as she observes above "If we taste the bitter we appreciate the sweet when it comes along." And so, all our experiences, bitter as well as sweet, are necessary to our perfection. She was one of the pure in heart, and a dear female friend who knew her well said to me she was an almost perfect woman, if any can be found. Having received all the ordinances and endowments, she has made her calling and election and exaltation sure. If I meet her again in glory, I must do the same. With all my troubles and sorrows concerning her, I thank Our Father for her, and pray I may so live as to retain not only her but all whom God has given me.

October 8, 1902—Up to this time we have been very busy taking care of our fruit, selling some and drying and preserving as much as we could. Our peaches were so plenty on the trees that many broke down, as did also Apricots. We had besides apples, pears, plums and a few almonds. We gave away one or two wagon loads of peaches, and many bushels wasted on the ground.

[page 229]

October 17, 1902—I have also been doing some mapping for various persons Lyman having recently written to me that he wished to buy my survey and draughting instruments. I wrote accepting his offer, and telegraphed him for money to come to Utah.

I am much hampered for money in consequence of the cessation of my pension since last June. The Pension Commissioner wrote saying my pension would be discontinued, because I had been actually in Mexico in the war of 1846–8, nor even on the way to "the front." I answered that I had been on the way there, traveling 1300 miles to Newport Barracks, where I was discharged in July 1848, and had also served on Recruiting Service. To date I have received no reply.

October 12, 1902—To day Gertrude had suddenly a fearful convulsion and for a long time we feared she would die any moment, by cessation of heart action; but by the power of the priesthood and our Father's blessing she was finally saved to us. She has had many such attacks,—always striking her in an instant, beginning at the pit of her stomach.

November 27, 1902—Bp. J. C. Bentley and his wife Gladys desiring me to bless and dedicate their home, I did so to day, a numerous company being invited. We all had thanksgiving dinner. Susan walked there and back, resting several times on the way. Rheumatism in her knees, tired her much.

~~Nov. 1~~ Friday, October 31, 1902—Started with Gertrude to St Luke's hospital, in El Paso. Texas. Carried her on a bed to Dublan, 16 miles, over rough road. I blessed her before starting, that she might endure the journey, for it was feared the shaking and jolting might kill her. But the Lord blessed her so that she stood the journey much better than we hoped.

As we entered Dublan, I met Prest Helaman Pratt, who desired me to stay and survey for platting the contemplated line of canal to fill the natural reservoirs, for Dublan fields.

November 1 ~~2~~, 1902—Sat. I worked on Survey to day and on Monday 4th It is probably the last surveying I will do. My dear Susan wishes me to quit surveying, as too hard and too much exposure for me: and when I ask—"how will I get means to support us all," she says "Some other way will open."

[page 230—see Appendix 5 for letter from daughter Gertrude inserted here.]

November ~~4~~ 3, 1902—I trust He will. I know the Lord loves her, and I believe her faith and prayers will avail much in my behalf. Returned home and found all well. On the 2nd (Saturday) Gertie went on to El Paso, on the R. R. train, arriving at the Hospital very much fatigued by the long day's travel, and Changing transit at Ciudad Juarez to cross to El Paso. Before she left Dublan, in the morning, I blessed her again, for the day's journey, and the Lord honored my ministration in her behalf. She and her companion, Mrs. Caroline Saville Telford were given a room to themselves, and were kindly received by the Surgeon and nurses. (All this should have been noted earlier)

November 30, 1902—Sunday. Last day of Stake Conference, at which Apostles Hiram Smith, Golden Kimball, Pres^{t} Jo^{s} E. Taylor of Salt Lake, Sisters Hyde and Brixen from S. L. City were present. I blessed both those sisters at their request. After the last meeting I dedicated and blessed our house & home. Susan's brother Sixtus E. Johnson & wife and others of the family being present.

[written in margin]

Sell city lot. to E. F. T.

A few days previously I sold half my residence lot, the upper city lot and Calf pasture adjoining to Ed^{d} F. Turley, Anna's husband, for a home for her, that she might be near us.[1] The price was $1200 [$28,031], payable as follows:—Jan. 1. 1903, $300.$^{\underline{00}}$ [$7,008] July 1, 1903 $400.$^{\underline{00}}$ [$9,344] Jan. 1, 1904, $500.$^{\underline{00}}$ [$11,680] with interest from Jan. 1. 1903 @ 10 o/c pr annum.

We intend that Gertrude shall live in our house until Guy can build a home for her, he being now heavily involved, through a serius [series] of ill fortunes, in loss of stock &c Thus we may be near each other for mutual help and comfort.

December 1, 1902—Monday. Finished preparations for journey to Logan. Until the very last I could not make up my mind to go. tho' Lyman had sent me money for the journey, ($50.^{00}) & I could leave Susan well provided for, in money—$50. [$1,168] an order on the Tithing Office, some $70. [$1,635] due from Harly [could be Harry] Johnson, board money from James Johnson, who boards with us and should pay $2.50 [$58] per mank [month] (equal to about 1$ Amer. money [$23] besides what Guy will help on Gertie's account.

[page 231]

But I had a dread of leaving Susan to bear alone the care of Gertrude, and a dread of leaving my dear wife, such as I have never before felt. Is it because I am never to return? But I have asked our Father concerning my proposed journey several times, in view of going to labor for the dead, and the answer every time has been "Go, and you shall be blessed upon your journey, and in your labors while in Utah, and shall not be hurt by chang to that cold climate. And Susan and Gertrude, and your home shall be blessed in your absence, even as if you were present with them, for they are in my hands, and my blessing shall be upon them."

And such being the inspiration of the Holy Spirit to me I fear not to go would forfeit me the promised blessings. But the parting is sad to me.

December 2, 1902—Susan and I sat up all night until 5 A.M. of Tuesday Dec. 2 to take the mail wagon to the R. R. Station, except about 2 hours sleep for me.

I left Nueva Casas Grandes about 8 A.M. arriving in El Paso about 5 P.M. Went at once to see Gertrude. Found her much improved, and looking well in feature and color.

December 3, 1902—Cashed Lyman's Check and spent some time with dear Gertrude. Got oranges & bananas &c for her, and left $4.$^{\underline{00}}$ [$93] to get some things for Susan. Blessed her in the evening and left El Paso at 9.15 P.M. on the Santa Fe R. R. Took sleeper.

December 4, 1902—Awoke next morning near Albuquerque. & took breakfast there. Los Vegas 1.45 P.M. Trinidad 9.30 P.M. and changed car, but not train

December 5, 1902—Pueblo 6.15 A.M. and lay by until 11.55 A.M. Here I met Apostle A. O. Woodruff, just returning from New Orleans. We had a very pleasant time together all the way to S. L. City, relating mutually our experiences. He also invited me to dine on the train

December 6, 1902—Sat. Arr^{d} in S. L. City 10.30 A.M. I went to Bp. Preston's and met a warm welcome.

[page 232]

December 7, 1902—Sunday. Visited Eliza and went to Virginia's, 9th South 942 West, close to Jordan river. She rushed out to meet me, looking in fine health. The children are fine looking and intelligent, and I feel proud—I should say—thankful for them. Edward Sudbury, her husband, in clerking in Scofield

December 8, 1902—Visited Mrs. Woodmansee,[2] and was warmly received, as I could tell her about her daughters in our village. Sherman was taken with sore throat, and as diphtheria is very prevalent and fatal,

1 Clarence F. Turley and Anna Tenney Turley, *History of the Mormon Colonies in Mexico (The Juarez Stake), 1885–1980* (Salt Lake City: Publishers Press, 1996), 111, 212.

2 The Woodmansees in the Church are of British heritage.

Genie was much alarmed. We were up with him till nearly 1 A.M.

December 9, 1902—The doctor Came, and said it was only tonsilitis. I wrote to Gertie and Uncle Benjamin, Prayed for Sherman and felt he would soon recover.

December 12, 1902—Snoing [snowing] heavily this morning. Winter is come. Genie went and bought Christmas things for the children, also 3 neck ties for me.

December 13, 1902—I tested my Aneroid[3] at the U. S. weather bureau.

December 14, 1902—Stake Conference, Preaching on priesthood by Pres^{t} Smith

December 16, 1902—Went to the temple, & presented names for baptism. Laman^{s} [Lamanites]

December 19, 1902—Saw Pres^{t} J. F. Smith about my book of "Pearls." Left it with him for examination and approval.

Yesterday, 18th I met Pat^{h} John Smith. He gave me permission to bless in Cache Co. Said I should ask $2.00 [$47] for blessing, stationery and recording, and giving copy. I told him I had never made any charge, and that not one in ten had ever given me anything. He said "the laborer is worthy of his hire." I have always as gladly blessed one who was unable to give anything, as though he had given gold. I esteem it a high honor and privilege to be permitted to seal a blessing upon any one in the authority of the holy patriarchal priesthood, whether I receive anything in return or not. My great anxiety is that I may be <u>worthy</u> for so high and holy a privilege.

Br. Smith also gave me a key by which to know an Ephraimite when not sealing a blessing upon him

December 21, 1902—Sunday, Memorial service for Joseph the Prophet.[4] Visited Eliza again & invited her to Christmas dinner

[page 233]

December 22, 1902—Sent magazine to Susan. I am sorry I have nothing else to send for a christmas gift—except my blessing & love

December 25, 1902—Christmas, but not much of one for me, because my dear wife is not with me. Gean had a nice dinner. I wrote to Susan and others a christmas greeting, having nothing else to send—no money in purse. I have helped Gean's table at times, when she had no money for marketing. In the evening Br. Sudbury and his daughters, Mrs. Jos. E Taylor (Clara) Lavina, Gr. dau. Ruth and Sissidore & Fred. spent a sociable evening.

December 27, 1902—By invitation took dinner with Pres. Ja^{s} E. Taylor's family. Also attended a funeral by his request.

January 1, 1903—The Sudbury's all came to visit us, also Mr. & Mrs. Peterson (Tip). A pleasant time.

Regulated my Barometer by that in U. S. weather Office, making mine read like that in the office.

JANUARY 1903

January 3, 1903—Ed^{d} Sudbury came home from Scofield.

January 5, 1903—Spent an hour or more in Pres^{t} J. F. Smith's office looking over my Book of "Pearls." Saw Prers^{ts} Lund & Winder.

Got a ruby set placed in Susan's ring. Price of stone $10.00 [$225].

January 6, 1903—Received permission from the Presidency to baptize over a hundred Lamanites,—Aztecs, and other Mexican indians, Auracanians, and Incas of Peru, also North American indians. Edward & Gean gave me a suit of his clothes, also $7.00 [$157] Money to pay on ring.

January 8, 1903—My 51st Wedding Anniversary. but my dear companion not with me, and this makes it not a pleasant one. To night I leave Gean's, to sleep at Bp. Preston's so I may take the early train for Logan. I hated to leave Gean, who is lonesome and fearful of burglars and robbers. She has been good and kind to me, and I have been happy with her. Ed. will go back in 2 or 3 days to Scofield, to the store in which he is a clerk.

January 9, 1903—Left S. L. City 7 A.M. At Logan 11 A.M. Found all the family but Lilla well.

[page 234]

January 9, 1903—Visited Frank and Lilla. She is almost perfectly deaf and I can hardly make her

3 This is a mechanical barometer, a mechanical means of measuring atmospheric pressure.

4 The memorial service honored Joseph Smith's birthday on December 23.

understand. She often is at a loss, in talking, for a word she needs. She can read well, but cannot write or spell at all.

Sunday, January 11, 1903—At First Ward meeting and Spoke.

January 12, 1903—Wrote to Dr. Robert Nichol, at Miñaca, to pay the bill of $41.^00 [$921] for repair of my transit which he broke.

Went with Nephi to his home. Cold weather. found them all well. Howard had run away again.

Their baby—James Gaston Martineau, was born April 21. 1901. One of twins. The other one died.

Nephi has nine children in all—living and dead. Lyman 8, Charles 6, Lilla 5, Gean 5 = 33

To those in Arizona and Mexico. 41, Hagberg 6 = 80

January 14, 1903—Leveled a canal line for Nephi.

January 16, 1903—Returned to Lyman's, Had a very pleasant visit with Nephi and family. Aurelia, the eldest girl, is attending the Brigham Young Academy, Howard is away.

January 17, 1903—Sent pension papers, hoping my pension may be renewed, although the Pension Commissioner said it must cease. In answer to my prayer I am told it shall be continued, and <u>increased</u>. I believe it.

Rec^d a letter from Jo^s F. Smith, President, inserted in previous page.

Sunday, January 18, 1903—Joined the 1st Ward in Logan, that I may continue in close touch with the Church. Found Walter Lamoreaux and wife. Sister J. C. Bentley (Maggie) specially charged me to hunt them up, as Sister Lamoreaux is her sister—Edith May (Ivins) Lamoreaux.[5] They were glad to see one who knew their sister in Mexico, and I like their spirit very much.

[written in margin]

Florence born to T.

January 14, 1903—By letter I learn Theodore and Josephine Thurstons baby girl, named Florence—was born Jan. 14 1903 at 10.45 A.M. About 20 miles south of Miñaca in State of Chihuahua, Mexico

January 17, 1903—My cousin, Anna (Mrs. Wm A. Mears) Mears, of Portland, Oregon came to visit us, to stay several days.

[page 235]

January 26, 1903—On 26 Lyman took us to see "Corianton," a mormon play. Very cold weather and snow about 8^in deep. Good play.

January 27, 1903—We visited the Agricultural College

Received pension (back) $48^00 [$1,078] Thus is verified the word of the Spirit to me. Thus I am learning His voice.

January 28, 1903—With Lyman, Alley, Cousin Mears I went to a Ball of the Social Club, then to Will & Kate Preston's reception.

January 29, 1903—Cousin Anna Mears went on home to Portland, well pleased with her entertainment in Logan.

January 31, 1903—Finished my biographical notes for publication in Jensen's new Biographical Work, according to Jensen's request.[6]

FEBRUARY

February 5, 1903—Sent my notes to Jensen.[7]

February 7, 1903—Blessed Robert & wife and daughter. Very cold weather. 13 degrees below zero.

[written in margin]

*Tithing paid. $5.^00* [$112]

February 4, 1903—Paid $5.^00 Cash tithing

February 14, 1903—Got my temple robes finally completed, all except cap.

February 20, 1903—Endowed to day for Elias Martineau.

Searched for family names and record in Genealogical Record in the temple. Mears' Genealogy found in

Joslin's history of Poultney Vt.	page 311
Keim Genealogy	page 400
Mears' Genealogy of 1873	31 pages
Savages Genl Dictionary vol. 3	p. 192

5 The Lamoreaux family are described as farmers, carpenters, builders, and laborers (Ray Somers, *History of Logan*, [Logan, UT: Somers Historic Press, 1993], 64).

6 This is a reference to Andrew Jenson's chronicles of Church history.

7 Entries in this part of the journal are out of chronological order.

Secomb's History of Amhurst N.H. 689
Smith's Hist^{y} of Peterborough 143
Stiles " " Windsor vol. 2 p. 492

February 23, 1903—Blessed W$^{\underline{m}}$ B. Preston Jun.

Tuesday, February 24, 1903—I was Baptized today for 27 Aztec princes & chiefs.

February 25, 1903—I was Endowed for Gaston Martineau

February 26, 1903—I was Endowed for John Martineau

February 27, 1903—I was Endowed for Peter Martineau

MARCH

March 2, 1903—Searched again for family names in Records.

[page 236]

March 3, 1903—I weighed myself today = 177 lbs. the heaviest in my life.

I was baptized for 87 Aztec Kings, princes and Chiefs.

March 4, 1903—I Endowed Peter Martineau, Born 1727

March 6, 1903—I Endowed Stephen Martineau Born 1773

March 7, 1903—Blessed Martin D. Cranney

[written in margin]

Note

March 4, 1903—Son-in-law Frank Nebeker went with others to Mexico desiring me to stay at his house while he is absent.

March 10, 1903—I endowed Peter Haughout, B. 1765.

Nephi endowed Lord Hutchinson B. 1680

March 12, 1903—I endowed Cornelius Martineau

Nephi endowed Stephen Martineau

March 13, 1903—My 75$^{\underline{th}}$ Birthday. My days are drawing to a close. I was invited to dinner at 6 P.M. by Br. W. S. Lamoreaux & Edith. Had a pleasant time. They gave me as birthday present a copy of the New History of the Church. This was the only remembrance received by me.

I endowed James Guyon, Nephi End^{d} Dirk Haughout

I rec^{d} from Genl Robt T. Burton an old commission of mine, as Capt in Top^{l} Engineers, Genl D. H. Wells. Staff dated in 1857.

March 15, 1903—Rec^{d} notice from Com^{r} of Pensions that my pension is disallowed by him. A great loss—my only revenues—only \$8.$^{\underline{00}}$ [\$180] per month, but my only income. He gave no reason

March 16, 1903—I wrote to Senator Thos Kearns about it.[8]

March 18, 1903—I endowed Peter M. Haughout, Nephi End$^{\underline{d}}$ Stephen Keteltas

March 19, 1903—Nephi Endowed Jacobus Haughout

I Endowed Egbert Haughout

W. S. Lamoreaux end^{d} Peter Haughout.

In the afternoon and evening had 3 severe chills. Some said they were Congestive Chills. I don't know I was quite sick all night

March 20, 1903—Sick in bed all day

March 21, 1903—Lilla gave me as birth day [birthday] present a pair of slippers and \$10.$^{\underline{00}}$ [\$225] cash. Very acceptable in my needs.

Rose this morning, but am still quite weak. Lyman administered to me, Felt blessed.

[page 237]

March 22, 1903—Feel much better today. Blessed Jean Spencer, who is visiting at Lyman's from S. L. City

March 23, 1903—Still very weak. Sought names in Genl Record.

March 24, 1903—Nephi was baptized to day for 80 Aztecs & Peruvian Kings, Princes and Chiefs.

March 25, 1903—Sent \$20$^{\underline{00}}$ [\$550] to Susan as part of R. R. fare from Mexico to S. L. City. Only one third enough, but all I could get.

March 26, 1903—I endowed Nicholas Haughout, 27$^{\underline{th}}$ Vincent Haughout

March 31, 1903—Blessed John A. Gordon rec^{d} \$1.$^{\underline{00}}$ [\$22] Am not well today.

....

8 Thomas Kearns (1862–1918) was the Republican U.S. senator representing Utah from 1901 to 1905. He was instrumental in Utah's mining business (Newell G. Bringhurst, "Thomas Kearns: Irish-American Builder of Modern Utah," *Journal of the West* 31 [April 1992]: 24–32).

APRIL 1903

April 2, 1903—Blessed Walter S. Lamoreaux.

Friday, April 3, 1903—I moved from Lilla's to Lymans, to be early to the train.

April 4, 1903—Feel quite unwell

Sunday, April 5, 1903—Started to S. L. City with Lyman & Alley. Arr[d] at noon & went to Bp. Preston's. Snow last night. Conference.

April 6, 1903—Attended Conference. On the [7th][continued in next entry]

April 7, 1903—Attended Special (private) Priesthood meeting, where some special instructions were given relative to temple work and garments, aprons &c Proceedings not to be public.

April 8, 1903—Edward Sudbury returned to Castle Gate.

April 10, 1903—Spent the day trying to get employment. Tried McCartney Chf. Eng. Las Angeles, San P. & S. L. R. R. Nothing to be done. Also Doremus, State Engineer, same answer; Twin Falls Co. (Idaho) same; also Sur. Gen. Anderson, for U. S. Contract for Land Survey. Nothing definite there now.

April 13, 1903—Sent to Caygell for pen ($1.62) [$36] Arranged with Br. A. Jenson for extension of time for payment of my genealogical record in his book.

April 15, 1903—Attended funeral of Brigham Young. Met Mrs Herbert White, daughter of Orson Hyde

April 17, 1903—Rec[d] letter from Eliza Belle Johnson (Martineau (Jesse's wife) with account of her ancestry as far as she knows:—

HER

Great Grandfather, William Johnson, Born Dec 2.1785 & (wife) Nancy, born June 28. 1788. Also his son, her Grandfather, William Eaton Johnson (Eldest Child) Born 24 Jan. 1812 (Their other children were Dewitt C. Johnson. Born 9th Feb. 1813.

[page 238]

April 16, 1903—

Ansil L.	Johnson,	Born	14 Aug. 1814
David B.	"	"	14 Feb. 1816 (Daniel B.)
Welcome W.	"	"	26 Oct. 1817
Harty J.	"	"	16 May 1819
David M.	"	"	7 Oct. 1821
John L. H.	"	"	3 Feb. 1826
Warren	"	"	5 Mch. 1830

[written in margin]

Note

Note. Warren was an officer in the Confederate Army & has not been heard of since the Civil War.

Her Grandfather William Eaton Johnson married Mary W. Dickinson in 1832, of South Williamstown Mass. They had four children, as follows:—Her Father

William Warren Johnson. Born 10 Nov. 1832. Died at Sharon, Wis. 18th July 1862, a private in 13th Wisconsin Res

Caroline H. Born 18th Sep. 1836. Now living in Hadley Mass.

Eliza Mills, " [born] 11 July 1834 Died 18 Mch. 1843

Edward Eaton, " [born] 21st Aug. 1845. Now in Los Angeles, Cal.

[written in margin]

Note.

~~~ Her Grandfather, William Eaton Johnson died 16 Jan. 1889. Her Grandmother died in 1872

HER MOTHER WAS

Mary E. Leavitt, Born in Stark. N. H. 24 July 1839 and was married in Delavan, Wisconsin, 1st Jan. 1857. Her children were

Carrie B. Johnson, born 24th Dec. 1857, Died 28 Feb. 1858

Willis Eaton, Born 8 Dec. 1859. Lives now in Passadina Cal.

Eliza Belle Johnson (Martineau) Born 21st Dec. 1861, in Sharon, Wisconsin.

Her uncle Edward has family genealogy back to 1626, when William Johnson married Nancy Eaton, in
~~~

London England. All the Johnsons were early Settlers in Mass. One of them was named Barrykiah.

Her Grandmother Leavitt's maiden name was Sarah Spaulding, a descendant of Hannah Dustin of early indian War (in Hadley) fame.

Five cousins have now joined the church.

April 18, 1903—Not well. In bed all day.

April 23, 1903—I endowed Garrett Cozine

[page 239]

April 23, 1903—Lilla was nearly burned to death to day, while burning waste paper &c in the yard. A gust of wind caugh[t] a flame on her apron. She tried to extinguish the flames, but could not pull off the burning clothing. Then she ran into the house, but the hired girl was too excited to help her any. So Lilla ran out doors hoping some one would help her, and fighting the flames all the time. Fortunately a man came to her rescue & put out the flames, which had burned both arms and shoulders, right hand very deeply, also her back and side. Her corsets had partially preserved her vitals. Her eyebrows and front hair were burned, but her face escaped. Had she not been dressed in woollen skirts and underclothes she would surely have been burned to death. It happened in the forenoon, and all day she passed form one chill into another, and the doctors feared, that in her weak previous condition, the shock would kill her, but by the great blessing of the Lord & administrations of priesthood, she was saved. Prompt surgical assistance was at hand and all was done to ease her pains.

April 24, 1903—I endowed Mr. Beatty today. Heard of Lilla's burn and tried to get to the train in time but failed to do so.

April 25, 1903—Went to Logan to see Lilla

April 26, 1903—She is resting easily as could be expected, and was glad to see me. Poor girl! She met me with a smile.

April 27, 1903—Rec^{d} letter from Senator Kearns relative to the Stop-page of my pension. He advised a special pension bill for me in next session of Congress. I wrote him a full Statement of my case in return.

April 29, 1903—I endowed Peter Cozine

Thursday, April 30, 1903—I endowed Covas Cozine. Received letter from Susan. She is in S. L. City, having arrived last Wednesday at Midnight, with Ed^{d} Sudbury.

May 1, 1903—Went to S. L. City, and found Susan well. I was very thankful to have her with me again after 5 months saporation [separation]. We have become necessary to each other.

[page 240]

May 1, 1903—Susan was four days on her journey, being detained 12 hours on the way at Pueblo. She came in company with John M. Cannon and Bp. Benion. Br. Cannon was as kind and attentive all the way as a son could have been, doing all that was possible for her comfort. May Our Father ever bless him and his. She was joined at Castle Gate, Utah, by our son-in-law Edward Sudbury, who took her to his house in S. L. City on arrival at midnight. They had never met previously. She said Gertrude, while desiring her mother to go, dreaded her absence, saying "Oh Ma, no one can pray for me and do for ~~you~~ me as you do." Susan had prayed for guidance as to going, and felt it right and expedient to go now, and that Gertie would suffer no ill by her going away. She was also told she should make the journey in peace, safety and comfort, and no accident should occur, all which was verified. I myself, had the same testimony in answer to my inquiry. What a blessed privilege to be able to ask Our Father for guidance, and be taught! In this privilege my dear Susan is greatly blessed, as has been shown many times to my own knowledge.

[written in margin]

May 1. 1903. A girl born to G. A. & Emma Martineau in Chuichupa, Mex. We named her Anita, Mexican pet name for Anna, on July 8th 1903.

Saturday, May 2, 1903—I entered temple work in my record. Susan and Virginia and myself visited Bp. W. B. Preston's, but all were absent except Alley Martineau, my gr-daughter. After getting back to Gean's Susan had a sinking spell such as she has had before. Blessed by administration.

May 4, 1903—Edward returned to Castle Gate. Sherman, his son, who has been very sick for about ten days, is about well.

May 5, 1903—I found my adopted son Nels L. Hagberg to day. I had not seen him for ten years.

Thursday, May 12, 1903—Visited ~~Br. &~~ Sis. H. A. White, and blessed ~~them~~ her.

Sunday, May 17, 1903—Visited at White's, and blessed him and his daughter Hazel White. Went to Gean's in a storm of rain and snow.

Tuesday, May 19, 1903—Went to Sur. Gen[l] Ed. H. Anderson to obtain a survey Contract, and to ascertain prices for work.[9] I find there must be surveyed 63 full townships, 58 fractional to. connection lines 100, besides base lines, meridians, standard parallels, and meander lines, in all about 9000 miles of lines. including some resurveys, & boundaries.

[page 241]

[written in margin]

Note

May 1, 1903—I learn by letter that a baby girl was born to ~~Nephi &~~ Albert & Emma on Friday May 1. She weighed 11 lbs.

May 19, 1903—Cont[d] By letter from Charles—he says he is called on a Mission to the Middle States, to go in October next.

To day I went with Hagberg and visited his burial lot in S. L. City cemetery, and found also our own graves.

May 20, 1903—Wed. Began work in S. L. temple. I endowed Robert Blake

May 21, 1903—Endowed Thomas Blake. Heavy rain. Eliza endowed Lady Lucy Rachel Stanhope.

May 22, 1903—Today Charles came to S. L. City and began work in Oregon Short Line R. R. Shop.

May 25, 1903—Monday. To day made bid for survey in Uinta indian Reservation as follows:—

For Subdivision township lines, per mile	$16.00
" Connecting lines	17.00
" Township Exteriors	18.00
" Meridian lines	22.00
" Standard Parallels	23.00
" Base, and Meander lines	24.00
	[$16 = $359 to $24 = $539]

Up to this time I have tried in many ways to get employment of some kind, but unsuccessfully so far.

But in answer to my prayer that my way may be opened to obtain means for our support I have received an answer that it shall be, and speedily; but how I cannot tell. I have small hope of obtaining a U. S. Survey contract, as there are more applicants than contracts to be let, and I am now unknown here,—a new generation has grown up who are known in the Sur. General's Office.

May 29, 1903—Friday. To day Pres[t] T. Roosevelt visited the city. A grand reception was given him, both in street parade and in the Tabernacle, where he spoke to 12000 people.[10]

JUNE 1, 1903

Monday, June 1, 1903—Attended dedication of Barrett Hall. Grand.

[page 242]

June 2, 1903—By invitation Susan and I went to visit John M. Cannon, in Granite Stake, and had a pleasant time.

Wednesday, June 3, 1903—I endowed W[m] Pitt (Earl Chatham) Susan endowed our dear Dora, and Eliza End[d] Lois Hutchinson.

I had Eight couples sealed. (See temple record)

June 4, 1903—I endowed Rob[t] Pitt, Susan End[d] Louisa Grenville. We visited Susan West Smith, widow of Geo. A. Smith

June 5, 1903—I end[d] Tho[s] Pitt. Susan end[d] Hester Pitt.

We visited Br. Herbert A. White and remained all night. Bp. John Neff of Forest Ward was present, a good man, full of the Spirit. We blessed each other and had a glorious time. The Lord said to Sister Mary Hyde White concerning us who were present, that we were "One with God and His son Jesus Christ."

[written in margin]

June 9. 1903. A girl baby born to Nephi and Emma

June 6, 1903—Sat. I blessed their daughter, Urania White, who had greatly desired a blessing from under my hands. Also blessed Sisters Lena Bell (Mrs. Davis) and C. W. Peterson Lenard. Had a time of rejoicing. Went to Gean's.

Tuesday, June 9, 1903—Mother, Gean and I went to Saltair bathing resort.

9 Surveyor-General Edward H. Anderson had received orders from the federal government to proceed with the survey contract.

10 Theodore Roosevelt was the twenty-sixth U.S. president, serving from 1901 to 1908.

Wednesday, June 10, 1903—I Endowed Charles Sprague. Too wet for Susan to go.

June 11, 1903—I Endowed Joseph May. Susan could not go.

June 12, 1903—I Endowed Richard Dexter. Susan End[d] Elizabeth Mears.

I had Sealed Mr. & Mrs. Robert Pitt

" " " W[m] & Mrs. W[m] Pitt

" " " Tho[s] & Mrs. Thomas Pitt

Saturday, June 13, 1903—Rec[d] letter from Lyman, with $5.00 [$112]. Wants to Come to Logan tomorrow, with Scandinavian excursion.

Saw President Joseph F. Smith and gave him, for his father, Hyrum Smith, my sister Lucretia, to be Hyrum's wife.

He also gave me permission to endow Lamanites for whom I have been endowed.

While in the city I had baptisms performed of 20 females of our family kindred. Sisters White and Peterson came to visit us before we should leave.

Sunday, June 14, 1903—We went to Logan with excursion. Virginia also.

June 15, 1903—Gean returned home.

June 16, 1903—Letter from Henry, who is very sick in city of Chihuahua, Mex.; he fears he may die.

[page 243]

Wednesday, June 17, 1903—I end[d] [endowed] John Dexter, Dominic Bodrero end[d] John Louis Pascal, a Piedmontese Martyr.

June 18, 1903—I end[d] Rob[t] Oguier Martyr

June 19, 1903—I end[d] John Dexter

June 24, 1903—To night Lilla Nebeker's little Marjorie was lost. A large number hunted with lanterns through the city and big canal, the alarm bell rang, and there was quite an excitement until nearly 3 A.M. when she was found asleep and safe. An anxious time indeed. We feared she was drowned in the Canal.

June 25, 1903—I end[d] Philip Henry Stanhope

June 26, 1903—Susan and I went to Nephi's, at Riverside on visit.

JULY 1903

July 8, 1903—We returned to Logan.

July 10, 1903—I end[d] Mr. Burrows, Sister Willard Cranny End Mrs. James Mears.

July 15, 1903—I end[d] Rob[t] Greenhow, Susan, Mrs. Sarah Hutchinson. Mrs. Cranney, Bethia Hutchinson

I had Sealed

Rich[d] Dexter and Mrs. Rich[d] Dexter

John Dexter and Mrs. John Dexter

[written in margin]

Susan sick

July 15, 1903—This evening at 7 P.M. while at dinner Susan was taken suddenly with a very severe Chill. We got her to bed with severe headache and hot fever. I sat up all night and fanned and attended her as best I could

July 16, 1903—Susan very sick all day and night.

July 17, 1903—Susan has congestion of the lungs with very hot fever, and is threatened with pneumonia. Lyman called Dr. Budge, who pronounced her in much danger. Does not know if she can live. I am with her every hour, night and day, doing all I can. The thought that she may leave me is agonizing.

July 18, 1903—Susan Seems a little better,—fever not so hot.

I am notified a contract as U. S. Dep. Surveyor is mine.

July 19, 1903—Wrote to Sur. Gen[l] Anderson about contract.

July 20, 1903—Susan a little better. I laid down and slept about an hour—my first since Susan was taken sick. I have eaten scarcely anything, and Susan nothing except a little milk.

[page 244]

July 21, 1903—Susan some better. I laid down 4 hours, a great help to me. Lyman has sat up twice, half or more the night which enabled me to lie down.

July 22, 1903—Susan better. An agent of a bonding company came to me, to let them be my bondsman, to amount of $9000.[00] [$202,148] on my Survey Contract, which is for $4453.[00] [$100,018] I made arrangements for bonds, and must pay the Company $22.50 [$505] premium. Notified to go at once to S. L. City to file [the word "execute" written above "file"] Contract and bonds.

July 23, 1903—Borrowed $6.00 [$135] from Frank, to go to the city

July 24, 1903—Went to the city. Signed contract, and received the "Manual" of instructions for the survey. Went to Gean's but she was gone to Castle Gate. So I went to White's who received me with much joy. remaining all night. By request I blessed him and her.

July 25, 1903—Filed my bond for $8906.[00] [$200,037] My bondsmen are United States Fidelity and Guaranty Comp, Baltimore, Md.

My contract binds me to make full returns of my survey on or before Sept. 30. 1904. Cannot get any money at any bank. Returned to Logan.

[written in margin]

Eva's baby born

At 7:40 P.M. Eva & Charles' little boy was born. All was well with Eva. Charles was in S. L. City.

Sunday, July 26, 1903—Quarterly Conference. Susan much better.

July 27, 1903—Wrote to Coz N. B. Van Slyke to borrow money to carry on my survey.

[written in margin]

Blessing on 26th

Before starting home yesterday I visited Pres[t] J. F. Smith and asked a blessing from him, that I may be blessed in performing my contract and for blessings in general.

He said "Yes, I love to bless a good man." He closed the doors and with Pres[t] J. R. Winder gave me a grand blessing, according to my desire, ending by saying "my last days shall be among my very best days." I was greatly comforted & strengthened.

July 28, 1903—Susan sat up a little while for the first time.

July 29, 1903—A letter from Albey L. Sherman, Susan's [Susan Julia's] cousin saying help to Survey may be had among his sons and family.

[page 245]

July 31, 1903—Old Folks Party in Logan, A very fine entertainment.

Afternoon, I went to Nephi's to level for a canal for him.

AUGUST.

August 1, 1903—Leveled for him all day, and formed a route by which he may bring waste water to his land. Mosquitoes!

Sunday, August 2, 1903—Returned to Logan. Found special instructions for my survey, which I am to sign and return.

August 3, 1903—Signed and mailed instructions. Made sketch of the ground to be surveyed. My work includes approx[1]

Base line	4 miles
Guide Meridian (special)	17 "
Township Boundaries	39 "
Section lines, subdivision	200 "
	260 miles

It consists of T.1N.—R.1E. T.4N.—R.1E. T.1N.—R.2E. T 2N —R.2E T.1N —R.1W. T 2N.—R.1E. T.2N.—R.1W. T 3N —R.1W T.3N.—R.1E Much of it joins E. bdy. of Uintah Indian Reservation, and it extends North into foothills of the Uintah Mountain range," peaks of which are 13000 ft.

August 4, 1903—Susan had a relapse today. We, Lyman and I, administered, and she at once became better

Received word from Sur. Gen[l] Anderson my contract and bonds are accepted, all right. Susan dresses herself.

August 10, 1903—At this date Susan is well in lungs and body, but is very weak in her knees, and hardly able to walk. Her bosom had been blistered 15 times and she had taken much medicine to relieve congestion of the lungs. I am very thankful she is thus spared to me. We went today by invitation to Patriarch Lorenzo H. Hatch, where we blessed each other and our wives, and had a day to be remembered. We also blessed br Hatch's daughter, who was visiting there, and comforted her much.

[written in margin]

My Blessing

11 The Uintah and Ouray Indian Reservation is in the far northeastern corner of Utah, bordering Colorado.

MY BLESSING BY BR. L H HATCH

Beloved Brother James, in the name of Jesus Christ of Nazareth I have placed my hands upon thy head in accordance with the desire of thy heart, and Seal upon thee a patriarchal blessing.

[page 246]

August 10, 1903—Behold I say unto thee the Lord is well pleased with thy labors and the integrity of thy heart. His guardian Angels have watched over thee, and thy life has been wonderfully preserved. Thou hast received great blessings and manifestations. The Lord has heard thy prayers and there is a crown of eternal life prepared for thee, and a mansion which has been prepared also, and in thy ministry thou hast been greatly blessed. And in thy calling as a Patriarch in the church it is the will of the Lord that you should lift up your voice as with the sound of a trumpet and bless the congregations of Israel, and lay your hands upon those who desire blessings and fear not, for whatsoever you seal on earth shall be acknowledged in the heavens. For this purpose thy life has been preserved, and the Lord will remember thee in thy labors and He will lengthen out thy days till thou art satisfied, For thou art entitled to every blessing that has been conferred upon thee, and thy enemies shall be confounded. The Lord is well pleased with thy labors in His holy temples. Lay the charge and responsibility for the continuation of this great work upon your sons and daughters. The Holy angels will yet minister unto them and they shall obtain the names of thy kindred, and the chain of the priesthood shall be made perfect. This day shall be a day of memorial to thee. The Lord has given unto thee a numerous posterity, and of thy increase there shall be no end. They are heirs to the fullness of the priesthood, and they shall become obedient, if it needs be, with the things they suffer. Rejoice and be exceeding glad, for this blessing is given to comfort thy heart. Thou shalt be blessed, and shall never lack for friends or means. For all things are in the hands of thy Heavenly Father. I seal all these blessings with thy former blessings, and say unto thee thou shalt obtain them unto the fullness, even unto the Godhead, For this blessing has been sealed upon thee, to reign and rule in the house of Israel forever.

[page 247]
There is no good gift that shall be withheld from thee. And I rebuke the power of the Enemy and say unto thee live humble and these words shall all be verified. I pronounce these blessings by the authority of the holy priesthood and in the name of Jesus Christ. Amen.

SUSAN'S BLESSING, SAME TIME & PLACE.

Beloved Sister Susan in the name of Jesus Christ of Nazareth I have placed my hands upon thy head, and I seal upon thee a patriarchal blessing in connexion with all the blessings that have been promised unto thee by thy Father and the Patriarchs, and say unto thee they are renewed upon thy head this day. The Lord has watched over thee and thy tribulations. He has witnessed thy tears, and thy husband has been greatly blessed by ~~thy~~ the prayers you have offered up in his behalf. Your children and your children's children shall be remembered unto the latest generation, and there shall be not one of them lost, For thou hast received all the blessings of the house of the Lord. When thou hast been in great peril the angel of the Lord has gone before thee in thy journeys. They that would have destroyed thy life have been turned aside. Lift up thy voice with thanksgiving and encourage thy children to go forth and perform their duties. Thou hast been a great comfort, & thy words have encouraged many to walk uprightly before the Lord. Thy name is recorded in the Lamb's Book of Life. Thou art a descendant of Joseph that was sold into Egypt and through the loins of Ephraim. This day shall be a day of remembrance, and these words shall be handed down to thy posterity. Thou shalt stand in thy lot and place with thy husband, and the holy ordinances that have been conferred upon thee shall all be verified, and thou shalt be associated and reign as a Queen and priestess ~~with~~ and be exalted with thy husband & inherit the mansion that has been prepared for thee in the celestial kingdom.

[page 248]

August 10, 1903—Continue to pray for thy husband and thy prayers shall be heard, and the Lord will watch over him in his labors, and he shall find favors with those who employ him, & everything shall be overruled for his good. I seal all these blessings with every blessing thy heart can desire in righteousness with thy former blessings by the authority of the holy priesthood and in the name of Jesus Christ. Amen.

In these two blessings the Spirit of revelation has been powerfully exhibited. Br. Hatch, knowing almost nothing of events in my life in the last 20 years has spoken as if well informed about them,—for instance, in my having had my life "wonderfully preserved," also Susan's and mine preserved when in "great peril,"—which was when, in the last great Apache raid Susan made me promise to kill her myself, rather than she should fall alive into their hands. Also in several other matters. These two blessings, therefore, are an additional and very great help to my faith, and I thank God for them.

August 16, 1903—By invitation Susan and I visited the new home of Bishop Wm B. Preston, on his farm on Bear river & spent the night there. Also Lyman took us to his farm, beyond Bear river, leaving us at Nephi's home in Benson Ward next day, where we spent a few days pleasantly.

August 19, 1903—I blessed, of Nephi's family his sons Leigh Edward, James Gaston, and baby daughter Anita.

August 22, 1903—Called to S. L. City by Sur. Genl Anderson to sign papers pertaining to my Survey contract. Returned to Logan next day.

August 24, 1903—I gave note payable to Cache Valley Banking Co. for $600.^00 [$13,477] payable in 8^month Lyman and Frank Nebeker Endorsed it. I was hard work to get the money, and I could not, without Lyman's help.

[page 249]

August 26, 1903—Susan and I left Logan, I for my Survey, She to visit Gean awhile, then to visit Sariah, in Virgin city Had my chains and transit tested by Sur. General

August 29, 1903—Finished testing instruments, and received all papers, maps, instructions &c for my Survey.

I state here, that I was greatly worried as to how I would be able to get the necessary bondsmen for my contract, amounting to $9006.^00 [$202,282] But to my great astonishment I received a letter from a Great U.S. Bonding Company, in Baltimore, offering to act as such. I had never heard of them before. That Co. became my surety, I paying them $22.50 [$505] premium. Thus the Lord opened my way, when it seemed to be firmly closed against, me. And thus was, in part, fulfilled the blessing I had received from President J .F. Smith and J. R. Winder.

Today Susan started alone on the railway to visit her sister Sariah Workman, in Virgin City. Washington Co. Utah,—a long and tedious journey for her, in her lameness and feeble condition, nearly 300 miles by rail and about 70 by wagon, over horrible roads.

I dreaded the journey for her, but she had faith she would go all right, and she did. At Lund, where she ~~found~~ left the Railway, she found her nephew Jacob Workman and wife, with a one seated buggy, waiting for her, and in that crowded little trap went to her sister's—two long days ride, over rough roads. After visiting Sariah awhile she and Sariah went to St. George, meeting there her brother Nephi & wife Maggie, They took a room together, and spent some days working in St George temple, and enjoying a nice family union, though Seth and Sixtus were absent. Then she returned to Virgin City and on Oct. 4 left for S. L. City, arriving at Lund .8.30 P.M. Oct. 6, and arrived S. L. City 9.30 A.M. Oct. 7th pretty used up by so tedious a journey, sitting up all the last night on the train. But she testified that while away her way was continually opened before her, and she was blessed all the time, just as had been her faith, from the first.

[page 250]

August 1903—While Susan and I were in S. L. City, previous to her journey south, we stayed at Herbert A. White's No 462 E. 7th South S. L. City, and one night with Sister Lena B. Davis, another dear friend.[12]

August 31, 1903—Nephi and Howard, who will help on Survey, started with Ether Tarbet on train for Price. I was detained.

September 1, 1903—I left S. L. City, for Price, via D & R. G. R. R. arriving there about 6 P.M.

September 2, 1903—I went to Huntington to hire men, not finding them at Price, as I had expected.

12 Herbert White was among the elders with Apostle John W. Taylor when the Colorado Mission was organized on December 15, 1896. At this writing there was no information on Lena B. Davis.

This place is 22 miles S. W. of Price. I stayed at my brother-in-law Albey L Sherman. In the evening all his family came to see me, and spent the evening pleasantly.

September 3, 1903—Returned to Price, having engaged 6 men, sons of Albey, most of them, also Wagon & 4 horses.

September 4, 1903—Left Price by wagon, for my field of labor, 120^{m} dist.

September 5, 1903—Camped at Brocks, in the mountains. In the night a tempest raged, of wind and rain, which wet us through very cold and dismal

September 6, 1903—Crossed another range, in cold rain, wind & snow.

September 7, 1903—Camped on Duchesne river. Cold and Cheerless

September 8, 1903—Arrived at Ft. Duchesne about 1 P.M. and camped. Heard alarming reports of threatened Ute indian uprising,—rounding up Survey camps by them. Most of my Company were badly scared. In answer to prayer I received a testimony that no harm should come to us. All to be well with us; which so was proved in the end.

September 9, 1903—Went 14^{m} to Whiterocks Indian Agency, near which my work lies, and Camped near by.

I spent several days trying to find an old Survey Corner, at which to begin my work, hindered also by heavy rains and finally snow, which broke down my tent one night upon Nephi and me, as we lay asleep.

Soldiers had been sent out to bring in bands of refractory indians. The Utes do not want their reservation surveyed and opened to the whites.

[page 251]

~~August~~ September, 1903—They say "Pretty soon white man get all land, Injuns have no home by 'and by." They are not to blame for thinking so, judging by past experience. No white man could live or stay on the reservation (Uintah Res^{n}) without permission, so I had presented to Capt Mercer, the Agent, my letter from the Commissioner of Interior authorizing me and my party to enter the reservation and make my survey, which was duly endorsed by Capt. Mercer, with authority to fish with hook and line, but not to kill game or prospect for minerals. Those not obeying these regulations liable to arrest by indian police, and punished.

Saturday, September 12, 1903—Found an old U. S. Survey Corner, so now we may begin work of Survey, having now a starting point.

I had previously sent Royal Sherman to Brown's camp to get some necessary notes of his survey, and on return of Sherman he got lost, the trail being covered with snow, but was found in the night by two Ute indians, who put him on the way to the Camp at the Agency. We had been much alarmed at his non-return two days.

Sunday, September 13, 1903—To day four of the men from Huntington deserted me, taking the two teams and wagon. Said our food was not good enough, though I had plenty of flour, bacon, canned tomatoes, beef, rice, sugar, coffee, tea, dried peaches &c,—far more and better than they had at home. I think it was fear of indians and of Storms that frightened them, and because of one of them—David Sherman, who was always sulky and surly from the beginning, who led his brothers away.

So I was left, flat,—no team or wagon, helpless. I had paid for their teams, for hay and grain \$16^{00} [\$359] since leaving Price—only 10 days.

September 16, 1903—I started to Vernal, 40^{m} distant, to hire new men arrived there about 5 P.M. going through a desolate land

September 17, 1903—Hired several men, bought supplies on credit of the Vernal Co-op Store.

September 17, 1903—Returned to camp. Tested transit on Polaris at night. Find var. of magnetic needle is 15° 36' E.

[page 252]

September 19, 1903—Two of my three men whom I had hired came to day. I sent one back to bring another man.

September 20, 1903—Moved camp about 8 miles to a point on Uinta river near which we had bound the old-survey township Corner

Monday, September 21, 1903—Spent the day and following night, taking observations on Polaris at its eastern elongation, to obtain true north, and to find Latitude, and ascertain variation of the needle at this point, so I can begin my survey.

Tuesday, September 22, 1903—Began Survey of my Contract lands, No. 265

After a few days of good weather, we had many days of rainy weather, causing at times cessation of Survey.

Quite often we were caught in cold drenching rains, miles from Camp, getting back at night cold and wet, to make our beds upon wet ground, for tho I had tents to cover us, the ground was soaked. This caused me to become almost helpless, days at a time, with severe lameness and pains in my loins, almost unbearable when the slightest motion was made by me, in trying to lie down, move in bed, rise or dress myself. But with nine men drawing pay each day, four or five horses to feed with expensive hay and grain, and the Company to feed, work or no work, I could not afford to lay by and wait until better able to work. Many days—weeks—I was on Survey line working, when every step I took or motion I made was in pain. But it might have been worse: I might have been unable to do any thing, even in pain, so I had no cause to complain.

This kind of weather continued with occasional changes for the better until early in October.

Our work was very arduous. In the lower part of my work we had miles at a time of dense cedars through which constant use of the axes was required and one or two miles advance in a day was all we could accomplish; and when near the top of the Uintah range of mountains, where about half my work must be done we had to contend with the most dense undergrowth of pines and aspens I ever saw in all my life,—so dense that a man could hardly get through it on foot.

[page 253]

September 22, 1903—So we had to cut every foot of the way a path through the thicket. And all this was made still more impassible for men, and totally so for horses in many places by fallen trunks of timber lying every way, over which it was often difficult to pass. Sometimes heavy labor all day gave us only a mile advance. In other places, where was no timber, we had to go over huge boulders with no earth among them, making it difficult to pass on foot;—totally impassible for horses or mules.

I had a horse to ride, but much of the time had to tie him and go all day clambering over fallen trees or boulders, or forcing my way through dense thickets, and all this, much of the time over ground so steep that to up or down it was very tiresome and sometimes dangerous. I had a sure footed, strong man to carry my transit, (which I could not safely do myself,) and even then had many falls sometimes quite painful ones among the rocks. One especially, I was carefully making my way down a steep slope of the mountain, elevation 12000 feet above the sea, when in clambering over a high breastwork of dead timber I fell headfirst down the mountain. As I fell I caught at a small bush, which partially broke my fall, so that instead of striking my head upon the rock below and probably killing me, I only nearly broke my leg, As they helped me to get up, I found myself scarcely able to stand or walk, my left knee being apparently badly injured. But I had to walk a long distance to camp, pain or no pain. This injury was painful to me for about 5 weeks. I think the bones were cracked or otherwise injured. For weeks I was unable to rise without help, nor could I mount a horse without efficient help from a strong man. Thus this injury caused me ~~to~~ pain in every movement I made each day. Had I been at home I would not have thought of doing anything, or even of walking about.

[page 254]

October 1903—But when we work in rough mountains we must expect hard knocks and make the best of them. It was a great blessing to me that heavy fall did not kill me, leaving my work not half completed, and a strong probability my dear wife would receive no material benefit from what I had already accomplished.

It was mostly for her sake I undertook such work at an age of almost 76 years. I wished she might not be left dependent should I pass away before her, and feel herself a burden upon our children. For, to one who for many years had presided in her own home, to become an inmate of that of some one else, with nothing to do or say about matters, must be anything but pleasant or agreeable.

Some of our work was in places actually dangerous and sometimes our lines lay across gorges and defiles[13] actually impassible—so precipitous & sheer. This is notably the case in the Whiterocks river cañon, a tremendous gorge about 2000 feet, or more deep; its

13 A defile is a narrow gorge or pass that restricts lateral movement.

sides bordered for miles with precipices from 100 to 600 or 700 feet in height. In the bottom of this cañon, in one place, are a number of beaver dams and artificial ponds, with acres of aspens cut down by them, lying in all directions. One of our party caught a beaver, which we ate The beaver tail is counted a great delicacy. We saw tracks of deer, but did not hunt any, as contrary to regulations, but our boys caught many fine brook trout, a pleasant addition to our larder.

The foregoing general description applies to work not only in October, but to all our work in general, till in November, when forced to discontinue survey by snow.

October 12, 1903—Was unable to rise from my bed on account of sever pain and lameness in my loins and back, which caused excruciating pain at the least and slightest movement. This continued several days; in this interval Nephi ran the transit on open grounds and was a considerable help to me.

[page 255]

October 15, 1903—To day I attempted to go out on line, and did so, but became worse again, and unable to leave my bed.

October 18, 1903—Able to sit up. Nephi says he must go home to save his crop of potatoes and other vegetables. How can I spare him? is the question with me. Two other men left me.

October 19, 1903—To day Nephi started home. I was able to go with him to the Indian Agency, to see him off, riding in a spring seat.

And now, with the absence of Nephi and the two other men, I am unable to go on with my survey, the five remaining being too few.

October 31, 1903—I was promised two men—said they were sure to come—but after waiting some days in vain, I went again to Vernal, to hire more, with a Mr. Washington Caldwell, staying at his house in Vernal. They were all very desirous to receive patriarchal blessings from me, and I accordingly gave them to Br. Caldwell, his wife Almira, daughter Pearl, and sons Earl and Alonzo. Also to the woman who wrote for us, Sister Holgate, her son, and daughter. I was able by the blessing of the Lord, to help them and do them much good, as they all testified to me time and again. And so I felt much blessed myself. Brother Caldwell left of liquor, tea, coffee and tobacco, on his own volition, altho for many years a user of them all. I pray that he may be able to continue to the end.

November 1, 1903—I obtained three men, and resumed survey on return to camp Nov. 5th

November 11, 1903—Went to work this morning, snowing gently. It soon became a regular blizzard, with piercing wind. We had often to stop, light a fire and thaw ourselves out from our benumbed condition. We did not reach camp till dark—glad indeed when we saw our camp fire [through] the blinding snow, and terribly tired. We were at an elevation of over 12000 feet all day—an elevation cool in the heat of summer,—how, then in winter, which had set in some time ago!

November 12, 1903—Still snowing, with prospect of a long continuance. My men, familiar with the mountains and climate at this time of the year, decided we could hope for nothing more favorable, and that we were in great danger of being snowed in, unless we immediately broke camp and sought the low lands.

[page 256]

November 12, 1903—This was afterwards proved correct, as one survey party had to be dug out by settlers, from snow five feet deep; and another party was snowed in eleven days, on very light rations all that time.

We accordingly broke camp, loading all upon our pack horses, and began our toilsome way. It required a labor of over half a day to go a little over 3 miles to lower altitude, reaching there utterly tired and worn,—but out of the deep snow and safe. I looked back up to the higher mountains we had left, and was glad indeed to be out of them for the time, but very sorry the snow had come to stop the survey; for the snow fallen will remain until next summer, besides that which will yet fall.

November 13, 1903—Moved camp today down into the open valley, hoping to continue the survey in lower altitude, and did a few days work, But the days are now so short we can at best put in but a half day's work, at cost of a full day-expense daily of party for food for men and five horses. And as we cannot under any circumstances finish the survey this season, but must come again next year, I concluded it best to stop survey now, & did so.

November ~~17~~ 18, 1903—I took final oaths of my men, and disbanded.

Saturday, November 21, 1903—We started for Price, by Caldwell's wagon and team.

Tuesday, November 24, 1903—arriving at Price on Wednesday Nov. 24th We had very cold weather all the way, in an open wagon, camping long after dark.

November 23, 1903—At The Well, where we camped one night a Mrs. Odekirk, hearing I was a Patriarch, was anxious to obtain a Blessing under my hands, which I sealed upon her on Monday 23d.

Before leaving the Agency I gave my note to the Store of W. P. Coltharp & Co, for $245.90 [$5,523] payable on or before July 1. 1904, with 10 o/c interest from maturity. My indebtedness at Vernal store is $216.16 [$4,855], while I owe my men about $500.00 [$11,230] payable when my work is finished and paid me.

[page 257]

November 24, 1903—I have paid them in all about 250 or $300.00 [$6,738] dollars. And I paid the Price Store for supplies about $80.00 [$1,797].

There was no grass for our horses on the whole time of survey, so I had to buy several thousand pounds of oats and hay to feed them all the time much of which cost me $40.00 [$898] to $60.00 [$1,348] per ton, and thus, in connexion with over 20 days lost by desertion of men, my expenses have been abnormal—far too much. But I was unable to help myself, and my men took advantage of it.

November 25, 1903—I reached S. L. City, with Howard, Nephi's son, and was overjoyed meet again my beloved wife and my daughter Virginia, and be again in a pleasant home for the time, to sit at a table, on a chair, not exposed to chilling wind nor stifling smoke, nor the many other discomforts of camp life in winter time,—for it was winter in the Uinta elevated plateau and mountains—the highest in Utah.

Susan said she never, for years, had seen me look so worn, thin and haggard as when I entered the house, and when I felt that a time of rest had come I nearly collapsed, but in a few days was all right again, my long continued worry and anxiety being over for the time.

December 7, 1903—Susan and I remained at Virginia's until Dec. 7th and on that day went to Lyman's, in Logan, and met a warm reception there

December 10, 1903—We went to Nephi, in Benson Ward, and had a very pleasant visit there until Thurs. Dec. 17

December 17 [or 18], 1903—Returned to Lyman's

December 24, 1903—Susan sick in bed with severe cold and cough.

December 25, 1903—Christmas at Lyman's. A pleasant day & good dinner.

December 28, 1903—Letter from Co-op store in Mexico, showing I have a stock interest in the store of about $1100.00 [$24,707].

December 30, 1903—This morning Susan was able to come down to breakfast for the first time since she was sick, but came down yesterday to dinner. I am very thankful.

[page 258]

JOSEPH'S PROPHECY. MAY 6. 1843.

"

December 31, 1903—I find among my papers a copy of a prophecy of the Prophet Joseph, copied from the original in possession of Samuel W. Richards by Mary Eliza Brown Jones (Martineau) I have been for many years acquainted with the brother Edwin Rushton, and believe his words are true:—[14]

"A prophecy by Joseph Smith Jr. related to Edwin Rushton and Theodore Turley, on or about May 6. 1843.[15]

A grand review of the Nauvoo Legion was held in Nauvoo. The Prophet, Joseph Smith, complimented them for the good discipline and evolutions performed. The weather being hot he called for a glass of water. With the glass of water in his hand he said "I will drink you a toast to the overthrow of the mobocrats." Which he did in language as follows:—"Here's wishing they were in the middle of the sea, in a stone

14 Samuel W. Richards served as the European Mission president twice in the 1850s. Edwin Rushton was an English convert to the Church who served in the Nauvoo Legion and moved to Salt Lake City.

15 The alleged "White Horse Prophecy" deals with the wars and difficulties of the last days. Joseph F. Smith labeled the story ridiculous (see Conference Report, October 1918, 58), but rumor and controversy persist.

coffin with iron paddles (padlocks) and a shark swallow the coffin, and the Devil swallow the shark, and him locked up in the northwest corner of hell, the key lost, and a blind man hunting for it."

The next morning a man who heard the prophet give the toast visited the mansion of the Prophet, and so abused him with bad language that he was ordered out by the prophet. It was while the two were out that my attention was attracted to them, and hearing the man speaking in a loud voice I went towards them, the man finally leaving. There were then the prophet Joseph Smith, Theodore Turley, and myself. The Prophet began talking to us of the mobbings and drivings, the persecutions we as a people had endured. "But," said he, "we will have worse things to see. Our persecutors will have all the mobbings they want. Don't wish them any harm, for when you see their suffering you will shed bitter tears for them." While the conversation was going on we stood near his south wicker gate in a triangle. Turning to me he said "I want to tell you something. In the future I will speak in parables, like John the Revelator." (Little did I think then the Prophet of the Lord would so soon be slain in cold blood.)

[page 259]

Continuing, he said

"You will go to the Rocky mountains, and you will see a great and mighty people established, which I will call the White Horse of Peace and Safety." When the Prophet said "you will see" I asked him where he would be at that time. He answered—"I shall never go there. Your enemies will continue to follow you with persecution, and they will make obnoxious laws against you in Congress, to destroy the White Horse, but you will have a friend or two to defend you, and throw out the worst part of the laws, so they will not hurt much. You must continue to petition Congress all the time, but they will treat you as strangers and aliens, and they will not give you your rights, but will govern you with strangers and Commissioners. You will see the Constitution of the United States almost destroyed; it will hang by a thread, and that thread as fine as the finest silk fibre."

At this point the Prophet's countenance became sad, as he said "I love the constitution. It was made by the inspiration of God, and it will be preserved and saved by the efforts of the White Horse and the Red Horse, who will combine in its defense The White Horse will raise an ensign on the mountains of peace and safety, where all the nations may flee for safety. The White Horse will find the mountains full of minerals, and they will become very rich. You will see silver piled up in the streets."

(At this time it must be remembered that it was not known that the precious metals existed either in the Rocky mountains or in California.) "You will see gold shoveled up like sand. Gold will be of but little value, even in a mercantile capacity. For the people of the world will have something else to do in seeking for Salvation. The time will come when the banks in every nation will fail, and only two places will be safe, where the people can deposit their gold and treasures. The places will be with the White Horse and England's vaults. A terrible revolution will take place in the land of America, such as has never been seen before; for the land will be left without a supreme government, and every species of wickedness will run rampant; it will be so terrible that father will be against son and son against father; mother against daughter, and daughter against mother.

[page 260 duplicate heading at page break]

JOSEPH'S PROPHECY, MAY 6. 1843 (CONT^D^

The most terrible scenes of murder, and bloodshed and rapine that has ever been looked upon will take place. Peace will be taken from the earth, and there will be no peace, only in the rocky mountains. This will cause hundreds and thousands of the honest in heart of the world to gather there, not because they would be saints, but for safety, & because they would not take up the sword against their neighbors. They will be so numerous that you will be in danger of famine, but not for the want of seed time & harvest, but that so many will have to be fed. Many will come with bundles under their arms to escape the calamities, and there will be no escape, only by fleeing to Zion. Those that come to you will try to keep the laws & be one with you, For they will see your unity and the greatness of your organizations. The Turkish Empire, or the Crescent, will be one of the first powers that will be disrupted as a power, For freedom must be given for the gospel to be preached in the holy land. The Lord took of the best blood of the nations and planted them on the small island now called England, or Great Britain, and gave them great power in the nations for a thousand years, and their power will continue with them that they may keep the balance of power; that they may keep Russia from usurping power all the world. England and France are now bitter enemies, but they will be allied together in order to keep Russia from Conquering the world. The two popes, Greek and Catholic, will come together & be united. The protestant religions do not know how much they are indebted to Henry 8th for throwing off the pope's rule and establishing the protestant faith. He was the only monarch that could do so at that time, and he did it because the nation was at his back to sustain him. One of the peculiar features in England is the established red coat, a uniform making so remarkable a mark to shoot at, and yet, they have conquered wherever they have gone. The reason for this will be known by them some day.

[page 261]

The Lion and the Unicorn of England is the ensign of Israel. The wisdom and statesmanship of England comes from there being so much of the blood of Israel in the nation. While the terrible revolution of which mention has been made is going on, England will be neutral until it becomes so inhuman that she will interfere to stop the shedding of blood. England and France will then unite together and come with the intention to make peace, not to subdue the nation. They will find the nation so broken up, and so many claiming government. Still, there will be no responsible government. Then it will appear to other nations or powers as though England had taken possession of the country. The Black Horse will flee to the invaders and join with them for they will have fear of becoming slaves again, knowing England did not believe in slavery; fleeing to them, they believed, would make them safe. Armed with British bayonets the doings of the Black Horse will be terrible, so the Prophet said he could not bear to look longer upon the scene as shown him in his vision, that he asked the Lord to close the Scene. Continuing, he said

"During this time the great White Horse will have gathered strength, sending out elders to get the honest in heart among the Pale Horse, or people of the United States, to stand by the Constitution of the United States, as it was given by inspiration of the Lord. In these days, God will set up a kingdom never to be thrown down. For other kingdoms to come unto, and those kingdoms that will not let the gospel be preached will be humbled until they will. England, Germany, Norway, Denmark, Sweden, Switzerland, Holland and Belgium have a considerable amount of the blood of Israel among their people which must be gathered. These nations will submit to the kingdom of God. England will be the last of these kingdoms to surrender, but when she does, she will do it as a whole, in Comparison as she threw off the Catholic power. The nobility know the gospel is true, but it has not enough pomp and grandeur and influence for them to embrace it. They are proud, and will not acknowledge the kingdom of God or come into it until they see the power which it will have.

[page 262 duplicate heading at page break]

JOSEPH'S PROPHECY. MAY 1843

Peace and safety in the Rocky mountains will be protected by a Cordon band of the White Horse and the Red Horse. The Coming of the Ten Tribes (illegible for a space)

The coming of the Messiah will be so natural that only those who see Him will know He has come; but He will come, and give the law unto Zion, and minister unto His people. This will not be His coming in the clouds of heaven to take vengeance on the wicked of the world. The temple in Jackson Co. will be built in this generation. The saints will think there will not be time enough to build it, but with all the great help you will receive you can put up a great temple quickly. You will have all the gold, silver and precious stones, for these things only, will be used for beautifying the temple. All the skilled mechanics you want, and the Ten Tribes of Israel to help you build it. When you see this land bonded with iron you may looks towards Jackson County."

At this point he made a pause, and looking up as though the vision was still in view, he said—

"There is a country beyond the rocky mountains that will be invaded by the heathen Chinese. Great care & protection is given [blank]" Speaking of heathen nations he said "Where there is no law there is no condemnation; this will apply to them. Power will be given the White Horse to rebuke nations afar off, and they will obey, not that they will be one with the White Horse, but when goes forth they will obey, For the law will go forth from Zion. The last great struggle Zion will have to contend with will be when the whole of America will be made the Zion of our God. Those opposing will be called 'Gog and Magog. The nations of the world will be led by the Russian Czar, and this power ~~will be great~~, but all opposition will be overcome, and this land will be the Zion of our God."

[page 263]

These words of the Prophet made a strong impression upon me, which I have never forgotten. In about two weeks later I was at a meeting where he preached a sermon which he said would be the greatest of his life. On that occasion he reiterated the matter which I have now written, so that the subject became firmly rooted in my memory and I know them to be true. Now therefore I testify these are the inspired words of the Prophet Joseph Smith as he stood looking up into heaven. His countenance became white and transparent He looked as if he had as much of the heavenly influence as he could bear, and stay with the Saints. His voice was powerful, and his words cut like a two edged sword

(signed) Edwin Rushton

Witness Signature

A. G. Giauque

I have skipped several pages in my journal to write the foregoing prophecy, and now continue my journal.

December 31, 1903—Susan mending rapidly, and will, I hope, soon be well.

1904

January 1, 1904—January 1st Had an enjoyable day, but would much rather have been, with Susan, at our own Mexican home.

January 19, 1904—Am Still without my pension, which was dropped last March, without any reasonable Cause. To day I wrote to Senator T. Kearns, asking his help to have it renewed.

January 27, 1904—In the Logan temple, to day endowed Herbert Martineau Lyman end^{d} Henry Martineau, and Alley, his wife, endowed Bethia Martineau

January 28, 1904—I end^{d} A. Y. Thompson; Lyman, Peter Martineau; Alley, Hannah Hutchinson; Ann Hymers, Mrs. Sarah Martineau

~~Feb.~~ January 30, 1904—Gean's baby girl born to day, weight 8½ lbs. All doing well.

I secured affidavits from Drs. Calderwood & Budge, as to my need of pension, through infirmity.

Yesterday (29th) we came back to Lyman's to stay awhile.

February 2, 1904—Sent Affidavits to Kearns.

January 29, 1904—I Endowed David Martineau Blackburn; Lyman, John Martineau Blackburn; Alley, Abagail Hutchinson; Ann Hymers, Mrs. Susannah Archer.

[page 264]

February 6, 1904—Blessed Emeline B. Rich

February 8, 1904—This morning I dreamed of holding a cup while one poured into it, long after it was full, but not running over the while. I had the interpretation, which was for good to me.

March 12, 1904—We moved to Eva's, by her invitation

March 13, 1904—My 76th Birthday. Lyman & Alley made a nice family dinner, all our family in Cache being present. Good time.

March 16, 1904—I endowed John Scott

March 17, 1904—I endowed Francis Martineau

March 18, 1904—I endowed Ed^{d} Marsh Martineau

~~APRIL~~ 1904

~~April 19th~~ March 29, 1904—Gave Lyman a deed for an alley, on my old place. I had previously, by his help, obtained \$50.^{00} [\$1,082] for right to use it, by Logan Journal Co. which was great help to me

APRIL.

April 1, 1904—Blessed Br. and Sister Harrison

April 2, 1904—Blessed Br. Guy Thatcher and Florence, his wife

April 3, 1904—Blessed Sister Needham. (widow)

April 4, 1904—Susan and I went to Gean's, in S. L. City

April 5, 1904—Attended special meeting in the new Barratt Hall

April 6, 1904—Genl Conference. Manifesto again sustained by u. vote

April 7, 1904—Visited H. A. and M. A. H. White and blessed them

April 10, 1904—Met Jesse N. Smith and his wife, friends of my youth. Had not seen them for about 40 years. Happy meeting. Blessed Albey and Mary Sherman, Susan Julias, brother

April 11, 1904—Wrote to Senator Smoot, about my renewal of pension.

April 12, 1904—Lyman enabled me to borrow $600.00 [$12,983] of the Utah Natl Bank. He and Prest Anthony Ivins signing my note as Sureties, on my first assigning my property to them, security.

April 13, 1904—Albey and Mary Sherman returned home to Huntington.

Note. I assigned as security on note for $600.00 the following:—[note Juárez home value]

Stock in Union Mercantile Store,	Dublan Mex.		$1100.00
" " Tannery,	Juarez	"	150.00
My home (house & ½ lot) Juárez val. in Mex. money			1200.00
			$2450.00
Value, American money			$1225.00 [$26,507]

Note: 10 o/c interest from date.

[page 265]

April 20, 1904—Recd word Congress, by special act, renewed my pension at rate of $12.00 [$260] per month. Previously it was at $8.00 [$173] and on the

April 22, 1904—I sent my old pension papers to Pension Agt, John R. King. D.C.

April 26, 1904—Opened an account with Utah Natl Bank.

April 28, 1904—Gave check for $300.00 [$6,492] to apply on my $600 [$12,983] note due in the Cache Valley Bank.

MAY. 1904

May 5, 1904—Susan and I met, at Whites, with Bp. John Neff, and Christina Pyper. Had a glorious time. Blessed each other. The voice of the Holy Ghost said we were "One with the Lord and his Son Jesus Christ." It was a glorious time, never to be forgotten.

May 6, 1904—Blessed Esther, Vilate, Albert & Lorenzo Elggren, also E. Iverson, Alice Schied, a little girl 7 years old, who desired it.

May 7, 1904—Blessed A. Lewis Elggren, Yesterday blessed Br. & Sis. Elggren. Susan anointed and blessed Sis. ~~Peterson~~ Brown, For confinement.

May 8, 1904—Blessed Mary E. Bassett, and Sister Brown, whom Susan had anointed and blessed the day previous. She had been, for 5 months under care of doctors with a complication of several serious disorders, and her case declared entirely hopeless, without taking into account her near confinement, through which it would be impossible for her to pass. She lay very low and lifeless, but Susan, in blessing her, said she should be blessed in her confinement and have the easiest time that she had ever had with any of her children; and that should soon be fully healed. Sister Brown desired me to give her a patriarchal blessing, which I did, and without knowing what Susan had promised her, gave her substantially the same.

[written in margin]

Note.

I will say here, that all this was fulfilled to the very letter, to the great joy of herself & husband, and wonder of all the doctors, who had said she must die. It was a great testimony to Susan and me.

May 9, 1904—Blessed David Brown, her husband. Also Mrs. Sainsbury and sealed Susan's anointing and blessing upon Mrs. Peterson Also blessed Br. Sainsbury.

May 16, 1904—Got my final papers from Sur. Genl Anderson. Got a Bro. Snarr, of Sonora, Mex. to help Susan on her way home, as she wishes to go home to Mexico.

[page 266]

May 17, 1904—To day I Started for my Survey, to finish it up, leaving Susan, who will start for Mexico in a few days. It was a trial for us to part, she to journey near 2000 miles without my help and company, but it had to be. How glad will I be when we can part no more. God grant that time may soon come.

I went by the Denver and Rio Grande R. R. to Price 130m From Price I went by Stage 130 miles to Vernal, Uinta Co, to get my company and supplies. Fare $12.50 [$270].

May 23, 1904—Started out with 2 wagons and teams and 10 men. Drove to Deep Creek, about 26 miles

May 24, 1904—Started Survey of the Uintah Special Base Line, finished next day, 3 miles, over very rough ground & in rain.

May 26, 1904—Susan started home 8.05 P.M. Had to walk alone 2½ blocks which was very hard for her to do. No one helped her.

From the 24th inst. I continued my survey, the ground being exceedingly bad. The lower and more level parts were covered with a dense growth of Cedars, making progress very slow. The mountains, on which most of my work lay, was exceedingly rough & precipitous, covered, almost totally—with pine or quaking aspens, and in many places almost impassible for dense growth of young pines, one to two inches diameter, 10 to 20 ft high, and so thick as to be almost impenetrable, so that we had to cut a passage every foot of the way. Also large areas were covered with fallen timber, impossible to get a horse through without much chopping. In other places, great tracts of huge boulders were almost impossible to cross on foot. The altitude 12000 to 13000 feet, made warm, heavy winter clothing necessary, even in July while the clouds of mosquitoes were almost unbearable to men or our horses. We also had much heavy rain and cold sleet, Although my men were robust, strong frontiersmen, inured all their lives to hardship three of them broke down and quit for sickness, Many wondered how I, at 77, stood these hardships so well, without breaking down also.

[page 267]

MY SURVEY

1904—It was a simple thing:—In the morning I asked the Father to bless and strengthen me for the days work. And He did. The others neglected this—never thought of it, I suppose. but trusted in their own strength. Sometimes, for miles at a time it was very difficult to get over the ground because of the dense mass of fallen timber, crossing in every way. Even in July we crossed old snow. Sometimes our way was along slopes so hard, smooth and steep that it was only with great difficulty I could pass, even afoot, with a possible slide or tumble of a thousand feet. Added to all this, two cañons crossed one Township, each of them over 2000 feet deep, with slopes inaccessible in many places;—huge precipices 500 to 800 feet—barring the way. At one point, the only one to get from the bottom of the Whiterocks river Cañon to the top of it, the trail we made was very steep, so much so, that in ascending it with my pack train, one of the horses fell backwards down the mountain. Although the oaken, strong pack saddle was between the body of the horse and the pack, it was broken into small pieces. I rode up this trail the previous fall, being unable to ascend it afoot, but it was a very dangerous thing to do: Many times my life was in extreme danger in the mountains, but through faith I was preserved,—by the mercy of the Lord alone.

Having finished my field work, as I supposed, I came back to S. L. City, and was there informed I had left out a small, separate tract I had not known of, and must return and Survey that also, as I will not farther on.

While in the city I gave patriarchal blessings to quite a number, visited and blessed the sick, and worked very hard and late on my Survey notes for Sur. General's office.

August 14, 1904—Today I was received as a member of the 2nd ward, Liberty Stake, as I wish always to be in touch with the church, in every place, when I can.

September 16, 1904—To day I started back to Uintah, to finish my field work going by wagon, with Br. Harden Benion.[16] Our road was all in all in the

16 Harden Bennion (note spelling) was a Utah State senator from 1899 to 1906 and secretary of state from 1917 to 1921.

mountains, and occupied 5 days hard and late driving, cold nights, and much bad road. Arrived at Vernal at 9 P.M. just ahead of a great tempest which caused me four or five days detention in Vernal, while I was engaged in getting up a new survey party.

[page 268]

1904—On the journey to Vernal, I noted elevations at points on the way, established by the U. S. Geological Survey party, on metal plates set on iron posts:—as follows:—

Ridge, (on wagon road, south of city, Park City,	7310 feet
" at S. E. entrance of Strawberry valley	8100 ft.
1st crossing of Duchesne river =	5517
2d " " " "	5378
at Lake Fork bridge	5170
" Uintah river bridge, Fort Duchesne	4994
" Sand ridge 5 m. from " "	5305
" Vernal	5500

September 27, 1904—Started out from Vernal with only 5 men and 1 team & wagon, as my alterations of corners and additional work will not need much time or labor, Reached the Forks in Whiterocks Cañon on next day, 28th and began work same day.

I arranged with Dep. U. S. Surveyor Wm Dallas to Survey the small tract north of my Survey (now finished) to save time, and finished the few corrections required on Oct. 8th

October 8, 1904—Arriving in Vernal, and started on return home Oct. 9th

October 9, 1904—by Stage to Price, 130 miles. In this short period of work I had a hard time, being at times drenched with cold, sleety storms, but had no accidents. I visited Kirkpatrick, the U .S. Land Examiner, and had a pleasant time

My journey from Vernal to Price, 130 miles in 2 days by a miserable stage, in very cold weather, in rains, snow storms and mud, driving long after dark and starting in the morning long before sunrise in the cold, was very hard and tedious, but might have been worse.

October 11, 1904—Arrived at Virginia's in S. L. City pretty tired, but well.

October 13, 1904—Quite sick all night, with severe pain. Lyman came to see me. Said Bp. Preston has asked for me many times, as he has long been sick, almost unto death, wishing me to administer to him, and to give him a patriarchal blessing Said the Bishop remarked "I dont know of any man in the Church whom I would rather bless me. He is one of the few honest men in the world, and I'm trying to be another." I felt much gratified for his confidence in me. Truly, I [am] striving with my might to live as a true L. D. Saint, but I know I fall short of what I should be.

[page 269]

October 13, 1904—I pray continually that I may become one with the Lord, even as was Enoch of old.

October 20, 1904—I blessed Bp. Preston and comforted him much. He shed tears of joy and said "That has the right ring, that sounds right." His blessing will be dependant upon his own faith and the blessing of the Lord.

November 9, 1904—I went to the temple to day, to A. W. Morrison's wedding, and endowed David Martineau (no. 177) Morrison Endd another David Martineau for me. In the evening attended wedding receptions at Elgreen's.

November 17, 1904—I Endowed Edwd Wansey

November 18, 1904—Finished my writing of field notes, giving the rest of it to a Mr. John Benson to be type written.

Up to this time I have labored every day, writing, at my table, continuing at night until 11 P.M. to 2 A.M. Much of this time is occupied in Complicated calculations, making my labors, so long continued, very exhausting, bodily and mentally. The days noted above, and Sundays, were the only days Exempt.

November 19, 1904—Blessed Bishop John Neff and his daughters Frances and Eugenia, the latter about to go on a mission. Sister Mary A. Hyde White also blessed the two girls in tongues. We had a delightful time.

November 22, 1904—Up to this time I have visited and blessed the sick daily, and today I blessed Sister Sears with P. Blessg

November 24, 1904—Thanksgiving Day. Lyman's family being invited to Preston's and Gean's to Andersons, I was left alone, so took my dinner at Br. & Sis. H. A. White's friendly table, and in evening visited Preston's, who apologized for not inviting me with Lyman.

December 5, 1904—To day put all my Survey notes in Sur. Gen[l] office & sent my pension papers to Washington.

December 8, 1904—My son-in-law E. Guy Taylor, from Canada, Called to see me.

December 10, 1904—Sold my transit to Joel for $300.[00] Mexican Money equal to $150.[00] [$3,246] American, and less than half it cost me, being in perfect order. Sell him my drawing instruments at same rate. he to pay as he can, from time to time.

December 20, 1904—Sent transit to Joel by express.

[page 270]

December 20, 1904—Paid John Benson in full for type writing field notes &c $33.75 [$730], making total paid him, $78.75 [$1,704]. His total bill was $83.75 [$1,812], but he deducted $5.00 [$108] It was all I could do to raise the money for him.

To day I removed from Virginia's (who is going soon to Castle Gate for awhile) to Lyman's.

[date out of order]

December 12, 1904—I learn by "El Progreso" newspaper that my grandson James Edward, Moroni's eldest son, was married on 12th to Myrtle Clark, daughter of Joseph Clark, of Colonia Chuichupa, Chihuahua State, Mexico.

December 25, 1904—Albert was released from his mission in Kansas where he presided over that state Conference.

I spent Christmas at Lyman's

December 29, 1904—Lyman & Alley and children, and I, spent afternoon by invitation of Bp. Preston and wife, at their house, in celebrating Lyman & Alley's wedding day—the 23[d] one.

1905

January 1, 1905—At Lyman's, Bp. Preston, Moyle and families present.

January 2, 1905—Bp. Preston took me through the new L. D. S. Hospital, the finest West of Chicago, and best appointed.

January 4, 1905—With Sister Mary Hyde White visited her Sister Zina Virginia Hyde Bull, widowed recently, who has cataract growing over her eyes and is losing her sight. She wished me to rebuke blindness and to bless her, which I did. Her sister Mary also blessed her in tongues, with the interpretation. I know Zina may be healed, through faith. She felt very happy. I enjoyed my visit very much, as I always do in visiting and blessing the sick.

Ever since I was free from my press of survey notes and mapping, I have rarely missed a day when I was not visiting & administering to the sick, or giving blessings, and I know I have given great comfort & help to many. Especially do I delight to visit and bless the poor. The rich can (they think) take care of themselves, and need no special blessings from a Patriarch. I never accept any remuneration from the poor for blessing, and the rich very seldom give me anything, so I spend much time in recording blessings and making copies for people.

[page 271]

January 4, 1905—I do not make, nor wish to—my holy office of Patriarch a matter of dollars. It is too sacred and holy a labor for that, and a precious privilege from our Father, to have a right to seal blessings upon others,—an office which reaches into the eternities,—the only office I have desired. I have never desired an office which would require to Sit as a Judge over others. I desire rather, to be as a Father—eventually, to become as a Father in heaven, as those who have gone before.

Paid $2.00 [$43] tithing, which covers all my increase for 1904, as I have not yet received anything for my last year's work.

January 7, 1905—Sent 111 names to Anna Woods, at Manti, to baptize and endow [left blank]

January 8, 1905—Gean's baby Marjorie quite sick, I went to her

January 11, 1905—Marjorie getting well, and I return to Lyman's

January 16, 1905—I went to Bp. Neff's at East Mill Creek by his request, and ~~bles~~ remained until the 18th Bp. Neff told me he heard apostle John W. Taylor prophecy, on his return from Mexico that "The time will come when ships of war commanded by officers wearing the Mexican uniform will be seen in New York harbor."

January 21, 1905—Blessed Sisters Neff, Spencer, Elaine, and Br. and Sister Hixon, Rec[d] $1.[00] [$22]

January 22, 1905—Attended (our) Liberty Stake Conference

January 25, 1905—I endowed (No.197) Richard Martineau

January 26, 1905—I endowed (199) Meadows Martineau

January 27, 1905—I endowed (205) James Martineau Lee

[written in margin]

On Jan. 31st 1905 I had 146 Males Baptized in S. L. Temple

FEBRUARY

February 1, 1905—I endowed Philip Martineau. Ollie came home from New York

February 2, 1905—I endowed Meadows Martineau No.237

February 3, 1905—I endowed John Martineau

February 4, 1905—Lyman and I went to Logan with Legislature to Ag. College

February 8, 1905—I endowed Edward Mears No 253

February 9, 1905—I endowed Robert Mears No 254 I blessed Sister Majors and her daughter Clara J M Larson; also Beatrice Sears.

February 10, 1905—I end[d] Oliver Mears No 255, Blessed Estella Sears.

February 11, 1905—Was at Sister Harriet A Preston's 66th birthday dinner. Was notified of error in one corner stone, of my Survey in the Uintah Reservation.

[page 272]

February 12, 1905—Attended meeting in Emerson Ward. Very cold,—below Zero

February 13, 1905—Presented papers to draw $11.74 [$254] sent by mail from Mexico. Could not get it. Some trickery, I fear.

[written in margin]

1905 Feb. 14. My son Nels L. Hagberg died in the L. D. S. Hospital S. L. City of an operation. I had not known he was sick. He was true as steel to the truth.

February 15, 1905—I end[d] John Mears No. 256

February 16, 1905—I end[d] Nathaniel Mears, No. 257

February 17, 1905—I end[d] Oliver M. Hyde

February 18, 1905—Rec[d] a blessing from Apostle John H. Smith. Visited

February 19, 1905—I worked all day on my temple records.

February 20, 1905—I gave 56 names of males and females for temple baptism. 33 men 23 women. This makes 202 in all, baptized this year. By request I visited and blessed Sister Isabel P. Kenner. At the temple I was told of Hagberg's death. Poor fellow. he had much grief in his life time. His first wife Josephine Rodhine left him when her baby was only [blank] days old, deserting it, and it soon died. His next wife, Sarah Westwood died in Childbirth & her baby also, about 14 months after marriage. His next wife Emilia Sophia [blank] died next. He thus lost by death 2 wives and four children, leaving one boy only; about 12 years old, of all his family. He was a true L. D. Saint, had done much missionary work in Sweden, and was a good, industrious man. His mother was sealed as my wife, and he sealed to me as Son. A letter of his gives particulars of himself and family.

February 21, 1905—Went to Mrs. Zina V. Hyde Bull's to meet her sister, Mrs Lulla Hyde Hess, of Farmington, who has come to the city for me to administer to her in Blessing, she being in very bad health. her kidneys almost without action, and threatened with dropsy and some other severe complications, making her a great sufferer. She had fasted 3 days for this occasion, and one day also her sisters Mary A. Hyde White and Zina Virginia. Her husband also Came. After prayer we all laid hands upon her, I being mouth, and a good blessing was sealed upon her causing her to shed tears of joy. Then we blessed each other, and had a time of heavenly rejoicing. I hope she will recover

[page 273—see Appendix 5 for letter from N. L. Hagberg inserted here.]

February 22, 1905—I endowed Richard Webb, next day Peter Haughout on 23[d] inst.

February 23, 1905—

Mrs. Clara J M Larson	End[d]	Alice Hutchinson
Mrs. Mary Ann Owen	"	Mehitable Hutchinson
Mrs. Mary E. L. Neff	"	Alice Barnett and
Mrs. Amelia L. M. Turner	"	Sarah Baker

February 24, 1905—I endowed Nicholas Haughout. To day Cora's son, Joseph Hyrum Robinson, was sealed to her and to me by Ass^{t} President Mattison, Sister Wilcox, as proxy for Cora and J B Adlard as proxy for the child. Now Cora, knowing she has her child secure, may rejoice exceedingly, and I am thankful also.

February 26, 1905—Sunday. Attended the funeral of my dear friend—one of the friends of my youth, L. John Nuttall.[17] His sudden death was a shock to all, to me especially. It seems as if all my old friends are leaving me.

MARCH. 1905.

March 1, 1905—I endowed David C. Lyon, husband of my sister Henrietta. He was a Presbyterian minister in high standing in his church, an honorable man, who treated me very kindly when I visited him in 1879. He believed in many of the principles of our faith—all except plural marriage an[d] the divine mission of Joseph Smith, the Seer. He has now received the work of God in Paradise—the Spirit World, Of this I have testimony.

I also sealed him and Henrietta, Christina M. F. Ericson proxy for my sister, I for him.

Also sealed Lord William Russell & Rachel Russell.

Also sealed Louis Paschal & Camilla Guarina (martyrs)

March 2, 1905—I End^{d} my uncle Charles Sprague Mears. Also D. Murphy. Sealed Uncle Charles S. Mears ~~and~~ to his father James & mother Lois Sprague Mears, my mother's parents. Maria W. R. Wilcox, proxy for Lois S. Mears. I for grandfather.

March 3, 1905—I end^{d} John Russell (Lord) Sealed Danl Murphy and Alicia Murphy, old friends of mine. Also sealed Lord John Russell and Lady Frances Anna Maria Russell. Also had sealed to me Lilla Dean, distant relative, unmarried, as all have been whom I have thus taken to wife by the holy ordinance of Sealings.

[page 274]

March 8, 1905—I endowed John Grant, Father of Mrs. Jane S. Hill, a friend; and she endowed for me Mrs. Hawkins.

March 9, 1905—I endowed Capt Hawkins, Father of Samuel & Elizabeth Hawkins, and husband of my father's first Wife, Sarah Stanhope, daughter of the Earl of Stanhope. He was Captain in the British Navy. The Earl of Stanhope disinherited his daughter Sarah, for marrying out of the nobility.

By my father she had Julia and Lucretia, my ½ sisters and died in Baltimore soon after father returned from England. Samuel became an officer in the American navy and was in Commodore Wilkes' Exploring Expedition in 1839–40–41 during which the Antarctic continent was discovered. Elizabeth married, but all trace of her is lost

As I have Sealed the wife and two children of Capt Hawkins to my father, I seal a Miss Bloomfield to him as wife, she being dead also, and believe they will accept the ordinance.

Sisters Jane S. Hill, Mary E. L. Neff, Nancy N L Neff and—Mary Ann Brown also endowed for names for me, as shown in Sealing and endowment record.

March 10, 1905—I end^{d} Capt. James Johnson.

In the Sealing of John Grant and wife for Jane S. Hill, I was proxy for him and she for the wife.

MARCH 1ST (OVERLOOKED)

Mch. 1

Fig. 10.2—Drawing of hand pointing to March 1 entry.

March 1, 1905—I sealed Julia and Lucretia Martineau, my half sisters to father, John Martineau and Sarah Stanhope, widow of Capt. Hawkins, noted on previous page. M. W. R. Wilcox proxy for her, I for father, Evelina L. Babbitt for Julia and Eliza D. Fletcher for Lucretia.

17 L. John Nuttall was secretary to President John Taylor. He was also his son-in-law.

March 10, 1905—(Continued) Sisters Owens, Neff, Williams, Neff, and Larson also worked for me.

Monday, March 10, 1905—Gave 8 more names for baptisms, making 210 in all.

March 15, 1905—I end[d] Mr. Winslow, husband of my sister Julia. I have lost all trace of them since their marriage in the 30[s] (Years) I believe he was a printer, and lived in Boston.

Sealed Cap[t] Hawkins & Miss Bloomfield

" Samuel Hawkins & Lucy Mears

" David M. Blackburn & Elizabeth Martineau

[page 275]

March 15, 1905—Sealed Samuel and Elizabeth Hawkins to Cap[t] and Mrs. Bloomfield Hawkins.

Also Sealed to William Sprague and Lois Hutchinson Sprague their children, as follows:—

Seth	Sprague	proxy	J. B. Adlard
John	"	"	J. C. Petersen
William	"	"	George Burt
James	"	"	William Hodge
Daniel	"	"	Peter A. Burt
Jesse	"	"	John James
Ester	Sprague (Babcock)	Proxy	Evelina L. Babbitt
Eunice	Sprague (Crittenden)	"	Eliza D. Fletcher
Lois	Sprague (Mears) (my gr. mother)	proxy	Elizabeth M. Cooper

March 16, 1905—I End.[d] Andrew Y. Thompson, my aunt Laura Mears Van Slyke's f Second husband. Also I

Sealed Elie and Marguerite Barbesson, our Norman ancestors, of Dieppe, France, I proxy for Elie & M. W. R. Wilcox For Marguerite, Also Sealed to them their children

1 Marie Martineau (Columbine, Proxy, Evelina L. Babbitt

2 Gaston Martineau proxy J. B. Adlard

Also Sealed to Peter & Maria Martineau Columbine

Ann	Columbine (Hilyard)	proxy	E. L. Babbitt
Francis	Columbine	"	Jabez B. Adlard
Mary	" (Rand)	"	Eliza D. Fletcher
Paul	Columbine	"	Jens C. Petersen
David	Columbine	"	Geo. Burt
Peter	Columbine	"	William Hodge

March 17, 1905—Sealed Andrew Y. Thompson & Mrs. A. Y. Thompson

Sealed Oliver M. Hyde & Julia Sprague and

Endowed Mr. Maturin, a martyr (Waldensees)

Sealed Gaston Martineau and Miss Hoyle & children

Gaston	Martineau	proxy	J. B. Adlard
John	"	"	J. C. Petersen
Fanny	" (Holland)	"	E. L. Babbitt
Susan	" (Cunningham)	"	E .D. Fletcher

Sealed to David & Elizabeth Finch Martineau their children, as follows:—

[page 276]

March 17, 1905—

Peter	Martineau	Proxy	J. B. Adlard
Mary	Martineau (Martineu)	"	Eliza D. Fletcher
Elizabeth	" (Blackburn)	"	Evelina L. Babbitt
Daniel	" —	"	J. C. Petersen
Peter	" —	"	— Burt
Hannah	" (Blackburn)	"	Elizabeth M. Cooper

March 18, 1905—Paid my tithing up to date, in full, in Liberty Stake

Blessed Zina Hyde Bull and Jane S. Hill, widows

I rec[d] recommend from Bp. Iverson to change my Membership to Emerson Stake, it being close to my present home, Lyman's house, so I can attend Ward meetings.

Sunday, March 19,1905—Joined Emerson Ward

March 20, 1905—Harriet's baby girl born, My Gr. Gr. Child at 11.40 P.M. the baby was born, 9 lbs. Hard time.

~~Wed.~~ Thursday, March 23, 1905—I endowed Peter Haughout. Sealed

Robert Mears and Abagail Hutchinson

Nathaniel " " another Abagail Hutchinson
John Mears " " Hannah Hutchinson

Friday, March 24, 1905—I End. Egbert Haughout also Seal

John Martineau & Nelly Haughout

Egbert " " Elenor Garebrantz

also Sealed

To John Martineau (my father) and Eliza Mears Martineau (mother)

Caroline Martineau Babcock } children born to my mother
Cha[s] Sprague Babcock } by her second husband William Babcock.

Caroline died about 3 years old. Charles S. died a soldier in the Union Army, near Stone river battlefield, of dysentery. He has been endowed, and a wife sealed to him.

Sealed to William Sprague & Mrs. W[m] Sprague their Children

William Sprague Jun. proxy J B Adlard, M. W. R. Wilcox acting for Mrs. William and I for him.

March 25, 1905—Sent answer to Sur. General's Office about my Survey, which is to be altered somewhat, Uinta Res[n]

[page 277]

March 27, 1905—Copied plats in Sur. Gen[l] Office. Administered to Bp. W[m] B. Preston who is again quite ill.

March 28, 1905—Went to theatre, free ticket to Old Folks. Enjoyed it.

March 29, 1905—I end[d] Nicholas Haughout

March 30, 1905—I end[d] Wynant Haughout Sealed Spragues' to fathers

March 31, 1905—To Edward & Mrs. Edward Sprague

William Sprague proxy JB Adlard

To William and Mrs. William Sprague

Anthony proxy JB Adlard

To Anthony and Mrs. Anthony Sprague

Jeremiah Sprague proxy J B Adlard

To Jeremiah and Mrs. Jeremiah Sprague

William Sprague proxy J B Adlard

who was husband of Lois Hutchinson, my gr. gr. gr mother

This carries an unbroken line of ten generations, including my great-grand-children, to the year 1600 A.D.

My Gr. Gr. mother Lois Hutchinson, was Gr. dau. of Lord Hutchinson; also a relative of Gov. Hutchinson, of Mass.

APRIL 1905.

April 1, 1905—Attended Priesthood meeting in Granite Stake house:

April 4, 1905—Joel, Annie & Sister Thurston and two children from Mexico.

Received the following from my son Nephi, which I insert, as testimony of his spiritual standing and love:—

"King April 1. 1905.

Dear Father. I received your welcome letter and felt sorry that you have to make another trip to Uintah, as it will be very hard on you to ride that long distance ~~on~~ over such a rough road and through such a bleak country, to say nothing of the expense. I can see that you are worried, but go ahead and you will do good on your trip. Your work will be received and you will get your pay, and your trip will be of a benefit to you. I feel impelled to write you these words, & they will be fulfilled to the very letter. You feel down, but the Lord hasn't forgot you and mother. You cannot measure the good you do.

[page 278]

April 1, 1905—You have great knowledge in the things of the Lord, few men equal you in sound judgment, and by coming in contact with men your influence is felt, and the Lord is glorified through your precept and example. I feel to bless you with life, health, an[d] an increase both temporally and spiritually. Your last days shall be your best days, with power to be saved in our Father's kingdom. Amen. Peace be to you dear Father, may our love for one another grow stronger through time and all eternity From Nephi.

P.S. Tell Joel and family to come along. I cannot come down."

This letter gave me great comfort. His words of promise are exactly in line with blessings I have received from the holy priesthood, and I believe they will be fulfilled.

April 5, 1905—I end[d] Richard Williment. Also Sealed David C. Lyon, my brother in law to Eliza Shiland, his first wife

At the conference to day it was said there are 55 stakes and 629 Bishop's wards

April 9, 1905—Joel and Company went North to visit Thurston's relatives.

April 12, 1905—Worked all day on my temple record

April 13, 1905—I end[d] William Williment family—children to parents. Also Endowed Simeon Mears, and sealed him & Mrs. Simeon Mears.

Gave blessings to Maria W. R. Wilcox, Evelina L. Babbitt and Eliza D. Fletcher, dear friends who have helped me in my temple work. They are women whom God loves.

Saturday, April 15, 1905—Quite unwell to day—kidneys—and lay in bed all day.

Sunday, April 16, 1905—Still in bed all day. Obstruction in urinating

Monday, April 17, 1905—Still in bed all day. Obstruction in urinating Have eaten almost nothing for 3 days. No appetite.

Tuesday, April 18, 1905—Feel stronger, but kidneys no better. Went up town, but was tired, and accomplished nothing.

Wednesday, April 19, 1905—Still weak, and kidneys apparently dead. I must again go up town. Lyman wants me to see a doctor.

Yester[day] I got from Susan Joel's recommend to temple, and to day I sent it to him in Charlie's care. Logan.

[page 279]

April 20, 1905—Rec[d] a demand from Cache Valley Bank to pay $358.49 [$7,757] with interest at 10o/c. Can't pay it—no money.

[written in margin]

sick

April 21, 1905—Lyman's 46th birthday. Preston and wife came. Named and blessed Harriet's baby, Lyman spokesman. Named her Harriet Louise. I was just able to get around, by holding to things My kidneys seem absolutely dead. No power to pass urine. Unless this can be changed, it means death by dropsy, or the filling up of my body with fluid.

I got my blessings and read them. Much in them still remains to be fulfilled. I prayed the Father to make known to me if I have forfeited any of them, or if they are still for me. I received answer that altho I have come short in many way, I have <u>not</u> forfeited any of my blessings,—they are still all mine by promise. Therefore, to fulfill them I must live and be healed. And so I received faith, an actual, living faith, to ask in faith that my kidneys renew their action and pass the fluids from my system. I went to sleep, and on awakening found it possible to urinate, & not with the severe pain, as before, but in a natural manner.

Sunday, April 23, 1905—Then I thought of my sister-friend Zina V. H. Bull, who has power in healing. I went to her, and asked her to bless me. She did so, and spoke in power. I felt better at once and the next day felt like a new man.

April 25, 1905—Went to Gean's.

[written in margin]

26th, Lilla's baby born

Wednesday, April 26, 1905—Went to temple and end[d] Jan Haughout and Jo[s] Hutchinson next day. I sealed Jan & Elizabeth Haughout, also sealed children to Hewett Rand. on Thurs. 27th

Friday, April 28, 1905—Endowed John Hutchinson, and Sealed family D. Columbine and Paul Columbine, also two couples in marriage.

Saturday, April 29, 1905—Visited Gean's with Mary A Freeze and her daughter.

Sunday, April 30, 1905—Wrote to Susan, and looked over my temple work.

May 2, 1905—Attended by Special invitation of Bp. Iverson the reunion held in honor of Pat[h] J. Leach, age 90. Banquet, speeches and flowers.

May 4, 1905*—Blessed Phebe Woodruff Snow, wife of Pres[t] Snow. She said had greatly desired it of me. Also blessed her daughter Florence Snow Critchlow and Mary Forster. I endowed Jo[s] Sprague sealed 3 couples *Yesterday sealed 3 families.

[page 280]

May 5, 1905—I end[d] Tho[s] Hutchinson. Had 2 women helping. Ford & Hansen also and they endowed 2 women

May 6, 1905—Lyman, member of Commercial Club, went with them to Los Angeles, on Excursion, by invitation of Senator Clark. I am still quite feeble from my late attack of kidney disorder. Was in home all day.

May 8, 1905—Gave 40 names for Baptism in the temple. males. paid 40¢

May 9, 1905—Rain and Snow

May 11, 1905—End^{d} Wm Mears. Ford End^{d} Ann Hutchinson, Eva H. for Susan H.

May 10, 1905—Not well yet. Visited Gean, who will go to Castle Gate to live tomorrow, taking cow, and some furniture, May Stay there a year.

May 11, 1905—End^{d} Wm Mears. Eva Hanson end^{d} Rishworth. Ed & Gean went in a cold rain storm. I blessed Zina Hyde Bull.

May 12, 1905—End^{d} Jo^{s} Sprague. 8 Sisters worked for me in temple.

May 13, 1905—Lyman returned home.

May 15, 1905—Gave 21 female names For baptism for Sister S. J. Russell also 4 males & paid for same.

Blessed Miss Afton Young, who is very lame, rheumatism of 5 years standing, and much money spent. A cripple. Gave a comforting blessing to Eva K. Hanson

May 17, 1905—End^{d} Abraham Taylor and Mr. Abrams on 18th Sisters Bassett Brown, Maddox assisting in Endowments For women.

May 19, 1905—I end. F. J. Blake. Assisted by Sisters Brinton, Pierce, Murphy, Bassett, Henderson, Carter, Maddox, and Reed and Jenkinson. Sealed Stanhope & family, 3 daughters. Blessed Lucille Critchlow, daughter of Florence, and Gr. Dau. of Pres^{t} Snow, a little girl, who had greatly desired a blessing from me.

May 20, 1905—Got garments and hose for Susan

May 22, 1905—Gave names of 2 men, & 5 women For Baptism in temple. Joel, Mary Ann, his wife, 2 children, Sister Thurston & her father came.

May 23, 1905—Gave 20 female names for baptism in temple

May 24, 1905—End^{d} David Martineau, Joel for T. A. Corlett. Sisters Bassett, Henderson and Maddox assisted For female dead.

May 25, 1905—End^{d} John Hilyard, Joel's wife End^{d}, also Bassett, Hanson, Madox, Perreninal, Henderson & Naylor.

Sister Wooley, very low, sick over a year, wished me to come and administer to her at her house. Sent me word.

[page 281]

May 25, 1905—I sealed Blake family, David Martineau family and P. M. [Martineau] family to day. Sisters Pierce and Fletcher assisted. End 2 women.

May 26, 1905—I End. Henry Columbine

May 29, 1905—Sister Badger came with carriage to take me to her sister Mrs Wooley who had wished me to come, and who is low and feeble—ner. [nervous] prostrations For more than a year. I went, blessed her, also Sister Badger. Also went to Mary A. H. White, who last night stuck a garden rake tooth into her foot two inches; then administered at homes of E. K. Hanson, who has diabetes, Sister Ford, rupured [ruptured]. Sister Jane Hill & V. Zina Hyde Bull, who has cataract growing over her eyes. Then went over 6 miles and gave P. blessing to Helen Babbitt. Got home 9.30 P.M.

May 30, 1905—Went up town and saw grand decoration parad[e]. Then to Saltair.

May 31, 1905—End^{d} Henry Columbine. Mary Bassett for Susan Hutchinson. Also Sealed 3 couples. Pat^{l} Blessing to Evadne Henderson Hart

June 1, 1905—End^{d} Philip Stanhope. Sisters Stevens, ~~Larsen~~, Iverson, Gave P. Bl. to Sister Cooper and Langton. Gave Langton $1.^{00} [$22] for some Huguenot Martineau names she found in her Huguenot record

June 2, 1905—I endowed Marinus, Duke of Rome, year 720. Marinus is same as Martinus, (Latin for Martineau). Sister Bassett for Farnun. I Sealed 3 families.

In the evening attended closing, graduation exercise of the High School, Class of 1905, of which Royal is head. Over 70 graduates. In S. L. Theatre, which was full. All Lyman's family but Harriet & Gowan were there.

June 3, 1905—Graduation exercises in Theatre again tonight. Royal is head of Class for 1905, graduating with highest honors and a record of 98 out of possible 100 points in all his branches of Study. He has studied indefatigably to accomplish it & has succeeded.

June 20, 1905—Went to Lagoon, on Nauvoo Legion excursion, 16^{m} 25¢. Met my old friend—Wm K. Rice—with whom I lived in 1850 and with whom I went South and helped settle Iron Co. in Spring of 1851. Saw also his eldest daughter, Mrs.

Lucy A. Clark, also of Farmington, now a matron of 55, then, a little baby. Br. Rice is now over 80, and very feeble.

June 21, 1905—By invitation of David Hess and wife of Farmington, visited them in Company with Sisters Zina Hyde Bull and Mary Hyde White, sisters of Mr. Hess. The widow of Orson Hyde was present. whom I blessed, and gave a Patriarchal Blessing to Sister David Hess, her daughter. Had a very pleasant time.

[page 282]

June 22, 1905—Again went to Farmington and Brigham City on Old Folks Excursion, 22 passenger cars—all filled—1148 people.

June 24, 1905—Visited and blessed my patients, as tomorrow I go away.

June 25, 1905—Started for Uintah reservation to do a little work. Price

June 26 & 27, 1905—On the road from Price to Vernal 130 miles—very bad ones.

June 29, 1905—Start out with survey party and camp at Dry Fork. 15^{m}

June 30, 1905—Drove to forks of Whiterocks river and camped.

July 1, 1905—Lay by, waitting [waiting] for one of my men.

July 2, 1905—Moved down to Farm Creek and Camped. Begun work.

July 3, 1905—Surveyed, also next day, 4th

July 4, 1905—To day I was preserved from death by the direct aid of my Guardian Angel. I had to ascend a high mountain, very steep—too steep for me to climb on foot, so I started to ride up. I came to a wide belt of flat rocks, sloping downwards, and as I could see no way round it, attempted to ride up over it, but after a little my horse began slipping, got scared and lost his wits and fell with me repeatedly, I sticking to him as he fell and rose again, doing my best to control him. Each time he fell, we tumbled farther down the rocks, the horse plunging frantically. After his last fall I found myself lying full length upon the rocks, at the horse's back, and above him. How I was laid there so carefully, without his falling upon my leg, or my brains not being dashed out, or any bones broken, and how my feet were loosed from the stirrups I cannot even guess, only that my Guardian Angel did it all, during all the plunging, falling, getting up, and falling again down the rocks. Had my feet hung in the stirrups nothing could have saved me, and had I fallen under my horse, as was seemingly unavoidable, I might have lain there, crushed, till death.

I was somewhat to blame. For years, when about to ride over or along a dangerous place, as many times I have had to do, I always blessed my horse, that he might not stumble, fall, or cause me any hurt, but this day, I never once thought of doing it, and paid penalty.

In my tumbles I got some bruises, and a severe wrench over my middle caused not by falling but by struggles of the horse.

[page 283]

July 4, 1905—It shows how careful we should always be, even about what we may esteem small things. My miraculous escape shows to me that I have still some work to do here on Earth. That is why my life was spared, by the mercy of Our Father.

July 6, 1905—Must go to Vernal and take one of my men who fell down the rocks on foot yesterday and got badly hurt, reaching Vernal on the 7th.

July 8, 1905—Broke up party and engage a new one, as several quit. Some of my party were taken as Jurors, causing me loss of 4 days more, so that my man's fall cost me about \$30.^{00} [\$649].

July 13, 1905—Start out again, finishing my work and returning to Vernal on the 17th

July 17, 1905—We had to camp on Water (Deep Creek) full of alkali and tasting like a cow yard. Nearly all my me[n] were made sick by it, excepting me,—another blessing from the Lord.

July 19, 1905—Started home to City, reaching Castle Gate on the 20th and there I stayed two days with my daughter Virginia, husband & family, & reaching City on the 23^{d}

July 23, 1905—Found Lyman's family away, camping, Harriet, baby and husband Chas A. Gowan, at Lyman's house—baby with whooping cough.

July 30, 1905—To date have been writing up my field notes etc. Has been very hot,—one death from heat in the city. Had a good celebration on the 24th but very hot, and I felt, too, a stranger among the 20,000 people that day in the Park. Visited Lagoon.

AUGUST 1905

August 1, 1905—Went to Whites. Sisters A. M. Musser and Carter desired me to bless them, which I did. Sister White had just blessed them, too.

August 2, 1905—Lyman took me to Barnum's circus. I then went to Bp. Preston's to see his sister Annis Chantrel, who had come from Cache Co. for me to bless and administer to her for a great swelling on her neck, which surgeons say cannot be operated upon for fear of certain death. I blessed her, with Bp & Sister P. assisting.

August 10, 1905—Up to date I have been working on my field notes. To day got word from Washington that part of my survey = $540.70 [$11,700] is ready for payment. I shall be glad to pay even part of my debt.

August 14, 1905—Sister Julia Woolley, widow, Sent carriage for me to come to her, some miles, and bless her, sick, very, for 15 months. I promised her recovery, through faith.

Rec[d] check for $540.70 from Govt. Sent. I paid Cache Valley Bank for $300.[00] [$6,492] and with $72.79 [$1,575] interest. Glad it is paid.

[page 284]

August 15, 1905—A few days ago I received Several letters from Susan dated in June and July, one contained a dream that to her seemed very impressive:—as follows:—"I thought I was living in a house in a canyon with very large trees whose branches were interlaced overhead. They seemed to be oaks, only they seemed to be so tall. I heard a strange sound and looked out of the window and saw one of those trees rise from the ground, and I went to the door and heard the sound of cracking limbs overhead, and saw 3 other trees rise up from the ground, their limbs still entwined together, and they sailed away in a southerly direction and were soon lost to sight. x x x The impression I had was that some of our leaders would leave us suddenly, Strong, sturdy oaks represent men and their leaving no roots shows that their families were left behind." Study and see if you can get the same feeling I have about it."

I believe it was a true dream, and that her interpretation is correct. I believe Changes will take place among our leading men, but whether by death or by some other way I cannot tell. But this is the work of our Father, and He knows just how to carry it on to a successful finish, so I have no fear or doubt,—only that I may be true to the end, according to promises made to me.

Went to Calder's Park with temple workers to reunion of the B. Young family. Pres[t] Smith spoke, with others. I became acquainted with many there and enjoyed myself much.

August 19, 1905—Bought shoes, 3.50$ [$75.74] and pants 4.00$ [$87] First I have bo't for years.

August 20, 1905—To Farmington, and saw my old friend W[m] K. Rice, with whom I lived in 1850, when he had only 2 Children, William & Lucy A, the latter being only a few (6) months old. He and I went and helped Settle Iron Co. in the spring of 1851, and had times of great danger with indians. Also with him when he brought Cora aged 9 yrs, and got Moshiem, age 4 or 5 yrs. We talked of old times. He is 2 or 3 yrs. older than I, and very feeble.

[page 285]

August 23, 1905—Went by invitation to Saltair on Butcher's & Grocers outing. About 20,000 there during the day. Had a fine bath in the lake, first for over 20 years. Had an enjoyable time with friends.

August 24, 1905—Blessed Eva Hanson, who is ill with diabetes—quite low.

August 25, 1905—Lyman and Allie went to Portland. I felt impelled to go to Br. H. A. Whites and there found Sisters A. M. Musser and Carter, They said they were hoping I would come, desiring blessings from me, which I gave them, Also blessed Sister White, who is quite ill. At 3 P.M. met with temple workers and Stake and Ward officers at G. A. Kenner's house, to its dedication. About 40 present. Bro Tollman, Patriarch dedicated the house, I opening by prayer, and later being placed in Charge of the meeting by Bp. Warburton, who had to go. We had a grand time. Sisters Babbitt, W. W. Phelps, A. M. Musser, M. A. White and others spoke in power, also the few brothers there. Br. Foster and I blessed by request Several of the sisters. One was deaf and desired hearing restored, another desired children, others were ill. Three other sisters have come to me for blessing that they may become mothers,—Francis Neff Smith, Florence Thatcher, of Logan, Florence Snow Critchlow, daughter of Pres[t]

Lorenzo Snow and gr. dau. of Pres[t] Woodruff. I pray their desires may be granted.

August 28, 1905—Blessed Several sisters to day

August 29, 1905—Sent $5.[00] [$108] for Wilson Ear Drum. My hearing is so poor Blessed Sisters Cummings and Knight. Also some others

August 31, 1905—Quite unwell all day.

SEPTEMBER. 1905.

September 2, 1905—Paid $5.[00] [$108] Cash tithing. Lyman and Alley got home.

September 5, 1905—Royal Martineau went to Harvard College. Bp & Sis. Preston were here. He blessed Royal, and I gave him patriarchal blessing having his father lay on hands with me.

September 6, 1905—Got word I must return to Uintah Reservation and make Some Changes in the Survey.

September 7, 1905—Blessed Mrs. Zina Hyde Bull, for her threatened blindness by cataract growing over both eyes. Doctors say She must get blind. My faith is—she shall not become blind, For she may be healed through faith

September 8, 1905—Visited temple. Administered to Julia Woolley, very sick for almost two years.

[page 286]

September 9, 1905—Sister Woolley sent for me again. She is very low. Can speak only in a whisper. I blessed her again.

Sunday, September 10, 1905—Blessed J. Woolley again. Bp Sheets sent urgent request to bless his little boy, whose legs are paralyzed. I went and blessed him and believe he will be perfectly healed.

Tuesday, September 12, 1905—Went to Farmington, to funeral of Mary T. Richards, widow of Willard Richards. She was a dear friend of mine, who assisted me very many times in my Logan temple Sealings.

Wednesday, September 13, 1905—Worked in temple for Joseph Hutchinson. Next day for John Hutchinson. Miss Afton Young worked for Lois Martineau, Henry's daughter. Also she assisted me in Sealing 3 couples,—1506 + 921–1547 +1009 and 313 + 918. (numbers on names in my temple record.)

Friday, September 15, 1905—End[d] Bartholomew Hutchinson. Blessed Fanny Palmer.

September 16, 1905—Had my teeth (11 of them) Extracted. Only 5 left. Visited Evelina Babbitt, who is sick. While there blessed Margaret Caine and Jessie T. Y. Driggs.

September 17, 1905—Recorded blessings. Visited Sisters Woolley and Fanny Blair Stringham and blessed them.

September 20, 1905—In answer to my prayer this morning, before day, I received a glorious blessing. I desired, among other things, that I might [have] good weather while upon my next trip to Uintah valley, Surveying, and not be caught in a equinoctial storm while camping out. Was told my prayer should be granted.

September 21, 1905—Visited and blessed sister Babbitt, who is very sick. Learn that Charles baby was born Aug. 10. 1905

Tuesday, September 26, 1905—I start for Uintah 10 P.M. Ride all night and arrive at Mack in Colorado 7 A.M. There I took Uintah R.y. 54½ m. to Dragon So named from the Dragon Asphaltum mine. This R. R. Crosses the Book Cliff Mts. at Baxter Pass, Elev. 8500 ft. This road has an ascent of 450 ft per mile, with 60° curves and one of 70°, the line ascending the steep mountain side in a series of letter S lines, like this,

Fig. 10.3—Sketch of ascending mountain trail.

as many as four lines at once being one above another.

September 28, 1905—Leave Dragon by Stage 7 A.M. and reach Vernal 7 P.M. after 65 miles drive over a rough mountainous country. Just as I entered the house in Vernal, the rain fell in a deluge, continuing all night and for two days and nights, during which time I made up another survey party, and started anew on Oct 2[d] to

October 2, 1905—finish alterations required.

[page 287]

October 3, 1905—Began work in the Deep Creek country; finishing there on the 12th I moved up into Whiterocks Cañon, and finished my work up in the mountains locality, over 10000 ft altitude, and finished Oct. 20th and returned to Vernal.

October 20, 1905—Here I remained several days working up my notes.

During all my survey the promise made me before I started—that I should have good weather and no Storm of snow or rain while on my work was literally fulfilled, though at times storms seemed inevitable, Storming all around us, but not upon us, and we returned to Vernal on ground dry, not wet, as had been promised me. For all this, all praise be to Our Father, who condescended to hear the prayer of one so small as I am.

For some days the weather was intensely cold, –22° below zero, and I had to dress in a double suit of underclothing and over clothing too. But I took no hurt, even as I had been promised. To Our Father be all the praise.

During this work I had extraordinary experiences of deep anxiety and dread, followed by corresponding joy and peace.—fear, lest I had been mistaken,—misled by false spirits causing me to think their whisperings were the voice of the Holy Spirit, or that what I supposed to be the voice of the Holy Spirit was not; and thus, how should I ever learn to know His voice. This was to teach me how to know and judge the Spirits which operate upon me.

The Holy Spirit, in His influence, brings peace, joy, trust, faith and courage and trust in God; desire to do His will and to works of righteousness. The evil spirit incites exactly to the opposite. I was told that when filled with fear, doubt and dread to rebuke that evil influence in the name of Jesus, & it should depart. And I found this true.

When I inquired why I should be thus troubled & afflicted I was plainly shown by a simile or parable by the Spirit, who said to me "Which is the better seaman, he who has all his life been only upon a small, unruffled lake, where he had no storm or danger to confront him,—or a sailor, upon a tempestuous ocean, exposed often to hurricanes, shipwreck, and constant danger, accustomed to meet and overcome danger and death?" The comparison and the answer—both plain as the noon-day sun, Satisfied me completely.

[page 288]

October 20, 1905—I see it is absolutely needful to meet and learn to overcome difficulties if we would reach perfection and victory. Thus was I strengthened in faith, and in courage to strive for victory, and to learn to know the voice of the Holy Spirit, to be my strength, guide and comfort, as has long been my constant prayer.

During this time, when praying, I received many great and priceless promises, often while lying awake at night in Camp while all others slept; promises so great that I dare not write them now, but which were promised or foreshadowed in my patriarchal blessings, especially the last one given by Patriarch Chas W. Hyde, who foresaw what was in store for me, but feared to tell me, and whe[n] he desired me to bless him, which I did, very unwillingly, fearing I was doing something I had no right to do, as I was not then a Patriarch except to my own family, causing me great dread until he said to me "Br. Martineau, that is word for word the blessing sealed upon me by Hyrum Smith in Nauvoo." I had told him things it seemed to me to be impossible of fulfillment, and thought I had been misled by an evil spirit for acting in an office not appointed me.

And so, although a hard and expensive trip, there has blessing been because of it. Truly "God moves in a mysterious way."

October 27, 1905—Left Vernal 7 A.M. Dragon 7 P.M. Next day to Mack

October 28, 1905—Took D & R. G. train 4 P.M. and arrived in City next morning

October 29, 1905—at about 4 A.M., a long and tedious night ride & no sleep. Elev. of Mack. Col. = 4540 ft. Distance to S. L. City = 271m to Denver 469m

October 30, 1905—Was sent for to administer to Julia Woolley, sick for 2 years nervous prostration. Also visited and blessed Sisters Ford and Hansen.

October 31, 1905—Registered to vote at Election.

November 7, 1905—Up to date I have gone to administer to the sick every day Sometimes to Several. One, a little boy 3 years old, paralyzed in both legs—limp as rags when I blessed him just before I left for Uintah the last time, can now stand on his legs.

[page 289]

November 7, 1905—And when I blessed him yesterday said "Now I can walk" & got down on floor and did walk several steps. To God be all the praise and oh! how thankful I am that God deigns to show His mercy and power through one so weak and sinful as I. The boy will be fully healed, I fully believe, for he has great faith, tho so small. And Miss Afton Young, who was so almost helpless when first I blessed her is now very much improved and will soon be healed of the rheumatism, which for 5 years has resisted all the power of the doctors. Thus is the one great desire of my soul being granted—the power to bless, comfort and help the sick and the afflicted, the sad and weary of Our Father's children.

I would do good, if possible, to the wickedest of men, those who would even desire my death, yet, to every son & daughter of Our Father. If they Sin, let Our Father judge them, not ~~I~~ me.

Today was election, and Lyman has gained great prestige as the Chairman and leader—manager of the Democratic party in S. L. City. He is credited with having made a magnificent fight against great odds, and great generalship, the Gentiles (American) party were victorious. To Lyman, personally, it is a great victory politically, and his party give him unstinted praise.

The "American," party, gotten up by the apostate, adulterer, and whoremonger Frank Cannon,[18] is now in power, enemies to the Church. But God has permitted it, and He will not suffer His Church to be overthrown. He will continue and finish His work, no matter what may be the desire of our enemies.

[written in margin]

Note

I think I should record here a comforting vision or dream given me about day break, Nov. 6, I had been praying, about 3 am For health and power to do great good, and that I might be fully healed and strengthened in my kidneys, which have long been Seriously affected. The dream or vision was short, but marvlously effective, showing perfect health and power in those organs, with promise never to have kidney disease.

At times the Father has given me other instruction and comfort in the same manner, a scene but momentary, but full of Significance, and so I have been helped when in deep distress of mind.

[page 290]

November 11, 1905—This morning I received words of comfort and blessing that filled my soul with gladness,—that the Father approves my ministry as Patriarch—a Father among the Saints, and will open my way that I may greatly increase in power to do good in healing, comforting, blessing and helping the saints and in my work for the dead and the living, with approval of my Survey by the Government, and means in abundance, so I may devote the rest of my days to the work of the Lord & to the living and the dead, with other promises, in connection with the Lamanites and the Three Nephites so great that I hesitate to write them. Oh that I may have power to do good to the fullness of my desires. I believe that I shall, for so said the voice of the Spirit to me, and I know He deceiveth not.

By letter from Susan, received to day I find we have 10 great-great grand Children:—5 from Elvira's Son Joseph, 3 from Bertha, Henry's eldest daughter; and 1 from Harriet, Lyman's daughter, and one from James Edward. Moroni's eldest son. Truly God blesses me greatly. I pray all the time that I may increase all the time in heavenly gifts & in power to do good.

November 16, 1905—Ed^{d} Sudbury came, with Florence. He gave me 2 prs. Each of undershirts, drawers and garments, which came very seasonably, as I had only one old, ragged undershirt and 1 old pair of drawers. I was very glad, and blessed him, that he shall never be without good clothing, which may God grant.

[written in margin]

Note

Lyman R. my son, was ordained High Priest by Apostle Moses Thatcher in Nov. 1881, on his appointment as President of the M. I. M. I Association [MIA] of Cache Co. of 32 wards.

18 Frank J. Cannon, son of George Q. Cannon, was a prominent reporter and newspaper editor. He was active in politics and elected as Utah's first senator. He later became a critic of the Church, authoring anti-Mormon works and lecturing against the Church (Kenneth W. Godfrey, "Frank J. Cannon: Declension in the Mormon Kingdom," in *Differing Visions: Dissenters in Mormon History*, ed. Roger D. Launius and Linda Thatcher [Urbana: Univ. of Illinois Press, 1994], 241–59).

November 21, 1905—Blessed Lillian V. Jones and Miss McKnight.

November 24, 1905—Attended Priesthood meeting of Granite Stake and was invited to Speak, which I did

November 25, 1905—At Quar. Conference of the Stake. A grand time and a good dinner with visiting officials of the Church.

November 21, 1905—To day by invitation of little Mary White, 2 years old to day, I attended her "Birf day party," originated by herself. She invited br. Motino, Aunty Kenner, Sister Sears and Fido (the dog) Several others came also. A pleasant time.

[page 291]

November 21, 1905—Tho only 2 years old little Mary has prayed daily for me. I think it is because I brought bananas for her at times, when she could not eat anything else, hardly, and she could not get them. She prayed at various times to God for "Nannas," and it was so that always shortly after, I was impressed to bring her some, & this, to her, was an answer to her prayer. I believe it was . She has wonderful faith, naturally born in her.

November 25, 1905—Rec[d] a letter from my Cousin Napolion B. Van Slyke, one of my few remaining relatives of the olden time. He is 83, shortly (born Dec. 21. 1822) still an active business man. He sent me information relative to his progenitors and family, and of my Sister Lois M. Voswinkel's family, which I insert here.

Children of

Lois Elenor Martineau, born Aug. 10, 1838 and John Peter Voswinkel, married 1860

Fredrick William Voswinkel, B. Jan. 27 1862. Died Feb. 25 1895

Bertha Martineau Voswinkel, B. Jan 9, 1864 —[no death date]

Adlienne Voswinkel, B. May 26 1866 Died July 22 1866

Louis Voswinkel, B. May 15 1868 Died Sept. 11 1868

Caroline Whittlesey Voswinkel, B. Sep. 13. 1869 ———[no death date]

Alexander Voswinkel, B. Dec. 25, 1870 D. July 1 1871

William Voswinkel, B. June 2 1872 D. Aug. 5, 1872

Jenny Louise Voswinkel, B. —[no month] 22 1873 ——[no death date]

(married Donald Roderick Osborn July 28. 1878. has 2 children)

Lois Elenor Voswinkel, B. June 26 1876 ———[no death date]

Note. She (Lois) says our half brother Charles Augustus, died in the last year of the civil war, before Richmond, of disease.

COUSIN NAPOLEON BUONAPARTE VAN SLYKE'S FAMILY.

He was Son of Daniel Van Slyke and Laura Mears. Daniel was Born about [blank] Died 1831, Daniel Van Slyke's record.

His father Daniel's parents were Garrett and Catherine: their Children were John, Peter, Catherine & Daniel, in the order above.

Napoleon's first wife was Laura Sheldon. His next wife is Annie Corbett, still living. Their Children—by Laura were Laura, Maie dead, Sheldon dead, and James, [blank space] by Annie [...] names of other 2 not given in letter

Napoleon's Grandchildren,—James' Children:—

[page 292]

November 25, 1905—Children of James Van Slyke:—

Ruth, age 18, B 1887

John, 16, 1889

Maie, 13, 1892

Elizabeth 5 yrs of age, 1900

November 27, 1905—Winter commences to day—Rain, followed by Snow storm.

December 3, 1905—We all went to Bp. Preston's for family dinner. Pleasant.

December 4, 1905—By invitation I visited Sister Maria W. Richards Wilcox, sister of Sam[l] W. Richards, and while there blessed her two daughters, Matilda W. Wilcox—Cummings and Ellen A. W. Wilcox Hyde, also Br. Horace H. Cummings. Also administered to Sister Wilcox, suffering from indigestion. Had a pleasant time.

December 16, 1905—Visited Sister Zina Hyde Bull, who has cataract, and can hardly see. She said, "Oh! I'm so glad you've come." She wanted me to bless her; also to bless her sister Delia Ellis, who has joined the Christian Science nonsense, and is now visiting her, from Seattle, Oregon. She said her sister, still feeble from a recent hospital operation, wished me to bless her, for her health. I did so, having asked Our Father about it, and being told to do so, and that she should be blessed. I then visited a widow, Jenny Hill who also was very glad I came. She was very sad,—husband, daughter and son taken by death. I was full of pity, and sealed a comforting blessing upon her, and she was blessed indeed. I then walked about 2 miles or more (to save car fare, which is scarce with me now) to see Sister White. Found her children sick, and blessed them. Then walked about a mile to see a little boy of 3 years, whose legs are paralyzed, and blessed him. Then walked about 2 miles home, several hours after dark.

I give this day's work as a sample of what I have done for two years in this city, few days passing without visiting and blessing the Sick. Often so tired, but always glad to help and comfort others. It is what I live for. I wish to live no longer than I can do good to others, and God has greatly blessed me and my labors in this. All praise be to His holy name, for all good is from Him.

December 19, 1905—Visited Sister Hill, who feels much happier since I blessed her a few days ago. Mrs. Delia Ellis and Zina Hyde Bull were also there.

[page 293]

December 19, 1905—Mrs. Ellis wished me to bless her, that her knees might be healed—weak and painful from her operation in hospital. She said she was very much better since I blessed her some days before & believed she could be blessed now. So I blessed her again, and believe God will bless and heal her, and hope she may come back again to the Church.

To day I finished the following verses, and sent to Susan in place of other Christmas gift, which I am unable to Send:—

LINES TO MY WIFE, FOR OUR WEDDING DAY. JAN 8. 1852

Susana querida! Thou wife of my youth
How blessed was the day in its dawning,
When, youthful, we plighted our love and our truth
In the brightness of Life's early morning.

How changeful the scenes since the hour we met—
Grim darkness the light oft succeeding!—
Gay laughter so joyous—then our pillow soon wet
With tears that would come without seeking.

The friends of our youth—from Earth they are gone—
From this sphere now so darksome and dreary;
While we who remain feebly totter along
To our haven of rest, worn and weary.

But there is a clime—oh! blissful and bright!
Where dwelleth our Father and Mother,
Where beameth Forever that radiant light
That shineth in heaven forever

Then let us take courage—in Father we'll trust
Whose acts are all pure, just and holy
When our work here is finished gain heavenly rest
With our Savior—once homeless and lowly

[page 294]

December 23, 1905—Visited and blessed Julia Woolley, who said "Oh! I'm glad you have come! You have done me so much good—more than one has ever done." She gave me a handkerchief to send to Susaying [Susan saying] "Tell her I love her, tho I never have seen her." She said "She is a good woman,—pure in spirit as this handkerchief, and I love her."

December 24, 1905—Visited Gean's after Tabernacle meeting.

December 25, 1905—Christmas again. I wonder if I will see any or many more in my life. I had a few presents. Bp. Preston fell down stairs early this morning, and was unconscious when picked up. I hope nothing serious may result. Wrote letters to nearly all my children.

JANUARY 1906.

January 8, 1906—To day is the anniversary—54th—of our marriage, Susan E. Johnson's and mine. But no beloved wife was near nor any one to care for it, seemingly, but I felt lonely all day. Well, when we both go to the "other side" sad lonely lives and partings will be no more for us. What a comforting thought! 54 years is a good while for people to live together as husband and wife, and in all these years she never, even once, gave me any wrong or evil counsel, but always her counsel was for good, not evil.

January 11, 1905—I started to day to go to administer to Bp. Preston, but felt to stop by the way and see Sister Maud Patterson, a widow. I did not know where she lived, but felt I must go there.

When I found her house I found why I went there. A woman, Lydia E. Carter White was in an agony—four days and nights,—peritonitis[19] in dangerous form, and some internal complication—female—also dangerous in nature.

When I came in the women exclaimed "Oh! I'm so glad you have come! The Lord has surely sent you to help." I found the doctor had just gone, his last words were—"If the pain continues, don't wait for me—get to the hospital just as quick as you can, if you would live, and have an operation at once." I asked our Father about her case. The answer was,—"She is not appointed unto death, but may be healed by my power and not by that of man, nor need go through any surgical operation."

[page 295—see Appendix 5 for letter from son Joel inserted here.]

1906—I told Sister White this and asked if she believed it. She said. I then administered to her, and she was healed almost instantly of all pain, which till then, had caused her to writhe in agony. Peritonitis was perfectly healed, and the trouble in her abdomen, But she still felt she must go to the hospital for an operation, But I said she could be healed without it, by faith. And she was, & is now, a month later, well. praise be to our Father above for to Him belongs all the praise and glory.

19 Peritonitis is an inflammation of the peritoneal cavity, which holds the intestines.

January 18, 1906—Attended a Social meeting of temple workers, at Knight's Pleasant time. I spoke and felt blessed

January 14, 1906—Was invited by Br. and Sister Morris B. Young to bless their children, and was urgently desired to go and administer to a young woman, Miss Stella Wickel, very sick and in agony. I went there from Young's and found Stella in great pain in her loins, one doctor said—appendicitis, another—inflammation of the ovaries. Both said she must have surgical operation if she wished to live. I obtained a testimony regarding her like that of Lydia E. W. Carter, (see previous page), told Stella, she said she believed, was prayed for, and amended from that time, & is now well—and no surgeon required.

While with Stella, another woman sent urgently for me. I found her in a very dangerous condition, she fearing lest she lose her unborn babe. I blessed her also, and she felt better at once, and is now doing well.

I record these cases—all desperate ones—that my children may see how our Father blesses those who put their trust in Him, and that they make great faith also

During the past month I have given patriarchal blessings to many—40 or 50, and scarcely a single day has passed that I did not visit and administer to the sick, often 3 to 5 a day, traveling miles at night on foot, in mud or snow, while it was counted very dangerous to do so because of thugs & murders committed almost every night. But I had a promise, by the voice of the Holy Spirit saying no one would harm or molest me, and thus far, it has been so.

[page 296]

February 2, 1906—To day a woman Mrs. Langton came from home several miles distant & brought her married daughter Mrs. Elizabeth Driggs For me to bless and help if I could, she being in a very bad condition, enciente, broken down, bloodless, and so nervous she shook all over like one in a heavy chill, and afraid she was going crazy.

She had been told she must have an operation to get rid of her babe—unborn—was told she would be justified, as it was lawful to kill a babe to save its mother's life. I could not consent to this, but she quoted examples in town, and felt it must be done. After, or while administering to her she felt much better and her nervous spasms and jerks ceased. I gave her then a Patl

Blessing, and she went away like an entirely different person, and could Smile & even laugh. The change was wonderful indeed, all praise to our Father in heaven.

February 4, 1906—I blessed Sister Maud Patterson, her two children and Lydia Carter's little girl, who asked for a blessing.

February 6, 1906—I was called to visit Sis. Stillman, who was in great need of help, soon to be confined, and at times unable to talk, or use words she wished—could not remember her own name, and feared she would lose her mind. I blessed her, and she was at once much better, her mind clear, and filled with hope and faith. and I feel sure all will be well with her in her confinement.

And thus I am called for continually, and I thank Our Father I am enabled, by His blessing, to do some good.

February 9, 1906—Attended a meeting of temple workers at the house of the Maorie prince lately deceased. About 40 present and a lovely time. His widow and family very much pleased. Several were administered to. Mrs. Ida White wished me to bless her, that she might have children, I did so.

February 10, 1906—I visited Sister Eliz[th] Driggs, whom I blessed on the 2[d] and the change in her, for good, was astonishing to me although I had fully expected her to be healed. She was another woman—no one would think she had been sick. Words could not express her joy and thankfulness. It was a great testimony to me also.

[page 297]

February, 1906—By recent letter from Susan, I learn that Moroni's Son, James Edward's wife's maiden name is Myrle Clark

His baby boy is named Edward Bernard Martineau and was born Oct. 6. 1905 in Chuichupa, Chihuahua Mex.

February 11, 1906—Sunday. Visited and blessed Sister Julia Woolley, also her daughter Jessie, whose eyes are very weak. Then to our Ward meeting, then to Eliz[th] Driggs, who is doing finely. Got home quite late at night, as Driggs lives about 6 or 7 miles off.

February 14, 1906—A Mrs. Murdock, unknown by me, phoned for me to come and bless her. I found her, weak and feeble, and troubled because of a tumor in her body, which she was told must be removed at the hospital—a place she dreaded to visit. Her husband, James B. Murdock, is not a Mormon, but seems a good man.

I blessed her and her mother. She is promised her tumor shall pass away naturally, and she become healthy and strong as she was in girlhood, through faith. She said she believed. If she does and continues she shall be fully healed, without any Surgery or knife.

On my way home I visited and blessed Fanny Blair Stringham, an old friend, who had phoned, also, for me to come and visit and bless her. She is feeble, with a boy a few weeks old. She has a swelled neck, and har[d] of hearing, For which she wished to blessed and healed. I did so, and belive [believe] she will be fully healed. Some 2 months ago, she wished me to bless her for her approaching confinement, feeling then greatly in fear of that trial, I blessed her that she should have the quickest, easiest and best confinement she ever had had. She now told every word of my blessing at that time had been fulfilled. Oh! how thankful I am to Father for blessing the sick, fearful and suffering and showing forth His power & goodness through so weak a one as I, and that He enables me to help and comfort those who need it!

February 15, 1906—By letter from Susan and Gertrude I learn G. is getting well. How thankful I shall be, when she is well and my dear wife be relieved from the wearing care and anxiety she has borne so long.

[page 298]

February 17 and 18, 1906—Attended Quarterly Conference of Granite Stake. Spoke Sunday 18. Conference continued. A grand time. Pres[t] J. F. Smith spoke in mighty power. He wept, I, and others also. He spoke of Ruth's Covenant with Naomi, in power, at close of meeting I took his hand and blessed him. He pressed my hand. I then said to him. "Brother Smith, the covenant Ruth made with Naomi I make with you." He pressed my hand so warmly! and gave me such a look! I cannot describe it, but it was full of love, glad surprise and joy. Afterwards I felt as John when he baptized Jesus—it was for him to bless me, not for me him—the less to bless the greater. But it was done on the inspiration of the moment.

I afterwards asked the Father about it, and the answer was "It was right, and was pleasing to thy brother."

Friday, February 23, 1906—Blessed Victor and Norma Cummings. Heavy snow.

Sunday, February 25, 1906—Ward meeting. Assisted in blessing and setting apart several sisters, as officers in Relief Society, also for washing and anointing the sick, and other duties. Then about 6 miles to visit a very sick woman who had sent for me to visit her, a Mrs. Jenny Brooks. She was very sick, weak and frail, hardly able to walk or even talk—Cancer in both breasts, I tried to cheer her, and blessed her, to be healed, live & labor in the temple to be built in Zion—Jackson Co. Mo.

I had obtained this testimony before I went. She was very much better when I left her. I thank thee, oh God for the privilege thou hast given me to comfort & heal the afflicted. After meeting to day, I was requested to go and bless two sisters, who are in precarious health, South and Kimball.

MARCH 1906

March 1, 1906—Heavy snow storm, worst of the winter. Snow nearly 1 ft deep. I am quite ill with rheumatism, and can hardly walk.

March 2, 1906—Alley's birth day.

March 6, 1906—Am better, but walking hurts me a little. Visited Sister Brooks. A desperate condition. In constant, heavy pain in breast and stomach (she thinks indigestion) hardly able to breathe, and each breath with much pain, can only talk a little and in whisper very faintly. Blessed her again, to be healed. I believe she will be.

[page 299]

March 8, 1906—E Guy Taylor came, on his way home from Canada. With him came a young woman, introduced to me as Miss Watts. They spent the Evening with us and went on to Mexico at 11 P.M.

Sunday, March 11, 1906—A hard day for me. Started out after breakfast, and spent most of the day visiting the sick. Walked several miles to get to the afternoon meeting, and then to the sick again. Got home at about 10 P.M. But I was greatly blessed, in giving comfort to those sisters who needed it so badly, so very ill and low with disease.

March 12, 1906—Was told in the Sur. Gen[l] office they could not approve my Survey. It was owing to erroneous work of a Mr. Brown, who Surveyed the Bdy. line of the Uintah Ind. Reservation upon which my work joined. I felt much distressed, for to go over part of it again could not be done before next June because of snow at so great an elevation (over 10000 feet), and the trip would cost over \$200.[00] [\$4,328]—which I knew not how to obtain; and I would be unable to pay the \$3000.[00] [\$64,916] I already owe, to those who need it, and gave me help in my survey. But worst of all, I feared I had been misled by some delusive spirit, for in answer to prayer I had been told I should <u>not</u> have to go again to make any corrections, and that my survey should speedily be accepted and paid in full. And now it seemed as if I had been deceived by some evil power. and how can I learn to know the true from the false! How can I know, as I bless one, that I am led by a good and not by an evil spirit! It seems all very dark to me as I pray during the night.

March 13, 1906—But as I wake I seem to see a letter from the Land Commissioner in Washington, saying my work <u>is</u> accepted there, and will be paid. If so, then I know I have been led by the true spirit and not the false one, and that when I bless, that my words are dictate by the Holy Spirit.

Cold, stormy and snowing. Well <u>any</u> weather is better than none, but it seems dismal, to me.

My 78th Birthday! And I used to think I would never be older that 45 or 50! It is truly the blessing from the Lord.

March 12, 1906—Yesterday, I was called to see a sister who fears miscarriage, and had faith I could help her. I blessed her that all will be well with her, and her frequent miscarriages shall cease from this time forth. Her mother, Sister Maria W. Richards Wilcox told me that she herself was perfectly healed of indigestion since I blessed her and rebuked it.

[page 300]

March 13, 1906—She had for years suffered from it, could eat scarcely anything, and even <u>that</u> put her in excruciating pain. I blessed her about Jan. 10th and she is now perfectly healed, even from that very day. She is full of life & like a young woman, tho now about my age. Thanks to to Thee! oh, my Father in Heaven, that Thou hast permitted me to be an instrument through whom to show Thy power, mercy and goodness to her and so many others! And I thank Thee for the power to do good, for that is all I desire to live for! Help me to continue and increase in doing good, my Father, and all the glory be to Thee forever, Amen.

March 14, 1906—My survey notes were sent to Washington today.

March 17, 1906—For several days I have been almost sick, with very bad cold and cough. To day I was phoned to go to Walnut Ave to see some unknown person, presumably sick. Altho I was quite unwell I went, and found a sister with a heart trouble—leakage of the heart. I blessed her that she should be healed. Also present another sister in sore trouble whom I comforted all I could.

March 18, 1906—After visiting Virginia I went to the Tabernacle meeting and met a sister Sharp. who wished me to go with her and bless some one. I went to Mr. Murdock's and met two young ladies and a Brother Paradise who desired P. Blessings. I blessed them all, and felt well.

March 20, 1906—Went to Logan, and went to Lilla's to stay. Have a very bad cough and cold. Cold and stormy,—snow.

March 21, 1906—Visited Charles and family, also Lamoreaux's and Will Preston's. Very cold and stormy. Snow all over valley

March 22, 1906—Quite unwell. In house all day. Lilla had her tooth drawn yesterday, and is now better. She had feared a stroke of paralysis, last Sunday.

March 23, 1906—Nephi came from Benson Ward. Roads almost bottomless I visited Aurelia, his eldest daughter, training as nurse in the hospital.

March 24, 1906—Spent day at Charles's

March 25, 1906—At meeting. Spoke, and felt well. After meeting a letter from Susan, saying Gertrude is very low—fading away. and I must come soon if I would see her again. Still rainy.

[page 301]

March 26, 1906—Return to S. L. City at noon. Find that Virginia is very sick—danger of miscarriage. Went to her after dinner. Next, I bid good bye to some dear friends in Emerson Ward & others.

March 27, 1906—Still quite unwell. In bed all day till 5 P.M. then walked to LeGrand Young's to see Afton, whom I had before blessed for her rheumatism. Found her greatly improved. I blessed her again. She, her father and mother were very glad I came. Still raining, cold and muddy. Walked over two miles.

March 28, 1906—Visited Gean, also Eliza Jones, and blessed the last, for heart disease, from which she has suffered 8 years. Was also sent for to Forest Dale, to administer to Sis. Gardner, for heart trouble. Also blessed a sister Brown for cancer in the breast. Thus I have visited and blessed parties many miles apart.—have walked some miles, but feel better.

March 29, 1906—Sent for again, to Forest Dale. Blessed Alice Grover, who has had 3 bones taken from her spine, and suffers much. Thence I went about 6 or more miles to see Sis. Bliss (cum) threatened with miscarriage. Found her mother, M. W R Wilcox very sick. Blessed her. Thence 5 miles home to Lyman's. tired.

March 30, 1906—Went to see Gean, who is rather worse to day. Thence to Preston's From there to Whites. Found her and Hazel very sick. Blessed them. Then to Eva Hanson, very sick—diabetes. Then to Matilda Ford, very weak from severe operation in hospital. Blessed her, then to Lyman's at night. 9 P.M.

There are so many sick who desire my help, though I am quite ill myself. but the Lord blesses my labors.

SUNDAY APRIL 1ST 1906

April 1, 1906—Snowing heavily all day, and last night. I am still quite unwell, and did not get up for breakfast, lying abed till noon. Was called by telephone to go to Sis. Julia Woolley. I went up to town 4 miles, got two sisters to accompany me & we then went about 4 miles to Sis. Woolley's. Blessed her, then went to Fanny Blair Stringham, blessed her for swelling on her neck and deafness. Thence (snow nearly a foot deep) about 5 miles up City Creek Cañon to Br. F. E. Barker's, whose wife fears a miscarriage, blessed her, and her son, who has a hot fever. Then to Sis. Anderson, whose left arm is totally paralyzed and her side and leg partially, blessed

[page 302]

April 1, 1906—Started home but stopped to White's and found her very ill, also her baby. Blessed both; then went to Eva Hanson who is very low, and blessed her; also Sis. Ford, who is very weak from a severe operation in the hospital, and blessed her. Thence home, quite late—10 or 11 P.M. Thus I have often gone, traveling miles at night, sometimes in mud,—snow—or rain. when men were sandbagged and robbed almost every night. Lyman's family were worried lest I come to grief, but I trust in the blessing of the Lord, in doing His work among the sick, and so I have no fear. Still quite ill with cold on my lungs.

April 3, 1906—Lay all day in bed till 5 P.M. Thought of Afton Young, who is still rheumatic. Arose and visited and blessed her, returning home about 9 P.M. Walked two miles. She and her parents were very glad I came, as all are whom I visit.

April 4, 1906—Attended funeral of my dear Sister, Eva Hanson. Spoke and was blessed in so doing, and believe others felt well.

April 5, 1906—Went about 6 miles Lydia Brooks, who fears miscarriage & blessed her. Then visited Sis. Driggs, whom I had blessed previously, and found her wonderfully improved. Home.

April 6, 1906—Attended Conference. Then to Bp. Sheets, and blessed his son partially paralyzed, but greatly improved since my last visit. Blessed him. He can now walk, and play out of doors. Was entirely paralyzed when I first blessed him. To God be all the praise, for His mercy to the boy I walked all the way home, 4 miles. In the evening I went to Kimball's and gave Pat[l] Blessing to his wife, Miss M. M. Merrill and a Sister Harper. Home 10:30 P.M.

Albey & Mary Sherman, and daughter Elvira Came.

April 7 & 8, 1906—Conference. 3 new Apostles chosen, two dropped from Apostleship,—M. F. Cowley and J. W. Taylor. About 15000 present at Conference.

April 11, 1906—In temple, to do a work for Susan Julia's (my wife) father Lyman R. Sherman and his wife (Susan's Aunt) Delcena D. Johnson-Sherman, who have long been waiting for their blessings. He died in 1839, Jan[y] a martyr, as Pres[t] H. C. Kimball told me, also Pres[t] G. A. Smith, his death caused by the exposure and hardships consequent upon his constant labors in guarding and protecting Joseph Smith and the Saints in the persecution of 1838.

[page 303]

April 11, 1906—He and she had never been sealed as husband and wife, though married by the law of the land, in the Church. He had not been endowed, she, his widow, was endowed in Nauvoo. In addition, I have greatly desired their 2nd A, feeling they were worthy if any are. and I made application to Pres[t] Jo[s] F. Smith in their behalf. He desired something written, in support of my application, and I wrote what I knew in favor, and said I would hold myself responsible. Last evening I was told over the phone my wish is granted.

I endowed Nathanial Hutchinson, Albey Sherman end[d] Seth, his brother, Mary Sherman End[d] Amy Johnson and Elvira Cox end[d] Eliz[th] Blackburn. Also Sister Wessman end[d] Eliz[th] H. Freak for me.

Mary Elvira, Albey, Seth and Susan Julia, L R Sherman's Children, were sealed to him and Delcena, his wife. I acted for the father, & Mary E. Cox for the mother.

April 13, 1906—To day two infant children were also sealed to L. R. and D. D. Sherman, viz. Alson, a boy, and Sarah, each about 1 yr. of age.

I also had the unspeakably great pleasure to act as proxy for Lyman R. Sherman, and Mary E. S. Cox as proxy for Delcena Diadama Johnson Sherman, in the holy 2[d] A.

Words cannot tell my joy. Now, they are united never to Sever; their children are now theirs, Susan, my wife, now has father and mother legally in the line of the priesthood: Now they have gained their exaltation and glory. How wonderfully good Our Father has been to me, in permitting me to bring all this to pass, Albey giving his assent, he being legal heir to labor for his father, but not eligible to act in the last & highest ordinance given on Earth.

Lyman Sherman joined the church in 1831, Was the first who ever spoke in tongues in this dispensation. Pres[t] Kimball told me that L. R. S. was the sweetest singer in tongues in the church, and was Joseph's "right hand man." in Missouri.

Pres[t] Smith said L. R. S. was appointed an apostle, but his untimely death occurred before there was opportunity for his ordination.

[page 304]

April 13, 1906—While Widow Sherman lived in Nauvoo, Joseph Smith came to see her, while Susan, her little daughter (my wife) was sick and bribed the child to take some medicine by promise of a plate with letters around the edge, as she sat upon his lap. Joseph had a Sister—Almera—sealed to him as wife, Sister of Delcena Sherman,—my wife's Aunt. She died in Parowan about 1878 if I remember the date rightly. She had married a Mr. Barton.

And so this is a grand "red-letter" day in my life, this 13th day of April 1906. Father, I thank Thee for thy goodness.

To day Albey endowed his father, and Mary S. end^{d}—Hutchinson

This finishes for the present, my temple work here & I took leave of some of my fellow laborers.

April 12, 1906—Blessed Frances A Langton

April 14, 1906—Busy in Sur. Genl Office. Sent my last Sur. Notes.

April 15, 1906—Sunday Adm^{d} to Lydia Smith, Julia Woolley, Pat. Bl. to her son Claude. Adm^{d} to Fanny B. Stringham, also to Walter Sheets (paralyzed partially) Thence Home, I had walked 4 miles and was tired.

April 16, 1906—Mon. Sent additional items of life of Lyman R. Sherman to Prest. Jo^{s} F. Smith, taken from life of H. C. Kimball, who says Sherman was appointed an apostle in place of Tho. B. Marsh by the Prophet Joseph while he was in Liberty Jail, date, Jan 16. 1839. Sherman was sick at the time and died in a few days. (about Feb 15, 1839. before he could be ordained.

In the evening, at 6.30 P.M. went several miles in Br. Best's carriage to bless his wife, bed fast 9 yrs. in Heavy rain storm, in Winder Ward. Attended Dr Keate's funeral, and spoke.

April 17, 1906—Visited Gean and family for good-bye. Then to Br. Best's Gave her Pat^{l} Blessing, also to Br. R. S. Horne, adm^{d} to Sis L. whose feet are partially paralyzed. Thence 7 miles to Sis. H. A. Ensign, very sick, & adm^{d} to her, then to Mary White Bld. [blessed] her and Hazel. Home 10.30 P.M.

[page 305]

April 17, 1906—Felt a slight Earthquake shock about 5 P.M. but did no damage.

April 18, 1906—Visited LeGrand Young and family & Bld. Afton. Her chronic rheumatism is almost healed. Sick 5 years.

April 19, 1906—Paid San Pedro R. R. $21.55 [$466] for half rate ticket to Colton 781 miles. Also $5.50 [$119] for Pullman berth; $1.25 [$27] to get baggage to depot; also $2.60 [$56] for 50 lbs excess weight.

In the afternoon Bp. W. B. Preston and wife, Gean, and Sister Moses Thatcher visited me. Sis. Preston gave me $15.$^{\underline{00}}$ [$325] and Lyman lent me $25.00 [$541], making a little more than R. R. fare with what I had before. I blessed Lyman and his family, and dedicated his house, also Dr. Chas Gowans (Harriet's husband)

April 20, 1906—At 10 P.M. Went to Depot and left Friday morning, midnight 12^{h} 1' A.M. Lyman helped me till train started. He and Alley also Gean gave me a good lunch, also some hdks [handkerchiefs], ties, hose &c for Susan, Anna and Gertrude. We all felt bad at Parting.

April 21, 1906—Awoke near Lynn. Arr$^{\underline{d}}$ at Colton 10.30 A.M. 5 hours behind time. Road washed badly. Took S. Pacific train at 3 P.M. for El Paso, 755 miles. Arr^{d} Yuma 9 P.M.

Sunday, April 22, 1906—and El Paso 1 P.M. I crossed into Mexico, at Juarez, and stopped at Pierce's. Just in time to attend a meeting of the few L. D. S. in that vicinity. Spoke. In evening I gave Pat^{l} Blessing to Br. I. W. Pierce and his wife.

April 23, 1906—Left Juarez 9.30 A.M. Arr^{d} Casas Grandes 6 P.M. and home in Col^{a} Juarez 10.30 P.M.

Found family better than I expected. Gertrude some better, but unable to sit up. My dear Susan seemed much broken down by Constant care, anxiety and watching with Gertrude for almost 2 years.

April 26, 1906—Visited Sis. Ivins and adm^{d} to her. Quite sick. Also visited my children Anna, Emma, Theo & wife came.

April 29, 1906—At meeting and spoke.

MAY 1906.

May 6, 1906—To day I became a member again, of the Juarez Ward by vote, as usual.

May 8, 1906—Susan and I visited Apostle Teasdale & wife. This the first time Susan has walked so far, for years. Had a pleasant visit with them.

[page 306]

May 9, 1906—Gertrude had a nervous chill, quite serious, by prayer and what else we could do she passed a good night.

Blessings received by Gertrude, not yet recorded herein. Patriarchal Blessing by Patriarch James N. Skowson given in Col[a] Juarez, Mex. upon Gertrude Martineau Taylor:—

Dear Sister, in the name of Jesus Christ I place my hands upon your head and give you a patriarchal blessing. Thou art a daughter of the House of Israel thru the loins of Ephraim, and a legal heir to all the blessings of the holy priesthood according to your sex. Rejoice, dear Sister, that you are placed on mother Earth in the fullness of times, when God has again spoken from the heavens thru Jo[s] Smith the Prophet. You are a legal heir to all the blessings that have ever been pronounced upon the daughters of Zion, according to your sex. Thy Guardian Angel shall follow thee by day and by night, and thou shalt live so that in a short time God will permit thee to walk upon Mother Earth like the rest of the daughters of Zion, even thou shalt walk on the streets of the New Jerusalem, and be troubled no more of the infirmity of your body, and God is well pleased with you because of the integrity of your heart. Thou art barren for the present, but the time will come when your offspring shall be great and numerous, like the stars of the heavens. You shall have no sorrow on Mother Earth, only for the sins of your fellow beings. The Gospel shall be sweeter unto you day by day, Thou shalt have visions and dreams, and the Eternal World shall be opened to thy vision, & you shall behold the great glories of the Heavenly Host. If you be taken before the Son of Man come I seal you up to eternal life, to receive all the glories and exaltation of a priestess and queen, and receive them under the crown of your husband. If it is the will of the Father that you shall wait till the Son of Man Come you shall be changed from Mortality to immortality & shout hosannah in His glorious presence., all these blessings, and all your former blessings I seal upon you by authority of the holy priesthood in the name of Jesus Christ. Amen.

[page 307]

Blessing by Pat[h] Wm. R. R. Stowell given in Col[a] Juarez. Mex. June 6. 1897.

Sister Gertrude, I place my hands upon your head in the name of the Lord Jesus Christ, and by authority of the holy priesthood vested in me, in ~~in~~ my office as a Patriarch in Israel I pronounce upon you a blessing, and pray God my heavenly Father that the words which I may speak may be dictated by the holy Spirit, and be a comfort and a pleasure to you, both now and hereafter. You are of the blood of Israel and have been reserved in the world of Spirits to come forth in this, the dispensation of the fullness of times. You have been born of goodly parents, and are an heir to all the blessings of the gospel, even the new and everlasting covenant, pertaining to your sex. Your Guardian Angel has watched over you from your infantile moments, and preserved you from dangers, both seen & unseen. You have had many afflictions, but do not despair, nor think that the arm of the Lord is shortened. Think over the many afflictions that the Saints of God have passed through in the past, and the many kind blessings from the hand of the Lord which you have enjoyed. Turn to the bright side of the picture & reflect upon the future, and ask God in humble prayer that your physical nature may be strengthened, that you may be able to endure and prove faithful to your covenants which you have made with God, to the end of your days. You have been permitted, dear sister, to come to this Earth for a wise purpose. You are one of those noble spirits now tabernacled in the flesh, & when you have finished your earthly career, you, through your faithfulness, will be entitled to many great, noble and grand blessings and positions, You shall be numbered with the Queens of Israel, also with the princesses, and enjoy those grand blessings that you have so long desired.

[page 308]

Gertrude's Blessing Con[d]

Let your aspirations be high. Your natural inclination and disposition is to acquire knowledge and intelligence, that you may enjoy the highest position of womanhood. Do not despair of these noble ideas. God is able to bring about all His noble purposes, and to your great astonishment the future shall bring to you blessings that you have almost despaired of. Ask God for wisdom, take the advice and counsel of your parents, whose object is to counsel you in righteousness, Your life shall be spared on the Earth and you will live as long as you desire life; and you shall overcome the weakness of nature and the pain and afflictions that you are and have been subject to in the past. And you shall rejoice and be comforted, and feel to acknowledge the hand of God in all things. Many blessings are for you, & you shall rise up in the strength and power of God, & shall see many happy days, and when you have finished your earthly career you shall go as a shock of corn fully ripe to the garner, with a hope and bright prospect of the future. I seal these blessings upon your head, & reseal every blessing that has hither to been conferred upon you, and seal you up to come forth in the morning of the first ressurrection, clothed with glory, immortality and eternal life in the kingdom of God, with many friends and kindred, through your faithfulness, in the name of Jesus Christ, Amen.

Recorded in his book A, page 149.

Blessing by Pat[h] Alex. Jameson upon Gertrude. M. Taylor, given Aug. 20. 1904.

Sister Gertrude, by virtue and authority of the holy priesthood and in the name of Jesus Christ I lay my hands upon thy head and shall proceed to bless thee, agreeable to the mind and will of the Lord, and I seal upon thee thy former blessings that have been given thee thru the channel of the holy priesthood, & say unto thee, thou art of Ephraim, and no blessing that belongs to his posterity shalt thou be deprived of unless it be that the Lord thy God should order otherwise, but I say unto thee thy sins are forgiven thee, for thy [thou] has come up before the Lord, and thou art accepted of Him, and if thou wilt continue to hold fast to the faith & be willing in thy heart to multiply blessings unto thy husband, and falter not in faith in the Lord I say unto thee thou shalt stand with him in Holy places.

[page 309]
These blessings are given to thee as an aim & object upon which thou mayest look forth in hours of affliction in order that thy faith may not falter for thy comfort and thy blessing: and by virtue of my calling as a Patriarch, and in the name of Jesus Christ our Lord do I rebuke the powers and influences that have preyed upon your system, and command them to depart from thee, and bless thee from the crown of thy head to the soles of thy feet, that thy heart, thy stomach, thy head & blood in thy arteries and veins maybe filled with the vigors of life, and with the blessing of health, peace and contentment in thy mind, to the end that thou mayest be comforted, yea, and be made whole, These are thy blessings at this time, and I seal them upon thee and seal thee up unto eternal life, even to a part in the glorious ressurrection of our Lord, there to enjoy all that thou hast merited, forever, even so. Amen.

Blessing by Winslow Farr, given Aug. 28. 1904

Sister Gertrude M. Taylor, in the authority of the holy Melchisedek priesthood and in the name of Jesus Christ of Nazareth I place my hands upon thy head and seal a Patriarchal blessing, and desire that God our Eternal Father dictates by His Spirit the words that may be used in this blessing. Thou art a chosen vessel of the Lord, selected from the Courts of heaven, and given the privilege to choose thy parentage and dispensation to come forth on the earth, and thy Guardian Angel that was given thee at thy birth has watched over thee and for a wise purpose thy life has been preserved.

[page 310]
Thy lineage is of Joseph, through the loins of Ephraim, born a legal heir to the keys of the priesthood and the blessings of the Gospel according to thy sex; and I say unto thee, dear Sister, if thou wilt exercise faith, the blessing thou so much desire shall come to pass, even to be healed in body and mind, and become a Mother in Israel, that you might be able to answer the measure of thy creation, and bring joy to thy household. The Lord is well pleased with thy mission on the Earth, and will sanctify thy afflictions to thy good. Thy faith shall increase and thy heart made to rejoice. Thou shall have power over this disease and live to fill a good mission on the Earth. Thou shalt be blessed with exceeding faith and wisdom and understanding to comprehend the things of God. Thou shalt have power over evil influences & unclean Spirits. Thou shalt have the privilege of going into the temple of God and assist in redeeming the dead who died without the gospel. Thou shalt have visions and dreams to comfort thee. The time shall come that you shall comprehend the things you desire of the Lord, and as thy days so shall thy strength

be, for thou shalt stand as Queen to thy husband in the kingdom of God. Thou shalt be comforted, and shall receive all blessings promised. If thy faith fail not it is thy privilege to live to see Zion redeemed, in power and influence here on the Earth. I say unto thee, dear Sister, cling to the promises made unto thee, For thou shalt live as long as life shall be desirable. Thy name is written in the Lamb's Book of Life. Thou shalt stand as a Savior on Mt. Zion and wear the crown of eternal Life. I bless thee with health and strength, with power to overcome this disease and affliction, and I bless thee with the blessings of Abraham, Isaac and Jacob, with power to come forth in the morning of the first ressurrection, and say unto thee let thy faith fail not and all of these blessings shall be fulfilled on thy head. I confirm all of thy former blessings and this blessing, for I seal them upon thee in the name of Jesus Christ.

[page 311—see Appendix 5 for letter from Gertrude inserted here.]

[written in margin]

Note

When Br. Farr gave this blessing he said Pres[t] Snow said "in 50 years the Savior will be here and he will visit from house to house, just like we are now." Br. Farr says this was said by Pres[t] Snow 3 or 4 years ago. (1902—or 1901)

[written in margin]

also

That 54 years will complete the 6000 years according to the chart of the Pyramid.

May 16, 1906—Up to date Gertrude seemed to be much better & talked, laughed, curled her hair, and seemed quite well, except her weakness, which made her unable to sit up any.

But to day she seems much worse, and talks in a faint voice, and but very little during the day, with much pain in her head.

May 21, 1906—Gertrude very low. Can not bear to hear the clock lick [tick] so we stop it. She seems near to death

May 23, 1906—Somewhat better to day. Ate a few mulberries.

As an invitation from the Young Ladies Journal for Personal Recollections of the Prophet Joseph, Susan contributed her "recollections" in the following:—

MY RECOLLECTIONS OF THE PROPHET JOSEPH SMITH.

I was born in Kirtland in 1836, and as a child often saw the prophet in the Sunday meetings in the temple and also at the house of my father Joel H. Johnson, but my more distinct recollections begin about 1841, when we lived in Ramus, afterwards named Macedonia, about 20 miles from Nauvoo, where father was Presiding Elder. The Prophet frequently came to our house and sometimes stayed over night, but usually with his uncle John Smith, who was Patriarch in S. L. City up to 1854. On one occasion Joseph, with H. C. Kimball, Jedediah M. Grant and some others from Nauvoo whose names I do not now remember, partook of a Christmas dinner at my Father's; and standing at the head of the table he carved the turkey. Fearing his clothing might accidentally be soiled my step mother, Susan Bryant Johnson tied a long apron upon him.

[page 312]

May 23, 1906—He laughed and said it was well, for he did not know what might happen to him. My brother Seth and I were in the room, admiring, in our childish way, him whom we thought the greatest man on Earth.

My father was present when Joseph received the "Word of Wisdom", and testified to the day of his death, 1883, that instead of "hot drinks," the words as received were "tea and coffee," which at that time were the only "hot drinks" in common use. Also, that the change in language was on suggestion by Oliver Cowdery who said "Why not write it "Hot drinks? That will cover it." He also said Joseph afterwards regretted having allowed the change, as it led to controversy even in his day.

The revelation given in Sec. 131 Doc. & Cov. was given in my father's house in Ramus, when Joseph came, to preach next day.

It was in Ramus that Joseph taught my father and grandmother, Julia Hills Johnson the principle of plural marriage, both of whom accepted it; and Joseph sealed my grandmother to his uncle, John Smith, afterwards Patriarch. She was sealed as his second wife for eternity. The Prophet married my Aunt Almera Johnson as a plural wife with my father's consent, to my certain knowledge, living as such until his martyrdom. She died a few years ago in Parowan, Iron Co. Utah, and was proud of her union with him.

May 24, 1906—Visited and blessed three sick children.

[written in margin]

Anna's baby born

May 25, 1906—At 12.30 A.M. Anna's boy baby was born, in severe labor he weighed 9½ lbs. and is a fine well-developed child. Se is getting along all right. Susan was with her.

May 26, 1906—I was left thus with Gertrude, who suddenly collapsed and at 2 A.M. had a collapse, and thought she was dying I thought so too, and sent for Guy's wife Minna. She and his wife Lilly remained all night, doing all we knew how and she gradually improved a little. Guy also came.

[page 313]

May 26, 1906—Picked the last of our early cherries. Others are just beginning to ripen. We also have ripe mulberries.

I blessed my Grandson, George, Albert's Son, as he is about to go to Temosachic, to obtain employment.

May 29, 1906—Gertrude is much better, and does up her hair, and has sung a little. She has wonderful faith still.

JUNE 1906.

June 4, 1906—Gertrude had a fit at 10.30 P.M., another next day at 6.20 P.M. with two other light ones.

June 6, 1906—Emma came to see how much Albert owes me. We found the amount due, on June 12th next to be $262.97 [$5,690] bearing 10 o/c [percent] interest pr annum.

June 7, 1906—Today and at night Gertrude had 8 fits, most of them light ones. In the morning she said she heard singing not of Earth, and said to her mother "Cant you hear it, I hear it plainly."

June 8, 1906—She had a bad fit, and 4 others at various hours.

June 9, 1906—She had a light attack at 11 A.M.

June 10, 1906—She was very bright and cheerful this morning and all day until 6 P.M. when she suddenly felt like death, and wanted Guy, Minna and Lilly sent for, thinking she was dying. They all came. We were with her all night. She said, "I want to kiss you all while I can." Her pulse almost ceased, and she wanted us to dedicate her so she might be released. We did so. Then she rested, and seemed to sleep till morning.

June 11, 1906—Very weak this morning, but seemingly better.

June 13, 1906—Began picking Apricots, and sell them at 8 cts per kilo, (kilo = 2 ½ lbs)

Lyman writes me he has engaged a Mr. Stewart to go to the Uintah Survey, and remedy an incorrect closing Corner, which will save me considerable expense, by not having to go myself from Mexico, to do the work.

June 14, 1906—Went to home of John W. Taylor, and blessed his wife Rhoda. She sent her carriage to bring Susan & me, also sent us home in the same way. She had also present Sister Saville and daughter, and Prest J. E. Robinson and wife.

[page 314]

June 14, 1906—He is President of the California Mission. We had a pleasant time.

June 15, 1906—Gertrude said that last Sunday, when she sank away, a feeling like death came upon her, unlike anything she ever felt before, and some one told her she must die. It seemed horrible to her, but after she had prayed a long time all dread ceased, and she felt at peace. She could see her body lying on the bed, dead, and had a glimpse of heaven, and Saw Dora and others of our dead.

It was on that morning she heard the Singing. She says a change for her is coming, and is willing for any.

June 15 & 16, 1906—Quarterly Conference. Apostles Teasdale & Clawson were present. Susan went on the second day by the kindness of the sisters J W Taylor, who gave us use of their carriage, and took us to their home for dinner.

June 19, 1906—Gertrude had a bad fit at 9.40 P.M. Guy and Minna went to El Paso yesterday

June 20, 1906—She Seems passing away.

June 25, 1906—She had a fit 1 A.M. Very weak all day.

I went to Heber F. Johnson's and gave Blessings to him and four of his family. At 10 P.M. G had another fit, also several light ones.

June 26, 1906—She had two, 6.20 P.M. and 10.30 P.M.

June 27, 1906—She had 8 fits from 1 A.M. until 10.40 P.M.

June 28, 1906—She had one at 5 A.M, 9 A.M. and 11 P.M.

June 29, 1906—She had one at 12.30. She gave me names for temple work for Alex. von Wenden, our friend, whose sweetheart Margaret Leavitt, a Scotch girl whom he loved when he was in Scotland at age of 20, died of a broken heart, because his parents forbade their marriage. Gertrude wants Margaret to be Sealed to von Wenden.

We obtained these data by a remarkable way. A young woman, Isabel Fowler, came from Ireland with Frank Stowell, whose Mother was Margaret's aunt Barbara Leavitt by name. She told Gertrude how her cousin Margaret Leavitt had loved a young Russian Nobleman, but whose father prevented their marriage, and she died of grief.

[page 315]

June 29, 1906—And we found she was the same girl von Wenden had told us of. It seems brought about by the Lord.

Gertrude still very weak.

June 30, 1906—Gertrude Another sinking spell at about noon. She said "Do plead with the Lord for my release. I can't endure it." Guy and I did so, praying God to release her. She then lay for hours as if asleep, but was not really so.

JULY 1906.

July 1, 1906—To day Apostle Teasdale blessed Anna's baby with the name Aubrey Franklin Turley, and said he was much impressed to give him a great blessing, as he did.

Gertrude rallied some in the night, but is very weak.

July 2, 1906—I was taken suddenly with cholera morbus.[20] I continued so, in bed on 3d and 4th Rainy Season began with heavy rain all night.

We have found, from a Miss Isabel Fowler, the name of the girl the Baron Alex. Von Wenden loved and wished to marry, but was prevented by his parents. She was the cousin of Miss Fowler, her name Margaret Leavitt, age about 17 or 18, lived in Kirkaldy, near Edinburg, Scotland. She died of a broken heart. I wish to have her united with the Baron, her lover, in the holy order of marriage. It seems as if our meeting with Miss Fowler, lately from G. Britain, was ordained by the Lord that the union may be brought about.

Wednesday, July 11, 1906—Susan's 70th Birth day. Had a nice dinner, with Anna, Edward Turley and Ida, Emma, Albert's wife. I thank thee Oh Father, she is preserved to me thus long, a blessing and comfort to all who know her, filled with faith and beloved of the Lord.

Gertrude had a fit at 3.15 P.M. the first in 13 days. Up to this time she had seemed very bright and cheerful. For several days after, she was very low and weak.

[page 316]

July 15, 1906—Emma paid me $265.00 [$5,734] which Albert has been owing so long, for my cattle sold him.

July 20, 1906—Albert came home from Sonora, where he has been grading on a railroad several months.

Gertie had a light fit, on 16th Also 1 at 10 P.M. to day

July 21, 1906—Gertie had a light fit 5 A.M., 9.30 P.M. and 3.20 P.M.

July 22 & 23, 1906—Slight fits 10 P.M. 23d fits 2.45 A.M. 10.45 A.M. 11.20 A.M. 1.15 P.M. 3.30 PM. 5.30 P.M. 6.35 P.M. 11.0 P.M.

July 24, 1906—fit 5.0 A.M. Recd [sum] from Colthorp & Co $378.46 [$8189] per F. G. Luke Collector for Merchants Protective Assn I wrote him I am unable to pay till Govt pays me.

Susan and I visited Alberts. Gertrude. F. at 6.30 P.M

July 31, 1906—Blessed Helen M. Clark

AUGUST 1906

August 1, 1906—I was suddenly attacked with inflam.y rheumatism.

August 6, 1906—I Able to sit up a little to day.

20 Cholera morbus is acute gastroenteritis.

Rec[d] statement from Co-op. Mercantile Ist. thus:—

"May 1st 1903	By E. Turley	{	$ 110.00
Oct. 1st	($1048.00)		938.00
Dec. 15 1904	Dividend	$ 47.16	
April 1 "	"	120.49	167.65
Total Capital Stock			$ 1215.65 [$26,305]

August 8, 1906—Gertie fit 9. P.M. Sent letter to F. G. Luke. Wrote Lyman. Sur. Gen[l] tells me all my survey accepted but 2 P P S. Wrote to Afton Young, to be Endowed for Margaret Leavitt.

August 9, 1906—Gertie F. 5 A.M. 10.00 P.M. Sent Express receipt to Lyman for my chain and pins

August 10, 11, 12, 1906—Gertrude a fit each day.

August 13, 1906—Gertrude 3 fits to day 14th 2 fits

August 22, 1906—Gertrude fit 6 P.M. 23[d] 24th & 25th a fit each day

August 25, 1906—I sent draft $1.25 [$27] for Ladies Home Journal. Bt [bought] Bedstead & M.[mattress]

August 30, 1906—Received the following letter from a sister who had been confined in bed two years and given up to die three times, with nervous prostration. I had visited and blessed her many times, having testimony she could be healed. She said I was the first and only one who had ever promised she should be healed.

[page 317]

1906—It is a sample of others from my "patients" in the City (Salt Lake) whom I had administered to, and whom the Lord had healed; some of deadly tumors others of deadly disease when the doctors said they must surely die, or have an operation in the hospital,—many marvelous healings of paralysis and kidney diseases, goitre Etc.

I insert this to show how my labors there, in visiting the sick were appreciated:—

Salt Lake City Aug. 18. 1906

Dear Brother Martineau

Not another day shall pass till I write you a note. I have been thinking of you all day and for several days. Your teachings and counsels came to me every day, and the promises Our Father made me through you. I am so very thankful to you for the faith & hope & patience you instilled into me. I am getting better just as you said I would, and can again walk around the house and look after my children a little. They are glad that I can eat at the table with them, and ride, and I can also go to Sunday School, and have been to meeting several times. I am so thankful for these blessings, dear Father Martineau, for I look upon you as a Father. What could I have done without you some days! I cannot tell how just and merciful is our Heavenly Father. He alone knows what his children need, at least this is so in my case. I have not stopped wavering yet, but I sleep pretty well and can often sleep in the day time. I wish you lived near. I would enjoy having you come and talk to me on those sacred principles. It seems people have so little time for such things here. We would so love to hear from you. I will take this letter to your son's wife and get your address. You have my faith and prayers, as also your dear wife. I shall never forget how you expressed your love for her. Br. Martineau accept my thanks and the gratitude of my heart For your kindness and care over me. x x I was very much disappointed at not seeing you before you left, and not seeing you again.

With kind love Julia S. Woolley
1169 S., 3[d] East S. L. City. Utah"

[page 318]

August 30, 1906—I take no credit for my ministrations, as I only had power as God in his mercy to the sick made manifest through me,—a privilege, which to me is of inestimable worth For very many years my greatest desire has been for power to do great good to all who will receive it. And the only office in the Priesthood I have desired was that of Patriarch, which would give me power to seal blessings upon others.

SEPTEMBER 1906

September 3, 1906—Paid Tannery Comp[y] $21.78 [$471] for Capital Stock, which makes our interest in the business $200.[00] [$4,328].

September 6, 1906—Today Guy Taylor moved Gertrude to his house She stood the change very well in her wheel reclining Chair. To her mother and me the change was a sad one, For she has lived at home with us all her life.

[written in margin]

Alone again, we two

Now, after about (or over) 54 years of married life, Susan and I are alone again,—just us two. For years our family increased until in Logan we ate at a long table—18 of us. Then as children married and left the family hive we decreased until now we are but two again. I hope the time may never come when there shall be but One. Far better for both to pass away together. We have become so necessary to each other that for either to be left alone would be dreadful.

Anna's little boy Freddy is still very sick with a hot fever,—now about two weeks.

By letter from Lyman I learn my last corrective work is finished. Glad

[page 319]

September 10, 1906—My left leg is still lame with rheumatism, and feels cold, numb and lifeless, which seems to me to threaten paralysis, but I hope not, as I am promised renewed health and strength, and that I shall labor in the temple to be built in Zion.

Phyllis, Anna's eldest daughter, comes to stay at night, and to help Susan.

September 26, 1906—To this date we have been very busy drying fruit, & selling some, at 3¢ per pound. Agreed to let Gruel have my apples at 6¢ per pound.

September 29, 1906—Sat. Left home for S. L. City, and to finish up my Survey business. Started 2.30 A.M. by mail wagon. Reach the Sierra Madre R. R. at Nueva Casas Grandes at Sunrise and reach Ciudad Juarez and El Paso at 3 P.M. Got my ticket to the city, via California, (return ticket) $43.05 [$996]. Sleeper to Colton $5.00 [$108]. Too tired to go on tonight and stayed in El Paso.

September 30, 1906—Sunday. Start 8.45 A.M. Colton, Cal. next day.

October 1, 1906—Monday 11.15 A.M. 2 hrs. late 884 miles. Found 2 women of our party stranded at Colton,—lost their train and did not know what to do, never having traveled, and but little money, I let my train go on and remained to help them through. We had hot weather here, 108° in shade. Left Colton at midnight.

October 2, 1906—Tues. Summit of mountains 2 A.M. at 8.30, Haydn, Cal. Caliente 6.20 P.M.

October 3, 1906—Arr[d] in S. L. City 7.10 A.M. Very cold—40°—Found Lyman's family and Virginia's well. Met Charles also.

October 5, 1906—At 5.30 A.M. My Great-gr. dau. Ruth Crismon, dau. of Ollie, Lyman's eldest dau, was born, but lived only 4 hours. Was delayed 2 weeks in birth, and lacked vitality. Allie was dangerously ill in confinement.

I visited two of my "patients," Julia S. Woolley and Fanny Blair Stringham, and blessed both. They are getting well.

Little Ruth's funeral was at 12.30 P.M.

October 6, 1906—Visited several "patients," as I call them, persons sick, and blessed them. I thought this was better than going to church. One, Sister Driggs, who had been in so desperate and hopeless condition when I blessed her last April, when the doctor said she must die in her approaching confinement, or her child must be taken instrumentally, and that, if she lived, after She would be a helpless invalid all her life, but whom I had blessed, saying she should go her full time, be blessed in her confinement, and her son should be a child of promise and she become healthy and well, even as in your young day

[page 320]

October, 1906—I found her well and strong, her babe a Son, as promised, whom they had named Arthur Martineau Drigs [Driggs], a large 12 lb. boy. Thus was fulfilled, exactly, a promise given by inspiration of the Comforter, but which seemed at the time almost presumptuous. To Our Father be all the honor.

By all who knew the circumstances, it was called an absolute miracle. I had been shown to her in dream before she had ever seen me, as one who would heal her, and this gave her faith when I blessed her, and me, also.

October 10, 1906—In Temple to day. Afterwards visited and blessed Sis. Gorringe, nearly a lunatic, who became quiet. Then to Eve Winberg, who is about to undergo an operation in the hospital which she dreads. Blessed and Comforted her and her mother. Gave P.

blessing to Br. Dixon and wife, who live about 7 miles from "home," as I style Lyman's while I am with him and Alley.

October 11, 1906—Blessed Sis Driggs for a special purpose. Met F. A. Mitchell and agree to go to Cache Valley and make a Survey for him.

October 12, 1906—Visited and blessed J. S. Woolley, who is still improving. Lives in the country, near Waterloo. Weather very cold & cloudy.

Spent 13th and 14th in visiting and blessing the sick.

October 15, 1906—Went to Logan and began Survey for Mitchell. Cold

October 16, 1906—Surveyed line over high, rugged hills. Very cold & windy.

October 17, 1906—Too stormy to work. Paid some debts and wrote letters. Next day Nephi came to see me. Still very cold to 19th

October 20, 1906—Snow 4 ins. deep in morning, and snowing all day. I am staying in Logan with Lilla (Nebeker) who is very good to me. She is still badly affected in speech and hearing.

October 29, 1906—Return to S. L. City. Found letter from Land office. Part of my Survey allowed to amount of $2316.43 [$50,124] and am't disallowed $186.89 [$4,044] from account sent by Sur. Gen[l] of Utah. It should have not been disallowed by the clerks in Washington.

[page 321]

October 31, 1906—Paid ~~Budge~~ Gowans $10.[00] [$216] also S. L. Herald $1.[05] [$23] in full.

Blessed Zina Bull and Jenny Hill, also went, as sent for to bless Nelly Nicholson, said to be dying of quick consumption. She is 24 yrs. of age, has cough and bad bleeding of the lungs, also great pain her lungs. All say she cannot live much longer. I asked a testimony, and was told she could be healed by administration. I told her she could be, and she said she believed. I blessed her with that promise, and she at once felt better, both in lungs and mind—was actually happy. So was I.

November 1, 1906—In temple, End[d] Ed[d] Wells. Sister Watson, a temple worker, took me in afternoon, to see and bless a sad case,—Lillie Anderson, who has for weeks wished for me. She seems melancholy—mad, almost, Deserted by her husband, poor and ill. I did all I could for her, but with little effect. Also went to and bl[d] Nelly Nicholson, who is better, pain less, bleeding less.

November 2, 1906—I end[d] Sylvander Hutchinson. Dyar LeBaron end[d] Joseph Hutchinson: Rich[d] S. Horne end[d] Benjamin Hutchinson.

I visited and blessed Nelly and Lilly. Gave patriarchal blessing to Nelly Nicholson and to Grant M. Weiler.

November 3, 1906—Visited and blessed Nelly N. who is improving daily. Then to Eve Winberg, who has returned from hospital. Said my blessing had been literally fulfilled. She is rapidly recovering. She and Nelly live about 6 miles from Lyman's, and I have to walk several miles, in visiting my "patients," who sometimes do not live on a Car line. I get tired, my lame leg causing me to limp. It feels lifeless below the knee, and sometimes I fall suddenly as my knee gives out without warning.

November 4, 1906—Sun. Visited and bl. Nelly N. Went to Gean's, visited and blessed Lilly Anderson, but she will not cease to yield to evil spirits, though she says she knows she ought to do so. They tell her to do wrong, and not to do right, and she yields. I cannot do her any good while she yields to such powers.

November 5, 1906—Went to Fanny Wessman and blessed her. She is recovering from typhoid fever. She and her mother have endowed 20 femals [females] for me. May Our Father ever bless them. Visited and blessed Nelly, who is better day by day and is getting well. Bleding [bleeding] only once or twice a day and pain in lungs almost ceased. Thanks to Our Father

[page 322]

November 5, 1906—Was caught in a heavy cold sleety rain at Wessman's over Jordan, and nearly fell, several times, in the mud.

November 6, 1906—Election day. Republicans win. Visited and blessed Nelly, Lilly, Eve, Hazel White and Sister Coulam, miles separated. Walking snowy, muddy, and slippery.

November 7, 1906—Took my last Survey notes to the office. Bl. [blessed] Nelly Ann Coulam. Visited Sister Ash by request. It was a Surprise party in my honor. My leg still weak. Fell down on way home.

November 8, 1906—Signed my last Survey notes in Office. Adm[d] to Nelly W. also to ~~Ann~~ Mary Wickel, who fears miscarriage.

November 9, 1906—Was invited to visit Sisters Bull, white and hill—close friends—at Sister Bull's home. Instead, I found it was a surprise party for me, the house full of ladies, mostly temple workers and friends of mine, with several of high standing whom I had not known before. It was given as a parting testimony of regard for me, in view of my soon return to Mexico. A nice lunch, pleasant time. A small parcel was given me, instructed not to open till I got home. It contained $10.[00] [$216] given by various ones. I felt unworthy so much honor. Four of Pres[t] B. Young's daughters were there, also Sis. McCune, Julia Smith and Dougall. Patriarch Lawson also there. I had to go before over, to visit and bless Nelly N. and to be at a Relief Society entertainment to which I was invited in Emerson Ward 5 miles away, which I reached at 8.30 P.M. Home about 11 P.M. Somewhat tired, having walked several miles, with nearly 10 miles street Car.

November 10, 1906—In temple a little while to bid good bye to many there. Visited and blessed Sisters Kimball, Barker, Sharp, Hazel White, and Lydia White, 3 to 5 miles separate necessitating much walking, but warmly greeted, as I always am, and blessed myself always in blessing others.

November 11, 1906—Went to Elgren's in 2[d] Ward, and gave Pat[l] Blessings to A. W. Morrison, Martha Elggren and D. F. Wissman.

Next to Br. Saniger, 3 miles distant, and gave P. blessings to his Children L. M. Saniger and Violet Saniger. Then to see Nellie Nicholson, who says she is now well. I gave her a parting blessing.

[page 323]

November 11, 1906—Then to 2[d] Ward and adm[d] to Hazel White, Urania White, and Lewis Elggren. So I have had a busy day. But I am sent for, for miles around, & have to spend dollars for Car fare, besides much walking.

Monday, November 12, 1906—Adm[d] to Nelly once more, because of sudden change in weather for heavy snow storm. Also adm[d] to Urania White and Mary Wickens, 5 miles apart.

Tuesday, November 13, 1906—Bl[d] Fanny B. Stringham, who had me go with her 6 miles to adm. to her daughter, Mrs. Mainwaring, who is in danger of miscarriage. Gave patriarchal blessing to Fanny. Thence to Geans 4 miles away, and stayed all night. Cold storm.

November 14, 1906—Wed. Bld. [blessed] Nelly Nicholson once more. Gave P. [Patriarchal] blessing to C. Eden Richards her nurse

November 15, 1906—End[d] Nathaniel Hutchinson. Mrs. Wessman End [Endowed] Mary Hutchinson. Sealed Margaret Leavitt and Alex. Von Wenden to each other, I proxy for him, Afton Young proxy for her. I am very glad.

This was brought about, I believe, by the power of God, and in a wonderful manner. In 1895 the Russian Baron Alex. Von Wenden, who boarded for a time with us told of his visiting Scotland when he was twenty years old, & there fell in love with a Scotch girl—Maggie, he called her, but never gave her full name—and would have married her; but his father hearing of it came from Riga, Russia, and took him home, unwilling for him to marry one not of noble blood. He often spoke of her with sorrow for his blighted love. He died in 1897.

In 1901 a girl came from Ireland, a new convert—named Isabel Fowler—came direct to Colonia Juarez, our home, and related that a cousin of hers, Margaret Leavitt, of Leith, near Edinburg, met there a young Russian nobleman who fell in love with Maggie, & would have married her, but his father came and took him from her, and she pined away and died of a broken heart. We found she was the girl von Wenden had spoken of. Miss Fowler remained with us only a short time, went to Utah, and we never heard of her after. The Lord sent her to us, who of all, were the only ones who knew von Wenden's story—and she gave all data needful to complete the story—then departed.

[page 324]

November 15, 1906—By E. Guy Taylor, my son-in-law, von Wenden was endowed Oct. 4. 1897 in S. Lake temple. On Sept. 11. 1906 Margaret Leavit was endowed by Miss Afton Young, on Nov. 15th they were sealed in marriage. Thus was finally finished a love story, giving us all very great joy.

Since then I have had testimony that both he and she accepted with joy what we had done for them.

I endowed Nathaniel Hutchinson 1518. Mrs. Wessman End[d] Mrs. Jane Taylor

Visited and blessed Maria Y. Dougal & dau. Clarissa who were both much pleased. Heavy rain Storms began at eve.

November 16, 1906—I end[d] Bartholomew Hutchinson. Snowy today. Visited Nelly Nicholson to see if Storm made her worse. It did not.

Saturday, November 17, 1906—Snowed all night and till 10 A.M. 7 [in] deep

Sunday, November 18, 1906—Blessed Violet and Lona Saniger (Patriarchal) Went to see Nelly Nicholson. She says she is fully healed, but weak yet.

November 19, 1906—Visited and blessed Virginia Zina Bull. She blessed me.

November 20, 1906—Visited and blessed Jenny Hill also went to Sis. Julia Woolley and blessed her, farewell.

Wednesday, November 22, 1906—Went to Temple and got my temple clothes. Bid good bye to many. Sis. Dougall bl. [blessed] me and I her. Bl. Nelly. Got some things for Susan. Also Pullman car ticket $5.50 [$119]. Spent some time with Gean. Got temple record from Afton Young. For 21 names she endowed for me.

November 24, 1906—Got my return ticket via San Pedro R. R. 43.05 to El Paso Blessed Mary A. H. White. In afternoon Bp. W. B. Preston and Wife, Ed[d] Sudbury & Gean, Gowans & Harriet, Crismon and Allie met at Lyman's who is absent in Star Valley, Wyo. as a farewell to me. Dined at 7 P.M. & then went to trains.

Sunday, November 25, 1906—Left city at 3 A.M, 5 hrs. behind time. Awoke near Milford. Snow all the way, 130 miles

Monday, November 26, 1906—Arrived at Colton, 58 m. east of Los Angeles & took SPRR train at 3 P.M.

Tuesday, November 27, 1906—Arrive El Paso 3.15 P.M.

Wednesday, November 28, 1906—Arrive home 4 P.M. Found all well as usual. "There's no place like home, be it every so humble.

[written in margin]

Nephi's baby boy

I learn Nephi's baby boy was born Nov. 20

[page 325]

November 28, 1906—I learn that Theodore & Josephine's girl baby was born & died Oct. 13. 1906. Her name given was Mary Ellen Martineau. It was a difficult birth, but the mother lived,—a blessing.

November 29, 1906—Thanksgiving day. We had a family dinner, with Anna and her children, and Emma and hers. A pleasant time. It was sad our dear Gertrude, still confined to her bed, cannot be with us. But we sent her some of our dinner. She seems stronger than when I went to the City.

December 31, 1906—Sat as a High Councilor in a case to day. Settled tithing amounting to $75.48 [$1,633]. I have not yet received my Survey money from the Gov[t] hence my tithing account is Small. But was in full, as I always pay, year by year.

Since my home coming nothing beyond usual home matters has occupied my attention. I have administered to the sick around me, and given some Patriarchal blessings. and spent some time examining my survey maps, of my Mexican work. For one thing especially I feel thankful—that Our Father has so greatly blessed me during the past year in my ministrations among the Sick, and for the dead, a work for which I would exchange uncounted gold. Gold is fleeting—the work I have done is for an eternity, and eternal.

JANUARY 1907.

January 1, 1907—Had a nice family dinner to day.

Lyman's daughter Harriet's child was born, I believe, Jan. 2[d]

January 8, 1907—Our 55th wedding day. When a young man I believed that I would never reach the age of fifty,—felt sure of it—and I have instead reached my 55th wedding anniversary, through the special blessing of the Lord, whose angel saved my life in the Uintah Mountains while on my Survey, when my horse fell with me on his back down the steep rocky side of the mountain. Nothing but the special power of God saved my life, and in a miraculous manner. We had a nice dinner again, and Anna and Emma gave us presents.

In December last I sold my land in Chuichupa to Henry, for $875.[00] [$18,934] payable in two years,

Interest 10 o/c [percent] from date. There was 92 ½ acres farm land and a vacant city lot. I sold cheaper to him than I would to others not of the family.

[page 326]

January 8, 1907—The sale was made Dec. 18. 1906. The land was worth full $1000[00] [$21,639] but I am too infirm to handle it.

55 years ago I stood alone. Now head of a family of about 150, including 100 grandchildren and 14 Gr-Gr. Chil[n] Truly has God blessed us, tho both of us are quite infirm. I having not yet recovered the full use of my left leg, from the rheumatism of last Summer. But we might be much worse—sick, perhaps.

January 15, 1907—Leveled for a canal in the Canyon for Pres[t] Ivins. Very tired, walking so much among rocks and sand.

January 16, 1907—Leveled another canal for him in our town.

January 17, 1907—Made estimates of cubic yds. in proposed canal.

January 18, 1907—finished estimates. & received $21.[00] Mex.

FEBRUARY 1907.

Sunday, February 3, 1907—To date have spent much time revising my maps.

Sunday, February 12, 1907—Received word from Sur. Gen[l] Hull my survey contract is approved in full. Approved Jan. 8. 1907.

February 16, 1907—Letter from Lyman, says he has rec[d] a draft from Govt. on my Survey, for $2334.50 [$50,515], and has paid my bank a/c of $1119.[00] [$24,214] which has long been drawing interest

February 23, 1907—Had telephone put in to day. Costs $1.50 [$32.46] per month Susan and [I] both sick with Lagrippe.

March 4, 1907—Just able to be about, but must go to El Paso to file papers. Stayed all night with Jo[s] Cardon, in Dublan. Blessed his wife, who fears cancer near the eye and nose.

March 5, 1907—Reached El Paso late in afternoon, Very tired.

March 6, 1907—Finished my business. Met Mr. Boyd. who wishes me to do some surveying for him at Carretas Hacienda.

March 8, 1907—Start home. Stop off at Dublan to attend Quar. Conference.

March 9 & 10, 1907—Conference in Dublan. Aposte H. J. Grant present. Very good Visited and blessed Sister Josephine M[c]M. Hilton who is very low.

March 11, 1907—Got home late to day. Found letter from Lyman, which causes me to return at once to El Paso. Must start 2.30 A.M, so I did not take any sleep, but started out, in cold night for Station.

March 12, 1907—Reached Nueva Casas Grandes before sun rise. Soon took train and reached El Paso about 5.0 P.M. nearly worn out with 2 days and one night, without sleep and almost constant travel.

[page 327—see Appendix 5 for letter from Lyman to his father inserted here.]

March, 1907—Fixed up my business same evening, very tired. Met Albert in Cuidad Juarez, on his way home from Sonora, where he is working on the new railway along the Pacific Coast. Emma, his wife, went there to meet him with me.

March 15, 1907—Reached home again. No place like home.

March 19, 1907—Got letters from Lyman and Allie, Gean, ~~Niece~~ Gr. daugher [daughter] Susan Martineau (Nephi's dau) and son Theodore, Congratulating me on my 79th birthday, which occurred while I was in El Paso. All were full of love and good wishes.

Up to this time I have visited among the sick & administered to them, and have spent much time in working on maps of Surveys I have made here, to correct any possible errors. So that who may come after me as a Surveyor here may find nothing to my discredit as an Engineer.

March 27, 1907—On the 5th inst. I went to El Paso to file pension papers and again, about a week after, on Survey business, and there met Albert, just on his way home on a visit from Sonora.

Today I bought Some fruit trees, to replace those killed this winter by the cold snap. Up to this time I have ministered to the sick and have worked on the new maps of my Surveys here I am making for the Colonization Company. Gertrude is much better, and I believe she will yet recover. If so, it will indeed be a veritable miracle to all who have known her. She is now able to go out short distances in her invalid chair.

APRIL 1907.

April 1, 1907—Have been awake all night. Insomnia. I lately got a letter from Sister J. S. Woolley, S. L. City, telling how wonderfully God has fulfilled to her the promises I made in blessing her, and her unbounded Joy for it. It gives me great joy also, showing I have been led by the Holy Spirit in my ministrations as a Patriarch, God has been wonderfully good to me

April 23, 1907—Obliged to go to El Paso again on my Pension business. and on Sunday 28 attended meeting in private house in Ciudad Juarez. Spoke and felt well. Blessed Lulu Johnson, dau. of Coz. W. D. Johnson, of Diaz.

[page 328]

May 5, 1903 [1907]—Got home again, and found all about as usual. Soon after getting home I became very lame, all through back and legs, continuing so about two weeks.

May 27, 1907—Made mining survey for J. C. Peterson.

June 6, 1907—Start to Col[a] Diaz, to Conference, to camp out on way

June 7, 1907—Arrive 4.30 P.M. Spent two following days in Confern [Conference] Blessed (Patriarchally) eight persons, who gave me $3.[00] [$65] in all, arrived home, camping on Casas Grandes river Cold night. I stood the whole trip very well, although on leaving home I could hardly climb into the wagon.

June 18, 1907—Received a letter from Young Woman's Journal asking me to become a contributor, per Ann M. Cannon Editor

JULY 1907

July 11, 1907—To day a number of relatives and friends came as a Surprise party in honor of my dear Susan's 71st birth day. She is certainly worthy. Born in Kirtland, tried in all the Church tribulations to this date, she has always been true to Mormonism, a great blessing & help to me. May she see many more birth days.

AUGUST 1907.

August 1, 1907—Quite ill with a flux, which is prevalent now.

August 15, 1907—Sent articles to Y. W. Journal. Poem "Boyhood's Days" and "A Sunday dance."

August 28, 1907—Received word that Joel's baby girl, born Aug. 28th /07 died in birth. She was named Ruth. Joel and his family are in Madera, a new mountain town. He is superintending 30 carpenters working for the Green-Silver Co. at that place. Annie, his wife, nearly died.

Up to this date I have done considerable mapping for the Colonization Comp. [Company] A.W. Ivins, Manager, and have done much administering to sick and injured, some whose condition seemed hopeless. But by the mercy and goodness of the Lord they recovered. One was Sister Charles Whipple, thrown to the ground in a run away, her spine so injured her least move caused exquisite pain. Through faith and prayer she was healed. I have visited the sick when myself hardly able to walk, but always was blest in doing so.

[page 329]

September 21, 1907—Heard the sad news of my son's wife, Allie Preston Martineau, who expired on 13th almost instantly, from something affecting her head. I here insert a letter received since from Lyman. (Insert below extracts from his letter.)

She was loved by all who knew her, and those who knew her best loved her most. She blessed the poor and did more good, unostatiously, than many who attain 80 or 90 years.[21]

September 24, 1907—Went to El Paso, on pension business. Regulated my barometer by the U. S. weather office. Returned 27th.

Found letter from Y. W. Journal, enclosing $3.00 [$65] and a letter expressing pleasure from my articles sent for publication relating to early scenes in settlement of Utah, privations, troubles with indians, etc.

Extracts from Lyman's letter of Sept. 21st 1907

x x "Just returned from Logan where we laid her (Allie) away in my family plot by the side of our two little girls. Oh! how I mourn! Oh what anguish of

21 "Mrs. Martineau Is Stricken," *Ogden Standard Examiner*, September 20, 1907; Utah Digital Newspapers.

Soul her loss has brought to us all. Words of course utterly fail me. I am crushed, I am undone utterly. x x x She died Sunday* morning at half past 7 o'clock, of the breaking of a blood vessel in her brain.

[written in margin]

**(Note 15th)*

You must know that for a number of days we had been arranging for Allie and Kenneth to go to Philadelphia on the 15th at noon, where Kenneth was to enter Jefferson Med[l] College, Also, that Royal was to go East for his 3[d] year in Harvard on the 19th inst. x x x On Friday the 13th we dined with May and Oscar Moyle. On Saturday evening some of the family were up to see us & stayed till 9 o'clock. Alley was feeling more cheerful than usual, altho all day Saturday I was much distressed in mind without knowing why. I went home early but felt awfully bad. x x x Alley awoke at 6.30 on Sunday and spoke to me. I arose and went down stairs to make a fire telling her not to hurry, but she soon got up and came down stairs and began to prepare breakfast. I staid 15 or 20 minutes with her, and Royal and Martha came in the room as I was excusing myself to go up stairs to take my morning cold bath. I turned the cold water on but before I undressed I was startled by Martha calling me to hurry to her mother who "was fainting."

[page 330]

1907—I was at her side in less than two minutes, but too late to hear her last words to Royal as she sank in his arms "Oh Royal." We thrust her feet in hot water, gave her some whiskey, prayed for her and phoned for the doctor all at once, almost, for Allie came to our rescue also. But all was of no avail. She expired without regaining consciousness She did not expect it I am sure, nor did she suffer more than one or two seconds. The doctors Richard, Stephen, & Gill soon came but said nothing could have saved her. Oh, dear Father, how I thought of you and wished you were here! I seemed to be utterly alone, lost! To lose my darling, my companion of 25 years! She and I had spent a happy life together. We were mated and loved each other devotedly, as you and Aunt Susan and all know. What to do seems a harrowing uncertainty. I shall have to have time and the Lord's help to heal the wounds, and the scar can never be effaced. I think Will's sudden death on Aug. 13th caused her so much grief that it finally took her away. Now if I can only live to be worthy of her hereafter I shall be so thankful. x x x

Praying God to bless you all. Your loving son L. R. Martineau.

October 1, 1907—Took observations on Polaris and find Var. of needle is 11° 54' E.

Wrote to Pres[t] J. R. Winder to see if he approves of sending names to the Temple, to be worked for there by temple workers. Received answer approving, also blanks for names.

October 2, 1907—Wrote to Cyril Martineau to see if we are kindred.

October 3, 1907—Rec[d] complimentary letter from Young Woman's Journal and a check for \$3.[00] [\$65], which last was unexpected by me.

August 25, 1907—Susan was suddenly taken with bleeding at the nose in a stream and it took two hours to entirely stop it. She lost fully 2 pints of blood, and was very faint and weak

I learn by letter that Harriet's baby girl Allie Martineau Gowans was born May 12. 1907.

October 8, 1907—Sent a genealogical article to Deseret News

October 21, 1907—Albert came home from his R. R. work in Sonora for a visit and to pay for his house and lot here.

[page 331—see Appendix 5 for letters from the *Young Woman Journal* editor inserted here.]

October 9, 1907—Old Folks reunion. A pleasant time and nice dinner, Susan was the only one who had ever been in Kirtland, and but a few who had ever seen Joseph the Seer or Nauvoo. The Pioneers and veterans are rapidly passing away.

November 12, 1907—Received answer to my letter to Cyril E. Martineau and a beautifully gotten up Genealogical record, dating back in unbroken line to the year 1450, when Romain Martineau Seigneur or Sieur de Romas, in middle age was one of the court of King Charles 7th of France and of Louis 11th, and in the time of Jeanne D Arc. He was of the ancient nobility. This record gives unbroken line of descent for me from 1450 to the present date, giving me knowledge of seven generations antedating my former records, and supplying the one name that was needful to make the connection complete.

This name was Francis Martineau, living in 1700, who with his Father Denis Martineau came to America from Holland, Amsterdam, to which place he fled in the persecutions of the huguenots in 1685–1690. No words can express my joy for this record, compiled by David Martineau, who is one year older than I, and was assisted by a noted French Genealogist in his researches in France.

I regard the coming of this record as a miracle, for I had no knowledge either of Cyril or David. I simply saw the name—Mrs. Cyril E. Martineau, as the name of a lady guest in a Woman's Club in New York City, and wrote on a mere chance that she would get my letter, as I knew not her address, but directed to her in New York City or New Jersey. She sent my letter to London and instantly the volume was sent me, with nearly or fully a thousand names. Thus Our Father opens the way for the redemption of the dead, and to Him be all the honor and glory. The address of him in London is

"David Martineau Esq. No. 122 King's Avenue. Clapham Park, London S. W. England.

November 22, 1907—About midnight Susan awoke struggling for breath and for over an hour I was struggling for: she in her agony was fighting for breath,—I praying for her. I was alone, could not go for help nor call any one. It was either congestion of the Lungs or pneumonia.

[page 332]

November 22, 1907—Her life was saved only by the mercy of the Lord. She could [not] lie down, and sat up all night, I with her. Albert and Emma came early, staid all day and all night, all next day and night, before they could leave her.

I also, for two weeks have been hardly able to move about or rise from a chair without help—a pain and weakness in my back. We are a couple of almost helpless cripples.

November 26, 1907—So helpless, suffering acute pain on the least motion Albert had to undress me for bed like a little child.

November 29, 1907—To night Gertrude went to a Social party—the first time in years. She is greatly improved in health, greatly to the wonder of all who know her, for no one thought she could live. It is all by the blessing of the Lord, administration and her wonderful faith.

DECEMBER.

December 2, 1907—Albert and Emma gave a social dinner to which Susan, Gertrude and I went, Albert bringing us in a carriage.

I learn from the newspaper of the birth of another Gr-Grand Child, a daughter of Henry's eldest daughter Bertha Farnsworth, who was born Nov. 2nd, last month.

[written in margin]

Nov. 2

December 3, 1907—Rec[d] a letter from a Miss Mary Bruyeré Wikoff, Cream ridge, N. J. who had read my genealogical article in the Des. News of Nov. 26, and desired information relative to temple work. Thus is interest increasing in this holy work. I rec[d] some mail, a letter on the same subject from Utah who also had read my article.

December 5, 1907—Letters from Persis L. Y. Richards and others asking particulars of my temple work, for indians and those of their families. Thus my article published in the "News" is bringing forth increased interest in the work for the dead. Thanks to God.

December 8 & 9, 1907—Quarterly Conference. Present from S. L. City Apostles G. A. Smith and Geo. F. Richards, also H. H. Cummings Gen. Supt. Church Schools and Sister E. C. M[c]Cune, A good time. Pleasant visits with Br. Cummings. Blessed him, that his wife Barbara shall know the Law of Plural Marriage is true and from God. Br. C. was greatly rejoiced & happy.

[page 333]

December 9, 1907—Had a good interview with Sister M[c]Cune about temple work. She was glad to see and talk with me.

December 10, 1907—Blessed Sister I. W. Pierce who was distressed in mind, and she was made happy. It makes me happy to make others so.

December 23, 1907—Rec[d] of Pres[t] A. W. Ivins store orders for mapping, amounting to $118.[00] [$2,553] Paid tithing $64[00] [$64 = $1385] and all other debts and had $17^{00} [$368] left. Thankful to be able to do so.

December 25, 1907—Susan and I took dinner at Guy Taylor's. Gertrude able to sit at the table. Albert also brought us some nice eatables.

December 30, 1907—Sent a temple sheet, male names, to Nephi, also a list to him of women, hoping he may get some to endow them. I hope so—

During the past month I have spent most of my time arranging my names for baptism and endowment, and hope I may interest my children warmly in the holy work.

JANUARY 1908

January 1, 1908—Spent the day quietly and wrote letters.

January 3, 1908—Sent 60 female names and 20 male, to temple (S. L. City) for baptism. Rain, and warm weather.

January 6, 1908—Surveyed for Allred

January 11, 1908—Sent 20 male names to B. S. Johnson for bap. & End^ts

January 15, 1908—Electric lighting began

January 16, 1908—Albert returned to his R. R. work in Sinaloa, Mex.

January 22, 1908—Electric lights finally in working order.

January 25, 1908—Sat in High Council, hearing 3 cases.

January 27, 1908—Susan suddenly very sick. Billious attack.[22] Went to Bp. J. C. Bentley's and blessed his wife for her confinement. Promised a boy baby, being thus impressed to do.

Went 10 miles to measure cub. metres in a reservoir dam of Gov. Terrazas,[23] a dispute as to true contents.

January 27, 1908—Again at the dam. Susan still sick, but better

January 31, 1908—Susan able to sit up most of the day.

22 Biliousness is nausea, abdominal pains, and constipation. It can be associated with liver disease.

23 This is Mexican governor Luis Tarrazas, Chihuahua (Mark Wasserman, "The Social Origins of the 1910 Revolution in Chihuahua," *Latin American Research Review* 15, no. 1 [1980], 15–38; see also Turley and Turley, *History of the Mormon Colonies in* Mexico, 14).

FEBRUARY

February 8, 1908—Sent 20 female names to Jennie S. Hill, S. L. City for baptism and Endowment. Rec^d from temple the list of 80 males and females baptized there.

[page 334]

February 15, 1908—Wrote to Pres^t J. F. Smith about removing to S. L. City, so I may be near the temple and genealogical records, for I wish to spend my last days in the work for the dead.

MARCH

March 20, 1908—Sent temple sheet to Sister Amanda Wessman, for her to endow for me, 20 female names.

F. R. Society entertainment. Very pleasant. Gertie went in her wheel chair, and was very happy. Letter from 1st Presidency, who say come to the City if you wish, in reply to my letter.

APRIL

April 8, 1908—Went to El Paso to file my pension papers, returned

April 10, 1908—home, 11 P.M.

April 18, 1908—Rec^d my pension check for last 6 months $72^{00} [$1,502].

April 20, 1908—Rec^d 5 o/c [%] dividend from Store ($1240^{00} stock) [$25,874] $62.00 [$1,294].

April 23, 1908—Surveyed pasture line of G. C. Wilson 1 day[24]

April 24, 1908—Surveyed plat of land for B. Y. Whipple 1 day

MAY

May 1, 1908—Rec^d my temple sheet from Mrs. Wessman, work all done, most of it by Mrs. M. W. R. Wilcox. God bless them.

24 This could be Guy C. Wilson, who was instrumental in educational developments of the colony (Turley and Turley, *History of the Mormon Colonies in* Mexico, 89–90).

Fig. 10.2—James Henry Martineau family in front of Mexico home. Back row: Lillie Susannah Hicks Taylor, Ida Elizabeth Eyring Turley, Selina Vermina Cardon Turley, Edward Franklin Turley, Aubrey Franklin Turley, Phyllis Walser, Annie Sariah Martineau Turley, Theodore Martineau, Charles Henry Martineau, Sixtus Johnson Martineau, Joel Hills Martineau, James Edward Martineau, Edward Bernard Martineau, Ernest Martineau; second row: Ernest Guy Taylor, unidentified, unidentified, Gertrude Martineau Taylor, Melissa Editha Johnson Martineau, Theodore Martineau Jr., Henry Augustus Martineau, Josephine Thurston Martineau, Susan Ellen Johnson Martineau, Adelaide Martineau, Anne Martineau, James Henry Martineau, Mary Ann Thurston Martineau, Alice Myrtle Clark, Elzada Martineau, Leland Allred Martineau, Sarah Sophia Johnson, Amon Douglas Martineau, Emma Pauline Allred Martineau, Wilma Martineau; front row: Vermina McCray Taylor, Jesse Elmer Taylor, Theodore Stanley Martineau, Carl Pierre Martineau, Henry Eyring Turley, Clarence Franklin Turley, Bernard Edward Martineau, Edward Vernon Turley, unidentified, Leland Knowlton Martineau, Florence Martineau, Clara Turley, unidentified, Aula Martineau, Nola Martineau.

May 5, 1908—Received temple sheet (20 names) from Jane S. Hill, work all done. May Our Father ever bless her.

MARCH 13, 1908

March 13, 1908—My 80th Birth day. Most of our children came from the mountains. We had a very nice dinner and an enjoyable time. We sat in a group for a photograph,—about 50 in number, including my two sons in law, E. Guy Taylor and E. F. Turley and their families.

MAY

May 24, 1908—I will here note two cases in my ministrations to the sick wherein two young women given up to die by the doctor and relatives were healed in a marvelous manner by the power of the Lord. The first was a daughter of R. C. Haney ill with typhoid pneumonia, age about 17 years. Sent for. I asked the Father if it was His will for her to live and if He would bless my ministration to her. (This as I always do) An affirmative answer by the Holy Spirit gave faith to bless her with full assurance of healing for her. I blessed her that she should be healed, and amend from that hour, all of which was fulfilled to the letter, and to the astonishment of the doctor, a man of great experience.

[page 335]

May, 1908—He said "I can't understand how she could live. Nothing to build hope upon."

The other Case was that of Mary Pierce, age 22, sick unto death with dropsy at the heart combined with rheumatism.

I obtained a favorable answer for her, that she should live and be perfectly healed. I blessed her accordingly & she revived so she could speak and said she believed. Next day she relapsed, and was apparently dying, suffocating with the water around her heart and lungs. Sent for again and told she was dying, I said to myself "Have I been misled by my sympathy for her in pronouncing upon her, life, health and speedy recovery? Has some other spirit—not of God—deceived me? How then shall I know the true voice of the Holy Ghost—the Comforter! I prayed to know how it was, and received a plain answer from the spirit—"You have not been deceived, The voice which spake yesterday to you was truly the voice of the Comforter. She shall be fully healed. Fear not to bless her with recovery for thy words of blessing shall be ratified in the heavens." I found the family in deep distress, with her father, mother and other relatives sent for from Diaz. I told them not to fear—she should be healed. Mary said she believed me. I then blessed her that she should amend from that hour and be perfectly healed. Next day I found a wonderful change. She seemed an entirely new woman, the dropsy nearly gone and all pain. Next day dropsy entirely gone, and she sitting up, and on the next morning went home by wagon to Diaz 70 miles distant, camping out one night on the way. How merciful is Our Father! To Him be all the praise.

May 24, 1908—Visited and blessed Br. and Sis. Longhurst and Eliz[th] Johnson. Not feeling well myself, in bed all forenoon,

May 19, 1908—This morning about 3 A.M. my father and his mother visited me either in dream or vision I know not which, and approved my temple work in their behalf.

May 29, 1908—Susan and [I] by invitation went to Dublan Old Folks party. Visited Iris Call, suffering from an operation for apendicitis and in a dangerous condition from inflamation of kidneys and rheumatism. I had testimony she should be healed but the hospital surgeon wrote Br. Call to bring her back to the hospital, as an abscess was forming and must be removed before too late.

[page 336]

May 29, 1908—She (Iris 17 yrs old) had faith to be healed,—and was healed, for the pain ceased before we removed our hands from her head. This was at noon, and that evening came to the reunion (Ward) seeming perfectly well, and danced once. Next evening she danced every time,—as well as the other girls. How good and merciful is Our Father.

I also visited Julia Jones, the blind woman of 20 yrs continuance, and she said "When you was here last time (6 weeks) I could only distinguish a chimney or window of a house: now I can see writing." I thank Thee oh God.

I also blessed a boy who had fits and a woman who was suffering from apparent appendicitis.

June 1, 1908—Visited Sister Longhurst—very sick and much pain—and she felt better immediately and soon was well

June 20, 1908—Up to this time I have been quite unwell & very feeble, lying in bed much of the time, but visiting the sick when asked for. One case of special note—Eva, the daughter of Joseph Cardon, who has been very ill for 14 months, most of the time in bed, eating nothing but a little Mellen's infant food. She was in bed, too weak to sit up longer than a few minutes at a time. But after administration she felt stronger, and when I visited her next day she was walking about in the garden, much stronger and better every way. She said she was no longer taking any of the doctors medicine. All praise to Our Father.

Albert came and told us to get ready to go to the mountains tomorrow, and have a change for our good.

May 21, 1908—Started 8 A.M. Over a very rough road, which shook up Susan very badly. Twenty miles of our route was in the mountains—ridges to cross and deep gorges. Reached Sister Sarah Lunts and had a warm welcome. Susan could hardly get out of the wagon.

May 22, 1908—Arrived at Theodore's, in Garcia, 8 miles over mountain. Remained in Garcia until 30th and enjoyed our selves very much, with Change of Climate and associations.

[page 337]

June, 1908—Gave 16 patriarchal blessings, and were invited out to dinner 5 or 6 times. Garcia is a beautiful Gem of the mountains—a scene of rare sylvan beauty, with an altitude of over 6000 feet above the sea. A village, only.

May 30, 1908—Went 40 miles to Chuichupa over high mountain ranges of the Sierra Madre Mts, some passes of over 8500 feet altitude. Pine timber all the way, with occasional beautiful grassy glades. Reach Henry's home about 9 P.M.—gladly received by all & glad to get to a resting place. It is just the beginning of the "rainy season." Chuichupa's altitude is over 8000 ft.—on the top, so to speak, of the Sierra, though peaks rise about us 2000 feet higher, notably, the Candelaria's.

This altitude gives pleasant days and cool nights, and one can eat and sleep well, with pine scented air and clear mountain water

While here, enjoying the society of our Children and grand and great grand children we felt at rest and spent 25 days very pleasantly. It rained a while almost every day—an hour or so at a time. I blessed many & went out a few times to dinner. I spent much time in getting indian names for baptism, from an ethnological work of the U. S. Government—Several hundred.

July 25, 1908—Started homeward, and reached Garcia at sunset.

Monday, July 27, 1908—This evening, at 10 P.M. Josephine, Theodore's wife, presented us with another grand child—a girl—8 lbs.—all being well with mother and Child

August 4, 1908—I Blessed and named the baby Lucilla, after my most ancient Martineau, who died in Syria in the year A.D. 70, her marble tomb still intact in the desert between Damascus and Alleppo, as noted previously in my journal. She was "the beloved daughter of Martinus, Roman General." So says the inscription on her tomb.

August 5, 1908—Start home and camped at Kartchener's camp.

August 6, 1908—Reached home. "No place like home." Theodore brought us home, and started back, soon returning & going to the summer school until 22d Aug.

[page 338]

September 7, 1908—Start to El Paso to file pension papers. Stayed over night in Dublan and administered to Eva Cardon who is very sick.

September 8, 1908—In El Paso. Remained until the 10th and came home.

September 12 & 13, 1908—Quarterly conference in Cola Juarez.

Joel's wife and children—Annie—came on Tuesd 8th from Madera, Joel remaining there to close up affairs. She will stay in our house, and relive [relieve] Susan of the housework, which is hard for her, she being so lame.

September 18, 1908—Henry returned home. I loaned him $15.00 [$313].

September 29, 1908—Started to S. L.City with Conference Company,

October 1 (2), 1908—arriving 2d Oct. in a cold rainy time. Went to Gean's who made me welcome. Visited a few of the family & on

October 4, 1908—attended Conference, also on 5th and 6th

October 10, 1908—Up to this time I have been very busy, visiting the sick and giving several blessings. Especially, visited Sister Alice Bowman, near the L. D. S. Hospital, in a very precarious state of health for several years. She desires children, but the doctors tell her that to conceive is to invite almost certain miscarriage and if not miscarriage, death at time of confinement. Consequently very despondent. Blessed her with promise she shall conceive, go safely her full time, be blessed in confinement, and all shall be well. Sister Margaret Sharp, whom I brought with me, blessed her also, confirming the same which I had sealed on her.

October 16, 1908—Attended a reunion of Temple workers, at which the wid. of W. W. Phelps was present and spoke in tongues.[25]

October 28, 1908—Today, in the Temple, Pres[t] Madsen took my hand and blessed me, saying;—"You shall never want for a dollar when you need it." This promise rejoices me very much, for I believe it will be fulfilled.

October 30, 1908—I learned to day that the name of Romain Martineau's father was Francois Martineau; and the name of my Romain Martineau was Madaleine Bucher, her father's name being Denis Bucher, with wife Mrs. Genevieve Bucher.

November 2, 1908—Had 80 male names in temple for baptism, and paid $15.[00] [$313] for endowment of 20 males. Also $20[00] [$417] endment [endowment] of 40 women by Sis. Wessman.

[page 339]

November 13, 1908—Adm[d] to Sister Wetzel, who lies very dangerously ill. She shall be healed, and this I sealed upon her. Also Sister Quist, that she need not be operated upon in hospital for removal of tumor in abdomen. (note: Fulfilled, both cases.)

December 21, 1908—Up to this time have spent my time in the Temple or the Genealogical Rooms, obtaining names of our dead. Also, nearly every day visiting and administering [to those] afflicted, and in giving many Pat[l] blessings. Have had many endowed, and many baptisms for the dead.

December 31, 1908—Attended social party at Pres[t] Winder's—I being the only man present, a lovely time and holy spirit. After close of meeting Pres[t] J. F. Smith's wife Edna asked me to bless a sister M[c]Donald—in great distress—which I did. I learned Sister Marie Young Dougall—a dear friend, was in Los Angeles in a very dangerous condition, and her sisters Susa and Zina wished me to bless and write to her, which I did next day, promising she should be healed & greatly blest.

25 William W. Phelps was an early leader in the Church, a scribe for the Joseph Smith. He was excommunicated in 1838 and returned to the Church in 1841, dying March 7, 1872.

JANUARY 1909.

January 1, 1909—Went to Lilla's, in Logan. Spent much time visiting and blessing the sick, and had temple work done for about 100 persons. I had previously joined the genealogical Society as a life member. I sent money, $8.00 [$173 + 2.00 [$43] = $10[00] [$216] also for a life membership for Susan.

January 25, 1909—Learn from Susan that Anna's boy was born Nov. 8, 1908,—named Lawrence Edward Turley.

January 31, 1909—At conference in Logan I blessed Pres[t] J. F. Smith. He was pleased, and told me to go on with my work for Lamanites—baptisms and sealings of husbands and wives & children.

February 11, 1909—Rec[d] word from Union Mercantil Co. Mexico, that my stock of 1240.[00] [$26,845] had dividend of 10 o/c [%], making my stock $1364.00 [$29,525].

I learn from my eldest daughter—that her dau. Gertrude Johnson Roberts has a son—Tillman Snowden Roberts—born 19 Feb. 1808 [1908], at Buckeye Arizona. Blessed 31 March 1908 by Elvira's husband—B. Samuel Johnson.

Her son Joseph & wife Cora Allred, have 7 children.

March 13, 1909—My 81st birth day, a sorrowful time, as Charlie's baby Dorothy is very sick. I spent the day visiting the sick. Up to this date I have obtained over 2000 new names of the dead.

[page 340]

Sunday, March 14, 1909—To day was held funeral of Charlie and Eva's baby Dorothy who died on 11th aged about 18 months.

March 23, 1909—Worked on my temple records, but still ill with la grippe.

March 24, 1909—In bed all day.

March 25, 1909—Better. Visited and blest the sick

March 27, 1909—Gave Pat[l] Blessings to Aileen, Eldon and George, children of Charles and Eva.

April 1, 1909—Went to S. L. City and went to Jean's [Gean's].

April 3, 1909—Was present at reception of Admiral Robby Evans and the review of High School Cadets, of which Gean's son Sherman is a member.

April 6, 1909—At banquet at Social Hall—"Founders Banquet"—Interesting time, and on 8th at temple party at Bp. Brinton's

April 12, 1909—Temple workers reunion at Bp. Brinton's. Good time

April 21, 1909—Lyman's 50th birth day. Visited and blessed him.

April 28, 1909—Heavy snow storm

May 8, 1909—Went to Logan, who is struck with paralysis, but better

May 15, 1909—Lilla is healed of her paralysis, but still weak. I went to Nephi, at Benson. Cold.

May 16, 1909—Snowing and dismal, but good for crops sown. Nephi had all his family at home, including Susa's husban [husband] Wm Chantrill. Went and looked at his late purchase of 380 A. [acres] of land, with good brick house & flowing wells.

May 18, 1909—Returned to Charles' in Logan.

May 20, 1909—Got three Martineau names—a side line as follows,

Edwarde Martinewe, & wife Thankfulle Martinewe who died in London Eng. May 5. 1545. He was son of Edwarde & Cecilia, son of John and Genevieve, son of Francois Martineau & Madaleine—

I knew long ago that Martineau's had come to England before the sons of Elie & Margarite came in 1685, but did not know how to connect them with the main Romain line.

From records in Genealogical Library I find that I am by marriage connected with Oliver Cromwell through the line the French family Bucher, wife of Romain 1st B. 1410 & Margarite Bucher B. 1420, as follows:—

"Sir James Bucher, of Filsted, Eng. had daughter, Elizabeth Boucher, who married Oliver Cromwell, who was then 21yrs of age."[26]

[page 341]

May 1909—I find also that a Martin (Martineau) came over to England with William the Conqueror, and became a Lord of a large domain in Wales, where he build a large castle.

[written in margin]

Note

The Family name in the old Roman empire, held by a Roman General in Syria A. D. 70 was Martinus, (male) and Martina (female) at which date he erected a marble tomb in honor to the "Manes" (Spirit) of his daughter Lucilla who died there. The tomb is still in that land.

The British Encyclopedia gives the following as the names, translated in various languages:—Latin Martinus, Italian and Spanish, Martino; Portuguese, Martinho, German, English and French—Martin. How did the name become Martineau in France? For centuries much intercourse occurred between Italy and France & Italian Martineaus who removed to France adopted the French—eau (o) in their new spelling, using "eau" (the French Sound of "O" But others, not moving from Italy spelled the name Martin, as St. Martin, tutelary Saint of France.[27] So all named Martin in England, Germany, and France, are of the same Martinus stock of old Rome,

From other records I learn that a Grandson of Columbus married a Martineau, and by my father's marriage with the daughter of the Earl of Stanhope he became connected by marriage with the Earls Mints Chesterfield, Bedford, Halifax and Lord Chatham, the most noble of the aristocracy of England, & by an intrigue of Geo. the Second, with him and his mistress,—a thing not to boast of, however.

Saturday, May 22, 1909—My Daughter Lilla Nebeker again a mother—a girl born 12.30 A.M. She had been several weeks very ill, was greatly blessed at delivery.

I returned to S. L. City, I have been quite ill for several days, but not enough to be in bed.

Lyman came to me at Gean's, and invited me to come and stay at his home. Moved there next day to 918 Logan Ave. Still quite feeble.

May 30, 1909—By invitation attended meeting of Genl Board Y. M. I. A. at the home of Marie Y. Dougall Pleasant time.

26 Oliver Cromwell (1599–63), Lord Protector of England, was a skillful politician and was driven by his Puritan religious convictions (S. R. Gardiner, *Cromwell's Place in History* [London: Longmans Green, 1897]).

27 A tutelary saint has the position of guardian and protector of a person, place, or thing.

[page 342]

May 31, 1909—Blessed Sister Bennett, also her daughter, who desires Children. Also blessed several others.

June 1, 1909—Sent 800 names of indians to Manti temple for baptisms

Went with sister M. Y. Dougall & Mary White to see Julia S. Woolly, long very ill and feeble. Admistered to her, each of us. Had great outpouring of the Holy Spirit.

June 2, 1909—By request of Sis[r] Dougall I was to day endowed for one of her father's family—Pres[t] Brigham Young's—a Mr. John Young.

June 3, 1909—Jos. F. Smith's wife Julina sent for me to visit her daughter Donetta who is very Sick. Administered.

June 4, 1909—Went again, found aughter [daughter] much better. It was a painful tumor on an Ovarian tube or vein to the uterus. Julina asked me to come every day and dine with her family and Pres[t] Smith.

My gr. dau. Alle M. Crissmon's baby, named Jefferson. He was born Feb. 4 1908 in Philadelphia P.A.

About this time Sis[r] Dougall ~~who~~ had been very sick & I went to see her. She was only able to sit up, but had not been out of doors,—very feeble. She said how much she wished she could go to a Committee meeting tomorrow but she dared not go out of doors yet. I asked the Father if she could go safely to the meeting, & got answer she could, (privately) So I said to [her] yes, you can go to the meeting and anywhere else you desire from this time henceforth, and not take any hurt." She said "I believe you. I'll go." She went next day without detriment & from that time was well and strong. God was merciful because of her faith, and He healed her.

A few days later she wished me to go with her to the hospital to see a friend there, who had had a severe operation performed. We went, administered to the woman and to three others who heard I was there and believed I could help them, and they truly were very greatly blessed and left the hospital much sooner than the surgeons thought possible. God healed them very speedily.

Shortly after this Sis[r] Dougall took me to see her friend—Mrs. Wright, of Ogden, in a very desperate condition, who had come to have two severe operations in the hospital.

[page 343]

June 1909—She had been ill five years and for last five month had her stomach pumped out every day. The opening from Stomach to bowels was closed, & must be cut open. Also, she had a tumor in her Uterus, large and painful. The doctor came daily to see if she was strong enough to go through these two severe operations, she being in bed, unable to dress herself. I asked and got a testimony she could be healed of all her troubles by the power of God and without having any surgical operations at all. Sister Dougall also had the same testimony. So we blessed Sis.[r] Wright, telling her she could & should be healed by administration. It was hard for her to have faith, for the surgeons said she could not live without surgical aid. She prayed all that afternoon and night, and when we came next day to bless her again she was greatly changed for the better and said she had faith to be healed. She had dressed herself, came down stairs without help, could walk about lively—entirely like another woman. We blessed her again, and in three days dismissed her doctor and went home feeling fine.

From Sister Wright we went about a mile to a woman very sick with appendicitis—going next day to be operated upon for that disease. Having testimony I sealed health & recovery upon her—without operation in hospital. She said "I believe—I know I'll be healed." And she was. A few days after this she came to see me—said she felt no pain from that moment (blessing)—was perfectly well & going on a pleasure trip to California tomorrow.

From her we went to another very sick woman and blessed her. She was healed immediately.

All these miracles were simply manifestations of the power and goodness of God, and to him be all the glory and honor. I, of myself, could do nothing.

[page 344]

June 1909—I have given so detailed an account of these cases as a sample of almost daily experiences for now & as I am sent for constantly, when hope from doctors fail people. The blind have been made to see, the paralyzed to instantly walk, ossification[28] of joints in a case (Miss Afton Young) which for years had dified [defied] the efforts of the most skillful surgeons in the United States; seven persons with tumors the surgeons said must be removed surgically, all healed by administration and the power of God, without going to a hospital; one woman given up by doctors and relatives to die of consumption speedily healed,—oh, so many cases, too many for enumeration. People from town north and south of S. L. City coming & being healed. To Father be all glory.

I cannot express how thankful I am to be the poor humble, unworthy instrument in the hands of Father in healing & comforting the afficted and sad. It is all I live for, this, and helping the dead, of course, first of all, I must labor for my <u>own</u> salvation.

Time not thus occupied I spend in hunting the names of dead kindred in the genealogical library, and have thus obtained thousands, I have expended considerable time and money in getting Temple work done for me, and have scrimped in food, going many days without dinner to save money to be used for the dead, but fasting thus has not hurt me any. I am feeble, and walk with difficulty, my legs below the knees being partially paralized & without feeling, except that my feet are always very cold. I have fallen several times on the side walks, as the least thing causes it. But—I might be sick in bed! So I can't complain, but only be thankful to be as well as I am. There but a very few men so greatly blessed as I, though poor financially. I am laying up my treasure in heaven, where no one can cheat or rob me, as many have done here. But I have not contended. I trust my Father to bless me if He thinks best to do so

[page 345—see Appendix 5 for letter from the Grand Army of the Republic inserted here.]

1909—From Cousin Napoleon B. Van Slyke's last letter I learn that my Cousin Laura Pool Starin [died] in 1898, and her husband John Starin in 1909. I learn from others that Coz. Van Slike died in 1908. I am now the last living member of our extensive circle of relatives.

June 23, 1909—Invited to a reunion of the Genealogical Society at the old "Lion House," Pres[t] Youngs old residence

June 29, 1909—Attended "Old folks Day." About 3000 dined on the Tabernacle grounds.

July 13, 1909—Visited and blessed a Sister Hinkley who was very ill with appendicitis, & going soon to hospital for operation. Was in much pain which instantly ceased, & she was perfectly healed, as she told me a few days later as she was about to go on a pleasure trip to California. Also blessed another that she might conceive.

July 22, 1909—I learn that my gr. daughter Bertha's (Henry's daughter) last child was born June 2 1909; also that my Gr. Son James Edward's son was born June 17, 1909. 22 Gr. Grands.

August 2, 1909—Visited G. A. R. [Grand Army of the Republic] headquarters to see if there is to be any place in the Grand Parade on Aug. 11 for Mexican war veterans. Was told by Col. Stetson, manager, that he would give me a carriage in the procession and tickets for the grandstand.

August 5, 1909—Visited Sis[r] Adkins sick baby, which three doctors say cannot live. Had testimony the child should be healed by administration. Met there Sisters Dougall and Sharp and Levi Richards. I was speaker, in blessing, and sealed life upon the child, who immediately opened his every eyes with new life & was healed soon. To Father be all the honor and glory for it.

August 11, 1909—At 8 A.M. a carriage came for me to go to the place where the procession was to form, four miles distant. Our procession was full two hours in passing a given point—Thousands of the veterans of the civil war, U. S. troops from Camp Douglas and the Utah military organization, more than 30 Brass Bands A grand display. Two other Mexican War veterans were also in the procession. A grand event.

August 16, 1909—Sent for at day light to bless Sis[r] Knight, very sick with typhoid fever.—104°. She was instantly healed. [writing is deteriorating with age]

[page 346]

August 17, 1909—Visited and blessed Sis[r] Grover. Weak, dangerous flooding.

28 Ossification is the hardening or calcification of soft tissue into bonelike material.

Went to see her next day and found her healed of her trouble.

August 20, 1909—Sent for to bless Sis[r] Stevens, of Ogden, who came for this purpose. She has cancer in the womb. Sealed full healing upon her, and she believed. I had previously blessed a friend of hers, Sis[r] Wright, of Ogden, who had cancer in the womb and serious stomach trougle, said to require surgical operation, who had been healed, the cancer quickly healing & disappearing

August 25, 1909—Went to Logan, to Moses Thatcher's funeral. Returning, I got off at Ogden to see my patient, Mrs. A. T. Wright. Found her in fine spirits and looking well

August 30, 1909—Visited Sis[r] Dougall. Found two of her family sick, one nealy [nearly] blind. Blessed them. Sis. Dougall, very glad, said "Surely the Lord must have sent you in this, our time of need." To Him be all honor.

August 31, 1909—Met Miss Marian E. Martins, of Eng.—one of our Martineau kindred

September 29, 1909—Attended a reunion in 19th ward in honor of the widow of W. W. Phelps, a veteran of Missouri persecution times. She spoke in tongues, interpreted by a daughter of Orson Hyde, Sis M. White.

Was then taken to see a Sister very ill. Blessed her & she was well next day. Found there a young girl of 17 years, from Mexico. She Came to have her leg amputated above the knee. I had testimony she could be healed of the tuberculosis of the knee by the power of God, and without amputation, and blessed her to that End. It seemed pitiful for a young girl to go through life with only one leg.

Received telegram from my beloved wife, saying she will meet me here Oct. 1 at 630 A.M. Oh how thankful I am for it.

October 1 [or 14], 1909—Susan came at 6.30 to the R. R. Station. I was not able to meet her, being in bed, quite weak, but Lyman met her & brought her to me. Now I believe I shall become stronger For weeks I have been scarcely able to walk without some one to hold to. I am partially paralyzed below the knees, But before this, for over 6 months, my legs have been very bad in condition—swollen and almost without sensation to the touch. An Osteopath, by examination, says my spinal cord is affected. It has been all I could do ever since April last to walk a block or two and climb the stairs to the Gen[l] Library rooms, which I have never missed doing a single day, except when called to visit the sick.

[page 347]

1909—This I am constantly called to do, usually when the person has been given up by the doctors. I have thus prevented seven persons, whose tumors must be removed, the doctors said, by surgical operation. All of them were healed—the tumor gradually disappeared. Many other wonderful manifestations of the power and goodness of God have occurred in my experience here, which I have not noted in any memorandum, and so cannot tell of them here, even if I wished to, which I do not care to do, only as a testimony of the Gospel Ordinances, & that God is to day, as of old, able and willing to bless His people.

December 31, 1909—Sister Nelson telephoned me saying Lura was worse, and suffering much pain in her knee. She had also fallen and hurt her hip very badly. I asked Susan to ask for a testimony concerning her. I did not wish to have her leg amputated. I had visited her several times, with Sisters Dougall, Sharp, Susan and Clayton, and we had blessed her that she should be fully healed by the power of God, for such was the testimony to us all. Could it fail?

I asked God to give to me and to Susan testimony concerning Lura. After a time I asked if She had an answer. She said Yes. What was it I asked. She said "She shall be healed by my power, for there is no other way. Therefore fear not. All shall be well."

The answer to me was: "Fear not concerning thy Sister. She shall be perfectly healed by my power, and not by any surgical operation."

I wrote this to Sister Dougall, hoping she could convey it to Sister Weston, to strengthen her faith which she did. I am unable, for the last 2 months to go out, as I cannot stand alone nor walk without holding to some one, so I could not go to see the poor girl. When I had visited her before I had to cling to my companion to enable me to walk,—could not alone.

[page 348]

1909—My trouble is in my legs and feet below my knees, which are paralyzed, the doctor says and he calls it Locomotor Ataxia,[29] and says nothing can be done, as it is an affection of the spinal cord, When he said this, a voice said to me, "You shall be healed by my power saith the Lord," and from that moment began to grow in my heart. I have had the gift to heal the sick, but not for myself, hence I could not pray for myself in real faith as I could for others. I believe I shall be healed, and if I am not, it will be because of failure in me and not in the Lord. My great desire is to live & bring souls to God, who has been so wonderfully good and merciful to me, and that I may help and bless the living. All else earthly is as nothing to me, save my beloved wife. I have gone scores of times to visit the sick when I was scarcely able to stand, but glad to do so because I could thus make others happy, as was always the case. Letters have come to me from Ogden, Logan and Los Angeles from those whom I have administered to, full of joy that my words were fulfilled in their cases, all of them desperate—internal cancers and one of severe internal complication of long standing. To Our Father be all the honor and glory.

December 25, 1909—Christmas, and many tokens of remembrance from almost all my dear ones. Thankful I am. I was admitted, with Susan, as members of Emerson Ward, S. L. City about the middle of December, and paid $7.50 [$162] tithing, accrued since I came from Mexico, having previously sent money to Bp. Bently, of Juarez, Mexico to pay my tithing in full there. I can say, thankfully I have paid full tithing all my church life,—almost 60 years, and in the early 50's I consecrated all I had to the Church, by deed, as required at that time.

[page 349]

1910 TRIBUNE CONSPIRACY

January 1, 1910—Before commencing my daily record for this year I will narrate how the Lord, through my humble labors,

In the 70's the "Tribune" clique of our enemies laid a plan to either destroy the church or drive us from Utah, by bringing upon us another army. To accomplish this they published daily reports that we were organizing for rebellion and were secretly drilling every night for an uprising.

Every day were published letters purporting to come from every town and hamlet, almost, in Utah crying for help, saying every night might be their last, for in each place Mormons were preparing to massacre them all. These letters were all written in the Tribune office. Every Mormon town or Village was in perfect peace, and there was no thought of evil to any non-Mormon, anywhere. There was no no friction—no cause for trouble. The Tribune continually called upon Government for help by an army to be sent quickly, or all non-Mormons in Utah would be killed.

Before Sending an Army the President Sent Gen. Crook to invistigate, before expending millions in a military crusade which might be needless.

I was a resident of Logan and one day received a telegram from Gen[l] Kimball,[30] U. S. Surveyor General, requesting me to visit him at once, but giving no reason. I went to him in the next day in his private office. He said:—Martineau, there is a great deal of talk about a Mormon uprising. I know you are one of the leading Military Men in Cache Co. and will know as much or more than anybody about the matter, and I want you to tell me what you know about it. You and I were comrades in the Mexican War, and I know I can depend upon what you tell me.

[page 350 duplicate heads at page break]

CONSPIRACY CONT[D]

1910—Now, is there any truth in these reports about a Mormon uprising"?

I smiled and replied "Do you think Brigham Young is a fool"? He said "No he is no fool, leaving religion out of question he is by far the smartest and most able man in the U. States" "Do you think" said I "that he would be so foolish as to attempt to accomplish what 12 great states attempted, with millions of money, men, munitions of war and the sympathy of all Europe, and attempted in vain? What could Brigham do with 8000 or 10000 militia, undisciplined, no arms of any value, ammunition for not to exceed half an

29 Locomotor Ataxia is a loss of coordination due to an infection of the spinal cord (see journal entry, February 14, 1910, [p. 360]).

30 Nathan Kimball (1822–98) was the surveyor general of Utah and the postmaster for the city of Ogden. He served in the Mexican War and the Civil War.

hour's firing, no supplies of ammunition, food, transportation ~~supplies of food~~ or clothing—not enough for a week's campaign! What could such a force do in opposition to the United States, with its millions of men and means? Do you think Brigham Young such an idiot as that"? "No," said he "I don't believe it for a moment, but I thought that where there was so much smoke there might be some fire." Gen Kimball, said I, "you may depent [depend] upon what I tell you. I am next in authority to Genl Hyde who is the Brig. Genl commanding in the Cache Militia District, a Brigade of two full regiments of infantry and one of mounted men, termed by us "Minute Men" expected to go any hour, day or night, against the indians, and as Chief of Staff receive reports from every company and regiment. Every military order pertaining to the Brigade or District is written by me. Therefore I know all that is going on in the whole District, more perfectly than any one else. If you doubt, come to Logan and inspect our military records and you will have no room for doubt."

"I believe you" said he. "I'll put a stop to all this infernal business.

[page 351]

1910—I'ts all that infernal Tribune Clique,—they ought to sent to Hill—they want an army here so they can take the property and homes of the Mormons, and get rich out of army contracts for supplies of all kinds. But I'll block their game. Genl Crook is on the way here to investigate. He and I were bosom friends in the civil war. I'll go and meet him, and post him about the whole thing." He thanked me warmly for my coming a 100 miles to see him, and, true to his word, soon started to meet Gen. Crook, which he did at Cheyenne, and fully explained to him the situation. At Ogden a special train was awaiting Gen. Crook with some 35 or 40 of the Tribune Conspirators ready to pump him full. He declined for the present to talk of the uprising, was tired by the journey and would talk later. Which he did. In two or three days the Tribune Clique called him a "Jack Mormon"—"bought with mormon gold" etc. etc.

So vanished the roseate[31] hopes of a few bold bad men, anxious for wealth, even if it be obtained by injustice to a whole community, always loyal and true to the Government.

While at Corinne on some Engineering business one day, a non-mormon whom I met at the railroad station who supposed me to be a Gentile, took me [to] one side and said "Somehow I've taken a liking to you, and I want to put you on to something perhaps you don't know, for it isn't made public yet." Any money in it" said I, "if there is, I'd like to know about it. I want money myself, just now." "I will tell you, but don't talk about [it] to any one you don't fully know. We're going to have a big army here before long and the Mormons have got to get out. They cant sell out for we wont need to buy. We'll just take such places as we like and they can't help themselves.

[page 352 duplicate headings at page breaks]

GOV. AXTELL

January 7, 1910—Some of my friends and I have picked out some good places. The best ones are rapidly being chosen already, and if you dont hurry up you'll lose some good chances."

"Well," said I, "I hope no one has picked out my home." "Your home"? said he "Where is your home?" "I[n] Logan city" I said "and if any body tries to take my home I'll kill him if I can." "Why," said he, "You are not a Mormon"! "Yes: I'm a full blooded mormon," and I tell you right now, if you or your chums try the game you are telling me about, you'll never live to enjoy it nor the plunder you hope to get."

His countenance underwent a sudden change and he muttered "It's all a joke" and got away speedily as possible.

To my personal knowledge there was at one time in Logan assertions by a Presbyterian minister resident there and by some apostate Mormons, that they would take the Tabernacle and the Temple, and devote the Temple to various secular uses.

The foregoing sketch should have been inserted years ago, also my experience with Gov. Axtell in 1875 which I now write:—

About the middle of June 1875 the County Court, and Logan City Council, of which I was a member, determined to invite Gov, Axtell to visit with his friends. Cache valley. I being appointed to write the invitation, as I did, soon receiving from the Governor a note ~~oth~~

31 *Roseate* means overoptimistic.

of thanks and acceptance. Apostles Brigham Young, Moses Thatcher and I were appointed a Committee to wait upon him and go with him through Cache County, But before his arrival to Logan both Elders Thatcher and Youn[g] were unavoidably compelled to be absent; therefore Pres[t] W. B. Preston and Judge M. D. Hammond were appointed in their places.

[page 353]

Gov. Axtell arrived in Logan June 22/75 and took apartments prepared for him at the Blanchard Hotel. During the Governor's visit we visited many towns in the county in his company, at all of which he addressed large audiences, and was specially desirous to see the children, which wish of his was gratified, the school or Sunday school children being marshaled before him for his inspection. In addressing them, he spoke always as would a L. D. Saint elder,—told them to avoid profanity, liquor, obscene language, tea, coffee or tobacco as being injurious to health; to observe and keep holy the sabbath day, to honor the aged and to be good, true citizens obedient to the laws. Any one not know who was speaking would have thought him a Mormon elder. And he was sincere, as I found in my personal interviews and conversations during his visit. He was not a member of any church, but was one of the "Honorable men of the Earth," full of broad minded integrity.

But our last and most pleasant interview occurred the day previous to his departure. He said to me "Mr. Martineau, I am satisfied the highest and most perfect ~~examples~~ type of the Anglo-Saxon race will be found in three or four generations among you mormons." I thought—that's taffy, because he's among us to day—so I said "Why do you think so"? He replied in a manner which surprised me beyond measure.

"Well", said he, "I see it this way. I don't know anything practically about polygamy, but I can understand that if a man has several wives he can only be present with one at a time, which would place the others in the position of spinsters or widows for the time being, placing upon them the responsibility of governing and teaching their children, planning their welfare, and in short, bring into exercise faculties otherwise lying dormant because of disuse.

[page 354]

GOV. AXTELL

Now back East where I came from such women are just as good "business men", so to speak, as men—often more so. And simply because they exercise their faculties A tailor, who wields only a needle or a pressing iron has not so muscular an arm as a blacksmith, who swings all day a heavy sledge or other heavy tool.

In like manner mental faculties become weak and dwarfed for lack of exercise. Women who thus exercise their mental faculties endow their children at birth with mental faculties above the average through natural laws; and their children produce a generation still superior; and so upon natural principles, a few generations should show a surpassing excellence, far above the average of the human race—at the very head of all."

I saw he was a man of profound thought. He had unwittingly given a powerful, philosophic testimony in favor of the Law of Plural marriage.

He told me of his early life, and how he first became ambitious to obtain education. His father, a well-to-do but uneducated farmer, thought that a little country school education was all a man needed, and he gave his son little opportunity for instruction.—no candle or lamp light for Study at night, so pitch pine knots burning in the fire place had to furnish the light for study. The final impetus for education came one day in the corn field. Tired and perspiring from hoeing corn he was resting in the shade of the rail fence when two gentlemen came slowly along the road, one of whom—a Jude [Judge] of the Supreme Court, related how he had attained his high position, his father giving him no encouragement. He had spent every spare dollar he could earn for books which he studied by firelight; had gained a place as Errand boy and general help in a lawyer's office who finally became interested in him,—made him clerk and finally admitted him to partnership and to general prosperity.

[page 355]

GOV. AXTELL

1910—Gov. Axtell said that the Judge told his story the thought came to him "—if one boy can do that so can I;" and from that time never ceased the struggle till he too, had gained the goal of his ambition,—first, a lawyer—next, Governor of Utah.

Before leaving Logan he gave me another and most agreeable bit of information. Said he "I will tell you why I wanted to see the children in every place I visited. I had been told in the East that the Mormon Children, especially polygamous children, were very inferior, mentally and physically, to the children of Non-Mormons and I wanted to see for myself." I said "Gov[r] what do you think of the children you saw?" "I never saw finer," said he, healthy, intelligent, and bright; and a high school teacher of seven years experience and eleven years in public schools of Chicago told me he could bring the Mormon children up to a point in two thirds the time required by the gentile children. I asked him his theory, and he said he had no theory, but knew it was true," I said, "Well, Governor, what is your theory"? He answered "I'm like the other fellow. I have no theory but I know I'm correct."

Gov. Axtell was all unknown to himself, a natural born Mormon, a man of true integrity.

I have thought it right to insert the foregoing two retrospects even at this late date, in honor of Gen. Kimball and Gov. S. B. Axtell.

January 8, 1910—To day is the blessed anniversary of Susan E.[s] and my marriage—58 years ago. Nothing done in remembrance—none is needed. She is with me.

January 18, 1910—This is the anniversary of my marriage with Susan Julia Sherman, who died 35 years ago in her comparative youth of 39 years. But she has escaped many years of Sorrow and Care, and for many years rejoiced with the just & in the companionship of her loved ones.

[page 356]

January 18, 1910—She obeyed cheerfully every law of God made known to her, and will go on to her exaltation as one of the Queens of Heaven, and in due time become Eve to an Earth, peopled by her spiritually born children, over whom she will preside forever as a Priestess and Queen, having received every ordinance that of the 2nd A, by Susan E. in Logan temple.

She is to be greatly congratulated—not mourned for she has passed all danger,—her exaltation is sure. Our faithfulness is yet to be proved.

[dates out of order]

Friday, January 13, 1910—This morning, while awake about 3 A.M. as I often do, I was wondering whether my place, as capable for doing the most good, is here in S. L. City or in Mexico, seeing that I am not able now to go about as before among the Sick, or to do any work in the temple, and as having no real home here for myself and Susan, I asked for a testimony, and received this answer plainly given by the Holy Spirit:—

"James, My Son, thy prayer is heard & accepted and thou also art accepted. For I know the secret desires of thy heart, for they are all for good & none for evil, and that thy great desire is to do good to the living and the dead, even to all who will receive it at thy hand; and there are not too many who have so great a desire to do so. Be of good cheer, for all shall be well for thee, for thou shalt remain here, near to the temple and the records of the dead, that thou mayest do a great work for them in the future as thou hast in the past. For thou wast appointed and set apart for this work before thou didst take thy temporal body because thou wast valiant for thy Father when Lucifer drew away so many after him. Thou shalt live and labor many years in this holy work, though Satan desires to hinder thee, and has brought thine affliction upon thee for this purpose, but the power of thy Father is still greater, and thou shalt do the work appointed thee yet many years to come.

[page 357]

January 18, 1910—Thou shalt labor not only here but in my holy house in Jackson county, even until the coming of my beloved Son. Thy way shall open up before way to thine own wonder. Thou shalt not lack for a comfortable home nor for means to obtain abundant help in thy temple work, even to the fulness of thy desires, for thou shalt be fully healed of all thy present infirmities and become strong as in thy prime. Amen.

This gave me much joy. I know it was from the Lord by the Holy Spirit, and if it is not fulfilled it will be because I prove myself unworthy of these blessings promised.

January 19, 1910—Sister Needham from Logan visited me and said her daughter, Mrs. Mae Earl, sick so long, was much better. My words of blessing had been fulfilled, also, in the case of Miss Marian Martines, whom I had blessed, to the least particular.

These things give me great joy and strengthen my faith, as showing my ministrations were approved of the Lord.

January 26, 1910—This morning at 1.10 A.M. my dear Virginia Sudbury's girl baby was born, all being well.

February 8, 1910—Received my temple sheets from St George, 599 Baptisms for me.

February 7, 1910—To day Sisters Bull, White and Hill visited me. I had at times greatly blessed them in times of trouble and sorrow, and we are dear to each other. I blessed Virginia, the little daughter of Sister Bull for diseased throat.

Sis. Hill pleased me greatly in telling me her dau-in-law is pregnant, after years of longing for a child. This was in fulfillment of a promise I had sealed upon her last summer.

[page 358]

February 7, 1910—I had met the young wife at the home of Sis. Bull, and she had unburdened her trouble to me of "hope deferred" and apparently vain, for motherhood. A few days later I felt so strongly impelled to visit and seal upon her her conception and motherhood, that went several miles to her and told her and husband what I had come to do, if they desired it, and had faith in the holy ordinance of blessing. They were both greatly pleased and said they believed.

I sealed upon her the promise she should become a mother to a noble spirit and should be greatly blessed in child bearing. Sister Bull told me all is being literally true and great is my joy that Our Father enables me thus to help and comfort others, and deigns to make known His will to one so little and unworthy as I am.

How could I dare to make such a promise? I had so promised, by blessing, several times before, and my words had literally been fulfilled. I asked the Father to thus bless them if it was His will so to do, and if so, to manifest it to me by the Holy Spirit. I received testimony it was His will, and not to fear, but bless the woman to that end and to fear not, for my words should be fulfilled. And so they were. I never go to administer to the sick without asking first for a testimon[y] concerning the Sick one, & when I obtain it, I speak as one having authority, and if the sick have faith, they are healed, even at the gates of death. All praise to Our Father, from whom all good comes.

February 8, 1910—Sister Pola brought Sister Newton and her baby 3 months old apparently blind,—born so. She wished me to bless her baby to restore or give sight. I did so. The result is with the Lord.

[page 359]

February 8, 1910—In the afternoon Sis. Alice Bowman came with her baby—a fine one—which she claimed as a child of promise in answer to a blessing sealed upon her by me, after physicians had declared she could never become a mother, or if she should become pregnant, she surely would die in confinement, her system so disorganized.

She is now the picture of health, more so, she says, than in many years.

She brought her niece, who desired & obtained a Patriarchal blessing.

February 10, 1910—Sis. Maria Dougall telephones to me that our friend, Sister Wright, is perfectly recovered from her cancer in Uterus and her closed stomach, which doctors all said must each be operated upon to save her life. Her recovery is a miracle.

February 13, 1910—Lyman received from my cousin, Mrs. W. A. Mears, of Seattle, Washington, data which will enable me to join the "Sons of the Revolution, as follows:—my great gr. father, John Mears, was born in Connecticut in 1734 or 1735 and served in the American Army in Capt. Joseph Boynton's Comp. Col. Nathanial Wade's regiment from June 26. 1778 to Jan. 6. 1779 (including 100 miles travel home) 6[mo] 11[d], His name is on the muster rolls of the Company on Nov. 6. 1778 at North Kensington R. I.; also in East Greenwich, R. I. Sept. 17 & 28; Nov. 6th to 12th, and Dec. 1778 and Jan.1. 1779. He died in Poultney Vt. He was a Sergeant. Our Mears tradition, told me by his son—my Gr. father James Mears, said he was at the execution of Maj. Andre, on a detail from each Reg[t]

February 11, 1910—Filed application with Indian War Commission for pension, for Ind. War Service in 1860.

February 19, 1910—Sent 940 names to be baptized for in St George temple. This number baptized for me there about 2000

[page 360]

February 23, 1910—My gr. daughter Alle M. Crismon and son Jefferson, who is nearly 3 years old Started to go to rejoin her husband Kenneth, who is studying medicine there. A sad parting. Will she see me again in this life? Who can tell.

February 23, 1910—Sent to Local Branch of "Sons of American Revolution," to ascertain how to obtain membership.

In searching the genealogical records of our Society I find the name of Romain Martineau (1st) was Francois Martineau, born about 1376, his wife's name Madeleine.

Also, that one of the family came to England with William the Conqueror in 11th century, and conquered for himself a part of Wales and erected two castles, the ruins of which still exist.

From "Gibbon's Dec. [Decline] & fall of Roman Empire" I learn of an ancestor—General Martinus, who served under the great Roman general Belisarius, A.D. 538. Also of a Byzantine (Eastern Roman empire, Constantinople) Empress Martina daughter of Heraelius, Exarch (Viceroy) of Africa at Alexandria, and wife of his son Heractius Emperor, living A.D. Another Martin was an officer serving under the Roman Emperor Maximim.

February 14, 1910—Sent 940 names for baptism at St George. Had previously had 599 baptized there, recently beside several hundreds previously.

In making out these lists, with all data, I was so weak I could hardly hold a pen or write legibly. Could not stand alone or walk alone.

When Dr. Richards pronounced my trouble a disease in spinal column, Locomotor ataxia, and said the nerves branching from it and giving life and sense of feeling to my legs & feet below the feet were dead, and nothing could be done. The same cause made me unable to balance and stand alone.

[page 361]

PEDIGREE.

February 23, 1910—When he said I was incurable a voice said to me "You may be healed by the power of God." Then faith sprang up in my heart. This was in January last/10. Since then I have gained considerably so that to day, Feb. 23d I can walk across the floor without touching any thing with my hands, and I believe I shall be healed. All honor to Father.

March 2, 1910—I walked about 40 rods to day alone, first time without help since Oct. 1. 1908

March 4, 1910—Florence Sudbury, (gr. dau.) was accidentally shot by her brother Lyman, with 22 Caliber gun. Hit at base of nostril, thru roof of mouth. "Didn't know gun was loaded," as usual. Lyman went to her and stayed all night.

TRACING BACK MY PEDIGREE.

March 5, 1910—I have now completed my Pedigree back for many generations, both Paternal and maternal, & God has blessed me wonderfully in doing so.

On my father's side I have been aided by the work of Basil and David Martineau, of London, who had spent thousands of pounds in their researches, David, especially, who employed the best experts in France, discovering that my French ancestry of 14th and 15th Centuries were of most eminent nobility, in the French Court, and one was a Knight of St John (or Malta. Also that a grand son of Columbus married a Martino.

The following is Paternal lineage from myself to year 1376, an unbroken line.

{ John Martineau (my Father Born 22 Mch. 1793 D. 1838
Eliza Mears. B. 13 Apr. 1806, in Fabius, N.Y. D. 1848

son of

Stephen Martineau B. 22 Mar. 1761 N.Y. 1st Gr. father
Elenor Haughwout B— D. 1832

son of

Stephen, B. 22 Mar. 1727 1st Great Grand Father
Mrs. Stephen Martineau

son of

[page 362]

PEDIGREE CONTD

March 5, 1910—
[written in margin]*2d G G F*
Cornelius Martineau B. 1704, Staten isld N. Y.
Mrs. Cornelius Martineau B. 1704

son of
[written in margin]*3d G G F*

Cornelius Martineau B. 1676 Holland
Mrs. " " 1677 "

son of
[written in margin]*4th G G F*

Denis Martineau B. 1651 France
Mrs. " " 1656

son of
[written in margin]*5th G G F*

Sieur Pierre Martineau 1624 France of
Lady " " 1630 Peronne

son of
[written in margin]*6th G G F*

Sieur (Lord) Francis Martineau B. 1597 France
Lady (Demoiselle) " " 1605 of Peronne

son of
[written in margin]*7th G G F*

Sieur Louis Martineau 1570 France
Lady Catherine Allearrme 1574 of Peronne

son of
[written in margin]*8th G G F*

Sieur Francois Martineau 1532 France
Lady Claude de Boulay 1533 of Peronne

son of
[written in margin]*9th G G F*

Sieur Denis Martineau 1493
Lady Marie de Chartier 1500

son of
[written in margin]*10 G G F*

Sieur Romain Martineau 1470
Lady Marie Chartelier 1468

son of
[written in margin]*11th G G F*

Sieur Jean Martineau 1440
Lady Genevieve— 1445

son of
[written in margin]*12 G G F*

Sieur Romain Martineau 1415
Lady Marguerite 1420

son of
[written in margin]*13 G G F*

Sieur Francois Martineau 1376
Lady Madeleine 1380

[written in margin]
note

In ancient France, Sieur corresponded to German "Baron" or English "Lord." Demoiselle, feminine title, of not less than nine generations of nobility, direct descent.

[page 363]

March 5, 1910—The term "Damsel" applied to unmarried ladies of less noble standing or to the comonalty [commonality].

The men noted "Sieur" were high officials of the court and one was a "Chevelier" in the celebrated order of the "Knights of St John" (or "Knights of Malta."

HUTCHINSON LINE. AND SPRAGUES.

James Mears (my Gr. father) B. Sharon Conn. 11 Apr. 1774 D. 1864
Lois Sprague Mears (Gr. mother) B. Lebanon, Conn 26 feb 1779

dau. of

William Sprague B. 1740 U.S.
Lois Hutchinson 1745 "

dau. of

Jeremiah Sprague 1700 "
Mrs. Jeremiah Sprague abt. 1705 "

dau. of

Anthony Sprague 1660 "
Mrs. Anthony Sprague abt. 1665 "

dau. of

William Sprague 1620 Eng.
Mrs. William Sprague abt. 1625

dau. of

Edward Sprague 1607 "
Mrs. Edward Sprague abt. 1605 "

dau. of

Edward Sprague 1579 Upway Dorset. Eng
Christiana Sprague 1574 Upway Dorset. Eng.

HUTCHINSON PEDIGREE OF LOIS MEARS SPRAGUE

she was dau. of

{ William Sprague (noted above) and B. 1740
Lois Hutchinson B. 1745 My 2^{d} Gr. Mother

dau. of

no. 2251 { Stephen Hutchinson B. 14 Aug. 1714
no. 2252 Abigail Haskins B. 1720 My 3 Gr. Mother

dau. of

[page 364]

March 5, 1910—

[written in margin]
320.2056

{ Richard Hutchinson B. 10 May 1681
Rachel Bance (My 4th Gr. Mother) 1694

dau. of

No. 1408 { Joseph Hutchinson B. 1658
Mrs. Joseph Hutchinson
5th Gr. Mother 1662

dau. of

No. 1300 { Richard Hutchinson B. 1633 D. 22 Oct 1680
Alice Bosworth 6th Gr. Mother 1635

[written in margin]
Note

NOTE

Stephen Hutchinson (No. 2251) had Chil^{n}
Lois B. 1739 (my ancestor) Stephen 1740
Daniel B. 1742— Richard 1744— Lydia 1746, Abigail 1748— Joseph 1750— Joseph 1752.

March 6, 1910—Before I arose I received a holy testimony regarding my Gr. dau. Florence Sudbury, age 11, who was accidentally shot on afternoon of 4th inst., the ball entering at base of nostril and passing through roof of mouth, and for which it is feared blood poisoning will ensue. I asked to know the will of the Father concerning her, and also others, partly or wholly blind, barren, tumors and cancers, for whom I had administered & blessed to be healed and the barren to be fruitful.

The answer came to me, that all who I had blessed thus should be healed; that Florence should not have blood poisoning but be fully healed; that my sisters, now barren shall bear noble spirits, that the tumor of Sister Pola shall disappear and not, as she has feared, injure her newborn babe; also that Gertrude shall be perfect healed, strong and healthy and be mother to a Son of Promise; that Freddy and Elzadie, and all others whom I had blessed through faith and the power of God. Also that Susan, my beloved wife, shall be healed, by the power of God and not by medicines, and that I, too, shall be healed and live to do a great work for the living and the dead, to the fullness of my desires, especially the work for the living and the dead, as far back as shall be needful, for names now unknown to me shall be made known.

[page 365]

March 6, 1910—This was by the still small voice of the Spirit, the Holy Ghost, who deceiveth not. I know that all this may be fulfilled through faith, hindered only by transgression not repented of. Other precious promises also were given. Help us, Oh Father, in our weakness, that we may become strong and receive what is our privilege to receive.

My mother had following Uncles and Aunts:—

1 Seth Sprague B. 1764 lived in N.Y. State
2 John " " 1766 Pa.
3 William " " 1768 died in Elbridge N. Y.
4 James " " 1770
5 Daniel " " 1772 died 1857 Vt. had wife Hannah Maxon
6 Jesse B. " B. 1774
7 Esther " " 1776 had hus. I. Ichabod Babcock. F. of Wm Bab^{k}
8 Eunice " " 1777 (hus. Crittenden
9 Lois " " 1779 (my Gr. mother (hus. James Mears, my gr. father

Daniel & Hannah Maxon had chil^{n}:—

1 Harriet Sprague, B. 1796 (hus Henry Stanley
2 George " " 1798
3 Isaac Newton " " 1800 (my mother's coz. sent pedigree)
4 Mary Ann " " 1803 (hus. Benj. Withwell of Mich.
5 Julia " " 1805 (hus. Oliver M. Hyde. He died 1867 Mich.
She had Chil^{n} Henry and Lewis, living 1879, Springfield Mass

March 29, 1910—Filed application for membership in "Sons of Amer. Revolution" paid $5.00 [$108] fee. The annual fee is $1.50 [$32].

March 31, 1910—Rec[d] $5.[00] [$108] (U.S. cur.) from Joel, on a/c of things sold him. Susan and I went to funeral of Pres[t] J. R. Winder.

Henry Came to day.

April 7, 1910—At conference with Susan

Sent 1340 names for baptism to St George

April 19, 1910—Attended Banquet of "Sons of Amer. Revolution."

[page 366]

March 13, 1910—(omitted by accident) My 83 birth day. Lyman gave dinner, In the evening Patriarch Jo[s] E. Taylor and Miss Afton Young (dau. of Le Grand Young) called to see me

March 9, 1910—Met Sister Robinson to day, in perfect health. I administered to her for cancer of the uterus when doctors said she must die. She was healed by the power of God immediately. Also received a letter from a Sister Stevens, of Ogden, who came to me for administration. She says she is perfectly healed, She also had Cancer in the Womb, and doctors ~~she~~ said she could not live over three months. I blessed her only twice. To God be all honor and glory.

Baptisms not noted in proper place, St George temple Nov. 1909, 820:—Apr. 1–1910 1340;—March 680;

April 30, 1910—Rec[d] letter from Gen[l] Registrar of Society of "Sons of Amer. Rev." in Washington D.C. saying my application is accepted and I am now a member, my number is 19322. I take pride in this membership of an Association acknowledged by Special act of Congress. My number [in] the Utah State Branch of the Society is 122.[32]

I visited and blessed LeGrand Young.[33] Severely injured by a horse stepping on his breast and foot. He healed immediately, to surprise of himself & all.

May 5, 1910—Received notification from Washington D.C. that I may obtain gold badge of the Society of "S. of A. Rev. with the number inscribed "19322."

Ichabod Babcock, B. Dec. 12 1731 was Father of Ichabod, who married my Great Aunt Ester Sprague He was born Jan. 15 1758 in Westerly R. I. He had Son William Babcock, my stepfather, who died 1864

May—Rec[d] $5.[00] [$108] (gold) from Joel on a/c.

May 24, 1910—Susan and I went to Old Folks theater—free

May 15, 1910—Henry returned home to Mexico

April 30, 1910—Sent 1200 names to St George for baptism

April 28, 1910—Rec[d] note from Joel for 375.[00] (Mex.= half that U.S. gold) $187.50 [$4059] (gold) also May 26 $10[00] Mex.= $5.00 [$108] U.S.

May 20, 1910—Total number names of my dead in my records = 27233 Of these about 16,000 have been added since I came from Mexico last time. Of those added over 4,000 have been baptized, most of them in the St George temple, some in Manti, Logan and Salt Lake temples, also many sealed.

[page 367]

May 1910—During the long winter, when unable to walk about unassisted, and hardly able to hold a pen, I made all or most of these baptismal records. For all these names dates of birth, & death, where born, when baptized and relationship were required to be sent to a temple, & again to be noted in my temple record. From first to last each name must be recorded 5 or 6 times:—1st, record, baptism, endowment, sealing; also, in some cases, 2nd Anointing. So that to date my list shows a great deal of time and labor—a labor of love indeed, to accomplish which I have expended considerable money—treasure laid up in Heaven, where no thief can steal. I have positive testimony that all, thus far, have received my temple work in their behalf—recompense to me in full, yes, far more than full.

May 22, 1910—Two light Earthquake shocks, rattled dishes, some plaster fell in houses. No one hurt. Time 7.25 A.M.

In trying to trace Susan's ancestry, back from her father—Joel Hills Johnson, Son of Ezekiel, born 12th Jan. 1776, in Uxbridge, Mass. Died 1848 in Nauvoo Ill. He was son of [blank] Johnson, who was killed in

32 Martineau's membership in the Sons of the American Revolution was approved March 30, 1910, national number 19322, state number 122. His application for membership contains his "Pedigree . . . Paternal Line" and lists his occupation as "civil and hydraulic engineering."

33 This is likely Judge LeGrand Young, Brigham Young's nephew.

battle of Bunker Hill, 1775. His widow [blank] remarried [blank] and they removed to Canada. Since then all trace of her family is lost.

I learn from my daughter Elvira Martineau Johnson that her son Joseph Johnson became father to twins on April 13, 1910, a boy named (2^0) Barnard Lavern, the first born, a girl named Verde Viralia, The wife of Joseph is Cora Johnson. They have eight children, Grandchildren to Elvira, Great Gr. Children to making, to me in all 22 Gr. Gr[d] Children.

Early arrivals in America of Mears & Johnsons noted in the Gen[l] Library;—

[written in margin]
hus. and wife

Suzan Johnson, B. 1612, Eng. in ship "Abigail" in 1634
John Johnson B. 1612 " " "
Edmond Johnson B. 1612 " " "James" in 1635
[last line not readable]
[words in margin, but unreadable]

[page 368]

May 1910—

Edmond Johnson (see previous page, bottom)
Mrs. Suzan Johnson, Born 1611 Eng. in ship "James." 1635
Eliza Johnson their child. (There were husband. Wife & Child)

— — —— ————

William Johnson, of London Eng. came 1635 in ship "Robert Bonaventura"

Neile Johnson. 1635, ship "John & Sarah."
Edward Johnson, 1635, " " (from Sandwich, Eng.)
Susan, his wife, 7 children and 3 servants 1635 (from Sandwich, Eng.)

Abram Johnson, of London, came 1634

— ——

John Johnson, came 1634 in ship "Hopewell"
John Johnson " " age 23 [yr] "
Robert Johnson " " " 26 " "
James Johnson " " " 28 " "

MEARS FAMILY.

Robert Mere B. 1592 came 1635 age 43 yrs. ship "Abigail" to Boston
Mrs. Elizabeth Mere (wife) B. 1605 [1635] age 30 yrs chil.
Samuel Mere B. 1630 age 3 yrs.
John Mere B. 1635 age 3 months

Note Mears is spelled in old records in more than 15 ways as noted by genealogists.

In reply to my letter to Orrin P. Allen, Genealogist, of Palmer, Mass. relative to the Johnson ancestry, he says no doubt Joel H. Johnson, my wife's Father, are descendants of William Johnson, who in 1634 or 1635, sett[l]ed in Charlestown, Uxbridge or Boston. Probably descended from William Johnson, of Charlestown, Mass. Came 1635 From London, ship "Rob[t] Bonaventura." His posterity all settled in eastern Mass, in vicinity of Uxbridge Mass.[34]

Those who defended Bunker Hill in militia, Farmers, who lived near at hand,—not regular soldirs—organized. And undoubtedly Gr. Gr[d] F. Johnson, who fell in that battle, lived near by, in or near Uxbridge.

Mr. Allen gives names of other early Johnson settlers:—John William Jun. came 1634, of Charlestown; Edward of Woburn Mass.—John, of Roxbury;—John. of Ipswich Mass. and Dea. Solomon Johnson, Sudbury, Mass. He died 1687.

June—Lyman wishes to go to his farm near Benson to day until school recommences in Sept, so Susan and I are to go to Logan on Sat. June 10th

June 9, 1910—Sister R. J. Grant sent for me to come and bless and name her baby, 8 days old. I did so.

[page 369]

June 9, 1910—This was a child of promise. Doctors had told her she could never conceive again, but I had blessed her last year that she should again become a mother, and she soon became pregna[n]t in response to her Faith. To Our Father be all praise.

This is the sixth case in which my blessing has been verified in like manner, in all of which doctors said it

34 Orrin P. Allen was a professional genealogist of the time.

could not be. And at this time (July 15. 1910) I have caused 18 persons to have no hospital operation performed by blessing them to be healed without any surgical operation. In every case doctors declared the operation was imperative, or death would surely result. No doubt such would have been the case, leaving the power of God out of consideration. I am more thankful than I can express that God has made one so weak as I ~~am~~ am the instrument of God's goodness and mercy. To Him be all honor and praise.

June 10, 1910—Saturday. Went to Logan, to my Son Charles and wife Eva.

June 20, 1910—who made us Welcome. On 20th June went to stay a few days with Nephi and Emma, Benson Ward.

June 23, 1910—Received $61.38 [$1,329], dividend for past year on my $1364.00 [$29,525] stock in the "Union Mercantile" store in Dublan, Mexico.

My sons Nephi and Charles have rented for Susan & me a small house in Logan, For $8.00 [$173] pr month. I fit it with furniture, so this money comes in good time.

June 25, 1910—Sent article for "Era" on the "Death Valley" tragedy of 1849.

JULY 1910

July 5, 1910—Recd check from Joel and Guy Taylor $17.50 [$379] and $25.00 [$541] (U.S. gold

July 9, 1910—Began getting furniture. To date July 15th $91.05 [$1,971], pd by me, besides several dollars for provisions, etc. since moving into our house July 11th 1910, We left Nephi's place July 8th

July 11, 1910—Susan's 74th Birth day. Eva made a dinner but I was not able to attend, having to be with men at the house.

I pray my dear wife may have many more & happier birth days, for she is worthy, if any woman is

A few days ago I wrote to Prest. J. F. Smith, asking that my Bro-in-law Sixtus E. Johnson may be ordained Patriarch, reciting his eminent worthiness, also told the visit of Nephi, the Nephite apostle who, the indians said visited them in Nevada, at the time of the "Ghost Dances" some years ago, and suggested that Sixtus be asked to write a statement of what the indians told him.

[page 370]

July 1910—In reply Prest Smith said he would have the first apostle who shall visit Mexico ordain him, and interview Sixtus about Nephi's visit to the indians.

He also said he had mailed my book "Pearls" which he had been examining.

July 15, 1910—Yesterday and last night, rain, first for several months.

July 24, 1910—To day Susan and I were admitted members of the 1st Ward in Logan,—Cache Stake.

August—Sent several hundred names to St George for Baptism in the Temple.

August 26, 1910—Lyman and family returned from his Preston farm to S. L. City.

August 27, 1910—Letter from Prest Jos F. Smith. Says he has left my book of "Pearls" with his Son Jos F. S. Jun, for examination by a Church Committee as I wished

October 2, 1910—My Gr. Son James Henry Johnson, son of B. S. Johnson & my eldest daughter Susan Elvira, and his wife Stella Clark, have their first child born & blessed in Mesa Ariz.

October 7, 1910—Lyman's dau. Harriet Gowan's baby girl born. 12.30 AM

October 24, 1910—Up to this date there have been born to us, besides Harriet's daughter just above noted eight Gr. Grand children during 1910 to date, as follows: some of Whom are noted above:—also in 1909

To Chas H. Martineau, dau. born 27 Sep. 1910, Chu[i]chupa,
" Saml J. Johnson, twins, Bernard Lavern and Verde Visalia Johnson, B. 13th April, Buckeye, Ariz.
" Edward Martineau, Ivans, B. 12 June 1909, Panguich
" James H. Johnson, a dau. (?) B. 10 Sep. 1910 Mesa, Ariz.
" Edward F. Turley, Lawrence B. 1909 Juarez Mex.
" T. G. Roberts, son Tillman S. Roberts B. 1909 Buckeye Ariz.
" " dau. B. 1910 " "
" James H. Johnson, Louise Elvira (?) B. Oct. 3 1910 Mesa "
" Ray Farnsworth, dau B. 1909 Chuichupa, Mex.
" William Chantril, dau. Annis B. 27 Sep.1910 Benson Utah

Besides these births Several other Grandchildren have married in 1910:—Howard Martineau & Mary Clark married in Logan temple, Utah, 29 Sep. 1910, and Emma Vilate Johnson & Chas Morton Lewis, were married in Salt Lake temple 24th Sept 1910.

[page 371]

October, 1910—Thus is being fulfilled the blessing promised of a mighty posterity. I Pray all may be true and faithful.

October 24, 1910—Up to date I have been confined much in the house, but am gradually gaining in health, tho Dr. Richards declared that as my infirmity is Locomoter Ataxia, nothing could be done for its healing. This may be true, usually, but I know the Lord is able to heal me entirely, if it be His will. If not His will, be it done, for it is always best.

I have been able to administer to some, and they have been healed by the power of the Lord.

One woman came to me from Salt Lake City for me to administer to her, 6 doctors saying she must be operated up[on], But she does not need any doctor, being on the way to speedy recovery.

Also a little girl, very low with typhoid fever, is now almost entirely well. To God be all honor.

October 24, 1910—Blessed my Great Grandchild Annis, dau. of Susan, Nephi's dau. and Wife of William Chantril. She is the first Gr. Grand Child of our 29, that I have blessed. By marriage Annis is Gr. dau. of Bp. WB Preston's Sister Annis Chantril.

[written in margin]

Mabel (Oct. 9)

I should have noted that on Oct. 9. 1910 Nephi's daughter Mabel married James Chantril in Logan temple. He, also William, were Sons of Annis Preston Chantril.

Rec^d my certificate of membership of Society of "Sons of the American Revolution from Washington D.C.,

October 30, 1910—Pres^t F. M. Lyman advised me to have my name and sons in the Book of Utah Pioneers.

November 10, 1910—Rec^d from Gr. Son Chas Henry $25.^00 [$541] on land account. His baby girl is named Lois,—my sister's and Gr. Mother Mears first names.

November 15, 1910—Rec^d letter from Señor Galan C. Porfirio Diaz of Mexico relative to his land for sale. which Susan's cousin Wm D. Johnson is endeavoring to colonize.

[page 372]

November 24, 1910—Ate our Thanksgiving dinner at Charlie's & Eva's.

December 12, 1910—Sent my petition for an increase of my "Invalid" pension as a Mexican War Soldier to Congressman Joseph Howell.[35]

December 19, 1910—Susan suddenly very sick, Charles and Eva Came I was up nearly all night with her, until she began to amend.

December 22, 1910—This evening a miracle was wrought in my behalf through faith and a blessing by Susan. For about ten years I have had an incipient rupture in left groin, a break being in the envelope of the bowels, which were prevented from emerging through the opening by a truss. By a strain by lifting and displacement of the truss my bowel gushed out forming a large swelling upon the abdomen with agonizing pain. I was unable to force it back through the small opening of about two inches or move the bowel in the least, and a light pressure upon it caused excruciating pain. All effort failing, I asked Susan to pray that the bowel might be replaced, knowing she had great faith and that she was beloved of the Lord.

She had prayed not longer than a minute, when some power—supernatural—forced the bowels back through the aperture manifestly too small for its passage, as if forced through by considerable force and yet without the least pain. I know this was done by some personage of the Spirit world, probably my Guardian Angel, who has saved me from death so many times before. And to God be all praise.

Now, I thank the Lord for this experience, though so powerful a one, for it gave me a faith to pray for healing of this affliction I did not have before, for I had never had faith before to hope for its healing by faith and prayers.

And thus, also, have I learned by many trials to trust in the Lord and to know the voice of the Holy Spirit far better than before.

35 Congressman Joseph Howell (1857–1918) was best known for the establishment of the Grand Canyon National Game Preserve. He served as a Republican Congressman from Logan from 1903 to 1917 (Christian C. Young, *In the Absence of Predators: Conservation and Controversy on the Kiabab Plateau* [Lincoln, NE: Univ. of Nebraska Press, 2002).

[written in margin]

Dec. 23 1910 Sent \$5$^{\underline{00}}$ [\$108] to help pay for name in Pioneer Book

[page 373—see Appendix 5 for letter from Geo. F. Gibbs and copy of family photo inserted here.]

December 24, 1910—The Relief Society sent us a chicken and other things for our Christmas dinner. Quite unexpected.

[written in margin]

Dec. 23d Sent \$5$^{\underline{00}}$ [\$108] to Frank Eshom, S. L. City to apply for space in "Pioneer Book." to be published soon

December 25, 1910—Susan and I ate our dinner alone, save Vere, a son of Charles, who happened in. Charles family were sick and Nephi too far away-at Benson.

December 26, 1910—Sent my pedigree to St George temple, going back, on father's side to 1376, and on my mother's side, Spragues, to 1255, in the reign of King Edward 1$^{\underline{st}}$ This I did that others in the Church might be able make connection of their lineage with mine, for scores thus are connected by intermarriage with my ancestry.

1911

January 6, 1911—Sent my genealogical record for publication in the "Pioneer Book" to Lyman to give to the publisher.

January 10, 1911—Received letter of thanks from Pres^{t} Lund for sending him an account of the discovery of the bodies of Dr. Whitmore and Robt McIntire, killed by Navajoe indians.

Deep snow last night.

January 8, 1911—On our 60$^{\underline{th}}$ wedding day Nephi and Charles and wives dined with us.

January 21, 1911—Wedding dinner of Charles & Eva—their 25$^{\underline{th}}$ ann^{y}

January 19, 1910—By letter from Henry learn his daughter Ida married [blank] on Jan. 19 1910

January 31, 1911—Susan began using obesity belt, on trial

Bertha's (Farnsworth) baby born Jan. 19th 1911

FEBRUARY 1911

February 27, 1911—By letters from Mexico I find my stock in Tannery Co. is \$248$^{\underline{00}}$ [\$5,177].

February 28, 1911—By invitation went to S. L. City to banquet of the "Sons of Amer$^{\underline{n}}$ Revolution," in which I am numbered 17322

Still very feeble. Can hardly walk. During much of the winter I have been confined to my bed the most of the time. Charles has been very good to us, sweeping snow paths, bringing in coal & water, for all which may our Father bless him and his forever. I do not know what we would have done without him & Eva [. . .]

[page 374]

March 1, 1911—Snow 4$^{\underline{in}}$ deep. Still very feeble, scarcely walk.

March 3, 1911—Walked round the city block. Fell, but was helped by a woman who saw me fall.

Administered to several who were ill.

March 4, 1911—A brother (church) came to see me. He blessed me, saying I <u>shall</u> be healed of Locomotor Ataxia, the only man with faith to say so. His name is A. Clark, of Idaho. I believe him.

March 8, 1911—Up to this date I have blessed several sick every day, as they come to me for help, & God has thus healed them all. To Him be all praise.

[written in margin]

Preston Married

This evening Lyman's son Preston married Miss Eleanora Herringer, a Catholic girl, much the surprise of his father and all of us. He is the first of my family to marry out of the church, His father was much displeased.

March 9, 1911—Before I was up a messenger came for me to go to see a woman very sick—Typhoid fever. Her temperature 105½°. Her fever instantly abated & was absolutely normal in 20 minutes, and in less than an hour she was perfectly healed. God is merciful.

March 10, 1911—Sister Julia S. Woolley & dau. Lucille came. Lucille has goitre of long standing. Blessed her. She will be healed, for she has faith. Her mother took me to Dr. Gamble, she gave me ortheopath treatment, which helped my lameness.

March 11, 1911—Visited and bessed [blessed] Maria Y. Dougal, dau. of Pr^{r}. Young also bl$^{\underline{d}}$ her daughter Catherine, whose heart beat was 160 a minute, and she very ill. Bl[d] & promised her perfect recovery: Her heart beat was soon reduced to 80.

March 16, 1911—Blest Sis[r] Witzell, also her son having "St Vitus Dane [Dance]" very badly. Note. He was healed perfectly Also blessed Mrs. that she may conceive. Also a woman, for her insanity, and another for approaching confinement, as I have several others lately; in every case words fulfilled.

[page 375]

March 17, 1911—At Relief Society. A sister who had long been childless and whom I had blessed to become a mother, came up to me with a baby, saying "Here's the baby you promised me. Every word you uttered came true." I was so thankful God had been merciful to her, and heard my prayer.

March 19, 1911—Visited Sis[t] Pola. She showed me her promised baby boy—a large, fine one. Learned of Susan is very ill. Applied for pass to go home.

March 24, 1911—Home 8 P.M. Susan had lost much blood, bleeding a stream from the nose for two days. But it had left her very feeble and bedfast. Better.

March 23, 1911—Bls[d] Mrs. King, very sick, Typhoid, soon to be be confined, Also Emma S. Hughes, sick 7 months very low, soon a mother, if she lives. Doctors say she cannot survive the ordeal in her weak state. I had promise for good for both, and blessed both with safe deliverance They both had faith.

March 28, 1911—I feared for the little unborn ones, their mothers having been sick so long—so little nourishment for the little ones, and by consent of the mothers of each baby and their mothers, I blessed each child in the womb, with promise they should be born safely, speedily and perfect in body and mind, (afterwards exactly fulfilled, for mothers and babies. In the case of Emma, the doctor declared it a miracle. It was the power and goodness of God alone.

March 30, 1911—At this date I have blessed the sick, several every day, and they have been healed.

March 31, 1911—Susan and I went to Lyman's in City.

April—Attended one meeting of Conference, Susan & I too feeble to go.

April 17, 1911—Susan taken very sick. Since we came I have administered to many, some every day.

Her sickness is erysipelas, great swelling in face and neck and violent pain.[36] (See p. 378)

[page 376]

1911—During our stay in Logan numbers have come to me for Patriarchal blessings, and very many administrations for healing the sick, in which the power and goodness of God has been shown in mighty power. In one case a Sister having heart disease for a long time was healed at once.

March 4, 1911—To day a Bro. A. Clark felt impelled to come and bless me, though a stranger, promising I shall be fully healed. I felt better immediately.

March 8, 1911—Got medal as "Indian War Veteran" from Gov. Spry. Should have had it earlier. Blessed 3 persons suffering from sickness.

My grandson Preston (Lyman's 2[d] son) was married to Eleanora Henager,—a good girl, but not a member of the church—a Catholic. I am sorry, but she may finally receive the Gospel. The wedding was at her fathers house, and most of the guests strangers to me

March 10, 1911—Sis. Julia S Woolley took me to Dr. Mary Gamble an Osteopath, for a trial treatment. She feels sure it will benefit me. I think it did, and she gave it freely. May God bless her.

March 11, 1911—Visited Catherine Dougall Platt, dau. of Sister Maria Young Dougall, She has goitre with a pulse 160 per minute. I blessed her that she shall be healed by the power of God, she has great faith and has before been greatly blessed, in becoming a mother, where was no hope of it.

March 13, 1911—Three women came for blessings for motherhood and conception.

March 14, 1911—Blessed Sis. Jewkes for confinement. Almost weekly, women come for blessing, that they may conceive and bear children. Many have done so previously, and had their blessings fulfilled in every case. So the Lord has been wonderfully good to me, in giving me power to bless and comfort my sisters, barren, but desirous of motherhood.

36 Erysipelas is an acute streptococcal infection characterized by inflammation of the skin and mucous membranes.

[page 377]

March 15 & 16, 1911—Blessed Irene Adkins and Mrs. Amot [or Arnot] who expect to be soon confined that all may be well. I will note here, that all was well, as promised. Also blessed Son of Sis. Wetzell, who has St. Vitus dance.[37] (St. Anthony's dance, so called. Also blessed Mrs. Peterson, barren, that she may conceive, and a Mrs. Horton for insanity which she fears.

March 20, 1911—Up to this time I have blessed from 2 or 3 to 6 or 7 daily, and Our Father has greatly blessed me in blessing others.

[written in margin]

Albert's boy baby

By letter I learn that Albert & Emma his wife are the happy parents of another son, born Mch. 15, 1911. All well. at 5.30 A.M. Born in Colonia Juarez. Chih. Mexico.

March 21, 1911—Susan phoned she was dangerously bleeding from the nose, for two days. Got to Logan same day, 8 P.M. I found the doctor had stopped the bleeding, but she was very weak, having lost a great deal of blood. She is now out of danger but very weak.

March 28, 1911—Administered & blessed Emma Smith Angus, about to be confined. Very sick for seven months, and legs much swollen. Dr. says if she ~~can~~ can be confined & live it will be a miracle in very deed—no strength or vitality. I obtain good testimony for her, that she shall live and be safely confined and all be well with her. Next day I thought of her poor unborn child all this time of its mother's illness, and on the next day

March 29, 1911—Went and blessed the baby in the womb, that it may be blessed, perfect in body and mind. Also blessed three women from Box Elder County

March 30, 1911—Bl. Mrs. McCrary from Box Elder County. For the last week Aurelia, Nephi's eldest daughter, who has helped us all last week, went home, she has greatly blest us.

March 31, 1911—Susan & I went to Salt Lake city for conference. She is still very weak, but I hope will be able to go. Very cold and heavy blizzard, arrived safely in the city, met by Lyman and went to his house.

APRIL 1911.

April 1, 1911—Blessed son of Sister Wetzell for St. Vitus, He has greatly improved, and I hope will soon be healed.

[page 378]

April 2, 1911—Blessed Cath. D. Platt for heart & goitre. Also to Sis. Burton (Sis. Dougal's niece) for general debility. Also to M. Y. Dougal.

April 27, 1911—Drs. S. L. Richards and [blank] opened the gathring [gathering] on Susan's face, she had suffered greatly up to this time, and I, in my feeble state nearly worn out with anxiety & little sleep.

MAY 1911

May 4, 1911—Lyman's hired girl left to day, and we had to go to Virginia's to stay. We moved in Sister Burton's Auto, as Susan could not get in carriage.

May 10, 1911—Mrs. Dr. Gamble gave Susan Osteopath treatment for severe pains in her legs. Susan growing worse all the time in her whole body, also on the 11th, 12th, & 13d by which time all pain in legs was gone.

May 15, 1911—Dr. Richards said she must get to the hospital quick as possible, she is in great danger.

In the night she saw her mother in vision who died when Susan ~~4~~ was four years old.

Susan saw herself small and dressed as a little girl of that age, just as her mother saw her last, She stood looking upward among the exceedingly white and beautiful clouds like flowers and trees, and standing between two trees that arched over her stood her mother robed in robes of exquisite whiteness, looking down at Susan a little while, then all vanished. All was far whiter and more clear than snow.

It troubled me, fearing her mother had come for her, though I said nothing. All who saw her thought she was beyond all hope.

37 St. Vitus Dance is a disease occurring chiefly in children and is associated with rheumatic fever. It is actually a version of chorea, a disease of the nervous system characterized by jerky, involuntary movements, chiefly of the face and extremities.

Lyman came with auto and took her to the hospital at 6 P.M. None but I thought she would ever return alive. She was very near death.

May 18, 1911—Susan very low, almost unconscious and able to articulate with difficulty and a strange, weird look in her eyes.

[page 379]

May 18, 1911—She told me afterwards she could die, but felt one little spark of life in her breast, Then thought of me—alone—no one to care for me as she could, and she decided to stay—for my sake. From that time she began slowly to mend. May the choice blessings of heaven be her's forever!

May 21, 1911—She seems a little better, but can hardly speak yet. Learned our house in Logan is sold, & our things carried to Charlie's and piled under a shed. Must go to Logan. I blessed and dedicated her, that all may be well with her while I am away.

May 22, 1911—Went to Logan. Visited & blessed 2 women and babies also another on 23rd and to Emma S. Hughes whose milk had totally ceased, through cold, and doctors said nothing could be done to restore. Had ceased 7 weeks. She was blessed that her breasts shall be renewed and supply abundant and healthy milk for this and all her future children. She believed.

May 24, 1911—To S. L. City. Found Susan still very low. I fear. Her eyes have so strange a look. Can scarcely speak. I got my [Cluthe] truss.

May 28, 1911—Susan better. But very weak. I visit her every day at 2 P.M. from the very first, but can stay but 2 hours.

JUNE

June 2, 1911—Susan now able to sit up a little, if lifted from bed. Henry and Melissa, Charles his son and wife Florence Whetton came to Hospital. It gave Susan new life They had just come from Mexico.

June 7, 1911—Charles baptized, also Melissa 20 men & 15 females (dead) and 8th were endowed for John Mears and Martha Mears. Charles & Florence baby Lois, born previous to their sealing in S. Lake temple (they having married in Mexico) was sealed to her parents.

June 10, 1911—Moved Susan to her niece Margaret Smith Jensen in Auto, by Nebeker's auto. We hire room there. Margaret nurses her tenderly, our meals free.

[page 380]

June 12, 1911—Susan now able to walk to next room and sit at table. I am obliged to go to Logan to day.

June 13, 1911—Visited Emma Hughes again. Her milk had gain [again] filled her breasts as promised, and she and baby doing finely. The doctor had tested her milk and found it perfect. Was astonished and "Can't understand it! It's a miracle." His mistak[e]—the power and goodness of the Lord To Him be praise.

I also Blessed three others the same day

June 14, 1911—At Old Folks Party in Agricultural Bldg. but did [not] remain to end. Felt impressed to leave, and found and blessed 5 persons, who had been seeking me anxiously.

June 15, 1911—Returned to City and found another swelling on Susan's face becoming very serious. The doctor said it must be lanced at once or serious consequences would follow. Susan and [I] objected feeling it was not necessary. She sits up a little.

June 18, 1911—The doctor again insisted on an operation, but we declined. Seth Johnson and family visited. Dr. Richards sent his bill $ [blank] Hospital bill $78.40 [$1,636]—Graft, too much for so poor atten[d]ance at the hospital (L. D. S. Groves)

June 26, 1911—As our room was let to another person before we took it, we went to board with Widow Robinson, to whom I had administered (and healed) for cancer of the womb. While living with her we applied [antophlo giston], to Susan swelling, and it healed it. We had one room in the 18th Ward, S. L. City. Lyman sent total bills for Susan's Sickness;—Richards $62.00 [$1,294] Hospital $79.40 [$1,657].

JULY

July 1, 1911—Nephi's daughter Aurelia married F. W. Stock.

[written in margin]

Note

Elvira's dau. married—Emma Vilate Johnson to Charles Lewis 13 Sep. 1910 Arizona.

July 11, 1911—Susan's 75th birthday. Henry dined with us May she have as many more as she shall wish in increased health, strength and prosperity.

[page 381]

July 13, 1911—We removed to Charlie's, Logan, to stay until Nephi can be ready for us on his farm a few miles north of Logan. Found all well.

July 24, 1911—Susan and I went to 24 Celebration in the Logan Tabernacle in an auto. This is the first time she has been out anywhere, being still quite feeble, and the first day she has left the bandages on her face necessitated by the last abcess on it.

AUGUST 1911

August 2, 1911—Had my photo taken for insertion in "Pioneer Book of Utah."[38]

August 7, 1911—Moved to Nephi's farm between Logan and Hyde Park, in Greenville Ward.

August 29, 1911—Up to this time since the 24th all Nephi's horses (3) have died, leaving only a small pony.

I learn Albert has exchanged all my stock in the "Union Mercantile" store in Dublan, Mexico for land in Sonora, Mexico, value $1364.00 [$28,471] and its dividend at 8 o/c [percent] is $55.12 [$1,151] total value $1419.12 [$29,623] and this without my knowledge or consent. It places me in straightened circumstances.

SEPTEMBER 1911

September 9, 1911—By letter from Gr. son James Johnson I learn that his sister Gertrude Johnson Roberts has a son—3d child born 3d Sept. 1911 at Buckeye Ariz.

September 12, 1911—Sixtus ordained Patriarch, at San Jose, Sonora by Apostle Richards

September 18, 1911—Albey Sherman, my bro-in-law, died 7.30 P.M. in Huntington, Utah, aged 78.

September 21, 1911—Lyman Royal Jr, my Gr. Son, married Zayde E. Bothwell, and next day they went to Harvard College, Mass. He has a year yet in [law] course

[written in margin]

Note 12th

Geo. Albert, my son to day ordained Bishop of San Jose, Sonora, Mex. by Apostle Richards

Signor di Martins, Italian Charge de affairs at Constantinople may be of our family.

[page 382]

October 7, 1911—Went to Salt Lake City, and went to my son-in-law Frank K. Nebeker and Lilla by Frank's invitation

October 8, 1911—At Church conference next day met Henry and Seth Johnson, Susan's brother from southern Utah.

October 2, 1911—Administered to and blessed Clara, dau. of Maria Young Dougall, for blessing approaching maternity who fears miscarriage,

October 13, 1911—Blessed Sis. Bull, Anna Knight & boy and Mrs. Wickel and her child, also Irene Adkins.

October 14, 1911—Blessed Sis. Billings

October 16, 1911—Blessed Sister M. Y. Dougall, also Sis. Burton, and son Julian, who is in great danger from blood-poison.

October 17, 1911—Attended funeral of Prest J. Henry Smith

October 20, 1911—To date have been continually blessing the sick

October 21, 1911—Gave Prest Lund an account of the visit of Nephi, of ancient days, to the indians of Southern Nevada. The account was given by them to my bro-in-law Sixtus E. Johnson, who for over 60 years, has been a trusted friend to them. They said this visitor said his name was Nephi; he told the Mormons were their friends—not to steal from them; told them of ancient Nephites and Lamanites, and taught them many days. Messengers were sent to gather indians for hundreds of miles around, in several states.

Prest Lund was greatly pleased.

October 30, 1911—Up to date I have been daily administering to the sick, many of them seriously, but all are healed, & it is by the goodness and power of God, not by me.

I start home, staying all night with Charles. I blessed Sis. Ellen Nibley, Str [Sister] Moses Thatcher and daughter

October 31, 1911—At home and found all well.

38 These records are at the Church Historian's Office.

NOVEMBER.

November 16, 1911—After a stay with Nephi of about 3 months we remove to Salt Lake City, to make it our final home, as Lyman has rented a house for us, and we go to the city, staying in Logan a few days, part of the time with Sister Ellen Nibley. but most of the time with our son Charles, who was quite ill with a swollen leg.

[written in margin]

home Salt Lake Nov. 17 1911

[page 383]

November 25, 1911—Saturday, Arrived in the city, and Lyman took us to our new home 545½ E. 6th S. which he & Alli, his daughter had made habitable with our furniture and some furnished by them; 3 rooms, bath and pantry. A nice, pleasant place, 3 rooms & toilet &c.

[written in margin]

Note

I note here that during our 5 days in Logan I gave several blessings, admd to several severe cases of kidney and womb disease, and blessed Jessie Knowles, sick for 5 weeks and recently with inflammatory rheumatism all over her body. All these were healed at once, by the power of the Lord. Blessed also Mrs. Afton Knowles, in critical condition, who was wonderfully benefited. She was pregnant & fearing.

DECEMBER (ERROR, TOO SOON)

December 2, 1911—To day Lyman presented me a new suit of clothes.

December 17, 1911—Sunday attended High Priests meeting of Liberty Stake. We are members of 9th Ward, Bp. Woolley.

[written in margin]

too soon

December 31, 1911—Up to this time have lived quietly, knowing very few of our neighbors, occasionally giving a blessing or visiting the sick

November

[written in margin]

Note

November 20, 1911—My gr. dau. Ida Martineau Jesperson's baby girl, her first child, was born in Chuichupa, Mexico. She is Henry's daughter.

JANUARY 1912

January 6, 1912—Became almost totally deaf, could scarcely hear my own voice, Susan blessed me, and I soon regained my hearing. She has great faith.

January 8, 1912—Our 60th Wedding day. Made dinner for Lyman, Lilla and Gean (Elizth and Virginia)

January 11, 1912—Visited Widow of Prest W. Woodruff and blessed her. My cousin Wm A. Mears and wife met me in Hotel Utah—first time I ever saw either. They were returning home to Seattle Wash, from a business trip (Panama Canal) in Washington D.C.

[page 384]

1912

January 12, 1912—Received a letter from Mrs. Anna Louise Mears Thompson, of Washington D. C. She is Natl Secy of "Daughters of American Revolution" in Washington D. C. Her address is 715 Pine St. She wrote me that a Mears (John Mears) fought under Paul Jones in "Bon Homme Richard" against the Serapis in Rev. War. Also that a Mears came to England with William the Conqueror in 1066.

I have since seen the record of the battle of Hastings, when three French Lords (Mears) fought with their Knights and retainers.

January 13, 1912—Joel wrote. Wishes to buy our home in Juarez.

[written in margin]

Note

I learn that Susan's mother (Anna Pixley Johnson) was born Aug 7 1800 in Canaan N. H. she married George G. Johnson, and [blank] Sarah Sophie Johnson Apr. 22, 1820, Keen, Essex Co. N. Y.

January 22, 1912—As requested by cousin Annie W. Mears I began search for family names of her line of Whipple and others, intermarried. She is not a Mormon, but has spent much time and money in genealogical research also in the Mears line of her husband, my cousin, Wm A. Mears. She found the name of John Mears, who served in the army in the Burgoyne

Campaign, 1777, under Gen. Gates. By this I obtained membership in the Society of "Sons of the American Revolution of which I am proud. I will state here, that I have since found other names, Samuel and Thomas Mears, both in the battle of Lexington, my mother's Grand uncles, also one who was with Washington, at Valley Forge, a boy of only 16 years. I have also a record of 3 others, French Lords with William Conq[r] at battle of Hastings, 1066, one of whom gained an estate in Wales and built three castles now in ruins. Another, a Martino, was a Knight of St John of Jerusalem, a crusader. His crest or armorial bearing was a shield, argent (silver) with three towers, sable. (black).[39]

[page 385 is left as a blank page]

[page 386]

1912

January, 1912—Three Roman generals, one under Emperor Maximus, one under Belisarius, and another in Syria—Catullus Martinus, A.D. 70, where his daughter Lucilla died A.D. 70, age 18 years. Her marble tomb still stands with ancient ruins as seen by a Mormon elder some years ago, who described it to me as like this:

Fig. 10.3—Lucilla Martinus Tomb.

It is more fully described with its inscription in a former entry of this record.

February 24, 1912—Susan had nose-bleed—started suddenly, 1 pint up with her all night.

March 3, 1912—Administered to Jessie Sterling, a young woman who 15 years has been badly twisted bodily by paralysis. Also blessed two others

March 12, 1912—Blessed Mrs. Kirkpatrick for falling of uterus to the open air. Believe she will be healed

39 Argent is a metal tincture used in heraldry to give a silvery appearance.

April 9, 1912—Blessed Clara Bergstrom, lately confined that her milk should be returned. It <u>was,</u> almost at once Also Blessed her sister, Catherine Platt, (both were gr. daughters of Pres[t] Brigham Young) that she might conceive, which soon occurred. She had long been barren and hopeles[s]. I had thus previously blessed her sister Clara, as noted above, who had been told by physicians she could never again conceive since the birth of a son years before. For all that all praise be to God, for He brought all to pass.

[written in margin]

Note

April 28, 1912—I find my maternal Gr. mother Mears was daughter of Stephen Hutchinson, 2[d] son of Lord Hutchinson, who was an officer killed at the massacre of the British garrison of Fort George by Montcalm's indians, 1757

Genealogical. On a tomb of Catacomb of Rome is the body of Aurelia Martina, Christian martyr inscribed "To the well deserving the chamber of Aurelia Martin a wife most chaste & modest who lived in wedlock 23 years 11 ~~months~~ days.

[page 387]

1912

April 1912—To the well deserving one who lived 40 years, 11 months, 13 days. Her burial was on the third Nones[40] of October, Nepotianus and Farundus [Faranundus] being conjuts [consorts]. In peace. A.D. 360 [...] (From the Cemetery of Calixtus, Pope and Martyr.

[written in margin]

Note

The name of the mother of Lucilla Martinus wife of Gen. Catullus Martinus, was <u>Sempronia</u>

MAY 1912

May 1, 1912—Up to this date I have administered to the sick or troubled in mind almost all the time since coming to the city to live, many have been desperate

40 The ninth day before the ides of a month; in the ancient Roman calendar, this was the seventh day of March, May, July, or October and the fifth day of the other months.

cases, given up to die by the doctors, but almost all have been healed by faith & the power of God, to whom be all the praise. Several cases of Cancer of the womb, falling of the same, quick consumption, blindness, paralysis, appendicitis, barrenness, typhoid fever and other troubles.

Elizabeth (Lilla Nebeker) has sent food to us weekly for the last two months, a great help to us. May God bless & heal her.

May 3, 1912—Fred[k] J. Holton called to see me today, as the U. S. Surveyor who in 1877 noted land as "Mineral" where he is now tunneling for gold. He said it was shown him in a dream several times, and he found the ground just as he dreamed.

I finished my family list of names for the "Pioneer Book" of early Utah Settlers.

May 4, 1912—Kenneth Crismon came home from Medical College in Philadelphia, where graduated at the head. He is Lyman's Son-in-law.

JUNE 1912

June 11, 1912—Learn that a son was born to Nephi and Emma on [blank] weighed 8 ½ lbs.

June 19, 1912—Went to Lagoon with Susan. Beautiful place.

June 25, 1912—Went to Hooper on excursion Ind. war Veterans

June 26, 1912—Went to Wandamere, [41] "Old folks excursion.

June 27, 1912—At 2.30 A.M. Susan taken very sick, and continue so till July 6th. Then I took my turn

[pages 388 and 389 are blank]

[page 390]

JULY 1912

July 8, 1912—My cousin W[m] A Mears sent me $10[00] [$209] for Genealogical names of Mears ancestry I sent him.

July 10, 1912—Susan's sister Janet Johnson Smith, the widow of my dear Bro. Jesse N. Smith, & several daughters came from St. Johns, Ariz.

July 11, 1912—Susan's 76 birth day. Aged in years but to me always young. May she have many more, with the choice blessings of heaven.

July 13, 1912—Miss. Marian E. Martins gave me treatment with electric Vibrator, and lent it [to] me

July 24, 1912—I am still very feeble

AUGUST 1913

August 1913—My electric stove cost $8.00 [$167] burns El[c] power 80 Watts per hour. Iron 80 Watts. We use the electric heater to save coal.

August 15, 1912—Our first letter from Annie since she, with 60 of my family, was driven from homes in Mexico. All had good homes some worth $25.000[00] to $300.000[00] [$521,836 to $6,262,034] She had a nice brick residence well furnished, orchard of 3 acres choice fruit, cows fowls, and plenty. Left her home as it stood, herself and 7 children, taking 1 trunk, 1 pillow and 7 quilts & the clothes they stood up in. Escaped to El Paso, Texas lived weeks under open shed, no privacy and at last given money by U. S. government to come, finally to Logan, Utah

My other children and married Grand children are scattered I know not where in, Arizona, Texas & New Mexico

August 21, 1912—finished paying for 2[d] hand sewing machine $15.[00] [$313] price. Administered to Mrs. Dorothy Kenner, suffering greatly in her whole arm for several weeks. She instantly was healed. Her mother gave me $5.00 [$104].

[page 391]

AUGUST

August 29, 1912—Letter from Joel. Sent my damage list (Rebel plunder) but not in full. I want him not to return to Mexico till peace is fully restored.

SEPTEMBER

September 4, 1912—Am very unwell and nearly helpless.

September 16, 1912—The Kindergarten children & teachers came as a surprise to us. Sang songs & gave us their little presents—an apple, a few grapes, a flower, etc. It was sunshine to us.

41 Wandamere Gardens in Salt Lake City.

September 27, 1912—George and Ernest, my grandsons, with each a girl they would marry, came & saw us a few hours. They married in Salt Lake temple, to Miss Langford & [blank]

September 30, 1912—Went to the fair. Very tired & feeble.

OCTOBER

October 2, 1912—Georg[e] and Lilly May Langford, and Ernest and Stella May Jones, and blessed both

October 4, 1912—girls Oct. 4

October 16, 1912—Learn Henry's dau. Bertha Farnsworth has boy baby born Sep. 27 27 1912

October 30, 1912—Snow this morning.

NOVEMBER

[See Appendix 3 for receipt for payment of article inserted here.]

November 3, 1912—Got letter from Albert, from Douglas Ariz. Sent $10.^{00}$ [$209] on amount due me.

November 4, 1912—Mrs. Martins has endowed 20 of my dead. Gave her 20 more names to endow for me.

November 5, 1912—Susan and I voted.

November 16, 1912—Elzada, Albert's daughter, came to stay with us.

During the past week I got about 500 names for baptism. Elzada was baptized for 40, I also sent 620 to St George temple for baptism.

I am very feeble—hardly able to in the house.

Phyllis, Anna's daughter, was married to William J. Preston.

November 19, 1912—Anna came with 6 children from refugee camp in El Paso, and in afternoon went to Logan, 4 P.M.

[page 392]

November 1912—It was a time of rejoicing, tho she had left a good home, with 3 acres of choice fruit trees, cows, chickens, and good furniture, dishes &c. She and her 7 children left home in haste with 7 quilts, 1 pillow and one trunk, left fruit cooking on the stove & fruit jars to be filled. Word had come to get away as quickly as[to] not risk death by Mex. Bandits. She and 4000 others had shelter for a time in an old and open lumber shed, with no privacy, lying on a quilt spread on bare ground—one quilt as cover.

El Paso people gave clothing, bedding, milk for children, and were very kind, & the U. S. government gave R. R. transportation free to any part of United States.

The Church gave $5.00 [$104] to each person.

Anna felt well—not murmering. I blessed her her son Louis Osborn. I learn that my Grandson Joseph Johnson & Sara have another daughter born Aug 17, 1912.

November 24, 1912—David Johnson my wifes brother came, He gave $10 [$209] for a life membership in the Genealogical Society and some money to use to do Temple ~~wor~~ work for his Mothers family the Bryants of Vermont. I paid for his membership in the Genealogical Society Later sent it to him

November 30, 1912—First snow, Bro C H Dunn has been baptized in the temple for 20 dead

December 14, 1912—Sick in bed with very bad cough

December 19, 1912—still in bed, Susan suddenly taken very sick with La grippe. Our neighbors were very kind to give us food & doing good in many ways.

December 25, 1912—A sorry Christmas both feeble but able to be up & about the house, Lyman invited us to dinner but we were unable to go,

December 30, 1912—I went out to day first time for about 3 weeks walked 2 blocks administer to a sick woman, though still feeble,

[page 393]

1913

January 1, 1913—Lillie invited us to dinner but we were too feeble to accept the invitation

[Penmanship has been difficult to read in the last few pages, denoting the feeble condition of James Henry. The handwriting changes at this point as if he is dictating to someone else to write for him.]

January 8, 1913—Our 61st wedding day. Several friends not our relatives remembered us and brought picnic and we had a very pleasant time.

January 25, 1913—Mrs Fowkes, who has had no children for seven years, and desiring to become a mother, and whome I have blessed that She Should be came and brought to Show me a fine boy as in fulfillment of the promise.

January ~~30~~ 20, 1913—Recieved a letter from Mrs. Sterling in Alberta Canada Saying She Saw our picture in the Deseret News and remembered that 33 years ago She arrived late one night in Logan on a R. R. traine and found no one to meet her as She expected and did not know where to go. She said we took her home and cared for her till her friends came and She had never forgotten it. Susan and I had forgoten it long ago.

January 29, 1913—Attended banquet of Sons of American Revolution.

FEBRUARY

February 5, 1913—Blessed a child for curvature of the Spine.

February 25, 1913—Received lists of 620 names baptized for in St George Temple. The Sisters in the temple had voluntary endowed 154 female names without charge. May God bless them forever.

[page 394]

OCTOBER 1913

October 3, 1913—My granddaughter Elzada my Son Alberts daughter who has been with us about a year went home to her perants in Arizona.

October 6, 1913—Phyllis Preston. Annies daughter has a girl born Sept 26 1913 in Pima Arizona.

October 9, 1913—My brother in law Nephi Jenson has examined the records in Charlston, Marlboro, Haverhill, ~~Leving~~ Leominster, Southboro, Worcester Longhill in Mass. Also in Truro N. S.

Up to this date there has been little daily change. The Sick and troubled have come almost daily to be administered to, meny [many] cases being very dangerous but almost every one departed feeling greatly blessed. And I have visited a great meny habitions [habitations] of the afflicted and troubled and God has greatly blessed my labors. To Him be all the honor praise and glory.

NOVEMBER

November 4, 1913—Elzada was babtised for a 133 names.

DECEMBER

December 12, 1913—David W. Johnson my brother in law desires me to assist him in doing temple work for his mothers family. Her fathers name was Charls [Charles] Bryant and his wifes name Susan Fuller. There childrens names were Daniel, Alfreda, Charls Martha Asa and Willard

[page 395]

DECEMBER ~~1914~~ 1913

December 16, 1913—Cousin William A. Mears writes me that his wife, Annie O. Mears died Dec 4 1914 in Seattle Wash. She had done much in obtaining the genealogy of her fathers family and had given me help in my enealogy [genealogy]. It was through her investigation that I was able to find out the connection of my ancestors with the Revolutionary war. I found that my Great Grandfather John Mears Served in the Burgoyne campaign in 1777 and that another grand uncle John Mears was with Paul Jones in his battle with the Serapis on the coast of England. In obtaining her information she had spent much time and money.

JANUARY 1914

January 20, 1914—Bought a Sewing Machine price $65 [$1,279] payable monthly installments. [handwritten in, apparently later] Due $44.00 [$866].

FEBRUARY 1914

February 6, 1914—My Grand Son Royal Martineau's son was born weighed ten pounds.

February 27, 1914—Dressed My Self today all but coat vest and Shoes having for months been unable to do so either to dress or undress my self for nearly a year. Some of the time I could not even wind my watch or feed my Self. Kidney trouble

[page 396]

[Handwriting again changes as if a different scribe was used.]

NOVEMBER 23, 1914.

November 23, 1914—Today removed to No. 1 Gudgells Ct. We were compelled to move as the owner of the present residence was going to demolish it & build a new house. Our new residence was more pleasant than the other. Rent. $15.^{00}$ [$295] month. Close to street car line & near the 2nd Ward Chapel.

June 14, 1915—Rec'd information that my pension had been increased to $30.^{00}$ [$590] a month instead of $12; [$236] for which we were very thankful, as our former pension of $12 was insufficient. The increase was obtained by Senator Reed Smoot. I pray that he may never need a friend, without having one & that he may be greatly prospered. Susan has had a very severe fit of sickness & Mrs. Steele a lodger in the same house has been very good & attentive every day. She is not a Morman but is a good woman & I pray that the choice blessings of Heaven may rest upon her. I also had a very severe attack & very dangerous one of bladder trouble, but was relieved by surgical aid. In other respects our daily life has been about the same as usual. My time being mostly spent in visiting the sick & blessing & comforting those who came to me, for help in their afflictions, bodily & mentally; many in a very serious condition, but all who came in sorrow & distress left me in smiles & peace of mind. Oh Father in Heaven, I thank thee for this power to bless those sad or afflicted in mind; and numbers of these afflictions were very serious indeed. I will state one case: A young woman came to me about 10:30—her mother very sick & in great pain, desiring me to go to her mother's assistance. The side walks were icy & I did not dare to go in the dark for fear of falling. I said to her, "Do you ever pray?"

[page 397]

She said, "You bet I do." I said "Put your hands upon her head & ask God in the name of Jesus Christ to heal her & I believe it will do her good." She came early next morning. I said, "What did you do?" She said, "I just put my hand on mother's head & said 'Be healed in the name of Jesus Christ, Amen. She was." All pain instantly ceased & she was instantly healed. Thus God hears & answers the prayers of faith. Many other cases equally serious have been healed by faith in my experience. One young woman paralyzed from head to foot unable to move, healed perfectly by one administration. A woman stone blind twenty years her sight perfectly restored. Two woman, each with an internal cancer (one sentenced to die in three months & the other in five months, by counsels of doctors) were both perfectly healed, one in two days & the other in three. Many other cases of healing were miraculous. In all this, all the praise & honor & glory be ascribed to our Father in Heaven, for He it was not me who showed forth His power & mercy. I have been repaid in my labors in the joy that I have experienced in helping to make others happy. One of my greatest delights is this.[42]

November 21, 1918—I come now to the saddest occurance in my life. A week before Thanksgiving Day (1918) having a chicken someone sent us & Susan said "We'll have our Thanksgiving dinner today."

November 22, 1918—Daughter Annie & husband Alvin J. Hawkes & son Louis Osborn Turley, together with my granddaughter Clara Turley & Elzada Martineau Jackson & her husband Hyrum Jackson were here to a big dinner, which Annie brought down in honor of Clara's 17th birthday, but Susan couldn't partake of it. Her stomach was upset. Her trouble was a clogging of the bowels which caused an entire stoppage of the contents of the bowels so that they couldn't be moved.

[page 398]

And the two doctors had no hope for her from the start. She suffered agonizing pains almost without cessation. Her daugh[ter] Annie & granddaughter Elzada, myself & others were unceasing in attempts to help her. During the last four days she was partially unconsious, with occasional short spells when she was consious & in one of those consious moments; as

42 Although Martineau's journal writing was slowing with his age, he continued to write for the newspapers. Two articles of history appeared this year: "J.H. Martineau, "Pioneer Incidents—A Mystery of Desert," *Deseret Evening News*, September 30, 1916, and "Veteran Engineer and Survivor Tells of . . . Days in Long and Active Life," *Deseret Evening News*, April 2, 1916 (inside marginal notes indicated this may have come from the *Herald Republic*); Journal History.

I sat by her constantly fanning her; she looked up with an expression of joy beyond measure saying "Oh how lovely, how beautiful everything is up there, so beautiful, so lovely, no words can tell." A glimpse of a better world had been opened & the day before she said as I said by her she was consious for a short time & she lay pointing with her fingers up to the Heavens with an expression upon her countenance of infinite joy. I said "Susan, what do you see?" She said, "I see the face of my Savior," & then she became again unconsious & slept for several hours as peacefully as a little baby, breathing naturally but a little quicker than usual, taking apparently full breath when suddenly she stopped breathing the next day at 4:10 P.M. & was gone. (The awful death gurgle was in her throat from 5 A.M. till 4:10 Dec. 5, 1918. While in her semi-consious state I sang several of our old familiar songs to her, hoping it might tend to quite [quiet] her excited nerves & it did, for although she was unconsious the sound of my voice seemed familiar to her & several times she weakly joined in with me & repeated one or two lines that I had sung. Now she can sing with the angels of Heaven.

[page 399]

Thus was fulfilled the blessing she received in 1865 from Patriarch Chas. W. Hyde, who told her she should live to be eighty and three years old, & should see the face or the coming of the Savior. She did die in her 83rd year & did see the face of her Savior.

I had often wondered in reading her blessing how it could be fulfilled & did not expect the coming of the Savior so soon as that; but to fulfill the promises of the patriarch did show her His face by vision.

No one can realize except by experience such a loss to me, but gain to her. For sixty-seven years lacking a few days had we been united. She only 15½ yrs. old & I twenty three when we married. In all that time she never once gave me evil counsel, nor held me back from my duty, when at times it is difficult to obey them. Numbers of times we faced death together from the Indians; once when she reentered the house she saw her little daughter Elvira, about 6 years old, crouching down on the floor crying bitterly, an Indian holding above in one hand, threatening to kill her with a big butcher knife. Unarmed she flew at him like a tigress, seizing him by the shoulders, dragged him from her child & with a piece of stove wood beat him over the head & face, until he was glad to escape on the run. And for a year Indians came from a distance to see & admire the white 'squaw' who beat an Indian. Upon another occasion she rescued a little child two years old, which a squaw had concealed under her blanket & was carrying away. She passed our house & was about to enter the willows, from which if once safe there, she couldn't be found.

[page 400]

The child was a Curtis boy & is a grown man today. She desired & was granted a badge as an Indian war veteran.

She recieved every ordinance of the church. The highest that was given, and will sit upon a throne of glory as one of the queen's of Heaven; to become mother to innumerable spirits born, who will eventually people a new earth & pass through an experience similiar [similar] to ours as we have done, & as Our Father in Heaven has done; who in His earthly experience feared & trembled lest He should fail.

[In the following paragraph, the original writing was crossed out and the other words were written over the top in a very shaky hand.]

In 1915, ~~one evening~~ I suddenly awoke at 3 A.M. and as I lay ~~reading in bed~~ I felt a strange sensation & plainly saw about an inch of thumb & fore finger which turned out the light & I said "What is all this?" A voice answered, "I am your son John W^{m}. Don't you remember your little Johnny who died so long ago? (He died in 1863 at the age of 5 years.) He said "I came to visit you first, because I died first. Della was come next, because she died next to me." He told me much that would happen, much of which I have forgotten, which I should of written. But he said as I well remember that mother should live to be eighty-three & should die in peace without any pain, which she did, & that I should live twenty years longer & should die in ~~smoke~~ fire, but without pain. I said, "Will I burn?" He said "No, you'll die just as if asleep." Then he said, "I must go now" & I again saw his thumb & finger seize & turn on the switch of the lamp relighting it. [in shaky hand the next part was added] which I was unable to do

[page 401]

I feel very sad to be left alone, once I had fourteen at the table, now I sit alone. I have many children who are good & loving, but they cannot fill the place of wife. I pray thee O Father in Heaven to help and comfort me the rest of my days & that I may be able in due time to rejoin my loved ones, never more to separate.

During her sickness and after her death, my son Lyman was of very great assistance to me, but in care for her while living & in arranging details of her funeral. My daughter Annie was also present & also my granddaughter Elzada; also my sons, Nephi from St. Anthony Ida. & Joel from Mexico. She was buried Dec. 7, 1918 in the City Cemetary; Nephi & Joel paying the funeral expences of more than two hundred dollars. Inasmuch as all this occured during the influenza scourge, during which schools & churches were closed, her funeral was not public but private attended by especial loved friends. Lyman took me to his own house & gave me a room for my own comfort, with Annie's daughter Clara to assist; for which I am to pay him \$35.[00] [\$689] a month. For a long time I have been almost helpless myself. For a long time unable to undress myself alone, but now so able to do so, but with difficulty of putting on my coat & vest. I can't stand or walk alone, but expect to be finally healed, that I may do the work which is appointed me in the future,

Add [written in shaky hand]

[See Appendix 6 for numerous newspaper clippings, family letters, certificates, and documents from dignitaries such as Hyrum G. Smith, Joseph F. Smith, William B. Preston, Lorenzo Snow, and Wilford Woodruff inserted following Martineau's final journal entry.]

Fig. 10.4—"The subject of building a temple at Juárez, Mexico was first suggested by Bro. James H. Martineau. He noted that it cost about $750 in Mexican money for a couple to come from the Mexican colonies to Salt Lake City to be married or do other temple work. President L. Snow favored the building of the Endowment House in Mexico, and perhaps another in Canada and also one in Arizona." From minutes of a meeting at the Salt Lake Temple 11:45 a.m., December 9, 1897. Present Presidents W. Woodruff, G. Q. Cannon, J. F. Smith, and L. Snow; Elders J. H. Smith, G. Teasdale and H. J. Grant.

APPENDICES

In providing context for the journals, the editors and family have provided family group sheets. Those of Martineau's immediate family are found on pages xxxi–xxxvi, and the extended family group sheets are in Appendix 1.

The remaining appendices relate to a variety of materials Martineau inserted as reminders. It appears that these were items that he had later intended to insert, describing within his narrative. The editors have included many of these here to facilitate future research.

APPENDIX

1

MARTINEAU FAMILY COAT OF ARMS AND EXTENDED FAMILY GROUP SHEETS

A1.1
THIS COAT OF ARMS WAS OFFICIALLY ADOPTED BY THE JAMES HENRY MARTINEAU ORGANIZATION.

Martineau Coat of Arms

In the 12th century Europe, knights and nobles began painting their shields to identify themselves while wearing full armor. These early coat of arms clearly showed the person's family identity. Symbolism and choice of color was very important. Unique heritage, noble deeds, and personal traits were placed on the family shields as a record for future generations information.

Our coat-of-arms has its origins within the royal lineage of France.

The coat of arms itself can be described as a quarterly shield with the 1st and 4th quarters each containing a gold cross on a field of white. **The 2nd and 3rd quarters** contain bordure shields containing a holly leaf on a field of red, overlaid on a gold shield on a field of green. **The center bordure shield** contains three castles in a lozenge field. A crown with three plumes is set upon the helmet at the top of the master shield. **The colors of three plumes are azure (blue), vert (green), and gules (red). The master shield is divided into four parts or quarters.**

The **1st and 4th quarters** contain a cross each. The **two crosses** are of strong Christian significance. They were awarded to families who engaged in the Crusades. The **three castles** or towers prominently set in the center of the master shield represent grandeur, society, and wealth. They can also represent towns or land tracts/kingdoms that may have been owned by the Martineau family. The **2nd and 3rd quarters are bordure shields** or a shield superimposed upon another. According to the *Glossary of Heraldic Terms* (Kyl MacKay Glenrakon) a bordure shield represents honor. It is of strong significance the bordure shield is represented not twice but three times in the coat of arms.

The two holly leaves represent 'truth' (*Guide to Medieval Terms* - Arkenberg). They are placed on a gules (red) field that represents 'warriors in battle, martyrs, and strong military strength'. The outer gold or 'Or' field that the holly shield is placed is on a field of **vert (green)**. The 'Or' field represents generosity. The **green or vert represents fidelity**. The helmet is significant of royal birth. The visor and mouth slit form a Crusader cross outlined in gold on a silver face plate. The helmet carries the heraldic interpretation of wisdom and reliable defense. The gold crown on the helmet prominently displays three feathered plumes - blue, green, and red. The gold crown itself represents the regal or senior authority, also 'heavenly reward' (*Heraldry Glossary,* Parker - 1894).

The colors in coat of arms are of high significance. Colors can help tell the history of the family, qualities of character and personality, and personal accomplishments by family ancestors. The **azure (blue) plume** represents strength and loyalty. The **vert (green) plume** means hope and loyalty in love. The **gules (red) plume** signifies military leadership. The three plumes together can symbolize the ancient Martineau family motto - **loyalty, fidelity, noble leadership, and hope.**

Note: This research provided to JHMFO by Paul McCarty

A1.2
JOHN AND ELIZA MEARS MARTINEAU FAMILY
PARENTS AND SIBLINGS OF JAMES HENRY MARTINEAU

John Martineau

Birth: 22 Mar 1793, Port Richmond, Staten Island, Richmond County, New York
Death: 6 Apr 1838, Elbridge, Onondaga County, New York
Buried: Elbridge, Onondaga County, New York
Married: 29 Apr 1824, Florida, Montgomery County, New York

Eliza Mears

Birth: 13 Apr 1806, Fabius, Onondaga County, New York
Death: 6 Jul 1848, Elbridge, Onondaga County, New York
Buried: Elbridge, Onondaga County, New York

Children:

1. ***Emily Henrietta Martineau***
Birth: 18 Oct 1825, <Huntsville, Madison County, Alabama>
Death: 21 Jul 1899, place unknown

2. ***James Henry Martineau***
Birth: 13 Mar 1828, Port Jackson, Montgomery County, New York
Death: 24 Jun 1921, Salt Lake City, Salt Lake County, Utah
Buried: 26 Jun 1921, Logan, Cache County, Utah

3. ***Charles Augustus Martineau***
Birth: 19 Jan 1831, New York City, New York County, New York
Death: 27 Feb 1831, New York City, New York County, New York

4. ***Francis Eliza Martineau***
Birth: 31 Sep 1831, Elbridge, Onondaga County, New York
Death: 15 Jun 1847, Victory, Cayuga County, New York

5. ***Harriet Martineau***
Birth: 26 May 1835, Elbridge, Onondaga County, New York
Death: 16 Oct 1837, Elbridge, Onondaga County, New York

6. ***Lois Elenor Martineau***
Birth: 10 Aug 1838, Elbridge, Onondaga County, New York
Death: 4 May 1919, Tomah, Monroe County, Wisconsin

7. ***male baby Martineau (stillborn)***
Birth: 5 Jul 1848, Victory, Cayuga County, New York
Death: 5 Jul 1848, Victory, Cayuga County, New York

A1.3
JOEL HILLS JOHNSON FAMILY
PARENTS AND SIBLINGS OF SUSAN ELLEN JOHNSON, FIRST WIFE OF JAMES HENRY MARTINEAU

Joel Hills Johnson

Birth: 23 Mar 1802, Grafton, Worchester County, Massachusetts
Death: 25 Sep 1882, Johnson, Kane County, Utah
Buried: 27 Sep 1882, Johnson, Kane County, Utah

Father: Ezekiel Johnson
Mother: Julia Hills

First Wife: Anna Pixley Johnson

Birth: 7 Aug 1800, Grafton, Worchester County, Massachusetts
Death: 11 Sep 1840, Macedonia, Hancock County, Illinois
Buried: 16 Sep 1840, Ramus, Hancock County, Illinois
Married: 2 Nov 1826, Pomfret, Chautauqua County, New York

Father: Timothy Johnson
Mother: Anna Pixley

Children:

1. Julia Ann Johnson

Birth: 2 Oct 1827, Pomfret, Chautauqua County, New York
Death: 18 Jul 1829, Pomfret, Chautauqua County, New York

2. Sixtus Ellis Johnson

Birth: 8 Oct 1829, Pomfret, Chautauqua County, New York
Death: 4 Jun 1916, Benson, Cochise County, Arizona
Buried: 5 Jun 1916, Pomerene, Cochise County, Arizona

3. Sariah Anna Johnson

Birth: 18 Feb 1831, Amhurst, Lorain County, Ohio
Death: 27 Mar 1925, Hurricane, Washington County, Utah
Buried: Mar 1925, Hurricane, Washington County, Utah

4. Nephi Johnson

Birth: 12 Dec 1833, Kirtland, Geauga County, Ohio
Death: 21 Jun 1919, Mesquite, Clark County, Nevada
Buried: Jun 1919, Mesquite, Clark County, Nevada

5. Susan Ellen Johnson

Birth: 11 Jun 1836, Kirtland, Geauga County, Ohio
Death: 5 Dec 1918, Salt Lake City, Salt Lake County, Utah
Buried: 7 Dec 1918, Salt Lake City, Salt Lake County, Utah

6. Seth Guernsey Johnson

Birth:	6 Mar 1839, Carthage, Hancock County, Illinois
Death:	22 Dec 1927, Cannonville, Garfield County, Utah
Buried:	24 Dec 1927, Georgetown, Garfield County, Utah

Second Wife: Susan Bryant

Birth:	28 Aug 1812, Vergennes, Addison County, Vermont
Death:	7 Apr 1896, Colonia Díaz, Chihuahua, Mexico
Married:	20 Oct 1840, Nauvoo, Hancock County, Illinois

Father:	Charles Bryant
Mother:	Susan Fuller

Children:

1. Nancy Maria Johnson

Birth:	2 Aug 1841, Ramus, Hancock County, Illinois
Death:	5 May 1842, Ramus, Hancock County, Illinois

2. Emily Johnson

Birth:	20 Nov 1842, Ramus, Hancock County, Illinois
Death:	20 Nov 1842, Ramus, Hancock County, Illinois

3. Joel Hills Johnson Jr.

Birth:	2 Jun 1844, Ramus, Hancock County, Illinois
Death:	20 Feb 1846, Ramus, Hancock County, Illinois

4. Julia Ann Johnson

Birth:	20 Feb 1847, French Creek, Hancock County, Illinois
Death:	9 Apr 1879, Parowan, Iron County, Utah
Buried:	12 Apr 1879, Parowan, Iron County, Utah

5. David William Johnson

Birth:	12 Feb 1849, Millcreek, Salt Lake County, Utah
Death:	20 Mar 1924, Mesa, Maricopa County, Arizona
Buried:	Mar 1924, Mesa, Maricopa County, Arizona

6. Mary Susan Johnson

Birth:	27 Nov 1850, Cottonwood, Salt Lake County, Utah
Death:	10 Mar 1851, Millcreek, Salt Lake County, Utah

7. Joel Hills Johnson

Birth:	27 Nov 1850, Millcreek, Salt Lake County, Utah
Death:	17 Jun 1902

8. Almon Babbitt Johnson

Birth: 21 Feb 1855, Johnson, Iron County, Utah
Death: 23 Nov 1890, Colonia Díaz, Chihuahua, Mexico

Third Wife: Janet Fife

Birth: 17 Feb 1828, Leith, Midlothian, Scotland
Death: 18 Jun 1911, Snowflake, Navajo County, Arizona
Buried: 20 Jun 1911, Snowflake, Navajo County, Arizona
Married: 25 Oct 1845, Snowflake, Navajo County, Arizona

Father: James Fife
Mother: Margaret Mathison

Children:

1. Janet Mauretta Johnson

Birth: 17 Dec 1848, Millcreek, Salt Lake County, Utah
Death: 21 May 1933, Snowflake, Navajo County, Arizona
Buried: 24 May 1933, Snowflake, Navajo County, Arizona

2. Margaret Johnson

Birth: 19 Mar 1850, Salt Lake City, Salt Lake County, Utah
Death: 19 Dec 1879

3. James Fife Johnson

Birth: 25 May 1852, Enoch, Iron County, Utah
Death: 20 Feb 1905, Hillsdale, Garfield County, Utah
Buried: 22 Feb 1905, Hillsdale, Garfield County, Utah

4. Joseph Elmer Johnson

Birth: 22 Jan 1855, Cedar City, Iron County, Utah
Death: 18 Oct 1857

5. Hyrum Johnson

Birth: 27 Nov 1856, Cedar City, Iron County, Utah
Death: 27 Nov 1856, Cedar City, Iron County, Utah

6. Carlos Johnson

Birth: 27 Nov 1857, Cedar City, Iron County, Utah
Death: 9 Oct 1866, Cedar City, Iron County, Utah

Fourth Wife: Lucinda Alzina Bascom

Birth: 26 Oct 1815, Brookfield, Madison County, New York
Death: 18 Oct 1885, Provo, Utah County, Utah
Married: 25 Oct 1845, Grafton, Worchester County, Massachusetts

Father: Ezekial Bascom
Mother: Sarah Pate

Children:

1. ***Joel Andrew Johnson***
   Birth: 22 Jul 1847, Oglesby, LaSalle County, Illinois
   Death: 7 Jun 1926, Provo, Utah County, Utah
   Buried: 9 Jun 1926, Provo, Utah County, Utah

Fifth Wife: Margaret Threlkeld

Birth: 22 Jul 1840, St. Mary, Carlisle, Cumberland, England
Death: 25 Dec 1914, Tropic, Garfield County, Utah
Buried: 28 Dec 1914, Tropic, Garfield County, Utah
Married: 11 Oct 1860, Salt Lake City, Salt Lake County, Utah

Father: John Threlkeld
Mother: Elizabeth Barker

Children:

1. ***Esther Ellis Johnson***
   Birth: 23 Dec 1861, Virgin, Washington County, Utah
   Death: 4 Aug 1949, Parowan, Iron County, Utah
   Buried: 7 Aug 1949, Parowan, Iron County, Utah

2. ***Mary Elizabeth Johnson***
   Birth: 17 Aug 1864, Virgin, Washington County, Utah
   Death: 27 Mar 1877

3. ***Joseph Hills Johnson***
   Birth: 1 Dec 1866, Virgin, Washington County, Utah
   Death: 23 Dec 1908, Tropic, Garfield County, Utah
   Buried: 25 Dec 1908, Tropic, Garfield County, Utah

4. ***Ezekiel Johnson***
   Birth: 16 Apr 1869, Bellevue, Washington County, Utah
   Death: 25 Feb 1957, Fruita, Mesa County, Colorado
   Buried: 28 Feb 1957, Salt Lake City, Salt Lake County, Utah

5. *Almera Woodward Johnson*

Birth: 25 Oct 1871, Bellevue, Washington County, Utah
Death: 19 Aug 1937, Provo, Utah County, Utah
Buried: 21 Aug 1937, Delta, Millard County, Utah

6. *Jeremiah Johnson*

Birth: 9 Apr 1874, Bellevue, Washington County, Utah
Death: 8 Feb 1879, Bellevue, Washington County, Utah
Buried: Feb 1879, Bellevue, Washington County, Utah

7. *Margaret Hannah Johnson*

Birth: 16 Apr 1876, Bellevue, Washington County, Utah
Death: 10 Dec 1917, Roosevelt, Duchesne County, Utah
Buried: 13 Dec 1917, Roosevelt, Duchesne County, Utah

8. *Amos Partridge Johnson*

Birth: 26 Mar 1878, Bellevue, Washington County, Utah
Death: 25 May 1895
Buried: May 1895, Bellevue, Washington County, Utah

9. *John Henry Johnson*

Birth: 7 Jan 1881, Johnson, Kane County, Utah
Death: 15 Sep 1972, Farmington, Davis County, Utah
Buried: 20 Sep 1972, Tropic, Garfield County, Utah

A1.4
LYMAN ROYAL SHERMAN FAMILY
PARENTS AND SIBLINGS OF SUSAN JULIA SHERMAN, SECOND WIFE OF JAMES HENRY MARTINEAU

Lyman Royal Sherman

Birth: 22 May 1804, Monkton, Addison County, Vermont
Death: 27 Jan 1839, Far West, Caldwell County, Missouri
Married: 16 Jan 1829, Pomfret, Chautauqua County, New York

Father: Elkanah Sherman
Mother: Asenath Hurlbut

Delcina Diadamie Johnson

Birth: 19 Nov 1806, Westford, Chittenden County, Vermont
Death: 21 Oct 1854, Salt Lake City, Salt Lake County, Utah
Buried: Oct 1854, Salt Lake City, Salt Lake County, Utah

Father: Ezekiel Johnson
Mother: Julia Hills

Children:

1. Elvira Sherman

Birth: 1829, Jamestown, Chautauqua County, New York
Death: Nov 1850, Kanesville, Pottawattamie County, Iowa

2. male baby Sherman

Birth: abt 1830, Chautauqua County, New York
Death: bef 31 Jul 1831, Chautauqua County, New York

3. Mary E. Sherman

Birth: bef 31 Jul 1831, Pomfret, Chautauqua County, New York
Death: 19 Aug 1850, Council Bluffs, Pottawattamie County, Iowa
Buried: Aug 1850, Council Bluffs, Pottawattamie County, Iowa

4. Albey Lyman Sherman

Birth: 30 Oct 1832, Jamestown, Chautauqua County, New York
Death: 18 Sep 1911, Huntington, Emery County, Utah
Buried: 20 Sep 1911, Huntington, Emery County, Utah

5. Seth Guernsey Sherman

Birth: 30 Jun 1836, Kirtland, Geauga County, Ohio
Death: Nov 1850, Council Bluffs, Pottawattamie County, Iowa

6. Daniel Sherman

Birth: 1837, Kirtland, Geauga County, Ohio
Death: bef 1849, Nauvoo, Hancock County, Illinois

7. Susan Julia Sherman

Birth: 21 Oct 1838, Far West, Caldwell County, Missouri
Death: 28 Jan 1874, Logan, Cache County, Utah
Buried: 29 Jan 1874, Logan, Cache County, Utah

A1.5
EZEKIEL AND JULIA HILLS JOHNSON FAMILY
AUNTS AND UNCLES OF SUSAN ELLEN JOHNSON, FIRST WIFE OF JAMES HENRY MARTINEAU

Ezekiel Johnson

Birth: 12 Jan 1773, Uxbridge, Worchester County, Massachusetts
Death: 13 Jan 1848, Nauvoo, Hancock County, Illinois
Buried: Jan 1848, Nauvoo, Hancock County, Illinois
Married: 12 Jan 1801, Grafton, Worchester County, Massachusetts

Julia Hills

Birth: 26 Sep 1783, Upton, Worchester County, Massachusetts
Death: 30 May 1853, Council Bluffs, Pottawattamie County, Iowa
Buried: May 1853, Council Bluffs, Pottawattamie County, Iowa

Children:

1. Joel Hills Johnson

Birth: 23 Mar 1802, Grafton, Worchester County, Massachusetts
Death: 24 Sep 1882, Johnson, Kane County, Utah
Buried: 27 Sep 1882, Johnson, Kane County, Utah

Spouses:

First Wife: Anna Pixley Johnson
Birth: 7 Aug 1800, Canaan, Grafton County, Massachusetts
Death: 11 Sep 1840, Macedonia, Hancock County, Illinois
Buried: 16 Sep 1840, Ramus, Hancock County, Illinois
Married: 2 Nov 1826, Pomfret, Chautauqua County, New York

Second Wife: Susan Bryant
Birth: 28 Aug 1812, Vergennes, Addison County, Vermont
Death: 7 Apr 1896, Colonia Díaz, Chihuahua, Mexico
Married: 20 Oct 1840, Macedonia, Hancock County, Illinois

Third Wife: Lucinda Alzina Bascom
Birth: 26 Oct 1815, Brookfield, Madison County, New York
Death: 18 Oct 1885, Provo, Utah County, Utah
Married: 25 Oct 1845, Nauvoo, Hancock County, Illinois

Fourth Wife: Janet Fife
Birth: 17 Feb 1827, Leith, Midlothian, Scotland
Death: 18 Jun 1911, Snowflake, Navajo County, Arizona
Buried: 20 Jun 1911, Snowflake, Navajo County, Arizona
Married: 25 Oct 1845, Kirtland, Lake County, Ohio

Fifth Wife: Margaret Threlkeld
Birth: 21 Jul 1840, Carlisle, Cumberland, England
Death: 25 Dec 1914, Tropic, Garfield County, Utah
Buried: 28 Dec 1914, Tropic, Garfield County, Utah
Married: 11 Oct 1860, Salt Lake City, Salt Lake County, Utah

2. *Nancy Mariah Johnson*

Birth: 1 Aug 1803, Grafton, Worchester County, Massachusetts
Death: 30 Oct 1836, Kirtland, Geauga County, Ohio
Buried: Oct 1836, Kirtland, Geauga County, Ohio
Married: 10 Feb 1827, Grafton, Worchester County, Massachusetts

Spouse: Joseph J. Clark
Birth: 1803, Massachusetts

3. *Seth Guernsey Johnson*

Birth: 14 Feb 1805, Royalton, Windsor County, Vermont
Death: 19 Feb 1835, Kirtland, Geauga County, Ohio
Buried: Feb 1835, Kirtland, Geauga County, Ohio

Spouse: Sophia Stone
Birth: 1805, Dana, Worchester County, Massachusetts

4. *Delcina Diademie Johnson*

Birth: 19 Nov 1806, Westford, Chittenden County, Vermont
Death: 21 Oct 1854, Salt Lake City, Salt Lake County, Utah
Buried: Oct 1854, Salt Lake City, Salt Lake County, Utah
Married: 16 Jan 1829, Pomfret, Chautauqua County, New York

Spouse: Lyman Royal Sherman
Birth: 22 May 1804, Monkton, Addison County, Vermont
Death: 27 Jan 1839, Far West, Caldwell County, Missouri

5. *Julia Ann Johnson*

Birth: 9 Nov 1808, Westford, Chittenden County, Vermont
Death: 17 Oct 1857, Crescent City, Pottawattamie County, Iowa
Buried: 24 Oct 1857, Council Bluffs, Pottawattamie County, Iowa
Married: 23 Nov 1833, Kirtland, Geauga County, Ohio

Spouse: Almon Whiting Babbitt
Birth: 1 Oct 1813, Cheshire, Berkshire County, Massachusetts
Death: 24 Oct 1856, East of Fort Laramie, Goshen County, Wyoming

6. David Partridge Johnson

Birth: 10 Sep 1810, Westford, Chittenden County, Vermont
Death: 3 Oct 1833, Kirtland, Geauga County, Ohio
Buried: Oct 1833, Kirtland, Geauga County, Ohio

7. Almera Woodward Johnson

Birth: 12 Oct 1812, Westford, Chittenden County, Vermont
Death: 4 Mar 1896, Parowan, Iron County, Utah
Buried: Mar 1896, Parowan, Iron County, Utah
Married: 16 Nov 1845, Nauvoo, Hancock County, Illinois

Spouse: Reuben Barton
Birth: 9 Jan 1812, Plainfield, Hampshire County, Massachusetts
Death: 2 Apr 1891

8. Susan Ellen Johnson

Birth: 16 Dec 1814, Pomfret, Chautauqua County, New York
Death: 16 Mar 1836, Kirtland, Geauga County, Ohio
Buried: Mar 1836, Kirtland, Geauga County, Ohio

9. Joseph Ellis Johnson

Birth: 28 Apr 1817, Pomfret, Chautauqua County, New York
Death: 17 Dec 1882, Tempe, Maricopa County, Arizona
Buried: 18 Dec 1882, Mesa, Maricopa County, Arizona

Spouses:

First Wife: Harriet Eloise Snider
Birth: 4 Sep 1823, Toronto, York, Ontario, Canada
Death: 17 Jun 1905, Tempe, Maricopa County, Arizona
Buried: 18 Jun 1905, Mesa, Maricopa County, Arizona
Married: 6 Oct 1840, Nauvoo, Hancock County, Illinois

Second Wife: Hannah Maria Goddard
Birth: 2 Jul 1828, Schuylkill County, Pennsylvania
Death: 20 Oct 1919, San Diego, San Diego County, California
Buried: 22 Oct 1919, San Diego, San Diego County, California
Married: 2 Dec 1850, Council Bluffs, Pottawattamie County, Iowa

Third Wife: Eliza Saunders
Birth: 19 Feb 1840, London, Middlesex, England
Death: 22 Mar 1903, Salt Lake City, Salt Lake County, Utah
Buried: 23 Mar 1903, Salt Lake City, Salt Lake County, Utah
Married: 1856, Council Bluffs, Pottawattamie County, Iowa

10. Benjamin Franklin Johnson

Birth: 28 Jul 1818, Pomfret, Chautauqua County, New York
Death: 18 Nov 1905, Mesa, Maricopa County, Arizona
Buried: 20 Nov 1905, Mesa, Maricopa County, Arizona

Spouses:

First Wife: Melissa Bloomfield LeBaron
Birth: 28 Jan 1817, Leroy, Genesee County, New York
Death: 4 Sep 1860, Santaquin, Utah County, Utah
Buried: 6 Sep 1860, Santaquin, Utah County, Utah
Married: 25 Dec 1841, Kirtland, Geauga County, Ohio

Second Wife: Mary Ann Hale
Birth: 11 Aug 1826, Whitestown, Oneida County, New York
Death: 17 Dec 1910, Mesa, Maricopa County, Arizona
Buried: 18 Dec 1910, Mesa, Maricopa County, Arizona
Married: 12 Oct 1844, Macedonia, Hancock County, Illinois

Third Wife: Flora Clarinda Gleason
Birth: 2 Aug 1819, Tolland, Hampden County, Massachusetts
Death: 13 Aug 1900, Monroe, Sevier County, Utah
Buried: Aug 1900, Monroe, Sevier County, Utah
Married: Jan 1846, Nauvoo, Hancock County, Illinois

Fourth Wife: Harriet Naomi Holman
Birth: 28 Jan 1834, Leroy, Genesee County, New York
Death: 1 Aug 1914, Raymond, Alberta, Canada
Buried: 2 Aug 1914, Raymond, Alberta, Canada
Married: 17 Mar 1850, Salt Lake City, Salt Lake County, Utah

Fifth Wife: Sara Melissa Holman
Birth: 18 Nov 1838, Kirtland, Geauga County, Ohio
Death: 5 Oct 1901, Mesa, Maricopa County, Arizona
Buried: Oct 1901, Mesa, Maricopa County, Arizona
Married: 3 Feb 1856, Salt Lake City, Salt Lake County, Utah

Sixth Wife: Susan Adaline Holman
Birth: 7 Oct 1841, Nauvoo, Hancock County, Illinois
Death: 5 Feb 1919, Mesa, Maricopa County, Arizona
Buried: Feb 1919, Mesa, Maricopa County, Arizona
Married: 8 Feb 1857, Salt Lake City, Salt Lake County, Utah

Seventh Wife: Sarah Jane Spooner
Birth: 1 Oct 1839, Cardiff, Glamorganshire, South Wales
Death: 5 Nov 1911, Mesa, Maricopa County, Arizona
Buried: Nov 1911, Mesa, Maricopa County, Arizona
Married: 5 Apr 1859, Salt Lake City, Salt Lake County, Utah

11. Mary Ellen Johnson

Birth: 7 Feb 1820, Pomfret, Chautauqua County, New York
Death: 11 Jun 1845, Nauvoo, Hancock County, Illinois
Buried: Jun 1845, Nauvoo, Hancock County, Illinois
Married: 7 Feb 1842, Macedonia, Hancock County, Illinois

Spouse: George Deliverance Wilson
Birth: 28 Dec 1807, Shelburne, Chittenden County, England
Death: 18 Oct 1887, Hillsdale, Garfield County, Utah
Buried: 20 Oct 1887, Hillsdale, Garfield County, Utah

12. Elmer Wood Johnson

Birth: 26 May 1821, Pomfret, Chautauqua County, New York
Death: 14 Sep 1822, Pomfret, Chautauqua County, New York
Buried: Sep 1822, Pomfret, Chautauqua County, New York

13. George Washington Johnson

Birth: 19 Feb 1823
Death: 22 Jan 1900, Moab, Grand County, Utah
Buried: 25 Jan 1900, Moab, Grand County, Utah

First Wife: Maria Jane Johnston
Birth: 28 Oct 1824, Wartrace Creek, Bedford County, Tennessee
Death: 14 Feb 1911, Huntington, Emery County, Utah
Buried: 17 Feb 1911, Huntington, Emery County, Utah
Married: 14 Apr 1844, Macedonia, Hancock County, Illinois

Second Wife: Eveline Burdick
Birth: 19 Sep 1832, Jamestown, Chautauqua County, New York
Death: 13 Feb 1911, Provo, Utah County, Utah
Buried: 14 Feb 1911, Provo, Utah County, Utah
Married: 1 Oct 1851, Salt Lake City, Salt Lake County, Utah

Third Wife: Clarice Maxwell
Birth: <1827>, <Pomfret, Chautauqua County, New York>

14. William Derby Johnson

Birth: 27 Oct 1824, Pomfret, Chautauqua County, New York
Death: 13 Apr 1896, Colonia Díaz, Chihuahua, Mexico
Buried: 15 Apr 1896, Colonia Díaz, Chihuahua, Mexico
Married: 2 Nov 1848, Nauvoo, Hancock County, Illinois

Spouse: Jane Cadwallader Brown
Birth: 5 Jun 1832, Birmingham, Erie, Ohio
Death: 19 Jan 1908, Colonia Díaz, Chihuahua, Mexico
Buried: 21 Jan 1908, Colonia Díaz, Chihuahua, Mexico

15. Esther Melita Johnson

Birth: 12 Jan 1828, Pomfret, Chautauqua County, New York
Death: 15 Mar 1876, Salt Lake City, Salt Lake County, Utah
Buried: Mar 1876, Salt Lake City, Salt Lake County, Utah
Married: 28 Mar 1844, Macedonia, Hancock County, Illinois

Spouse: David Tulley LeBaron
Birth: 24 Nov 1822, Leroy, Genesee County, New York
Death: 31 Aug 1905, Mesa, Maricopa County, Arizona
Buried: 2 Sep 1905, Mesa, Maricopa County, Arizona

16. Amos Partridge Johnson

Birth: 15 Jan 1829, Pomfret, Chautauqua County, New York
Death: 9 May 1842, Macedonia, Hancock County, Illinois
Buried: May 1842

A1.6
ELKANAH SHERMAN FAMILY
AUNTS AND UNCLES OF SUSAN JULIA SHERMAN, SECOND WIFE OF JAMES HENRY MARTINEAU

Elkanah Sherman

Birth: 1780, Monkton, Addison County, Vermont
Death: after 1817
Married: about 1802

Asenath Hurlbut

Birth: 2 Aug 1780, Norwich, Hampshire County, Massachusetts
Death: 1854, Salt Lake City, Salt Lake County, Utah

Children:

1. Almon Worthy Sherman

Birth: <9 May 1803>, <Monkton, Addison County, Vermont>
Death: 30 Dec 1869, Oak Lake, Becker County, Minnesota
Married: 14 May 1835, Geauga County, Ohio

Spouse: Lois Huntington Cutler
Birth: 2 Mar 1811, Upper Lisle, Broome County, New York
Death: 11 Apr 1880, Oak Lake, Becker County, Minnesota

2. Lyman Royal Sherman

Birth: 22 May 1804, Monkton, Addison County, Vermont
Death: 27 Jan 1839, Far West, Caldwell County, Missouri
Married: 16 Jan 1829, Pomfret, Chautauqua County, New York

Spouse: Delcina Diademie Johnson
Birth: 19 Nov 1806, Westford, Chittenden County, Vermont
Death: 21 Oct 1854, Salt Lake City, Salt Lake County, Utah
Buried: Oct 1854, Salt Lake City, Salt Lake County, Utah

3. George Sherman

Birth: about 1806, Vermont

4. Martin Joshua Sherman*

Birth: 22 Nov 1807, Monkton, Addison County, Vermont
Death: 20 Sep 1889

5. Elberta Jane Sherman

Birth: abt 1808, Vermont
Death: bef 1815

6. Male baby Sherman

Birth: abt 1809, <Monkton, Addison County, Vermont>

7. Cornelia Jane Sherman

Birth: 11 May 1812, Kirtland, Lake County, Ohio
Death: 26 Jun 1882
Married: abt 1832, <Kirtland, Lake County, Ohio>

Spouse: Edmond Fisher
Birth: 7 Jul 1803, Massachusetts
Death: 5 Sep 1872

8. Electa Elenor Sherman

Birth: 5 May 1816, Kirtland, Lake County, Ohio
Married: 9 Apr 1835, Kirtland, Lake County, Ohio

Spouse: John Alexander Whitesides
Birth: 19 May 1811, North Carolina
Death: 1886

** Martin Joshua Sherman is not found in FamilySearch.org but is included in some families in Ancestry.com.*

APPENDIX

INSERTS BEFORE VOLUME 1

A2.1
THIS CERTIFICATE IS A FORM THAT WAS FILLED OUT BY HAND. ITALICS SHOW HANDWRITTEN PARTS.

CERTIFICATE

TO WHOM IT MAY CONCERN:

This Certifies That *James Henry Martineau*
Susan Ellen. Jesse N. George Albert. Julia Henrietta.
Joel Hills. Elizabeth. Virginia. Gertrude. Theodore
Anna Sariah
are Members of the Church of Jesus Christ of Latter-day Saints, in *Logan First* Ward, of the Cache Valley Stake of Zion, in full fellowship, and as such we recommend *them* as worthy to ~~receive~~ *Join any*
Ward they may desire
~~blessings in the house of the Lord.~~

B. M. Lewis.. Per W. G. B Bishop.
W. G. Burton Clerk ~~President.~~

Logan Sep[tr] 12th 188*4*
JHM is an High Priest.
Jessie N. is an Elder
Joel H. is a Priest
P.S. Dora a child under 8 Years of age

A2.2

THIS FORM WAS FILLED IN BY HAND. ITALICS SHOW THE HANDWRITTEN PARTS. IT IS FOUND IN THE FRONT OF JOURNAL 1.

B-4-P.83-

Sep 26

This form [of blank] is to be used in giving information required for baptisms or endowments; other blanks are provided for sealings. Writing should be plain and legible, and information as complete and accurate as possible. The Saints should make themselves familiar with the instructions issued concerning temple ordinances, printed copies of which can be obtained from the doorkeeper.

Name of Heir, or Friend, at whose instance this work is done *James H. Martineau*

NAMES IN FULL	BORN DAY / MONTH / YEAR	WHERE BORN TOWN / COUNTY / STATE OR COUNTRY	DIED DAY / MONTH / YEAR	BAPTIZED DAY / MONTH / YEAR	ENDOWED DAY / MONTH / YEAR	NAMES OF PROXIES	RELATIONSHIP OF ABOVE NAMED TO THE DEAD
2457 Mr. Meers	*1669*	*London Eng.*		*Sep 26 1916*		*Henry A Martineau*	*Rel.*
2468 William Meers	*--- --- ---*	*" "*	*15 June 1761*				*"*
2462 Edward Meerz	*1644*						
2464 Edward Meerze	*22 Oct. 1675*						
Thomas Meerze	*22 Mch. 1679*						
Henry Meerze	*26 May 1685*						
2470 John Meerze	*11 Feb 1702*						
2473 Richard Meerze	*17 Mar 1705*			[sets of initials are listed in the "Baptized" column]			
Edward Meerze	*8 apr 1707*	*all noted in Record*					
2075 John Meers	*1672*						
2076 John Meers	*1743*			*CAM*			
2486 Thomas Meeerz	*1717*			*BJ*			
Mr. Mears (abt)	*1750*			*AAQ*			
John V. Mears	*16 Aug 1750*			*WAI*			
2483 Mr. Mears	*1587*			*H*			
2456 Mr. Blague	*1582*						
2743 Edward Meares	*1690*			[across these in shaky handwriting is]			
2779 Peter Smith	*1812*						
2781 William Stevens	*1770 [or 1776]*			*Ready for Bap*			
2782 Thomas Mears[e]	*1795*						
Edward Meerze	*8 apr 1707*						
2075 John Meers	*1672*						
2076 John Meers	*1743*						
2486 Thomas Meeerz	*1717*						
Mr. Mears (abt)	*1750*						
John V. Mears	*16 Aug 1750*						
2483 Mr. Mears	*1587*						
2456 Mr. Blague	*1582*						
2743 Edward Meares	*1690*						
2779 Peter Smith	*1812*						
2781 William Stevens	*1770 [or 1776]*						
2782 Thomas Mears[e]	*1795*						

A2.3
PAGE SHOWING NOTES HANDWRITTEN BY MARTINEAU IN SHAKY HANDWRITING

1st death in [illegible]

Jan. 23 1853 Dr. Wm A Morse died [illegible] by [illegible]

April 15 1853 Trapped by Walker - [illegible]

Party J A Little, J [illegible] Barry Carter, O Lewis

[illegible] Burton J. L. Hyatt and Clyde Lot. [illegible]

Also A. [illegible] + [illegible] Mirk

Johnson Springs — Ind name = Pah [illegible]

Sunday Oct 2 1854 Br [illegible] began teaching new alphabet.

Col Dame appointed me Regt Adjutant

Brass Band org ~~Oct. 10 (Tuesday)~~ (date Oct 18 [illegible]

April 5 1855 Arapeen, Utes Chief, refused the request of
Col. Steptoe to sell Utah lands to the whites. Said
was willing whites should live here, but dedicated himself &
tribe to the Lord. Steptoe annoyed.
Steptoe had been [illegible] to and healed by Arapeen & other medicines. [illegible] Steptoe testified to [illegible].
Barry Ward interpreted.

X I was ordained H Priest by Geo A Smith & Jo L Smith & was
set apart as 1st Counselor to Pres J C L Smith
Monday May 21 1855

Dec 26 Jan 1855 [illegible] Parowan [illegible] Lake

Jan 1 [illegible] R. [illegible] End - 30 [illegible] [illegible] Apr 14 29
Apr 27

A2.4
HANDWRITTEN DOCUMENT SIGNED BY BRIGHAM YOUNG AND WILLARD RICHARDS.

Utah Territory
Executive Department

Whereas, a vacancy has occurred in the Office of Judge of Probate in Iron County, in consequence of the resignation of Calvin C. Pendleton, the former incumbent of said office

Therfore, I, Brigham Young, Governor of said Territory, by virtue of the Authority vested in me do hereby appoint John Steele of said County, Judge of Probate of said County, to fill said vacancy, and to hold said Office until superceded by due course of Law.

Done at Great Salt Lake
City, this Twenty fifth
day of August, in the year
of our Lord one thousand
Eight Hundred and Fifty
three, and of the Independence
of the U. S. of America the Seventyes

Brigham Young
Governor

Brigham Young

W. Richards
Secretary Pro Tem
Appointed by the Governor

A2.5
NEWSPAPER CLIPPING.

EPISTLE
OF
ELDER WILFORD WOODRUFF,
ONE OF THE TWELVE APOSTLES.

To the Church of Jesus Christ of Latter-day Saints, and to all the world, Greeting:—

the earth. This testimony I bear to all nations under heaven, and I know it is true by the inspiration of Almighty God, and the decision of the Supreme Court of the United States bears me out in the opinion that the constitution gives me the privilege of enjoying my belief, and faith and opinion in religion, *if I do not act.* Therefore the acts and execution of all these tremendous events I leave for the God of heaven to execute, which he most assuredly will. What I have spoken I have spoken, and I excuse not myself, and "though the heavens and the earth pass away, my words will not pass away, but will all be fulfilled," saith the Lord of Hosts. I subscribe myself an Apostle of the Lord Jesus Christ, and member of the Church of Jesus Christ of Latter-day Saints.

WILFORD WOODRUFF.

A2.6
CLIPPING SHOWING SIGNATURES OF FRANKLIN D. RICHARDS, HEBER J. GRANT, AND JOHN HENRY SMITH.

Franklin D. Richards
Heber J. Grant
John Henry Smith

A2.7
HANDWRITTEN LETTER BY THOMAS BULLOCK.

James H. Martineau

Sir

You are hereby cited to be and appear before the High Council in Great Salt Lake City, in the 13th ward vestry room, on Wednesday April 9, 1862, at 10 a.m. and bring and have with you, on a trial between Thomas Bose and Seth M. Blair, all books and accounts showing the transactions between said Bose and Blair— and give evidence in said case.

Herein fail not.

Thomas Bullock

Clerk of High Council

Great Salt Lake City

March 18/62

Bro. T. Bose will pay you for your loss of time.

A2.8
HANDWRITTEN NOTE.

Parowan November 6th 1860
This is to certify that James H. Martineau
his [is] a member of the High Priests Quorum
in Parowan and as [has] been since December 22nd 1855
and having removed North we recommend him
to any Quorum of the High Priesthood he
may wish to join
Calvin C. Pendleton Prest
High Priests Quorum
Parowan Stake

A2.9
HANDWRITTEN RECEIPT FOR TITHING.

Parowan Tithing Office April 19th 1860
This is to Certify that James H. Martineau has paid
his Tithing in full to Jany.1.1860 and we recommend
him to the confidence of the Saints where he may be
located,

Wm. G. Warren
Bishop

A2.10
HANDWRITTEN NOTE FROM WILFORD WOODRUFF.

There must be order observed in the House
of God in regard to these Ordinances for the dead
or confusion of the gravest character may arise.
A little reflection will show this to you.
With Kind regards
Your Brother.
Wilford Woodruff

[The following is a note in the corner of this sheet, but it doesn't appear to belong with anything on the page.]

I
bought
March 14. 1871
Logan. Cache Co
U. T.
[unreadable alphabet letter]

A2.11
HANDWRITTEN LETTER ON CHURCH STATIONERY.

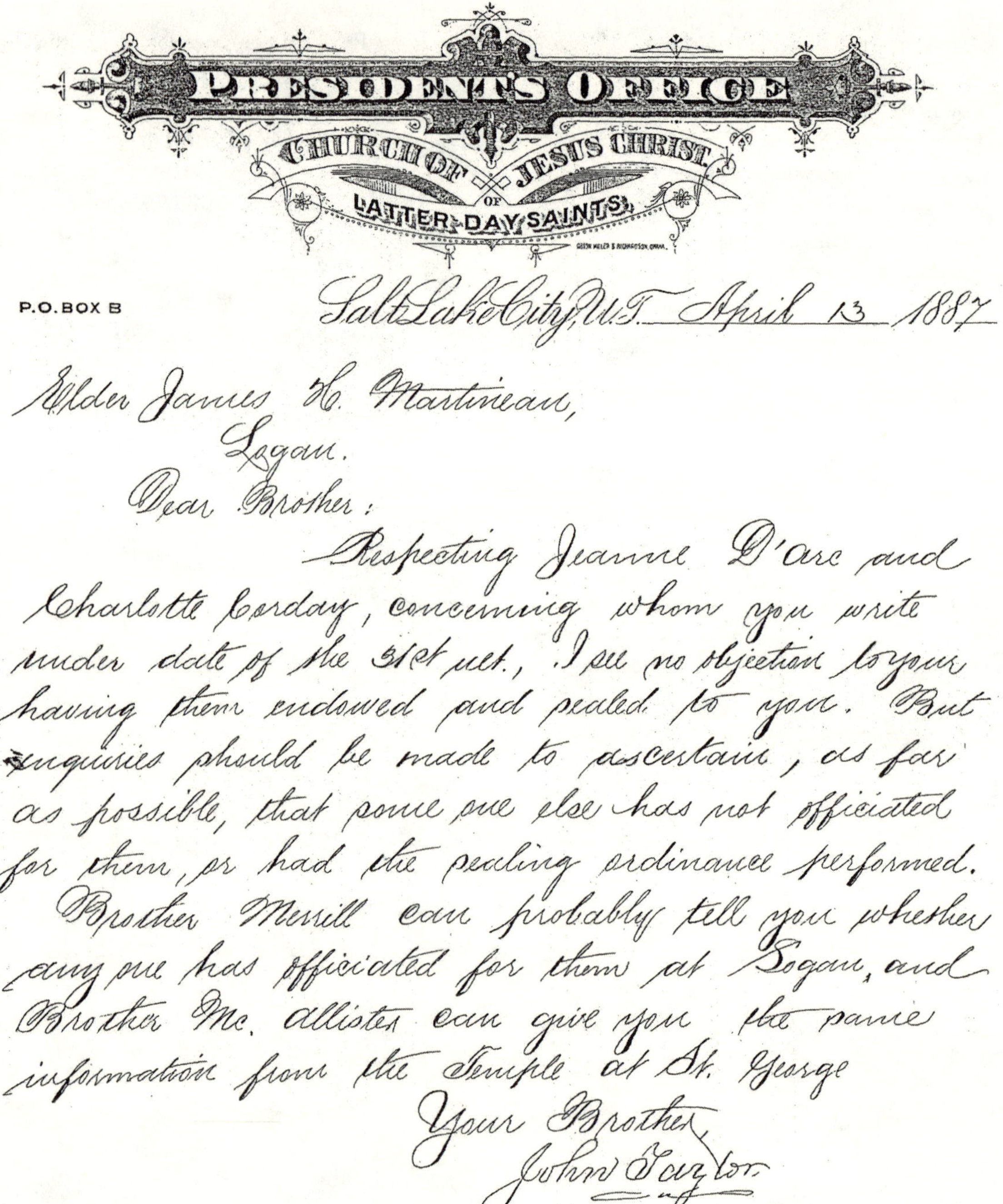

PRESIDENT'S OFFICE
CHURCH OF JESUS CHRIST OF LATTER-DAY SAINTS.

P.O. BOX B

Salt Lake City, U.T. April 13 1887

Elder James H. Martineau,
Logan.

Dear Brother:

Respecting Jeanne D'arc and Charlotte Corday, concerning whom you write under date of the 31st ult., I see no objection to your having them endowed and sealed to you. But enquiries should be made to ascertain, as far as possible, that some one else has not officiated for them, or had the sealing ordinance performed.

Brother Merrill can probably tell you whether any one has officiated for them at Logan, and Brother Mc. Allister can give you the same information from the Temple at St. George

Your Brother
John Taylor

A2.12
TWO-PAGE LETTER WRITTEN IN A DIFFERENT HAND THAN THE ONE WHO SIGNED IT.

[page 1]
G. S. L. City, April 11, 1859

Elder James Martineau

Dear Brother:— I am in receipt of your report of Excommunicated members, which I am happy to state, is as correct, legible and full as any received, and a great deal more so than the generality. There is only on improvement which I would suggest, instead of "unchristian conduct" I should like a more explicit statement of the crime, where it can be made more specific. This you can attend to in your future reports.

The weather is still [unreadable words, as sheet appears to have been torn] it has been snowing to day. Spring backward, cattle very poor, Feed and bread scarce, and the prospect for another crop is exceedingly dull. Winter wheat in some places is killed. Our Christian friends very hostile. We had a good Conference, excellent discourses from the Presidency and other Elders. News from the East indicates a storm cloud of war hanging over Europe. Congress adjourned without passing the post office appropriation bill leaving Mr Buchanan to carry the letters for the ensuing year on credit.

Prest. Y. in good health & Spirits. ~~We~~

[page 2]
It has been understood that about 100 families are calculating to leave for a Christian country in the Spring

Quite a number of brethren are going to the States on business but they have not been able to get through the mountains yet.

The Eastern mails have been ~~intercepted~~ interrupted by the storm but last mail came through in time.

Congress appropriated $15,000,000 for the support of the army, being $3.000.000 less than Secretary Floyd's estimates. $200,000 is especially appropriated for Dragoon horses for the service.

Geo A. Smith

A2.13
NEWSPAPER CLIPPING ON DORA'S DEATH.

COLONIA JUAREZ, MEXICO

ANOTHER FINE SCHOOLHOUSE

Disastrous Fire—Serious Accident
Dublan's Growth and Prospects.—

Colonia Juarez, Chihuahua, Mexico, Feb. 4.–The recent death of Miss Dora Martineau, daughter of James H. and Susan E. J. Martineau, was a sad bereavement to her relatives. She was a little more than 19 years of age, in character gentle and refined, and exceptionally endowed by nature with talent in music and drawing. She was never heard to utter a disparaging word against any, nor could she endure to hear evil said of others.

A few days ago the house of Mr. Alfred Baker of Chuichupa was destroyed by fire with all its contents while the family was absent. The origin of the fire is unknown, except that it was not incendiary. The people of Chuichupa immediately subscribed a generous sum to build another home, which with what will be furnished from other colonies here, will provide the family with food, clothing, furniture, etc.

Mr. Daniel Skowson of this place recently met with a severe accident, in which his hand was badly mangled and crushed between a wagon wheel and the rack of a heavily laden wagon. At one period danger was feared from blood poisoning, but at present we understand he is ina fair way to speedy recovery.

Civil Engineer J. H. Martineau has just finished the survey at Dublan of extensive farm lands, and a city plat about two miles in width by two and a half in length. These lands will be watered from extensive natural reservoirs about five miles distant, which will be filled from the Casas Grandes river by a canal about seven miles long.

The people of Dublan have completed a very fine cut stone foundation wall for the erection of an up-to-date school building fifty feet wide and one hundred and thirty in length, including the vestry room and tower. The brick for it are burned and work on the superstructure will begin in the near future.

Dublan will undoubtedly become a large city, having plenty of farm and pasture land, excellent well water at moderate depth, a salubrious and delightful climate, and by location a natural business center. Already the co-operative store is extensively patronized by people from San Isidro, Nueva Casas Grandes, Guadalupe, San Jose, Galeana, El Valle, Casas Grandes (old), Juarez and the settlements in the mountains and Sonora.

Prospects are extremely bright for an early extension of the Sierra Madre railroad from its present terminus at Terazas, through this town and up into the mountain towns and mining and timber regions, an extension greatly desired by all as it will render available for settlement a great amount of valuable land now without inhabitant.

A2.14
MISSION CERTIFICATE.

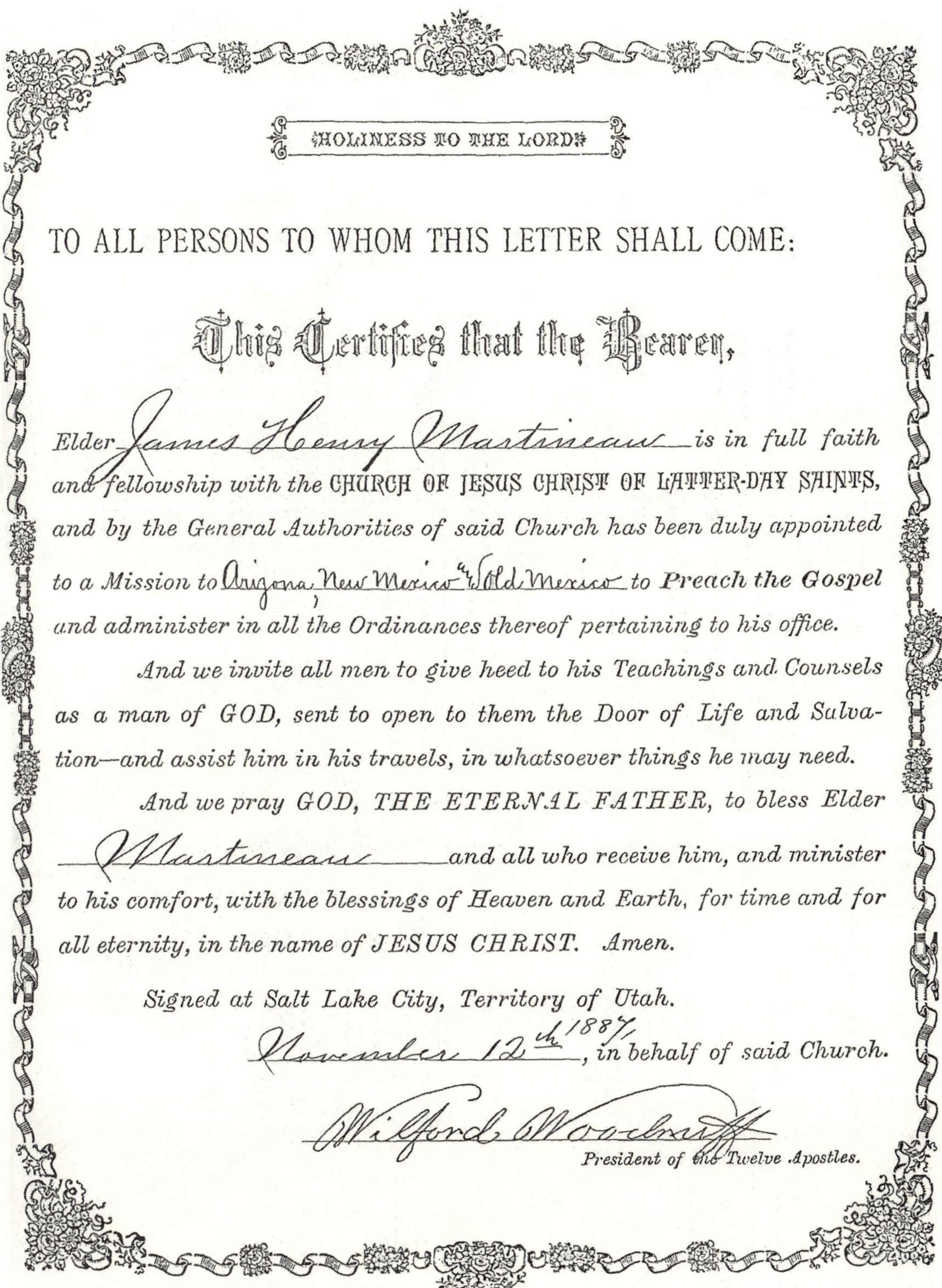

HOLINESS TO THE LORD

TO ALL PERSONS TO WHOM THIS LETTER SHALL COME:

This Certifies that the Bearer,

Elder James Henry Martineau *is in full faith and fellowship with the* CHURCH OF JESUS CHRIST OF LATTER-DAY SAINTS, *and by the General Authorities of said Church has been duly appointed to a Mission to* Arizona, New Mexico & Old Mexico *to* **Preach the Gospel** *and administer in all the Ordinances thereof pertaining to his office.*

And we invite all men to give heed to his Teachings and Counsels as a man of GOD, sent to open to them the Door of Life and Salvation—and assist him in his travels, in whatsoever things he may need.

And we pray GOD, THE ETERNAL FATHER, to bless Elder Martineau *and all who receive him, and minister to his comfort, with the blessings of Heaven and Earth, for time and for all eternity, in the name of JESUS CHRIST. Amen.*

Signed at Salt Lake City, Territory of Utah.

November 12th 1887, *in behalf of said Church.*

Wilford Woodruff
President of the Twelve Apostles.

A2.15
HANDWRITTEN LETTER ON LOGAN TEMPLE LETTERHEAD.

HOLINESS TO THE LORD

Office of the Logan Temple.
–P. O. Box D–

Logan, Utah, *30th Nov* 189*8*

To All Concerned,

This Certifies that Elder James Henry Martineau has this day been Ordained and set apart a Patriarch, in the Church of Jesus Christ of Latter-day Saints, by Apostle M. W. Merrill in the Logan Temple.

Samuel Roskelley. Recorder Logan Temple
Witness.

A2.16
NEWSPAPER CLIPPING ON DORA'S FUNERAL.

It is with sorrow I inform you of the recent death of the beloved daughter of Mr. and Mrs. J. H. Martineau, Dora Martineau, after an illness of twelve days.

Her desease [disease] was lung fever. She was a young lady of refined and artistic temperament, remarkably endowed by nature with a gift in music, having a very clear sweet voice in song and a tender and artistic touch as an organist, with much native talent in drawing. Although for some four years she had poor health, she was helpful to her full ability in assisting in the labors of the household, and in doing all the good she was able to perform. She lived a most pure and exemplary life and never in all her nineteen years of life did she indulge in gossip or scandal or unkind remarks about any one, for all this she abhorred.

At her funeral, which occurred last Friday, the 20th inst, her remains were followed from her father's abode to the school house by a long procession of young ladies, and her coffin was carried with wreaths of beautiful flowers. Very consoling remarks were made by Elders J. J. Walser, Hyrum Harris and Louis P. Cardon and the music by the choir was most tender and sweet. Thus passed to her rest one who has proved her right to a holy ressurrection [resurrection] among the just.

APPENDIX

3

INSERTS FROM VOLUME 1

A3.1

SHAKY HANDWRITTEN NOTE INSERTED BETWEEN PAGES 66 AND 67.

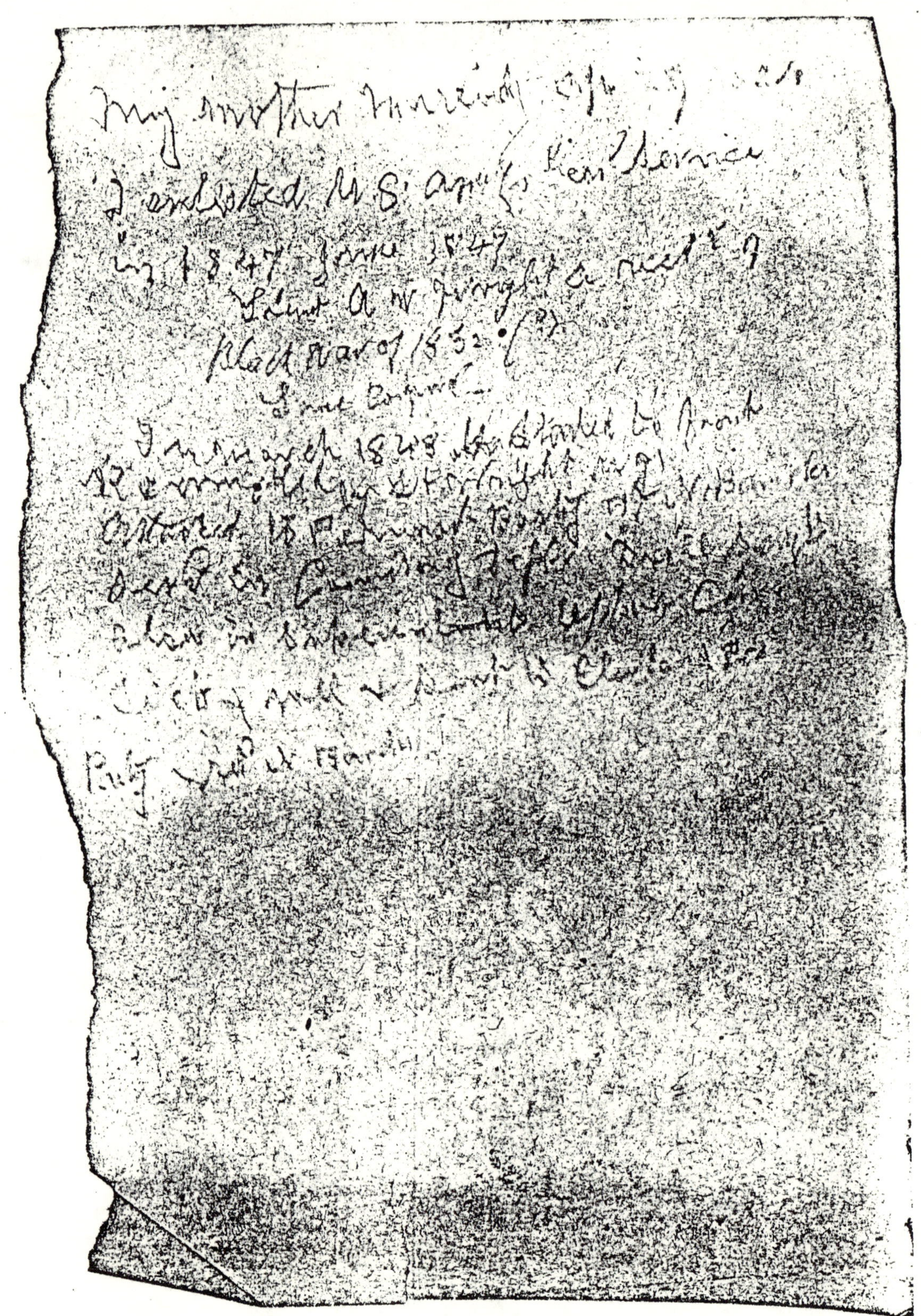

My mother married [illegible]

I enlisted U.S. Army Gen'l Service

in 1847 June 1847 [illegible]

Lieut A W Wright [illegible]

Black War of 1832 [illegible]

[illegible]

I in March 1848 [illegible]

[illegible]

[illegible] 18 February 1849 [illegible]

[illegible]

[illegible]

[illegible]

[illegible]

A3.2

THE FIRST ITEM IS THE OUTSIDE OF A LETTER IN TWO DIFFERENT HANDWRITINGS. THE HANDWRITING AT THE TOP APPEARS TO BE MARTINEAU'S, AND THE HANDWRITING IN THE MIDDLE IS GEORGE A. SMITH'S. THE SECOND ITEM IS A HANDWRITTEN LETTER IN SMITH'S HANDWRITING. THE ITEMS WERE FOUND BETWEEN PAGES 88 AND 89 OF JOURNAL 1.

[first item]

Letter from Geo. A. Smith
Dec. 1835

[second item]

Pres. John C. L. Smith
Parowan
Iron Co

A3.2

[transcription of second item]

Filmore Dec 15. 1855

Br Haight has Presented A
Petition for the [removal] of the
County Seat of Iron to Cedar
If the Citizens of the North
Part of the County are opposed
they had better get up A
[Remove here] to the measure
~~to it~~ for my part I have
no objection to it. Butt would
like to know how the people
feel on the Subject of it
they are aquainted [with] what
is going on concerning it
on the subject Please [write]
& make any [Sugestion] on the
Subject by the mail an [and] any
other & they [will] be [Received] with
Pleasure yours [&]
GeoA Smith

A3.3
THIS SECTION WAS HANDWRITTEN BY MARTINEAU AND FOUND BEFORE PAGE 179 OF JOURNAL 1.

[page 1]

Jas. H. Martineau born near midnight Mar. 13 1828. in the village of —— New York

Father, John, born 1793 – son of Stephen Martineau, whose ancesters came from France at the expulsion of the Huegunots.

Mother, Eliza Mears was descended on her mothers side from the Allens family a grand-niece of Ethan Allen. She was born in Fabius, New York Apr. 13, 1806. Died July 6, 1848. Her father and mother Jas: – Lois Mears were born in Berkshire Co., Mass, moving in early life to Elbridge, Onondago Co, N.Y.

Grandfather served a short time as a militia man in the war of 1812 and was at the battle of Sacketts Harbor.

About 1860 he & his wife moved to Madison, Wis. He died at the age of 93 and his wife at 91.

My great-grandfather was a major in Washingtons army and his father and officer in the French & Indian war My grandmother was descended from the Hutchison family. Her grandfather being Lord Hutchison. His sons my grandmothers uncle was in French & Indian War. Was killed by the Indians at the massacre of Fort William Henry in N.Y. Sept 1754

My mother was left a widow in in 1830

My father's first wife was daughter of the Earl of Stanhope. Her too children Samuel and Elizabeth, Samuel became an under officer in the U.S. navy and was in Com Wilkes expedition 184[...]

My fathers ancestors came to France from Italy and were related to the Columna family

[page 2]

My father had been apprenticed to a hatter but desiring to get a better education ran away to England where he remained seven years

He married there Mrs Hawkins. He had four children. Returned to America two of the children died. Julia & Lucretia lived & grew to maturity

On the death of his 1st wife father married my mother. His bro Peter married my mother's sister Mary Mother was married Apr. 29, 1824.

My father practiced medicine & sur [surgery] for year[s] but was attracted to Civil E. He was an Eng. on some of the first R.R. in the U.[S.] larges bridges & finally acted as engineer on the N.Y. Croton Aqueduct. Thro exposure he contracted consumption of which he died in 1838 at Elbridge, N.Y.

My mother was born in 1806 in Vermont. She had six children by my father, Emily Henrietta born 1825. Jas. H., 1828, Chas Augustus, born 1831, died 1831, Francis Eliza 1831, died 1847, Harriet born 1835, died 1837, and Lois Elenor born 1838.

After Father's death she lived a widow several years, then married William Babcock, by him she had one son, Chas who at 17 ~~died a soldier near~~

Mother died 1848 July 6 and was buried at Elbridge

[page 3]

In 1835 we lived on Staten Island [In] 1837 Father failed in business, real estate so moved back to Elbridge where he soon died.

In 1840 my Uncle William Mears a merchant living at Fultonville Montgomery Co, N.Y. sent for me My journey 143 mi by rail alone was my first experience in traveling The journey took 3 days. I lived with him about a yr. In 1843 spent another year with him. On returning home I went to Munro Academy with my sister Henrietta until 1845 when I went into my Uncle Peter's store as clerk in the village of Sennett, Cayuga Co N.Y.

When I left the academy I had a good knowledge of Eng & Latin grammar, Arithmetic, Geography, History, Natural Philosophy Algebra Chemistry and Geology. At yearly examinations always rece'd prizes.

When about 12 yrs old there was a revival of religion in Elbridge by Baptists & Presbyterians. My mother & I joined the Baptists

In 1846 I went to Auburn to learn the art of printing. I remained here some time until I was overcome by the desire to become a soldier and I enlisted as such to serve in the Mexican War But my mother demanded my release because I was under age. I subsequently got a chance to join the Navy as Midshipman but thro her tears gave that up too.

In 1847 I went to Milwaukee to live with my uncle Peter

[page 4]

I did not live long with Uncle Peter not liking him and went to work in the office of the Milwaukee Sentinel Could not resist the sound of drum & fife and soon enlisted again under [A.] A. W. Wright

Early in March our party started to Newport Barracks, Ky by way of Lake Michigan. I served as drill sergeant, as clerk in the commissary office & finally as clerk in the Supts office, Cinn. I remained here until an illness necessitated my going to the Hosp On coming out as I was too weak to drill so I was sent on recruiting service to Cleveland Ohio. Soon after arriving peace was declared and we were mustered out.

July 6 1848 as I was on my way home my Mother died.

I went into the large bookstore Hale & Chapman where I remained until the Spring 1849

I determined to go to Cal. to the gold mines - thence to travel round the world. This my relatives opposed but as I was resolved Uncle Peter bot the land I had rece'd from Govt as Military bounty 160 acres giving me $160 dollars. It was located near Madison, Wis. I started across the plains with a Methodist preacher & his wife & an Irish gentleman named Russel. Left Milwaukee by steamer to Chicago then by ox team thro Ill. Crossing the Miss. to Palmyra in Mo. Thence to St. Jos. where we found the emigrant companies had left the frontier and we were advised no to cross the plains alone.

I soon got situation to teach where I taught three quarters

[page 5]

The Spring of 1850 [with two men] I decided to start for Cal. We [crossed] the Mo river May 13, 1850.

We arrived at the So. Pass July 7th 1850 and in the night was a heavy snowstorm. Here we debated as to where to go by Fort Hall or by S.L.City

We wanted to see the "Mormons so we took the Salt Lake road.

We entered S.L. valley thro Parley's canyon

I settled with Keener & Russell & decided to remain in S.L. I hired out to to Mrs. Daniel Jones at $1.50 a day

Jan 19th, 1851, I became a member of the Church of J. C. of L.D.S. being baptized by Wm McBride. This incurred the displeasure of my relatives.

About this time decided to go to Iron Co to help make a settlement there

Mar 5th 1850 started for Iron Co about 260 miles from S.L.

April 9 1851 we arrived at Parowan

Nov. 1851 I taught school about a mo.

1,8,52/ 1852 This day myself Susan Ellen Johnson were married at Fort Johnson

Nov. 4 1852 Henry Augustus was born

Aug 29– 1851 appointed Tithing clerk

January 10 1853 Today I began teaching school

A3.4
FIVE-DOLLAR BILL, CONFEDERATE STATES OF AMERICA.

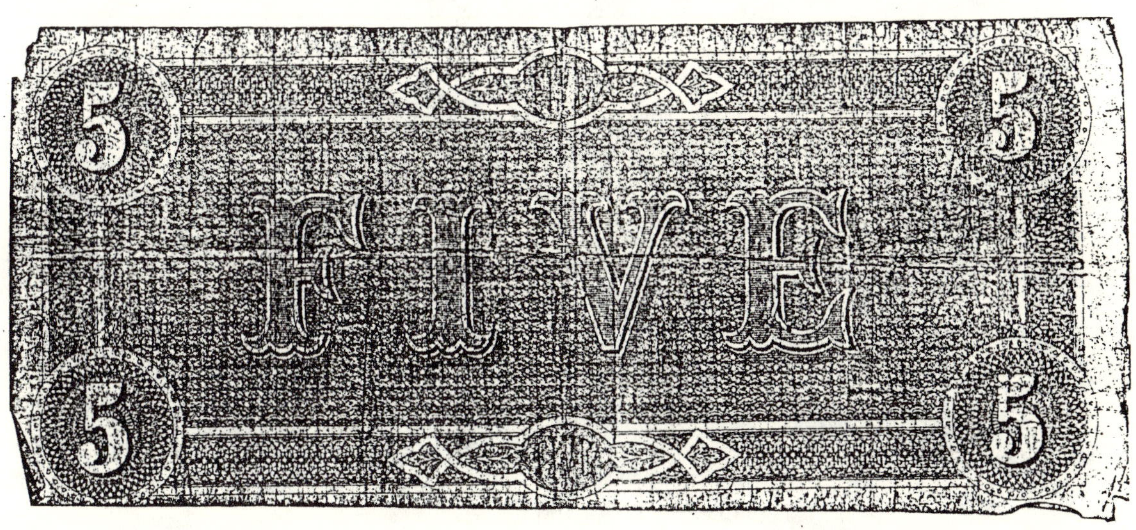

A3.5
TWO-PAGE HANDWRITTEN LETTER FOUND BETWEEN PAGES 231 AND 232 OF JOURNAL 1.

Council Chamber
Gr. S, L, City Dec 30/65

J H, Martineau Esq
Dear Brother,
Yours of Dec, 7th
and the accompanying report of our Brigade came safe to hand, the Lt. Generel expressed himself sattisfied, I asked him about the number of our Brigade. he did not give me any satisfaction said theres was a number which were not as yet numbered, he was much pleased to learn of our success—and the spirit that prevailed during our three days drill,

Our Legislative Business is Progressing—a Committee are at work Compiling, and revising the Laws,

We have also another setting which Consists of Brig. Gen. and Col.[1]

[Page 2]

trying to arrange a more suitable Law on Military affairs

On Christmas day Pres. Young was out in his mammouth Sleigh drawn by 6 grey horses and containing about 20 persons, made ~~about~~ a very imposing appearance.

Captain Bennet is arrested some say because he is friendly to the mormons—and Col. Smith is banished to Bridger while his Command stay here—

Please write and give us the news, I remain your friend and Brother in the Gospel

E. T. Benson

A3.6
NEWSPAPER CLIPPING INSERTED AFTER PAGE 370.

Thoughts on Leaving Logan.

BY A WANDERER,

To his Friends and Pupils in Logan.

Good-by, my friends, good-by! The
 words were said
While with a cheerless smile I checked
 a tear;
And with a beating, heavy heart I sped
From cherish'd scenes and friends I
 loved most dear.
 'Tis scarce three years that I with
 dread approached
 The very place I'm now so loth to
 leave;
 Such are the changes wrought on
 human hearts
 When love and friendship deign their
 spells to weave.

The happy scenes of innocence and
 mirth,
Where with sweet music many an hour
 were passed,
Where love and harmony made heaven
 of earth—
These scenes within my thoughts must
 ever last.
 And when I've heard those little
 ones, a host—
 With voices sweet like angels from
 above,
 Sing those sweet songs which pleased
 their fancy most,
 How could I hear and still withhold
 my love?

And then to know by looks and actions
 kind,
What place I held within each childish
 heart.
Could I be mortal, with a heart and
 mind,
And with these loved ones not be loth
 to part?
 Ah! ye who pass the children proud-
 ly by,
 As if unworthy of a look or smile,
 Ye lose a treasure ye should value
 high
 A child's pure love without deceit or
 guile.

This I have treasured; and 'tis worth
 to me
More than the gold I've earned with
 irksome toil;
'Twas this, O Logan, made me cling to
 thee,
And not thy wealth, thy palaces, or
 soil.
 And in thee, too, I've found two lov-
 ing hearts,
 Which seemed to beat in friendship
 with my own;
 Who sought to turn aside the stinging
 darts
 Which at myself or efforts have been
 thrown.

Such friends made life a highly treas-
 ured boon,
Which else had been but very scant of
 cheer;
They cool'd my fevered brow in sum-
 mer noon,
They warmed my heart when wintry
 days appeared.
 And in the heart they warmed they
 still shall live,
 Though I should absent be for many
 a year,
 And all I ask of them is but to give
 A place in theirs for him who holds
 them dear.

I thank ye not for gold or flattering
 praise,
For these alone would leave my heart a
 blank;
But for each smile, kind act, o kindly
 phrase,
Each deed of love, for these my heart
 cries, Thanks!

WILLARD, March 1st, 1882.

A3.7
LETTER FROM FRANKLIN D. RICHARDS INSERTED AFTER PAGE 375.

L. D. S. Historian's Office,
P. O. Box 1678,
Salt Lake City, Utah, Feb. 21- 1896

Rec'd Feb 25 1896.

Elder James H. Martineau -
Tucson - Arizona

Dear Brother -

In reply to your note of the 16th inst. I may say that I have never before known of a Patriarch sealing a blessing upon any other person without being present with the person and having his hand on the person's head. I do not say such a thing could not be but that I have not known of such an occurrence.

It is a very consistent idea that a Patriarch in Israel may know what shall happen to his posterity by the revelations of the Holy Ghost for so it was given to our great father Adam in the Valley of Adam-ondi-Ahman, and he had them together with him there.

I see no objection to a man writing a blessing if it be revealed to him by the Holy Spirit and sending it to the one for whom it is intended; but, the sealing it upon that person is quite another thing, while such a blessing dictated by revelation will just as surely come to a fulfilment as if it had been sealed upon the person.

"The power of Godliness is revealed through the Ordinances of the Gospel and since the Lord has so abundantly appointed ordinances for young and old in every condition for the living and the dead it is quite superfluous for us to institute new methods by which to convey his blessings from one to another.

The Priesthood is given to bless and not to curse mankind and so far as we can, it is not only our privilege to do good to all as we have opportunity and especially to the household of faith, but it is our duty also, without dishonoring the Truth or casting our Pearls before those who can not appreciate them. Your Bro. in the Gospel with love & blessing F. D. Richards.

A3.8
NOTES FOLLOWING PAGE 375.

I cannot find the date of death of Charles Babcock, only know that he died, a soldier, of disease, before Richmond, the last year of war—
Do not know the date of marriage of either Henrietta, or James—

(Children of Lois Eleanor Brunkel and John Peter Brunkel—

Frederic William Born Jan 27, 1862.
Died Feb 25-1895.

Bertha Whitman Born Jan 9 1864.

Adrienne Born May 26, 1866
died July 22, 1866.

Louis Born May 15- 1868
died Sept 11. 1868

Caroline Whittery. Born Sept 13. 1869

Alexander Born Dec 25-1870
died July 1. 1871

over

William. Born June 2nd 1872.
died Aug 5th 1872.

Jenny Louise. Born 22nd 1873
Married to Donald Roderick Osborn
July 25th 1898. has two children.

Lois Eleanor. Born June 26th 1876

Sister Lois' family record from her.

She Born Aug, 10. 1838
Married John Peter Brunkle—about 1860

A3.8
TWO-PAGE HANDWRITTEN LETTER FOUND BETWEEN PAGES 375 AND 376.

[transcription of page 1]
I cannot find the date of death
of Charles Babcock, only know that
he died, a soldier of disease before
Richmond, the last year of war—
Do not know the date of marriage of
either Henrietta, or James—

(Children of Lois Eleanor Voswinkel
and John Peter Voswinkel—)

Frederick William	Born Jan. 27. 1862.
Died Feb 25. 1895.	
Bertha Martineau	Born Jan 9 1864.
Adrienne	Born May 26, 1866
died July 22, 1866.	
Louis	Born May 15 1868
	died Sept 11. 1868
Caroline Whittling.	Born Sept 13. 1869
Alexander	Born Dec 25. 1870
	died July 1. 1871

over

[transcription of page 2]

William	Born June 2nd 1872.
	died Aug 5th 1872.
Jenny Louise	Born 22nd 1873

Married to Donald Roderick Osborn
July 28th 1898. his two
children.

Lois Eleanor	Born June 26th 1876

Sister Lois' family record from her
She Born Aug. 10. 1838
Married John Peter Voswinkel—about 1860

A3.9

QUOTE INSERTED AFTER PAGE 375.

A3.10

BIRTHDAY NOTE INSERTED AFTER PAGE 403.

Logan Utah.
March 13th 1878

To our
Esteemed friend and brother
James H. Martineau
with the
Compliments & Congratulations
of
Joseph C. and Annie L. Hyde
upon this
your Fiftieth Birth day—
Hoping
that you may live to enjoy very
many happy returns of the day.
And beg that you will accept the
enclosed token as a slight memento
of our good wishes for you and yours

A3.11
LETTER FROM EDWIN HUNTER INSERTED AFTER PAGE 409.

S L City July 18/81

Ja H Martineau Esqr

Dr Sir

Edward is out at Silver City
with Mr J H Smoot & Dorman
I expect a Job of 2 or 3 Years, or
he would be pleased to be with You
I will send him Your Card
very warm weather, I hope all is
well with You Remember to Your
Good Lady & Family

Respt Yours Edwin Hunter

N B our Country is filled with
Surveyors the whole Country
will be surveyed, call if at S L C
E H

A3.12
HANDWRITTEN LETTER FOUND BETWEEN PAGES 409 AND 410 OF JOURNAL 1.

S. L. City July 18/81

Ja[s] H Martenuo esq.

D[r] Sir

Edward is out at Silver City
with Mr J H Smith & [Do...]
I expect a Job of 2 or 3 Years, or
he would be pleased to be with you
I will send him Your Card
Verry warm weather, I hope all is
well with You Remember to Your
Good ladey & Family

Resp[l] Yours   Edw[d] Hunter

[If] [B] our Countrey is filled wtih
Surveyors the whole Country
will be surveyed, call if at S L C

E H

A3.13
RECEIPT INSERTED AFTER PAGE 441.

ISSUED MONTHLY $1.00 PER YEAR

OFFICE OF
YOUNG WOMAN'S JOURNAL
ORGAN OF THE Y. L. M. I. A.
PUBLISHED BY THE GENERAL BOARD
33 BISHOP'S BUILDING
BOTH PHONES
EDITORIAL DEPT.

Salt Lake City, Utah. Nov. 5, 1912.

James H. Martineau.
Salt Lake City.

Dear Bro Martineau,

Enc losed find c hec k in payment for your poem Little ones Gone. We think many mothers will be comforted by it.

Respectfully,

Mary E. Connelly.

A3.14
LETTER FROM CHRISTOPHER CLAYTON INSERTED AFTER PAGE 526.

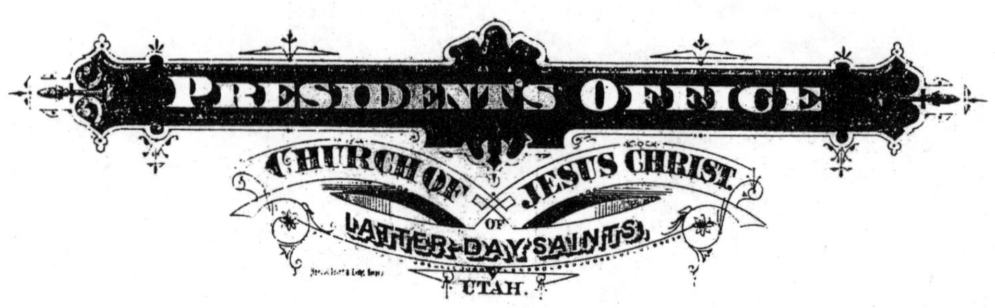

P.O. BOX B.

Salt Lake City Feb 3rd 1883

Elder James H. Martineau,
Logan.

Dear Brother:

I suppose that you will have been informed that I have been appointed to preside over a stake to be organized in Southern Arizona and that you are appointed as one of my Counsellor

Owing to the peculiar circumstances in which the people are placed, I have thought it best to make an early start, say about the 12th of this month, so that I can be there in time to put in grain for this season, and also be in a position to counsel others in regard to their settlements and the cultivation of the soil, as it would seem very much better for the people to raise their living from the earth than to obtain it by freighting I have been desirous to make an early start that we may not be behind hand in regard to our operations for the coming season. I have been negotiating with two railroads for the transportation of teams, furniture and other household affairs. I find that I can do much better with the C.P. than the U.P. The C.P. engages to furnish a car for this purpose to Maricopa for the sum of $350. They also allow us to put in three pair of horses if we wish. I thought we would take two teams, 1000 lbs of lucern seed, 1000 lbs of early wheat, and 1000 lbs of barley. I have also ordered a farm wagon, and a light buggy wagon to be unloaded at Bowie Station, the best place, I think, to unload. I am in hopes of getting the car a little cheaper than the above named price.

If convenient, I shall be glad if you can meet me in Salt Lake City on the 10th, when we could be set apart together. If this time is not convenient, please say when you can meet me in the city and I will arrange to keep the appointment. Please answer immediately by telegram to Kaysville, & oblige

Your Brother

C. Layton,

A3.15
NEWSPAPER ARTICLE INSERTED AFTER PAGE 526.

SALT LAKE CITY, UTAH.

A SECOND ALAMO.

That Will Bring Light and Liberty to the Mexican People.

TEMOCHIA, MEXICO, ANNIHILATED.

Excessive Taxation, Extortion by Officials and Government Influence in Religious Belief, Cause an Awful Massacre.

EL PASO, Tex., Oct. 27.—The news of the annihilation of the Temochians, a people who inhabit the village of Temochia and who are nearly pure Aztecs, received here last evening is more circumstantial than was first indicated. Temochia is situated on the direct road to Guerrero and Jesus Maria, in the mountains of southeastern Chihuahua, Mexico, and it has been in open rebellion against the state and federal government for more than a year on account of excessive taxation, extortion by government officials and government interference in their religious belief.

Two months ago the government sent the 110th battalion, in command of General Ranjel, to make the people pay the tax required and accept the government officials appointed to take charge or kill every one of them. This alternative was openly boasted of by officers in Chihuahua before the troops started for the town, and when the Temochians heard of it they decided to fight it out, as they knew even should they receive the soldiers peaceably they would be shot on the slightest provocation.

When the soldiers made the descent on the village they were met and driven off with officers and fourteen men killed, while two officers and forty-five men were taken prisoners. The prisoners were confined on the top of an adobe church, General Ranjel being the only officer who escaped. When news of this affair reached the ears of President Diaz he decided to annihilate the village, and when the people were notified they answered "God is with us and we will not be taken."

The soldiers left Chihuahua two weeks ago and formed a junction with others from Pinos Altos and Guerrero to the number of 1,200, and on Monday an attack was made on all sides. The Temochians, with their families, took refuge in the church awaiting the attack which, when it did come, was made on all sides, and the slaughter was terrible. At dusk the soldiers gained entrance to the church and a terrible hand to hand fight took place, in which the soldiers completed the massacre with 368 of their number killed and many wounded. The village next day presented a terrible view, the street leading to the church was filled with bodies and blood seemed to flow in torrents. Not a man of the Temochians was left, except those who happened to be out in the mountains; but the government has paid dearly for its victory.

The Temochians were, sometime ago, a very wealthy people in cattle and farms, but lack of rain and failure of their crops had brought them to poverty, and they were unable to exist under the extortion of the government and its petty officials and were brought near to starvation. They were very hospitable and several weeks ago when several parties of Americans passed through from Guerrero to Chihuahua they were treated kindly and well cared for, though government officials objected to their going, they saying the Temochians were bandits. The feeling against the government is very strong, and the incident has been called a second Alamo, which will bring light and liberty to the Mexican people as it did to those of Texas.

A3.16
PENSION APPLICATION INSERTED AFTER PAGE 630.

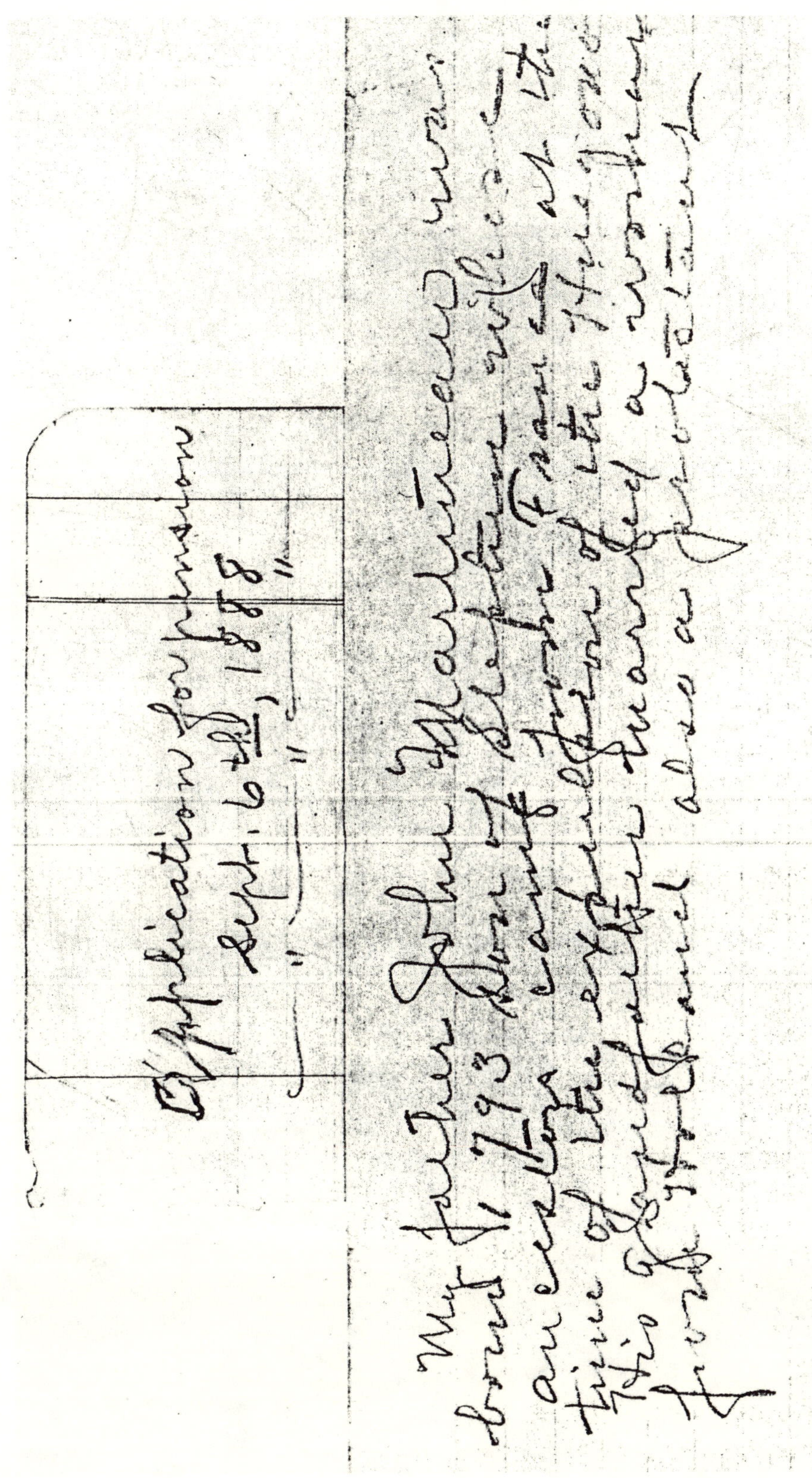

Application for pension
Sept. 6th, 1888
" " "

My father John Martineau was born 1793 Son of Stephen whose ancestors came from France at the time of the expulsion of the Huguenots. His grandfather married a woman from Holland also a protestant.

A3.16

[transcription]

Application for pension
Sept. 6th, 1888
—/—/—/—

My father John Martineau was born 1793 son of Stephen whose ancestors came from France at the time of the expulsion of the Huegonot[s] His grandfather married a woman from Holland also a protestant

A3.17
HANDWRITTEN LETTER INSERTED AFTER PAGE 684.

[page 1]
Bern
Mar. 19th 1891
Elder Jesse N. Martineau

Dear Bro.
At last I am enabled to give you the information which brings Joy to the heart of every elder who has labored faithfully in the Missionary field for a number of years. President B. Young has sanctioned your release to return home.

You are therefore honorable released from your labors in this Mission to return home with the next company of Saints, which will leave Mannheim about the 20th of April or the early part of May time of departure is not yet definitely set.

No doubt the time you have spent in the ministry in this Mission has been an excellent school for you as it is for every elder, you have seen much and experienced much and seen the hand of the Lord made manifest in your behalf. You can

[page 2]
now return home with the satisfaction of having done your duty to the best of your ability and may the lessons you have learnt prove a lasting benefit to you for time and eternity. May the spirit of your holy calling, the priesthood you hold, be and abide with you and enable you to remain in the harness after your return home, where to labore for the building up of the Kingdom of God and the establishment of truth and righteousness upon this earth. Then you will allways look back upon the two years & a half spent here in the service of God with joy and pleasure; and grow stronger in the testimony of Jesus from day to day. My prayer is that God our heavenly Father may bring you home in safety and bless you abundantly with His Holy Spirit that you may become a shining light among the elders of Israel and be a comfort and a joy to your esteemed father.

With love to yourself & the Saints
I remain your Brother in Christ
Theo Brandley.

A3.18
HANDWRITTEN DOCUMENT INSERTED AFTER PAGE 718.

[Written vertically along left side]
June,—Time Files [Flies] as a Bird.

Hark to the voice of the Shepherd
Calling his flock as of old
List to His voice and be gathered
Safely and sure to his fold.
Haste for the wolves are about thee
Raging and fierce to destroy thee
Fly, for the arms that await thee
Would thee so gladly enfold
Oh would the[y] so gladly unfold,

Why will ye wander in dan[ger]
Sorrow, and darkness and [. . .]
Come, be no longer a ranger,—
Come to thy Father again.
He in his love will [comfort]
He with His might will [defend]
He in the end will exalt [thee]
Ever with Him then shalt [re...]
O Even with Him thou shalt reign

Tucson Nov. 22 1889
J. H. M.

A3.19
ITALICS SHOW HANDWRITTEN PARTS OF A LETTER INSERTED AFTER PAGE 718.

P. O. BOX B.
Salt Lake City, U.T. *June 22nd* 188 *7*

Elder James H. Martineau
Logan.

with Kind regards,
Your Brother.
John Taylor.

A3.20

HANDWRITTEN LETTER ON OFFICIAL CHURCH LETTERHEAD. BELOW THIS IS PART OF A DIFFERENT LETTER WITH DIFFERENT HANDWRITING. IT IS INSERTED AFTER PAGE 718.

PRESIDENT'S OFFICE
CHURCH OF JESUS CHRIST
OF
LATTER-DAY SAINTS

P. O. BOX B.
Salt Lake U. T. 15 April 1887

Dear Bro. Martineau,—

Some years ago Sister Josephene Ursenbach was baptized for quite a long list of deceased french ladies of note, amongst them, according to my best recollection, Empress Josephene, Marie Antoinette, Ninon D. Euclos, Madame de Manlenon, Jeanne D'Arc, and Charlotte Corday. I also have the impression that she had them sealed to different brethren, but of this I am not so certain, as I am of their baptism. Of course no endowments were given them at that time, as such work was not done in the Endowment House. If the records were [come]-atable I would make sure on these points for your satisfaction, but they are beyond my reach.

Endeavor has lately been made to prove that Jeanne D'Arc was not burned by the English, but married and lived to a good old age, receiving a pension, the entries of the payment of which are said to be still in existence.

Your Brother, Geo. Reynolds.

With love I am your
Brother in the New Covenant
G. M. Lyman

A3.21

THIS INSERT HAS THREE SEPARATE DOCUMENTS. THE FIRST AND SECOND ARE THE END OF LETTERS WITH SIGNATURES. THE THIRD IS A HANDWRITTEN LETTER. IT IS INSERTED AFTER PAGE 718.

[First document.]
spirit of progression in this direction, manifest
in your communication
I am Brethren
Yours very Truly
Daniel H. Wells
Lieut General Nauvoo Legion

[Second document, copied vertically to the others.]
With kind regards,
Your Brother,
Wilford Woodruff

[Third document.]
Anna's first letter [Note in upper left corner.]
lyman folks are all well and so are Nephis
folks and emma and sister farr

to Nephi and to to emma this is
the first chance I hav had to write
to you so I thought I would write
to you all the letters hov [have] been full so
I Dident hav a chance this havent told
you much News but I like to write
so Well now. I hav wrote so ~~mu~~ much
this last ~~w~~ week Nettie is practising
We have made lots of molasses candy since I have
been sick and it made me so sick I
could not eat it I am sick of
molasses ~~candy~~ that is a about all
we hav to eat now Nettie are joel cant
eat it they are sick of it to gean
and trude ~~cant eate~~ and theodre
is a bout all that can eat it
o yes [...] lillie she eats it to Dora
is growing quite big now I can not
~~lift her~~ hardly lift here now I cant
think of much more to write we got
a letter from lyman Thursday he says
alley got the babys photo~~graph~~graph
taken good by from Annie

A3.22

THIS INSERT CONTAINS TWO DOCUMENTS. THE FIRST IS A HANDWRITTEN NOTE. THE SECOND IS A PRINTED CERTIFICATE FILLED IN BY HAND. ITALICS SHOW HANDWRITTEN PARTS. THIS IS INSERTED AFTER PAGE 718.

[First document.]
This is to certify that James H. Martineau
was elected Notary Public of Iron county
by the Joint Assembly of the territory of Utah
on Thursday January 18. 1859.
See page 169 of laws of Utah.

Thomas Bullock
Chief Clerk House of Rep.[s]

[Second document.]

Salt Lake City, Utah, *Nov. 20th* 188*7*

Central Pacific Railroad Company:

THIS CERTIFIES

That the bearer, Elder *James H Martineaux*
is a Missionary of the Church of Jesus Christ of Latter-day Saints
now on the way *from* his field of labor in *Arizona*

John Taylor. President of the Church of Jesus Christ of Latter-day Saints.

A3.23
LETTER FROM JOHN TAYLOR INSERTED AFTER PAGE 718.

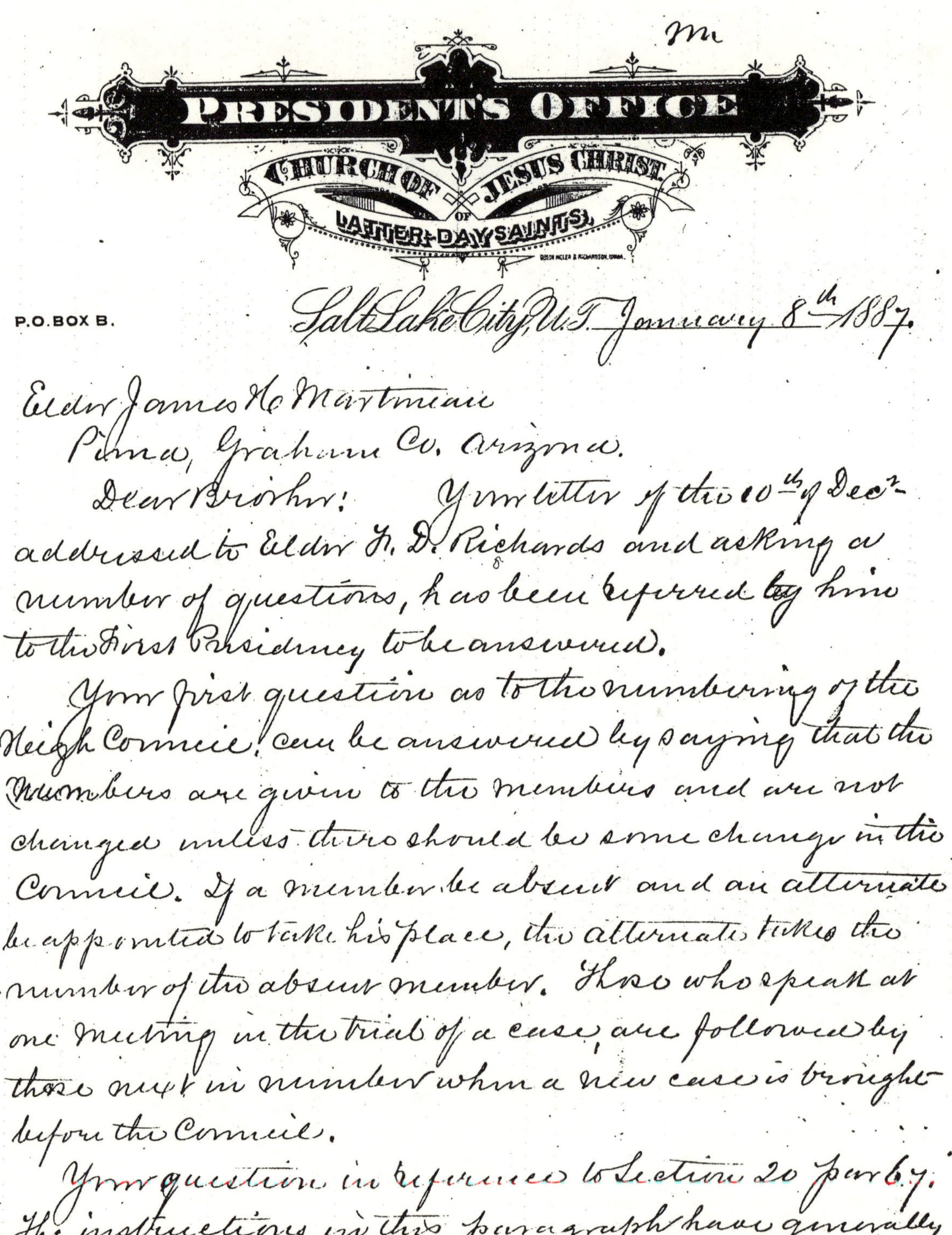

PRESIDENT'S OFFICE
CHURCH OF JESUS CHRIST OF LATTER-DAY SAINTS.

P.O. BOX B. Salt Lake City, U.T. January 8th 1887.

Elder James H. Martineau
Pima, Graham Co. Arizona.

Dear Brother: Your letter of the 10th of Decr. addressed to Elder F. D. Richards and asking a number of questions, has been referred by him to the First Presidency to be answered.

Your first question as to the numbering of the High Council, can be answered by saying that the numbers are given to the members and are not changed unless there should be some change in the Council. If a member be absent and an alternate be appointed to take his place, the alternate takes the number of the absent member. Those who speak at one meeting in the trial of a case, are followed by those next in number when a new case is brought before the Council.

Your question in reference to Section 20 par 67. The instructions in this paragraph have generally b.... followed. For instance, The First Presidency

Presidency, acted also as the Presidency of the Stake, and it was possible for them to sit and try the case of a Bishop if necessary. At the present time Stakes have multiplied and the Presidency of the Stake performs many of the duties which formerly devolved upon the First Presidency of the Church, and among other duties is that of trying local Bishops in their Stake should they be in transgression.

As there is no probability, at present, of the President of the Church being tried, we think it unnecessary to say anything about Sec 107 par 82.

The Quorums of Elders, Priests, Teachers and Deacons are numbered in their own Stakes. A Bishop presides over the Priests; and over the other quorums their Presidents preside.

These are the general rules, there may be exceptions under certain peculiar circumstances, which until they arise cannot be explained.

With kind regards

Your Brethren, John Taylor
Geo. Q. Cannon

for a certain ward. We have generally instructed the Presidency of the Stake and the High Council to select the names of the most eligable men in the ward for these positions, and prayerfully consider them; and when they have decided who they shall be, to send the names to us, and if approved by us the Presidency of the Stake are required to submit them to the people of the Ward for their vote, and if they accept them, instructions are given for them to be ordained.

In regard to the selection and ordination of High Priests. When brethren are deemed worthy to receive the High Priesthood it would be well for the Presidency of the Stake to bring the names to the attention of the High Council, and if they feel that they can recommend them to this high and important office, their names can then be submitted to the First Presidency with the recommendation of the Presidency of the Stake and the High Council in their favor. If the First Presidency approve of their Ordination, the names should then be submitted to the Quarterly Conference of the Stake, and if voted for by the Conference they can then be ordained.

In reference to Sec. 68. par. 22. The First

A3.24
TWO-PAGE HANDWRITTEN DOCUMENT WITH NOTES TO BE WRITTEN IN THE JOURNAL FOUND AFTER PAGE 718.

[First page.]
Sept 8 1872 Theodore was born.
Sept 18, S

Dec 24 was taken with malignant diptheria
Jan 3rd Fully recovered.

Mar 27. 1875.

This evening about dusk Theo fell into the well which is about 15 ft. deep and narrowly escaped death The [hap]—door covering the will [well] (which is in the kitchen) was up. Charlie had just drawn a pail of water & turned his back. Theo fell head first striking ~~strick~~ edge of the floor fell feet first into the water which is 2 ft. deep. As soon as he was missed Moroni ran to the well & got him out of the water

July 17, 1877

Came home & found Theodore who had slight attack of scarlet fever last week about well.

Sept. 7, 1882

Today Theodore. was baptized by Bro Larson and confirmed by myself and Jos. Goddard.

Sept 22 1884 En route to Arizona with family bot hat for Theo at San Francisco

Sun Jan 4 1885 ordained Deacon
Feb. 9, 1886 Albert & Theo went to St David for the mare

[Second page.]
1888 Nov. 28 In Mexico

Sent to San Francisco for suit for Theo. too small - sent for another

Oct 3 1891

Started with Theo & J. M. Macfarlan surveying Corrales Boundary line.

Theo killed a wild turkey.
Oct 9 Started survey of east boundary running South. Theo killed fine deer.

Oct 13. Some more men came from Pacheco, making 11 in all. We moved camp climbing difficult steeps with our 5 pack horses, not knowing where we'd find water. Camped at dark in a deep canyon but Theo & H. Porter were not in came [camp]. We fired guns shouted and I went up on a hill side & kept a large fire burning

A3.25
TWO HANDWRITTEN PAGES OF NOTES FOUND AFTER PAGE 718.

[First page.]
Jas Mears (mothers father) born in
Sharon, Conn. Apr. 11 1774

Lois Sprague (Mears (his wife) born Lebanon, Conn. Feb 22 1779

Grandmother was granddaughter of a son of Ld [Lord] Hutchinson

[Second page.]
Royal began to walk Oct 23 1887

A3.26
NEWSPAPER CLIPPING. THERE ARE FOUR COPIES OF IT FOUND AFTER PAGE 718.

[In the original a picture is above the article with the caption "Lyman R. Martineau."]

LYMAN MARTINEAU
DIES IN SALT LAKE
Banker, Church Worker,
Official Falls to
Heart Attack.

Lyman R. Martineau, 67, prominent Church worker, and business man of Utah, died at his home 918 Logan avenue Monday night. Death was a result of heart failure aggravated by a long period of ill health. Mr. Martineau had not been in good health since he suffered from influenza in 1920, but had carried on his regular business activities until a few days before his death.

Mr. Martineau was born in Parowan April 21, 1859 the son of James Henry and Julia Sherman Martineau. He moved to Logan in 1860 where he became county assessor and treasurer in 1882 at the age of 23. He held these positions for five years and later became a member of the Logan city council. During his long career he also served as a trustee of the Brigham Young college of Logan, a member of the board of trustees of the Industrial school at Ogden and in other positions.

At one time he was chairman of the democratic state committee. He was also a candidate for Congress on the Democratic ticket in 1908 and was subsequently mentioned for governor. He was a member of the Sons of the American Revolution.

In a business capacity Mr. Martineau served as a director of Thatcher Brothers bank at Logan and was connected with the Federal Farm Loan bank for several years as appraiser. During the past few years he had been in business in Salt Lake, being chiefly interested in real estate, stock raising and agriculture. He with his family moved to this city from Logan in 1904.

Mr. Martineau filled a mission to England from 1879 to 1881. He was actively engaged in M. I. A. work for more than 50 years. He served as a high councilmen [councilman] in Cache stake from 1884 to 1904, also as stake superintendent of the Y. M. M. I. A. of Cache stake. For a number of years he had been a member of the general board of the Y. M. M. I. A.

Surviving are his widow, Mrs. Emmeline Cannon Martineau, whom he married Sept. 30, 1913, and four children by the surviving wife as follows: Jeanne, Emma, Vilate and Marion Martineau.

In 1881, he married Alley Preston at Salt Lake and the following children survive from that union: Mrs. Alley M. Crismon, Los Angeles; Mrs. Harriett A. Gowans, L. R. Martineau, Jr., and Mrs. Martha C. Snow, Salt Lake; Preston Martineau, Spokane; and Dr. Allen S. Martineau, New York.

A3.27
LETTER INSERTED AFTER PAGE 719.

G. S. L. City March 2. 1856

To the Presidents Bishops and Brethren in the Counties of Iron and Washington

I write to inform you that the persons who can get their endowments must be those who pray, who pay their tithing from year to year, who live the lives of Saints from day to day, setting good examples before their Neighbors, men and women, boys and girls over 16 years of age, who are living the lives of Saints, believe in the plurality, do not speak evil of the authorities of the Church, and possess true integrity towards their friends. can come up after their Spring crops are sown, and their case shall be attended to.

Brigham Young
Heber C. Kimball
J. M. Grant.

P.S. Send us word ten days before you send your company, that we may have the rooms vacant for them

(This is the writing of Thomas Bullock, many years Clerk of the High Council, Salt Lake City, Utah. J. H. M.)

APPENDIX

4

INSERTS BEFORE VOLUME 2

A4.1
NEWSPAPER ARTICLE INSERTED BEFORE JOURNAL 2.

FIRST WHITE CHILD BORN IN THIS COUNTRY

Editor Deseret News—I wish to correct a statement in last Saturday's News in reference to the first white child born in Utah, as published in the Placer County Republican of Auburn, Cal., claiming that Mrs. Harriet Ann Scott was entitled to that distinction. This is incorrect in every particular.

The first white child born in Utah was Young Elizabeth Steele, daughter of John and Elizabeth Steele, born in Salt Lake City shortly after their arrival in 1847, with others of the Mormon Battalion, who first joined the pioneers after their entrance in July, 1847. Mrs. Elizabeth Steele was one of the few women who accompanied her husband with the battalion. I lived for years their intimate friend and neighbor after their removal to Parowan, Irion county, Utah, when that town was founded Jan. 19, 1851, by Elder George A. Smith.

John Steele served as first counselor to President John C. L. Smith until called to a foreign mission, dying finally in Toquerville, leaving a numerous posterity who can vouch, if necessary, for the truth of my statements.

The statement that the party of California emigrants with which the parents of Mrs. Scott traveled reached the Sierra Nevadas, turned back and wintered at Salt Lake, planted and harvested a crop of corn there and then resumed their journey to California, is absolutely incorrect. No party of California emigrants ever did such a thing; the only land available was occupied by those who had diverted the canyon waters for irrigation, without which nothing could grow and mature.

Mrs. Scott's informants evidently erred as to the location of their winter camp, very easily, depending upon a memory of things long past, and no doubt believed themselves correct.

JAMES H. MARTINEAU.

A4.2
NEWSPAPER ARTICLE INSERTED BEFORE JOURNAL 2.

LAID TO REST.

The Last Rites of Little Retta Martineaus Full of Tenderness and Tears.

Tender hands and warm hearts laid the precious remains of little Rietta Martineau to their final rest, on Thursday.

The balm of sweet flowers, the tears of friends, the incense of soft music were tendered, as well as the benedictions and prayers of Holy men.

Presidents Orson Smith, S. M. Molen, and Isaac Smith, Bishop Lewis and Seth Langton spoke feelingly of the lost jewel,—not lost but wandered to its heavenly home, and offered such consolation to the stricken parents and relatives as the hope of the Resurrection gives.

Beautiful and impressive music was rendered by Messrs. Easton, Adams, R. W. Sloan, Thatcher and Mrs. Harris.

The musical selections were as follows:

"Go to thy rest in peace."
"God of mercy hear my prayer."
"Welcome wanderer."
"When the swallows homeward fly."

The tributes of roses, callow lillies and other flowers were many and beautiful.

Other Utah News.

The Republicans of Provo have decided upon Reed Smoot for Mayor.

A bill has been introduced in the Provo city council making it a misdemeanor to build corrals within a distance of fifty feet of the sidewalk.

The liberals of Provo have nominated the following ticket: Mayor, H. W. Davis; marshal, Newel Knight; recorder J. J. Knight; assessor and collector, R. Hills; treasurer, R. S. Hines.

A4.3
WEDDING ANNOUNCEMENT.

Mr Edward Ma tineat and Miss Myrtle Clark. of Chuichupa, were married by Prest. A. W. Ivins at the home of Jos. Clark Esq. the bride's father, on Monday December 12th. We offer sincere congratulations, to the young couple and wish them every blessing.

A4.4
THIS INSERT HAS TWO HANDWRITTEN LETTERS. AT THE TOP WAS THE RIGHT HALF OF A LETTER, COPIED VERTICALLY AND LABELED BY "LEGRAND YOUNG [S.] L. CITY UTAH JULY 20. 1909." IT IS NOT INCLUDED. THE SECOND LETTER IS BELOW. THIS IS FOUND AFTER PAGE 2.

Salt Lake City June 12th 1901
Dear Grandpa I thought I would write you a
few lines to let you know how we are getting along. We are
all right and I hope you are the same. Mamma is writing
to Papa and I am [rest of line in missing because of a fold in
the paper when it was copied.]
Pigons. Tell grandma I am 9 the 23rd of June and Lyman is
8 the 5th of July. Florence has a cold and the rest of us
are all right. The weather is very cold and [chambil] to-
day. How are all the folks there. I was very glad
to hear from you and Grandma. I have some new
shoes last night. Lyman try's to write you but h [he]
gets started and stops. I would like to come and see
you for a month. Well I can not say and [any] more
for this time and write soon again.

Good by
Your loing [loving] grandson
Sherman Sudbury
942 W. 9th south

[note written diagonally across the bottom right side:]
His first letter to me. J. H. M.

A4.5
HANDWRITTEN LETTER FOUND AFTER PAGE 2.

Colonia Juarez

September 22, 1900.

Dear Teacher

I feel it a great privilege to write to you these
few words for it is so hard to write anything. I am
trying my best to think of something, for they say
if you try you surely can do something, for I know
for my own self that you can whether anyone else
thinks so are [or] not, for we all have a great work to
perform. And Just think of the hundards [hundreds] and
may be thousands of missionaries in the field who
have to work nearly all the time during the time
they are there, besides, that isent [isn't] all they have to
do for they have many other works to preform [perform] before
they can return home to there families and friends.
For we all are united as one people and we belive [believe]
that there is a god and we ought to be thankful
for the blessings he has bestowed upon us for I
think that we all are trying to live are religion
the best we know how. We are having a lovely
little shower now as we have hade [had] lovely weather
all during this month and I still hope that we
will have more rain than we ever had before
for it is surely doing lots of good. Dora Martineau.

A4.6
A TYPEWRITTEN DOCUMENT. THE RIGHT SIDE OF THE PAGE IS SLIGHTLY CUT OFF. IT IS FOUND AFTER PAGE 2.

A MISSIONARY BLESSING,

Pronounced upon the head of Elder Theodore Martineau, in the Salt Lake Temple, April 9, 1900, by Apostle Reed Smoot.

--------------------------oOo---------------------------

Brother Theodore Martineau, in the name of the Lord Jesus Christ, we, the servants of the Lord, lay our hands upon your head and ordain y[ou] a Seventy in the Church of Jesus Christ of Latter-day Saints and we sea[l] upon you all the blessings pertaining to this calling and all the keys [...] gifts and powers thereof, and we ask our Heavenly Father to ratify the same in the heavens as we, His servants, do upon the earth.

We also set you apart for a mission to the Southern States, and w[e] ask our Heavenly Father to look upon you in tender mercy; that His hol[y] angels may be with you at all times to guard you from everything that would prevent you from fulfilling an honorable mission. We ask our Heavenly Father to quicken your understanding; that you may have a testimony of Him and that you may be able to bear it to the people with w[hom] you come in contact, that they may know that you are laboring for God [...] cause. We ask our Heavenly Father to bless you with health and stren[gth] and to take charge concerning you from this very time, that you shall have success in your mission and in going and returning, and we feel [at] this time to warn you of the many temptations that shall come to you, we admonish you to be humble at all times, that you may have power to overcome them; and we bless you to the end that you shall be satisfie[d] with your mission, provided you observe the laws of God. We also f[eel] to say unto you that you should at all times realize that God giveth [and] that He also taketh away, and whatever the will of the Lord may be y[ou] must submit thereto.

We seal these blessings upon your head in the name of the Lord [Jesus] Christ, amen.

Martin S. Lindsay,
Reporter.

A4.7
TWO-PAGE HANDWRITTEN INDEX TO MARTINEAU'S POEMS FOUND AFTER PAGE 2.

[Page 1.]

Vol.

Poems. Book 1.

———— // ————

[Page 2.]

[Numbers are written here and there below this part. In the middle of the index is written "Tomb of Luella Martinus Vol. 2 p 109 109"]

[. . .] Vol. 2

A4.8
LETTER FROM SUSAN E. FOUND AFTER PAGE 2.

Colonia Juarez
August 4. 1905.

My dear James.

why dont you write to me I have written + sent you 3 letters + have had only one in return from Vernal. Wrote you to see if you could have some work done for Moroni He was faithful + true + believed in the principle of Plural Mariage + would have entered into that order if he could have had an opportunity + I think you should have wives sealed to him if you have any left unsealed

Moroni H Martineau Born Parowan Iron Co. Utah Sept. 12. 1854. Look in your record for date of his death

I sent you Lois + Edies record also can you have them endowed they can be sealed to someone hereafter There are quite a number cases of Typhoid fever in town John Walser + 4 children are down several other families are also afflicted. Our Coop Store will soon have a Bank + Millinery department also a Tailor shop + dress making all combined hope they will make a success of it. I would like to meet you at Ciudad Juarez when you come in you can buy goods there free of duty. the Custom house is at the Bridge. The free zone has been abolished + no duty after you leave El Paso but a heavy one at the Bridge so dont get anything that you can buy this side

Hoping to hear from you soon I am as ever Susan, with love

A4.8

[transcription of page 1]
Colonia Juarez ~~July~~

My dear James August 4, 1905.
why don't you write to me I
have written & sent you 3 letters
& have had only one in return from
Vernal. Wrote you to see if you could

have some work done for Moroni
He was faithful & true & believedd
in the principle of Plural Marriage
& would have entered into that
order if he could have had an
opportunity & I think you
should have wives sealed to him
if you have any left unsealed

Moroni H. Martineau Born Parowan
Iron Co. Utah Sept. 12, 1854. Look in your
record for date of his death

[transcription of page 2]
I sent you Lois & Edies record also
Can you have them endowed they
can be sealed to someone hereafter
There are quite a number cases of
Typhoid fever in town John Walser
& 4 children are down several other
families are also afflicted. Our Coop
Store will soon have a Bank a Milin-
-ery department also a Tailor Shop
& dress making all combined
hope they will make a success of
it, I would like to meet you at
Ciudad Juarez when you come in
you can buy goods there free of
duty, the Custom house is at the
Bridge, The free zone has been
abolished & no duty after you
leave El Paso but a heavy one at
the Bridge so don't get anything
that you can buy this side ~~in~~
Hoping to hear from you soon
I am as ever Susan, with love

room, upon a table, while the company occupy seats along the sides formed of rough boards covered with quilts and upheld by blocks and benches. The younger part of the company show unmistakable signs of impatience until the Bishop, in humble prayer, asks the blessing of God upon the evening's enjoyment. He ceases, and expectation lights up every eye. "Numbers one to twelve," cries the floor manager, and all holding those numbers rush for their partners. The numbers, by the way, were drawn, lottery fashion, from a hat passed around at the commencement. But one of these dancers was a youth evidently new to social functions of this kind, and was a picture of embarrassment and unrest as he sat casting covert glances towards "his girl"—his first boyish love perhaps—watching the moment when he could lead his partner to the floor unobserved by any one, and she apparently a little flurried too. Here a couple of tall gawky youths are just bowing awkwardly to their partners, but unluckily they stand back to back and are a little too near each other. The result is a collision entirely spoiling the dignity of their salute, and causing a titter in those lucky enough to witness the scene, much to the inward wrath of the unlucky youth. But the music and "circle all" quickly banish all remembrance of the incident, and away they go. How delicious to watch this elderly couple who are just learning to dance! The only thing they seem to have really learned is how to make the most mistakes in a given time. But no one laughs at them, as they evidently are doing their best, and friendly hands pull them this way or push them the other until the figure is finished, and they stand, the picture of pleasure and content, as having got through, thus far, a very difficult undertaking.

Most young men in those days considered that the greater the number of "steps" they could execute to the second, the greater their skill as dancers, and so the boys' feet flew and the girls' skirts swished in marvelous fashion. But such violent "skill" brings copious moisture to the brow, which the few who are lucky enough to possess a handkerchief remove by its use; while others, not so favored by fortune, use their shirt sleeves. To wear a coat on such an occasion would sadly intefere with this convenience—a coat being an article of no real use, and always in one's way. Besides this, most of the boys didn't own a coat, but wore shirts of linsey or flannel, with two big pockets on the bosom. The second figure being finished, the caller cries "Promenade all—you know where," and each swain proudly leads his partner to her seat. But new arrivals have filled all vacant places, so one girl holds another on her lap, the boys looking on enviously and wishing they could hold them instead.

him, even if she has to marry him to accomplish it. [illegible]

The dance is dismissed with benediction, and all have enjoyed it; not an unkind word or oath has been heard; not a single breath tainted with liquor; peace and good will have reigned supreme.

And now, while the mothers gather their pans and baskets, a crisis is approaching which, to the inexperienced, is appalling, while it is to others a delightful anticipation,—the pairing off and seeing the girls home. See those two youngsters,—timid where girls are concerned, but brave as lions when facing Indians or grizzlies. They both secretly watch the same girl and try to meet her at the door, fondly believing no one notices them. Vain thought! She sees them both, and secretly rejoices, as she perfectly understands, while seemingly utterly unconscious of all. She carelessly delays, to give them opportunity, and is trying to decide which of them to favor as they approach. Thus, it may be, she may be unconsciously settling, for good or for ill, the most important event of her life; a union that may endure through all the eternities, or may result in final and eternal separation.

This description of an old time party is not a fancy sketch, but will be recognized by many of the older readers of the NEWS as a true picture, and bring to their remembrance many happy reunions in days long past, with friends who long ago have passed behind the vail. But I will confidently assert that no more real enjoyment can today be found in a dancing party or a Bradley-Martin ball than those of olden time within the log walls and upon the rough floor of our primitive schoolhouse.

J. H MARTINEAU.

Colonia Juarez, Chihuahua, Mexico.

THE MORMON CHURCH

HOLDS BALANCE OF POWER IN UTAH STATE.

Resident Of Salt Lake Explains Why the Mormons Vote Together and Claims That the Church Is the Dominant Factor In Politics.

The Mormon church of Utah has shown its power in the election. It has made the state republican notwithstanding four years ago Bryan had 51,000 out of 63,000 votes," said J. S. Wilston, who is here from Salt Lake. Mr. Wilston who has traveled all over Utah, knows the state thoroughly. He is a stanch republican and what is known in Utah as a "gentile," the name given those not members of the dominant church. He says he is glad that President McKinley has been re-elected and that the state ticket went through.

Several days ago R. C. Hammond of Salt Lake stated before the election that there was no doubt that the church would throw the state to McKinley.

"That has been done," said Mr. Wilston this morning. "The state would have gone democratic had it not been for the aid of the church; there need be no question about it. The Mormon church does, or at least it can, control the politics of Utah, as is shown in this election. It is a religio-political organization, just as it always has been.

"I am not pleased with the methods employed in Utah, notwithstanding that I am a republican. I hold that the separation of church and state are of more importance than mere party success.

"If the Mormon church had good government in view when it aids one party or the other in Utah I would not protest, but there is nothing in view but its own purposes. If the church managers believed that the country would suffer if President McKinley was not reelected, if their motives were patriotic, there would not be so much reason to find fault.

"Those who control the church vote believe that a fierce effort will be made at the coming session of congress to pass an anti-polygamy amendment to the constitution. At the last sesssion an attempt was made to pass an amendment disfranchising every person who had more than one wife. There are in Utah many men who have two, three and four wives. I do not say that this system of polygamy is as general as many outsiders imagine, but the polygamists are the influential church officials, the wealthy men who can support several establishments and numerous progeny. They control the rank and file of the church.

"Why, President Snow, the head of the church, the pretended prophet, has four or six wives. George Q. Cannon and Joseph Smith, the next in authority, the president's councilors, each have several wives. Cannon has four that I know of.

"These men don't want to be disfranchised. That is but natural. Why last year, John Henry Smith, another high official, a polygamist with four wives, was sent to Washington to work against the amendment.

"The leaders of the church believe that [illegible] publi[illegible] the [illegible] They [want the help] of the administration [in] defeating the anti-polygamy amendment to the constitution which will surely be introduced at the coming session of congress. They will go to Senator Hanna.

"'Did we not make Utah republican? True, you didn't need it, but you might have needed it. Now we want the administration's aid to defeat this amendment.'

"That will be their argument."

PROMINENT MORMON

Replies To Statements Of a Man From Salt Lake.

COLONIA JUAREZ, Mex., Nov. 17, 1900:

Editor El Paso Herald:—Your issue of the 14th inst. contains an article contributed by one J. S. Wilston, hailing from Salt Lake, Utah, and as it contains some inaccuracies I beg leave to make some corrections. He charges the Mormon church with having caused Utah to go republican at the recent election, a charge without the slightest foundation in fact. Mormons, like Baptists, Presbyterians, Methodists, Catholics or members of any religious community under heaven have their individual political beliefs and predictions, no more, no less—and have the same right to express them at the election booth.

No man loses his right to the elective franchise by reason of his religious belief or unbelief, because a union of church and state is antagonistic to the true spirit of republicanism and individual liberty. This is a cardinal point in the political and religious creed of the Mormons and has been so always. They are divided on political lines as republicans, democrats and populists, just like other states and communities and the members of either party are just as energetic in advocating their principles as other people.

Why should they not? Religion or atheism has nothing to do with the matter.

Mr. Wilston notes as very strange, that Utah, democratic in 1896 was republican in 1900; how about other states, Nebraska, for instance, and others far moore politically important, which changed their pluralities from democratic to republican? Take New York, for instance, which has swung like a pendulum from side to side for many years.

The cause the change in Utah is not difficult to discover. In 1896 "Free Silver" was the battle cry of democracy which swept all before it in the silver producing states; but that doctrine met its Waterloo in that year when McKinley was elected, and the nation signified its disapproval of the principle. Unprecedented prosperity, manufacturing and commercial flooded the nation, and the United States took a mighty upward leap in the scale of nations. Men differ as to the causes of this great prosperity and advancement but the indisputable fact remains, and "nothing is so successful as success." Bryan forced the insertion of the "free silver" plank—repudiated by the nation in 1896—into the democratic platform—and it more than any one thing else defeated him.

The Mormon democrats could see this as clearly as others—could understand just as clearly the folly of fighting longer for a "lost cause," and had they continued the fight for "16 to 1" might justly have been charged with blind political fanaticism.

Mr. Wilston intimates that the secret cause of the change in Utah was the fear of further anti-polygamy legislation in the next session of congress. They have no such fear; should such legislation be enacted it would merely supplement the provisions of the constitution of the state of Utah, which

A4.10
FOUR-PAGE HANDWRITTEN LETTER FROM JESSE MARTINEAU.
THE LETTER IS FOUND AFTER PAGE 2.

This old Castle in right side of the city is where the [illegible] of Germany was imprisoned by his son

Oct 26th/89

Dear, Father!

I wrote you some time ago but I thought perhaps you might like to see how your boy looks by this time and also how I am getting along;

This paper I bought in Bingen when I was down there last month but have not used it before because it did not hold as much as I wanted to write. This is a very good picture of Bingen & also the Castle of Rhinstein. So you can form some idea of what Bingen on the Rhine looks like. Oh! I forgot to ask your opinion of the Photographs. I think they are very good. Oh yes while I think of it I had a letter from Bro Stucki & He sent his regards to you. when He comes He always asks about you. and is just like a father to us boys!

Well Father last Wednesday I had the privilage of baptizing two more a young man & his Frau which makes six that I have baptized in all

and I hope next year to be able to baptize many more but of course a person can not say how that will be I have baptized more here in this branch than have been baptized in two years before I came here but of course it is not due to my smartness as the Apostle Paul says I planted & watered but God gave the increase. Now I know if I plant good seed & water well God will bless the crop and perhaps I can reap a good harvest. I tell you the crop is great in this land there are thousands & thousands who have never heard of Mormonism I have met many myself. Now just think of the 45000000 of people in this land & only about one Dozen Missionaries. and then to think of Russia & Austria with their millions who have never heard of the Gospel a Person can first understand what a great work rests upon the Latter Day Saints.

I had a letter from Charl a few days ago & He says they are all well & have moved into their new house and how proud they were to think they have a house of their own.

I also learned from Wm B.P. Jr who is now in Berlin that Aunt Susan is in Logan but have heard nothing further as they do not write as often as they might. It is now more than 3 weeks since I have had a letter from Logan but am now expecting one every day for Alley is very good about writing she has written me more letters than O.F. Eva Nephi Emma & Gean & Lillie together sehr gut [illegible] or in our own way of speaking very good is it not?

Well Father I dont know what to write about for I dont know what would interest you. But I hope and pray that the Lord will bless you with Health & Strength & let His Holy Spirit be with you Continually & with the hope of hearing from you soon I am as ever your loving son

Jesse N. Martineau

Lebewohl

A4.10
TRANSCRIPTION OF LETTER FROM JESSE MARTINEAU.

[written above castle image on stationery]
This old castle in right side of the city is where the 4th of Germany was imprisoned by his son.

[transcription of page 1]
Oct 26th/89
Dear Father!
I wrote you
some time ago but I
thought perhaps you might
like to see how your boy
looks by this time and
also how I am getting along;
This paper I bought in Bingen when I
was down there last month but have not
used it before because it did not hold as
much as I wanted to write. This is a very
good picture of Bingen & also the Castle
of Rheinstein. So you can form some
idea of what Bingen on the Rhine
looks like. Oh! I forgot to ask your opinion
of the Photographs. I think they are very
good. Oh! yes while I think of it I had
a letter from Bro Stucki & He sent his
regards to you. when He comes he
always asks about you and is just
like a father to us boys!
Well Father last Wednesday I had the
privilege of baptizing two more a
young man & his Frau which makes
six that I have baptized in all

[transcription of page 2]
and I hope next year to be
able to baptize many more
but of course a person Can
not say how that will be
I have baptized more here
in this branch then have
been baptized in two years
before I came here but of course
it is not due to my smartness
as the Apostle Paul says I plan—
ted & watered but God gave the
increase. Now I Know if I
plant good seed & water well
God will bless the crop and
perhaps I can reap a good
harvest. I tell you the
Crop is great in this land
there are thousands & thousands
who have never heard of
Mormonism I have met many
myself. Now just think of
the 45 000 000 of people in
this land & only about one
Dozen Missionaries. and then
to think of Russia & Austria

[transcription of page 3]
with their millions who have
never heard of the Gospel
a Person can first understand
what a great work rests upon
the Latter.Day.Saints.
I had a letter from Charl[es]
a few days ago & He says
they are all well have moved
into their new house. and
how proud they were to
think they have a house
of their own.
I also learned from Wm B. P. Jr
who is now in Berlin
that Aunt Susan is in
Logan but have heard
nothing further, as they
do not write as often as
they might It is now more
then 3 weeks since I have
had a letter from Logan
but am now expecting
one every day for Alley

[transcription of page 4]
is very good about writing
she has written me more
letters then O. F. Eva Nephi
Emma & Gean & Lillie together
[four German words written here] or in our
own way of speaking Very good
is it not?
Well Father I don't Know what
to write about for I don't
Know what would interest
you. But I hope and
pray that the Lord
will bless you with
Health & Strength & let
His Holy Spirit be with
you continueally [continually] & with
the hope of hearing from
you soon I am as ever
your loving son
Jesse N. Martineau
[...] [...]

APPENDIX

INSERTS FROM VOLUME 2

A5.1

LETTER FROM SUSAN E. INSERTED AFTER PAGE 26.

Tucson Ariz July 11, 1895.

J H Martineau

Many thanks for your lovely present & to show that I apreciate it I will use it first in writing to you My dear husband & may our fathers blessing ever attend you & may your future be filled with happiness & peace

May we ever retain the mutual affection we have kept pure through the cares & trials of life & may our love grow & increase until the perfect day

Your Loving Wife

Susan

A5.2
POEM WRITTEN FOR SUSAN E.'S 82ND BIRTHDAY. INSERTED AFTER PAGE 56.

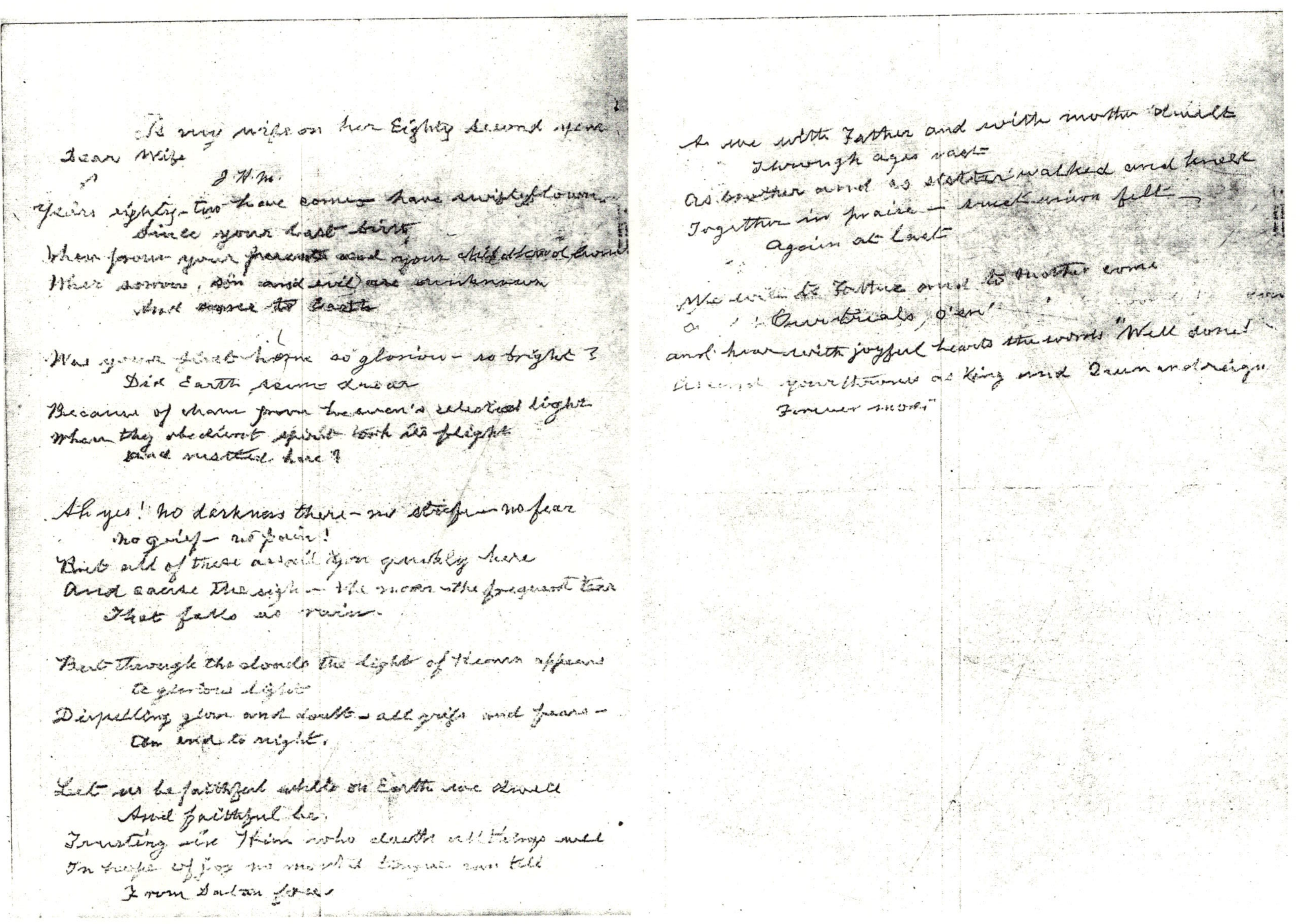

To my wife on her Eighty second year
Dear Wife
J.W.M.

Years eighty-two have come – have swiftly flown
Since your last birth
When from your parents and your childhood home
Where sorrow, sin and evil are unknown
And came to Earth

Was your first home so glorious – so bright?
Did Earth seem drear
Because of shame from heaven's celestial light
When thy obedient spirit took its flight
And nestled here?

Ah yes! No darkness there – no strife – no fear
No grief – no pain!
But all of these assail you quickly here
And cause the sigh – the moan – the frequent tear
That falls as rain.

But through the clouds the light of Heaven appears
A glorious light
Dispelling gloom and doubt – all grief and fears –
An end to night.

Let us be faithful while on Earth we dwell
And faithful be.
Trusting in Him who doeth all things well
In hope of joy no mortal tongue can tell
From Satan free.

As we with Father and with mother dwelt
Through ages vast
As brother and as sister walked and knelt
Together in praise – such union felt –
Again at last

We will to Father and to mother come
[illegible]
Our trials o'er
And hear with joyful hearts the words "Well done!
[illegible] your thrones as King and Queen and reign
Forever more"

A5.2
TRANSCRIPTION OF THE TWO-PAGE HANDWRITTEN POEM FOUND AFTER PAGE 56.

To my wife on her Eighty second year
Dear Wife J. H. M.

Years eighty-two have come—have swiftly flown
Since your last birth
When [forever] your parents and your children [...]
Where sorrow, sin and evil are unknown
And came to Earth

Was your first home as glorious—so bright?
Did Earth seem drear
Because of harm from heaven's celestial light
When thy obedient spirit took its flight
and rested here?

Ah yes! no darkness there—no strife—no fear
no grief—no pain!
but all of these assail you greatly here
and cause the sigh—the moan—the frequent tear
That falls as rain.

But through the clouds the light of Heaven appears
A glorious light
Dispelling gloom and death—all griefs and fears—
An end to night.

Let us be faithful while on Earth we dwell
And faithful be,
Trusting in Him who doeth all things well
In hope of joy no [mo...] & tongue can tell
From Satan free—

As we with Father and with mother dwelt
Through ages vast—
As brother and as sister walked an knelt
Together in praise—[...] [...] felt—
Again at last—

We will to Father and to Mother come
Our trials o'er
and hear with joyful hearts the words "Well done!
[...] your thrones as King and Queen and reign
Forever more."

A5.3
CLIPPINGS FOUND AFTER PAGE 150.

IN OLD SALT LAKE.

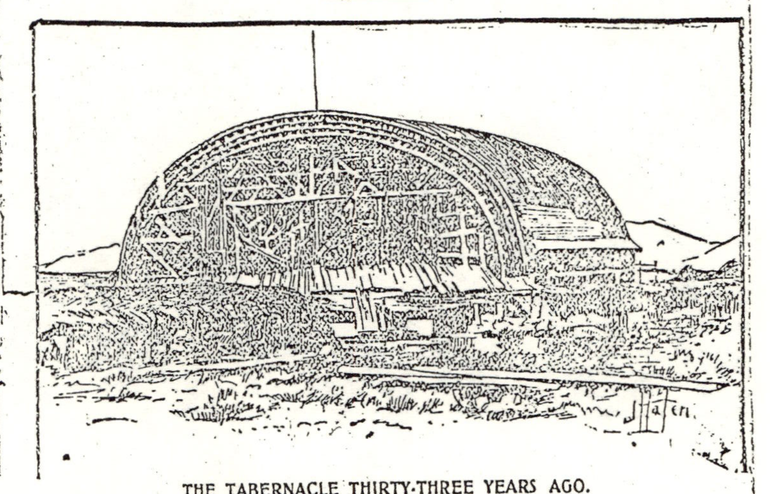

THE TABERNACLE THIRTY-THREE YEARS AGO.

THE above picture shows what was a familiar sight to Salt Lakers of the past generation during the several years the Tabernacle was in course of construction. The idea of a great assembly hall, with a self-supporting roof, a hall which should be large enough to accommodate the people in their Semi-Annual Conferences, originated with President Brigham Young, and work on the great building was begun on July 26th, 1864; it was dedicated October 6th, 1867, the Semi-Annual Conference being held there. It was at this Conference that President Joseph F. Smith was called to the Quorum of the Twelve, to succeed Amasa M. Lyman. The gallery was added to the interior, and the final finishing touches added in the year following. The dimensions of the Tabernacle are as follows: Length, 250 feet; width, 150 feet; height of ceiling, 70 feet; height of entire structure, 80 feet; its actual seating capacity is about 8,000, though 10,000 have often been crowded within its walls. The great organ, which stands at the west end, is world-famed, not only on account of its peculiar richness of tone, but because of its being built entirely of Utah timber, and by a Utah builder, Joseph H. Ridges being its constructor. The building is lighted by both gas and electricity and heated by steam. On concert occasions, when it is filled with a fashionable audience, lit up with the glare of hundreds of jets, it presents a scene of brilliance and beauty rarely excelled by any other auditorium in the world. The acoustic properties of the building are wonderful; though when crowded with people, it requires a good pair of lungs and clear enunciation to make a speaker intelligible in every part. The Tabernacle has been the scene of some notable historic events. The celebrated discussion between Rev. John P. Newman and Apostle Orson Pratt, on the question, "Does the Bible Sanction Polygamy?" took place there, August 12th, 1870; and Adelina Patti made a memorable appearance there, April 1st, 1884. The architect of the Tabernacle, under President Young, was Henry Grow, wh superintended the construction.

THE DESERET NEWS.

(SEMI-WEEKLY.)

Organ of the Church of Jesus Christ of Latter-day Saints.

LORENZO SNOW, TRUSTEE-IN-TRUST.

PUBLISHED EVERY TUESDAY AND FRIDAY. Corner of South Temple and East Temple Streets, Salt Lake City, Utah.

Charles W. Penrose, - - - Editor.
Horace G. Whitney, Business Manager.

SUBSCRIPTION PRICES.

One Year,	in advance	$2.00
Six Months,	"	1.00
Daily News, per year,	"	8.00
Daily News, per month,	"	.75

Correspondence and other reading matter for publication should be addressed to the EDITOR.
Address all business communications THE DESERET NEWS, Salt Lake City, Utah.

SALT LAKE CITY, - MAY 5, 1899.

A PUBLIC LOSS.

The killing of the valiant Ogden police officer is a great calamity, and his popularity and the lawlessness which led to his death naturally aroused the people of his native city to anger. Threats of lynching, however, indicate a spirit of lawlessness something akin to that which occasioned his murder. They ought not to be indulged in by civilized people. The law has been violated, let the law be vindicated in a lawful manner.

If the culprit had been slain in the battle on Sunday it would have been all right. The dead bandit met his just deserts. The probability is that the living criminal will share his fate. But, having been lawfully captured, he must be lawfully tried, and, if found guilty, be lawfully executed. There must be no mobocracy in Utah.

Captain William A. Brown was an efficient and faithful public servant. He came of an excellent family. His father was one of Ogden's leading and most respected citizens. Francis A. Brown lives in the memory of the people as an honest, fearless and useful man, who spent his life in doing good. The slain officer was stalwart in mind and body, beloved by his family and friends, and relied upon by the public and his chief. His taking off is a calamity to the city of Ogden, and there should be some substantial recognition

the other will be soon in a position to dictate the terms to the land powers, and under the circumstances few European powers, if any, would venture a war with either. On the contrary, they should be glad to know that there is an impartial court to which to refer their possible disputes for a peaceful adjudication.

We hope the American delegates will be heard on the momentous question now before the world. Our country has always been an advocate of peace, and should go on record again as the champion of international arbitration.

IN THE FROZEN SOUTH.

A telegram was received a few days ago in Christiania, Norway, from Captain Borchrevink, stating that the explorer had reached the Antarctic continent. He left the shores of civilization so unostentatiously that comparatively few people took any notice of the daring enterprise.

Mr. Borchrevink was born in 1864 in Christiania. For some time he lived in Australia, where he became teacher of surveying and natural science at Cooewull college, New South Wales. It was then that he conceived the idea of launching an expedition in the southern Polar regions, but lack of funds prevented him from carrying out his plans until recently.

His ship, the Southern Cross, is a bark rigged vessel with an auxiliary screw, constructed somewhat upon the lines of Nansen's Fram. She can stand a good deal of crush in the ice. She is well provisioned for several years.

The expedition is also provided with all that is needed for a journey over the frozen fields of the extreme south. It has tents, alpenstocks, ropes, spades, hammers, shovels and folding lanterns in great abundance, and a collection of dogs, obtained at great expense among the Samoyeds. Suits of special clothing fill the wardrobes of the vessel, suitable for winter and summer use. The sleighs are a kind of cross between a sled and a canoe, each giving room for one person and provisions for a couple of weeks. They are so constructed that they right themselves when capsized.

Several expeditions have gone to the Antarctic region but none so well equipped as this. In 1774 Captain Cook crossed the 71 parallel and traversed the southern sea sufficiently to ascertain that if there is a continent it must be almost entirely within the Antartic Circle. In 1823 Weddel sailed three degrees further to the south. In 1841 Sir James Ross discovered Victoria land and some adjacent islands, traced a coast line for 500 miles, and encountered an ice wall which barred all fur-

A5.4
CLIPPINGS FOUND AFTER PAGE 158.

Y, MARCH 9,

OUR NEIGHBORS.

COLONIA JUAREZ, MEXICO.

CHANCE FOR HOMESEEKERS.

Exceptional Opportunities for the Industrious—The Poor Man's Country.

Special Correspondence.

Colonia Juarez, Mexico, Feb. 26.—In a former letter, dated Batipito, Sonora, Feb. 4th, 1900, reference was made to the new colony just established at that place, and a few additional items may be of interest, historic and otherwise. Presidents A. W. Ivins and Helaman Pratt, with J. H. Martineau as engineer and surveyor, arrived on the ground of the future colony January 25th, and on the next day began the survey of several trial canal lines. While this work was in progress other colonists came in, among whome were two ladies—the sisters Christina and C. S. McCall, whose names I record as the first female colonists of Batipito.

On Sunday, January 28, 1900, the first religious meeting held in Batipito convened in the rude shelter reared by Samuel Lewis, a "Mormon" battalion veteran, and for the first time in 1,500 years, probably, songs of praise ascended to the heavens. The opening prayer was by J. H. Martineau, and the speakers were Presidents Ivins and Pratt and Elder Martineau. The congregation numbered 23 persons, including visitors, but though few in number it was an enjoyable occasion.

On Sunday, February 12th, 1900, a branch of the Oaxaca ward was organized with Lorenzo S. Huish as presiding Elder, E. A. Huish as clerk of branch, and S. J. Jarvis and Elders Hunsaker and Snarr as a committee to oversee and direct canal building and other necessary labors. All the officials nominated were sustained by unanimous vote.

The surveys of city plat and farm land were finished February 16th, 1900, and President Ivins and party returned home immediately. Only a small part of the farm land was subdivided, as President Ivins was notified of the coming of Apostles Grant and Clawson and party from Salt Lake City, and hurried home to meet them.

Colonia Batipito offers exceptional advantages to such as wish to build up homes for themselves. There are thousands of acres of very rich land with great depth of soil. The bottom lands are covered with a heavy growth of coarse grass, which grows from four to seven feet high, and through which in consequence, it was very difficult to run survey lines. To break up this soil requires a strong team and a strong plow; I think a railroad plow would be best for the work, the first plowing. The gently sloping bench land has a growth of mesquite trees and brush on it, which will require considerable labor to clear, but the value of the wood for fuel will far exceed the cost of its removal. In fact, each man who takes up his land on the Baptipito creek will have his farm and his fuel near at hand for years to come. Misquite wood is very hard, and of the very best quality as fuel.

The Bavispe river is a large stream, pure, free from mineral and unexcelled for drinking, fordable only on the riffles, between which it is from five to fifteen feed deep and the habitat of large catfish and fish of other kinds.

Another great advantage this colony possesses is its fine climate, very much like that of southern California, though not warm enough, perhaps, to raise oranges; but without doubt pomegranates, olives, figs, almonds and other fruits adapted to a semi-tropical climate will do well; also those adapted to a climate like that of Utah.

Mexico is truly the place for those who have little worldly gear, for in this land there is no inclement winter to eat up the summer's earnings; but instead there are twelve months in which to do a year's work instead of six or seven as in the north, and a man can earn as much in the winter as in the summer.

But as every place has some disadvantages so has Batipito, the principal of which is the lack of good saw timber near at hand, but with rich land, abundant fuel, water and fine climate, this place is, in generals terms, very desirable for such as are brave enough to cut loose from a well developed country to build up a new one. But the settlement of this land as for hardship, is nothing, compared to that of Utah in the beginning. We often receive letters of inquiry concerning Mexico. I would say to all such, come and see for yourselves, look through your own spectacles and act upon your own judgment.

I will state that a canal one and three-quarters mile long will bring the water upon the farm land, at a cost of about $3.00 per acre, and this without any dam in the river. To bring out the waters of the Batipito creek upon its adjacent lands will be but a trifle.

We have just enjoyed a great treat in the visit of Apostles Grant and Clawson, President Kimball and Elder Maeser, with Sister Grant. The special conference just terminated is one to be long remembered. The instructions given by the speakers were dictated by the Holy Spirit, consequently, just what we needed. There was a goodly attendance from Colonial Diaz, Dublan, the mountain towns, and Oaxaca and all seemed to be well paid for their journeys to the conference.

General good health, peace and prosperity prevail in all the settlements, with constant accessions to our numbers, evidenced by the fact that in this Stake there are 1,591 teachers and pupils enrolled in the Sunday school organizations, with a general attendance of 80 per cent. Zion flourishes like a bay tree, and the rude blasts intended to uproot her only cause her roots to take a stronger hold.

A5.5
CLIPPINGS FOUND AFTER PAGE 158.

DESERET SEMI-W

the Mr. Wheelwrights to loan him his pocket knife, which he did, and as soon as the storekeeper saw the knife he recognized it as being one of those stolen. On being asked whom he got it from the man named a certain party, and the police were notified of the discovery and in a few hours they had three young boys about 16 years of age, sons of respectable families, under arrest, and a great deal of the plunder was also recovered from various places where they had disposed of it. The parents of the boys are very desirous of keeping the matter from the courts and to keep the names of the boys from the public and if a satisfactory arrangement can be made with the police and Wheelwright Bros., the boys will get off this time with a severe reprimanding.

CASES CONTINUED.

Before Judge Rolapp in the Second district court:

State of Utah vs Ralph Pidcock; continued for the term.

A. J. McNish vs O. S. L. R.R. Co.: continued for the term.

Emil Olsen et al vs O. S. L. R. R. Co.; continued for the term.

All jurors who were summoned to appear on March 8, 1900, have been excused until March 10th.

A SMALL BLAZE.

The fire department was called out to a small fire on Jefferson avenue, the damage will amount to about $50.

ARRESTED FOR STEALING A WATCH.

Three young men were arrested by the police today on the charge of stealing a watch from Fred Woodmansee, last Saturday night. According to the report the men entered his room on the lower Twenty-fifth street, while he was asleep and stole the watch.

There will be a most interesting lecture given next Saturday at the county teachers' meeting at the court house, by Prof. Stewart, of the State University.

PROVO.

UTAH COUNTY BUSINESS.

Busy Session of the Provo City Council—Jail Delivery.

Special Correspondence.

Provo, March 5.—The county board of commissioners met today in regular session and transacted the following business:

The matter of selecting a matron for the county infirmary was called up and the names presented to the board as applicants for the position were Mrs. D. L. Rogers and Mrs. L. A. Hurd, of Salt Lake; F. W. C. Hathenbruck, Mrs. M. A. McLean, Mrs. Wilmirth White, of Provo.

The only name voted upon was that of Mrs. McLean who received the support of all the commissioners and was declared appointed. The lady for a great many years was the matron of the State insane asylum under Dr. W. H. Pike and is considered qualified in every way. The lady will not assume her new duties until the building is completed, which will be some time yet. The salary for the matron was placed at $50 per month.

County Treasurer Malmberg reported the financial condition of the county to be as follows:

General fund—Balance on hand Feb. 1, 1900	$4,321.30
Received during month	1,898.36
Total	$6,219.66

A5.6
PHOTO OF BRIGHAM YOUNG FOUND AFTER PAGE 162.

PRESIDENT BRIGHAM YOUNG. FOUNDER OF THE B. Y. COLLEGE.

A5.7
OBITUARY CLIPPED AND FOUND AFTER PAGE 162.

LYO—In this city, on the 21st instant, ...ily Henrietta, relict of the late ...v. David C. Lyon, of St. Paul, ...nnesota; aged 73 years.

Th... funeral will take place TO-DAY (Sun...y) at 12:15 p.m. from St. Joseph's hospital. Friends will please accept this intimation. Aug. 21. 1899

(St. Paul, Minn., papers please copy.)

A5.8
LETTER FROM GERTRUDE FOUND AFTER PAGE 196.

Box 78

Mr. E. E. Taylor
Raymond
Alberta N. W. T.
Canada
via
Great Falls Mont.

We send letters from here via Great Falls Montana otherwise they go way round by New York or Montreal and some times San Francisco which takes so much longer to reach their destination.

Dear Pa I recid your good letter last mail from Whiterocks & enjoyed it so much. Take good care of your self & dont overdo. I am glad you are there at last so that dreaded part will soon be over. We are all so anxious for the time to come when you can come home where we can take care of you and appreciate you as you aught to be after what you have done for us all. I am getting better the spells seem to be passing away as I have been promised they should do and every day brings the time nearer when I shall be well and time flies for here it is the middle of July. I'll try to write you a long letter soon. May God bless & prosper you is the prayer of

Your Loving - Gertrude

A5.9

LETTER FROM GRANDCHILD INSERTED AFTER PAGE 196.

Fletcher Jan. 30. 1897

My dear Grandma.

I am glad you are comming to see us.

Pa has not come yet.

It rained very hard last night.

Leland is not very well.

I am going to school now.

But it will be out in about one month.

If you can read this I will write again.

From your loving grandson

George A Martineau

Little George: Alberts oldest child's first letter recieved Feb. 10. 1897.

A5.10
LETTER FROM GERTRUDE INSERTED AFTER PAGE 230.

Juarez Aug. 5 – 83

Mr. J. H. Martineau

My dear father

Your good letters of July 29 just came and we are so glad to know you are back in the City again and settled. I thank Providence you won't have to go into the Mountains again and the Surveyor genl is a mormon so maybe he will help you to get your work thru much sooner so you can soon come home. at least by Conference time. I do hope you can come not later than Oct. so you will miss the cold stormy weather there. I have my glasses & thank you for getting them fixed. The glass is just right. The reason I wanted to know the cost especially was that I feared you might not have money enough to pay for them as I had no idea what it would cost. You are perfectly welcome to all the money left over and I'm glad there was some left. I never want it back. Some time when you get real rich I wish you would send me one of those little Temple pamphlets 15 cts at the News Book store

Its so hard to get U. S. stamps here to send out for things. There is a dear good man here just a few months younger than you Patriarch Skousen who calls to see me often and is always full of blessing & words of comfort and has done me so much good. About 2 months ago he was here & when leaving got out-side the door he came back in without a word put his hands on my head and said "These spells that afflict you shall get less & less & will soon die away and afflict you no more" & it is so for the affliction is dying away & are nothing like they used to be. It is now four years that I have been bed fast almost all the entire time but every day brings the time nearer when I shall be well. It is so hard to even imagine being well and up and around like other people it would seem so strange but its coming. May the Lord bless & prosper you & soon bring you home is the constant prayer of your loving

Gertrude

A5.11
LETTER FROM N. L. HAGBERG INSERTED AFTER PAGE 272.

Bingham December 2d 85.

J. H. Martineau Esq:
Dear Father!

Your letter dated Oct 23d 85 have I received with great pleasure for I am wery glad to hear from you, more so when I hear you contented and satisfied with your Country and Circumstances. I think and really believe: it was the wery best Exchortation you could give me in my deep sorrow: when you said in your letter (The Great thing for us is to live so, as to go where our loved ones are) The desire of my heart is to live so. and do right, so far as I know and understand it. I do hope and trust in the Lord that he will help me through all trying circumstances that I may gain the victory – for I myself is a weak and helpless mortal whatsoever the Lord does, we may aknowledge as right. He gives, and He takes, Blessed be his Holy name.

Now I will give you the particulars you are asking for.

I am born the 26 of July 1840. in St: Olof pronounces (Sanct Olof) Christianstads Co Sweden. Baptised the 10th of December 1871. Greflunda Christianstads Co Sweden Ordanined a Preest in April 1872. by P. B. Holmgreen. and on a Conferens held in Malmö the 4 and 5 of June Ordained an Elder by Paul Dehlin and apointed to fill a mission to Landskrona. Sweden, and efter was removed from one place to another so I have traveled all around in the Conferens of Skåne Sweden. Emigrated in June 1875. Landed in S. L. City in July 1875. Since I came here I have never filled any Ofices or Apointments. the reason I think is, that I all the time been in the mountains working, so I am in reallity known of but wery few. I and my first wife Josephine Rodihne was Endowed and

Paul Dehlin:

Sealed by D. H. Wells. in S. L. City the 26 of Juli 1875.

Our first and Only Child. Mary Charlotte was born 22nd of February 1877. Blessed of P. Pettersson. Mount Pleasant San Pepe Co Utah

Died in West Jordan S. L. Co the 26th of Sept 1878. the Mother had departed from me and left the Child the 10th of Sept the same Year.

Efter these I been single op to the 16th of July 1884. when I was sealed to Sarah Westwood. she was born the 29th of Jan: 1863. Hull. Yorkshire England Baptised and Confirmed the 2nd of March 1878. in the same Town and Co by Elder John Meatcaff

Died in S. L. City the 4th of Sept 1885. in Child bed. there was two Doctors and the said at first it was impossible to safe the Child, but would try to safe the mother, agordingly the Child was killed in the mothers womb. yust when it was to be born. if the Mothers Organism had been in the right Order the Child had surely been born alive. Now is the quistion? Is it wrong or is it right to give the Child a name, and record it as if it had been born alive. We both agreed to call him Nephi if it was a boy. and it was a fine and Noble looking boy. Please write to me soon and let me know your ideas about it.

Before I Emigrated I went to the Minister for to get what Geneaology that was possible. and I found in a book, the name of a Sister of mine (her father unknown.) Her name was Johanna born Oct 28th Died Nov 2nd 1846. in Mellby Christianstads Co Sweden. aged 4 days.

I am well and hope you enjoy the same blessings as these lives me. I close my letter with the kindest love. and best wishes for you and all. from yours humble and efectionate son in the Everlasting Covenant

N. L. Hagberg.

when you come to Utah. please let me know when, or where; for I am longing for to se you.

A5.12
LETTER FROM JOEL INSERTED AFTER PAGE 294.

Guerrero Jan 8 1906

Mr Jas. H. Martineau

819 Logan Ave S.L. City

My dear Father

To day is the 54 anniversary of your marriage. and I wish you many, many happy returns of the day: I Pray our heavenly father to bless you and strenghten you that you may be still a wise counsellor to your family.

I thank the Lord for good, kind and faithful parents and that I am born heir to the priesthood and I feel in my heart to bless you for I realize as I get older what blessed parents I have and I hope I may emulate your example in all things good. I do not possess eloquence to portray in beautiful language the depth and intensity of my love for you but perhaps my poor weak way may at least comfort you in knowing at least it is true.

2

I am in Guerrero on business for Mr. G. Webb and have just bought for him 1500 hectolitros of corn 100 of beans and all the baled hay. lucerne and straw I can find amounting to over $6,000.00 and will be here nearly a week shipping it I also expect to send up to the camps $1000.00 worth of merchandise. He asked me to come and attend to this part and then I will ship it on mules from the end of the track to the camps beyond Bocoyna for he has confidance in my ability to do the business properly. after I have distributed this lot will come here or Miñaca and send up another lot and let my partner Capt Coetzee distribute it while I run in home for a short visit for I havent been but ten days at home since last february now almost a year. We are having so much snow here that tiemaking is almost at a standstill.

I hope to rent about ten thousand acres of timber land tomorrow so we can make some ties for the Mex Central.

My partner has started a camp 11 Kilometers beyond Bocoyna and is clearing off the right of way as the road runs through a forest for over 100 miles. we will not make very much this winter as the snow is too deep but as soon as Spring opens we will make things hum.

For a month we have been in the snow and New Years day my partner and I left our snug little log cabin and went to Bocoyna in a blinding snow storm and I returned next day when it was worse than ever. I hated to go up there but had promised to look after Bro. Wilsons camp while he is in home and will have to make another trip soon to pay off the men for the month and audit his accounts and see that his camp has supplies.

2

This work keeps me out of mischief and I cant bear to be idle anyhow.

Now Father dear this is nearly all about me and I hope you will tell me all about you for I love to hear from you. I often think of the blessed temple work and long to be there again. There is nothing so ennobling and enjoyable as the work of the gospel and I am striving to show by precept and example to the natives that there is something better and nobler than they possess and the leaven is slowly working and some day will bear fruit.

Father, may God Bless you in all your labors, your eating and drinking and sleeping to give you health and strength of body; in your blessings and ministrations and counsels to give you strenghth of mind and spirit; in your temple work and prayers and ordinances that you may become a prophet and elect of God. Affectionately Joel

A5.13
LETTER FROM GERTRUDE INSERTED AFTER PAGE 310.

Colonia Juarez Feb. 4

Mr. J. H. Martineau

My dear father

Your dear good letter came last mail and gave us so much pleasure as your letters always do, we appreciate your advice and instructions so much, and try to profit by them. Your letters always give me new hope & courage to bear my trials for sometimes my soul gets so weary of pain and I get so hungry to go to meeting where I can get Spiritual food I crave it so. I cant read much or be read to for it makes my head and eyes ache so I just starve but I am getting well I am better in many ways in fact in every way than I have been since I have been sick almost five years now. I cling to the promises I have recieved and know they will be realized in time but I get impatient I want to be doing something

useful but perhaps its all in the pro-
gram. I believe if you were here to
bless me often I should gain much
faster. Good men who are visiting here
call in and bless me occasionly which
does me much good and sometimes
6 or 8 men will come in (fasting) to
administer to me which of course is
powerful. Every body thinks it is a
miracle I have lived thru it all and
come out with my senses and we all
know it is only thru faith & the power of
the Lord and I'll soon be well now.
Guy will be home in about a week
to stay he has sold everything in
Canada it is so far away. Dublan is
going to build an ice plant this year
and we have a dynamo for electric light
mabe we will soon have street car
just imagine. We all long to see
your dear face and pray earnestly
that you may soon be able to come home
to stay where you will be appreciated so much.
Always your own loving Kid
Gertrude

A5.14
LETTER FROM LYMAN INSERTED AFTER PAGE 326.

LYMAN R. MARTINEAU
RESIDENCE
818 LOGAN AVENUE

SALT LAKE CITY, 2/13 1907

Col J. H. Martineau
Colonia Juarez
Mexico.

Dear Father:— If my dates are not mixed this is your 79th birthday. I congratulate you on reaching such an age possessed with unusual mental & physical vigor. I hope the Future holds out for you the choicest blessings, and that you may see many recurring anniversaries. Your family record would indicate that you ought to live 10 or 15 years longer & if you are careful why shouldn't you?

I want to include Aunt Susan in my congratulations & good cheer because you have lived so long together that your lives are closely interwoven and so coalesce, that all but a physical unity, makes you one. She suffers when you suffer and shares your joys & hopes. May she live long, & retain all her mental & physical powers. The Lord bless you both, & also Gertie, Anna & all, is my most earnest prayer. With love and a birthday kiss Your son Lyman 80

A5.15
LETTER FROM YOUNG WOMAN'S JOURNAL *INSERTED AFTER PAGE 330.*

Salt Lake City, Utah, Sept.28,1907.

James H.Martineau,

Col.Juarez,Chihuahua,Mex.

Dear Brother:-

We do greatly appreciate your articles. It seems wonderful that you are able to write them at your age. Will you kindly send us a brief account of your life of about five or six lines so that we can use them as a foot note to one of your articles. It would add to the value if the girls knew something about the aged writer.

Your "Night of Anxiety"appears in the October Journal. Enclosed please find check for $3.00 as a slight token of appreciation. We will send the paper you ask for.

Your articles about the Pioneer and the early experiences with the Indians will be very interesting. We should be glad to receive more of them.

May God's blessings attend you. I remain,

Yours very sincerely,

Mary E. Connelly,
Editor.

A5.16
LETTER FROM YOUNG WOMAN'S JOURNAL *INSERTED AFTER PAGE 330.*

ISSUED MONTHLY $1.00 PER YEAR

OFFICE OF

YOUNG WOMAN'S JOURNAL

ORGAN OF THE Y. L. M. I. A.
PUBLISHED BY THE GENERAL BOARD
535 CONSTITUTION BUILDING
BOTH PHONES 566

Salt Lake City, Utah, Feb.2,1908.

James H.Martineau,

Col.Juarez,Mex.

Dear Brother Martineau:

Enclosed please find check for $1.25 in payment for your article "A Dance On Sunday"which appears in the February Journal. It is a slight recognition of your valuable articles. We were so much interested with the short sketch of your life that we desire a longer one,if it is not asking too much of you. We would like one that would fill about trhee pages of the Journal,and if you have a good photograph of yourself we would be glad to have that also.

We hope you will send us some more articles regarding your experiences in the settlement of the southern country.

Trusting that yourself and wife are enjoying health and strength, and that the year 1908 will be a happy one ~~to~~ for you both, I remain,

Yours very sincerely,

Mary E. Connelly
Editor.

A5.17

LETTER FROM THE ARMY INSERTED AFTER PAGE 344.

FORTY-THIRD NATIONAL ENCAMPMENT

EXECUTIVE OFFICERS

CHAIRMAN
MAYOR JOHN S. BRANSFORD

FIRST VICE CHAIRMAN
GOV. WM. SPRY

SECOND VICE CHAIRMAN
W. J. HALLORAN

TREASURER
HEBER M. WELLS

EXECUTIVE DIRECTOR
FRANK M. STERRETT

SECRETARY
FISHER HARRIS

EXECUTIVE COMMITTEE

J. S. BRANSFORD	F. C. SCHRAMM
WM. SPRY	F. S. STEPHENS
W. M ROYLANCE	LEON SWEET
GEO. A. BLACK	HEBER M. WELLS
R. G. SLEATER	J. G. BARNES
JOHN C. CUTLER	GEO. A. EATON
A. R. HEYWOOD	ELMER I. GOSHEN
W. J. HALLORAN	S. H. BABCOCK
A. J. DAVIS	W. H. KING
A. W. CARLSON	THOMAS KEARNS
JOHN DERN	EDWIN F. HOLMES
M. M, KAIGHN	S. X. SMITH
EZRA THOMPSON	D. H. CHRISTENSEN
E. F. COLBORN	A. L. THOMAS
JOY H. JOHNSON	O. W. POWERS
H. VANCE LANE	HENRY GARDNER
R. P. MORRIS	E. W. ROBINSON
JAMES G. MC DONALD	E. T. HULANISKI
WM. NELSON	

AUGUST 9, 1909 — SALT LAKE CITY — AUGUST 14, 1909

HEADQUARTERS
232-233 COMMERCIAL CLUB BUILDING

August 2, 1909

Mr. James H. Martineau,

919 Logan Ave.,

City.

Dear Sir:

I am instructed by Col. Sterett, Executive Director, to say to you that a carriage will be sent to your place of residence, 919 Logan Ave., City, about 8 or 9 o'clock, Wednesday morning, August 11, in which you will be given a seat during the parade. You will also be furnished with at least one ticket possibly two to the Grand Stand. You will present this letter to the driver of the carriage when he calls.

Yours truly,

Jas. W. O'Neall
Asst. Exc. Director, G A R

A5.18
LETTER FROM CHURCH FIRST PRESIDENCY INSERTED AFTER PAGE 372.

OFFICE OF
The First Presidency
of the
Church of Jesus Christ
of
Latter-day Saints

P.O. Box B.

Salt Lake City, Utah, January 9th, 1911

Elder James H. Martineau,

Logan.

Dear Brother:-

President Lund duly received your communication of the 12th ult. and thanks you for it, and directs me to say to you that any further communication at any time you may be prompted to make on matters historical will be appreciated. He wishes you to know that the Historian's Office has verified the date of the murder of Dr. Whitmore and Robert McIntire, as given by you.

Yours, &c.,

Geo. F. Gibbs

Secretary.

A5.19
FOUR GENERATIONS PHOTO, CIRCA 1920, INSERTED AFTER PAGE 372.

APPENDIX

6

INSERTS AFTER VOLUME 2

A6.1
NEWS CLIPPING ON ANNIVERSARY.

Sixty-One Eventful Years Spent Happily as Man and Wife

1913

1913

Aaron 1914

MR. AND MRS. JAMES H. MARTINEAU.

Mr. and Mrs. James H. Martineau, residing at 545½ east Sixth South street, on Wednesday last quietly observed the sixty-first anniversary of their wedding day. A number of friends from various wards in the city called upon the aged couple, making the anniversary pleasurable to them beyond their expectation.

Mr. Martineau was born in 1828 in Amsterdam, N. Y., and in his boyhood became a printer. He operated the first Hoe power press used in the city of New York, as well as the first in existence. When the Mexican war broke out he enlisted in the United States army, and after the war began a transcontinental trip to California. Reaching Salt Lake in 1850, he became interested in "Mormonism," and joined the Church in the same year, remaining in this city.

Mrs. Martineau was born in Kirtland, O., July 11, 1836. She was the daughter of Joel H. Johnson, one of the first elders in the Church, an intimate friend of the Prophet Joseph, who was present at the time of the Word of Wisdom was given, and who made the shingles with which the Kirtland temple was covered. Mrs. Martineau came to Utah in 1850, two years after her father had come, and resided in Salt Lake for some time.

In 1852 Mr. Martineau was sent to Iron county, to help colonize that place. Mr. Johnson had also been sent there, with his family, and it was at that place that the couple met and were married. After residing there nine years, they removed to this city, and from here to Logan, where Mr. Martineau became the first county surveyor of Cache county, and served the city of Logan as recorder and also as alderman. He surveyed all the towns of Cache county in 1860 and laid out many canals. He was on the survey of the Utah Northern railroad from Ogden to Cache valley, and later into Idaho. He also assisted in surveying the Union Pacific railroad from Echo canyon into the state of Nevada. He was adjutant in the Cache military district, and was a minute man for 20 years.

After spending 25 years in Logan, the family moved to Arizona, where Mr. Martineau engaged in surveying, laying out six towns and two large canals. They then moved to Colonia Juarez, Mexico, and assisted in the colonization of that place. Here they spent the next 20 years, and established considerable possessions. The aged couple returned to this city three years ago, leaving their children in Mexico. During the recent trouble his family became scattered and the members are now located in the states of Utah, Idaho, Arizona, New Mexico and Texas. They have eight living children, 76 grandchildren and over 30 great-grandchildren. Both enjoy fairly good health, Mr. Martineau, although he is 85 years old, being able to read without spectacles.

The accompanying photographs show Mr. Martineau in his seventy-eighth year, and Mrs. Martineau a few years befo—

A6.1

Mrs. Elizabeth C. McCune, President Daughters of Pioneers.

Dear Madam:

The publication in the Deseret News of genealogical and temple work has already been productive of much good, several known to the writer having thus received valuable information relative to their kindred living or dead; and as I have had a work done more or less complete for several thousand names, I find in my record those of many now living in the Church connected by intermarriage. It may be that for some of them a work has also been performed by others. To avoid such possible chance for error in time to come, I give a sketch of my family connections, and temple work performed.

So far as I know, I am the only Martineaux ever baptized into the Church from the outside world. If there be others I would like to know and correspond with them, as thus missing genealogical links may be supplied both parties.

My father, John Martineau, born March 22, 1793, was a son of Stephen, born March 22, 1761, son of Stephen, born March 22, 1827, descendants of Elie and Marguerite Farbesson of Dieppe, France. They were Huguenots, and by the revocation of the edict of Nantes in 1682 became victims of a persecution so deadly that multitudes—all who could—fled to Switzerland, Holland, Germany, England and America for refuge. David, son of Elie noted above, escaped with his family to England and became head of the English branch of Martineaux. I here remark that some years ago my son, Lyman R. Martineau, when in London, met and obtained from Mr. Basil Martineau, an eminent barrister, a complete record of the family and connections back to Elie, 1682. To obtain these names and dates Basil had expended over $10,000, and my son obtained all simply by copying a thousand or more names. The ways of our Father are wonderful, in thus opening a way to salvation for those who never heard the gospel; for all these have had temple work performed for them.

My father went to England at the age of 19 years; went to college and graduated as a physician, surgeon and civil engineer, and there married as his first wife the widow of Capt. Hawkins of the royal navy, who left at his death a son, Samuel Hawkins, and daughter, Elizabeth. She was a daughter of the Earl of Stanhope, disowned because she had married one not of the nobility. By her my father had two daughters, my half sisters Julia and Lucretia. Julia married a Mr. Winslow of Boston, since when all trace of her is lost. Lucretia died young.

My father's second wife, my mother, was Eliza Mears, daughter of James Mears and Lois Sprague Mears, born 1806, and married at the age of 17 years. After father's death she married William Babcock of Vermont. All her children are dead except myself and Mrs. Lois E. Voswinkel of Tomah, Minn.

By my father's first marriage he became connected with some of the most noble families of Great Britain—the Earls of Bedford, Minto and Stanhope, Lords Chatham, Chesterfield, Russell and Halifax.

Because of this connection I have performed for them all a work in the holy temple, as complete as possible, with those of their families whose names I could obtain.

After the conquest of Gaul (France) by Julius Caesar, it became Romanized by multitudes of Romans who were granted lands there. Among these were my Roman ancestors, their name in Latin being Martinus, masculine, and Martina, feminine. The British Encyclopedia gives the change of name from the Latin to other nationalities as follows: Spanish and Italian—Martino; German and English—Martin; French—Martineau; Portuguese—Martinho. The name in Latin was also by some branches of the family spelled Marinus, the letter t being omitted. The family was prominent from early times, five popes being of the family and many others high in authority in the Catholic church. In A. D. 235 one of the family, a girl of 15 years—Martina—suffered death by burning rather than sacrifice to the Roman pagan gods. She is now a Catholic saint—Santa Martina. The most ancient family name I have found is that of a daughter of a Roman General Martinus. Her marble tomb still stands among others among the ruins of an ancient fortified Roman post between Aleppo and Damascus, in Syria. In that climate where rain seldom falls the inscription upon the tomb is still legible; it reads, as translated from Latin into English that the tomb was erected "in honor of the manes of Lucilla, beloved daughter of Martinus imperator (general)." The word manes is equivalent to our word soul or spirit, and conclusively proves the general and his family were pagans, not having embraced Christianity, for Christians never used the word manes nor paid any religious or other honors to the spirits of their dead. The date upon the tomb was about A. D. 70 or 90, the first figure being a little indistinct. This tomb was discovered by a Greek Mormon missionary—Locander—while on a mission in Syria many years ago, and described by him in a letter published in the "News." Since then I met the elder in Mexico, receiving from him full particulars. A work has been performed for her after so long a wait of many centuries and she has undoubtedly received it with joy. I mention these things to illustrate how our Father makes known scattered names, which in due time will all be connected together.

On my mother's side I have unbroken record back to 1600. Her father, James Mears, born 1774, was a soldier in the war of 1812. His father, John Mears, served under Washington, and was present at the execution of Major Andre. His father, also John Mears, served in the "French and Indian" war of 1756-7, and was taken prisoner by Montcalm, the French general when he captured Fort Oswego. The name of the family is variously spelled in ancient records, as Meers, Meares, Myers, etc. I think the family was of Welsh origin.

My maternal grandmother's ancestry were Hutchinsons, descendants of a younger son of Lord Hutchinson of England, who founded a family in the early settlement of Massachusetts, about the year 1624. They were all Puritans, prominent in early days and valiant as soldiers. Several were killed in various Indian wars, Mrs. Ann Hutchinson and her children in 1627; William, in 1643; Edward Hutchinson, killed in "King Philip's" war, 1675; Nathaniel in 1693 and Moses Hutchinson, wife and child, in 1704.

My great-grandmother, Lois Hutchinson, married William Sprague; her daughter Lois Sprague married James Mears, my grandfather in 1796, removing from Berkshire, Mass., to central New York, then an unbroken forest. He died at the age of 93, his wife, three years previously.

Among my ancestry there is no record of any disreputable in any manner, all being devout according to the little light they possessed.

The following are namese for whom I have had temple work done:

Males—Hilyard, [illegible] Blake, Howes, Brewer, Marsh, Wilde, May, Jardine, Fletcher, Sprague, Hutchinson, Mears, Cooley, Burt, Crittendon, Barlow, Hale, Hadlock, Leavitt, Taylor, Morrill, Shuman and many others. [illegible]—Ferguson, Russell, Dean; Simmons[illegible], Beatty, Christopher, Webb, Neave, [illegible], Stewart, Harris, Clark, Scott, Smith, Jardine, Day, Taylor, Parry, Rogers, Stephens, Pierce, Langdon, Foster, Louise, La Valliere, Davenport, Anderson, Baker, Wood, Leavitt, Sprague, Cole, Brown, Morrill, Morris, Parker, Button and many others.

Parties interested may receive information of work done by sending an envelope, self addressed, with stamp, to me at Colonia Juarez, Chihuahua, Mexico.

Many years ago the writer was blessed by patriarchal authority at three several times to lead forth and do a great work for the Lamanites, a prophecy at that time very distasteful, as I was filled with hatred against them; but our Father in His mercy took from me that hatred by a dream or vision, I know not which, and gave me instead love and desire for their redemption through the ordinances of His holy house. Authorized by the presidency, I have acted in behalf of several hundred of the blood of Lehi, including all the noted Lamanites of the United States, Mexico, the Incas of Peru, and a noble line of Auracanian chieftains of South America who for centuries defied the efforts of Spain to conquer them. The Mexican names include the Montezuma emperors, their wives and children, with many subject kings, princes and chieftains; also Hidalgo, Allende, Morelos, Guerrero and others who died for their country, and President Benito Juarez, their second liberator.

JAMES H. MARTINEAU.

A6.2
THREE-PAGE HANDWRITTEN BIRTHDAY LETTER FROM GRANDDAUGHTER VEE. IT IS FOUND AFTER PAGE 401.

Salt Lake City,
March 13, 1920.

Dear Grandfather:—

This letter will be late in reaching you on your birthday, but nevertheless, all the good wishes and love go with it.

We hope you are feeling O. K. and that you will get stronger when the nice spring weather comes.

Vere, Mary and myself are all fine and dandy.

Yesterday we inquired how Uncle Lyman was feeling and found that he is improving. He is getting impatient having to stay in bed, but if he will only wait until he gets much stronger he will get along alright. The chief thing now is for him to just be patient.

I just know how glad you were to see Uncle Jesse. We hope to have him up to dinner the first of next week.

We hope all the folks up there are well.

Congratulating you again on your 92nd birthday,

I remain
Lovingly,
Vee.

Vere joins me in sending love and best wishes.

A6.3

TWO-PAGE HANDWRITTEN LETTER FROM SON JOEL, 1920. IT IS FOUND AFTER PAGE 401.

Moran Texas Mar 11 1920

My dear Father

I am thinking of your birth anniversary which marks the 92nd milestone of your long and eventful life and in looking back over your past my heart swells with pride at the splendid record you have made in temple work and of the many times the spirit and power of God have been made manifest in wonderful healings and in prophetic blessings through you. The Lord has been gracious to you and though you never amassed wealth you received something infinitely greater, a worthy family.

Our ancesters spent much money gathering data and
publishing it in book form so we may read and enjoy knowing some of their achievements in the past. I would love to assist in compiling a complete history of each of your children to date also their children
and grandchildren that may be a foundation for later generations to build on that we may in future years still
honor you as the founder of a great family that will yet make a mark in the world for good.

Your own achievements on the frontier as a minute man, a railroader and builder of canals that have helped develope the west into a great empire are worthy of being recorded where your posterity may have access to it to read it. While some of the family are noted in finance and politics others are known as missionaries and pioneers
and all are worthy in their place and the generation of your grandchildren now arriving at manhood promise to maintain the good name of Martineau.

There is still a great work for us to do to do the work
for our dead and I am sure as soon as the present supply of names is finished, more will be found in some manner that we may continue right on.

Dear Father I wish you joy and contentment on this anniversary and may you be strengthened in body and in spirit till your labors here are done and you go to join the loving ones waiting to receive you. I would love to be with you and hear your counsels and receive of your wisdom.

May the Lord bless you prolong your days is my fervent prayer.

Your affectionate son Joel.

P. S. I also send my love to Brother Charley and Sister Eva and may the Lord reward their love and devotion to you. J.

A6.4
LETTER FROM PRESIDING BISHOP.

Presiding Bishop's Office,

Salt Lake City, Utah, Feby 5th 1885

Bishop J. H. Martineau

Dear Brother.—Your name has been selected by the Presiding Bishopric, and approved by the First Presidency of the Church, to act as our agent in the St Joseph Stake of Zion. You are therefore authorized to enter upon the labors and duties of that office; and in placing this responsibility upon you, we desire to call your attention to some matters pertaining to this position.

It becomes your duty to take a general supervision of all the tithing matters in your Stake, counseling with and advising the Bishops as to the best means of taking care of all tithes that may be paid, and to see that proper and convenient storehouses, hay sheds, cellars, yards, etc., are provided, according to the requirements of the ward where they are situated, and encourage the Bishops to have the tithing properties kept clean and in good repair, thus setting an example in the ward, and also stimulate the Bishops to have all the accounts connected with their offices kept in a plain, straight, business form, so that a person of ordinary intelligence could understand them.

We wish it distinctly understood that the Bishop's Agent is not to interfere with the duties and responsibilities of the Bishops in their respective wards, but in your visiting around among the people of the different wards, lay before them the requirements of the Lord to pay their tithing in the kind and in the season thereof, so that they may have a right to the blessings that are promised from a faithful performance of that law.

We desire you to keep us posted upon matters associated with your labors, and where questions arise as to your duties, advise with us in relation thereto.

Respectfully, your brethren and co-laborers in the Gospel,

Wm B. Preston, *Presiding Bishop.*

R. T. Burton
Jno. Q. Cannon } *Counselors.*

A6.5
NEWS CLIPPING.

Prest. L. Snow.

PRESIDENT LORENZO SNOW addressed the Conference. He said, in substance: "I marvel that I have ventured out today, but I have something to say to you, and I trust that I may have sufficient strength of voice, and time enough to say it. And I hope you will give me your faith and prayers that I may address you.

I am delighted to hear that there has been such a good spirit at the Conference—a spirit that has enabled the brethren to speak of the glorious progress the Saints have made. The Saints have not been idle during the past six months. They have done their duty to a great extent. They have exercised their faith in behalf of the brethren during this conference more than at the other conferences. They are improving in this respect. And if they continue to improve in this, the brethren at the next conference will have still more of the Spirit by which to speak to them.

During the past day or two I have had a distressing cold, rendering me hoarse; and I feared that I should be unable to be here at all. But through the blessings of the Lord and your faith and prayers, I am here.

I want to say something to you about a very important subject, a subject that deeply concerns the Priesthood—you Presidents of Stakes, you Bishops of wards, and you Elders, High Priests, and the High Councilors. I wish you to remember what I say. It is of interest to all the officers in the Church. There are fifty Stakes in Zion, presided over by a president and counselors. In each of these Stakes there is an average of at least eight wards, each having a Bishop at its head. Now, this means a tremendous responsibility. The details of all these organizations depend on the fifty presidents. There is something, therefore, for each of them to do. There is a great deal for them to accomplish. This responsibility is sacred and extensive. Though these presidents have been faithful, they have not been as faithful as they could be—as they ought to be. They have not sensed their responsibilities as they should do.

The Church is now seventy-two years old, and during this period we have improved. This is right. We ought to be doing greater things than we did in our youth. The Lord is coming one of these days. He is interested in what you officers are doing. You presidents of Stakes should attend to the affairs in your districts. Look after the interests of the people whom you oversee as you would look after the interests of your own families—your own wives and children. You should think of them day and night. When you go to rest you should devote half an hour before you sleep in thinking of their welfare. Try to find out where you can help them. See wherein you can advise them in their spiritual and material affairs. Ascertain whether they are spending too much or too little, and whether they can spend their money to better advantage. Then, too, the Bishops have to be looked after. Bishops, however wise—and many of them are wise—have to be cared for. This is the duty, not of the Apostles, but of the presidents of Stakes. It is the duty of the High Priests, Elders, Priests, Teachers and Deacons to look after the interests of the Church in Zion. Do not lay this duty on the Apostles. They have too much already. They ought to look to these things of which I have been speaking occasionally at least.

Now, the Lord has ordained a certain channel through which He is going to exalt His children, overcome wickedness, and uplift righteousness. This channel is the holy Priesthood—His authority to men. And the Priesthood has various officers the duties of whom He has clearly shown. The special duty of the Seventies and the Apostles is to look after the world. The duty of the High Priests and Elders is to lool after our home interests—to build up the waste places of Zion. The time is coming when you cannot have the Twelve to depend upon—when you will have to do these things yourselves. They will have other duties to perform. I want you to remember this.

It is a tremendous responsibility, this matter of the Priesthood. You presidents of Stakes, know how the Lord is obeyed in your district of country. Know whether the people keep the Sabbath day, whether they profane the name of Deity, whether they pay their tithes, use tobacco, build meeting houses and school houses—know everything they do. God will help you in this; for it is what He requires of you. But when you are depending on the Apostles to do these things you are doing what you have no business to do. Let the High Council visit the wards with you, that they also may know what is the condition of the people. Be lively in performing these duties.

God bless you all, brethren and sisters. I am glad to see such a vast multitude of people. I am delighted, as I said in the beginning, at the good spirit that has been poured out upon you. I thank you for exercising your faith and prayers in my behalf. When I got up here, I did not think I could say half a dozen words. But I have been enabled to say what I had on my mind. Of course a great deal more might be said. It might be expanded and made much more of.

There is another subject that I wish to speak of. I am getting along in years now, being nearly 88 years old. I have had only one counselor since President Cannon died. I have chosen another counselor. I have sought the guidance of the Lord in the matter, and the Lord has directed the choice. I have chosen a strong, energetic man, and I think he will be a great help to myself and President Smith; I hope therefore you will sustain him. God bless you all.

---

prohibits polygamy in that state now and forever, and which are possible for repeal only by the congress of the United States. Also the civil code of the state makes polygamy a crime liable to severe punishment. No new plural marriages have been contracted in Utah since it was solemnly and officially announced by the leading church officials that the church would accept the decision of the U. S. supreme court relative to polygamy and obey the law of congress prohibiting it.

Mr. Wilston says leading churchmen in Utah still have several wires; if this be so, doubtless they are men who married plural wives before any law had been enacted by congress prohibiting it and therefore when not a criminal offense; and while it would be unlawful now to take plural wives no honorable man would refuse to support and educate those whom the law made practically widows and orphans—women who had married him in good faith, and whose children would naturally be as dear to him as any others.

I do not charge Mr. Wilston with intentional unfairness and only notice his article so that both sides may be heard.

J. H. Martinean.

AN OLD TIME DANCING PARTY

Graphic Description Which Brings Again the Old Familiar Scenes—Candles as Cash for the Admission Price—Dearth of Candlesticks, With a Resort to Pocketknives, Potatoes and Turnips.—"On With the Dance"—Awkwardness of Youth—The Uselessness of Coats—An Envious Longing—Recess For Picnic—Sweetmeats and Happiness—The Home Going.

To the Editor:

Those who today attend a ball in Utah expect to enter a fine hall, well lighted and tastefully ornamented, and to dance to the best of music, because this is the general rule. But it was not always so in Utah, as many of our elderly people will recollect. To illustrate the difference I give a sketch of one which I attended in early days.

It was in Parowan, Iron county, in the fall of 1851. The largest house in the place was a log building used for Sunday meetings, schools, dancing and other public assemblies, and in this the merrymakers met. As this party was to be rather a "swell" affair, extra exertion was made to obtain the best of music regardless of expense, and so two fiddlers were engaged instead of one, the usual number, and each gentleman was expected to bring two candles to pay for his ticket, those not burned to go to the musicians as their pay. This was no small matter, as candles were very scarce, and generally were kept in reserve for cases of sickness or other extra occasions.

This wise arrangement as to candles promised a brilliant room, but unfortunately, when the time arrived to light up it was found no one had brought a candlestick. The committee, their minds overburdened with the magnitude of the affair, had entirely forgotten this necessary appendage to a candle. But when was Young America hindered from dancing by so slight an impediment?" Some took their jack knives, stuck a blade into a log, and this, when partly closed, would hold a candle very well; others rushed home and brought large potatoes or turnips which were transformed quickly into candlesticks by slicing off the bottom for a base and by making a hole in the top to hold the candle; and shingles stuck between the logs at intervals made very good brackets for them.

Then we come to the dance. The musicians are seated at one end of the

After a while a rest is called; some one sings a song or speaks a few words until all are rested—then, "on with the dance!" About 11 p. m., many glances are cast towards a corner where many baskets, pails and pans are piled, and the younger ones whisper "When will they have the picnic?" Reproved by their elders, their eyes still plead, though their tongues are silent; for you know, boys are always hungry. But others, too, are hungry, and soon the eatables are all spread by the sisters, and eaten with a relish.

Let us examine the contents of this pan. Here is a cake—a little dark in color, perhaps. Well, that is because it is sweetened with home-made molasses made from corn stalks, beets, melons or parsnips, each of which will make a passable syrup. Here are cakes with dried service berries in them—rather tasteless—but it is the best we have and good enough for anybody. Sugar is almost unknown, raisins and spices entirely so. But, luckily, happiness does not depend upon delicacies, and all are happy without them.

Again the dance goes on, and by this time the candles are becoming short and flaring. What is that fellow doing? Oh, just scraping off, as much as possible, the grease that has dripped upon his only coat, as he sat under one of the candles. He says nothing, but his eyes speak volumes of wrath. Poor fellow! He only wears his coat upon the most momentous occasions, and we must excuse his ill-feeling. But oh, the perversity of human nature! His mind becomes serene as he beholds a rival engaged in a similar manner; or, the girl who had refused his escort to the dance, scraping the tallow from her best dress—the girl whom he has idolized in secret for the last three weeks. "S'rve her right," he says to himself. She, noting his look of exultation at her trouble, vows inwardly to get even with

A6.6
NEWS CLIPPING.

THE SEVEN LINES.

An Interesting Article From Edward Stevenson.

The seven lines of Characters which the JOURNAL presents to its readers in this issue represents the engraving which were coppied by the hand of Joseph Smith in Harmony, Pennsylvania, in the years 1827, when he was in the 22nd, year of his age. They were copied from a book of gold plates which he found hidden in a stone box nicely pointed together and set in cement. The six slabs of stone, forming the box were dressed so that they were smooth and square on the inside but rough on the outside, so much so that the cap stone was crowning and very much looked like a cable stone, and was laid bare when he found it, that is to say only just enough to see a small portion of it protruding from the hill side.

No one unless he was in possession of the knowledge of what was therein, would have paid any attention to it in causually passing that way.

Most certainly it was very engeniusly constructed and hidden in a very choice spot of ground. It was found first in spring of 1823. The young man who found it was only in the 17th year of his age. He was too young at that time to be trusted with such a valuable find, for it must be in weight about 40 lbs. and of pure gold, in sheets that were very thin like unto thin sheets of tin plate, and they were covered with engravings of a very curious workmanship, showing great skill by those who were the engravers. There were several different ones who did the work. They contained a history which reached out over a period of 1,000 years, beginning at a point of time 600 years B. C., and continuing on until 420 years A. D. The history necessarily had to be very brief, and when translated became the Book of Mormon, that is the portion which was translated, for there is a portion of them which is yet held in reserve, which was sealed with three extra rigns which is reserved to yet and in due time of the Lord to be translated.

All of these plates were fastened together with three great rings, so that each plate could be turned over on these rings as if they were hinged together, so we are led to see that the people were very skilled and were very choice in preserving their history to bring to light who the people were who left so many ruined cities, towers, temples, and other rellics, many of which are found with hyresgliftics of a similar character to their 7 lines presented in this issue. Having in reserve another article with an engraving, and giving the history of where those engravers came from. I will leave that part of my narative for the future, anticipating shortly to publish in pamphlet form 4 chapters of lectures, all of them illustrated with 6 or 7 engravings. As I was saying those plates which were translated makes a book of 623 pages, called the Book of Mormon, and is at the present time printed in about 20 different languages. With those gold plates, and in the same box, was a breast plate of gold valued at about $500.00. Attached to this breast plate was a Urim and Thumim,—or interpreter. They were in form like unto a pair of old fashioned spectacles, 2 clear stones set in rims of silver. I have conversed with the man who handled them, and he said that he had placed them as he would a pair of spectacles but they were to large for him, as if for a much larger race of people than we are. This Urim and Thumim was similar to what we read of in the Bible of olden times, and which only belonged to Seers, Revelators and Prophets. These were hid up with the book so as to help the one to whom they should be entrusted to translate them into the English language, as has been done.

The hill side from whence those plates were taken, is fully described in an article with a beautiful engraving of the hill, in the Utah Monthly Magazine in this year 1892. It is situated in the North West part of the state of New York, [illegible] miles South of Palmyra, and

I will vouch for the correctness of the characters as I have compared them with the identical lines, which I have handled as they are still in existence infact, just as they were when Martin Harris took them (as a messenger) to Professor Anthon of N. Y. with the translation of them as they were translated by the Prophet Joseph Smith. They were first traced with tracing paper from the exact coppy from which this engraveing has been made by Mr. Held of Salt Lake City.

Twenty-two years ago (in the year 1871) I was favored with the privilege of bringing Martin Haris to Utah from Kirtland Ohio while an hour journey [I had] many opportunities of conversing with him on the subject as well as many other incidents which occurred at the early period of the translation, as he aided the young Prophet as a scribe, etc., in writing some of the translation to the learned gentleman, Professor Anthon, who, after examining them carefully, gave him a certificate stating that they were Egyptian characters and that the translation was correct. Martin, with the certificate, started homeward, but when he had advanced as far as the door, the Professor called to him, asking him where he obtained those plates; to which Martin replied

"In a hill near Palmyra, N. Y."

"Then bring the book to me and I will translate the plates for you."

"I cannot do so," said Martin, "for a part of them is sealed."

"Then," replied Mr. Anthon, "I cannot read a sealed book."

Caractors

A6.7

COPY OF THE ANTHON TRANSCRIPT SHOWING CHARACTERS FROM THE GOLD PLATES. IN FEBRUARY 1828, MARTIN HARRIS VISITED PROFESSOR CHARLES ANTHON AT COLUMBIA, WHO CERTIFIED THAT THESE CHARACTERS COPIED FROM THE GOLD PLATES WERE "ANCIENT SHORTHAND EGYPTIAN." LATER PROFESSOR ANTHON DENIED HE HAD MADE THE STATEMENT (JOHN W. WELCH, ED., REEXPLORING THE BOOK OF MORMON [SALT LAKE CITY: DESERET BOOK; PROVO, UT: FARMS, 1992], 73).

A6.8
CERTIFICATE OF ORDINATION.

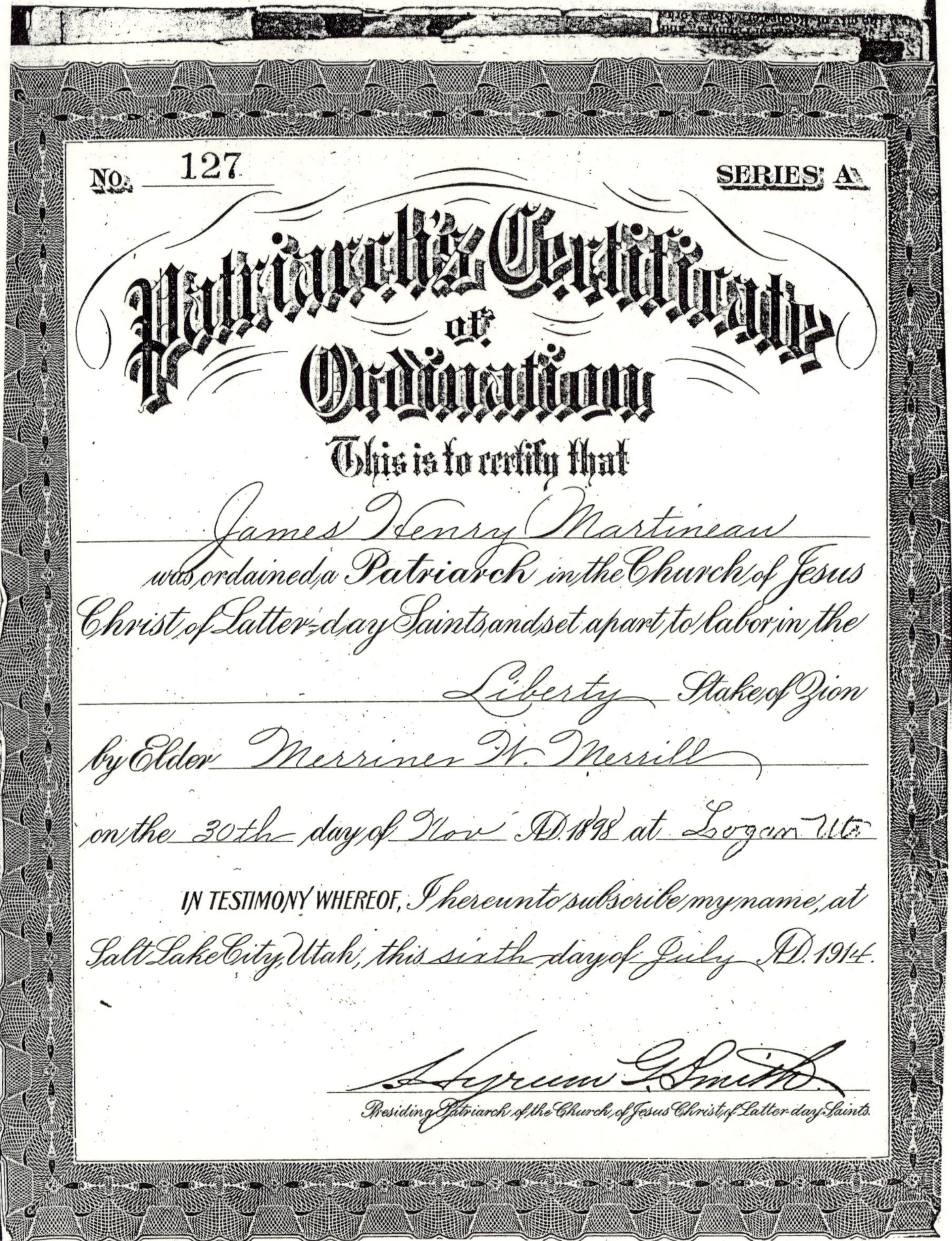

No. 127 SERIES: A

Patriarch's Certificate of Ordination

This is to certify that

James Henry Martineau

was ordained a Patriarch in the Church of Jesus Christ of Latter-day Saints, and set apart to labor in the

Liberty Stake of Zion

by Elder Merriner W. Merrill

on the 30th day of Nov A.D. 1898 at Logan Ut

IN TESTIMONY WHEREOF, I hereunto subscribe my name, at Salt Lake City, Utah, this sixth day of July A.D. 1914.

Hyrum G. Smith
Presiding Patriarch of the Church of Jesus Christ of Latter-day Saints.

A6.9
LETTER REGARDING MOVE TO UTAH.

P.O. Box B. Salt Lake City, Utah, March 13th, 1908.

Elder James H. Martineau,

Colonia Juarez.

Dear Brother:-

We certainly misunderstood the purport of yours of the 14th ult. if, as you say in yours of the 4th inst. that your letter was only intended as one of inquiry and advice.

Inasmuch as you desire to change your residence from Colonia Juarez to this city, we know no reason whatever why you should not do so, and as far as we are concerned therefore you may consider yourself at perfect liberty to come and live here.

With kindest regards and best wishes, we are,

Your Brethren,

Joseph F. Smith
John R Winder
Anthon H. Lund

A6.10
PAPER ADDRESSED BY HAND TO JAMES MEARS IN NY. IT IS FOUND AFTER PAGE 401.

Mr James Mears
Elbridge, Onodaga Co:
N. York.

A6.11

HANDWRITTEN LETTER FROM SON JOHN, NEW YORK, IN 1831. THERE WAS A FOLD IN THE PAPER WHEN IT WAS COPIED, SO SOME WORDS ARE MISSING. IT IS FOUND AFTER PAGE 401.

New York Nov 7th 1831

Dear Father

I [write you] after a long interval which you must not impute [...] intentional neglect, so much as to other causes, such as not [...] [...aving] to say of a favourable nature [rel...] to my circumstance[...] no news &c &c. One object of this letter is to say to you [tha...] in my opinion you would do well to be here soon, as then, to be a letting on the Rariton & Delaware Canal at New Brunswick.

I had understood from Chauncy both when at his House and more lately, (he being now in my employ on the Camiden & Amboy R Road as my assistant engineer) that you was desirous to be engaged in some business, Now, If you are not here in time to attend the letting. Chauncy, [...] myself will attend & if any job can be obtained on proper terms we will take one for you either wholly or in Connection with us, or one of us

Should nothing be accomplished here [...] I would advise you to come, as I am pretty certain that I can carve out some business for you connected with the Camiden & Amboy R. Road. that will pay something if not a good proffit. I think if nothing prevents, you had better come immediately, you would of course call at Our House in New York 407 Hudsen St. from which place you will have no further travelling expenses to incur. I write a note to the Captain Seymour of the steam Boat New Philladelphia, I am acquainted with capt Seymour, & have a right to ask him to allow you a passage free of [cost], as coning on to be engaged on the R. Road of which the owners of the North River Line of steam Boats [are] principal stockholders & President

In haste yours with affectionate regard

John Martineau

A6.12
HANDWRITTEN LETTER TO SUSAN ELLEN FROM SON JOHN. THERE IS NO DATE, BUT IT LOOKS LIKE IT ACCOMPANIES THE NOVEMBER 7, 1831, LETTER FROM JOHN TO MARTINEAU. IT IS FOUND AFTER PAGE 401.

Dear Mother

I have on the other page written to father partly on business & this page I propose to Devote to you to tell you how much I want to see you Father & All the family. I think it was particularly unfortunate that we could not meet at Chauncy's when we were so near it. I am glad to hear that you are in good health at Elbridge & that Laura's health is on the mend, Have just heard from Daniel & was surprised to find that he had had a severe fit of the bilious fever

Chauncy is with me as assistant Engineer on the Camiden & Amoy R Road, he is a good sturdy fellow [for] the business I assure you, I am sure I can, if Father comes on, carve out some business for him that will afford a moderate compensation, so you must not object to his coming, if you could come [...] it would be highly gratifying to us Eliza [...] coming to Elbridge in the spring & make you a good long visit I shall not disappoint her I assure you

We are all in good health. Eliza eats more like a horse [is] an alligator than a woman. I Donot think I should know either Louisa or May give my love to them all & [...] me [t...]

Yours with affectionate regards

J. W. Martineau

A6.13
HANDWRITTEN LETTER DATED NOVEMBER 1831. IT IS FOUND AFTER PAGE 401.

Capt Seymour—

D[r] Sir— The [bea...] [W...] James Mears is coming on to Amboy to engage in the employ of the R road Co: should you think it right not to charge him for his passage it would much oblige

Sir [...] [...] [...]

John Martineau

New York Nov[r] 8th 1831

A6.14
HANDWRITTEN LETTER ON PROVO WOOLEN MILLS COMPANY LETTERHEAD, DATED 1901. IT IS FOUND AFTER PAGE 401.

OFFICE OF
PROVO WOOLEN MILLS COMPANY,
MANUFACTURERS OF
ALL KINDS OF

HIGHEST CASH PRICE PAID FOR WOOL	WOOLEN GOODS, PLAIN AND FANCY CLOTH DOESKIN, JEANS, LINDSEYS.	KERSEY TWEED. Etc. PLAIN & FANCY COLORED FLANNELS, AND YARNS OF ALL DESCRIPTION.

Provo City, Utah Jany 30 1~~8~~9*01*

Mr. Jas, H. Martineau
Dear Brother
With this Mail
I Send you a volume of the "Preston Family Geneology" which I have succeeded in Compiling. Bro. Wilson assisting me— You being much interested in geneologies I send you this volume with the Compliments of the Century hoping You May enjoy, just as much of it as you may wish.
All are usually well—with Kind regards & good wishes—your brother in the Gospel Wm B Preston

A6.15
LETTER FROM LORENZO SNOW FOUND AFTER PAGE 401.

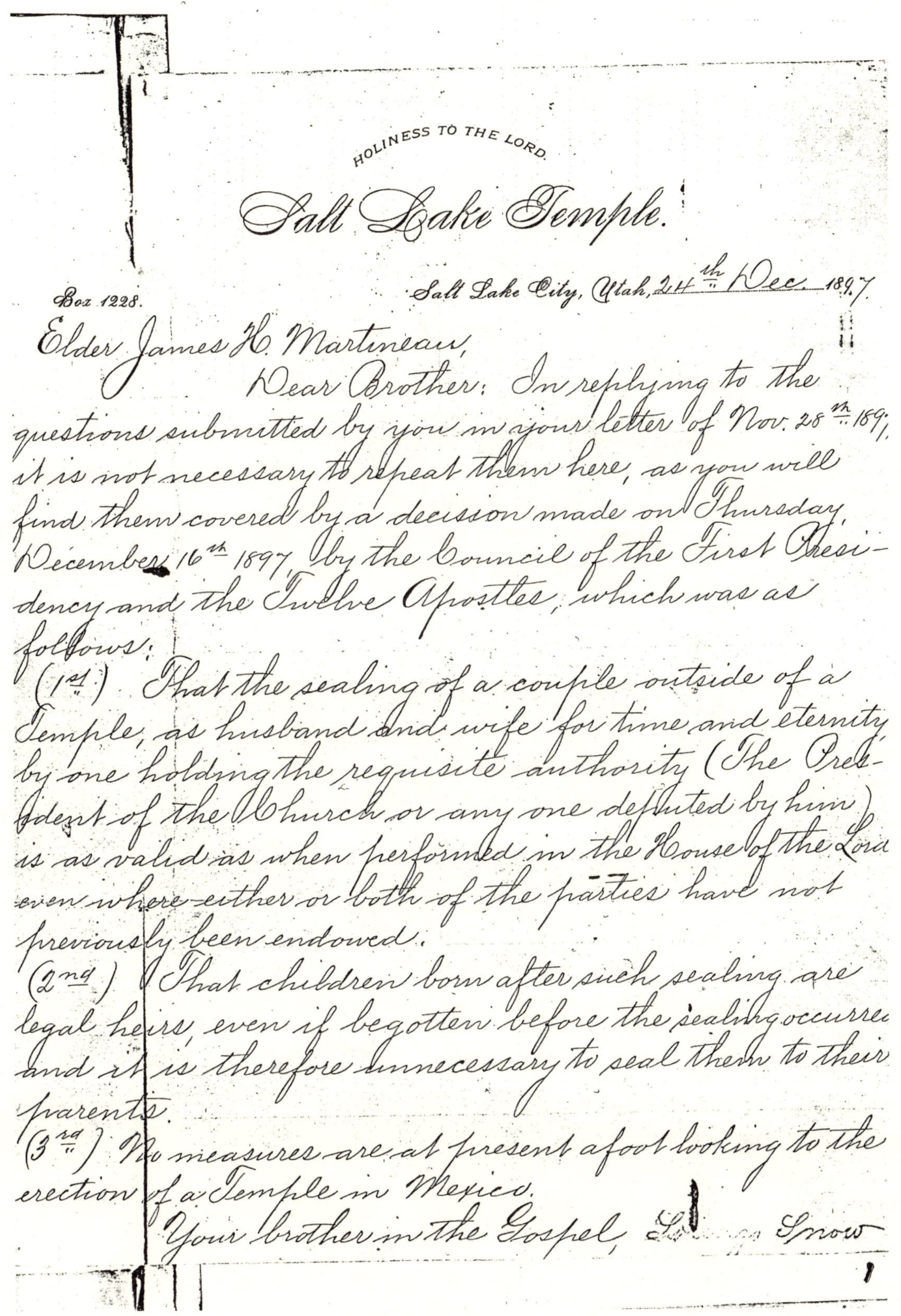

HOLINESS TO THE LORD.

Salt Lake Temple.

Box 1228. Salt Lake City, Utah, 24th Dec. 1897.

Elder James H. Martineau,

Dear Brother: In replying to the questions submitted by you in your letter of Nov. 28th 1897, it is not necessary to repeat them here, as you will find them covered by a decisson made on Thursday, December 16th 1897, by the Council of the First Presidency and the Twelve Apostles, which was as follows:

(1st) That the sealing of a couple outside of a Temple, as husband and wife for time and eternity by one holding the requisite authority (The President of the Church or any one deputed by him) is as valid as when performed in the House of the Lord even where either or both of the parties have not previously been endowed.

(2nd) That children born after such sealing are legal heirs, even if begotten before the sealing occurred and it is therefore unnecessary to seal them to their parents.

(3rd) No measures are at present afoot looking to the erection of a Temple in Mexico.

Your brother in the Gospel, Lorenzo Snow

A6.15
TRANSCRIPTION OF LETTER FROM LORENZO SNOW.

HOLINESS TO THE LORD.
Salt Lake Temple.
Box 1228. Salt Lake City, Utah 24th Dec. 1897

Elder James H. Martineau,

Dear Brother: In replying to the questions submitted by you in your letter of Nov. 28th 1897 it is not necessary to repeat them here, as you will find them covered by a decision made on Thursday, December 16th 1897, by the Council of the First Presidency and the Twelve Apostles, which was as follows:

(1st) That the sealing of a couple outside of a Temple, as husband and wife for time and eternity by one holding the requisite authority (The President of the Church or any one deputed by him) is as valid as when performed in the House of the Lord even where either or both of the parties have not previously been endowed.

(2nd) That children born after such sealing are legal heirs, even if begotten before the sealing occurred and it is therefore unnecessary to seal them to their parents.

(3rd) No measures are at present afoot looking to the erection of a Temple in Mexico.

Your brother in the Gospel, Lorenzo Snow

A6.16
LETTER FROM JESSIE H. GRIEVE (HER PEN NAME WAS "JESSIE RUSSELL."). IT IS FOUND AFTER PAGE 401.

Letter from J. H. R. A. [illegible]

1860 Central Avenue
Alameda. Cal.
Nov. 30, 1887.

My dear Friend,

You surely have not received two letters which I sent to you. One addressed Great Western Hotel, Sacramento, and the other to Vallejo. In my last I wanted to see you and tell you fully why I thought it safer not to go South with you. D.P.A. sent to Vallejo a long letter telling everything. how they found it out I know not, and they sent to know if I were there and my aunt telegraphed back to him that I was not there, that I had been & gone again, and that she knew nothing about me. They say if they find you, they will make you suffer, you know in what way I presume. That was the motive for me acting as I have done since I knew of that D.P.A.'s letter. My aunt thought also it was better for me to go away, so that she would feel free, should any thing serious take place.

I have been expecting to see you all week, but my friend did not come. I have felt very impatient at times, almost forget what I was about, I would be so very absent-minded. Will you my friend send me Bp. W. Bassett's address, so that I can write to Ma without sending it to the house. Did you see Ma or Mrs. Russell last time you were at the City. I have sent to Bowie for my freight 2 boxes both weighing 525 lbs. marked J. H Greive, Smithville, Arizona via Bowie Station S. P. R.R. via C. P. R.R. they were prepaid before I left, I sent for them on the 9th inst. but I have not received any word from the freight agent. You might make inquiry about them, and you confer a favor upon me by so doing When you write, sign as formerly. I was surprised that morning when I was asked about you, and they wished to know if it was so, so that she might know what was best to be done. It was immediate action for we knew not the hour that some one might enter in to intercept me. We went to S. F. C. spent the day there it being Thursday on, Saturday I started for Alameda and here I am still. I do feel so lonely at times with no one to talk to about things that are nearest and dearest to one. You know what it is, having been in the same position yourself, yet I can always find a refuge in prayer, oh, never forget me at any time, even though we are separated by distance. I think the old adage is true "Absence makes the heart grow fonder". Don't you think that California is a great Sabbath breaking State, I think it is really worse than the European Continent, hardly any one here observes the Sabbath; last Sunday I rode on the train to Alameda wharf. I had my book and writing tablet with me, I did feel so refreshed while sitting on the end of the pier with the sea breeze blowing upon my temples. It finally drove all my headache away. Each one seems to go to the most places of amusement on Sunday. All week here it has been raining off & on

My written address is Miss Jessie Russell, c/o Mrs. Wertheimer 1860 Central Avenue, Alameda, Cal. You may guess why I take this name. I am having a little experience just now, which I think may do me good in after life, I hope you will find every one well in the South, also Gertrude's leg improving. Write me a long letter as soon as you can. Tonight I felt I could not go to sleep without writing you a few lines. If we taste the bitter beforehand we shall appreciate the sweet, when it comes along. I am well, hoping you & the others are the same I am your a.b.c.

P.S. Address all letters to the following address until I tell you to change. a.b.c.

Miss Jessie Russell
c/o Mrs. Wertheimer
1860 Central Avenue
Alameda
Cal.

[In Martineau's shaky handwriting]
Letter from J. H R A G.

[transcription of page 1]
1860 Central Avenue
Alameda. Cal.
Nov. 30, 1887.
My dear Friend,
You surely have not
received two letters which I sent to you.
One addressed Great Western Hotel, Sacramento,
and the other to Vallejo. In my last I wanted to
see you and tell you fully why I thought it
safer not to go South with you. D.P.A. sent to
Vallejo a long letter telling everything, how they
found
it out I know not, and they sent to know if I were
there and my aunt telegraphed back to him that
I was not there, that I had been & gone again,
and that she knew nothing about me.
They say if they find you, they will make you
suffer, you know in what way I presume.
That was the motive for me acting as I have
done since I knew of that D.P.A.'s letter.
My aunt thought also it was better for me to go
away, so that she would feel free, should
any thing serious take place.

[transcription of page 2]
I have been expecting to see you all week, but my
friend did not come. I have felt very impatient
at times, almost forget whatI was about, I would
be so very absent-minded. Will you my friend
send me Bp. W. Bassett's address so that I can
write to Ma without sending it to the house.
Did you see Ma or Mrs. Russell last time you were
at the City. I have sent to Bowie for my
freight 2 boxes both weighing 525 lbs. marked
J. H Grieve, Smithville, Arizona via Bowie Station, S.P.R.R.
via
C.P.R.R. they were prepaid before I left. I sent for
them on the 9th inst. but I have not received any word
from the freight agenet. You might make inquiry
about them, and you confer a favor upon me by so doing
When you write sign as formerly. I was surprised
that morning when I was asked about you, and
they wished to know if it was so, so that she might
know what was best to be done. It was immediate
action for we knew not the hour that some
one might enter in to intercept me. We went
to S. L. C. spent the day there it being Thursday
on Saturday I started for Alameda and

[transcription of page 3]
here I am still. I do feel so lonely at times with no one to talk to about things that are nearest and dearest to me. You know what it is, having been in the same position yourself, yet I can always find a refuge in prayer, oh, never forget me at any time, even though we are separated by distance. I think the old adage is true "Absence makes the heart grow fonder". Don't you think that California is a great Sabbath breaking State, I think it is really worse than the European Continent; hardly any one here observes the Sabbath; last Sunday I rode on the train to Alameda wharf. I had my book and writing tablet with me. I did feel so refreshed while sitting on the end of the pier with the sea breeze blowing upon my temples. It finallly drove all my headache away. Each one seems to go to the most places of amusement on Sunday. All week here it has been raining of & on

[transcription of page 4]
My written address is Miss Jessie Russell, c/o Mrs. Wertheimer
1860 Central Avenue, Alameda, Cal. You may guess why I take this name. I am having a little experience just now, which I think may do me good in after life, I hope you will find every one well in the south, also Gertrude's leg improving. Write me a long letter as soon as you can. Tonight I felt I could not go to sleep without writing you a few lines.
If we taste the bitter beforehand we shall apapreciate the sweet, when it comes along.
I am well, hoping you & the others are the same
I am your a.b.c.
P. S. Address all letters to the following address until I tell you to change. a.b.c.

Miss Jessie Russell
c/o Mrs. Wertheimer
1860 Central Avenue
Alameda
Cal.

A6.17 NEWS CLIPPING.

A Meeting With Fremont

PIONEER EXPERIENCES

For The Saturday News by Col. J. H. Martineau.

ABOUT the fifteenth of February the people of Parowan were astonished by the sudden arrival of Col. Fremont with a party [illegible] whites and 11 Delaware Indians. The party was in an almost starving condition, having been nearly three months in the snows of the Rocky and Wasatch mountains, and on the day previous to their arrival one of the men fell from his horse from starvation and hardship and died. Having no means to dig a grave his comrades spread a blanket over his body and left it to the mercy of the elements and wild beasts. When this sad event became known, a party of colonists went out and discovered his body and buried it.

The night previous to his arrival the party encamped near a band of Ute Indians from whom, by a payment at an exorbitant price in ammunition and blankets they obtained about 50 pounds of flour and a small dog. The flour was divided equally among the 25 persons, and the dog being killed, made about a mouthful to each of the party. They were all taken in by the colonists and received the most tender care which their limited means would permit for about three weeks until sufficiently restored to continue their journey to California. The colonists furnished Col. Fremont horses and other needed supplies to the amount of $3,000, receiving nothing in payment, but a promise from the colonel of full payment as soon as he should reach the coast, when he would send payment in full. But he never paid one dollar.

Tell Story of Journey.

I had many interesting conversations, not only with Fremont himself, but with most of his party, both whites and Indians, the latter of whom spoke English passably well, and their reports of the journey were in complete unison.

They had joined the party during the autumn and had expected to cross the mountains before any snow should fall; but they did not enter the mountains until Dec. 1, being delayed by several trips of Fremont to the eastern states made by the colonel. They told me they believed he made these delays purposely, and that he intended to cross the mountains during the winter season, but kept his intentions secret, fearing his men would refuse to make the trip in the winter. In conversation with the colonel he admitted this was the fact for he knew his men would refuse to go if they would have to encounter the snows and storms of winter. But as his point of departure was at the foot of the mountains and his men had no means of travel independently they were compelled to go on. He told me it was his special and sole desire to test the possibility of locating a railroad line across the mountains that would be practicable for traffic in the winter, or whether the snows would be too deep.

He employed the Indians as hunters in the expectation that plenty of game killed would obviate the necessity of taking a large supply of meat along. In this he was greatly disappointed, scarcely any game was seen and none at all was killed, as the elk and deer had sought lower levels to escape the snows.

Their progress was toilsome in the extreme, struggling through the snows with excessive labor their pack animals soon began to give out and when at length a mule or horse did succumb it was killed and eaten, everything except hair, bones, and the contents of the entrails. All his men declared that he did not favor himself in the least, either in choice bits of food or quantity, but on their arrival in Parowan he appeared to me as the best, physically, of any of the party—"tough as a knot."

Used a Camera.

In order to make his explorations of the mountains of greater value, he daily took photographs to the front and rear, thus giving a perfect view of his entire line of march until, compelled by lack of transport animals, he abandoned his photographic outfit and much other valuable property, and finally when within a few days' march of deliverance from their toils and arrival to the lowlands, he cached all of his property not absolutely necessary, amounting in value to more than a thousand dollars, consisting of blankets and articles intended for trade with the Indians to procure horses or other things necessary.

He appeared very grateful to the colonists for their kindly assistance and I believe that much of his former hostility to the "Mormons" had eased.

The valuable cache of goods referred to was the cause of a tragedy. One of his men, a Spaniard, Carvalho by name, refused to accompany him as he continued his journey from Parowan and remained for some time, for the purpose, as I believe, of obtaining possession of the goods cached. As none of the colonists would go with him to obtain the property, saying that they would not steal it, he made an agreement with some Ute Indians, who agreed to go with him and get the prize upon the condition of having one-half of the plunder. They went with him and found the goods, but evidently concluded it better to keep the whole without the bother of dividing it. This they did and killed him. This was the report the Indians made some months afterwards. They said they were many and needed the goods, and that he being neither a "Mormon" nor an Indian, had no need of any of it. Thus the greed of Carvalho was his undoing.

Sees Military Drill.

It happened that while the colonel was in Parowan, one of our usual company and battalion drills occurred, in which I acted as military instructor. As one of the veterans, the war with Mexico in 1846-48 had given me experience. I felt much annoyed, as to their presence on the occasion, for he was an officer used to seeing men standing in stiff military order—"eyes front," while our boys on such occasions were apt to talk, stand unsteadily and lean forward to look up and down the line. We went through our evolutions all right, and upon dismissal of the men, I invited him to accompany me home and have something to eat, which he very willingly did.

I excused our unmilitary appearance on drill, but he cut me short saying, "Mr. Martineau, if I had five thousand men like those I saw on drill today, I could march through Mexico, and with ten thousand, I could conquer Mexico." "Why," said he, "they move just like that," moving his finger to and fro. It appeared to me as if he did not notice our unmilitary style of drill but that in some way he felt the spirit of unity. He expressed a very ardent desire to see a railroad connecting the east and the west, and I am glad he lived long enough to see his wish fulfilled.

While at my house he said to me, "I never eat the whole of any meal. I save a piece in my pocket in case I accidentally miss my next meal, which has happened a number of times on expeditions like my present one. A number of times the piece saved at breakfast was all I had for supper. I have made this my invariable rule on my long trip, the bit saved from one meal was all I had for the next."

Since then I have found it best in my own experience to always keep at least "one shot in the locker."

A6.18
TWO NEWSPAPER CLIPPINGS ABOUT THE DEATH OF ALLIE PRESTON MARTINEAU.

[First article]

MRS. MARTINEAU
CLAIMED BY DEATH

Wife of Prominent Salt Lake Business Man Suddenly Stricken Sunday Morning.

Mrs Allie Preston Martineau, wife of Lyman R. Martineau, died suddenly at the family residence, 918 Logan avenue, shortly after 7 o'clock yesterday morning. The end came wholly unexpectedly, as Mrs. Martineau was seemingly in usual good health when she arose. While engaged in the preparation of

breakfast she was seized with a pain in her head, and fell into the arms of her son Lyman, who was standing by, and expired within a very short time. Endolism, caused by a stoppage of blood in one of the veins of the head, was given as the cause of death.

MOST ESTIMABLE WOMAN.

The demise of Mrs. Martineau will bring widespread sorrow, especially in Logan, her former home. She was a most estimable woman, kind and loving in her disposition, and she was greatly beloved by all who were acquainted with her. She was born in that city and lived there all her life, until removing to Salt Lake a short time ago.

Mrs. Martineau was the eldest daughter of Bishop William B. Preston and his wife Harriet Thatcher Preston. She was 44 years of age on March 2, last. Dec. 29, 1881, she became the wife of Lyman R. Martineau. Eight children were the issue of the marriage, six of whom survive their mother. They are: Mrs. K. A. Crismon, Mrs. C. A. Gowans, L. R. Martineau, Jr., Preston Martineau, Martha Martineau and Allen Martineau.

William B. Preston, Jr., who was drowned in Bear river a few weeks ago was a brother of Mrs. Martineau. She took his death much to heart, and it is believed that the tragic occurrence hastened her own end.

Mr. Martineau is well known in business and political circles. He is state chairman of the Democratic party, is largely engaged in real estate affairs, and is the treasurer of the Nelden Drug Company.

The funeral of Mrs. Martineau will be held tomorrow at the family residence, commencing at 12 o'clock. Later in the day the remains will be taken to Logan, and there interment will take place on Wednesday.

[Second article]

INTERMENT AT LOGAN.

Funeral Services of Mrs. Martineau Held at Salt Lake Residence.

The last sad rites to the memory of the late Allie Preston Martineau, wife of Hon. L. R. Martineau, took place at the family residence on Logan avenue at noon today. The place was thonged with mourners, many friends and relatives from Logan being in attendance. The services were presided over by Bishop Atwood, and the speakers were Elders J. Golden Kimball, Heber

J. Grant, Orson F. Whitney, Francis M. Lyman, John Henry Smith, President John R. Winder and President Joseph F. Smith. The addresses were brief but full of feeling and consolation, and the tributes paid the departed were most eloquent. The prayers were pronounced by Elders Hugh S. Gowans and George A. Smith, the music of the occasion being rendered by Messrs. Pyper, Whitney, Spencer, Ensign and E. P. Kimball, the songs were "Nearer, My God to Thee," "Dear Refuge of the Weary," "When the Swallows' Homeward fly," and "Sometime We'll Understand." At the conclusion of the funeral the remains were conveyed to the O. S. L. depot, and thence to Logan where the interment will take place tomorrow.

A6.19

TWO PAPERS COPIED ONTO ONE PAGE. THE FIRST IS A FORM FROM THE LOGAN TEMPLE, FILLED IN BY HAND. THE SECOND IS THE END OF A HANDWRITTEN LETTER AND A SIGNATURE. JUST TO THE RIGHT OF IT IS A NOTE WRITTEN BY MARTINEAU.

[first paper]

HOLINESS TO THE LORD

Office of the Logan Temple,
P. O. Box 8

Logan, Utah, *21st Apl* 1893

Received of James H. Martineau and his
wife Susan E. J. Martineau Vol 1, parts 1 & 2 a[nd]
Vol. 2, parts 1 & 2 of the Lives and Times
of the Roman Pontiffs, a donation to the Log[an]
Temple Library. Valued at Eight ($8.[00]) dol[lars]

James A. Leishman

Thanks *Librarian*

[second paper]

with kind regards

Your Brother.

Wilford Woodruff.

Written in his
90th year, to me
J. H. M.

A6.20
LETTER FROM FIRST PRESIDENCY.

OFFICE OF
The First Presidency
of the
Church of Jesus Christ
of
Latter-day Saints.

P.O. Box B. Salt Lake City, Utah, Nov. 22, 1898.

Elder James H. Martineau,

Logan.

Dear Brother:-

Your recent letter asking the privilege of being ordained a patriarch has received our favorable consideration, and we have written to Prest. M. W. Merrill authorizing him to ordain you to that priesthood.

Praying the Lord to give you grace and wisdom to faithfully fulfil the duties of this important calling, and with kindest regards, we remain,

Your Brethren,

Lorenzo S[now]

Geo. Q. Cannon

Jos. F. Smith

To explain the above; Prest. M. W. Merrill of Logan Temple said he wished me to be ordained a Patriarch, but desiring full approbation of the First Presidency, told me to write them, asking the privilege. I said I did not like to do so. He said "Write, and say I told you to do so." Against my own will, as seemingly presumptuous, I did so, and the above came, and Prest. Merrill ordained me. Prest. Merrill said Prest. Young told him to ordain just such men as me, to be patriarchs. James H. Martineau
So the office came to me, unsought.

A6.21
NEWSPAPER CLIPPING.

GENEALOGY.

Instructions to all Interested in Getting Names From Genealogical Library—Manti Temple Lists.

All communications for this department should be addressed to Mrs. Elizabeth C. McCune, chairman general committee of Daughters of Pioneers, corner Main and North Temple streets, Salt Lake City.

Many letters are received by this department asking what can be learned in regard to this or that family, in the genealogical library here in Salt Lake City. We will here endeavor to give a brief summary of sources of information contained there, and if all concerned will study this article carefully, they will be able to write direct to the society, and will know just what to ask about. The most of the books contained now in this society were obtained by purchase in England, and in Boston. There are about 400 English books and a like number of American books. The choice books of reference in the English department are: First, Burke's Commonors, and Burkes' Landed Gentry. These four bulky volumes contain brief notes about all the old established English families, and they are remarkably reliable. Then, there are the 30 odd volumes published by the Harleian society. These among other things contain the various visitations to the counties of England. That is, in the sixteenth, and seventeenth centuries, royal messengers, or heralds, now called census takers, visited the counties and obtained the pedigrees of all the county families. Therefore, they are called "visitations." Then this society has published such volumes as the London Marriages, Births and Deaths. Also, many parish registers, and the registers of many old or famous churches. These necessarily contain much scattered information of great value to Latter-day Saints. For it will ever be found that this people have sprung from the very bone and sinew of every nation. There are also some family genealogies, or pedigrees. The history of Scottish families is given in four bulky volumes, called the Scottish Nation. Other English books are the genealogical magazines, and similar publications.

In the American section, there are first, Savage's Genealogical Dictionary. This volume contains the briefest pedigrees of a great majority of the early American families, with names and some dates. Then, there are the splendid series of volumes of New England Genealogical Magazines, over 60 in number, and they come regularly now. Also, the New York Biographical and Historical Magazine, which has reached its thirty-eighth volume. These magazines publish all sorts of valuable genealogical data, and in some instances, whole pedigrees of famous families are herein given. These contain excellent indexes, without which such books are almost valueless. Then, there are county records of the births, marriages and deaths, with church and parish registers. Town and county histories, all these are mines of information for the eager genealogist. Added to these, there are books with detailed information, such as English Surnames; homes of family names; also many English and Scotch catalogues in which all English and Scotch genealogical books are noted; a book treating on the subject of genealogy; and last, and most important of all, there are the English guide, and the American Index. Indeed, these last are the first books a searcher after genealogy would open. For instance, if a person asks me what there is in the Library in regard to the Bigelows, I would take up Munsell's American Index and turn to the B's. Here I would find Bigelow. And following the name would appear the title of all the American books now published which contain references or pedigrees of the Bigelows. This would begin with Mr. Howe's "Bigelow Genealogy," and then would follow the list of the various town and county histories with the volumes of the New York and New England magazines, which contain scattered information about the Bigelows; and indeed every published work which contains any degree of genealogical information about the Bigelow family would be here listed or catalogued. Then, I would gather all the books in this list which are contained in the library, and with pencil and note-book in hand I would begin to copy out every scrap of information as it came under my hand. If it were the English family Bigelows, I would ask for the Guide, and there would find Bigelow under the letter B, and would find every book listed in the Guide which contains genealogical information about the English family of Bigelow. The way most of us do, we take the books by shelves, searching every single book through its index for any mention of the name we are after.

This, in brief, is the line of procedure in the work of getting genealogies. We would here address a word to our numerous correspondents. Please be patient! This work is a labor of love, and the busy woman who conducts this department has a family to "do for." She is a regular temple worker, beside having a round half dozen public offices, with consequent duties. And she cannot get to the genealogical library to answer your questions as often as she would like; while the letters now come in so fast that they must begin to take their turn, as there is not time or space in these columns for all of them to receive public notice. Yet, we do wish to express delight at the interest taken in this work, and to thank all our friends who write to us; we will do our best to meet your wishes; only be patient, and bear with us! Stamps for written answers are acceptable.

BRACE—Elder Thomas Evans of Rexburg, Ida., wishes information in regard to his sister Sarah, who married Edward Brace, born in Herefordshire, England. Any relatives would oblige by writing to Elder Evans.

YOUNGS—All members of the Young family are invited to come to the temple on Thanksgiving day and give their dead relatives a glorious cause for Thanksgiving, especially are the male members of the family invited. If you can't come, send your donation to Richard W. Young, Templeton building, Salt Lake City.

The following incident will prove of general interest to temple workers:

PROPHECY FULFILLED.

It may interest readers of the genealogical department of the Deseret News to see how wonderfully a prophecy uttered by President Daniel H. Wells in 1877, in the hearing of the writer, was fulfilled in relation to the work for the dead. Preaching in the Fifteenth ward he urged the saints to greater diligence in that holy work, since Joseph the seer declared "the greatest responsibility in this world that God has laid upon us is to seek after our dead." (See sermon of Joseph Smith, Jr., April 6, 1844, in vol. 5-6 Times and Seasons.) President Wells said: "Go to the Endowment house and be baptized for your dead. Perhaps you will say 'I have only a few names, not enough to bother with.' I say if you have but half a dozen names, be baptized for them and you shall never want for names."

This struck me very forcibly. After I joined the church, 27 years previously, I had written many time to my relatives in the east for information relative to my deceased kindred and ancestry, asking for dates of birth, death, etc., but they would not give me the least information. They said I had disgraced the honorable family name by joining the Mormons, and utterly disowned me during all that period.

But I believed the promise given by President Wells and was baptized by Elder Samuel H. B. Smith for eight names—all I could give any data for; and found afterwards that two of them were wrong, leaving only six that were valid. Now see how wonderfully the promise was fulfilled.

Shortly after this a cousin, who had utterly ignored me, sent me a long list of names with dates of birth and death, saying perhaps I would like them. Elder B. F. Cummings at that time in New York City engaged in genealogical research, sent me several hundred names gleaned from records of births, marriages, wills, deaths, etc, of Staten Island near New York City, where my paternal ancesters first settled early in the seventeenth century. Then I received from a man in Michigan who claimed to be a cousin to my mother—a Mr. Newton Sprague—an unbroken record of names of the Sprague family (my material grandmother's name being Lois Sprague) back to the year 1,600, they being some of the first settlers of Massachusetts. And while upon a mission in England in 1880 my son, Hyrum R. Martineau, met in London a celebrated lawyer or barister, Mr. Basil Martineau, and from him obtained over 1,000 names of the English branch of the family. To compile this record Basil had expended over $10,000, though born in England and enjoying exceptional facilities for such an undertaking. From genealogical works in the Logan Temple and in Salt Lake City many more names have been obtained, also from other sources, until now my temple record amounts to almost 3,000, for whom work more or less complete has been performed; with many hundred husbands and wives, parents and children, reunited. I believe that as time passes many more names will be added, the first six will grow to thousands.

Thus has the prophecy of President Wells been wonderfully and miraculously—as it seems to me—fulfilled.

I know also others who have received from persons often unknown by them, records of their dead kindred, sometimes thousands of names at a time, which parties influenced by a holy impulse, had been led to gather and send to those who could perform a holy work for them.

If the Lord thus finds it needful to cause unbelievers to assist in the redemption of the dead, unwittingly in most cases, how imperative is the obligation resting upon the Latter-day Saints who desire to become saviors upon Mount Zion to be diligent and constant in their labors in this holy work. Can we become such in any other manner? The Prophet Joseph Smith has declared "Baptism for the dead is the only way that men can appear as saviors on Mount Zion." (See lecture by Elder Joseph F. Smith, Jr., Deseret News, March 28, 1907.) He further declares that "those saints who neglect it in behalf of their deceased relatives, do it at the peril of their own salvation."

To those who profess to believe in the divine mission of Joseph Smith, prophet, seer and revelator, what more can be said?

JAMES H. MARTINEAU

A6.22
LETTER FROM THE FIRST PRESIDENCY

Office of
The First Presidency
of the
Church of Jesus Christ
of
Latter-day Saints.

P.O. Box B.

Salt Lake City, Utah, Nov. 7th, 1900.

Elder James H. Martineau,

Juarez.

Dear Brother:-

On the 31st of October your sister, Francis Eliza Martineau, was sealed to my father, Hyrum Smith in Salt Lake Temple by Elder John R. Winder, presiding there, and Julia Henrietta was sealed to me, I acting for my father in the first place, and my wife, Edna L. Smith acting for and in behalf of your sister and daughter, done in the presence of Bishop George Romney and William W. Riter, as witnesses.

With kindest regards, I am,

Your Brother,

Jos. F. Smith

I hope to be among the good people of Mexico again for a short time, before long. Sincerely &c.

J. F. S.

A6.23
TWO NEWSPAPER CLIPPINGS AND THE SIGNATURES OF THE FIRST PRESIDENCY.

[First item]

An interesting event of the week was the celebration on Tuesday of the 80th birthday anniversary of Mrs. Susan E. Martineau, wife of J. H. Martineau, a large number of friends and relatives calling at the home and others sending messages of love and esteem. The rooms were bright also with floral offerings from her many friends. She is one of the pioneers of Utah, having arrived here in 1850. She was born in Kirtland, Ohio, and is the mother of 12 children, 78 grandchildren and 53 great-grandchildren.

[Second item]

Veteran Civil Engineer,
Age 92 Years, Comes in
For Railroad Celebration

One of the conspicuous features of the railroad jubilee celebration in this city Saturday, to commemorate the completion of the Utah Central line between Ogden and Salt Lake 50 years ago, was the presence of James H. Martineau of Logan. This veteran is 92 years of age, and he came down from Cache valley especially to attend the celebration.

Mr. Martineau was one of the foremost civil engineers that did the work of surveying for the Utah Central. He was called to do this work by President Brigham Young largely because he had had previous experience in connection with the building of the Union Pacific. Mr. Martineau is said to be the oldest living civil engineer in Utah.

[Third item]

Your Brethren, [typed]

Joseph F. Smith
John D. Winder
Anthon H. Lund
First Presidency.

SELECTED BIBLIOGRAPHY

A Historical and Biographical Record of the Territory of Arizona. Chicago: McFarland and Poole, 1896.

Alexander, Thomas G., and Leonard J. Arrington. "Camp in the Sagebrush: Camp Floyd, Utah, 1858–61." *Utah Historical Quarterly* 34 (1966): 3–21.

Allen, James B., Ronald K. Esplin, and David J. Whittaker. *Men with a Mission: The Quorum of the Twelve Apostles in the British Isles, 1837–1841*. Salt Lake City: Deseret Book, 1992.

Alter, J. Cecil. *Early Utah Journalism: A Half Century of Forensic Warfare, Waged by the West's Most Militant Press*. Salt Lake City: Utah State Historical Society, 1938.

Anderson, John C. *Mackinaws Down the Missouri*. Edited by Glen Barrett. Logan, UT: Western Text Society, 1973.

Anderson, Nels. *Desert Saints: The Mormon Frontier in Utah*. Chicago: Univ. of Chicago Press, 1966.

Arrington, Leonard J. *Brigham Young: American Moses*. Urbana: Univ. of Illinois Press, 1986.

———. *Charles C. Rich: Mormon General and Western Frontiersman*. Provo, UT: Brigham Young Univ. Press, 1974.

———. *Great Basin Kingdom: An Economic History of the Latter-day Saints, 1830–1900*. Cambridge, MA: Harvard Univ. Press, 1958.

———, ed. *The Presidents of the Church: Biographical Essays*. Salt Lake City: Deseret Book, 1986.

Arrington, Leonard J., and Davis Bitton. *The Mormon Experience: A History of the Latter-day Saints*. Urbana: Univ. of Illinois Press, 1992.

Arrington, Leonard J., Feramorz Y. Fox, and Dean L. May. *Building the City of God: Community & Cooperation Among the Mormons*. 2nd ed. Urbana: Univ. of Illinois Press, 1976.

Bancroft, Hubert Howe. *History of Arizona and New Mexico, 1530–1888.* San Francisco: History Company, 1889.

———. *History of the Northwest Coast*. San Francisco: A. L. Bancroft, 1884.

———. *History of Utah, 1540–1886*. San Francisco History Company, 1889.

Barrett, Swynn W. "Dr. John Bernhisel: Mormon Elder in Congress." *Utah Historical Quarterly* 36 (Spring 1968): 143–67.

Bartlett, Richard A. *Great Surveys of the American West*. Norman: Univ. of Oklahoma Press, 1962.

Beecher, Maureen Ursenbach. "The Eliza Enigma." *Dialogue: A Journal of Mormon Thought* 11 (Spring 1978): 30–43.

Bennion, Lowell B. "A Bird's-Eye View of Erastus Snow's St. George, Utah." *Utah Historical Quarterly* 45 (Spring 1979): 311–27.

Bertell, Allen and Cherrel B. Weech. *A History of Mount Graham*. Safford, AZ: 2000.

Bodsworth, C. *Sir Henry Bessemer: Father of the Steel Industry*. London: Institute of Materials, 1998.

Bradley, Martha Sonntag. *A History of Kane County*. Salt Lake City: Utah State Historical Society, 1999.

———. and Mary Brown Firmage Woodward. *Four Zinas: A Story of Mothers and Daughters on the Mormon Frontier*. Salt Lake City: Signature Books, 2000.

Bringhurst, Newell G. "Thomas Kearns: Irish-American Builder of Modern Utah." *Journal of the West* 31 (April 1992): 24–32.

Britsch, R. Lanier. *Unto the Islands of the Sea: A History of the Latter-day Saints in the Pacific*. Salt Lake City: Deseret Book, 1986.

Brooks, Juanita. *The Mountain Meadows Massacre*. Norman: Univ. of Oklahoma Press, 1991.

Bruce, Dwight H., ed. *Onondaga's Centennial: Gleanings of a Century*. Boston: Boston History Company, 1896.

Buerger, David John. *The Mysteries of Godliness: A History of Mormon Temple Worship*. San Francisco: Smith Research Associates, 1994.

Burns, Barney T., and Thomas H. Naylor. "Colonia Morelos: A Short History of a Mormon Colony in Sanora, Mexico." *Smoke Signal* 27 (Spring 1977): 142–80.

Campbell, Eugene E. "The Mormon Gold Mining Mission of 1849." *BYU Studies* 1, no. 2 (Autumn 1959/60): 20–31.

Card, Brigham Y., Herbert C. Northcott, John E. Foster, Howard Palmer, and George K. Jarvis. *The Mormon Presence in Canada*. Edmonton: Univ. of Alberta Press, 1990.

Carmack, Noel A. "Labor and Construction of the Logan Temple, 1877–1844," *Journal of Mormon History* 22, no. 1 (Spring 1996): 52–79.

———. "Running the Line: James Henry Martineau Survey's in Northern Utah, 1860–1882," *Utah Historical Quarterly* 68 (Fall 2004): 292–312.

Clark, James R., comp. *Messages of the First Presidency*, Salt Lake City: Bookcraft, 1965.

Cole, Helen R., ed. *One Hundred Years in Thatcher, 1883–1983.* Thatcher, AZ: Town of Thatcher, 1983.

Cornwall, Rebecca Coster, and Leonard J. Arrington. "Perpetuation of a Myth: Mormon Danites in Five Western Novels, 1840–90." *BYU Studies* 23, no. 2 (Spring 1983): 147–65.

Creer, Leland Hargrave. *The Founding of an Empire: The Exploration and Colonization of Utah, 1776–1856.* Salt Lake City: Bookcraft, 1947.

Davies, J. Kenneth. *Mormon Gold: The Story of California's Mormon Argonauts.* Salt Lake City: Olympus, 1984.

Dodge, Mildred Kempton. *Our Family Book: Dodge, Kempton, Bingham, Bryce*. Salt Lake City: Publishers Press, 1999.

Eicher, John H., and David J. Eicher. *Civil War High Commands*. Palo Alto, CA: Stanford Univ. Press, 2001.

Emery, Edwin, and Henry Ladd Smith. *The Press and America*. New York: Prentice-Hall, 1954.

Ericksen, Bess, ed. *Snowflake Stake: 100 Years of Faith and Service, 1887–1987.* Snowflake, AZ: Snowflake Stake, 1987.

Froissant, Jean. *Chronicles*. Translated by Geoffrey Brereton. New York: Penguin Classics, 1978.

Gardiner, S. R. *Cromwell's Place in History, Founded on Six Lectures Delivered in the University of Oxford*. London: Longmans, 1897.

Garr, Arnold K., Donald Q. Cannon, and Richard O. Cowan, eds. *Encyclopedia of Latter-day Saint History*. Salt Lake City: Deseret Book, 2000.

Gibbons, Francis M. *John Taylor: Mormon Philosopher, Prophet of God.* Salt Lake City: Deseret Book, 1985.

Godfrey, Audrey M. "'The Queen of Inventions': The Sewing Machine Comes to Utah." *Journal of Mormon History* 32, no. 3 (Fall 2006): 82–103.

Godfrey, Donald G. *Philo T. Farnsworth: The Father of Television*. Salt Lake City: Univ. of Utah Press, 2001.

———. "Zina Presidia Young Williams Card: Brigham's Daughter, Cardston's First Lady." *Journal of Mormon History* 23, no. 2 (Fall 1997): 107–27.

——— and Brigham Y. Card, eds. *The Diaries of Charles Ora Card: The Canadian Years, 1886–1903.* Salt Lake City: Univ. of Utah Press, 1993.

——— and Kenneth W. Godfrey, eds. *The Diaries of Charles Ora Card: The Utah Years, 1871–1886.* Provo, UT: Religious Studies Center, Brigham Young University, 2006.

Godfrey, Kenneth W. "Moses Thatcher and Mormon Beginnings in Mexico." *BYU Studies* 38, no. 4 (1999): 139–55.

———. "Moses Thatcher in the Dock: His Trials, the Aftermath, and His Last Days." *Journal of Mormon History* 24 (Spring 1998): 54–88.

Granger, Byrd H. *Arizona's Names: (X Marks the Place).* Tucson: Falconer, 1983.

Green, Doyle L. "The Church and Its Magazines." *Ensign*, January 1971, 12–15.

Greever, William S. *Arid Domain: The Santa Fe Railway and Its Western Land Grant.* Palo Alto, CA: Stanford Univ. Press, 1954.

Gurney, Alan. *Below the Convergence: Voyages toward Antarctica, 1699–1839.* New York: Penguin, 1998.

Hardy, Blaine C. "The Mormon Colonies of Northern Mexico: A History, 1885–1912." PhD diss., Wayne State Univ., 1963.

Hill, Donna. *Joseph Smith: The First Mormon.* Garden City, NY: Doubleday, 1977.

Hilton, Hope A. *"Wild Bill" Hickman and the Mormon Frontier.* Salt Lake City: Signature Books, 1988.

Hodge, Hiram C. *Arizona as It Is; or, The Coming Country.* New York: Hurd and Houghton, 1877.

Hodgson, Barbara. *In the Arms of Morpheus: The Tragic History of Morphine, Laudanum and Patent Medicines.* Buffalo, NY: Firefly Books, 2001.

Holzapfel, Richard Neitzel. *A History of Utah County.* Salt Lake City: Utah State Historical Society, 1999.

Huchel, Frederick M. *A History of Box Elder County.* Salt Lake City: Utah State Historical Society, 1999.

Hudson, A. James. *Charles Ora Card: Pioneer and Colonizer.* Cardston, Alberta: privately printed, 1963.

Hughston, Caroline Mary. *Old Fort Lowell.* Tucson, AZ: Arizona Silhouettes, 1964.

Jenson, Andrew, comp. *Church Chronology: A Record of Important Events Pertaining to the History of the Church of Jesus Christ of Latter-day Saints.* 2nd rev. ed. Salt Lake City: Deseret News, 1914.

———. *Encyclopedic History of the Church of Jesus Christ of Latter-day Saints.* Salt Lake City: Deseret News, 1941.

———. *Latter-day Saint Biographical Encyclopedia: A Compilation of Biographical Sketches of Prominent Men and Women in the Church of Jesus Christ of Latter-day Saints.* Salt Lake City: Andrew Jenson History Company, 1901–1936.

Johnson, Annie Richardson. *Heartbeats of Colonia Diaz.* Salt Lake City: Publishers Press, 1972.

Johnson, Benjamin F. *My Life's Review.* Independence, MO: Zion's Printing and Publishing, 1947.

Journal History of the Church of Jesus Christ of Latter-day Saints. Salt Lake City: Church Historian's Office.

Karolevitz, Robert F. *Doctors of the Old West: A Pictorial History of Medicine on the Frontier.* Seattle: Superior, 1967.

Kimball, Stanley B. *Historic Sites and Markers along the Mormon and Other Great Western Trails.* Urbana: Univ. of Illinois Press, 1988.

Louder, Dean R., and Lowell Bennion. "Mapping Mormons across the Modern West." In *The Mormon Role in the Settlement of the West,* edited by Richard H. Jackson, 135–67. Provo, UT: Brigham Young Univ. Press, 1978.

Ludlow, Daniel H., ed. *Encyclopedia of Mormonism.* New York: Macmillan, 1992.

Madsen, Brigham D. *Glory Hunter: A Biography of Patrick Edward Connor.* Salt Lake City: Univ. of Utah Press, 1990.

McClintock, James H. *Mormon Settlement in Arizona: A Record of Peaceful Conquest of the Desert.* Phoenix: Manufacturing Stationers, 1921.

McIntyre, Myron W., and Noel R. Barton. *Christopher Layton.* Salt Lake City: Christopher Layton Family Organization, 1966.

McLaws, Monte Burr. *Spokesman for the Kingdom: Early Mormon Journalism and the* Deseret News, *1830–1898.* Provo, UT: Brigham Young Univ. Press, 1977.

Meinig, D. W. "The Mormon Culture Region: Strategies and Patterns in the Geography of the American West, 1874–1964." *Annals of the Association of American Geographers* 55 (1965): 191–221.

Miller, Mark E. "St. John's Saints Interethnic Conflict in Northeastern Arizona, 1880–1885." *Journal of Mormon History* 23, no. 1 (Spring 1997): 87.

Mills, Elizabeth H. "The Mormon Colonies in Chihuahua after the 1912 Exodus." *New Mexico Historical Review* 29, nos. 3–4 (1954): 165–310.

Morgan, Dale L. "The State of Deseret." *Utah Historical Quarterly* 8 (1940): 65–251.

Naylor, Thomas S. "Colonia Morelos and the Mexican Revolution: Consul Dye Inspects an Evacuated Mormon Colony, 1912." *Journal of Arizona History* 20 (1979): 101–20.

Newman, Peter Charles. *Caesars of the Wilderness.* Markham, Ontario: Viking, 1987.

Olsen, Nolan Porter. *Logan Temple: The First 100 Years.* Providence, UT: Keith W. Watkins and Sons, 1978.

Packer, Boyd K. *The Holy Temple.* Salt Lake City: Bookcraft, 1980.

Peterson, F. Ross. *A History of Cache County.* Salt Lake City: Utah State Historical Society, 1997.

Powell, Allan Kent, ed. *Utah History Encyclopedia.* Salt Lake City: Univ. of Utah Press, 1994.

Pratt, Parley P. *Autobiography of Parley P. Pratt.* Salt Lake City: Deseret Book, 1980.

Pratt, Rey L. "History of the Mexican Mission." *Improvement Era,* April 1912, 489.

Ramsaye, Terry. *A Million and One Nights: A History of the Motion Picture.* New York: Simon and Schuster, 1964.

Reilly, P. T. *Lee's Ferry: From Mormon Crossing to National Park.* Logan, UT: Utah State Univ. Press 1999.

Ricketts, Norma Baldwin, ed. *Arizona's Honeymoon Trail and Mormon Wagon Roads.* Mesa, AZ: Cox, 2001.

———. *The Mormon Battalion: U.S. Army of the West, 1846–1848*. Logan, UT: Utah State Univ. Press, 1996.

Ricks, Joel E., and Everett L. Cooley, eds. *The History of a Valley: Cache Valley, Utah–Idaho*. Logan, UT: Cache Valley Centennial Commission, 1956.

Roberts, B. H. *The Autobiography of B. H. Roberts*. Edited by Gary James Bergera. Salt Lake City: Signature Books, 1990.

Roberts, Richard C., and Richard W. Sadler. *A History of Weber County*. Salt Lake City: Utah State Historical Society, 1997.

Robinson, Phil. *Sinners and Saints: A Tour across the States, and round Them; with Three Months among the Mormons.* Boston: Roberts Brothers, 1883.

Romney, Thomas Cottam. *The Mormon Colonies in Mexico.* Salt Lake City: Univ. of Utah Press, 2005.

Schwartz, Seymour I. *The French and Indian War, 1754–1753: The Imperial Struggle for North America*. New York: Simon & Schuster, 1994.

Schwendiman, Anita Martineau. *Nephi Martineau and Emmeline Knowles Martineau*. Rexburg, ID: Ricks College Press, 1987.

Seegmiller, Janet Burton. *A History of Iron County: Community above Self*. Salt Lake City: Utah Historical Society, 1998.

Serpico, Phil. *Santa Fe Route to the Pacific*. Santa Fe: Omni, 1988.

Shirts, Morris A., and Kathryn H. Shirts. *A Trial Furnace: Southern Utah's Iron Mission.* Provo, UT: Brigham Young Univ. Press, 1991.

Sillitoe, Linda. *Welcoming the World: A History of Salt Lake County*. Salt Lake City: Salt Lake County, 1996.

Simmonds, A. J. *The Gentile Comes to Cache Valley: A Study of the Logan Apostasies of 1874 and the Establishment of Non-Mormon Churches in Cache Valley, 1873–1913*. Logan: Utah State Univ. Press, 1976.

Snyder, Robert W. *Voice of the City: Vaudeville and Popular Culture in New York*. New York: Oxford Univ. Press, 1989.

Somers, Ray. *History of Logan*. Logan, UT: Somers Historic Press, 1993.

Sorenson, Isaac. *Isaac Sorensen's History of Mendon: A Pioneer Chronicle of a Mormon Settlement*. Edited by Doran J. Baker, Charles S. Peterson, and Gene A. Ware. Logan, UT: Cache County Historical Preservation Commission, 1988.

Stott, Clifford L. *Search for Sanctuary: Brigham Young and the White Mountain Expedition*. Salt Lake City: Univ. of Utah Press, 1984.

Stout, Wayne Dunham. *A History of Thatcher, Arizona*. Salt Lake City: W. Stout, 1975.

Stubbs, Glen R. "A Biography of George Albert Smith, 1870–1951." PhD diss., Brigham Young Univ., 1974.

Taylor, B. Kim. *The Great New York City Trivia and Fact Book*. New York: Cumberland, 1998.

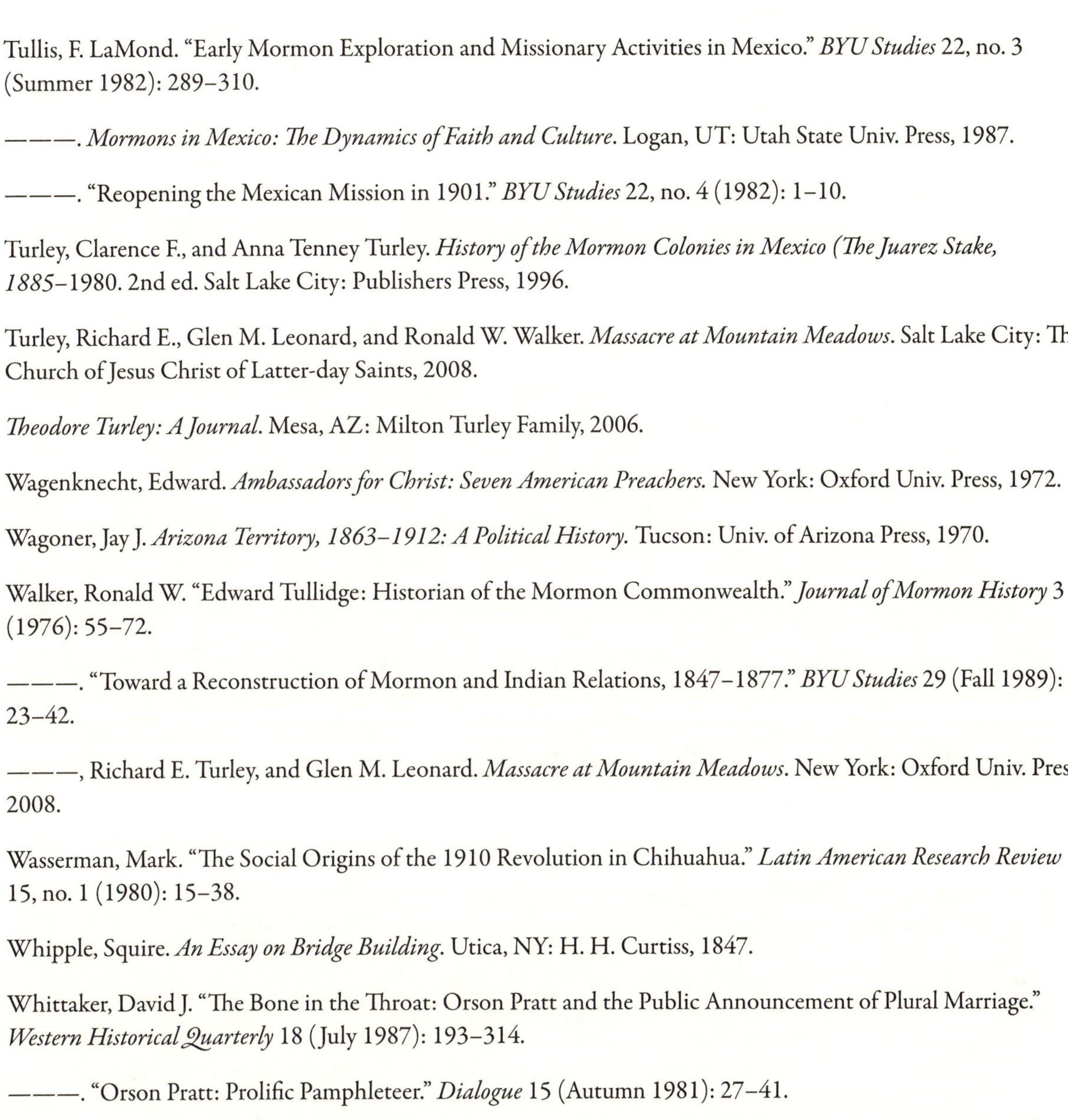

Tullis, F. LaMond. "Early Mormon Exploration and Missionary Activities in Mexico." *BYU Studies* 22, no. 3 (Summer 1982): 289–310.

———. *Mormons in Mexico: The Dynamics of Faith and Culture*. Logan, UT: Utah State Univ. Press, 1987.

———. "Reopening the Mexican Mission in 1901." *BYU Studies* 22, no. 4 (1982): 1–10.

Turley, Clarence F., and Anna Tenney Turley. *History of the Mormon Colonies in Mexico (The Juarez Stake, 1885*–1980. 2nd ed. Salt Lake City: Publishers Press, 1996.

Turley, Richard E., Glen M. Leonard, and Ronald W. Walker. *Massacre at Mountain Meadows*. Salt Lake City: The Church of Jesus Christ of Latter-day Saints, 2008.

Theodore Turley: A Journal. Mesa, AZ: Milton Turley Family, 2006.

Wagenknecht, Edward. *Ambassadors for Christ: Seven American Preachers.* New York: Oxford Univ. Press, 1972.

Wagoner, Jay J. *Arizona Territory, 1863–1912: A Political History.* Tucson: Univ. of Arizona Press, 1970.

Walker, Ronald W. "Edward Tullidge: Historian of the Mormon Commonwealth." *Journal of Mormon History* 3 (1976): 55–72.

———. "Toward a Reconstruction of Mormon and Indian Relations, 1847–1877." *BYU Studies* 29 (Fall 1989): 23–42.

———, Richard E. Turley, and Glen M. Leonard. *Massacre at Mountain Meadows*. New York: Oxford Univ. Press, 2008.

Wasserman, Mark. "The Social Origins of the 1910 Revolution in Chihuahua." *Latin American Research Review* 15, no. 1 (1980): 15–38.

Whipple, Squire. *An Essay on Bridge Building*. Utica, NY: H. H. Curtiss, 1847.

Whittaker, David J. "The Bone in the Throat: Orson Pratt and the Public Announcement of Plural Marriage." *Western Historical Quarterly* 18 (July 1987): 193–314.

———. "Orson Pratt: Prolific Pamphleteer." *Dialogue* 15 (Autumn 1981): 27–41.

Winchester, Benjamin, ed. *The Gospel Reflector, in which the Doctrine of The Church of Jesus Christ of Latter-Day Saints is Set Forth, and Scriptural Evidence Adduced to Establish It*. Philadelphia: Brown, Bicking & Guilber, 1841.

Woodford, Frank B. *Lewis Cass: The Last Jeffersonian*. New Brunswick, NJ: Rutgers Univ. Press, 1950.

Young, Christian C. *In the Absence of Predators: Conservation and Controversy on the Kiabab Plateau*. Lincoln: Univ. of Nebraska Press, 2002.

PERIODICALS AND NEWSPAPERS

James Henry Martineau wrote many articles for local papers; they are noted in the text:

Deseret Evening News

Salt Lake City Herald

Salt Lake Tribune

Contributor

Tullidge's Quarterly Magazine

INTERNET SOURCES

Online sources that proved useful for studying James Henry Martineau are below:

Hubert Howe Bancroft's *History of Utah, 1540–1866* is a primary source of biographical sketches. http://www.utlm.org/onlinebooks/bancroftshistoryofutah_index_a.htm.

BYU Studies has full text information at http://byustudies.byu.edu.

The International Society—Daughters of Utah Pioneers provides an online card index at http://www.dupinternational.org.

FamilySearch (http://www.familysearch.org) is an open genealogical index provided by The Church of Jesus Christ of Latter-day Saints. Some caution must be taken with the accuracy of files of this service.

"Glossary of Medical Terms Used in the 18th and 19th Centuries" helped decipher the Martineaus' heath conditions: http://www.thornber.net/medicine/html/medgloss.html.

The Journal of Mormon History has general search information online: http://www.mhahome.org/index.php.

The Inflation Calculator provides insight as to comparative dollar values and is found at http://www.westegg.com/inflation/infl.cgi.

LDS Library (http://search.ldslibrary.com/) is a database of thousands of Latter-day Saint historical documents. It requires a minimal fee.

The Martineau family Website is www.martineaus.org.

BYU's Mormon Literature Database provides a diverse collection of history: http://mormonlit.lib.byu.edu.

Saints Without Halos (http://www.saintswithouthalos.com/b/_bios.phtml) provides biographical sketches.

Utah Collections Browsers provides a coordinated Utah library service at http://www.uen.org/cgi-bin/websql/ucme/ucme.hts.

Utah Digital Newspapers is an invaluable full-text source: (http://www.lib.utah.edu/digital/unews/).

An online edition of Allan Kent Powell's *Utah History Encyclopedia* can be found at http://www.media.utah.edu/UHE/UHEindex.html.

Utah History to Go provides bibliographies, facts, and historical photographs: http://historytogo.utah.gov/index.html.

The Utah State Historical Society has a searchable catalog at http://history.utah.gov/index.html.

ARCHIVE AND MANUSCRIPT COLLECTIONS

Arizona Historical Society

L. Tom Perry Special Collections, Harold B. Lee Library, Brigham Young University, Provo, UT

Church History Library, The Church of Jesus Christ of Latter-day Saints, Salt Lake City

University of Nevada, Reno Library, Special Collections

Western Americana; Special Collections, J. Willard Marriott Library, University of Utah, Salt Lake City

Utah State Historical Society

INDEX

Martineau's spelling varies and often involves initials and abbreviations. Look freely for alternative spellings, cross-references, and alternative topical citations. Most married women are listed by maiden names with married names in parentheses.